THE ROUGH GUIDE TO

The Greek Islands

written and researched by

Nick Edwards, John Fisher, John Malathronas,
Carol Palioudakis and

**ROUGH
GUIDES**

roughguides.com

Contents

INTRODUCTION   4

Where to go	5	Things not to miss	13
When to go	11	Itineraries	22

BASICS   24

Getting there	25	The media	41
Getting around	29	Festivals	42
Accommodation	33	Sports and outdoor pursuits	44
Food and drink	36	Culture and etiquette	45
Health	40	Travel essentials	46

THE GUIDE   54

1 Athens and the mainland ports	54	5 The Dodecanese	260
2 The Argo-Saronic Islands	76	6 The East and North Aegean	346
3 The Cyclades	104	7 The Sporades and Évvia	420
4 Crete	196	8 The Ionian Islands	454

CONTEXTS   516

History	517	Music	550
Archeology	542	Books	555
Wildlife	546	Greek	561

SMALL PRINT & INDEX   572

Introduction to
The Greek Islands

It would take a lifetime of island-hopping to fully appreciate the 227 inhabited Greek islands scattered across the Aegean and Ionian seas. With sapphire water lapping at rocky coastlines sprinkled with secret coves and sandy beaches, they are the stuff of dreamy travel-posters, the very definition of the eulogized Greek summer of sun, sea and sand. Easy as it is to wax lyrical in general terms, however, the islands are by no means a homogeneous holiday cluster – no Bahamas or Seychelles here. Each one has its distinctive personality, architecture and flora as well as its own loyal tourist base.

The sea, surprisingly **unpolluted** and beautifully clear, is undoubtedly the major selling point: as well as offering gorgeous swimming, there are **watersports** galore, from snorkelling and kayaking to banana boating and windsurfing – indeed, the Greek islands are home to some of the best windsurfing spots in the world. Yacht charter, whether bare-boat or skippered, is big business, particularly out of Rhodes, Kálymnos, Kos, Lefkáda, Páros and Pireás. When the sea is less welcoming during the spring and winter months and the crowds have abated a little, there's plenty of land-based activity including **walking** through lush, wild flower-strewn meadows, **hiking** and **rock-climbing** to enjoy.

But the islands are far from simply good-looking outdoor playgrounds: like the rest of Greece, they exude a colossal sense of **history**, sheltering vestiges of occupying foreign forces. Romans, Arabs, Byzantines, Genoese, Venetians, French, English, Italians and Ottomans have all controlled different islands since the time of Alexander the Great, and countless monuments have been left behind by these waves of power: frescoed Byzantine churches, fortified Venetian towns, conventional castles built by the Genoese and Knights, Ottoman mosques and the Art Deco edifices of the Italian administration make up this historical patchwork. Couple these with the lovely cities and temples of ancient Greece itself and the fascinating jumble is complete.

ABOVE FROM LEFT COLOURFUL HOUSES, FISKÁRDHO, KEFALONIÁ; PRIEST STROLLING IN KÁLYMNOS; CHEZ LUCIEN, ATHENS; **OPPOSITE** WINDMILL, ÍOS

The biggest surprise – for the first-time visitor at least – is the ecologically sensitive absorption of mass tourism, from the untainted beaches to the traditional, still inhabited, inland capitals. Of course, there are overblown resorts, tavernas aplenty, sophisticated bars and clubs, even the obligatory Irish pub. But, with a few loutish exceptions, the sense of history, accompanied by stringent planning regulations, has ensured that life on the islands more or less goes on as it has for centuries. This is becoming even more pronounced in the second decade of the tumultuous, debt-ridden twenty-first century as more and more Greeks eschew their urban jails and change to a lower gear by starting new lives where their ancestors began their long cultural journey so long ago.

Where to go

After an almost mandatory stop in **Athens** – the big, sprawling capital of Greece – perhaps the best approach for first-time visitors is to sample islands from neighbouring archipelagos. Crete, the Dodecanese, the Cyclades and the northeast Aegean are all reasonably well connected with each other, though the Sporades, Argo-Saronic and Ionian groups offer limited possibilities for island-hopping, and usually involve a long mainland traipse to get to.

If time and money are short, head for well-preserved, atmospheric **Ýdhra** in the Argo-Saronic Gulf, just a short ride from **Pireás** (the main port of Athens); nearby **Spétses** has similar architectural charm and more accessible beaches. Of the Sporades, **Skýros** and **Skópelos** remain the most traditional and attractive, with forests, pale-sand beaches and well-preserved capitals. Among the Cyclades, cataclysmically volcanic **Santoríni** (Thíra) and **Mýkonos** with its perfectly preserved harbour-town rank as must-see spectacles, but mountainous **Náxos** and gently rolling **Sífnos** have a life independent of cruise-ship tourism and are better for longer stays. Cliff-bound **Amorgós** and **Folégandhros**, rocky **Sýros** with its Italianate main town, artistic **Tínos**, secluded **Sérifos** and lonely **Anáfi** with its balmy, south-facing beaches are less obvious but equally satisfying choices. **Crete** can fill an entire Rough Guide itself, but the highlights have to be Knossos plus the nearby archeological museum in Iráklion, the other Minoan palaces at Phaestos and Ayía Triádha, and the west in general – Réthymnon and Haniá, whose hinterland extends to the relatively unspoilt southwest coast, reachable via the remarkable Samarian gorge.

Rhodes, with its unique Old Town, is capital of the Dodecanese, but picturesque, Neoclassical **Sými** and austere **Pátmos**, the island of St John's Revelation, have beaches just as lovely. **Kárpathos**, marooned between Rhodes and Crete, has arguably the best coastline in the Dodecanese, while **Léros** and **Níssyros** will appeal to those looking for unspoilt islands. From Pátmos or Léros, it's easy to continue north via **Sámos** – one of Greece's most attractive islands – or **Híos**, with its striking medieval architecture, to balmy, olive-cloaked **Lésvos**, perhaps the most traditional of all islands in its way of life.

The Ionian islands are primarily package-holiday territory but, especially if you're exiting Greece towards Italy, be sure to stop at **Corfu**, which along with neighbouring **Paxí** islet escaped damage from the 1953 earthquake that devastated the southern Ionians. Little **Itháki**, most easily reached from the mainland, is relatively untouristy, given its lack of beaches, though big brother **Kefaloniá** is well and truly in the spotlight owing to spectacular scenery – and (over)exposure in Louis de Bernière's *Captain Corelli's Mandolin*.

BEST ISLAND FOR...

Watersports Kárpathos, p.292. The *meltémi* winds are the best and strongest here, so grab your windsurfer and hit the water.

Food and drink Lésvos, p.384. As this island is the main producer of both olive oil and ouzo, you can expect top-quality ingredients served up in the tavernas and bars.

Parties Mýkonos, p.144. From energetic superclubs to chilled, sophisticated beach bars, the nightlife here is seriously hot – be prepared to party hard.

Classical sights Crete, p.209, p.217, p.213 & p.231. Knossos, Mália, Phaestos, Zákros…and there's many more. Take your pick from a number of Cretan classics.

Seclusion Skópelos, p.429. If you're keen for some peace and quiet, this traditional little island has it in spades.

Luxury Ýdhra, p.93. With mule the only way of getting around, this cute and charming island hasn't escaped the attention of the rich and famous, so expect pricey boutique hotels and chic restaurants, and indulge your sophisticated side.

ABOVE VLYHÓS, ÝDHRA **OPPOSITE** PYRGÍ, HÍOS

When to go

Most islands and their inhabitants are far more agreeable, and resolutely Greek, outside the **busiest period** of early July to late August, when crowds of foreigners or Greek mainlanders, soaring temperatures and the effects of the infamous **meltémi** can detract considerably from enjoyment. The *meltémi* is a cool, fair-weather wind which appears during daytime from around mid-July to mid-August but disappears at night. It originates in high-pressure systems over the far north Aegean, gathering momentum as it travels southwards and ending up in gusts by the time it reaches Crete. North-facing coasts there, and throughout the Cyclades and Dodecanese, bear the full brunt; its howling is less pronounced in the north or northeast Aegean, where continental landmasses provide some shelter for the islands just offshore. In the Ionian archipelago, an analogous northwest wind off the Adriatic is called the *maïstros*.

You won't miss out on **warm weather** if you come between late May and the end of June, or in September, when the sea is warmest for swimming, though at these times you'll find little activity on the northernmost islands of Thássos, Límnos and Samothráki. During October you'll probably hit a week's stormy spell, but for much of that month the "little summer of Áyios Dhimítrios", the Greek equivalent of Indian summer, prevails. While restaurants and nightlife can be limited in spring and autumn, the light is softer, and going out at midday becomes a pleasure rather than

GODS AND MONSTERS

A high proportion of the ancient sites still seen in Greece today were built as **shrines and temples to the gods**. They include spectacular sites such as Delphi and the Acropolis in Athens, but also many other sanctuaries, great and small, throughout the islands – everywhere, in fact, because the gods themselves were everywhere.

There were many lesser and local gods like the Nymphs and Pan, but the great gods known to all were the **twelve** who lived on **Mount Olympus**, including **Zeus** and his wife and sister, **Hera**. They had human form, and were born and had sexual relations among themselves and humankind, but they never ate human food nor did they age or die.

As well as fearsome gods, tales of **monsters** and demons proliferate from the Greek islands, of which the half-bull, half-man **Minotaur** (see p.209) is probably best known. Dwelling within the Cretan labyrinth at Knossos, in the grounds of his father's palace, he was fed a diet of youths and maidens until Theseus turned up and destroyed him. The Minotaur's notoriety is equalled by the **Cyclops**, one-eyed giants who were said to live on the island of Sérifos (see p.115) and supplied Zeus with regular thunderbolts. The three horrifyingly ugly **Gorgon** sisters with snakes as their hair and a gaze that could turn a mortal to stone, Euryale, Stheno and (the ill-fated) Medusa, were feared to such a degree that their figures were carved onto buildings throughout the Greek islands; check out the pediment on the Temple of Artemis in the Archeological museum in Corfu (see p.463). Add to this motley crew the giant, winged **Sirens**, who lived on the rocks in the sea and reputedly lured sailors to their watery deaths, and one thing is for sure – the Greeks certainly had imagination.

an ordeal. The most reliable venues for late autumn or early winter breaks are Rhodes and balmy southeastern Crete, where it's possible to swim in relative comfort as late as November.

December to March are the **coldest** and least reliably sunny months, particularly on the Ionian islands, typically the rainiest area from November onwards. The high peaks of northerly or lofty islands wear a brief mantle of snow around the turn of the year, with Crete's mountainous spine staying partly covered well into April. Between January and April the glorious lowland **wild flowers** start to bloom, beginning in the southeast Aegean. April weather is more reliable, the air is crystal-clear and the landscape green. May is generally settled, though the sea is still a bit cool for prolonged dips.

Another factor that affects the timing of a Greek island visit is the level of tourism and the related amenities provided. Service standards occasionally slip under peak-season pressure, and room rates are at their highest from mid-July to the end of August. If you can only visit during midsummer, it is wise to reserve a package well in advance, plan an itinerary off the beaten track and buy all your ferry tickets beforehand. Between November and Easter, you'll have to contend with pared-back ferry and plane schedules plus skeletal facilities when you arrive. However, you should be able to find adequate services to the more populated islands, and at least one hotel and taverna open in the port or main town of all but the tiniest isles.

TOP GORGON, MOSAIC IN RHODES TOWN

Author picks

Our authors hopped from island to island, testing out the best beaches, sampling the tastiest tzatziki, taking to the water on boats, kayaks or windsurfers and exploring countless ancient ruins. Here are their highlights:

Best arrival Looking at the bare granite cliffs of Ýdhra, wondering whether it was wise to holiday here and then turning suddenly into the fabulous horseshoe of its harbour. See p.93

Killer views There's nothing like standing on the vertical cliffs of Santoríni, topped by the icing of the whitewashed Cycladic houses, gazing over the submerged caldera. See p.186

Most outlandish meal The *Sirocco* taverna on Mílos uses the hot volcanic sand to slow-bake casseroles of lamb, veal and fish in clay pots overnight. See p.128

Abba homage Take a swim at Kastáni Bay, Skópelos, where *Mamma Mia!* was shot, and unashamedly mime "Does Your Mother Know" on the beach. See p.432

Surprise walk The one-hour Dovecote Trail on Tínos leads you to its giant pigeon houses which are decorated with unrivalled skill. See p.139

Wildest surf Located in a vast, cliff-flanked bay, Vassilikí in Lefkádha is one of Europe's biggest but also most atmospheric windsurfing centres. See p.484

Alien landscape Visit the seemingly extraterrestrial Stéfanos crater floor on top of Níssyros's dormant volcano and imagine yourself on a different planet. See p.311

Our author recommendations don't end here. We've flagged up our favourite places – a perfectly sited hotel, an atmospheric café, a special restaurant – throughout the guide, highlighted with the ★ symbol.

FROM TOP KASTÁNI BEACH, SKÓPELOS; DOVECOTE, TÍNOS; WINDSURFING AT VASSILIKÍ, LEFKÁDHA

things not to miss

It's not possible to see everything that the Greek Islands have to offer in one trip – and we don't suggest you try. What follows, in no particular order, is a selective taste of the region's highlights, including beautiful beaches, outstanding Classical monuments, charming seaside towns and unforgettable wildlife and outdoor experiences. All the highlights have a page reference to take you straight into the guide, where you can find out more.

1 VÁΪ BEACH
Page 230
Sunbathe on this superb beach, fringed by Europe's only natural wild date-palm grove.

2 MÝKONOS NIGHTLIFE
Page 144
Soak up the electrifying atmosphere of the Greek party capital – this is the most frenetic nightlife east of Ibiza.

3 NÁXOS ACTIVITIES
Page 162
Whether you climb Mount Zas, or kitesurf on Orkós, this is the activity playground of the Cyclades.

4 KNOSSOS PALACE
Page 209
Visit the most spectacularly restored, vividly coloured and most exciting of Crete's Minoan palaces.

5 KLÉFTIKO, MÍLOS
Page 128

Two hours by boat from Adhámas, this otherwise unreachable cove is as close to being marooned on a desert beach as you will get.

6 THE CLIFFS OF KÁLYMNOS
Page 326

The island's limestone cliffs and dry weather attract climbers from all over the world.

7 DELOS
Page 146

Pay your respects to the most sacred site of the Eastern Mediterranean and the biggest port of the Cyclades in the ancient world.

8 SÝMI
Page 295

Take a leap into the past and stroll among the grand mansions of Sými's picturesque harbour, built with wealth from the sponge trade.

9 AUGUST 15
Page 136

The Assumption of the Virgin provides a spectacular explosion of Orthodox devotion in the Cyclades, especially on Tínos.

10 CHURCH OF EKATONDAPYLIANÍ, PÁROS
Page 156

Built by St Helen in the fourth century AD over an old pagan temple, this may well be the most continuous place of worship in Europe.

11 HANIÁ HARBOUR
Page 244
Crete's most charming city, Haniá displays the haunting vestiges of its Venetian and Ottoman past with pride.

12 SHIPWRECK BAY, ZÁKYNTHOS
Page 510
Lie back and enjoy the unforgettable scenery of one of Greece's poster beaches.

13 ISLAND WINES
Pages 38, 192, 214
Try wine tasting in the vineyards of Santoríni, Crete or Sámos and sample the delights of local grape varieties.

14 KÝTHIRA
Page 510
An inspiration for artists, this is also the ultimate family destination, with plenty of hiking opportunities and golden sand beaches.

15 ÓLYMBOS VILLAGE, KÁRPATHOS
Page 294
The majestic view south from windswept, remote Ólymbos across the rugged coast of unspoilt northern Kárpathos is goosebump-inducing.

19

20

16 CORFU OLD TOWN
Page 459

With its elegant Venetian architecture and fine museums, Corfu's capital is the beating heart of the Ionian Islands.

17 THE OTHER ACRÓPOLIS
Page 278

From the Hellenistic Acropolis of Líndhos, high above the modern village, look north along the length of Rhodes Island for one of the most stunning views of the Dodecanese.

18 PÁTMOS, MONASTERY OF ST JOHN
Page 340

Built around the cave where St John wrote the Book of Revelation, this monastery is a warren of fresco-strewn courtyards, arcades and roof terraces.

19 MARINE PARK, ALÓNISSOS
Page 439

The sea around the island is a haven for the endangered Mediterranean monk seal.

20 MELISSÁNI CAVE, KEFALONIÁ
Page 495

Visit the underwater Melissáni Cave to admire the rock formations and play of light on the cave walls.

21 SAMARIÁ GORGE
Page 251

The 16k descent of this leafy gorge enclosed by high rock faces is an unforgettable hike.

Itineraries

Although there are as many itineraries as there are islands, the ultimate Greek summer experience is island-hopping, and in particular around the Cyclades. If you want to combine some history with blissful beach living, then head for the Dodecanese, while if you haven't got your sea legs and prefer driving to sailing, take the Cretan Circuit for your perfect holiday. The other islands, especially the Ionians, are best explored individually.

HOPPING AROUND THE CYCLADES

Ferry routes connect all of these islands; in the summer months be sure to book tickets in advance and check the most recent timetables. You'll need at least 2–3 weeks to cover this itinerary depending on ferry frequency.

❶ **Ándhros** Green and fertile, with some terrific walking trails and a fantastic selection of beaches, this is a great introduction to the Cyclades. **See p.132**

❷ **Mýkonos** The party island for as many sensuous, fun-filled days as your body can take and your wallet can stand. **See p.140**

❸ **Páros** A little bit of everything – beautiful beaches, pretty fishing harbours, graceful monasteries and an energetic nightlife defined by its "happy hours". **See p.154**

❹ **Náxos** The activity centre of the Cyclades, this is the place to go trekking, diving or kitesurfing. **See p.162**

❺ **Santoríni** Don't forget your camera – the crater that makes up this island is particularly photogenic at sunset. **See p.186**

❻ **Mílos** Join a boat ride around the island and swim in some of its inaccessible, kaleidoscopic coves. **See p.124**

❼ **Sérifos** Glorious beaches and with a breathtaking inland capital, Sérifos is a perfect chill-out zone. **See p.115**

DISCOVERING THE DODECANESE

The starting point for this itinerary, Rhodes, is served by several flights daily, while all the other islands are connected by regular ferries. The whole itinerary should take a minimum of 2–3 weeks depending on how often ferries are running.

❶ **Rhodes** With its lovely medieval Old Town and numerous sandy beaches, this is rightfully one of the most visited of the Greek islands. See p.264

❷ **Sými** The sheer coastal range of this island is astounding; golden sand, small pebble, wide shingle or steep cliff – Sými has them all. See p.295

❸ **Tílos** Quiet, volcanic and part-protected with a national park, this is the most relaxing of the Dodecanese. **See p.302**

❹ **Níssyros** Home to a dormant volcano, there are some rather unearthly moonscape panoramas to enjoy here. **See p.306**

❺ **Kálymnos** The sponge capital of the Mediterranean has reinvented itself as a rock-climbing, hiking and scuba-diving destination. **See p.326**

❻ **Pátmos** Despite the awe-inspiring cave where St John the Divine wrote the Book of Revelation, beaches are still the island's principal attraction. **See p.337**

A CRETAN CIRCUIT

Fly into one of three Crete airports, rent a car and spend at least 2 weeks on the road.

❶ **Haniá** Vying for the title of the most attractive town in Greece, this is the ultimate destination for *flâneurs*. **See p.244**

❷ **Samariá Gorge** The most popular hike on the Greek islands and as perfect a one-day excursion as you can hope for. **See p.251**

❸ **Réthymnon** A fascinating city with a beach offering views of a skyline of Ottoman minarets and Venetian mansions. **See p.234**

❹ **Iráklion** Crete's capital is the best base for exploring the outstanding ruins at Knossos and for hiking on the Lassíthi plateau. **See p.201**

❺ **Paleóhora** Pleasant resort town with a pebble beach and a fun social scene centring on some decent restaurants and bars. **See p.254**

❻ **Váï** You'd be forgiven for thinking you were in the Caribbean lying on this fine-sand beach lined with exotic palm trees. **See p.230**

SARONIC SAILING

If you don't have time for long ferry trips, enjoy a taster of Greece's island flavours around the Saronic Gulf. One week minimum.

❶ **Égina** The closest island to Athens also sports the beautiful Temple of Aphaea, one of the most visually compelling in Greece. **See p.81**

❷ **Póros** Popular with foreigners as well as Athenians, this is the place to head for if you want a simple beach holiday with some nightlife to boot. **See p.90**

❸ **Ýdhra** The most dramatic of the Argo-Saronic islands, the amphitheatric setting of the town is as beautiful as any in Greece. **See p.93**

❹ **Spétses** A family holiday island with developed infrastructure, good beaches and excellent, upmarket tavernas. **See p.99**

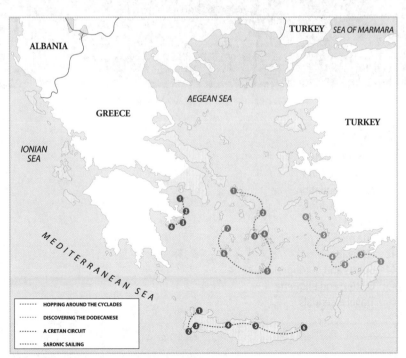

TOUR BOATS, SPINÁLONGA, CRETE

Basics

25 Getting there
29 Getting around
33 Accommodation
36 Food and drink
40 Health
41 The media
42 Festivals
44 Sports and outdoor pursuits
45 Culture and etiquette
46 Travel essentials

Getting there

By far the easiest way to get to the Greek Islands is to fly. An increasing number of islands have international airports that see charters and occasional scheduled flights from Britain, Ireland and the rest of northern Europe. Other islands can be reached on domestic flights, connecting with international scheduled arrivals in Athens and Thessaloníki. Even if your starting point is North America, Australia, New Zealand or South Africa, the most cost-effective way to Greece may well be to get to London – or Amsterdam, Frankfurt or another northern European hub – and pick up an onward flight from there.

Airfares are highest in July, August and during Easter week. But May, June and September are also popular, and since far fewer flights operate through the winter, bargains are rare at any time.

When **buying flights** it always pays to shop around and bear in mind that many websites don't include charter or budget airlines in their results. Be aware too that a **package deal**, with accommodation included, can sometimes be as cheap as, or even cheaper than, a flight alone: there's no rule that says you have to use your accommodation every night, or even at all.

Once in Greece, a vast **ferry** network, connects even the smallest of islands (see p.29). Details of the main ports are covered in the "Athens and the ports" chapter (see p.54).

Overland alternatives from the UK or Northern Europe involve at least three days of nonstop travel. If you want to take your time over the journey, then **driving** or travelling **by train** can be enjoyable, although invariably more expensive than flying. We've included only brief details of these routes here.

Flights from the UK and Ireland

The only **direct flights** to the islands are with budget or charter airlines. The latter mostly offer flight-only seats in much the same way as budget operators, albeit with clunkier booking systems and often less convenient flight times; most of them fly only in the summer months, from May to September. Regular scheduled flights include easyJet from Gatwick to Corfu, Haniá (Chania, Crete), Iráklion (Heraklion, Crete), Kos, Mýkonos, Ródhos (Rhodes), Thíra (Santoríni) and Zákynthos, **from Liverpool to** Ródhos, and from Manchester and Bristol to Iráklion and Corfu; Jet2 (Ⓦjet2.com) **from Manchester to** Iráklion, Kos and Ródhos, and from East Midlands, Leeds and Newcastle to Iráklion and Ródhos; and Ryanair (Ⓦryanair.com) from Stansted to Corfu and Ródhos and Liverpool to Ródhos. In addition charter operators go from a variety of UK regional airports to all of the above, plus **Kefaloniá**, **Skiáthos**, **Sámos**, **Lésvos** and **Límnos, as well as Kavála** (for Thássos), **Vólos** (for the Sporades) and **Préveza** (for Lefkádha) on the Greek mainland (see map, p.58). The main charter operators with whom you can book direct are Monarch (Ⓦmonarch.co.uk), Thomas Cook (Ⓦflythomascook.com), Thomson (Ⓦthomson .co.uk) and Torair (Ⓦflytorair.com); others may be available indirectly, through travel agencies or third-party websites.

Don't expect any of the above to be cheap: unless you book far in advance, there are few bargain **fares** to Greece or its islands. Seats are available on the budget airlines for less than £50 each way, but you'll have to move very fast indeed (or travel way out of season) to find fares this low. Realistically you can expect to pay £75–150 each way at most times of the year.

Indirect flights

If you can't get a direct flight, or the island you're heading for has no airport, you'll have to make at least one stop along the way and continue by **domestic flight** – with Aegean, Olympic or Sky Express – or **ferry**. Most obviously this means via Athens, but there are also plenty of connecting flights to the islands from Thessaloníki, while ferry connections may be better from nearby islands: if

A BETTER KIND OF TRAVEL

At Rough Guides we are passionately committed to travel. We feel that travelling is the best way to understand the world we live in and the people we share it with – plus tourism has brought a great deal of benefit to developing economies around the world over the last few decades. But the growth in tourism has also damaged some places irreparably, and climate change is exacerbated by most forms of transport, especially flying. All Rough Guides' trips are carbon-offset, and every year we donate money to a variety of charities devoted to combating the effects of climate change.

you're travelling to Pátmos, for example, look at flights to Kos or Ródhos; for Skópelos consider Skiáthos or Vólos (on the mainland). Details of how to get to and through Athens and the other mainland ports can be found in chapter 1 (see p.54), where there's also a map showing airports with domestic flights.

Scheduled flights include Aegean and British Airways from Heathrow to Athens; British Airways and easyJet from Gatwick to Thessaloníki; and Viking Hellas from Manchester to Athens. From **Dublin to Athens**, Aer Lingus have three direct flights a week from April to September, with fares starting at around €100 each way, though you can easily pay twice that. Almost all airlines, including charter operators, allow you to book one-way tickets at no extra cost, so you can fly into Athens with one, leave from an island with another.

Travelling from Ireland or a regional airport in the UK, it can pay to think laterally: one of the best routings from Dublin, for example, is on Malev Hungarian airlines (Ⓦ www.malev.com) via Budapest – with good prices and convenient connections to Athens and other Greek airports.

Flights from the US and Canada

Direct **nonstop** flights from New York to Athens – daily for much of the year – are operated by Delta (Ⓦ delta.com), Hellenic Imperial (Ⓦ hellenic airways.com), both from JFK, and Continental (Ⓦ continental.com) from Newark. Between May and October, US Airways (Ⓦ usair.com) also flies daily from Philadelphia to Athens. Code-sharing airlines can quote through fares with one of the above, or a European partner, from virtually every major US city, connecting either at New York or a European hub such as London or Frankfurt. From Athens, Aegean, Olympic and Sky Express offer reasonably priced add-on flights to the islands (see p.30).

Fares vary greatly, so it's worth putting in a little time on the internet, or using a good travel agent; book as far ahead as possible to get the best price. The lowest starting point is around US$900 for a restricted, off-season round-trip flight from the east coast, rising to about $1400 for a similar deal in summer; from the west coast, expect to pay ten to twenty percent more. The lower fares are rarely on the most direct flights, so check the routing to avoid lengthy delays or stopovers. Remember too that you may be better off getting a domestic flight to New York or Philadelphia and heading directly to Athens from there, or buying a cheap flight to London (beware of changing airports) or another European city, and onward travel from there.

As with the US, airfares **from Canada** vary depending on where you start your journey, and whether you take a direct service. Air Canada (Ⓦ aircanada.com) flies to Athens out of Toronto, with a stop in Montreal, from one to four times weekly depending on the time of year. Air Transat (Ⓦ airtransat.com) also have seasonal weekly flights from Toronto and Montreal to Athens. Otherwise you'll have to choose among one- or two-stop itineraries on a variety of European carriers, or perhaps Delta via New York; costs run from Can$900 round-trip in low season from Toronto to more than double that from Vancouver in high season.

Flights from Australia and New Zealand

There are **no direct flights** from Australia or New Zealand to Greece; you'll have to change planes in Southeast Asia or Europe. Tickets purchased direct from the airlines tend to be expensive; travel agents or Australia-based websites generally offer much better deals on fares and have the latest information on limited specials and stopovers. For a simple return fare, you may also have to buy an add-on internal flight to get you to the international departure point.

Fares **from Australia** start from around Aus$1800, rising to around Aus$2600 depending on season, routing, validity, number of stopovers, etc. The shortest flights and best fares are generally with airlines like Thai (Ⓦ thaiair.com), Singapore (Ⓦ singaporeair.com), Etihad (Ⓦ etihadairways.com) and Emirates (Ⓦ emirates.com) that can fly you directly to Athens from their Asian or Gulf hubs, though you'll also find offers on Swiss (Ⓦ swiss .com), KLM (Ⓦ klm.com) and other European carriers. **From New Zealand**, prices are significantly higher: rarely less than NZ$2200, rising to over NZ$3000 for a more flexible high-season flight.

If Greece is only one stop on a longer journey, you might consider buying a **Round-the-World** (RTW) fare, although Greece never seems to be included in any of the cheaper deals, which means you might have to stump up around Aus$3500/NZ$4000 for one of the fully flexible multi-stop fares from One World or the Star Alliance. At that price, you may be better off with a cheaper deal and a separate ticket to Greece once you get to Europe.

Flights from South Africa

There are currently no direct flights from **South Africa** to Athens, though Hellenic Imperial plan to restart one. Alternative routes include EgyptAir (W egyptair.com) via Cairo, Emirates (W emirates .com), Etihad (W etihadairways.com) or Qatar Airways (W qatarairways.com) via the Gulf, or just about any of the major European airlines through their domestic hub. Prices start at R6500–7000 for a good low-season deal, to double that in high season or if the cheaper seats have gone.

FLIGHT AGENTS

Charter Flight Centre UK ☎ 0208/714 0010, W charterflights .co.uk. Booking for a huge range of charter flights from the UK and Ireland.
Flight Centre W flightcentre.com. Low-cost airfares worldwide from their local websites, plus rail passes and more.
North South Travel UK ☎ 01245/608291, W northsouthtravel .co.uk. Friendly, competitive flight agency, offering discounted fares worldwide. Profits are used to support projects in the developing world, especially the promotion of sustainable tourism.
Skyscanner W skyscanner.net. Comprehensive flight search site that includes charter and budget airlines.
STA Travel UK ☎ 0871/2300 040, US ☎ 1-800/781-4040, Australia ☎ 134 782, New Zealand ☎ 0800/474 400, South Africa ☎ 0861/781 781, W statravel.com. Worldwide specialists in independent travel; also student IDs, travel insurance, car rental, rail passes, and more. Good discounts for students and under-26s.
Trailfinders UK ☎ 0845/054 6060, Ireland ☎ 021/464 8800, Australia ☎ 1300/780 212, W trailfinders.com. One of the best-informed and most efficient agents for independent travellers.
Travel CUTS Canada ☎ 1-800/667-2887, US ☎ 1-800/592-2887, W travelcuts.com. Popular, long-established student-travel organization, with good worldwide offers; not only for students.

Trains

As a result of the economic crisis, all international and some domestic **Greek rail routes** have been **suspended**. However, that doesn't necessarily mean that you can't travel to Greece by train (though of course the train won't take you to any of the islands); the most practical route **from Britain** was always in any event to cross France and Italy before embarking on the ferry from Bari or Brindisi to Pátra (Patras), and that remains unaffected. Many of the ferries from Italy call at Corfu on the way (see box below), and this route is relatively handy for the rest of the Ionian islands too; for anywhere else there are connecting buses from Pátra to Athens and the rest of the ferry network.

The journey takes two-and-a-half days at least and will almost always work out more expensive than flying. It also takes a fair bit of planning, since there's no through train and tickets have to be bought from several separate operators. However, you do have the chance to stop over on the way, while with an InterRail (for European residents only; W interrailnet.com) or Eurail (for all others; W eurail .com) pass you can take in Greece as part of a wider rail trip around Europe. Booking well in advance (essential in summer) and going for the cheapest seats on each leg, you can theoretically buy individual tickets to Athens for less than £150 each way (marginally less to Corfu), not including the incidental expenses along the way. Using rail passes will cost you more, but give far more flexibility. For full details, check out the Man in Seat 61 website (W seat61.com).

ITALY–GREECE FERRIES

Sailing from **Italy to Greece**, you've a choice of four ports; ferries run year-round, but services are reduced December to April. The shortest routes and most frequent ferries link Bari and Brindisi with Corfu, Igoumenítsa (the port of the western Greek mainland) and Pátra (at the northwest tip of the Peloponnese). Ferries also sail from Ancona and Venice to Pátra via Igoumenítsa/Corfu. These longer routes are more expensive, but the extra cost closely matches what you'll pay in Italian motorway tolls and fuel to get further south. On most ferries you can stop over in Corfu for no extra charge. For direct access to Athens and the Aegean islands head for Pátra, from where you can cut across country to Pireás.

The following companies operate ferries: schedule and booking details for all of them are also available at W openseas.gr and W viamare.com.

Agoudimos W agoudimos-lines.com. Bari and Brindisi to Corfu and Igoumenítsa.
ANEK W anek.gr. Ancona and Venice to Corfu, Igoumenítsa and Pátra.
Endeavor Lines W endeavor-lines.com. Brindisi to Corfu, Igoumenítsa and Pátra.
Minoan Lines W minoan.gr. Ancona and Venice to Corfu, Igoumenítsa and Pátra.
Superfast Ferries W superfast.com. Ancona and Bari to Corfu, Igoumenítsa and Pátra.
Ventouris Ferries W ventouris.gr. Bari and Brindisi to Corfu, Igoumenítsa, Kefaloniá and Zákynthos.

Car and ferry

Driving to Greece can be worth considering if you want to explore en route, or are going to stay for an extended period. The most popular **route** is again down through France and Italy to catch one of the Adriatic ferries (see box, p.27); this is much the best way to get to the Ionian islands, and to Athens for ferries to most other islands. The far longer alternative through Eastern Europe (Hungary, Romania and Bulgaria) is fraught with visa problems, and only makes sense if you are heading for the northeast Aegean islands or want to explore northern Greece on the way.

Tour operators

Every mainstream **tour operator** includes Greece in its portfolio. You'll find far more interesting alternatives, however, through the small **specialist agencies**. As well as traditional village-based accommodation and less-known islands, many also offer **walking** or **nature holidays** and other special interests such as **yoga**, **art** and above all **sailing**, with options ranging from shore-based clubs with dinghy tuition, through organized yacht flotillas to bareboat or skippered charters.

PACKAGE OPERATORS

Grecian Tours Australia ☎ 03/9663 3711, ⓦ greciantours
.com.au. A variety of accommodation and sightseeing tours, plus flights.
Greek Sun Holidays UK ☎ 01732/740317, ⓦ www.greeksun
.co.uk. Good-value package holidays mainly in smaller islands of the
Dodecanese, northeast Aegean and Cyclades; also tailor-made
island-hopping itineraries.
Hidden Greece UK ☎ 020/8758 4707, ⓦ hidden-greece.co.uk.
Specialist agent putting together tailor-made packages to smaller
destinations at reasonable prices.
Homeric Tours US ☎ 1-800/223-5570, ⓦ homerictours.com.
Hotel packages, individual tours, escorted group tours and fly/drive deals.
Good source of inexpensive flights.
Inntravel UK ☎ 01653/617001, ⓦ inntravel.co.uk. High-quality
packages and tailor-made itineraries and fly-drives to unspoilt areas of
Crete and smaller islands; also walking and other special-interest holidays.
Olympic Holidays UK ☎ 0800/093 3322, ⓦ olympicholidays
.com. Huge package holiday company serving a wide variety of islands;
all standards from cheap and cheerful to five-star, and often a good
source of last-minute bargains and cheap flights.
Simply Travel UK ☎ 0871/231 4050, ⓦ simplytravel.co.uk.
Although part of the vast TUI organization, Simply still manages a personal
touch, and has plenty of excellent, upmarket accommodation in Crete and
the Ionian islands.
Sun Island Tours Australia ☎ 1300/665 673, ⓦ sunisland
tours.com.au. Greece specialist offering an assortment of
island-hopping, fly-drives, cruises and guided land-tour options, as
well as tailor-made.
Sunvil Holidays UK ☎ 020/8758 4758, ⓦ sunvil.co.uk/greece.
High-quality outfit with a wide range of holidays to many islands.

VILLA AND APARTMENT AGENTS

Cachet Travel UK ☎ 020/8847 8700, ⓦ cachet-travel.co.uk.
Attractive range of villas and apartments in the more unspoilt south and
west of Crete, plus Híos and remote corners of Sámos.
CV Travel UK ☎ 0870/606 0013, ⓦ cvtravel.co.uk, US
☎ 1-866/308-1343, ⓦ cvtravelusa.com. Quality villas and luxury
resorts, principally in the Ionian islands and Crete.
Greek Islands Club UK ☎ 020/8232 9780, ⓦ gicthevilla
collection.com. Specialist in upmarket villas with private pools,
especially in the Ionian islands.
Pure Crete UK ☎ 01444/881 402, ⓦ purecrete.com. Lovely,
converted cottages and farmhouses in western Crete, plus walking,
wildlife and other special-interest trips.
Simpson Travel UK ☎ 0845/811 6502, ⓦ simpsontravel.com.
Classy villas, upmarket hotels and village hideaways in selected areas of
Crete, the Ionians, Skópelos, Sámos and more.
Travel à la Carte UK ☎ 01635/33800, ⓦ travelalacarte
.co.uk. Villas and apartments on Corfu, Skiáthos, Paxí, Sými and
more, plus painting, photography, yoga and creative writing courses
on Paxí.

SMALL GROUP TOURS AND YOGA HOLIDAYS

Astra US ☎ 303/321-5403, ⓦ astragreece.com. Very personal,
idiosyncratic tours, some women-only, led by veteran Hellenophile
Thordis Simonsen, during spring and autumn.
Hellenic Adventures US ☎ 1-800/851-6349 or 612/827-0937,
ⓦ hellenicadventures.com. Small-group escorted tours led by
enthusiastic expert guides, as well as itineraries for independent
travellers, cruises and other travel services.
True Greece US ☎ 1- 800/817-7098, ⓦ truegreece.com.
Upmarket escorted travel and custom-made trips including special
interests such as cooking.
Free Spirit Travel UK ☎ 01273/564230, ⓦ freespirituk.com.
Yoga and meditation in western Crete, plus some walking holidays.
Yoga Plus UK ☎ 01273/276175, ⓦ yogaplus.co.uk. Ashtanga yoga
courses in a remote part of southern Crete.
Skyros Holidays UK ☎ 01983/865566, ⓦ skyros.com. Holistic
yoga, dance, art, music, "personal growth" and more on the island of
Skýros, as well as well-regarded writers' workshops.

WALKING AND CYCLING

ATG Oxford UK ☎ 01865/315678, ⓦ atg-oxford.co.uk. Somewhat
pricey but high-standard guided walks on Crete and select Cyclades
islands.
Classic Adventures US ☎ 1-800/777-8090, ⓦ classic
adventures.com. Spring or autumn rural cycling tours on Crete.
Exodus UK ☎ 0845/287 7511, ⓦ exodus.co.uk. Week-long treks
exploring southern Évvia.

Explore Worldwide US ☎ 1-800/715-1746, Can ☎ 1-888
/216-3401, UK ☎ 01252/760 000, ⓦ exploreworldwide.com. A
variety of tours, many combining hiking with sailing between the islands.
Freewheeling Adventures Canada & US ☎ 1-800/672-0775,
ⓦ freewheeling.ca. Eight-day cycling tours of Crete.
Jonathan's Tours ☎ 0033/561046447, ⓦ jonathanstours.com.
Family-run walking holidays on Crete and smaller islands.
Ramblers Holidays UK ☎ 01707/331133, ⓦ ramblersholidays
.co.uk. Walking trips including spring hiking in Crete, Dodecanese
island-hopping and combined island and mainland treks.
Sherpa Expeditions UK ☎ 020/8577 2717, ⓦ www.sherpa-
walking-holidays.co.uk. Self-guided and escorted 8-day outings on Crete.
Walking Plus UK ☎ 020/8835 8303, ⓦ walkingplus.co.uk.
Enthusiastic Gilly and Robin Cameron Cooper offer guided and
self-guided off-season walks in the Cyclades.

WILDLIFE HOLIDAYS

Naturetrek UK ☎ 01962/733051, ⓦ naturetrek.co.uk. Fairly pricey
but expertly led one- or two-week natural history tours; offerings include
springtime birds and flora on Sámos, and wildlife of Crete.
The Travelling Naturalist UK ☎ 01305/267994, ⓦ www
.naturalist.co.uk. Wildlife holiday company that runs excellent
birdwatching and wild-flower-spotting trips to Crete and Lésvos.

SAILING AND WATERSPORTS

Northwest Passage US ☎ 1-800/RECREATE, ⓦ nwpassage.com.
Excellent sea-kayaking tours in Crete and the islands, including
island-hopping by kayak; also yoga, hiking and art in Crete.
Nautilus Yachting UK ☎ 01732/867445, ⓦ nautilus-yachting
.co.uk. Bareboat yacht charter, flotillas and sailing courses from a wide
variety of marinas.
Neilson UK ☎ 0844/879 8155, ⓦ neilson.co.uk. Half a dozen
excellent beach activity clubs, plus flotillas and bareboat charter.
Seafarer Cruising & Sailing UK ☎ 020/8324 3118,
ⓦ seafarercruises.com. Ionian and Argo-Saronic flotillas, beach club,
bareboat charter, courses and small-boat island cruises.
Sportif UK ☎ 01273/844919, ⓦ sportif.travel. Windsurfing
packages and instruction on Crete, Kos, Rhodes, Sámos, Lésvos and
Kárpathos.
Sunsail UK ☎ 0870/112 8612, ⓦ sunsail.com. Beach club, flotillas
and bareboat mainly in the Ionians and Sporades.
Swim Trek US ☎ 1-877/455-SWIM, UK ☎ 01273/739 713,
ⓦ swimtrek.com. Week-long tours of Náxos and the small islands
around it, swimming between the islands.
Valef Yachts US ☎ 1-800/223-3845, ⓦ valefyachts.com.
Small-boat cruises around the islands and luxury crewed yacht or
motor-boat charter.

Getting around

**Inter-island travel mostly means taking
ferries, catamarans or hydrofoils, which
will eventually get you to any of the**
sixty-plus inhabited isles. Internal flights
are relatively expensive, but can save
literally days of travel: Athens–Rhodes is
just two hours return, versus 28 hours by
boat. The standard public transport on
the Greek islands is the bus, although
services vary from rudimentary to quite
comprehensive. The best way to supplement buses is to rent a scooter, motorbike
or car – in any substantial town or resort
you will find at least one rental outlet.

By sea

There are several varieties of sea-going vessels:
ordinary ferries; the new generation of "**high-
speed**" boats (*tahyplóö*) and catamarans, which
usually carry cars; **roll-on-roll-off** short-haul barges,
nicknamed *pandófles* ("slippers"), **hydrofoils**,
similarly quick but which carry only passengers; and
local **kaïkia**, small boats which do short hops and
excursions in season.

Ferry connections are indicated both on the
route **map** (see p.58) and in the "Arrival and
Departure" sections throughout the book.
Schedules are notoriously erratic, however, and
must be verified seasonally; details given are for
departures between late June and early September.
When sailing in season from **Pireás** to the Cyclades
or Dodecanese, you should have a choice of at least
two, sometimes three, daily departures. **Out-of-
season** departure frequencies drop sharply, with
less populated islands connected only two or three
times weekly.

Reliable departure information is available from
the local **port police** (*limenarhío*) at all island and
mainland harbours of any size; around Athens there
are offices at Pireás (☎ 210 45 50 000), Rafína
(☎ 22940 28888) and Lávrio (☎ 22920 25249). Busier
port police have automated phone-answering
services with an English option for schedule information. Many companies produce annual
schedule booklets, which may not be adhered to
as the season wears on – check their **websites** (if
any) for current information, or refer to ⓦ gtp.gr or,
even better, ⓦ openseas.gr.

Ferries

Except for some subsidized peripheral routes where
older rust-buckets are still used, the Greek **ferry
fleet** is fairly contemporary. **Routes and speed** can
vary enormously, however; a journey from Pireás to
Santoríni, for instance, can take anything from five
to ten hours.

Tickets are best bought a day before departure, unless you need to reserve a cabin berth or space for a car. During holiday periods – Christmas/New Year, the week before and after Easter, late July to early September – and around the dates of elections, ferries need to be booked at least ten days in advance. Ticketing for most major routes is computerized and you cannot **buy** your ticket on board. Many companies allow you to reserve places and pay online but tickets must still be picked up at the port at least fifteen minutes before departure.

The cheapest **fare class**, which you'll automatically be sold unless you specify otherwise, is *ikonomikí thési*, which gives you the run of most boats except for the upper-class restaurant and bar. Most newer boats seem expressly designed to frustrate summertime travellers attempting to sleep on deck. For long overnight journeys, it's worth considering the few extra euros for a **cabin bunk**; second-class cabins are typically quadruple, while **first-class** double cabins with en-suite bathrooms can cost as much as a flight.

Motorbikes and cars get issued separate tickets; the latter have risen in price dramatically of late to as much as five times the passenger fare, depending on size. For example Sámos–Ikaría costs around €12 per person/€40 per car, while Sámos–Pireás is about €28/€100. It's really only worth taking a car to the larger islands like Crete, Rhodes, Híos, Lésvos, Sámos, Corfu or Kefaloniá, and only if staying a week or more. Otherwise, it is cheaper to leave your car on the mainland and rent another on arrival.

Hydrofoils, catamarans and high-speed boats

Hydrofoils – commonly known as *dhelfínia* or "Flying Dolphins" – are at least twice as expensive as ordinary ferries, but their network neatly fills gaps in ferry scheduling, often with more convenient departure times. Their main drawback is that they are the first vessels to get cancelled in bad weather and even in moderate seas are not for the seasick-prone. Many don't operate – or are heavily reduced in frequency – from October to June. Hydrofoils aren't allowed to carry scooters or bicycles.

Catamarans and high-speed boats (tahýplia) are ruthlessly air conditioned, usually without deck seating and with Greek TV blaring at you from multiple screens – paying extra for *dhiakikriméni thési* (upper class) merely gets you a better view. Car fares are normal, though passenger **tickets** are at least double a comparable ferry journey, ie similar to hydrofoil rates. Similarly, many don't run between October and April.

Small boats

In season, small boats known as **kaïkia** and **small ferries** sail between adjacent islands and to a few of the more obscure satellite islets. These are extremely useful and often very pleasant, but seldom cheaper than mainline services. The more consistent *kaïki* links are noted in the text, though the only firm information is to be had on the quayside. Swarms of **taxi boats** are a feature of many islands; these shuttle clients on set routes to remote beaches or ports which can only be reached arduously, if at all, overland. Costs on these can be pretty stiff, usually per person but occasionally per boat.

By plane

Scheduled Greek **domestic flights** are operated by national carrier Olympic Airlines (including its subsidiary Olympic Aviation; ☎801 11 44 444, ⓦwww.olympicairlines.com), Aegean Airlines (☎801 11 20 000, ⓦwww.aegeanair.com) and Sky Express (☎281 02/23 500, ⓦwww.skyexpress.gr). They cover a broad network of island destinations, though most routes are to and from Athens or Thessaloníki. Aegean often undercuts Olympic fare-wise, and surpasses it service-wise, though services are less frequent; Sky Express, established 2007, is pricey and restricted to various routes between Iráklio (Crete) and certain Aegean islands. All three airlines are geared to web and call-centre **e-ticket sales**, there being few walk-in town offices. Tickets bought through travel agencies attract a minimum €10 commission charge.

Fares to/between the islands cost at least double the cost of a deck-class ferry journey, but on inter-island routes poorly served by boat (Rhodes–Sámos, for example), consider this time well bought, and indeed some subsidized peripheral routes cost less than a hydrofoil/catamaran journey. The cheapest web fares on Aegean are non-changeable and non-refundable, but with Olympic you can **change** your flight date, space permitting, without penalty up to 24 hours before your original departure.

Island flights are often full in peak season; if they're an essential part of your plans, make **reservations** at least a month in advance. Waiting lists exist and are worth signing on to, as there are almost always cancellations. Many Olympic flights use small prop planes which won't fly in strong winds or (depending on the airport) after dark, so beware of leaving tight connections with connecting international flights; Aegean and Sky

Express use more robust jets. A 15kg baggage **weight limit** can be strictly enforced; if, however, you've just arrived from overseas or purchased your ticket outside Greece, you're allowed the standard international limits (20–23kg).

By bus

On the islands there are usually buses to connect the port and main town (if different) for ferry arrivals or departures. The national network is run by a syndicate of private operators based on each island, known as the **KTEL** (*Kratikó Tamío Ellinikón Leoforíon;* ❸ 14505 premium call charge and no national online timetable).

In island capitals or large cities in Crete the **ticketing** is often computerized, sometimes with assigned seating, but otherwise it's first-come, first-served, with some standing allowed, and tickets dispensed on the spot by a conductor (*ispráktoras*). Prices are fixed according to distance and there are no cheap advance booking fares; Iráklio–Haniá costs €13.80, for example, but no other island except Évvia will have fares much in excess of €5.

By car, motorcycle and taxi

The islands are blessed with dramatic coastal and mountain scenery, which is undoubtedly a joy to drive through. You should, however, bear in mind that it has one of the highest fatal **accident rates** in Europe. Local driving habits can be atrocious; overtaking on bends, barging out from side roads and failing to signal manoeuvres are common practices. **Drunk driving** is also a major issue, especially on Sunday afternoons, public holidays or late at night. **Road conditions** can be very poor, from bad surfaces and inadequate signposting to unmarked railway crossings. There is a limited but

growing number of **motorways** on which tolls (€2–3) are levied, adding over €30, for example on the drive from Athens to Thessaloníki. **Fuel**, whether regular unleaded (*amólyvdhi*), super or diesel, is currently over €1.65 per litre across the country, often €1.80-plus in remoter areas. Be aware that many petrol stations close after 8pm and on Sundays, meaning quite a hunt in rural areas at those times.

Parking in almost every mainland town, plus the biggest island centres, is uniformly a nightmare owing to oversubscription. **Pay-and-display** systems, plus residents-only schemes, are common, and it's rarely clear where you obtain tickets.

Rules of the road

As in all of continental Europe, you **drive on the right** in Greece. Uphill drivers demand their **right of way**, as do the first to approach a one-lane bridge; **flashed headlights** usually mean the opposite of what they do in the UK or North America, here signifying that the other driver insists on coming through or overtaking. However, this gesture rapidly repeated from someone approaching means they're warning you of a police control-point ahead.

Seat-belt use (and helmet wearing on scooters and motorcycles) is compulsory and children under the age of 10 are not allowed to sit in the front seats of cars; infractions of these rules are punishable by fines. It's illegal to drive away from any kind of **accident** – or to move the vehicles before the police appear – and where serious injury has resulted to the other party you can be held at a police station for up to 24 hours.

Car rental

Car rental in Greece starts at around €300 a week in peak season for the smallest vehicle from a one-off outlet or local chain, including unlimited

---

SIX MEMORABLE JOURNEYS

Kefaloniá's West Coast The road route north from Argostóli offers vistas of the Lixoúri Peninsula, Mýrtos beach and picturesque Ássos. See p.496.

The approach to Samothráki The ferry from Alexandhroúpoli allows Samothraki's profile, dominated by majestic Mount Fengari, to loom into focus. See p.408.

Mount Psilorítis, Crete Drive via Týlissos and Anóyia for sweeping views of the fertile valleys around Mount Psilorítis. See p.218.

Náxos to Amorgós Take the ferry from fertile Náxos via the delightful minor Cyclades to the imposing coast of Amorgós. See p.173.

Mastic villages, Híos Glimpse the alluring Mastic coast and marvel at the unique architecture of the villages on a drive through southern Híos. See p.377.

The Zákynthos circuit The anti-clockwise boat tour of the island takes you to the famous Blue caves and Shipwreck Bay. See p.502.

mileage, tax and insurance. At other times, at smaller local outfits, you can get terms of €30 per day, all inclusive, with even better **rates** for three days or more – or prebooked on the internet. Rates for open **jeeps** vary from €65 to €100 per day.

Rental prices in Greece almost never include **collision damage waiver** (CDW) and personal insurance. The CDW typically has a deductible charge of €400–600, which may be levied for even the tiniest scratch or missing mudguard. To avoid this, it is strongly recommended that you pay the €5–7 extra per day for full coverage. Frequent travellers should consider **annual excess insurance** through Insurance 4 Car Hire (🔵www.insurance4carhire.com), which will cover all UK- and North America-based drivers.

All agencies will require a blank **credit card** slip as a deposit (destroyed when you return the vehicle safely); minimum **age requirements** vary from 21 to 23. **Driving licences** issued by any European Economic Area state are honoured, but an **International Driving Permit** is required by all other drivers (despite claims by unscrupulous agencies). You can be arrested and charged if caught by the traffic police without an IDP if you require one.

Avance, Antena, Payless, Kosmos, National/Alamo, Reliable, Tomaso and Eurodollar are dependable Greek, or smaller international, chains with branches on many islands; all are cheaper than Hertz, Sixt or Avis. Specific local recommendations are given in the guide.

Bringing your own car

If you intend to **drive your own car to and within Greece**, remember that insurance contracted in any EU state is valid in any other, but in many cases this is only third-party cover. Competition in the industry is intense, however, so many UK insurers will throw in full, pan-European cover for free or for a nominal sum, for up to sixty days. Those with proof of AA/RAC/AAA membership are given free road assistance from ELPA, the Greek equivalent, which runs **breakdown services** on several of the larger islands; in an emergency ring ☎10400.

EU citizens bringing their own cars are free to circulate in the country for six months, or until their home-based road tax or insurance expires, whichever happens first; keeping a car in Greece for longer entails more paperwork. **Non-EU nationals** will get a car entered in their passport; the carnet normally allows you to keep a vehicle in Greece for up to six months, exempt from road tax.

Scooter and motorcycle rental

Small **motor scooters** with automatic transmission, known in Greek as *mihanákia* or *papákia* (little ducks), are good transport for all but the steepest terrain. They're available for rent on most islands for €12–18 per day. Prices can be bargained down out of peak season, or for a longer rental period. Only models of 80cc and above are powerful enough for two riders in mountainous areas, which includes most islands.

True **motorbikes** (*mihanés*) with manual transmissions and safer tyres are less common than they ought to be. With the proper licence, bikes of 125cc and up are available in many resorts for around €20 per day. **Quads** are also increasingly offered – without doubt the most stupid-looking and impractical conveyance yet devised, and very unstable on turns – make sure helmets are supplied.

Reputable establishments demand a full **motorcycle driving licence** (Class B) for any engine over 80cc (Greek law actually stipulates "over 50cc"). You will usually have to leave your passport as a deposit. Failure to carry the correct licence on your person also attracts a stiff fine, though some agencies still demand this rather than a passport as security.

Many rental outfits will offer you (an often ill-fitting) **crash helmet** (*krános*), and some will make you sign a waiver of liability if you refuse it. Helmet-wearing is required by law, with a €185 fine levied for failure to do so; on some smaller islands the rule is laxly enforced, on others random police roadblocks do a brisk commerce in citations, to foreigners and locals alike.

Before riding off, always check the **brakes** and **electrics**; dealers often keep the front brakes far too loose, with the commendable intention of preventing you going over the handlebars. Make sure also that there's a kick-start as backup to the battery, since ignition switches commonly fail. If you **break down** on a scooter or motorcycle you're often responsible for returning the machine, although the better outlets offer a free retrieval service.

Taxis

Greek **taxis** are among the cheapest in the Mediterranean – so long as you get an honest driver who switches the meter on and doesn't use high-tech devices to doctor the reading. Use of the meter is mandatory within city or town limits, where Tariff 1 applies, while in rural areas or between midnight and 5am Tariff 2 is in effect. On certain islands, set rates apply on specific fixed routes – these might only depart when full. Otherwise, throughout Greece the meter starts at €0.85, though the minimum **fare** is €1.75; baggage in the boot is charged at €0.35 per piece. Additionally, there are surcharges of €2 for leaving or entering an airport (€3 for Athens), and €0.80 for leaving a harbour area. If you summon a taxi by phone on spec, there's a €1.50 charge; the meter starts running from the moment the driver begins heading towards you. All categories of supplemental charges must be set out on a card affixed to the dashboard. For a week or so before and after Orthodox Easter, and Christmas, a *filodhórima* or gratuity of about ten percent is levied.

By bike

Cycling in Greece is not such hard going as you might imagine (except in summer), especially on one of the mountain bikes that are now the rule at rental outfits; they rarely cost more than €8 a day. You do, however, need steady nerves, as roads are generally narrow with no verges or bike lanes and Greek drivers are notoriously inconsiderate to cyclists.

If you have your own bike, consider taking it along on the **plane** (it's free if within your 20–23kg international air allowance, but arrange it in writing with the airline beforehand to avoid huge charges at check-in). Once in Greece you can take a bike for free on most ferries and in the luggage bays of buses. Any small spare parts you might need are best brought along, since specialist shops are rare.

Accommodation

There are vast numbers of tourist beds throughout the Greek Islands, and most of the year you can rely on turning up pretty much anywhere and finding something. At Easter and in July and August, however, you can run into problems unless you've booked in advance, especially in the more popular resorts and islands. The economic crisis and subsequent loss of domestic tourism has tended to depress prices, and what you pay may depend on how far you are willing to bargain.

Many of the big hotels and self-catering complexes are pre-booked by package-holiday companies for the whole season. Although they may have vacancies if you just turn up, non-package visitors are far more likely to find themselves staying in

smaller, simpler places which usually describe themselves simply as "**rooms**", or as apartments or studios. Standards here can vary from spartan (though invariably clean) to luxurious, but the vast majority are purpose-built blocks where every room is en suite, and where the minimal furnishings are well adapted to the local climate – at least in summer.

Seasons

There are typically three **seasons** which affect prices: October to April (low), May, June and September (mid) and July and August (high) – though **Easter** and the first two weeks of August may be in a higher category still. Urban hotels with a predominantly business clientele tend to charge the same rates all year. Elsewhere, places that have significant domestic tourism, such as Náfplio, the Pelion or the Argo-Saronic islands, frequently charge significantly more at weekends.

Many of the smaller places offering rooms **close from October to April**. In winter, then, you may have to stay in hotels in the main towns or ports. On smaller islands, there may be just one hotel and a single taverna that stays open year-round. Be warned also that resort or harbour hotels which do operate through the winter are likely to have a certain number of prostitutes as long-term guests; licensed prostitution is legal in Greece, and the management may consider this the most painless way to keep the bills paid.

Hotels

The tourist police set official **categories** for hotels, starting with L (Luxury) and then from A down to the rarely encountered E class; all except the top category have to keep within set price limits. The letter system is being slowly replaced with a star grading system; L is five-star, E is no-star, etc. Ratings correspond to the facilities available (lifts, dining room, pool etc), a box-ticking exercise which doesn't always reflect the actual quality of the hotel; there are plenty of D-class hotels which are in practice smarter and more comfortable than nearby C-class outfits.

C-class hotels and below have only to provide the most rudimentary of continental breakfasts – sometimes optional for an extra charge – while B-class and above will usually offer a buffet breakfast including cheese, cold meats, eggs and cereals.

Single rooms are rare, and generally poor value – you'll often have to pay the full double-room price

ACCOMMODATION PRICES

The price we quote is for the establishment's **cheapest double room in high season** – there may well be other rooms that cost more. For much of the year, however, you can expect to pay a bit less.

Prices are for the room only, except where otherwise indicated; fancier places often include breakfast in the price – we indicate this in the listing, but check when booking.

By law, **prices must be displayed** on the back of the door of your room, or over the reception desk. You should never pay more than this, and in practice it is rare to pay as much as the sign says. If you feel you're being overcharged, threaten to make a report to the tourist office or police, who will generally take your side in such cases.

or haggle for around a third off; on the other hand, larger groups and families can almost always find triple and quadruple rooms, and fancier hotels may have **family suites** (two rooms sharing one bathroom), all of which can be very good value.

Private rooms and apartments

Many places categorized as apartments or rooms are every bit as comfortable as hotels, and in the lower price ranges are usually more congenial and better value. At their most basic, **rooms** (*dhomátia* – but usually spotted by a "Rooms for Rent" or Zimmer Frei sign) might be literally a room in someone's house, a bare space with a bed and a hook on the back of the door, and washing facilities outside; the sparse facilities offset by the disarming hospitality you'll be offered as part of the family. However, these days almost all are purpose-built, with comfortable en-suite accommodation and balconies – at the fancier end of the scale you'll find studio and apartment complexes with marble floors, pools, bars and children's playgrounds. Many have a variety of rooms at different prices, so if possible always ask to see the room first. Places described as studios usually have a small kitchenette – a fridge, sink and a couple of hotplates in the room itself – while apartments generally have at least one bedroom and separate kitchen/living room.

Areas to **look for rooms**, along with recommendations of the best places, are included in the guide. The rooms may also find you, as owners descend on ferry or bus arrivals to fill any space they have, sometimes with photos of their premises. This can be great, but you can also be in for a nasty surprise – usually because the rooms are much further than you had been led to believe, or bear no relation to the pictures. In some places the practice has been outlawed. In the more developed island resorts, where package holiday-makers predominate, room owners may insist on a minimum stay of a few days, or even a week.

Rooms proprietors usually ask to keep your **passport**: ostensibly "for the tourist police", but in reality to prevent you leaving with an unpaid bill. Some may be satisfied with just taking down the details, and they'll almost always return the documents once you get to know them, or if you need them for changing money.

If you are **stranded**, or arrive very late in a remote village, you may well find someone with an unlicensed room prepared to earn extra money by putting you up. This should not be counted on, but things work out more often than not.

Villas and longer-term rentals

Although one of the great dreams of Greek travel is finding an idyllic coastal villa and renting it for virtually nothing for a whole month, there's no chance at all of your dream coming true in

HOT WATER AND AIR CONDITIONING

When checking out a room, always ask about the status of **hot water** and **air conditioning**. Most modern rooms and apartments have air conditioning (indicted by a/c in our listings), but it's frequently an optional extra and you'll be charged an additional €5 or so a night to use it. Just occasionally you may also be asked to pay extra for hot water. A more likely problem is that there won't be enough: rooftop solar heaters are popular and effective, but shared solar-powered tanks tend to run out of hot water in the post-beach shower crunch around 6–7pm, with no more available until the next day. A heater, either as a backup or primary source, is more reliable.

SIX SPECIAL PLACES TO STAY

Heaven on Naoussa, Páros Individually decorated rooms, crisp white sheets and views to die for at this heavenly B&B. See p.159

Karimalis Winery, Ikaría A winery and organic farm running wine and cooking courses on little-visited Ikaría. See p.369

Miliá Mountain Retreat, Crete A beautiful eco retreat in Crete's White Mountains offering plenty of activities and fresh organic food. See p.256

Mýlos tou Markétou, Mílos A sixteenth-century windmill converted into a stylish apartment. See p.127

Polikandia, Folégandhros A well-priced, well-designed boutique hotel on one of Greece's less discovered islands. See p.184

Spirit of the Knights, Rhodes Exquisite B&B with a lovely courtyard tucked away in Rhodes old town. See p.272

---

modern Greece. All the best villas are contracted out to **agents** and let through foreign operators. Even if you do find one empty for a week or two, renting it locally usually costs far more than it would have done to arrange from home. There, specialist operators (see p.28) represent some superb places, from simple to luxurious, and costs can be very reasonable, especially if shared between a few people. Several of the companies listed will arrange stays on two islands over two weeks.

Having said the above, if you do arrive and decide you want to drop roots for a while, you can still strike lucky if you don't mind avoiding the obvious coastal tourist spots, and are happy with relatively modest accommodation. Pick an untouristed village, get yourself known and ask about; you might still pick up a wonderful deal. Out of season your chances are much better – even in touristy areas, between October and March (sometimes as late as April and May) you can bargain a very good rate, especially for stays of a month or more. Travel agents are another good source of information on what's available locally, and many rooms places have an apartment on the side or know someone with one to rent.

Hostels and backpackers

Over the years most traditional youth **hostels** in the islands have closed down; competition from inexpensive rooms meant that in general they were simply not cost-effective. However, those that survive are generally very good, and there's a new generation of youth-oriented **backpackers** on the more popular islands, where social life and a party atmosphere may take precedence over a good night's sleep. Few of them are members of any official organization – though an IYHF card or student ID may save you a few euros – and virtually

none will have a curfew or any restrictive regulations. Prices for a dorm bed vary from as little as €12 in a simple, traditional hostel to as much as €25 in the fancier backpackers.

If you're planning to spend a few nights in hostels, **IYHF membership** is probably a worthwhile investment. By no means all Greek hostels offer discounts, but there are other membership benefits and the card may be accepted as student ID, for example. At official hostels you may be able to buy membership on the spot; otherwise visit ⓦhihostels.com from where you can apply via your local youth hostel association. For booking youth hostels online try either ⓦhihostels.com or ⓦhostelworld.com.

Camping

Officially recognized campsites range from ramshackle compounds to highly organized and rather soulless complexes, often dominated by camper vans. Most places cost in the region of €5–7 a night per person, plus €5–6 per tent or €6–8 per camper van, though at the fanciest sites rates for two people plus a tent can almost equal the price of a basic room. You will need at least a light sleeping bag, since even summer nights can get cool and damp; a foam pad lets you sleep in relative comfort almost anywhere. The website of the official Greek camping organization (ⓦpanhellenic-camping-union.gr) lists all authorized campsites, with booking for many of them.

Camping outside an official campsite (with or without a tent) is against the law – enforced in most tourist areas and on beaches. If you do camp rough, exercise sensitivity and discretion. Police will crack down on people camping (and especially littering) if a large community of campers develops. Off the beaten track nobody is very bothered, though it is always best to ask permission in the local taverna or café, and to be aware of rising crime, even in remote areas. If you want to camp near a beach, the best strategy is to find a sympathetic taverna, which in exchange for regular patronage will probably be willing to guard small valuables and let you use their facilities.

Food and drink

Although many visitors get by on moussaka or kalamári almost every night, there is a huge range to Greek cuisine, not least its wonderful mezédhes, seafood and juicy, fat olives. Despite depressed wages, most Greeks still eat out with friends or family at least once a week. The atmosphere is always relaxed and informal, with pretensions rare outside of the more chichi parts of Athens and certain major resorts. Drinking is traditionally meant to accompany food, though a range of bars and clubs exists.

Breakfast

Greeks don't generally eat **breakfast**, more often opting for a mid-morning snack (see below). This is reflected in the abysmal quality of most hotel "continental" offerings, where waxy orange squash, stewed coffee, processed cheese and meats, plus pre-packaged butter, honey and jam (confusingly called *marmeládha*), are the rule in all but the top establishments. There might be some fresh fruit, decent yoghurt and pure honey, if you are lucky. The only egg-and-bacon kinds of places are in resorts where foreigners congregate, or where there are returned North American- or Australian-Greeks. Such outlets can often be good value (€4–7 for the works, including coffee), especially if there's competition.

Picnics and snacks

Picnic ingredients are easily available at supermarkets, bakeries and greengrocers; sampling produce like cheese or olives is acceptable. Standard white **bread** is often of minimal nutritional value and inedible within a day of purchase, although rarer brown varieties such as *olikís* (wholemeal), *sikalísio* (rye bread) or *oktásporo* (multi-grain) fare better. Olives are ubiquitous, with the Kalamáta and Ámfissa varieties usually surpassing most local picks in quality.

Honey is the ideal topping for the famous local **yoghurt**, which is widely available in bulk. Sheepmilk yoghurt (*próvio*) is richer and sweeter than the more common cow's-milk. **Feta cheese** is found everywhere, often with a dozen varieties to choose from, made from goat's, sheep's or cow's milk in varying proportions. Harder *graviéra* is the second most popular cheese.

Greece imports very little produce from abroad, aside from bananas, the odd pineapple and a few mangoes. **Fruit** is relatively expensive and available mainly by season, though in more cosmopolitan spots one can find such things as avocados for much of the year. Reliable picnic fruits include cherries (June–July); *krystália*, small, heavenly green pears (Sept–Nov); *vaniliés*, orange- or red-fleshed plums (July–Oct); and kiwi (Oct–May). Less portable, but succulent, are figs, whose main season is August and September. Salad **vegetables** are more reasonably priced; besides the famous, enormous tomatoes (June–Sept), there's a bewildering variety of cool-season greens, including rocket, dill, enormous spring onions and lettuces.

Restaurants

Greek cuisine and **restaurants** are usually straightforward and still largely affordable – typically €12–20 per person for a substantial meal with house wine. Even when preparation is basic, raw

---

FAST FOOD GREEK STYLE

Traditional hot **snacks** are still easy to come by, although they are being elbowed aside by Western fast food at both international and nationwide Greek chains such as *Goody's* (burgers, pasta and salad bar), *Everest*, *Grigoris* and *Theios Vanias* (baked pastries and baguette sandwiches), and various pizzerias. Still, thousands of kebab shops (*souvladzídhika*) churn out *souvlákia*, either as small shish on wooden sticks or as *yíros* – doner kebab with garnish in pítta bread. Other snacks include cheese pies (*tyrópites*), spinach pies (*spanokópites*) and, less commonly, minced meat pies (*kreatópites*); these are found either at the baker's or some of the aforementioned chains.

TAVERNA TIPS

Since the idea of **courses** is foreign to Greek cuisine, starters, main dishes and salads often arrive together unless you request otherwise. The best strategy is to order a selection of mezédhes and salads to share, in local fashion. Waiters encourage you to take *horiátiki saláta* – the so-called Greek **salad**, including feta cheese – because it is the most expensive. If you only want tomato and cucumber, ask for *angourodomáta*. Cabbage-carrot (*láhano-karóto*) and lettuce (*maroúli*) are the typical cool-season salads.

Bread is generally counted as part of the "cover" charge (€0.50–1 per person), so you have to pay for it even if you don't eat any. Though menu prices are supposedly inclusive of all taxes and service, an extra **tip** of around five percent or simple rounding up of the bill is in order.

materials are usually wholesome and fresh. The best strategy is to **go where Greeks go**, often less obvious backstreet places that might not look much from outside but deliver the real deal. The two most common types of restaurant are the **estiatório** and the **taverna**. Distinctions are slight, though the former is more commonly found in the larger island towns and emphasize the more complicated, oven-baked casserole dishes termed *mayireftá* (literally, "cooked").

As one might expect, the identikit tavernas at resorts dominated by foreigners tend to make less effort, bashing out speedily grilled meat with pre-cut chips and rice containing the odd pea. You should beware of overcharging and bill-padding at such establishments too. In towns, growing numbers of pretentious "**koultouriárika**" restaurants boast fancy decor and Greek nouvelle (or fusion) cuisine with speciality wine lists, while producing little of substance.

Greeks generally eat very late in the evening, rarely venturing out until after 9pm and often arriving at midnight or later. Consequently, most restaurants operate flexible hours, varying according to the level of custom, and thus the **opening times** given throughout the listings should be viewed as approximate at best.

Estiatória

With their long hours and tiny profit margins, **estiatória** (sometimes known as *inomayiría*, "wine-and-cook-houses") are, alas, a vanishing breed. An *estiatório* will generally feature a variety of *mayireftá* such as moussaka, macaroni pie, meat or game stews, stuffed tomatoes or peppers, the oily vegetable casseroles called *ladherá*, and oven-baked meat and fish. Usually you point at the steam trays to choose these dishes. Batches are cooked in the morning and then left to stand, which is why the food is often **lukewarm**; most such dishes are in fact enhanced by being allowed to steep in their own juice.

Tavernas and psistariés

Tavernas range from the glitzy and fashionable to rough-and-ready beachside ones with seating under a reed canopy. Really primitive ones have a very limited (often unwritten) menu, but the more elaborate will offer some of the main *mayireftá* dishes mentioned above, as well as standard taverna fare: **mezédhes** (hors d'oeuvres) or **orektiká** (appetizers) and **tís óras** (meat and fish, fried or grilled to order). **Psistariés** (grill-houses) serve spit-roasted lamb, pork, goat, chicken or *kokorétsi* (grilled offal roulade). They will usually have a limited selection of mezédhes and salads (*salátes*), but no *mayireftá*. In rural areas, roadside *psistariés* are often called *exohiká kéndra*.

The most common **mezédhes** are *tzatzíki* (yoghurt, garlic and cucumber dip), *melitzanosaláta* (aubergine/eggplant dip), fried courgette/zucchini or aubergine/eggplant slices, *yígandes* (white haricot beans in hot tomato sauce), *tyropitákia* or *spanakopitákia* (small cheese or spinach pies), *revythókeftedhes* (chickpea patties similar to falafel), octopus salad and *mavromátika* (black-eyed peas).

Among **meats**, *souvláki* and chops are reliable choices; pork is usually better and cheaper than veal, especially as *pansétta* (spare ribs). The best *souvláki*, not always available, is lamb; more commonly encountered are rib chops (*païdhákia*); lamb roasted in tin foil (*exohikó*) is another favourite. *Keftédhes* (breadcrumbed meatballs), *biftékia* (pure-meat patties) and the spicy, coarse-grain sausages called *loukánika* are cheap and good. Chicken is widely available but typically battery-farmed. Other dishes worth trying are stewed goat (*gídha vrastí*) or baked goat (*katsíki stó foúrno*) – goat in general is typically free-range and organic.

Fish and seafood

Seafood can be one of the highlights of a trip to Greece, though there are some tips to bear in mind when ordering fish at a taverna or *psarotavérna*

VEGETARIANS

Vegetarians will find scarcely any dedicated meat-free restaurants at all in Greece. That is not to say that they cannot enjoy excellent food, however. The best solution in tavernas or ouzerís is to assemble a meal from vegetarian *mezédhes* and salads and, in *estiatória* especially, keep an eye open for the delicious *ladhera*, vegetables baked in various sauces.

(specialist seafood restaurant). The standard procedure is to go to the glass cooler and pick your specimen, then have it weighed (uncleaned) in your presence. Overcharging, especially where a printed menu is absent, is not uncommon; have weight and price confirmed clearly. Taverna owners often comply only minimally with the requirement to indicate when seafood is **frozen** – look for the abbreviation "kat", "k" or just an asterisk on the Greek-language side of the menu. If the price, almost invariably quoted by the kilo, seems too good to be true, it's almost certainly farmed. The choicest varieties, such as red mullet, *tsipoúra* (gilt-head bream), seabass or *fangrí* (common bream), will be expensive if wild – €45–70 per kilo. Less esteemed species tend to cost €20–35 per kilo but are usually quoted at €6–9 per portion.

Fish caught in the summer months tend to be smaller and drier, and so are served with *ladholé-mono* (oil and lemon) sauce. An inexpensive May–June treat is fresh, grilled or fried *bakaliáros* (hake), the classic UK fish-and-chip shop species. *Gávros* (anchovy), *atherína* (sand smelts) and *sardhélles* (sardines) are late-summer fixtures, at their best in the northeast Aegean. *Koliós* (mackerel) is excellent either grilled or baked in sauce. Especially in autumn you may find *psarósoupa* (fish soup) or *kakaviá* (bouillabaisse).

Cheaper **seafood** (*thalassiná*) such as fried baby squid (usually frozen); *thrápsalo* (large, grillable deep-water squid) and octopus are summer staples; often mussels, cockles and small prawns will also be offered at reasonable sums (€20–30 per kilo).

Wine

All tavernas will offer you a choice of bottled **wines**, and most have their own house variety: kept in barrels, sold in bulk (*varelísio* or *hýma*) by the quarter-, half- or full litre, and served in glass flagons or brightly coloured tin "monkey-cups". Per-litre prices depend on locale and quality, ranging from €4 (Skýros) to €10–11 (Santoríni, Rhodes). Non-resinated wine is almost always more than decent; some people add a dash of soda water or lemonade. Barrelled **retsina** – pine-resinated wine, often an acquired taste – is far less common than it used to be, though you will find bottled brands everywhere: Yeoryiadhi from Thessaloníki, Liokri from Ahaïa and Malamatina from central Greece are all quaffable.

Among **bottled wines** available throughout the islands, Cambas Attikos, Zítsa and Rhodian CAIR products are good, inexpensive whites, while Boutari Naoussa and Kourtakis Apelia are decent, mid-range reds. For a better but still moderately priced red, choose either Boutari or Tsantali Merlot, or Averof Katoï from Epirus.

Travelling around **wine-producing islands** such as Límnos, Lésvos, Santoríni, Kefaloniá, Náxos, Ikaría, Rhodes and Crete you will also have the chance to sample local bottlings. Curiously, island **red wines** are almost uniformly mediocre, so you are better off ordering mainland varieties from Carras on Halki-dhikí, and various spots in the Peloponnese and Thessaly. Particularly notable local vintages are mentioned throughout the guide. The best available current **guide** to the emerging Greek domaines and vintners is Konstantinos Lazarakis' *The Wines of Greece*.

Finally, CAIR on Rhodes makes "champagne" ("naturally sparkling wine fermented en bouteille", says the label), in both brut and demi-sec versions. It's not Moët & Chandon quality by any means, but at about €6 per bottle, nobody's complaining.

Cafés and bars

A venerable institution, under attack from the onslaught of mass global culture, is the **kafenío**, still found in every Greek town but dying out in many resorts. In greater abundance, you'll encounter **patisseries** (*zaharoplastía*), swish modern **cafeterias and trendy bars**.

Kafenía, cafeterias and coffee

The **kafenío** (plural *kafenía*) is the traditional Greek coffee-house. Although its main business is "Greek" (Middle Eastern) **coffee** – prepared unsweetened (*skétos* or *pikrós*), medium (*métrios*) or sweet (*glykós*) – it also serves instant coffee, ouzo, brandy, beer, sage-based tea known as *tsáï vounoú*, soft drinks and juices. Some *kafenía* close at siesta time, but many remain open from early in the morning until late at night. The chief summer socializing time for a pre-prandial ouzo is 6–8pm, immediately after the afternoon nap.

Cafeterias are the province of fancier varieties of coffee and **kafés frappé**, iced instant coffee with sugar and (optionally) condensed milk – uniquely Greek despite its French name. Like Greek coffee, it is always accompanied by a glass of water. *Freddoccino* is a newer, cappuccino-based alternative to the traditional cold frappé. "Nes"(café) is the generic term for all instant **coffee**, regardless of brand. Thankfully, almost all cafeterias now offer a range of foreign-style coffees – filter, dubbed *fíltros* or *gallikós* (French); cappuccino; and espresso – at overseas prices. Alcohol is also served and many establishments morph into lively bars late at night.

Ouzería, mezedhopolía and spirits

Ouzería, found mainly in select neighbourhoods of larger island towns, specialize in ouzo and mezédhes. In some places you also find *mezedhopolía*, a bigger, more elaborate kind of *ouzerí*. These places are well worth trying for the marvellous variety of mezédhes they serve. In effect, several plates of mezédhes plus drinks will substitute for a more involved meal at a taverna, though it works out more expensive if you have a healthy appetite. Faced with an often bewilderingly varied menu, you might opt for a *pikilía* (assortment) available in several sizes, the most expensive one usually emphasizing seafood.

Ouzo is served by the glass, to which you can add water from the accompanying glass or ice to taste. The next measure up is a *karafáki* – a 200ml vial, the favourite means of delivery for *tsípouro*. Once, every ouzo was automatically accompanied by a small plate of **mezédhes** on the house: cheese, cucumber, tomato, a few olives, sometimes octopus or a couple of small fish. Nowadays "ouzomezés" is a separate, pricier option. Often, however, this is "off-menu" but if you order a *karafáki* you will automatically be served a selection of snacks.

Sweets and desserts

The **zaharoplastío**, a cross between café and patisserie, serves coffee, a limited range of alcohol, yoghurt with honey and sticky cakes. The better establishments offer an amazing variety of pastries, cream-and-chocolate confections, honey-soaked Greco–Turkish sweets like *baklavás*, *kataïfi* (honey-drenched "shredded wheat"), *loukoumádhes* (deep-fried batter puffs dusted with cinnamon and dipped in syrup), *galaktoboúreko* (custard pie) and so on. For more dairy-based products, seek out a **galaktopolío**, where you'll often find *ryzógalo* (rice pudding), *kréma* (custard) and locally made *yiaoúrti* (yoghurt). Both *zaharoplastía* and *galaktopolía* are more family-oriented places than a *kafenío*. **Traditional specialities** include "spoon sweets" or *glyká koutalioú* (syrupy preserves of quince, grape, fig, citrus fruit or cherry) .

Ice cream, sold principally at the parlours which have swept across Greece (Dhodhoni is the posh home-grown competition to Haägen-Dazs), can be very good and almost indistinguishable from Italian prototypes. A scoop (*baláki*) costs €1.20–1.50; you'll be asked if you want it in a cup (*kypelláki*) or a cone (*konáki*), and whether you want toppings like *santiyí* (whipped cream) or nuts.

Bars, beer and mineral water

Bars (*barákia*) are ubiquitous throughout the islands, ranging from clones of Spanish bodegas to musical beachside bars more active by day than at night. At their most sophisticated, however, they are well-executed theme venues in ex-industrial premises or Neoclassical houses, with both Greek and international soundtracks. Most Greek bars have a half-life of about a year; the best way to find current hot spots, especially if they're more club than bar, is to look out for posters advertising bar-hosted events in the neighbourhood.

Shots and **cocktails** are invariably expensive at €5–8, except during well-advertised happy hours: beer in a bar will cost €4–5, up to €12 for imports in trendier parts of Athens. **Beers** are mostly foreign

---

THE STRONG STUFF

Ouzo and the similar **tsípouro** (some north Aegean islands) and **tsikoudhiá** (Crete) are simple spirits of up to 48 percent alcohol, distilled from the grape-mash residue of wine-making. The former is always flavoured with anise, the latter two may be unadulterated or also have a touch of anise, cinnamon, pear essence or fennel. There are nearly thirty brands of ouzo or *tsípouro*, with the best reckoned to be from Lésvos and Sámos. Note that ouzo has the peculiar ability to bring back its effect when you drink water the morning after, so make sure you don't plan to do anything important (not least driving) the next day.

lagers made locally under licence at just a handful of breweries on the central mainland. **Local brands** include the palatable Fix from Athens, milder Mythos and Veryina from Komotiní. Athens also has a **microbrewery**, Craft: they produce lager in three grades (blonde, "smoked" and black), as well as a red ale, distribution of which is on the rise, even in the islands. Genuinely **imported** German beers, such as Bitburger, Fisher and Warsteiner (plus a few British and Irish ones), are found in Athens and at busier resorts.

The ubiquitous Loutraki **mineral water** is not esteemed by the Greeks themselves, who prefer various brands from Crete and Epirus. In many tavernas there has been a backlash against plastic bottles, and you can now get mineral water in glass bottles. Souroti, Epsa and Sariza are the principal labels of naturally **sparkling** (*aerioúho* in Greek) water, in small bottles; Tuborg club soda is also widespread. Note that despite variable quality in taste **tap water** is essentially safe all over Greece, though persuading restaurants to provide it can be difficult on many islands.

Health

There are no required inoculations for Greece, though it's wise to ensure that you are up to date on tetanus and polio. The main health risks faced by visitors involve overexposure to the sun, overindulgence in food and drink, or bites and stings from insects and sea creatures.

British and other EU nationals are entitled to free medical care in Greece upon presentation of a European Health Insurance Card (see box below). The US, Canada, Australia and New Zealand have no formal healthcare agreements with Greece (other than allowing for free emergency trauma treatment), so insurance is highly recommended.

Doctors and hospitals

For serious medical attention you'll find English-speaking **doctors** (mainly private) in all the bigger towns and resorts: if your hotel can't help, the tourist police or your consulate should be able to come up with some names if you have any difficulty. There are hospitals on all the bigger islands, and some kind of medical centre on virtually every one. For an ambulance, phone ☎ 166.

Pharmacies, drugs and contraception

For minor complaints it's enough to go to the local **pharmacy** (*farmakío*). Greek pharmacists are highly trained and dispense a number of medicines which elsewhere could only be prescribed by a doctor. In the larger towns and resorts there'll usually be one who speaks good English. Pharmacies are usually closed evenings and Saturday mornings, but all should have a schedule on their door showing the night and weekend duty pharmacists in town.

If you regularly use any form of **prescription drug**, you should bring along a copy of the prescription, together with the generic name of the drug; this will help you replace it, and avoids problems with customs officials. In this regard, you should be aware that **codeine** is banned in Greece. If you import any you might find yourself in serious trouble, so check labels carefully; it's a major ingredient of Panadeine, Veganin, Solpadeine, Codis and Nurofen Plus, to name just a few.

Contraceptive pills are sold over the counter at larger pharmacies, though not necessarily the brands you may be used to; a good pharmacist should come up with a close match. **Condoms** are inexpensive and ubiquitous – just ask for *profylaktiká* (less formally, *plastiká* or *kapótes*) at any pharmacy, sundries store or corner *períptero* (kiosk). Sanitary towels and **tampons** are widely sold in supermarkets.

THE EUROPEAN HEALTH INSURANCE CARD

If you have an EHIC (ⓦ www.ehic.org.uk, ⓦ ehic.ie) you are entitled to free consultation and treatment from doctors and dentists – there may be small charges for secondary treatments (such as x-rays), however. At hospitals you should simply have to show your EHIC; for free treatment from a regular doctor or dentist, you should call the IKA (the Social Insurance Institute, who administer the scheme) on their national appointments hotline, ☎ 184. For prescriptions from pharmacies in the state scheme you pay a small fixed charge plus 25 percent of the cost of the medicine; if you are charged in full, get a receipt and keep the original prescription to claim it back. You can also claim back for private treatment; take the original receipts and your EHIC to the IKA within one month, and they will reimburse you up to the limit allowed for similar treatment by the IKA.

Common health problems

The main health problems experienced by visitors – including many blamed on the food – have to do with **overexposure to the sun**. To avoid these, cover up, wear a hat, and drink plenty of fluids to avoid any danger of **sunstroke**; remember that even hazy sun can burn. **Tap water** meets strict EU standards for safety, but high mineral content and less than perfect desalination on many islands can leave a brackish taste not suited to everyone. For that reason many people prefer to stick to bottled water (see opposite). Hayfever sufferers should be prepared for a pollen season earlier than in northern Europe, peaking in April and May.

Hazards of the sea

To avoid hazards by the sea, goggles or a dive mask for swimming and footwear for walking over wet or rough rocks are useful. You may have the bad luck to meet an armada of **jellyfish** (*tsoúkhtres*), especially in late summer; they come in various colours and sizes ranging from purple "pizzas" to invisible, minute creatures. Various over-the-counter remedies are sold in resort pharmacies to combat the sting, and baking soda or diluted ammonia also help to lessen the effects. Less vicious but far more common are spiny sea urchins, which infest rocky shorelines year-round. If you're unlucky enough to step on or graze against one, an effective way to remove the spines is with a needle (you can crudely sterilize it with heat from a cigarette lighter) and olive oil. If you don't remove the spines, they'll fester.

Bites and stings

Most of Greece's insects and reptiles are pretty benign, but there are a few that can give a painful bite. Much the most common are **mosquitoes**: you can buy repellent devices and sprays at any minimarket. On beaches, sandflies can also give a nasty (and potentially infection-carrying) sting. Adders (*ohiés*) and scorpions (*scorpií*) are found throughout Greece. Both creatures are shy, but take care when climbing over drystone walls where snakes like to sun themselves, and – particularly when camping – don't put hands or feet in places, like shoes, where you haven't looked first.

Finally, in addition to munching its way through a fair amount of Greece's surviving pine forests, the pine processionary **caterpillar** – which takes its name from the long, nose-to-tail convoys which individuals form at certain points in their lifecycle – sports highly irritating hairs, with a venom worse than a scorpion's. If you touch one, or even a tree-trunk they've been on recently, you'll know all about it for a week, and the welts may require antihistamine to heal.

If you snap a **wild-fig shoot** while walking, avoid contact with the highly irritant **sap**. The immediate antidote to the active alkaloid is a mild acid – lemon juice or vinegar; left unneutralized, fig "milk" raises welts which take a month to heal.

The media

Greeks are great devourers of newsprint – although few would propose the Greek mass media as a paradigm of objective journalism. Papers are almost uniformly sensational, while state-run TV and radio are often biased in favour of whichever party happens to be in government. Foreign news is widely available, though, in the form of locally printed newspaper editions and TV news channels.

Newspapers and magazines

British newspapers are widely available in resorts and the larger towns at a cost of €2–3 for dailies, or €4–5 for Sunday editions. Many, including the *Guardian*, *Times*, *Mail* and *Mirror*, have slimmed-down editions printed in Greece which are available the same day in the main resorts; others are likely to be a day old. In bigger newsagents you'll also be able to find *USA Today*, *Time* and *Newsweek* as well as the *International Herald Tribune*, which has the bonus of including an abridged English edition of the same day's *Kathimerini*, a respected Greek daily, thus allowing you to keep up with Greek news too. From time to time you'll also find various English-language magazines aimed at visitors to Greece, though none seems to survive for long.

The main local English-language newspaper, available in most resorts, is the *Athens News* (weekly every Friday, online at ⓦathensnews.gr; €2.50), in colour with good features and Balkan news, plus entertainment and arts listings.

Radio

Greece's airwaves are cluttered with **local and regional stations**, many of which have plenty of music, often traditional. In popular areas many of them have regular news bulletins and tourist information in English. The mountainous nature of much of the country, though, means that any sort of radio reception is tricky: if you're driving around you'll find that you constantly have to retune. The two state-run networks are ER1 (a mix of news, talk and pop music) and ER2 (pop music).

The BBC World Service no longer broadcasts to Europe on short wave, though Voice of America can be picked up in places. Both of these and dozens of others are of course available as internet broadcasts, however, or via satellite TV channels.

Television

Greece's state-funded **TV stations**, ET1, NET and ET3, nowadays lag behind private channels – Mega, Star, Alpha, Alter and Skai among others – in the ratings, though not necessarily in quality of offerings. Most foreign films and serials are broadcast in their original language, with Greek subtitles; there's almost always a choice of English-language movies from about 9pm onwards, although the closer you get to the end of the movie, the more adverts you'll encounter. Although hotels and rooms places frequently have TVs in the room, reception is often dire: even where they advertise satellite, the only English-language channels this usually includes are CNN and BBC World.

Festivals

Most of the big Greek popular festivals have a religious basis, so they're observed in accordance with the Orthodox calendar: this means that Easter, for example, can fall as much as three weeks to either side of the Western festival.

On top of the main religious festivals, there are scores of local festivities, or **paniyíria**, celebrating the patron saint of the village church. Some of the more important are listed below; the *paramoní*, or **eve of the festival**, is often as significant as the day itself, and many of the events are actually celebrated on the night before. If you show up on the morning of the date given you may find that you have missed most of the music, dancing and drinking. With some 330-odd possible saints' days, though, you're unlikely to travel round for long without stumbling on something. Local tourist offices should be able to fill you in on events in their area.

Easter

Easter is by far the most important festival of the Greek year. It is an excellent time to be in Greece,

both for the beautiful and moving religious ceremonies and for the days of feasting and celebration which follow. If you make for a smallish village, you may well find yourself an honorary member for the period of the festival. This is a busy time for Greek tourists as well as international ones, however, so book ahead: for Easter dates, see opposite.

The first great ceremony takes place on **Good Friday** evening as the Descent from the Cross is lamented in church. At dusk, the *Epitáfios*, Christ's funeral bier, lavishly decorated by the women of the parish, leaves the sanctuary and is paraded solemnly through the streets. Late **Saturday** evening sees the climax in a majestic Mass to celebrate Christ's triumphant return. At the stroke of midnight all the lights in each crowded church are extinguished and the congregation plunged into the darkness which enveloped Christ as He passed through the underworld. Then there's a faint glimmer of light behind the altar screen before the priest appears, holding aloft a lighted taper and chanting *"Avtó to fos…"* ("This is the Light of the World"). Stepping down to the level of the parishioners, he lights the unlit candles of the nearest worshippers, intoning *"Dévte, lévete Fós"* ("Come, take the Light"). Those at the front of the congregation do the same for their neighbours until the entire church – and the outer courtyard, standing room only for latecomers – is ablaze with burning **candles** and the miracle reaffirmed. The burning candles are carried home through the streets; they are said to bring good fortune to the house if they arrive still burning.

The lighting of the flames is the signal for celebrations to start and the Lent fast to be broken. The traditional greeting, as fireworks and dynamite explode all around you in the street, is *Khristós Anésti* ("Christ is risen"), to which the response is *Alithós Anésti* ("Truly He is risen"). On **Easter Sunday** there's feasting on roast lamb.

The Greek equivalent of **Easter eggs** is hard-boiled eggs (painted red on Holy Thursday), which are baked into twisted, sweet bread-loaves (*tsourékia*) or distributed on Easter Sunday. People rap their eggs against their friends' eggs, and the owner of the last uncracked egg is considered lucky.

Name days

In Greece, everyone gets to celebrate their birthday twice. More important, in fact, than your actual birthday, is the "**Name Day**" of the saint who bears the same name. Greek ingenuity has stretched the saints' names (or invented new saints) to cover almost everyone, so even pagan Dionysos or Socrates get to celebrate. If your name isn't covered, no problem – your party is on All Saints' Day, eight weeks after Easter. If you learn that it's an acquaintance's name day, you wish them *Khrónia Pollá* (literally, "many years").

The big name day celebrations (Iannis/Ianna on January 7 or Yioryios on April 23 for example) can involve thousands of people, and traditional naming conventions guarantee that families get to celebrate together. In most families the eldest boy is still named after his paternal grandfather, and the eldest girl after her grandmother, so all the eldest cousins will share the same name, and the same name day. Any church or chapel bearing the saint's name will mark the event – some smaller chapels will open just for this one day of the year – while if an entire village is named after the saint, you can almost guarantee a festival. To check out when your name day falls, see Ⓦ sfakia-crete.com.

Festival calendar

JANUARY

January 1: New Year's Day (Protokhroniá) In Greece this is the feast day of Áyios Vassílios (St Basil). The traditional New Year greeting is "Kalí Khroniá".

January 6: Epiphany (Theofánia/Tón Fóton) Marks the baptism of Jesus as well as the end of the twelve days of Christmas. Baptismal fonts, lakes, rivers and seas are blessed, especially harbours (such as Pireás), where the priest traditionally casts a crucifix into the water, with local youths competing for the privilege of recovering it.

FEBRUARY/MARCH

Carnival (Apokriátika) Festivities span three weeks, climaxing during the seventh weekend before Easter. The Ionian islands, especially Kefaloniá, are also good for carnival, as is Ayiássos on Lésvos, while the outrageous Goat Dance (see p.440) takes place on Skýros in the Sporades.

Clean Monday (Kathará Dheftéra) The day after Carnival ends and the first day of Lent, 48 days before Easter, marks the start of fasting and is traditionally spent picnicking and flying kites.

March 25: Independence Day and the feast of the Annunciation (Evangelismós) Both a religious and a national holiday, with, on the one hand, military parades and dancing to celebrate the beginning of the revolt against Ottoman rule in 1821, and, on the other, church services to honour the news given to Mary that she was to become the Mother of Christ. There are major festivities on Tínos, Ýdhra and any locality with a monastery or church named Evangelístria or Evangelismós.

APRIL/MAY

Easter (Páskha: April 15, 2012; May 5, 2013; April 20, 2014; April 12, 2015) The most important festival of the Greek year (see opposite). The island of Ýdhra, with its alleged 360 churches and monasteries, is the prime Easter resort; other famous Easter celebrations are held at Corfu, Pyrgí on Híos, Ólymbos on Kárpathos and St John's monastery on Pátmos, where on Holy Thursday the abbot washes the feet of twelve monks in the village square, in imitation of Christ doing the same for his disciples. Good Friday and Easter Monday are also public holidays.

April 23: The feast of St George (Áyios Yeóryios) A big rural celebration for the patron saint of shepherds, with much feasting and dancing at associated shrines and towns. At the mountain town of Asigonía in Crete, this is a major event. If it falls during Lent, festivities are postponed until the Monday after Easter.

MAY/JUNE

May 1: May Day (Protomayiá) The great urban holiday when townspeople traditionally make for the countryside to picnic and fly kites, returning with bunches of wild flowers. Wreaths are hung on their doorways or balconies until they are burnt in bonfires on St John's Eve (June 23). There are also large demonstrations by the Left for Labour Day.

May 21: Feast of St Constantine and St Helen (Áyios Konstandínos & Ayía Eléni) Constantine, as emperor, championed Christianity in the Byzantine Empire; St Helen was his mother. It's a widely celebrated name day for two of the more popular Christian names in Greece.

May 20–27: Battle of Crete The anniversary of one of the major World War II battles is celebrated in the Haniá province of Crete with veterans' ceremonies, sporting events and folk dancing.

Whit Monday (Áyio Pnévma) Fifty days after Easter, sees services to commemorate the descent of the Holy Spirit to the assembled disciples. Many young Greeks take advantage of the long weekend, marking the start of summer, to head for the islands.

June 29 & 30: SS Peter and Paul (Áyios Pétros and Áyios Pávlos) The joint feast of two of the more widely celebrated name days is on June 29. Celebrations often run together with those for the Holy Apostles (Áyii Apóstoli), the following day.

JULY

July 17: Feast of St Margaret (Ayía Marína) A big event in rural areas, as she's an important protector of crops. Ayiá Marina village on Kássos will be en fête, as will countless other similarly named towns and villages.

July 20: Feast of the Prophet Elijah (Profítis Ilías) Widely celebrated at the countless hilltop shrines of Profítis Ilías.

July 26: St Paraskevi (Ayía Paraskeví) Celebrated in parishes or villages bearing that name.

AUGUST

August 6: Transfiguration of the Saviour (Metamórfosis toú Sotíros) Another excuse for celebrations, particularly at Khristós Ráhon village on Ikaría, and at Plátanos on Léros. On Hálki the date is marked by messy food fights with flour, eggs and squid ink.

August 15: Assumption of the Blessed Virgin Mary (Apokímisis tís Panayías) This is the day when people traditionally return to their home village, and the heart of the holiday season, so in many places there will be no accommodation available on any terms. Even some Greeks will resort to sleeping in the streets at the great

CULTURAL FESTIVALS

Festivals of music, dance and theatre take place in summer throughout the islands, many at atmospheric outdoor venues. Some are unashamedly aimed at drawing tourists, others more seriously artistic. Some of the more durable include:

Domus Festival, Náxos July–early Sept
Ⓦ naxosfestival.com
Ippokrateia Festival, Kos July
Iráklion Festival July–Aug
Kornaria Cultural Festival, Sitía, Crete July–Sept
Lató Cultural Festival, Áyios Nikólaos, Crete
July–Sept

Lefkádha Arts and Folklore festivals Aug
Ⓦ lefkasculturalcenter.gr
Philippi Festival, Thássos July–Aug Ⓦ philippifestival.gr
Réthymnon Wine Festival July
Ⓦ rethymnowinefestival.gr
Sými Festival July–Aug Ⓦ symifestival.com
Thíra Music Festival Aug–Sept

pilgrimage to Tínos; also major festivities at Páros, at Ayiássos on Lésvos, and at Ólymbos on Kárpathos.

August 29: Beheading of John the Baptist (Apokefálisis toú Prodhrómou) Popular pilgrimages and celebrations at Vrykoúnda on Kárpathos. On Crete a massive name-day pilgrimage treks to the church of Áyios Ioánnis on the Rodhópou peninsula.

SEPTEMBER

September 8: Birth of the Virgin Mary (Yénnisis tís Panayías) Sees special services in churches dedicated to the event, and a double cause for rejoicing on Spétses where they also celebrate the anniversary of the battle of the straits of Spétses. Elsewhere, there's a pilgrimage of childless women to the monastery at Tsambíka, Rhodes.
September 14: Exaltation of the Cross (Ípsosis toú Stavroú) A last major summer festival, keenly observed on Hálki.
September 24: Feast of St John the Divine (Áyios Ioánnis Theológos) Observed on Níssyros and Pátmos, where at the saint's monastery there are solemn, beautiful liturgies the night before and early in the morning.

OCTOBER

October 26: Feast of St Demetrios (Áyios Dhimítrios) Another popular name day; in rural areas the new wine is traditionally broached on this day, a good excuse for general inebriation.
October 28: Óhi Day A national holiday with parades, folk dancing and speeches to commemorate prime minister Metaxas' one-word reply to Mussolini's 1940 ultimatum: Ohi! ("No!").

NOVEMBER

November 7–9: Arkádhi The anniversary of the 1866 explosion at Arkádhi monastery in Crete is marked by an enormous gathering at the island's most revered shrine.
November 8: Feast of the Archangels Michael and Gabriel (Mihaíl and Gavriíl, or tón Taxiárhon) Marked by rites at the numerous churches named after them, particularly at the rural monastery of Taxiárhis on Sými, and the big monastery of Mandamádhos, Lésvos.

DECEMBER

December 6: Feast of St Nicholas (Áyios Nikólaos) The patron saint of seafarers, who has many chapels dedicated to him.

December 25 & 26: Christmas (Khristoúyenna) If less all-encompassing than Greek Easter, Christmas is still an important religious feast, and one that increasingly comes with all the usual commercial trappings.
December 31: New Year's Eve (Paramoní Protohroniá) As on the other twelve days of Christmas, a few children still go door-to-door singing traditional carols, receiving money in return. Adults tend to sit around playing cards, often for money. A special baked loaf, the vassilópitta, in which a coin is concealed to bring its finder good luck throughout the year, is cut at midnight.

Sports and outdoor pursuits

The Greek seashore offers endless scope for watersports, from waterskiing and parasailing to yachting and windsurfing. On land, the greatest attraction lies in hiking; often the smaller, less developed islands are better for this than the larger ones criss-crossed by roads. As for spectator sports, the twin Greek obsessions are football (soccer) and basketball, with volleyball a close third. You'll see youths playing impromptu games everywhere, but except on Crete there are few top-flight teams on the islands.

Watersports

Windsurfing is very popular around Greece: the islands' bays and coves are ideal for beginners, with a few spectacularly windy spots for experts (see opposite). Board rental rates are reasonable and instruction is generally also available. **Waterski** boats spend most of their time towing people around on bananas or other inflatables, though you usually can be waterski or wakeboard as well, while parasailing (*parapént* in Greek) is also on offer at all the big resorts. **Jet skis** can be rented in many resorts, too, for a fifteen-minute burst of fuel-guzzling thrills.

A combination of steady winds, appealing seascapes and numerous natural harbours has long made the islands a tremendous place for **sailing**. All sorts of bareboat and flotilla yacht trips are on offer (see p.29), while dinghies, small cats and motor boats can be rented at many resorts. For yachting, spring and autumn are the most pleasant seasons; *meltémi* winds can make for nauseous sailing in July and August when you'll also find far higher prices and crowded moorings. The Cyclades suffer particularly badly from the *meltémi*, and are also relatively short on facilities: better choices are to explore the Sporades from Skiáthos; to set out from Athens for the Argo-Saronic islands; or to sail around Corfu and the Ionians, though here winds can be very light.

Because of the potential for pilfering submerged antiquities, **scuba diving** is still restricted, though relaxation of the controls has led to a proliferation of dive centres across the Dodecanese, Ionians, Cyclades and Crete. There's not a huge amount of aquatic life surviving around Greece's over-fished shores, but you do get wonderfully clear water, while the rocky coast offers plenty of caves and hidden nooks to explore.

Walking and cycling

If you have the time and stamina, **walking** is probably the single best way to see the quieter islands. The bigger islands offer greater choice, especially the well-organized Corfu Trail (see p.475), mountainous Évvia and above all Crete, with its famous gorge descents. This guide includes some of the more accessible hikes, from gentle strolls to long-distance mountain paths; there are also plenty of companies offering walking holidays (see p.29). In addition, you may want to acquire a countrywide or regional **hiking guidebook** and some detailed **maps** (see p.50).

Cycling is less popular with Greeks, but in an increasing number of resorts you can hire **mountain bikes**, and many of the rental places lead organized rides, which again vary from easy explorations of the countryside to serious rides up proper mountains. Summer heat can be fierce, but spring and autumn offer great riding and walking conditions. Again, there are specialist companies offering cycling breaks in Greece (see p.29).

Culture and etiquette

In many ways, Greece is a thoroughly integrated European country, and behaviour and social mores differ little from what you may be used to at home. Dig a little deeper, however, or travel to more remote, less touristed areas, and you'll find that traditional Greek ways survive to a gratifying degree. It's easy to accidentally give offence – but equally easy to avoid doing so by following a few simple tips, and to upgrade your status from that of tourist to xénos, a word that means both stranger and guest.

In general, Greeks are exceptionally friendly and curious, to an extent that can seem intrusive, certainly to a reserved Brit. Don't be surprised at being asked personal questions, even on short acquaintance, or having your **personal space** invaded – conversation is often held at close quarters, with plenty of touching involved. On the other hand, you're also likely to be invited to people's houses, often to meet a large extended family. Should you get such an invitation, you are not expected to be punctual – thirty minutes late is normal – and you should bring a small **gift**, usually flowers, or cakes from the local cake shop. If you're invited out to dinner, you can offer to **pay**, but it's very unlikely you'll be allowed to do so, and too much insistence could be construed as rude. If someone in a bar or café offers you a drink, again they'll pay, but here you should get the next one.

Dress codes and cultural hints

Though **dress codes** on the beach are entirely informal, they're much less so away from the sea; most Greeks will dress up to go out, and not doing so is considered slovenly at the least. There are quite a number of **nudist** beaches in remote spots, with plenty of locals enjoying them, but on family beaches, or those close to town or near a church (of

---

**FIVE OF THE BEST
WINDSURFING SPOTS**

Vassilikí on Lefkádha island (see p.484)
Sánta María, Páros (see p.159)
Áyios Yeóryios, Náxos (see p.166)
Kokkári, Sámos (see p.358)
Kouremenos, eastern Crete (see p.230)

SHHHH! SIESTA TIME

The hours **between 3 and 5pm**, the midday **siesta** (*mikró ýpno*), are sacrosanct – it's not acceptable to visit people, make phone calls to strangers or cause any sort of loud noise (especially with motorcycles) at this time. Quiet is also legally mandated **between midnight and 8am** in residential areas.

---

which there are many along the Greek coast), even toplessness is often frowned on. Most monasteries and to a lesser extent churches impose a fairly strict **dress code** for visitors: no shorts, with women expected to cover their arms and wear skirts (though most Greek women visitors will be in trousers); the necessary wraps are sometimes provided on the spot.

Two pieces of **body language** that can cause unintentional offence are hand gestures; don't hold your hand up, palm out, to anybody, and don't make an OK sign by forming a circle with your thumb and forefinger – both are extremely rude. Nodding and shaking your head for yes and no are also unlikely to be understood; Greeks use a slight forward inclination of the head for yes, a more vigorous backward nod for no.

Bargaining and tipping

Most shops have fixed prices, so **bargaining** isn't a regular feature of tourist life. It is worth negotiating over rooms – especially off season – or for vehicle rental, especially for longer periods, but it's best not to be aggressive about it; ask if they have a cheaper room, for example, rather than demanding a lower price. **Tipping** is not essential anywhere, though taxi drivers generally expect it from tourists and most service staff are very poorly paid. Restaurant bills incorporate a service charge; if you want to tip, rounding up the bill is usually sufficient.

Smoking also deserves a mention. Greeks are the heaviest smokers in Europe, and although legally you're not allowed to smoke indoors in restaurants, bars or public offices, in practice the law is almost universally disregarded. Effective no-smoking areas are very rare indeed.

Women and lone travellers

Thousands of **women** travel independently around the islands without being harassed or feeling intimidated. With the westernization of relationships between unmarried Greek men and women, almost all of the traditional Mediterranean macho impetus for trying one's luck with foreign girls has faded. Foreign women are more at risk of **sexual assault** at certain notorious resorts (including Kávos in Corfu; Laganás in Zákynthos; Faliráki in Rhodes) by northern European men than by ill-intentioned locals. It is sensible not to bar-crawl alone or to accept late-night rides from strangers (**hitching** at any time is not advisable for lone female travellers). In more remote areas intensely traditional villagers may wonder why women travelling alone are unaccompanied, and may not welcome their presence in exclusively male *kafenía*. Travelling with a man, you're more likely to be treated as a *xéni*.

Travel essentials

Costs

The **cost of living** in Greece has increased astronomically since it joined the EU, particularly after the adoption of the euro and further increases in the VAT rate in 2011. Prices in shops and cafés now match or exceed those of many other EU member countries (including the UK). However, outside the chintzier resorts, travel remains affordable, with the aggregate cost of restaurant meals, short-term accommodation (see p.34) and public transport falling somewhere in between that of cheaper Spain or France and pricier Italy.

Prices depend on where and when you go. Larger cities and the trendier tourist resorts and small islands (such as Sými, Ýdhra, Mýkonos, Paxí and Pátmos) are more expensive and costs everywhere increase sharply during July–August and during other holiday periods such as Easter.

On most islands a daily per-person **budget** of €50/£44/US$72 will get you basic accommodation and meals, plus a short ferry or bus ride, as one of a couple. Camping would cut costs marginally. On €100/£88/US$144 a day you could be living quite well, plus sharing the cost of renting a large motorbike or small car.

A basic taverna **meal** with bulk wine or a beer costs around €12–20 per person. Add a better bottle of wine, pricier fish or fancier decor and it could be up to €20–30 a head; you'll rarely pay more than that. Even in the most developed of resorts, with inflated "international" menus, there

DISCOUNTS

Full-time students are eligible for the **International Student ID Card** (ISIC; ⓦ www.isiccard .com), which entitles the bearer to cut-price transport and discounts at museums, theatres and other attractions, though often not accepted as valid proof of age. If you're not a student but aged under 26, you can qualify for the **International Youth Travel Card**, which provides similar benefits to the ISIC. Teachers qualify for the **International Teacher Identity Card** (ITIC), offering insurance benefits but limited travel discounts.

Seniors are entitled to a discount on bus passes in the major cities; Olympic Airways also offer discounts on full fares on domestic flights. Proof of age is necessary.

is often a basic but decent taverna where the locals eat.

Crime and personal safety

Greece is one of Europe's safest countries, with a **low crime rate** and a deserved reputation for honesty. Most of the time if you leave a bag or wallet at a café, you'll probably find it scrupulously looked after, pending your return. Nonetheless theft and muggings are becoming increasingly common, a trend only likely to be increased by the economic crisis. With this in mind, it's best to lock rooms and cars securely, and to keep your valuables hidden, especially in cities. **Civil unrest**, in the form of strikes and demonstrations, is also on the increase, but while this might inconvenience you, you'd be very unlucky to get caught up in any trouble as a visitor.

Though the chances are you'll never meet a member of the national **police force**, the Elliniki Astynomia, Greek cops expect respect, and many have little regard for foreigners. If you do need to go to the police, always try to do so through the **Tourist Police** (❶ 171), who should speak English and are used to dealing with visitors. You are required to carry suitable ID on you at all times – either a passport or a driving licence.

The most common causes of a brush with the law are beach nudity, camping outside authorized sites, **public inebriation** or lewd behaviour. In 2009 a large British stag group dressed as nuns was arrested in Mália and held for several days, having managed to combine extreme drunkenness with a lack of respect for the church. Also avoid taking **photos in forbidden areas** such as airports (see p.51).

Drug offences are treated as major crimes, particularly since there's a mushrooming local addiction problem. The maximum penalty for "causing the use of drugs by someone under 18", for example, is life imprisonment and an astronomical fine. Foreigners caught in possession of even small amounts of marijuana get long jail sentences if there's evidence that they've been supplying the drug to others.

Electricity

Voltage is 220 volts AC. Standard European two-pin plugs are used; adaptors should be purchased beforehand in the UK, as they can be difficult to find locally; standard 5-, 6- or 7.5-amp models permit operation of a hair dryer or travel iron. Unless they're dual voltage, North American appliances will require both a step-down transformer and a plug adaptor (the latter easy to find in Greece).

Entrance fees

All the major **ancient sites**, like most **museums**, charge **entrance fees** ranging from €2 to €12, with an average fee of around €3. Entrance to all state-run sites and museums is **free** on Sundays from November to March.

Entry requirements

UK and all other EU nationals need only a valid **passport, which remains unstamped,** to enter Greece. US, Australian, New Zealand, Canadian and most non-EU Europeans receive mandatory entry and exit stamps in their passports and can stay, as tourists, for ninety days (cumulative) in any six-month period. Such nationals arriving by flight or boat from another EU state not party to the Schengen Agreement may not be stamped in routinely at minor Greek ports, so make sure this is done in order to avoid unpleasantness on exit. Your passport must be valid for three months after your arrival date.

Unless of Greek descent, or married to an EU national, visitors from **non-EU** countries are currently not, in practice, being given extensions to tourist visas by the various Aliens' Bureaux in Greece. You must leave not just Greece but the

AVERAGE MONTHLY TEMPERATURES AND RAINFALL

	Jan	Feb	Mar	Apr	May	Jun	Jul	Aug	Sep	Oct	Nov	Dec
Athens												
Maximum °C/°F	13/55	14/57	16/61	20/68	25/77	30/86	33/91	33/91	29/84	24/75	19/66	15/59
Minimum °C/°F	6/43	7/45	8/46	11/52	16/61	20/68	23/73	23/73	19/66	15/59	12/54	8/46
Rainfall mm	62	37	37	23	23	14	6	7	7	51	56	71
Cyclades (Náxos)												
Maximum °C/°F	15/59	15/59	16/62	20/68	23/73	26/79	27/81	28/82	26/79	24/75	20/68	17/63
Minimum °C/°F	10/50	10/50	11/52	13/55	16/62	20/68	22/72	22/72	20/68	18/64	15/59	12/54
Rainfall mm	91	73	69	19	12	11	2	1	11	45	48	93
Crete (Iráklio)												
Maximum °C/°F	16/62	16/62	17/63	20/68	23/73	27/81	29/84	29/84	27/81	24/75	21/70	18/64
Minimum °C/°F	9/48	9/48	10/50	12/54	15/59	19/66	22/72	22/72	19/66	17/63	14/57	11/52
Rainfall mm	95	46	43	26	13	3	1	1	11	64	71	79
Dodecanese (Rhodes)												
Maximum °C/°F	15/59	16/62	17/63	21/70	25/77	30/86	32/90	33/91	29/84	25/77	21/70	17/63
Minimum °C/°F	7/45	8/46	9/48	12/54	15/59	19/66	21/70	22/72	19/66	15/59	12/54	9/48
Rainfall mm	201	101	92	23	21	1	1	0	15	75	114	205
Ionians (Corfu)												
Maximum °C/°F	14/57	15/59	16/62	19/66	23/73	28/82	31/88	32/91	28/82	23/73	19/66	16/61
Minimum °C/°F	6/43	6/43	8/46	10/50	13/55	17/63	19/66	19/66	17/63	14/57	11/52	8/46
Rainfall mm	196	132	100	70	41	14	4	20	95	184	237	259

entire Schengen Group – essentially the entire EU as it was before May 2004, minus Britain and Eire, plus Norway and Iceland – and stay out until the maximum 90-days-in-180 rule, as set forth above, is satisfied. If you overstay your time and then leave under your own power – ie are not deported – you'll be hit with a huge fine upon departure, and possibly be banned from re-entering for a period of time; no excuses will be entertained except (just maybe) a doctor's certificate stating you were immobilized in hospital. It cannot be overemphasized just how exigent Greek immigration officials have become on this issue.

Greek embassies abroad

Australia 9 Turrana St, Yarralumla, Canberra, ACT 2600 ☎ 02/6273 3011, ⓦ mfa.gr/sydney.
Britain 1A Holland Park, London W11 3TP ☎ 020/7221 6467, ⓦ mfa.gr/london
Canada 80 Maclaren St, Ottawa, ON K2P 0K6 ☎ 613/238-6271, ⓦ mfa.gr/ottawa
Ireland 1 Upper Pembroke St, Dublin 2 ☎ 01/676 7254, ⓦ mfa.gr/dublin
New Zealand 5–7 Willeston St, Wellington ☎ 04/473 7775, ⓦ mfa.gr/wellington
South Africa 1003 Church Street, 0028 Hatfield, Pretoria ☎ 012/434-7351, ⓦ mfa.gr/pretoria
USA 2217 Massachusetts Ave NW, Washington, DC 20008 ☎ 202/939-1300, ⓦ mfa.gr/washington

Gay and lesbian travellers

Greece is deeply ambivalent about **homosexuality**: ghettoized as "to be expected" in the arts, theatre and music scenes but apt to be closeted elsewhere. "Out" gay Greeks are rare, and "out" local lesbians rarer still; foreign same-sex couples will be regarded on most islands with some bemusement but accorded the standard courtesy as foreigners – as long as they refrain from public displays of affection, taboo in rural areas. There is a sizeable gay community in Athens, plus a fairly obvious scene at resorts like Ýdhra, Rhodes and Mýkonos. Skála Eressoü on Lésvos, the birthplace of Sappho, is (appropriately) an international mecca for lesbians. Even in Athens, however, most gay nightlife is underground (often literally so in the siting of clubs), with no visible signage for nondescript premises.

Insurance

Even though EU healthcare privileges apply in Greece (see box, p.40), you should consider taking out an **insurance policy** before travelling to cover against theft, loss, illness or injury. Before paying for a whole new policy, however, it's worth checking whether you are already covered: some home insurance policies may cover your possessions when overseas, and many private medical schemes (such as BUPA or WPA in the UK) offer coverage extensions for abroad. **Students** will often find that their student health coverage extends during the vacations.

After exhausting these possibilities, you might want to contact a **specialist travel insurance** company, or consider the travel insurance deal we offer (see box below). A typical policy usually provides cover for the **loss** of baggage, tickets and – up to a certain limit – cash, cards or cheques, as well as **cancellation** or curtailment of your journey. With baggage cover, make sure that the **per-article limit** will cover your most valuable possession. Unless an extra premium is paid, most exclude "**dangerous sports**": in the Greek islands this means motorbiking, windsurfing and possibly sailing, and on the mainland this could mean rafting, skiing or trekking.

Make any claim as soon as possible. If you have medical treatment, keep all receipts for medicines and treatment. If you have anything stolen or lost, you must obtain an **official statement** from the police or the airline which lost your bags – with numerous claims being fraudulent, most insurers won't even consider one unless you have a police report.

Internet

Rates at **internet cafés** tend to be about €2–4 per hour and any town or major resort will have at least one. Most hotels and an increasing number of cafés offer free wi-fi internet access to patrons.

Laundry

Laundries or *Plindíria*, as they're known in Greek, are available in the main resort towns; sometimes an attended service wash is available for little or no extra charge over the basic cost of €8–10 per wash and dry. Self-catering villas will usually be furnished with a drying line and a selection of plastic wash-tubs or a bucket. Most hotels will charge for laundry services.

Living in Greece

EU (and EEA) nationals are allowed to stay indefinitely in any EU state, but to ensure avoidance of any problems – eg, in setting up a bank account – you should, after the third month of stay, get a **certificate of registration** (*vevéosi engrafís*). Residence/work permits for **non-EU/non-EEA nationals** can only be obtained on application to a Greek embassy or consulate outside of Greece; you have a much better chance of securing one if you are married to a Greek, are of Greek background by birth or have permanent-resident status in another EU state.

As for **work**, non-EU nationals of Greek descent and EU/EEA native speakers of English (ie Brits and Irish) have a much better chance than anyone else. **Teaching English at a private language school** (*frontistírio*) is still a relatively well-paid option but almost impossible to get into these days without a bona fide TEFL certificate.

Many people find **tourism-related work**, especially on the islands most dominated by foreign visitors, April and May being the best time to look around. This is often as a rep for a package company, although they recruit the majority of staff from the home country; all you need is EU nationality and the appropriate language, though knowledge of Greek is a big plus. Jobs in bars or restaurants are a lot easier for women to come by than men. Another option if you have the requisite skills is to work for a **windsurfing** school or **scuba** operation.

Mail

Post offices are open Monday to Friday from 7.30am to 2pm, though certain main branches are also open evenings and Saturday mornings.

Airmail letters take 3–7 days to reach the rest of Europe, 5–12 days to North America, a little longer for Australia and New Zealand. Postal rates for up to 20g are a uniform €0.75 to all overseas destinations. For a modest fee (about €3) you can shave a day or two off delivery time to any destination by using the **express service** (*katepígonda*). **Registered** (*systiméno*) delivery is also available for a similar amount but is slow unless coupled with express service. Stamps (*grammatósima*) are widely available at newsagents and other tourist shops.

Parcels should (and often can) only be handled in the main provincial or county capitals. For non-EU/EEA destinations, always present your box open for inspection, and come prepared with tape and scissors.

Ordinary **post boxes** are bright yellow, express boxes dark red, but it's best to use those adjacent to an actual post office, since days may pass between collections at boxes elsewhere.

Maps

The most reliable **general touring maps** of Greece are those published by Athens-based Anavasi (**W** anavasi.gr), Road Editions (**W** road.gr) and newcomer Orama (**W** nakas-maps.gr). Anavasi and Road Editions products are widely available in Greece at selected bookshops, as well as at petrol stations and general tourist shops countrywide. In Britain they are found at Stanfords (**T** 020/7836 1321, **W** stanfords.co.uk) and the Hellenic Book Service (**T** 020/7267 9499, **W** hellenicbookservice .com); in the US, they're sold through Omni Resources (**T** 910/227-8300, **W** omnimap.com).

Hiking/topographical maps are gradually improving in quality and availability. Anavasi publishes a series covering the White Mountains and Psiloritis on Crete and Mt Dhýrfis on Évvia. The map-and-guide booklets published by Marengo Publications (**T** 01485/532710, **W** marengowalks .com) in England also prove very useful for areas including Crete, Corfu, Kálymnos, Lésvos, Sámos, Sými and Thássos.

Money

Greece's currency is the **euro** (€). Up-to-date **exchange rates** can be found on **W** xe.com. Euro notes exist in denominations of 5, 10, 20, 50, 100, 200 and 500 euros, and coins in denominations of 1, 2, 5, 10, 20 and 50 cents and 1 and 2 euros. Avoid getting stuck with **counterfeit euro notes** (€100 and €200 ones abound). The best tests are done by

the naked eye: genuine notes all have a hologram strip or (if over €50) patch at one end, there's a watermark at the other, plus a security thread embedded in the middle. If you end up with a fake note, you'll have no recourse to a refund. Note that shopkeepers do not bother much with shortfalls of 10 cents or less, whether in their favour (especially) or yours.

Banks and exchange

Greek **banks** normally open Monday to Thursday 8.30am–2.30pm and Friday 8.30am–2pm. Always take your passport with you as proof of identity and expect long queues. Large hotels and some travel agencies also provide an exchange service, though with hefty commissions. On small islands with no full-service bank, "authorized" bank agents will charge an additional fee for posting a travellers' cheque to a proper branch.

A number of authorized brokers for exchanging foreign cash have emerged in Athens and other major tourist centres. When changing small amounts, choose those bureaux that charge a flat percentage commission (usually 1 percent) rather than a high minimum. There is a small number of 24-hour **automatic exchange machines**, but a high minimum commission tends to be deducted. There is no need to **purchase euros** beforehand unless you're arriving at some ungodly hour to one of the remoter frontier posts. **Travellers' cheques** (best in euros rather than dollars), can be cashed at most banks, though rarely elsewhere. Cashing the cheques will incur a minimum charge of €1.20–2.40 depending on the bank; for larger amounts, a set percentage will apply.

ATMs and credit cards

Debit cards have become the most common means of accessing funds while travelling, by withdrawing money from the vast network of Greek **ATMs**. Larger airports have at least one ATM in the arrivals hall and any town or island with a population larger than a few thousand (or substantial tourist traffic) also has them. Most accept Visa, MasterCard, Visa Electron, Plus and Cirrus cards; American Express holders are restricted to the ATMs of Alpha and National Bank. There is usually a charge of 2.25 percent on the sterling/dollar transaction value, plus a commission fee of a similar amount. Using **credit cards** at an ATM costs roughly the same; however, inflated interest accrues from the moment of use.

Major credit cards are not usually accepted by cheaper tavernas or hotels but they can be essential for renting cars. Major travel agents may also accept them, though a **three-percent surcharge** is often levied on the purchase of ferry tickets.

Opening hours and public holidays

It's difficult to generalize about Greek **opening hours**, which are notoriously erratic. Most shops open 8.30/9am and close for a long break at 2/2.30pm. Most places, except banks, reopen around 5.30/6pm for three hours or so, at least on Tuesday, Thursday and Friday. Tourist areas tend to adopt a more northern European timetable, with supermarkets and travel agencies, as well as the most important archeological sites and museums, more likely to stay open throughout the day. If you find yourself needing to tackle Greek bureaucracy, you can't count on getting anything essential done except from Monday to Friday, between 9.30am and 1pm.

As far as possible, times are quoted in the text for tourist sites but these change with exasperating frequency, especially since the economic crisis. Both winter and summer hours are quoted throughout the guide, but to avoid disappoint-ment, either phone ahead or time your visit during the core hours of 9am–2pm. **Monasteries** are generally open from approximately 9am to 1pm and 5 to 8pm (3.30–6.30pm in winter) for limited visits.

Phones

Three **mobile phone networks** operate in Greece: Vodafone-Panafon, Cosmote and Q-Telecom/WIND Hellas. **Coverage** is good, though there are a few "dead" zones on the most mountainous islands or really remote islets. Contract-free plans are heavily promoted in Greece, so if you're here for more than a week or so, buying a **pay-as-you-go** SIM card (for €15–20) from any of the mobile phone outlets will pay for itself very quickly. Top-up cards – starting

from €8–10 – are available at all *períptera* (kiosks). Roaming charges within the EU are capped at €0.51 equivalent per minute (or €0.26 to receive calls). North American users will only be able to use tri-band phones in Greece.

Land lines and public phones are run by OTE who provide phone cards (*tilekártes*), available in denom-inations starting at €4, from kiosks and newsagents. If you plan on making lots of international calls, you'll want a **calling card**, all of which involve calling a free access number from either certain phone boxes or a fixed line (not a mobile) and then entering a twelve-digit code. OTE has its own scheme, but competitors generally prove cheaper. Avoid making calls direct **from hotel rooms**, as a large surcharge will be applied, though you will not be charged to access a free calling card number.

Photography

You can feel free to snap away pretty much anywhere in Greece, although some churches display "No photography" signs, and museums and archeological sites may require permits at least for professional photographers. The main exception is around **airports** or **military installations** (usually clearly indicated with a "No pictures" sign). The ordeal of twelve British plane-spotters who processed slowly through Greek jails and courts in 2001–2 on espionage charges should be ample incentive.

Time

Standard Greek time is always two hours ahead of GMT. For North America, the difference is usually seven hours for Eastern Standard Time, ten hours for Pacific Standard Time. Greek summer time begins at 2am on the last Sunday in March, when the clocks go forward one hour, and ends at 2am the last Sunday in October when they go back. This change is not well publicized locally, and visitors miss planes and ferries every year.

PUBLIC HOLIDAYS

January 1 New Year's Day.
January 6 Epiphany.
February/March Clean Monday
 (*katharí dheftéra*), 7 weeks before Easter.
March 25 Independence Day.
April/May Good Friday and Easter Monday
 (see p.43).

May 1 May Day.
May/June Whit Monday, 7 weeks
 after Easter.
August 15 Assumption of the Virgin Mary.
October 28 Ohi Day (see p.44).
December 25/26: Christmas Day/
 Boxing Day.

PHONE CODES AND NUMBERS

All Greek phone numbers require dialling of all ten digits, including the area code. Land lines begin with 2; mobiles begin with 6. All land-line exchanges are digital, and you should have few problems reaching any number from either overseas or within Greece. Mobile phone users are well looked after, with a signal even in the Athens metro.

PHONING GREECE FROM ABROAD

Dial ☎0030 + the full number

PHONING ABROAD FROM GREECE

Dial the country code (below) + area code (minus any initial 0) + number

Australia	☎0061	UK	☎0044
New Zealand	☎0064	Ireland	☎00353
Canada	☎001	USA	☎001
South Africa	☎0027		

GREEK PHONE PREFIXES

Local call rate	☎0801	Toll-free/Freefone	☎0800

USEFUL GREEK TELEPHONE NUMBERS

Ambulance	☎166	Police/Emergency	☎100
Fire brigade, urban	☎199	Speaking clock	☎141
Forest fire reporting	☎191	Tourist police	☎171 (Athens);
Operator	☎132 (Domestic)		☎210 171 (elsewhere)
Operator	☎139 (International)		

Toilets

Public toilets are usually in parks or squares, often subterranean; otherwise try a bus station. Except in tourist areas, public toilets tend to be filthy – it's best to use those in restaurants and bars. Remember that throughout Greece, you drop paper in the adjacent wastebins, not the toilet bowl.

Tourist Information

The **National Tourist Organization of Greece** (Ellinikós Organismós Tourismoú, or EOT; Visit Greece abroad, ⓦvisitgreece.gr) maintains offices in most European capitals, plus major cities in North America and Australia. It publishes an array of free, glossy, regional pamphlets, invariably several years out of date, fine for getting a picture of where you want to go, though low on useful facts.

In Greece, you will find official **EOT offices** in many but by no means all of the larger islands where, in addition to the usual leaflets, you can find weekly **schedules** for the inter-island **ferries** – rarely entirely accurate, but useful as a guideline. EOT staff may be able to advise on **bus** and **train** departures as well as current opening hours for local sites and museums and occasionally can assist with accommodation.

Where there is no EOT office, you can get information from municipally run tourist offices – these can be more highly motivated and helpful than EOT branches. In the absence of any of these, you can visit the **Tourist Police**, essentially a division (often just a single room) of the local police. They can sometimes provide you with lists of rooms to let, which they regulate, but they're really the place to go if you have a **serious complaint** about a taxi, or an accommodation or eating establishment.

Greek national tourist offices abroad

Australia & New Zealand 51 Pitt St, Sydney, NSW 2000 ☎02/9241 1663, ⓔhto@tpg.com.au.
UK 4 Conduit St, London W1R 0DJ ☎020/7495 4300, ⓔinfo@gnto.co.uk.
USA 305 E 47th St, New York, NY 10017 ☎212/421-5777, ⓔinfo@greektourism.com.

Travellers with disabilities

In general the **disabled** are not especially well catered for in Greece though, as relevant EU-wide legislation is implemented, the situation is gradually improving. In cities, wheelchair ramps and beeps for the sight-impaired are rare at pedestrian crossings, and outside Athens few buses are of the "kneeling" type. Only Athens airport, its metro and airline staff in general (who are used to handling wheelchairs) are disabled-friendly. Ancient monuments, one of the country's main attractions, are usually inaccessible or hazardous for anyone with mobility impairments.

Some advance planning will make a stress-free holiday in Greece more likely. The Greek National Tourist Office is helpful; they also publish a useful questionnaire that you might send to hotels or self-catering accommodation. Before purchasing **travel insurance**, ensure that pre-existing medical conditions are not excluded. A **medical certificate** of your fitness to travel is also extremely useful; some airlines or insurance companies may insist on it.

Travelling with children

Children are worshipped and indulged in Greece, and present few problems when travelling. They are not segregated from adults at meal times, and early on in life are inducted into the typical late-night routine – kids at tavernas are expected to eat (and up to their capabilities, talk) like adults.

Outside of certain all-inclusive resorts with children's programmes, however, there are very few amusements specifically for them – certainly nothing like Disney World Paris. Water parks, tourist sites and other places of interest that are particularly child-friendly are noted throughout the guide.

Luxury hotels are more likely to offer some kind of **babysitting or crèche service**. All the same basic baby products that you can find at home are available on the islands, though some may be more expensive, so it can pay to load up on nappies, powders and creams before leaving home.

Most domestic ferry-boat companies and airlines offer child **discounts**, ranging from fifty to one hundred percent depending on their age; hotels and rooms won't charge extra for infants, and levy a modest supplement for "third" beds which the child occupies by him/herself.

Athens and the mainland ports

56 Athens and Pireás

68 Alexandhroúpoli

69 Astakós

69 Áyios Konstandínos

69 Igoumenítsa

70 Kalamáta

70 Kavála

71 Kyllíni

71 Lávrio

72 Neápoli

72 Pátra

73 Rafína

73 Thessaloníki

74 Vólos

75 Yíthio

CAFÉ LIFE, THISSÍO, ATHENS

Athens and the mainland ports

Although a growing number of islands have their own airports served by direct international flights, the majority still have to be reached by ferry. In this chapter you'll find survival guides to all the significant ports on the Greek mainland; how to get there, where to find the ferries, and suggestions for places to stay and to eat if you need to do so.

Most commonly, you'll find yourself travelling to or from the islands via **Athens**, and here you may well want to break your journey to take in the exceptional array of ancient sites and museums, while sampling some of the country's best food and nightlife. A couple of nights' stopover will allow you to take in the Acropolis and the other major sites and museums, and get a feel for a few of the city's neighbourhoods. Even in a single day, a morning arrival would give you time for a look at the Acropolis and Pláka before heading down to the port of **Pireás** (Piraeus) to catch an overnight ferry.

Athens and Pireás

ATHENS is home to more than a third of Greece's population, and, while its history looms large, the twenty-first-century capital is a vibrant, hectic place, buzzing with life into the early hours of its warm summer nights. While on first acquaintance it may not be a beautiful city, Athens is starting to make the most of what it has, with new roads, rail and metro, along with extensive pedestrianization in the centre. The clamorous port at **Pireás** is quickly and easily reached from the centre or airport.

The vestiges of the ancient Classical Greek city, most famously represented by the **Parthenon** and other remains that top the **Acropolis**, are an inevitable focus, along with the magnificent **National Archeological Museum**. Even on a brief stopover, though, you should take the time to explore some of the city's **neighbourhoods** too. **Eating out** is great, with establishments ranging from traditional tavernas to gourmet restaurants. In summer, much of the action takes place outdoors, from dining on the street or clubbing on the beach, to **open-air cinema**, **concerts** and **classical drama**. There's a diverse **shopping** scene, too, ranging from colourful bazaars and lively street markets to chic suburban malls. And with good-value, extensive public transportation allied to inexpensive taxis, you'll have no difficulty getting around.

The Acropolis

Daily: April–Sept 8am–6.30pm; Oct–March 8am–4.30pm • €12 • Metro Akrópoli

The **rock of the Acropolis**, crowned by the dramatic ruins of the Parthenon, dominates almost every view of Athens. Surrounded by **pedestrianized streets**, it can be appreciated from almost every angle.

Entering via the monumental double gatehouse, the **Propylaia**, you'll see the elegant, tiny **Temple of Athena Nike** on a precipitous platform to the right, overlooking Pireás and the Saronic Gulf. In myth, it was from here that King Aegeus threw himself to his death, thinking that his son Theseus had failed in his mission to slay the Minotaur on

Acropolis approaches and tickets p.60   Bus, metro and tram tickets p.66

THE PARTHENON, ATHENS

Highlights

❶ Acropolis, Athens Rising above the city, the great rock of the Acropolis topped by the Parthenon symbolizes not just Athens, but the birth of European civilization. **See p.56**

❷ National Archeological Museum, Athens Quite simply the world's finest collection of ancient Greek art and sculpture. **See p.61**

❸ Psyrrí, Athens The heart of Athenian nightlife, a tiny quarter packed with cafés, bars and restaurants that are buzzing till late at night. **See p.61**

❹ Pireás The port of Athens is constantly alive with the movement of ferries and cruise liners – if this is not enough, the small boat harbours boast some of the city's best fish restaurants. **See p.64**

❺ Áno Póli, Thessaloníki In the city's Upper Town, restored Ottoman architecture vies for space with Roman and Byzantine remains, and it's also home to a burgeoning nightlife scene. **See p.74**

❻ Archeological Museum, Thessaloníki Home to the Gold of Macedon exhibition, displaying finds from the royal tombs at Vergina. **See p.73**

HIGHLIGHTS ARE MARKED ON THE MAP ON P.58 & P.63

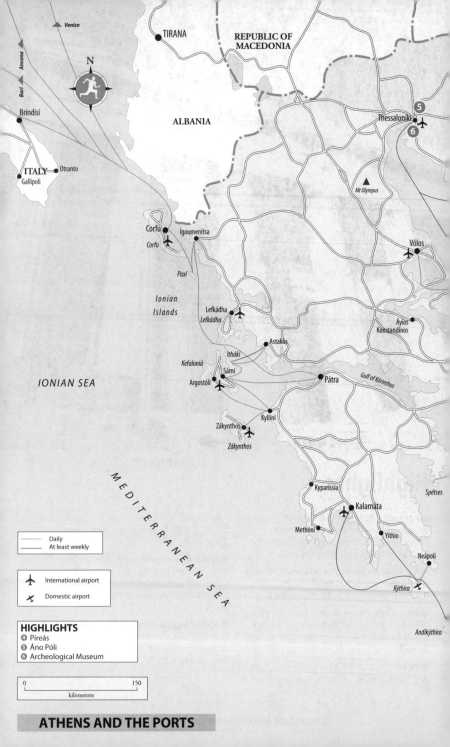

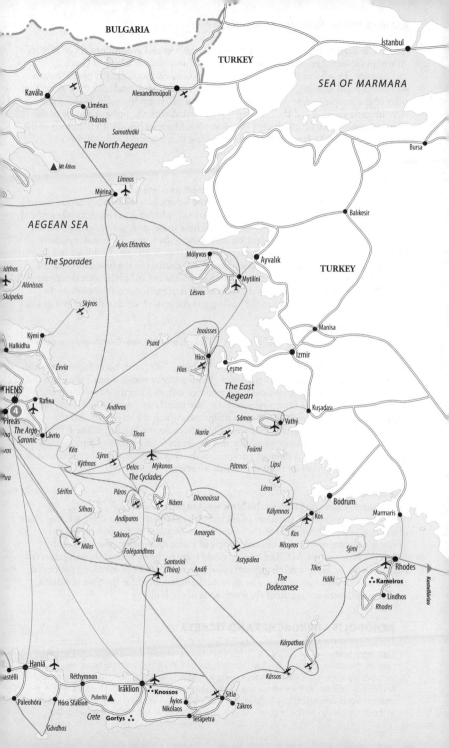

1

Crete. The **Parthenon** is the highlight, though, the first and greatest project of Pericles' Athenian Golden Age, and arguably the finest achievement of Classical Greek architecture. To achieve the appearance of perfection, each column (its profile bowed slightly to avoid seeming concave) is slanted inwards by 6cm, while the steps along the sides of the temple incline just 12cm over a length of 70m. Originally the columns were brightly painted and the building was decorated with the finest sculpture of the Classical age, also lavishly coloured (see Acropolis Museum below). To the north of the Parthenon stands the **Erechtheion** and its striking Porch of the Caryatids, whose columns form the tunics of six tall maidens.

The South Slope of the Acropolis

Daily: April–Sept 8am–6.30pm; Oct–March 8.30am–3pm • €2 or joint Acropolis ticket • Metro Akrópoli

The dominant structure on the **South Slope of the Acropolis** is the second-century Roman **Herodes Atticus Theatre** (Odeion of Herodes Atticus), which has been extensively restored but is open only for shows; at other times you'll have to be content with spying over the wall. Nearby, the much more ancient **Theatre of Dionysos** is one of the most evocative locations in the city. Here the masterpieces of Aeschylus, Sophocles, Euripides and Aristophanes were first performed. Between the two theatres lie the foundations of the **Stoa of Eumenes**, originally a massive colonnade of stalls erected in the second century BC. Above the *stoa*, high up under the walls of the Acropolis, extend the ruins of the **Asklepion**, a sanctuary devoted to the healing god Asklepios built around a sacred spring.

The Acropolis Museum

Dhionysíou Areopayítou 15 • Tues–Sun 8am–8pm, last admission 7.30pm, late opening Fri till 10pm • €5 • ⓦ theacropolismuseum.gr • Metro Akrópoli

The new **Acropolis Museum** is a magnificent building, filled with beautiful objects, with a wonderful sense of space and light and a glass top storey with a direct view up to the Parthenon itself. The displays include magnificent statues from the Acropolis sites, while on the top floor, a fifteen-minute video (alternately in English and Greek) offers a superb introduction to the **Parthenon sculptures**, which are set out around the outside of the hall, arranged as they would have been on the Parthenon itself. Only a relatively small number are original; the rest are represented by plaster copies which seem deliberately crude, a pointed reference to the ongoing campaign for the return of the so-called Elgin Marbles from the British Museum.

The ancient Agora

Daily: summer 8am–6.30pm; winter 8.30am–3pm • €4 or joint Acropolis ticket • Metro Monastiráki

The **Agora** or market was the heart of ancient Athenian city life; the chief meeting place of the city, where orators held forth, business was discussed and gossip exchanged. Today it's an extensive and confusing jumble of ruins, dating from the sixth century BC to the fifth century AD. The best overview is from the exceptionally well-preserved **Hephaisteion**, or Temple of Hephaistos, where there's a terrace overlooking the rest of the site and an explanatory map. For some background, head for the **Stoa of Attalos**, where a small **museum** occupies the lower level of the building.

ACROPOLIS APPROACHES AND TICKETS

The summit of the Acropolis can be entered only from the west, where there's a big coach park at the bottom of the hill: bus #230 from Sýndagma will take you almost to the entrance. On foot, the obvious approach is from Metro Akrópoli. Entry is by a multiple ticket which also includes the Theatre of Dionysos, Ancient Agora, Roman Forum, Hadrian's Library, Kerameikos and Temple of Zeus, so if you visit any of them before the Acropolis, be sure to buy this multiple ticket rather than an individual entry; the tickets can be used over four days. Crowds at the Acropolis can be horrendous – to avoid the worst come very early in the day, or late.

Pláka

1

The largely pedestrianized area of **Pláka**, with its narrow lanes and stepped alleys climbing towards the Acropolis, is arguably the most attractive part of Athens, and certainly the most popular with visitors. Although surrounded by traffic-choked avenues, Pláka itself provides a welcome escape from concrete and exhaust fumes. With scores of **cafés and restaurants** to fill the time between museums and sites, and streets lined with touristy **shops**, it's an enjoyable place to wander. Of the sights, don't miss the **Folk Art Museum** (Kydhathinéon 17; Tues–Sun 9am–2.30pm; €2; ⓦmelt.gr), with five floors devoted to displays of weaving, pottery, regional costumes and embroidery along with other traditional Greek arts and crafts, or the **Roman Forum** (daily: summer 8.30am–6.30pm, winter 8.30am–3pm; €2 or joint Acropolis ticket), built during the reign of Julius Caesar and his successor Augustus as an extension of the Greek Agora.

Monastiráki and Psyrrí

Monastiráki, to the north of Pláka, is substantially less touristy than its neighbour. The area has been a marketplace since Ottoman times, and still preserves, in places, a bazaar atmosphere; from Platía Monastirakíou you'll see signs in both directions that proclaim you're entering the famous **Athens Flea Market**. **Psyrrí**, northwest, is home to Athens' busiest nightlife as well as some quirky shops. This is also a great place to **eat and drink**: between them, Monastiráki and Psyrrí probably have more eating places per square metre than anywhere else in Athens.

Sýndagma

All roads lead to **Sýndagma** – you'll almost inevitably find yourself here sooner or later for the metro and bus connections. With the Greek Parliament building (the Voulí) on its uphill side, **Platía Syndágmatos** – Constitution Square – is the political and geographic heart of Athens; the principal venue for mass demonstrations and political rallies. In front of the **Voulí**, goose-stepping **evzónes** in tasselled caps, kilt and woolly leggings change their guard at regular intervals before the **Tomb of the Unknown Soldier**, while behind it spread the shady **National Gardens** (sunrise–sunset; free) – a luxuriant tangle of trees whose shade and duck ponds provide palpable relief from the heat of summer.

Omónia and the bazaar

While Pláka and Sýndagma are resolutely geared to tourists and the Athenian well-heeled, **Platía Omonías** (Omónia Square) and its surroundings represent a much more gritty city, revolving around everyday commerce and trade. The **bazaar area** around Odhós Athinás is home to a bustling series of markets and small shops spilling into the streets and offering some of urban Athens' most compelling sights and sounds, as well as an ethnic mix that is a rare reminder of Greece's traditional role as a meeting place of East and West. It's also a neighbourhood being increasingly recolonized by the drug addicts and prostitutes who were cleared out in time for the Olympics; a process accelerated by the economic crisis.

The National Archeological Museum

Patissíon 44 • Mon 1.30–8pm, Tues–Sun 9.30am–4pm • €7 • ⓦ namuseum.gr • Metro Viktorías or Omónia, also dozens of buses, including trolleys 2 and 5 – look for those labelled Mousseio

The **National Archeological Museum** is an unrivalled treasure trove of ancient Greek art. You could easily spend an entire morning or afternoon here, but it's equally possible to scoot round the highlights in an hour or two; arriving early in the morning or late in

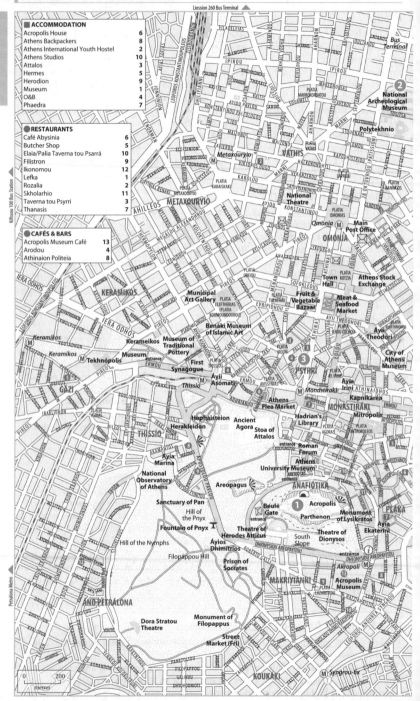

Liossion 260 Bus Terminal

■ **ACCOMMODATION**
Acropolis House	6
Athens Backpackers	8
Athens International Youth Hostel	2
Athens Studios	10
Attalos	3
Hermes	5
Herodion	9
Museum	1
O&B	4
Phaedra	7

● **RESTAURANTS**
Café Abysinia	6
Butcher Shop	5
Elaia/Palia Taverna tou Psarrá	10
Filistron	9
Ikonomou	12
Lefka	1
Rozalia	2
Skholarhio	11
Taverna tou Psyrri	3
Thanasis	7

● **CAFÉS & BARS**
Acropolis Museum Café	13
Arodou	4
Athinaion Politeia	8

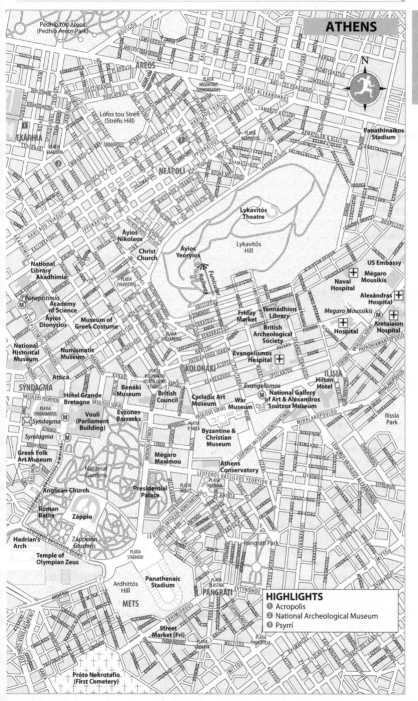

ATHENS

N

Pedhío tou Áreos
(Pedhío Áreos Park)

ÁREOS

Lófos tou Stréfi
(Stréfis Hill)

Panathinaïkos
Stadium

EXÁRHIA

NEÁPOLI

Lykavitós
Theatre

Lykavitós
Hill

Áyios
Nikolaos

Christ
Church

Áyios
Yeóryios

Funicular
Railway

US Embassy

National
Library
Akadhimía

Panepistímio
Academy
of Science

Áyios
Dionýsios

Museum of
Greek Costume

Friday
Market

Yennádhion
Library

British
Archeological
Society

Mégaro
Mousikís

Naval
Hospital

Aléxandras
Hospital

Megaro Moussikis

Aretaíaion
Hospital

National
Historical
Museum

Numismatic
Museum

Evangelismós
Hospital

Hospital

Attica

SYNDAGMA

Syndagma

Hôtel Grande
Bretagne

Benáki
Museum

British
Council

Cycladic Art
Museum

War
Museum

Evangelismos

National Gallery
of Art & Aléxandros
Soútzos Museum

ILÍSIA

Hilton
Hotel

Syndagma

Vouli
(Parliament
Building)

Evzones
Barracks

KOLONÁKI

Byzantine &
Christian
Museum

Ilissia
Park

Greek Folk
Art Museum

Mégaro
Maximou

Athens
Conservatory

Anglican Church

National
Gardens

Presidential
Palace

Roman
Baths

Záppio

Hadrian's
Arch

Zappeíon
Gardens

Pangráti Park

Temple of
Olympian Zeus

Ardhittós
Hill

Panathenaic
Stadium

PANGRÁTI

METS

Street
Market (Fri)

HIGHLIGHTS
❶ Acropolis
❷ National Archeological Museum
❸ Psyrrí

Próto Nekrotafío
(First Cemetery)

1

the afternoon should mean you won't be competing with the tour groups for space. Highlights include the **Mycenaean halls** – where the gold **Mask of Agamemnon**, arguably the museum's most famous piece, is almost the first thing you see – and a vast collection of Classical **sculpture**, following a broadly chronological arrangement around the main halls of the museum. Don't ignore, either, the less well-known collections hidden away at the rear of the museum and upstairs. These include the **Stathatos collection**, with some truly exquisite jewellery; a wonderful **Egyptian** room; the **bronze collection**; hundreds of **vases**; and a display on the excavations of Akrotíri on Santoríni (p.193), including some of the famous **Minoan frescoes** discovered there.

Pireás

PIREÁS (Piraeus) has been the port of Athens since Classical times, when the so-called Long Walls, scattered remnants of which can still be seen, were built to connect it to the city. Today it's a substantial metropolis in its own right. The port and its **island ferries** are the reason most people come here; if you're spending any time, though, the real attractions of the place are around the small-boat harbours of **Zéa Marina** and **Mikrolímano** on the opposite side of the small peninsula. Here, the upscale residential areas are alive with attractive waterfront cafés, bars and restaurants offering some of the best seafood in town, and there's an excellent archeological museum and a small beach – all are accessible by local trolley bus #20 from the metro station.

ARRIVAL AND DEPARTURE

BY PLANE

Eleftheríos Venizélos Airport (☎210 353 0000, ⓦaia.gr) is at Spáta, 33km southeast of the city. Modern and efficient, its facilities include free wi-fi (for 60min), ATMs and banks with money-changing facilities on all levels, the usual array of travel agencies and car rental places, plus luggage storage with Pacific (☎210 353 0160, ⓦpacifictravel.gr) and both national and municipal tourist offices.

Destinations Aegean (ⓦaegeanair.com), Olympic (ⓦolympicairlines.com) and Sky Express (ⓦskyexpress.gr) operate daily flights in summer to the following island destinations: Haniá (Crete), Híos, Ikaría, Iráklion (Crete), Kálimnos, Kárpathos, Kefaloniá, Kérkyra (Corfu), Kos, Kýthira, Léros, Límnos, Mílos, Mýkonos, Mytilíni (Lésvos), Náxos, Páros, Ródhos (Rhodes), Sámos, Skiáthos, and Thíra (Santoríni). There are also regular departures to Astypálea, Sitía (Crete), Skýros, Sýros and Zákynthos.

FROM THE AIRPORT INTO TOWN

By metro and rail The metro and suburban trains share a station at the airport. Metro Line 3 (every 30min, 6.35am–11.35pm) takes you straight into the heart of the city in 45min (€8 single, €14 return, discounts for multiple tickets) where you can change to the other lines at either Monastiráki or Sýndagma. The suburban train (same fares) offers direct trains to the northern suburbs and Corinth, but for Laríssis station in the centre, and Pireás, you have to change at Áno Liósia.

By bus Buses can be slower than the metro (1hr–1hr 30min), especially at rush hours, but they're also cheaper,

more frequent (at least 2–3 per hr), run all night and offer direct links to other parts of the city: the #X95 runs to Sýndagma square; #X96 to the port at Pireás via Glyfádha and the beach suburbs; #X93 to the bus stations. Tickets cost €5 from a booth beside the stops or on board – be sure to validate your ticket on the bus. There are also regional bus services to local destinations including the ports of Rafína (hourly; 6am–9pm; €5; ticket on the bus) and Lávrio (20 daily; 6.30am–10pm; €6).

By taxi Taxis can take anything from 35min to 1hr 35min (at rush hour) to reach the centre; there's a fixed fare to the centre of €35, or €50 at night, and no extras should be added. The fare to Rafína should be similar, Pireás or Lávrio €10–15 more.

BY FERRY FROM PIREÁS

Hundreds of ferries leave Pireás daily, so it's perhaps not surprising that a comprehensive list is hard to find: even the tourist office simply look up individual queries online (at ⓦopenseas.gr). There are also smaller ferry terminals at **Rafína** (see p.73) and Lávrio (see p.71).

Getting there The easiest way to travel between the port and central Athens is on metro line 1; the journey takes about 20min from Omónia. Alternatively, there are buses: #40 (about every 10min from 5am–midnight; hourly 1–5am) runs to and from Sýndagma, while #49 from Omónia (roughly every 15min from 5am–midnight; hourly 1–5am) will drop you slightly closer to the ferries. Both are very slow, however – allow an hour to be safe. From the airport, you can take express bus #X96 (around 1hr 20min). Taxis cost about €10 at day tariff from the centre of Athens.

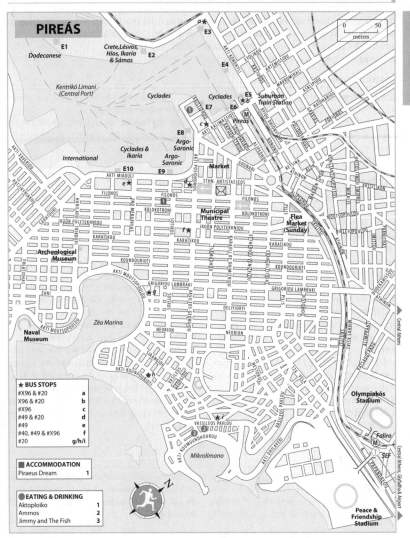

PIREÁS

E1 Dodecanese

Crete, Lésvos, Híos, Ikaría & Sámos E2

E3

E4

Kentrikó Limani (Central Port)

Cyclades

Cyclades

E5

E7 E6

Suburban Train Station

Pireás

International

Cyclades & Ikaría

E8 Argo-Saronic

Argo-Saronic

E10 E9

Market

AKTI MIAOULI

FILONOS

FILONOS

FILONOS

ETHN. ANTISTASSEOS

KOLOKOTRONI

KOLOKOTRONI

Municipal Theatre

IRÓON POLYTEKHNIOU

KARAÏSKOU

KARAÏSKOU

KARAÏSKOU

Archeological Museum

KOUNDOURIOTI

AKTI MOUTSOPOULOU

KOUNDOURIOTI

Flea Market (Sunday)

GRIGORIOU LAMBRAKI

GRIGORIOU LAMBRAKI

Zéa Marina

NEORION

DELIYIORY

NEORION

Naval Museum

LIRANGIOU

AKTI KOUNDOURIOTI

Mikrolímano

VASSILEOS PAVLOU

AKTI KOUMOUNDHOUROU

AKTI DHILAVERI

Olympiakós Stadium

Faliro

SEF

Peace & Friendship Stadium

Central Athens

Central Athens, Glyfadha & Airport

0   50
metres

★ BUS STOPS

#96 & #20	a
X96 & #20	b
#X96	c
#49 & #20	d
#49	e
#40, #49 & #X96	f
#20	g/h/i

■ ACCOMMODATION

| Piraeus Dream | 1 |

● EATING & DRINKING

Aktoploiko	1
Ammos	2
Jimmy and The Fish	3

It can be hard to get a taxi amid the throng disgorging from a ferry.

Ferry tickets There's no need to buy ferry tickets for conventional ferries before you get here, unless you want a berth in a cabin or are taking a car on board; during Greek holidays (August and Easter especially) these can be hard to get and it's worth booking in advance – the big companies have online booking. Flying Dolphin hydrofoil reservations are also a good idea at busy times, especially Friday night/Saturday morning out of Athens, and Sunday evening coming back. In general, though, the best plan is

simply to get to Pireás early and check with some of the dozens of shipping agents around the metro station and along the quayside Platía Karaïskáki (there are plenty of agents in central Athens too). Most of these act only for particular lines, so for a full picture you will need to ask at three or four outlets.

Departure points Boats for different destinations leave from a variety of points around the main harbour: it can be helpful to know the gate number, though these are primarily for drivers. Free, airport-style buses run from gate E5, near the metro, as far as E1, for the big ferries to Crete,

1

the Dodecanese and the northwest. The main gates and departure points are marked on our map, but always check with the ticket agent as on any given day a ferry may dock in an unexpected spot. They all display signs showing their destination and departure time; you can't buy tickets on the boat, but there's usually a ticket hut on the quayside nearby.

INFORMATION AND TOURS

Greek National Tourist Office Dhionysíou Areopayítou 18–20, just by the entrance to the South Slope of the Acropolis (Mon–Fri 9am–7pm, Sat & Sun 10am–4pm; Ⓦ gnto.gr; Metro Akrópoli). This is a useful first stop and they have a good free map as well as information sheets on current museum and site opening hours, bus schedules and so on. If you are arriving by plane, you can save time by calling in at the airport branch.

Athens City Tourism Provides an infopoint at the airport and an excellent website, Ⓦ breathtakingathens.com – check out the interactive maps.

GETTING AROUND

By metro The expanded metro system is much the easiest way to get around central Athens; it's fast, quiet and user-friendly. Trains run from roughly 5.30am to midnight (later on Line 1). When travelling on the metro you need to know the final stop in the direction you're heading, as that is how the platforms are identified; there are plenty of maps in the stations. Further information on Line 1 at Ⓦ isap.gr, other lines at Ⓦ amel.gr.

By bus The bus network is extensive, but crowded and confusing; most buses run from around 5am to midnight, with just a few – including those to the airport – continuing all night. Easiest to use are the trolleybuses: #1 connects the Laríssis train station with Omónia, Sýndagma and Koukáki; #2, #4, #5, #9, #11 and #15 all link Sýndagma with Omónia and the National Archeological Museum. There's excellent city bus information at Ⓦ oasa.gr.

By tram Athens' tram is a great way to get to coastal suburbs and the beach, running from around 5.30am to 1am, or 2.30am on Friday and Saturday. The tram heads from Sýndagma to the coast, where it branches: northwest towards Pireás, terminating at SEF, an interchange with metro line 1 and within walking distance of Pireás's leisure harbours; southwest along the coast to Glyfádha and Voúla, giving access to numerous city beaches. The tram doesn't automatically stop at every station, so push the bell if you're on board, or wave it down if you're on the platform. Details at Ⓦ tramsa.gr.

By taxi Athenian taxis can seem astonishingly cheap – trips around the city centre will rarely run above €5 and Pireás is €9–12 from the centre, the exact amount determined by traffic and amount of luggage. One legitimate way that taxi-drivers increase their income is to pick up other passengers along the way. There is no fare-sharing: each passenger (or group of passengers) pays the full fare for their journey. So if you're picked up by an already-occupied taxi, you'll pay from that point on, plus the €1.16 initial tariff. When hailing an occupied taxi, call out your destination, so the driver can decide whether you suit him or not.

ACCOMMODATION

HOTELS

Acropolis House Kódhrou 6, Pláka ☎ 210 322 2344, Ⓦ acropolishouse.gr; Metro Sýndagma. A rambling, slightly dilapidated 150-year-old mansion much loved by its regulars – mostly students and academics. Furnishings are individual and some rooms have (sole use) baths across the hall; there's a/c and free wi-fi throughout. Breakfast included. **€70**

BUS, METRO AND TRAM TICKETS

The easiest and least stressful way to travel is with a **pass**. A **one-day imerísio** costs €4 and can be used on buses, trolleybuses, trams, metro and the suburban railway in central Athens (everything except the airport route and some long-distance bus lines). You validate it once, on starting your first journey, and it is good for 24 hours from then. A **weekly pass** costs €14. A single ticket, valid for 90 minutes on all forms of transport (and transfers between them), is €1.40; a single ticket for one journey by bus or tram only is €1.20. Tickets must be validated at the start of your journey – in the machines at the top of the stairs in metro stations, on board buses, or on the platform or on board for trams.

Tickets and passes can be bought from any metro ticket office, machines at tram stations, blue-and-yellow bus ticket booths (near most major stops) and many newsstands – you can buy several at once and then validate them as necessary.

1

Athens Studios Veïkóu 3a, Makriyiánni ☎ 210 923 5811, ⓦ athensstudios.gr; Metro Akrópoli. Furnished apartments for up to six people, with kitchen, sitting room, TV, free wi-fi, a/c and linen provided. Associated with *Athens Backpackers* (see below), and includes use of their bar and facilities. From **€90**

Attalos Athinás 29, Monastiráki ☎ 210 321 2801, ⓦ attalos.gr; Metro Monastiráki. Modern from the outside but traditional within, the *Attalos* has bright, comfortable rooms, well insulated from the noisy street, all with a/c, TV and free wi-fi (also free computer terminals in the lobby). Some balcony rooms on the upper floors have great views – there's also a roof-terrace bar in the evenings – but rooms facing the internal courtyard at the back are generally larger and quieter. **€85**

Hermes Apóllonos 19, Pláka ☎ 210 323 5514, ⓦ hermeshotel.gr; Metro Sýndagma. Friendly and welcoming three-star with marble bathrooms and polished wood floors, plus TV, a/c, fridge and wi-fi (small charge). Some rooms are rather small; others have big balconies. Breakfast included. **€120**

Herodion Robérto Gálli 4, Makriyiánni ☎ 210 923 6832, ⓦ herodion.gr; Metro Akrópoli. Lovely four-star hotel – albeit not quite as luxurious as the exterior and lobby might lead you to believe – with an enviable position right behind the Acropolis. **€130**

Museum Bouboulínas 16 ☎ 210 380 5611, ⓦ museum -hotel.gr; Metro Viktorías/Omónia. Very pleasant, international-style hotel (part of the Best Western chain), right behind the National Archeological Museum and the Polytekhnío. Rooms in the new wing, which has triples, quads and small suites, are more luxurious but slightly more expensive. **€75**

O&B Leokoríou 7, Psyrrí ☎ 210 331 2950, ⓦ oandbhotel .com; Metro Thissío. Understated designer hotel with exceptional service and just 22 rooms, including a couple of large suites with private terrace and Acropolis views; all have free wi-fi and satellite TV, as well as DVD and CD players. Friendly and comfortable as well as elegant, plus a great location on the fringes of Psyrrí. **€150**

Phaedra Herefóndos 16, cnr Adhrianoú, Pláka ☎ 210 323 8461, ⓦ hotelphaedra.com; Metro Akrópoli. Small, simple rooms with bare tiled floors, TV and a/c, not all en suite (but you get a private bathroom). Polite, welcoming management looks after the place well and it's quiet at night. **€65** separate bathroom, **€80** en suite

HOSTELS

Athens Backpackers Mákri 12, Makriyiánni ☎ 210 922 4044, ⓦ backpackers.gr; Metro Akrópoli. Very central Athenian-Australian-run hostel with few frills, but clean rooms, communal kitchen, internet access, bar, fabulous rooftop view and great atmosphere. Dorms from **€22**

Athens International Youth Hostel Víktoros Ougó 16, Metaxouryío ☎ 210 523 2540, ⓦ athens -international.com; Metro Metaxouryío. A huge affair, with 140 beds over 7 floors in 2-, 4- and 6-bed dorms, all a/c and en suite, some women-only. Recently given a fresh coat of paint, it is cheap and always busy. Dorms from **€13**

PIREÁS

Piraeus Dream Fílonos 79–81 & Notára 78–80, Pireás ☎ 210 411 0555, ⓦ piraeusdream.gr; Metro Pireás. It's easy to get from the centre to Pireás, but if you do have a very early departure this friendly hotel, handy for ferries, has quiet, recently refurbished rooms (with spectacular lighting), a/c and TV. Buffet breakfast included. **€70**

EATING AND DRINKING

Athens has arguably the best and most varied **restaurants** and **tavernas** in the country, though most tourists, sticking to the obvious central choices, never discover that. While Pláka's hills and narrow lanes can provide a pleasant, romantic evening setting, they also tend to be marred by high prices and tourist hype: areas like Psyrrí and Thissío (or Gázi and Exárhia a little further afield) are where the locals go for a meal out. The pleasure harbours of **Pireás**, meanwhile, are a favourite Sunday lunchtime destination.

RESTAURANTS, TAVERNAS AND OUZERÍS

Butcher Shop Persefónis 19, Gázi ☎ 210 341 3440. As the name and the decor – a modernist take on a traditional butcher shop – suggest, this is not one for the vegetarians. Instead there's all sorts of high-quality meat, from lamb chops (€15.40) to game birds (€12) plus a huge variety of burgers (€10–12.50), exotic sausages (€7.50–9) and the fanciest *yíros* in town (with shank and pancetta of free-range pork, €11.50). Great chips too. Daily noon–1am.

Café Abysinia Kynétou 7, Platía Avysinnías, Monastiráki ☎ 210 321 7047. With two floors and a delicious, modern take on traditional Greek cooking (wild

boar meatballs €15, or mussel pilaf for €10.50), *Café Abysinia* is always busy, popular with a local alternative crowd. Live music most weekday evenings and weekend lunchtimes. Tues–Sat 11am–1am, Sun 11am–7pm.

Elaia/Palia Taverna tou Psarrá Erekhthéos 16 at Erotókritou, Pláka ☎ 210 324 9512/321 8733. Though they appear to be separate restaurants, these two actually share a menu and kitchen; given that, the best place to sit is on the roof terrace at Elaia, with wonderful views; there are also plenty of tables below, both inside and on a tree-shaded and bougainvillea-draped pedestrian crossroads. You're best making a meal of the mezédhes (€6–9). Live

1

music Thurs–Sat eves, open lunchtime till late.

Filistron Apóstolou Pávlou 23, Thissío ☎ 210 342 2897. Somewhat touristy, but worth it for the roof terrace with great Acropolis view. Short menu of tasty, well-presented mezédhes from all over Greece (small plates €5–8.50, large ones €8–13.50), which means some interesting and unusual dishes. Tues–Sun noon–midnight.

Ikonomou Tróon 41, cnr Kydhantidhón, Áno Petrálona ☎ 210 346 7555. Wonderful, traditional taverna with home-cooked food served to packed pavement tables in summer. No menu, just a dozen or so inexpensive daily specials: check out what others are eating as the waiters may not know the names of some of the dishes in English. Mon–Sat dinner only.

Lefka Mavromiháli 121, Neápoli ☎ 210 361 4038. Marvellous traditional taverna with great fáva (hummus-like bean purée), black-eyed beans and baked and grilled meat with barrelled retsina. Summer seating in a huge garden enclosed by barrels. Lunch & dinner Mon–Sat, lunch only Sun.

Rozalia Valtetsíou 58, Exárhia ☎ 210 330 2933. Ever-popular mid-range taverna, with excellent chicken and highly palatable barrelled wine. You order mezédhes from the tray as the waiters thread their way through the throng; there's also a regular menu of grilled fish and meat. Garden seating in summer. Daily lunch & dinner.

Skholarhio Tripódhon 14, Pláka ☎ 210 324 7605. Attractive, split-level ouzerí with a popular summer terrace. It has a great selection of mezédhes (all €3–6) brought out on trays so that you can point to the ones that you fancy. The house red wine is also palatable and cheap. All-inclusive deals at €14 a head. Daily 11am–2am.

Taverna tou Psyrri Eskhýlou 12, Psyrrí ☎ 210 321 4923. Some of the lowest prices and tastiest food in Psyrrí, so unsurprisingly popular. Starters like stuffed aubergine for €4 and simple dishes including moussaka and meatballs for €5.50, but be sure to check out the day's specials in the kitchen, many of them traditional country dishes like rabbit stifado or an earthy goat soup (€7). Daily lunch & dinner.

Thanasis Mitropóleos 69, Monastiráki. Reckoned to serve the best souvláki and yíros in this part of Athens, where there's plenty of competition. Inexpensive, and always packed with locals at lunchtime: there's no booking, so you'll have to fight for a table. Daily 11am to late.

CAFÉS AND BARS

Acropolis Museum Café Dhionysíou Areopayítou 15. A wonderful space in this magnificent modern museum: food is simple – salads, sandwiches, cakes and drinks – and portions aren't huge, but the quality is superb and prices low by Athens standards (€4 for sandwiches, €2.50 for a cappuccino), making this one of the best-value places in the city. Try the delicious píta me fakés, a traditional lentil pie. Open museum hours: Tues–Sun 8am–8pm, late opening Fri till 10pm.

Arodou Miaoúli 22, cnr Protoyénous, Psyrrí ☎ 210 321 6774. Miaoúli, leading up from the metro into Psyrrí, is packed with bars and crowded with people every evening. Arodou is right at the heart – a hugely popular place with plenty of space both outside and in. Drink prices are very reasonable and excellent, well-priced meze (€2.50–6, shared plates from €9) are also available. Daily till late.

Athinaion Politeia Akamántos 1, cnr Apóstolou Pávlou, Thissío. An enviable position in an old mansion, with stunning views from the terrace towards the Acropolis, makes this café a popular meeting place and a great spot to relax over a frappé. Daily 9am–3am.

PIREÁS

If you're looking for food to take on board a ferry, or breakfast, you'll find numerous places around the market area and near the metro station, as well as all along the waterfront. There are plenty of bakeries and souvláki joints here, including a handy branch of Everest on the corner of Aktí Kalimassióti by the metro. Otherwise there's little good food in the port area, but some superb fish tavernas over at Mikrolímano.

Aktoploiko Aktí Tsélegi 4. Less manic than most around the port, this café/restaurant has tables outside on a pedestrianized part of the waterfront just off Platía Karaïskáki and serves breakfast and light meals – souvláki, salads, pasta – throughout the day. Daily till late.

Ammos Aktí Koumoundhoúrou 44, Mikrolímano ☎ 210 422 4633. Ammos goes for an island feel, with hand-painted tables and beach scenes. The menu is predominantly fish (drunkard's mussels €7.80, grilled prawns or fisherman's pasta €15), but there's also a wide variety of meze (€5–9) and a younger crowd than many of its neighbours. Book at weekends. Daily lunch & dinner.

Alexandhroúpoli

The modern city of **ALEXANDHROÚPOLI**, almost on the Turkish border in the northwest corner of Greece, has daily ferries and summer-only hydrofoils to Samothráki. It's not the most exciting of places, but there's a lively seafront promenade and, if you have a few hours to spare, the excellent **Ethnological Museum** (March–Sept Tues–Wed 9am–3pm, Thurs–Fri 9am–3pm & 6–9pm, Sat–Sun 10am–3pm; Oct–Feb Tues–Sat 9am–3pm, Sun 10am–3pm, €3), about 500m north of the ferry terminal, is one of the best in Greece.

ARRIVAL AND DEPARTURE

By plane The airport, with 3 or 4 daily flights from Athens (1hr), is 4km west of town. Frequent local buses stop by en route to town.
By train The train station is next to the port; there are 2 daily services to Thessaloníki.

ACCOMMODATION AND EATING

Erika K Dhimitríou 110, just east of the port entrance ☎ 25510 34115, ⊛ hotel-erika.gr. Smart seafront hotel, recently upgraded, with comfortable rooms and a decent breakfast included. **€60**

ALEXANDHROÚPOLI

By bus The KTEL station is at Venizélou 36 (☎ 25510 26479), several blocks inland from the port; Thessaloníki (6 daily; 5hr).
By ferry Alexandhroúpoli is the only access port for ferries to Samothráki (1–3 daily, 2hr 30min).

Okeanis K Paleológou 20–22, six blocks northwest of the port ☎ 25510 28830. Renovated hotel, stylishly furnished in dark wood and fabrics, with comfortable, average-sized rooms. **€55**

Astakós

ASTAKÓS ("Lobster") is a small port on the western mainland with a ferry to Kefaloniá every weekday lunchtime, plus a Sunday evening departure to Itháki and Kefaloniá. Despite the name there's no lobster served at any of the mediocre tavernas lining the quay; around the marketplace many Neoclassical buildings from the 1870s hint at a more prosperous past.

ARRIVAL AND DEPARTURE

ASTAKÓS

By bus The KTEL is at the end of the quay; buses from Athens should coincide with the ferry.
By ferry Weekday departures to Kefaloniá at around noon

(Sámi; early May to mid-Sept only), Sun evening to Itháki and Kefaloniá; ☎ 26460 38020 for current details.

ACCOMMODATION

Stratos By the quay ☎ 26460 41911. The only hotel, overlooking the tiny, gravelly town beach, is overpriced;

in peak season cheaper rooms are available elsewhere. **€80**

Áyios Konstandínos

ÁYIOS KONSTANDÍNOS is the closest port to Athens for the Sporades islands, with daily departures to Skiáthos, Skópelos and Alónissos. There's little to hang about for and, with frequent buses along the coastal Athens–Lamía motorway, no real need to do so.

ARRIVAL AND DEPARTURE

ÁYIOS KONSTANDÍNOS

By bus The bus station is located about 200m south of the ferry landing; KTEL buses run to and from Athens' Liossíon terminal hourly (2hr 30min) and there's a daily service to Pátra (3hr 30min); ferry operators also run buses from central Athens in high season, timed to coincide with ferries.

By ferry Three or four ferries, fast cats and hydrofoils in high season daily to Skiáthos (1hr 35min–2hr 45min), Skópelos, both ports (2hr 15min–4hr) and Alónissos (3hr–5hr). Operators are Hellenic Seaways (⊛ hsw.gr) and NEL (⊛ nel.gr); local agents Bilalis (☎ 22350 31614, ⊛ bta .gr) and Alkyon (☎ 22350 32444, ⊛ alkyontravel.com).

Igoumenítsa

IGOUMENÍTSA is Greece's third passenger port after Pireás and Pátra, with frequent ferries to **Corfu** and **Italy**. It's also the country's leading cargo port, so away from the waterfront it's far from attractive; levelled during World War II, it was rebuilt in bland utilitarian style. You should hopefully be able to get a ferry out immediately; every day in season there are sailings to Italy in the morning, and throughout the evening. If you

1

end up stuck for the day, you're better off taking an excursion out of Igoumenítsa than hanging around.

ARRIVAL AND DEPARTURE   IGOUMENÍTSA

By bus The KTEL is inland from the Corfu/Paxí quay on Minermoú, corner Arhilóhou.
Destinations Athens (5 daily; 8hr); Ioánnina (9 daily; 2hr); Párga (5 daily; 1hr); Préveza (2 daily; 2hr 30min).
By ferry Almost all international ferries (see p.27) depart from the New Port Egnatía at the far south end of town, although a few do still use the old port; you must check in at least 2hrs before departure. Local ferries operate from the domestic ferry quay just north of the new terminal;

tickets for these services are purchased at waterside booths.
International destinations Ancona (1–2 daily;15hr–15hr 30min); Bari (1–2 daily; 9hr–10hr 30min); Brindisi (1–3 daily; 6hr 30min–8hr); Venice (every day except Wed 22–25hr).
Domestic destinations Corfu (5 daily; 1hr 15min–1hr 45min); Pátra (1–2 daily; 5hr 45min); Zákynthos, (1 weekly; 6hr 15min).

ACCOMMODATION AND EATING

Egnatia Eleftherías 2 ☎ 26650 23648. Inland, at the southeast corner of the main platía, stands this comfortable, air conditioned hotel. Ask for a rear room facing the pine grove, and take advantage of unrestricted street parking out back. Breakfast extra. **€50**

Emily Akti Roudou 13, cnr Agion Apostolon ☎ 26650 23763. This simple taverna is much more authentic than the usual choices along the strip. The menu has all the Greek standards, plus fresh catch of the day, for around €10 a head. Daily lunch & dinner.

Kalamáta

KALAMÁTA, famous for its olives, is by far the largest city in the southern Peloponnese; quite a metropolitan shock after the small-town life of the rest of the region. With time to kill it's worth visiting the **Kástro** (Mon–Fri 8am–2pm, Sat & Sun 9am–3pm; free), a small Byzantine fortress twenty minutes' walk north of the centre. An **amphitheatre** at its base hosts summer concerts. There are also a couple of small **museums**, as well as the simple pleasures of eating at tavernas among the Neoclassical houses on the waterfront.

ARRIVAL AND DEPARTURE   KALAMÁTA

By air The airport (☎ 27210 69442) is 10km west of town on the highway; you'll need to get a taxi into town.
By bus The bus station (☎ 27320 23145) is nearly 1km north of the centre along Nédhondos; again it's easiest to get a taxi down to the port (Athens 28 daily, 4hr 30min;

Pátra 2 daily, 4hr).
By ferry One or two departures weekly with Lane Lines to Kýthira (4hr 30min) and Kastélli, Crete (8hr 30min); ⓦ lane.gr.

ACCOMMODATION AND EATING

Haïkos Navarínou 115 ☎ 27210 88902, ⓦ haikos.gr. Trim, modern hotel with plush rooms but basic bathrooms. All rooms have balconies and a/c and there's internet access. Rooms on the beach side can be noisy. **€85**
Rex Aristomenous 26 ☎ 27210 94440, ⓦ rexhotel.gr. Convenient and historic hotel situated in the old town. Rooms are on the small side, but fresh and well appointed, some with balconies, in a fine Neoclassical building, facing

the palm-lined promenade. There's also a restaurant and a café, the former using all local ingredients, including real Kalamáta olives. Breakfast included. **€100**
Routsis Navarínou 127 ☎ 27210 80830. Old-fashioned taverna with dishes featuring fresh local olives, home-made feta, steamed greens, catch of the day or fish soup (mains aorund €12). Seating along the strip, or in a garden terrace on the beach side. Daily lunch & dinner.

Kavála

KAVÁLA, the second-largest city in Macedonia, is the chief access point for Thássos and also has regular ferries to the other islands of the northeast Aegean. Although its attempt to style itself as the "Azure City", on account of its position at the head of a wide bay, is going a little overboard, it does have a characterful centre, focused on the harbour area and the few remaining tobacco warehouses. A picturesque citadel looks down from a rocky promontory to the east, and an elegant Ottoman aqueduct leaps over modern buildings into the old quarter on the bluff.

ARRIVAL AND DEPARTURE
KAVÁLA

By plane Kavála's "Megas Alexandhros" airport, with frequent direct connections to the UK (Thomsonfly) and Athens (3–4 daily; 1hr), lies 29km southeast. There is no convenient bus, and taxis cost at least €40.

By bus The main bus station, with hourly services to Thessaloníki (2hr) and four a day to Alexandhroúpoli (3hr), is on the corner of Mitropolítou Khryssostómou and Filikís Eterías, an easy walk from the port.

By ferry Several operators ply to Thássos; long-distance services are operated by NEL (℗ nel.gr). Details from the port authority (☎ 2510 223 716) and tickets from harbourfront agencies such as Zolotas (☎ 2510 835 671).
Destinations Híos (2–3 weekly; 12hr); Ikaría (1 weekly; 17hr); Lésvos (2–3 weekly; 10hr); Límnos (2–3 weekly; 5hr); Sámos (2 weekly; 15hr); Thássos (Skála Prínou; 6 daily; 1hr 15min).

ACCOMMODATION AND EATING

Esperia Erythroú Stavroú 42 ☎ 2510 229 621, ℗ esperiakavala.gr. A decent hotel offering comfortable rooms with a/c – ask for the quieter side or back ones. Breakfast, served on a terrace, included. **€55**

Imaret Poulídhou 6 ☎ 2510 620 151, ℗ imaret.gr. This expertly refurbished Ottoman medrese offers rooms and suites that have been faultlessly fashioned. Services

include a traditional hammam with massage, a restaurant serving Ottoman dishes and a womb-like indoor pool. **€300**

Tembelhanio Poulídhou 33b ☎ 2510 232 502. Cosy ouzerí serving a tasty range of mezédhes, involving both meat and seafood, to a soundtrack of eclectic Greek and Middle Eastern sounds. Daily noon–2am; Sun closes 6pm.

Kyllíni

The small port of **KYLLÍNI**, south of Pátra, is the main departure point for the Ionian island of Zákynthos and also has boats to Póros and Argostóli on Kefaloniá. But it's not a particularly attractive place, and there's little point in staying, if you time things right.

ARRIVAL AND DEPARTURE
KYLLÍNI

By ferry Operators are Ionian Ferries (℗ ionianferries.gr), to all destinations, and Strintzis (℗ strintzisferries.gr) for Póros.
Destinations Zákynthos (4–7 daily; 1hr); Kefaloniá, Póros (5 daily summer, 2–3 daily winter; 1hr 15min–2hr 15min),

Kefaloniá Lixoúri–Argostóli (1 daily summer; 2hr–2hr 30min).

By bus Buses from Athens (2–3 daily; 4hr) and Pátra (1–3 daily; 1hr) continue on the ferry to Zákynthos.

Lávrio

LÁVRIO lies close to the southern tip of Attica, some 60km from the centre of Athens; easily accessed from there or direct from the airport. Its ferries mainly serve **Kéa** and **Kýthnos**, but there are also services to the northeast Aegean and to many of the Cycladic islands via Sýros. There are plenty of cafés and restaurants around the harbour, a major yachting centre, and an excellent archeological museum (Tues–Sun 8.30am–3pm), but given the frequent connections there's absolutely no need to stay here.

ARRIVAL AND DEPARTURE
LÁVRIO

By bus KTEL buses run between Lávrio and Athens airport (20 daily; 30min), as well as the Mavrommatéon terminal in Athens (hourly; 1hr 40min).

By ferry Operators are Goutos Lines (☎ 22920 26777), Karystia (☎ 22920 26040) and NEL (℗ nel.gr).

Destinations Kéa (at least 3 daily; 1hr); Kýthnos (at least one a day; 1hr 40min); also twice or more a week to Áyios Efstrátios (5hr), Límnos (8hr) and Kavála (14hr), and to Psará (5hr) and Híos (6hr 30min); and to many of the Cycladic islands via Sýros (5hr).

1

Neápoli

A small port at the southern foot of the Peloponnese, **NEÁPOLI** is a mix of old buildings and modern Greek concrete behind a grey-sand beach with views of Kýthira and Elafónissos islands. For such an out-of-the-way place, it is surprisingly developed, catering mostly to Greek holiday-makers.

ARRIVAL AND DEPARTURE NEÁPOLI

By bus KTEL buses from Athens (3 daily; 7hr) stop on Dhimokratías, the main road down towards the sea.

By ferry Daily to Kýthira (1hr 15min); tickets from Vatika

Bay Shipping (☎ 27340 24004, ⓦ vatikabay.gr), just west of the pier.

ACCOMMODATION

Aïvali Akti Voion 164 ☎ 27340 22287, ⓦ aivali-neapoli .gr. This clean, unpretentious and very friendly, family-run hotel is right on the seafront, near the ferry for Kýthira. Rooms have balconies, all facing the water, plus a/c and wi-fi. Breakfast included. **€50**

Vergina ☎ 27340 23443, ⓦ verginahotel.com. This hotel is more quietly situated, one block away from the harbour. It's modestly modern, with internet access, a/c, and basic rooms with balconies. Breakfast included. **€50**

Pátra

PÁTRA (Patras) is the largest city in the Peloponnese and, after Pireás, the major port of Greece; it's the chief terminal for **ferries from Italy** as well as having connections to most of the **Ionian islands**. The city is also a hub of the Greek-mainland transport network, with connections throughout the Peloponnese and, via the ferry at Río, across the straits to Delphi or western Greece. Unless you arrive late in the day from Italy, you shouldn't need to spend more than a few hours in the city.

ARRIVAL AND DEPARTURE PÁTRA

By bus Buses for the Peloponnese, Athens, Ioánnina, Thessaloníki and Vólos depart from the main bus station (☎ 26106 23886), on the waterfront just south of the port. Buses for Zákynthos go from Óthonos & Amalías 47 (☎ 26102 20993); for northern Greece, Kefaloniá and Crete from Óthonos & Amalías 58 (☎ 2610 274 938); and for destinations in the Peloponnese from Nórman 5 (☎ 26104 21205).

Destinations Athens (every 20min daily, 2.30am–9.45pm; 3hr); Itháki (1 daily, via Kefaloniá; 6hr); Kalamáta (2 daily; 4hr); Kefaloniá (3 daily; 4hr); Lefkádha (2 weekly; 3hr); Thessaloníki (4 daily; 7hr); Vólos (1 daily, except Sat; 6hr); Zákynthos (4 daily; 2hr 30min including ferry from Kyllíni).

By train The train station is on Óthonos & Amalías, south of the port. Trains (replacement bus part of the way) travel

north and east to Kórinthos and Athens (7 daily; 3hr 30min).

By ferry Ferries leave from or near the Triándi Jetty (Gate 6), at the end of Norman Street; ticket agencies are also located along here, on the waterfront street. Italy-bound ferries (see box, p.27) leave from early afternoon to midnight. You must check in with the agent's embarkation booth at least 2hrs before departure.

International destinations Ancona (2–3 daily; 19hr 30min/20hr 30min); Bari (1–2 daily; 14hr 30min/16hr); Brindisi (1 daily; 14hr 30min); Venice (1 daily; 1day 7hr/1day 7hr 30min).

Domestic destinations Corfu (1–2 daily; 6hr 15min/6hr 45min); Igoumenítsa (3–5 daily; 4hr 45min–7hr); Kefaloniá and Itháki (1–2 daily; 3hr 20min/3hr 45min).

ACCOMMODATION AND EATING

Don't expect too much of Pátra's **hotels**; most cater for a very passing trade and don't try too hard. The pedestrianized seaward end of Ayíou Nikoláou is a very lively area at night, with busy cafés spread across the street.

Adonis Kapsáli 9, cnr Záïmi ☎ 26102 24213, ✉ hoteladonis@pat.forthnet.gr. This large high-rise hotel is well furnished and maintained. Most room balconies overlook the harbour, though bathrooms are

small. Free wi-fi throughout. Buffet breakfast €5/person extra. **€60**

Apanemo Óthonos & Amalías 107. Seafood taverna opposite the fishing harbour, with good fresh fish and noted for its *galaktoboúreko* (custard pudding). Fresh fish priced by the kilo, otherwise expect about €15/person. Daily lunch & dinner.

Galaxy Ayíou Nikoláou 9 ☎ 26102 75981, ⓦ galaxy hotel.com.gr. This is a well-placed hotel, newly refurbished, with a sleekly modern lobby and handsome rooms that include wi-fi and a flat-screen TV. Good buffet breakfast included. **€80**

Youth Hostel Iróön Polytekhníou 62 ☎ 26104 27278, ⓦ patrasrooms.gr/hostel.htm. A handsome stone mansion (used as Nazi headquarters in World War II) set in a garden opposite the marina, but a 1.5km walk from the centre. No curfew; open all year. Dorm beds **€10**

Rafína

The port of **RAFÍNA**, about 30km from central Athens, has fast ferries and catamarans to the **Cyclades**, as well as to nearby **Évvia**. Many Athenians have summer homes overlooking the attractive, rocky coast, but the beaches are tricky to reach even with a car, so for visitors the chief attraction, ferries aside, is gastronomic. Overlooking the harbour is a line of excellent **seafood restaurants**, many with roof terraces and a ringside view of the comings and goings at the harbour. The pedestrianized square above the harbour is also a lively place, ringed with cafés and rather cheaper eating options.

ARRIVAL AND DEPARTURE RAFÍNA

By bus Rafína is connected by KTEL bus with the Mavrommatéon terminal in Athens (every 30min; 1hr) and also has direct buses to the airport (13 daily; 40min). The bus terminal is right on the seafront at the outer edge of the harbour, facing the sea; get your ticket on the bus.

By ferry The main destinations served (most at least twice a day) are Ándhros, Tínos, Páros, Mýkonos, Íos, Thíra and Náxos, plus at least five daily to Marmári on Évvia (1hr): the vast majority of ferries leave either early morning or late afternoon and there are ticket agents for the dozens of operators all round the port.

ACCOMMODATION AND EATING

Hotel Akti Arafinidhón Alón and Vithinías ☎ 22940 29370, ⓦ aktihotel-rafina.gr. Recently refurbished, with some sea views, new soundproofing and a/c, the *Akti* is very pleasant, though some bathrooms are almost comically cramped. Good deals often available. **€80**

Ouzeri Limeni Platía Plastíra 17 ☎ 22940 24750. The best choice on the lively square above the harbour, with

excellent meze and Greek standards. Daily lunch & dinner.

Ta Kavoúria tou Asimáki Rafína harbour ☎ 22940 24551. The pick of Rafína's seafood restaurants is the first as you descend towards the harbour from the square; though it looks fancier than its neighbours, with linen tablecloths and proper wine glasses, it's no more expensive. Daily lunch & dinner.

Thessaloníki

Greece's second city and capital of the north, **THESSALONÍKI** – or Salonica, as it is sometimes known to English-speakers – has a distinctly Balkan feel but also an unusually wide ethnic mix and a prosperous air, stimulated by a major university, an international trade fair and a famously avant-garde live music and entertainment scene. The food is generally better than in the rest of the country, too: there are some very sophisticated restaurants, but also flavoursome traditional fare on offer in a great number of old-fashioned ouzerís and Turkish-influenced tavernas.

Though in no way a tourist resort, the city has plenty to offer: **churches**, **Ottoman buildings** and excellent **museums** above all. Of the latter, the undoubted champion is the **archeological museum** (June–Oct Mon 1.30am–8pm, Tues–Sun 8am–8pm; Nov–May Tues–Sun 8.30am–3pm; €6), which displays many of the finds from the royal tombs of Philip II of Macedon (father of Alexander the Great). Monumental highlights include the **White Tower (Lefkós Pýrgos)**, the city's graceful symbol; Roman remains including the **Arch of Galerius** and **Rotónda** (now the church of **Áyios**

1

Yeóryios); the many Ottoman survivals in the heart of the Upper Town or **Áno Póli**; and Byzantine churches, above all **Ayía Sofía** (daily 7am–1pm & 5–6.30pm; free) and **Áyios Dhimítrios** (Mon 12.30–7pm, Tues–Sat 8am–8pm, Sun 10.30am–8pm; free).

ARRIVAL AND DEPARTURE

THESSALONÍKI

By plane Thessaloníki "Makedonia" airport (☎2310 985 000, ☎2310 411 977 for flight information, ⓦthessalonikiairport.gr) is located 15km south of the city centre. City bus #78 shuttles back and forth from the airport to the KTEL bus terminal via the town centre once or twice hourly all day and #78N goes once an hour through the night. A taxi ride into town comes to €14, plus extras.
Destinations Athens (12–14 daily; 50min); Corfu (1 weekly; 1hr); Haniá, Crete (1–2 daily; 1hr 30min); Híos (4 weekly; 1hr 10min–2hr 45min); Iráklion, Crete (2–4 daily; 1hr 15min); Lésvos (1–2 daily; 1hr–1hr 50min); Límnos (5 weekly; 50min); Rhodes (2–4 daily; 50min); Sámos (4 weekly; 1hr 20min).
By train The train station is on the west side of town, with convenient bus links and a taxi rank. If you want to buy tickets or make reservations in advance, the OSE office at

Aristotélous 18 (Mon & Sat 8am–3pm, Tues–Fri 8am–9pm) is far more central and helpful than the station ticket-windows.
Destinations Alexandhroúpoli (2 daily; 5hr 45min–6hr 15min); Athens (7 daily; 4hr 15min–7hr).
By bus Most KTEL buses use the main terminal ("Makedonia"), 3km west of the city centre at Yiannitsón 194 (☎2310 500 111, ⓦktel-thes.gr); local buses #1, #31 & #78 go to the train station and Egnatía.
Destinations Alexandhroúpoli (6 daily; 5hr); Athens (11 daily; 7hr); Kavála (hourly; 2hr 15min); Vólos (4 daily; 4hr).
By ferry All ferries leave from the port located at the western end of the seafront. The most convenient all-round agent, selling tickets for all companies, is Zorpidis, near the port at Salamínas 4 (☎2310 555 995, ⓦzorpidis.gr). Currently, only one reliable route operates to Límnos, Lésvos, Híos and Sámos (1 weekly).

ACCOMMODATION

Augustos Ptoleméon 1 ☎2310 522 550, ⓦaugustos .gr. Charming if slightly faded 1920s hotel on a quiet corner near Egnatía, with all en-suite high-ceilinged rooms and wi-fi in the spacious lounge. **€30**
Capsis Bristol Oplopíou 2 ☎2310 506 500, ⓦcapsisbristol.gr. Thessaloníki's original boutique hotel, with twenty period-furnished rooms and suites in an impeccably restored 1870 building. Good Italian/Argentinian restaurant and lavish buffet breakfast included; best booked online. **€130**
Electra Palace Platía Aristotélous 9 ☎2310 294 000,

ⓦelectrahotels.gr. In one of the town's most prestigious positions and as palatial inside as out, this five-star has large, lavishly furnished rooms and a good restaurant, albeit with a slightly dated air. **€175**
Kinissi Palace Egnatía 41 ☎2310 508 081, ⓦkinissipalace.gr. The smartest hotel in the area, its comfortable rooms have all mod cons but cramped bathrooms and noisy a/c. There's a sauna, hammam and massage service, plus a bar and a decent restaurant, the Averof. Breakfast included. **€70**

EATING

Iy Gonia tou Merakli Avyerinoú, alley off Platía Áthonos, ☎2310 287 726. Inexpensive seafood, better than average portions, a quality free dessert and highly palatable barrelled wine make this the best of several ouzerís in these atmospheric surrounding lanes. Daily noon–2am.
Molyvos Kapodhistríou 1, ☎2310 555 952, ⓦmolyvos .gr. Ouzo and mezédhes combos for €12–15 from Crete, Lésvos, Cyclades and Istanbul are among the regional specialities served at this first-floor taverna-ouzerí, with an attached shop selling ouzo and olive oils. Daily 11am–2am.

Myrovolos Smyrni In arcade in the Modhiáno off Komninón 32 ☎2310 274 170. Friendly, crowded ouzerí, also known as Tou Thanassi. Typical dishes include cheese-stuffed squid, Smyrna-style meatballs, stuffed potatoes and grilled baby fish. Reservations recommended. Daily noon–2am, closed Sun eves.
Ta Bakaliarakia tou Aristou Katoúni 3, Ladhádhika, ☎2310 542 906. Heapings of cod and chips, served on greaseproof paper for around €6–7, make this joint in a pedestrianized portside alley quite memorable. Second branch one block away. Daily 9am–7pm.

Vólos

VÓLOS is the major port of Thessaly, in central Greece, with frequent ferries and hydrofoils to the **Sporades – Skiáthos, Skópelos** and **Alónissos**. The industrial outskirts give little hint of a mythological past, but 4km west lies the site of ancient Iolkos, from where Jason and the Argonauts legendarily embarked on their quest for the Golden Fleece. Nowadays, University of Thessaly students make it a lively place, so it's not a bad spot to spend a few hours or even a night while waiting for a boat. The most attractive place to linger is along the eastern **waterfront esplanade**, between landscaped **Platía Yeoryíou** and the **archeological museum**.

ARRIVAL AND DEPARTURE
VÓLOS

By air The airport is 26km southwest of the city. Buses generally meet flights and transfer passengers to Vólos.
By train The train station is just off Platía Ríga Feréou, a short walk to the waterfront and ferries.
Destinations Athens (1 daily express service via Lárissa; 4hr 30min); Lárissa on the main Athens – Thessaloníki line (15 daily; 52min).
By bus The KTEL city bus terminal is on Sekéri, just off Grigoríou Lambráki, a 10min walk southwest of the main

square, Platía Ríga Feréou. There is a taxi rank outside.
Destinations Athens (11–12 daily; 4hr 30min–5hr); Thessaloníki (8–9 daily; 3hr).
By ferry Hellenic Seaways (ⓦhsw.gr) flying cats and ferries run twice daily for most of the year – more in mid-summer – to Skiáthos (1hr 30min/2hr 30min), Skópelos (2hr 45min/3hr 45min) and Alónissos (3hr 15min/4hr 30min); the local agent is *Sporades Travel* at Argonaftón 33 (ⓣ24210 23400).

ACCOMMODATION, EATING AND DRINKING

Iasson Pávlou Melá 1 ⓣ24210 26075. Facing the waterfront, this basic, bright yellow modern choice offers double-glazed windows, a/c, a small elevator and balconies. Rooms and bathrooms are generally on the small side, but clean. **€35**
Nikos Iasonos 118. You can always count on the freshly grilled *souvlákis*, chicken or pork, served here. You'll find it near the Art Deco cinema back from the port. €10/person

or less for a freshly prepared, simple meal. Daily noon–midnight.
Xenia Domotel Plastíra 1 ⓣ24210 92700, ⓦdomotel xeniavolouhotel.gr. This crisply modern seafront luxury resort has a pool, spa, fitness centre, plush rooms in Grecian blue and white, with free wi-fi and free use of a laptop, as well as a range of other amenities and a copious buffet breakfast. **€130**

Yíthio

YÍTHIO (Gythion), Sparta's ancient port, is the eastern gateway to the dramatic Máni peninsula, and one of the south's most attractive seaside towns in its own right. Its low-key harbour, with **ferries to Pireás** and **Kýthira**, gives onto a graceful nineteenth-century waterside of tiled-roof houses. There are beaches within walking distance, and rooms are relatively easy to find. In the bay, tethered by a long, narrow jetty, is the islet of **Marathoníssi**, ancient Kranae, where Paris of Troy, having abducted Helen from Menelaus's palace at Sparta, dropped anchor, and where the lovers spent their first night.

ARRIVAL AND DEPARTURE
YÍTHIO

By bus The bus station (Athens, 6 daily; 5hr) is close to the centre of town, with the main waterfront street, Vassiléos Pávlou, ahead of you.

By ferry Weekly service to Kýthira (2hr 30min), Andikýthira (4hr 30min) and Kastélli (Crete; 6hr 30min); ⓦlane.gr.

ACCOMMODATION AND EATING

Gythion Vassiléos Pávlou 33 ⓣ27330 23452, ⓦgythionhotel.gr. A fine old (1864) hotel with period decorated rooms, all with views of the waterfront, located above *Dodoni* ice cream parlour. Guests can use the Gythion Bay campsite's facilities. Breakfast included, with fresh orange juice. **€65**
Poulikakos ⓣ27330 22792. Located on the main square, this cosy, traditional taverna is simple but offers

delicious food in large portions and at good prices. Full meals run about €10–15. Daily lunch & dinner.
Saga Tzanetáki ⓣ27330 23220, ⓕ27330 24370. Comfortable seafront *pension* run by a friendly, knowledgeable French-Greek family, with a good restaurant on the ground floor, overlooking the Marathoníssi islet. **€45**

The Argo-Saronic Islands

80 Salamína

81 Égina

87 Angístri

90 Póros

93 Ýdhra

99 Spétses

TEMPLE OF APHAEA

The Argo-Saronic Islands

The rocky, partly volcanic Argo-Saronic islands, most of them barely an olive's throw from the mainland, differ to a surprising extent not just from the land they face but also from one another. The northernmost island of the Argo-Saronic group, Salamína, is effectively a suburb of Pireás, with its narrow strait, barely a kilometre across, crossed by a constant stream of ferries. There's little to attract you on the other side, however, and the island is covered only briefly here. Égina, important in antiquity and more or less continually inhabited since then, is infinitely preferable: the most fertile of the group, it is famous for its pistachio nuts and home to one of the finest ancient temples in Greece. Tiny Angístri is often treated as little more than an adjunct of Égina, but it's a lovely place in its own right, ideal for a few days' complete relaxation. The three southerly islands – green Póros, tiny, car-free Ýdhra and upmarket Spétses – are comparatively infertile, and rely on water piped or transported in rusting freighters from the mainland.

Given their proximity to Athens and their beauty, the Argo-Saronics are hugely popular destinations, with Égina (Aegina) almost becoming a city suburb at weekends. Póros, Ýdhra (Hydra) and Spétses are similar in the summer, though their visitors include a higher proportion of foreign tourists. More than any other group, these islands are best out of season and midweek, when visitors (and prices) fall dramatically and the port towns return to a quieter, more provincial pace. You'll also notice a significant difference between Ýdhra and Spétses, the furthest of the islands, and those closer to Athens – because of the distance, and because they're accessible only by hydrofoil and catamaran rather than the cheaper conventional ferries, they're markedly more expensive and exclusive, with significant expat populations. The islands were not extensively settled until medieval times, when refugees from the mainland established themselves here, adopting seagoing commerce (and piracy) as livelihoods. Today, foreigners and Athenians have replaced locals in the depopulated harbour towns; windsurfers, water-taxis and yachts are faint echoes of the massed warships, schooners and *kaïkia* once at anchor.

GETTING THERE

By ferry Virtually all services from Pireás to the Argo-Saronic islands leave from between gates E8 and E9; there are ticket booths here. For all of these islands, hydrofoil or catamaran services are faster and more frequent than ferries, though they cost around twice as much. Friday evening and Saturday morning sailings, as well as the returns on Sunday night, can be very busy; for these, or if you hope to bring a vehicle for the weekend on a regular ferry, reserve your trip well in advance.

Tickets and agencies Contact details for Pireás are as follows (local island agencies are given in the island accounts): Aegean Flying Dolphins (to Égina and Angístri) ☎ 210 412 1654, ⓦ aegeanflyingdolphins.gr; Alexandros (fast ferry to Souvála and Ayía Marína, Égina) ☎ 210 482 1002, ⓦ alexcruises.com; Ayios Nektarios Eginas (ferry to Égina) ☎ 210 422 5625, ⓦ anes.gr; Hellenic Seaways (ferries, hydrofoils and Flying Cat to all points) ☎ 210 419 9000, ⓦ hsw .gr; Nova (ferry to Égina) ☎ 210 412 6181, ⓦ novaferries.gr.

The Battle of Salamis p.81
Excursions to the Peloponnese p.92
Ýdhra's festivals p.97

Ýdhra's inland walks p.98
Sotírios Anáryiros p.100
Hiking across Spétses p.103

SPÉTSES ISLAND

Highlights

❶ Temple of Aphaea, Égina The best-preserved ancient temple on any island, in an evocative setting on a wooded hill with magnificent views towards the mainland and Athens. **See p.85**

❷ Angístri Island Little known to outsiders, this dot of land is less than an hour from Athens by hydrofoil, yet preserves the feel of an unspoilt hideaway. **See p.87**

❸ Póros Town Climb to the clocktower of this small island's capital to look down over the Argo-Saronic Gulf and the Peloponnese; the shipping in the narrow strait between here and

the mainland offers an ever-changing spectacle. **See p.91**

❹ Ýdhra Town Ydhra's perfect, horseshoe-shaped harbour, surrounded by grand eighteenth-century mansions and genuinely traffic-free streets, is one of the most perfect in all of Greece. **See p.95**

❺ Zoyeriá Beach, Spétses Some of the most alluring beaches in the Argo-Saronics can be found along Spétses' pine-speckled coastline; at hard-to-reach Zoyeriá is a wonderful, isolated taverna, most of whose customers arrive by boat. **See p.102**

HIGHLIGHTS ARE MARKED ON THE MAP ON P.80

Salamína

SALAMÍNA is the quickest possible island-hop from Pireás, and indeed much of its population commutes to the city to work. The island itself, however, is highly developed, has few tourist facilities, and is close enough to the Athenian dockyards to make swimming unappealing. The island's port is at **Paloúkia**, facing the mainland, just a short hop across a narrow, built-up isthmus to **Salamína Town** on the west coast. Five kilometres or so beyond Salamína Town, **Eándio** has the island's cleanest and most attractive beaches. A similar distance from Salamína Town to the north, the **monastery of Faneroméni** (daily 8.30am–12.30pm & 4pm–sunset) is a working nunnery with impressive frescoes, beautifully sited amid pine woods overlooking the mainland.

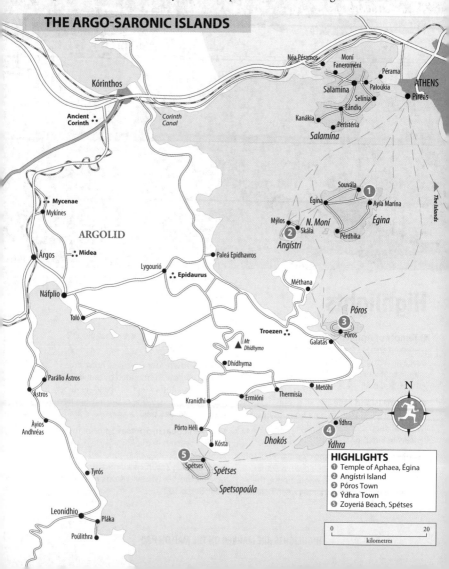

THE ARGO-SARONIC ISLANDS

HIGHLIGHTS

① Temple of Aphaea, Égina
② Angístri Island
③ Póros Town
④ Ýdhra Town
⑤ Zoyeriá Beach, Spétses

THE BATTLE OF SALAMIS

Perhaps the main reason for heading to Salamína is for the boat trip itself, through an extraordinary industrial seascape of docks and shipworks. The waters you cross were the site of one of the most significant **sea battles** of ancient times; some would say of all time, given that this was a decisive blow in preventing a Persian invasion and allowing the development of Classical Athens, and with it modern Western culture.

In 480 BC, the Greeks were in full retreat from the vast Persian army under Xerxes, following the defeat of the Spartans at Thermopylae. Many Greek cities, including Athens, had been sacked and burned by the invaders – indeed smoke from the ruins on the Acropolis probably formed a backdrop to the **Battle of Salamis**. The Greeks had roughly 370 triremes supplied by around twenty cities, the bulk from Athens, Corinth and Aegina; the Persian fleet was twice the size, with heavier ships, but even more diverse, with many from subject nations whose loyalty was questionable.

Through false information and strategic retreats, the Greeks managed first to tire many of the Persian crews – who rowed all night to cut off a non-existent escape attempt – and then to lure them into the narrow strait off Salamína. Crowded in and unable to manoeuvre, and with the wind in the wrong direction, the Persians found themselves at the mercy of the more nimble Greek triremes, and the battle eventually became a rout. Some two hundred Persian ships were sunk, against forty-odd on the Greek side, and few of their heavily armoured crews or marines survived.

ARRIVAL AND DEPARTURE SALAMÍNA

By boat There are half-hourly small passenger boats from Pireás throughout the day (Gate E8; 45min), and a constant stream of small boats and roll-on, roll-off car ferries, day and night, from Pérama, on the mainland directly opposite (5min). Pérama is easily reached by bus: #843 from Pireás, G18 or B18 from Omónia in central Athens. There are also ferries every 20min or so between Faneroméni and Néa Péramos (aka Megára) on the mainland.

GETTING AROUND

By bus Salamína has a pretty impressive bus system, with departures from the ferry dock in Paloúkia to Salamína Town every fifteen minutes. Buses also run hourly to numerous other destinations on the island, including Eándio and Faneroméni.

Égina

A substantial and attractive island with a proud history, less than an hour from Pireás, **ÉGINA (Aegina)** is not surprisingly a popular weekend escape from Athens. Despite the holiday homes, though, it retains a laidback, island atmosphere, especially if you visit midweek or out of season. Famous for its **pistachio orchards** – the nuts are hawked from stalls all around the harbour – the island can also boast substantial ancient remains, the finest of which is the beautiful fifth-century BC **Temple of Aphaea**, commanding superb views towards Athens from high above the northeast coast.

ARRIVAL AND DEPARTURE ÉGINA

By ferry and hydrofoils Those to Égina Town dock at parallel quays, pretty much at the heart of things; the *Angístri Express* (☎ 694 71 18863) can be found among the pleasure and fishing boats a short distance to the south. The schedule summaries below are for summer weekday services; sailings are more frequent and significantly busier at weekends (Fri–Sun), less regular from mid-Sept to June. Ayía Marína and Souvála are linked to Pireás once or twice daily, with an extra early morning run to Souvála only in high season.

Tickets and agencies Immediately in front of the docks in Égina Town is a row of cabins selling tickets for Aegean Flying Dolphins (to Pireás and Angístri ☎ 22970 25800, ⓦ aegeanflyingdolphins.gr), Ayios Nektarios Eginas (ferry to Pireás ☎ 22970 25625, ⓦ anes.gr), Hellenic Seaways (ferries, hydrofoils and Flying Cat to Pireás and Angístri, ferry to Póros ☎ 22970 24456, ⓦ hsw.gr) and Nova (ferry to Pireás ☎ 22970 24200, ⓦ novaferries.gr). Alexandros

2 Angístri

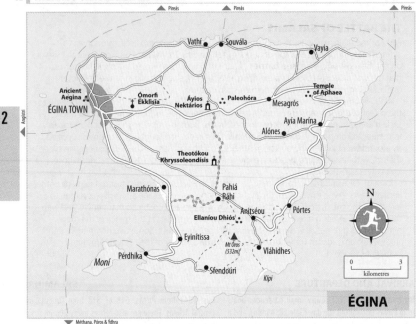

ÉGINA

Ferries (to Pireás from Ayía Marína ☎ 22970 52210 and Souvála ☎ 22970 32234, ⓦ alexcruises.gr) has quayside booths open an hour or so before departure.
Destinations Angístri (6 hydrofoils and 1 or 2 ferries daily, plus Angístri Express 2–3 daily except Sun; 15min); Pireás (from Égina Town 12 hydrofoils and 15 ferries daily, 40min–1hr 30min; from Ayía Marína 1–2 ferries daily, 1hr 15min; from Souvála 1–3 daily, 40 min); Póros (via Méthana 2–3 ferries daily; 1hr 15min).

INFORMATION

Services There are numerous banks around Égina Town harbour, many with ATMs. The post office is at the rear of Platía Ethneyersías, where the buses stop. Most of the harbourfront cafés have wi-fi; Global Internet Café at Fanerómenis 7, just off the southern end of the waterfront, has plenty of terminals and fast connections.
Newspapers Foreign-language papers and a few books from Kendrou Typou, on Eákou at the corner of Spýrou Ródhi.

Useful website There's no tourist office, but ⓦ aeginagreece.com is a useful resource.
Travel agent Aegina Island Holidays (☎ 22970 26430, ⓦ aeginaislandgreece.com), on the Égina Town waterfront near the church of Panayítsa, offers excursions to the mainland and islands, including to the Epidaurus festival, as well as help with accommodation should you need it.

GETTING AROUND

By bus The bus station is on Platía Ethneyersías, immediately north of the dock; buy your tickets at the little booth, in summer located on the waterfront, the rest of the year in the square by the bus stop. At least five buses a day (mostly in the morning) head to Souvála and to Ayía Marína, at least six along the coast to Pérdhika; on arrival they turn round and head straight back. All buses towards Ayía Marína stop at Áyios Nektários and most at the Temple of Aphaea; on the return journey, they all stop at both.
By car and motorcycle Several places on and behind Égina Town's main waterfront rent scooters, cars,

motorbikes and mountain bikes – Égina is large and hilly enough to make a motor worthwhile for anything other than a pedal to the local beaches: Trust (☎ 22970 27010), one of the first you come to behind the harbour, has the best prices, though some of their mopeds are fairly battered. There are also hire places in Ayía Marína.
By taxi The taxi rank is at the base of the ferry jetty, opposite the ticket cabins; taxis meet ferry arrivals in Ayía Marína and Souvála too.

Brief history

Inhabited from the earliest times, ancient **Aegina** was a significant regional power as early as the Bronze Age. It traded to the limits of the known world, maintained a sophisticated silver coinage system (the first in Greece) and fostered prominent athletes and craftsmen. The Aeginian fleet played a major role in the Battle of Salamis (see p.81). After this, however, the islanders made the political mistake of siding with the Spartans, giving Athens a pretext to act on long-standing jealousy; her fleets defeated those of the islanders in two separate sea battles and, after the second, the population was expelled and replaced by more tractable colonists.

Subsequent history was less distinguished, with a familiar pattern of occupation – by Romans, Franks, Venetians, Catalans and Ottomans – before the War of Independence brought a brief period of glory as seat of government for the fledgling Greek nation, from 1826 to 1828. For many decades afterwards Égina was a penal island, and you can still see the **enormous jail** undergoing restoration on the edge of town; the building was originally an **orphanage** for victims of the independence struggle, founded by first president Kapodhístrias in 1828.

Égina Town

ÉGINA TOWN, the island's capital, makes an attractive base, with some grand old buildings around a large, busy harbour. The Neoclassical architecture is matched by a sophisticated ethos: by island standards this is a large town, with plenty of shopping and no shortage of tempting places to eat and drink. Life revolves around the **waterfront**, where ferries come and go, yachts moor, fishermen tend their nets and *kaïkia* tie up to sell produce from the mainland.

The Markellos Tower

The restored **Pýrgos Markéllou**, or Markellos Tower, is an extraordinary miniature castle which was the seat of the first Greek government after independence. Despite appearances, it was built only around 1800 by members of the Friendly Society (see p.533) and the local politician Spýros Márkellos. You can't go inside except during the occasional special exhibition, but walking here, through the cramped inland streets, is enjoyable in itself.

Folklore Museum

Spýrou Ródhi 16 • Wed & Thurs 8.30am–2.30pm, Fri 8.30am–2.30pm & 4.30–7.30pm, Sat 10am–1pm & 4.30–7.30pm, Sun10am–1pm • Free

Égina's **Folklore Museum** is a lovely example of its type, housed in a nineteenth-century mansion. Its upper rooms are packed with fine old furniture, traditional costumes, and many of the trappings of island life a century ago, along with a small local historical archive. Downstairs are rooms devoted to fishing, with model boats and fishing gear, and to agricultural life, with a collection of the basics of village life.

Ancient Aegina

Daily 8.30am–3pm, museum closed Mon • €3

The site of **Ancient Aegina** lies north of the centre on a promontory known as **Kolóna**, after the lone column that stands there. The extensive remains, centring on a Temple of Apollo at the highest point, are well signed, and some reconstruction makes it easier to make out the various layers of settlement from different eras. Near the entrance, a small but worthwhile **archeological museum** houses finds from the site, along with information on the island's ancient history. Highlights of the display include a room of Minoan-influenced Middle Bronze Age pottery, rescued from a nearby building site.

The beaches

On the north edge of town, between the port and Kolóna, there's a tiny but popular **beach** with remarkably shallow water. This was the site of the ancient city's harbour,

2

of which various underwater remains are clearly visible. You can swim south of town, too, but there are more enticing spots further north – immediately beyond Kolóna there's an attractive bay with a small, sandy **beach**, while other small coves lie off the road heading further out of town in this direction. Just a couple have any facilities, with loungers and beach bars; **Kamares Paradise** is among the more attractive.

ACCOMMODATION   ÉGINA TOWN

Aeginitiko Archontiko Thomaïdhou and Ayíou Nikólaou ☎ 22970 24968, �🌐 aeginitikoarchontiko.gr. Brick-red Neoclassical mansion opposite the Markellos Tower, lovingly restored with period furnishings and a conscious attempt to preserve traditional island culture. About as far from a bland business hotel as you can get – there's lots of lace, old pictures on the walls, creaking, springy beds and a wonderful breakfast (included) with home-made preserves, cakes and pastries. The suite has painted ceilings; other rooms can be pretty basic, though all have a/c, TV and fridge. **€70**

Brown Waterfront ☎ 22970 22271, �🌐 hotelbrown .gr. Rather dated 3-star hotel, housed in a former sponge factory dating from 1886, on the southern part of the harbour. Some rooms have great views of the harbour activity, though the garden bungalows are quieter; a galleried family suite sleeps four. Breakfast included. **€65**

Elektra Leonándrou Ladhá 25 ☎ 22970 26715, ⚖aegina-electra.gr. Friendly, quiet establishment, directly inland from the ferry quay on the street with Piraeus Bank on the corner, whose compact but comfortable rooms come with small balconies and free wi-fi. **€55**

Pavlou Eyinítou 21 ☎ 22970 22795. Old-school rooms establishment set behind Panayítsa church, with very plain, stone-floored rooms not all of which are en suite; they do all have fans, a/c (extra charge), fridge and TV though. **€40**

⭐ **Plaza** Kazantzáki 4 ☎ 22970 25600, ⚖plaza -aegina.gr. One of a series of small waterfront hotels close to the town beach. Rooms have been newly refurbished, with quality bathrooms and elegant dark-wood decor, plus double-glazing, a/c and TV. There are great sea views from the marginally more expensive rooms at the front, and little balconies from which to appreciate them. **€55**

EATING AND DRINKING

There are plenty of good places to eat and drink in Égina, particularly at the south end of pedestrianized Panayióti Irióti behind the fish market, and at the far ends of the waterfront – fussy Athenian patronage keeps the standards fairly high. The cafés near the ferry jetty and in the centre of the waterfront tend to be less good value. Numerous bakeries are in the backstreets – Papayionis, by Trust motorbike hire up the first alley off the seafront, is excellent, while Melenio, close to the Markellos Tower, is an exceptional modern *zaharoplastío*, with fine ice cream and beautiful displays of cakes and sweets.

⭐ **Agora** (also known as Yeladhakis) Panayióti Irióti ☎ 22970 27308. The best of three rival seafood ouzerís behind the fish market (the others are very good too). Not the most attractive location, but serves wonderful, inexpensive (around €8 per fish plate), authentic Greek food: accordingly it's usually mobbed and you may have to wait for a table. Summer seating in the cobbled lane, winter up in the loft inside. Daily, evening only.

Avli Panayióti Irióti 17 ☎ 22970 26438. Big place in an alley behind the harbour, popular with expats and open all day serving coffee, breakfast (€4–8), lunch and dinner (mains €6–9; spaghetti and pizza as well as Greek dishes and pricier steaks), while in the early hours it transforms into a bar with Latin/jazz sounds. Daily 10am–late.

Elia Koumoundhoúrou 4 ☎ 22975 00205. Modern taverna in an alley that emerges close to the Markellos Tower with a Mediterranean menu including salads, pasta (carbonara

€7.50) and unusual meze (chicken satay €6.50) as well as traditional Greek dishes (daily special €8.50); live music many evenings. Wed–Sat lunch and dinner, Sun lunch only.

Flisvos Kazantzáki 8 ☎ 22970 26459. An excellent spot for grilled fresh fish and traditional dishes at fair prices (moussaka or *souvláki* €7.50, swordfish steak €12), towards the end of a line of similar establishments behind the town beach. Good-value lunchtime specials. Daily lunch & dinner.

Posto Grillo Panayióti Irióti ☎ 22970 28687. A modern kebab place behind the fish market with a wide variety of grills, from excellent *yíros píta* (€1.70) to chops and *souvláki*; takeaway or eat in. Daily 11am–midnight.

Skotadis Harbourfront ☎ 22970 24014. The best of a cluster of taverna-ouzerís just south of the market, popular with locals. A short menu, predominantly fish and meze at €6–7 a dish, but what it does it does well. Daily 10am–1am.

NIGHTLIFE AND ENTERTAINMENT

Athenian visitors are largely responsible for a surprisingly ample choice of nightlife given a town of about nine thousand souls. As well as bars and clubs there are three summer open-air cinemas – Anesis on Eákou close to the Pýrgos Markéllou,

Olympia on Faneroménis opposite the football ground, and Akroyiali out beyond this on the Pérdhika road; indoor Titina, opposite the Pýrgos Markéllou, is open year-round.

Ellinikon Seaside Aktí Hatzí 10 ☎ 22976 00448 or 693 61 11 213. A big, enjoyable, somewhat touristy club on the southern fringe of town, near the Cine Akroyiali, with mainstream and Greek dance music. Nightly in summer from 10pm.

En Aigini Spýrou Ródhi 44 ☎ 22970 22483 or 694 85 33 060. Upstairs bar with live Greek music from around 11pm every weekend; they also host big-name visiting artists – look out for posters, and book if you want to secure a table. Fri–Sat from around 9pm, plus special events.

Maska Mitropóleos 8 ☎ 22970 22280. Restored stone-walled, high-ceilinged building that makes a pleasant spot for a quiet, early drink – later there's often a DJ playing oldies and classic dance tracks. Daily from 9pm.

Across the island

Two main routes lead east towards Ayía Marína and the Temple of Aphaea: you can head directly **inland** from Égina Town across the centre of the island or follow the **north coast** road via Souvála. Along this north coast there are plenty of scruffy beaches and clusters of second-home development, between which is a surprisingly industrial landscape, with boatyards and working ports. Souvála itself is something of an Athenian resort, with a couple of direct daily ferries to Pireás but little other reason to stop.

Áyios Nektários

On the route inland you'll pass the modern convent of **Áyios Nektários**, whose vast church is said to be the largest in Greece. The convent was founded by Saint Nektarios, who died in 1920 and was canonized in 1961. His tomb lies in the chapel of the original monastery, Ayía Triádha. Miracles surrounded Nektarios from the moment of his death, when nurses put some of his clothing on an adjacent bed, occupied by a man who was paralyzed; the patient promptly leapt up, praising God.

Paleohóra
Unrestricted • Free

On the hillside opposite Áyios Nektários is the ghost-town of **PALEOHÓRA**, the island capital through the Middle Ages. Established in early Christian times as a refuge against piracy, it thrived under the Venetians (1451–1540) but was destroyed by Barbarossa in 1537. The Turks took over and rebuilt the town, but it was again destroyed, this time by the Venetians, in 1654, and finally abandoned altogether in the early nineteenth century. The place now consists of some thirty stone chapels dotted across a rocky outcrop, an extraordinary sight from a distance. Little remains of the town itself – when the islanders left, they simply dismantled their houses and moved the masonry to newly founded Égina Town. At the entrance a helpful map shows the churches and the paths that lead up the hill between them; many are semi-derelict or locked, but plenty are open too, and several preserve remains of frescoes. Despite their apparent abandonment, many have candles burning inside, and prayers left alongside the icons. If you climb right to the top you're rewarded with wonderful views in all directions – you can also appreciate the defensive qualities of the site, from which both coasts can be watched, yet which is almost invisible from the sea.

The Temple of Aphaea
Summer daily 8am–7pm, winter Tues–Sun 8am–5pm; museum Tues–Sun 8am–2.15pm • €4

The Doric **Temple of Aphaea** stands on a pine-covered hill 12km east of Égina Town, with stunning views all around: Athens, Cape Soúnio, the Peloponnese and Ýdhra are all easily made out. Built between 500 and 480 BC, it slightly predates the Parthenon, and is one of the most complete and visually complex ancient buildings in Greece, its superimposed arrays of columns and lintels evocative of an Escher drawing. Aphaea was a Cretan nymph who, fleeing from the lust of King Minos, fell into the sea, was caught by some fishermen and brought to ancient Aegina; her cult, virtually unknown anywhere else, was established on the island as early as 1300 BC. Two hundred years ago the temple's pediments were intact and essentially in perfect condition. However, like the Elgin marbles, they were "purchased" from the Turks – this time by Ludwig I of Bavaria – and they currently reside in Munich's Glyptothek museum. A small **museum** offers a great deal of information about the history and architecture of the temple. A well-signed path leads from the temple to Ayía Marína; an easy walk down, slightly tougher coming up.

Ayía Marína and around

The island's major beach resort, **AYÍA MARÍNA**, lies steeply below the Temple of Aphaea on the east coast. There's a good, clean, sandy beach that shelves very gently, pedaloes to rent and plenty of places to eat, many of them catering to day-trippers – direct boats arrive from Pireás daily. The place has clearly seen better days, as the number of empty premises and the ugly, half-built hotel overshadowing the beach attest, but package tourism seems to be on the up, and it can be lively and enjoyable in a bucket-and-spade sort of way, with plenty of hotels and rooms, and a main street lined with shops, bars and pubs; the occasional summer beach party sees an overnight invasion of young Athenians.

Pórtes

PÓRTES, 8km south of Ayía Marína, is a hamlet with a distinctly end-of-the-road feel, a partly sandy beach with decent snorkelling and a couple of good tavernas. From here, the road climbs steeply inland, beneath the island's highest peak, heading back towards Égina Town via the villages of **Anitséou** and **Pahiá Ráhi**. The latter, with fine views eastwards, has been almost entirely rebuilt in traditional style by foreign and Athenian owners.

ACCOMMODATION AND EATING

AYÍA MARÍNA AND AROUND

AYÍA MARÍNA

Argo Spa Hotel ☎ 22970 32266, ⟲ argohotel.com. With a great position directly above the bay as you come into town, the *Argo* has a pool and small "spa" (sauna, hot tub) and often offers good, all-in deals; refurbished, modern rooms mostly have sea views. **€65**

Barracuda Beach Bar ☎ 694 55 33 693. With a precarious wooden terrace hanging over the beach, the *Barracuda* also offers service on the beach itself. Milkshakes, coffee and sandwiches by day; cocktails and a DJ at night. Daily 11am–3am.

Hotel Liberty 2 ☎ 22970 32105, ⟲ hotelliberty2.gr. An ochre-coloured building overlooking the end of the beach; simple and old-fashioned, with marble floors, but all rooms have sea views as well as a/c and TV. **€40**

Neromilos ☎ 22970 32198. Just above the tiny fishing harbour, Neromilos (the "Watermill") is a big, popular place with a terrace above the water serving inexpensive no-nonsense Greek food – starters €3–5, mains €5–9. Daily lunch & dinner.

PÓRTES

Akroyiali ☎ 22970 31335. A fine *psarotavérna* with a terrace above the sea, close to the beach. Good fish and mezédhes attract visitors from around the island at weekends. Nearby *Thanasis* offers a slightly more meaty menu. May–Sept lunch & dinner daily, plus winter weekends.

The west coast

The road south of Égina Town, along the **west coast** of the island, is flat and easy. Sprawling **Marathónas**, 5km from Égina, has the biggest if not the prettiest of the west coast's sandy beaches, offering fine views and loungers, along with a scattering of rooms, tavernas and cafés. The next settlement, **Eyinítissa**, has a popular, sheltered cove backed by eucalypts and a beach bar.

Pérdhika

PÉRDHIKA, scenically set on a little bay packed with yachts at the end of the coastal road, is the most picturesque village on the island. The pedestrianized waterfront esplanade at the southern edge of the village, overlooking Moní islet and the

Peloponnese, is the heart of tourist life. From the harbour, you can take a boat to **Moní** (10min; €5 return), most of which is fenced off as a nature conservation area and is worth the trip for a swim in wonderfully clear water. Pérdhika Bay itself is shallow and yacht-tainted, though you can swim from the rocky shore further round.

On the headland opposite the harbour, along with crumbling wartime bunkers, is a **Camera Obscura** built by two Austrian artists. In the darkened interior twelve narrow slits project an inverted 360-degree image of the landscape outside. If you have your own transport, a couple more **cove beaches** are accessible beyond Pérdhika, where new holiday homes are reached by steep concrete tracks.

ACCOMMODATION AND EATING   THE WEST COAST

MARATHÓNAS

Ostria ☎ 22970 26738. An idyllic setting, with tables set out under the trees at the southern end of the beach and the water lapping almost to your feet. The food is great too, especially the calamari and the cheese pies. Daily lunch & dinner.

PÉRDHIKA

Andonis ☎ 22970 61443. One of a long line of tavernas along the front, this is the best of the bunch for fish; plenty of Athenian and yachtie patronage, so prices are a little higher than its neighbours – fish is priced by the kilo. Daily lunch & dinner.

Antzi Studios ☎ 22970 61446, ⓦ antzistudios.gr. Large studio and apartment complex with a good-sized pool. The modern apartment units with separate kitchens,

some for four people, are greatly preferable to the older studios. €50, new apartments €90

Hermes At the furthest extremity of the esplanade, this café-bar is Pérdhika's busiest late-night spot, probably because its position means it can afford to turn the music up louder than its neighbours. Daily 10am–late.

Hotel Hippocampus ☎ 22970 61363, ⓦ hippocampus -hotel-greece.com. Friendly, simple two-star hotel built around a garden courtyard. All rooms have balcony, a/c and TV, and there's a small roof terrace. €50

To Proreon ☎ 22970 61577. Proreon stands out thanks to its many potted plants and old-fashioned atmosphere. Excellent Greek food including home-made cheese (€3.50) or pumpkin (€6) pies, standards like moussaka (€6) and fish by the kilo. Daily lunch & dinner.

Angístri

ANGÍSTRI, fifteen minutes by fast boat from Égina, is a tiny island, obscure enough to be overlooked by most island-hoppers, though the visitors it does have are a diverse mix: Athenian weekenders, retirees who bought and restored property here years ago, plus a few British and Scandinavian package holidaymakers. There's a small, not terribly attractive strip of development on the north coast facing Égina, but the rest of the island is pine-covered, timeless and beautiful – albeit with very few beaches. It's also strangely schizophrenic: holiday weekends can see hordes of young Greeks camping out on otherwise empty beaches, while in Skála a few small, classy hotels are juxtaposed with cafés serving English breakfasts to the package-trippers.

ARRIVAL AND DEPARTURE   ANGÍSTRI

By ferry There are ferries and hydrofoils to and from Pireás via Égina; ferries dock at Skála (twice daily in the week, three from Fri–Sun; 25min/1hr 30min); hydrofoils at Mýlos (12 daily in summer, 6 out of season; 10min/1hr). The Angístri Express (☎ 694 71 18 863) calls at both on its route

to and from Égina (2–3 daily; 15min).

Ferry operators Hellenic Seaways (ferry and hydrofoils; ☎ 22970 91171, ⓦ hsw.gr) and Aegean Flying Dolphins (hydrofoils; ☎ 22970 91221, ⓦ aegeanflyingdolphins.gr).

GETTING AROUND

By bus In summer, the island bus connects Skála and Mýlos with Dhragonéra, Limenária and Apónissos several times a day; the day's timetable (timed to match ferry and hydrofoil arrivals) is chalked up at its starting point, outside the church in Skála.

By scooter and bike Scooters and mountain bikes are available for rent from several outlets in Skála and Mýlos; Kostas Motorent in Skála (☎ 22970 91021) is particularly helpful. It is less than 10km to the furthest point of the island, so in cooler weather you can comfortably cross Angístri by

2

pedal power – albeit with a couple of steep climbs.
On foot The island is small enough to cross on foot, via
Metóhi along a winding dirt track through the pines.

By water-taxi Water-taxis (☎697 76 18 040; about €30
per boat from Skála to Dhragonéra, for example) serve the
beaches and Égina.

Skála and around

SKÁLA is Angístri's main tourist centre, its sandy beach backed by a straggle of modern development. Thanks to the weekending Athenian youth, there are lively bars and cafés here, and an unexpectedly busy nightlife; in summer, there's even an open-air cinema. The beach, and most of the new development, lies to the right (west) from the jetty, beyond the big church, but there are some far more attractive places to stay, looking out over a rocky coastline, if you turn left.

From the paved road's end in this direction, beyond the *Alkyoni Hotel*, a path leads along the clifftop to secluded **Halikiádha**. This pebble beach, backed by crumbling cliffs, is predominantly nudist; at busy weekends there may be crowds of young Greeks camping nearby, the rest of the time it's almost deserted. The scary scramble down is rewarded by the island's best swimming in crystalline water. On the main town beach, you can rent sun-loungers, pedaloes and kayaks.

METÓHI, the hillside hamlet just above Skála, was once the island's main village, but now consists chiefly of holiday homes. If you can face the steep climb there are wonderful views out towards Égina.

ACCOMMODATION   SKÁLA

Aktaion Hotel ☎22970 91222, ⊛hotelaktaion.gr. Close to the jetty and the best of the options in town, with a small swimming pool. Most rooms have sea views and big balconies; some are a little dilapidated, others refurbished. Also small apartments with kitchen. **€55**

★ **Alkyoni Hotel** ☎22970 91377, ⊛alkyoni-agistri.gr. Turn left (southeast) from the jetty to find these large, stone-floored rooms; those on the seafront side have balconies directly above the water with stunning views. Best of all are the duplex rooms on the upper floor, big enough for a family with a raised sleeping area and kitchenette below. There's also a friendly coffee/breakfast bar. **€50**

Rosy's Little Village ☎22970 91610, ⊛rosyslittle village.com. Delightful spot on the rocks southeast of the jetty with a variety of rooms, most with sea view, direct access to its own rocky swimming spot, free kayaks and bikes for guests, and a small sail-boat and motorboat for hire, plus a good restaurant. **€60**

EATING, DRINKING AND NIGHTLIFE

Quattro ☎ 22970 91447. Beachside café/bar that trumps its neighbours by offering not just free wi-fi, but a laptop brought to your table. Open all day for breakfast, coffee and cocktails, plus good, chilled out sounds at night. Daily 10am–late.

Saronis ☎ 22970 91394. Blue-and-white checked tablecloths lend a relaxed feel to this long-established restaurant beside the church, with a more interesting and authentic menu than many here; stuffed mushrooms, horta and saganaki feature, as well as fresh fish, prawns and octopus. Daily lunch & dinner.

Taboo Main road on the western edge of town ☎ 22970 91181. The one real club on the island, which can be packed, sweaty and thumping or can be deserted, depending on the visiting crowds – watch out for posters advertising special events like beach parties and funk and soul nights. Summer Fri–Sun from 11pm, plus special events year-round.

Taverna Parnassos Metóhi ☎ 22970 91539. The roof terrace here, close to the village's highest point, has perhaps the best views on the whole island, and there's excellent, home-cooked traditional food to appreciate while you enjoy them. Daily lunch & dinner.

To Kyma ☎ 22970 91622. Behind the beach in the midst of the beachfront cafés, To Kyma has a charcoal grill out front where kebabs and squid are grilled, plus a good, traditional Greek menu with plenty of vegetable dishes. Daily lunch & dinner.

Mýlos

The least attractive aspect of Angístri is the windblown road along the coast between Skála and **MÝLOS (Megalohóri)**. Mýlos itself has an attractive, traditional village centre with a church and platía, but there's only a tiny beach, so relatively few people stay here. Access to the rest of the island is easy, however, and there are plenty of rooms and tavernas.

ACCOMMODATION AND EATING — MÝLOS

Fotis ☎ 22970 91325. This year-round taverna on the main street in the village centre is also the local butcher, so the meat here is particularly good. It's worth checking out the day's specials in the kitchen – they're often absolutely delicious. Daily lunch & dinner.

Kouros Café with a lovely position looking out over the goings-on of the harbour; breakfast, ice cream and waffles served as well as full meals, and there's free wi-fi. Daily 10am–10pm.

Meltemi Studios ☎ 22970 91057, ⓦ meltemistudios .gr. Purpose-built studios in a prime position with views back along the coast towards Skála as well as over the harbour. Rooms are clean and cheerful, and there's a tiny deep pool that operates as a pool bar in high season. **€50**

Rest of the island

There's basically just one road on Angístri, running from Skála and Mýlos round the west coast to the bottom of the island. Midway around, **Dhragonéra** is a beautiful but rocky pine-fringed beach with a dramatic panorama across to the mainland; other small coves are accessible across the rocks. Despite the warning signs, many people camp in the woods around these beaches. **LIMENÁRIA**, a small farming community at the edge of a fertile plateau in the southern corner of the island, is largely unaffected by tourism. The closest swimming is a few hundred metres east down a cement drive, then steps, at **Máriza**, where a diminutive concrete lido gives access to deep, ice-clear water. The little anchorage of **Apónissos** lies 2km west, past a shallow salt marsh; there's lovely swimming here in a tiny, warm lagoon, idyllic when uncrowded, or off the rocks in deeper, cooler water.

EATING AND DRINKING — REST OF THE ISLAND

Aponisos Taverna Apónissos. A matchless beachside setting for this simple ouzerí, whose wooden chairs are set on a terrace above the water. Simple meze dishes are the order of the day. June–Sept lunch & dinner daily.

O Tasos Limenária ☎ 22970 91362. Hugely popular with visiting mainlanders – and hence packed at weekend lunchtimes – O Tasos produces traditional cooking using local produce. Pricier than you'd expect for the location. Daily lunch & dinner.

2

Póros

Separated from the mainland by a 350m strait, **PÓROS** ("the ford") barely qualifies as an island at all. Popular with Brits and Scandinavians – more than any other Argo-Saronic island, Póros attracts package-holiday operators – it is also busy with weekending Athenians, who can get here by road (via Galatás) or on cheap ferries from Pireás, and with yachties taking advantage of the extensive mooring. There are in fact two islands, **Sferiá** (Póros Town) and the far larger **Kalávria**, separated from each other by a miniature canal spanned by a bridge. The town is a busy place, with constant traffic of shipping and people: if your stay is longer than a couple of nights you may want to base yourself on Kalávria for a little more peace, coming into town for the food, nightlife and shopping.

ARRIVAL AND DEPARTURE
PÓROS

By ferry In addition to regular ferry and hydrofoil connections with Pireás and the other Argo-Saronics, Póros has frequent, almost round-the-clock passenger boats shuttling across from the mainland port of Galatás (5min; €1) to Póros Town, plus a car ferry every half-hour. Small passenger boats tie up among the yachts and other small vessels on the southerly side facing Galatás, hydrofoils next to them near the northwestern end of the waterfront, ferries further round at the northern end of town.
Destinations Pireás via Méthana and Égina (2–3 ferries daily; 2hr 15min; plus 4–6 hydrofoils and flying cats; 1hr); Spétses (4–6 hydrofoils and flying cats; 1hr 30min); Ýdhra (4–6 hydrofoils and flying cats; 35min).
Tickets and agents All hydrofoils and catamarans serving the island are operated by Hellenic Seaways (w hsw.gr), whose local agents, both on the waterfront, are Marinos Tours (☎22980 23423) for hydrofoils, and Askeli Travel (☎22980 24900, w poros-accommodation .gr) for conventional ferries.

INFORMATION

Services A couple of banks with ATMs and the post office are on Platía Iroön in the centre of Póros Town. Many of the waterfront cafés have free wi-fi; terminals at Kendrou Typou (see below) or Fight Club, on the southeastern waterfront beyond *Taverna Naftis*.
Newspapers and books Available in English from Kendro Typou, opposite the ferry dock.
Useful website Check w poros.com.gr for information on the island, and for accommodation listings.

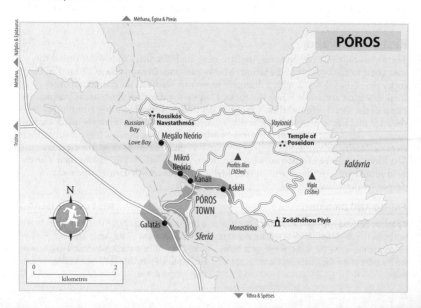

GETTING AROUND

By bus Buses (€1.50) depart to Kalávria, west to Russian Bay or east to the monastery, hourly on the hour from the road across from Platía Iroön (less frequent out of season).

By taxi The taxi rank is close to Platía Iroön; a taxi to the beaches is less than €5.

By car or bike Travel agents in town can rent you a car, or a quad-bike or scooter, though for the latter much the best service and prices are from Fotis (☎ 22980 25873); their office is over the bridge, on the road towards Askéli, but if you call they can deliver a bike to you.

Island tours In high season, thrice-weekly boat trips around the island depart from the central waterfront while a *trenaki* offers a variety of tours from the car park by the ferry dock, including a regular evening haul all the way up to the Temple of Poseidon.

Póros Town

PÓROS TOWN rises steeply across the western half of tiny volcanic Sferiá, a landmark clocktower at its summit. There's a two-room **archeological museum** on the waterfront (Tues–Sun 8.30am–3pm; €2) whose local finds will fill a spare half-hour, but otherwise few sights. This is a place to eat, drink, shop and watch the world go by. Away from the waterfront you'll quickly get lost in the labyrinth of steep, narrow streets, but nowhere is far away and most of the restaurants reasonably well signed. For a fine view over the rooftops and the strait, climb up to the **clocktower** (signed Roloï) – the tower itself is structurally suspect and fenced off, but you can still enjoy the outlook.

ACCOMMODATION   PÓROS TOWN

Rooms in Póros Town itself can be in very short supply at weekends and holiday times, when prices are inevitably high (they can be dramatically lower out of season); some noise is always likely too. Over on Kalávria (see p.92) there's considerably more choice, with plenty of apartments and small hotels in the touristy enclaves of Askéli – close to good beaches – or less attractive Mikró Neório.

Dionysos ☎ 22980 23511, ⓦ hoteldionysos.eu. An imposing mansion on the waterfront directly opposite the ferry dock, with large, newly refurbished rooms; most have bare stone walls, some with four-poster beds and wonderful old baths. Great value. **€50**

Manessi ☎ 22980 22273, ⓦ manessi.com. Classy place on the waterfront in the centre of town, with lots of dark wood and designery touches. The larger rooms have impressive power showers, while those at the front have fabulous views; new windows mean they're well soundproofed too. **€60**

Nikos Douros ☎ 22980 22633, ⓦ poros.com.gr /nikos-studios. Rooms and apartments in a number of houses, which means facilities and quality vary, but all are clean and comfortable, with a/c and TV, and prices are good. Try to see the room before you check in. **€40**

Villa Tryfon ☎ 22980 25854, ⓦ poros.com.gr/tryfon -villa. Cheerful blue-and-white studio rooms with kitchenette, near the main square on the clocktower side of the hill. Facilities are somewhat basic, but they do all have a/c, stunning views and an exceptionally friendly welcome. **€50**

EATING, DRINKING AND NIGHTLIFE

The central waterfront is mostly given over to competing cafés, all of which are open from breakfast till late, bars and souvenir shops: the better tavernas lie towards the southeastern end of the waterfront or up in the steep streets of the hilltop town. The southeastern end of the waterfront is also the place for good-value cafés – on Platía Dhimarhíou, for example, or next to the archeological museum. The better bars and clubs are in this direction too, becoming livelier as you head out along the coast road, though nightlife is highly seasonal. The open-air Cine Diana, functioning in the summer only, is on the northern waterfront towards the ferry dock.

★ **Karavolos** ☎ 22980 26158. Rightly popular with locals and expats, friendly *Karavolos*, above and directly behind Cine Diana (see above), serves excellent traditional cuisine such as *kolokythokeftédhes* (courgette and cheese fritters) or pork roasted with garlic; the name means snail, and you'll also find these on the menu. Daily, evenings only.

Kyma ☎ 22980 22793. Simple, good-value kebab and grill place on the waterfront just beyond the archeological museum. There are plenty of *yíros* joints in town, but this has a waterfront terrace with a setting to match the fanciest restaurant. Daily 11am–1am.

Luna Piena Platía Iroön ☎ 694 85 94 928. Greek-influenced Italian food, a step up in price and quality from its neighbours; try the excellent spaghetti with king prawns (€16.50), for example. Also pasta and pizzas. Daily lunch & dinner.

Malibu ☎ 22980 22491. One of the first of the bars you

come to on the southeastern harbourfront, and the most reliably open year-round. Popular with expats and tourists, and a good place to start your evening. Daily 9pm–late.
Naftis ☏ 22980 23096. Excellent *psarotavérna* with an attractive waterside terrace overlooking the yachts, south of the centre. As the evening wears on, the owners have been known to put on an impromptu Greek dancing display. Daily, evenings only.
Platanos ☏ 22980 25409. On the main square of the upper town, *Platanos* serves earthy, rural food on a

vine-covered terrace, washed down with powerful retsina. The owners also have a butcher's shop, so charcoal-grilled meat is the speciality – *kondosoúvli* (hunks of pork roasted on a spit) or pricier steaks. Daily, evenings only.
★ **Yiahni Sokaki** ☏ 693 64 48 568. Old-fashioned *mayireftá* establishment in the alley behind the fish market. Take a look at the kitchen to see what's been prepared that day – meatballs, moussaka or more original dishes like chicken roasted with potatoes and cherry tomatoes, all for €6–7. When it's all gone, they close. Daily, lunchtime only.

Kalávria

KALÁVRIA, Póros's "mainland", is covered in pine forest and barely inhabited, though there are a couple of fertile plateaus on the northern side with olive terraces, vineyards and magnificent panoramic views.

Western Kalávria

Kanáli and **Míkro Neório**, immediately across the canal from Póros Town, are overdeveloped, though they do have some good seafront restaurants looking back toward town. The first place worth a stop in its own right, though, is **MEGÁLO NEÓRIO**, arguably the island's most pleasant resort, small-scale, with a sandy beach, an excellent waterski centre with courses to professional level (☏ 22980 42540, ⓦ passage.gr), and some fine beachside tavernas. **Love Bay**, immediately west, has a lovely sandy beach, but is unfortunately tiny and always packed; there's a friendly seasonal *kantína*, and kayaks and snorkel gear can be hired here.

The **Rossikós Navstathmós** on Russian Bay, a crumbling Russian naval base dating from the early nineteenth century, marks the end of the route for the westward bus. There's a hard-packed, mostly shadeless beach here, with lots of small craft anchored offshore.

Askéli

Askéli, with its strip of hotels and villas, is the first place you reach as you head east on Kalávria. There are plenty of cafés and places to eat, many overlooking the narrow, crowded beach. A good watersports centre hires out kayaks and small sailing boats, and they also have a powerboat for ringo rides and the like.

EXCURSIONS TO THE PELOPONNESE

Take one of the boats shuttling constantly to and from Galatás and you're on the mainland Peloponnese, where there are numerous potential excursions. Local travel agents run a variety of tours, or you'll see hire cars on offer in Galatás from around €25 a day.

Troezen Ancient Troezen is an unenclosed site near the modern village of Trizína, barely 10km from Galatás. Legendary birthplace of Theseus, the scattered site is most easily understood if you purchase a map in the village – this also recounts the stories of Theseus's life. A short walk up a gorge from the site takes you to the spectacular natural rock arch of the Dhiavoloyéfyro, the Devil's Bridge.

Epidaurus (Epídhavros) Most famous for its fourth-century BC theatre, one of the finest ancient monuments in Greece, Epidaurus is also an extensive sanctuary to Asklepios, god of healing. The theatre is used for productions of Classical Greek drama on Friday and Saturday nights from June to August as part of the annual Athens & Epidaurus Festival (ⓦ greekfestival.gr; organized excursions from many island travel agents). Daily summer 8am–7.30pm, winter 8am–5pm; €6.

Náfplio A long day-trip, but arguably the most rewarding destination in the Peloponnese, Náfplio is a gorgeous nineteenth-century town in a stunning coastal setting protected by forbidding fortresses. There are plenty of excellent restaurants and cafés.

Monastiríou

The eighteenth-century **monastery of Zoödhóhou Piyís** (daily sunrise–1.30pm & 4.30pm–sunset), next to the island's only spring, is the terminus of Póros's eastward bus. Steps from the bus stop lead down to the pleasant sandy beach of **Monastiríou**, overlooked by pine-covered slopes. Perhaps the island's best beach, it is, surprisingly, usually one of the least crowded – though hardly empty as the two tavernas here will testify.

Temple of Poseidon

Daily 8am–2.30pm • Free • ⓦ kalaureia.org

The remains of the **Temple of Poseidon** overlook the island's northern and western coasts, with great views towards Égina. The temple lay at the heart of ancient Kalaureia, whose heyday was in the fourth century BC, and it's an extensive site. Despite plenty of new signage and an ongoing Swedish excavation there's not a great deal to see above ground level, however – many of the stones were carted off to be used as building materials in the seventeenth and eighteenth centuries (much of it ended up on Ýdhra), and some of the more interesting sections are roped off while they are excavated. It was here that Demosthenes, fleeing from the Macedonians after encouraging the Athenians to resist their rule, took poison rather than surrender.

Vayioniá

Vayioniá, just about the only accessible beach on the island's north shore, was the port of ancient Kalaureia. The bay is beautiful when viewed from above; close up the pebbly beach is narrow and can be windy, but it's still a very pleasant spot, with a seasonal beach bar/café, and loungers to rent.

ACCOMMODATION AND EATING   KALÁVRIA

MEGÁLO NEÓRIO

★ **Pavlou** ☎ 22980 22734, ⓦ pavlouhotel.gr. Family-run hotel with pool, tennis court and restaurant, right on one of the island's best beaches (where they also have a great restaurant). The decor is plain but comfortable, with big balconies, half of which have great sea views. Breakfast included. **€50**

MIKRÓ NEÓRIO

Aspros Gatos Waterfront ☎ 22980 25650. Friendly taverna serving good seafood on a waterfront terrace with views back over Póros Town; try the rice pilaf with mussels and pine nuts, for example. Only about twenty minutes' walk from town, or they offer free water-taxi service for groups of five or more. Daily lunch & dinner.

MONASTIRÍOU

Sirene ☎ 22980 22741, ⓦ sireneblueresort.gr. Large, modern hotel with pool and tennis courts, spectacularly sited on a steep slope above the sea, with a small private beach below. The stunning location ensures fabulous views from the balconies, though the refurbished rooms are small. Good off-peak deals. **€140**

VAYIONIÁ

Paradisos ☎ 22980 23419. Well signed on the main road just east of the turning down to Vayioniá, this rural taverna serves plenty of local produce, including rabbit stifado or spit-roasted pork, plus charcoal-grilled squid or lamb, washed down with local retsina and home-made bread. Daily noon–midnight.

Ýdhra

The island of **ÝDHRA (Hydra)** is one of the most atmospheric destinations in Greece. Its harbour and main town preserved as a national monument, it feels like a Greek island should, entirely traffic-free (even bicycles are banned) with a bustling harbour and narrow stone streets climbing steeply above it. Away from the main settlement the rest of the island is roadless, rugged and barely inhabited. The charm hasn't gone unnoticed – Ýdhra became fashionable as early as the 1950s, and in the Sixties characters ranging from Greek painter Nikos Hatzikyriakos-Ghikas to Canadian songster Leonard Cohen bought and restored grand old houses here. There's still a sizeable expat community, which contributes to a relatively sophisticated atmosphere, and also noticeably high

2

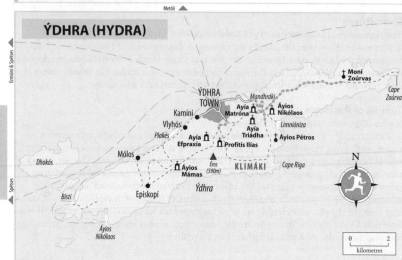

prices. But even the seasonal and weekend crowds, and a very limited number of beaches, can't seriously detract from the appeal. When the town is overrun, it's easy enough to leave it all behind on foot or by excursion boat. The interior is mountainous and little-visited, so with a little walking you can find a dramatically different kind of island – one of rural cottages, terraces of grain to feed the donkeys, hilltop monasteries and pine forest.

ARRIVAL AND DEPARTURE   ÝDHRA

By ferry Hellenic Seaways hydrofoils and flying cats connect Ýdhra to Pireás (1hr 20min) via Póros (35min) at least 5 times a day, more in midsummer. In the other direction they continue to Spétses (5 daily; 45min), some via Ermióni or on to Pórto Héli on the mainland. Small passenger boats also cross to Metóhi (4 daily; 15 min) on the nearby mainland.

Tickets and agencies The local agent for Hellenic Seaways tickets (w hsw.gr) is Hydreoniki Travel (t 22980 54007, w hydreoniki.gr), located in an alley at the eastern end of the harbour. Metóhi boats are operated by Hydra Lines (t 694 73 25 263, w hydralines.gr).

INFORMATION

Services Several banks with ATMs can be found round the waterfront, while the post office is on the market square just inland. There's free wi-fi at many cafés; terminals at the shop immediately behind the waterfront Alpha Bank.

Newspapers Foreign-language papers, and some books, are sold at a shop on N. Votsi, off the waterfront between the church and Pirate bar.

GETTING AROUND

On foot There's only one paved road on Ýdhra, leading east from the harbour to Mandhráki just a couple of kilometres away, so to explore the island you either walk or take a boat (see below). The largely shadeless trails mean that in midsummer walking can be a mercilessly hot experience. There are excellent, part-cobbled tracks leading west of town to the beaches at Kamíni (about 20min), Vlyhós (30min) and Plákes (40min). Steeper, rougher paths lead into the interior and towards the south coast (see box, p.98).

By boat Small boats shuttle constantly from the harbour to the beaches, at prices ranging from about €2.50 per person one-way to Mandhráki or Vlyhós, to €12 return to Bísti. You can also hire private water-taxis – good value for groups at around €15 per boat to Vlyhós or €55 to Bísti, for example.

By mule If you are carrying luggage, or might struggle on the sometimes steep cobbles in Ýdhra Town, you can hire a mule at the harbour; fixed prices for various destinations are posted. The fancier hotels may provide a mule if they know when you are arriving – or more likely a porter with a handcart for your luggage.

Ýdhra Town

ÝDHRA TOWN, with tiers of grey-stone mansions and humbler white-walled, red-tiled houses rising from a perfect horseshoe harbour, makes a beautiful spectacle. Around the harbour, trippers flock to cafés and chic boutiques, but it's also worth spending time wandering the backstreets and narrow alleys – one thing you may notice while doing so is that even more than most Greek island towns, Ýdhra is overrun with wild cats, probably because there are so many "cat ladies" who feed them.

The waterfront mansions were mostly built during the eighteenth century on the accumulated wealth of a remarkable merchant fleet, which traded as far afield as America and – during the Napoleonic Wars – broke the British blockade to sell grain to France. In the 1820s the town's population was nearly 20,000 – an incredible figure when you reflect that today it is under 3000 – and Ýdhra's merchants provided many of the ships for the Greek forces during the War of Independence, and consequently many of the commanders. At each side of the harbour, cannons facing out to sea and statues of the heroes of independence remind you of this place in history.

The mansions

The **mansions** of the wealthy eighteenth-century merchant families are still the great monuments of the town; some labelled at the entrance with "*Oikía*" ("Residence of …") followed by the family name. Among the finest are the two **Koundouriótis mansions**, built by two brothers: Yíoryios, whose former home is periodically open for art exhibitions, was a leading politician of the fledgling Greek nation and grandfather of Pávlos, president of Republican Greece in the 1920s; older brother Lázaros was prominent in the independence wars.

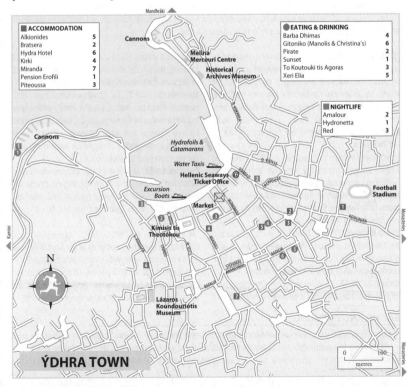

Lázaros Koundouriótis Museum

Daily 10am–2pm, July & Aug also 5.30–8.30pm • €4

The **Lázaros Koundouriótis Museum** is the large ochre building high on the western side of town. The hot climb up the stepped alleyways is rewarded with great views down over the town and port, and a lovingly restored interior that looks ready to move into. The red-tiled floors, panelled wooden ceilings and period furnishings outshine the contents of the museum – paintings, folk costume and independence paraphernalia.

Historical Archives Museum

Daily 9am–4pm, July & Aug also 7.30–9.30pm; €5

On the eastern waterfront, the **Historical Archives Museum** occupies one of Ýdhra's great houses. It's a small, crowded and enjoyable display of clothing, period engravings, and ships' prows and sidearms from the independence struggle. The **Melina Mercouri Centre**, next door, often has interesting temporary art exhibitions.

Kímisis tís Theotókou

Museum Tues–Sun 10am–2pm, Aug also 7–9pm • €2

The most obvious and important of Ýdhra's many churches is **Kímisis tís Theotókou** by the port, with its distinctive clocktower. The cloistered courtyard houses the small but rich collection of the **ecclesiastical museum** – silver-bound books, icons, vestments, bejewelled crosses and the like.

ACCOMMODATION   ÝDHRA TOWN

Most accommodation in Ýdhra Town is high quality, though prices tend to be equally high. Midweek or out of season you should be able to negotiate significant reductions on the official rates. The nature of the old buildings and the closely packed streets mean that some noise is inevitable, especially near the waterfront. Addresses and street signs are almost nonexistent, so ask for directions when you book, or refer to our map.

★ **Alkionides** ☎ 22980 54055, 🌐 alkionidespension .com. Lovely pension, quietly tucked away yet central, with an attractive courtyard and helpful management; the rooms are extremely comfortable and well equipped, especially the slightly more expensive ones that have been newly refurbished, and there's a wonderful studio apartment with its own roof terrace. €65, studio €100

★ **Bratsera** ☎ 22980 53971, 🌐 bratserahotel.com. Classy four-star hotel that occupies a stylishly renovated former sponge factory; the extensive common areas (including bar, restaurant and courtyard pool) serve as a museum of the industry with photos and artefacts. Lovely rooms have flagstone floors and beamed ceilings, though only superior and above have balconies. €150

Hydra Hotel ☎ 22980 53420, 🌐 hydra-hotel.gr. Stunning boutique hotel in a mansion high above the harbour, with glorious views from many rooms. Each room is different, from simple doubles up to a split-level family apartment. €150

Kirki ☎ 22980 53181, 🌐 hydrakirki.gr. Unprepossessing entry leads to a delightful old house, with a small courtyard garden and simple, island-style rooms; all have a/c and balconies, though the attractive large terraces at the back do get some early morning noise from the market. €60

Miranda ☎ 22980 52230, 🌐 mirandahotel.gr. An 1810 mansion converted into a popular hotel, with highly individual rooms; best are nos. 2 and 3, both with painted, coffered ceilings and large sea-view terraces. Large breakfasts in the shaded courtyard are another big plus; there is a basement bar for winter. €120

Pension Erofili ☎ 22980 54049, 🌐 pensionerofili.gr. Simple but spacious rooms around a courtyard, all with a/c, fridge and television; quiet, friendly and relatively inexpensive. A small apartment upstairs has its own kitchen. €55

★ **Piteoussa** ☎ 22980 52810, 🌐 piteoussa.com. Named after the three giant pines at the front, this small inn is exceptional value, with modern units equipped with iPod speakers, CD and DVD players and Korres toiletries in the marble-floored bathrooms. Downstairs rooms are larger, but all have balconies and designer touches. €65

EATING AND DRINKING

The permanently busy quayside cafés and bars offer an incomparable people-watching experience – albeit at a price – but there are few worthwhile restaurants on the harbour. If you want something to take down to the beach with you, there's an excellent bakery, with *tyrópittes* and cakes, tucked into the western corner of the harbour by the *Pirate* bar.

Barba Dhimas ☎ 22980 53306. Tiny place with just half a dozen tables set out in an alley. There's a short, daily menu of Italian food; mixed antipasto (€8) or spaghetti *vongole* (€18), for example. May–Sept 7pm–midnight.

★ **Gitoniko (Manolis & Christina's)** ☎ 22980 53615. Hidden away inland, near Áyios Konstandínos church, this traditional taverna serves excellent, well-priced *mayireftá* at lunch (stuffed marrow €7) – which runs out early – plus grills (including succulent fish) in the evening; extensive roof-terrace in summer. Daily lunch & dinner.

Pirate ☎ 22980 52711. Café by day and an increasingly lively bar as the evening wears on, *Pirate* has a young crowd and Western music. Among the best prices on the waterfront for coffee, breakfast and sandwiches. Daily 10am–2am.

Sunset ☎ 22980 52067. Behind the cannons on the western edge of town, *Sunset* offers an incomparable setting for an end-of-holiday treat or romantic tryst; the modern Greek and Italian cuisine is on the pricey side (pasta dishes €10–18, steak €25), but the views justify the cost. Daily lunch & dinner.

To Koutouki tis Agoras. Rickety-tabled, inexpensive tradesmen's ouzerí behind the market. The place makes no concessions at all to tourists, but the titbits served with drinks, ranging from *pastourmás* (cured meat) to octopus, can be exceptional. At its best in the early evening. Daily noon–9pm.

Xeri Elia ☎ 22980 52886. Large, busy taverna with a lovely setting in a vine-shaded inland platía. All the standards are served, along with good seafood, and there's often live music in the evenings. Daily lunch & dinner.

NIGHTLIFE

Nightlife is tame on the whole, though a number of bars do play music into the early hours; there's also an open-air cinema in summer.

Amalour Laidback cocktail bar with an eclectic playlist – plenty of Latin and jazz – and 30-to-40-something crowd. Almost always the busiest place in town in the early evening; sometimes hosts special events or theme nights. Daily 6pm–2am.

Hydronetta The classic sunset-watching bar, with steps down the rocks into the water, where the music carries on into the small hours. Limited seating gives it an exclusive,

chill-out vibe. The place is also open during the day, for swimming, coffee and an early start on the drinking. Daily 9am–2am.

Red The closest thing you'll find to a dance club in town, *Red* is a late-night joint right on the waterfront playing sixties and seventies rock plus a few dance tunes and the odd Greek number. Fri–Sun 10pm–3am, plus some weekdays in summer.

Beaches

There's no big sandy beach on Ýdhra, just a series of small, mainly shingly, coves. **Mandhráki** is the closest to town, dominated by the *Miramare Hotel* which occupies the imposing former shipyard of independence war hero Admiral Miaoulis. Despite appearances, the sandy beach is open to all, with windsurfing, waterskiing, pedaloes to hire and floating trampolines.

Walk west from Ýdhra Town and you'll find several spots where you can clamber down to swim from the rocks in crystal-clear water, but the first tiny pebble beach lies just beyond the picturesque village of **Kamíni**. Next up is a popular swimming cove at **Kastéllo** and then **Vlyhós**, a small hamlet with a rebuilt nineteenth-century bridge and a shingle beach with loungers and umbrellas; there's pleasant swimming in the lee of an offshore islet here. **Plákes**, a long, pebbly stretch with loungers, palapa shelters and a small resort hotel,

---

ÝDHRA'S FESTIVALS

Over the weekend closest to June 21, Ýdhra Town celebrates the **Miaoulia**, in honour of Admiral Andreas Miaoulis whose fire boats, packed with explosives, were set adrift downwind of the Turkish fleet during the War of Independence. The highlight of the celebrations is the burning of a boat at sea as a tribute to the sailors who risked their lives in this dangerous enterprise.

Orthodox Easter is also a colourful and moving experience, especially on the evening of Good Friday when the fishermen's parish of Áyios Ioánnnis at Kamíni carries its *Epitáfios*, or symbolic bier of Christ, into the shallows to bless the boats and ensure calm seas.

2

ÝDHRA'S INLAND WALKS

To explore the island's interior and south coast, head out of Ýdhra Town on the street that leads past the *Miranda* hotel or around the eastern edge past the *Piteoussa*: as you start to climb, a left turn leads to Áyios Nikólaos, keeping right heads to Profítis Ilías.

Profítis Ilías and Mount Éros The monastery of Profítis Ilías and nearby convent of Ayía Efpraxía are about an hour's climb above Ýdhra Town. What must be the longest stairway in Greece (or alternatively a zigzag path) constitutes the final approach to Profítis Ilías (closed noon–4pm, but water and *loukoúm* are hospitably left at the gate). If you want to go further, a rather tougher, harder-to-follow trail continues left behind the monastery to a saddle overlooking the south coast. From here a pathless scramble brings you within twenty minutes to the 590m summit of Mount Éros, the Argo-Saronic islands' highest point, but the path itself branches: right to the chapel of Áyios Mámas, on whose feast day of September 2 there's a pilgrimage of people and animals to be blessed; left eventually circles down to the sea at the tiny hamlet of Klimáki, a couple of hours' walk in all.

Áyios Nikólaos The path from Ýdhra Town towards deserted Áyios Nikólaos monastery offers spectacular views back down over the harbour before reaching, at the top, a broad, easy dirt track heading straight across a high plateau towards the monastery. Just beyond Áyios Nikólaos is a small settlement, from where you can in theory head down to Limnióniza, a scenic cove on the south coast an hour and a quarter from Ýdhra Town. However, it's a steep scramble on a path which is hard to find and there are no boats back unless you arrange to be picked up by water-taxi. A far easier alternative is to follow the broad track down from Áyios Nikólaos to Mandhráki, where you can have a swim before taking the boat back to town.

Cape Zoúrva This is Ýdhra's eastern tip and is about three hours' walk from town, on a path that heads east from Áyios Nikólaos. There are several small chapels along the way, along with the substantial Moní Zoúrvas. Perhaps the best way to do this trip is to take an early morning water-taxi to the cape, and walk back to town along the island's spine.

marks the end of the easy path. At the western tip of the island, virtually inaccessible except by boat, are two coves sheltering perhaps the island's best beaches: **Bísti** has a smallish, white-pebbled beach surrounded by pine trees that offer shade; **Áyios Nikólaos** is larger and sandier, but with less shade and fewer boats. A path leads over the cape between the two; both have seasonal snack bars as well as loungers and kayaks to rent.

ACCOMMODATION, EATING AND DRINKING   BEACHES

MANDHRÁKI

Mandraki 1800 ☏22980 52112. Above a tiny cove as you enter Mandhráki, where they have loungers and umbrellas, free for customers, this café/ouzerí serves good fresh fish as well as meze and drinks.

Miramare Hotel ☏22980 52300, ⊛miramare.gr. Restaurant, beach-bar and hotel right on the beach. The rather crude beachside bungalows are not great value, but you can eat or simply have a coffee on a beautiful waterside terrace, and they have their own boat to town. **€70**

KAMÍNI

Antonia ☏22980 52481. Just one delightfully old-fashioned room and one apartment for up to five people, both with balconies hanging right over the sea; with no frills at all (though there is a/c), and virtually no English spoken, this feels like the Greece of thirty years ago. **€60**

Pension Petrolekka ☏22980 52701. Immediately behind Antonia, with just a couple of well-equipped apartments, simply furnished but with wi-fi and a/c; the larger and more expensive one has two rooms with separate bathroom and kitchen and huge balcony. **€80**

Taverna Kodylenia ☏22980 53520. With a beautiful terrace overlooking the little harbour, *Kodylenia* is famous for its seafood and wonderful sunset views. Crowds of weekend trippers mean slightly higher-than-average prices: moussaka for €9, seafood spaghetti €15, pork with mushroom and wine sauce €12.

VLYHÓS

Antigone ☏22980 53228, ✉antigone@freemail.gr. Just above the jetty where the boats drop you, *Antigone* has good-value apartments; small ones with bedroom and living room/kitchenette, larger with two bedrooms and separate kitchen. There's also a decent restaurant and snack bar. **€65**

PLÁKES

Four Seasons ☎22980 53698, **ⓦ**fourseasonshydra
.gr. An incongruously luxurious small suite hotel in this
isolated spot, complete with a decent restaurant and

organized beach. Accommodation is in beautiful,
spacious suites and studio apartments, sleeping up to
four people, with modern facilities including wi-fi and
satellite TV. **€170**

Spétses

A popular, upmarket escape for Athenians, **SPÉTSES** had brief fame and a vogue as a
package destination, largely thanks to John Fowles, who lived here in the early 1950s
and used the place, thinly disguised, as the setting for his cult novel *The Magus*. But the
island never developed the mass infrastructure – or the convenient beaches – to match.
Today, the town is much the biggest in the Saronic islands, with apartments and villas
spreading for several kilometres along the northeast coast, while the rest of the island
remains almost entirely uninhabited, with pine forest inland and numerous excellent
small beaches around the coast.

ARRIVAL AND DEPARTURE   SPÉTSES

By ferry At least five daily Hellenic Seaways hydrofoils
and flying cats connect Spétses with Pireás (2hr 20min)
via Ýdhra (45min) and Póros (1hr 25min). Around three a
day call at mainland Ermióni en route, and in the other
direction continue to Pórto Héli. A car ferry and seasonal
passenger boats also run several times daily to Kósta on

the nearby mainland (though you can't bring a car to the
island). All of them dock pretty much in the heart of
town at the cannon-studded main harbour known as the
Dápia.

Tickets The local agent for Hellenic Seaways is Bardakos
(**☎**22980 73141, **ⓦ**hsw.gr), on the east side of the Dápia.

INFORMATION

Services There are banks with ATMs all around the Dápia.
Many of the harbour cafés have free wi-fi, but *Café 1800*, on
the waterfront towards Kounoupítsa, is the only central
internet café.

Travel agents Mimoza Travel (**☎**22980 75170) and
Alasia Travel (**☎**22980 74098, **ⓦ**alasiatravel.gr), both on
the waterfront immediately east of the Dápia, can help
with accommodation and local information.

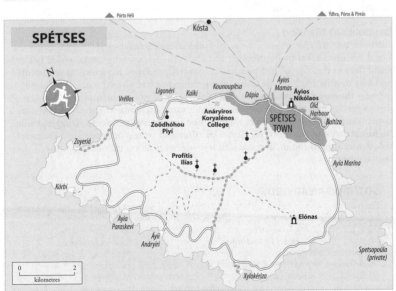

2

GETTING AROUND

By bus There are two bus services to the beaches in high season: west to Kounoupítsa, Ligonéri and Vréllos from the waterfront by the *Hotel Poseidonion*; east and then around the island to Áyii Anáryiri and Ayía Paraskévi from behind the town beach.

By boat Seasonal *kaïkia* offer shuttles to the beaches (€9 return to Áyii Anáryiri, for example) or round-the-island trips, and there are plentiful water-taxis (€15–80 per boatload depending on destination).

By bike Bike Center (☎ 22980 74009), about halfway along the shopping street behind the seafront hotels, has good mountain bikes for €6 a day, plus maps and suggested routes.

By scooter and motorbike Several rental places can be found behind the town beach; try Labros (☎ 693 23 33 014), often the cheapest if you bargain (from €15 a day), or Nautilus (☎ 22980 72107). Stanathiotis (☎ 22980 75364) on Bótasi, the main street inland, generally has the newest machines.

Spétses Town

SPÉTSES TOWN shares with Ýdhra a history of late eighteenth-century mercantile adventure and prosperity, and a leading role in the War of Independence, which made its foremost citizens the aristocrats of the new Greek state. Plenty of fine old homes and public buildings survive, but here there's been little restriction on new building, which spreads along the shore in both directions. And although most cars are banned in town you won't notice it, as they're replaced by thousands of mopeds and scooters that pay little attention to whether a street is pedestrianized or not. In short, it's much less pretty than Ýdhra Town, but also a great deal more lively and earthy, and full of pricey shops, bars and restaurants.

For most visitors, shopping, eating and drinking are the principal attractions of Spétses, but it's a very enjoyable place to wander, with majestic old houses and gardens scattered through the narrow streets. The harbour, the **Dápia**, marks pretty much the centre of town, with the main square tucked in behind. To the east lies the **town beach** of Áyios Mámas and beyond that – a lovely walk around the point – the **Old Harbour**, upmarket focus of the island's nightlife, where private yachts moor up. West of the Dápia is **Kounoupítsa** – much of the simpler accommodation is here, and there are small beaches and waterfront tavernas. It's a big place; to walk from Kounoupítsa to the far end of the Old Harbour will take at least forty minutes.

Bouboulína's Mansion

Guided tours (30min) up to a dozen times daily; times are posted outside and on boards around town • €6

Local heroine **Laskarína Bouboulína** was a wealthy widow who commanded her own small fleet in the War of Independence, reputedly seduced her lovers at gunpoint, and was shot in 1825 by the father of a girl her son had eloped with. Her former home – the so-called **Bouboulína's Mansion** – signed not far behind the Dápia, is now a private museum. On the entertaining tour you'll hear the story of how she spent much of her fortune on ships and men for the independence struggle, while highlights among the arms, furniture, pictures and correspondence are a gorgeous wooden ceiling in the main room and a model of Bouboulína's flagship, the *Agamemnon*.

SOTÍRIOS ANÁRYIROS

The man most responsible for Spétses' appearance today is **Sotírios Anáryiros**, a descendant of a once grand Spetsiot family who emigrated in 1868 and returned, thirty years later, having made a fortune selling Turkish tobacco in the United States. His most obvious legacy is the landmark waterfront **Hotel Poseidonion**, but he also built and endowed **Anáryiros Koryalénos College**, a curious Greek re-creation of an English public school, where John Fowles taught (behind College beach), and a kitsch, Neoclassical private residence, now gradually falling into disrepair alongside the Bouboulína mansion. Most importantly, however, he was responsible for replanting the island's **pine forests**, depleted by generations of shipbuilders.

Spétses Museum

Tues–Sun 8.30am–2.30pm • €3

Spétses' enjoyable local **museum** is housed in one of the town's grandest mansions, the Hatziyánnis Méxis family home above the east side of town. Apart from the house itself, highlights include magnificent polychrome wooden ships' prows from the revolutionary fleet, as well as its flag, plus (out of sight in a plain wooden ossuary) the bones of Laskarína Bouboulína.

ACCOMMODATION   SPÉTSES TOWN

2

Accommodation, especially at the cheaper end of the range, tends to be widely scattered. On busy weekends and in August it can be in short supply, so it may make life easier to arrange it through an agency (see p.99). The rest of the season, though, you're likely to be met off the hydrofoil by people offering rooms. In town prices range from high, at comfortable studio complexes, to jaw-droppingly expensive at some of the boutique hotels; at quiet times, big discounts can be negotiated.

Kastro Apartments ☎22980 75152, ⓦkastro -margarita.com. An attractive complex of studios and duplex apartments towards Kounoupítsa, behind Café 1800. Comfy accommodation with kitchen, a/c, TV and balcony is arranged around a small pool and bar. **€100**

Klimis ☎22980 72334, ⓔklimishotel@hol.gr. Right on the front, 200m east of the Dápia, *Klimis* may be a little run-down, but is convenient, open all year and excellent value given its position, with wonderful views from the balconied rooms at the front and some kind of sea view from almost every room. Downstairs there's a superb, old-fashioned *zaharoplastío* with excellent ice cream, where breakfast (included) is served. **€60**

Poseidonion ☎22980 74553, ⓦposeidonion.com. Vast, imposing, fin-de-siècle edifice immediately west of the Dápia which reopened in 2009 after years of meticulous refurbishment. Grand, high-ceilinged rooms in the main building, many with free-standing, claw-foot baths; bungalows at the back, behind the pool, and an amazing cupola suite in the tower. Prices to match, unfortunately. **€200**

Roumani ☎22980 72244, ⓦhotelroumani.gr. Prime location right on the Dápia, which means rooms at the front have stunning views – though they can also be noisy

and are overdue for a refurb. Hence the reasonable prices. **€65**

★ **Villa Christina** ☎22980 72218, ⓦvillachristina hotel.com. Friendly, well-maintained restored inn occupying a rambling old building with two courtyards, in a quiet location 200m inland from the Dápia, just off Bótasi. A/c rooms and studios (with kitchens) for up to four people; breakfast in the courtyard usually included. **€60**

Villa Orizontes ☎22980 72509, ⓦvillaorizontes.gr. Simple hotel in a quiet spot, high up (500m directly uphill from the back of Platía Oroloyíou – look for the large veranda and blue shutters), with a variety of different-sized rooms and apartments with fridge, a/c and TV; more than half have knockout views across town and out to sea. **€50**

Zoe's Club ☎22980 74447, ⓦzoesclub.gr. Lovely, designer-decorated studios, apartments and houses around a large pool, 200m east of the Dápia on a quiet inland corner. All have flat-screen satellite TV, DVD players and espresso machines in the fully equipped kitchens, and almost all have a great sea view. Fully booked for Aug and summer weekends and almost empty the rest of the time, though few bargains even then. **€195**

EATING AND DRINKING

Brace yourself for some of the steepest food and drink prices in the Greek islands outside of Mýkonos and Rhodes – especially in the cafés around the Dápia and romantic spots on the old harbour.

★ **Akroyialia** ☎22980 74749. Excellent seafood taverna on the waterfront towards Kounoupítsa with reasonable prices (cheese-stuffed biftékia €9, grilled prawns €16) and a wonderful setting, with candlelit tables on the beach and the water lapping almost to your feet as you eat. Daily lunch & dinner.

Cockatoo ☎22980 74085. Basic kebab and *yíros* place in a narrow alley between the Dápia and Platía Oroloyíou, serving some of the cheapest food in town; stick to the basics, and it's delicious. Daily noon–midnight.

Exedra Old Harbour ☎22980 73497. A smarter, older crowd enjoys standard dishes like moussaka, *angináres ala políta* (artichokes with dill sauce, both €7.50) and fresh fish in an unbeatable waterside seating. Despite the upmarket image, prices are just a little higher than at neighbouring establishments. Daily noon–4pm & 7pm–midnight.

Kafeneion Dápia. Pebble mosaics underfoot and sepia photos indicate that this was the island's first watering hole; a prime people-watching spot, open all day for coffee and snacks, progressing later to a full range of mezédhes, or just a drink while waiting for a hydrofoil. Daily 10am–1am.

Lazaros Bótasi ☎ 22980 72600. A stiff climb 500m uphill leads to this most traditional of tavernas, its cavernous interior decked out with an old jukebox, dangling gourds and wine barrels; it serves a limited but savoury menu of grills, goat in lemon sauce, superior *taramás* and decent barrelled wine. Evening only, late March–early Oct.

Patralis Kounoupítsa ☎ 22980 75380. Old-fashioned, bourgeois *psarotavérna*, very popular with Greek visitors, which can mean slow service and a wait for a table. The fish is excellent, though, and there are plenty of less expensive meaty alternatives (lamb chops €7) plus good barrelled wine if you don't like the prices on the extensive wine list. Better value for fish and sea views than the Old Harbour. Daily lunch & dinner.

To Liotrivi Old Harbour ☎ 22980 72269. The "old olive oil press" offers an upmarket, Greek-Mediterranean menu – pirate risotto, grilled prawns, *Spetsiot fish* – to a Latin and jazz soundtrack, with occasional live music. Some tables enjoy a stunning position on a jetty that extends right out into the harbour. Daily lunch & dinner.

To Nero tis Agapis Kounoupítsa ☎ 22980 74009. Virtually adjacent to *Patralis* (see above) and with a similar seafood-based menu (excellent seafood spaghetti), "The Water of Love" could hardly be a greater contrast in style and decor – self-consciously modern, island-style, with decent music and enthusiastic young staff. Crayfish €17, black tagliatelle with squid €15, zarzuela fish stew €18. Daily lunch & dinner.

NIGHTLIFE

Late-night nightlife is mostly centred on Baltíza, the furthest of the inlets at the old harbour – here there are several seasonal clubs, though even in August they only really come to life at the weekend. Closer to town, Áyios Mámas beach also has a couple of lively music bars. Two cinemas operate in summer, close to the main square – Titania (with a roof for shelter, but open sides) and open-air, rooftop Marina.

Balkoni The elegant alternative to nearby *Socrates*; sip your wine or cocktails on a candlelit balcony overlooking the waterfront east of the Dápia; also open for coffee during the day. Daily 10am–2am.

Bar Spetsa Áyios Mámas. Chilled-out bar playing decent retro rock, mainly 60s and 70s. Strong drinks and a great craic most nights. Nightly 8pm–3am.

La Luz Old harbour. Classy music bar spreading over two upstairs floors in a beautifully restored mansion with plenty of exposed brickwork. Open from 4pm for coffee and drinks, but the main action is late at night – live music or DJs most weekends from 11.45pm. Daily 4pm–late.

Mama's Beach Café Áyios Mámas beach. Lively café and lunch spot by day, with sandwiches, milkshakes and waffles, while at night the upstairs music bar (playing summer party stuff) takes over. Daily 10.30am–2am.

Socrates English-pub-style bar on the waterfront east of the Dápia (main entry from the shopping street behind) serving draught beer, including Guinness, and showing big-screen sports. A popular hangout for local expats, especially on football nights. Daily 7pm–2am.

The beaches

A single paved road circles Spétses, mostly high above a rocky coast but with access to beaches at various points. You can also get to many of the beaches by excursion boat.

Kaïki or **College Beach** is just twenty minutes' walk west of town, with a frequent bus service and extensive facilities including loungers, bars and a waterski outfit that also rents jet-skis. **Vréllos**, a small, pebbly cove in a pretty, wooded bay, is the end of the line for buses heading west out of Spétses. Thanks to paved access and a beach cocktail bar pumping out loud Greek rock it's almost always packed at weekends.

At the western extremity of the island, **Zoyeriá** is reached down a track that soon degenerates into a path (which doesn't stop locals riding their scooters) past a series of rocky coves – following this you eventually climb over a small headland to arrive at a sandy beach with a large and popular summer-only taverna, *Loula*. Many of the patrons here arrive the easy way, by boat.

The bay of **Ayía Paraskeví**, on the southwest coast, shelters a part-sand beach that is almost always quieter than its near neighbour, Áyii Anáryiri. The end of the eastern bus route, it has a seasonal café/bar, but no other development at all.

Áyii Anáryiri is the largest and most popular beach on Spétses: a long, sheltered, partly sandy bay, with an offshore swimming pontoon and a watersports centre offering kayaks, pedaloes, windsurfers and catamarans to rent, as well as a waterski boat. At the

HIKING ACROSS SPÉTSES

If you want to explore Spétses on foot, you can strike directly across the island to many of the beaches. Follow Bótasi out of town, past the *Lazaros* taverna, and as you leave town a sign (the only one you'll see) points you up a paved road. The paving soon runs out, but a good broad track heads up towards the heights. At the top there are no signs at all: one track leads directly down the other side, to rejoin the road halfway between Áyii Anáryiri and Xylokériza (the other end of this track is optimistically signposted "Profítis Ilías 5", but in practice is virtually impassable, on two wheels or four). The better option is to turn right along the spine of the island, with increasingly impressive views across towards the mainland over both coasts; before long there's an obvious (unsigned) path heading down towards Áyii Anáryiri. Continue beyond this and there's a less obvious path to Ayía Paraskeví, while the main trail curls back around towards the north, eventually descending to the coast road near Vréllos.

end of the beach concrete steps lead round to the Bekiris Cave, a low-ceilinged, shallow cavern; you can clamber in through a narrow entrance at the back and then swim out, though best to have something on your feet for the sharp rocks.

Almost at the southern tip of the island a long, steep concrete track leads down to a cove of pale-coloured pebbles at **Xylokériza**. There's no sand at all here, but it's a beautiful spot, surrounded by pines and phoenix palms, and rarely crowded. There's a café and volleyball court.

Ayía Marína or Paradise Beach is a busy, almost suburban beach, within walking distance of the eastern edge of Spétses Town. Packed with loungers, it also has a popular bar-restaurant and a watersports operation offering kayaks and waterski and ringo rides. There are views offshore towards the tempting but off-limits islet of **Spetsopoúla**, the private property of the heirs of shipping magnate Stavros Niarchos.

2

The Cyclades

109 Kéa

112 Kýthnos

115 Sérifos

118 Sífnos

124 Mílos

129 Kímolos

132 Ándhros

136 Tínos

140 Mýkonos

146 Delos

149 Sýros

154 Páros

162 Náxos

170 Lesser Cyclades

173 Amorgós

177 Íos

180 Síkinos

182 Folégandhros

186 Santoríni

194 Anáfi

SANTORÍNI AT SUNSET

The Cyclades

Named from the circle they form around the sacred island of Delos, the Cyclades (Kykládhes) offer Greece's best island-hopping. Each island has a strong, distinct character based on traditions, customs, topography and its historical development. Most are compact enough for a few days' exploration to show you a major part of their scenery and personality in a way that is impossible in Crete, Rhodes or most of the Ionian islands.

The islands do have some features in common. The majority (Ándhros, Kéa, Náxos and Tínos excepted) are arid and rocky, and most also share the "Cycladic" style of brilliant-white cuboid architecture, a feature of which is the central **kástro** of the old island capitals. The typical kástro has just one or two entrances, and a continuous outer ring of houses with all their doors and windows on the inner side, so forming a single protective perimeter wall.

The impact of mass tourism has been felt more severely in the Cyclades than anywhere else in Greece; yet whatever the level of tourist development, there are only three islands where it completely dominates their character in season: **Íos**, the original hippie island and still a paradise for hard-drinking backpackers, the volcanic cluster of **Santoríni** – a dramatic natural backdrop for luxury cruise liners – and **Mýkonos**, by far the most popular of the group, with its teeming old town, selection of gay, nudist and gay-nudist beaches, and sophisticated restaurants, clubs and hotels. After these, **Páros**, **Náxos** and **Mílos** are the most popular, their beaches and main towns packed at the height of the season. The once-tranquil **Lesser Cyclades** southeast of Náxos have become fashionable destinations in recent years, as have nearby **Amorgós**, and **Folégandhros** to the west. To avoid the hordes altogether the most promising islands are **Kýthnos** or **Sérifos** and for an even more remote experience **Síkinos**, **Kímolos** or **Anáfi**. For a completely different picture of the Cyclades, try the islands of **Tínos** with its imposing pilgrimage church and **Sýros** with its elegant Italianate townscape, both with a substantial Catholic minority. Due to their proximity to Attica, **Ándhros** and **Kéa** are predictably popular weekend havens for Athenian families, while **Sífnos** remains a smart, chic destination for tourists of all nationalities. The one UNESCO site, **Delos** – once a great religious centre for the Cyclades – is certainly worth making time for, visited most easily on a day-trip from Mýkonos. One consideration for the timing of your visit is that the Cyclades is the group worst affected by the *meltémi*, which scatters sand and tablecloths with ease between mid-July and mid-August. Delayed or cancelled ferries are not uncommon, so if you're heading back to Athens to catch a flight, leave yourself a day's leeway.

ARRIVAL AND DEPARTURE

BY PLANE

There are airports on Páros, Mýkonos, Santoríni, Sýros, Mílos and Náxos. In season, or during storms when ferries are idle, you have little chance of getting a seat on any flight at less than three days' notice, and tickets are predictably expensive. Expect off-season (Nov–April) frequencies to drop by at least eighty percent.

A brief history p.109
Ancient Karthaia p.111
The Monastery of Khryssopiyí p.122
Mílos boat tour p.125
Panayía Panakhrándou p.135
The Dovecote Trail p.139

Old Delos Days p.148
Náxos Music Festival p.164
Climbing Mount Zas p.169
Homer's tomb p.180
The wineries p.192

FOLÉGANDHROS

Highlights

❶ **Beaches of Mílos** Spectacular shorelines characterized by multicoloured rocks and volcanically heated sand. **See p.127**

❷ **Mýkonos Town** Labyrinthine lanes crammed with restaurants, boutiques and nightlife. **See p.142**

❸ **Delos** The Cyclades' sacred centre and holiest ancient site, birthplace of Apollo and Artemis. See p.146

❹ **Ermoúpolis, Sýros** The elegant capital of the Cyclades, an Italianate architectural jewel and once Greece's busiest port. **See p.150**

❺ **Church of Ekatondapylianí, Parikiá** An imposing and ornate Paleochristian church on Páros, incorporating a number of impressive architectural styles. **See p.156**

❻ **Mount Zas, Náxos** The only must-do trek in the Cyclades: climb the archipelago's highest mountain. **See p.169**

❼ **Hóra, Folégandhros** The "town of five squares", free of traffic and sitting atop a spectacular cliff, arguably the most beautiful inland island capital. **See p.183**

❽ **Caldera of Santoríni** The geological wonder of a crater left by a colossal volcanic explosion, offering unforgettable sunset views. **See p.188**

HIGHLIGHTS ARE MARKED ON THE MAP ON P.108

BY FERRY

Most of the Cyclades are served by main-line ferries from Pireás. Boats for Kéa, and seasonally elsewhere, depart from Lávrio. There are regular services from Rafína to Ándhros, Tínos and Mýkonos, with seasonal sailings elsewhere. All three ports are easily reached by bus from Athens. Between May and Sept there are also a few weekly sailings to the most popular islands from Crete and the eastern Aegean.

Agents and tickets Routes are covered by Aegean Speed Lines (ⓦaegeanspeedlines.gr), ANEK lines (ⓦanek.gr), Blue Star ferries (ⓦbluestarferries.gr), Hellenic Seaways (ⓦhsw.gr), SeaJets (ⓦseajets.gr) and NEL (ⓦnel.gr). All agents are required to issue computerized tickets, to conform to EU regulations and prevent the ferry overcrowding. In high season (particularly Easter, August and during elections),

popular routes will be booked up, so it is important to check availability upon arrival in Greece and book your outward and inbound pre-flight ferry tickets well ahead (particularly those returning to Pireás from the most popular islands). That said, agents may have little advance information on ferry schedules, and purchasing a ticket too far in advance can lead to problems with delayed or cancelled boats. There is usually more space on ferries sailing between islands than to and from Pireás.

Timetables The frequency of Pireás, Lávrio and Rafína sailings given in the chapter is from June to August, and the timings are for both direct and indirect services. For other islands the listings are intended to give an idea of services from late June to early Sept, when most visitors tour the islands. During other months, expect schedules to be at or below the minimum level listed, with some ferries cancelled entirely.

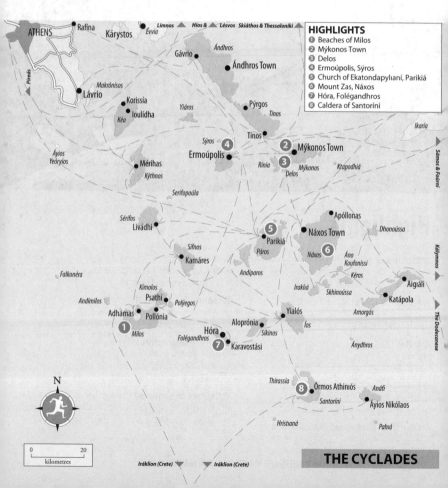

HIGHLIGHTS
- ❶ Beaches of Milos
- ❷ Mýkonos Town
- ❸ Delos
- ❹ Ermoúpolis, Sýros
- ❺ Church of Ekatondapylianí, Parikiá
- ❻ Mount Zas, Náxos
- ❼ Hóra, Folégandhros
- ❽ Caldera of Santoríni

THE CYCLADES

A BRIEF HISTORY

The Cyclades are the most quintessentially Greek of all the islands and their long history reflects that. The mining of **obsidian**, the black, sharp-edged volcanic glass used for making implements, originated on Mílos; shards dating to 11,000 BC have been found deep in the Peloponnese, demonstrating early seaborne Paleolithic trade. The Bronze Age started here around 2800 BC and with it came the **Cycladic civilization**, notable for its sought-after geometric, minimalist figurines made of marble from **Páros** or **Náxos**. **Mining** for copper, silver and gold, combined with the islands' strategic position, turned them into trading centres.

By 2000 BC the Cretan Minoans had become influential in the area, particularly on **Santoríni**. Such influence, however, came to an end with a catastrophic volcanic eruption around 1600 BC. The Ionian Greeks arrived around 1000 BC and within two hundred years the first cities had appeared. **Delos** became a great religious centre in antiquity.

During and after the Persian wars, **Athens** gradually stripped away the wealth and influence of the **Delian Confederacy**. The Cyclades only regained prosperity during the Hellenistic period, as demonstrated by the construction of numerous large, impressive watchtowers, most notably on Náxos. The subsequent Roman occupation converted Delos back into a successful commercial centre, until a series of raids from the east eventually destroyed it. Under **Byzantine** rule, with little control or support from distant Constantinople, the islands were vulnerable to **pirates**, and settlements moved from the open coast to inland, defensive **Kástros**, where you find them today.

With the fall of Constantinople to the Crusaders in 1204, the Cyclades came under **Venetian** control and were divided up by adventurers under **Marco Sanudo** who set up the Náxos-based Duchy of the Aegean. Catholicism prospered, some vestiges of which are still found today on Sýros and Tínos. Most of the islands were taken by the **Ottomans** from the 1530s onwards, though Tínos held out until 1715. As they rightly considered the West a bigger threat, the Turks encouraged the Orthodox Church to fight a resurgence against the former Catholic majority.

After the revolution against the Ottoman Empire in 1821, the Cyclades became part of the Greek state in 1832 and **Sýros**, in particular, prospered, as the new state's largest port and a major industrial base. However, the development of **Pireás** and the 1893 opening of the **Corinth Canal** led to a sharp industrial and commercial decline. This was only reversed in the 1960s when the discovery of the pleasures of **Mýkonos** kick-started the tourism boom that continues unabated today.

Catamaran and small-boat services These operate during the summer season from Pireás and Rafína, replacing winter ferries on some routes. Catamaran travel is expensive, but when time is an issue these high-speed craft are a welcome addition to the conventional fleet. The slower *Express Skopelitis* sails daily in season between Náxos and Amorgós, overnighting at the latter and connecting Irakliá, Skhinoússa, Koufoníssi and Dhonoússa – for current info call ☎ 22850 71256.

Kéa

KÉA (Tziá), the nearest of the Cyclades to the mainland, is extremely popular with Athenian families in August and at weekends year-round; their impact has spread beyond the small resorts, and much of the coastline is peppered with holiday homes built with the locally quarried green-brown stone. Because so many visitors self-cater, there is a preponderance of villa accommodation and not as many tavernas as you might expect. However, outside August or weekends, the island, with its rocky, forbidding perimeter and inland oak and almond groves, is an enticing destination for those who enjoy a rural ramble: ten separate walking paths have been earmarked and are well signposted.

ARRIVAL AND DEPARTURE   KÉA

By ferry There are regular ferry connections to and from Lávrio on the mainland; ferries dock at Korissía. Only a few agents in Athens sell ferry tickets from Lávrio to Kéa, so you will probably need to get these in Lávrio.

Destinations Ándhros (1 weekly; 5hr 40min); Folégandhros (1 weekly; 12hr); Kýthnos (1–4 weekly; 1hr 15min); Lávrio (2–4 daily; 1hr); Mílos (1 weekly; 12hr 20min); Náxos (1 weekly; 6hr 40min); Páros (1 weekly; 5hr 20min); Sýros (1–4 weekly; 3hr 40min); Tínos (1 weekly; 3hr 50min).

INFORMATION

Tourist office At the seafront in Korissía (Mon–Fri 8.30am–2pm).

Services There are two banks and three ATMs in Korissía. Ioulídha has one bank and three ATMs. The island's only post office is opposite the archeological museum (see opposite) in Ioulídha.

Travel agents Kea Paths (☎22880 22651, ⊛keapaths .gr) in Korissía offers a different walking tour or excursion around the island every day; €8–15 per person depending on the length of the trip.

GETTING AROUND

By bus Buses always meet the boats, and from mid-June to September there's a regular fixed schedule around the island (every 30–45min). Most visitors bring their cars along, so there are not many extensive bus services. You may need one of the six taxis available.

By car and motorcycle There is only one, expensive rental outlet, so it's best to rent a car or motorcycle in Athens – or the airport, which is very close to Lávrio – and take it to Kéa, like Athenians do. The island has three petrol stations, all on the road to the port.

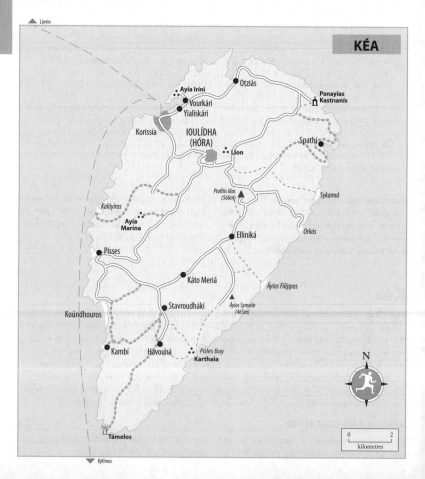

ANCIENT KARTHAIA

The only remains of any real significance from Kéa's past are fragments of temples of Apollo and Athena at **ancient Karthaia**, tucked away on the southeastern edge of the island above Póles Bay, with an excellent deserted twin beach. It is a good ninety-minute round-trip walk from the hamlet of Stavroudháki (on the paved road linking Ioulídha and Havouná), and the inland paved road is worth following along the island's summit from Ioulídha, as it affords fine views over the thousands of magnificent oaks, Kéa's most distinctive feature. Kea Paths (see opposite) offers a walking trip (June–Sept Sat only).

Korissía

The small port of **KORISSÍA** is unlike any other in the Cyclades; with its red-tiled roofs and Neoclassical houses, it could be Pláka-by-the-Sea. It is very convenient as a base; from there you can easily get by bus to Otziás (6km), Ioulídha (6km) or Písses (16km). Although the port beach, **Áyios Yeóryios**, is adequate, there is better swimming at **Yialiskári**, a small, eucalyptus-fringed cove after the eastern promontory on the road to Vourkári.

3

ACCOMMODATION

KORISSÍA

Brillante Zoi ☏ 22880 22685/86, ⓦ hotelbrillante.gr. A comfortable hotel on the middle of the port beach, with a beautifully overgrown garden, idiosyncratic furnishings, spacious rooms and a sumptuous breakfast. The chatty, welcoming owner will feel more like an old acquaintance than your landlady. **€70**

Karthea ☏ 22880 21204, ⓦ hotelkarthea.gr. Dated 1970s hotel, but very centrally located at the beginning of the port beach. Followers of modern history would be interested to learn that this is where Greek junta leaders were held under house arrest in 1974. Breakfast included. **€75**

★ **Keos Katoikies** ☏ 22880 84002, ⓦ keos.gr. Cool, contemporary minimalist studios, each one with its own large balcony in a dramatic setting overlooking Korissía bay. Make sure you watch the sunset in the adjoining café. The room price includes an excellent English buffet breakfast. Free wi-fi at reception. Easter–Oct. **€120**

Porto Kea ☏ 22880 22870, ⓦ portokea-suites.com. Luxurious hotel behind the main road and by the church of Áyios Yeóryios, with a large swimming pool and complimentary internet access. It has its own trendy bar, Ammos, on the beach in front offering free chairs for hotel clients. Breakfast included. Easter–Oct. **€160**

EATING AND DRINKING

En Plo ☏ 694 86 05 176. Opposite the ferry disembarkation point, this snack bar-café serves delicious desserts. Try the chocolate soufflé with a cappuccino for €5 while watching the world go by and the ferries dock. It's a lively spot in the early evening. April–Oct daily 8am–1am; Nov–March Fri–Sat 8am–1am.

★ **Fillipas** ☏ 22880 21690. Built in local Kéa stone and sitting on the hill above Keos Katoikies, this is the best grill restaurant on the island. Although often booked for functions, they will always find you a table

and serve you promptly. Try the giant steaks or its signature beefburger filled with local cheese (€8). April–Oct daily 6pm–1am; Nov–March Fri–Sat 6pm–1am.

Magazés ☏ 22880 21104. The best in the cluster of the port restaurants, this traditional taverna with a small but tasty range of Greek dishes also offers fresh fish, often caught by the speargun of the owner. If you crave meat instead, try the baked pork with potatoes for €9. April–Oct daily 9am–midnight.

Ioulídha

Kéa's capital, **IOULÍDHA** (Hóra), with its winding flagstoned paths, is beautifully situated in an amphitheatric fold in the hills. It is by no means a typical Cycladic town, but is architecturally the most interesting settlement on the island. Accordingly it has numerous bars and bistros, much patronized in August and at weekends, but during other times the town is quiet, its atmospheric, labyrinthine lanes excluding vehicles.

The lower reaches of the town stretch across a spur to the **kástro**, a tumbledown Venetian fortress incorporating stones from an ancient temple of Apollo. Ioulídha's **archeological museum** (Tues–Sun 8.30am–2.30pm; €3) displays extensive finds from the four ancient city-states of Kéa, its highlight being thirteen female Minoan-style statues. Fifteen-minutes' walk northeast of Ioulídha on the path toward Otziás, you pass the **Lion of Kéa**, a sixth-century BC sculpture carved out of an outcrop of rock, 6m long and 3m high – the effect is most striking from a distance.

ACCOMMODATION AND EATING

En Lefko ☎ 22880 22155. On the street between Hóra's two squares, this coffee shop has one of the most romantic gardens, suspended over the cliffs and overlooking the port and beyond. Dimly lit, this is the perfect place to snuggle up with a cappuccino (€4). April–Oct daily 8am–2am.

Hotel Serie ☎ 22880 22355, ⓦ serie.gr. Only 100m from the Ioulídha bus stop and employing a tasteful colour combination of blue and orange throughout – from the stone building itself to the furnishings – this is maybe the best-situated boutique hotel on the island with views both of Ioulídha itself and the valley below. Easter–Oct. **€80**

★ **Rolandos** Main square ☎ 22880 22224. The chef, Rolandos, comes from Corfu and serves a traditional Greek menu with an Ionian flavour. His moussaka (€8) – using courgettes instead of potatoes – is as famed as his house wine. Easter–Oct daily 10am–2am.

The northwest coast

Kéa's northwest coast attracts the most visitors. **VOURKÁRI**, strung out around the next bay, a couple of kilometres northeast of Korissía, is a fishing village, arguably more attractive than Korissía, serving as a hangout for the yachting set. Another 4km further, **OTZIÁS** has a beach that's bigger and better than any on the northern shore, though more exposed to prevailing meltémi winds.

The eighteenth-century monastery of **Panayías Kastrianís** (June–Sept sunrise–sunset) is 7km along a surfaced road from Otziás. From here you can take the pleasant walk on dirt tracks and occasional paths to Ioulídha in another two hours. Further on, **Spathí**, only reachable by car 3km away from the monastery on a dirt road, is by far the island's finest beach.

ACCOMMODATION AND EATING

Anemousa Otziás ☎ 22880 21335. A modern cluster of villas alternating the brown-gold Kéa stone with whitewashed walls. The colour scheme extends to the tasteful furnishings inside the spacious studios. April–Oct. **€55**

Aristos Vourkári ☎ 22880 21475. Don't be fooled by the look of this sleepy fish and seafood taverna at the entrance to the village; it is renowned for its crayfish spaghetti (€20–30) drawing customers from all over the island. April–Oct daily noon–midnight; Nov–March Fri–Sat noon–midnight.

Otziás Otziás beach ☎ 22887 70500. You can relax in the taverna's beach deckchairs for €4/day in the morning before retiring under its roof to sample a variety of grilled meat and fish from only €8 for lunch when the sun gets really scorching. Easter–Oct daily noon–8.30pm.

Strofi tou Mimi Vourkári ☎ 22880 21480. The locals are almost equally divided on whether this place, on the corner of the road towards Otziás, or *Aristos* (see above) is the best fish taverna on the island. You'll have to make up your own mind by dining in both. *Strofi tou Mimi* is only slightly cheaper. April–Oct daily 7pm–midnight.

The south

The road southwest of Ioulídha twists around a scenic agricultural valley and emerges at a large sandy beach at **Písses**. Beyond here, the asphalt peters out at the end of the 5km road south to **Koúndhouros beach**, consisting of two sheltered coves popular with yachters. A further 2km south, at **Kambí**, there's a nice little beach and a good taverna of the same name.

Kýthnos

One of the lesser known and most low-key of the larger Cyclades, **KÝTHNOS** is an antidote to the overdevelopment you may encounter elsewhere, so much so that credit cards are still not accepted in many places. Few foreigners visit, and the island – known also as Thermiá, after its renowned hot springs – is even quieter than Kéa, particularly to the south where drives or long hikes from **Dhryopídha** to its coastal coves are the primary diversion. This is truly a place to sprawl on sunbed-free beaches without having to jostle for space.

ARRIVAL AND DEPARTURE

By ferry Boats dock at the west-coast in Mérihas. There is a frequent service to Lávrio and Pireás, but ferries to nearby Kéa, Sérifos or other islands are sparse.

Destinations Ándhros (0–1 weekly 4hr 30min); Folégandhros (1–2 weekly; 8hr 30min); Íos (1–2 weekly; 7hr); Kéa (2–4 weekly; 1hr 10min); Kímolos (3–5 weekly;

KÝTHNOS

3hr); Lávrio (1–2 daily; 1hr 40min–2hr 30min); Mílos (1–2 daily; 4hr); Náxos (1 weekly; 5hr); Páros (1 weekly; 4hr); Pireás (4–5 weekly; 3hr); Sérifos (4–8 weekly; 1hr 30min); Sífnos (4–8 weekly; 2hr 15min); Síkinos (1 weekly; 7hr 30min); Sýros (2–4 weekly; 2hr 20min); Tínos (1 weekly; 2hr 30min).

INFORMATION

Tourist office A good and helpful information office is open by the jetty during ferry arrivals even on Sundays or late at night.

Services There is one bank and two ATMs in Mérihas: one up the steps near the disembarkation point, and a second on the harbour road. These are the only ATMs on the island,

and hotels or restaurants do not as a rule accept credit cards. Hóra has the island's only post office (Mon–Fri 9.30am–2pm).

Activities Aqua Team (☎ 22810 31333, ⓦ aquakythnos .com), opposite the spa in Loutrá, offer PADI, ANDI and IAHD diving courses.

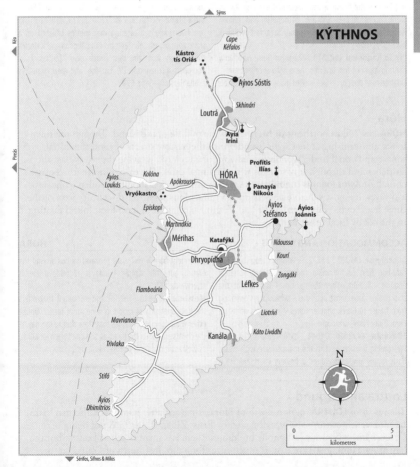

GETTING AROUND

By bus Buses run from Mérihas port around six times daily from early June to September, serving Hóra (15min), Loutrá (30min), Dhryopídha (30min) and Kanála (45min).
By boat There is a *kaïki* from Mérihas (4 daily; ☎ 22810

32104) to the northern beaches of Apókrousi and Kolóna.
By car and motorcycle Halivelakis rental agency (☎ 22810 32506, ⓦ halivelakis.gr) operate a manned stand at the port during ship arrivals.

Mérihas and around

MÉRIHAS is an attractive ferry and fishing port – but not really the place to base your stay. The closest beach of any repute is the fine sandy cove of **Martinakia**, a ten-minute stroll north of the port, while **Episkopí**, a 500m stretch of clean grey sand, is thirty minutes' walk further north. About an hour's walk northwest of Episkopí are the vastly better and more popular beaches of **Apókroussi** and **Kolóna**, the latter a very picturesque sand spit joining Kýthnos to the islet of **Áyios Loukás**.

ACCOMMODATION AND EATING   MÉRIHAS AND AROUND

Martinos Studios ☎ 22810 3246, ⓦ martinos-studios .com. Good-sized rooms, only 30m from the sea and overlooking the harbour, with local Kýthnos furnishings, stone floors, fridge, a/c, TV, kitchenette and phone. Reception is closed in the afternoon. Breakfast included. May–Sept. **€50**

★ **To Kandouni** ☎ 22810 32220. For those who fancy meat in a sea of fish tavernas: here is an excellent grill – situated near the port police – with many different starters

and salads as well as specialities such as *sfoungáto* (local cheese croquettes) for €6. The owners also rent studios above the restaurant. April–Oct daily noon–1am. Studios **€50**
Villa Elena Martinakia ☎ 22810 32275, ⓦ villa-elena .gr. Two-storey self-catering maisonettes situated on a slope with superb sea views over the Aegean and a stone's throw away from the best beach near Mérihas. Fully equipped kitchenette, TV, parking and port transfers available. April–Sept. **€70**

Hóra

HÓRA lies 7.5km northeast of Mérihas, in the middle of the island. Though the town looks unpromising at first sight, wander into the narrow streets beyond the initial square and you'll find a wonderful network of alleyways, weaving their way past shops, churches and through tiny squares with colourful cafés. The early nineteenth-century church of **Áyios Ioánnis Theológos** is worth a visit for its elaborate wooden iconostasis. However, its most valuable possession is a miraculous seventeenth-century icon of the three matriarchs (Elisabeth, Anne and Virgin Mary), said to have been found floating in the sea by local fishermen.

ACCOMMODATION AND EATING   HÓRA

Apocalypse ☎ 22810 31272. Relatively cheap (beer €3) café-bar, next to the main church of – appropriately enough – St John. When the bar closes at midnight, the club of the same name opposite – which plays anything from trance to Greek popular tunes – opens its doors till 6am. Daily 7am–midnight.
Filoxenia ☎ 22810 31644, ⓦ filoxenia-kythnos.gr. Welcoming *pension* next to the main square with clean, basic rooms arranged around a flowery courtyard. It's a

convenient base if you want to travel by bus around the island, but still sample whatever nightlife there is afterwards. **€50**
Messaria ☎ 22810 31620. Large restaurant that offers the Hóra speciality of rabbit in wine sauce for €9. Unlike other establishments in Hóra that close during the day as the clients are out on the beaches, this one's open for lunch, as well as dinner. Daily noon–midnight.

Loutrá and around

The resort of **LOUTRÁ**, 4.5km north of Hóra, is named after its mineral thermal baths. Its nineteenth-century spa was designed by Ernst Ziller, the architect of many of Greece's finest Neoclassical public buildings. There is a small beach at Loutrá, but the bay of **Ayía Iríni**, just 1km east, is much nicer for a dip. Just north of Loutrá, at

Maroula, Mesolithic graves dating to about the eighth millennium BC suggest Kýthnos may have been one of the earliest inhabited Cycladic islands; other sites indicate copper mining and smelting. About a ninety-minute walk from Loutrá, on Cape Kéfalos, lie the picturesque ruins of the medieval capital **Kástro tís Oriás**, once home to around 5000 people, but now abandoned.

ACCOMMODATION — LOUTRÁ AND AROUND

Meltemi ⓣ 22810 31271, ⓦ meltemihotel-kythnos.gr. Fully renovated hotel on the road out of Loutrá that offers dependable good value, with beautifully tiled walls, a landscaped garden and different colour schemes in each room. It organizes daily excursions all over Kýthnos. Credit cards accepted; breakfast included; free wi-fi available; free pick-ups from Mérihas offered. April–Oct. **€65**

★ **Porto Klaras** ⓣ 22810 31276, ⓦ porto-klaras.gr. A hotel worth making the trip to Loutrá just to stay in; its rooms are huge, with decorated carved recesses and large, sculpted beds, while its balconies – some of which come with sofas – have great port views. Free wi-fi, safebox, and, for those who dislike a/c, there are ceiling fans, as well. April–Oct. **€70**

EATING AND DRINKING

Araxovóli ⓣ 22810 31082. A fish taverna conveniently situated in the middle of the quay that also offers tasty cooked meals (dish of the day €10). If you want to eat calamari, octopus, crayfish or lobster on the island, this is the place to make a beeline for. Daily 8am–1am.

Sofrano ⓣ 22810 31436. A waterfront restaurant for the yachting jet-set, this is the most romantic establishment on the island complete with candle-lit tables, flower-filled vases, pink tablecloths and bundles of atmosphere. Thankfully the food (mains €12) matches the decor. March–Nov daily 9am–midnight.

Dhryopídha and the south

From Hóra you can drive south to **DHRYOPÍDHA**; more visually appealing than Hóra by virtue of spanning a well-watered valley, its red-tiled roofs are reminiscent of Spain or Tuscany. It was once the island's capital, built around one of Greece's largest **caves**, the Katafýki, that served as a hiding place from corsairs. South of Dhryopídha, **KANÁLA** is a relaxed alternative to Loutrá, with its **Panayía Kanála** church set in a tiny but pleasant pine woodland and home to a miracle-working icon by the seventeenth-century Cretan master, Skordhilis.

ACCOMMODATION AND EATING — DHRYOPÍDHA AND THE SOUTH

Bouritis Kanála ⓣ 22810 32350. Large self-catering apartments and studios on the beach, all with balcony sea views, a/c, TV and kitchen, sharing a delightfully tended garden with a BBQ. There is also a well-stocked supermarket in the premises. **€60**

Mílas Rooms Áyios Dhimítrios ⓣ 22810 32815. Modern villa complex at the end of Áyios Dhimítrios beach decorated in schist stone and marble and comprising large suites with separate, fully equipped kitchens. The owners also operate a restaurant nearby, whose *sfoungata* (€6) have won a Greek gourmet prize. May–Sept. **€40**

Sérifos

SÉRIFOS has long languished outside the mainstream of history and modern tourism. Little has happened here since Perseus returned with Medusa's head in time to save his mother, Danaë, from being ravished by the local king Polydectes – turning him, his court and the green island into stone. Many would-be visitors are deterred by the apparently barren, hilly interior, which, with the stark, rocky coastline, makes Sérifos appear uninhabited until the ferry turns into postcard-picturesque Livádhi Bay. This element of surprise continues as you slowly discover a number of lovely **beaches** around the island.

Sérifos is also great for serious **walkers**, who can head for several small villages in the under-explored interior, plus some isolated coves. Many people still keep livestock and produce their own cognac-red wines, which are an acquired taste.

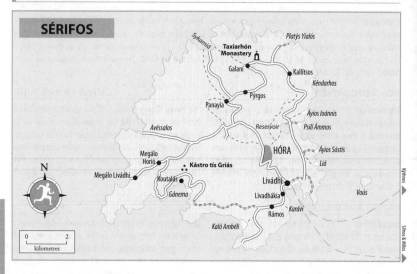

SÉRIFOS

Sykamiá
Platýs Yialós
Taxiarhón Monastery
Galaní
Kallítsos
Kéndarhos
Pýrgos
Panayía
Áyios Ioánnis
Avéssalos
Reservoir
Psilí Ámmos
HÓRA
Megálo Horió
Áyios Sóstis
Kástro tís Griás
Lid
Megálo Livádhi
Koutalás
Livádhi
Gánema
Livadhákia
Voús
Rámos
Karávi
Kaló Ambéli

N

0   2
kilometres

Kýthnos
Sífnos & Mílos

ARRIVAL AND DEPARTURE
SÉRIFOS

By ferry There is a fast catamaran service to Pireás taking only two hours and there are good connections in the summer to many other islands. The port is at the Livádhi promontory.

Destinations Ándhros (1 weekly; 4hr); Folégandhros (2–4 weekly; 2hr); Íos (1–2 weekly; 2hr); Kímolos (3–5 weekly; 3hr 30min); Kýthnos (4–8 weekly; 1hr 20min); Mílos (4–6 weekly; 1hr 45min); Mýkonos (1 weekly; 3hr 45min); Páros (1 weekly; 2hr 40min); Pireás (6–8 weekly 4hr); Sífnos (1–3daily; 45min); Síkinos (1–2 weekly; 3hr 10min); Sýros (1–3 weekly; 3hr 20min); Tínos (1 weekly; 3hr).

INFORMATION

Services There are two ATMs along the seafront in Livádhi. The island's post office is in the lowest quarter of Hóra. For internet access try *Malabar* pub (☎ 22810 52333) in Livádhi inside the shopping arcade (€4/hr); it also attracts the local youth in numbers because of its pool table (daily 10am–1.30pm & 6pm–1am).

Travel agents Krinas Travel (☎ 22810 51488; daily 9am–9pm) opposite the disembarkation point has become by default the starting point for help to visitors on the island.

Activities Avlómonas beach (see opposite) is the headquarters of Sérifos Scuba Divers (☎ 693 25 70 552, ☜ serifosscubadivers.gr), who operate scuba-diving and snorkelling trips plus day-long boat excursions during July and August.

GETTING AROUND

By bus The bus stop and timetable are at the base of the yacht- and fishing-boat jetty. There is a circular bus route serving Panayía–Galaní–Kéndarhos–Áyios Ioánnis–Psilí Ámmos (2–7 daily; circular route 1hr), Hóra (every 30min in summer; 15min; the last weekend bus from Hóra is after midnight) and Panayía–Galaní–Áyios Ioánnis–Psilí Ámmos–Méga Livádhi–Koutalás (2 daily; 30min).

By car and motorcycle For car and motorcycle rental try Blue Bird (☎ 22810 51511, ☜ rentacar-bluebird.gr), next to the filling station on the main street of Livádhi, or from Kartsonaki Bros (☎ 22810 51534) at Livadhákia.

Livádhi and around

Most visitors stay in the port, **LIVÁDHI**, set in a wide greenery-fringed bay and handy for most of the island's beaches. The usually calm bay here is a magnet for island-hopping yachts, to take on fresh water which, despite its barren appearance, Sérifos has in abundance. Livádhi and the neighbouring cove of Livadhákia are certainly the easiest places to find rooms in, along with any amenities you might need, which are scarce elsewhere.

Beaches

The very attractive curve of **Avlómonas**, the long Livádhi town beach, has the advantage of overlooking the inland capital, so that when you are swimming in the sea you have a great inland view. Heading away from the dock, climb over the southerly headland to reach **Livadhákia**, a golden-sand beach, shaded by tamarisk trees. A further ten-minutes' stroll across the low headland to the south brings you to the smaller **Karávi** beach, with its blue-green clear waters, but which has no shade or facilities.

North of Livádhi Bay and accessible by bus in summer – or a 45-minute walk (3km) along a (mostly) surfaced road – is **Psilí Ámmos**, a long, sheltered, award-winning white-sand beach, backed by a large reservoir, and considered the island's best. It is possible to continue on the road, then by path for ten minutes to the larger, but more exposed, **Áyios Ioánnis** beach. Additionally, two more sandy coves, **Liá** (naturist) and **Áyios Sóstis**, hide at the far eastern flank of the island opposite the islet Voús; they are popular with the locals, and accessible via a dirt track off the road to Psilí Ámmos.

3

ACCOMMODATION · LIVÁDHI

Areti ☎22810 51479, ⓦaretihotel.com. Attractively positioned hotel on the headland overlooking Livádhi, with a lovely communal terrace fronting a tiny beach and the entrance to the bay. They also have studios and apartments further out for around €50. April–Oct. €60

Coralli Camping at Livadhákia Beach ☎22810 51500, ⓦcoralli.gr. Superbly located and managed camping with a communal pool, restaurant, bar, mini-market and free wi-fi. This has been named by the Greek *Vima* newspaper as the best campsite in Greece. They also run the more modern four-person *Coralli Studios for €100*, closer to town. April–Oct. €11

★ **Maïstráli** ☎22810 51220, ⓦhotelmaistrali .com. Seventies-built and furnished hotel but, being the tallest building in town, it has balconies (many

frequented by nesting birds) with the best views. At the start of the beach, it is situated conveniently for everything: nightlife, beach and restaurants. Breakfast included. April–Oct. €55

Naïás ☎22810 51749, ⓦnaiasserifos.gr. A slightly dated, but comfortable, good-value hotel on the headland between Livádhi and Livadhákia, with a sociable owner; come here to make friends, not just pass through. All rooms with balconies, some with sea views. Breakfast included. €55

Vasso ☎22810 51346. Very spacious, spotless rooms – some with kitchens – looking inwards into a common courtyard, right on the asphalted road from Livádhi to Livadhákia. If airiness and roominess is your thing, look no further – these are simply exceptional value. €40

EATING AND DRINKING

Kalís Waterfront ☎694 24 67 987. One of the most popular ouzerí, where you may have to queue to get a table; you may be tempted to stuff yourself with just its excellent mezédhes, but hang on and try the delicious crayfish spaghetti for €14. Daily 1am–1am.

Metalleio Livádhi ☎22810 51755. Hidden behind the coastal road, this is one of the few restaurants in the Cyclades where you may have to book. Great service and food without having to break the bank; imaginative mains

from €12; and desserts that can't be finished. After midnight it becomes a nightclub with occasional live bands. Easter–Oct daily 6pm–1am.

★ **Sail** ☎22810 52242. German-managed beach café-bar in the middle of Livádhi beach that transforms itself into a sophisticated first-rate restaurant at night, with a chef from Salonika who cooks excellent and varied European or Greek food (mains €9). Easter–Oct daily 8am–2am.

NIGHTLIFE

Nightlife is lively and mostly clustered in or near the Livádhi seafront mini-mall.

Shark Livádhi ☎693 24 11 657. Set in a conspicuous roof garden above the mini-mall, where all nightlife seems to be clustered, this is an institution on the island playing mostly Top 10 hits. It has a good selection of bottled beers for €5 and some strong cocktails from €7. April–Oct daily 9pm–5am.

Yacht club Livádhi Beach ☎22810 51888, ⓦyachtclubserifos.gr. Hard to imagine that this was the first and only taverna in Livádhi back in 1938. It seems that every person under 30 on the island will come here to be seen at some point during the night, every night. Easter–Oct daily 8am–4am.

Hóra

Quiet and atmospheric, **HÓRA** – only 2km from Livádhi – is one of the most unspoilt villages of the Cyclades. The best sights are in the precarious upper town: follow signs to the kástro to reach the top via steep and occasionally overgrown stairways. The central square, Ayíou Athanasíou, just northwest of the summit, has an attractive church and a small but colourful Neoclassical town hall. From the main bus stop, starting from the *Tap Bar* (see below), a circular signposted loop "route A" takes you to Áyios Konstandínos where on a clear day you can see as far as Sífnos.

EATING AND DRINKING   **HÓRA**

Alóni ☎ 22810 52603. A restaurant with superb westerly views over Livádhi that offers tasty Mediterranean specialities (including rabbit in lemon sauce for €8). More locals than tourists frequent it at weekends because of its live Greek music evenings. Daily 6pm–1am.

Stou Stratou ☎ 22810 52566, ⓦ stoustratou.com. An atmospheric café on the main square with a poetry-strewn menu which offers a nice alternative to eating on the busy seafront down below. Its chocolate cake (€5) is renowned all over the island. Daily noon–2am.

Tap ☎ 22810 52513. Just up from the final bus stop, this is a cosy alternative rock pub for people who just want to drink cold beer, sit at the bar and listen to the bass bouncing off the walls and down their solar plexus. June–Sept daily 9am–5am.

The north and west

If you venture north from Psili Ámmos (p.117) your best bet for a swim is the sheltered cove of **Platýs Yialós** at the extreme northeastern tip of the island, reached easily by a partly paved road. Immediately after the Platýs Yialós turn is the fortified fifteenth-century monastery of **Taxiarhón**, once home to sixty monks but currently inhabited by only one. Treasures of the monastic **catholicon** include an ivory-inlaid bishop's throne, silver lamps from Egypt (to where many Serifiots emigrated during the nineteenth century) and the finely carved **iconostasis**. Call before you arrive (☎ 22810 51027) to arrange a visit; a donation is expected.

If you drive north from Hóra, you reach a junction in the road; follow the signs west for Megálo Horió and on to **Megálo Livádhi**, a remote but lovely beach resort 10km west of Hóra. Iron and copper ores were once exported from here, via a loading bridge that still hangs over the water. At the north end of the beach, there is a monument to four workers killed in 1916 in one of Greece's first protest strikes for better pay and conditions.

An alternative turning just below Megálo Horió leads 3.5km to the small mining and fishing port of **Koutalás**, a pretty sweep of bay with a church-tipped rock and a long, if narrow, beach. Above the port are the scant ruins of the medieval **Kástro tís Griás**. The winding track above the village leads east back to Livádhi, but there are no places to buy refreshments on the two-hour journey back. A side-track en route leads down to the very pretty but shadeless **Kaló Ambéli** beach.

Sífnos

SÍFNOS is prettier, tidier and more cultivated than its northern neighbours. In keeping with the island's somewhat high-class clientele, camping rough is forbidden, while nude sunbathing is not tolerated. The island's modest size makes it eminently explorable. The areas to head for are the port, **Kamáres**, the island's capital **Apollonía**, as well as the east and south coasts. There is nothing in the north worth a peek, except maybe the small fishing village of **Herrónisos**, but even that is too far and offers too little for the first-time visitor. Sífnos has a strong tradition of pottery (as early as the third century BC) and has long been esteemed for its distinctive cuisine, with sophisticated casseroles baked in the clay-fired *gástres* (pots), from where the word gastronomy derives. The island is perhaps best appreciated today, however, for its many beautifully situated **churches** and **monasteries**, and for the beautiful scenery around **Vathý** in the far southwest (see p.123).

ARRIVAL AND DEPARTURE SÍFNOS

By ferry Sífnos is better connected with the mainland and with the rest of the Cyclades than its northern neighbours. Ferries dock at the port in Kamáres.

Destinations Ándhros (1 weekly; 5hr 30min); Folégandhros (1–2 weekly; 1hr 30min–4hr); Íos (1–3 weekly; 3hr); Kímolos (2–5 weekly; 1hr 45min); Kýthnos (1–3 weekly; 2hr–15min); Mílos (5–7 weekly; 1hr); Mýkonos (1 weekly; 5hr); Páros (2 weekly; 3hr); Pireás (2–4 daily; 3–5hr); Santoríni (2 weekly; 4hr 30min); Sérifos (1–3 daily; 40min–1hr); Síkinos (2 weekly; 2hr); Sýros (2–3 weekly; 2hr 30min–5hr 30min).

INFORMATION

Tourist office There is an information centre opposite the disembarkation point (Mon–Fri 8am–3.30pm).

Services There are three banks and four ATMs in Apollonía; the post office is beside the central square. *Stavros Hotel* (see p.120) in Kamáres operates an internet and fax hub available to non-residents at €4/hr.

Travel agents Katsoularis Travel on Stenó in Apollonía (daily 9.30am–2pm & 6–9.30pm; ☎ 22840 31004) can help you find accommodation, tours and ferry tickets. Aegean Thesaurus (☎ 22840 33527), on Kamáres main street, can arrange accommodation across the island.

GETTING AROUND

By bus The bus service is excellent, most of the roads are good, and there's a vast network of paths that are mostly easy to follow. Buses leave regularly from Kamáres to Apollonía/Artemónas (8–10/day; 20min); for all other destinations you have to change at Apollonía. Buses leave for Kamáres (8–10 daily) from Apollonía's central square, Platía Iróon. There is a second station by the *Anthoússa hotel* (see p.121) hotel for Platys Gialós (6–8 daily; 30min),

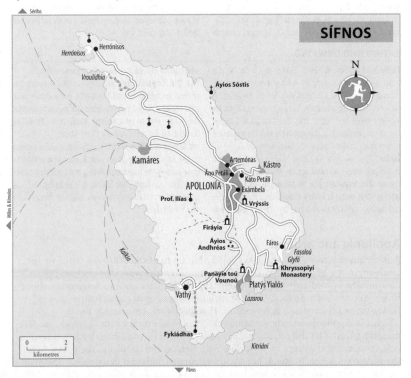

Fáros (5–6 daily; 20min), Kastro (5–6 daily; 20min), Vathý (3–4 daily; 50min) and Herrónisos (3 daily; 1hr).

By car and motorcycle For rental try Stavros Hotel (see

below) and No1 (☎ 22840 33791/33793, ⓦ protomotocar .gr) right by the disembarkation point in Kamáres.

Kamáres

KAMÁRES, the island's port, with its gorgeous, clean beach, is tucked away in a long, steep-sided valley that cuts into the cliffs of the island's western side. A compact resort, though with concrete blocks of accommodations edging up to the base of the hill-slopes, Kamáres' seafront road is crammed with bars, travel agencies, ice-cream shops and restaurants.

ACCOMMODATION   KAMÁRES

Boulis ☎ 22840 32122, ⓦ hotelboulis.gr. If you want to wake up and head straight for a swim, this hotel – arranged around a hedged and vine-covered courtyard in the middle of Kamáres beach – is the place for you. Optional breakfast (€8) in the adjoining, atmospheric café. Easter–Oct. **€65**

Dina's rooms Ayía Marína ☎ 22840 32364. On the furthest side of the beach, these spotless rooms have the best views in Kamáres and are suited for those who prefer quieter, more secluded accommodation. "Rooms" here is a misnomer – there are hotels that offer much less. May–Sept. **€60**

Makis ☎ 22840 32366, ⓦ makiscamping.gr. A campsite on Kamáres beach with excellent facilities such as a café-bar, free wi-fi, minimarket and a laundry open to

non-guests. The obliging, friendly owner is a mine of information about the island. There are also on-site double studios. May–Sept. Camping **€10**, studios **€50**

Myrtó bungalows ☎ 22840 32055 ⓦ hotel-myrto.gr. Opposite the junction to Ayía Marína, this is what you envisage as the ultimate Cycladic hotel: whitewashed, stone-paved, comfortable rooms with balconies and, up from the port as it stands overlooking Ayía María, beautiful beach views. Breakfast included. April–Oct. **€60**

⭐ **Stavros** ☎ 22840 33383, ⓦ sifnostravel.com. A first-class, extremely helpful and reasonably priced hotel on the harbourfront with spacious rooms, free wi-fi and internet facilities. With a wide range of services, it can serve as a one-point information and booking centre for trips and the like. May–Sept. **€60**

EATING AND DRINKING

Follie Ayía Marína ☎ 22840 31183. Is it a bar? Is it a beach club? Is it a nightspot? A bit of everything really; Athenian-owned and operated, it is full for breakfast, is rather muted in the afternoon, but packs them in again for evening drinks and dinner (€8). Don't let all this multi-functioning confuse you, though; the food in the restaurant is very good. Easter–Sept daily 8am–3am.

Ísalos Ayía Marina ☎ 22840 33716. Café-bar and restaurant with a shaded terrace offering more classy cuisine than anywhere else on the island. Its Greek and International menu is highly imaginative, matching the assiduously sophisticated decor. Try its marinated fish

selection for €10. Easter–Sept daily 8am–midnight.

The Old Captain Bar ☎ 22840 31990. A beach bar offering deckchairs during the day, it really comes alive after sunset when a DJ plays eclectic rock music catering for the young people who haven't made it to Apollonía. Cocktails €8. Easter–Oct daily 11am–3am.

⭐ **Simos** ☎ 22840 32353. Family-run, popular taverna on the Kamáres main street with a reputation second to none among the islanders, offering meat and vegetables from their own farm. Their Sunday split-pea soup (€7) is as traditional as it is tasty and an absolute must. Daily noon–midnight.

Apollonía and around

A steep bus ride from Kamáres takes you 5.5km up to **APOLLONÍA**, the centre of an amalgam of five hilltop villages that have merged over the years into one continuous community: immediately north is **Áno Petáli**, which then runs into **Artemónas**, about fifteen minutes away on foot. With white buildings, stepped paths, belfries and flower-draped balconies, it is very scenic, though not self-consciously so.

Sights in Apollonía include numerous churches, while on the central square, the **folk museum** (April–Oct daily 9.30am–2pm & 6–10pm; €1), with its collection of textiles, lace, costumes and weaponry, is worth a visit. Behind and parallel to the square runs the pedestrian street, **To Stenó**, lined with restaurants, bars and fancy shops. The main pedestrian street north from the square leads via Áno Petáli to Artemónas, past the eighteenth-century church of **Panayía Ouranofóra**, incorporating fragments of a seventh-century BC temple of Apollo and a relief of St George over the door.

Taking the road south to **Katavatí** you'll pass, after a few minutes, the beautiful empty monastery of Firáyia and – fifteen minutes further along– there is a turning to a vast Mycenaean archeological site (Tues–Sun 8.30am–3pm; free). Next to it, there is the church of **Áyios Andhréas**, from where there are tremendous views over the neighbouring islands.

ACCOMMODATION

APOLLONÍA AND AROUND

Anthoússa Hotel ☎22840 31431, ⓦhotelanthousa -sifnos.gr. A good and solid enough hotel with comfortable rooms, balconies with views and tasteful light blue decor, plus a terrific patisserie below: try its home-made cakes, chocolates and ice cream for breakfast, if you dare. Free wi-fi. Easter–Nov. **€60**

Mrs Dina ☎22840 31125. A string of well-furnished rooms and studios in a peaceful position with panoramic views, next to the four-star *Petali Village* (see below) in the cathedral area but at a fraction of the price. The landlady is almost never there and will leave you to chill out in peace. May–Oct. **€45**

★ **Petali Village** Áno Petáli ☎22840 33024, ⓦhotelpetali.gr. A luxurious hotel in a quiet position, easy to fall in love with, offering parking, jacuzzi, pool and free wi-fi. Its nautical decoration and verandas overlooking the east of the island offer relaxation worth the price tag. Breakfast included. **€125**

EATING AND DRINKING

Mamma Mia ☎22840 33086. On the Ano Petali steps, this is the surprising meeting point of the island's teenage youth, but don't let that put you off. If you find yourself tired of moussaka and pastitsio and, of course, fish, then have a large wood-fired pizza here for €10; that's what the Sifniots themselves do. June–Sept daily 7pm–2am.

Okýalos ☎22840 32060. Established as the in-place to dine, with Hard Rock Café-style music while you eat, this restaurant on the main street is worth making a reservation for the roof garden – if you can. The casseroles here (€15) are worth sampling, especially if they are the dish of the day. Daily 7pm–late.

Tou Apostóli to Koutoúki To Stenó ☎22840 33186. One of the better eating establishments but rather pricey, offering island and other Greek specialities. This is the best place to try the Sifniot casseroles; choose either from its selection of veal- or pork-baked dishes (€13). April–Sept daily 7am–11am.

NIGHTLIFE

Argó Stenó ☎22840 31114, ⓦargobar.gr. Long-standing island club, refurbished in 2009 and playing everything from classical music to modern rock. While weekdays are mostly the realm of young tourists with their drink antics, the live music shows on Fridays and Saturdays attract all ages and are considerably better behaved. April–Oct daily 11pm–late.

Cosí Stenó ⓔcosisifnos@gmail.com. Club with live DJs playing soul and R&B. Its mostly 18–30 clientele tends to sit down outside, where you can hardly walk through the chairs and tables sometimes, but there is much less of a crush on the large indoors dancefloor, should you want to boogie. June–Sept daily 11pm–late.

The east coast

Most of Sífnos's coastal settlements are along the less precipitous **east coast**, within a modest distance of Apollonía and its surrounding cultivated plateau. **Kástro** may be more appealing than the resorts of **Fáros** and **Platýs Yialós**, which can get very overcrowded in July and August.

Kástro

KÁSTRO, the ancient capital of the island, retains much of its medieval character. It's essentially a sinuous main street along the ridge of a hilltop, the houses on either side, all of the same height, forming the outer defence wall. Their roofs slope inwards in order to collect rainwater inside in case of siege. There are some fine sixteenth- and seventeenth-century churches with ornamental floors; Venetian coats of arms, ancient wall fragments and cunningly recycled Classical columns are still on some of the older dwellings, while the occasional ancient sarcophagus lies incongruously on the pavement. In addition, there are the remains of the ancient acropolis, as well as a small **archeological museum** (Tues–Sun 9am–3pm; free) operating in a former Catholic church in the higher part of the village.

You can walk along Kástro's northeastern peripheral path overlooking the picture-postcard church of the **Eptá Martyres** (Seven Martyrs), which juts out into the sea. There's nothing approximating a **beach** near Kástro, as defence and not easy access was the aim of the inhabitants. For a swim you can use the Eptá Martyres rocks, or possibly the rocky cove of **Serália**, just south of Kástro, or the small shore at **Panayía Pouláti**, 1.3km to the northwest; both have facilities.

The fantastic views over the valley below might inspire you to tackle two well-signposted walks to Fáros (1hr 30min) and to Vrússis monastery (50min) that start from the Konáki snack bar (see below).

ACCOMMODATION AND EATING   KÁSTRO

Aris & Maria ✆ 22840 31161, ⓦ arismaria -traditional.com. Rooms and studios in six century-old houses all over Kástro, fully renovated, but retaining all of the traditional Cycladic features such as wooden ceilings and stone floors. As no cars are allowed inside Kástro, you will need to carry your luggage for about 100m uphill to the reception following the signs to "Ancient Wall". **€55**

★ **Konáki** ✆ 22840 33165. With a striking pink decor, this café-cum-snack bar has good, strong cappuccino and

home-made local pastries (€5). Shaded with comfortable seats, it is the perfect place to laze about and gaze across to Apollonía beyond the valley below. April–Oct daily 9am–10pm.

To Astro ✆ 22840 31476. The oldest taverna in the village, feeding people since 1969. Enjoy your food slowly and unhurriedly to match the service, but you can speed it up by choosing from the day's *gastra* dishes (€12) that should already have been prepared. May–Sept daily noon–midnight.

Fáros

To the south of Kástro, the small fishing village of **FÁROS** is a possible fall-back base, though the beaches are relatively small. The main beach is partly shaded and crowded in season while **Fasoloú**, a 400m walk to the southeast past the headland is better and shaded by many tamarisk trees. Head off west through the older part of the village to find the picturesque **GLYFÓ** beach, arguably the best of the three.

ACCOMMODATION   FÁROS

Sifnéïko Arhontikó Fáros ✆ 22840 71422, ⓦ sifneiko-arxontiko.gr. Don't be taken in by its Greek name (Sífnos Manor); this modern hotel is not housed in an old mansion, but was built in 1992 in typical Cycladic style. Rather hard to find because it's not signposted, but worth tracking down, as it offers the most comfortable option in Fáros – convenient both for the buses and the

beach. April–Sept. **€50**

Thalatta Glyfó ✆ 22840 71485. Built on a slope and inaccessible to vehicles, this villa complex is as close to pure solitude as you can hope for – although you do have access to a minimarket, bars and several tavernas within 200m. Four nights minimum stay. May–Sept. **€65**

THE MONASTERY OF KHRYSSOPIYÍ

From the beach at Glyfó (see above), a fifteen-minute hillside path leads to the longer beach of **Apokoftó**, with a couple of good grill tavernas. Flanking Apokoftó to the south, marooned on a sea-washed promontory, the seventeenth-century **Khryssopiyí Monastery** features on every poster of the island. According to legend, the cleft in the rock (under the entrance bridge) appeared when two village girls, fleeing to the spit to escape the attentions of menacing pirates, prayed to the Virgin to defend their virtue. To celebrate the story, a large festival takes place forty days after Easter and involves the spectacular arrival of a holy icon on a large high-speed ferry, and its – often dramatic – transfer to a small boat to be brought ashore.

EATING AND DRINKING

Gorgóna ☎ 22840 71461. A lively hippy and alternative commune that also offers rooms. Don't be put off by the tattooed arms on display, or the rock music blasting out of the speaker; this is the hangout of mellow souls who welcome strangers. May–Sept daily noon–late. Rooms €60

Yórgos-Dimítris Fasoloú ☎ 22840 71493. An excellent and well-priced taverna offering only produce from its own farm and good house wine. The shady location under the tamarisk trees and the nearby parking facilities make it the best beach eating option in this part of the island (mains start from €5). Easter–Sept daily noon–midnight.

Platýs Yialós

PLATÝS YIALÓS is 12km away from Apollonía, near the southern tip of the island, and has a long stretch of beach that takes four bus stops to cross in its entirety. Buffeted by occasional strong winds, a continuous row of buildings – many of them pottery workshops – lines the entire stretch of beach, which can be slightly off-putting. Still, it should be on everyone's radar, because it offers some of the best food on the island. A five-minute walk from the last bus stop over the southwestern headland brings you to **Lazárou Beach**, a tiny pebble bay entirely occupied by the eponymous beach bar and restaurant behind the water's edge.

ACCOMMODATION AND EATING

PLATÝS YIALÓS

Alexandros ☎ 22840 71300, ⓦ hotelalexandros.gr. Getting off at the first bus stop at Platýs Yialós, you encounter this unmistakeably luxurious – as the large swimming pool indicates – but surprisingly affordable hotel where the focus is on room size rather than elaborate reception areas. Large, home-made buffet breakfast included. May–Sept. €70

★ **Ariadne Beach** ☎ 22840 71277. An excellent restaurant in a shady courtyard under the beach salt cedar trees near bus stop #3. It is featured regularly in every Greek gourmet publication, specializing in octopus macaroni, lobster spaghetti and seafood risotto (€11). March–Oct daily noon–midnight.

Cyclades Beach ☎ 22840 71276, ⓦ cycladesbeach.gr. Reputable hotel by the third beach bus stop that has been operating since 1979 and offering the best-priced rooms on the island. Its restaurant, open to non-residents, has a good buffet breakfast for €4 and, later, traditional Greek food for €8 till midnight. The owners also organize trips around Sífnos. €45

Vathý

A fishing village on the shore of an almost circular, almost enclosed bay, **VATHÝ** is the most attractive base on the island, with little to do but relax on the beach or in a waterfront taverna. Even the surfaced road and the opening of the luxury *Elies* resort (see below) seems not to have destroyed the character of this previously remote spot; a character accentuated by the poster-pretty all-white monastery of Taxiárhis on the promontory bisecting the beach.

ACCOMMODATION

VATHÝ

Elies Resort ☎ 22840 34000, ⓦ eliesresorts.com. Gated, and protected by its own security staff, this top-class resort – where every employee is disconcertingly attired in white clothes, giving it a semblance of the village in the *Prisoner* TV series – offers luxurious surroundings and claims to have the largest pool in the Cyclades. Drop in to play spot-the-VIP, as it is frequented by celebrities, politicians and industrialists. May–Oct. €250

Studios Nikos ☎ 22840 33244, ⓦ sifnosrooms.com. A villa compound dead on the beach with attractive, comfortable studios sharing a front grass garden with uninterrupted views to the sea. With large balconies and verandas, separate kitchens and a lot of room inside for three or four people, they are great value for a family self-catering stay. April–Nov. €50

EATING AND DRINKING

To Tsikali ☎ 22840 71177. One of the better-known family tavernas on Sífnos, it has the best spot on the seafront beyond the monastery and can occasionally surprise the most discerning of palates with its home-made cheese, mezédhes, chunky chips, goat *gástres* and lemony rabbit dishes (€7). Easter–Oct daily noon–midnight.

Tou Koutsouná ☎ 22840 71156. Signposted just before the hairpin that descends to the village, this is a grill restaurant that claims with good reason to have the best views over Vathý. It has some imaginative croquettes based on courgettes, tomatoes and chick peas (€6) which are all worth sampling before moving to its traditional lamb stew *mastélo*. Take it easy and don't hurry the two old dears who own it. Daily noon–midnight.

Mílos

Volcanic **MÍLOS** is a geologically diverse island with weird rock formations, hot springs and odd outcrops off the coast. Minoan settlers were attracted by obsidian; this and other products of its volcanic soil made it one of the most important of the Cyclades in the ancient world. Today, the quarrying of many rare minerals has left huge scars on the landscape but has given the island a relative prosperity which today translates into several gourmet restaurants with better wine lists than many of its neighbours. With some 75-odd **beaches** and sensational views Mílos hasn't had to tart itself up to court tourism – indeed, the wealthy mining companies that employ a quarter of the population are happy to see tourism stay at low levels. It helps that the western half of Mílos, as well the other islands around it, including **Kímolos**, is a nature reserve protecting three endemic species: the extremely rare **Mediterranean seal**, the **Mílos viper** and the one you are most likely to encounter, the long, crocodile-shaped **Mílos wall lizard**. Note that the importance of the archeological finds, museums and sites here is only surpassed by Delos and Santoríni.

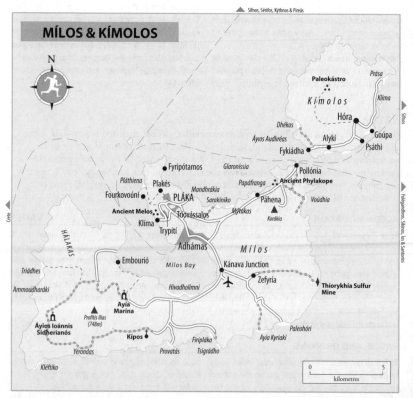

MÍLOS & KÍMOLOS

ARRIVAL AND DEPARTURE

MÍLOS

By plane The tiny airport is 5km southeast of the port and served by Olympic with flights to Athens (1–2 daily; 45min).

By ferry Ferries dock at the port of Adhámas. A small car ferry to Kímolos leaves from Pollónia, a quicker and cheaper option than the larger ferries.

Destinations Amorgós (1 weekly; 5hr 30min); Anáfi (1–2 weekly; 7hr); Ándhros (1 weekly; 6hr); Iráklion/Lassithi (2 weekly; 9hr); Folégandhros (1–3 daily; 2hr); Íos (3–5 weekly; 3hr 30min); Kárpathos and Kássos (2 weekly; 14–26hr); Kímolos (5–7 daily from Pollónia; 20min); Kýthnos (1 daily; 3hr); Mýkonos (3–4 weekly; 6–9hr); Náxos (1–2 daily; 6hr); Páros (3 weekly; 6hr 30min); Pireás (1–3 daily; 6hr); Rhodes and Hálki (1–2 weekly; 27–36hr); Santoríni (1–2 daily; 2–5hr); Sérifos (1–3 daily; 1hr 30min); Sífnos (1 daily; 2hr); Síkinos (2–3 weekly; 3hr 30min); Sýros (2–3 weekly; 5–10hr); Tínos (1 weekly; 6hr).

INFORMATION

Tourist office Situated opposite the ferry dock (☎ 22870 22445, ⊛ milos.gr; daily 9am–5pm & 7–11pm), with daily updated list of available rooms around the island, maps, plus detailed bus and ferry timetables.

Services There are several banks and ATMs behind the main square in Adhámas, while the post office is by the main square. Internet Café (April–Oct daily 9am–5pm & 7–11pm), at the start of the Pláka road, is well priced at €1.50/hr. Pláka has a post office near the archeological museum.

GETTING AROUND

By bus Services start from the main square by *Hotel Portiani* and are sometimes inconveniently timed in the shoulder season: Pláka/Tripití (9–10 daily; 20min), Pollónia (2–3 daily; 30min), Paleohóri via Zefyría (2–4 daily; 30min), Hivadholímni (8–10 daily; 15 min), Sarakíniko (1–2 daily; 30min).

By taxi Taxis seem to be used on Mílos more than on other islands. The taxi rank is near the bus stop (☎ 22870 22219). The fare to Pollónia is around €12.

By car and motorcycle Rental is available on the waterfront near the jetty from many places including Sophia (☎ 22870 21994) and Tomaso (☎ 22870 24100, ⊛ tomaso.gr).

Adhámas

The lively main port of **ADHÁMAS** was a small hamlet until it was populated by refugees from a failed rebellion in Crete in the 1840s. Because it is so recent, you may find it architecturally disappointing compared to some of the Cycladic ports, despite the marble-paved esplanade around its natural headland. There is an ill-defined centre just inland of the esplanade, at the junction of the Pláka road and the Mílos Bay coastal road, where restaurants, cafés and shops abound.

Ecclesiastical Museum

April–Oct Mon–Sat 9.15am–1.15pm & 6.15–10.15pm • Free

The unmissable **Ecclesiastical Museum** is housed in the ninth-century church of Ayía Triádha just behind the quayside. It has a superb collection of liturgical paraphernalia and rare icons that arrived in Adhámas when the inland capital, Zefyría, was

---

MÍLOS BOAT TOUR

One of the absolute must-dos on Mílos is a **boat tour**, either down the bizarre western coastline, making several stops at otherwise inaccessible swimming spots like the magnificent **Kléftiko**, or to **Kímolos** and **Períaigos** to spot the rare Mediterranean seal. Weather permitting, the boats normally leave at 10am from the Adhámas quayside and return at 6–7pm.

Chrysovalándou ☎ 6944 587 574. Offers two shorter excursions per day.

Excellent Yachting ☎ 22870 41292, ⊛ e-y.com. Provides alternative "snorkel safaris" aimed at younger travellers for €50 including lunch and free drinks.

★ **Panormos** ☎ 694 57 78 809, ✉ skipper20@in.gr. Excursions to sheltered coves whatever the weather and the wind direction.

abandoned. This is the place to admire the work of the Cretans Emmanouel Skordhílis and his son, Antonis, two of the prime icon makers in eighteenth-century Greece.

Mining Museum of Mílos

Daily 9am–2pm & 5.30–9.30pm • €3 • ⓦ milosminingmuseum.gr

On the seafront east of town, about 500m from the centre, the well-organized **Mining Museum of Mílos** gives an interesting insight into how mining has shaped the island, with an extensive collection of mining equipment, mineral samples and geological maps of Mílos, plus informative displays on the extraction, processing and uses of minerals. The museum is well worth a visit at the start of your stay in order to make more sense of the island's appearance and economy. Don't miss the two moving short films where old miners describe their working conditions (English subtitles).

ACCOMMODATION   ADHÁMAS

★ **Aeolis** ☎ 22870 23985, ⓦ aeolis-hotel.com. Great-value hotel with palatial rooms and designer furniture but a bit difficult to find: behind the main square, in the street by the dry rivulet. Built with modern specifications, it provides baby cots on request and has two rooms specially adapted for disabled travellers. Minimum stay two nights in the summer. **€70**

Meltémi ☎ 22860 41425, ⓦ hotelmeltemi.gr. Basic, centrally positioned hotel behind the main square, clean, a bit noisy (ask for a room at the back) but with all amenities, this is the cheapest option in town. Suffers from occasional water pump pressure, so your showers may be quite lengthy. **€60**

Ostria ☎ 22870 28127, ⓦ ostria-hotel.gr. A beautiful and comfortable hotel in a quiet position to the east of town (near the mining museum) with excellent breakfast. The ivy-covered common areas and its candle-lit roof garden are as relaxing as the rooms themselves. May–Sept. **€120**

Portiani ☎ 22870 22940, ⓦ hotelportiani.gr. The most central hotel (in the main square), partly renovated, with excellent buffet breakfast, free wi-fi and a spectacular seaview terrace. The reception can organize everything for you, from car rental to daily excursions. It can be a bit noisy, though, if you are an early sleeper. **€100**

EATING AND DRINKING

Aggeliki ☎ 694 24 75 162. A waterfront café that will appeal to lovers of ice cream, with its selection of extremely delicious home-made products. Turn your back on your hotel breakfast to have a strong cup of cappuccino (€3) and a piece of mouthwatering chocolate cake. Daily 9am–2am.

★ **Flisvos** ☎ 22870 22275. An award-winning restaurant in the same family for three generations. Wide menu offering everything from fried calamari to grilled

meats (€8) and a variety of savoury filo pastries accompanied by a good wine list of Santoríni vintages. April–Oct daily noon–midnight.

Kinigós ☎ 22870 22349. A popular place to eat, with a varied menu and excellent people-watching potential. Its specialities are the various meatball dishes (€7) made with a secret house recipe, as well as its famed moussaka (€6.50). Come early to find a table. April–Oct daily noon–midnight.

Pláka and around

PLÁKA, the capital of the island, is the largest of a cluster of traditional villages that huddle beneath a small crag on the road northwest of Adhámas. Steps beginning near the *Fóras* taverna lead up to the **kástro**, its upper slopes clad in stone and cement to channel precious rainwater into cisterns. The **Folk Museum** (Tues–Sat 10am–2pm & 6–9pm, Sun 10am–2pm; €3) has a well-presented array of artefacts related to the history of arts, crafts and daily life on Mílos. The small church of the **Dormition** nearby offers one of the best views in the Aegean, particularly at sunset.

On a long ridge 1km south of Pláka, the narrow, attractive village of **Trypití** ("perforated"), which takes its name from the cliffside catacombs nearby, is less busy with traffic than lower Pláka. At the very bottom of the cliff edge and accessed via a road from the southern end of Trypití or steps down from the catacombs, **Klíma** is the most photogenic of the island's fishing hamlets, with its picturesque boathouses tucked underneath the colourful village dwellings.

Archeological Museum

Tues–Sun 8.30am–3pm – it does not always look open, even when it is • €3

Behind the lower car park in Pláka, this Neoclassical jewel of a building, built by Ernst Ziller (see p.114) in the 1840s, contains numerous Neolithic obsidian implements, plus a whole wing of finds from ancient Phylakope (see p.128); highlights include a votive lamp in the form of a bull and a Minoan-looking terracotta idol, the **Lady of Phylakope**. You'll also recognize the plaster-cast copy of the **Venus de Milo**, the original of which was found on the island in 1820. It is not clear whether it was discovered with the arms already separated from the torso, or if they were broken off in a skirmish between French sailors and locals.

Catacombs and Ancient Melos

Tues–Sun 8am–3pm • €2 • Groups of ten allowed at a time

From Pláka's archeological museum, signs point you towards the **early Christian catacombs**, 1km south of Pláka and just 400m from Trypití; steps lead down from the road to the inconspicuous entrance. Some 5000 bodies were buried in three tomb-lined corridors with side galleries, stretching 200m into the soft volcanic rock, making these the largest catacombs in Greece. Bear in mind that only the first 50m are illuminated and accessible by boardwalk and the guided tour lasts only about fifteen minutes.

Just above the catacombs, extending down from Pláka almost to the sea, are the ruins of **Ancient Mílos** whose focal point is a well-preserved Roman **amphitheatre**. En route to the theatre from the surfaced road is the signposted spot where the *Venus de Milo* was found in what may have been the compound's gymnasium.

ACCOMMODATION

PLÁKA AND AROUND

★ **Mýlos tou Markétou** Tripití ☎ 22870 22147, ⓦ marketoswindmill.gr. A sixteenth-century windmill on the furthest, eastern side of the village that has been fully adapted to a four-bed apartment (€170). The adjoining auxiliary buildings have been converted to more conventional studios; all with a fantastic view of the Mílos bay. May–Oct. **€70**

Spíti tis Mákhis ☎ 22870 41353/22129. A hotel with refurbished rooms employing cherry-wood furniture and bright orange colours that make a difference from the Cycladic blue, it occupies the house where the *Venus de Milo* was hidden following its discovery. Conveniently situated for the bus, but set back from the main road, it also has plenty of parking space. June–Oct. **€75**

EATING AND DRINKING

Arhontoúla ☎ 22870 21384, ✉ arhontoula3@yahoo .gr. One of the oldest and more reputable family restaurants in Pláka occupying the same spot for over 100 years offering Greek and International cuisine – even Indian curry dishes – plus a carefully selected wine list. Mains start from €7. April–Nov daily noon–midnight.

Foras ☎ 22870 23954. An old-style *mezedhopolío* like they don't make them any more. Greek coffee, a variety of ouzo bottles, many small-plate mezédhes (€6) and an elderly clientele that has been coming here to enjoy the food for decades. Daily noon–midnight.

The south

The main road to **SOUTHERN MÍLOS** splits at Kánava junction, near the large power station. The sea there contains underwater hot vents resulting in fizzy hotspots that locals use for jacuzzi-like baths. The eastern fork leads to **Zefyría**, which was briefly the capital until an eighteenth-century earthquake (and subsequent plague) drove out the population. There is little to see in the old town, but a magnificent seventeenth-century church with beautifully painted walls and ceilings. The original iconostasis was transferred to the church of the Dormition in Adhámas, while the icons are displayed in the Ecclesiastical museum.

South of Zefyría, it's a further 8km down a winding, surfaced road to the coarse sand of **Paleohóri**, one of the island's best beaches, warmed by underground volcanism. A little rock tunnel leads west to a second beach, which is backed by extraordinarily coloured cliffs and where steam vents heat the shallow water. **Ayía Kyriakí**, further to the west of Paleohóri, is a pebble beach under imposing sulphurous and red oxide cliffs.

ACCOMMODATION AND EATING THE SOUTH

Artémis Paleohóri ☎ 22870 31222. A restaurant and apartment complex, difficult to categorize because its fish taverna (with an excellent wine list) is as good and as well known as its comfortable lodgings. May–Oct daily 9am–6pm. Apartments for 2–3 people **€100**

★ **Sirocco** Paleohóri ☎ 22870 31201. An institution on the island, using the hot volcanic sand – that reaches a constant temperature of 100°C only 30cm below the surface – to bake casseroles of lamb, veal, pork and fish (€10) in clay pots overnight. May–Oct daily noon–10pm.

Hivadholímni and the west

The westerly road from the Kánava junction leads past the airport entrance to **HIVADHOLÍMNI**, the best beach on Mílos bay itself. Behind the beach is a salty lagoon, where in May and September you can observe migrating birdlife. Just before Hivadholímni, you can fork south to **Provatás**, a short beach, closed off by multicoloured cliffs to the east. It's easy to get to so it hasn't escaped development.

Forking to the east before Provatás, the road leads to the trendy and very popular beach of **Firipláka**. Further east, on a dirt road, sandy **Tsigrádho** is excellent for swimming and usually uncrowded. Going west from the Kanava junction the surfaced road ends at **Ayía Marína**, although a dirt road continues into **Hálakas** and the small fishing village of **Embourió** with a perfectly acceptable beach.

For the most part, the southwestern peninsula of Hálakas centred on the wilderness of Mount Profítis Ilías (748m) is an uninhabited nature reserve with unsurfaced, dirt tracks, two of which lead to the fine, unspoilt beaches of **Triádhes** and **Ammoudharáki Kléftiko** in the southwest corner. It is only reachable by boat, but repays the effort to get there with its stunning rock formations and semi-submerged tunnels.

ACCOMMODATION HIVADHOLÍMNI

Milos Camping ☎ 22870 31410, ⊚ miloscamping.gr. Large campsite overlooking Mílos Bay and above Hivadholímni beach; its minibus meets ferries, and in summer there are frequent buses to and from Adhámas. There is a decent restaurant next door with a swimming pool. Ask for special deals (five days get a sixth free). May–Sept. **€13**

The north coast

From either Adhámas or the Pláka area, good roads run roughly parallel to the **NORTH COAST** which, despite being windswept and sparsely inhabited, is not devoid of geological interest. **Sarakíniko**, in particular, is an astonishing sculpted inlet with a sandy sea bed and gleaming white rocks popular with sunbathing local youth. Nearby **Mýtakas** is another good beach, accessible via a 500m dirt road, with dramatic views west along the rocky coastline.

Eastwards you reach another of Mílos's coastal wonders, **Papáfranga**, a short ravine into which the sea flows under a rock arch – the tiny beach at its inland end is accessed by rock-carved steps. To the right of the Papáfranga car park, the remains of three superimposed Neolithic settlements crown a small knoll at **Phylakope** (Tues–Sun 8.30am–3pm; free). **Pollónia**, the end of the road 12km northeast of Adhámas, is a small harbour within a semicircular bay with a long, curved, tamarisk-lined beach. This is where you take the small ferry to Kímolos (see opposite).

INFORMATION THE NORTH COAST

Activities Pollónia is immensely popular with windsurfers and divers; the Apollon Dive Centre (☎ 22870 41451) offers PADI courses, snorkelling trips and equipment rental.

ACCOMMODATION

Andréas ☎ 22870 41262, ⓦ andreas-rooms.gr. Villa complex at the western edge of Pollónia with triple studios, stunning views and easy access to the quiet neighbouring bay, plus its own boat, *Perseas*, bookable for trips and fishing expeditions to nearby islands. Help yourself to vegetables from the garden. **€60**

Kapetán Tásos ☎ 22870 41287, ⓦ kapetantasos.gr. One of the more luxurious options in the quay area that has been fully renovated; the "superior" suites are as big as a two-bedroom flat. Free transfers, wi-fi, mini-gym and optional breakfast until 2pm. April–Oct. **€110**

EATING AND DRINKING

★ **Armenáki** Pollónia ☎ 22870 41061. Claiming never to use anything frozen and nothing but olive oil, this is one of the best restaurants on Milos, packed day and night, so it is wise to make a reservation. Its fish casseroles (€12) and seafood pasta go down well with its diligently chosen white wines. April–Oct daily noon–late.

Yialós Pollónia ☎ 22870 41208. Small but stylish restaurant with a well-thought-out menu and a wide range of seafood and fish dishes. Try the fish soup, or crab (€18), and follow that with an imaginative dessert such as caramelized strawberries. April–Oct daily noon–midnight.

3

Kímolos

Of the three islands off the coast of Mílos, only rugged, scenic **KÍMOLOS** is inhabited. Volcanic like Mílos, it profits from its geology and used to export chalk (*kimolía* in Greek) until the supply was exhausted. Bentonite is still extracted locally, and the fine dust of this clay is a familiar sight on the northeastern corner of the island, where mining still outstrips fishing and farming as an occupation. Apart from the inhabited southeast, the rest of the island is a nature reserve, which explains the lack of surfaced roads.

Even in August Kímolos isn't swamped by visitors. Just as well, since, although there are around 450-odd beds on the whole island, there is little in the way of other amenities. There is only one bus, no car or motorbike rental (rent your vehicle from Mílos) and few restaurants. Those visitors who venture here come for the tranquillity and for trekking in pristine nature.

ARRIVAL AND INFORMATION

KÍMOLOS

By ferry Whether you arrive from Adhámas or from Pollónia on Mílos (see p.127), you'll dock at the tiny port of Psáthi. Ferry tickets for onward journeys – unless bought in advance up in Hóra (see below) – are only sold an hour or so before the arrival of the boat. Larger ferries call briefly on their way to and from Adhámas, but the best option for Milos is the ferry *Panagia Faneromeni* (☎ 22870 51184, ⓦ kimolos-link.gr) that serves Pollónia (see opposite). Destinations Folégandhros (2 weekly; 1hr); Kýthnos (2–5

weekly; 3hr 30min); Mílos, Adhámas (2–8 weekly; 1hr); Mílos, Pollónia (7 daily; 20min); Santoríni (2 weekly; 3hr); Sérifos (2–5 weekly; 2hr 30min); Sífnos (2–5 weekly; 2hr); Síkinos (2 weekly; 1hr 30min).

Travel agents There are two shipping agencies, both highly reputable: Kimolos Travel (☎ 22870 51219) and Maganiotis (☎ 22870 51000).

Services There is one bank and one ATM in Hóra; the island's post office is in the west of the village.

GETTING AROUND

By bus There is one regular bus in high season to Hóra (8–10 daily; 10min) from the port as well as connecting with the ferries.

On foot The capital, Hóra, can be reached on foot in about thirty minutes from the port. Other destinations around the island are on paths that are 2–3 hours on foot from Hóra.

Hóra

Dazzlingly white **HÓRA** (known locally as Horió) is perched on the ridge above Psáthi behind a few old windmills overlooking the bay. The magnificent, two-gated, sixteenth-century **kástro** was built against marauding pirates. The perimeter houses are still intact and inhabited, though its heart is a jumble of ruins except for the small church of **Christós** (1592) and the chapel of the island's own saint **Ayía Methodhía**, beatified in

1991. Just outside the kástro to the north stands the conspicuously unwhitewashed, late seventeenth-century church of **Khryssóstomos**, the most beautiful on the island. Near the church is the **archeological museum** (July–Sept Tues–Sun 8.30am–3pm; free), displaying pottery from the Geometric to the Roman period. In a restored house near the eastern gateway is the privately run **Folk and Maritime Museum** (July–Sept daily 9am–1.30pm; €1).

ACCOMMODATION   HÓRA

★ **Meltemi** ☎ 22870 51360. A superlative option in the west of the village, with modern, recently renovated rooms, airy balconies and an excellent view across to Hóra. The owner is the captain of the *Panagia Faneromeni* and can arrange for your pickup at Psáthi. There is also an excellent restaurant below where you can taste island dishes such as *tomatokeftédhes* (€6), something like

tomato bhajis. €50
Villa Maria ☎ 22870 51392. Central hotel, right by the entrance to Hóra, with rooms and studios that are up there with the most comfortable in the Cyclades; however, check carefully (and then reconfirm) whether it is block-booked, something that happens often. €50

EATING AND DRINKING

★ **Panorama** ☎ 22870 51351. This is the best place to eat on the island near the northeastern gate of the kástro. It offers well-cooked dishes (mains €6) with fresh ingredients, a tasteful marine decor and a pretty veranda. Most importantly in an island as sleepy as this, the place is consistently open. Daily noon–midnight.

To Kyma Psáthi ☎ 22870 51001. An excellent taverna midway along the beach, specializing in fresh seafood (€8) and vegetarian dishes that come directly from their own farm. This is the place to try fried rather than the normally grilled octopus. April–Oct daily noon–late.

Rest of the island

The hamlet of **Alykí** on the south coast is about thirty minutes' walk on the paved road that forks left from Psáthi; it is named after the saltpan that sprawls behind a pebbly beach. Here you can indulge in some serious birdwatching or to spot the rare, endemic Mílos wall lizard. If you stroll west one cove, you arrive at **Bonátsa** which has better sand and shallower water. Passing another cove you come to the even more attractive beach of **Kalamítsi**, with decent shade.

There are three clearly signposted beaches next to each other starting from the dirt track at the end of the asphalted road off **Fykiádha**, a 45-minute walk west of Alykí. The first one, dotted with caves and ancient tombs, is **Dhékas**. It is divided by a low bluff from the long coarse-sand beach of **Elliniká**, itself divided by a rocky promontory from **Mavrospiliá**, which provides the best spot to watch the sunset. There are no facilities on any beach.

Some 7km northeast from Hóra is **Prása**, arguably the best easily accessible beach on the island, with crystal-clear water, fine sand and, to top it all, radioactive thermal springs. The route takes in impressive views across the straits to the island of **Políaigos**, and there are several peaceful coves where it's possible to swim in solitude. In the northwest, on Kímolos's 361m summit, are the scant ruins of a Venetian fortress known as **Paleókastro** which can be reached after a reasonable trek (2hr 30min) from the dirt road off Prása. The road forks by the peak to Sklavos with one branch leading to **Skiadhi**, an odd rock formation like a mushroom which has been adopted as the island landmark.

ACCOMMODATION AND EATING   REST OF THE ISLAND

Bonátsa Studios Bonátsa ☎ 22870 51429, ⊕ bonatsa .gr. Right behind a string of salt cedars, this apartment complex offers studios of exceptional quality in bright red and yellow colours. A good restaurant belonging to the owner operates next door. June–Sept. €90
Kimolía Yi Prássa ☎ 22870 51192, ⊕ kimoliagi.gr. Set

at 200m from the beach, this is the only, but still pretty good, accommodation option here, eye-catchingly decorated, with much ornamental bric-a-brac on show. Children under the age of four pay nothing. Breakfast included. April–Sept. €90
Sardis Alykí ☎ 22870 51458. Comfortable hotel with

enormous rooms 50m from the sea. Recommended for birdwatchers especially outside the peak season as the saltpan (Alykí) that gives the beach its name attracts many waders. Good restaurant on-site. June–Sept. **€60**

Ándhros

ÁNDHROS, the second largest and northernmost of the Cyclades, is also one of the most verdant, its fertile, well-watered valleys and hillsides sprouting scores of holiday villas. Still home to a very hospitable people, an attractive capital, numerous good beaches, plus some idiosyncratic reminders of the Venetian period – such as the *peristereónes* (dovecote towers) and the *frákhtes* (dry-stone walls) – Ándhros has a special charm. Driving is also a joy, with precipitous coastal roads offering panoramic views over the Aegean.

The only cloud in your enjoyment of the island may be the current shutdown of all state museums on Ándhros; check if they have opened before you visit.

ARRIVAL AND INFORMATION   ÁNDHROS

By ferry All ferries and catamarans arrive at the main port, Gávrio.
Destinations Lávrio via Kéa/Kýthnos (1 weekly; 5–6hr); Mýkonos (1–3 daily; 2hr 30min); Náxos (4 weekly; 4hr); Rafína (2–3 daily; 1–2hr); Sýros (4 weekly; 3hr); Tínos (1–3 daily; 1hr 30min).
Tourist offices A tiny converted dovecote by the disembarkation point in Gávrio houses an unmanned information booth. There's also an unmanned but signposted info kiosk by the jewellers' in Batsí.
Services There are two banks and three ATMs on the

waterfront in Gávrio, and the post office is at the southern end. *Carlito's* café-bar (☎ 22820 71442; daily 9am–3am) also at the waterfront offers free wi-fi as well as internet facilities (€2.50/hr). Batsí has an ATM behind the *Dodóni* café-bar. There are several banks and ATMs in Hóra, and the post office is on the main street. There is one ATM in Southern Ándhros, on Yeoryíou Psálti, parallel to the esplanade.
Travel agents Batis (☎ 22820 71489), Kyklades Travel (☎ 22820 72363) and Porto Andros (☎ 22820 71222), all operate near the centre of the port.

GETTING AROUND

By bus Buses run from the port's waterfront where the schedules are posted: Batsí (6–8 daily; 20min); Hóra (4–6 daily; 50 min); Kórthi (2–3 daily; 1hr).
By car and motorcycle Gávrio is the easiest place on the island for car rental, with several competing

establishments. Try the reliable and friendly Euro Car (☎ 22820 71312, ⊛ rentacareuro.com) right in front of the disembarkation point. As the island is very large and tricky to explore, and the bus services limited, you are advised to book your transport before arriving.

Gávrio and around

GÁVRIO is a pleasant enough small town set in an oval bay, but it has more tavernas and bars than good hotels, which generally tend to be out of town. There is an adjacent town beach, but there are more attractive alternatives 5km northwest of the port: beautiful **Fellós** is very popular with the self-catering holiday community, while **Kourtáli** hidden beyond the headland is as popular but with fewer facilities.

Head inland and south from Gávrio, and you reach the best beaches on the island in a row: **Áyios Pétros** attracts the young because of the lively beach bar; **Khryssí Ammos** is long, sandy and very popular with families; **Kyprí** is a long stretch of fine sand; and **Áyios Kyprianos**, just before you reach the major resort of **Batsí**, is located in a small sheltered cove of the same name.

ACCOMMODATION   GÁVRIO AND AROUND

Andros ☎ 22820 71444, ⊛ campingandros.gr. A very pleasant campsite, 300m behind the centre of town, with a minimarket, café and excellent communal kitchen facilities. The swimming pool partly compensates for the fact that it is not very close to the sea. Free pickups to and

from the port. As the reception is not always open, make sure they are waiting for you. May–Oct. **€10**
★ **Andros Holidays** ☎ 22820 71384, ⊛ androsholiday hotel.com. Luxury hotel on the headland side road south of town with lovely sea views from its garden terraces and

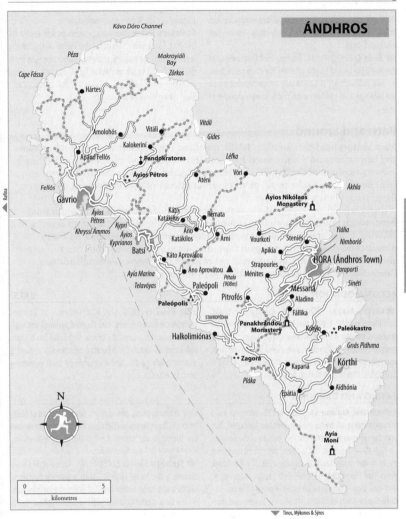

ÁNDHROS

Kávo Dóro Channel

Péza
Cape Fássa
Hártes
Makroyiáli Bay
Zórkos
Amolohós
Vitáli
Vitáli
Gídes
Kalokerini
Apáno Fellós
† Pandokrátoras
Áyios Pétros
Léfka
Vóri
Áténi
Fellós
Ákhla
Gávrio
Áyios Pétros
Áyios Nikólaos Monastery
Khryssí Ámmos
Kypri
Áyios Kyprianos
Batsí
Káto Katákilos
Áno Katákilos
Remáta
Árni
Vourkotí
Steniés
Yiália
Nimborió
Apikía
Káto Aprováíou
Áyia Marína
Telavóyas
Áno Aprovátou
Paleópoli
Pétalo (908m)
Strapouriés
Ménites
HÓRA (Ándhros Town)
Paraporti
Sinéti
Paleópolis
Pitrofós
Messariá
Aladíno
Fállika
STAVROPÉDHA
Panakhrándou Monastery
Kóryío
Paleókastro
Halkolimiónas
Gríds Pídhima
Zagorá
Kapariá
Kórthi
Pláka
Épátia
Aïdhónia
N
Ayía Moní
0   5
kilometres

▲ Rafína

3

▼ Tínos, Mýkonos & Sýros

arched verandas. With a large pool, a bar, and a private cove in front, its rooms are exceptional value. Breakfast included. During the last week of June it holds a renowned English Creative Writing workshop. April–Oct. **€80**

Galaxias ☎ 22820 71228. Labelled "basic but clean", this hotel right at the centre of the port feels like living in one of the faceless blocks of flats in Central Athens. However, it is very cheap and, due to its location, it can serve as a late-arrival fallback. **€35**

Perrakis ☎ 22820 71456, ⓦ hotelperrakis.com. Top hotel in white and gold – matching the local stone it is built with – that offers great views from even its standard-rate rooms. Situated between Khryssí Ámmos and Kyprí, it houses the headquarters of Andros Surf Club (ⓦ windsurfingingreece.com) as well as one of the most creative restaurants on the island (open to non-residents) with mains around €15. April–Oct. **€80**

EATING, DRINKING AND NIGHTLIFE

Marabou Áyios Pétros beach ☎ 693 71 01 695, ⓦ marabouclub.gr. High on a promontory and facing

west, this is the main late-night option for a predominantly young crowd dancing to Western pop, although many choose to spend the nights in the garden simply sipping drinks (€6–8). Fri–Sat, plus July–Aug Thurs–Sun midnight–late.

★ **Sails** ☎ 22820 71333. An excellent fish taverna at the northern end of Gávrio offering the daily catch from its own fishing boat (€12). Highly recommended by all the locals and, as you will soon find out, by a clowder of local stray cats. Daily noon–midnight.

St Peter's Beach Bar Áyios Pétros beach ☎ 697 03 06 792. A friendly, youthful bar with lively, chatty international staff and a studenty atmosphere. It rents deckchairs and beach umbrellas for €6 and sells beer and cocktails while lulling you with lounge music. May–Sept daily 10am–8pm.

Batsí and around

Most visitors head 8km south to **BATSÍ**, the island's main resort with its hotels, rooms and bars set around a fine natural harbour. The beautiful though often crowded beach curves twice around the bay, and the sea is cold, calm and clean. South of town, a coastal road leads to the small, picturesque sandy cove of **Ayía Marína** and, further on, the gorgeous beach of **Telavóyas**.

There's a good archeological site of the ancient city of **Paleópolis**, 8km south from Batsí, which flourished from the sixth century BC to the end of the eighth century AD, covering a large area just southwest of the modern village. It is reached via a very pleasant and shady signposted path from the village to the eponymous beach. You may also be interested in the archeological site of **Zagorá** on west-coast headlands near Paleópolis, but access is not straightforward without a map.

ACCOMMODATION   BATSÍ

★ **Chryssí Akti** ☎ 22820 41236, ⊛ hotel-chryssiakti .gr. Right behind the main beach, this hotel, which depends mainly on domestic package tours, is solid, central, efficient and comfortable. Good swimming pool, and even better interior café-bar with a first-class range of patisseries. Breakfast included. April–Oct. **€60**

Villa Rena ☎ 22820 41024, ⊛ villarena.gr. Reached both by car from the ring road (limited parking) and via a five-minute climb from the beach, this hotel has a super collection of tastefully decorated apartments around a sloping shady garden and a surprisingly deep swimming pool. March–Oct. **€60**

EATING AND DRINKING

Balkoni tou Aigaiou ☎ 22820 41020. Accessed via a narrow, winding hill road to the village of Áno Aprovátou, 3km from the highway south of Batsí, the "Balcony of the Aegean", set high above the coast, has superior, well-priced rural food; try its home-made Ándhros sausage (€9). The panoramic views are legendary. Easter–Oct daily noon–4pm, 6–11pm, Nov–Easter Fri–Sat noon–4pm, 6–11pm.

Café Scala Batsí ☎ 22820 41656. The largest and most popular hangout in the village with a DJ playing easy-listening music after sunset. Good selection of beers from €5. Don't forget to check out the hilarious Adam and Eve theme in the toilets. Easter–Oct daily 9am–5am, Nov–Easter Fri–Sat 9am–5am.

★ **Stamátis** Batsí ☎ 22820 41283. An old-style family taverna – the locals' choice – with a balcony for balmy nights and a large indoor area for when the *meltémi* hits. Try the Batsí speciality, chicken roll with local cheese for €9. Daily noon–1am.

Hóra and around

Stretched along a rocky spur that divides a huge bay 32km from Gávrio, the capital **HÓRA** (also known as **ÁNDHROS TOWN**) is the most attractive town on the island. Paved in marble and schist from the still-active local quarries, the buildings near the bus station are grand nineteenth-century edifices, and the squares with their ornate wall fountains and gateways are equally elegant. The old port, Plakoúra, on the west side of the headland, has a yacht supply station and a former ferry landing from where occasional boats run to the isolated but superbly idyllic **Ákhla** beach in summer. More locally, there are beaches on both sides of the town headland, **Nimborió** to the north and the less developed **Parapórti** to the southeast, though both are exposed to the *meltémi* winds in summer – the reason Gávrio (see p.132), on the other side of the island, became the main port instead.

From the Theófilou Kaïri square, right at the end of Hóra's main street, Embiríkou (aka "Agorá"), you pass through an archway and down through the residential area of Paleá Póli past the town theatre to **Ríva Square**, with its Soviet-donated statue of an unknown sailor scanning the sea.

The tidy village of **Apikía**, north of Hóra, is the source of the Sáriza mineral water brand. An uphill turn at the southwestern end of the village leads, via a signed fifteen-minute path, to the **Rematiá Pytháras**, a pretty wooded stream with small waterfalls. The road continues to **Vourkotí** and, after a turn-off to **Ákhla** (a dirt track continuing for 8km), it then becomes a broad, mostly unused highway, via Árni, to the west coast. There are some wonderful views of the northeast from along this road, particularly where it crosses the **Kouvára ridge** at an altitude of 700m.

Archeological museum
Currently closed; check if open

Inside the **archeological museum**, on the main street near Kaïri, the displays, mostly from Paleópolis (see opposite), are well laid-out and clearly labelled: there are funerary stellae, a kouros and a torso of Artemis, but its prize item is the fourth-century *Hermes of Ándhros*, reclaimed from a prominent position in the Athens archeological museum. This is a remarkably preserved Roman copy of the Hermes of Praxiteles, one of antiquity's greatest sculptors.

Goulandhrís Museum of Contemporary Art
June–Sept Wed–Mon 10am–2pm • €6 • Oct–May Sat–Mon 10am–2pm • €3 • Temporary exhibitions also open evenings 6–8pm • Ⓦ moca-andros.gr

Behind the archeological museum (see above) there is the private **Goulandhrís Museum of Contemporary Art** in the street of the same name. A four-storey mansion, it has a permanent collection with works by prominent Greek sculptors as well as international artists such as Hundertwasser, Warhol, Rodin and Giacometti, plus regular temporary exhibitions.

ACCOMMODATION   HÓRA AND AROUND

Alcióni ☎22820 23652/23805, Ⓦalcioni.gr. These pink-and-cyan studios right by Nimborió beach have been expanded to fill all available space, cutting down on common areas, such as reception; consequently they are on the large side, with local wooden furniture, though some tend to be a bit noisy from the traffic in front. April–Oct. **€70**

Iró ☎22820 22905. Just one block away from the main road, behind Nimborió beach, you can hear a pin drop in these huge, well-furnished studios with their own kitchenette – the best priced in Hóra. Easter–Oct. **€50**

Onar Residence Áchla beach ☎693 25 63 707, Ⓦonar -andros.gr. Extremely difficult to reach and a pain to get to

– 40km from Gávrio including 8km on a dirt road – but worth it. This is an eco-lodge in the middle of one of the best beaches of Ándhros with self-catering bungalows composed of stone, wood and reeds, but supplied with all modern facilities; as close to feeling stranded on a desert island as you could dream of. May–Oct. **€150**

Paradise Hotel ☎22820 22187, Ⓦparadiseandros.gr. If you have your own transport, this hotel, though far from the beach and the town centre, is an exclusive holiday sanctuary with modern art paintings in the common areas, a striking swimming pool, a tennis court, free wi-fi, regal furnishings and even a small folklore museum next door. Easter–Sept. **€90**

PANAYÍA PANAKHRÁNDOU

Two hours' pleasant walk from Hóra via the village of Fállika, or via a signposted turn-off on the road to Kórthi, you arrive at the finest monastery on the island, **Panayía Panakhrándou** (closed 1–4.30pm). Founded around 961 and with an icon said to be by St Luke, it's still defended by massive walls but is occupied these days by just one monk. From the entrance door, a long passageway leads in past gushing springs to the atmospheric catholicon dedicated to the Dormition of the Virgin with its impressive and colourful iconostasis. Its lower decoration with **Ottoman Iznik tiles** is unique in the Aegean and it represents a gift to the monastery by Patriarch Dionysius III in the 1660s.

EATING AND DRINKING

Madoúris Nimborió ☎22820 24620. Simple and unassuming, you'll wonder why its tables are all taken while the surrounding tavernas are empty. Then you'll taste the fresh fried calamari with portions that feed two adults (€9) and you'll understand. April–Sept daily noon–midnight.

Vegéra Nimborió ☎698 02 20 171. You've heard it before: an establishment that starts as a beach bar at 10am, continues as a pretty decent restaurant after 2pm (mains €8) and ends up as a club with a live DJ after 10pm (drinks €7). Yes, there may be many bars like that, but not as stylish in each incarnation. May–Sept daily 10am–late.

The south

If you're exploring **the south** from Hóra, take the road that runs through the dramatic **Dipotámata** valley; at the seaward end, the fine, sheltered cove of **Sinéti** is worth a detour, though the access road is somewhat steep. Two kilometres further, the entry road to Kohýlo village forks: the left goes 2km (partly surfaced) to **Paleókastro** (aka Kástro Faneroménis), a ruined Venetian castle perched on a rocky crest at 586m, with amazing views overlooking Kórthi Bay. Legend has it that an old woman, who betrayed the stronghold to the Turks, jumped from the top in remorse, and she remains as a column of rock in the sea off **Griás Pídhima** beach where she landed. A short distance further south, the resort of **Kórthi** (or Órmos Korthíou or simply Órmos) is a small town, with a new seafront esplanade, waking up to its tourist potential and popular with windsurfers; this is where the Greek Olympic team practises. Set on a large bay, isolated from the rest of the island by the high ridge and relatively unspoilt, it is pleasant enough to merit a stay. Lovely Griás Pídhima beach is accessible via a signed road and dirt track from near the northern end of the esplanade, while **Kandoúni** beach covers the southern half of the main bay.

EATING AND DRINKING   THE SOUTH

Lithodhomí ☎22820 61130. One of those surprise finds that make your heart beat faster with excitement: a restaurant in the middle of the Kórthi esplanade with great rustic stone decor, an inventive menu offering many vegetarian options (€10), good service, fresh ingredients and a great wine list. A must if you've come all this way. Daily 8am–1am.

Tínos

TÍNOS still feels like one of the most Greek of the larger islands in the Cyclades. A few foreigners have discovered its beaches and unspoilt villages, but most visitors are Greek, here to see the church of **Panayía Evangelístria**, a grandiose shrine erected on the spot where a miraculous icon with healing powers was found in 1822. A local nun, now canonized as Ayía Pelayía, was directed in a vision to unearth the relic just as the War of Independence was getting under way, a timely coincidence that served to underscore the links between the Orthodox Church and Greek nationalism. Today, there are two major annual pilgrimages, on March 25 and August 15, when Tínos is inundated by the faithful, and at 11am, the icon bearing the Virgin's image is carried in state down to the harbour.

The Ottoman tenure here, and on adjoining Sýros, was the most fleeting in the Aegean. **Exóbourgo**, the craggy mount dominating southern Tínos and surrounded by most of the island's sixty-odd villages, is studded with the ruins of a Venetian citadel that defied the Turks until 1715, long after the rest of Greece had fallen; an enduring legacy of the long Venetian rule is a **Catholic minority**, which accounts for almost half the population. Hills are dotted with distinctive and ornate **dovecotes**, even more in evidence here than on Ándhros. Aside from all this, the inland village architecture is striking, and there's a flourishing folk-art tradition that finds expression in the abundant local marble.

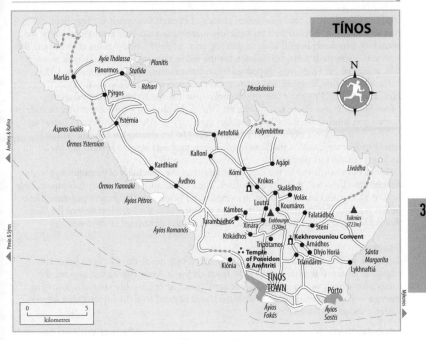

ARRIVAL AND DEPARTURE

TÍNOS

By ferry All ferries dock at Tínos Town at any one of three different marinas; one for yachts, one for catamarans and one for normal ferries, all next to each other.

Destinations Ándhros (2–6 daily; 1hr 30min); Iráklion (0–1 weekly; 4hr); Íos (2–4 weekly; 2hr); Lávrio via Kéa/ Kýthnos (1 weekly; 5hr 30min); Mýkonos (2–6 daily; 30min); Náxos (5–6 weekly; 1hr 30min); Páros (1–2 daily; 1hr); Pireás (2–4 daily; 4–5hr); Rafína (3–5 daily; 2–4hr); Santoríni (5 weekly; 3hr); Sýros (2–4 daily; 30min–1hr 20min).

TOURS AND INFORMATION

Services There is no shortage of banks or ATMs in Tínos town.

Travel agents Windmills Travel (☎22830 23398, ⓦ windmillstravel.com) on the front towards the new jetty can help with information as well as tour bookings to Delos and hotel bookings both here and on Mýkonos.

Day-trip to Delos In season (July–Sept) there are day-trips by boat to Delos (Tues–Sun; €50 round trip); this makes it possible to see Delos (see p.146) without the expense of staying overnight on Mýkonos. The time on Delos itself (about 2hr 30min) is the same from wherever you sail off.

GETTING AROUND

By bus Buses leave from a small parking area on the inner quay and serve: Áyios Fokás (5 daily; 15min); Falatádos/ Stení (6 daily; 20min); Kalloní via Xinára (3 daily; 20min); Kiónia (hourly; 10min); Pánormos via Pýrgos (5 daily; 45min); Kalloní (3 daily; 45min); Pórto (6 daily; 20min).

By car and motorcycle Not only a much more reliable means of exploring the island than bus, especially in the shoulder season, but also the only way to reach some of the beaches of the island. Vidalis at 2 Ierarhon St (☎22830 23400, ⓦ vidalis-rentacar.gr) is an excellent rental agency – there are four other rental outlets in Tínos Town.

Tínos Town and around

Tínos Town is large and commercial, possessing a unique mixture of religion and commerce: trafficking in devotional articles certainly dominates the streets leading up from the busy waterfront to the Neoclassical church of **Panayía Evangelístria** (daily 8am–8pm) that towers above. Approached via a massive marble staircase, the famous **icon** inside the church is completely buried under a dazzling array of jewels; below is the crypt (where the icon was discovered) and a mausoleum for the sailors drowned when the Greek warship *Elli*, at anchor off Tínos, was torpedoed by an Italian submarine on August 15, 1940.

The shrine aside, the port has many good examples of nineteenth-century Neoclassical buildings and you might make time for the **archeological museum** (Tues–Sun 8.30am–3pm; €2) on the way up to the church, whose collection includes a fascinating sundial from the local Roman sanctuary of Poseidon and Amphitrite (see below). If you have a sweet tooth you may want to try the highly calorific Tiniot specialities: *amygdalotó*, a marzipan-style sweet, and *loukoumia* (Turkish delight), sold by street vendors or patisseries.

Kiónia, 3km northwest of the capital, is the site of the **Sanctuary of Poseidon and Amphitrite** (Tues–Sun 8.30am–3pm; free). The excavations yielded many columns (*kiónia* in Greek), but also a temple, baths, a fountain and hostels for the ancient pilgrims. The **beach** is a long thin strip, lined with rooms to rent and snack-bars, but west of the *Tinos Beach Hotel* you can follow an unpaved road to a series of isolated sandy coves.

Beaches

There are several first-class but mostly unshaded beaches at the southern tip of the island. In order of proximity to Tínos Town they are: **Áyios Fokás**, just beyond the eastern headland, which is a good, fine sand beach after a pebbly start, shallow **Áyios Ioánnis** at Pórto (served by six daily buses), and beyond that the idyllic **Pahiá Ámmos**, with a view of Mýkonos.

ACCOMMODATION — TÍNOS TOWN AND AROUND

Ávra Konstandínou 4–6 ☎ 22830 22242, ⓦ avrahoteltinos.gr. Charming Neoclassical building on the waterfront with fully renovated spacious rooms and modern bathrooms, some with balconies and an attractive plant-filled communal atrium area. Port transfers, breakfast and free wi-fi included. May–Oct. **€55**

Cávos Áyios Sóstis ☎ 22830 24224, ⓦ cavos-tinos.com. Well situated for the beach and adorned with flowers and palm trees, these large apartments and suites can sleep up to four people and are ideal for families; everything from a baby cot to laundry services can be provided. April–Nov. **€80**

Favie Suzanne Antoníou Sókhou 22 ☎ 22830 22693, ⓦ faviesuzanne.gr. An attractive hotel about 200m from the waterfront fully renovated with facilities for disabled guests, marble balconies, large swimming pool plus free jacuzzi and wi-fi. Breakfast included. March–Oct. **€70**

★ **Tínion Hotel** Alavánou 1 ☎ 22830 22261, ⓦ tinionhotel.gr. A 1920s Neoclassical hotel just back from the waterfront, full of faded grandeur and resonating with history; a Greek prime minister once resigned in the dining room in a fit of pique. Spacious rooms, some with balconies. Port transfers, free wi-fi and breakfast included. March–Nov. **€55**

Tinos Beach Kiónia ☎ 22830 22626, ⓦ tinosbeach.gr. Typical 1970s-built hotel that dominates the beach, offering comfortable rooms with verandas. Good swimming pool, large breakfast, fair pricing, a range of facilities and regular shuttle into town makes this rather anonymous resort a more attractive option than expected. April–Oct. **€75**

Tinos Camping Ten-minute walk south of port ☎ 22830 22344, ⓦ camping.gr/tinos.html. One of the nicer and more laidback campsites in the Cyclades, shady and roomy very close to the centre of town, but reception only open 8am–4pm. En-suite doubles studios are also on offer. May–Oct. Camping **€11**, studios **€40**

EATING AND DRINKING

Symposion Evangelistrias 13 ☎ 22830 24368, ⓦ symposion.gr. Sophisticated restaurant at the top of a converted Neoclassical house offering an imaginative menu (€14) that makes no concessions to normal meagre pilgrim fare as is usual around town. It's worth trying its huge English brunch for €17 at least once during your stay. April–Oct daily 9am–4pm & 7.30pm–midnight.

★ **To Koutouki tis Elenis** G. Gafou 5 ☎ 22830 24857. A gem of a restaurant with a creative chef who mixes international and traditional cooking with superb results. Try its artichoke pie for a starter, the pork with feta (€9) as a main and finish with its irresistible cheesecake with Tiniot sour cheese. Daily noon–midnight.

THE DOVECOTE TRAIL

Drive up Evangelistrías, turn right and follow the signs to **Tripótamos** where you can visit the only still functioning clay pot workshop on the island. Nearby **Ktikádhos** is a fine village with two superb churches and a very good taverna. Heading northwest from the main road junction beyond Ktikádhos, you can see several beautifully restored **dovecote houses** on the turn-off to **Tarambádho**– it's worth stopping there and following an hour-long signed path through the village, to get as close to these dovecotes as possible, as they are the most photogenic you are likely to encounter.

Driving further north from the Tarambádho turn-off, you can break your trip at **Ystérnia** by turning off to **Órmos Ysterníon**, a pretty compact beach, and even prettier Skhináki beach at the far end.

There are a number of eating options en route; here are the best:

Drosia Ktikádhos ☎ 22830 21087. A good, vine-shaded, sea-view taverna with mains around €8. One of the few that still offers baked pigeons (*pitsounia*), the age-old traditional Tínos staple food and the *raison d'être* of the dovecotes, if booked in advance. April–Oct daily noon–midnight.

To Thalassaki Órmos Ysterníon ☎ 22830 31366, ✉ tothalassaki@gmail.com. Award-winning fish taverna right on the beach providing exceptional range and quality of food for something so out of the way. Most dishes (€13) are marinated in an infusion of herbs before cooking. Just its extensive ouzo selection is worth making a detour for. March–Oct daily noon–midnight.

3

The north

A good beginning to a foray into **NORTHERN TÍNOS** is to drive the so-called **Dovecote Trail** (see box above). The ornate dovecotes are mostly found in the villages off the main road between **Tínos Town** and **Ystérnia**.

Pýrgos and around

Five daily buses along the Dovecote Trail (see box above) finish up at **PÝRGOS**, a few kilometres beyond Ystérnia and in the middle of the island's marble-quarrying district, as can be surmised by the magnificently crafted marble bus stop. The artisans of this beautiful village are renowned throughout Greece for their skill in producing marble ornamentation; ornate fanlights and bas-relief plaques fashioned here adorn houses throughout Tínos. Pýrgos is also home to a School of Fine Arts, and the **museum of Tiniot artists** (daily 10.30am–2.30pm & 5.30–7pm) contains numerous representative works from some of the island's finest pupils. Nearby, the **Yiannoúlis Halepás museum** (same hours; €3 for both) is devoted exclusively to the work of the artist who spent many years here and is generally recognized as the most important Neoclassical Greek sculptor. The small cemetery up and left from the main square offers a free showcase of the villagers' talent over the ages.

The marble products were once exported from **Pánormos** harbour, 4km northeast of Pýrgos, with its small, shaded **Stafída** beach. The village itself gives access to a number of good beaches reachable on foot: **Róhari** is to the southeast, facing north with deep clear waters and massive waves, while **Ayía Thálassa** and **Kaválargos** are much more sheltered on the northwest side of the bay.

EATING   PÝRGOS AND AROUND

Marina Pánormos ☎ 22830 31314. A seaside ouzerí with a great ouzo and mezédhes selection; spoilt for choice, you may want to order a starters platter (€7) but, unless there are two of you, wait until you've finished before you venture into a main; the portions are quite large. May–Sept daily 10am–midnight.

Myrónia Pýrgos ☎ 22830 31229. The best of the tavernas and patisseries on the attractive main village square, with seats around the 150-year-old plane tree. It still serves baked pigeon with pasta (€8) if you pre-order; but there are some excellent vealburgers if you want something more conventional. Easter–Oct daily noon–midnight.

Tis Irinis Pýrgos ☎ 22830 31165. A friendly, popular taverna opposite the stunning marble bus stop that offers good, traditional family favourites such as pastitsio (€6) and a quick turnaround service for those pressed for time to visit the museums opposite. Easter–Oct daily noon–midnight.

Around Exóbourgo

The ring of villages around the mountain of **EXÓBOURGO** is a worthwhile visit. The fortified pinnacle itself (570m), with the ruins of three Venetian churches and a fountain, is reached by steep steps from **Xinára** (near the island's major road junction), the old seat of the island's Roman Catholic bishop. Most villages in north-central Tínos have mixed populations, but Xinára and its immediate neighbours are purely Catholic; the inland villages also tend to have a more sheltered position, with better farmland nearby – the Venetians' way of rewarding converts and their descendants.

At **Loutrá**, an almost deserted village north of Xinára (population 7), there's an Ursuline convent, and a small **folk art museum** (daily 9.30am–2.30pm; free) in the seventeenth-century Jesuit monastery. From Krókos, 1km northwest of Loutrá, you can turn to tiny **Voláx**, the most spectacular village on the island: a windswept oasis surrounded by hundreds of giant granite boulders, as far from a typical Greek landscape as you can get in the Cyclades. Alternatively you can continue to **Kómi**, 5km beyond Krókos, where you can take a detour for **Kolymbíthra**, a magnificent double beach: one part wild, huge and windswept and the other balmy and sheltered.

From either Skaládho or Voláx you go on to **Koúmaros**, towards the agricultural villages of **Falatádhos** and **Stení**, which appear as white speckles against the fertile Livádhia valley. Falatádhos has a number of whitewashed churches, including Áyios Ioánnis, notable for its marble decoration. From Stení, which has fewer amenities but plenty of postcard-perfect whitewashed buildings to admire, you can catch the bus back to Tínos Town.

EATING AND DRINKING   **AROUND EXÓBOURGO**

To Katöï Falatádhos ☎ 22830 41000. A good restaurant that draws customers from all around the island, based in a low-ceilinged old warehouse that reminds you of Central European Bierkellers; it specializes in grills (€12) and meat on the spit. June–Sept daily 7pm–midnight.

Mýkonos

MÝKONOS has become the most popular, the most high profile and the most expensive of the Cyclades. Boosted by direct air links with Europe, it sees several million tourists a year pass through, producing some spectacular August overcrowding on the island's 85 square kilometres. But if you don't mind the tourist hordes, or you come in the shoulder season, its striking capital is still one of the most photogenic Cycladic towns with whitewashed houses concealing a dozen little churches, shrines and chapels.

The sophisticated nightlife is hectic, amply stimulated by Mýkonos's former reputation as *the* gay resort of the Mediterranean, although today gay tourists are well in the minority. While everywhere on the island is at least gay-friendly, gay tourists prefer to congregate in Mýkonos Town itself or the beaches of Super Paradise and Eliá. The locals take it all in their stride, ever conscious of the important revenue generated by their laissez-faire attitude. When they first opened up to the hippy tourists who began appearing on Mýkonos in the 1960s, they assumed their eccentric visitors were sharing cigarettes due to lack of funds. Since then, a lot of the innocence has evaporated, and you shouldn't come for scenery, solitude or tradition, but Mýkonos offers lively beaches and a party lifestyle next to none.

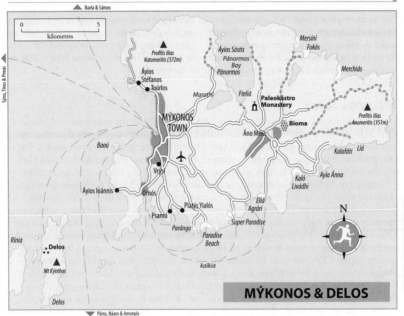

MÝKONOS & DELOS

ARRIVAL AND DEPARTURE

MÝKONOS

By plane The airport is twenty minutes outside Mýkonos Town in the centre of the island.

Destinations Athens (2–5 daily with Aegean and Olympic; 55min); Thessaloníki (1–2 daily with Aegean; 1hr); Santoríni (daily with Sky Express; 30min); Vólos (2 daily; 1hr with Sky Express).

By ferry Most visitors arrive by ferry at the old port jetty at the north end of town. Cruise ships and the occasional overflow anchor at the new port, which is 1km further out. Check your ticket before leaving to see if you have an old or a new port stamp. Boats for Delos leave from the waterfront in town.

Destinations Amorgós (0–1 weekly; 2hr 15min); Ándhros (1–2 daily; 2hr 15min); Folégandhros (1 daily; 5hr); Iráklion (1 weekly; 4h 30min); Ikaría (1 weekly; 2hr min); Íos (6 weekly; 1hr 15min–5hr 30min); Mílos (1–2 weekly; 6hr); Náxos (2–3 daily; 45min–3hr); Páros (2–3 daily; 1hr 30min); Pireás (3–4 daily; 4hr–5hr 30min); Rafína (1–3 daily; 2hr 10min–3hr); Sámos (6–7 weekly; 4hr 40min); Santoríni (2–4 daily; 2hr 15min–7hr); Sérifos (1 weekly; 3hr 30min); Sífnos (1 weekly; 3hr 30min); Sýros (2–5 daily; 45min–1hr 15min); Tínos (2–5 daily; 30min).

INFORMATION

Services There is no shortage of banks or ATMs in Mýkonos Town. The island post office is near the south bus station. There are countless advertiser-based tourist publications circulating throughout Mýkonos during high season, the best of which is the free Mýkonos Sky Map, available from some agents and hotels.

Activities Kalafáti (see p.146) is the activity centre of the island with no less than three watersports facilities based there: Kalafati Watersports for waterskiing and wakeboarding (☎ 694 52 61 242 ⍇ mykonoswatersports .t35.com), Kalafati Dive Center (☎ 22890 71677, ⍇ mykonos-diving.com) for scuba diving, and Pezi-Huber (☎ 22890 72345, ⍇ pezi-huber.com) for windsurfing. Alternatively, behind Paradise beach (see p.145), Dive Adventures (☎ 22890 26539, ⍇ diveadventures.gr and ⍇ divemykonos.gr; April–Oct) offer introductory scuba and a full range of PADI.

GETTING AROUND

By bus The north bus station for Toúrlos, Áyios Stéfanos, Kalafáti, Eliá and Áno Méra is located by the old port; the south bus station for all western and the popular southern beaches is just outside the pedestrianized area at the other end of town. If you choose to use public transport to the beaches from Paránga to Paradise, you certainly won't be alone – on any sunny day in season the beaches and transport range from busy to overcrowded. Buses to

Paradise run every hour through the night in high season.

By car and motorcycle Rental agencies are concentrated around the two bus stops. The only free parking area near the town is by the north bus station. Parking spaces at most beaches are inadequate and signposting surprisingly poor.

By taxi Taxis run from Mantó square on the main seafront and from the south bus station; the rates are fixed and quite reasonable; try Mykonos Radio Taxi (☏ 22890 22400).

By boat Kaïkia head from town and Orkós to all of the southern beaches.

Mýkonos Town

Don't let the crowds put you off exploring **MÝKONOS TOWN**, the quintessential image of the Cyclades. In summer most people head out to the beaches during the day, so early morning or late afternoon are the best times to wander the maze of narrow streets. The labyrinthine design was supposed to confuse the pirates who plagued Mýkonos in the eighteenth and early nineteenth centuries, and it has the same effect on today's visitors.

Getting lost in the convoluted streets and alleys is half the fun of Mýkonos, although there are a few places worth seeking out. Coming from the ferry quay you'll pass the **archeological museum** (Tues–Sun 9.30am–3pm; €2) on your way into town, which was specially built in 1905 to display artefacts from the cemeteries on Rínia island, opposite Delos (see p.148). The town also boasts a **Maritime museum** displaying various nautical artefacts and ship models as well as an 1890 lighthouse lantern re-erected in the back garden (April–Oct Tues–Sun 10.30am–1pm & 6.30–9pm; €4). Next door is **Lena's House** (Mon–Sat 4.30–8.30pm; free), a completely restored and furnished merchant home from the turn of the twentieth century. Near the base of the Delos jetty, the **Folklore museum** (Mon–Sat 4.30–8.30pm; free), housed in an eighteenth-century mansion, crams in a larger-than-usual collection of bric-a-brac, including a basement dedicated to Mýkonos's maritime past. The museum shares the promontory with Mýkonos's oldest and best-known church, **Paraportianí**, a fascinating asymmetrical hodgepodge of four chapels amalgamated into one (and a gay cruising area after dark).

Beyond the church, the shoreline leads to the area known as **Little Venice** because of the high, arcaded Venetian houses built right up to the water's edge on its southwest side. Together with the adjoining **Alefkándhra** district, this is a dense area packed with art galleries, trendy bars, shops and clubs. Beyond Little Venice, the famous **windmills** look over the area, renovated and ripe for photo opportunities.

ACCOMMODATION   **MÝKONOS TOWN**

The scrum of room-owners by the old port jetty can be intimidating, so if you arrive by ferry press on 100m further, where you will find two accommodation offices; one deals with hotels (☏ 22890 24540, ⓦ mha.gr) and the other with rented rooms (☏ 22890 24860).

K Group Vrýsi ☏ 22890 23415, ⓦ myconiancollection .gr. A cluster of hotels, Kalypso, Kochyli, Korali and Kyma about 1km south of town. Many of the comfortable rooms have wonderful views and there's also a pool and restaurant. Often available when smaller places are fully booked. Breakfast included. Easter–Oct. **€150**

★ **Leto** Old Port ☏ 22890 22207/22918, ⓦ letohotel .com. The best of the luxury town hotels, slightly raised above the small town beach with a large swimming pool that becomes the focus both in the daytime and, fully lit, at night when the hotel restaurant – one of the best on the island – lays its tables around it. Breakfast included. **€250**

Mantó Evangelistrías 1 ☏ 22890 22330, ⓔ mantohotel1@yahoo.gr. Situated in a small side street, the hotel's exterior belies its Tardis-like interior expanse. Good, simple rooms with a/c and fridge for those who are

always on the move and just want a comfortable bed to crash in afterwards. March–Nov. **€75**

Matogianni Matogianni Str ☏ 22890 22217, ⓦ matogianni.gr. Living proof that it's possible to stay in Mýkonos Town without mortgaging your home, this is a comfortable hotel with classically minimalist decor and as peaceful as can be in the buzz of the backstreets. **€60**

Stelios Above the old port ☏ 22890 24641. This whitewashed Mykoniot-style building is an excellent-value pension in a prime location overlooking the old port. Only hitch may be hauling your luggage up the steep steps behind the OTE office. April–Oct. **€90**

Tagoo Tangoú ☏ 22890 22611, ⓦ hoteltagoo.gr. Top-quality hotel overlooking the sea, about a 700m walk north of the archeological museum. Attentive service, spacious rooms, roof pool with panoramic views and

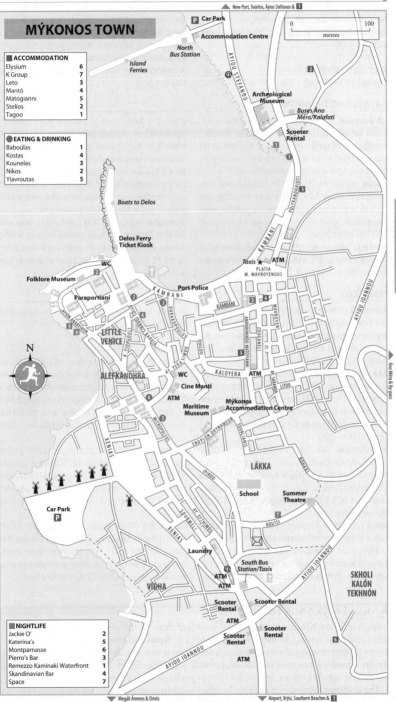

MÝKONOS TOWN

■ ACCOMMODATION

Elysium	6
K Group	7
Leto	3
Mantó	4
Matógianni	5
Stelios	2
Tagoo	1

● EATING & DRINKING

Baboúlas	1
Kostas	4
Kounelas	3
Nikos	2
Yiavroutas	5

■ NIGHTLIFE

Jackie O'	2
Katerina's	5
Montparnasse	6
Pierro's Bar	3
Remezzo Kaminaki Waterfront	1
Skandinavian Bar	4
Space	7

restaurant with specialist sushi chef. Booking for a minimum four nights in July–Aug. Breakfast included. May–Oct. **€450**

GAY AND LESBIAN
Elysium By the School of Fine Arts ☎ 22890 23952, ⓦ elysiumhotel.com. Exclusively gay hotel with beautiful views, boasting a poolside bar open to non-residents, a popular setting for an early evening party complete with go-go dancers and drag shows. Occasional all-night parties in conjunction with international DJs. Breakfast included. May–Oct. **€250**

EATING AND DRINKING
★ **Baboúlas** Kaminaki Waterfront ☎ 22890 26804. Ouzerí that offers the best coal-grilled seafood mezédhes on Mýkonos, all personally supervised by Petroúla, the owner and chef. Try the mussels cooked in seawater (€13) and marvel. April–Nov daily noon–midnight.

Kostas Mitropoléos 5 ☎ 22890 23326. Buried deep within Alefkándhra, this restaurant serves everything from seafood to grills with a good wine list including wine straight from the barrel. Competitive prices for mains start at €12. Daily 6pm–2am.

Kounelas Svorónou ☎ 22890 28220. Seafood taverna set in an appealing garden, with a reputation for offering the freshest fish on the island. Very popular with the gay crowd, it is tucked away in a narrow street but easily signposted. May–Oct daily 8pm–2am.

Nikos Ayías Monís square ☎ 22890 28220. One of the most famous tavernas on the island, strong on the catch of the day but also serving traditional Greek cuisine (€15). Every centimetre of its side of the square is packed with customers after 10pm, which sometimes has a detrimental effect on service. April–Oct daily noon–2am.

Yiavroutas Mitropoléos 11 ☎ 22890 23063. Open until the early morning, this basic taverna has been serving clubbers with the munchies for decades with Greek dishes around €8. For those who prefer, above all, quantity over quality. April–Oct daily noon–7am.

NIGHTLIFE
Katerina's Little Venice ☎ 22890 23084. Owned by the first female captain in the Greek navy, Katerina, this low-key bar-restaurant with sea and sunset views from the balcony, is one of the most laidback places for a drink (cocktails €10). April–Oct daily noon–late.

Remezzo Kaminaki Waterfront ☎ 22890 28999. Stylish music club, offering alternative sunset views to those at Little Venice. Split into two sections and bars: one for the early birds with lounge music outside, and a second one with stronger beats for the night owls indoors. April–Oct daily 8pm–late.

Skandinavian Bar Áyios Ioánnis Barkiá ☎ 22890 22669, ⓦ skandinavianbar.com. For some serious drinking, head for the *Skandinavian*, which has been thumping out dance music and cocktails (€8) until the early hours since 1978. VIP table service can be booked. May–Sept daily 8pm–late.

Space Lákka ⓦ spacemykonos.com. The largest dance club in town, Space Mykonos has become a world brand in dance circles. Resident DJs from Greece and Italy play feelgood house tunes with the best sound system this side of Ibiza. Entrance €8 includes first drink. May, June & Sept Fri–Sat midnight–8am; July–Aug daily midnight–8am.

GAY AND LESBIAN
Jackie O' Near Paraportianí ☎ 22890 17968, ⓦ jackieomykonos.com. The busiest gay club in town, it attracts a crowd of all sexual persuasions who like to dance to relentless funky house mixed with the occasional disco hit. On two floors, although trying to reach the top bar through the crowd is sometimes impossible. Daily 10pm–6am.

Montparnasse Ayíon Anargýron 24, Little Venice ☎ 22890 23719 ⓦ pianobar.com. With great cocktails (€8) and a balcony over the sea, this gay piano bar is a very good place to warm up for the night ahead. Sunset views followed by cabaret and live music. May–Oct daily 8pm–3.30am.

Pierro's Bar Ayías Kyriakís Square ☎ 22890 22177 ⓦ pierrosbar.gr. Legendary gay bar and club that has thrived since the 1960s, with innovative dance music. Despite its longevity, it is still trendy with its finger on the pulse of the gay scene. May–Sept daily 9pm–late.

Around Mýkonos Town
The closest **beaches** around Mýkonos Town are those to the north, at **Toúrlos** (only 2km away but not up to the usual standard) and **Áyios Stéfanos** (3km away, much better), both developed resorts and connected by a very regular bus service to Mýkonos Town. There are tavernas and rooms (as well as package hotels) at Áyios Stéfanos. You'll need your own transport, a bus or *kaïki*, to get to most of them.

The undistinguished but popular beaches southwest of the town are tucked into pretty bays. The nearest, 1km away, is **Megáli Ámmos**, a good but often windy beach backed by flat rocks and pricey rooms, but nearby Kórfos Bay is unpleasant, thanks to the town dump and machine noise. Buses serve **Ornós**, a package resort on a low-lying area between the rest of the island and the Áyios Ioánnis peninsula. The south side has a reasonable beach, plus *kaïkia* to other beaches, a handful of tavernas, and numerous accommodation options.

Two kilometres west is **Áyios Ioánnis**, the island's westernmost bay and small, namesake church, overlooking Delos – the tiny public beach achieved a moment of fame as a location for the film *Shirley Valentine*. Accessed by a 500m dirt track northwest from Áyios Ioánnis is the small but popular beach at **Kápari**, with good views of Delos and the sunset.

ACCOMMODATION | **AROUND MÝKONOS TOWN**

Best Western Dionysos Ornós ☎ 22890 23313, ⓦ dionysoshotel.gr. Easily the most comfortable hotel in the area with a pool and adjoining bar, free wi-fi, satellite TV, children's area and a fitness room, as well as parking space – mission impossible in Ornós. Breakfast included. May–Oct. €100

Manoúlas Beach Áyios Ioánnis ☎ 22890 22900, ⓦ hotelmanoulas.gr. A surprisingly affordable high-class hotel, blindingly set in white against the background of the deep blue of the Aegean. The panoramic view of its restaurant (€12) across to Delos is breathtaking. Breakfast included. May–Oct. €120

The south coast

The western half of the south coast is the busiest part of the island. *Kaïkia* and buses head from town to all of its beaches; drivers will find that car-parking spaces at most beaches are inadequate and signposting surprisingly poor. You might begin with **Platýs Yialós**, 4km south of town: one of the longest-established resorts on the island, where the sand is monopolized by end-to-end hotels. **Psaroú**, just a steep hairpin road away to the west, is much prettier – 150m of white sand backed by foliage and reeds.

Just over the headland to the east of Platýs Yialós lies **Paránga**, actually two beaches separated by a smaller headland, the first of which is quieter than its neighbour. Next is the golden crescent of **Paradise beach**. Here, as on many of Mýkonos's most popular beaches, it can be difficult to find an opening big enough to fit a towel in high season, and any space clear of people is likely to be taken up by straw umbrellas, rentable (usually along with two accompanying loungers) for about €16 per day.

The next bay east contains **Super Paradise beach**, accessible by *kaïki*, or by a surfaced but extremely steep access road. It is one of the most fun spots on the island with its main beach bar staging a party every evening at 6pm. The eastern half gets progressively more gay as you walk towards the hills, below which the beach is almost exclusively gay and nudist. The more secluded **Agrári** beach is 300m to the east.

One of the more scenically attractive beaches on Mýkonos is **Eliá**, the last port of call east for the *kaïkia*, also reachable via an inland road. A broad, sandy stretch, with plenty of parking and a mountainous backdrop at the eastern end, it's the longest beach on the island, though divided by a rocky area, and almost exclusively gay later in the season.

East from the Eliá road is **Kaló Livádhi** (seasonal bus service), long and sandy, fronting an agricultural valley scattered with little farmhouses.

ACCOMMODATION | **THE SOUTH COAST**

★ **Mykonos Camping** Paránga ☎ 22890 24915/6, ⓦ mycamp.gr. This small campsite, a short distance from the second Paránga beach, has one of the most pleasant settings on the island. It offers a wood-fired pizzeria, a pool

with an adjoining cocktail bar and a minimarket, as well as relative peace and quiet from the relentless Mykoniot buzz. May–Oct. €7.50

Paradise Beach Resort Paradise ☎ 22890 22852,

W paradise-greece.com. An industrial-size (and feel) campsite operating since 1969, also offering cabins for €30 and bungalows for €54. Totally self-sufficient with a restaurant, various bars, a clothes shop and its own club with resident DJs. April–Oct. €15

NIGHTLIFE

★ **Cavo Paradiso** Paradise ☎ 22890 27205, W www .cavoparadiso.gr. The after-hours club in the Cyclades, regularly voted as one of the Top 10 in the world, where die-hard party animals of all persuasions come together, united by world-famous DJs. €20 entrance includes first drink, but check for discounts/guest list online. June– Sept (opening nights vary during the week) 12.30am–9am.

The east and north

The main road **east** via the unexciting village of **Áno Méra** leads to **Ayía Ánna**, on a double-headed headland with a shingle beach and taverna, just before the larger, more attractive **Kalafáti**, the island's cleanest beach. **Liá**, roughly 4.6km east by road from Áno Méra, is smaller than Kalafáti, but as pleasant and with as clear water.

The **north coast** suffers persistent battering from the *meltémi* and for the most part is bare, brown and exposed. The deep inlet of **Pánormos Bay** is the exception to this, with the lovely, relatively sheltered beaches of **Pánormos** and **Áyios Sóstis**; although not served by buses, they are becoming increasingly popular, but still remain among the least crowded on the island. At the southern, inner end of the bay, **Fteliá** is a good windsurfers' beach and legendary burial site of Ajax, one of *The Íliad's* mythical heroes. If you are driving there, stop by at the only – but excellent – vineyard on the island, **Bíoma** (☎ 22890 71883), for some wine tasting.

ACCOMMODATION AND EATING   THE EAST AND NORTH

★ **Aphrodite Beach** Kalafáti ☎ 22890 71367, W aphrodite-mykonos.gr. A four-star hotel 18km from Mýkonos Town, and completely self-sufficient should you want to sample Mýkonos without the crowds. There is also a selection of hostel-style accommodation with four bunk beds per room, so it draws a very hip young crowd. April– Nov. Dorms €35, doubles €120

La Luna Liá ☎ 22890 72150. The furthest restaurant east, but don't let that deter you if you have your own transport.

Once there, you will be surprised as to how busy it is, but once you sample the Italian menu (€12) you'll understand. April–Sept daily 10am–9pm.

Thalassa Kalafáti beach ☎ 22890 72081. One of the best places to eat on Mýkonos and worth making the trip for dinner only. Its pork in thyme-honey (€18) is one of the top gastronomic experiences on the island. All this and free wi-fi, too. May–Sept daily noon–midnight.

Delos

The remains of **ANCIENT DELOS (Dhílos)**, the Cyclades' sole UNESCO Heritage Site, manage to convey the past grandeur of this small, sacred isle a few kilometres west of Mýkonos. The ancient town lies on the west coast on flat, sometimes marshy ground that rises in the south to **Mount Kýnthos**.

ARRIVAL AND DEPARTURE   DELOS

By boat In season, excursion boats to Delos leave from the west end of Mýkonos harbour Tues–Sun at 9am, 10am and 11am, returning from the site at 1pm, 2pm and 3pm (€17 return from a kiosk at the front). Guided day-trips are also possible from Tínos (see p.137). Note that it is illegal to remove anything from Delos – not even a stone as a souvenir – as well as anchor, swim or dive at or near the island.

The site

Tues–Sun 9am–3pm • €5

As you disembark from the boat, the Sacred Harbour is on your left, the Commercial

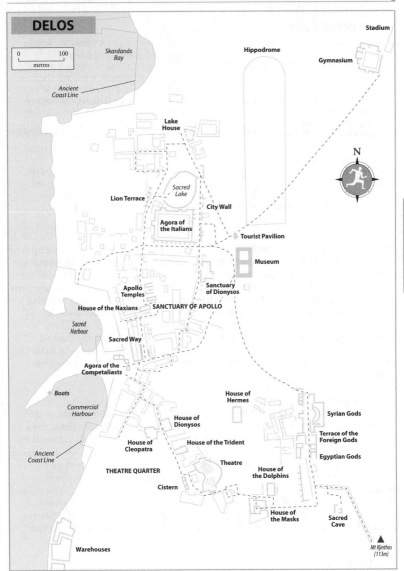

Harbour on your right and straight ahead lies the **Agora of the Competaliasts**. The Competaliasts were Roman merchants who worshipped the Lares Competales, the guardian spirits of crossroads; offerings to Hermes would once have been placed in the middle of the agora (market square), their positions now marked by one round and one square base.

Sacred Way and Sanctuary of Apollo

The **Sacred Way** leads north from the far left corner of the Agora of the Competaliasts.

3

OLD DELOS DAYS

Delos's ancient fame arose because **Leto** gave birth to the divine twins **Artemis** and **Apollo** here, although the island's fine, sheltered harbour and central position in the Aegean did nothing to hamper development from around 2500 BC. When the Ionians colonized the island about 1000 BC it was already a cult centre, and by the seventh century BC it had also become a major commercial and religious port. Unfortunately Delos attracted the attention of Athens, which sought dominion over this prestigious island; the wealth of the **Delian Confederacy**, founded after the Persian Wars to protect the Aegean cities, was harnessed to Athenian ends, and for a while Athens controlled the Sanctuary of Apollo. Athenian attempts to "purify" the island began with a decree (426 BC) that no one could die or give birth on Delos – the sick and the pregnant were shipped to the neighbouring island of **Rínia** – and culminated in the simple expedient of banishing the native population.

Delos recovered in Roman times and reached its peak of prosperity in the third and second centuries BC, after being declared a free port by its Roman overlords; by the start of the first century BC, its population was around 25,000. In the end, though, its undefended wealth brought ruin: first **Mithridates**, of Pontus (88 BC), then the pirate **Athenodorus** (69 BC) plundered the treasures, and the island never recovered since.

Formerly lined with statues and the grandiose monuments of rival kings, walk up it to reach the three marble steps of the **Propýlaia** leading into the **Sanctuary of Apollo**. On your left is the Stoá of the Naxians, while against the north wall of the House of the Naxians, to the right, a huge statue of Apollo (c.600 BC) stood in ancient times; parts of it can be seen behind the **Temple of Artemis** to the left. In 417 BC the Athenian general Nikias led a procession of priests across a bridge of boats from Rínia to dedicate a bronze palm tree whose circular granite base you can still see. Three **Temples to Apollo** stand in a row to the right along the Sacred Way: the massive Delian Temple, the Athenian, and the Porinos, the earliest, dating from the sixth century BC. To the east stands the **Sanctuary of Dionysus** with its colossal marble phallus.

Lions' Quarter

Northwest of the Sanctuary of Dionysus, behind the small **Letóön** temple, is the huge **Agora of the Italians**, while on the left are replicas of the famous **lions**, their lean bodies masterfully executed by Naxians in the seventh century BC to ward off intruders who would have been unfamiliar with the fearful creatures. Of the original lions, three have disappeared and one – looted by Venetians in the seventeenth century– adorns the Arsenale in Venice. The remaining originals are in the site **museum** whose nine rooms include a marble statue of Apollo, mosaic fragments and an extensive collection of phallic artefacts. Opposite the lions, tamarisk trees ring the site of the **Sacred Lake**, where Leto gave birth, clinging to a palm tree. On the other side of the lake is the City Wall, built – in 69 BC – too late to protect the treasures.

Theatre Quarter

Bear right from the Agora of the Competaliasts and you enter the residential area, known as the **Theatre Quarter**. The remnants of impressive private mansions are now named after their colourful main **mosaic** – Dionysus, Trident, Masks and Dolphins. The **theatre** itself seated no fewer than 5500 spectators; just below it and structurally almost as spectacular is a huge underground cistern with arched roof supports. Behind the theatre, a path leads towards the **Sanctuaries of the Foreign Gods**, serving the immigrant population. It then rises steeply up Mount Kýnthos for a **Sanctuary of Zeus and Athena** with spectacular views out to the surrounding islands. Near its base, a small side path leads to the **Sacred Cave**, a rock cleft covered with a remarkable roof of giant stone slabs – a Hellenistic shrine to Hercules.

Sýros

SÝROS is a living, working island with only a fleeting history of tourism, rendering it the most Greek of the Cyclades. There's a thriving, permanent community, the beaches are busy but not overflowing and the villages don't sprawl widely with new developments. As well as being home to a number of excellent restaurants, the island is known for its numerous shops selling *loukoúmia* (Turkish delight), *mandoláta* (nougat) and *halvadhópita* (soft nougat between disc-shaped wafers). In addition Sýros still honours its contribution to the development of **rembétika** music: Markos Vamvakaris, one of its prime proponents, hailed from Áno Sýros where a square has been named after him.

The island's sights – including the best beaches – are concentrated in the south and west; the north is unpopulated and barren, offering little interest. Most people tend to stay in Ermoúpolis, which offers better connections to a variety of beaches, none further than 15km away.

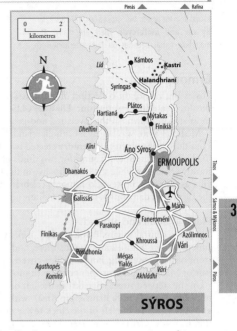

ARRIVAL AND DEPARTURE

SÝROS

By plane The island is served by Athens (via Olympic, 1 daily; 45min). There is no bus service from the airport, and you will have to take a taxi.

By ferry All ferries dock at Ermoúpolis.

Destinations Amorgós (3–4 weekly; 5–6hr); Anáfi (3 weekly; 10hr); Ándhros (2–3 weekly; 2hr 30min); Astypálea (1 weekly; 6hr 30min); Folégandhros (5 weekly; 5hr 30min); Ikaría (6–7 weekly; 3hr); Íos (3–5 weekly; 4hr); Koufoníssi/Lesser Cyclades (3 weekly; 3hr–7hr

30min); Lávrio via Kéa/Kýthnos (2–4 weekly; 4hr); Mílos/ Kímolos (3–5 weekly; 5–7hr); Mýkonos (2–5 daily; 1hr); Náxos (2–5 weekly; 2hr); Páros (2–5 weekly; 1hr 10min– 1hr 30min); Pátmos (1 weekly; 3hr 30min); Pireás (2–3 daily; 3–4hr); Sámos (6 weekly; 4hr 30min); Santoríni (3–5 weekly; 5–7hr); Sérifos (3 weekly; 2–5hr); Sífnos (3 weekly; 2hr 30min–6hr); Síkinos (3–5 weekly; 5hr); Tínos (2–6 daily; 30–50min).

INFORMATION AND TOURS

Tourist office TeamWork (☎ 22810 83400, ⓦ teamwork .gr), at Aktí Papágou 18 on the waterfront in Ermoúpolis, is a useful source of information and is able to help with your accommodation, excursion and ticket needs. In the summer there is an accommodation kiosk on the waterfront open during ferry arrivals.

Services There are several banks and about a dozen ATMs in Ermoúpolis, mostly around the waterfront. The post office is on Protopapadháki street. Laundry facilities are

available at Krinos, Protopapadháki 34 (☎ 22810 88554). In Spot, on the seafront at Papágou, has internet but requires that you become a member, the cheapest option being €5 for 3hr. It is open 24/7.

Tours Starting from Platía Miaoúli in Ermoúpolis a small tourist train runs a 40min tour of the town's main sights (€4), while horse-drawn carriages (☎ 22810 81517) start from the centre of the waterfront in season, doing city tours of various durations (€10–50).

GETTING AROUND

By bus The buses inside the city are free, but there are moves to start charging soon. Buses run on the main beach loop road south (to Galissás, Fínikas, Mégas Yialós, Akhládi,

Vári and Azólimno) hourly in high season, until late.

By taxi Sýros drivers tend not to use the taximeter, so insist. If you are unsuccessful, a fare inside the city should cost around

€3 and from the port to Áno Sýros €5 (☎ 22810 86222).

By car and motorcycle There are many car and motorbike rental agencies on the waterfront such as

Gaviotis, Papagou 20 ☎ 22810 86610. Note that the police are pretty stringent here about giving drivers alcohol tests or fines for speeding.

Ermoúpolis

Possessing an elegant collection of grand townhouses that rise majestically from the bustling, café-lined waterfront, **ERMOÚPOLIS** – once Greece's chief port – is one of the most striking towns in the Cyclades, and is certainly worth at least a night's stay.

Medieval Sýros was largely a Catholic island, but the influx of refugees from Psará and Híos during the nineteenth century created two distinct communities. Today, the Orthodox community accounts for two thirds of the population; Lower Ermoúpolis is mostly Orthodox while the Catholics live in the Upper Town and in the majority of the villages. They do, however, commonly celebrate each other's festivals (including Easter on the Orthodox dates only), lending a vibrant mix of cultures that gives the island its colour.

Platía Miaoúli and around

The long, central square, **Platía Miaoúli**, is named after an admiral of the War of Independence whose statue stands there, and in the evenings the population parades in front of its arcades. The bougainvillea-covered pedestrian street of Roïdi and side streets east of Miaoúli square are peppered with most of the better eating options.

Up the stepped street (Benáki) to the left of the town hall is the small **archeological museum** (Tues–Sun 8.30am–3pm; free), with three rooms of finds from Sýros, Páros and Amorgós. To the left of the clock tower more steps climb up to **Vrondádho**, the hill that hosts the Orthodox quarter. The wonderful church of the **Anástasis** stands atop the hill, with its domed roof and panoramic views over Tínos and Mýkonos.

Below Miaoúli square, and down a side street you can find the elaborate **Casino** and the **Church of the Dormition** (Sept–March 7.30am–12.30pm & 4.30–5.30pm; April–Aug 7.30am–noon, 5.30–6.30pm; free), which contains the town's top art treasure: a painting of the Assumption by **El Greco**, executed while he was around 20 years old.

Vapória

Up from the right of Miaoúli square is the **Apollon Theatre**, built like an Italian provincial opera house, which occasionally hosts performances (during morning rehearsals you can enter and watch for free or visit its small museum for €1.50). Further on up, the handsome Neoclassical Orthodox church of **Áyios Nikólaos** was built in 1848–70, with an impressive marble iconostasis (7am–2pm & 5–8pm). Beyond it lies the **Vapória** district, where the island's wealthiest shipowners, merchants and bankers built their mansions.

Áno Sýros

On the taller hill to the left from Miaoúli square is the intricate medieval quarter of **Áno Sýros**, with a clutch of Catholic churches below the cathedral of St George. Just below it lies the **Capuchin monastery of St Jean**, founded in 1535 to do duty as a poorhouse. Once up here it's worth visiting the local art and rembétika exhibitions, as well as personal items of the man himself at the **Markos Vamvakaris museum** (June–Sept daily 11am–2pm & 7–10pm; €1.50).

ACCOMMODATION	**ERMOÚPOLIS**

Hermes Kanári Square ☎ 22810 88011, 🖰 hermes -syros.com. Modernist sixties hotel in a prime location, overlooking the port and home to a very popular seafront restaurant (mains €10). Ask specifically for a room with sea

views. Breakfast included. **€85**

Kastro Kalomenopóulou 12 ☎ 22810 88064. Spacious rooms in a beautiful old mansion near the main square, with access to a communal kitchen. These are the

ERMOÚPOLIS

cheapest – but far from disagreeable – lodgings in town. **€35**

Omiros Omírou 43 ☎ 22810 84910, ⓦ hotel-omiros.gr. One of the most romantic options in town, on a quiet road above the Orthodox Cathedral, in the direction of Áno Sýros. Classically styled rooms set in an elegant nineteenth-century mansion once owned by Tiniot sculptor Yeóryios Vitalis. Breakfast €7.50. **€80**

Palladion Proïou 3 ☎ 22810 86400, ⓦ palladion-hotel .com. Not far from the Casino, yet quiet, clean, recently renovated and with rooms overlooking a garden; overall excellent value. **€55**

Paradise Omírou 3 ☎ 22810 83204, ⓦ hotel-paradise -syros.com. Basic en-suite rooms in a quiet part of town. All rooms have access to a pleasant shaded courtyard, while rooms on the top floor have good views. Breakfast €7. **€45**

Sea Colours Apartments Athinás 10 ☎22810 81181. Traditionally decorated apartments for up to six people, with sea views, just above the swimming platforms of Áyios Nikólaos, a 5min walk from Platía Miaoúli. April–Nov. **€65**

★ **Sýrou Mélathron** Babayiótou 5 ☎22810 85963, ⓦsyroumelathron.gr. Regal hotel, recently renovated, set in a restored 1856 mansion in the quieter Áyios Nikólaos area of town. Has suites as well as spacious rooms, some with sea views. **€100**

EATING

Amvix Aktí Papágou 26 ☎22810 83989. Owned by Roberto, an Italian chef from Padua, since 1995, this trattoria offers a taste of real Italy. Best pizzas on the island for €12. Daily noon–midnight.

Archontariki tis Maritsas Roïdi 8 ☎22810 86771. Very popular rustic taverna that serves island specialities, including its signature dish of casserole of mushrooms and spicy local sausage with peppers (€8). Daily noon–midnight.

Cotton Fresh Platia Miaouli ☎22810 82781. The best of the central square cafés, this is one to visit for a coffee and a snack, and it even uses its own home-made filo pastry for sweet and savoury pies (€4). Try a piece of the *karydhópita* (walnut pie with honey). Daily 8am–3am.

Lilis Ano Syros ☎22810 82100. An institution in the old town, with an unmatched view by the Kamares entrance, this is the taverna where Vamvakaris (see p.149) played. It's still going since 1953, offering Greek specialities from Asia Minor (€9). March–Oct daily noon–midnight.

★ **Stin Ithaki tou Aï** ☎22810 82060, ⓦithakitouai .gr. Welcoming taverna at Klonos and Stefanou corner, serving traditional ladherá dishes (various vegetables cooked in oil), as well as a good, cheap *souvláki* (€10). Daily noon–midnight.

Yiánnena Kanári Square ☎22810 87865. Popular, friendly spot, seemingly unchanged since the 1950s, serving great seafood and other Greek standards (€7). A smaller branch is on Venizelou 2. March–Oct daily 11am–1am.

NIGHTLIFE

Casino Aigeou Proïou 74 ☎22810 84400, ⓦcasinosyros .gr. Large casino that draws in well-dressed punters (no T-shirts, shorts or flip-flops) from as far as Russia. Minimum bid roulette €2.50; Black Jack €5; slot machines open 24/7. Sun–Thurs 8pm–3.30am, Fri–Sat 8pm–5.30am.

Piramatikó Platía Miaoúli ☎22810 83734. Busy, sophisticated bar, playing a varied and eclectic mix from indie rock to house music. Starts off as a café and ends up as a club. Cheap beers start at €3. Daily 9am–4am.

Theia Methi Chiou 43 ☎690 85 20 165. If you want to hear rembétika now, then take an early seat at this *mezedhopolío* on the western side of Platía Miaoúli, which has free live music most days after 9.30pm, order your mains (€8) and enjoy the show. Daily 7pm–late.

Beaches

The first stop on the beach round-trip from Ermoúpolis is well-developed **Galissás**, the largest beach on the island, and the home of its only **campsite** (see p.154). If you feel the urge to escape the crowds, you can rent a scooter, or walk ten minutes over the southern headland to the small nudist beach of **Armeós**. A longer walk (1hr 15min plus) goes, rather steeply, over the ridge to the southeast and down to the **sea-cave** of Áyios Stéfanos.

A rural forty-minute walk, or a ten-minute bus ride south from Galissás, brings you to the more mainstream resort of **Fínikas**, with its long and narrow beach protected from the road by a row of tamarisk trees. Fínikas is separated by a small headland from its neighbour **Posidhonía** (or Delagrazia after the local Madonna della Grazia church), a nicer spot with some idiosyncratically ornate mansions and a bright-blue church right on the edge of the village. It's worth walking ten minutes further south, past the naval yacht club and its patrol boat, to **Agathopés**. This is the best sandy beach on the island, facing a little islet, Skhinónisi, just offshore. **Komitó**, at the end of the road leading south 500m from **Agathopés**, is a small, quiet sandy bay below a private olive grove.

From Posidhonía the road swings southeast to **Mégas Yialós**, a diffuse, elongated resort. There are two beaches, Mégas Yialós and Ambélia; the long, eponymous beach is lined with shady trees and there are pedal boats for hire.

The cove of **Akhládhi** is sheltered and family-friendly, while **Vári**, just beyond, is more – though not much more – of a town, with its own small fishing fleet. As it is the most sheltered of the island's bays – something to remember when the *meltémi* is up – it

FROM TOP SÝROS (P.149); BEACH ON NÁXOS (P.167) >

attracts mostly families and little children; the younger crowd are attracted by the beach bars of Agathopés and Komito above.

The final resort on the circular tour is **Azólimnos**, accessed by a narrow road from Vári, or a wider one from the northern end.

ACCOMMODATION

Brazzera Fínikas ☎ 22810 79173, ⓦ www.brazzera.gr. Modern, well-situated hotel close to the beach, whose green furnishings tastefully match the green of the salt cedars in front. Large rooms with tiled floors adorned with flowers make this one of the most pleasant stays outside Ermoúpolis. April–Oct. **€85**

Dolphin Bay Galissás ☎ 22810 42924, ⓦ dolphin-bay .gr. Luxurious hotel, amphitheatrically built with impressive views over the bay from its large swimming

BEACHES

pool and bar. The complex includes an excellent restaurant (mains €15). Breakfast included. May–Oct. **€90**

Two Hearts Galissás ☎ 22810 42052, ⓦ ww.twohearts -camping.com. The only camping on the island, it is well organized with a minimarket, internet access, a currency exchange plus a car and motorcycle rental office. It offers bungalows that sleep two and have their own WCs, as well as pickups from the ferries. May–Sept. Camping **€8**, bungalows **€20**

EATING AND DRINKING

Niriídhes Akhládhi ☎ 697 88 30 332. Fish taverna, the beach offshoot of the Archontariki tis Maritsas (see p.152) in Ermoúpolis, which specializes in imaginative seafood dishes such as shrimp omelette, yet still has a place for time-honoured platters like grilled octopus (€9). May–Oct noon–midnight.

To Iliovasilema Galissás ☎ 22810 43325. A small

seaside taverna with an inventive menu, it punches well above its weight in the reputation stakes. The owner has his own boat and nothing from the catch goes to waste: small fish are used for the bouillabaisse, shellfish are added to the pasta sauce, while the larger items are grilled with lemon and herbs. April–Oct noon–midnight, Nov– March 7pm–midnight.

Páros

With a gentle and undramatic landscape arranged around the central peak of Profítis Ilías, **PÁROS** has a little of everything one expects from a Greek island: old villages, monasteries, fishing harbours, nice beaches and varied nightlife. However, Parikiá, the capital, can be touristy and expensive, and it is very difficult finding rooms and beach space here in August, when the other settlements, the port of **Náoussa** and the satellite island of **Andíparos**, handle most of the overflow. Drinking and carousing is many people's idea of a holiday on Páros, so it's not surprising that both Parikiá and Náoussa have a wealth of pubs, bars and discos, offering staggered happy hours.

ARRIVAL AND DEPARTURE

PÁROS

By plane The island is served by regular flights from Athens (via Olympic; 2–3 daily; 55min). The airport is 12km south of Parikiá. There are buses waiting for the flights during the summer months.

By ferry Parikiá is a major hub for inter-island ferry services and serves almost all islands in the Cyclades. There are two ferries to Andíparos: the first is a passenger ferry from Parikiá and the second is a car ferry from Poúnda, 7km south of Parikiá (see opposite). The latter leaves every 30–45min during the summer months; 7.15am–1.30am (€1.15 per person, €6.15 per car).

Destinations Amorgós (2–3 weekly; 3hr); Anáfi (1–3

weekly; 6hr 30min); Andíparos (hourly in season; 40min); Astypálea (1–4 weekly; 4hr 50min); Iráklion (5–6 weekly; 3hr 30min); Dhonoússa (daily; 2hr); Folégandhros (2–4 weekly; 3hr 30min); Íos (2–3 weekly; 2hr–3hr 45min); Lávrio via Kéa/Kýthnos (1 weekly; 8hr); Mílos (2–3 weekly; 5hr); Mýkonos (1–2 daily; 45min–1hr 40min); Náxos (2–3 daily; 35min–1hr); Pireás (3–5 daily; 3–4hr); Santoríni (1–3 daily; 3hr); Sérifos (1–2 weekly; 3–5hr); Sífnos (2 weekly; 2hr 30min); Síkinos (2–4 weekly; 3hr); Skhinoússa (2–4 weekly; 2hr 20min–6hr); Sýros (6–8 weekly; 2hr 40min); Tínos (1–2 daily; 1hr 10min).

INFORMATION

Tourist office There is no official tourist office on the island; bus timetables are posted by the bus station in

Parikiá and there is a kiosk by the windmill with general accommodation information on the island. Your best bet is

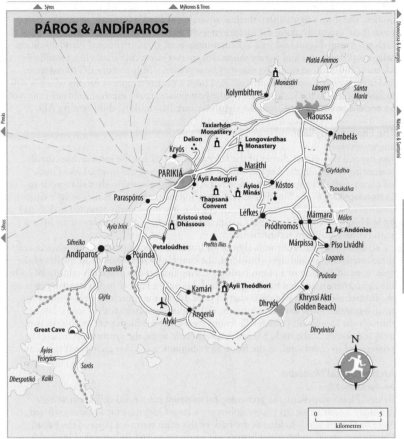

to go to a travel agent (see below).

Services There is no shortage of banks or ATMs in Parikiá. The island's only post office is west of the windmill, past the ancient cemetery. Cybercookies (☏ 22840 21610, ⓦ cybercookies.gr; €3/hr) off the main square is the best internet café. Luggage can be left at various travel agents

(look for signs) along Parikiá's watefront.

Travel agents Polos Tours (☏ 22840 22092, ⓦ polostours .gr) in Parikiá is one of the friendlier travel agencies, issuing air tickets for Olympic, and acting as agents for virtually all the boats.

GETTING AROUND

By bus The bus station is 100m or so west of the ferry dock. Note that there are two places called Poúnda on Páros, one being the west-coast port (see p.158), the other a beach on the east coast (see p.160). Náoussa (hourly through the night in high season; 20min), Poúnda for Andíparos (20min), Dhryós (1hr).

By car and motorcycle Rental outfits include European

(☏ 22840 21771, ⓦ paroscars.gr) and Avant Travel (☏ 22840 22302, ⓦ europcar-paros.com) on the western and eastern waterfronts respectively. Note that traffic rules are strictly enforced, and that various streets are one-way. Parking is only allowed in designated areas and parts of the Parikiá seafront are closed to traffic during summer evenings.

Parikiá and around

Bustling **PARIKIÁ** sets the tone architecturally for the rest of Páros, its ranks of typically Cycladic white houses punctuated by the occasional Venetian-style building and church domes. The town's sights apart, the real attraction of Parikiá is simply to wander the town itself, especially along the meandering **old market street** (Agorá) and adjoining Grávari. Arcaded lanes lead past Venetian-influenced villas, traditional island dwellings, ornate wall-fountains and trendy shops. The market street culminates in a formidable **kástro** (1260), whose surviving east wall incorporates a fifth-century BC round tower and is constructed using masonry pillaged from a nearby temple of Athena which is still highly visible. On the seafront behind the port police are the exposed, excavated ruins of an **ancient cemetery** used from the eighth century BC until the third century AD.

The Ekatondapylianí
Daily 7am–9pm • Free

Just beyond the central clutter of the ferry port, Parikiá has the most architecturally interesting church in the Aegean – the **Katopoliani** (facing the town). Later Greek scholars purified the name and connected it with past glories, so they changed it to **Ekatondapylianí** ("The One Hundred Gated"), a nickname that baffles today's visitors. Tradition, supported by excavations, claims that it was originally founded in 326 AD by St Helen, mother of Emperor Constantine, but what's visible today stems from a sixth century Justinian reconstruction.

Enclosed by a great front wall, sign of an Imperial-built church, the church is in fact three interlocking buildings. The oldest, the chapel of **Áyios Nikólaos** to the left of the apse, is an adaptation of a pagan building dating from the early fourth century BC. On the right, there is another building attached, housing a Paleochristian **baptistry**, where the initiate used to dip in a cross-shaped pool. Inside the church courtyard, there is a small **Byzantine museum** (church hours; €2) displaying a collection of icons. Look through the iconostasis (which still retains its ancient marble frame) to observe two unique features: at the back, a set of amphitheatric steps, the **synthronon**, where the priests used to chant, and, at the front, the **ciborium**, a marble canopy over the altar.

Archeological Museum
Tues–Sun 8.30am–2.30pm • €2

Behind Ekatondapylianí, the **archeological museum** has a good collection and is definitely worth a visit. Its prize exhibits are a large Gorgon, a fifth-century winged Nike by **Skopas** and – hidden at the back of the main room – a piece of the **Parian Chronicle**, a social and cultural history of Greece up to 264 BC engraved in marble.

Áyii Anárgyiri monastery
If you're staying in Parikiá, you'll want to get out at some stage. The shortest **excursion** is the 2.5km along the road starting from the northern end of the ring-road up to the **Áyii Anárgyiri** monastery. Perched on the bluff above town, this makes a great picnic spot, with cypress groves, a gushing fountain and some splendid views.

Beaches near Parikiá
Less than 1km north of the harbour lies the twin crescent of **Livádhia** beach, with shallow waters and shaded by salt cedars; further on lies **Kriós** beach, much better, served by *kaiki* from just to the right of the ferry terminal (€4). The beaches south along the asphalt road are even better: the first unsurfaced side-track leads to the small, sheltered **Dhelfíni**; fifteen minutes further on is **Paraspóros** near the remains of an ancient temple to Asklepios, the god of healing. Continuing for 45 minutes (or a short hop by bus) brings you to arguably the best of the bunch, **Ayía Iríni**, a palm-fringed beach with fine sand, a taverna and a beautiful **campsite** (see p.158).

Petaloúdhes
Not far from the turning to Ayía Iríni, is the "Valley of the Butterflies", a walled-in private oasis where millions of Jersey tiger moths perch on the foliage in summer

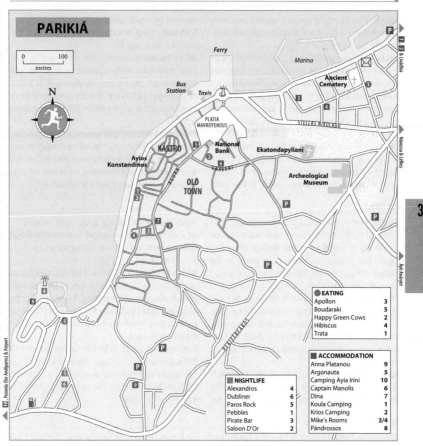

PARIKIÁ

0 — 100 metres

N

Ferry

Bus Station — Taxis

Marina

Ancient Cemetery

PLATIA MAVROYENOUS

KASTRO

Áyios Konstandínos

National Bank

Ekatondapylianí

STELLAS NIKOLAOU

GRAVARI

OLD TOWN

Archeological Museum

DEXAMENON

PERIFERIAKOS

EATING
Apollon	3
Boudaraki	5
Happy Green Cows	2
Hibiscus	4
Trata	1

ACCOMMODATION
Anna Platanou	9
Argonauta	5
Camping Ayía Iríni	10
Captain Manolis	6
Dina	7
Koula Camping	1
Krios Camping	2
Mike's Rooms	3/4
Pándrossos	8

NIGHTLIFE
Alexandros	4
Dubliner	6
Paros Rock	5
Pebbles	1
Pirate Bar	3
Saloon D'Or	2

Poúnda (for Andíparos) & Airport

3

Naoussa & Léfkes

Ayía Anarhyri

(May–Sept 9am–8pm; €2). The trip can be combined with a visit to the eighteenth-century nunnery of **Áyios Arsénios**, at the crest of a ridge 1km to the north. Only women are allowed in the sanctuary, although men can wait in the courtyard. Petaloúdhes can also be reached from Parikiá by bus during the summer months.

ACCOMMODATION   PARIKIÁ AND AROUND

Anna Platanou ☎ 22840 21751, ⓦ annaplatanou.gr. This smart, family-run and family-friendly hotel 600m southwest of the port has clean, refurbished rooms in a peaceful location overlooking a garden. The owners also have much larger studios, and apartments at the junction of the Alykí-Poúnda roads for €50. Port transfers available. April–Oct. **€60**

Argonauta ☎ 22840 21440, ⓦ argonauta.gr. Stylish hotel in the white-and-blue Cycladic fashion with smart rooms arranged around a beautiful stone courtyard next to the National Bank. There is a good restaurant underneath. April–Oct. **€70**

Camping Agia Iríni Ayía Iríni ☎ 22840 91496,

ⓦ campingai.gr. One of the most atmospheric campsites in the Cyclades: you are right on the beach, but it feels like you are camping in someone's overgrown garden. It has its own cheap taverna, although the olive, citrus and summer-ripening fruit trees can provide you with free sustenance. Bus transfers organized. May–Sept. **€18**

★ **Captain Manolis** ☎ 22840 21244, ⓦ paroswelcome .com. Central – behind the National Bank – but unbelievably quiet; all rooms have ivy-covered balconies facing the garden, as well as a/c and fridge. Free wi-fi. May–Oct. **€40**

Dina ☎ 22840 21325, ⓦ hoteldina.com. Small family pension, right in the middle of the night action in the Agorá opposite the Ayía Triádha church. There is only occasional

3

noise from the *Pirate's Bar* opposite, so either come home when they close at 3am or ask for a room at the back. May–Oct. **€50**

Koula Camping 📞 22840 22081, 🖥 campingkoula.gr. For those who need to be very close to the town, this campsite, 900m along the seafront east of the bus stop, is a reasonable choice for a night or two, with 24/7 reception, a wide range of cabins or bungalows, and even a covered area for just sleeping bags. The owners also operate a cheap but good restaurant next door. April–Oct. **€6**

★ **Krios Beach Camping** 📞 22840 21705, 🖥 krios -camping.gr. Excellent facilities in a shady, flat site, 2km east from Parikiá, supplemented by a cool beach bar next door. Occasional Greek parties, which include plate

smashing, see crowds specially bussed in from Parikiá; they finish early enough so that you can enjoy your sleep. Free wi-fi, pool. May–Sept. **€8**

Mike's Rooms 📞 22840 22856, 🖥 roomsmike.com. Clean, comfortable studios opposite the ferry dock with hospitable staff, and a recommendations diary as long as the Encyclopedia Britannica. Mike, the owner, is a tirelessly enthusiastic source of information and assistance. May–Sept. **€35**

Pándrossos 📞 22840 22903, 🖥 pandrossoshotel.com. Perched magnificently on a high hill overlooking the port and beyond, this four-star hotel has a good restaurant, a deep swimming pool and colourful rooms with balconies offering exceptional sunset views. March–Oct. **€75**

EATING

Apollon Off *Agorá* 📞 22840 24691. Housed in a converted 1920s olive press with a large garden near the market, this is one of the island's classiest restaurants. Despite high prices, its popularity never wanes. Try the chicken with prunes (€18), highly recommended. April–Oct daily 7pm–late.

★ **Boudaraki** 📞 22840 22297. The locals rate this restaurant at the southern beachfront by the bridge as the best one on Páros. Expect good service even when packed, an excellent selection of mezédhes and mains (€12), as well as home-made baklava to finish the meal off. Easter–Sept daily noon–1am.

Happy Green Cows 📞 22840 24691. Remarkably eclectic vegetarian restaurant in a side street behind the National Bank with some concessions to carnivores that

include chicken and fish. Not cheap (mains around €17), yet imaginative, with unexpected local ingredients that make you want to play "name that vegetable". April–Oct daily 7pm–2am.

Hibiscus 📞 22840 24691. One of the oldest restaurants on the island, in a great, central spot on the waterfront south of the windmill, overlooking the sea; it offers the usual Greek dishes, but is famed mainly for its selection of generous-sized, wood-oven-baked pizzas for €10. April–Oct daily 6pm–2am.

Trata 📞 22840 24651. Behind the ancient cemetery off the road heading out of town, this popular, family-run taverna specializes in serving large plates of tasty seafood and grilled meats (€12) in a vine-covered patio. April–Oct daily noon–midnight.

NIGHTLIFE

Alexandros The best possible location for a sophisticated evening drink in a fabulously romantic spot around a real windmill. Set apart from the town, on an elevated promontory at the southern end of the promenade, it has wonderful sunset views which you can enjoy while listening to classical music. Cocktails €9. June–Sept daily 6.30pm–3am.

Dubliner/Paros Rock 📞 22840 21113. Large, brash and youthful dance complex thankfully set back from the main drag just off the seafront bridge, thus avoiding scrutiny of the antics of the 18–30 crowd dancing to mainstream hits. It comprises four loud bars – opening gradually as the summer hots up – a main club and an outdoors chillout area. Entrance with first drink €5. June–Sept daily 11pm–6am.

★ **Pebbles** Upstairs bar at the seafront, east of the

windmill and up the steps from the kiosk, playing jazz and lounge music, with good sunset views and excellent cocktails (€7). It attracts a mixed-age crowd, who pack the place to watch the sunset around 8pm and then return after midnight. Daily noon–3am.

Pirate Bar Popular, established jazz and blues bar near the town hall, opposite Dina's. It is rather small, so it's convenient for smokers as most of its clientele tend to stand outside. Cocktails €8. April–Oct daily 10am–2pm & 6.30pm–3am.

Saloon D'Or Rowdy but fun spot on the seafront south of the windmill, with cheap drinks and lounge/chillout music. It offers shishas in various flavours, as well as comfortable Oriental divans and settees to sink in and enjoy them. Cocktails €7. May–Sept daily 8.30pm–3.30am.

The southwest

There's little to stop for southwest of Parikiá until **Poúnda**, 6km away, the watersports centre of the island. A further 6km south, past the airport, you reach **Alykí**, a pretty resort on a picturesque bay with two beach sections: one pebbly and bare and the other sandy and shaded.

Skorpios Cycladic Folk Museum

Daily May–Sept 9.30am–2pm • Free

A fascinating and deeply idiosyncratic private museum with a collection of model boats and miniatures of various typical buildings from the Cyclades. You can find here painstakingly reconstructed examples, from the dovecotes of Tínos to Náxos cereal grinding mills, and from the Lion Avenue of Delos to the windmills of Mýkonos.

INFORMATION   THE SOUTHWEST

Activities Paros Watersports in Poúnda (☎ 22840 92229, ⓦ paros-watersports.gr) offers courses and rents equipment for all levels of kitesurfing, wakeboarding and scuba diving leading to a PADI certification course.

ACCOMMODATION AND EATING

Galatis Alykí ☎ 22840 91355, ⓦ galatishotel.com. This is the best hotel outside Parikiá and Náoussa, several notches up from merely comfortable, offering a pool, a restaurant and (mostly) sea-view rooms. Free wi-fi. Breakfast included. April–Nov. **€75**

Náoussa and around

Many consider **Náoussa** as a more fashionable alternative to Parikiá. Although a major resort town, with modern concrete hotels and attendant trappings, it has developed around a charming little port whose layout has not been adversely affected. The local festivals are still celebrated with enthusiasm, especially the re-enactment on August 23 of a naval victory over the pirates, followed by a fireworks display.

Although the nightlife is on a par with that of Parikiá, most people are here for the local beaches. **Áyii Anárgyri** is just off the path that goes east of Náoussa's harbour, while **Pipéri** is a couple of minutes' walk west. To the northwest, 4km on the road around the bay brings you to **Kolymbíthres**, with its wind- and sea-sculpted rock formations. A few minutes beyond, **Monastíri beach**, below the abandoned Pródhromos monastery, is similarly attractive for diving and snorkelling. A regular summer *kaïki* service connects them for €6 return.

Go northeast of town and the sands are better still: after the glorious sandbank of **Xínari** you reach the barren **Viglákia** headland, also reached by *kaïki*. It is dotted with good surfing beaches such as **Platiá Ámmos** that lies on the northeastern tip of the island and **Lángeri** which is backed by dunes; a walk ten minutes south of the main beach brings you to the mostly gay section. The best surfing beach, though, is at **Sánta María**, an expanse of sand 6km by road from Náoussa.

Ambelás, 3km southeast of Náoussa, has a safe, sheltered beach, as you might guess from the number of fishing boats moored here. It is also the start of a long, rough coastal 6km track that leads south, passing several undeveloped shady coves on the way such as **Glyfádha** and the almost deserted **Tsoukália** until you reach the impressive spread of **Mólos beach**, never particularly crowded. From here you can pick up again the asphalted road straight back to Náoussa or through the **inland villages** back to Parikiá.

ACCOMMODATION   NÁOUSSA AND AROUND

Astir of Paros ☎ 22840 51976, ⓦ www.astirofparos.gr. Superb and lavish five-star resort on the road to Kolymbíthres with marble baths, huge balconies and excellent service. Its sixteen-acre site includes two restaurants, large pool, tennis court, three-hole golf course, heliport and even two small chapels for weddings. April–Oct. **€250**

Christiana Ambelás ☎ 22840 51573, ⓦ christiana hotel.gr. A good-value hotel, with great fresh fish and local wine in the in-house restaurant and extremely friendly proprietors; they have both rooms and fully equipped apartments, all with balconies facing the beach. Breakfast included. May–Sept. **€45**

★ **Heaven** ☎ 22840 51549, ⓦ heaven-naoussa.com. As it is difficult to find (walk up the steps above the bus station car park), this feels like a true discovery: an elegant, cool, gay-friendly and spotlessly clean boutique hotel belonging to a Scandinavian Greek and his family. Internet and parking available. May–Sept. **€60**

Sea House ☎ 22840 52198. This was one of the first places in Náoussa to let rooms and has one of the best locations above Pipéri beach with beautiful views from all of its balconies. Recommended for those who prize location over extravagance. April–Oct. **€60**

Stella ☎ 22840 53617, ⊚ hotelstella.gr. Out of season, you should be able to haggle for reduced prices at this basic but well-located hotel with rooms arranged around its own garden, several blocks inland from the old harbour. **€55**

Surfing Beach Village Sánta María ☎ 22840 52493, ⊚ surfbeach.gr. A well-organized campsite where surfers rub shoulders with families. In late June–July it runs a summer camp for 7–14-year-olds. Also offers beach huts and bungalows with a/c and private WC (€55). Courtesy minibus to and from Parikiá. June–Sept. Camping **€8**, beach huts **€15**

EATING AND DRINKING

Meltemi ☎ 22840 51263. On the quiet side of the bridge, this excellent grill restaurant offers Cretan specialities (€12) with a smile. The owner is friendly and chatty and you'll undoubtedly be offered a free shot of *tsikoudiá* "for digestion". Easter–Oct daily 6pm–late.

Ouzerí ton Naftikón ☎ 22840 51662. Probably the best *mezedhopolio* in the harbour area. Offers fresh fish and a rather standard Greek menu (mains €8), but has a

reputation second to none. Come before 9pm or else you won't find a seat. April–Oct daily 6.30pm–late.

Yeméni ☎ 22840 51445, ⊚ yemeni.gr. Popular family restaurant in the winding streets of central Náoussa, offering well-cooked, traditional Greek dishes for around €10. Everything comes from the family farm – from the pork and chicken to the oil you will pour on your salad. Easter–Oct daily 6pm–late.

NIGHTLIFE

Barbarossa ☎ 22840 51391. Chic bar bathed in candlelight at the far end of the harbour (not to be confused with the expensive restaurant at the opposite end). Frequented mostly by twenty-something Greeks, this may be the place to try your language skills. Cocktails €10. April–Oct daily 6pm–4am.

Shark ☎ 693 73 06 037. On a first-floor balcony overlooking the harbour, this is a bar for alternative rockers

and where ale rather than cocktails is the drink of choice. A good selection of bottled beers on offer (€5). May–Sept daily 9pm–3am.

Vareladhiko Potami. Classic club playing pop hits and frequented mainly by under-thirties. The script is predictable: beer will flow, patrons will dance on the tables and holiday romances will blossom. It's still great fun, though. Mid-June to mid-Sept (days vary) 11pm–6am.

The southeast coast

The coast southeast of the inland junction at **Marpíssa** – itself a maze of winding alleys and ageing archways overhung by floral balconies – is comparatively off the tourist radar, yet it is easily reachable by regular buses during the summer and boasts some magnificent beaches.

The first resort you reach, **Píso Livádhi**, was once a quiet fishing village, but it is now dominated by open-air car parks and relatively indifferent tavernas. However, between here and **Dhryós** to the south there are no fewer than four excellent beaches. **Logarás** just over the promontory from Píso Livádhi has a superb stretch of sand, while the next

---

THE INLAND VILLAGES

Most people bypass Páros interior, but on a cooler day try walking the **medieval flagstoned path** that once linked both sides of the island. Start from the main square of the village of **Mármara** and go west. First up is **Pródhromos**, an old fortified farming settlement with defensive walls girding its nearby monastery. **Léfkes** itself, 5km from Pródhromos, is perhaps the most unspoilt settlement on Páros. The town flourished from the seventeenth century on, its population swollen by refugees fleeing from coastal piracy; indeed it was the island's capital during most of the Ottoman period. Léfkes's marbled alleyways and amphitheatrical setting are unparalleled – and undisturbed by motor vehicles, which are forbidden in the middle of town. Another 5km towards Parikiá and you hit **Maráthi**, from where Parian marble was supplied to much of Europe. Considered second only to Carrara marble, the last slabs were mined here by the French in 1844 for **Napoleon's tomb** in Les Invalides. Just east of the village, marked paths lead to two huge entrances of ancient marble mines which can be visited with an organized tour only (ask at Polo Tours, see p.155). From Maráthi, it's easy enough to pick up the bus on to Parikiá.

beach, **Poúnda** (not to be confused with the port of the same name on the west coast), is home to a beach club with parties that go on well into the night. The final two are the twin windsurfing beaches of **New** and **Old Khrissí Akti** (Golden Beach), which have been established as the main resorts of the southeast.

Dhryós, the end of the bus routes, is the only settlement of any size in this part of Páros. Although the village is mostly modern and characterless, it has an attractive, quiet beach.

ACCOMMODATION AND EATING
THE SOUTHEAST COAST

Fisilánis Logarás ☎ 22840 41734, ✉ fysilanisgr@hol .gr. In operation since 1964, this is an outstanding value family hotel and taverna (mains €6) worth experiencing if only for a few days. Well-stocked rooms with sea views, friendly service and unbeatable prices. April–Oct. **€40**

Golden Beach Khrissí Aktí ☎ 22840 41366, ⓦ goldenbeach.gr. The dominant hotel on the "Old" Golden Beach with windsurfing facilities available next door, an adjoining restaurant open for breakfast through to dinner and a beach bar open until 2am (beer €3). Free wi-fi and breakfast included. April–Oct. **€80**

Andíparos

3

ANDÍPAROS is no longer a secret destination: the waterfront is lined with new hotels and apartments, and in high season it can be full, though in recent years families have displaced the former young, international crowd. However, the island has retained its friendly backwoods atmosphere and has a lot going for it, including good sandy beaches and a remarkable cave. Furthermore, rooms and hotels here are much less expensive than on Páros.

ARRIVAL AND INFORMATION
ANDÍPAROS

By ferry There are two ferries going to two different places on Páros: the passenger-only ferry goes to Parikiá (see p.155) and the car ferry goes to Poúnda, 7km below Parikiá (see p.158).
Destinations To Páros, Parikiá (hourly in season; 40min); Páros, Poúnda (every 30min in season; 20min).
Services There is a bank at the waterfront, as well as a small post office.

Travel agents Oliaros Tours (☎ 22840 61231, ⓦ antiparostravel.gr) in the main shopping street can help with accommodation, boat and plane tickets, excursions and car rental. They also operate a currency exchange and a postal courier service.
Activities Blue Island Divers (☎ 22840 61767, ⓦ blueisland -divers.gr) on the waterfront offer two-day PADI diving courses (€200). They also rent underwater scooters.

GETTING AROUND

By bus The stop is by the disembarkation point. Cave (30min); Áyios Yeóryios (50min).
By car and motorcycle Europecar (☎ 22840 61346,

ⓦ antiparos-cars.com) is a good rental outlet near the ferry dock.

Andíparos Town

Most of the population live in the large low-lying **ANDÍPAROS TOWN**, across the narrow straits from Páros, the new development on the outskirts concealing an attractive traditional settlement. A long, flagstoned pedestrian street forms its backbone, leading from the jetty to the Cycladic houses around the outer wall of the kástro. It was built by Leonardo Loredano in the 1440s as a fortified settlement safe from pirate raids – his family coat of arms can still be seen on a house in the courtyard. The only way in is through a pointed archway from the main square, where several cafés are shaded by a giant eucalyptus. Inside, more whitewashed houses surround two churches and a cistern built into the surviving base of the central tower. The town has also developed into a prime diving centre.

ACCOMMODATION
ANDÍPAROS TOWN

Camping Antiparos ☎ 22840 61221, ⓦ camping -antiparos.gr. This fully equipped campsite is a 10min

walk northeast of town along a track, next to its own nudist beach; the water here is shallow enough for campers to wade across to the neighbouring islet of Dhipló. June–Sept. €8

Koúros Village ☎ 22840 61084/5, ⓦ kouros-village.gr. If any proof were needed that Andíparos is value for money you need only visit this extensive resort. Large, clean pool, a restaurant with a panoramic view (mains €6), an open-air dancefloor and apartment-sized rooms. Breakfast included. Easter–Oct. €70

Mantaléna ☎ 22840 61206, ⓦ hotelmantalena.gr. In 1960 a Greek film, *Mantalena*, was shot on Andíparos by director George Roussos. Three years later his brother built this hotel north of the jetty, which is still run by his family. This is one of the more exclusive places on Andíparos and offers large rooms and balconies with wi-fi and satellite TV – plus some apartments in the old town. Breakfast included. Easter–Oct. €70

EATING AND DRINKING

Anárgyros ☎ 22840 61204. Taverna with the most central location in the port where you can rest assured that the daily special (around €8) will be also be consumed by the owner's family later. Also offers basic, clean rooms at the back for €50. June–Sept daily 10am–midnight.

Yannis Place ☎ 22840 61469. A restaurant that mutates into a late-night bar. This is a laidback place for the young and the very young and will make you feel nostalgic for your salad days, if you are but over 30. June–Sept daily 8pm–midnight.

Beaches

Andíparos's **beaches** begin right outside town: **Psaralíki**, just to the south with golden sand and tamarisks for shade, is much better than **Sifnéïko** on the opposite side of the island. Villa development is starting to follow the surfaced road down the east coast, but has yet to get out of hand. **Glýfa**, 4km down, is another good beach, while, in the southeast of the island, **Sorós** is by far the most bewitching beach on the island. On the southwest coast there are some fine sand dunes at **Áyios Yeóryios**, the end of the surfaced road. From there, one *kaïki* makes an 11am daily trip to the uninhabited, but archeologically rich, island of **Dhespotikó**, opposite.

ACCOMMODATION AND EATING

BEACHES

Delfini Áyios Yeóryios ☎ 22840 24506, ⓦ dolphinantiparos.gr. Newly renovated studios sleeping up to four people, with large verandas. There is a café-bar for breakfast and lunch as well as a grill for dinner. Although off the beaten track, this is a lively establishment, offering a range of excursions and activities. May–Sept. €80

The Great Cave

Summer daily 11am–3pm • €3

The great **cave** in the south of the island is the chief attraction for day-trippers. In these eerie chambers the Marquis de Nointel, Louis XIV's ambassador to Constantinople, celebrated Christmas Mass in 1673 while a retinue of five hundred, including painters, pirates, Jesuits and Turks, looked on; at the exact moment of midnight explosives were detonated to emphasize the enormity of the event. Although electric lights and cement steps have diminished its mystery and grandeur, the cave remains impressive. Check out the historical graffiti carved over the centuries.

Náxos

NÁXOS is the largest and most fertile of all the Cyclades islands and with its green and mountainous highland scenery it appears immediately dissimilar to its neighbours. The difference is accentuated by the **unique architecture** of many of the interior villages: the Venetian Duchy of the Aegean, headquartered here from 1204 to 1537, left towers and fortified mansions scattered throughout the island, while medieval Cretan refugees bestowed a singular character upon Náxos's eastern settlements.

Today Náxos could easily support itself without visitors by relying on its production of potatoes, olives, grapes and lemons, but it has thrown in its lot with mass tourism, so that parts of the island are now almost as busy as Páros (see p.154) in season. The island has plenty to see if you know where to look: the highest mountains in the Cyclades, intriguing central valleys, a spectacular north coast and long, marvellously sandy beaches in the southwest. It is also renowned for its wines, cheese and *kítron*, a sweet liqueur distilled from the leaves of this citrus tree and available in green, yellow or clear varieties depending on strength and sugar level.

ARRIVAL AND DEPARTURE NÁXOS

By plane Náxos is served by regular flights from Athens (via Olympic, 1–2 daily; 45min). The airport is a 10min bus ride south from Náxos Town (€12).

By ferry Ferries dock in the northern harbour quay of Náxos Town.

Destinations Amorgós (7–9 weekly; 3–4hr); Anáfi (3 weekly; 7hr); Ándhros (2–4 weekly; 4hr); Astypálea (1–4 weekly; 3hr); Dhonoússa (3–7 weekly; 1hr 30min); Folégandhros (1–4 daily; 4hr); Íos (4–5 weekly; 1hr 30min); Iráklia (2–5 weekly; 1hr 30min); Koufoníssi (3–7 weekly; 2hr 30min); Mýkonos (1–3 daily; 3hr); Páros (2–3 daily; 45min); Pireás (2–3 daily; 4hr–5hr 30min); Rafína (4–8 weekly 3–6hr); Santoríni (1–2 daily; 1hr 30min–3hr 30min); Sérifos (1 weekly; 2hr 30min); Sífnos (1 weekly; 3hr 30min); Síkinos (3–5 weekly; 2–5hr); Skhinoússa (2–4 weekly; 2hr); Sýros (4–5 weekly; 2hr 30min); Tínos (4–8 weekly; 1–2hr 30min).

3

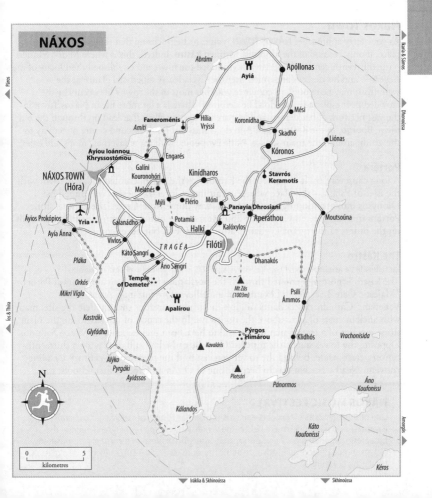

INFORMATION

Services The post office is north of the Town Hall square in Náxos Town.

Travel agents Excursions around Náxos and to other islands are conveniently booked at Zas Travel (☏ 22850 23330) on the seafront near the jetty. Further down the promenade Naxos Tours (☏ 22850 23043, ⓦ naxostours .net) can also help with all kinds of arrangements.

Activities Flisvos Sportsclub (☏ 22850 22935, ⓦ flisvos -sportclub.com) is based at Áyios Yeóryios beach, offering windsurfing courses and other activities.

GETTING AROUND

By bus The bus station (☏ 22850 22291) is opposite the main dock. Printed timetables are available.
Destinations Aperáthou via Filóti and Halkí (4–5 daily; 1hr); Apóllonas (2–3 daily; 1hr; 2hr via scenic coastal route); Ayía Marína – Zas (4–5 daily; 1hr); Áyios Prokópios/ Ayía Ánna (half hourly; 7.30am–midnight; 15min); Pláka (half hourly; 7.30am–midnight; 30min); Kastráki-Pyrgáki (3 daily; 45min).

By car and motorcycle Auto Tour Rent-a-Car by the bus station in Náxos Town (☏ 22850 25480) rents cars and offers a wealth of information as well as accommodation advice. In town parking immediately next to accommodation is not always possible. The best one-day drive is Halkí–Filóti–Aperáthou–Apóllonas returning via the northern coastal route.

By taxi The central taxi call number is ☏ 22850 22444.

Náxos Town

As your ferry approaches **NÁXOS TOWN**, you can't help sensing that this a really special place, if only because of the looming, fortified **kástro**. Indeed, this is where Marco Sanudo – the thirteenth-century Venetian who founded the town and established the Duchy of the Aegean – and his descendants ruled over the Cyclades. A superficial glance at the waterfront may be enough to convince you that most of the town's life occurs by the crowded port esplanade, but don't be deceived. There is a lot more life in Náxos Town in the vast network of backstreets and low-arched narrow alleys that lead up through the old town, **Boúrgo**, to the **Kastro** itself. And don't miss out on the second centre of activity to the south, around the main square, **Platía Evripéous**, with more tavernas, shops and cafés.

Portára

A long causeway, built to protect the harbour to the north, connects Náxos Town with the islet of Palátia – the place where, according to legend, Theseus was duped by Dionysos into abandoning Ariadne on his way home from Crete. The famous stone **Portára** that has greeted visitors for 2500 years is the portal of a temple of Apollo, built on the orders of the tyrant Lygdamis around 530 BC, but never completed.

The Kástro

Tours offered by the Venetian museum at 11am Tues–Sun in season • €15, includes entrance to all the kástro museums

The kástro is normally entered through the **north gate** (also known as the Traní Pórta or "Majestic Gate"), a splendid example of a medieval fort entrance. A few of the Venetians' Catholic descendants still live in the old mansions that encircle the site, many with ancient coats of arms above the doorways. In the centre of the kástro are the plain stone remains of a rectangular tower, said to have been the residence of Marco Sanudo. Opposite the tower stands the restored Catholic cathedral, still displaying a thirteenth-century crest inside. Behind the tower you can find the seventeenth-century Ursuline convent. Nearby is what was to become one of Ottoman Greece's first schools, the

---

NÁXOS MUSIC FESTIVAL

One of the highlights of Naxiot evenings is the Domus Festival of classical, jazz, choral, Byzantine and traditional music held at the Venetian Museum in either the garden or the basement, depending on the season and weather (ⓦ naxosfestival.com/naxos-domus-festival). Tickets should be booked in advance at the museum (☏ 22850 22387) and include a glass of local wine or *kítron*.

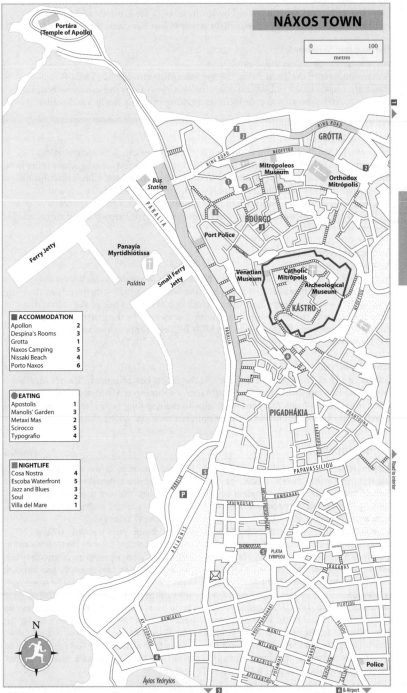

NÁXOS TOWN

Portára (Temple of Apollo)

0   100
metres

GRÓTTA

RING ROAD

NEOFYTOU

RING ROAD

Bus Station

Mitropoleos Museum

Orthodox Mitrópolis

PARALIA

BOÚRGO

Port Police

Ferry Jetty

Panayía Myrtidhiótissa

Palátia

Smaill Ferry Jetty

Venetian Museum

Catholic Mitrópolis

Archeological Museum

KÁSTRO

PARALIA

PIGADHÁKIA

FRANTOUNA

EKATODAPILIANI

PAPAVASSILIOU

PARALIA

P

ARIADNIS

SKHINOUSSAS

DAMBANAKI

IRAKLIDHON
PROTOPAPADHAKI

DHONOUSSAS

PLATIA EVRIPEOU

TRAGAÉAS

FILOTIOU

KOMIAKIS

AY. YORGOU

PROTOPAPADHAKI

MONIS

MELANON

SANGRIDHI

POTAMIAS

ENGAROU

FENDIOU

APEIRANTHOU

Police

N

Áyios Yeóryios

Road to interior

& Airport

ACCOMMODATION

Apollon	2
Despina's Rooms	3
Grotta	1
Naxos Camping	5
Nissaki Beach	4
Porto Naxos	6

EATING

Apostolis	1
Manolis' Garden	3
Metaxí Mas	2
Scirocco	5
Typografio	4

NIGHTLIFE

Cosa Nostra	4
Escoba Waterfront	5
Jazz and Blues	3
Soul	2
Villa del Mare	1

French Commercial School; opened by Jesuits in 1627 for Catholic and Orthodox students alike, its pupils included, briefly, writer Nikos Kazantzakis (see p.200 & p.557).

The Venetian Museum
Daily 10am–3pm & 7–10pm (to 11pm in July–Aug) • €3

A mansion next to the Traní Pórta, the **Venetian Museum** (Domus Della-Rocca-Barozzi), is open to the public and offers the best views from the kástro, with concerts (see box, p.164); the guided tour includes a tasting from the family's wine cellar.

The Archeological Museum
Tues–Sun 8.30am–2.30pm • €3

The French Commercial School building now houses an excellent **archeological museum**, which includes an important collection of Early Cycladic figurines (note how most of the throats were cut in some kind of ritual), Archaic and Classical sculpture, pottery dating from Neolithic to Roman times, as well as obsidian knives and spectacular gold rosettes. Sadly, labelling is mostly in Greek. On the terrace, a Hellenistic period mosaic floor shows a Nereid (sea nymph) astride a bull surrounded by deer and peacocks.

Mitropóleos Museum
Tues–Sun 8.30am–3pm • Free

In front of the Orthodox cathedral, the **Mitropóleos Museum** has walkways over a recently excavated tumulus cemetery from the Mycenaean era – thirteenth to eleventh century BC – with funerary remnants including a *hermax*, a pile of the stones that were traditionally thrown behind on leaving a cemetery. In the general area, items dating from the early Cycladic period (3200 BC) right through to late Roman (300 AD) have been found.

Town beaches
Grótta, just to the northeast of the town, is the easiest beach to reach. It's not ideal for swimming but snorkellers can see the remains of submerged Mycenaean buildings. The other town beach, **Áyios Yeóryios**, is an improvement: a long sandy bay fringed by the town's southern accommodation area, within ten minutes' walking distance from Platía Evripéous.

ACCOMMODATION   **NÁXOS**

Apollon Fontana ☎ 22850 22468, ⓦ apollonhotel -naxos.gr. Comfortable, modern doubles, all with balconies, in a quiet spot near the Mitropóleos Museum (see above) and convenient for the port, the nightlife and Grótta beach. Breakfast included. **€60**

Despina's Rooms Boúrgo ☎ 22850 22356. Hidden (but well signposted) beneath the castle; you'll need to climb some distance to reach it. The rooms are small but clean and airy, some with shared bathroom, and balconies with sea views. The owner organizes boat trips to the Lesser Cyclades. **€35**

★ **Grotta** Grótta ☎ 22850 22215, ⓦ hotelgrotta.gr. Welcoming hotel in a good location, with fabulous sunset views. Offers comfortable rooms, an indoor jacuzzi, a fantastic breakfast (included) with pies cooked fresh daily, free pickups plus free wi-fi and cable internet access. **€75**

Naxos Camping Áyios Yeóryios ☎ 22850 23500, ⓦ naxos-camping.gr. At the southern end of Áyios Yeóryios – but close to the highway – this is the cheapest option for those who want to combine the beach with nightlife. They also offer wooden cabins for two. June–Sept. Camping **€7**, cabins **€30**

Nissaki Beach Áyios Yeóryios ☎ 22850 25710, ⓦ nissaki-beach.com. One of the most luxurious options on the island, oozing minimalist but comfortable Cycladic elegance. If the palm trees around the pool area don't tempt you, then the boundless views to the Aegean surely will. Buffet breakfast included. April–Oct. **€240**

Porto Naxos Áyios Yeóryios ☎ 22850 25710, ⓦ porto -naxos.gr. If you have your own transport, this five-star hotel with parking space, a swimming pool and a tennis court by the Náxos circular road – but only 200m from the beach – is highly recommended. Breakfast included. April–Oct. **€90**

EATING

★ **Apostolis** Old Market, Hóra ☎ 22850 26777. Always busy, a sign of its regard in the town, with invariably excellent family dishes and grills (€8). Good selection of local wines. Beware its side salads (€5) – they are a meal in themselves. Daily noon–midnight.

Manolis' Garden Boúrgo ☎ 22850 25168. Popular taverna, located in a large yet cosy garden in the old town, with a small but well-considered menu (mains €8). Although not vegetarian it has many vegetable-only options. May–Oct daily 6pm–1am.

Metaxí Mas Boúrgo ☎ 22850 26425. Friendly ouzerí serving excellent, well-priced food (€7) on a little street heading up to the kástro. Service is friendly and unhurried,

and even the fussiest demands are met with a smile. April–Oct daily noon–midnight.

Scirocco Platía Evripéous ☎ 22850 25931, ⍟ scirocco -naxos.gr. Well-known restaurant popular with locals and tourists alike for its well-priced traditional dishes such as meatballs in tomato sauce (€7) – hence the occasional long queue to get in. Daily noon–midnight.

Typografio Hóra ☎ 22850 22375. Superb central location, delicious local cuisine and reasonable prices for a menu (mains €9) as imaginative as the wine list. This is the place to go for a romantic tête-à-tête (book in advance one of the tables with the best views in front). Daily 6pm–midnight.

NIGHTLIFE

Cosa Nostra Old Market. On a huge balcony above the harbourfront but entered from Old Market street, this bar plays funk/soul/rock and attracts a young clientele all year long. It's often difficult to find standing space, let alone a seat, after 11pm. Wide range of cocktails starting from €8. April–Oct daily 8pm–5am.

Escoba Waterfront ☎ 22850 23567. The best option in the cluster of bars and clubs in the southern waterfront, it serves large cocktails (€8), and is bigger than its neighbours, so there is less of a crush. Normally plays Latin music, but it has a popular rock night on Tuesdays. June–Sept daily 6pm–1am.

Jazz and Blues ☎ 694 47 01 215. A petite jazz bar, with the occasional live performance thrown in, tucked away on a street behind the port police. It has classy

drinks much cheaper (€5) than the rest of the surrounding bars. April–Oct daily 10am–2pm & 8.30pm–3am.

Soul Halfway up the road to Grótta, this is the town's biggest and most cavernous club, but also managing to contain intimate corners, nooks and crannies. It is frequented by a regular, mixed-age crowd dancing to European hits. Entrance €10 with a free first drink. June–Aug Fri & Sat midnight–6am.

Villa del Mare With a large terrace facing west, *Villa del Mare* opens just before the sunset and closes earlier than most, dumping its clientele in the bigger club, *Soul*, below. Good value cocktails at €7 and a relaxed pre-dinner atmosphere. June–Sept daily 8pm–3.30am.

3

Beaches

Lying just 4km from Náxos Town, **Áyios Prokópios** is a long line of sand dotted with lagoons that's regularly voted among Greece's top beaches. The village itself lies in the southern part of the main road and on the bus route, but the best and quieter part of the beach is closer to Náxos Town, at the base of the distinct double cone of Stelídha hill. Rapid development along the southwestern stretch means that Áyios Prokópios has blended into the next village, **Ayía Ánna**, further along the busy southern highway. Beyond the Ayía Ánna headland is 5km-long **Pláka beach**, a vegetation-fringed expanse of white sand accessed by a flat, unsurfaced road from the north where purely for convenience this part of the beach is called **Marágas**. Some parts of Pláka are naturist where shielded from the road by dunes, and at the southern end is **Orkós**, the playground of the young and intrepid with plenty of wind- and kitesurfers in high season. You'll find more windsurfers along the coastal stretch from Pláka through remote **Glyfádha** down to **Alykó** and nearby **Pyrgáki**, where the coastal road ends and the asphalted highway to Náxos begins. On the juniper-covered promontory by **Alykó** there is another nudist beach, known locally as **Hawaii** for the vibrant blue colour of its waters, while 4km beyond by unsurfaced road is the **Ayiassós** beach – this is where Marco Sanudo landed, in 1207 to conquer the island from the Byzantines and promptly burned his ships so that there could be no way back.

ACCOMMODATION

Finikas Pyrgáki ☎ 22850 75230, ⓦ hotelfinikas.gr. At the end of the coastal dirt road and away from it all, this is a fully self-sufficient hotel, offering everything from a restaurant and free wi-fi to a sauna and a gym. It also organizes watersports activities. Breakfast included. May–Sept. **€165**

Marágas Ayía Anna ☎ 22850 24552, ⓦ maragas camping.gr. A suitably laidback shaded campsite with a taverna, beach bar and watersports facilities. There is a regular bus service to Náxos. April–Oct. Camping **€7**, cabins **€45**

Naxos Imperial Resort and Spa Stelídha ☎ 22850 26620, ⓦ naxosimperial.com. The best deluxe hotel of many on the Stelídha peninsula, it is also close to the best section of Áyios Prokópios beach. There's volleyball, gym, spa, restaurant, bar and a pool. Breakfast included. May–Nov. **€160**

BEACHES

Orkos Beach Orkós ☎ 22850 75194, ⓦ orkosbeach .gr. Next to the Flisvos Kite Center, with a cool pool and even cooler customers. Its garden alone is perfect to laze in. Internet, wi-fi, parking and breakfast included. May–Oct. **€70**

Plaka Pláka ☎ 22850 42700, ⓦ plakacamping.gr. Near the beginning of the Cyclades' longest beach, this is the newest camping on Náxos with a swimming pool, restaurant and café. It is flanked by its imaginatively named Plaka I and Plaka II sister hotels (€45–60). Bus service to Náxos Town available. April–Oct. **€9**

Stella Ayía Anna ☎ 22850 42526, ⓦ stella-apartments -naxos.gr. Clean and close to the sea but not far from the village itself, these studios with kitchenette and bougainvillea-bursting balconies are possibly the best option south of Náxos Town. Wi-fi in the reception only. May–Oct. **€50**

EATING AND DRINKING

Gorgóna Ayía Anna ☎ 22850 41007. Cool, large, shaded, family-run beach bar that becomes a fish restaurant with reasonable prices (€10) in the evening and continues functioning as a late-night bar until the morning. Known locally for its delicious home-made *rizógalo*, a spiced rice pudding. Daily 8am–3am.

Mólos Áyios Prokópios ☎ 22850 26980. Fish taverna offering only fresh fish caught on the day and assorted seafood – which tends to be fried, however, rather than grilled. Occupying the best spot on the beach, it is unsurprisingly popular. Two deckchairs plus one umbrella €10. May–Oct daily 9am–1am.

Central Náxos

After its beaches, **Central Náxos** is the island's second unique selling point with lush green valleys, mountains, painfully picturesque villages, historic churches, old forts and Classical sites. Because of the sheer size of the island these are best enjoyed via two day-long drives: one short and one much longer. The short drive is Náxos–Galanádho–Sangrí–Halkí–Moní–Kinídharos–Flério–Náxos, while the longer drive is Náxos–Galanádho–Sangrí–Halkí–Filóti–Aperáthou–Apóllonas–Náxos via the northern coastal road.

Galanádho and Sangrí

From Náxos Town, head for the market village of **Galanádho** to reach the twin villages of **Sangrí**, on a vast plateau at the head of a long valley. On the way have a look at the domed eighth-century church of **Áyios Mámas**, neglected since the Ottoman conquest. Káto Sangrí has the ruins of a Venetian castle, while Áno Sangrí is an attractive little place, all cobbled streets and fragrant courtyards. It's also only about ninety minutes' walk to the Byzantine castle of **Apalírou**, at 474m, which held out for two months against the besieging Marco Sanudo. Its fortifications are relatively intact and the views magnificent. Thirty minutes' stroll away, on a path leading south out of the village, or 3km by surfaced lane, are the partially rebuilt remains of a **Classical temple of Demeter** (Tues–Sun 8.30am–3pm; free) from 530 BC, over which was constructed an early Christian basilica.

The Tragéa and Halkí

From Sangrí, the road twists northeast into the **Tragéa** region, scattered with olive trees and occupying a vast highland valley. The area is the only part of the Cyclades to have a regular winter snowfall, and the only part with traditional songs about snow. It's a good jumping-off point for all sorts of exploratory rambling. **Halkí**, 16km from Náxos Town, is a fine introduction of what is to come; set high up, it's a quiet town with some lovely churches, including the **Panayía Protóthronis** church (daily 10am–1pm; free), with its eleventh- to thirteenth-century frescoes. Just behind is the restored seventeenth-century Venetian **Grazia-Barozzi Tower**, and nearby is the distillery (1896) and shop of **Vallindras Naxos Citron**, whose charming proprietors explain the process of producing *kítron* followed by a little tasting session.

Moní, Kinídharos and Flério

Driving from Halkí to Moní you pass the sixth-century church of **Panayía Dhrosianí** (daily 11am–5pm; donation expected), historically the most important church on the island with some of the oldest frescoes in Greece. Moní itself, at an altitude of 550m, enjoys an outstanding view of the Tragéa and Mount Zas, and has numerous woodcarving workshops. From Moní you can loop back to Náxos Town, and the first village you encounter on the way is **Kinídharos**, with its marble quarries and daily folk evenings; it has a reputation of staging one of the best carnivals in the Cyclades. Five kilometres beyond is the village of **Flério**. Nearby is the most interesting of the ancient marble quarries of the seventh- to sixth-century BC on Náxos, home to two famous **koúroi**, left recumbent and unfinished; even so, they're finely detailed figures, over 5m in length. The Koúros Flerioú (Koúros Melánon), from around 570 BC, is a short walk along the stream valley; the Koúros Farangioú (Koúros Potamiás) is a steeper walk up the hillside. Both are well signposted.

Aperáthou and the south

At the far side of the gorgeous Tragéa valley, Filóti, the largest village in the region, lies on the northwestern slopes of Mount Zas, which at 1001m is the highest point in the Cyclades. **APERÁTHOU** (officially Apíranthos), 8km beyond Filóti, is hilly, winding and highly picturesque; it shows the most Cretan influence of all interior villages and gave Greece one of its prime ministers, **Petros Protopapadakis** (it's unfortunate that he was executed for high treason in 1922). Its location high in the mountains means it is noticeably cooler and greener than the coast. There are two Venetian fortified mansions, Bardáni and Zevgóli, and, amazingly, four small private museums: Natural History, Geological, Fine Arts and a Folklore museum (April–Oct daily 10.30am–2.30pm; 7.30pm June–July; 9pm Aug; €2 for all); as well as a state Archeological museum (Tues–Sun 8.30am–3pm; free). There is some good **shopping** in Aperáthou, as well: **Epilekton** in the main street is an excellent delicatessen with a selection of local cheeses, hot peppers and sun-dried aubergines.

A turning at the southern end of Filóti is signposted to the **Pýrgos Himárrou** (12.5km), a remote 20m-high Hellenistic watchtower – one of the tourist landmarks of the island – and onward (another 12km) to the deserted but excellent in all respects **Kalandó** beach on the south coast. Bring your own water and food supplies if you're planning to stop here.

CLIMBING MOUNT ZAS

If you are arriving by bus and intend to climb **Mount Zas** you should start from the steps opposite the taverna *Baboulas* at the main square. This is a round-trip walk of three to four hours on partly marked trails to the summit, a climb that rewards you with an astounding panorama of virtually the whole of Náxos and its Cycladic neighbours. The initial path out of the village climbs up to rejoin the road to Apóllonas. The final approach trail begins beside the small Ayía Marína chapel. You can return to Filóti via the trail to the 150m-deep Zas Cave, which is also accessed by a separate route through **Ariés**, ten minutes' drive from Filóti.

If you have your own transport, you can drive all the way to Ayía Marína and continue on from there.

EATING AND DRINKING

CENTRAL NÁXOS

Leftéris Aperáthou ☎ 22850 61333. A restaurant with an unmatched reputation on Náxos and, as a bonus, not as full as others closer to the main road, which are always busy. At the end of your meal (mains €13) try the home-made *glyká koutalioú*, stewed syrupy fruit which are so sweet that a few teaspoonfuls constitute a serving. April–Oct daily 10am–1am.

Panorama Moní ☎ 22850 31070. Small family restaurant with exceptional views. Whatever the dish of the day is (€6), order it; it will most likely involve some kind of meat, as this part of Náxos is famous for its tender beef and veal. Daily 11am–11pm.

Plátanos Aperáthou ☎ 22850 61192. Rare mountain decor, good balcony views and food standards to rival *Leftéris* (see above). This is one of those old-fashioned Greek restaurants where you can go in the kitchen to check what's available (mains €9) and whether you like the look of it. April–Oct daily 9am–11pm.

Yannis Halkí ☎ 22850 31214. A traditional grill, under a vine-covered roof, which is always busy with customers stopping at the nearby Vallindras distillery. Try the local mountain sausage in tomato sauce (€7) or order the locally sourced beefburger. Daily noon–midnight.

Northern Náxos

The route to **Northern Náxos** through the mountains from Aperáthou to Apóllonas is very scenic, and the road surface is in reasonable condition all the way. Jagged ranges and hairpin bends confront you after **Kóronos**, past **Skadhó**, to the remote emery-miners' village of **Koronídha** – the highest village on the island.

Apóllonas is a small resort with two good beaches: a tiny and crowded stretch of sand backed by a line of cafés and restaurants, and a longer and quieter stretch of shingle, where *Kouros Hotel* lies. The major attraction in Apóllonas is a 12m-long **koúros**, approached by a path from the main road just above the village. Lying *in situ* at a marble quarry, this is the largest of Náxos's abandoned stone figures, but less detailed than those at Flério. The return to Náxos Town is via the northern coastal road which is spectacularly beautiful, set high above the sea for most of the way.

ACCOMMODATION

NORTHERN NÁXOS

Kouros Apóllonas ☎ 22850 67000, ⊚ hotelkouros .blogspot.com. Relaxing, dreamy hotel standing alone in the middle of the shingle beach with spacious, quiet rooms and a well-stocked beach bar. Despite it being out of the way, it attracts a surprisingly young clientele. May–Sept. **€60**

Lesser Cyclades

Four of the six small islands in the patch of the Aegean between Náxos and Amorgós have slid from obscurity into fashion in recent years. Inhabited since prehistoric times, the group is known commonly as the **Lesser Cyclades** and includes **Irakliá**, **Skhinoússa**, **Áno Koufoníssi** and **Dhonoússa**. The islands' popularity has hastened the development of better facilities and higher prices, but, with only limited ferry services, they've managed to avoid mass tourism.

GETTING THERE

LESSER CYCLADES

By ferry Apart from slower direct connections to Pireás, the fast Blue Star ferries call at Náxos linking up with the smaller *Express Skopelitis* which serves the Lesser Cyclades and Amorgós.

Day-trip from Náxos A boat trip from Náxos takes in

Irakliá and Áno Koufonísi. If you stay in the latter, you can travel by boat for a swim to the uninhabited Káto Koufonísi, but not to Kéros which is out of bounds; the whole island is an archeological area (much like Delos) which is still being excavated.

INFORMATION

Health Note that there are no pharmacies on any island, but some drugs are dispensed from the rural GP practices.

In case of emergency there are speedboats on call 24/7, so make sure you have good travel insurance.

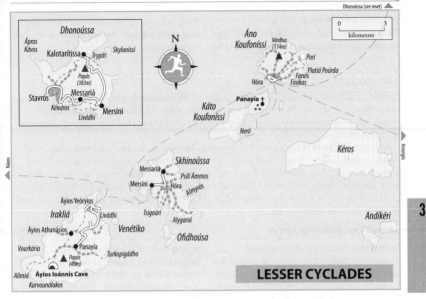

LESSER CYCLADES

Irakliá

Irakliá, the westernmost of the Lesser Cyclades, and with the least spoilt scenery, has just over 150 permanent residents. As the first stop on the ferry service from Náxos, the island is hardly undiscovered by tourists, but with fewer amenities than some of its neighbours, it retains the feel of a more secluded retreat.

The port of **Áyios Yeóryios** is a small but sprawling settlement behind a sandy tamarisk-backed beach that gets quite crowded in August. **Livádhi**, a big, shallow beach, is 2km southeast of the port and its crystal-clear waters are the main tourist attraction of the island. The asphalted road continues 3km on to the tiny capital **Panayía (Hóra)**, which has no lodgings to speak of. In season, a local boat sails from the port at 11am to make a tour of the island, stopping at the small sandy beach at **Alimiá** and the nearby pebble beach of **Karvounólakos**.

ARRIVAL AND INFORMATION   IRAKLIÁ

By ferry Ferries call at Áyios Yeóryios.
Destinations Áno Koufonísi (1–2 daily; 2hr); Amorgós (1–2 daily; 1hr 45min); Dhonoússa (1–2 daily; 3hr 30min); Náxos (1–2 daily; 1hr); Páros (2–4 weekly; 2hr 15min); Pireás (2–3 weekly; 7hr); Skhinoússa (2–3 daily; 15min); Sýros (2 weekly; 7hr 10min).

Services There are no banks in Irakliá, but there is an ATM at Áyios Yeóryios. The post office is a short distance above the *Perigiali* taverna (see p.172).
Travel agents Aegeon (☎ 22850 71561) should take care of all your travel and ticket needs.

ACCOMMODATION

Anna's ☎ 22850 74234. Family lodgings on the slope at the back of the village with great views offering rooms with own bathroom, plus some luxurious studios (€60) higher up the hill. Not all rooms have air conditioning, so check. **€35**

Iliovasílema ☎ 22850 71486, ⓦ sunset-iraklia.gr. Four very large apartments on top of a small hill 500m from the port and with magnificent sunset views, a/c, TV, fridge and WC; cooking facilities are shared. May–Sept. **€35**

EATING AND DRINKING

Maïstrali ☎ 22850 71807. The best place to eat on the island with a menu of seafood, goat stew – the Lesser

Cyclades' signature dish – and moussaka (€6). The veranda has a good view of the port below and there is free internet

available for clients. May–Sept daily 6pm–midnight.
Perigiali port ☎ 22850 71118. Small ouzerí with great fish and seafood meze platters (€15) caught daily by the

family boat; nice, cosy atmosphere with tables around a large central salt cedar tree and friendly service. Daily noon–midnight.

Skhinoússa

A little to the northeast of Irakliá, the island of **Skhinoússa** is just beginning to awaken to its tourist potential. Its indented outline, sweeping valleys and partly submerged headlands – such as the sinuous, snake-like islet Ofidhoúsa (Fidoú) – provide some of the most dramatic views in the group.

An asphalted road leads up from the port of **Mersíni** to the capital, **Hóra** (also called **Panayía**), for 1.2km. From Hóra you can reach no fewer than sixteen beaches dotted around the island, accessible by a network of dirt tracks. **Tsigoúri** is a ten-minute track walk downhill from northwest Hóra and gradually being developed. The locals' preferred choice of beaches are **Alygariá** to the south, **Psilí Ámmos** to the northeast, and **Almyrós**, half an hour southeast.

ARRIVAL AND INFORMATION · SKHINOÚSSA

By ferry Boats dock at the small port of Mersíni.
Destinations Amorgós (1–2 daily; 1hr 30min); Áno Koufonísi (6–8 weekly; 30min); Dhonoússa (1–2 daily; 3hr 40min); Irakliá (2–3 daily; 15min); Náxos (1–2 daily; 1hr 45min); Páros (4 weekly; 4hr 30min); Pireás (2–3

weekly; 7hr 45min); Sýros (3 weekly; 5hr).
Services There are no banks, but there is an ATM at Hóra, and four minimarkets, four bars and several tourist shops. There's also a post office and a Western Union branch at Hóra.

GETTING AROUND

There are no buses or taxis on the island; hotels will organize your transport to and from the port. There is also no car rental.

ACCOMMODATION AND EATING

Grispos Villas Tsigoúri ☎ 22850 71930, ⓦ grisposvillas .com. Perched above Tsigoúri beach at the northwest end, this complex offers everything – from rooms with continental breakfast to large studios with cooking facilities; they also sell ferry tickets in season. There's a half-board option for €14 per adult, €10 per child. **€60**

Iliovasilema ☎ 22850 71948, ⓦ iliovasilemahotel.gr. Well-priced friendly hotel, comfortable rather than luxurious, whose veranda bar enjoys spectacular views of the harbour. They operate a free shuttle to and from every beach for their customers. May–Oct. **€60**

Áno Koufoníssi

ÁNO KOUFONÍSSI (usually referred to simply as Koufoníssi) is the flattest, most developed and most densely inhabited island of the group. With some of the least-spoilt beaches in the Cyclades, the island is attracting increasing numbers of Greek and foreign holidaymakers and as it's small enough to walk round in a day, it can feel overcrowded in July and August. The best views are not of Koufoníssi itself, but out across the water to mountainous Kéros island.

The old pedestrian street of **HÓRA**, crossing a low hill behind the ferry harbour, has been engulfed by new room and hotel development, but the town still retains its affable, small-island atmosphere. All the good **beaches** are in the southeast of the island, improving as you go east along a road that skirts the gradually developing coastline along the edge of low cliffs. **Fínikas**, a fifteen-minute walk from town, is the first of four wide coves with gently shelving golden sand. The next beach, **Fanós**, is the youngsters' favourite, because of the beach bar that dominates the stretch of sand. Next is **Platiá Poúnda**, where caves have been hollowed out of the cliffs. Further east, the path rounds a rocky headland to **Porí**, a much longer and wilder beach, backed by dunes and set in a deep bay. It can be reached more easily from the town by following a dirt road heading inland through the scrub-covered hills.

ARRIVAL AND INFORMATION

By ferry Boats dock at the jetty below Hóra.

Destinations Amorgós (1–3 daily; 1hr); Dhonoússa (4–5 daily; 2hr 30min); Irakliá (2–4 daily; 45min); Mílos (1–2 weekly; 4hr 15min); Mýkonos (3 weekly; 2hr); Náxos (1–2 daily; 2hr 20min); Páros (4–5 weekly; 5hr); Pireás (6–8 weekly; 7–8hr); Skhinoússa (1–2 daily; 30min); Sýros

ÁNO KOUFONÍSSI

(3 weekly; 6hr).

Services There is a post office up a street by the *Hotel Roussetos*, with an ATM.

Travel agents The Koufonissia Tours ticket agency (☎ 22850 74091, ⓦ koufonissiatours.gr) is on the main pedestrian street.

ACCOMMODATION

Aeolos ☎ 22850 74206, ⓦ aeoloshotel.com. Modern, exceptionally well-designed hotel with a great pool overlooked by bougainvillea-draped balconies and large rooms in bright colour schemes. Free wi-fi and big breakfast buffet included. June–Sept. **€100**

Kéros Icons ☎ 22850 71600, ⓦ keroshotel.gr. Smart

hotel complex, technologically up to date with intelligent a/c, electronic card keys, memory mattresses and massage showers. Even if the cherry and ebony furniture doesn't satisfy your romantic streak, the rooms with four-poster beds will. Breakfast included. June–Oct. **€110**

EATING AND DRINKING

Capetan Nicolas ☎ 22850 71690. Cheaper than most, but still the best place to eat on the island. At the west of the bay, it offers a fine array of fresh, grilled seafood and home-made taramasalata that bears no resemblance to any supermarket varieties. May–Oct daily noon–late.

Remezzo ☎ 22850 74203. Family fish taverna above the ferry jetty with excellent food, not all seafood-based – try the chef's delicious savoury pastries (€6) – and a cosy atmosphere. The terrace tables have an incomparable view to Kato Koufoníssi. June –Sept daily noon–late.

Dhonoússa

Dhonoússa is a little out on a limb compared with the other Lesser Cyclades, and ferries call less frequently. Island life centres on the pleasant port settlement of **Stavrós**, spread out behind the harbour and the village beach. Most sunbathers head for **Kéndros**, a long and attractive stretch of shadeless sand twenty minutes over the ridge to the east; a World War II wreck can be easily spotted by snorkellers. The village of **Mersíni** is an hour's walk from Stavrós, while a nearby path leads down to **Livádhi**, an idyllic white-sand beach with tamarisks for shade. In high season a beach-boat runs from the port to all beaches, many of which are nudist; the locals don't seem to mind.

ARRIVAL AND DEPARTURE

By ferry Ferries dock at Stavrós.

Destinations Amorgós (1–2 daily; 1hr); Áno Koufoníssi (2–4 weekly; 1–3hr); Irakliá (1–2 daily; 3hr); Náxos (1–2

DHONOÚSSA

daily; 1hr 10min–5hr); Páros (4–5 weekly; 2hr 30min–5hr); Pireás (4 weekly; 7hr); Skhinoússa (1–2 daily; 30min); Sýros (3 weekly; 6hr).

ACCOMMODATION AND EATING

Chrýssa ☎ 22850 51575, ⓦ donoussarooms.gr. Set back from Stavrós, a pension with basic but large rooms and balconies overlooking the port. Every room has its own kitchenette and cooking implements but not all have a/c. May–Oct. **€45**

Corona Borealis Beach bar that slowly becomes the soul of the party in Stavrós playing alternative indie rock until the early hours. Young clientele, because, well, there are not many other places to go. June–Sept daily 10am–3am.

Amorgós

AMORGÓS, with its dramatic mountain scenery and laidback atmosphere, is attracting visitors in increasing numbers. The island can get extremely crowded in midsummer, the numbers swollen by film buffs paying their respects to the film location of Luc Besson's *The Big Blue*, although fewer venture out to Líveros at the island's western end to see the wreck of the *Olympia* which figures so prominently in the film. In general it's a low-key, escapist clientele, happy to have found a relatively large, interesting, uncommercialized and hospitable island with excellent walking. Families tend to stay around Katápola, while younger tourists prefer Aigiáli.

This is the island to try *rakómelo* – a kind of fermented grappa with honey, herbs and spices, drunk in shots as an aperitif.

ARRIVAL AND DEPARTURE   AMORGÓS

Most ferries and catamarans call either to Katápola in the southwest or Aigiáli in the north, while some dock at both. Be aware that it is those destinations, rather than "Amorgós", that are named on ferry schedules. There are more onward connections from Katápola than Aigiáli.

KATÁPOLA

By ferry The ferries stop at the town jetty; some continue on to Aigiáli (15min).

Destinations Áno Koufoníssi (1–2 daily; 40min); Dhonoússa (3–4 weekly; 1hr 30min); Irakliá (1–2 daily; 1hr 50min); Folégandhros (6–7 weekly; 2hr 30min); Íos (1 weekly; 5hr 20min); Kos (1 weekly; 5hr); Léros (1 weekly; 3hr 20min); Mílos (0–3 weekly; 3hr 30min); Mýkonos (0–3 weekly; 2hr 20min); Náxos (1–2 daily; 3hr); Páros (4–5 weekly; 4hr 15min); Pátmos (0–1 weekly; 2hr); Pireás (1–2 daily; 9hr); Rhodes (1 weekly; 8hr); Skhinoússa (5–6

weekly; 1hr 25min); Sýros (3 weekly; 7hr).

AIGIÁLI

By ferry Ferries stop at the town jetty; some continue on to Katápola (15min).

Destinations Áno Koufoníssi (4–5 weekly; 25min); Astypálea (4 weekly; 1hr 30min); Dhonoússa (1–2 daily; 50min); Irakliá (1 daily; 2hr 45min); Náxos (1–2 daily; 3–4hr); Páros (4–5 weekly; 4hr 30min); Pireás (4 weekly; 6hr); Skhinoússa (5 weekly; 2hr 20min); Sýros (2 weekly; 7hr 30min).

INFORMATION

Services Internet is available at the Teloneio rock café in Katápola.The island's main post office is in the upper square in Hóra. There's no bank in Aigiáli, but you'll find an ATM near the ferry dock.

Travel agents Prekas (☎ 22850 71256) in Katápola,

just along from the ferry dock, is the one-stop boat-ticket agency (as well as an ouzerí). Aegialis Tours (☎ 22850 73393, ⓦ www.aegialistours.com) in Aigiáli can help you with tickets, transfers, car rental and accommodation.

GETTING AROUND

By bus A bus shuttles between Katápola and Hóra, the island capital; several times daily it continues to Ayía Ánna

via Hozoviótissas monastery, and 2–7 times weekly (9.45am) out to the "Káto Meriá", made up of the hamlets

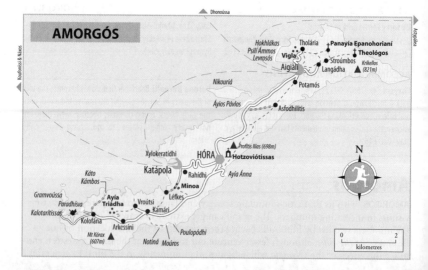

of Kamári-Vroútsi, Arkessíni and Kolofána. From Aigiáli there is a bus service up to Langádha and Tholária, the two villages east of and 200m above Aigiáli bay, with 3–8 departures daily up and down (a timetable is posted by the harbour bus stop).

By boat There's a *kaïki* service from Katápola to the nearby beaches at Maltézi and Plákes (€3 return) and a daily

excursion *kaïki* to the islet of Gramvoússa off the western end of Amorgós (€8 return).

By car and motorcyle There are several car/bike-rental outfits, but the one that has been around the longest is Thomas (☎ 22850 71777, ✆ thomas-rental.gr) in Katápola. In Aigiáli, Aegialis Tours (see opposite) can help; Thomas Rental also has a branch here (☎ 22850 73444, ✆ thomas-rental.gr).

Katápola and around

KATÁPOLA, set at the head of a deep inlet, is actually three separate villages: **Katápola** proper on the south side, **Xylokeratídhi** on the north shore, and **Rahídhi** on the central ridge. There is a beach in front of Rahídhi, but Káto Krotíri beach to the west of Katápola is better, though not up to the standards of Aigiáli in the northeast.

ACCOMMODATION   KATÁPOLA AND AROUND

Anna Studios ☎ 22850 71218, ✆ studioanna -amorgos.com. Well signed and difficult to miss because of its height, this hospitable *pension* with a garden setting has some very good views to the sea from the top floors. Laptops with internet connections available. **€45**

Camping Kastanis ☎ 22850 71012, ✆ kastanis.com .gr. 1km up towards Hóra this is a fully modern, shaded campsite with free wi-fi, offering a scale of accommodation that includes studios with their own WC, kitchenette and balcony with sea views. Camping **€8**, studio **€35**

Minoa-Landéris ☎ 22850 71480, ✆ hotelminoa.gr. Twin neighbouring two-star hotels in the waterfront square under the same management with smart, comfortable and contemporary rooms, as well as internet access. *Minoa* is the older, traditional one, *Landéris* the modern one (built 2006). **€55**

Sofia ☎ 22850 71493, ✆ pensionsofia.gr. Super little pension in the east of Katápola with large, bright rooms; the ones on the top floor have balconies with views while those on the ground floor have individual garden yards. Free wi-fi. **€40**

EATING AND DRINKING

Mourayio Katápola ☎ 22850 71518. The most popular taverna in town, cooking a wide range of seafood including a good fish soup, cheap lobster and marinated octopus (€12), all worth the wait while you sample the waterfront views. April–Oct daily noon–late.

Vitzentzos Xylokeratídhi ☎ 22850 71011. Traditional Amorgós dishes that include island goat in the oven with potatoes and a range of vegetable dishes cooked in oil and tomato sauce (€6). Daily noon–midnight.

NIGHTLIFE

Teloneio Café Bar ☎ 22850 71721. A loud, youthful alternative rock café on the main town drag with live DJ, this is the life and soul of Katápola. Atmospheric interior

with local quarried stone if it's too windy, and tables outside for those with a low decibel threshold. Daily 11am–late.

Hóra and around

HÓRA is one of the better-preserved settlements in the Cyclades, with a scattering of tourist shops, cafés, tavernas and rooms. Dominated by an upright volcanic rock plug, wrapped with a chapel or two, the thirteenth-century Venetian fortifications look down on nearly thirty other churches, some domed, and a line of decapitated windmills beyond. The nearest beach at **Ayía Ánna** is small but more than adequate. If you skip the first tiny coves, where the car park is larger than the sand, the path will take you to the nudist bay of Kambí; bring food and water for the day. For alternatives to Ayía Ánna, head west to **Kamári** and down to the adjacent beaches of **Notiná**, **Moúros** and **Poulopódhi**, all of them clean, crystal clear and calm.

Three kilometres further west of Kamári is **Kolofána**. From here the surfaced road leads towards the far western tip of the island, branching north to Ayía Paraskeví above **Paradhísia beach** (20km from Hóra), or 3km further west to spectacular **Kalotarítissas Bay**, its tiny fishing jetty and small sand and pebble beach partly enclosed and sheltered by a rocky headland and the islet of **Gramvoússa**. About 1.8km before Kalotarítissas, the **wreck of the Olympia** is visible down to the right, in **Líveros Bay**.

Monastery of Hotzoviótissas

Daily 8.30am–1pm & 5–7pm • Donation expected

The spectacular **Monastery of Hotzoviótissas**, gleaming white at the base of a towering, vertical orange cliff, can be reached by bus or on foot from a wide cobbled 8km-path by the upper telecoms tower. Modest dress is required; the sign advises that trousers are not suitable for women, but you will find that most female Greek visitors wear them. Only a handful of monks occupy the fifty rooms now, but they are quite welcoming considering the crowds who file through; you can see the miraculous icon around which the monastery was founded, along with other treasures. Tradition has it that between the ninth and eleventh centuries AD, a precious icon of the Virgin was brought here by beleaguered monks from the monastery of **Khotziba** in Palestine, who settled here to escape Arab raids. Sitting and admiring the view from the *katholikón*'s terrace while being treated to a shot of *rakómelo* and a sweet by the monks is one of the highlights of visiting Amorgós.

ACCOMMODATION AND EATING

HÓRA AND AROUND

Liotrivi ☎ 22850 71700. With a roof terrace facing the kástro, this taverna, down the steps from the bus stop, is where you should try the local casseroles such as veal with aubergines (€8) or lamb pie. Its home-made *rakómelo* makes it the most popular in Hóra. May–Oct daily noon–midnight.

Panorama ☎ 22850 74016, ⊕ panorama-studios .amorgos.net. Rooms and studios in two different sites in Hóra, large and comfortable with fitted and kitted kitchens; some have balconies with western views towards the kástro. **€50**

Aigiáli and around

The road from Hóra to **Aigiáli (Eyiáli)**, 15km away, is one of the most impressive in the Cyclades, overlooking several beautiful small coves. The town itself is smaller and more picturesque than Katápola, and so tends to be more popular. The main Aigiáli beach is more than satisfactory, getting better and better as you stroll further north. A trail here leads over various headlands to three bays: **Levrosós**, which is sandy and nudist (20min walk), **Psilí Ámmos** (30min walk), which is mixed sand and gravel, and **Hokhlákas** (20min) where naturism is also tolerated; there are no facilities here so bring along what you need. The best of all beaches north, however, is **Áyios Pávlos**, 5km away, reachable by bus.

ACCOMMODATION

AIGIÁLI AND AROUND

★ **Aegialis** ☎ 22850 73393, ⊕ amorgos-aegialis.com. High on the hillside on the far side of the bay, this is the largest hotel on the island with an Olympic-size pool, spa with thalassotherapy treatments, using salt water and natural marine products, sauna, jacuzzi, gym and a superb restaurant (mains €15). **€130**

Aegiali Camping ☎ 22850 73500, ⊕ aegialicamping.gr. Usually busier than the one in Katápola but not necessarily better, this is a huge, tree-covered campsite with spots to suit everybody, 100m from the beach on the road to Tholária.

A WALK INLAND

Climb up the well-made cobblestone path that starts by the tiny cave-church of Ayía Triádha in Aigiáli to reach the picturesque village of **Langádha** about 200m above. Beyond Langádha, turn left off the main onward path towards the pretty, monastery-like Panayía Epanohorianí, then continue around the hillside to **Tholária**, named after vaulted Roman tombs. They were found around Vígla, the site of ancient Aegiale, on a hill opposite the village, where you can still see the bases of statues and traces of city walls incorporated into later terracing. A descending cobblestone path from the village car park towards Aigiáli goes back to the end of the town beach. The whole walk should take 2–3 hours.

Free wi-fi in the restaurant next door. April–Oct. **€9.50**

Karkisia 🕿 22850 73180, 🖳 karkisia-hotel.gr. Well-priced option that's very comfortable and easy on the eye, near the Aigiáli beach over which all studio balconies have views. Every double room has a sofabed that can be used to sleep a third person at no extra cost. Breakfast buffet €5 per

person. April–Oct. **€40**

Pension Christina 🕿 22850 73236, 🖳 christina-pension.amorgos.net. A family pension 200m from Aigiáli beach offering bright, cheerfully painted rooms and simple furnishings, as well as studios with fully equipped kitchens. April–Oct. **€45**

EATING AND DRINKING

Barba Yánnis Áyios Pávlos 🕿 22850 73011. Fish taverna on the beach offering generous portions of salads and seafood spaghetti as well as at least one meat or vegetable

casserole as a dish of the day. The owner bakes his own bread in a traditional wood-fired oven. June–Sept daily noon–9pm.

Íos

Though not terribly different – geographically or architecturally – from its immediate neighbours, no other Greek island attracts the same vast crowds of young people as **Íos**. Although it has worked hard to shake off its late-twentieth-century reputation for alcohol excesses and to move the island's tourism one class up with some success, Íos is still extremely popular with the young backpacker set who take over the island in July and August.

The only real villages – **Yialós** (for families), **Hóra** and **Mylopótas** (for the 18–25s) – are clustered in a western corner of the island, and development elsewhere is restricted by poor roads. As a result there are still some very quiet beaches with just a few rooms to rent. Most visitors stay along the arc delineated by the port – at Yialós, where you'll arrive, in Hóra above it, or by the beach at Mylopótas. Despite its past popularity, sleeping on the beach on Íos is strictly banned these days and so is nudism.

ARRIVAL AND DEPARTURE   ÍOS

By ferry Ferries dock in Yialós, an easy 20min trek from the capital, Hóra.

Destinations Amorgós (1 weekly; 3hr); Anáfi (1–2 weekly; 4hr); Folégandhros (4–6 weekly; 1hr); Kéa/Lávrio (1 weekly; 11–12hr); Kímolos (3–4 weekly; 3hr); Kýthnos (1–2 weekly; 8hr 30min); Mílos (3 weekly; 4hr); Mýkonos

(1–2 daily; 1hr 40min); Náxos (4–5 weekly; 45min–3hr); Páros (2–4 weekly; 5hr); Pireás (1–2 daily; 3hr 20min); Rafína (1 weekly; 4hr); Santoríni (2–3 daily; 1hr 30min); Sérifos (1 weekly; 6hr 30min); Sífnos (3 weekly; 3hr 30min–5hr 30min); Síkinos (1–2 daily; 20min); Sýros (3–5 weekly; 5hr 30min); Tínos (5 weekly; 2hr).

INFORMATION AND TOURS

Tourist office The unofficial tourist information office is Aktaion right in the middle of the port (daily 9am–2pm & 5–9pm), which also has a branch in Hóra.

Services An ATM is near the quay. The post office is in the new town of Hóra, a block behind the town hall.

Travel agents Aktaion Travel (🕿 22860 91343) has a

branch (closed 2–5pm) in the main church square in Yialós.

Tours For a quick escape from the packed beaches at the height of the season, try one of the daily excursions around quieter nearby beaches on the wooden Leigh Browne sailing vessel moored in the harbour (€25), available on demand.

GETTING AROUND

By bus Buses constantly shuttle between Yialós, Hóra and Mylopótas (every 20–30min 8am–midnight). There are occasional public and private buses running to the beaches at Manganári and Ayía Theodhóti; they sell return tickets only and are quite pricey (€6).

By boat From Yialós, daily boats depart at around 10am (returning in the late afternoon; €12 return) to the beaches

on the south coast

By car and motorcycle Hiring cars is not as necessary as on other islands; the main strip, Yialós to Mylopótas, is walkable and a very nice stroll. To rent your own transport in Hóra try Vangelis Bike Rental (🕿 22860 91919) or Jacob's Car & Bike Rental (🕿 22860 91700, 🖳 jacobs-los.gr) in Yialós.

Hóra and around

HÓRA (also called Íos Town) is a twenty-minute walk up behind Yialós port, and is one of the more accessible picturesque towns in the Cyclades, filled with meandering arcaded lanes and whitewashed chapels. Still, it gets pretty raunchy when the younger crowd moves in for the high season, and the laddish logos and inscriptions available on T-shirts and at tattoo parlours clash with its superior aspirations. The main road divides it naturally into two parts: the old town climbing the hillside to the left as you arrive, and the newer development to the right. The **archeological museum** (Tues–Sun 8.30am–3pm; free), in the yellow town hall, is part of an attempt to attract a more diverse range of visitors to the island. It contains some interesting finds from ancient **Skárkos**, a few kilometres inland from Yialós.

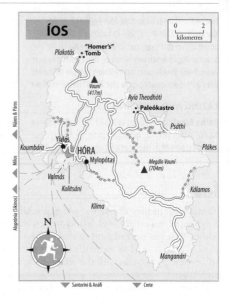

Yialós – with its surprisingly peaceful and uncrowded beach – isn't in the same league as Hóra above, but it provides a refreshing, breezy escape from the hot, noisy capital. Alternatively there's the popular **Mylopótas**, the site of a magnificent beach, lots of water activity outlets and surprisingly little nightlife.

ACTIVITIES
HÓRA AND AROUND

Meltemi Watersports ☎ 693 21 53 912, ⓦ meltemi watersports.com. Outlets on Mylopótas and Manganári beaches, offering waterskiing, windsurfing and wakeboarding lessons. They also hire out canoes, pedaloes, snorkelling equipment and sailboats.

ACCOMMODATION

HÓRA

★ **Francesco's** ☎ 22860 91223, ⓦ francescos.net. An excellent hostel made up mostly with super-clean doubles (€40) and relatively few dorm beds. With free pickups and wi-fi, a bar, a pool and jacuzzi plus spectacular views over the port, it offers the best value for money on the island. May–Sept. **€17**

Lofos new quarter ☎ 22860 91481. Right up from the archeological site, this family-owned, shaded room complex, with simple but well-furnished rooms, is very convenient for access both to the bus stop and Hóra's nightlife opposite. Best of all, for something so close to the action, it's quiet. May–Oct. **€40**

Lofos Village new quarter ☎ 22860 92481, ✉ lofosvillagehotel@yahoo.com. A luxurious set of modern villas further up the hill with panoramic views over Hóra from its common swimming pool. Currency exchange, free port transfers, jacuzzi and parking are some of the many facilities on offer. May–Oct. **€80**

YIALÓS

Brothers' Hotel ☎ 22860 91508, ⓦ brothershotel .com. A relaxed family-friendly option set far back from the beach with spacious rooms, studios and a pool; it is co-managed by a Geordie lady who has made her Shirley Valentine dream come true. Free wi-fi. April–Oct. **€70**

Galini Rooms ☎ 22860 91115, ⓦ galini-ios.com. A good, quiet choice, in a rural setting just over 200m down the lane by the centre of the beach; relaxing in the well-tended large garden is as big a delight as lying on the beach. April–Oct. **€70**

Golden Sun ☎ 22860 91110, ⓦ www.iosgoldensun .com. Family-owned hotel about 300m up the road to Hóra with meticulously clean, brightly painted rooms offering nice views over the bay and large, well thought-out common areas around a swimming pool. Mid-May to Sept. **€60**

Yialós Beach ☎ 22860 91421, ⓦ yialosbeach.gr. Stylish hotel, just behind the hospital, offering smart doubles and studios with their own private gardens, built around a large pool with a children's pool nearby. Minimum two nights stay in high season. May–Oct. **€65**

MYLOPÓTAS

Dionysos ☎ 22860 91215, ⓦ dionysos-ios.gr. Both attractive and luxurious, with buildings arranged around a swimming pool, this complex has rooms rather on the small side, but it comes up trumps on location and services offered including free wi-fi, children's pool, a fitness studio and tennis courts. May–Oct. **€120**

Far Out Beach Club ☎ 22860 91468, ⓦ faroutclub .com. Large campsite with well-organized facilities, including a pool, laundry, internet, bungalows and a good-value cafeteria. However, it can get very noisy and crowded in August. May–Sept. Camping **€9**, dorm **€18**, bungalow **€50**

Íos Palace ☎ 22860 92000, ⓦ iospalacehotel.com. Luxury hotel that has appropriated part of the beach with its own deckchairs (free to residents). Despite its opulent looks, this is a place for all budgets offering a range of differently priced rooms from basic and undersized, to massive suites with their own balcony pool. May–Oct. **€90**

Purple Pig (ex-Stars) ☎ 22860 91302, ⓦ purple pigstars.com. A friendly, laidback hostel and camping complex by the road up to Hóra, with a range of facilities, including its own club, minimarket, pool and poolside bar. It offers film shows, twice-weekly live music and watersports rental. Call to check the latest rates.

EATING

HÓRA

Lord Byron ☎ 22860 92125. A *mezedhopolío* off the main square that tries hard to re-create a traditional atmosphere, with old rembétika music, a good, Greek menu (mains €12) and a well-chosen Santoríni wine list. Extremely popular, so make a booking or come early. Daily 6pm–1am.

★ **The Nest** Old Town ☎ 22860 91778. Signposted from everywhere in Hóra, this is where the locals go to eat and you will soon find out why: from the moment you sit down the service and sociability are exceptional. Try the *yiuvétsi* (veal baked in pasta), a snip at €7. April–Oct daily noon–1am.

YIALÓS

Octopus Tree ☎ 697 27 54 365. A warm, intimate space a bit out of the way by the fishing boats on the Yialós waterfront, which serves fresh seafood caught by the owner. With mains starting at €12 it is not exactly cheap but you pay for the freshness. Daily 9am–3pm & 7pm–1am.

MYLOPÓTAS

Drákos ☎ 22860 91281. Right at the water's edge, this is the best fish taverna on Mylopótas offering mostly fried seafood dishes (€10). If you want to challenge your tastebuds, try its cod in garlic sauce, which is thankfully based mostly on mashed potato. May–Sept daily noon–2am.

Mários ☎ 22860 91130. Perched alone on a curve on the road to Hóra at the top of the steps to the beach, this chalet-like restaurant has spectacular views, excellent service and enormous pizzas for €9. Daily noon–midnight.

NIGHTLIFE AND ENTERTAINMENT

Every evening during the summer, Hóra is the centre of the island's nightlife, its streets throbbing with music from ranks of competing discos and clubs – mostly free, or with a nominal entrance charge, and inexpensive drinks. Most of the smaller bars and pubs are tucked into the narrow streets of the old village on the hill, offering something for everyone, and you'll have no trouble finding them.

CLUBS

Fun Pub Old Hóra ⓦ funpubios.com. An early starter and late finisher, this is a lively, Irish-themed and Irish-owned pub in the narrow backstreets of Hóra. From karaoke, quiz nights and internet to free films and a pool table, you can come here seven nights a week and still be entertained. April–Oct daily 6pm–3am.

Íos Club ⓦ iosclub.gr. In the same spot since 1969, this snack bar at the top of the stairs leading to Yialós starts off the evening with classical music while the clients sit back and enjoy the sweeping sunset views over Yialós. May–Sept daily 6pm–late.

Skorpion Cavernous club on the road to Mylopótas, with an excellent sound and lighting system; its frenetic atmosphere is up there with the best on Mýkonos. This is where everyone ends up when the clubs in Hóra close, so large queues start forming around 3am. €10 with first drink. June–Sept daily midnight–8am.

THEATRE

Odysséas Elýtis ⓦ los.gr. An outdoor theatre behind the windmills provides a beautiful setting in which to enjoy concerts and plays (July & Aug).

Beaches

The best beach on the Yialós side is **Koumbára**, a twenty-minute stroll over the headland, where the scenery is rockier and more remote. There is also a smaller beach

> ### HOMER'S TOMB
>
> **Homer's tomb** can be reached by car or motorbike (signposted from the road to Ayía Theodhóti, 4.5km from Hóra). An ancient town has long since slipped down the side of the cliff, but the rocky ruins of the entrance to a tomb remain, as well as some graves. There is certainly an ancient tradition, from Pausanias and Pliny, that Homer was buried on the island; furthermore, Hellenistic coins from Íos bear his name and his head. However, it was Dutch archeologist Pasch van Krienen who first discovered these tombs in 1771 and immediately claimed one of them as Homer's – in reality, though, it probably dates only to the Byzantine era.

further on with a cove backed by extraordinary green cliffs and a rocky islet to explore. Its western-facing setting and string of palm trees makes it ideal to watch the sunset, and attracts many amateur photographers.

On the south coast, there's a superb beach at **Manganári** easily reached by boat or bus (see p.177). Another decent beach is at **Kálamos**: get off the Manganári bus at the turning for Kálamos, which leaves you with a 4km walk, else take a *kaïki* from Yialós. There's more to see, and a better atmosphere, at **Ayía Theodhóti** up on the east coast. You can get there on a paved road across the island – the daily excursion bus costs €6 return. A couple of kilometres south of Ayía Theodhóti is **Paleókastro**, a ruined Venetian castle which encompasses the remains of a marble-finished town and a Byzantine church.

In the unlikely event that the beach is too crowded, try the one at **Psáthi**, 14km to the southeast, although you may need your own transport.

EATING   BEACHES

KUMBÁRA

Polídoros ☎ 22860 92072. This grill taverna is one of the better places to eat on Íos offering coal-grilled meats and local specialities such as pork with celery casserole (€12). Unfortunately, it has a very short opening season. Mid-June to mid-Sept daily noon–10pm.

AYÍA THEODHÓTI

Koukos ☎ 22860 92420. A very good family restaurant, rated highly by the locals, because it offers produce such as honey, milk products, eggs and chickens from its own farm next door (mains €8). Accompanied by bread baked in a wood-fired oven, organic food never tasted so good. May–Sept daily noon–8pm.

Síkinos

SÍKINOS has so small a population – around 240 – that the mule ride or walk from the port up to the capital was only replaced by a bus in the late 1980s. At roughly the same time the new jetty was completed; until then Síkinos was the last major Greek island where ferry passengers were still taken ashore in launches. With no dramatic characteristics and no nightlife to speak of, few foreigners make the short trip over here from neighbouring Folégandhros or Íos. The end result, however, is the most unspoilt rural countryside in the Cyclades where the clichéd image of a priest riding a donkey can suddenly materialize from over a hill.

ARRIVAL AND INFORMATION   SÍKINOS

By ferry Ferries dock at the far end of the port of Aloprónia. There are fewer connection options than in many of the neighbouring islands.
Destinations Anáfi (2–4 weekly; 3hr); Folégandhros (6–8 weekly; 40min); Íos (4–6 weekly; 30min); Kéa/Kýthnos/Lávrio (1 weekly; 8–12hr); Kímolos (1–2 weekly; 2hr); Kýthnos (2 weekly; 7hr 30min); Mílos (3 weekly; 3hr);

Mýkonos (2 weekly; 5hr 30min); Náxos (3–5 weekly; 2hr 30min); Páros (3–6 weekly; 3hr); Pireás (2–3 weekly; 6–7hr); Santoríni (5–7 weekly; 2hr); Sífnos (2 weekly; 2hr 30min); Sýros (3–5 weekly; 4–7hr).
Services There is a bank with an ATM in Kástro, while the post office is at the entrance to Kástro.

SÍKINOS & FOLÉGANDHROS

GETTING AROUND

By bus There is a single island bus, which shuttles in the high season regularly (4–8 daily; 7.15am–11.45pm) between the harbour and Hóra. Note that the bus changes to a normal four-seater car out of season.

By car and motorcycle The island's only rental office is at the Eko petrol station 50m back from Aloprónia; it mostly rents scooters.

Aloprónia

Such tourist facilities that exist are concentrated in the little harbour of **Aloprónia**, with its crystal-clear water, sandy beach, breakwaters and jetty. Many of the few dozen houses around the bay are summer holiday homes owned by expat Sikiniots now resident in Athens or beyond.

ACCOMMODATION AND EATING   ALOPRÓNIA

Lucas ☎ 22860 51076, ⓦ sikinoslucas.gr. Family studios at the water's edge on the opposite side of the bay, as well as rooms and studios among a cluster of buildings at the back of the village, 700m from the harbour along the road to Hóra. The family also operate a taverna which in May and June is your only eating option in the port (mains €10). April–Oct. €50

Maïstrali 22860 51087, ⓦ maistrali-sikinos.gr. Modern hotel behind the lighthouse, unimaginatively built like a square, urban two-storey house, but offering large, well-furnished rooms with the best views over the port. April–Oct. €80

★ **Porto Sikinos** ☎ 22860 51220, ⓦ portosikinos.gr. The place to stay in Aloprónia, a pricey option but on the swish side, offering free wi-fi, fridge, TV, a/c, island furnishings and everything else you might require for a restful stay. May–Sept. €95

Hóra

HÓRA consists of the double village of **Kástro** and **Horió**. As you slowly drive or walk up from Aloprónia, the scenery turns out to be less desolate than initial views from the ferry suggest, while the village itself, draped across a ridge overlooking the sea, is a delightfully unspoilt settlement. Most of the facilities are in the larger, northeastern Kástro, whereas Horió is mainly residential. A partly ruined fortress-monastery,

Zoödhóhou Piyís ("Life-giving Fountain"), crowns the cliff-edged hill above, and is accessed by a stepped path out of the top of Kástro. The architectural highlight of the village is the **kástro** itself, a quadrangle of eighteenth-century mansions arrayed defensively around the blue-domed church of **Panayía Pantánassa** which opens for evensong at around 6pm. Although tourists don't tend to stay here, eating options cater for the locals and are surprisingly varied and better than in Aloprónia.

EATING AND DRINKING   HÓRA

★ **Anémelo** ☎ 22860 51216. A friendly café-bar with the only shade in town; it has only a few tables outside, but you can share a table with strangers. Good cup of coffee and a snack menu from omelettes (€5) to home-made syrupy desserts. May–Oct daily 10am–midnight.

To Stéki tou Garbí ☎ 22860 51215. Unpretentious and cheap with a first-class selection of traditional Greek island cooking (€6), along with its own barrel wine, which is still made in the same traditional way for generations. March–Nov daily noon–midnight.

Around the island

Ninety minutes' walk northeast from Hóra lies **Paleókastro**, the patchy remains of an ancient fortress. In the opposite direction, another ninety-minute walk takes you by an old path or higher road through a steeply terraced landscape to **Episkopí**, where elements of an ancient temple-tomb have been incorporated into a seventh-century church – the structure is known formally as the **Héroön**, though it is now thought to have been a Roman mausoleum rather than a temple of Hera. Note the weathered wooden door, and the cistern under long stone slabs in the courtyard.

The beaches of **Dhialiskári** and **Áyios Yeóryios** are reachable by road – though only the latter is asphalted – while **Málta** is only reachable by *kaïki* from Aloprónia. A more feasible journey by foot is to the pebble beach at **Áyios Pandeleïmonas**: just under an hour's trail walk southwest of Aloprónia, it is the most sheltered on the island, and is also served by a small boat in season.

Folégandhros

The sheer cliffs of **FOLÉGANDHROS** rise 300m from the sea in places, and until the early 1980s they were as effective a deterrent to tourists as they had historically been to pirates. Folégandhros was used now and then as an island of political exile from Roman times right up until 1969, and life in the high, barren interior was only eased in 1974 by the arrival of electricity and the subsequent construction of a road running from the harbour to Hóra and beyond. Development has been given further impetus by the recent increase in tourism and the ensuing commercialization. The island is becoming so trendy that Greek journalists speak of a new Mýkonos in the making, a fact that is reflected in its swish jewellery and clothes shops. Yet away from showcase Hóra and the beaches, the countryside remains mostly pristine. Donkeys are also still very much in evidence, since the terrain on much of the island is too steep for vehicles.

ARRIVAL AND INFORMATION   FOLÉGANDHROS

By ferry The recent popularity of Folégandhros has resulted in a slew of new ferry routes to almost every other port in the Cyclades. Ferries dock at Karavostási.

Destinations Amorgós (1–2 weekly; 2hr 15min–4hr); Anáfi (2–4 weekly; 4hr); Íos (4–8 weekly; 1hr 15min); Kéa/Lávrio (1 weekly; 10–11hr); Kýthnos (3 weekly; 9hr); Mílos (3–5 weekly; 2hr 30min); Mýkonos (0–2 weekly; 4hr); Náxos (3–6 weekly; 1hr 30min–2hr); Páros (2–4 weekly; 1hr 15min); Pireás (2–6 weekly; 3hr 30min–10hr);

Santoríni (3–5 weekly; 3hr); Sérifos (0–2 weekly; 2hr 30min); Sífnos (1–3 weekly; 1hr 30min); Síkinos (3–5 weekly; 40min); Sýros (3–4 weekly; 3hr 30min).

Services There is an ATM at Doúnavi square and the island's post office is at Poúnda square.

Travel agents Diaplous (☎ 22860 41158) and Maraki (☎ 22860 41211) – both closed 2–5pm – are between Doúnavi and Poúnda squares.

GETTING AROUND

By bus There are hourly buses daily in summer from Karavostási to Hóra, from where further buses run to Áno Meriá (6 daily; 30min) or Angáli beach (4 daily; 30min). Off-season the bus to Angáli leaves you 1km away on the road to Áno Meriá.

By car and motorcycle It may be worthwhile renting a car for a day – try Spyros's Motorbike Rental at Karavostási (☎ 22860 41448), which is cheaper than its counterparts in Hóra – but generally the buses will, as a rule, take you where you want to be. Lignós (☎ 22860 41346) rents motorcycles at the northern end of Hóra.

Karavostási and around

Karavostási, the port, serves really as a last-resort base. There are several hotels and plenty of rooms but compared to the beauty of Hóra, just above, hardly any atmosphere. The closest **beach**, other than the narrow main shingle strip, is the smallish, sand-and-pebble **Várdhia**, signposted just north over the tiny headland. Some fifteen minutes' walk south lies **Livádhi**, a family beach with tamarisk trees. Just before Livádhi are the much smaller but more romantic beaches of **Vitséntzou** and **Poundáki**, reached by steep paths.

Touted as the island's most scenic beach, **Kátergo** is a 300m stretch of pea-gravel with two offshore islets, on the southeastern tip of the island. Most visitors come on a boat excursion from Karavostási or Angáli, but you can also get there on foot (20min) from the hamlet of Livádhi, itself a fifteen-minute dirt-road walk inland from Livádhi beach. Be warned, though, that it's a rather arduous and stony trek, with a final 80m descent on loose-surfaced paths; there is no shade on the walk or the beach. The narrow sea passage between the beach's southern cliffs and the right-hand islet, **Makrí**, has very strong currents and swimming through is not recommended.

ACCOMMODATION AND EATING   KARAVOSTÁSI AND AROUND

Kalýmnios ☎ 22860 41146. Fish taverna said to have the freshest seafood on the island. Whether crab claws, fried calamari (€10) or lobster spaghetti, you order and pay by the kilo. Also open for breakfast. April–Oct daily 7am–1am.

Livadhi Camping Livádhi ☎ 22860 41204, ☼ www .folegandros.org. A friendly and more than adequate campsite with a café-restaurant, minimarket, and a rental

office for cars and motorbikes. They also rent apartments for two people (€50). June–Sept. **€9**

Vardia Bay Várdhia ☎ 22860 41277, ☼ vardiabay.com. Grand hotel with luxurious rooms and studios in a great location above the jetty, right on the beach of the same name. Everything is on the large side: from the rooms and the verandas with their stupendous seaviews to the breakfast buffet. **€80**

Hóra

The island's real character and appeal are rooted in the spectacular **HÓRA**, perched on a cliff-edge plateau, a steep 3km from the port. Locals and foreigners mingle at the cafés and tavernas under the trees of the five adjacent squares, passing the time undisturbed by traffic, which is banned from the village centre. Towards the northern cliff-edge and entered through two arcades, the defensive core of the medieval **kástro** neighbourhood is marked by ranks of two-storey residential houses, with almost identical stairways and slightly recessed doors.

From the cliff-edge Poúnda square, where the bus stops, a path zigzags up – with views along the northern coastline – to the wedding-cake church of **Kímisis tis Theotókou**, whose unusual design includes two little fake chapels mounted astride the roof. The church, formerly part of a nunnery, is on the gentlest slope of a pyramidal hill with 360m cliffs dropping to the sea on the northwest side and is a favourite spot for watching some of the Aegean's most spectacular sunsets. Beyond and below it hides the **Khryssospiliá**, a large cave with stalactites and ancient inscriptions, centre of a strange ancient youth cult, but closed to the public for archeological excavations. However, a minor, lower grotto can still be visited by excursion boat from the port. Towards the top of the hill are a few fragments of the ancient Paleókastro.

Hóra is inevitably beginning to sprawl at the edges, and the burgeoning **nightlife** – a few dance bars along with a number of music pubs and ouzerís – is to the south, away from most accommodation.

ACCOMMODATION HÓRA

Aegeo ☎ 22860 41468, ⓦ aegeohotel.com. A reasonably priced hotel option, just before Poúnda square, which includes free wi-fi and breakfast, but gets booked quickly. The same family manages a more basic option at *Evgenía* rooms (☎ 22860 41006) right next to the hotel; basic but immaculately clean. April–Sept. **€60**

Anemómilos Apartments ☎ 22860 41309, ⓦ anemomilosapartments.com. Wonderfully appointed at the cliff's edge with dramatic vistas, these are super-luxurious apartments from which watching the sunset becomes an artistic experience. "Blue" coded rooms have better views and are more expensive than "green" ones. April–Sept. **€190**

Chora Resort ☎ 22860 41590–4, ⓦ choraresort.com. Grand luxury resort at the northern end of town, spanning a couple of acres, that offers a large pool, fitness centre, designer rooms, minigolf and even its own church for weddings and baptisms. Larger rooms have their own jacuzzi. April–Sept. **€190**

★ **Polikandia** ☎ 22860 41322, ⓦ polikandia -folegandros.gr. Centred around a large swimming pool, this is a superbly designed boutique hotel before Poúnda square, paying great attention to detail: free wi-fi, communal jacuzzi and individual massage showers that have to be seen to be believed. April–Sept. **€110**

EATING AND DRINKING

Eva's Garden ☎ 22860 41110. If proof be needed that Folégandhros is sophisticated, this elegant restaurant-bar provides it with an unusually inventive menu (mains €8) in a very romantic atmosphere. Easter–Oct daily 6am–1am.

Kritikós ☎ 22860 41219. A Cretan grill in the fourth square with the best *dakos* (feta, crispy roll and tomato salad) in the

Cyclades and some good Cretan wines. Excellent barbecued and broiled steaks from €8. April–Oct daily noon–1am.

★ **Piazza** ☎ 22860 41274. By the third square, this is the best restaurant to try the local *matsáta* (hand-drawn tagliatelle with veal, chicken or goat) for €10. May–Oct daily noon–1am.

NIGHTLIFE

Astarti A very popular bar in the third square with an alternative feel, elegant furnishings, carefully chosen wooden decor and large cocktails. The clubbers come here and then continue to Beez, a few doors down, its sister club that stays open after everything else has closed. May–Sept daily 6pm–3am.

★ **BaRaki** On the same road as Astarti, this is a cosy, friendly bar with a good selection of cocktails for €7. Occasional music with a DJ whose booth takes up almost half the space inside – but, who cares, as everyone is out enjoying the pleasant nights. June–Sept daily 10pm–3am.

Áno Meriá and around

West of Hóra, a paved road threads its way along the spine of the island towards sprawling **Áno Meriá** – in fact a multitude of tiny hamlets. In the middle of the settlement stands the large parish church of Áyios Yeóryios (1905), with an unusual white, carved iconostasis. Ask the bus driver to drop you off at the long footpaths down to the beaches on the western half of the island. Muleteers await the buses here and will, for €5, transport tourists down dirt roads to the beaches at **Ambéli**, **Ligariá** and **Áyios Yeóryios**; the former are small and can get crowded, the latter is a much better beach but faces north and is only comfortable when the wind blows from the south. **Livadháki beach** is accessed by signed path from just beyond Taxiárhis.

The best swimming in this part of the island is at the attractive and popular sheltered south-coast beach of **Angáli**, where there are several tavernas. (Off-season the bus leaves you 1km away on the road to Áno Meriá.) Naturists should take the paths which lead twenty minutes east to **Firá** or west to **Áyios Nikólaos** beaches respectively. The latter is particularly fine, with many tamarisks, coarse sand and views back over the island. Although at Áyios Nikólaos, a lone taverna operates up by the namesake chapel, while Firá has no facilities.

ACCOMMODATION

Blue Sand Angáli ☎ 22860 41042, ⊕ bluesand.gr. A three-star boutique option in this well-connected beach with white, minimalist undulating staircases and rooms

ÁNO MERIÁ AND AROUND

with verandas offering mesmerizing sea views. Free wi-fi and port transfers. May–Sept. **€120**

EATING AND DRINKING

The best eating options lie at the end of the bus line at Taxiárhis.

Profítis Ilías Bakery At Profítis Ilías, a well-concealed, yet signposted, bakery is along a short lane to the left of the road. It offers the local cheese-and-onion pie called *kalasoúna* for €2. Mon–Sat 8am–3pm.

Synandisi ☎ 22860 41208. A taverna at the last but one bus stop in Áno Meriá with a bit of everything: fresh fish, home-grown vegetables and hotpots of local meat such as rabbit, goat or chicken (€9). This is the easiest place to find and try the local *kalasoúna* pies. May–Sept 10am–midnight.

3

Santoríni

As the ferry manoeuvres into the great caldera of **SANTORÍNI (Thíra)**, the land seems to rise up and clamp around it. Gaunt, sheer cliffs loom hundreds of metres above the deep blue sea, nothing grows or grazes to soften the awesome view, and the only colours are the reddish-brown, black and grey pumice layers on the cliff face of Santoríni, the largest island in this mini-archipelago. The landscape tells of a history so dramatic and turbulent that legend hangs as fact upon it.

These apocalyptic events, though, scarcely concern modern tourists, who come here to take in the spectacular views, stretch out on the island's dark-sand beaches and absorb the peculiar, infernal geographic features. The tourism industry has changed traditional island life, creating a rather expensive playground. There is one time-honoured local industry, however, that has benefited from all the outside attention: **wine**. Santoríni is one of Greece's most important producers, and the fresh, dry white wines it is known for (most from the *assýrtiko* grape for which the region is known) are the perfect accompaniment to the seafood served in the many restaurants and tavernas that hug the island's cliffs.

Brief history

From as early as 3000 BC, Ancient Thíra developed as a sophisticated outpost of Minoan civilization, until sometime between 1650–1600 BC when catastrophe struck: the volcano-island erupted some 60 cubic kilometres of magma over a period of months. The island's heart sank below the sea, leaving a caldera 10km in diameter. Earthquakes and tsunami reverberated across the Aegean – one full metre of ash was discovered on Rhodes – Thíra was destroyed, and the great Minoan civilization on Crete was dealt a severe blow by the ensuing ash fallout and tsunami. The island's history has become linked with the legend of Atlantis, all because of Plato. Although he dated the cataclysm to approximately 9500 BC, he was perhaps inspired by folk memories.

ARRIVAL AND DEPARTURE
SANTORÍNI

By plane The airport is on the east side of the island, near Monólithos. Buses are not frequent, so make sure you have arranged a pickup.

Destinations Athens (both Olympic and Aegean; 3–8 daily; 45min); Crete, Iráklion (Olympic, 1 daily; 30min); Rhodes (4–5 weekly; 45min); Thessaloníki (Aegean 1–2 daily; 1hr 5min).

By ferry All ferries dock at the port of Athiniós. The old ports of Skála Firás and Ammoúdhi for Ía in the north are only used by local excursion boats and cruise ships. The old, traditional route of 580 steps from Skála up to Firá is a difficult 45min walk; you can also go by mule (€5) or cable car (April–Oct daily 6.30am–11pm, every 20min; Nov–March daily 7.30am–10.30am & 2.30–4.30pm, every 30min; €4, luggage €2 extra).

Destinations Amorgós (1–3 weekly; 3hr); Anáfi (2–5 weekly; 1hr 20min); Astypálea (1 weekly; 3hr); Chálki

(2 weekly, 11hr); Iráklion (1–2 daily; 1hr 30min–5hr); Folégandhros (1–2 daily; 1hr 30min); Íos (1–3 daily; 30min–1hr); Kálymnos/Tílos (2 weekly; 5hr 30min–10hr); Kárpathos/Kássos (3 weekly; 6–8hr); Kéa/Lávrio (2 weekly; 13–14hr); Kímolos (2 weekly; 4hr); Mílos (4–6 weekly; 2hr); Mýkonos (1–3 daily; 2hr 30min); Náxos (2–4 daily; 1hr 30min); Níssyros (2 weekly; 8hr); Páros (1 daily; 3hr 30min–7hr); Pireás (3–5 daily; 4hr 30min–9hr); Rhodes (5–6 weekly; 9–12hr); Sífnos (1–2 weekly; 5hr); Síkinos (6–8 weekly; 2hr); Sýros (5–6 weekly; 5–8hr); Thirassía (4–6 daily from Órmos and 2–3 daily from Ammoúdhi; 15 min); Tínos (5 weekly; 3hr).

INFORMATION

Services There are many cafés clustered on Firá's main square; others offer free wi-fi to their customers all over the island. Penguin (☎22860 22168; 9am–9pm) laundry is on the main road to Ía about 100m up from the main square (from €6).

Travel agents There are many travel agents clustered around Firá's main square. Santo Star (☎22860 23082, Ⓦsantostar.gr) and Kamari Tours (☎22860 31390, Ⓦkamaritours.gr) organize excursions and trips to ancient Thíra, as well as day tours to Nea and Paleá Kaméni and Thirassía. Prices for the latter range from €10 for simple transport to about €30 for a more intimate guided tour on a traditional *kaïki*.

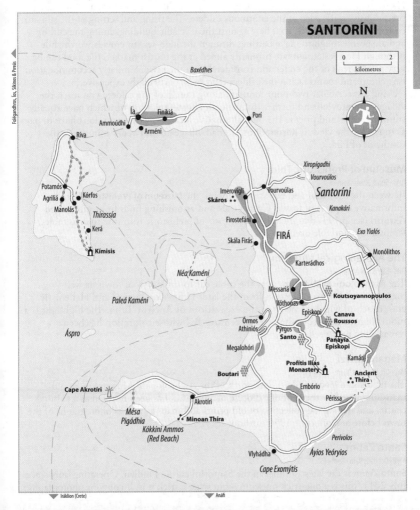

GETTING AROUND

By bus Buses leave Firá from just south of Theotokopoúlou Square to Períssa, Perívolos, Kamári, Monólithos (via the airport), Akrotíri, Órmos Athiniós and Vliháda. For the timetable consult ⓦ ktel-santorini.gr.

By taxi The island's taxi base (ⓣ 22860 22555) is near the Firá bus station, within steps of the main square. There are fewer than forty in the whole island, so make sure you have your onward transport arranged well in advance.

By car and motorcycle If you want to see the whole island in a couple of days, a rented motorbike or car will be essential. There are many rental places all over the island and your hotel or any travel agent can arrange it for you. Nomikos Travel (ⓣ 22860 24940, ⓦ nomikostravel.gr) opposite the OTE building in Firá is a good, reliable agency.

Day-trips The glass-bottom *Calypso* (ⓣ 22860 22958, ⓦ dakoutrostravel.gr) makes an excursion to the islands of the archipelago daily at 10.45am (€28) and hovers over the volcanic reefs at the end of each journey to allow passengers a peek into the dark depths of Santoríni's flooded crater. Ancient Thira Tours (ⓣ 22860 32474; €8; 2hr stopping time at site) also operate guided tours of the ruins of Ancient Thíra from Kamári (p.191).

Firá and around

Half-rebuilt after a devastating earthquake in 1956, **FIRÁ** (also known as Hóra) clings precariously to the edge of the enormous caldera. The rising and setting of the sun are especially beautiful when seen here against the Cycladic buildings lining the clifftop, and are even enough to make battling through the high-season crowds worthwhile. Although Firá's restaurants are primarily aimed at the tourist market, the food can be very good; views of the crater add considerably to the price. Similarly accommodation isn't cheap and rooms facing the caldera tend to be particularly expensive.

Using a spectacular two-hour footpath along the lip of the caldera you reach the village of **Imerovígli** and further to the north **Firostefáni**, both of which have equally stunning views and prices. The only alternative location, where you don't have to pay as much for the view, is **Karterádhos**, a small village about twenty minutes' walk southeast of Firá.

Museum of Prehistoric Thira

Tues–Sun 8.30am–8pm • €3

Between the cathedral and bus station in Firá, the **Museum of Prehistoric Thira** has informative displays of fossils, Cycladic art and astonishing finds from submerged Akrotíri (see p.193) that include plaster casts of prehistoric furniture such as tables, lamps and a portable oven.

The Archeological Museum

Tues–Sun 8.30am–3pm • €3

The **Archeological Museum**, near the cable car to the north of town, is well presented, and has a collection from the later Homeric Classical and Hellenistic eras, much of which came from the excavations of Ancient Thira. The highlight is a mourning woman from the seventh century BC whose coloration has been remarkably preserved.

Mégaro Ghýzi

May–Oct Mon–Sat 10am–4pm • €3

The handsome **Mégaro Ghýzi**, just north of the Archeological Museum in an old mansion owned by the Catholic diocese of Santoríni, has been restored as a cultural centre, and has a good collection of old prints and maps as well as photographs of the town before and after the 1956 earthquake.

Santo Zeum

April–Oct daily 9am–8pm • €5

Santo Zeum is the latest stunner in the Santoríni cultural milieu. Operating only since July 2011, this is a one-trick museum – but what a trick it is: it contains photographic reproductions (using a technique specially invented by Kodak) of the Akrotíri murals, which can be reasonably assumed to mark the beginning of the art of painting per se.

Lignós Folklore Museum

Daily 10am–2pm • €2

In a part of Firá called Kondohóri the extensive **Lignós Folklore Museum** features a completely furnished local "cave home" with period winery, chapel, garden and workshops, as well as a gallery and historical archive.

ACCOMMODATION   FIRÁ

Galini Firostefáni ☎ 22860 22095, ⓦ hotelgalini.gr. Possibly the cheapest hotel with a caldera view, situated in a relatively quiet spot a 10min walk from Firá. March–Nov. **€100**

Loucas ☎ 22860 22480, ⓦ www.loucashotel -santorini.com. Traditional caldera-side hotel below Ypapandís with rooms in caves carved into the cliffside with 180-degree views of the precipice below and a beautiful pool and jacuzzi. Breakfast included. April–Oct. **€150**

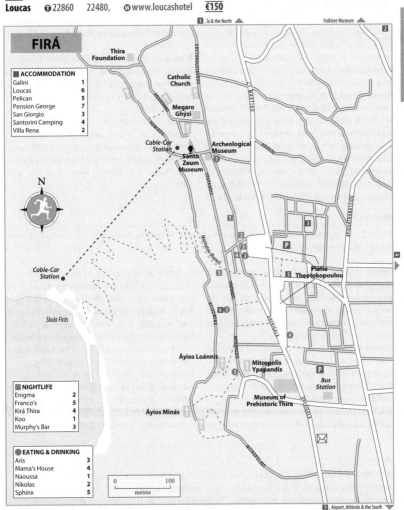

3

FIRÁ

1, Ía & the North

Folklore Museum

Thira Foundation

Catholic Church

Megaro Ghýzi

Cable-Car Station

Archeological Museum

Santo Zeum Museum

ACCOMMODATION
Galini	1
Loucas	6
Pelican	5
Pension George	7
San Giorgio	3
Santorini Camping	4
Villa Rena	2

N

Cable-Car Station

Skala Firás

Platía Theotokopoulou

Áyios Loánnis

Mitrópolis Ypapandís

Bus Station

Museum of Prehistoric Thira

Áyios Minás

NIGHTLIFE
Enigma	2
Franco's	5
Kirá Thira	4
Koo	1
Murphy's Bar	3

EATING & DRINKING
Aris	3
Mama's House	4
Naoussa	1
Nikolas	2
Sphinx	5

0   100
metres

7, Airport, Athiniós & the South

Pelican ☎ 22860 23113, ⓦ pelicanhotel.gr. Large hotel off the central square with spacious rooms; it's owned by a travel agency a few blocks away, so they can organize your stay completely. Free wi-fi, satellite TV, 24/7 reception, parking possible nearby. **€85**

Pension George Karterádhos ☎ 22860 22351, ⓦ pensiongeorge.com. Comfortable rooms and studios, pool and a good welcome, just a 15min walk from Firá. Unlike other hotels, this one also has a well-attended garden where you can relax among the palm trees. Free transfers. **€70**

★ **San Giorgio** ☎ 22860 23516, ⓦ sangiorgiovilla.gr. Tucked away to the left of parking next to the main square, you can find this hospitable, clean, hotel with simple rooms, all with balconies; excellent value for budget travellers. Also offers a ten percent discount for Rough Guide readers. April–Nov. **€50**

Santorini Camping ☎ 22860 22944, ⓦ santorini camping.gr. A shady campsite 300m east of the centre, with a pool, restaurant, games room, 24/7 reception, own security and free internet access. March–Nov. **€9**

Villa Rena ☎ 22860 28130, ⓦ renasplace.gr. Comfortable, friendly hotel, a 10min walk towards the Folklore Museum, whose rooms are furnished individually in bright, non-standard Cycladic colours, some overlooking a large pool. Minibus transfers available for a charge. April–Oct. **€70**

EATING AND DRINKING

Aris ☎ 22860 22480. Dependably good Greek and international food plus an excellent wine list in a relaxed, unhurried atmosphere, with a sensational view – and prices to match (€20); not always busy, as the steep steps down below *Hotel Loucas* act as a deterrent to some customers. April–Oct daily noon–midnight.

Mama's House Right below the main square, this is a cheap, backpacker-friendly spot with hearty Continental and English breakfasts, filling dishes (€8), a shaggy dog and the overwhelming chatty presence of Mama herself, a distinguished old lady straight out of the photo album of Greek stereotypes. March–Nov daily 8am–1am.

Naoussa ☎ 22860 24869, ⓦ naoussa-restaurant.gr. Good traditional Greek cuisine on the first floor of the shopping centre Lagoudhéra opposite the steps to old port.

Dishes as close to home-made as you'll get anywhere on Firá; start with the celebrated moussaka for €10. Easter– Oct daily noon–late.

Nikolas Erythroú Stavroú ☎ 22860 24550. An old and defiantly traditional taverna, insisting on using nothing frozen or not in season; the locals know this and prefer it, so it can be very hard to get a table. Mains around €15. Daily noon–midnight.

Sphinx Mitropóleos (Via d'Oro) ☎ 22860 23823, ⓦ sphinx.gr. On terraces overlooking the caldera, and offering home-made pasta dishes with a Greek twist, such as the addition of lobster, crayfish or octopus, at a price (€20). Its cellar boasts 150 different wines. April–Oct daily noon–1am.

NIGHTLIFE

Most of the first-rate nightlife is northwest of the central square, on Erythroú Stavroú, often not starting long before midnight and busiest between 1am and 4am.

Enigma Erythroú Stavroú ⓦ www.enigmaclub.gr. Long-established dance club with three large barrel-roofed arches and outdoor area with a palm-tree bar and facecheck security. Its VIP room has seen some of the most famous world celebrities and still attracts the island's *beau monde*. June–Sept daily midnight–late.

Franco's ☎ 22860 24428, ⓦ www.francos.gr. Exclusive, expensive cocktail bar in a fabulous location by the steps to the old port offering opera, champagne and sunbeds. Try the Maria Callas cocktail (€9) and watch the sunset listening to the Diva herself singing Norma. Easter–Oct daily 5pm–late.

Kirá Thíra Erythroú Stavroú. Going back more than three decades, this small, laidback venue with live DJs and music

has fanatic followers who pack the place to the rafters year after year, despite its less-than-ideal acoustics: it's cut in a cave so its sound is on the echoey side. May–Oct daily 8pm–late.

Koo Erythroú Stavroú ☎ 22860 22025, ⓦ kooclub.gr. In direct competition with *Enigma* (see above), it offers less frenetic chill-out and trance music, with candles and cocktails, three bars, and a reservation service if you want to book a table in the VIP room. June–Sept daily midnight–late.

Murphy's Bar Erythroú Stavroú ☎ 22860 22248. Reasonably priced Irish pub with all the obligatory hilarity; established in 1999 and hasn't looked back since. The wall of drinks behind the bar reaches to the ceiling and this is a rather tall venue. April–Oct daily noon–3am.

Ía

Ía (Oía), the most photographed town on the island, was once a major commercial centre in the Aegean, but it has declined in the wake of economic depression, wars, earthquakes and depleted fish stocks. Partly destroyed in the 1956 earthquake, the town has been sympathetically reconstructed, its white and cyan houses clinging to the cliff face. Apart from the caldera and the town itself, there are a couple of things to see, including the **Naval Museum** (Mon & Wed–Sun 10am–2pm & 5–8pm; €3) and the very modest remains of a Venetian castle. It is a quieter, though still touristy, alternative to Firá except during sunset, for which people are coached in from all over the island, creating traffic chaos and driving up prices. Public buses are extremely full around this time (after 6pm, although in the summer the sunset occurs around 8.30pm).

Below the town, two sets of 220-odd steps lead to two small harbours: one to **Arméni** for the fishermen, and the other to **Ammoúdhi**, where the excursion boats dock.

ACCOMMODATION ÍA

Much of the town's accommodation is in restored cave houses, with caldera views adding at least €100 to the rooms.

Andronis Suites ☎22860 72041, ⓦandronis-suites .com. With its central location, superlative views, spa, apartments carved deep into the cliffs, and balconies that can induce vertigo, this may well be the most prestigious spot in the Cyclades and the price reflects it. The apartments sleep up to five, mind you. April–Oct. __€600__

Oia Youth Hostel ☎22860 71465, ⓦsantorinihostel .gr. Well signposted from the bus terminal, this excellent

hostel has a terrace and a shady courtyard, laundry, a good café-bar and clean dormitories, but with a very short season, so call to check it's open. Mid-June to Sept. __€16__

Pension Delfini ☎22860 23016, ⓦdelfinihotel.net. By far the best middle-price option, this small boutique hotel offers rooms with jacuzzis and private balconies with caldera views. April–Nov. Doubles __€110__, 4-person suite __€180__

EATING AND DRINKING

Restaurant prices can be as steep as the cliffs, at the older, western end of town. In general the further east you go along the central ridge the better the price.

1800 ☎22860 71485. Regarded as one of the best restaurants on the island, and serving highly refined, French-inspired cuisine, its interiors have a fin-de-siècle feel and the roof garden offers unique unhindered views over the caldera. Its wines are excellent and, like the food (mains around €30), accordingly expensive. May–Oct daily 6.30pm–midnight.

King Neptune ☎22860 71294. With a rooftop bar to rival the best for views and dishes for €15 that don't break the bank, this is the best-value combination of good food, view and atmosphere in Ía. Come early for dinner before the sunset buses invade, get a front-row table and chill. April–Nov daily noon–late.

The east coast

Santoríni's **beaches**, on the island's east coast, are long black stretches of volcanic sand that get blisteringly hot in the afternoon sun. They're no secret, and in the summer the crowds can be a bit overpowering. Among the resorts lie the substantial and beautifully sited remains of **ancient Thira**.

In the southeast, the family resort of **Kamári** is popular with package-tour operators, and hence more touristy. Nonetheless it's quieter and cleaner than most, with a well-maintained seafront promenade.

Things are considerably scruffier at **Períssa**, around the cape. Because of its beach and abundance of cheap rooms, it's crowded with backpackers. The beach itself extends several kilometres to the west, through Perívolos to Áyios Yeóryios, sheltered by the occasional tamarisk tree and with beach bars dotted along at intervals. A new attraction in Períssa is the **Museum of Minerals and Fossils** (summer, daily 10am–2pm, winter Sun only; free), with exhibits that include rare palm tree fossils from pre-eruption Santoríni.

Ancient Thira

Tues–Sun 8.30am–2.30pm • €1.50 • Excursion minibuses depart from Kamári (see above); there are also donkey rides up (€20). Alternatively, walk the interminably looping cobbled road – Archaias Thiras – starting from Ancient Thira Tours

Kamári and Períssa are separated by the Mésa Vounó headland, on which stood **ancient Thira**, the post-eruption settlement, dating from 915 BC through to the

Venetian period. Starting from Períssa a stony shadeless path to the site passes a chapel dating back to the fourth century AD before skirting round to the Temenos of Artemidoros with bas-relief carvings of a dolphin, eagle and lion representing Poseidon, Zeus and Apollo. Next, the trail follows the sacred way of the ancient city through the remains of the agora and past the theatre. The path meets the paved road to Kamári at a saddle between Mésa Vounó and Profítis Ilías, the only remaining visible components of the pre-eruption landscape.

INFORMATION   THE EAST COAST

Activities Kamári is the base of Navy's Diving Centre (☎22860 31006, ⍟navys.gr), which offers PADI courses for beginners and volcanic reef diving for certified divers.

ACCOMMODATION

★**Chez Sophie** Kamári ☎22860 32912, ⍟chezsophie.gr. A stunningly designed boutique hotel with large rooms set around a swimming pool towards the southern end of the beach. Superb service that includes free wi-fi, parking, free air and ferry transfers, plus a delicious home-made buffet breakfast. May–Oct. **€90**

Ostria Kamári ☎22860 31727, ⍟villaostria.gr. A friendly, family-run oasis of studios and apartments at the foot of Mount Profítis Ilías that stands in pleasant contrast to the resort's many large hotel blocks. Parking available. April–Oct. **€100**

Perissa Beach Períssa ☎22860 81343. Right behind the coastal road, this campsite has plenty of space and shade, but is also next to a couple of noisy late-night bars, but if you choose to stay here you are more likely to be carousing rather than resting. Has special overflow space for sleeping bags only. **€9**

Rose Bay Hotel Kamári ☎22860 33650, ⍟rosebay.gr. A less pricey option than other luxurious hotels in the north part of town, with a pleasant pool setting, set back from the beach. Single rooms are as big as the doubles, too. April–Oct. **€120**

EATING AND DRINKING

Kamári is the centre of nightlife in the east coast: the best of the bars are towards the southern end of the beach offering staggered happy hours 8pm–midnight, and there is a good open-air cinema at the north end of the town, which is licensed and offers cocktails and drinks at reasonable prices during the film.

Kritikos Kamári ☎22460 4170. A taverna much frequented by locals, this is one of the better grill places to eat on the island (mains €15). It's a long way out of Kamári on the road up to Messariá, and too far to walk, but the bus stops outside. April–Nov daily noon–midnight.

Mistral Kamári ☎22860 32108, ⍟www.mistral-fishtavern.gr. Set in a quiet alley with tables in a large, tree-covered garden, this is rumoured to offer the best lobster spaghetti on the island (€30–40 for a platter for two). Also try the tomato salad with caper leaves, a Santoríni special. April–Nov daily noon–late.

THE WINERIES

Some of Santoríni's most important **wineries** are scattered around Pýrgos and the south, and offer excellent-value tours. Whichever tour you go on, none is complete without a taste of Santoríni's prized dessert wine, **vinsánto** (reminiscent of the Tuscan *vin santo*), which is among the finest wines produced in Greece and used by the Orthodox Church in Holy Communion. Tour prices at the smaller wineries usually include tastings, while samples are available for the larger wineries for a nominal fee.

Boutari Just out of Megalohóri ⍟boutari.gr. This is the Santorini branch of one of the largest wineries of Greece with an exceptional Estate Argyros Vinsanto, named Best Greek Wine 2009.

Canava Roussos Episkopí ⍟canavaroussos.gr. Making wines since 1836, this is one of the most traditional Greek family wineries producing a famed white called Nyktéri. May–Oct.

Koutsoyannopoulos Just outside Kamári ⍟volcanwines.gr. The best-known winery, it has a 300m-long cellar that's home to a wine museum offering a more intimate glimpse at the wine-making process (April–Oct daily noon–8pm; €4 includes tasting; on Fri evenings there are buffet meals with Greek dancing).

Santo Near Pýrgos. April–Nov, 10am–sunset; ⍟santowines.gr. Offers the most comprehensive tours (€2–3), complete with multimedia presentations.

Pýrgos

As you drive west of Kamári towards **PÝRGOS** you can't miss the sight of **Panayía Episkopí**, the most important Byzantine monument on the island. Built in the eleventh century, it was the setting of centuries of conflict between Orthodox Greeks and Catholics, but is most notable today for its carved iconostasis of light blue marble with a white grain.

Further west, Pýrgos is one of the oldest settlements on the island, a jumble of weather-beaten houses and alleys that form several concentric circles around the village kástro. It climbs to another Venetian fortress crowned by the seventeenth-century church of the **Presentation of the Virgin**. You can clamber around the battlements for sweeping views over the entire island and its Aegean neighbours.

EATING AND DRINKING

PÝRGOS

Kallisti Pýrgos ☏ 22860 34108. If you can't get a table at *Selene* (see below), worry not. This cosy, covered taverna on the main square has excellent cheap food and a tradition of good service; its lamb casserole (€6) literally melts in the mouth. April–Oct daily noon–midnight.

★ **Selene** Pýrgos ☏ 22860 22249, ⓦ selene.gr. Santorini's most famous restaurant, awarded Greece's top gastronomic accolade in 2011, has moved to Pýrgos from Firá, but still serves delicious, inventive food. Choose from dishes such as rabbit confit, piglet cheeks, cuttlefish in its own ink, vegetable risotto with feta powder (all around €20–€30) or the taster menu from €60 per person. Booking essential. April–Oct daily noon–11pm.

Akrotíri and the south coast

Evidence of the Minoan colony that once thrived here has been uncovered at the ancient site of Minoan Thira at **AKROTÍRI** (closed since 2005; check with the Museum

THE ARCHIPELAGO

The best and most popular day-trip from Firá is to the three islands of the inner archipelago. Most people stick to the still volcanically active Paleá and Néa Kaméni, although, if you have time, it is worth staying overnight in Thirassía for a glimpse of what Santoríni used to feel like before the cruise ships arrived.

PALEÁ AND NÉA KAMÉNI

Local ferries from either Skála Firás or Ía (Ammoúdhi), venture to the charred volcanic islets of **Paleá Kaméni** (active 46–1458 AD) and **Néa Kaméni** (active 1707–1950). At Paleá Kaméni you can swim from the boat to warm mineral-laden springs, while Néa Kaméni (€2 entrance fee), with its own mud-clouded hot springs, features a demanding hike to a smouldering, volcanically active crater.

THIRASSÍA

The boat excursions also continue to the relatively unspoilt islet of **Thirassía** (ⓦ thirasia.gr), which was once part of Santoríni until sliced off by an eruption in the third century BC. It's an excellent destination, except during the tour-boat rush of lunch hour. At other times, the island is one of the quietest in the Cyclades, with views as dramatic as any on Santoríni. The downside is that there is no proper beach and the tavernas in Kórfos close early after the last ferry has gone. There is an ATM at the Citizen's Service office (KEP) and credit cards are normally not accepted on the island.

Tour boats head for the village of **Kórfos**, a stretch of shingle backed by fishermen's houses and high cliffs while ferries dock at **Ríva**. There should be no problem taking a car or rental bike over, but fill up with petrol first. From Kórfos a steep, stepped path climbs up to **Manolás**, nearly 200m above, where donkeys are still used for transport. Manolás straggles along the edge of the caldera, an attractive small village that gives an idea of what Santoríni was like before tourism arrived there.

ACCOMMODATION

Zacharo Rooms Manolás ☏ 22860 29102. All rooms have a/c, private bathroom and TV with amazing views over both Manolás, Kórfos and Santoríni itself. No credit cards accepted. Easter–Oct. **€45**

of Prehistoric Thira in Firá; see p.188), at the southwestern tip of the island; the site was inhabited from the Late Neolithic period through to the seventeenth century BC.

Kókkini Ámmos (Red Beach) is about 500m from the site and is quite spectacular, with high reddish-brown cliffs above sand of the same colour. It's a better beach than the one below the site, but gets crowded in season. More secluded black-sand beaches lie under the surreal, pockmarked pumice stone that dominates the lunar coast around **Cape Exomýtis** at the island's southern extremity. Both **Vlyhádha** to the west and **Áyios Yeóryios** to the east of the cape are accessed by decent roads branching off from the main one to Embório, though no buses run here and there are no amenities to speak of. An hour's walk west of ancient Akrotíri, a lighthouse marks the tip of **Cape Akrotíri**, which offers better views of the caldera than even Ía itself.

ACCOMMODATION AND EATING	AKROTÍRI AND THE SOUTH COAST
Caldera View Resort Megalohóri ☎ 22860 82010, ⓦ caldera view-santorini.com. Situated 2km from Akrotíri and very near the Red Beach, this modern bungalow complex, only opened in May 2011, has arguably better sunset and caldera views than any other location on the island. June–Sept. **€90**	**Delfinia** Akrotíri ☎ 22860 81151. Wonderfully situated at the water's edge, just below the bus stop, this is a grill taverna that offers fresh seafood and the catch of the day. Try the lightly fried calamari (€15), which is perfectly cooked. Daily noon–10pm.

Anáfi

A ninety-minute boat ride to the east of Santoríni, **ANÁFI** is the last stop for ferries and is something of a travellers' dead end. It was so for the Argonauts who prayed to Apollo for some land to rest; he let the island emerge from the sea for their repose. If rest is what you crave, you'll have it here in abundance. Not that this is likely to bother most of the visitors, who come here for weeks in midsummer to enjoy exactly that: its seclusion. Although idyllic geographically, Anáfi is a harsh place, its mixed granite and limestone core overlaid by volcanic rock spewed out by Santoríni's eruptions. Apart from the few olive trees and vines grown in the valleys, the only plants that seem to thrive are prickly pears. The quiet, unassuming capital, **Hóra**, provides a daring dash of white in a treeless, shrub-strewn hillock, its narrow, winding streets offering protection from the occasionally squally *gharbís* wind that comes unencumbered from the southwest.

The beaches

The glory of Anáfi is a string of south-facing beaches starting under the cliffs at **Áyios Nikólaos**. These – along with two nearby monasteries – are accessible by bus,

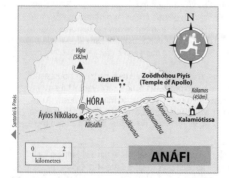

although walking is still an option. The nearest beach is **Klisídhi**, east of the harbour, which has 200m of gently shelving sand. The next big beach is **Roúkounas** with some 500m of broad sand rising to tamarisk-stabilized dunes; the craggy hill of **Kastélli**, an hour's scramble above the beach, is the site both of ancient Anáfi and a ruined Venetian castle. Beyond Roúkounas, it's another half-hour on foot to the first of the exquisite half-dozen coves at **Kateloumátsa**, of all shapes and sizes, and forty-five minutes to **Monastíri**, where the bus stops – all without facilities, so come prepared.

The monasteries

Monastíri in Anáfi means the **monastery of Zoödhóhou Piyís**. The bus stops only a few hundred metres before the building. A ruined temple of Apollo, supposedly built by the grateful Argonauts, is incorporated into the monastery, while the courtyard, with a welcome cistern, is the venue for the island's major festivals, celebrated eleven days after Easter and September 7–8. Go left immediately before the monastery to join the spectacular onward path to **Kalamiótissa**, another monastery perched atop the abrupt limestone pinnacle at the extreme southeast of the island. It takes another hour to reach, but is eminently worthwhile for the stunning scenery and views over the entire south coast – there is no accessible water up here, so bring enough with you.

ARRIVAL AND INFORMATION   ANÁFI

By ferry All ferries dock at the small port of Áyios Nikólaos. Buses always wait for ferries to take them to Hóra (5min). Destinations Chalki (1 weekly; 10hr); Iráklion (1 weekly; 3hr 30min); Folégandhros (4 weekly; 4hr 30min); Íos (4 weekly; 3hr); Kárpathos/Kássos (2–3 weekly; 5–10hr); Kéa/Lávrio (2 weekly; 14–15hr); Mílos (1 weekly; 7hr 30min); Mýkonos (1 weekly; 6hr 30min); Náxos (2–3 weekly; 5hr 30min); Páros (3 weekly; 6–7hr); Pireás (2 weekly; 9–11hr); Rhodes (2 weekly; 12hr); Santoríni (5–6 weekly; 1hr 30min); Síkinos (2–3 weekly; 3hr); Sýros (2–3 weekly; 7hr).

Pharmacy There is no pharmacy on the island (some drugs are dispensed from the GP's practice).

Services There is an ATM in Hóra, and the island's only post office.

Travel agents Jeyzed Travel (☎ 22860 61253, ✉ jeyzed @san.forthnet.gr) sell boat tickets and arrange excursions around the island.

GETTING AROUND

By bus There are buses from Hóra to Áyios Nikólaos (7–8 daily; 15min) and Monastíri (3–4 daily) via the beaches.
By car and motorcycle You can rent both cars and motorbikes at Margarita's (☎ 22860 61292) or Panorama (☎ 22860 61292).

ACCOMMODATION

Apollon Village Klisídhi ☎ 22860 28739, ✇ apollonvillage.gr. Fifteen minutes outside Hóra, this complex has twelve elegant maisonettes on the hillside overlooking Klisídhi beach each named after the 12 Olympian gods and every one designed accordingly. Breakfast included. May–Sept. €70

Ta Plágia Hóra ☎ 22860 61308, ✇ taplagia.gr. Rooms (with ceiling fans) and studios with kitchenette (and a/c) for up to four people (€70) with own balconies and unhindered pelagic views. Internet and good home-made breakfasts charged separately. May–Sept. €40

EATING AND DRINKING

Alexandhra Hóra ☎ 22860 61212. A good, solid restaurant, as laidback as the island itself, offering both grilled fresh fish and seafood by the kilo as well as casseroles and prepared dishes (€6). Daily 9am–11pm.
Liotrivi Hóra ☎ 22860 61209. A good family taverna where you are invited to come to the kitchen and choose among the prepared dishes (€9) or pick up the fresh ingredients for your own individual fish soup, which is then cooked on the spot. May–Sept daily noon–midnight.

3

Crete

200 Central Crete

219 Eastern Crete

234 Réthymnon and around

244 Western Crete

FALÁSARNA BEACH, WESTERN CRETE

Crete

Crete (Kríti) is a great deal more than just another Greek island. In many places, especially in the cities or along the developed north coast, it doesn't feel like an island at all, but rather a substantial land in its own right. Which of course it is – a precipitous, wealthy and at times surprisingly cosmopolitan one with a tremendous and unique history. At the same time, it has everything you could want of a Greek island and more: great beaches, remote hinterlands and hospitable people.

With enough land for agriculture (and some surprisingly good vineyards), it's one of the few Greek islands that could probably support itself without visitors. Nevertheless, tourism is an important part of the economy, particularly exploited along the **north coast**, where many resorts cater almost exclusively to rowdy young revellers lured by thumping bars and cheap booze. The quieter, less commercialized resorts and villages lie at either end of the island – west, towards **Haniá** and the smaller, less well-connected places along the south and west coasts, or east around Sitía. The **high mountains** of the interior are still barely touched by tourism.

Of the cities, sprawling **Iráklion** often gives a poor first impression of the island but is well worth a visit for its excellent archeological museum. It's also close to the fabulous Minoan sites of **Knossos**, **Phaestos** and **Ayía Triádha** to the south (with Roman Gortys to provide contrast). Further east, the upmarket resort of **Áyios Nikólaos** provides sophisticated restaurants and hotels, while quiet, lazy **Sitía** is a perfect base for exploring the eastern coastline. Heading west, **Réthymnon** boasts a pretty old town and an excellent beach, though **Haniá** in the extreme west arguably beats it in terms of style and atmosphere. South of here is the **Samariá Gorge**, one of the best hikes in the country.

In terms of **climate**, Crete has by far the longest summers in Greece, and you can get a decent tan here right into October and swim at least from May until early November. The one seasonal blight is the *meltémi*, a northerly wind, which regularly blows harder and more continuously here than anywhere else in Greece – the locals may welcome its cooling effects, but it's another reason (along with crowds and heat) to avoid an August visit if you can.

Brief history

Crete is distinguished above all as the home of Europe's earliest civilization, the **Minoans**. They had a remarkably advanced society, and formed the centre of a maritime trading empire as early as 2000 BC (see p.518). The island's strategic position between east and west has since continued to play a major role in its history. Control of the island passed from **Greeks** to **Romans** to **Saracens**, through the **Byzantine empire** to **Venice**, and finally to Turkey for more than two centuries. During **World War II**, Crete was occupied by the Germans and attained the dubious distinction of being the first place to be successfully invaded by paratroops.

Adventure sports p.202
The legend of the Minotaur p.209
Wine tasting in Crete p.214
Climbing Mount Psilorítis p.219

Island escape: Gaidhouronísi p.233
Hiking the Amári valley p.242
Festival island p.251
Ecotourism in Crete p.256

WINDMILL, LASÍTHI PLATEAU

Highlights

❶ Archeological Museum, Iráklion The world's foremost Minoan museum. Following a substantial renovation, the museum is set to reopen in 2012. **See p.204**

❷ Knossos The Minoan palace of Knossos is the standout archeological site on the island. **See p.207**

❸ Paleóhora With bags of charm and excellent strands, this resort in the far east of the island is well worth seeking out. **See p.254**

❹ Lasíthi Plateau This fertile high mountain plateau has picturesque agricultural villages and unique white-cloth-sailed windmills. **See p.225**

❺ The Dhiktean Cave Mythological birthplace of Zeus, stunningly situated on the Lasíthi Plateau. **See p.225**

❻ Haniá old town Atmospheric city centre where vibrant modern life coexists with the beautiful architectural legacies of Venetian and Turkish history. **See p.244**

❼ Samariá Gorge A magnificent gorge, offering a chance to see brilliant wild flowers, golden eagles and perhaps a Cretan ibex. **See p.251**

❽ Southwest coast Having made it through the Samariá Gorge, some of Crete's least-visited coastline awaits. **See p.253**

HIGHLIGHTS ARE MARKED ON THE MAP ON PP.200–201

ARRIVAL AND DEPARTURE

By plane Crete has two international airports, Iráklion (Heraklion) and Haniá (Chania), both served by direct flights from the UK and Europe between April and October. Daily flights from mainland Athens operate year-round to Iráklion, Haniá and Sitía with Aegean Airways and Olympic Air.

By ferry There are daily year-round ferry connections from Pireás to both Iráklion and Haniá with ANEK Lines and Minoan Lines, and there are also ferries to Kastélli in the west and Sitía in the east.

GETTING AROUND

By bus There are excellent connections across most of Crete, regular fast buses run along the north-coast highway, and the south coast is served, less frequently, with connections from the main hubs of Iráklion, Áyios Nikólaos, Réthymnon and Haniá.

By car or motorcycle The main routes across the island and south are generally well surfaced and fairly well signposted. Beware of heading off on unsurfaced roads, particularly on mountain tracks, which often just peter out before coming to a dead end.

INFORMATION

Maps The best maps for driving are the German-produced Harms-Verlag (⌖ harms-ic-verlag.de), which cover the island (east and west) in two separate maps at a scale of 1:100,000. For hiking try the 1:25,000-scale Crete Hiking Maps series (Anavasi; ⌖ mountains.gr); both are widely available from bookshops on the island.

Central Crete

The hub of central Crete is the capital city, **Iráklion**, a busy but convenient base for visits to the nearby Minoan palace of **Knossos**. The area immediately around the city is

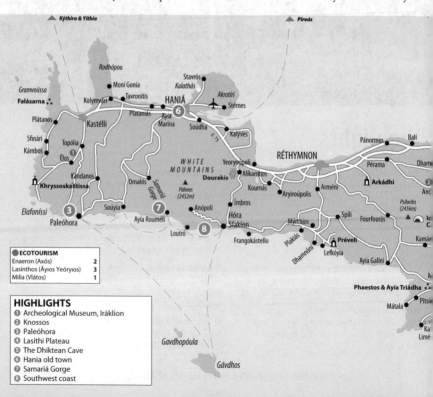

● ECOTOURISM

Enaeron (Axós)	2
Lasinthos (Áyios Yeóryios)	3
Milia (Vlátos)	1

HIGHLIGHTS

❶ Archeological Museum, Iráklion
❷ Knossos
❸ Paleóhora
❹ Lasíthi Plateau
❺ The Dhiktean Cave
❻ Hania old town
❼ Samariá Gorge
❽ Southwest coast

less touristy than you might expect, mainly because there are few decent beaches of any size on the adjacent coast. To the west, mountains drop straight into the sea virtually all the way to Réthymnon, with just two significant coastal settlements: **Ayia Pelayia**, and the more attractive **Bali**. Eastwards, the main resorts are at least 30km away, at Hersónissos and beyond, although there is a string of rather unattractive developments all the way there. **Inland**, there's agricultural country, some of the richest on the island, a cluster of Crete's better vineyards and a series of wealthy villages. To the south lie the sites of **Gortys**, **Phaestos** and **Ayía Triádha** which can all be visited in a day, with a lunchtime swim on the south coast at **Mátala** or Léndas thrown in.

Iráklion

Crete's biggest city, **IRÁKLION** (Heraklion) is a hectic place, a maelstrom of bustle, noise and traffic-congested thoroughfares. On the positive side, though, the city does have superb fortifications, a fine market, atmospheric old alleys and some interesting lesser museums. Virtually everything you're likely to want to see lies within the northeastern corner of the walled city. The most vital thoroughfare, **25-Avgoústou**, links the harbour with the commercial city centre. Further up 25-Avgoústou, **Kalokerinoú** leads down to Haniá Gate and westwards out of the city; straight ahead, **Odhós-1821** is a major shopping street, and adjacent **Odhós-1866** is given over to the animated street market, perhaps the best on the island. To the left, **Dhikeosínis** heads for the city's main square, **Platía Eleftherías**, paralleled by the pedestrian alley, **Dedhálou**, lined with many of the city's swankier fashion stores and the direct link between the two squares.

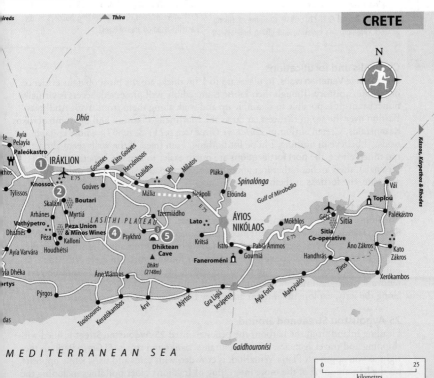

ADVENTURE SPORTS

With its temperate climate and varied topography Crete is a great place for **adventure holidays**, and there are numerous companies across the island offering everything from mountain biking and canyoning to trekking and horseriding. Here's a selection of what's on offer. Watersports and diving operators are also listed throughout the chapter.

CLIMBING/ADRENALINE SPORTS

Liquid Bungy ☎ 693 76 15 191, ⒲ bungy.gr. White-knuckle bungee jumping (Europe's second highest) at the Arádhena Gorge, Haniá.

Trekking Plan ☎ 28210 60861, ⒲ cycling.gr. Rock climbing, mountaineering, canyoning, rapelling, kayaking and mountain biking in Haniá province.

HORSERIDING

Melanouri ☎ 28920 45040, ⒲ melanouri.com. Horseriding holidays (one to seven days) from a stable near Mátala.

Odysseia ☎ 28970 51080, ⒲ horseriding.gr. One-to six-day guided and unguided horse treks from their base at Avdhoú near the Lasíthi Plateau.

Zoraïda's Horseriding ☎ 28250 61745, ⒲ zoraidas -horseriding.com. Horseriding holidays and treks from their stables in Yeoryoúpoli, Haniá.

WALKING AND CYCLING

Alpine Travel ☎ 28210 50939, ⒲ alpine.gr. Hiking, rock climbing, sea kayaking and biking holidays (or combinations thereof) in Haniá province.

Cretan Adventures ☎ 28103 33772, ⒲ cretan adventures.gr. Hiking, horseriding and jeep safaris throughout Crete.

The Happy Walker Tombázi 56, Réthymnon ☎ 28310 52920, ⒲ happywalker.com. Walking tours from one day to two weeks from €30 (for the day-hike which includes minibus from your hotel to start point).

Hellas Bike ☎ 28210 60858, ⒲ hellasbike.net. One- to seven-day bike tours from Ayía Marína in Haniá province.

Korifi Tours ☎ 28930 41440, ⒲ korifi.de. Hiking and climbing holidays in central, southern and western Crete.

Olympic Bike Adelianos Kampos 32, Réthymnon ☎ 28310 72383, ⒲ olympicbike.com. Guided bike tours from €139 for three one-day trips, or bike rental only from €20 per day.

Strata Walking Tours ☎ 28220 24336, ⒲ stratatours.com. Guided trekking holidays in the Kastélli Kissamou area of Haniá.

City walls and fortifications

The massive **Venetian walls**, in places up to 15m thick, are the most obvious evidence of Iráklion's history. Though their fabric is incredibly well preserved, access is virtually nonexistent. It is possible to scramble up and walk along them from Áyios Andhréas Bastion over the sea in the west, as far as the Martinengo Bastion and the **tomb of Nikos Kazantzakis**, Cretan author of *Zorba the Greek* (see p.211 & p.557), whose epitaph reads: "I believe in nothing, I hope for nothing, I am free." If the walls seem altogether too much effort, the **port fortifications** are much easier to see; the Venetian **arsenáli** (arsenals), their arches rather lost amid the concrete road system all around, and, opposite, the **fortress** at the harbour entrance.

Venetian fortress

The impressive sixteenth-century **Venetian fortress**, known by its Turkish name of **Koúles**, stands at the harbour entrance; emblazoned with the Venetian Lion of St Mark, it withstood a 22-year siege before finally falling to the Ottomans. Unfortunately the siege of time has caught up with the underwater foundations – in early 2011 the building was deemed unsafe and closed to visitors for an expected two- to three-year renovation programme; once completed, it should once again be possible to stroll out along the jetty, explore the interior and enjoy the views from the top floor.

25-Avgoústou Street and around

Heading inland from the harbour the pedestrianized **25-Avgoústou Street** is lined with shipping and travel agencies, a few restaurants, banks and stores. **El Greco Park**, to the right as you approach Platía Venizélou, is crowded with cafés and bars, while opposite, on the left, are some of the more interesting of Iráklion's older buildings including the

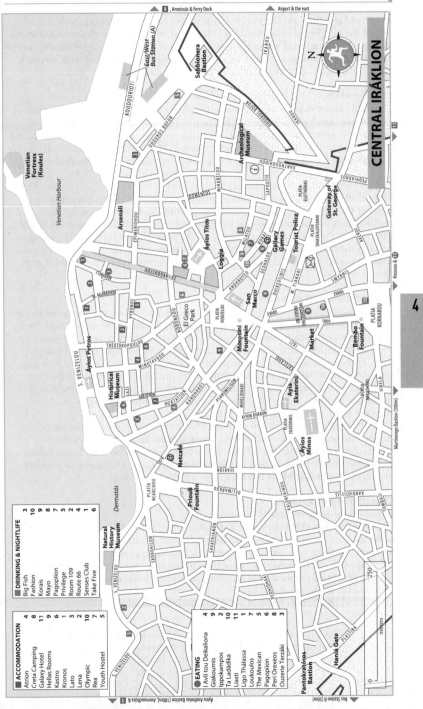

CENTRAL IRÁKLION

ACCOMMODATION

Atrion	4
Creta Camping	8
Galaxy Hotel	11
Hellas Rooms	6
Kastro	1
Kronos	3
Lato	2
Lena	10
Olympic	7
Rea	5
Youth Hostel	

DRINKING & NIGHTLIFE

Big Fish	3
Fashion	10
Korais	9
Mayo	8
Pagopiion	7
Privilege	5
Room 109	2
Route 66	4
Senses Club	1
Take Five	6

EATING

I Avli tou Deikaliona	4
Giakoumis	9
Ippokampos	2
Ta Ladadika	10
Liasti	11
Ligo Thálassa	1
Loukoulos	7
The Mexican	5
Pagopion	6
Peri Orexeos	8
Ouzerie Terzáki	3

church of Áyios Títos and the Venetian city hall with its famous **loggia**, both almost entirely rebuilt. Just above this, facing Platía Venizélou, stands the **church of San Marco**, its steps usually crowded with sightseers spilling over from the nearby platía. Neither of these last two buildings has found a permanent role in its refurbished state, but both are generally open to house some kind of exhibition or craft show.

Platía Venizélou

The focal **Platía Venizélou**, also known as **Liontária** or Lion Square, is crowded most of the day with locals patronizing its café terraces. The **Morosini Fountain** is not particularly spectacular at first glance, but on closer inspection is really a very beautiful work; it was built by Venetian governor Francesco Morosini in the seventeenth century, incorporating four lions which were some three hundred years old even then.

Platía Eleftherías

Platía Eleftherías, with seats shaded by palms and eucalyptuses, is the traditional heart of the city; traffic swirls around it constantly, on summer evenings crowds of strolling locals come to fill its café terraces, and most of Iráklion's more expensive shops are in the streets leading off here. At the southeastern corner of the platía an underground entrance to the **Gateway of St George** – a recently restored sixteenth-century tunnel and vault housing small art exhibitions – connects the platía with Ikárou Avenue.

The archeological museum

Xanthoudhídhou and Hatzidhaki, off Platía Eleftherías • May, June, Oct Mon noon–5pm; Tues–Sun 8.30am–5pm; July–Sept Mon 1–8pm, Tues–Sun 8am–8pm; Nov–April Mon noon–3pm, Tues–Sun 8.30am–3pm (check times with the tourist office) • €4 • ☎ 2810 224 630

Iráklion's **archeological museum** is one of Greece's largest; almost every important prehistoric and Minoan find on Crete is included in this fabulous, if bewilderingly large, collection. Hopefully, the current refurbishment (see box below) will be a huge improvement on the museum's previously dreary presentation. The size of the collection means that it's not possible to see everything in one visit, and the museum tends to be crowded – especially when guided tours stampede through – but it's certainly worth taking time over.

A number of the main exhibits from the collection are on display in the temporary museum annexe; highlights include the **"Town Mosaic"** and fragments of the spectacular **"Bull Leaping"** from Knossos, the famous **Festos disc** from Festos Palace, a **bull's head rhyton** (drinking vessel), the **snake goddess**, and a collection of jewellery including the **pendant of the two bees** from the Palace of Mália.

Church of Ayía Ekateríni

Ayía Ekateríni Square • Museum daily 9.30am–3.30pm • €2

The **church of Ayía Ekateríni**, an ancient building just below the new **Áyios Minas cathedral** off Kalokerinoú, has an excellent collection of icons in its **Ecclesiastical Museum**. The finest here are six large scenes by Mihaïl Damaskinos (a near contemporary of Cretan painter Doménikos Theotokópoulos, better known as El Greco), who fused Byzantine and Renaissance influences. Supposedly both Damaskinos and El Greco studied at Ayía Ekateríni in the sixteenth century, before the latter moved to Spain, when it functioned as a sort of monastic art school.

Iráklion's archeological museum closed in 2007 for complete **refurbishment**, with a temporary exhibition established at the rear of the building while work took place. The proposed two-year completion date proved hopelessly optimistic (it took four years just to approve the plans) but a section of the new museum is expected to open sometime during 2012 with full reopening pencilled in for 2013.

Historical Museum

Sófokli Venizélou 27 • May–Oct Mon–Sat 9am–5pm, Nov–April Mon–Sat 9am–3pm • €5 • ☎ 2810 283 219, ⓦ historical-museum.gr

The **Historical Museum** lies some 300m west of the harbour, on the waterfront. Its display gives a comprehensive view of Cretan history, incorporating sculptures and architectural pieces from the Byzantine, Venetian and Turkish periods as well as documents and photos of the German invasion of Crete, and folklore exhibits. Local memorabilia include the reconstructed studies of both Nikos Kazantzakis and Emanuel Tsouderos (the latter both Cretan statesman and former Greek prime minister). There's enough variety to satisfy just about anyone, including the only **El Greco** paintings on Crete, the small *View of Mount Sinai and the Monastery of St Catherine* and the even smaller *Baptism of Christ*.

Natural History Museum

Sófokli Venizélou • Mon–Fri 9am–4pm, Sat–Sun 10am–6pm • €6 • ☎ 2810 282 740, ⓦ www.nhmc.uoc.gr

Rehoused in a converted old power plant overlooking the bay of Dermatás, is the excellent **Natural History Museum**, operated under the framework of the University of Crete, and definitely worth a visit. Covering the ecosystems of the eastern Mediterranean, flora and fauna, exhibits over four floors detail the island's geological evolution, the arrival of man and the environment as it would have appeared to the Minoans. There's also an earthquake simulator and a planetarium, as well as a child-oriented Discovery Centre with interactive exhibits.

The beaches

Iráklion's **beaches** are a short way out, to both the east and west of town. **Ammoudhára** to the west has a large sandy beach that has been subjected to a degree of development, with hotels lining much of the coastal strip; at the far end there's an ugly power station and cement works. **Amnissós**, to the east, is the better choice, with several tavernas and the added amusement of planes swooping in immediately overhead to land at the nearby airport. This is where most locals go on their afternoons off; the furthest of the beaches is the best, although new hotels are encroaching. Little remains to indicate the once-flourishing port of Knossos here, aside from a rather dull, fenced-in dig.

ARRIVAL AND DEPARTURE
IRÁKLION

BY PLANE

Iráklion airport (Heraklion) (☎ 2810 397 111, ⓦ heraklion-airport.info) is right on the coast, 4km east of the city. Bus #1 goes to the city (every 20min until 11pm; €1.10); buy your ticket at the booth before boarding. Taxis can be found at the airport rank (about €14 into town); prices to all major destinations are posted here.

Airlines Aegean, Airport office (☎ 2810 330 475, ⓦ aegeanair.com), and Olympic, 25-Avgoústou 27 (☎ 2810 245 644, ⓦ olympic-airways.com), are the main scheduled airlines with connecting flights to Athens and other parts of Greece. EasyJet and Jet2 operate direct flights from the UK in summer. Charter airlines flying into Iráklion mostly use local travel agents as their representatives.

Domestic destinations Athens (12 daily with Olympic and Aegean; 50min); Rhodes (at least 2 daily on Olympic and Sky Express; 1hr); Thessaloníki (at least 2 daily on Olympic, Aegean or Sky Express; 1hr 15min).

International destinations Bristol, Leeds-Bradford, London Gatwick and Manchester (easyJet and Jet2 April–Oct).

BY FERRY

From the port cut straight up the stepped alleys behind the bus station onto Dhoúkos Bofór to Platía Eleftherías (about a 15min walk) or follow the main road west along the coast, past the bus station and the Venetian harbour, then cut up towards the centre along 25-Avgoústou.

Tickets Available from Minoan Lines, 25-Avgoústou 78 (☎ 2810 399 800, ⓦ minoan.gr), which handles the islands and Athens; and ANEK Lines, Dhimokratías 11 (☎ 2810 223 067, ⓦ anek.gr), for Athens only; or from any of the travel agents listed on p.208. For the latest timetables for domestic and international ferries to and from Crete visit ⓦ cretetravel.com, ⓦ ferries.gr or ⓦ greekislands.gr.

Destinations 2 ferries daily to Pireás (9hr); 1 daily fast catamaran to Thíra-Santorini (April–Oct; 2hr), also fast boats and hydrofoils (2hr 30min); 4–5 weekly ferries to Páros, Mýkonos, Íos and Náxos in season.

BY BUS

Bus station A Near the Venetian harbour. Use this station for buses to: west to Réthymnon, Haniá, east to Hersónissos, Mália, Áyios Nikólaos, Sitía, southeast to Ierápetra and points en route. Local bus #2 to Knossos also leaves from here.

Bus Station B Haniá Gate, at the beginning of 62-Martyrs street (a very long walk from the centre up Kalokerinoú, or jump on any bus heading down this street). Buses to: southwest to Phaestos, Mátala and Ayía Galíni, inland west to Týlissos, Anóyia.

Destinations Ayía Galíni (7 daily 6.30am–4.30pm; 2hr 15min); Áyios Nikólaos (19 daily 6.30am–10.30pm; 1hr 30min); Haniá (16 daily 5.30am–9pm; 2hr 50min); Ierápetra (8 daily 6.45am–7.30pm; 2hr 30min); Mátala (5 daily 7.30am–3.30pm; 2hr 30min); Phaestos (8 daily 7.30am–4.30pm; 1hr 30min); Réthymnon (16 daily 5.30am–9.30pm; 1hr 30min); Sitía (4 daily 7am–5.45pm; 3hr 15min).

GETTING AROUND

By bus Local buses serve the beaches (see p.205): to get to Ammoudhára, take #6 from the stop outside the *Astoria* hotel in Platía Eleftherías; for Amnissós, take #7 from the stop opposite this, under the trees of the platía.

By car Driving in busy Iráklion can be stressful. Follow the signs for car parking as soon as you enter the city centre; there's parking at the Museum car park (with another car park next door if this is full), just off Platía Eleftherías (well signed). There are plenty of car rental offices in town (see p.208).

Taxis Major taxi ranks are in Platía Eleftherías, Platía Kornarou and at the bus stations. Alternatively call ☎ 2810 210 102 or ☎ 2810 210 168. Prices should be displayed on boards at the taxi stands.

INFORMATION

Tourist office Xanthoudhídhou 1, just below Platía Eleftherías and opposite the Archeological Museum (Mon–Fri: May–Sept 9am–5pm; Oct–April 9am–2.30pm; ☎ 2810 246 298, ⊚ heraklion-city.gr). There's a secondary office at the airport (May–Sept daily 8am–8pm).

4 ACCOMMODATION

Finding a room can be difficult in high season. Inexpensive places cluster around Platía Venizélou, along Hándhakos and towards the harbour to the west of 25-Avgoústou. Other concentrations of affordable places are around El Greco Park and in the streets above the Venetian harbour. More luxurious hotels mostly lie closer to Platía Eleftherías and near the east- and westbound bus stations.

Atrion Hronáki 9 ☎ 2810 246 000, ⊚ atrion.gr. This attractive, modern, minimalistic-style hotel is in a handy location between the port and the centre, rooms are well-equipped with fridge, satellite TV, wi-fi and balcony. Breakfast included. **€80**

Galaxy Hotel Dimokratías 75 ☎ 2810 238 812, ⊚ galaxy-hotel.com. Located outside the old city wall, a 10min walk to the centre, this sleek, modern five-star hotel boasts a large pool, two gourmet restaurants and a wellness centre. Rooms are luxurious, with balcony, although some are rather small; allergy-friendly rooms are also available. Excellent buffet breakfast included. **€145**

Hellas Rooms Hándhakos 24 ☎ 2810 288 851, ⊜ hellasrooms24@yahoo.gr. A central hostel-type place, clean and friendly, with simple doubles, and dormitory rooms favoured by younger travellers. Facilities include a roof garden (with sea view) and snack-bar. The hotel is open May–Oct. Dorms **€14**

Kastro Theotokopoúlou 22 ☎ 82810 284185, ⊚ kastro-hotel.gr. The Kastro has undergone a contemporary restyle with comfortable a/c rooms, flat-screen TV and modern en-suite bathrooms. It's handily located on a side street behind El Greco park, but lacks decent views. Breakfast included. **€80**

Kronos Agárthou 2, west of 25-Avgoústou ☎ 2810 282 240, ⊚ kronoshotel.gr. Refurbished in 2011, this friendly two-star hotel is located on a busy street (so some traffic noise) by the central seafront. En-suite rooms with a/c, TV, fridge and balcony, some with sea view. **€50**

★ **Lato** Epomenídhou 15 ☎ 2810 228 103, ⊚ lato.gr. Stylish boutique hotel in a great central location opposite the Venetian harbour, with luxurious rooms sporting a/c, minibar, TV and fine balcony views over the port (the higher floors have better views). Breakfast included. **€103**

Lena Lahaná 10 ☎ 2810 223 280, ⊚ lena-hotel.gr. In a quiet, yet central, area, this efficient small hotel, north of El Greco park, offers rooms with balconies, both a/c en-suite rooms and rooms with shared bath and ceiling fan. TV and wi-fi. **€45**

Olympic Platía Kornárou, west of Platía Eleftherías ☎ 2810 288 861, ⊚ hotelolympic.com. One of the many hotels built in the 1960s, this one has been beautifully refurbished, and overlooks the busy platía and the famous Bembo fountain; facilities include a/c, TV, minibar and strongbox. Breakfast included. **€78**

Rea Kalimeráki 1 ☎ 2810 223 638. A good budget option, this friendly, comfortable and clean *pension* is in a quiet area just off Hándakos street. Some rooms with washbasin, others en suite. May–Oct. **€35**

Youth Hostel Vyronos 5 ☎ 2810 286 281, ✉ heraklio youthhostel@yahoo.gr. Formerly Iraklíon's official youth hostel, now privately operated, this is a reasonable and economical option. There's plenty of space, some private rooms as well as dormitories, with hot showers, breakfast and other meals available. May–Oct. Dorms **€10**

CAMPING

Creta Camping Káto Goúves, 16km east of the city ☎ 2897 041 400. Sits at the western end of the long sandy Káto Goúves beach, and offers some shady pitches (not all) and simple facilities. If you don't have your own equipment you can rent a tent or a cabin. **€25**

EATING

It's best to avoid the main tourist cafés around the platíes Venizélou and Eleftherias, which are generally both expensive and mediocre. Authentic and inexpensive **ouzerís** huddle near the 1866 market street and round Platía Dhaskaloyiánni (near the archeological museum), while other good **restaurants** are on, and just off, the seafront. For **snacks** and **takeaways**, a group of *souvláki* and other fast-food joints clusters around the top of 25-Avgoústou, and for *tyrópita* and *spanakópita* (cheese or spinach pies) and other pastries there is no shortage of bakery shops.

★ **Giakoumis** Fótiou Theodosáki 5, in the market ☎ 2810 284 039. Established in 1935, this is the city's oldest taverna and locals claim it serves up the best *païdhákia* (lamb chops) on the island – some tribute given the competition. You can wash them down with the hyma (house) wine produced by Lyrarakis, a noted Pezá vineyard. *Païdhákia* €7.50. Mon–Sat 10am–late.

★ **I Avli tou Deikaliona** Kalokairinoú 8, at the rear of the Historical Museum ☎ 2810 244 215. Popular taverna, with a lovely little terrace fronting the Idomeneus Fountain, serving up well-prepared meat and fish dishes. In high summer you may need to book to ensure an outdoor table. Grills from €6.50. Daily, dinner only.

★ **Ippokampos** Sófokli Venizélou, west of 25-Avgoústou, close to the Kronos hotel ☎ 2810 280 240. Deservedly popular with locals for lunch mezédhes as well as dinner, this fish taverna is often crowded late into the evening; turn up early to snag a table. Has a pleasant shaded terrace over the road on the seafront. Mon–Sat, lunch & dinner.

Liasti Miliara 7, south of the central zone ☎ 2810 343 490. At the end of an alley with a terrace under the trees – in the centre of town, just off Evans, yet away from the main hustle and bustle of traffic. This new *mezedhopolío* (formerly *Embolo*) produces many original dishes, with reasonable prices; try the pork shank with honey (€8), the house speciality. There's also indoor dining for the cooler months. Mon–Sat 1pm–1am.

Ligo Thálassa At the foot of Marinéli near the Venetian fort ☎ 2810 300 501. This small ouzerí is very popular with locals and serves up a good selection of seafood mezédhes, with a small street terrace facing the harbour. Daily 1pm–1am.

Loukoulos Koraí 5 ☎ 2810 224 435. With a leafy courtyard terrace and an Italian slant to its international menu, this is one of the better tavernas in Iráklion. However, the pricey food (mains from €15) and wine list seem aimed more at luring Iráklion's smart set than the casual visitor. Daily noon–1am.

The Mexican Hándhakos 71 ☎ 2810 220 334. The red and orange ethnic decor creates a warm atmosphere in this eatery, which serves inexpensive Mexican tacos, beers and jugs of sangria, complemented by salads and bean dishes. Daily lunch & dinner.

Ouzerie Terzáki Marinéli 17 ☎ 2810 221 444. This place is a favourite among local city-types, and serves mezédhes, pasta dishes and mains such as chicken fillet stuffed with spinach and mushrooms, on the outdoor street terrace. Mezédhes from €6. Daily noon–late.

★ **Pagopiion** Platía Áyios Títos ☎ 2810 346 028. This is the pricier restaurant of Iráklion's most original bar, serving Cretan and international dishes to a high standard; the wine list includes interesting bottles from little-known but excellent small vineyards around the island. Mains €15–20. Daily noon–late.

Peri Orexeos Koraí 10, almost opposite Loukoulos ☎ 2810 222 679. This popular small taverna is a good bet for creative Cretan cooking, with dishes such as burger stuffed with feta, red pepper and olives. Mains from €7. Daily noon–1am.

Ta Ladádika Tzikritzi 5, near the market ☎ 2810 346 135. Welcoming little ouzerí in a small pedestrianized street, with outdoor tables. Excellent mezédhes – try their *dolmadhákia* €4.50 – and local house wine from the barrel. Mon–Sat, 10am–late.

DRINKING AND NIGHTLIFE

As a university town, Iráklion has plenty of places to let your hair down. Young Cretans tend to be more into sitting and chatting over background music than energetic dancing; consequently large areas of **Koraï** and the surrounding pedestrianized streets are packed with alfresco cafés which transform into bars as the lights dim and the volume ramps up. In addition to the central zone nightlife, venues are also in the suburbs and out along the hotel strip to the west at Amoudhára.

BARS

Fashion Perdhíkari 3 ☎ 2810 241 903. A large, trendy music café-bar that's cloned numerous similar places nearby. On summer weekends, this is the place to be if you're under 30. Daily 9am–3am.

Korais Koraí 3 ☎ 2810 346 336. Glitzy open-air café with spacious plant-festooned terraces, overhead movie screens and soft rock music – highly popular with Iráklion's smart set. Daily 10am–3am.

Mayo Milátou 11, just north of Korai ☎ 2810 336 000. This extravaganza of a bar with spotlights, screens and music under a big canopy terrace is one of the places to be seen if you're part of Iráklion's student set. Its arrival has spawned a whole new set of bars and cafés along the same street. Daily 9am–3am.

Pagopiion (Ice Factory) Platía Áyios Títos ☎ 2810 346 028. Stunning bar with arty decor inside Iráklion's former ice factory. Much of the old building has been preserved, including a lift for hauling the ice from the basement freezer and a fascistic call to duty in German Gothic script on one wall – a remnant of Nazi occupation of the factory in World War II. Make sure to visit the toilets, which are in an artistic league of their own. Daily 9am–late.

Route 66 Hándakos 46. This small rock bar attracts a slightly older crowd, and blasts out rock classics into the night. Also opens as a café during the day, with a couple of tables on the pedestrianized street outside. Daily noon–late.

Take Five Arkoléontos 7, El Greco Park ☎ 2810 226 564.

One of the oldest bars in Iráklion, it began as a rock bar in the 1980s and is now a slick pavement café with an indoor bar, playing mainstream music that ramps up the volume as the night goes on. Daily 9am–4am.

CLUBS AND DISCOS

Discos and clubs proper tend to play Western music (and lots of techno) interspersed with Greek pop. Some of the clubs-proper don't open their doors before 11pm, with the crowds drifting in after 1am and dancing until dawn. For livelier, and earlier, partying head to one of the nearby resorts.

Big Fish Corner of Sófokli Venizélou & Makarios 17 ☎ 697 32 36 922. Popular late-night dance club, with theme evenings, international and Greek music, and occasional live performers. Daily 9pm–late.

Privilege Dhoúkos Bofór 7, down towards the harbour, below the archeological museum ☎ 2810 244 850. A glitzy mainstream club, which opens at midnight in the summer months – you can dance until the sun rises. Entrance €10 including a drink.

Room 109 Sófokli Venizélou 109 ☎ 2810 261 615. Fashionable and cool late-night bar on the seafront road, hosting various dance-themed nights, including Latin and house nights. Daily 9pm–late.

Senses Club Papandréou 277, Ammoudára ☎ 2810 824 059. A lively summer club with a party atmosphere, 5km west of the city, by Ammoudára beach, playing various international music including dance & R&B. Daily 9pm–late.

DIRECTORY

Banks There are ATMs all over town, but the main bank branches are on 25-Avgoústou.

Car and motorbike rental 25-Avgoústou is lined with rental companies, but you'll often find good deals on the backstreets nearby; it's always worth asking for discounts. For cars and bikes try: Blue Sea, Kosmá Zótou 7, just off the bottom of 25-Avgoústou (☎ 2810 241 097, ⊛ bluesea rentals.com), Kosmos, 25-Avgoústou 15 (☎ 2810 241 357, ⊛ cosmos-sa.gr), or the nearby Caravel, 25-Avgoústou 39 (☎ 2810 245 345, ⊛ caravel.gr); and Ritz in the *Hotel Rea*, Kalimeráki 1 (☎ 2810 223 638). All offer free delivery to hotels and airport.

Hospital The closest is the Venizélou Hospital, on the Knossós road south out of town (☎ 2810 368 000).

Internet Two central cafés are Netcafé, Odhós-1878 4 (daily 10am–2am), and Gallery Games, Koraï 14. Many cafés and hotels offer free wi-fi.

Laundry Washsalon, Hándakos 18 (Mon–Sat 8.30am–9pm), is reliable and also does service washes (around €7 for 6kg). The slightly cheaper (around €6 for 6kg) Laundry Perfect at Malikoúti 32, north of the archeological museum, is also good (Mon–Sat 9am–9pm).

Left luggage Offices in (bus) Station A (daily 6.30am–8pm; €2 per bag per day), but not Station B, as well as a commercial

agency at Hándakos 18 (daily 9am–9pm; €3 per large locker per day). Blue Sea, Kotzia 3 off Epimenidhou, near the Venetian harbour (daily 7am–11pm), is a reliable and similar outfit and stores bags for €3 per day. You can also leave bags at the youth hostel (see p.207); €3 per bag per day for guests, €5 per bag per day for non-guests.

Newspapers and books For English-language newspapers and novels, Bibliopoleio, almost opposite the Morosini Fountain on Platía Venizélou, is the most central. The excellent Planet International Bookstore, near the seafront at Hándakos 73, has the island's biggest stock of English-language titles and is a great place to browse.

Pharmacies Plentiful on the main shopping streets – at least one is open 24hr on a rota basis; the others will have a sign on the door indicating which it is. There are traditional herbalists in the market.

Post office Platía Dhaskaloyiánnis, off Platía Eleftherías (Mon–Fri 7.30am–8pm, Sat 7.30am–2pm).

Travel agencies Budget operators and student specialists include the extremely helpful Blavakis Travel, Platía Kallergón 8, just off 25-Avgoústou by the entrance to El Greco Park (☎ 2810 282 541). Ferry information and tickets from Paleologos Travel, 25-Avgoústou 5 (☎ 2810 346 185, ⊛ ferries.gr).

Knossos

Daily: May–June 8am–5pm; July–Sept 8am–8pm; Oct–April 8.30am–3pm • €6 • ☎ 2810 231 940

KNOSSOS, the largest and most important of the **Minoan palaces**, and the most visited, lies some 5km southeast of Iráklion. The mythological home of King Minos and the Minotaur, it dates from the second millennium BC, and its vast interconnected rooms and corridors provide a fitting backdrop to the legend.

The discovery of the palace is among the most amazing tales of modern archeology. **Heinrich Schliemann**, the German excavator of Troy, suspected that a major Minoan palace lay under the various tumuli here, but was denied the permission to dig by the local Ottoman authorities. It was left for **Sir Arthur Evans** who excavated and liberally "restored" the palace from 1900 onwards. His restorations have been the source of furious controversy among archeologists ever since. Even so, his guess as to what the palace might have looked like is certainly as good as anyone's, and it makes Crete's other Minoan sites infinitely more meaningful if you have seen Knossos first.

ARRIVAL AND INFORMATION   KNOSSOS

To avoid the hordes get to the site early morning, before the coach tours arrive, or late afternoon when they've left

By bus Local buses #2 and #4. Set off (every 10min) from Iráklion's city bus stands (adjacent to the eastbound Bus Station A), then proceed to Platía Eleftherías and out of town along Odhós-1821 and Evans).
From the centre of Iráklion a taxi will cost around €10.
By car There's a free car park immediately before the site entrance, which will enable you to avoid paying exorbitant rates for the private car parks dotting the road immediately before this (and whose touts will attempt to wave you in).

Guided tours Official guides can be hired at the site entrance; they are self-employed and expensive, but you can usually negotiate the price a little if you wish to use their services, and rope in other visitors to share the cost.
Websites The British School at Athens has a useful website dedicated to Knossos, with detail on its history and excavations in addition to a virtual tour; check out ⓦ bsa.gla.ac.uk/knossos/vrtour.

The site

As soon as you enter the **Palace of Knossos** through the West Court, the ancient ceremonial entrance, it is clear how the legends of the labyrinth grew up around it. Even with a detailed plan, it's almost impossible to find your way around the complex with any success, although a series of **timber walkways** channels visitors around the site, severely restricting the scope for independent exploration. If you haven't hired a guide and are worried about missing the highlights, you can always tag along with a group

---

THE LEGEND OF THE MINOTAUR

Knossos was the court of the legendary **King Minos**, whose wife Pasiphae, cursed by Poseidon, bore the **Minotaur**, half-bull, half-man. The **labyrinth** was constructed by Daedalus to contain the monster, and every nine years seven youths and seven maidens were brought from Athens as human sacrifice. Hearing of this, the Greek hero **Theseus** arrived on Crete vowing to venture into the labyrinth and slay the beast. **Ariadne**, daughter of the king, promptly fell in love with him and, as every cub scout knows, showed Theseus how to find his way back using a simple ball of thread. The legend has inspired writers from Homer to Dante, who famously depicts the best in his vision of Hell:

Into the chasm was that descent: and there
At point of the disparted ridge lay stretch'd
The infamy of Crete, detested brood
Of the feign'd heifer: and at sight of us
It gnaw'd itself, as one with rage distract.

Dante, Inferno, Canto XII

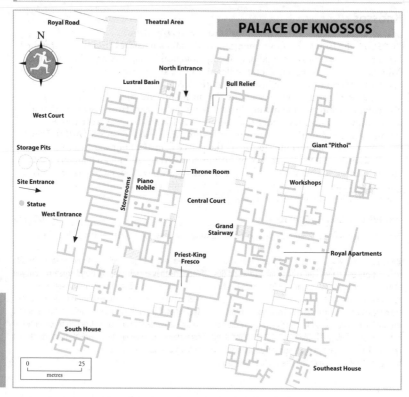

Map labels: Royal Road · Theatral Area · **PALACE OF KNOSSOS** · N · North Entrance · Lustral Basin · Bull Relief · West Court · Storage Pits · Giant "Pithoi" · Site Entrance · Piano Nobile · Throne Room · Workshops · Storerooms · Statue · Central Court · West Entrance · Grand Stairway · Royal Apartments · Priest-King Fresco · South House · Southeast House · 0 25 metres

for a while, catching the patter and then backtracking to absorb the detail when the crowd has moved on. You won't get the place to yourself, whenever you come, but exploring on your own does give you the opportunity to appreciate individual parts of the palace in the brief lulls between groups.

For some idea of the size and complexity of the palace in its original state, take a look at the cutaway drawings (wholly imaginary but probably not too far off) on sale outside.

Royal Apartments

The superb **Royal Apartments** around the central staircase are not guesswork, and they are plainly the finest of the rooms at Knossos. The **Grand Stairway** itself is a masterpiece of design, its large well bringing light into the lower storeys.

In the **Queen's Suite**, off the grand **Hall of the Colonnades** at the bottom of the staircase, the main living room is decorated with the celebrated **dolphin fresco** – it's a reproduction; the original is now in the Iráklion Archeological Museum (see p.204) – and with running friezes of flowers and abstract spirals. Remember, though, that all this is speculation; the dolphin fresco, for example, was found on the courtyard floor, not in the room itself, and would have been viewed from an upper balcony as a sort of trompe l'oeil, like looking through a glass-bottomed boat. A dark passage leads around to the queen's **bathroom** and a clay tub, the famous "flushing" toilet (a hole in the ground with drains to take the waste away – it was flushed by throwing a bucket of water down).

The much-perused **drainage system** was a series of interconnecting terracotta pipes running underneath most of the palace. Guides to the site never fail to point these out as evidence of the advanced state of Minoan civilization.

The Grand Stairway ascends to the floor above the queen's domain, and the **King's Quarters**; the staircase opens into a grandiose reception chamber known as the **Hall of the Royal Guard**, its walls decorated in repeated shield patterns. Immediately off here is the **Hall of the Double Axes** (or the King's Room); believed to have been the ruler's personal chamber, its name comes from the double-axe symbol carved into every block of masonry.

The Throne Room

At the top of the Grand Stairway you emerge onto the broad **Central Court**; on the far side, in the northwestern corner, is the entrance to another of Knossos's most atmospheric survivals, the **Throne Room**. Here, a worn stone throne – with its hollowed shaping for the posterior – sits against the wall of a surprisingly small chamber; along the walls around it are ranged stone benches, suggesting a king ruling in council, and behind there's a reconstructed fresco of two griffins.

The rest of the palace

Try not to miss the giant *pithoi* in the northeast quadrant of the site, an area known as the palace workshops; other must-see areas and features include the storage chambers (which you see from behind the Throne Room), the reproduced frescoes in the reconstructed room above it, the fresco of the Priest-King looking down on the south side of the central court, and the relief of a charging bull on its north side. Just outside the North Entrance is the **theatral area** (another Evans designation), an open space a little like a stepped amphitheatre, which may have been used for ritual performances or dances. From here the **Royal Road**, claimed as the oldest road in Europe, sets out. Circling back around the outside of the palace, you can get an idea of its scale by looking up at it; on the south side are a couple of small reconstructed Minoan houses which are worth exploring.

Inland from Iráklion

Heading south from Knossos, the zone around **Arhánes** and **Péza** is one of Crete's major wine-producing areas (see box, p.214). Nearby are some more Minoan sites at **Anemospiliá** and **Vathýpetro**, plus a few diverting villages. The main inland route southwest from Iráklion climbs through the mountains before winding down to **Áyii Dhéka** and the Messará plain. Here on the Messará, all within a 40km range of each other, lie the three major archeological sites of **Phaestos**, **Ayía Triádha** and **Gortys**. Once you get this far south you're within a short drive of the coastal resorts of **Mátala** and (accessed via a mountain road) **Léndas.**

GETTING AROUND   **INLAND FROM IRÁKLION**

By bus Iráklion (Bus station A) to: Arhánes (Mon–Fri hourly 6am–9pm, Sat hourly 7am–7pm, Sun 8am, 11am, 2pm, 5pm); Houdhétsi (Mon–Thur 6 daily 7am–3pm, Fri 7 daily 7am–8.15pm, Sat 4 daily 9.30am–3pm, Sun 7.30am only); Mátala – some change at Mires (4 daily 7.30am–3.30pm; 2hr 30min); Léndas (Mon–Fri; 12.30pm;

2hr). Iráklion (Bus station B) to: Phaestos (8 daily 7.30am–4.30pm; 1hr 30min).
By car When heading south from the Messará plain, the Asteroussia hills, which divide the plain from the coast, are surprisingly precipitous and the roads in these parts are slow going.

Myrtiá

MYRTIÁ is an attractive village, 15km south of Iráklion, and home to the small **Kazantzakis Museum** (March–Oct daily 9am–5pm; Nov–Feb Sun only 10am–3pm; €3), dedicated to the famous writer and philosopher, Nikos Kazantzakis (see p.202). The museum, a cluster of buildings in the village square, displays manuscripts, notes and first editions of the writer's works, as well as photographs and personal effects – expect to see plenty of models, costumes and other material from theatre productions of his works in Greece and abroad.

Arhánes

ARHÁNES, at the foot of Mount Yioúhtas, is a sizeable, wealthy farming town that was reasonably heavily populated in Minoan times. The main square has several tavernas, cafés and bars, while 100m to the north is the excellent **archeological museum** (Wed–Mon 8.30am–2.30pm; free), which displays finds from here and other excavations in the area, including a strange ceremonial dagger seemingly used for human sacrifice. The nearby site of **Anemospiliá**, 2km northwest of the town (directions are available from the archeological museum), is visitable, and has experienced huge controversy since its excavation in the 1980s: many traditional views of the Minoans, particularly that of Minoan life as peaceful and idyllic, have had to be rethought in the light of the discovery of an apparent human sacrifice. From Arhánes you can also drive (or walk with a couple of hours to spare) to the summit of Mount Yoúktas to see the imposing remains of a Minoan **peak sanctuary** and enjoy spectacular panoramic **views** towards Knossos (with which it was linked) and the northern coast beyond.

Vathýpetro

At **VATHÝPETRO**, some 4km south of Mount Yoúktas, is a **Minoan villa and vineyard** (Tues–Sun 8.30am–2pm; free), which once controlled the rich farmland south of Arhánes. Inside, a remarkable collection of farming implements was found, as well as a unique **wine press**, which remains *in situ*. Substantial portions of the farm's buildings remain, and it's still surrounded by fertile vines three-and-a-half-thousand years later – making it probably the oldest still-functioning vineyard in Europe, if not the world.

Houdhétsi

Some 2km southeast of **Vathýpetro** brings you to the agricultural village of **HOUDHÉTSI**, where you'll find the remarkable **Museum of Musical Instruments of the World** (March–Oct daily 8am–4pm; Nov–Feb Sun 10am–3pm; €3; ☏2810 741 027, ⓦlabyrinthmusic.gr). Founded by Irish *lýra* player Ross Daly, who is famed in Crete and lives in the village, the museum consists of a collection of mainly string and percussion instruments (many very rare) from across the globe. To get to the museum head for the pharmacy on the main road by the central square – the museum is opposite, housed in a mansion.

Áyii Dhéka

ÁYII DHÉKA is the first village on the fertile Messará plain on the main route south from Iráklion and for religious Cretans a place of pilgrimage; its name, "The Ten Saints", refers to ten early Christians martyred here under the Romans. The old Byzantine church in the centre of the village preserves the stone block on which they are supposed to have been decapitated, and in a crypt below the modern church on the village's western edge you can see the martyrs' (now empty) tombs. It's an attractive village to wander around, with several places to eat.

Gortys

Daily: July–Sept 8am–8pm; Oct–June 8am–3pm • €3 • ☏2810 226 470

Within easy walking distance of Áyii Dhéka (1km), sprawls the site of **Gortys**, ruined capital of the Roman province that included not only Crete but also much of North Africa. Evidence of a Minoan site has been unearthed on the acropolis, but the extant ruins date almost entirely from the Roman era.

At the main entrance to the **fenced site**, to the north of the road, are the ruins of the still impressive sixth-century **basilica of Áyios Títos**, and beyond this is the **odeion**, which houses the most important discovery on the site, the **Law Code**. Written in an obscure early Doric-Cretan dialect, they are, at 9m by 3m, the largest Greek inscription ever found. The laws set forth reflect a strictly hierarchical society: five witnesses were needed to convict a free man of a crime, only one for a slave; raping a free man or woman carried a fine of a hundred *staters*, a serf only five. A small **museum** in a loggia (also within the fenced area) holds a number of large and finely worked sculptures found at Gortys, more evidence of the city's importance. Next to the museum is a **café** (same hours as site).

Phaestos

Daily: June–Sept daily 8am–8pm; Oct–May 8.30am–3pm • €4, joint ticket with Ayía Triádha €6

The **Palace of Phaestos**, 35km west of Gortys, was excavated by the Italian Federico Halbherr (also responsible for the early work at Gortys) at almost exactly the same time as Evans was working at Knossos. Here, however, to the approval of most traditional archeologists, reconstruction was kept to an absolute minimum – it's all bare foundations, and walls which rise at most 1m above ground level. This means that, despite a magnificent setting overlooking the plain of Messará, the palace at Phaestos is not as immediately arresting as those at Knossos or Mália, but no less fascinating.

It's interesting to speculate why the palace was built halfway up a hill rather than on the plain below – certainly not for defence, for this is in no way a good defensive position. Psychological superiority over the peasants or reasons of health are both possible, but it seems quite likely that it was simply the magnificent view that finally swayed the decision. The site looks over Psilorítis to the north and the huge plain, with the Lasíthi mountains beyond it, to the east.

On the ground closer at hand, you can hardly fail to notice the strong similarities between Phaestos and the other palaces: the same huge rows of storage jars, the great courtyard with its monumental stairway, and the theatre area. Unique to Phaestos,

4

PALACE OF PHAESTOS

Tourist Pavilion
Entrance
Lustral Basin
Royal Apartments
Archive
Peristyle Hall
Peristyle House
North Court
Theatral Area and West Court
Propylon
Grand Stairway
Workshops
Storage Pits
Storerooms
Furnace
Office
Prince's rooms
Steep bank
First Palace Remains
Central Court
Classical Temple
Steep bank
N
0   25
metres

4

WINE TASTING IN CRETE

As well as the large Péza region near Knossos and the ancient vineyard at Vathýpetro (see p.212), there are also vineyards in eastern Crete, around Sitía, another major producer, and smaller vineyards in the west around Haniá. The main grape varieties grown on the island are the white Vilana and the red Mantilari, Kotsifari and Syrah grapes. Wine tasting and cellar tours can be undertaken during the summer months.

Boutari Skaláni, Iráklion ☎2810 731617, ⓦboutari.gr. On the road towards the village of Myrtiá lies the Fantaxometocho estate of the privately owned Boutari vineyard. Specializing in organic production methods, they make excellent wines. Tours €5. May–Oct daily 10am–4pm.

Dourakis Alíkambos, Vrýsses, near Haniá ☎28250 51761. On the main road, 4km from Vrýsses towards Hóra Sfákion, this small, friendly family-owned winery offers tasting and tours, and there's a small one-room museum of old farming implements. Tours €3. May–Oct Mon–Sat 10am–2pm & 4–6pm.

Minos Wines Péza, Iráklion ☎2810 741213, ⓦminoswines.gr. Milliarakis is the estate of another privately owned producer, Minos Wines. Tasting takes place in their large wine-tasting room, which is furnished as a traditional *kafenío*. Tours €2. May–Oct Mon–Fri 9am–4pm.

Peza Union Kalloní, Iráklion ☎2810 741945, ⓦpezaunion.gr. Beyond Péza village, 2km. The union of agricultural cooperatives of Péza produces olive oil as well as wine. A tour of their exhibition centre is followed by wine tasting and a small meze. Tours free. May–Oct Mon–Sat 9am–5pm.

Sitia Co-operative Géla, Sitía ☎28430 29991. On the main road towards Áyios Nikólaos, 1km from Sitía. The famous wines of Sitía OPAP are produced here. Tours include a tasting in the cellar and an audiovisual presentation. Tours €2. Mon–Fri 9am–3pm.

however, is the third courtyard, in the middle of which are the remains of a **furnace** used for metalworking. Oddly enough, Phaestos was much less ornately decorated than Knossos; there is no evidence, for example, of any of the dramatic Minoan wall-paintings.

Ayía Triádha

Daily: May–Sept 10am–4pm; Oct–April 8.30am–3pm • €4, joint ticket with Phaestos €6

Some of the finest artworks in the museum at Iráklion came from **Ayía Triádha**, 4km west of Phaestos. No one is quite sure what this site is, but the most common theory has it as some kind of royal summer villa. It's smaller than the palaces but, if anything, even more lavishly appointed and beautifully situated. In any event, it's an attractive place to visit, far less crowded than Phaestos, with a wealth of interesting little details. Look out in particular for the row of **stores** in front of what was apparently a marketplace, and the remains of a **paved road** that probably led down to a harbour on the Gulf of Messará. There's a fourteenth-century **chapel** – dedicated to Áyios Yeóryios – at the site, worth visiting in its own right for the remains of ancient frescoes.

Míres

The large market town of **MÍRES**, 20km west of Gortys, serves as a transport hub for buses further west and to the beaches of the south coast; if you're travelling to Mátala, or west beyond Phaistos, then you'll normally switch buses here. There are good facilities including a **bank**, a few **restaurants**, a couple of **rooms** places and a handy **internet** café, *Sirvitis*, right opposite the bus stop, though there's no particular reason to stay unless you are waiting for a bus.

Mátala

MÁTALA is best-known for its famous caves cut into the cliffs above beautiful sands. These are ancient tombs first used by Romans or early Christians, but more recently inhabited by a sizeable hippie community in the 1960s and 1970s (including some famous names such as Bob Dylan and Joni Mitchell). The caves have long since been cleared and cleaned up, and these days they are an archeological site, fenced off at night, but you can still wander around them freely in the daytime.

The resort still has a laidback feel outside of high summer, but July and August see the beach packed to overflowing in the early afternoon, when the tour buses pull in for their swimming stop. The town beach is beautiful, and if the crowds get excessive, you can climb over the rocks in about twenty minutes to another excellent stretch of sand, known locally as "Red Beach". It's best to stay a night here and enjoy the waterside bars and restaurants in peace once the tour buses have left.

ARRIVAL AND INFORMATION

MÁTALA

By bus Buses arrive by the beach car park. There are 5 services per day to Iráklion (2hr 30min).
By car In Mátala, park in the car park at the beach (€2 per day), on the right as you reach the town proper.
Services Internet is available at *Zafiria Café* opposite the main square.

ACCOMMODATION

A cluster of rooms places lies near to the *Zafiria* hotel, and the street to the left is known as "Hotel Street"; here you'll find several options.

Iliaki Hotel Street ☏ 28920 45110, ⓦ matala-holidays.gr. A small, immaculate *pension* with recently decorated rooms. All have a/c, TV, fridge and free wi-fi. A two-bedroomed apartment within the *pension* with its own patio garden is also available to rent (€75). May–Oct. **€45**

Matala Camping Next to the main beach, behind the car park ☏ 28920 45720. There's plenty of shade here to pitch your tent in the sand under the tamarisk trees, close to the beach, but the shower/wc facilities are very basic. June–Oct. **€12**

Matala View Hotel Street ☏ 28920 45114, ⓦ matala-apartments.com. Simple and clean rooms, studios and apartments (sleeps 4) with private bathroom, fan and fridge. Studios and apartments have kitchenette and some with a/c (€5/day extra). May–Oct. **€40**

★ **Nikos** Hotel Street ☏ 28920 45375, ⓦ matala-nikos.com. The friendly *Nikos* has pleasant a/c rooms with en-suite bathroom, TV and fridge, off a plant-filled patio. The "penthouse" room, which stands alone on the roof, has a stunning view. Some rooms with cooking facilities. Free wi-fi. May–Oct. **€45**

Zafiria Main street, just beyond the car park turn-off ☏ 28920 45112, ⓦ zafiria-matala.com. Here rooms (some with a sea view) come with a/c but no TV, and there's a pool. May–Oct. **€45**

EATING AND DRINKING

Alex and Anna A popular, simple taverna serving fresh home-cooked food, daily specials and grills, with tables on the road-side terrace in the main square. Mains from €5.50. May–Oct daily lunch & dinner.

Kafeneio Stylish café at the entrance to town, serving coffees, snacks, drinks and cocktails throughout the day and evening, and with wi-fi access. April–Oct daily 8am–1am.

Skala ☏ 28920 45489. A good fish taverna, perched above the sea at the far south end of the bay with a great view. Fresh fish, with seafood dishes from €7. May–Oct daily lunch & dinner.

NIGHTLIFE

Port Side ☏ 694 59 83 886. A cocktail bar with an enviable location, great views across the bay from the bar terrace, perched above the beach, and a café by day. May–Oct daily 9am–late.

Tommy's Music Bar Just beyond Port Side, this popular bar gets lively later on, with the crowds spilling into the street. May–Sept daily 8pm–late.

Léndas

LÉNDAS, east of Mátala, has a partly justified reputation for being peaceful though it suffers from considerable summer weekend crowds. From the ramshackle outskirts of the village take the cobbled paths leading down to the village square and to the small, grey-sand beach. The main attraction, however, is the vast and sandy beach on the other (west) side of the headland, **Ditikós** (or Diskós) beach; part of it is usually taken over by nudists, with a number of taverna/bars overlooking it from the road side.

Akti Léndas beach. Excellent, friendly taverna in a great location on the beach, serving freshly prepared meat, fish and Cretan dishes. April–Oct daily 11am–1am.

El Greco Léndas village ☎ 28920 95322. A particularly good restaurant with a large leafy terrace, serving home-made Greek dishes, as well as fresh fish and seafood. Try their *oktapódhi* (octopus; €8), or prime

Messará beef pepper steak. April–Oct daily lunch & dinner.

Villa Tsapakis Ditikós Beach ☎ 28920 95378, ⓦ villa -tsapakis.gr. These bougainvillea-fronted rooms above Ditikós beach come with a sea view, fridge and TV, and reductions for longer stays. They have their own decent taverna, *Odysseas*, nearby. April–Oct. **€35**

East of Iráklion: the package-tour coast

East of Iráklion, the main package-tour resorts are at least 30km away, at **Hersónissos** and **Mália**, although there is a string of rather unattractive developments all the way there; the merest hint of a beach is an excuse to build hotel and apartment complexes. That said, there are one or two highlights amid the dross, which are well worth a visit: the impressive **Cretaquarium** at Goúrnes, the **old villages** in the hills behind Hersónissos, and, beyond the clubbing resort of Mália, a fine **Minoan palace** that will transport you back three and a half millennia.

By bus Iráklion (Bus station B) to: Hersónissos and Mália (daily, every 30min 6am–10.30pm; 40min); Palace of

Malia (2 daily 9.15am, 3.15pm; 45min).

4

Cretaquarium

Daily: May–Sept 9.30am–9pm; Oct–Apr 9.30am–5pm • €8, children aged 5–17 €6 • ☎ 28103 37788, ⓦ cretaquarium.gr • Goúrnes, 15km from Iráklion

The only reason to visit the resort of Goúrnes is the **Cretaquarium**, a spectacular and sizeable marine aquarium converted from a US air base. Boasting thirty tanks (some huge), it houses everything from menacing sharks to dazzling jellyfish. Part of the Hellenic Centre for Marine Research, the venture is purely educational, scientific and non-profit making. Most of the island's fish and crustaceans are included among the 250 species and over 2500 specimens on display, and unless you're a marine biologist the audio-guide (€3; easily shared between two or three) is pretty well indispensable and gives loads of fascinating background information on the creatures you're looking at. The aquarium is well signposted on the road leading from Iráklion.

Hersónissos

The first of the really big resorts, **HERSÓNISSOS** was once just a small fishing village (Límin Hersoníssou); today it's one of the most popular of Crete's package resorts, a brash, sprawling place overrun with hotels, bars, touristy tavernas and nightclubs. Beach and clubs excepted, the main attractions are the **Lychnostatis Open-air Museum of Folklore** (Mon–Fri & Sun 9am–2pm; €5), a surprisingly rewarding museum of traditional Crete with imaginative reconstructions of island life past and present, and **Aqua World** (April–Oct daily 10am–6pm; €6 adults, €4 under-12s), a small aquarium. A short distance inland, the three pretty **hill villages** of Koutoulafári, Piskopianó and "old" Hersónissos present a glimpse of more traditional Crete and offer some attractive rooms and good tavernas.

Mália

Eight kilometres east of Hersónissos lies the package-resort town of **MÁLIA,** renowned for its wild, teenage, bar and clubbing scene. The town's focus is a T-junction, from where the beach road – a kilometre-long strip lined with bars, clubs, games arcades, tavernas and souvenir shops – heads north to the sea and beaches. South of this junction the **old town** presents a saner image of what Mália used to be; a labyrinth of narrow streets and whitewashed walls, but even here commercialism is making inroads.

The Palace of Malia
Tues–Sun 8.30am–3pm • €4 • ☎ 28970 31957

Much less imposing than either Knossos or Phaestos, the **Palace of Malia**, 2km east of Mália town, in some ways surpasses both. For a start, it's a great deal emptier and you can wander among the remains in relative peace. While no reconstruction has been attempted, the palace was never reoccupied after its second destruction in the fifteenth century BC, so the ground plan is virtually intact.

From this site came the famous **gold pendant** of two bees and the beautiful **leopard-head axe**, both of which are displayed in Iráklion's archeological museum. At the site, look out for the strange indented stone in the central court (which probably held ritual offerings), for the remains of ceremonial stairways and for the giant *pithoi*, which stand like sentinels around the palace. To the north and west of the main site, archeological digs are still going on as the large town which surrounded the palace comes slowly to light (part of this can be viewed via an overhead walkway).

Any passing **bus** should stop at the site, or you could even rent a **bike** for a couple of hours as it's a pleasant, flat ride from Mália town. Leaving the archeological zone and turning immediately right, you can follow the road down to a lovely stretch of clean and relatively peaceful **beach**.

West of Iráklion

Leaving Iráklion city to the west, the fast **E75 coastal highway** winds all the way to Réthymnon, a spectacular drive, the road being hacked into the sides of mountains which for the most part drop straight to the sea, though there are no more than a handful of places where you might consider stopping: the coastal settlements of **Ayía Pelayía** and the more attractive **Balí**, both sizeable resorts, and the smaller village of **Fódhele**, which claims to be the birthplace of **El Greco**. By contrast, the old roads inland are agonizingly slow, but they do pass through a whole string of **attractive villages** beneath the heights of the **Psilorítis** range.

Ayía Pelayía
Some 20km west along the highway from Iráklion lies the resort of **AYÍA PELAYÍA**. It looks extremely attractive from above but, once there, and especially in July and August, you're likely to find the narrow, taverna-lined beach packed to full capacity. Despite the high-season crowds, the resort maintains a dignity long since lost in Mália and Hersónissos, and even a certain exclusivity; one of Crete's most luxurious hotel resorts nestles on the headlands just beyond the main town beach.

Fódhele
Beyond Ayía Pelayía, there's a turning inland to the village of **FÓDHELE**, allegedly El Greco's birthplace. A plaque from the University of Valladolid (in Spain) acknowledges the claim and, true or not, the community has built a small tourist industry on that basis. There are a number of craft shops and some pleasant tavernas where you can sit outside along the river. A peaceful 1km walk (or drive) takes you to the spuriously titled **El Greco's House** (aka Museum of El Greco; May–Oct Tues–Sun 9am–7pm; €2), exhibiting a few poor reproductions of his works and not much more, while the picturesque fourteenth-century Byzantine **church of the Panayía** is opposite (usually locked). None of this amounts to very much, but it is a pleasant, relatively unspoilt village if you simply want to sit in peace for a while.

Balí

BALÍ, on the coast about halfway between Iráklion and Réthymnon, is a charming small resort with a beautiful setting and sandy beaches. The village is built around a trio of small coves, some 2km from the highway, and is similar to Ayía Pelayía except that the beaches are not quite as good and there are no big hotels, just an ever-growing proliferation of apartment buildings, rooms for rent and a number of smaller hotels. You'll have plenty of company here, and it has to be said that Balí has become a package resort too popular for its own good; it's a beautiful place to splash about, surrounded by mountains rising straight from the sea, but there's rarely a spare inch on the sand in high season.

Týlissos

Daily 8.30am–3pm • €2

TÝLISSOS, 11km inland and west of Iráklion, has a significant archeological site where three Minoan houses were excavated; unfortunately, its reputation is based more on what was found here (many pieces in the Iráklion Archeological Museum) and on its significance for archeologists than on anything which remains to be seen. Still, it's worth a look, if you're passing, for a glimpse of Minoan life away from the big palaces, and for the tranquillity of the pine-shaded remains.

Anóyia

ANÓYIA is a tempting place to stay, especially if the summer heat is becoming oppressive. It's a large village, with two centres, spilling prettily down a hillside below **Mount Psilorítis**. It looks traditional, but closer inspection shows that most of the buildings are actually concrete; the village was destroyed during World War II and the local men were rounded up and shot – one of the German reprisals for the abduction of General Kreipe by the Cretan resistance. The town has a reputation as a centre of **lýra** playing (many famous exponents were born here, most notably the late Nikos Xylouris) and also as a **handicrafts** centre. It's a thriving place today thanks to a buoyant sheep farming sector – farmers here are some of the richest in Greece; don't miss the **spit-roast lamb** if you're carnivorously inclined.

GETTING AROUND   WEST OF IRÁKLION

By bus Iráklion–Réthymnon line buses, running hourly along the main coastal highway, stop at the exit roads to Ayía Pelayía, Balí and Fódhele; you'll then have a 2–3km (hot) walk down to each village. Ayía Pelayía also has a limited direct service from Iráklion to the centre of the resort (3 daily, 8.30am, 9.15am, 2.30pm; 30min).

ACCOMMODATION AND EATING

AYÍA PELAYÍA

Most accommodation here is block-booked by package holiday companies, although in quieter times you shouldn't have any problems finding a bed. The Pangosmio travel agency (☎ 28108 11402) may be able to come up with something at the last minute.

Irini Beach road ☎ 28108 11455, ⓦ irini-hotel -apartments.gr. Cheery apartments, above a good snack-bar and café of the same name, and just a few metres from the beach. Apartments sleep 2–6, with a/c, balcony, TV, and kitchen. April–Oct. **€45**

Out of the Blue, Capsis Elite Resort ☎ 28108 11112, ⓦ capsis.gr. This five-star luxury resort complex sits on a private peninsula, comprising four hotels, seven pools, luxury villas with private pools and three private beaches. It even has its own zoo. April–Oct. From **€200**

Zorba's Beach road, near the beach ☎ 28102 56072, ⓦ zorbas.gr. Pleasant apartments and studios with balcony, located above a shop just seconds from the beach. Facilities include a/c, kitchenette and fridge. Wi-fi is also available. May–Oct. **€45**

BALÍ

Mira Mare ☎ 28340 94256. Good-value rooms located on the main thoroughfare, a short, but steep, walk from the beach, and above a supermarket, with a/c, fridge and balcony with sea views. May–Oct. **€35**

ANÓYIA

Aetos Upper village. A popular local meat taverna, specializing in lamb and goat (€7–8) cooked on the outdoor barbecue. Some good local cheeses too. Daily lunch & dinner.

CLIMBING MOUNT PSILORÍTIS

Climbing to the summit of **Mount Psilorítis**, for experienced and properly equipped hikers, is not at all arduous. The route, which diverts from the path to the Idean Cave just beyond a small chapel, forms a stretch of the E4 Pan-European footpath and is marked with the red arrows and the E4 waymarkers. It should be a 6–8hr return journey to the summit, although in spring, thick snow may slow you down. Don't attempt the walk alone as you could face a very long wait should you run into trouble, and mobile phones may not have a signal in places.

If you're prepared to camp on the Nídha plateau (it can be very cold), or rent a room at the *Taverna Nida*, you could continue on foot the next day down to the southern slopes of the range. It's a beautiful hike and also relatively easy, four hours or so down a fairly clear path to **Vorízia** where there is no food or accommodation, although **Kamáres**, 4km west, has both.

Aristea Upper village ☎ 28340 31459, ⊚ hotelaristea .gr. Simple en-suite rooms with TV and spectacular valley views from the terrace; also has studios and apartments, with open fireplace for winter stays, which sleep up to six. Breakfast included. **€45**

Rooms Aris Upper village ☎ 28340 31817, ⊚ aris .anogia.info. The flower-bedecked *Aris* has pleasant en-suite rooms with fabulous valley and mountain views.

Facilities include fridge, balcony and central heating for winter stays. **€40**

Taverna Skalomata Upper village, east. ☎ 28340 31316. Offers well-prepared taverna standards, including the usual barbecued meats and spit-roast lamb, with a fine view. Grills from €6. Daily lunch & dinner.

Mount Psilorítis

Heading for the mountains from Anóyia, a smooth road ascends 21km to an altitude of 1400m on the **Nídha Plateau** at the base of Mount Psilorítis. Here, at the end of the road and opposite the *Taverna Nida*, is the path up to the celebrated **Idean cave** (about a 15min walk) and the start of the way to the top of **Mount Psilorítis** (2456m), Crete's highest mountain.

Idean cave

The **Idean cave** (Idhéon Ándhron), a rival of that on Mount Dhíkti (see p.225) for the title of Zeus's birthplace, is certainly associated from the earliest of times with the cult of Zeus. The remnants of a major archeological dig carried out inside – including a miniature railway used by archeologists to remove tonnes of rock and rubble – still litter the site, giving the place a rather unattractive prospect. When you enter the cave down concrete steps into the depths, it turns out to be a rather shallow affair, with little to see.

ACCOMMODATION AND EATING   **MOUNT PSILORÍTIS**

Taverna Nida Nihda plateau ☎ 28340 31141. Serves up hearty mountain dishes featuring lamb, pork and chicken, and has a couple of simple rooms, which makes it a good base for hikes in the surrounding mountains. June–Sept daily; Oct–May Sat & Sun only. Breakfast included. **€30**

Eastern Crete

Eastern Crete is dominated by **Áyios Nikólaos**, a small cosmopolitan town and resort, and its close neighbour Eloúnda, the home of luxury hotel and villa complexes, and the gateway to the mysterious islet of **Spinalónga**. Inland from Áyios Nikólaos, **Kritsá** with its famous frescoed church and textile sellers and the imposing ruins of **ancient Lato** make for good excursions. Further inland, the extraordinary **Lasíthi Plateau** is worth a night's stay if only to observe its abidingly rural life. Far fewer people venture beyond the road south to **Ierápetra** and east to **Sitía**, where only the famous beach at **Váï** ever sees anything approaching a crowd.

Áyios Nikólaos

ÁYIOS NIKÓLAOS, known simply as "Áyios" to the locals, is set around a supposedly bottomless salt lake, now connected to the sea to form an inner harbour. It is supremely picturesque and has some style and charm, which it exploits to the full. The excellent **archeological museum** (Tues–Sun 8.30am–3pm; €3) on Paleológou north of the lake, and an interesting **Folk Museum** (Tues–Sun April–Oct 10am–2pm and 5–7pm; €3) near the tourist office are both worth seeking out. Both the lake and the harbour area are surrounded by charming restaurants and bars.

The small and busy **Kitroplatía beach** lies just around the southwest corner of the port and is lined with tavernas and cafés, while 1km beyond here, past the marina, lies the much larger, and well-kept, municipal beach. There are further swimming opportunities to the north around Eloúnda, and some great backcountry inland – perfect to explore on a scooter.

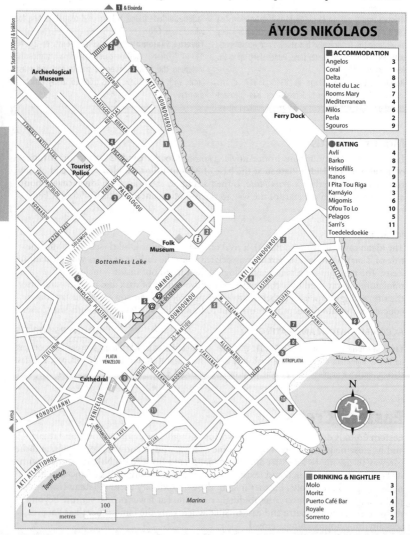

ÁYIOS NIKÓLAOS

■ **ACCOMMODATION**
Angelos	3
Coral	1
Delta	8
Hotel du Lac	5
Rooms Mary	7
Mediterranean	4
Milos	6
Perla	2
Sgouros	9

● **EATING**
Avlí	4
Barko	8
Hrisofillís	7
Itanos	9
I Pita Tou Riga	2
Karnáyio	3
Migomis	6
Ofou To Lo	10
Pelagos	5
Sarri's	11
Toedeledoekie	1

■ **DRINKING & NIGHTLIFE**
Molo	3
Moritz	1
Puerto Café Bar	4
Royale	5
Sorrento	2

Archeological Museum

Tourist Police

Folk Museum

Bottomless Lake

Ferry Dock

PLATIA VENIZELOU

Cathedral

KITROPLATIA

Town Beach

Marina

N

0   100
metres

ARRIVAL AND DEPARTURE

ÁYIOS NIKÓLAOS

By bus The station is situated to the northwest end of town near the archeological museum.
Destinations Eloúnda (20 daily; 20min); Iráklion (at least 20 daily, 6 via Iráklion Airport 6.15am–9.30pm; 1hr 30min); Kritsá (9 daily 6am–8.15pm; 20min); Lasíthi plateau (2 daily; 2hr); Pláka (7 daily 6am–7pm; 30min); Sitía (7 daily 6.15am–8.30pm; 1hr 45min).

INFORMATION AND ACTIVITIES

Tourist office Between the lake and the port (April–June & Oct 9am–5pm, July–Sept 8.30am–9.30pm; closed Sat; ☏ 28410 22357, �🌐 aghiosnikolaos.gr). One of the best on the island for accommodation information, they also exchange currency.

Boat trips Leave from the west side of the harbour to Spinalónga and Eloúnda (about €12–20 depending on the company, some include lunch).

Diving Pelagos Minos Beach Hotel, Eloúnda road, Áyios Nikólaos ☏ 28410 24376, �🌐 divecrete.com. This company also rents out sailing dinghies by the hour.

ACCOMMODATION

★ **Angelos** Aktí S. Koundoúrou 16 ☏ 28410 23501. Welcoming small hotel located on the seafront, offering excellent a/c balconied rooms with TV and fridge plus fine views over the Gulf. No breakfast but a supermarket sits directly beneath. **€40**

Coral Aktí S. Koundoúrou ☏ 28410 28363, ⌨ mhotels.gr. One of the best in-town hotels offering a/c rooms with sea view, fridge, balcony and satellite TV, plus a rooftop pool and bar. Out of high season, prices can fall by up to fifty percent. Breakfast included. **€115**

Delta Tselepi 1 Kitroplatia ☏ 28410 28893, ⌨ agiosnikolaos-hotels.gr. Modern, refurbished a/c studios and apartments overlooking Kitroplatiá beach, a 5min walk from the centre of town. Rooms at the front have sea-view balconies. Facilities include full kitchen and TV. **€55**

★ **Hotel du Lac** 28-Octovríou ☏ 28410 22711, ⌨ dulachotel.gr. Perhaps the most unexpected bargain in town, with classily renovated rooms and studios in designer style with all facilities including a/c, TV, wi-fi and (in studios) kitchenette in a prime location overlooking the lake. However, it's also in the heart of things so night-time noise is the only downside. **€60**

Mediterranean S. Dhávaki 27 ☏ 28410 23611. On a hill between the lake and the seafront, run by an Anglo-Greek couple, these clean, economical en-suite rooms come with fridges, a/c, TV, use of communal kitchen and some rooms with balcony. **€30**

★ **Milos** Sarolídi 2 ☏ 28410 23783. Sweet little pension east of the Kitroplatía beach, with some of the best rooms in town for the price. The spotless en-suite balcony rooms (number 2 is a dream) with a/c have spectacular sea views over the gulf. April–Oct. **€35**

Perla Salaminos 4 ☏ 28410 23379, ⌨ apartments-perla.gr. Chic en-suite apartments, close to the sea, on a hill to the north of the harbour, recently refurbished, with a/c, cooker, fridge, TV and wi-fi, and front rooms have sea-view balconies. **€50**

★ **Rooms Mary** Evans 13, near the Kitroplatía ☏ 28410 23760. Very friendly place with a/c (€5 extra) en-suite balcony rooms (some with sea view), access to fridge and use of kitchen. Also has some apartments nearby sleeping up to four. **€35**

Sgouros Kitroplatía ☏ 28410 28931, ⌨ sgourosgroup hotels.com. Good-value modern hotel with a/c, TV, fridge, balcony rooms overlooking one of the town's beaches, and close to plenty of tavernas. Breakfast included. **€70**

EATING

The places around the Kitroplatía are generally good, but you are paying for the location – the more authentic establishments tend to be less obvious, on the streets behind the tourist office, and near Platia Venizelou.

Avlí Odhós P. Georgíou 12 ☏ 28410 82479. Delightful garden ouzerí offering a wide mezédhes selection as well as more elaborate dishes. May–Oct daily 12.30–2.30pm & 7–11pm.

Barko Kitroplatía ☏ 28410 24610. This hip restaurant and bar, with a large terrace overlooking the beach, serves Greek dishes with flair; share a mix of mezédhes such as feta-stuffed red peppers, courgette pie and pork in wine. There's indoor seating too, in the smartly renovated building. Daily lunch & dinner.

Hrisofillís Aktí Themistokléous ☏ 28410 22705. Attractive, stylish and creative *mezedhopolío* with reasonably priced fish, meat and veggie mezédhes served on a pleasant sea-facing terrace fronting the east side of the Kitroplatía beach. Meze from €4.50. Daily lunch & dinner.

I Pita Tou Riga Paleológou 24, close to the lake. Excellent Lilliputian snack-bar/restaurant serving imaginative fare – salads, filled pitta breads and some Asian dishes; has a small terrace up steps across the road, shared with its sister restaurant, *Karnáyio* (below). Pitta club sandwich with pork €5.50. Daily noon–2am.

4

Itanos Kýprou 1. Popular with locals, this traditional taverna serves reasonably priced Cretan food such as *yemista* (rice-stuffed vegetables; €5), and barrel wine. It also has a terrace across the road. Daily 11am–midnight.

★ **Karnáyio** Paleológou 21 ☎28410 25968. Atmospheric traditional *kafenío* popular with a younger crowd and serving tasty *mezédhes* – try the *fava* (mashed split peas) – inside or on its pleasant terrace with lake view. A bonus here is some great *lýra* and *lauto* (lute) music most Fri and Sat evenings. Daily noon–3am.

Migomis Nikoláou Plastíra 22 ☎28410 24353. Pleasant café high above the bottomless lake with a stunning view. Perfect (if pricey) place for breakfast, afternoon or evening drinks. Their next-door restaurant enjoys the same vista and is pricier than the norm, but perhaps worth it if you've booked a table to feast on that view. Daily 9am–1am.

★ **Ofou To Lo** Kitroplatía ☎28410 24819. Best of the moderately priced places on the seafront here: the food is consistently good. Try their *loukánika me tirí* (spicy sausages with cheese; €5) starter. Daily lunch & dinner.

★ **Pelagos** Stratigoú Kóraka, behind the tourist office ☎28410 25737. Housed in an elegant mansion, this stylish fish taverna has an attractive leafy garden terrace which complements the excellent food. Pricey, but worth it. April–Oct daily lunch & dinner.

Sarri's Kýprou 15. Great little economical neighbourhood café-diner especially good for breakfast, also grills and *souvláki*, all served on a leafy terrace. Daily 9am–midnight.

Toedeledoekie Aktí S. Koundoúrou 24. Friendly, low-key Dutch-run café with international press to read; great sandwiches and milkshakes by day, chilled bar at night. Daily 9am–late.

DRINKING AND NIGHTLIFE

The one thing which Áyios Nikólaos undeniably does well is bars and nightlife. Music bars with terraces spread along Aktí Koundoúrou on the harbourfront. More raucous bars and clubs crowd the bottom of 25-Martíou (known as "Soho Street") as it heads up the hill.

Molo Aktí Koundoúrou 6. One of a bunch of popular glitzy café-bars looking out over the ferry dock on the east side of the harbour. A relaxed café during the day and a bar at night, open until the early hours. Daily 9am–late.

Moritz Aktí Koundoúrou 10. West of the harbour. Cosy, laidback café-bar along the seafront with a dressy clientele and jazz and soft-rock sounds. Daily 9am–late.

Puerto Café Bar Aktí I Koundoúrou. One of the row of café-bars on the harbourfront, with outdoor harbourside

seating and an indoor bar which pumps up the volume after dark. Daily 9am–late.

Royale 25-Martiou. The first of a row of bars proper, at the bottom of 25-Martíou, near the harbour. Daily 11pm- late.

Sorrento Aktí I Koundoúrou 23. On the west side of the harbour, near the tourist office. A long-established haunt of expats, loud and fun, if that's what you're in the mood for. Daily 9pm–late.

DIRECTORY

Car rental Good deals are available at Club Cars, 28-Oktovríou 24 (☎28410 25868), near the post office, or Economy (☎28410 22013) under the *Hotel Angelos*.

Internet access Peripou, 28-Oktovríou 25 (daily 9.30am–2am), and Café du Lac at no. 17 on the same street.

Travel agents Plora Travel, Corner of 28-Oktovríou and K. Sfakianáki (☎28410 82804).

Post office 28-Oktovríou (Mon–Sat 7.30am–2pm), halfway up, on the right.

Eloúnda and around

The village of **ELOÚNDA**, now a small-scale resort, lies about 8km from Áyios Nikólaos, along the coast road. Just before the centre of the village, a road (signposted) leads downhill to a natural causeway leading to the ancient "sunken city" of **Olous**. Here you'll find restored windmills, a short length of canal, Venetian salt pans and a well-preserved dolphin **mosaic**, inside a former Roman basilica, but nothing of the sunken city itself beyond a couple of walls in about 70cm of water. Swimming here is good – but watch out for sea urchins. Life in **Eloúnda** village focuses around the large square lined with cafés, tavernas and shops, in front of the picturesque harbour. Right next to the harbour is the sandy town **beach**, with other patches of sand stretching out north along the coast.

CLOCKWISE FROM TOP LEFT IRÁKLION MUSEUM (P.204); LÝRA MAKER, RÉTHYMNON (P.236); PALACE OF KNOSSOS (P.209) >

Pláka

PLÁKA, some 5km north of Eloúnda, stands on the shore directly across the sea from Spinalónga and used to be the colony's supply point. This small seaside village consists of a few **rooms** and a clutch of fish **tavernas** – a couple of which arrange boats excursions across to Spinalónga. The *Taverna Spinalonga*'s proprietor Aris also does boat trips to isolated beaches not reachable by road and fishing trips (€80/hr, up to four people). A small pebble beach lies to the north of the village.

Spinalónga

Daily: June–Sept 9am–7pm, Oct & April–May 9am–3pm, Nov–March Sat & Sun 9am–3pm • €2 • ☎ 28410 41773 • Boats run to Spinalónga every 30min in high season from Eloúnda (€10 return) and Pláka (€8 return); tickets can be bought at the signed dockside

As a bastion of the Venetian defence, the fortress-rock of **Spinalónga** withstood the Turkish invaders for 45 years after the mainland had fallen; the infamous part of the islet's history, however, is more recent; it served as a **leper colony** for five decades until 1957. Even today, despite the crowds of visitors, there's a real sense of the desolation of those years as you walk through the gated tunnel entrance and emerge on a narrow street below the castle, with the roofless shells of houses once inhabited by the unfortunate lepers all around. A short row of buildings here, which were once stores, has been restored and houses a small **museum** with photos and artefacts.

ARRIVAL AND INFORMATION

By bus Services run from Áyios Nikólaos to Eloúnda and Pláka from 6am to 7.30pm, every 2hr.
Services The friendly Olous Travel (☎ 28410 41324) on the

ELOÚNDA AND AROUND

main square in Eloúnda gives out information, can help with accommodation and changes money.

ACTIVITIES

Watersports Driros Beach (☎694 49 37 760, ⓦ spinalonga-windsurf.com. Windsurfing, waterskiing, kayaking and sailing courses at Driros Beach near Eloúnda. Also rents out outboard dinghies.

ACCOMMODATION

ELOÚNDA

★ **Akti Olous** On the Olous road, seafront ☎28410 41270, ⓦgreekhotels.net/aktiolous. This is one of the good mid-range hotel options, with a beach bar, restaurant and roof garden pool with panoramic view. Rooms have a/c, fridge and TV. May–Oct. **€70**
Elounda Bay Palace ☎28410 67000, ⓦeloundabay .gr. If you fancy indulging in a little luxury this swanky hotel has en-suite a/c rooms, suites and bungalows with TV, mini bar, three pools, spa and two private beaches with watersports. May–Oct. **€260**
Milos Upper part of town ☎28410 41641, ⓦpediaditis .gr. Ask at "The Bookshop" on the main square. Attractive,

clean and comfortable rooms, studios and apartments which come with sea views and a pool. May–Oct. Rooms **€45**, apartment **€60**
Oasis Off the square, on the road heading inland ☎28410 41076, ⓦpensionoasis.gr. This friendly place, just 100m from the centre in a rural setting, has en-suite rooms with kitchenette, fridge and TV. June–Oct. **€40**

PLÁKA

Taverna Spinalonga On the main street ☎28410 41804. Clean, simple rooms in the heart of the village, across the street from the taverna and with a view to the island. En-suite bath and fridge. Ask Aris at the taverna. **€40**

EATING, DRINKING AND NIGHTLIFE

ELOÚNDA

Aligos On the square. One of the livelier café-bars, open throughout the day until late, for drinks and snacks and, later, loud music. Daily 9am–late.
Ferryman ☎28410 41230. The ultra-chic *Ferryman* is one of the town's best (and priciest) tavernas. Freshly prepared starters, fish and meat dishes, and a lovely waterfront setting. April–Oct daily lunch & dinner.
★ **Megaro** ☎28410 42220. This friendly place serves

fresh, well-prepared fish, seafood and steaks, inside or on a pontoon terrace on the water. Salads and starters are delicious too – try the halloumi and aubergine salad, €6. April–Oct daily noon–late.
Vritomartes ☎28410 41325. Situated in a plum spot in the centre of the harbour, noted for the fish, which can be a bit pricey, but they also have more economical options such as the fish dish for two at €18.50. April–Oct daily lunch & dinner.

PLÁKA

Taverna Giorgos ☎ 28410 41353, ⓦ giorgos-plaka.gr. Serves good seafood, fish and traditional Cretan dishes on a large terrace facing out to sea opposite Spinalónga island. Daily lunch & dinner.

Taverna Spinalonga ☎ 28410 41804. With an outdoor terrace facing the sea and island, this taverna has perhaps the most economical fish meals, fresh from the day's catch. Daily lunch & dinner.

SHOPPING

Eklektos Papandreou 13. Guide books and reading matter in English, it also stocks walking guides and maps for the area. Located 100m uphill from the square in the direction of Áyios Nikólaos.

Lasíthi Plateau

Scores of daily tour buses visit the **LASÍTHI PLATEAU** to view the "thousands of white-cloth-sailed windmills" which irrigate the high plain. In fact there are very few working windmills left, although most roadside tavernas seem to have adopted many of those made redundant as marketing features. The drive alone is worthwhile, however, and the plain is a fine example of rural Crete at work, every inch devoted to the cultivation of potatoes, apples, figs, olives and a host of other crops; stay in one of the villages for a night or two and you'll see real life return as the tourists leave.

Lasíthi villages

Tzermiádho is the largest village on the plateau, on the northern edge, and one of the least touristy; here there's a number of tavernas and *kafenía* and a couple of places to stay. Travelling clockwise around the plateau, **Áyios Yeóryios** has a couple of tavernas and rooms and a lovely little-visited Folk Museum, while **Psykhró** is the most visited village on the plateau, as it's the base for visiting Lasíthi's other chief attraction: the birthplace of Zeus, the **Dhiktean Cave**.

The Dhiktean Cave

Daily: June–Sept 8am–7pm; Oct–May 8.30am–3pm • €4

In legend, Zeus's father, the Titan Kronos, was warned that he would be overthrown by a son, and accordingly ate all his offspring; however, when Rhea gave birth to Zeus in the **Dhiktean Cave**, she fed Kronos a stone and left the child concealed, protected by the Kouretes, who beat their shields outside to disguise his cries. The rest, as they say, is history (or at least myth).

The cave lies 1km southwest of Psykhró, where a signed road takes you up to a car park (€2); from here the cave is a ten-minute climb, or you can go up by mule (€15). The cave has been made more "visitor friendly" in recent years, with the introduction of concrete steps and electric lighting, so inevitably some of the magic and mystery have been lost, but it's still a worthwhile visit. The steps meander down to the bottom of the cave where there is a small lake surrounded by impressive stalactites and stalagmites.

ARRIVAL AND TOURS

LASÍTHI PLATEAU

By bus Services run around the plateau to Psykhró direct from Iráklion and from Áyios Nikólaos via Neápoli. Both roads offer spectacular views, coiling through a succession of passes guarded by lines of ruined windmills.

Wildlife tours Petros Zarvakis is a wildlife expert and leads guided wild-flower and bird-spotting hikes (April–Sept) into the mountains surrounding the plain, and also to the summit of Mount Dhíkti; Ask for him at the *Taverna Petros* at the Dhiktean Cave or call direct on ☎ 28440 31600 or 694 56 16 074.

ACCOMMODATION AND EATING

Dias Village Áyios Yeóryios ☎ 28440 31207. This economical and friendly hotel can offer basic rooms with shared bath, and there's a small taverna below with wholesome home-cooked food. The same family also rent out more superior en-suite rooms at their nearby sister hotel, *Maria*. April–Oct. €25̲

4

Zeus Psykhró ☎ 28440 31284 (or enquire at Taverna Halavro close to the cave car park). This small, seven-room hotel offers simple rooms just outside the main village, with views across the plateau. April–Oct. **€35**

Kritsá

KRITSÁ is a pretty mountain village about 10km inland from Áyios Nikólaos and despite some commercialization is a welcome break from resort life. On the way you'll find the **Church of Panayía Kyrá** and the ancient site of **Lato**, both worth a visit.

Kritsá is known for its local **crafts**, particularly weaving, ceramics, embroidery and olive wood carvings, which are sold along the main-street shops by the village women. Once you get past the touristy shops and explore the maze of streets winding up the hillside, and their wonderful valley views, you get a real sense of a genuinely Cretan village. The small platía at the centre of the village is the focus of life.

Church of Panayía Kyrá
Daily 8.30am–3pm • €3
On the approach road, about 1km before Kritsá, is the lovely Byzantine **church of Panayía Kyrá**, inside which survives perhaps the most complete set of Byzantine frescoes in Crete. The fourteenth- and fifteenth-century works have been much retouched, but they're still worth the visit. Excellent (and expensive) reproductions are sold from a shop alongside.

Lato
Tues–Sun 8.30am–3pm • €2
Just before Kritsá a surfaced road leads off for about 4km to the archeological site of **Lato**, where the substantial remains of a Doric city are coupled with a grand hilltop setting. The city itself is extensive, but largely neglected, presumably because visitors and archeologists on Crete are more concerned with the Minoan era. If you're interested in knowing more about the site and its history an informative booklet is on sale at the ticket office. Ruins aside, you could come here just for the views: west over Áyios Nikólaos and beyond to the bay and Olous (which was Lato's port), and inland to the Lasíthi mountains.

ARRIVAL AND DEPARTURE   KRITSÁ

By Bus Áyios Nikólaos to Kritsá (8 daily; 7am–8.15pm; 15min).

ACCOMMODATION

Argyro On the way into the village ☎ 28410 51174, ⓦ argyrorentrooms.gr. Clean, pleasant and economical en-suite rooms, some with TV and wi-fi – around a courtyard, with open views across the olive tree-lined valley. A/c €5 extra. **€35**

★ **The Olive Press** Close to the main church ☎ 28410 51296, ⓦ www.olivepress.centerall.com. A most attractive place to stay, this is a Belgian-run venture with pleasant rooms and apartments in a beautifully restored, stone-built olive-oil mill. Breakfast included. **€50**

EATING AND DRINKING

There are a number of decent places to eat in the small platía at the centre of the village, with more alternatives further up, as well as a couple of bakeries for tempting *tyrópita* (cheese pies) or currant breads.

East to Sitía

From Áyios Nikólaos the main road heads south and then east, a drive through barren hills sprinkled with villas and skirting above the occasional sandy cove. A newly completed stretch of the E75 continues past the site of **Gourniá**, slumped in the saddle between two low peaks, and from here on the road to **Sitía** is one of the most exhilarating in Crete. Carved into cliffs and mountain-sides, the road teeters above the coast before plunging inland at Kavoúsi. Of the beaches you see below, only the one at **Mókhlos** is at all accessible, some 5km below the main road.

Gourniá

Tues–Sun 8.30am–3pm • €3 • ☎ 28410 22462

GOURNIÁ, 20km east of Áyios Nikólaos, is the most completely preserved **Minoan town**. Its narrow alleys and stairways intersect a throng of one-roomed houses centred on a main square, and the rather grand house of what may have been a local ruler or governor. Although less impressive than the great palaces, the site is strong on revelations about the lives of the ordinary people – many of the dwellings housed craftsmen, who left behind their tools and materials to be found by the excavators. Its desolation today (you are likely to be alone save for a dozing guardian) only serves to heighten the contrast with what must have been a cramped and raucous community 3500 years ago.

Mókhlos

MÓKHLOS is a sleepy seaside village with a few rooms, a hotel or two and a number of **tavernas** along its tiny harbour. The village beach is very small and pebbly, but there's a slightly larger beach (also pebble) to the west. For those who stay there's not a great deal to do – hang out in the harbour taverna-cafés or swim out to the **islet of Mókhlos** just offshore, where there are remains of Minoan houses – but it's very easy to do nothing here in this laidback place.

ACCOMMODATION AND EATING — MÓKHLOS

Hermes ☎ 28430 94074. This clean and simple pension behind the waterfront offers the cheapest rooms in the village. Some en-suite rooms with a/c, others sharing bath. April–Oct. **€28**

Sofia Hotel ☎ 28430 94738. For a bit more en-suite luxury, and a harbourfront view, this friendly hotel has a/c rooms with fridge and TV, and is situated above its waterside taverna which serves good home-cooked dishes. April–Oct. **€40**

Sitía

SITÍA is the port and main town of the relatively unexploited eastern edge of Crete. It's a pleasantly scenic place, offering a plethora of waterside restaurants, a long sandy beach and a lazy lifestyle little affected even by the thousands of visitors in peak season. The town attracts a number of French, Italian and Greek tourists, and it grows on you, perhaps inviting a longer stay than intended. For entertainment there's the **town beach**, providing good swimming, windsurfing and diving. In town there's a small **folklore museum** (Mon–Fri 10am–1pm; €2), an excellent **archeological museum** (Tues–Sun 8.30am–3pm; €2) and a Venetian fort to explore. A colourful weekly **market** takes place on Tuesdays between 7am and 2pm along Odhós Itanou near the archeological museum.

ARRIVAL AND DEPARTURE — SITÍA

By plane Sitía's airport lies 1km north of the town and is currently served by domestic flights only, with Aegean Airways and Olympic Air.
Destinations Athens (5 weekly; 50min), Kárpathos (5 weekly; 1hr), Kássos (6 weekly; 25min), Rhodes (5 weekly; 1hr).
By ferry The ferry port lies 500m north of the town. Sitía to: Pireás via Iráklion (2 weekly; 16hr). Tues–Wed to: Kássos (2hr 30min), Kárpathos (4hr 20min), Mílos (9hr) Rhodes (9hr), Santoríni (7hr).

By bus The station is at the south end of Venizélou – the main entry road into town from the west.
Destinations Áyios Nikólaos (7 daily; 6.15am–8.30pm; 1hr 45min), Iráklion (6 daily; 5.30am–7.45pm; 3hr 15min), Ierápetra (5 daily; 6.15am–8pm; 1hr 30min), Palékastro (5 daily; 6am–2.30pm; 40min), Váï Beach (3 daily 9.30am–2.30pm; 1hr), Zákros (2 daily 6am & 2pm; 1hr 20min).

INFORMATION AND ACTIVITIES

Tourist office On the seafront, at the start of the beach road (Mon–Fri 9.30am–2.30pm & 5–9pm, Sat 9am–2.30pm; ☎ 28430 28300, ⊛ sitia.gr). Supplies accommodation lists, maps and local information.

Diving Universal Diver, Kornárou 140 (☎ 28430 23489, ⊜ pavlossimos@yahoo.gr). PADI-certified dive centre with courses for all levels.

4

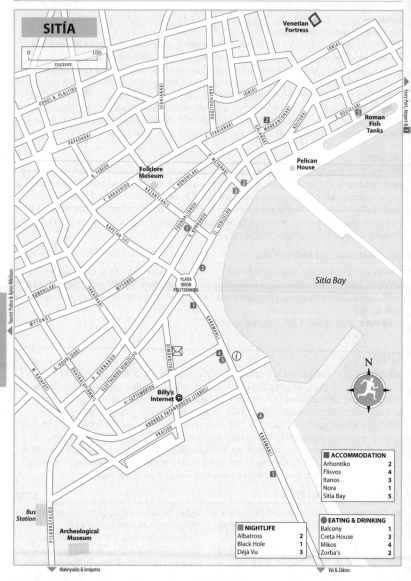

SITÍA

Venetian Fortress

Roman Fish Tanks

Pelican House

Folklore Museum

Sitía Bay

PLATIA IROON POLYTEKHNIOU

Billy's Internet

N

Bus Station

Archeological Museum

ACCOMMODATION
Arhontiko	2
Flisvos	4
Itanos	3
Nora	1
Sitia Bay	5

NIGHTLIFE
Albatross	2
Black Hole	1
Déjà Vu	3

EATING & DRINKING
Balcony	1
Creta House	3
Mikos	4
Zorba's	2

Makriyialós & Ierápetra

Vái & Zákros

ACCOMMODATION

Arhontiko Kondhiláki 16 ☎ 28430 28172. One of the best budget places in town, a couple of blocks back from the seafront (10min walk to beach), with clean, attractive rooms and a garden with communal terrace. One of the rooms is en suite. **€30**

Flisvos Karamanlí 4 ☎ 28430 27135, ⓦ flisvos-sitia .com. Refurbished hotel fronting the sea at the start of the Beach Road; simple, clean a/c rooms with TV, wi-fi and

fridge face either the sea or a patio garden behind. Breakfast included. **€60**

★ **Itanos** Platía Iroon Polytekhníou ☎ 28430 22900, ⓦ itanoshotel.com. Upmarket hotel by the town's main sea-front square, 200m along the harbour to the beach, with smart, a/c balcony rooms (those at the front with sea view), satellite TV and there's a rooftop bar. Breakfast included. **€60**

Sitia Bay Karamanlí ☎ 28430 24800, ⓦ sitiabay.com. A stone's throw from the town beach, this modern hotel-apartment complex offers tastefully furnished, comfortable a/c rooms and studios with kitchenette; all rooms have sea-view balcony and there's a pool. Optional breakfast is extra. **€90**

Nora Rouseláki 31 ☎ 28430 23017, ⓔ norahotel@yahoo .gr. Near the ferry port, this small female-run hotel has basic rooms with a/c, TV, balcony and shower and fine views over the bay. A 10min walk to the town centre. April–Oct. **€35**

EATING AND DRINKING

A line of enticing outdoor tavernas crowds the harbourfront, many displaying dishes and fresh fish to lure you in – though these places can be relatively expensive. Away from the water you'll find cheaper (and often more interesting) places to dine.

★ **Balcony** Kazantzákis & Foundalídhou ☎ 28430 25084. Stylish restaurant in the upper floor of an elegant townhouse. An eclectic menu has Mexican- and Asian-influenced dishes as well as Greek fusion cooking, such as the pork fillet with yoghurt and pilaf rice. Mains from €10. May–Oct daily lunch & dinner; Nov–March daily dinner only.

Creta House Karamanlí, next to the Hotel Flisvos. A reliable, if somewhat touristy, traditional taverna specializing in Cretan dishes; try the moussaka or lamb, all served on the large harbourside terrace. April–Oct daily lunch & dinner.

Mikos Karamanlí 14 ☎ 28430 22416. Tasty charcoal-grill meats (from €6) plus traditional Greek dishes are served up with very strong local wine at this popular diner with a seafront terrace. Daily lunch & dinner.

Zorba's Cnr El Venizélou & Kazantzákis. The oldest, biggest and most popular place on the seafront. Serves up much more authentic food than you might expect from its touristy appearance and is regularly frequented by locals. Daily lunch & dinner.

DRINKING AND NIGHTLIFE

Sitía's nightlife, mostly conducted at an easy pace, centres on the music bars and cafés at the northern end of Venizélou and along the beach road.

Albatross Venizélou 185. This modern café and bar is one of many along the harbourfront strip, with street and terrace seating. Daily 10am–late.

Black Hole Venizélou, far end. One of Sitía's most popular summer music bars, playing house and rock, a lively place with a large outdoor terrace and indoor bar. May–Sept 9pm–late.

Déjà Vu Venizélou 183. Glitzy, neon café-bar on the harbourfront, with comfy terrace seating, popular with young Sitians. Daily 10am–late.

The far east

Not long after leaving Sitía along the new main road a signed side road up to the left leads to **Váï** and the **Monastery of Toploú**. **Palékastro**, some 9km south of Váï, is a good place to stopover, with good beaches to explore and a **Minoan site**. Palékastro is also the crossroads for the winding road south to **Zákros** and **Xerókambos**, a beautiful drive, and having your own transport presents all kinds of beach and exploration possibilities.

Monastery of Toploú
Daily 9am–1pm & 2–6pm, Oct–March closes 4pm • €3

The **Monasterty of Toploú**'s forbidding exterior reflects a history of resistance to invaders, and doesn't prepare you for the gorgeous flower-decked cloister within. The blue-robed monks keep out of the way as far as possible, but in quieter periods their cells and refectory are left discreetly on view. In the church is one of the masterpieces of Cretan art, the **eighteenth-century icon** *Lord Thou Art Great* by Ioannis Kornaros, incorporating 61 small scenes full of amazing detail inspired by the Orthodox prayer "Lord thou art great …" In the monastery's shop you can buy enormously expensive reproductions of the work as well as olive oil and wine made by the monks.

Recently a €1 billion tourist resort and golf course was set to be built on monastery-owned land at Cape Sideros. The project, approved by the Abbot, was abandoned after vehement opposition by local residents and environmentalists.

Váï

Váï beach itself features alongside Knossos or the Lasíthi Plateau on almost every Cretan travel agent's list of excursions. Not surprisingly, it is now covered in sunbeds and umbrellas, though it is still a superb beach. Above all, it is famous for its **palm trees**, and the sudden appearance of the grove is indeed an exotic shock; lying on the fine sand in the early morning, the illusion is of a Caribbean island. There's a car park (€3), a café and an expensive taverna at the beach, plus toilets and showers. By day you can find a bit more solitude by climbing the rocks or swimming to one of the smaller beaches which surround Váï. **Ítanos**, twenty minutes' walk north by an obvious trail, has a couple of tiny beaches and some modest ruins from the Classical era.

Palékastro

PALÉKASTRO is an attractive large farming village with a good choice of tavernas, shops, a few bars and a small **folk museum** (May–Oct Tues–Sun 10am–1pm & 5–8pm; €2). The sea is a couple of kilometres to the east of town, where you'll find fine beaches which are highly popular with windsurfers. **ANGÁTHIA** village, smaller and quieter, lies less than 1km to the east of its neighbour, and closer to the beaches.

The beaches

Hióna beach, a good stretch of EU blue-flagged pebble and sand, to the south of a flat-topped hill named Kastrí which dominates the coastal landscape, lies a kilometre east of Angáthia and is the most popular local beach, though still far from crowded. The better sands are around the bay further to the south of Hióna, where for most of the year you can easily claim a cove to yourself. Also south of Hióna beach along the track running beside the sea, about 200m down on the right (signed "Peak Sanctuary"), a walking track will take you to the nearby **Petsofas peak** – a pleasant 3km hike. The best beach of all, **Kouréménos**, lies to the north of the Kastrí bluff and is one of Crete's top **windsurfing** spots. The long golden sand beach here has a number of tavernas and rooms along the beachfront road.

Palékastro Minoan site

Open daily during daylight hours • Free

Behind Hióna beach lies the main excavation area – known as Roussolákkos and left open – of Palékastro's **Minoan site**, one of the most important in eastern Crete. Only partly excavated (digging continues and new finds are coming to light) surveys indicate that the largest Minoan town yet discovered lies underground here, as well as a very large building which could be a palace.

Áno Zákros

ÁNO ZÁKROS (Upper Zákros) lies a little under 20km from Palékastro, a slow-moving country town with a couple of cafés, tavernas and one hotel. The beach and the Minoan palace of Zákros are actually at Káto ("lower") Zákros, eight winding kilometres further down an asphalted road towards the sea. If you prefer to walk, there's a magnificent hike down the impressive **Valley of the Dead gorge** (named after ancient Minoan tombs in its sides); follow the signs from the south end of town, opposite the *Taverna Napoleon*.

Káto Zákros

The delightful village of **KÁTO ZÁKROS** is little more than a collection of tavernas, some of which rent out rooms, around a peaceful beach with a minuscule fishing anchorage and another interesting Minoan palace. It's a wonderfully restful place, quiet most of the time, except in high season when rooms are rarely to be had on spec; at such times you'd be wise to ring ahead if you wish to stay.

Palace of Zákros

Daily: June–Oct 8am–5pm; Nov–May 8am–3pm • €3 • ☎ 28430 26897 • 100m behind Káto Zákros beach

The **Palace of Zákros** was an important find for archeologists; it had been occupied from about 1600 BC to 1450 BC, when it was abandoned hurriedly and completely. Later, it was forgotten almost entirely and as a result was never plundered. The first major excavation began only in 1960; all sorts of everyday objects, such as tools, raw materials, food and pottery, were thus discovered intact among the ruins. Although the site is set back from the sea, in places it is often marshy and waterlogged – partly the fault of a spring which once supplied fresh water to a cistern beside the royal apartments. In wetter periods you can keep your feet dry and get an excellent view down over the central court and royal apartments by climbing up the remains of narrow streets of the town which occupied the hill higher up.

Xerókambos

The newly asphalted road south of Áno Zákros descends through olive groves and giant greenhouses to run along a deep ravine. After 10km a brilliant turquoise sea and white sandy beaches divided by rocky outcrops appear below; here lies **XERÓKAMBOS**, as tranquil a getaway as you could wish for. This coastal settlement consists of one long "main" street, in the midst of fields and olive groves, with a few rooms and tavernas and a couple of minimarkets, but nothing at all in the way of after-dark diversions. The main beach is 2km of pristine shimmering sand, long enough to find seclusion should you want it, and if that isn't escapist enough, to the north and especially the south are wonderful isolated coves.

4

GETTING AROUND
THE FAR EAST

By bus Sitía to: Palékastro (5 daily 6am–2.30pm; 40min), Vái Beach (3 daily 9.30am–2.30pm; 1hr); Zákros (2 daily 6am & 2pm;1hr 20min); Káto Zákros site (2 daily 11am & 2pm; 1hr 30 min). There is no public transport south of Zákros.

By car and scooter Rental is available in Palékastro at Moto Kastri (☎ 28430 61477), on the eastern edge of the village along the Vái road.

INFORMATION AND ACTIVITIES

Tourist office On the Sitía road 50m from the square (April–Oct Mon–Fri 9am–9pm, Sat 9am–2pm ☎ 28430 61546).
Windsurfing Freak Windsurf ☎ 697 92 53 861,

🌐 freak-surf.com. Courses and board hire from a reliable company based at Kouremenos, Crete's best windsurfing locale, at the extreme east end of the island.

ACCOMMODATION

PALÉKASTRO

Hellas Hotel ☎ 28430 61240, 🌐 palaikastro.com. Comfortable en-suite rooms in the village centre with a/c, balcony, TV, fridge, and there's a taverna below. Reductions for longer stays. April–Oct. **€36**

★**Marina Village** Between Angathia and Kouremenos beach ☎ 28430 61284, 🌐 palaikastro .com/marinavillage. A peaceful haven 800m from the beach with well-furnished, a/c balcony rooms, surrounded by a garden of bougainvillea and banana plants. Buffet breakfast included. May–Oct. **€68**

Metochi Vai Village On the Vái–Palékastro road ☎ 28430 61546, 🌐 palaikastro.com/metohivai. Here shepherds' shelters, owned by the Monastery of Toploú, have been converted into well-furnished, traditional-style apartments, which retain many original features including Cretan stone arches, fireplaces and wooden beams. Rooms

come with a/c, fridge, cooker and TV. **€55**

Ostria ☎ 28430 61022, 🌐 ostria-itanos.gr. This brightly furbished hotel is set in gardens on the outskirts of the village on the Vái road. The modern, clean rooms have a/c, fridge and balcony. March–Oct. **€45**

ÁNO ZÁKROS

Hotel Zakros ☎ 28430 93379. A plain hotel with simple, economical rooms, some en-suite, with a/c, TV and great views across the Valley of the Dead gorge from its rear rooms; it also offers guests a free minibus service to the Minoan palace at Káto Zákros and beach. **€35**

KÁTO ZÁKROS

Coral & Athina ☎ 28430 26893, 🌐 kato-zakros.gr. These rooms sit right above the beach, with great sea views from their large communal terraces; en suites are clean, simply furnished and come with a/c, fridge and TV. March–Nov. **€45**

George Villas ☎ 28430 23739. George has spacious a/c studios in a lovely stone building with mature gardens, in a quiet spot at the back of the village (600m behind the archeological site, along a driveable track). Rooms come with kitchenette, terrace and views over the bay. April–Oct. **€60**

★ **Zakros Palace Apartments** ☎ 28430 29550, ⓦ katozakros-apts.gr. An attractive option on the hill, with superb views; all balconies overlook both the bay and gorge, rooms and studios are all a/c with large terraces, TV and kitchen corner. **€50**

XERÓKAMBOS

Asteras ☎ 28430 26787. Set in their own garden, above the olive groves, these modern a/c studio rooms and apartments all come with kitchenette, fridge and good sea views. April–Oct. **€45**

Liviko View ☎ 28430 27001, ⓦ livikoview.gr. These excellent rooms (and taverna below) are run by a couple of Greek-Australians. Rooms come with a/c and balcony sea view, and there are some more expensive apartments sleeping up to four. Internet access available. April–Oct. **€35**

EATING AND DRINKING

When it comes to eating, there are plenty of tavernas in the area. With the exception of Palékastro, there are few, if any, bars in these quiet villages.

PALÉKASTRO

Hellas Hotel Taverna On the main square ☎ 28430 61240. A good traditional taverna on the terrace beneath the hotel, in the heart of the village, serving Greek and Cretan dishes. April–Oct daily 10am–late.

Mythos On the main square ☎ 28430 61243. This popular family-run taverna serves good traditional food, with meat, fish and plenty of vegetarian options. Friendly service and economical prices. Daily 10am-late.

Taverna Vaios Angáthia ☎ 28430 61043. Up the hill from the bridge leading into the village, on the right. Makes a good lunch stop; their home-cooked food and charcoal-grilled meats (from €5.50) are served on a large roadside terrace in this quiet village. May–Oct daily lunch & dinner.

To Botsalo Kouremenos beach. Cretan dishes, fish and grills served on a large pleasant terrace facing the sea and shaded by tamarisk trees. May–Oct daily lunch & dinner.

★ **Xiona Taverna** Hióna beach ☎ 28430 61228. A great spot at the northern end of the beach; fresh fish and seafood (try the kalamari €7) are served on a shady terrace perched on the rocks above the sea. May–Oct daily lunch & dinner.

ÁNO ZÁKROS

Napoleon ☎ 28430 93252. This taverna serves

traditional Greek food and home-cooked pizza on a small road-side terrace overlooking the valley, with great views. Daily noon–1am.

Xyloporto Next to the petrol station. A good place for coffee, breakfast or a snack. If you need to check email there's internet and wi-fi. Daily 8am–midnight.

KÁTO ZÁKROS

★ **Akrogiali** On the beachfront ☎ 28430 26893. With a large shady terrace by the water's edge, this relaxed taverna serves good fish, seafood and charcoal-grill meats (€6). The friendly owner, Nikos, also acts as an agent for many room options nearby. March–Nov daily 9am–late.

XERÓKAMBOS

Akrogiali On the beachfront, at the south end. This taverna serves up fresh fish, seafood, salads and Cretan dishes on a large terrace set back from the beach with good sea views. April–Oct daily lunch & dinner.

Liviko View Below the apartments of the same name (see above). The cooking here, with organic ingredients grown on the family farm, is recommended and there is a wonderful terrace. Vegetarian dishes from €4. April–Oct daily lunch & dinner.

Ierápetra and the southeast coast

The main road across the island from Sitía to the south coast runs between the east and west ranges of the **Sitía mountains**. One of the first places it hits on the south coast is the sprawling resort of **Makryialós**, but from here to the bustling town and resort of **Ierápetra** there's little reason to stop; the few beaches are rocky and the coastal plain submerged under ranks of polythene-covered greenhouses. A more tranquil hideaway lies just west of Ierápetra, the charming resort of **Mýrtos**.

Ierápetra

IERÁPETRA itself is a bustling modern supply centre for the region's farmers, but despite an ongoing modernization programme, which has cleaned up the centre and revamped

---

ISLAND ESCAPE: GAIDHOURONÍSI

One way to escape the urban hubbub for a few hours is to take a boat to the **island of Gaidhouronísi** (aka Donkey Island or Chrissi Island) some 10km out to sea from Ierápetra. No one seems to know how the 5km-long island got its name as there are no donkeys; instead you'll find a cedar forest, the fabulous **"Shell Beach"** covered with millions of multicoloured mollusc shells, some good sandy beaches and a couple of tavernas. Excursion **boats** (May–Sept daily 10.30am & 12.30pm out, 4pm & 7pm return; €24, under-12s €12) leave from Ierápetra seafront harbour, and you can buy tickets on the boat or at any of the town travel agents in advance. The voyage to the island takes fifty minutes and the boats have an on-board bar.

---

the seafront, as a town, most people find it pretty uninspiring. The tavernas along the tree-lined seafront are scenic enough and there is a decent EU blue-flagged beach which stretches a couple of kilometres east. Although there has been a port here since Roman times, only the **Venetian fort** guarding the harbour and a crumbling Turkish minaret remain as reminders of better days. What little else has been salvaged is in the one-room **archeological museum** (Tues–Sun 8.30am–3pm; €2) near the post office.

Makryialós

MAKRYIALÓS, some 27km east of Ierápetra, was originally composed of two distinct villages. It has gobbled up its neighbour Análipsi to form a single resort, strung out along the coastal road. There are still quiet spots along the long beach, one of the best in the east, a strand of fine sand which shelves so gently you feel you could walk the two hundred nautical miles to Africa. To the west lies the village's small harbour, lined with tavernas. Many rooms and apartment places here are pre-booked by package tours, so while still a very pleasant place to stop for a swim or a bite, it can get pretty busy in high summer.

Mýrtos

MÝRTOS, 15km west of Ierápetra, lies just off the main road, and although developed to a degree, it nonetheless remains a tranquil and charming white-walled village kept clean as a whistle by its house-proud inhabitants, and most of the summer you'll find plenty of space on the long shingle-and-sand beach. A village **museum** (April–Oct Mon–Fri 3.30–7.30pm), located to the side of the church, houses some of the finds from a couple of excavated hilltop **Minoan villas**, Fournoú Korifí and Pýrgos (which can be found just off the road from Ierápetra a couple of kilometres east of the village, and signed), in addition to a folklore section.

ARRIVAL AND DEPARTURE   IERÁPETRA AND THE SOUTHEAST COAST

By bus Ierápetra bus station is on Lasthenous, north of town.
Destinations Áyios Nikólaos (8 daily 6.30am–8.30pm; 1hr), Iráklion (8 daily 6.30am–8.30pm; 2hr 30min),
Makrigialos (8 daily, 6.15am–8.15pm; 30 min), Mýrtos (6 daily 6.30am–8.15pm; 30min), Sitía (6 daily 6.15am–6.15pm; 1hr 30min).

INFORMATION AND TOURS

Tourist office In the seafront car park in Ierápetra. (Mon-Sat 9am–1pm ⓦierapetra.gr). Provides a detailed town map and leaflets.
Services Ierápetra Express travel agency, 100m north of
the town hall on Platía Eleftherías, is a good source of information.
Tours Prima Tours in Mýrtos (☎ 28420 51530, ⓦ sunbudget .net) offer guided walks and provide internet access.

ACCOMMODATION

IERÁPETRA

Camping Koutsounari 7km east of Ierápetra on the Makryialós road ☎ 28420 61213. Offers plenty of shade on
fixed camping positions right next to a long sandy beach, with access to the new pool bar next door. May–Sept. **€18**
★ **Cretan Villa** Lakérdha 16 ☎ 28420 28522,

Ⓦcretan-villa.com. Close to the bus station; sparkling a/c rooms with TV and fridge overlook the flower-bedecked patio of a beautiful 180-year-old stone house. **€54**

Ersi Platía Eleftherías 20 ☏ 28420 23208. Central hotel, recently refurbished, offering good-value rooms with fridge, TV, balcony; the owner also rents out seafront apartments nearby for not much more than the cost of a room. **€35**

Katerina Eastern seafront ☏ 28420 28345, Ⓦkaterina-rooms.gr. Recently refurbished inside (but in need of an outside refurbishment at the time of writing), smart rooms and studios with a/c, TV, wi-fi, fridge and balcony with sea view. **€50**

MAKRYIALÓS

★ **Maria Tsanakalioti Apartments** ☏ 28430 51557, Ⓦmakrigialos-crete.com. The friendly proprietor offers bright beach-front studio rooms and apartments – some with sea view and terrace – with kitchenette, a/c and TV. April–Oct. **€50**

Oasis Rooms Beachfront, before the harbour ☏ 28430 51918. Simple sea-view en-suite rooms with a/c, fridge and balcony, just 10m from the beach (just after the Roman villa). May–Oct. **€40**

★ **White River Cottages** ☏ 28430 51120, Ⓔwriver@otenet.gr. An abandoned hamlet of traditional stone dwellings (originally *Áspro Pótamos* or "White River") has been restored as a warren of charming a/c studios and apartments with kitchen and private terraces, set around a pool. It's located 900m up a signed track on the right as you enter the village from the east. April–Oct. **€68**

MÝRTOS

Big Blue West village, near the beach ☏ 28420 51094, Ⓦbig-blue.gr. Spacious studios and pricier apartments above the beach, sleeping two to four with en-suite bathrooms, a/c, kitchenette and sea view. April–Nov. **€45**

Mirtos Hotel Main thoroughfare behind the beach ☏ 28420 51227, Ⓦmirtoshotel.com. Friendly and good-value small hotel with comfortable a/c, en-suite rooms with balcony. They own the excellent taverna below, where breakfast (included) is served. Jan–Nov. **€42**

EATING AND DRINKING

IERÁPETRA

★ **Gorgona** Stratigou Samouil 12 ☏ 28420 26619. Near the harbour and fort, directly on the beach, this reliable, well-known taverna serves good fish, seafood (try the octopus €8) and Cretan dishes at reasonable prices and is very popular among the locals. March–Nov daily, breakfast, lunch & dinner.

Napoleon Stratigou Samouil 26 ☏ 28420 22410. Close to the *Gorgona* this is one of Ierápetra's oldest tavernas. Freshly cooked dishes, a good choice of appetizers and reasonable prices make this another favourite with locals. Daily lunch & dinner.

MAKRYIALÓS

Faros ☏ 28430 52456. Set in a great position overlooking the harbourfront, this taverna serves good fish ("fresh from our boat") as well as the usual taverna offerings. May–Oct daily lunch & dinner.

To Limani ☏ 28430 52457. This taverna serves fish, seafood and meat dishes on the waterfront terrace overlooking a tiny strip of beach by the harbour. May–Oct daily lunch & dinner.

MÝRTOS

Mirtos Taverna Main thoroughfare, below the Hotel Mirtos ☏ 28420 51227. An excellent, family-run taverna offering a range of home-cooked dishes and tasty mezédhes, with some outdoor tables along the pavement.. Jan–Nov daily breakfast, lunch & dinner.

Réthymnon and around

The province of **Réthymnon** reaches to Mount Psilorítis in the east and towards the White Mountains in the west. The fertile **Amari Valley**, with its pretty villages, lies in the central plain, while on the south coast, in particular around **Plakiás**, there are beaches as fine as any Crete can offer.

Réthymnon itself is an attractive and lively city, with some excellent beaches nearby, although the coastline to the east has seen a great influx of tourists, with the development of a whole series of large hotels extending almost 10km along the beach.

Réthymnon

RÉTHYMNON remains one of the most beautiful of Crete's major cities (only Haniá is a serious rival), with an enduringly provincial air. A wide sandy beach and palm-lined promenade border the old town, a labyrinthine tangle of Venetian and Turkish houses where ancient minarets lend an exotic air to the skyline. Dominating everything from the west is the superbly preserved outline of the **fortress** built by the Venetians after a series of pirate raids had devastated the town.

The beach

With a large sandy **beach** right in the heart of town, lined with cafés and tavernas, you don't need to stir too far. The sea here is dead calm, being protected by the breakwaters in front of the town, but there are disadvantages – the beach can be crowded and the

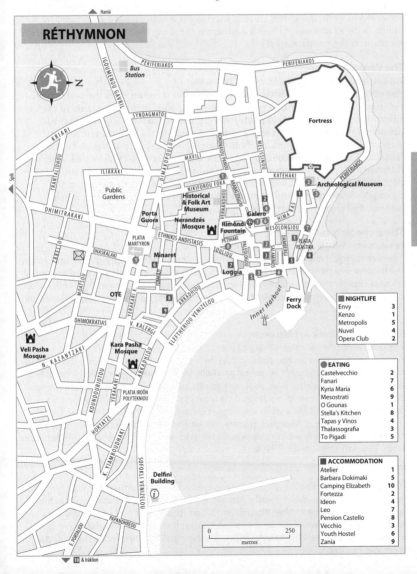

NIGHTLIFE

Envy	3
Kenzo	1
Metropolis	5
Nuvel	4
Opera Club	2

EATING

Castelvecchio	2
Fanari	7
Kyria Maria	6
Mesostrati	9
O Gounas	1
Stella's Kitchen	8
Tapas y Vinos	4
Thalassografia	3
To Pigadi	5

ACCOMMODATION

Atelier	1
Barbara Dokimaki	5
Camping Elizabeth	10
Fortezza	2
Ideon	4
Leo	7
Pension Castello	8
Vecchio	3
Youth Hostel	6
Zania	9

water none too clean. Less sheltered sands stretch for many kilometres to the east, crowded at first but progressively less so further out.

The Old Town

Away from the beach, the atmospheric **old town** lies immediately behind the attractive **inner** harbour. Almost anywhere here, you'll find unexpected old buildings, wall fountains, overhanging wooden balconies, heavy, carved doors and rickety shops, some still with local craftsmen – such as the lýra makers, the "national" instrument of Crete – sitting out front. Look out for the **Venetian loggia** which houses a shop selling Classical art reproductions; the **Rimóndi Fountain**, another of the more elegant Venetian survivals; and the **Nerandzés mosque**, the best preserved in Réthymnon but currently serving as a music school and closed to the public, with its **minaret**. Ethnikís Andístasis, the street leading straight up from the fountain, is the town's **market** area.

The Venetian fortress

Daily: May–Sept 8am–7pm; 10am–5.30pm Oct–April • €4 • ☏ 28310 28101

The massive Fortezza or **Venetian fortress** dominates the town from the west. Said to be the largest Venetian castle ever built, this was a response, in the last quarter of the sixteenth century, to a series of **pirate raids** (by Barbarossa among others) that had devastated the town. Inside is now a vast open space dotted with the remains of all sorts of barracks, arsenals, officers' houses, earthworks and deep shafts, and at the centre a large domed **mosque** complete with surviving *mihrab* (a niche indicating the direction of Mecca). The fortress was designed to be large enough for the entire population to take shelter within the walls. Although much is ruined, it remains thoroughly atmospheric, and you can look out from the walls over the town and harbour, and along the coast to the west.

The archeological museum

Top end of Himáras • Tues–Sun 8.30am–3pm • €3 • ☏ 28310 54668

The **archeological museum** occupies a building almost directly opposite the entrance to the fortress. This was built by the Turks as an extra defence, and later served as a prison; it's now entirely modern inside: cool, spacious and airy. Unfortunately, the collection is not particularly exciting, but worth seeing if you're going to miss the bigger museums elsewhere on the island.

Historical and Folk Art Museum

M. Vernárdhou 28 • Mon–Sat 9am–2.15pm • €3 • ☏ 28310 23398

A beautifully restored seventeenth-century Venetian mansion is the home of the small but tremendously enjoyable **Historical and Folk Art Museum**, close to the Nerandzés mosque. Gathered within four, cool, airy rooms are musical instruments, old photos, basketry, farm implements, traditional costumes and jewellery, lace, weaving and embroidery (look out for a traditional-style tapestry made in 1941 depicting German parachutists landing at Máleme), pottery, knives and old wooden chests. It makes for a fascinating insight into a fast-disappearing lifestyle, which survived virtually unchanged from Venetian times to the 1960s.

The public gardens

The old city ends at the Porta Guora at the top of Ethnikís Andístasis, the only surviving remnant of the city walls. Almost opposite are the quiet and shady **public gardens**. These are a soothing place to stroll, and in the latter half of July the **Réthymnon Wine Festival** is staged here; an enjoyable event, with local dancing as the evening progresses and the barrels empty. The nominal entrance fee includes all the wine you can drink.

ARRIVAL AND DEPARTURE

By bus The bus station in Réthymnon is by the sea to the west of the town centre just off Periferiakós, the road which skirts the waterfront around the fortress.

Destinations Arkádhi monastery (3 daily; 40min); Ayía Galíni via Spíli (4 daily 5.30am–2.15pm; 45min–1hr 30min); Haniá (16 daily 7.30–10.30pm; 1hr 30min); Iráklion (18 daily 6.30am–10.15pm; 1hr 30min); Plakiás (4 daily 6.15am–7.30pm; 50min).

RÉTHYMNON

INFORMATION

Tourist office Delfini Building, on the seafront (Mon–Fri 8am–2.30pm, Sat 10am–4pm; ☎28310 29148, ⓦrethymnon.com), provides maps, timetables and accommodation lists.

Services Galero Internet Café, Rimóndi fountain (daily 9am–midnight). Ellotia Tours, Arkhadíou 155, behind the seafront (☎28310 51981, ⓦrethymnoatcrete.com), is a reliable source of travel information and tickets.

ACCOMMODATION

There's a great number of places to stay in Réthymnon, and only at the height of the season are you likely to have difficulty finding somewhere, though you may get weary looking. The greatest concentration of rooms is in the tangled streets west of the inner harbour, between the Rimóndi fountain and the museums; there are also quite a few places on and around Arkadhíou and Platía Plastíra.

★ **Atelier** Himáras 25 ☎28310 24440, ⓦfrosso-bora.com/rooms. Attractive en-suite balcony rooms with a/c, fridge and plasma TV run by a talented potter, who has her studio in the basement and sells her wares in a shop on the other side of the building. **€45**

Barbara Dokimaki Platía Plastíra 14 ☎28310 24581, ✉alicedokk@yahoo.gr. Strange warren of a place, with one entrance at the above address, just off the seafront behind the Ideon, and another on Dambérgi; ask for the refurbished top-floor studio rooms, which have balconies and kitchenettes. April–Oct. **€45**

★ **Fortezza** Melissinoú 16, near the fortress ☎28310 55551, ⓦfortezza.gr. Fully renovated in 2011, this top-range hotel is styled with a mix of marble, chrome and wood, while cream furnishings complement the traditional wooden furniture in the rooms and suites, which have a/c, satellite TV and balcony. There is a swimming pool, two bars and a restaurant. Breakfast included. April–Oct. **€88**

Ideon Platía Plastíra 10 ☎28310 28667, ⓦhotelideon.gr. High-class hotel with a brilliant position just north of the ferry dock; little chance of getting one of their superior balcony sea-view rooms without prebooking in high season, though. Facilities include a swimming pool, bar and restaurant. Breakfast included. April–Oct. **€88**

Leo Vafé 2 ☎28310 26197, ⓦleohotel.gr. This elegant boutique hotel in a restored Venetian mansion offers luxurious individually styled rooms featuring exposed stonework and beautiful wooden floors,

equipped with a/c, fridge, satellite TV and wi-fi. Breakfast included. **€95**

Pension Castello Karaoli 10 ☎28310 23570, ⓦcastello-rethymno.gr. An attractive small pension in a renovated sixteenth-century Venetian-Turkish mansion; a/c en-suite rooms with fridge, TV and a delightful patio garden. Breakfast included. **€60**

Vecchio Daliani 4, near the Rimóndi Fountain ☎28310 54985, ⓦvecchio.gr. Elegant Venetian mansion tastefully transformed into an enchanting small hotel with a/c rooms (some with balcony) set around a pool. Breakfast included. May–Oct. **€85**

Youth Hostel Tombázi 41 ☎28310 22848, ⓦyhrethymno.com. The cheapest beds in town. Large, clean, very friendly and popular, it has food, showers, clothes-washing facilities, internet access and a multilingual library. **€11**

Zania Pávlou Vlástou 3 ☎28310 28169. Pension right on the corner of Arkadhíou in a well-adapted and atmospheric Venetian mansion. The airy high-ceilinged rooms come with a/c and fridge, but bathrooms are shared. May–Oct. **€40**

CAMPING

Camping Elizabeth 4km east of town ☎28310 28694, ⓦcamping-elizabeth.com. A pleasant, large site on the beach with all facilities and wi-fi. Special rates for long-term stays in autumn/winter. To get here take the bus for the out-of-town hotels (marked Scaleta/El Greco). **€20**

EATING AND DRINKING

The most touristy restaurants are arrayed immediately behind the town beach with menu picture boards outside – many of them overpriced and mediocre – and around the inner harbour there's a cluster of expensive and intimate fish tavernas. The most inviting and best-value places to eat tend to be scattered in less obvious parts of the old town.

Castelvecchio Himáras 29 ☎28310 55163. This long-established family taverna next to the fortress has a large pleasant terrace with stylish seating and a great view over the town. Try the succulent *kléftiko* lamb (€8). Offers quite a few vegetarian choices as well. May–Oct daily 1pm–late.

Fanari Makedhonías 5 ☎ 28310 50070. A good-value little taverna, below the fortress on a seafront terrace with wonderful open sea views, serves up tasty lamb and chicken dishes. Daily lunch & dinner.

Kyria Maria Moskhovítou 20 ☎ 28310 29078. Tucked down an alley behind the Rimóndi Fountain, this quaint, unassuming little taverna serves tasty mezédhes and good-value fish and meat dishes; after the meal, everyone gets a couple of Maria's delicious *tyropitákia* with honey on the house. May–Oct daily noon–late.

★ **Mesostrati** Yerakári 1. Just behind the church on Platía Martíron, this is a pleasant little neighbourhood ouzerí/taverna serving Cretan country dishes and mezédhes, on a small terrace. It's frequented by some of Réthymnon's (and Crete's) top *lýra* and *lauto* players who often hold impromptu jam sessions. Mon–Sat 11am–3pm & 6pm–2am, Sun 6pm–2am.

Stella's Kitchen Soulíou 55 ☎ 28310 28665. Great-value little diner tucked away in an alleyway, serving healthy, home-baked food and six daily specials (at least two of which are vegetarian, from €4); also good for breakfasts. Daily 9am–9pm.

Tapas y Vinos Melissinoú 14 ☎ 28310 58554. An expat from Málaga runs Réthymnon's authentic Spanish tapas bar, complete with ethnic decor, a great tapas range, excellent *jamón serrano* and superb Spanish wines. Daily 1pm–late.

★ **Thalassografia** Kefalogiánidon 33 ☎ 28310 52569. Near the fortress, this modish taverna perched on a cliff overlooking the sea is one of the "in" places for locals to dine out. Tables have sensational views, service is slick and dishes such as *arní sti stamna* (jugged lamb; €8) hit the spot. May–Oct daily 11am–late.

O Gounas Koronaiou 6 ☎ 28310 28816. Hearty, no-frills traditional cooking by a family who leave the stove to perform *lýra* every night, and when things get really lively the dancing starts. May–Oct daily dinner only.

★ **To Pigadi** Xanthoudhídhou 31 ☎ 28310 27522. Excellent taverna in the old town serving traditional dishes with a twist, such as pork with wild greens and lemon (€8). Reasonably priced and efficient service. The name is a reference to the ancient well (*pigádi*) on the attractive terrace. May–Oct daily lunch & dinner.

NIGHTLIFE

Nightlife is concentrated in the streets immediately behind the inner harbour. A relatively new café-bar scene popular with the local university student community has taken root around Platía Plastíra, above the inner harbour.

Envy Archadiou 226. Music and dance bar with a mix of house, techno and rock with a fun, casual atmosphere. Watch out for the explosive cocktail shots. Daily 11pm–dawn.

Kenzo Platía Plastíra ☎ 28310 51488. One of the row of trendy cafés above the Platía, with a young crowd, one of the sitting cafés rather than a bar. The large terrace looks out to sea, making it a good spot for a sunset drink. Daily 10am–late.

Metropolis Neárchou 24. In the small alley between the inner harbour and Arkhadíou, this loud music and dance bar plays 70s, 80s and rock music, with occasional performances by live bands. Mar–Nov daily 10pm–late.

Nuvel Inner harbour. Chic café bar with a large terrace by the harbourfront. Open all day, the music gets louder as night falls. Daily 9am–late.

Opera Club Salamínos 12 ☎ 694 43 33 282. One of the town's bigger dance clubs with an eclectic mix of Greek and western rock and lots of strobe pyrotechnics. May–Oct daily 11pm–dawn; Nov–April weekends only.

Around Réthymnon

To the southeast of the city the best-known, and still the most worthwhile, short trip that can be made is to the **monastery of Arkádhi**, some 25km and immaculately situated in the foothills of the Psilorítis range. Leaving Réthymnon to the west, the main road climbs for a while above a rocky coastline before descending to the sea, where it runs alongside sandy **beaches** for perhaps 14km. About 7km before **Yeoryioúpoli**, the beach widens and scattered hotel development appears along the coast. If you have your own vehicle, there are plenty of places to stop for a swim, some with hardly anyone else around – but beware of some very strong currents.

Monastery of Arkádhi

Daily 9am–8pm • €2 • ☎ 28310 83136

The **monastery of Arkádhi** is also something of a national Cretan shrine. During the 1866 rebellion against the Turks, the monastery became a rebel strongpoint in which, as the Turks gained the upper hand, hundreds of Cretan independence fighters and their families took refuge. Surrounded and on the point of defeat, the defenders ignited a powder magazine just as the Turks entered. Hundreds were killed, Cretan and Turk alike, and the tragedy did much to promote international sympathy for the cause of Cretan independence. Nowadays, you can peer into the roofless vault where the explosion occurred and wander about the rest of the well-restored grounds. The sixteenth-century **church** survived, and is one of the finest Venetian structures left on Crete; other buildings house a small **museum** devoted to the exploits of the defenders of the faith.

Yeoryioúpoli and around
On the coastal route, midway between Haniá and Réthymnon (on the provincial border of Haniá), **YEORYOÚPOLI** (Georgioúpoli) is very much a resort, packed with rooms to rent, small hotels, apartment buildings, tavernas and travel agencies, but everything remains on a small scale. As long as you don't expect to find too many vestiges of traditional Crete, it's a very pleasant place to pass a few days. Yeoryioúpoli's central beach is narrow and busy; walk east a few hundred metres for the quieter and wider sands.

Lake Kournás
KOURNÁS, Crete's only natural freshwater lake, is set deep in a bowl of hills just 4km inland from Yeoryioúpoli. The best scenic route is via the hamlet of **MATHÉS**, and if you are on foot there is a ramblers' path from here leading to the lake's northern edge. **Kournás** village proper lies 4km uphill from the lake. Spring is the best time to visit the lake; the peacefulness and the profusion of wild flowers are stunning. In high summer you could be in a completely different place, as the winter waters recede and the lake-shore "beach" is packed with umbrellas and sunloungers.

4

ARRIVAL AND DEPARTURE   YEORYIOÚPOLI AND AROUND

By bus Yeoryioúpoli is easily reached from both Réthymnon and Haniá; the main-line buses running hourly (6.30am–10.30pm) along the main highway stop here.

ACTIVITIES

Cycling Adventure Bikes (☎ 28250 61830, ⓦ adventurebikes.org) organize easy bike tours all around the western end of the island with transport to get you up the steep bits.
Diving Paradise Dive Centre, Petres Geraniou ☎ 28310 26317, ⓦ diving-center.gr. Beginners' and advanced scuba diving based near Yeoryioúpoli to the west of town. Will pick up from hotels in Réthymnon. PADI certificated.
Horseriding Zoraïda's (☎ 28250 61745, ⓦ zoraidas -horseriding.com), for horseriding, including organized rides along the beach or up to Lake Kournás.

ACCOMMODATION

YEORYIOÚPOLI
Andy's Rooms ☎ 28250 61394. Friendly place, shaded by eucalyptus trees, offering large good-value rooms and apartments with balcony, a/c, fridge and TV. Take the road towards the beach from the south end of the square and you'll find it opposite the church. **€45**
Anna ☎ 28250 61556, ⓦ annashouse.gr. Just across the river, this upgraded complex of stylish rooms, studios and apartments (sleeping up to seven) with balcony is set around a large pool. Facilities include fridge and satellite TV. May–Oct. **€85**

River House ☎ 28250 61141, ⓦ riverhouse.gr. A pleasant family-run complex of rooms and studios with balcony, kitchenette, a/c, satellite TV and free wi-fi access. There's also a pool and garden. May–Oct. **€48**

LAKE KOURNÁS
Villa Kapasa ☎ 28250 61050, ⓦ villa-kapasas.com. Comfortable, spacious, en-suite, a/c rooms in a restored old building which retains a number of its original stone features, with a cool, leafy garden. 50m uphill from *Taverna Mathes* (see p.240). May–Oct. **€40**

EATING AND DRINKING

YEORYIOÚPOLI
Taverna Babis-Fontas ☎ 28250 61760. This friendly traditional taverna down towards the beach is good for simple Greek and Cretan dishes; try their excellent rabbit stifado (€7.50). May–Oct daily lunch & dinner.
Taverna Paradise ☎ 28250 61313. A good taverna with

a large terrace garden, home-cooked Greek and Cretan dishes such as lamb stifado and pork with peppers (€8). May–Oct daily 7pm–late.

LAKE KOURNÁS

Eye of the Lake The lakeside view here is peaceful and the food is good; fresh starters and salads, grilled meats and home-cooked dishes. Well frequented by locals. May–Oct daily 10am–late, Nov–Apr weekends only.

★ **Kali Kardia** Kournás ☎ 28250 96278. This is a wonderful, simple but popular place. Sample the local lamb (€7) and *loukánika* (sausages), accompanied by fresh home-grown salad. All the produce is their own. May–Oct daily 10am–late, Nov–April weekends only.

Taverna Mathes Mathés ☎ 28250 61514. This peaceful place offers great terrace views over the bay of Yeoryioúpoli. Good food with traditional dishes, many made from their own produce. May–Oct daily 10am–late.

South from Réthymnon

There are a couple of alternative routes south from Réthymnon, but the main one heads straight out from the centre of town, an initially featureless road due south across the middle of the island towards the south coast and **Ayía Galíni**. About 23km out, a turning cuts off to the right for **Plakiás** and **Mýrthios**, following the course of the spectacular Kourtaliótiko ravine.

Plakiás

PLAKIÁS is an established, yet still quite low-key, resort with a satisfactory beach and a string of good tavernas around the dock. Relax and soak up the atmosphere, or if you're looking for **walks** there's plenty to explore along the coastline and inland. Some of the most tempting beaches in central Crete hide just to the east of Plakiás, though unfortunately they're now a very poorly kept secret. These three splashes of yellow sand, divided by rocky promontories, are within walking distance (40min) and together go by the name **Dhamnóni**.

Mýrthios

For a stay of more than a day or two, **MÝRTHIOS**, in the hills just behind Plakiás, also deserves consideration. There are some great apartments and wonderful views, and you'll generally find locals still outnumbering the tourists. It takes twenty minutes to walk down to the beach at Plakiás, a little longer to Dhamnóni.

Préveli monastery

April & May daily 9am–7pm; June–Oct Mon–Sat 9am–1.30pm & 3.30–7pm, Sun 9am–7pm; in winter, knock for admission • €3 • ⓦ preveli.org

PRÉVELI, lying some 7km southeast of Plakiás, takes its name from the **monastery** set high above the sea which, like every other in Crete, has a proud history of resistance, in this case accentuated by its role in World War II as a shelter for marooned Allied soldiers awaiting evacuation. There are fine views and a new monument commemorating the rescue operations and depicting a startling life-size, rifle-toting abbot and an Allied soldier cast in bronze.

Préveli "Palm Beach"

Préveli "**Palm Beach**" is a sandy cove with a small date-palm grove (recovering from fire damage in 2010) where an estuary feeds a little oasis. Although beautiful, the beach is often crowded with day-trip boats from Plakiás and Ayía Galíni. The turn-off for the beach is the newly asphalted road 1km before Préveli monastery (if travelling by bus you'll be dropped at this junction). This leads to a pay car park (€2) from where the beach is accessed via a steep climb down a path over the rocks (about a 10min descent and a sweaty 20min haul back up). Another path from the east side of the beach follows the river valley 2km back to a stone bridge, by the main road, where there are cafés.

Spíli

The pleasant country town of **SPÍLI** lies about 30km south of Réthymnon. A popular coffee break for coach tours passing this way, Spíli warrants a visit and there's some good hiking country in the nearby hills. Sheltered under a cliff are narrow alleys of ancient houses, all leading up from a platía with a famous 25-spouted **fountain** that replaced a Venetian original. It's a worthwhile place to stay, peacefully rural at night and with several good **rooms** for rent.

Ayía Galíni

AYÍA GALÍNI is a picturesque place nestling in a fold in the mountains. Once a small "fishing village", it is now so busy in high season that you can't see it for the tour buses, hotel billboards and package tourists. It also has a beach that is much too small for the crowds that congregate here. Even so, there are a few saving graces – mainly some excellent restaurants and bars, a lively nightlife scene, plenty of rooms and a friendly atmosphere that survives and even thrives on all the visitors. Out of season, when the climate is mild and the crowds have departed, it can be quite enjoyable too.

The Amári valley

An alternative route south from Réthymnon, and a far less travelled one, is the road which turns off on the eastern fringe of town to run via the **Amári valley**. There's little specifically to see or do (though a number of richly frescoed Byzantine churches are hidden away en route), but it's an impressive drive under the flanks of the mountains and a reminder of how, in places, rural Crete continues to exist regardless of visitors. The countryside here is delightfully green even in summer, with rich groves of olive and assorted fruit trees, and if you **stay** you'll find the nights are cool and quiet. It may seem odd that many of the villages along the way are modern: they were systematically destroyed by the German army in reprisal for the 1944 kidnapping of General Kreipeo, and many have poignant roadside monuments commemorating those tragic events.

GETTING AROUND   **SOUTH FROM RÉTHYMNON**

By bus Réthymnon to: Ayía Galíni via Spíli (4 daily; 1hr), Plakiás (4 daily; 1hr), Préveli (2 daily; 1hr).

HIKING THE AMÁRI VALLEY

A good base for touring the **Amári valley** is Thrónos, a sizeable village at the valley's northern end with an inviting place to stay, *Rooms Aravanes* (see below). The proprietor here – Lambros Papoutsakis – is a keen walker and conducts guided treks to the peak of **Mount Psilorítis**, which at 2456m is Crete's highest. Although he does guide groups up in the daytime, his preferred approach is during the full moons of June, July and August, which avoids the extreme summer temperatures. Phone in advance for details; it's not a difficult climb, but you'll need sturdy footwear and a sleeping bag. The summit is reached at around dawn, and the sunrise is always spectacular: on clear days the mountain offers a breathtaking view of the whole island and its four seas spreading in all directions.

Other hikes from Thrónos include a relatively easy path leading north through the foothills in a couple of hours to the monastery of Arkádhi (see p.238), while south from Thrónos is an easy stroll on a paved road running back into the main valley via Kalóyerosa. A map detailing these walks is available from *Rooms Aravanes*.

Rooms Aravanes Thrónos ☎ 28330 22760, ✉ aravanesthronos@yahoo.gr. The stone-built *Aravanes* has amazing panoramic views across the valley to Mount Psilorítis. The owners rent five en-suite rooms with large balconies and run the taverna below, together with a small shop selling mountain herbs and home-made honey. **€35**

ACTIVITIES

Boat trips from Plakiás and Ayía Galíni will get you to Préveli "Palm Beach" with a great deal less fuss.

Diving Kalypso Rock Palace Plakiás ☎ 28310, 20990, ⓦ kalypsodivingcenter.com. This PADI-certificated diving centre offers advanced and learner courses.

ACCOMMODATION

PLAKIÁS

Afrodite Off the inland road to the hostel ☎ 28320 31266, ⓔ kasel@hol.gr. The bougainvillea-draped *Afrodite* is in a quiet spot, 150m from the beach, and offers pleasant a/c rooms and apartments, with TV, fridge and large balconies with mountain views, plus a garden. April–Oct. **€30**

⭐ **Gio-ma** Western end of the seafront ⓦ gioma.gr. In a prime position on the seafront by the harbour, opposite the taverna of the same name, sea-view balcony rooms and studios with a/c, fridge and TV. April–Oct. **€40**

Ippokambos On the inland road parallel to the sea ☎ 28320 31525, ⓔ amoutsos@otenet.gr. Excellent simple and friendly rooms place with modern en-suite balcony rooms and fridge, along the backstreet, 200m from the beach. April–Oct. **€35**

Youth Hostel 500m inland, signed from the seafront ☎ 28320 32118, ⓦ yhplakias.com. A friendly, well-run hostel with gardens and a large shady terrace for breakfast, evening drinks and barbecues. Accommodation is in dorm bungalows sleeping four. April–Oct. Dorms **€10**

MÝRTHIOS

⭐ **Anna Apartments** Mýrthios ☎ 697 33 24 775, ⓦ annaview.com. These classy apartments, built with traditional stone and wood, are beautifully furnished and have fantastic views over Plakiás Bay. All come with kitchenette, balcony, a/c, satellite TV and wi-fi. **€48**

SPÍLI

Green Hotel On the main road, north of the square. ☎ 28320 22225. Comfortable en-suite rooms with TV and wi-fi. Rooms at the back have good valley views and the hotel has a small sauna and fitness room. Breakfast included. **€40**

Herakles Rooms Off the main road, below the Green Hotel ☎ 28320 22111, ⓔ heraclespapadakis@hotmail .com. This friendly pension has a/c en-suite balcony rooms with valley views and internet, situated in a quiet spot. The genial proprietor can advise on some superb walks in the surrounding hills and also rents out mountain bikes. **€35**

AYÍA GALÍNI

Camping No Problem ☎ 28320 91386. A big site with shady pitches, down by the river. Good facilities include a supermarket, taverna and large pool. A 10min walk from town along the beach. May–Oct. **€18**

Idi Opposite Minos Hotel ☎ 28320 91152. Friendly rooms place, simple and clean a/c rooms with TV, fridge and balcony – some of which have sea view. June–Oct. **€35**

Minos Hotel ☎ 28320 91292. Economical and great value with en-suite rooms, with TV and fridge, the south-facing rooms have superb views from the terrace. May–Oct. **€35**

⭐ **Neos Ikaros** ☎ 28320 91447, ⓦ neosikaros.gr. A more upmarket option towards the harbour; modern rooms come with a/c, fridge, satellite TV and large balconies, and there's a superb pool and gardens. Breakfast included. April–Oct. **€53**

EATING AND DRINKING

PLAKIÁS

Gio-ma ☎ 28320 32003. Right on the water's edge, this taverna is good for fish, seafood, home-cooked specials and grills. The kalamári is excellent (€7.50). April–Oct daily 9am–late.

Medousa At the east end of town. ☎ 28320 31521. Reached up the road inland from the post office and then right. A splendid traditional taverna with prices lower than those on the seafront, and they also serve breakfast. May–Oct daily 9am–11pm.

Nikos Souvlaki On the road inland from the post office ☎ 28320 31921. Dishes up the least expensive meals in town – excellent *souvláki* (€2) or even fish and chips, to eat in, at one of the small pavement tables, or take away. March–Oct Tues–Sun 6pm–11.30pm.

⭐ **Sofia** ☎ 28320 31226, ⓦ tavernasofia.gr. A long-established taverna, friendly with a good reputation. Try

their fresh daily specials (€5.50–8) or choose from the range of starters, fish and grills on their large menu. April–Oct daily 10am–late.

Tassomanolis ☎ 28320 31129. One of a line of waterfront places enjoying spectacular sunsets; this one has a blue-and-white nautical theme and specializes in fish caught by the proprietor from his own boat (from €22/kg – there are many more economical dishes too). April–Oct daily lunch & dinner.

MÝRTHIOS

Taverna Plateia ☎ 28320 31560. This long-established taverna on the central square has had a complete makeover but still serves up excellent traditional Cretan cooking, great wines, and has arguably the most spectacular terrace view of any taverna on the island. May–Oct daily lunch & dinner.

4

AYÍA GALÍNI

Onar Taverna Street ☎ 28320 91121. One of the best tavernas on this row, at the harbour end with a great rooftop terrace and views over the harbour, serving wholesome food; try their excellent charcoal-grilled fish and meat or specials such as meatballs with feta cheese (€6). May–Oct daily 10am–late.

To Petrino Off the harbour platía ☎ 28320 91504. A charming little stone-built (*Petrino*) street café-ouzerí serving up breakfasts, coffees and drinks during the day and tasty mezédhes at night. April–Oct daily 9am–late.

Western Crete

Crete's westernmost quarter is one of its least visited, partly because there are no big sandy beaches to accommodate resort hotels, and partly because it's so far from the great archeological sites. But for mountains, scattered coves and unexploited villages, it's unrivalled.

The city of **Haniá** (Chania) is an excellent reason to come here, but the immediately adjacent coast, especially to the west of the city, is overdeveloped and not particularly exciting; if you want beaches head for the south coast or the far west. Here, Paleóhora is the only place which could really be described as a resort, and even this is on a thoroughly human scale; others are emptier still. Elsewhere on the south coast, **Ayía Rouméli** and **Loutró** can be reached only on foot or by boat; **Hóra Sfakíon** sees hordes passing through but few who stay; **Frangokástello**, nearby, has a beautiful castle and the first stirrings of development. Behind these lie the **White Mountains** (Lefká Óri) and the famed walk through the **Samariá Gorge**. In the far west, great beaches at **Falásarna** and **Elafoníssi** are mostly visited only as day-trips.

Haniá

HANIÁ, as any of its residents will tell you, is spiritually the capital of Crete, even if the political title was passed back to Iráklion. It is also the island's most attractive city, especially if you can catch it in spring, when the White Mountains' snowcapped peaks seem to hover above the roofs. Although it is for the most part a modern city, you might never know it as a tourist. Surrounding the harbour is a wonderful jumble of **Venetian streets** that survived the wartime bombardments, while simply wandering the old town you will discover old city walls, Ottoman, Byzantine and Minoan ruins. Restoration and gentrification, consequences of the tourist boom, have made inroads of late, but it remains an atmospheric place.

The harbour

The **harbour** area is the oldest and the most interesting part of town, at its busiest and most attractive at night, when the lights from bars and restaurants reflect in the water and crowds of visitors and locals turn out to promenade. By day, things are quieter. Straight ahead from Platía Sindriváni (also known as Harbour Square) lies the curious domed shape of the **Mosque of the Janissaries**, built in 1645 (though heavily restored since) and the oldest Ottoman building on the island. It is usually open as a gallery, housing temporary exhibitions. Further east, on the inner harbour, the arches of sixteenth-century **Venetian arsenals**, a couple of them beautifully restored (and one housing a reconstructed Minoan ship), survive alongside remains of the outer walls.

Kastélli

The little hill that rises behind the mosque is **Kastélli**, site of the earliest habitation and core of the Minoan, Venetian and Turkish towns. There's not a great deal left, but archeologists believe that they may have found the remains of a Minoan palace, and the "lost" city of **Kydonia**, in the excavations being carried out – and open to view – along

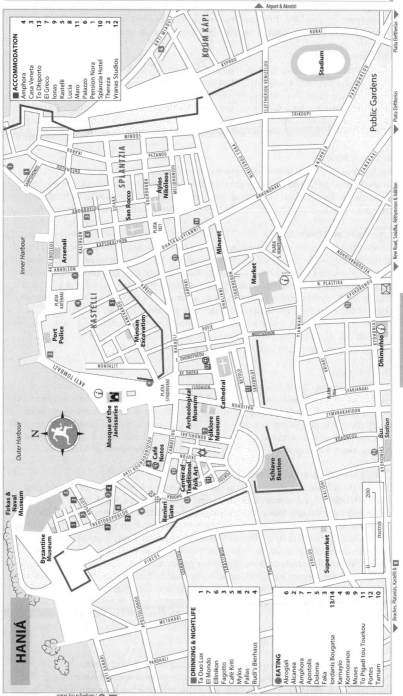

HANIÁ

Airport & Akrotiri

ACCOMMODATION
Amphora	4
Casa Veneta	3
To Dhiporto	13
El Greco	7
Ionas	9
Kastelli	5
Lucia	8
Maro	11
Palazzo	6
Pension Nora	1
Splanzia Hotel	10
Thereza	2
Vranas Studios	12

DRINKING & NIGHTLIFE
Ta Duo Lux	1
El Mondo	7
Ellinikon	6
Fagotto	3
Café Kriti	5
Mylos	8
Pallas	2
Rudi's Bierhaus	4

EATING
Akrogiali	6
Alcanea	2
Amphora	7
Apostolis	1
Doloma	5
Faka	3
Iordanis Bougatsa	13/14
Karnayio	4
Kormoranos	8
Muses	9
To Pigadi tou Tourkou	11
Portes	12
Tamam	10

Inner Harbour
Outer Harbour
N

KOÚM KÁPI
Stadium
Public Gardens

Firkas & Naval Museum
Byzantine Museum
Port Police
Arsenali
KASTELLI
Minoan Excavation
SPLANTZIA
San Rocco
Áyios Nikólaos
Mosque of the Janissaries
Café Notos
Renieri Gate
Center of Traditional Folk Art
Archeological Museum
Folklore Museum
Cathedral
Minaret
Market
Schiavo Bastion
Supermarket
Bus Station
Dhimarhío

Platía Eleftherías
New Road, Soudha, Réthymnon & Iráklion
Beaches, Platanias, Kandéli &

Camping & City Beach

4

Kanevárou. It's also here that you'll find traces of the oldest **walls**; there were two rings, one defending Kastélli alone, a later set encompassing the whole of the medieval city.

The Naval Museum

Daily: April–Oct 9am–4pm, Nov–March 9am–2pm • €3 • ☎ 28210 91875

The hefty bastion at the western end of the harbour now houses Crete's **Naval Museum**. The collection consists of model ships and other naval ephemera tracing the history of Greek navigation, plus a section on the 1941 **Battle of Crete** with fascinating artefacts, and poignant photos depicting the suffering here under the Nazis. From the **Fírkas**, the fortress behind the museum, the modern Greek flag was first flown on Crete, in 1913.

Byzantine Museum

Tues–Sun 8.30am–3pm • €2, combined ticket with Archeological Museum €3 • ☎ 28210 96046

At the back of the Naval Museum lies the **Byzantine Museum** (entrance at the top of Theotokopoúlou), located in the Venetian Chapel of San Salvatore, with an interesting collection of mosaics, icons and jewellery from the various periods of Byzantine rule.

City walls and backstreets

Beyond the Byzantine museum, follow Pireós inland outside the best-preserved stretch of the old city walls. Following the walls around on the inside is rather trickier, but far more enjoyable. This is where you'll stumble on some of the most picturesque little alleyways and finest Venetian houses in Haniá. Keep your eyes open for details on the houses, such as old wooden balconies or stone coats of arms. The arch of the **Renieri Gate**, at the bottom of Moschón, is particularly elegant. There are also lots of interesting art and craft stores around here, along Theotokopoúlou and the many alleys that run off, while between the Renieri Gate and Hálidhon are more such alleys, though here the emphasis is more on tavernas, bars and cafés.

The synagogue

Mon–Fri 10am–6pm • Free • ⓦ www.etz-hayyim-hania.org

At the end of a small alley off the west side of Kóndhilaki is Haniá's fifteenth-century Etz Hayyim **synagogue**, recently renovated. All but one of the city's Jews were rounded up by the Nazi occupation forces in 1944, but they met their end (along with around 500 members of the captured Cretan resistance) when the transport ship taking them to Auschwitz was torpedoed by a British submarine off the island of Mílos.

Odhós Hálidhon and beyond

Behind the harbour lie the less picturesque but more lively sections of the old city. **Odhós Hálidhon** is lined with touristy shops, in the midst of which you'll find the **archeological museum**, **folklore museum** and the modern **cathedral**. Behind the cathedral square are cafés and some of the more animated shopping areas, leading up to the back of the market: on **Odhós Skrídhlof** ("Leather Street") traditional leathermakers plied their trade, but today just one small workshop remains, the rest having been replaced with imported leather goods and souvenirs, but there are still leather bargains (shoes, bags and more) to be had. Further east behind the market, the **Splántzia** quarter is a maze of ancient alleys with tumbledown Venetian stonework and wooden balconies; there are a couple of **minarets** here, one on Dhaliáni, and the other attached to the church of Áyios Nikólaos in Platía 1821. A clutch of new, popular *mezedhopolía* and *ouzerís* along Dhaliáni have revitalized this area.

Archeological Museum

Odhós Hálidhon 28 • Tues–Sun 8am–3pm • €2, combined ticket with Byzantine Museum €3 • ☎ 28210 90334

A short way up Hálidhon, on the right, is Haniá's **Archeological Museum**, housed in the Venetian-built church of San Francesco. The building has been substantially restored and contains a fine display, covering the local area from Minoan through to Roman times. In the courtyard garden, a huge fountain and the base of a minaret survive from the period when the Ottomans converted the church into a mosque; around them are scattered various other sculptures and architectural remnants.

Folklore Museum

Odhós Hálidhon 46b • Mon–Sat 9.30am–3pm & 6–9pm • €2 • ☎ 28210 90816

The nearby **Folklore Museum** is worth a look as much for its setting, on a fine courtyard that is also home to Haniá's Roman Catholic church, as for its contents. This small museum replicates a "traditional" Cretan house, with furnishings, tapestries and artefacts on display.

The beaches

Haniá's beaches lie to the west of the city and on the Akrotíri peninsula to the northeast. The clean **city beach** (Néa Hóra) is no more than a ten-minute walk west, following the shoreline from the Naval Museum, but for more extensive spaces you're better off heading further west along the coast to the beaches of **Khrissi Akti**, **Áyios Apostólis and Kalamáki**. These beaches can get pretty crowded but they may be a considerable improvement over the beach in Haniá itself. Further afield there are even finer beaches at **Áyía Marína** (see p.251) to the west, or **Kalathás** and **Stavrós** (p.251) out on the Akrotíri peninsula, all of which can be reached by KTEL buses from the main station.

ARRIVAL AND DEPARTURE   HANIÁ 4

BY PLANE

Haniá Airport (Chania) lies 15km east of town on the Akrotíri peninsula and is served by domestic flights (Aegean Airways ☎ 28210 63366 and Olympic Air ☎ 28210 63264 and international flights with easyJet and charter airlines in the summer only. Airport buses to the city run frequently during the summer, less regularly in winter months (April–Oct 15 daily 6.40am–9.45pm, Nov–March 6 daily 6.40am–9.20pm; 25min; €2.40). Taxis (€20) are plentiful, from the airport taxi rank.

Destinations Athens (6 daily on Aegean and Olympic; 50min); Thessaloníki (1 daily on Aegean; 1hr 15min). London (easyJet – summer only).

BY FERRY

Arriving by ferry, you'll anchor about 10km east of Haniá at the port of Soúdha: take a bus (every 15 min; 20min; €1.60) or taxi (around €12) to the city. Tickets are available from ANEK line office (on Venizélou, right opposite the market;

☎ 28210 27500) or any travel agent.

Destinations Daily overnight (8hr 30min), with ANEK lines (ⓦ anek.gr), extra daytime sailing in July and Aug.

BY BUS

The bus station is on Kydhonías. For the latest timetables and complete route and fare information for Haniá buses, visit ⓦ bus-service-crete-ktel.com.

Destinations Elafonísi (daily at 9am; 2hr 30min); Falásarna (3 daily 8.30am–3.30pm; 1hr 30min); Frangokástello (daily at 2pm; 2hr 30min); Hóra Sfakíon (2 daily 8.30am & 2pm; 2hr); Iráklion via Réthymnon (hourly 5.30am–6.30pm, then 8pm & 9pm; 3hr); Kastélli (14 daily 6.30am–9.15pm; 1hr); Omalós (Samariá Gorge; 4 daily 6.15am–2pm; 1hr); Paleóhora (4 daily 5am–4pm; 1hr 30min); Soúyia (2 daily 5am & 2pm; 2hr); Stavrós (5 daily 6.50am–8.20pm; 30min).

INFORMATION, TOURS AND ACTIVITIES

Tourist office Kydhonías 29 (Mon–Fri 8am–2.30pm ☎ 28210 36155, ⓦ chania.gr). In the *dhimarhío* (town hall), with entrance at the side of the building, four blocks east of the bus station.

Boat tours A number of boats run trips from the harbour (around €10–12 for 2hr), mainly to the nearby islands of Áyii Theódori and Lazarétta, for swimming and *krí-krí* (ibex) spotting, also evening sunset cruises.

Diving Blue Adventures Diving, Arholéon 11, near the inner harbour (☎ 28210 40608, ⓦ blueadventuresdiving .gr), runs daily diving and snorkelling trips.

Waterpark Limnoupolis (ⓦ limnoupolis.gr), located close to the village of Varípetro, 8km southwest of the city, with slides taking advantage of a natural hillside (€11–23). Buses from the bus station depart daily at 10.45am and return at 6.30pm.

GETTING AROUND

Bike and car rental For bikes, Summertime, Dhaskaloyiánnis 7, slightly northeast of the market (☎ 28210 45797, ⓦ strentals.gr), including mountain bikes. For cars, try around the top of Hálidhon where Tellus Rent a Car (☎ 28210 91500, ⓦ tellustravel.gr) is one of many. El Greco Cars at the *El Greco* hotel (☎ 28210 60883, ⓦ elgreco.gr; see below) offer ten percent off to Rough Guide readers.

Taxis The main taxi ranks are on Platía 1866 and at the junction of Yiánnari and Karaiskáki. For radio taxis call ☎ 18300, ☎ 28210 94300 or 28210 98700.

ACCOMMODATION

There are thousands of rooms to rent in Haniá, as well as a number of pricey boutique hotels. Though you may face a long search for a bed at the height of the season, eventually everyone does seem to find something. Perhaps the most desirable rooms of all are those overlooking the **harbour**. Most are approached not direct from the harbourside itself but from the streets behind; those further back are likely to be more peaceful. Theotokopoúlou and the alleys off it make a good starting point. In the eastern half of the old town, rooms are far more scattered and in the height of the season your chances are much better over here. Try **Kastélli**, immediately east of the harbour, or around **Splántzia** and the streets around the cathedral.

HARBOUR AREA

★ **Amphora** 2 Párodos Theotokopoúlou 20 ☎ 28210 93224, ⓦ amphora.gr. Traditional hotel in a beautifully renovated Venetian mansion; the entrance is via a small alley but the hotel faces the harbour and lighthouse. Rooms and suites come with a/c, TV, fridge and some with balcony and sea view. Good harbourfront restaurant below. March–Nov. **€110**

Casa Veneta Theotokopoúlou 57 ☎ 28210 90007, ⓦ casa-veneta.gr. Well-equipped, comfortable studios and apartments with a/c, fridge, kitchenette, some with balcony, behind a Venetian facade along the quaint Theotokopoúlou street, and with a friendly owner. April–Oct. **€60**

El Greco Theotokopoúlou 47–49 ☎ 28210 94030, ⓦ elgreco.gr. Comfortable hotel with nicely furnished if rather compact rooms which include fridge, a/c, TV and wi-fi. Some have balconies and there's a seasonal roof terrace. Breakfast included. April–Oct. **€50**

Lucia Aktí Koundouriótou ☎ 28210 90302, ⓦ loukiahotel.gr. Harbourfront hotel with a/c rooms with TV and fridge; furnishing is basic at best, hence much less expensive than you might expect for one of the best views in town, and – thanks to double-glazing – reasonably soundproof. May–Oct. **€45**

Maro Párodos Portoú 5 ☎ 28210 97913. Probably the cheapest en-suite rooms in the old town, hidden away in a quiet, unmarked alley off Portou not far from the Schiavo bastion. Basic but friendly and clean; with a/c. May–Oct. **€35**

Palazzo Theotokopoúlou 54 ☎ 28210 93227, ⓦ palazzohotel.gr. This old converted mansion has wood-beamed ceilings and wooden floors. Good-sized, simply furnished rooms with a/c, TV, fridge, and most rooms come with balcony, plus there is a pretty roof terrace with harbour views and tasty breakfasts. Breakfast included. May–Oct. **€80**

Pension Nora Theotokopoúlou 60 ☎ 28210 72265, ⓦ pension-nora.com. Charming a/c rooms in a ramshackle wooden Turkish house, some very basic with shared bath, others relatively fancy, so look first. Pleasant breakfast café below. **€40**

Thereza Angélou 8 ☎ 28210 92798, ⓦ pensiontheresa .gr. Beautiful old house in a great position, with stunning views from the roof terrace and en-suite a/c rooms (some with TV); classy decor, too; unlikely to have room in high season unless you book. **€60**

THE OLD TOWN

Ionas Sarpáki, cnr Sórvolou ☎ 28210 55090, ⓦ ionashotel.com. Small boutique hotel in a lovingly restored Venetian mansion, set at the end of a small square in the heart of the old Splántzia quarter. Very comfortable rooms and beautiful architectural detail. May–Oct. **€90**

Kastelli Kanevárou 39 ☎ 28210 57057, ⓦ kastelistudios.gr. A comfortable, modern, reasonably priced *pension* that's very quiet at the back. All rooms come with a/c, TV, fridge, balcony and wi-fi. The owner is exceptionally helpful and also has a few apartments and a beautiful house (for up to five people) to rent nearby. **€45**

★ **Splanzia Hotel** Dhaskaloyiánnis 58 ☎ 28210 45313, ⓦ splanzia.com. Small friendly boutique hotel in a beautiful restored Venetian building, comfortable stylish en-suite rooms come with a/c, satellite TV and wi-fi. Breakfast, served in the pretty courtyard, is included. **€115**

To Dhiporto Betólo 41 ☎ 28210 40570, ⓦ todiporto .gr. In the alley one block in front of Odhós Skrídhlof (Leather Street). Refurbished, good-value en-suite rooms in a traditional renovated building, with a/c, TV, fridge and balcony; some triples and singles too. **€40**

Vranas Studios Ayíon Dhéka, cnr Sarpáki ☎ 28210 58618, ⓦ vranas.gr. Tucked away in a narrow street below the cathedral, these traditional-style, spacious, studio rooms have TV, a/c, kitchenette and wi-fi, with an internet café below. **€55**

CAMPING

Camping Hania Áyios Apostólis, 4km west of Haniá 📞 28210 31138, 🌐 camping-chania.gr. Served by local

bus. The site is rather small, and hemmed in by new development, but it has a pool and all the usual facilities just a short walk from some of the better beaches. May–Oct. **€20**

EATING

The harbour is encircled by a succession of pricey restaurants, tavernas and cafés which are usually better for a drink than a meal. Away from the water, there are plenty of slightly cheaper possibilities on Kondhiláki, Zambelíou and most of the streets off Hálidhon.

CAFÉS

⭐ **Alcanea** Angélou 2 📞 28210 75370. Small, relaxed terrace café at the quieter western tip of the harbour, beneath the hotel of the same name, next to the naval museum. Good for breakfast, coffee or evening drinks. Daily 9am–late.

Iordanis Bougatsa Branches at Kydhonías 96 and Apokorónou 24. Specializes in traditional creamy *bougátsa*, a sugar-coated cream-cheese pie to eat in or take away. Mon–Sat 8am–3pm.

Kormoranos Theotokopoúlou. This bakery/café/ouzerí serves pastries washed down by juices, herb teas and coffee during the day, and an ouzerí serving delicious meze to go with your drinks at night. May–Oct daily 9am–late.

Muses Platía Sindriváni. Pleasant café on the harbour square, in a prime position for people-watching, serves breakfasts, coffees, snacks and late drinks. May–Oct daily 7am–late.

RESTAURANTS

⭐ **Akrogiali** Aktí Papanikolí 19, Néa Hóra 📞 28210 73110. Opposite the city beach, with a summer terrace, this excellent, reasonably priced fish and seafood taverna is well worth the 15min walk or short taxi ride. Always packed with locals, so may be worth booking – though there are plenty of alternatives along the same street. Daily lunch & dinner.

Amphora Aktí Koundouriótou, under Hotel Amphora 📞 28210 93224. One of the most reliable places on the outer harbour seafront, across from the lighthouse, with good, simple home-cooked Greek food, fish and seafood. Mains €5.50–10. March–Nov daily 10am–late.

Apostolis 1 and 2 Aktí Enóseos 6 & 10, inner harbour 📞 28210 43470. The fish tavernas at the inner end of the harbour are rated much more highly by locals than those further round – some locals claim *Apostolis 2* is the best of all. The fish is excellent, but pricey. Daily lunch & dinner.

⭐ **Doloma** Kapsokályvon 5, behind the Arsenali 📞 28210 51196. Excellent little taverna set back off the

street, with a shady terrace, serving well-prepared and economical Cretan dishes with good local wine. Mains such as rice-stuffed tomatoes or *pastitsio* (spaghetti pie) from €4. Daily lunch & dinner.

Faka Arholéon 15 📞 28210 42341. Set back from the harbour in the small square behind the *Arsenali* building, this is significantly less touristy and less expensive than many near neighbours. Excellent traditional local food, often with live Greek music. May–Oct daily lunch & dinner.

Karnayio Platía Kateháki 8, next to the Arsenali 📞 28210 53366. Not right on the water, but one of the best harbour restaurants nonetheless. Excellent fish, traditional Cretan cooking and a fine selection of wines – all served on an inviting terrace – make this a winner. Mains from €5.50. May–Oct daily lunch & dinner.

⭐ **Portes** Portoú 48 📞 28210 76261. A small group of restaurants nestles under the walls along Portoú. *Portes* is smarter than most, with a particularly adventurous menu putting a modern twist on age-old dishes: rabbit with prunes (€9.50), cuttlefish with fennel (€8.50), and traditional pies with unusual fillings. April–Oct lunch & dinner.

To Pigadi tou Tourkou Sarpáki 1 📞 28210 54547, 🌐 welloftheturk.com. Greco-Moroccan restaurant (the name translates to "Well of the Turk") with an interesting menu combining the two cuisines along with dishes from the Middle East. Mains from €8. Wed–Sun dinner only; closed Dec.

⭐ **Tamam** Zambelíou 📞 28210 96080, 🌐 tamam restaurant.com. Popular place where the adventurous Greek menu includes much vegetarian food, with added spices giving an eastern flavour. The original restaurant is housed in an old Turkish baths, while opposite is the less atmospheric annexe, *Tamam II*; tables are squeezed into the alley between the two. Mains from €6. Daily noon–1am.

DRINKING AND NIGHTLIFE

The harbour area contains dozens of beautifully set but touristy bars. Locals head east, to the inner harbour and beyond to Koum Kápi, where the scores of bars and cafés lining Aktí Miaoúli are heaving by 11pm. In summer the action moves to the vibrant club scene on the coast west of town.

Café Kriti (Lyrakia) Kalergón 22, cnr Andhroyíou. Cretan music and dancing virtually every night at what is

basically an old-fashioned *kafenío*. Daily 7.30pm–late.
El Mondo Kondiláki 35 📞 28210 88044, 🌐 elmondo

bar.com. An old favourite, popular with tourists and occasional visiting military, this small but lively bar belts out a mixture of rock classics, dance music and latest tracks. May–Oct daily 9pm–4am, Nov–April Wed–Mon 8pm–2am.

Elliniko Aktí Miaoúli ☎ 28210 27729. One of the more popular and consistent of the bar-cafés on the Koum Kápi strip to the east, beyond the harbour, packed nightly with young locals: if this doesn't appeal, take your pick from its dozens of neighbours. Daily 10am–late.

★ **Fagotto** Angélou 16 ☎ 28210 71877. Laidback, indoor jazz bar off the quieter end of the harbour, often with live performances. Daily 8pm–late.

Mylos Main street, Plataniás ☎ 28210 60449. Large, buzzing summer nightclub with four indoor bars and a large dancefloor, on the coast 10km out of town, in the busy resort of Plataniás, popular with both locals and tourists. June–Sept midnight–6am.

Pallas Aktí Tombázi 15, near Port Police ☎ 28210 45688. Popular harbourfront café-bar with a terrace that's ideally placed to admire the sunset over the harbour. In winter the action moves indoors to the first-floor music bar. Daily 9am–late.

★ **Rudi's Bierhaus** Kalergón 16 ☎ 28210 50824. Austrian – and long-time Haniá resident – Rudi Riegler's bar stocks more than a hundred of Europe's finest beers. Excellent mezédhes to accompany them. Daily 8pm–late.

Ta Duo Lux Sarpidhónos ☎ 28210 52519. Comfy bar-café in a street full of similar places, just off the inner harbour, that attracts a slightly older crowd than nearby Aktí Miaoúli. Daily 10am–late.

DIRECTORY

Banks and exchange The National Bank of Greece is directly opposite the market with three ATMs, and there's a cluster of banks with more ATMs around the top of Halídhon. You'll also find plenty of out-of-hours exchange places on Hálidhon, in the travel agencies.

Internet access There are plenty of internet cafés including Vranas, Ayíon Dhéka beneath Vranas Studios (see p.248), Triple W, Odhós Balantínou just off the top of Hálidhon, and Café Notos (May–Oct) on the outer harbour under the *Hotel Lucia*.

Laundry Speedy Laundry (☎ 28210 88411), junction of Koronéou and Korkídhi, just west of Platía 1866, will collect and deliver your load if you call; the Old Town Laundromat, Karaóli 40; Oscar, Kanevárou, just off Platía Syndriváni.

Left luggage The bus station has a left-luggage office (6am–8.30pm).

Market and supermarkets The central indoor market has fresh fruit and vegetables, meat and fish, dairy stalls and a baker; on Saturday mornings there is a farmer's market (*laïkí*) with a wonderful line of stalls along Minóos, inside the eastern city wall, selling local produce. Several small stores by the harbour platía sell cold drinks and food; they are expensive but open late. Small supermarkets can be found on Platía 1866, and the larger Carrefour supermarket is at the top of Pireós, outside the western wall, close to the Schiavo bastion.

Post office The main post office is on Odhs Perídou just off the bottom of Kydhonías (Mon–Fri 7.30am–8pm, Sat 9am–1pm).

Travel agencies Concentrated around the top of Hálidhon and on Platía 1866, as well as around the bus station. Try Tellus Travel, Hálidhon 108 (☎ 28210 91500, ⊛ tellustravel .gr), or in the old town El Greco Travel, Theotokopoúlou 50 (☎ 28210 86015, ⊛ elgreco.gr).

Around Haniá

Northeast of Haniá, the **Akrotíri peninsula** loops around, protecting the Bay of Soúdha. The peninsula has a number of sandy beaches and coves on the northeast side; beyond the suburb of Kounoupidhianá lies the excellent sandy beach of **Kalathás** and, further out, lies **Stavrós** with its magnificent mountain soaring up out of the bay, while inland are the **monasteries** of **Ayía Triádha** and **Gouvernétou**.

The coast west of Haniá has considerable tourist development along much of the shore to Áyía Marína and **Plataniás**. Beyond, the road to **Kolymvári** runs through mixed groves of calamus reed (Crete's bamboo) and oranges; the windbreaks fashioned from the reeds protect the ripening oranges from the *meltémi*. You'll still find long, quiet stretches of sand here, between hotels and villages.

Ayía Triádha

Daily 7.30am–2pm & 5–7pm · €2 · ☎ 28210 63572

The majestic three-domed **Ayía Triádha** monastery, originally built in the seventeenth century on the ruins of an old church, is approached via an avenue of cypress trees and surrounded by olive groves and vines – all property of the monastery; it's a thriving

---

FESTIVAL ISLAND

The Cretans love a *glendi* (party) and **festivals** are celebrated with pleny of eating, drinking, live music and dancing. Here are some of those which celebrate local harvests (check locally for specific dates):

Chestnut Festival Élos and Prásses, West Crete, end of October. The village squares are packed with tables and chairs as the villages celebrate the local chestnut harvest with eating, drinking, dancing, and roast chestnuts, of course.

Sardine Festival Néa Hóra, Haniá. The first Monday in September is the date for this annual festival at the small harbour by the town beach, with plentiful free fish and wine with local musicians and dancers.

Sultana Festival Sitía, in August. The region is well known for its sultana production, and the harvest is celebrated with traditional Cretan music and dance in the main square, accompanied by food and wine.

Tsikoudiá (Raki) Festival Haniá, Iráklion and Voukoliés, mid-October and early November. At the end of the grape harvest the must-residue from the wine press is boiled and distilled to make *tsikoudiá*, the local fire water. Hot *tsikoudiá*, with an alcohol content as high as 60 percent, is scooped from the vats and proffered in shot glasses, and so the merriment begins.

---

commercial place, producing and selling organic olive oil and wine from its vast landholdings. By the entrance a small museum houses ecclesiastical heirlooms, including valuable sixteenth- and seventeenth-century icons.

Gouvernétou and Katholikó

Easter–Sept Mon, Tues & Thurs 9am–noon & 5–8pm, Sat & Sun 8–11am & 5–8pm • Oct–Easter afternoon hours are 4–7pm • Free

Gouvernétou is one of the oldest monasteries on Crete, dating back to around 1537, and it's a rather isolated, contemplative and strict place; visitors are expected to respect this. The monastery looks more like a fortress from the outside where two towers stand guard; originally there were four – one on each corner – but two have collapsed. Inside, there are fine frescoes in the ancient church, and a small museum. Next to the monastery a paved path followed by steep steps leads down to the amazing abandoned ruins of the **monastery of Katholikó** (25min walk down – longer to climb back up), built into a craggy ravine and, further on, the remains of its narrow harbour.

Stavrós

Stavrós beach, 15km from Haniá, is superb if you like the calm, shallow water of an almost completely enclosed lagoon; this one sits right beneath the imposing "Zorbas" mountain (*Zorba the Greek* was filmed here). It's not very large, so it does get crowded, but rarely overpoweringly so. There's a makeshift café/*kantína* on the beach, and a couple of tavernas across the road. For accommodation search 1km west of here, in the area around *Blue Beach* and beyond where there are plenty of apartment complexes.

Ayía Marína

AYÍA MARÍNA, 8km west of Haniá, is a developed resort of some size with many hotels, shops, tavernas and nightlife; it's also known for its trendy beach bars, pumping out sounds which attract hordes of young locals and tourists. The west end of the long sandy beach is quieter and there are good **watersports** facilities here, including jet skiing and paragliding. Just offshore, **Theodorou** island is said to be a sea monster petrified by Zeus before it could swallow Crete. Seen from the west, its "mouth" still gapes open.

The Samariá Gorge

May–Oct (in the first and last few weeks of opening period it may close if there's a danger of flash floods) • €6 • ☎ 28210 67179

From Haniá the spectacular **SAMARIÁ GORGE**, which claims to be Europe's longest (it's a 16km hike), can be visited as a day-trip or as part of a longer excursion to the south. It's strenuous – you'll know all about it next day – the path is rough and it's not a walk to be undertaken lightly, particularly in the heat of summer, and walking boots or solid shoes are vital.

The **gorge** begins at the *xylóskalo*, or "wooden staircase", a stepped path plunging steeply down from the southern lip of the Omalós plain. The descent is at first through almost alpine scenery: pine forest, wild flowers and greenery – a verdant shock in the spring, when the stream is at its liveliest. About halfway down you pass the abandoned village of **Samariá**, now home to a wardens' station, with picnic facilities and toilets. Further down, the path levels out and the gorge walls close in until, at the narrowest

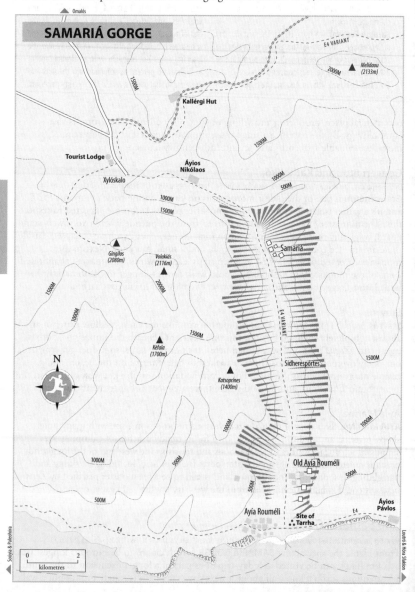

SAMARIÁ GORGE

Omalós

E4 VARIANT

Melídaou
(2133m)
2000M

1500M

Kallérgi Hut

1500M

1000M

Tourist Lodge

Áyios
Nikólaos

500M

Xylóskalo

1000M

1500M

Samariá

Gíngilos
(2080m)

Volakiás
(2116m)

2000M

E4 VARIANT

1500M

Kéfala
(1700m)

1500M

Sidherespórtes

1500M

Katsoprínes
(1400m)

1000M

1000M

1000M

500M

Old Ayía Rouméli

500M

500M

Ayía Rouméli

Áyios
Pávlos

E4

500M

Site of
Tarrha

E4

N

Soúyia & Paleohóra

0   2
kilometres

Loutró & Hóra Sfakíon

point (the *sidherespórtes* or "iron gates"), one can practically touch both tortured rock faces at once and, looking up, see them rising sheer for well over 300m.

At an average pace, with regular stops, the walk down takes between five and seven hours (though you can do it quicker); beware of the kilometre markers: these mark only distances within the **National Park** and it's a further 2km of hot walking before your reach the sea at **Ayía Rouméli**. On the way down there is plenty of water from springs and streams, but nothing to eat. The park that surrounds the gorge is a refuge of the Cretan wild ibex, the *krí-krí*, but don't expect to see one; there are usually far too many people around.

ARRIVAL AND DEPARTURE   THE SAMARIÁ GORGE

Tours to Samariá Gorge run from virtually everywhere on the island. The gorge walk ends on the south coast at Ayía Rouméli; from here you need to take a boat to Hóra Sfakíon, Soúyia or Paleóhora (see p.255) then catch a connecting bus. Return bus journeys are timed to coincide with the ferries and will wait for them – theoretically, no one gets left behind.

By bus From Haniá (4 daily at 6.15am, 7.30am, 8.30am & 2pm); from Soúyia (Mon, Wed, Sat; 6.15am); from Paleóhora (Mon, Wed, Sat; 7am).

ACCOMMODATION

Wardens ensure that no one remains in the gorge overnight, where camping is strictly forbidden. The nearest accommodation is at Omalós where you'll find the hotels listed below. Both have tavernas and also offer lifts to the top of the gorge in the morning if you stay overnight.

Hotel Gingilos ☎ 28210 67181. Slightly cheaper than the neighbouring *Neos Omalos* hotel and also very friendly. Modern en-suite rooms come with bath and balcony view. €30

Hotel Neos Omalos ☎ 28210 67269, ⓦ neos-omalos .gr. This is perhaps the best hotel; en-suite rooms all have balcony with views of the Lefká Óri, TV and central heating. €35

Omalós

OMALÓS lies in the middle of the mountain plain from which the Samariá gorge descends. The climate is cooler here all year round and the many paths into the hills surrounding the plateau are a welcome bonus; in season a profusion of wild flowers and birdlife is to be seen. There are plenty of **tavernas** and some surprisingly fancy **rooms** with all facilities, should you want to stay overnight to get an early start into the gorge. Another significant advantage to staying up here would be if you wanted to undertake some other **climbs** in the White Mountains; the **Kallérgi mountain hut** (☎ 28210 33199 or 697 34 00 777; €12 per person) is about ninety minutes' hike (signed) from Omalós or the top of the gorge.

The southwest coast

The ancient capital of the Sfakiá region, **Hóra Sfakíon**, lies 70km south of Haniá, reached via a spectacular twisting asphalted road over the mountains. It's the main terminus for gorge walkers, with a regular boat service west along the coast to **Ayía Rouméli** and **Loutro**, which are accessible only by foot or boat. **Frangokastello**, with its castle fortress and sandy **beaches**, lies a few kilometres east of Hóra Sfakíon, along the coastal road. Other main routes south over the mountains from Haniá are those to the small town of **Paleóhora** (from the north-coast highway at Tavronítis) and to the laidback seaside village of Soúyia (via Alikianós on the Omalós road).

Hóra Sfakíon

HÓRA SFAKÍON sees thousands of people passing through daily; those who have walked Samariá Gorge come striding, or staggering, off the boat from Ayía Rouméli to pile onto onward buses or waiting coaches. Relatively few stay, although there are plenty of great-value **rooms** and some excellent waterfront **tavernas**. Though there are a couple of pebbly coves, what is missing in Hóra Sfakíon is a decent beach. You could walk (or for much of the year take an excursion boat) west to Sweetwater, or there are numerous opportunities for a dip along the coast road east towards Frangokástello and beyond.

Loutró

For tranquillity, it's hard to beat **LOUTRÓ**, one-third of the way from Hóra Sfakíon to Ayía Rouméli and accessible only by boat or on foot. Like Hóra Sfakíon, the small pebbly bay in front of the village soon gets crowded. If you're prepared to walk, however, there are plenty of lovely **beaches** along the coast in each direction; these can also be reached by hired **canoe**, and some (particularly Sweetwater to the east and Mármara to the west) by regular excursion boats. For walkers, the **coastal trail** through Loutró covers the entire distance between Ayía Rouméli and Hóra Sfakíon (part of the E4 Pan-European footpath), and there's also a daunting zigzag path up the cliff behind to the mountain village of **Anópoli**.

   Loutró itself has a number of excellent **tavernas** and a fair few **rooms**, though not always enough of the latter in peak season. The season in Loutró runs from April to October, but in the winter months everything is closed.

Ayía Rouméli

AYÍA ROUMÉLI, a small coastal settlement lying at the end of Samariá Gorge, is visited daily by hundreds of weary walkers for whom the sea is a welcome shimmering mirage after their long hike. After an iced drink, a plunge in the sea to cool the aching limbs, and lunch at one of the cluster of tavernas, there's nothing much else to stay for, although you'll have no choice if you've missed the last boat, in which case you'll need to seek out one of the many **rooms** for rent along the beach.

Frangokástello

FRANGOKÁSTELLO is named after a crumbling Venetian attempt to bring law and order to a district that went on to defy both Turks and Germans. The four-square, crenellated thirteenth-century **castle**, isolated a few kilometres below a chiselled wall of mountains, looks as though it's been spirited out of the High Atlas or Tibet. The place is said to be haunted by ghosts of Greek rebels massacred here in 1829: every May, these *dhrossoulítes* ("dewy ones") march at dawn across the coastal plain and disappear into the sea near the fort. The rest of the time Frangokástello is peaceful enough, with a lovely beach and a number of tavernas and rooms scattered for some distance along the coast.

Paleóhora

The easiest route to the southwest leaves the north coast at Tavronítis, 22km west of Haniá, heading for **PALEÓHORA**, and although this road also has to wind through the western outriders of the White Mountains, it lacks the excitement of the alternatives to either side.

   The little town is built across the base of a peninsula, its harbour and a beach known as Pebble Beach on the eastern side, the wide sands (Sandy Beach) on the west. Above, on the outcrop, ruined Venetian ramparts stand sentinel. Though a resort of some size, Paleóhora remains thoroughly enjoyable, with a narrow main street that closes to traffic in the evenings so diners can spill out of the restaurants, and with a pleasantly chaotic social life.

Soúyia

A small village slowly on its way to becoming a resort, **SOÚYIA** is not, in all honesty, a particularly attractive place on first sight but it does grow on you; its best feature is the enormous swathe of bay with a long, grey pebble beach and sparkling clean water. At the far end of this bay most summers there's something of a nudist and camping community – known locally as the Bay of Pigs. Otherwise, sights are few – the local church has a sixth-century Byzantine mosaic as the foundation, although most of it is in Haniá's archeological museum – but there are a couple of fabulous walks: down the beautiful **Ayía Iríni Gorge** or a wonderful hour-long hike over to the nearby ancient site of **Lissós** with temples and mosaics.

There are a number of good tavernas, cafés and a couple of minimarkets in the village; the latter will exchange money.

GETTING AROUND   THE SOUTHWEST COAST

By bus Haniá to: Frangokástello (1 daily; 2hr 30min), Hóra Sfakíon (2 daily; 2hr), Paleóhora (4 daily 5am–4pm; 1hr 30min), Soúyia (2 daily 5am & 2pm; 2hr).
By boat Hóra Sfakíon to: Loutró/Ayía Rouméli (3 daily April–Oct; 15min/45min), Gávdhos (2–3 weekly; 3hr).

Ayía Rouméli to: Soúyia (2 daily April–Oct; 45min), Paleóhora (1 daily May–Oct; 1hr 20min). Paleóhora to: Elafoníssi (daily May–Oct), Soúyia (daily May–Oct; 30min).
Taxi boats can be hired in Loutró and Hóra Sfakíon to take you to local beaches and coves.

INFORMATION

Tourist office Paleohora Pebble Beach, close to the ferry harbour (June–Sept, Mon & Wed–Sun 10am–1pm & 6–9pm; ☎ 28230 41507) provides accommodation lists and a useful map with listings.

Services Notos Travel, Odhós Venizélou, Paleóhora (☎ 28230 42110), can book ferry tickets. There are also plenty of other travel agents along and around central Venizélos. There's a post office on the road behind Sandy Beach.

ACCOMMODATION

HÓRA SFAKÍON

Livikon ☎ 28250 91211, ⓦ sfakia-livikon.com. Has great views from the upper-floor rooms though some noise from the tavernas below. All rooms are en suite with a/c, balcony, sea view and TV. **€40**

Stavris ☎ 28250 91220, ⓦ hotel-stavris-chora-sfakion .com. Plain but comfortable en-suite rooms with balcony, some with side sea view. They also have smarter apartments on the edge of town. **€35**

Xenia ☎ 28250 91202, ⓦ xenia-crete.com. Has the best location in town with amazing views across the Libyan Sea. This former state-owned hotel, now refurbished, has en-suite rooms with a/c, fridge, satellite TV and balcony with sea view. April–Oct. **€50**

LOUTRÓ

Blue House ☎ 28250 91127, ⓦ bluehouse.loutro.gr. Simple, yet comfortable, sea-front en-suite rooms with balcony and a wonderful (slightly pricier) top-floor extension as well as a great taverna. April–Oct. **€45**

Nikolas ☎ 28250 91352. Thanks to its position right at the eastern end of the seafront, the simple rooms with a/c are probably the quietest you'll find in Loutró, some with balcony and sea view. April–Oct. **€40**

Porto Loutro ☎ 28250 91433, ⓦ hotelportoloutro .com. The only place with any pretensions at all, whose comfortable rooms with a/c and balcony spread across several attractive cubist white buildings by the beach (and more rooms by the ferry dock). Breakfast included. April–Oct. **€60**

AYÍA ROUMÉLI

Hotel Kalypso Western end of the village ☎ 28250

91231, ⓦ agiaroumeli.gr. Simple, airy rooms with a/c, fridge, TV and balcony, most with sea view, and there's a café below for coffee and breakfast (not included). April–Oct. **€40**

PALEÓHORA

Anonymous Homestay Off Odhós Venizélos ☎ 28230 42098, ⓦ anonymoushomestay.gr. Among the least expensive places in town, and something of a travellers' meeting place, with simple, en-suite rooms around a courtyard garden and a very friendly, far from anonymous, atmosphere. **€25**

Camping Paleohora 1km north of Pebble Beach ☎ 28230 41120. Set in a large olive grove with plenty of shade and decent facilities, next to a rather desolate stretch of beach. Opposite is the Paleochora Club (see p.257); although indoors and soundproofed, some noise from late-night revellers is inevitable when the club is open. May–Oct. **€16**

★ **Castello** Overlooking the southern end of Sandy Beach ☎ 28230 41143. Exceptionally friendly place, most of whose simple rooms have balconies overlooking the beach; otherwise enjoy the view from the excellent café. The alleys behind here, beneath the castle, have many more simple rooms places. April–Oct. **€30**

Sandy Beach Seafront at the southern end of Sandy Beach ☎ 28230 42138. The town's chicest hotel option, right opposite the beach, its a/c balcony rooms equipped with fridge, TV and sea view. Breakfast included. **€55**

Scorpios North end of Pebble Beach ☎ 28230 41058, ⓦ scorpios-rooms.gr. Comfortable rooms, most with sea views, and quieter than most thanks to a position near the end of the beach. Breakfast included. April–Oct. **€50**

4

Villa Marise Sandy beach ☎28230 41162, ⓦvillamarise.com. One of the best locations in town, right on the main beach and boasting a variety of good apartments and studios. The pool is shared with accommodation next door. April–Oct. **€60**

SOÚYIA

★ **Captain George** ☎28230 51133, ⓦsougia.info /hotels/captain_george. Clean and comfortable en-suite rooms, studios and apartments, set in gardens, a few hundred metres from the beach, with a/c, balcony, TV, fridge and kettle (kitchenette in studios/apartments). The owner also owns a couple of small cruise boats and books day-trips. April–Oct. **€45**

El Greco ☎28230 51186, ⓦwww.elgreco.sougia .info. The *El Greco* is tucked away off the main street in a

peaceful location, 200m from the beach (behind *Captain George*). It offers a/c balcony rooms with fridge and kettle, wi-fi, and some studios with kitchenette. April–Oct. **€40**

Santa Irene ☎28230 51342, ⓦsanta-irene.gr. Smart, modern studios and apartments in probably the best location. Rooms come with a/c, TV, kitchenette and balcony (some with sea view). Long-stay deals available in winter. **€50**

Syia ☎28230 51174, ⓦsyiahotel.gr. This modern hotel is the fanciest place in the village, although it doesn't boast the best location, bang on the noisy main street. Spacious boutique-style studios and apartments, with a/c, TV, fridge and coffee maker. Breakfast included. April–Oct **€80**

EATING AND DRINKING

LOUTRÓ

Blue House ☎28250 91127. This friendly taverna, beneath the rooms of the same name, has a good choice of fresh home-cooked Cretan and Greek dishes, all at reasonable prices. April–Oct daily 10am–late.

Ilios ☎28250 91160. Good seafood and fish, which is caught from their own boat, and reasonable prices. Try the excellent swordfish (€9). Standard taverna fare is also served. Located at the far eastern end of the bay, just beyond the beach. April–Oct daily 10am–late.

AYÍA ROUMÉLI

Taverna Tara ☎28250 91231. Under the same management as the *Hotel Kalypso*, this taverna offers the usual suspects – oven-baked lamb and stuffed aubergines, from €5, on a large seafront terrace by the ferry dock. April–Oct daily 10am–11pm.

PALEÓHORA

Atoli ☎28230 41645. Lively café-bar serving drinks and snacks – a good spot to catch the sunset – that has occasional live music, both Greek traditional and modern. Southern end of Sandy Beach. Daily 10am–late.

★ **Caravella** ☎28230 41131. Overlooking the harbour, this is Paleóhora's flagship seafood restaurant. The cooking and service are outstanding, as is their chilled *hýma* (barrelled wine) from a vineyard in the Kastélli Kissámou area. April–Oct daily lunch & dinner.

★ **The Third Eye** ☎28230 41234. An excellent vegetarian restaurant which includes plenty of Asian spices and ingredients you won't find anywhere else on the island, as well as the usual Greek veggie dishes and vegetarian curry (€7). Inland from sandy beach. April–Oct. Daily breakfast, lunch & dinner.

ECOTOURISM IN CRETE

Crete has an incredibly diverse landscape, flora and fauna, and a number of environmentally aware locals have set about preserving its natural and cultural heritage. A range of retreats and lodges has sprung up across the island, offering the chance to experience sustainable, eco-friendly living and participate in everything from hiking to making the local firewater *tsikoudhiá*.

Enagron Axós, Réthymnon ☎28340 61611, ⓦenagron.gr. These traditional-style, stone-built houses stand in the hills at the foot of Mount Psilorítis, surrounded by olive groves and vines. There's a farm and taverna, with activities including grape harvesting, cooking courses and botanical walks. **€95**

Lasinthos Áyios Yeóryios, Lasíthi Plateau ☎28440 89101, ⓦlasinthos.gr. At the foot of the Dikti mountains, this newly constructed eco-park and village rents traditionally furnished and well-equipped guest rooms. The farm cultivates olives, grapes and

vegetables, and there are workshops for ceramics, weaving and woodcarving, plus a still for making *tsikoudhiá*. **€60**

Miliá Vlátos, Haniá ☎28210 46774, ⓦmilia.gr. The most authentic of Crete's eco retreats, this renovated seventeenth-century settlement in the White Mountains uses only renewable energy sources, accommodation is in small cottages with solar power and candles, while the taverna uses fresh organic ingredients. Activities include walking and cooking. Breakfast included. **€75**

SOÚYIA

Omikron On the seafront ☎ 28230 51492. This French-run café and taverna has a more northern European flavour and offers some vegetarian choices. Snacks, salads, curry and pepper steak, among other offerings, are usually on the menu. April–Oct daily

breakfast, lunch & dinner.

★ **Rembetiko** ☎ 28230 51510. Home-cooked traditional dishes including plenty of vegetarian options such as rice-stuffed tomatoes and peppers (€5) are served on a pleasant garden terrace (halfway up the main street). April–Oct daily lunch & dinner.

NIGHTLIFE

PALEÓHORA

Nostos Pebble Beach, by the tourist office ☎ 697 48 93 355. Open as a café and bar throughout the day, Nostos is also the liveliest late-night joint in town, with a chilled club atmosphere. May–Oct daily 10am–late, Nov–March

weekends and bank holidays 10am–late.

Paleohora Club North end of Pebble Beach close to the campsite. The one real dance place, far enough from town to be able to make some noise, though still fairly restrained and mainstream. June–Sept daily 11pm–6am.

Kastélli and the far west

Apart from being Crete's most westerly town, and the end of the main coastal highway, **KASTÉLLI** (Kíssamos, or Kastélli Kissámou, as it's variously known) has little obvious appeal. It's a busy small town and port with a long seafront and a rocky central **beach** (there's also a small sandy beach to the west). The very ordinariness of Kastélli, however, can be attractive: life goes on pretty much regardless of outsiders, and there's every facility you might need. The town was important in antiquity, when the Greco-Roman city-state of **Kísamos** was a major regional power.

To the west of Kastélli lies some of Crete's loneliest and, for many visitors, finest coastline. On the far western tip, **Falásarna** has beautiful beaches and ancient ruins, while **Elafonísi's** "pink" beaches and lagoon lie in the southwest corner; the coastal road connecting them has little development along the way, just a couple of villages, rocky coves and patches of sand.

The archeological museum

Platía Tzanakáki • Tues–Sun 8.30am–3pm • €3 • ☎ 28220 83308

Kastélli's superb **archeological museum** houses stunning Roman-era **mosaics** on the upper floor; mosaic production was a local speciality, and many more are being excavated around town. Other exhibits include prehistoric and Minoan relics from excavations in the town and from nearby Ancient Polyrínia.

Falásarna

The ruins of an ancient city and port are ignored by most visitors to **FALÁSARNA** in favour of some of the best beaches on Crete, wide and sandy with clean water, though far from undiscovered. There's a handful of **tavernas** and an increasing number of **rooms** for rent, and plenty of people **camp** out here too. Although the beach can occasionally be afflicted by washed-up tar and discarded rubbish, this doesn't detract from the overall beauty of the place. Crowds of locals on summer weekends can always be escaped if you're prepared to walk, and the beaches are worth it.

Sfinári and Kámbos

Further south, the western coastline is far less discovered. **SFINÁRI** is a sleepy village with a number of rooms to rent on the road down to a quiet pebble beach, sandy in patches. At the bottom is a cluster of tavernas which offer free sunloungers to customers.

KÁMBOS is similar to Sfinári, but even less visited. Its stony beach is a good hour's walk down a well-marked gorge path – a branch of the E4 – starting from the village square. Alternatively there's a steep asphalted track, which is driveable.

Monastery of Khryssoskalítissa

Daily 8am–8pm • €2

Some 5km before Elafonísi the **monastery of Khryssoskalítissa** sits perched on a cliff with amazing views along the coastline. It is increasingly visited by tours from Haniá and Paleóhora, but worth the effort for its isolation. The name Khryssoskalítissa translates as **golden step**, and the faithful here believe that one of the 90 steps leading up to the monastery appears gold to those who are pure of spirit.

Elafonísi

The tiny uninhabited islet of **Elafonísi** lies marooned on the edge of a gloriously scenic turquoise lagoon that shares its name. The pinky-white sand, the warm, clear lagoon and the islet to which you can easily wade are magnificent, but you certainly won't have them to yourself unless you visit out of season.

There are a number of stalls selling cold drinks and basic food on the beach, but perhaps the best option is to bring your own supplies and have a picnic on the beach.

ARRIVAL AND DEPARTURE   KASTÉLLI AND THE FAR WEST

By bus Kastélli bus station is on Platía Tzanakáki. Destinations Haniá (14 daily 6.30am–9.30pm; 1hr 15min), Elafonísi (May–Sept 1 daily; 1hr 40min), Falásarna (May–Sept 3 daily; 40min), Sfinári (1 daily; 1hr).

By ferry The port of Kastélli lies some 3km to the west of town. Destinations Weekly (Thurs) to Andikýthira (2hr), Kýthira (4hr), Yíthio (8hr).

INFORMATION AND TOURS

Tours Daily boat trips run from Kastélli port to the beautiful beaches at Gramvoússa and Bálos Bay, at the far northwestern tip of Crete.

Services Travel agents (for ferry tickets, boat tours or car rental) lie east of the square along Skalídhi; another group can be found around nearby Platía Venizélou, on the main road through town.

ACCOMMODATION

KASTÉLLI

Argo Telonio beach ☎ 28220 23322, ⓦ papadaki.biz. Simply furnished rooms on the seafront with a/c, TV, fridge and balconies with sea view. April–Oct. €45

Galini Beach Hotel ☎ 28220 23288, ⓦ galinibeach .com. Located right by the beach near the football pitch, this family-run hotel has sparkling a/c, sea-view rooms with TV, balconies and free wi-fi in communal areas. April–Oct. €50

Vergerakis (aka Jimmy's) Platía Tzanakáki ☎ 28220 22663. Central rooms place, a few hundred metres from the beach; simple, clean rooms with shared bath and use of kitchen facilities, plus a few en suites. April–Oct. €25

FALÁSARNA

Pension Anastasia Stathis ☎ 28220 41480, ⓦ stathisanastasia.com. Spacious, modern, but simple, rooms with sea and mountain views from the balconies, located 300m from the beach (on the main road down to Falásarna). Facilities include a/c, fridge, and some rooms

with kitchenette. April–Oct. €45

Sunset ☎ 28220 41204, ⓦ sunsethotel.biz. One of the best locations right above the beach. Basic rooms with a/c, fridge and balcony with great sea views – and sunsets – with a good taverna below. April–Oct. €40

KÁMBOS

Rooms Hartzulakis On the edge of the village ☎ 28220 44445. Friendly rooms with taverna and dramatic views overlooking the gorge. A map here gives details of local walking routes around the area and coast, and the owner can provide further information. April–Oct. €30

ELAFONÍSI

Elafonísi 1km before the beach ☎ 28220 61274. Probably the best of Elafonísi's few rooms places, with a/c balcony rooms, TV and fridge. There is a good taverna below which uses many home-grown ingredients, and a minimarket. May–Oct. €40

EATING AND DRINKING

There are a number of tavernas on Kastélli's beach promenade. Around them are numerous cafés and bars, popular with young locals and hence livelier than you might expect, particularly at weekends.

★ **Kellari (The Cellar)** Telenio beach, eastern seafront ☎ 28220 23700. Popular seafront taverna with friendly service and delicious fresh dishes – such as beef *kritiko* (beef in a red wine and ouzo sauce; €8) – all cooked with their own olive oil. April–Oct daily lunch & dinner.

Papadakis ☎ 28220 22340. Good taverna with a large seafront terrace (same owner as the *Argo* rooms), serving fish, seafood and meat dishes. Try the excellent fish soup, the speciality of the house. April–Oct daily lunch & dinner.

Gávdhos

GÁVDHOS, some 50km of rough sea south of Hóra Sfakíon, is the southernmost island in Greece (and Europe if you don't count Spain's Canary Islands). Gávdhos is small (about 10km by 7km) and barren, but it has one major attraction: the enduring **isolation** which its inaccessible position has helped preserve. If all you want is a beach and a taverna to grill your fish, this remains the place for you. There's a semi-permanent community of campers and would-be "Robinson Crusoes" resident on the island year-round, swelling to thousands in August – but just six indigenous families.

Most people choose to base themselves near to one of the three largest beaches; at the most popular of all, **Sarakíniko**, there's a number of beachfront tavernas and cafés and a few rooms places. At **Áyios Ioánnis**, 2km to the northwest, there's a thriving hippy-type community of nudist campers. The third choice is pebbly **Kórfos**, south of the port and capital at **Karabé**.

ARRIVAL AND INFORMATION

GÁVDHOS

By ferry Check in advance, as the schedules change year to year, and be aware that in windy or bad weather the ferry will not go at all – even in high summer. The summer timetable is currently as follows: From Hóra Sfakíon: June–Aug; Fri, Sat & Sun 11.30am. From Paleóhora: via Soúyia and Ayía Rouméli May–Oct; Mon, Wed 8.30am.

Services There are well-stocked minimarkets at Sarakíniko and Áyios Ioánnis, but no banks on the island so remember to bring cash with you, and more than you might normally need, in case you get stuck on the island due to the weather.

GETTING AROUND

By bus From the harbour at Karabé, local buses head north towards Sarakíniko and south to Kórfos.

ACCOMMODATION AND EATING

If you turn up in August without a booking you may well find yourself camping on the beach. Travel agents in Paleóhora (see p.254) or Hóra Sfakíon (p.253) will arrange rooms.

Sarakiniko Studios Sarakíniko ☎ 28230 42182, ⓦ gavdostudios.gr. A collection of rooms and studios on the hillside above the bay, with kitchen, fridge and terrace. They will pick you up from the ferry if you've pre-booked. Satellite TV and internet are available at their taverna. May–Oct. **€45**

Vailakakis (Gerti & Manolis) Sarakíniko ☎ 28230 41103. Simple en-suite rooms with a/c. They also have

some new stone villas, split into apartments, for rent. Their taverna has probably the best food on the beach, with good-value seafood caught daily by Manolis. May–Oct. **€45**

Yiorgos and Maria's Kórfos ☎ 28230 42166, ⓦ gavdos-online.com. Friendly place with comfortable a/c rooms and an excellent taverna. Breakfast included. May–Oct. **€48**

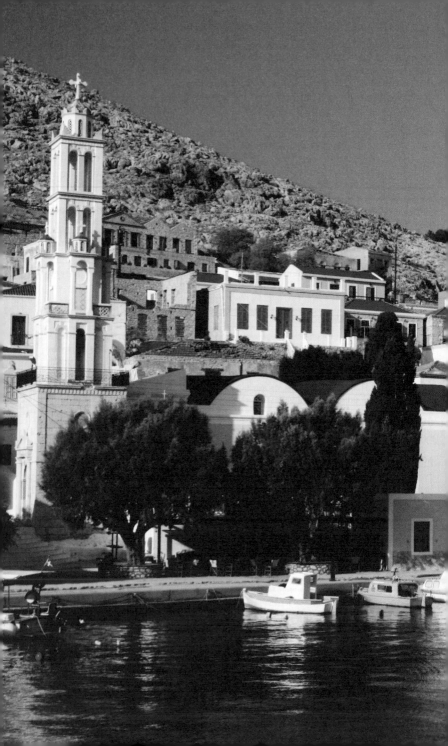

The Dodecanese

264 Rhodes

282 Kastellórizo

285 Hálki

287 Kássos

289 Kárpathos

295 Sými

302 Tílos

306 Níssyros

312 Kos

321 Psérimos

321 Astypálea

326 Kálymnos

332 Léros

337 Pátmos

342 Lipsí

344 Arkí

344 Agathoníssi

HÁLKI

5

The Dodecanese

Curving tightly against the Turkish coast, almost within hailing distance of Anatolia, the Dodecanese (Dhodhekánisos) are the furthest island group from the Greek mainland. They're hardly a homogeneous bunch. The two largest, Rhodes (Ródhos) and Kos, are fertile giants where traditional agriculture has almost entirely been displaced by a tourist industry focused on beaches and nightlife. Kastellórizo, Sými, Hálki, Kássos and Kálymnos, on the other hand, are essentially dry limestone outcrops that grew rich enough from the sea – especially during the nineteenth century – to build attractive port towns. Níssyros is a real anomaly, created by a still-steaming volcano that cradles lush vegetation, while Kárpathos is more variegated, its forested north grafted onto a rocky limestone south. Tílos, despite its lack of trees, has ample water, Léros shelters soft contours and amenable terrain, and further-flung Pátmos and Astypálea offer architecture and landscapes more reminiscent of the Cyclades.

Major Dodecanese attractions include the beaches on Rhodes and Kos; the wonderful medieval enclave of Rhodes Old Town; the gorgeous ensemble of Neoclassical mansions that surrounds the harbour on Sými; the rugged landscapes of Kálymnos, Kárpathos and Níssyros; the cave and monastery on Pátmos, where St John had his vision of the Apocalypse; and the hilltop village of Hóra on Astypálea. Each island has its own subtler pleasures, however; every visitor seems to find one where the pace of life, and friendly ambience, strikes a particular chord.

Thanks to their position en route to the Middle East, the Dodecanese – too rich and strategic to be ignored, but never powerful enough to rule themselves – have had a turbulent history. The scene of ferocious battles between German and British forces in 1943–44, they only joined the modern Greek state in 1948 after centuries of rule by Crusaders, Ottomans and Italians.

That historical legacy has given the islands a wonderful blend of **architectural styles** and **cultures**; almost all hold Classical remains, a Crusaders' castle, a clutch of vernacular villages and whimsical or grandiose public buildings. For these last the Italians, who held the Dodecanese from 1912 to 1943, are responsible. Determined to turn them into a showplace for Fascism, they undertook ambitious public works, excavations and reconstruction.

GETTING AROUND   THE DODECANESE

The largest islands in the group are connected by regular ferries and catamarans, as well as flights; only Kastellórizo and Tílos are relatively difficult to reach. Rhodes is the main transport hub, with connections for Crete, the northeastern Aegean, the Cyclades and the mainland too. The fastest, most useful connections are provided by twin catamarans, the *Dodekanisos Express* and the *Dodekanisos Pride*, which follow a busy schedule between Rhodes and Pátmos; see ⓦ 12ne.gr.

Windsurfing at Prassoníssi p.280
Hiking in northern Kárpathos p.295
Hiking on Sými p.301
Hiking on Níssyros Island p.311
Hippocrates p.318

Sponges and sponge-diving p.328
Italian architecture in
   the Dodecanese p.334
Saint John on Pátmos p.340

FRESCO, PÁTMOS

Highlights

❶ Rhodes Old Town One of Europe's most magnificently preserved medieval towns. **See p.266**

❷ Lindos Acropolis, Rhodes Occupied for over 3000 years, this hilltop citadel enjoys great views over the town and coast. **See p.278**

❸ Northern Kárpathos Old walking trails thread through a spectacular mountainous landscape to reach isolated villages. **See p.294**

❹ Sými Graceful Neoclassical mansions soar to all sides of Sými's gorgeous harbour. **See p.295**

❺ Níssyros Volcano Explore the still-bubbling craters of the volcano that created the island. See p.310

❻ Brós Thermá, Kos Relax in shoreline hot springs, which flow into the sea, protected by a boulder ring. **See p.318**

❼ Hóra, Astypálea Wrapped around a beautiful Venetian kástro, the windswept island capital perches proudly above the sea. **See p.323**

❽ Télendhos islet, Kálymnos Whether admired at sunset from western Kálymnos, or visited via local ferries, beach-fringed little Télendhos should not be missed. **See p.330**

❾ Hóra, Pátmos With its fortified monastery dedicated to St John of the Apocalypse, this is the Dodecanese's most atmospheric village. **See p.340**

HIGHLIGHTS ARE MARKED ON THE MAP ON P.264

5 Rhodes

RHODES (Ródhos) is deservedly among the most visited of all Greek islands. Its star attraction is the beautiful **medieval Old Town** that lies at the heart of its capital, Rhodes Town – a legacy of the crusading Knights of St John, who used the island as their main base from 1309 until 1522. Elsewhere, the ravishing hillside village of **Líndhos**, topped by

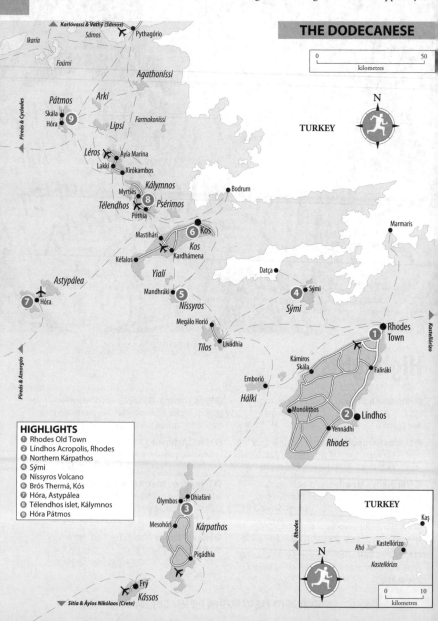

THE DODECANESE

0 — 50
kilometres

N

TURKEY

HIGHLIGHTS

1. Rhodes Old Town
2. Líndhos Acropolis, Rhodes
3. Northern Kárpathos
4. Sými
5. Níssyros Volcano
6. Brós Thermá, Kós
7. Hóra, Astypálea
8. Télendhos islet, Kálymnos
9. Hóra Pátmos

TURKEY

Rhó   Kastellórizo

Kastellórizo

0 — 10
kilometres

N

an ancient acropolis, should not be missed. It marks the midpoint of the island's long eastern shoreline, adorned with numerous sandy **beaches** that have attracted considerable resort development. At the southern cape, **Prassoníssi** is one of the best windsurfing spots in Europe. If you want to escape the summer crowds, take a road trip into the island's craggy and partly forested interior: worthwhile targets include the castles near **Monólithos** and **Kritinía**, and frescoed churches at **Thárri**, **Asklipió** and **Áyios Yeóryios Várdhas**.

Brief history

Blessed with an equable climate and strategic position, Rhodes, despite its lack of good harbours, was important from the very earliest times. The finest natural port served the ancient town of **Lindos** which, together with the other Dorian city-states **Kameiros** and **Ialyssos**, united in 408 BC to found a new capital, **Rodos** (Rhodes), at the windswept northern tip of the island. The cities allied themselves with Alexander, the Persians, Athenians or Spartans as conditions suited them, generally escaping retribution for backing the wrong side by a combination of seafaring audacity, sycophancy and burgeoning wealth as a trade centre. Following the failed siege of Macedonian general Demetrios Polyorketes in 305 BC, Rhodes prospered even further, displacing Athens as the major venue for rhetoric and the arts in the east Mediterranean.

Decline set in when the island became involved in the Roman civil wars and was sacked by Cassius; by late imperial times, it was a backwater. The Byzantines ceded Rhodes to the Genoese, who in turn surrendered it to the Knights of St John. After the second great **siege** of Rhodes, in 1522–23, when Ottoman Sultan Süleyman the Magnificent ousted the stubborn knights, the island once again lapsed into relative obscurity, though heavily colonized and garrisoned, until its seizure by the Italians in 1912.

ARRIVAL AND DEPARTURE   RHODES

BY PLANE

Rhodes' airport lies on the island's west coast, 14km southwest of Rhodes Town alongside Paradhísi village. Buses to and from town stop between the two terminals (turn left out of arrivals; frequent services 6.30am–midnight; €2.30). A taxi ride into town should cost around €22.

Destinations Olympic fly to and from the following islands: Astypálea (2–3 weekly); Athens (4–5 daily); Iráklion, Crete (2 daily); Kos (2–3 weekly); Léros (2–3 weekly); Thessaloníki (2 weekly); Kárpathos (1–2 daily); Kássos (1–2 daily); Sitía (1–2 daily). Aegean fly to Athens (4–7 daily) and Thessaloníki (1–2 daily).

BY FERRY

Ferries to Rhodes use two separate harbours in Rhodes Town. Large boats and catamarans dock at Kolóna, immediately outside the Old Town, while smaller vessels and excursion craft use the yacht harbour of Mandhráki facing the New Town.

Ticket offices ANES 88 Australis St (☏ 22410 37769, ⊛ anes.gr) for catamarans and hydrofoil to Sými; Dodhekanisos Seaways have a kiosk at their departure

point in Kolóna Harbour (☏ 22410 70590, ⊛ 12ne.gr); Tsangaris (☏ 22410 36170) for GA boats; Skevos, 111 Amerikis St (☏ 22410 22461, ⊛ bluestarferries.gr), for Blue Star; Zorpidhis (☏ 22410 20625) for LANE; Stefanakis, Alex Diakou St, for Sea Star and *Panayia Spiliani* (☏ 22410 78052, ⊛ tils.gr).

Destinations The following islands have regular connections: Anafi (1 weekly; 17hr); Astypálea (1 weekly; 9hr 10min); Crete (2 weekly; 12hr 30min); Hálki (4 weekly; 1hr 25min–2hr); Kálymnos (2–4 daily; 2hr 40min–8hr 15min); Kárpathos (4 weekly; 5hr); Kássos (4 weekly; 6hr 30min); Kastellórizo (3 weekly; 2hr 20min–3hr 40min); Kos (1–5 daily; 2hr 10min–6hr 15min); Léros (1–2 daily; 4hr–5hr 15min); Lipsí (6 weekly; 5hr 10min–8hr 20min); Milos (2 weekly; 23hr); Níssyros (4 weekly; 3hr 10min–4hr 45min); Pátmos (1–3 daily; 4hr 45min–9hr 45min); Pireás (1–4 daily; 12hr 30min–17hr); Santoríni (7 weekly; 7–20hr); Sitía (2 weekly; 9hr 20min); Sými (3–4 daily; 50min–1hr 40min); Sýros (2 weekly; 9hr); Tílos (7 weekly; 1hr 20min–2hr 15min). The tiny port at Kámiros Skála, 45km southwest of Rhodes Town, is used only by regular boats to Hálki (daily except Sun; 1hr 15min).

INFORMATION

Tourist offices The municipal tourist office is at Platía Rimínis, just north of the Old Town (June–Sept Mon–Sat 7.30am–9.30pm, Sun 9am–3pm; Oct–May daily 7.30am–3pm). A short walk from here up Papágou, on the

corner of Makaríou, the Greek National Tourist Office (Mon– Fri 8.30am–2.45pm) dispenses bus and ferry schedules.

Hospital/clinic The modern state hospital, just northwest of town, is understaffed and has a deservedly poor reputation;

5

especially if you're insured, head for the well-signed Euromedica clinic in Koskinoú, 6.5km south (24hr; English-speaking staff; ☎ 22410 45000 for their ambulances).

Activities For scuba diving, contact Waterhoppers (ⓦ waterhoppers.com) at Mandhráki quay; as well as running beginners' courses in the bay at Kallithéas beach, they offer more challenging deep-wall dives at Ladhikó, just south of Faliraki, and near Líndhos.

GETTING AROUND

By bus Buses from Rhodes Town to the west and east coasts leave from adjacent terminals on Avérof in New Town, immediately north of the Old Town just outside the Italian-built New Market. The main local operator is KTEL (☎ 22410 27706, ⓦ ktelrodou.gr).

By taxi The main taxi rank is at Platía Rimínis, immediately north of Rhodes Old Town, across from the bus stops. A taxi to the airport officially costs €22; the fare to Líndhos is €44. Taxi drivers won't normally enter Rhodes Old Town; expect to walk to your hotel from the nearest gate.

By car Major car rental chains have outlets at the airport. In Rhodes Town, try Just, Mandhilará 70 (☎ 22410 31811,

ⓦ just-rentacar.gr); Etos, Venizelou 33 (☎ 22410 22511, ⓦ etos.gr); or Kosmos, Papaloúka 31 (☎ 22410 74374, ⓦ cosmos-sa.gr). Driving is not permitted in Rhodes Old Town, while parking outside can be hard to find; the best bet is along Filellínon on the south side, between the Ayíou Athanasíou and Koskinoú gates.

By bike and motorcycle Outlets that rent bikes, scooters and motorcycles include Kiriakos, Apodhímon Amerikís 16 (☎ 22410 36047, ⓦ motorclubkiriakos.gr), which will deliver to Rhodes Old Town and shuttle you back once you've finished; Bicycle Centre, Griva 39 (☎ 22410 28315); and Mike's Motor Club, Ioánni Kazoúli 23 (☎ 22410 37420).

Rhodes Town

By far the largest town on the island, **Rhodes Town** straddles its northernmost headland, in full view of Turkey less than 20km north. The ancient city that occupied this site, laid out during the fifth century BC by Hippodamos of Miletos, was almost twice the size of its modern counterpart, and at over 100,000 held more than double its population.

While the fortified enclave now known as the **Old Town** is of more recent construction, created by the Knights Hospitaller in the fourteenth century, it's one of the finest medieval walled cities you could ever hope to see. Yes, it gets hideously overcrowded with day-trippers in high season, but at night it's quite magical, and well worth an extended stay. It makes sense to think of it as an entirely separate destination to the **New Town**, or **Neohóri**, the mélange of unremarkable suburbs and dreary resort that sprawls out from it in three directions.

It was the entrance to **Mandhráki** harbour, incidentally, that was supposedly straddled by the **Colossus**, an ancient statue of Apollo erected to commemorate the 305 BC siege. In front of the New Town, the harbour is today used largely by yachts and excursion boats.

Rhodes Old Town

Rhodes Old Town is an absolute gem, a superbly preserved medieval ensemble that's all but unique in retaining the feel of a genuine lived-in village, having neither grown to become a city nor been overly prettified for visitors. Still entirely enclosed within a double ring of mighty sandstone walls, it stands utterly aloof from the modern world.

Although the newly arrived Knights encircled the local population as well as their own castle within their fourteenth-century walls, they took the precaution of keeping whatever they needed for survival north of the straight-line street of **Sokrátous**, which could be sealed off in times of emergency. Broadly speaking that distinction remains, with the monumental district, now also scattered with Ottoman mosques and minarets, set somewhat apart.

While it does hold some fascinating sights and museums, however, what makes the Old Town so special is the sheer vibrancy of the place as a whole. Its busiest commercial lanes, packed with restaurants, cafés, and souvenir stores selling anything from T-shirts to fur coats, and gelati to jewellery, can be overpoweringly congested in summer – Sokrátous itself is the worst culprit – but it's always possible to escape into the time-forgotten tangle of cobbled alleyways that lie further south, and away from the sea.

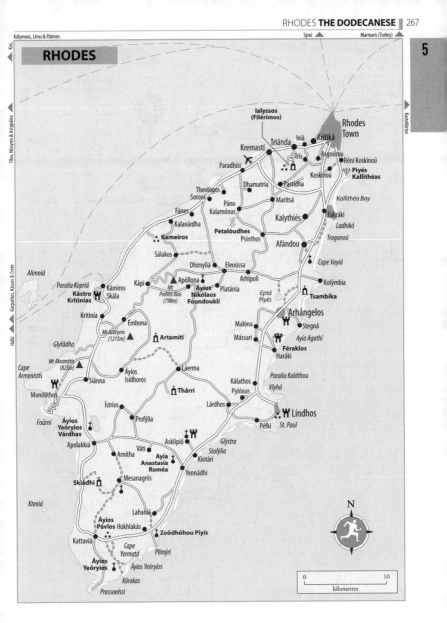

No map can do justice to what a labyrinth it all is, or quite how much is missing; mysterious ruins lie half-buried, amok with cats or wildflowers, while isolated Cyclopean arches suddenly rear into view, without a trace of the buildings they used to hold up.

Palace of the Grand Masters

Summer Mon 12.30–7.30pm, Tues–Sun 8am–7.30pm; winter Tues–Sun 8.30am–3pm • €6, free Sun Nov–March

The **Palace of the Grand Masters** dominates the northwestern corner of the Old Town's walls. Destroyed by an ammunition explosion in 1856, it was reconstructed by the

5

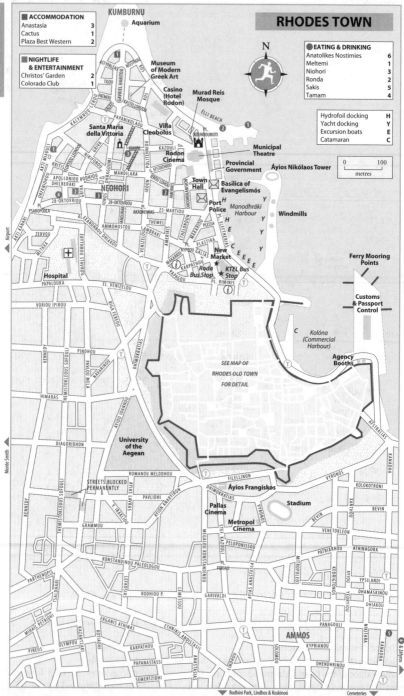

RHODES TOWN

ACCOMMODATION
Anastasia	3
Cactus	1
Plaza Best Western	2

NIGHTLIFE & ENTERTAINMENT
Christos' Garden	2
Colorado Club	1

EATING & DRINKING
Anatolikes Nostimies	6
Meltemi	1
Niohori	3
Ronda	2
Sakis	5
Tamam	4

Hydrofoil docking	H
Yacht docking	Y
Excursion boats	E
Catamaran	C

0 — 100 metres

Italians as a summer home for Mussolini and King Vittore Emmanuele III, although neither one ever visited Rhodes. While its external appearance, based on medieval engravings and accounts, remains reasonably authentic, free rein was given in its interior to Fascist delusions of grandeur.

The two splendid ground-floor galleries jointly constitute the best **museums** in town. They often close due to staff shortages; check whether they're open before you pay for admission, because otherwise there's precious little to see. One covers ancient Rhodes, documenting everyday life around 250 BC; highlights include a Hellenistic floor mosaic of a comedic mask. The other, across the courtyard, covers the medieval era, stressing the importance of Christian Rhodes as a trade centre. The Knights are represented with a display on their sugar-refining industry and a gravestone of a Grand Master; precious manuscripts and books precede a wing of post-Byzantine icons.

Street of the Knights

The Gothic, heavily restored **Street of the Knights** (Odhós Ippotón) leads east from Platía Kleovoúlou in front of the Palace of the Grand Masters. The various "Inns" along the way lodged the Knights of St John, according to linguistic and ethnic affiliation, until the Ottoman Turks forced them to leave for Malta in 1523. Today the Inns house government offices, foreign consulates or cultural institutions vaguely appropriate to their past. Several stage occasional exhibitions, but the overall effect of the Italian renovation is sterile and stagey.

Archeological Museum

Summer Tues–Sun 8am–7.30pm; winter Tues–Sun 8.30am–3pm • €6

At the foot of the Street of the Knights, the Knights' Hospital now houses the town's **archeological museum**. A very lovely complex in its own right, which takes at least an hour to explore, it consists of several galleries in the medieval hospital itself, plus a delightful raised and walled garden where extensions and outbuildings hold further displays. Rather too many rooms simply hold glass cases filled with small artefacts, displayed with little contextual information, but there's a lot of interesting stuff, including votive offerings from Egypt and Cyprus found in the Kamiros acropolis, and an amazing array of ancient painted pottery. The grandest hall upstairs is lined with the tomb slabs of fourteenth- and fifteenth-century Knights, but the light-filled gallery of **Hellenistic statues** nearby is the true highlight. *Aphrodite Adioumene*, the so-called "Marine Venus" beloved of Lawrence Durrell, stands in a rear corner, lent a sinister aspect by her sea-dissolved face that makes a striking contrast to the friendlier *Aphrodite Bathing*.

Decorative Arts Collection

Platía Aryirokastrou • Daily except Mon 8.30am–3pm • €2

The vernacular treasures in the **Decorative Arts Collection**, which occupies a single large room at the northern edge of the old town, were gleaned from old houses throughout the Dodecanese. Redolent of Byzantine and Italian influences, they reflect the islands' cosmopolitan past. Amid the fading embroidery and brightly painted plates, the most compelling artefacts are the carved cupboard doors and chest lids, depicting mythological or historical episodes.

Turkish Rhodes

Many of the mosques and *mescids* (the Islamic equivalent of a chapel) in which the old town abounds were converted from Byzantine churches after the Christians were expelled in 1522. The most conspicuous of all is the rust-coloured, candy-striped **Süleymaniye Mosque**, rebuilt during the nineteenth century on 300-year-old foundations. Like most local Ottoman monuments, it's not open to visitors, though the purpose-built (1531) **Ibrahim Pasha Mosque** on Plátonos, for example, is still used by the sizeable Turkish-speaking minority.

5

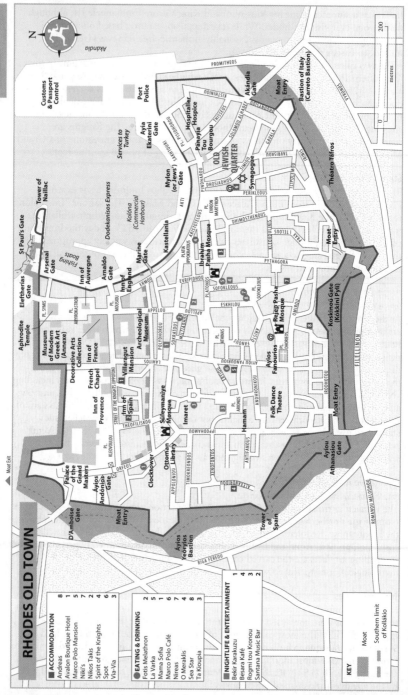

RHODES OLD TOWN

■ **ACCOMMODATION**
Andreas	8
Avalon Boutique Hotel	1
Marco Polo Mansion	5
Niki's	7
Nikos Takis	2
Spirit of the Knights	4
Spot	6
Via-Via	3

● **EATING & DRINKING**
Fotis Melathron	2
La Varka	5
Mama Sofia	1
Marco Polo Café	6
Nireas	7
O Meraklis	4
Sea Star	8
Ta Kioupia	3

■ **NIGHTLIFE & ENTERTAINMENT**
Bekir Karakuzu	1
Besara Kafé	4
Rogmi tou Kronou	3
Santana Music Bar	2

KEY
Moat
Southern limit of Kollakio

The Ottomans' most enduring civic contributions are the **Ottoman Library**, opposite the Süleymaniye (Mon–Sat 9.30am–4pm; tip custodian), which has a rich collection of early medieval manuscripts and Korans; the **imaret** (mess-hall) at Sokrátous 179, now an exceptionally pleasant café (*Palio Syssitio*); and the imposing 1558 **Mustafa Hammam** (Turkish bath) on Platía Aríonos (Mon–Fri 10am–5pm, Sat 8am–5pm, last admission 4pm; €5). Bring everything you need – soap, shampoo, towel, loofah – to enjoy separate, *au naturel* men's and women's sections.

Jewish Rhodes

Beyond the tiled central fountain in Platía Ippokrátous, Odhós Aristotélous leads to **Platía tón Evréon Martýron** ("Square of the Jewish Martyrs"), named in memory of the 2100 Jews of Rhodes and Kos who were sent to the concentration camps in 1944; a black granite column honours them. Of four synagogues that once graced the nearby Jewish quarter, only ornate, arcaded, pebble-floored **Kal Kadosh Shalom** (Mon–Fri & Sun 10am–3pm; donation) on Odhós Simíou, just south, survives. To one side, a well-labelled, three-room **museum** thematically chronicles the community's life on Rhodes.

The New Town (Neohóri)

What's now known as the New Town – in Greek, **Neohóri** – dates originally to the Ottoman era, when Orthodox Greeks excluded from the fortified city built their own residential districts outside the walls. Only **Kumburnú**, the area immediately north of the Old Town, at the tip of the headland, bears any relevance to visitors. On its eastern side, Mandhráki yacht harbour serves as the base for excursion boats and some ferry companies, while the streets immediately inland hold the workaday shops, offices and agencies that keep the town as a whole ticking along. The headland itself is surrounded by a continuous **beach** of gritty shingle (loungers, parasols and showers), particularly at **Élli**, the more sheltered east-facing section. Despite being so close to the city, the water offshore is exceptionally clean. That explains the many hotels and restaurants hereabouts, but judged on its own merits the New Town makes a poor holiday destination.

Aquarium

Daily: April–Oct 9am–8.30pm; Nov–March 9am–4.30pm • €5.50 • ⓦ hcmr.gr

Perched at the northernmost point of the island, Rhodes' **Aquarium** is as much a museum as a conventional aquarium. It does hold tanks of live fish, not necessarily captioned correctly, but most of its space is taken up with displays on the history and function of the building itself, as well as a monk seal buried as an ancient family's pet, and a stuffed Cuvier's beaked whale.

Museum of Modern Greek Art

Pl. G. Harítou • Tues–Thurs & Sat 8am–2pm, Fri 8am–2pm & 5–8pm • €3 • ⓦ mgamuseum.gr

Near the northernmost tip of the New Town, on what's colloquially known as "100 Palms Square", Rhodes' **Museum of Modern Greek Art** holds the most important collection of twentieth-century Greek painting outside Athens. All the heavy hitters – Hatzikyriakos-Ghikas, surrealist Nikos Engonopoulos, naïve artist Theophilos, neo-Byzantinist Fotis Kontoglou – are amply represented. Some of Kontoglou's greatest frescoes, dating from 1951–61, are in the **Evangelismós basilica** at Mandhráki.

What used to be the main, cramped home of the museum, on Platía Sýmis 2 in the Old Town, is now the **annexe** (Tues–Sat 8am–2pm, same ticket), devoted to maps, prints and special exhibits. Both premises have excellent gift shops.

Hellenistic Rhodes

A half-hour, 2km walk west and uphill from the Old Town – a hike best undertaken just before sunset, both for the views and the temperature – leads to the unenclosed

5

remains of the **acropolis of Hellenistic Rhodes**, atop Monte Smith. Formerly known as Áyios Stéfanos, this hill was renamed for a British admiral during the Napoleonic Wars. While the ruins cover an extensive area, there's not really all that much to see – a restored theatre and stadium, plus three columns of a temple to **Apollo Pythios**. It's striking to realize that the ancient city stretched from here all the way down to the sea, however.

The cemeteries

While the vast **municipal cemeteries** at Korakónero, just inland from Zéfyros beach 2km southeast of the centre, might not sound like a hot tourist destination, they can be strangely compelling. This is one of the very few remaining spots in the Balkans where the dead of four faiths lie in proximity, albeit separated by high walls. The easterly **Greek Orthodox section**, the largest, holds the fewest surprises. The small **Catholic section** is not only the last home of various north European expatriates, but also demonstrates that a fair number of Italians elected to accept Greek nationality and stay on after the 1948 unification with Greece. The **Jewish section** (Mon–Fri 8am–1pm) has, understandably, seen little activity since 1944, and is full of memorials in French to those who were deported. Opposite its gate, across the busy road, a small **Allied War graves** plot holds 142 burials. Just south of the Jewish section, the "**Muslim**" section (ie Turkish) is the most heavily used and best maintained of the three minority cemeteries.

ACCOMMODATION

RHODES TOWN

OLD TOWN

★ **Andreas** Omírou 28D ☎22410 34156, ⓦhotelandreas.com; see map, p.270. Perennially popular *pension*, imaginatively converted from an old Turkish mansion, with switched-on, international management. The eleven rooms vary in size and price; some sleep four, and there's a fabulous "penthouse". All have a/c; eight have en-suite bathrooms, while each of the other three has the key to its own dedicated bathroom, down the corridor. Excellent breakfasts (€6–8 extra) and evening drinks are served on the terrace bar, which has free wi-fi and great views. Two-night minimum stay, reservations essential. **€55**

Avalon Boutique Hotel Háritos 9 ☎22410 31438, ⓦavalonrhodes.gr; see map, p.270. Fourteenth-century manor house, tucked into a quiet courtyard very near the Grand Masters' palace, and stylishly re-modelled to hold six bright, modern and very luxurious suites, each with an open-air terrace. The friendly family team serve breakfast in your unit, the courtyard café, or the vaulted bar. **€215**

★ **Marco Polo Mansion** Ayíou Fanouríou 42 ☎22410 25562, ⓦmarcopolomansion.gr; see map, p.270. Superb conversion of an old Turkish mansion, opening off one of the old town's most charming lanes, with a hammam on site. All rooms are en suite, exquisitely furnished with antiques from the nearby eponymous gallery, and equipped with cotton pillows and handmade mattresses. The cheapest rooms face the garden. Large buffet breakfasts are provided in the garden snack bar, open to all later in the day (see opposite). Reservations and credit-card deposit mandatory. Closed Nov–March. **€100**

Niki's Sofokléous 39 ☎22410 25115, ⓦnikishotel.gr; see map, p.270. Attractive and very welcoming little hotel. All rooms are en suite, most have a/c, and those on the upper storey have fine views; there's also a shared roof terrace, and guests have use of a washing machine. Pay a little extra for a private balcony, or a room that sleeps three. Someone will wait up for late-night arrivals. Rates include breakfast. **€50**

Nikos Takis Panetíou 26 ☎22410 70773, ⓦnikostakishotel.com; see map, p.270. Miniature "fashion hotel" in a restored mansion close to the Grand Masters' palace. Set up by two of Greece's most celebrated fashion designers, whose flamboyant 1960s' work is on show throughout (and sold in the ground-floor boutique), its eight rather extraordinary units range through themes from Moroccan to medieval, with opulent furnishings, plush fabrics everywhere, stone arches and painted ceilings. Pebble-mosaic courtyard, with fine views over town, for breakfast and drinks. **€170**

★ **Spirit of the Knights** Alexandridou 14 ☎22410 39765, ⓦrhodesluxuryhotel.com; see map, p.270. Gorgeous traditional home in a very quiet back alleyway of the old town, in full view of a peaceful stretch of walls. Sensitively converted to create a lovely boutique hotel, it holds six exquisitely furnished and very distinct suites. Breakfast served in a pleasant garden courtyard that also holds a large jacuzzi. The front desk remains open around the clock, and nothing is too much trouble for the extended English family who own and run the place. **€200**

Spot Perikléous 21 ☎22410 34737, ⓦspothotel rhodes.gr; see map, p.270. The cheerfully painted a/c en-suite rooms in this custard-yellow modern building are festooned with artworks and textiles, and offer excellent value; triples available. An unlimited buffet breakfast, charged extra, is served on the rear patio, and there's also a roof terrace and free luggage storage. Closed Dec–Feb. **€90**

Via-Via Lysipoú 2 ☎22410 77027, ⓦhotel-via-via .com; see map, p.270. Efficiently but congenially run hotel on an alleyway off Pythagóra; most of the one-to-four-person rooms, all a/c, are en suite, but two share baths across the hall. All are simply and tastefully furnished with bedding and throw rugs in pastel hues. Roof terrace with pergola and divans for three grades of breakfast and an eyeful of the Ibrahim Pasha mosque opposite. **€70**

NEW TOWN

Anastasia 28-Oktovríou 46 ☎22410 28007, ⓦanastasia-hotel.com; see map, p.268. Italian-era mansion, with high ceilings and tiled floors, that's been converted to a congenial, family-run guesthouse. The rooms, which sleep up to four, are simple but have a/c and en-suite facilities; there's a bar in the garden, with its resident tortoises. Breakfast costs extra. **€45**

Cactus Kó 14 ☎22410 26100, ⓦcactus-hotel.gr; see map, p.268. The best-value beachfront hotel in the new town, an updated 1960s high-rise with graceful curving glass-fronted balconies, facing the best stretch of Élli beach near the tip of the headland and offering a street-side pool of its own. **€110**

Plaza Best Western Ieroú Lóhou 7 ☎22410 22501, ⓦrhodesplazahotel.com; see map, p.268. Crisp, modern four-star hotel, convenient for Mandhráki harbour, with a pool, garden and sauna. There's also a restaurant, and they offer buffet English breakfasts. **€115**

EATING AND DRINKING

While the Old Town holds a quite staggering number of restaurants, prices tend to be high, and both value and quality tend to improve away from the main commercial lanes. Most places are open long hours every night, serving couples with children from about 6.30pm, then tourists until perhaps 10pm, and Greeks until midnight or later.

OLD TOWN

Fotis Melathron Sokrátous 41 ☎22410 24272, ⓦfotisgroup.com; see map, p.270. Despite the address, this large restaurant opens onto a small square just south of the main pedestrian drag. Come at lunchtime, when the tables in the flowery gardens that surround the compound are all but irresistible, and you might never realize that the interior's charming too, rambling through an old town house that holds assorted dining rooms. Reckon on €70 for dinner for two. A good mixed mezédhes plate costs €10.50, while the sliced-up whole stuffed squid is excellent. Daily noon–10pm.

La Varka Sofokléous 5; see map, p.270. Indoor-outdoor ouzerí, with a table-filled terrace right on a busy bar-filled alleyway, and live Greek music of its own. The interior makes a cosy retreat in the cooler months. Good salads, pikilíes for 2 at €30, grilled thrápsalo, fried or salt-cured seafood titbits, cheapish ouzo and soúma by the carafe. Daily 11.30am–1am.

Mama Sofia Orfeos 28 ☎22410 24469; see map, p.270. Good, reasonably priced home cooking in a very friendly atmosphere, across from the clocktower and minaret in the northwest corner of the Old Town. Choose between the roof terrace or the plentiful street-level tables, which make for perfect people-watching. Open until 10pm nightly.

★ **Marco Polo Café** Ayíou Fanouríou 42 ☎22410 25562; see map, p.270. Very lovely, deservedly popular hotel restaurant, filling a garden courtyard; don't worry

about the lack of a street sign, they just want to keep the crowds down. Traditional adapted recipes, adeptly blending subtle flavours, include pilaf with lamb and raisins, turnovers with pastourmá, and psaronéfri with manoúri cheese, fig and red peppercorn sauce. Excellent wine list and desserts of the day. Closed Nov–March. Dinner only, daily until midnight.

★ **Nireas** Sofokléous 22 ☎22410 21703; see map, p.270. This long-standing, family-run fish specialist, in a quiet square just away from the bustle, has earned its sky-high reputation thanks to the hard work and friendly professionalism of its owners, its still-reasonable prices, and its atmospheric indoor/outdoor seating, making this a good choice for a treat. Individual seafood dishes, like mussels saganaki, cost around €10, and unusually they have a range of Italian desserts too. Around €70 for two including dessert and wine. Daily lunch & dinner.

O Meraklis Aristotélous 30; see map, p.270. One of the last Rhodian rough edges not yet filed smooth, this pátsatzídhiko (tripe-and-trotter-soup kitchen) caters for a pre-dawn clientele of clubbers, Turkish shopkeepers, gangsters and nightclub singers. Great free entertainment, including famously rude staff, and the soup's good, too: the traditional working man's breakfast and hangover cure. Open 1–8am only, at its peak 3–4am.

Sea Star Sofokléous 24 ☎22410 31884; see map, p.270. Quality seafood restaurant that's somewhat overshadowed by Nireas (see above) next door, but deserves mention in its own right for its perfectly grilled

5

fresh fish – the bream, at around €12.50, is out of this world – and mezédhes like *kápari* and salt-cured mackerel. Indoor seating in winter, otherwise outside on the little square. Daily lunch & dinner.

Ta Kioupia Menekleous 22 ☎ 22410 30192; see map, p.270. Friendly, high-quality restaurant, perched towards the top of the Old Town, slightly south of Sokrátous. Its contemporary twists on classic Greek cuisine are consistently delicious – you'll remember the smoked aubergine with feta, and the blue cheese mousse, for a long time. It all works out expensive, though, especially as they make a habit of charging for the various little bonus extra plates they bring to your table. Expect to pay around €40 per head. Daily lunch & dinner, closes 6pm Sun.

NEW TOWN

Anatolikes Nostimies Klavdhíou Pépper 109, Zéfyros Beach ☎ 22410 29516; see map, p.268. The name means "Anatolian Delicacies": Thracian Pomak/Middle Eastern dips and starters, plus beef-based kebabs. Beach-hut atmosphere, but friendly, popular and reasonably priced; post-prandial hubble-bubble on request. Daily noon–midnight.

★ **Meltemi** Platía Koundourióti 8, Élli beach ☎ 22410 30480; see map, p.268. Beachfront ouzerí, with a nicely shaded beach-level patio, offering such delights as *karavidhópsyha* (crayfish nuggets), octopus croquettes, chunky hummus, and superb roast aubergine with beans and onions to a local crowd; pleasant winter salon inside. Daily lunch & dinner.

Niohori Ioánni Kazoúli 29, Neohóri ☎ 22410 35116; see map, p.268. Alias "Kiki's" after the jolly proprietress, this homely, inexpensive local, across from the Franciscan monastery, is tops for meat grills, sourced from their own butcher/farm; veal liver costs €6, a mixed grill €8. There's usually a cooked vegetable dish like okra for the salad-averse. Most seating is indoors, but there's a little shaded courtyard at the side. Daily lunch & dinner.

Ronda Platía Koundourióti 6, Neohóri ☎ 22410 76944; see map, p.268. Built by the Italians as a waterfront spa complex, and every bit as round as the name implies, this large-domed room now houses a very spacious and rather expensive café. There's nothing remarkable about the food or drink, but it's a lovely place to sit, with views through its huge arched windows of the beach to one side and the harbour to the other. Daily 9am–1am.

Sakis Kanadhá 95, cnr Apostólou Papaïoánnou, Zéfyros ☎ 22410 21537, 🌐 tavernasakis.gr; see map, p.268. A friendly old favourite with pleasant patio and indoor seating, equally popular with Rhodians and foreigners. Known for its shellfish (such as limpets and snails), meat (chops, Cypriot *seftaliés*) and the usual starters. Mon–Sat 5pm–1am, Sun 12.30pm–12.30am.

Tamam Yeoryiou Leondos 1, Neohóri ☎ 22410 73522; see map, p.268. This small but enormously popular New-Town newcomer serves good but expensive traditional cuisine. Steaks cost €25–30 each, and there's a wine list to match. If you're happy to spend a lot, you'll have a real feast; show any reluctance, and the charming service turns off like a tap. Daily lunch & dinner.

NIGHTLIFE AND ENTERTAINMENT

In the Old Town, an entire alley (Miltiádhou) off Apellóu is home to a score of loud, annually changing music bars and clubs, extending towards Plátonos and Platía Dhamayítou, and frequented mostly by Greeks (in winter too). Two a/c cinemas show first-run action films year-round: the Metropol multiplex, at the corner of Venetokléon and Výronos (☎ 22410 28410), southeast of the Old Town opposite the stadium, and the nearby Pallas multiplex on Dhimokratías (☎ 22410 24475).

Bekir Karakuzu Sokrátous 76, Old Town; see map, p.270. The last traditional Turkish *kafenío* in the Old Town simply oozes atmosphere; its Oriental-fantasy interior is filled with wooden screens and has an ornate *votsalotó* floor. Yoghurt, *loukoúmi*, *alisfakiá* tea and coffees are on the expensive side – consider it admission to an informal museum. Daily 11am–midnight.

Besara Kafé Sofokléous 11–13, Old Town; see map, p.270. Congenial breakfast-snack café-cum-low-key bar run by Australian-Texan Besara Harris, with a mixed clientele and live jazz two nights weekly Oct–May. Daily 9am until late.

Christos' Garden Dhilberáki 59, Neohóri; see map, p.268. This combination art gallery/bar/café occupies a carefully restored old house and courtyard with pebble-mosaic floors throughout. Daily 10pm until late.

Colorado Club Orfanídhou 57, cnr Aktí Miaoúli, Neohóri ☎ 22410 75120, 🌐 colorado.com.gr; see map,

p.268. Triple venue, just back from the sea on the west side of the New Town, and comprising a "disco-house" dance club, a live music venue, and "Heaven", the top-floor chill-out bar. Daily 9pm until late.

Rogmi tou Kronou Platía Aríonos 4, Old Town ☎ 22410 25202; see map, p.270. Rock-oriented bar and music venue, taking up two storeys of a fine old house on one of the Old Town's most attractive squares – outside tables make this a great spot for a drink. Live music or DJs every night until late. Daily noon until late.

Santana Music Bar Miltiadou 4–8, Old Town ☎ 695 53 12 251; see map, p.270. Somewhat garish bar and music venue, on an alleyway just off Sokrátous – look out for the creeping flowers – which unlikely as it may seem is the one Old-Town spot where you may catch live, late-night rembétika and local music. Daily 9am until late, closed Sun–Thurs in winter.

The east coast

From the capital as far south as Líndhos, the **east coast** of Rhodes has been built up with a succession of sprawling towns and resorts. Some, such as **Faliráki**, have long since lost any charm they may once have possessed, but there are still some pleasant lower-key alternatives, including **Stegná** and **Haráki**.

Piyés Kallithéas

Daily 8am–8pm • €2.50

A prize example of orientalized Art Deco from 1929, the former spa at **Piyés Kallithéas**, 7km south of Rhodes Town, was the work of a young Pietro Lombardi who, in his old age, designed Strasbourg's European Parliament building. Accessed via a short side road through pines, the complex has an upmarket bar serving from inside artificial grottoes at the swimming lido, just below the dome of the **Mikrí Rotónda** in its clump of palms. The main **Megáli Rotónda** higher up is now a small **museum**, with changing modern art exhibits.

Faliráki

The overblown and unappealing resort of **Faliráki**, 10km south of the capital, is a town of two halves. The half-dozen high-rise family hotels in its northerly zone sit uneasily alongside the cheap-and-nasty southern zone, notorious for its drink-fuelled brawls, rapes and even murder. Since the island police forcefully curbed the local club-crawling culture, the place is now a shadow of its former self.

Faliráki's sandy sweep is closed off on the south by the cape of **Ladhikó**. For the best swimming, head for the main cove, south of the promontory. The scenic bay of "**Anthony Quinn**", on its northern flank, is named after the late Mexican American actor, whom Greeks took to their hearts following his roles in *Zorba the Greek* and *The Guns of Navarone*. Quinn bought much of this area and constructed the first road to the beach, but during the 1980s the Greek government swindled him out of his claim; legal battles continue to this day.

Afándou Bay

South of Ladhikó, the coastline is adorned, all the way to Líndhos, by striking limestone turrets that punctuate long stretches of beach. The first is the pebble-and-sand expanse of **Afándou Bay**, the least developed large east-coast beach, with just a few showers and clusters of inexpensive sunbeds. Spare a moment, heading down the main access road to mid-beach, for the atmospheric sixteenth-century church of **Panayía Katholikí**, paved with a *votsalotó* floor and decorated with frescoes.

Kolýmbia

Immediately north of the Tsambíka headland, 25km south of Rhodes Town, **Kolýmbia** was laid out by the Italians, not long before World War II, as a model farming village. Its original little grid of streets now serves a fast-growing resort that's become a favourite with more upscale package travellers. Reasonable beaches lie to either side of the low hill at road's end; the northern one holds more facilities.

Tsambíka and Stegná

The enormous promontory of **Tsambíka**, 26km south of town, offers unrivalled views along some 50km of coastline. From the main highway, a steep, 1500m cement drive leads to a small car park from where steps mount to the summit. On its September 8 festival childless women climb up – on their hands and knees in the final stretches – to an otherwise unremarkable **monastery** to be cured of their barrenness. Shallow **Tsambíka Bay**, south of the headland (2km access road), has an excellent if packed beach.

A kilometre or so south of Tsambíka Bay, a steep road drops for 3.5km down to the sea from the main highway, in huge sweeping curves. It ends at the scruffy but

5

appealing semicircular bay of **Stegná**, where for once no large hotels lurk behind the fine-gravel shore, just some relatively tasteful apartment complexes.

Haráki and around

Haráki is a very likeable little crescent bay, overlooked by the stubby ruins of **Feraklós castle**, the last Knights' citadel to fall to the Turks. There's no road along the shoreline, just a walkway beside a part pebble, part grey-sand **beach** that's backed by a solid row of small two- or three-storey studios, interspersed with the occasional café. It couldn't really be called a port, or a village, but it's a nice self-contained enclave.

The long straight shoreline south of Haráki is lined with beaches of sand and fine gravel, such as **Paralía Kaláthou**. It ends after 8km, just short of Líndhos, at the little cove of **Vlyhá**, which holds a couple of enormous hotels.

ACCOMMODATION   THE EAST COAST

Atrium Palace Paralía Kaláthou ☎ 22440 31601, ⓦ atrium.gr. Surprisingly unobtrusive despite its 300-plus luxurious rooms, this upscale hotel is one of the few developments on Kaláthou Beach, not far north of Líndhos. Its expensively landscaped grounds are dotted with pools, and the lawns extend down to the beach; the remoter villa wings, towards the spa, are best. Closed Nov–March. **€180**

Haraki Village Haráki ☎ 694 63 50 401, ⓦ haraki village.gr. Eight little pastel-coloured studios and apartments, all with balconies or outdoor space, at the north end of the beach below the castle. **€100**

Lindos Blu Vlyhá ☎ 22440 32110, ⓦ lindosblu.gr. Very opulent, very stylish modern resort hotel, tumbling down the slopes of a pretty bay immediately north of Líndhos, with a spa, infinity pools, and on-site restaurants. All seventy units have sea views, and are intended for adults only – villas/maisonettes have private pools. Minimum stay 4 nights in high season. **€420**

Panorama B&B Stegná ☎ 22440 22516, ⓦ stegna.gr. Laidback B&B, in a peaceful setting a short walk back from Stegná beach, with simple good-value a/c studios and rooms and a breezy shared terrace. **€50**

EATING AND DRINKING

Argo Restaurant Haráki ☎ 694 63 51 410. Behind its weathered, custard-yellow exterior, this seafront restaurant, squeezed among the toothy rocks at the southern end of Haráki beach, is surprisingly smart, and serves a good Greek menu, with mussels, chicken or shrimp main dishes priced at €8–12, with views across to the castle thrown in. Daily noon–10pm.

★ **To Periyiali** Stegná ☎ 22440 23444. The best taverna in Stegná, down by the fish anchorage. Greeks flock here for seafood, hand-cut round chips, home-made *yaprákia* and substantial salads ("Periyali" has caper greens and grilled aubergine) washed down by good bulk wine; the travertine-clad loos must be the wackiest, yet most charming, on the island. Daily lunch & dinner.

Líndhos

Set on a stark headland 50km south of Rhodes Town, **LÍNDHOS** is almost too good to be true. A classic Greek village of crazily stacked whitewashed houses, poised between a stupendous castle-topped acropolis above and sandy crescent beaches below, it's the island's number-two tourist attraction. Inevitably, it's so tightly packed with day-trippers in summer that you can barely breathe, let alone move along its impossibly narrow lanes. Almost all its immaculately whitewashed houses have long since been bought up by foreigners; most of those along the ancient agora, or serpentine main alleyway, are now run as restaurants, cafés and souvenir stores, while discreetly advertised rental properties lie to either side.

Arrive outside peak season, or if that's not possible at least in the early morning, and strolling through the village is still hugely atmospheric. The belfried, post-Byzantine **Panayía church** (Mon–Sat 9am–3pm & 6.30–8pm, Sun 9am–3pm) is covered inside with well-preserved eighteenth-century frescoes. The most imposing **medieval captains' residences** are built around *votsalotó* courtyards, their monumental doorways often fringed by intricate stone braids or cables supposedly corresponding in number to the fleet owned.

LÍNDHOS >

5

The acropolis

Mid-June to mid-Sept Mon 12.30–7.10pm, Tues–Sun 8am–7.10pm; mid-Sept to mid-June Tues–Sun 8.30am–2.40pm • €6

Although the dramatic battlements that circle the **acropolis** on the bluff directly above Líndhos belong to a **Knights' castle**, the precinct they enclose is much more ancient. A sanctuary dedicated to local deity Lindia was founded here in the ninth century BC, while the surviving structures were started by local ruler Kleoboulos three hundred years later.

A short climb up steep steps from the centre of the village, or a longer walk (or even donkey ride) up a gentler but more exposed pathway, brings you to the stairway to the castle itself. The relief sculpture of a ship's prow at its foot dates from the second century BC. Once you pass through the sole gateway, restrain the impulse to head straight for the summit, and explore the site from the bottom upwards instead. That way the temple of Athena Lindia at the top, set on a level platform that commands magnificent coastline views to both north and south, comes as a stunning climax. Almost all the buildings are recent reconstructions, replacing older restoration work now deemed inaccurate, though some ancient stones have been incorporated.

Come early or late in the day if you can, to avoid the crowds and enjoy the best light. And be warned that many of the stairways, parapets and platforms have precipitous, unrailed drop-offs.

Beaches

Líndhos's main **beach**, once the principal ancient harbour, tends to get very overcrowded; quieter options lie one cove beyond at **Pállas beach**. The small, perfectly sheltered **St Paul's harbour**, south of the acropolis and well away from town, has excellent swimming. According to legend, the Apostle landed here in 58 AD on a mission to evangelize the island.

ARRIVAL AND INFORMATION

LÍNDHOS

By car No cars are allowed in the village itself, and there's no vehicle access to the acropolis. Arriving drivers instead have to perform an elaborate U-turn at the tiny main square to reach car parks towards the beach, some of which, as clearly signposted, are free.

ACCOMMODATION

★ **Melenos** ☎ 22440 32222, ⓦ melenoslindos.com. The only hotel in Líndhos itself is an absolute gem, exquisite and highly exclusive, discreetly sited on the second lane above the north beach, by the school. No expense has been spared in laying out the twelve luxurious suites with semi-private, *votslaotó* terraces and tasteful furnishings; there's also a swanky garden-bar and restaurant. Open all year round. **€310**

EATING AND DRINKING

The lanes of Líndhos are crammed with run-of-the-mill restaurants, with a rapid turnover in ownership, but there are still a few stand-outs. Almost all have roof terraces, offering views up to the castle; whatever the decor may look like inside, most diners end up sitting on bare concrete patios in a parallel rooftop world.

Acropolis Roof Garden Trapeza 26 ☎ 22440 32160, ⓦ lindostreasures.com/village. The best option along the lanes, with a solid menu of Greek specialities such as rabbit stifhádo (€9.50) and a fine array of mezhédes, including tasty dolmádhes, all served on a castle-view terrace. Daily lunch & dinner.

★ **Mavrikos** Main Square ☎ 22440 31232. Prominent restaurant, on the fig-tree square where all traffic has to turn around. Starters such as yígandes in carob syrup (€7.50), sweet marinated sardines, or beets in goat-cheese sauce, are accomplished, as are fish mains such as skate timbale with sweetened balsamic, or superior traditional recipes like dolmádhes and tyrokafterí. Typical food charge of €23–30 per person. Daily noon–midnight.

Village Café ☎ 22440 31554, ⓦ lindostreasures.com /village. Friendly café and snack bar, set around a little pebbled courtyard, with a fine array of pastries, juices, sandwiches and snacks. Daily 10am–5pm.

The southeast coast

Until recently, tourist development petered out south of Líndhos, but these days Rhodes' **southeast coast** holds plenty of facilities for travellers seeking to escape the hectic atmosphere of the northern resorts. **Péfki** and **Yennádhi** are the best overnight stops, while **Prassoníssi** at the southern tip is popular with windsurfers. Even if you're not staying down here, it's worth touring in your own vehicle, stopping off perhaps in the villages just inland, like **Asklipió**, with its wonderful church.

Péfki

A couple of kilometres around the headland beyond Líndhos, **PÉFKI** was originally the garden annexe of its illustrious neighbour, but has now burgeoned as a resort in its own right. Its principal **beach**, a gorgeous little cove lined with sand and lapped by sparkling clear waters, inevitably becomes very crowded in summer, but other, more secluded little beaches are tucked at the base of the low cliffs to the west.

Lárdhos

Although the village of **LÁRDHOS** stands well in from the sea, it has lent its name to dense beachfront development a little further south. Its main beach, 2km south of the centre, is gravelly and heavily impinged upon by hotels; Glýstra cove, 3km south, is a small and more sheltered crescent that's at its best in low season.

Asklipió

Nine kilometres south of Lárdhos, close to the unexciting resort of Kiotári, a side road heads 3.5km inland to **ASKLIPIÓ**, a sleepy village enlivened by a crumbling Knights' castle and Byzantine **Kímisis Theotókou church.** Asklipió's central **Kímisis Theotókou church** (daily: summer 9am–6pm, spring/autumn 9am–5pm; €1) dates from 1060, and has a pebble-floored ground plan, to which two apses were added during the eighteenth century. Thanks to the dry local climate, the **frescoes** inside remain in breathtaking condition. Didactic "cartoon strips" extend completely around the church and up onto the ceiling, featuring Old Testament stories alongside the more usual lives of Christ and the Virgin. Half of the adjacent **Asklipió Museum** (same hours and ticket) is devoted to ecclesiastical treasures; the other, housed in a former olive mill, holds a folklore gallery, full of craft tools and antiquated machinery.

Yennádhi and Lahaniá

The drab outskirts of **YENNÁDHI**, 13km south of Lárdhos and the only sizeable settlement on the southeast coast, mask the attractive older village core inland. Though the present, barrel-vaulted structure of the village cemetery-church, **Ayía Anastasía Roméa**, dates from the fifteenth century, it's built on sixth-century foundations, and covered inside with post-Byzantine **frescoes**. Yennádhi's dark-sand-and-gravel **beach**, clean and offering the usual amenities, extends for kilometres in either direction.

Some 10km south of Yennádhi, then 2km inland, the tiny and picturesque village of **LAHANIÁ** was abandoned after a postwar earthquake, though since the 1980s its older houses have been mostly occupied and renovated by foreigners.

Prassoníssi

The main circular island highway doesn't run all the way down its southernmost tip. Branch south at Kattaviá, however, and a paved 8km spur road will bring you to **Prassoníssi**, a two-hour, 90km drive south of Rhodes Town. This gloriously desolate spot has become a major rendezvous for **windsurfers** (see box, p.280).

5

WINDSURFING AT PRASSONÍSSI

Situated at the very southern tip of Rhodes, **Prassoníssi** is regarded as one of the finest **windsurfing** sites in Europe. Strictly speaking the name refers to "Leek Island", the sturdy little islet just offshore, which is connected to the mainland by a long, low and very narrow sandspit through which a small natural channel frequently opens.

Not only do the waters here belong to different seas – the **Aegean** to the west of the spit, and the **Mediterranean** to the east – but in season they usually offer dramatically contrasting conditions. Thanks to the prevailing **meltémi** wind, and the funnelling effect of the islet, the Aegean side is generally much rougher, with head-high waves. On summer days it therefore becomes the area for expert windsurfers and daredevil kitesurfers. The Mediterranean side, meanwhile, tends to be much calmer, almost lagoon-like, and its shallow sandbars make it especially ideal for beginners.

The **season** at Prassoníssi lasts from May until mid-October. Of the three **windsurfing schools** that operate here, the Polish-run Prasonisi Center (late April–Oct; ☏ 22440 91044, ⓦ prasonisicenter.com) is the keenest and friendliest.

ACCOMMODATION   THE SOUTHEAST COAST

Effie's Dreams Yennádhi ☏ 22440 43410, ⓦ effiesdreams.com. Six serviceable, good-value a/c studios, overlooking a fountain-fed oasis at the northern end of Yennádhi, plus free wi-fi and a bar. **€55**

Lindian Village Lárdhos ☏ 22440 35900, ⓦ lindian village.gr. Sumptuous beachfront resort, 5km south of Lárdhos, and consisting of an attractive complex of individual bungalows that hold three grades of units (suites have their own plunge-pools), plus several gourmet restaurants, a spa/gym and a private beach. **€500**

Pefkos Blue Hotel Péfki ☏ 22440 48017, ⓦ dimitristudiospefkos.com. Good-value all-studio hotel on the hillside just above Péfki. 35 clean, comfortable apartments sleeping two to four, with kitchens, a/c and panoramic views. **€80**

Prasonisi Light House Prassoníssi ☏ 22440 91030, ⓦ prasonisilighthouse.com. Marginally the better of the two accommodation options at the island's southernmost tip, with a wide range of possibilities, from simple good-value "eco rooms" to larger rooms with sea-view balconies and fully-fledged apartments. Rates include breakfast and dinner in the reasonable on-site restaurant. **€92**

EATING AND DRINKING

Kyma Beach Restaurant Péfki ☏ 22440 48213. High-class restaurant at the midpoint of Péfki beach, with lovely sunset views, and serving delicious Greek specialities with a creative twist; try the octopus carpaccio. Reserve ahead in summer. Daily noon–10pm.

★ **Platanos** Lahaniá Prassoníssi ☏ 694 41 99 991, ⓦ achaniaplatanostaverna.com. On the tiny little main platía at the lower, eastern end of Lahaniá village, this welcoming rural taverna has superb mezédhes platters like hummus and *dolmadhákia*. Sit outside at the front, under the eponymous plane tree, or in the indoors dining room, overlooking a deep wooded valley. Daily lunch & dinner.

The west coast

While Rhodes' windward **west coast** is damp, fertile and forested, its beaches are exposed and often rocky. None of this has deterred development and, as on the east coast, the first few kilometres of the busy main road have been surrendered entirely to tourism. From Rhodes Town to the airport, the shore is lined with generic hotels, though **Triánda**, **Kremastí** and **Paradhísi** are still nominally villages, with real centres.

Kameiros

Tues–Sun: summer 8am–7.10pm; winter 8.30am–2.40pm • €4

The site of ancient **KAMEIROS**, which united with Lindos and Ialyssos to found the city-state of Rhodes, stands above the coast 30km southwest of Rhodes Town. Soon eclipsed by the new capital, Kameiros was only rediscovered in 1859, leaving a well-preserved Doric townscape in a beautiful hillside setting. Visitors can make out the foundations of two small temples, the re-erected pillars of a Hellenistic house, a Classical fountain, and the *stoa* of the upper agora, complete with a water cistern.

5

Kameiros had no fortifications, nor even an acropolis – partly owing to the gentle slope of the site, and also to the likely settlement here by peaceable Minoans.

Kámiros Skála

The tiny anchorage of **KÁMIROS SKÁLA** (aka Skála Kamírou), 45km southwest of Rhodes Town, is noteworthy only as the home port for a regular ferry service to the island of Hálki (see p.285). It does hold a handful of restaurants, however, while the off-puttingly named **Paralía Kopriá** ("Manure Beach") is 400m southwest.

Kástro Kritinías

From afar, **Kástro Kritinías**, 2km south of Kámiros Skála, is the most impressive of the Knights' rural strongholds; the paved access road is too narrow and steep for tour buses. Close up, it proves to be no more than a shell, albeit a glorious one, with fine views west to Hálki, Alimniá, Tílos and Níssyros.

Monólithos

The tiered, flat-roofed houses of **MONÓLITHOS**, high atop the cliffs 22km south of Kámiros Skála, don't themselves justify the long trip out, but the view over the Aegean is striking. Local diversions include yet another **Knights' castle**, out of sight of town 2km west, which is photogenically perched on its own pinnacle but encloses very little, and the sand-and-gravel beaches at **Foúrni**, five paved but curvy kilometres below the castle.

ACCOMMODATION AND EATING   MONÓLITHOS

Hotel Thomas ☎22460 61291 or 697 30 38 494, ⓦthomashotel.gr. Behind its somewhat grim exterior, this welcoming village hotel holds plain, fair-sized rooms with kitchen facilities and panoramic balconies. **€85**

O Palios Monolithos ☎22460 61276. The best of several tavernas in the village, opposite the church. Mains are a bit pricey but it's known for grilled meat and starters like wild mushrooms, *tyrokafterí* and mixed *dolmádhes*, accompanied by good bread and non-CAIR bulk wine. Open all year, weekends only off season.

Inland Rhodes

Inland Rhodes is hilly and still part-forested, despite the ongoing efforts of arsonists. You'll need a vehicle to take in the soft-contoured, undulating scenery, along with the last vestiges of agrarian life in the villages; no single spot justifies the expense of a taxi or battling with inconveniently sparse bus schedules. Most people under retirement age are away working in the tourist industry, returning only at weekends and during winter.

Ialyssos

Summer Tues–Sat 8am–7.10pm, Sun 8.30am–2.40pm; winter Tues–Sun 8.30am–2.40pm • €3

From the scanty acropolis of ancient **Ialyssos**, 10km southwest of Rhodes Town on flat-topped Filérimos hill, Süleyman the Magnificent directed the 1522 siege of Rhodes. Filérimos means "lover of solitude", after tenth-century Byzantine hermits who dwelt here; **Filérimos monastery** is the most substantial structure. Directly in front of the church sprawl the foundations of third-century temples to Zeus and Athena, built atop a far older Phoenician shrine.

Petaloúdhes

Daily: May–Sept 9am–6pm; April & Oct 9am–5pm • Oct to mid-June free, mid-June to Sept €5

The one "tourist attraction" in the island's interior, **Petaloúdhes** ("Butterfly Valley"), is reached by a 7km side road that bears inland between Paradhísi and Theológos. It's actually a rest stop for Jersey tiger moths, which congregate here between mid-June and September, attracted for unknown reasons by the abundant *Liquidambar orientalis* trees growing abundantly in this stream canyon. The moths, which roost in droves on the tree trunks and cannot eat during this final phase of their life cycle, rest to conserve energy, and die of

5

starvation soon after mating. When stationary, the moths are a well-camouflaged black and yellow, but they flash cherry-red overwings in flight.

Eptá Piyés to Profítis Ilías

Eptá Piyés ("Seven Springs"), 4km inland from Kolýmbia junction on the main east-coast highway, is an oasis with a tiny irrigation dam created by the Italians. A trail and a rather claustrophobic Italian aqueduct-tunnel both lead from the vicinity of the springs to the reservoir. Continuing on the same road, you reach **ELEOÚSSA** after another 9km, in the shade of dense forest. Built as the planned agricultural colony of Campochiaro in the mid-1930s, it's now a bizarre **ghost town**, with a central square lined by eerily derelict Italian structures that visitors can wander through at will. From the vast, yellow-trimmed Art Deco fountain-cum-pool just west of the village, stocked with endangered *gizáni* fish, keep straight 3km further to the gorgeous little late-Byzantine church of **Áyios Nikólaos Foundouklí** ("St Nicholas of the Hazelnuts").

Émbona

All tracks and roads west across Profítis Ilías converge on the road from Kalavárdha bound for **ÉMBONA**, a large but unremarkable village backed up against the north slope of 1215m **Mount Atávyros**. Émbona lies at the heart of the island's most important wine-producing districts. The small, family-run **Emery winery** (daily 9.30am–3.30pm; ⓦemery.gr) is highly regarded.

Thárri monastery

Accessible from Apóllona and Laerma to the north, or via a rough but passable road from Asklipió 11km south, the Byzantine monastery of **Thárri** is the oldest religious foundation on Rhodes, re-established as a vital community in 1990 by charismatic abbot Amfilohios. In the striking *katholikón* (daily, all day), successive cleanings have restored damp-smudged frescoes dated 1300–1450 to a pale approximation of their original glory.

ACCOMMODATION AND EATING   INLAND RHODES

★ **Elafos Hotel** Profítis Ilías ☎ 22460 22402, ⓦ hotel-elafos.gr. Rather splendid, restored Italian, 1929-vintage chalet-hotel, in a village west of Áyios Nikólaos church, where the high-ceilinged rooms ooze retro charm, and the arcaded ground-floor common areas include a restaurant and a sauna. **€95**

★ **Piyi Fasouli** Psínthos ☎ 22410 50071. Excellent taverna, at the edge of Psínthos village, 6km southeast of Butterfly Valley (see p.281), serving excellent grills and appetizers as well as a few tasty *mayireftá* at tables overlooking the namesake spring. Daily lunch & dinner.

Kastellórizo

Although **KASTELLÓRIZO**'s official name of Meyísti means "Biggest", it's actually among the very smallest Dodecanese islands; it's just the biggest of a local archipelago of islets. It's also extremely remote, located more than 100km east of Rhodes and barely more than a nautical mile off mainland Asia. At night its lights are outnumbered by those of the Turkish town of Kaş opposite, with which Kastellórizo has excellent relations.

The island's population has dwindled from around ten thousand a century ago to perhaps three hundred now. Having been an Ottoman possession since 1552, it was occupied by the French from 1915 until 1921, and then by the Italians. When Italy capitulated to the Allies in 1943, 1500 Commonwealth commandos occupied Kastellórizo. Most departed that November, after the Germans captured the other Dodecanese, which left the island vulnerable to looters, both Greek and British. By the time a fuel fire in 1944 triggered the explosion of an adjacent arsenal, demolishing half the houses on Kastellórizo, most islanders had already left. Those who remain are

KASTELLÓRIZO

supported by remittances from more than 30,000 emigrants, as well as subsidies from the Greek government to prevent the island reverting to Turkey.

Yet Kastellórizo has a future of sorts, thanks partly to repatriating "Kassies" returning each summer to renovate their crumbling ancestral houses as second homes. Visitors tend either to love Kastellórizo and stay a week, or crave escape after a day; detractors dismiss it as a human zoo maintained by the Greek government to placate nationalists, while devotees celebrate an atmospheric, little-commercialized outpost of Hellenism.

ARRIVAL AND DEPARTURE   KASTELLÓRIZO

By air Kastellórizo's airport, 1km above the harbour, is served by regular Olympic Air flights from Rhodes (4–6 weekly). A minibus shuttles once between town and airstrip at flight times (€2); excess passengers are accommodated in the island's lone taxi, at €6 per passenger.

By ferry Kastellórizo is connected to: Astypálea (1 weekly; 16hr); Kalymnós (2 weekly; 11hr 40min); Kos (2 weekly; 10hr);

Naxós (1 weekly; 20hr 30min); Níssyros (2 weekly; 8hr 30min); Páros (1 weekly; 22hr); Pireás (2 weekly; 28hr); Rhodes (3 weekly; 2hr 20min–3hr 40min); Sými (2 weekly; 3hr 50min–6hr 25min); Tílos (2 weekly; 7hr). Day-trips to Turkey leave regularly from the port in summer, for around €20.

Travel agents Papoutsis Travel sells all sea and air tickets (☎ 22410 70630, ⊛ kastelorizo.gr).

Kastellórizo Town

The island's population is concentrated in **KASTELLÓRIZO TOWN** on the north coast – neatly arrayed around what's said to be the finest natural harbour between Beirut and Fethiye on the Turkish coast – and its "suburb" of Mandhráki, just over the fire-blasted hill and boasting a half-ruined Knights' castle. In summer, it's what Greeks call a *klouví* (bird

5

cage) – the sort of place where, after two strolls up and down the pedestrianized quay, you'll have a nodding acquaintance with your fellow visitors and all the island's characters.

Most of the town's surviving original **mansions** are ranged along the waterfront, sporting tiled roofs, wooden balconies and blue or green shutters on long, narrow windows. Derelict houses in the backstreets are being attended to, and even the hillside is sprouting new constructions in unconventional colours, though the cumulative effect of World War I shelling, a 1926 earthquake, 1943 air-raids and the 1944 explosions will never be reversed. The black-and-white posters and postcards depicting the town in its prime, on sale everywhere, are poignant evidence of its later decline.

Archeological Museum and Lycian house-tomb

Mandhráki • Tues–Sun 8.30am–3pm • Free

The outer bulwark of Mandhráki's clifftop castle houses the island's worthwhile **archeological museum**. Displays include Byzantine plates, frescoes rescued from decaying rural churches and a reconstruction of an ancient basilica on the site of today's gaudy, crumbling Áyios Yeóryios Santrapé church at Horáfia. Immediately below and beyond the museum, facing across to Psorádhia islet, Greece's only **Lycian house-tomb** is hollowed into the cliff face. Steep unrailed steps lead up to its imposing Doric facade from the shoreline walkway.

ACCOMMODATION   KASTELLÓRIZO TOWN

★ **Karnayo** ☎ 22460 49266, ⓦ karnayo.gr. An excellent mid-range choice, off the platía at the west end of the south quay, spread over two quiet, sensitively restored buildings, and offering four double a/c en-suite rooms as well as two studios, one of which sleeps four. **€70**

★ **Kastellorizo Hotel** ☎ 22460 49044, ⓦ kastellorizohotel.gr. Right in the thick of things in the middle of west quay, this lovely hotel has friendly management and some of the best amenities on the island. All its fourteen individually styled suites have kitchenettes, four have balconies, and there's a thalasso-spa-pool as well as waterfront lido. March–Nov. **€130**

★ **Megisti Hotel** ☎ 22460 49219, ⓦ megistihotel .gr. Beautiful hotel in an unbeatable location, at the northwest corner of the harbour, with fabulous views

and fifteen spotless, attractively decorated rooms plus four large and very lavish suites. There's great swimming immediately off the spacious patio. Closed Oct–April. **€160**

Pension Mediterraneo ☎ 22460 49007 or 697 36 76 038, ⓦ mediterraneo-kastelorizo.com. Simple rooms at the end of the northwest quay, furnished with mosquito nets and wall art, some with sea view, plus an arcaded, waterside basement suite that's worth the extra cost for the privilege of being able to roll out the door and into the sea. Rates include breakfast. **€80**

Poseidon ☎ 22460 49257, ⓦ kastelorizo-poseidon.gr. Newly built houses in traditional style, set back from the platía at the west end of the south quay, and offering a total of sixteen well-appointed studios similar to the neighbouring Karnayo, some with balcony. **€70**

EATING AND DRINKING

Kastellórizo's harbour quayside is a wonderfully romantic spot to enjoy a leisurely meal, though taverna prices are significantly higher than elsewhere. The island has its own fish, goat meat and wild-fig preserves, and assorted produce is smuggled over from Kaş, but otherwise food and drinking water have to be shipped here from Rhodes. Incidentally, the mains water is contaminated by goat droppings, and not safe to drink.

★ **Akrothalassi** ☎ 22460 49052. The best of the waterfront tavernas, near the west end of the quay, dishing out large, great-value grills and salads. It's especially popular at lunch, as it offers the only shaded quayside seating. Daily lunch & dinner.

Iy Ypomoni Cheap, cheerful and popular waterfront taverna, two doors to the left of the arcaded market. Open for dinner only, it serves a limited seafood menu. Daily 7pm–late.

Ta Platania ☎ 22460 49206. Set well back from the sea, up the hill on the Horáfia platía, this welcoming place is festooned with film posters, and a good option for

daily-changing *mayireftá* and desserts, though the prices are much the same as down by the port. June–Sept only, daily lunch & dinner.

To Mikro Parisi ☎ 22460 49282. Long-established seafood specialist alongside the port, with succulent soups and stews and zestful meat and fish grills. Not the cheapest by any means, but good for a special occasion. Daily lunch & dinner.

Zaharoplastio Iy Meyisti Sweet shop and café by the harbour, serving a fine array of fresh-baked pastries and cakes. Just the place to linger over a fine breakfast or pudding. Daily 8am–6pm.

NIGHTLIFE

Faros ☎ 22460 49370. Bright yellow café-bar, alongside the mosque, where the roof terrace is the coolest place in town on long summer nights. While the sun's up, it's a "day-bar" with sunbeds on the quay. Daily noon–late.

Radio Café ☎ 22460 49029. Café with great views, close to the ferry jetty, which as well as coffee and breakfast offers internet access and *ouzomezédhes*. Daily 9am–late.

The rest of the island

Kastellórizo's austere **hinterland** is predominantly bare rock, flecked with stunted vegetation; incredibly, until 1900 this was carefully tended, producing abundant wine of some quality. A rudimentary paved road system links points between Mandhráki and the airstrip, and a dirt track heads towards Áyios Stéfanos, but there are few specific attractions, and no scooters for rent. Karstic cliffs drop sheer to the sea, offering no anchorage except at the main town, Mandhráki and Návlakas fjord (see below).

The shoreline

Swimming on Kastellórizo is made difficult by the total lack of beaches, and the abundance of sea urchins and razor-sharp limestone reefs. Once clear of the shoreline, however, you're rewarded by clear waters with a rich variety of marine life, and amphora shards that testify to the ancient wine trade. Many visitors simply dive in from the lidos on the northwest quay; otherwise the safest entries near town lie beyond the graveyard at Mandhráki and the cement jetty below the power plant at road's end. **Taxi-boats** can take you to otherwise inaccessible coves such as **Plákes**, along the western shoreline of the town bay, where the flat surfaces of a former quarry are equally good for sunbathing on, or swimming off.

Návlakas fjord and Perastá grotto

Halfway along Kastellórizo's southeastern coast, **Návlakas fjord** is a favourite mooring spot for yachts and fishing boats. Uniquely for the island, Návlakas is free of sea urchins. Freshwater seeps keep the temperature brisk, and there's superb snorkelling to 20m depths off the south wall.

Another popular stop for boat excursions, a little further south, **Perastá grotto** (Galázio Spílio) deserves a visit for its stalactites and strange blue-light effects. The low entrance, negotiable only by inflatable raft, gives little hint of the enormous chamber within, with monk seals occasionally sheltering in an adjacent cave.

Hálki

The little island of **Hálki**, a waterless limestone speck west of Rhodes, continues to count as a fully fledged member of the Dodecanese, even if its population has dwindled from three thousand to barely three hundred in the century since its Italian rulers imposed restrictions on sponge-fishing.

While visitation has brought the island back to life, except at the height of summer Hálki tends to be very quiet indeed. That said, in the middle of the day in high season, when day-trippers from Rhodes vastly outnumber locals in its broad quayside-cum-square, Emborió can feel more like a stage set than a genuine town.

ARRIVAL AND INFORMATION   HÁLKI

By ferry Hálki's port, Emborió, is connected with the following ports: Anáfi (2 weekly; 9hr 50min); Crete (2 weekly; Sítia 4hr 10min, Iráklion 7hr 20min); Kárpathos (2 weekly; 2hr 40min); Kássos (2 weekly; 5hr); Kos (2 weekly; 2hr 45min); Níssyros (2 weekly; 1hr 40min); Pireás (2 weekly; 20–24hr); Rhodes Kámiros Skála (daily except Sun; 1hr 15min); Rhodes Town (4 weekly; 1hr 25min–2hr); Santoríni (2 weekly; 11hr 20min); Sými (2 weekly; 2hr 20min); Tílos (2 weekly; 35min).

Ticket agency Zifos (☎ 22460 45028, ⍟ zifostravel.gr).

5

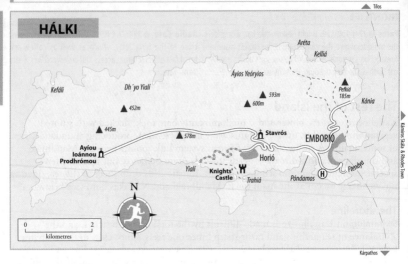

GETTING AROUND

By bus A sixteen-seat bus shuttles between the waterfront, Póndamos and Ftenáya.

Emborió

With its photogenic ensemble of restored Italianate houses rising from the waterfront, **EMBORIÓ**, facing east towards Rhodes from the head of a large bay, is a sort of miniature version of Sými (see p.295). Hálki's port as well as the only inhabited town, its skyline is pierced by the tallest freestanding **clocktower** in the Dodecanese, as well – a bit further north – as the **belfry** of Áyios Nikólaos, which holds a fine *votsalotó* (pebble-mosaic) courtyard. The waterfront has been paved with fieldstones, generally prettified and declared off-limits to vehicles in season.

Although there's no **beach** at Emborió, many visitors swim anyway, simply lowering themselves into the water from the quayside or shoreline rocks. If that doesn't suit you, two beaches lie within easy walking distance, both equipped with good seaside tavernas. The island's only sandy beach, long narrow **Póndamos**, a fifteen-minute walk west over the hilltop, along the grandly named Tarpon Springs Boulevard, fills with day-trippers in summer. The best alternative, the tiny pebble cove and the gravel sunbed-lido at **Ftenáya**, lies a few minutes south of Emborió, along a well-signposted path that starts behind the *Hiona Art Hotel*. It too can get heavily subscribed.

ACCOMMODATION   EMBORIÓ

Reserve accommodation in high season, whether in one of Emborió's handful of hotels, or in the many rental houses and villas. Some are divided into individual studios, while several perch right over the sea, with access ladders for swimmers. Both ⓦ nissiaholidays.com and ⓦ zifostravel.gr offer an extensive selection of properties.

★ **Captain's House** ⓣ 2246045201, ⓦchalkiholidays .gr. Three delightful en-suite a/c rooms, with a sea-view terrace, a shady garden, and the feel of an old French country hotel. Closed Nov–March. **€50**

Hiona Art Hotel ⓣ 22460 45244, ⓦhionaart.gr. Nicely refurbished, municipally owned hotel, in the splendid-looking old sponge factory on the south side of the bay, barely 5m from the sea. Tasteful en-suite rooms with

sea-view balconies, but haphazard service. Closed Nov–March. **€130**

Mouthouria House ⓣ 22460 45061, ⓦhalki mouthouria.com. Fine old pastel-orange mansion, perched above the harbour and decorated in rich antique flair, and rented out for longer stays. Sleeps four, in two bedrooms. **€90**

EATING AND DRINKING

The quayside at Emborió is lined with six full-service tavernas, bars and cafés, filled with leisurely holiday-makers every night in summer. There are also four well-stocked stores and a bakery.

★ **Lefkosia's Paradosiako** Known for her TV appearances, chef Lefkosia believes in making everything – from her cheese to her pasta – from scratch. Baked dishes are the highlights at her waterfont taverna, including a delicious moussaka as well as her speciality "Halki pasta", baked with onions and feta. Daily lunch & dinner.

Maria ☎ 22460 45300. Well-shaded café, tucked behind the post office, that's dependable for substantial portions of island staples such as lamb stew, or pasta baked with bubbling feta cheese. Daily lunch & dinner.

Remezzo ☎ 22460 45010. Simple little green-painted taverna, with a cluster of little tables outside, which as well as excellent *mayireftá* serves pretty much the gamut of tourist-favoured cuisines, from pizzas to Mexican. Daily noon–late.

Theodosia's Zaharoplastio ☎ 22460 45218. Also known as "The Parrot Café" on account of its resident bird, this friendly café, with a cushioned wooden bench facing the base of the jetty, serves puddings and home-made ice cream to die for, as well as good breakfasts. Daily 9am–late.

Horió and beyond

Still crowned by its Knights' castle, the old pirate-safe village of **HORIÓ**, looming 3km west of Emborió, beyond Pondamos, was abandoned in the 1950s. Except during the August 14–15 festival, the church here is locked to protect its frescoes. Across the valley, little **Stavrós monastery** hosts another big bash on September 14. There's little else inland, though Tarpon Springs Boulevard continues all the way across the island to reach the monastery of **Ayíou Ioánnou Prodhrómou** (festival Aug 28–29; *kantína* otherwise). The terrain en route is bleak, but compensated for by views over half the Dodecanese and Turkey. The monastery itself has a certain charm, with its central courtyard dominated by a huge juniper, and surrounded by an array of cells.

Trahiá and Aréta

Hálki's remotest **beaches** can be reached either on boat excursions from Emborió quay – for example, aboard the *Kristani* (☎ 693 61 16 229) – or via demanding hiking trails. **Trahiá**, directly below Horió's castle, and served by a very rough path from Yialí, consists of two coves to either side of an isthmus.

On the north coast, **Aréta fjord** is an impressive, cliff-girt place where seabirds roost and soar. There's some morning and afternoon shade, but only a brackish well for the inquisitive sheep with which you may share the small-pebble beach, so bring plenty of water. Experienced hillwalkers can get here on foot in around 1hr 30min.

Kássos

The southernmost Dodecanese island, less than 48km northeast of Crete, **KÁSSOS** is very much off the beaten tourist track. Ever since 1824, when an Egyptian fleet punished Kássos for its active participation in the Greek revolution by slaughtering most of the 11,000 Kassiots, the island has remained barren and depopulated. Sheer gorges slash through lunar terrain relieved only by fenced smallholdings of midget olive trees; spring grain crops briefly soften usually fallow terraces, and livestock somehow survives on a thin furze of scrub. The remaining population occupies five villages facing Kárpathos, leaving most of the island uninhabited and uncultivated, with crumbling old houses poignantly recalling better days.

ARRIVAL AND INFORMATION   KÁSSOS

By air The island's airport, 1km west of Frý, is connected to Kárpathos (1–2 daily); Rhodes (1–2 daily); and Sitía on

Crete (1–2 daily).

By ferry The island's port, Frý, is connected with: Anáfi

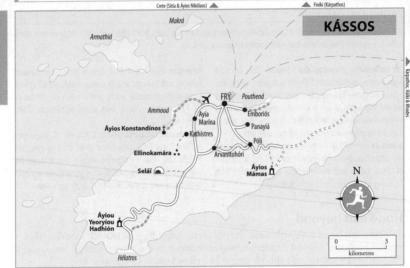

(2 weekly; 4hr 30min–10hr 30min); Crete (2 weekly; Sítia 2hr 30min, Iráklion 5hr 40min); Hálki (2 weekly; 4hr 30min); Karpathós (4 weekly; 1hr 20min); Mílos (2 weekly; 14hr 20min); Pireás (3 weekly; 14–20hr); Rhodes (4 weekly; 6hr 30min); Santoríni (2 weekly; 6–12hr). In season, to no fixed schedule, excursion boats also run to Frý from tiny Finíki on Kárpathos's west coast.

Tourist information The official island website is ⓦ kasos.gr.

Travel agent The main agent for ferry tickets is Kasos Maritime & Travel Agency (☏ 22450 41495, ⓦ kassos-island.gr).

GETTING AROUND

By bus A Mercedes van connects all the island's villages several times daily in summer, for a flat fare of €0.80.

By car and scooter Oasis in Frý rents out cars and scooters between June and September (☏ 22450 41746).

Frý

The capital of Kássos, **FRÝ** (pronounced "free"), is halfway along the island's north coast, with views towards northwest Kárpathos. It's a low-key little place, with most of its appeal concentrated in the **Boúka** fishing port, protected by two crab-claws of breakwater and overlooked by Áyios Spyrídhon cathedral. Inland, Frý is engagingly unpretentious, even down-at-heel in spots; there are few concessions to tourism, though some attempts have been made to prettify a scruffy little town that's quite desolate out of season.

There's no beach in Frý itself: what's generally regarded as the town beach is the sandy cove at **Ammouá**, a half-hour walk along the coastal track west, beyond the airstrip. The first section you reach is often caked with seaweed and tar, but keep going another five minutes and you'll find cleaner pea-gravel coves.

Determined swimmers also use the little patch of sand at **Emboriós**, fifteen minutes' walk east from Frý, where there's also a more private pebble stretch off to the right. Once you've got this far, however, it's worth continuing ten minutes along the shore, first along an old track, then on a path past the last house, for a final scramble to the base of the **Pouthená ravine**, which cradles another secluded pebble cove.

In high season, boat excursions head to far better beaches on two islets visible to the northwest, **Armáthia** and **Makrá**. Armáthia has five white-sand beaches to choose from, while Makrá has just one large cove. There are no amenities on either islet, so bring all you need.

ACCOMMODATION FRÝ

Angelica's ☎ 22450 41268, ⓦ angelicas.gr. Four bright, roomy kitchenette apartments in a converted mansion 200m above Boúka harbour, with traditional furnishings, and, courtesy of the owner's mother, some rather extraordinary floor-paintings. All have outside space, but only two enjoy sea views. **€50**

★ **Evita Village** ☎ 22450 41731, ⓦ evita-village.gr. Small complex of five impeccable and very spacious modern studios, 200m uphill from Emboriós, with comfortable new furnishings and plenty of room to spread out. **€60**

Fantasis Apartments ☎ 22450 41695, ⓦ fantasis -hotel.gr. Six plain en-suite rooms, four equipped with sea-view balconies, in a prominent yellow-trimmed modern structure five minutes' climb up from the port towards Panayía. **€40**

Flisvos ☎ 22450 41284. Very basic hotel, right on the seafront 150m beyond the harbour towards Emboriós. All rooms are en suite with sea-view balconies, and share use of a kitchen. **€50**

EATING AND DRINKING

Iy Orea Bouka Summer-only taverna with a small terrace overlooking the port at Boúka, and a good range of inventive and tasty Kassiot dishes, which you select by visiting the kitchen. June–Sept only, daily lunch & dinner.

O Mylos ☎ 22450 41825. Frý's finest full-service taverna, overlooking the ferry port, is also the only one that stays open year-round. Excellent food, with a selection of slow-cooked *mayireftá* at lunch, and grilled meat or fish by night. Daily lunch & dinner.

Taverna Emborios ☎ 22450 41586, ⓦ emborios.com. This lively and very welcoming taverna, facing the eponymous cove, is renowned for its fresh-caught seafood, supplemented with hand-picked local herbs and vegetables. Summer only, daily 11am–2am.

To Koutouki ☎ 22450 41545. This bustling little place, up the steps from the quayside at Boúka, deserves its reputation for sizeable servings of old-fashioned Greek cooking; succulent lamb is the house speciality. June–Sept only, daily lunch & dinner.

Ayía Marína and around

Several villages are scattered around the edges of the agricultural plain inland from Frý, linked to each other by road; all can be toured on foot in a single day. Larger and yet more rural than Frý, **AYÍA MARÍNA**, 1500m inland and uphill, is best admired from the south, arrayed above olive groves; its two belfried churches are the focus of lively **festivals**, on July 16–17 and September 13–14. Fifteen minutes beyond the hamlet of **Kathístres**, a further 500m southwest, the cave of **Ellinokamára** has a late Classical, polygonal wall blocking the entrance; it may have been a cult shrine or tomb complex.

Ayíou Yeoryíou Hadhión

Between Ayía Marína and Arvanitohóri, a paved road veers southwest towards the rural monastery of **Ayíou Yeoryíou Hadhión**. The entire route is 12km, and best tackled by scooter. Once you've skirted the dramatic gorge early on, you're unlikely to see another living thing aside from goats, sheep or an occasional falcon. Soon the Mediterranean appears; when you reach a fork, take the upper, right-hand turning, following the phone lines. Cistern water is always available in the monastery grounds, which only come to life around the April 23 festival.

Kárpathos

Despite being the third-largest Dodecanese island, poised halfway between Rhodes and Crete, long, narrow **KÁRPATHOS** has always been a wild and underpopulated backwater. The island's usually cloud-capped mountainous spine, which rises to over 1200m, divides it into two very distinct sections – the low-lying **south**, with its pretty bays and long beaches, and the exceptionally rugged **north**, where deeply traditional villages nest atop towering cliffs. If you prefer to stay in a sizeable town, then **Pigádhia** on the east coast, Kárpathos's capital and largest port, is a good choice, with a wide range of hotels as well

5

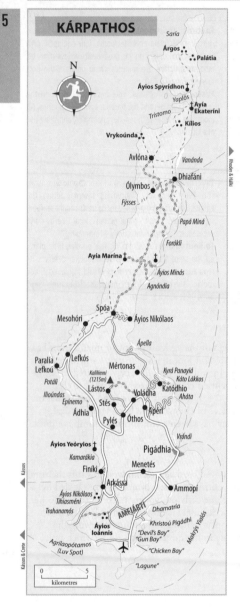

KÁRPATHOS

as a good beach, but several smaller resorts and isolated coves also hold lovely beachfront accommodation.

Touring Kárpathos's magnificent, windswept **coastline** is consistently superb, with its verdant meadows, high peaks, isolated promontories and secluded **beaches**, lapped by crystalline waters. The **interior**, however, isn't always as alluring: the central and northern forests have been scorched by repeated fires, while agriculture plays a minor role. The Karpathians are too well off to bother much with farming; emigration to North America and the resulting remittances have made this one of Greece's wealthiest islands.

Although the Minoans and Mycenaeans established trading posts on what they called Krapathos, the island's four Classical cities figure little in ancient **history**. Kárpathos was held by the Genoese and Venetians after the Byzantine collapse and so has no castle of the Knights of St John, nor any surviving medieval fortresses of note.

ARRIVAL AND DEPARTURE
KÁRPATHOS

By air Kárpathos's airport is on the flatlands at the island's extreme southern tip, 14km south of Pigádhia. It's served by Olympic Air flights to Athens (1 daily), Rhodes (1–2 daily), and Sitía at the eastern tip of Crete, via Kássos (daily except Fri). There's no bus service, so renting a car at the airport can save you a steep taxi fare (from €18 to Pigádhia).

By ferry The port at Pigádhia is connected with the following ports: Anáfi (2 weekly; 6hr 15min–12hr); Crete (2 weekly; Sitía 4hr 10min, Iráklion 7hr 20min); Hálki (2 weekly; 2hr 40min); Kássos (4 weekly; 1hr 20min); Mílos (2 weekly; 17hr 30min); Pireás (3 weekly; 21hr); Rhodes (4 weekly; 5hr); Santoríni (2 weekly; 12hr). One weekly ferry in each direction also calls at Dhiafáni on Kárpathos's north coast.

Travel agents The main ferry agent in Pigádhia is Possi Travel (☎ 22450 22235, ✉ possitvl@hotmail .com), who also sell day-trips to Hálki by ferry (Tues), and Kássos by air and ferry (Sat).

GETTING AROUND

By car The airport's only car rental outlet, Houvarda Maria (☎ 22450 61249), is the agent for Budget (✉ budgetkarpathos@yahoo.gr) and Drive

(✉ drivekarpathos@yahoo.gr). Several more agencies are based in Pigádhia. The only petrol stations are immediately north and south of Pigádhia, so it's impossible to tour the

whole island on a scooter.
By bus Pigádhia's "bus station" is a car park at the western edge of the town centre. Regular buses, run by KTEL (☎ 22450 22338), go to Pylés, via Apéri, Voládha and Óthos (3–4 daily); Ammopí (5–6 daily). Less frequent services run to Menetés, Arkássa, Finíki and Lefkos, with some continuing to Mesohóri; and to Kyrá Panayía, Ápella and Spóa.

By taxi Set-rate, unmetered taxis congregate two blocks inland from the harbour. Typical fares range from €10 to Ammopí up to €42 to Lefkos.
Boat excursions Boats offer day-trips from Pigádhia to isolated east-coast beaches. In addition, *Chrisovalandou III* (☎ 02410 51292) sails to and from Dhiafáni every day, typically leaving Pigádhia at 8.30am and Dhiafáni around 4.30pm, for a one-way fare of €15.

Pigádhia

The island capital of **PIGÁDHIA (Kárpathos Town)** lies on the southeast coast, at the southern end of scenic, 3km-long **Vróndi Bay**. The town itself makes little of its spectacular setting, typically reaching just one or two streets back from its long curving waterfront. All the main action is concentrated along its southernmost section. From the jetty where ferries and excursion boats dock, at the far end, the quayside curls north, lined initially by seafood restaurants and then an increasing number of cafés and music bars. The only buildings that catch the eye are a group of stately but fading Italian-era port police and county-government buildings, overlooking the port from a low bluff at its northern end. Beyond them, another hotel or two, most large but reasonably tasteful, seem to join the procession along the bay each year, stretching Pigádhia ever further northwards. While there's nothing special to see, Pigádhia does offer most conceivable facilities, albeit with a package-tourism slant.

ACCOMMODATION

PIGÁDHIA

A long line of beach hotels is snaking ever northwards along Vróndi Bay; the larger and newer ones tend to be dominated by package clients, but in any case you're likely to enjoy Pigádhia more if you stay closer to the harbour.

Amarylis Hotel ☎ 22450 22375, ⊛ amarylis.gr. Nice little budget hotel, on the hillside just above the bus terminal and central car park, with sixteen clean, whitewashed and surprisingly large studios and apartments. All have a/c, showers and kitchenettes, half have sea-view balconies. **€30**
Atlantis Hotel ☎ 22450 22777, ⊛ atlantis hotelkarpathos.gr. Welcoming little hotel in a great central location, facing the Italian "palace" just up from the port. Helpful management, and nice rooms. Cheaper rooms overlook the pool; pay €9 extra for a port view. **€63**
Electra Beach Hotel ☎ 22450 23256, ⊛ electra beachhotel.gr. Imposing modern hotel a 5min walk along

the beach from the harbour. Each of its somewhat small but very neat and tastefully modernized rooms has its own balcony, with dazzling views of the bay, and there's also a good pool. Buffet breakfasts included. In summer it tends to be filled with Scandinavian groups, but look for bargain low-season rates. **€100**
Elias Rooms ☎ 22450 22446 or 697 85 87 924, ⊛ eliasrooms.com. Simple little converted house, perched just above the *Hotel Karpathos* in the heart of town, with sea views from the balconies. Three plain little en-suite double rooms, two larger and slightly more expensive apartments that sleep four. Closed Nov–March. **€35**

EATING AND DRINKING

★ Mezedhopolio To Ellinikon ☎ 22450 23932. Serving what's unquestionably Pigádhia's finest food, this cosy indoor dining room is set back a block inland from the middle of the harbour. Diners are invited up to the raised kitchen to choose from daily specials like a fabulous stuffed aubergine for €5, or a substantial grilled bream for €12; expect free trimmings such as a rich tapenade. Open all year, daily lunch & dinner.
Orea Karpathos ☎ 22450 22501. The best all-round restaurant along the harbourfront strip, near the southern

end; almost nothing costs more than €10. *Trahanádhes* soup for €4.50, spicy sausages for €7.50, marinated artichokes, great spinach pie, and palatable local bulk wine. Locals use it as an ouzerí, ordering just mezédhes. Evenings only, closed Dec–Feb.
Sofia's Place ☎ 22450 23152. Sit and enjoy the life of the port from the blue chairs on the terrace of this pretty little restaurant in the heart of the action. Friendly service, good local seafood at above-average prices, and tasty grilled-meat specials. Daily noon–late.

5

The south

Immediately south of Pigádhia, reached by a detour off the main road down the other side of a low headland, the purpose-built resort of **AMMOPÍ** (also known as "Amoopi") is not so much a town as a succession of sand-and-gravel, tree- or cliff-fringed coves. There's no commercial centre to it, let alone anything that could be called authentic, but for a beach-side holiday any of the hotels here could make an appealing base. Keep going beyond them all to find some delightful little turquoise bays, usually deserted except at the height of summer.

Back on the main road, the further south you go, the flatter and more desolate Kárpathos becomes. The long windswept beach that leads all the way down to the airport has become popular with foreign **windsurfers**, who take advantage of the prevailing northwesterlies, especially during the annual summer European championships. As such, different segments are known these days by their windsurfing nicknames, such as Gun Bay.

For non-surfers, the best beach here is **Chicken Bay**, the southernmost, though it's a bit too exposed to spend a whole day here. Its shallow, impossibly turquoise waters begin within a few metres of the airport runway.

INFORMATION   **THE SOUTH**

Activities The most established surf school in southern Kárpathos is Pro Center Kárpathos (☎ 22450 91063 or 697 78 86 289, ⓦ Chris-Schill.com), which makes use of three separate bays, catering to different ability levels.

ACCOMMODATION AND EATING

Esperida Ammopí ☎ 22450 81002, ⓦ esperida.gr. Large, very welcoming taverna, set well back from the sea halfway down the approach road to Ammopí. Delicious local food, including island cheese, wine and sausage, roast aubergine, and pickled wild vegetables (look out for what they call "capers"). Main dishes cost around €8, mezes half that. They also offer clean, good-value rooms and apartments. **€50**

Irini Beach Hotel Gun Bay ☎ 22450 91000, ⓦ hotelirini24.com. Upscale hotel complex on the island's prime windsurfing beach, with large comfortable rooms, a good pool, equipment rental and instruction. **€65**

★ **Vardes Studios** Ammopí ☎ 22450 81111 or 697 21 52 901, ⓦ hotelvardes.com. Ammopí's most peaceful studios, set amid orchards 400m back from the beach. Ten comfortable units, all with shower and balcony; some sleep up to five. House fruit and jam for breakfast, plus a bar but no restaurant. **€73**

The west

Although it's much less developed than the area around Pigádhia, the western shoreline of Kárpathos holds several of the island's most attractive **beaches**. Small resorts such as Finíki and Lefkós make great bases for low-key holiday relaxation, amid scintillating scenery.

Arkássa

The main road from Pigádhia reaches the west coast at the little town of **ARKÁSSA**. Hardly anything survives of the original village, the rocky coastal frontage now consisting of unremarkable studios and tavernas. Head a few hundred metres south, and you'll come to the signposted side-road that leads to the whitewashed chapel of **Ayía Sofía**. Remains of a much larger Byzantine basilica here feature several mosaic floors with geometric patterns.

The finest beach hereabouts is also located just south of Arkássa. The broad 100m stretch of good-quality sand known as **Áyios Nikólaos beach** still feels pleasantly rural, even though a newly built hotel has just joined its long-standing taverna.

Finíki

A couple of kilometres north of Arkássa, facing it from the northern end of a long bay, the even smaller resort of **FINÍKI** is still very recognizable as the fishing village it used to be. A brief detour down from the main road, the port is arrayed along the curve of a minuscule beach, and holds several welcoming tavernas. In summer, excursion boats head across from here to Kássos.

Lefkós

To reach the attractive resort of **LEFKÓS** – also known as **Paralía Lefkoú** – take a side turning that drops back down from the main road as it climbs through the dense forest around 10km north of Finíki. While considerably more developed than Finíki, it too visibly started out as a fishing village. Its best tavernas are concentrated around the harbour, which also holds a great sheltered beach, and accommodation is plentiful too. Several more beaches lie nearby, separated by a striking topography of cliffs, islets and sandspits.

Mesohóri

The main road climbs northeast from Lefkos through the pine forest to the dramatically sited village of **MESOHÓRI**. Tumbling seaward along narrow, stepped alleys, Mesohóri comes to a halt at the edge of a bluff that's dotted with three tiny, ancient chapels, separated from the village proper by extensive orchards.

ACCOMMODATION THE WEST

Arhontiko Studios Finíki ☎ 22450 61473, ⊛ hotel arhontiko.gr. Simple, well-run hotel on the main coast road just above Finíki, where all six comfortable studios and six larger apartments have sea-view balconies. €60

Finiki View Hotel Finíki ☎ 22450 61400, ⊛ finikiview.gr. Pleasant modern hotel, dropping down towards the port from the coast road. Eighteen well-equipped studios and two apartments, set in attractive gardens and sharing use of a pool. Great views at sunset. Closed Nov–April. €70

Glaros Áyios Nikólaos, Arkássa ☎ 22450 61015, ⊛ glarosrestaurant-karpathos.com. Classic little beach taverna beside one of Kárpathos' nicest beaches, run by returned Karpathian-Virginians. Good open-air dining, plus

five tastefully furnished, good-value studios. €60

Hotel Krinos Lefkos ☎ 22450 71410, ⊛ hotel-krinos .com. Low-rise complex, just before the road reaches the centre of town, that's especially popular with returning German guests. All its mix of rooms, studios and apartments are en suite and have either balcony or terrace. Closed Nov–April. €55

★ **Pine Tree** Ádhia ☎ 697 73 69 948, ⊛ pinetree -karpathos.gr. Simple but very attractive and inexpensive rooms in an utterly gorgeous rural location, a short walk up the hillside from the *Pine Tree Restaurant* (see below), and enjoying long-range sea views. There's also a lovely stand-alone studio, complete with traditional sleeping platform, a little higher up, and free camping. €35

EATING AND DRINKING

Dhramoundana 1 Mesohóri ☎ 22450 71373. The finest eating option in this hillside village, but fiendishly difficult to find; it's near the church of Panayía Vryssianí, low down at the far north end. A couple of outdoor tables enjoy fabulous views, but the food indoors is the main attraction, featuring capers, sausages, home-made *dolmadhes* and marinated "sardines". Daily lunch & dinner.

Dhramoundana 2 Lefkos ☎ 22450 71373. The pick of the three restaurants grouped together at the western end of Lefkos's harbour is slap in the middle. Its friendly owner, whose wife runs the sister restaurant *Dhramoundana 1* (see above), is a Greek-American who lived in Baltimore – hence the fabulous crab cakes. Daily lunch & dinner.

Marina Finíki ☎ 22450 61100. Finíki's finest waterfront taverna, with a shady patio right by the beach. €5 buys a quarter chicken, otherwise most meat and fish dishes cost €8, though you'll pay more when there's fresh lobster. Live Greek music on summer evenings. Daily 9am–late.

Pine Tree Restaurant Ádhia ☎ 697 73 69 948, ⊛ pinetree-karpathos.gr. Delightful restaurant, set amid orchards and lush gardens in an isolated spot, just up from the sea, 7km north of Finíki. Relax on the flower-decked terrace and sample such delights as home-baked bread, lentil soup and octopus *makaronádha* (plus other *mayireftá*), washed down by sweet Óthos wine. Daily noon–9pm.

The centre

Central Kárpathos supports a group of villages blessed with commanding hillside settings, ample running water and a cool climate, even in August. Nearly everyone here

5

has "done time" in North America before returning home with their nest eggs; the area is said to have the highest per capita income in Greece.

You're more likely to take a driving tour through the interior than to spend much time in any one place. Villages to look out for include **ÓTHOS**, which is the highest (around 400m) and the chilliest, on the flanks of 1215m Mount Kalilímni, and is noted for its bread, sausages and sweet, tawny-amber wine. **VOLÁDHA**, downhill to the east, cradles a tiny Venetian citadel, while the most attractive, **PYLÉS**, faces west atop a steeply switchbacking road that branches from the main west-coast road 6km north of Finíki.

The north

Northern Kárpathos still feels very much a world apart. Despite repeated promises, the road north from Spóa has not been fully paved, and remains a hair-raising prospect for all but the hardiest mountain drivers. Most visitors therefore still arrive by boat at the little port of **Dhiafáni**, and then take a bus up to the traditional hilltop village of **Ólymbos**.

Spóa

The gateway to northern Kárpathos, where the unpaved road to Ólymbos branches off the main circle-island road, is the village of **SPÓA**, just east of the island's central spine. No road enters the village itself.

If you're heading this way along the east coast, you might prefer to take a break at the best beach in these parts, down at **Ápella**, though from the taverna at the road's end you still have to walk a short pathway to reach the scenic 300m gravel strand.

Dhiafáni

The sleepy seafront village of **DHIAFÁNI** only springs to life twice a week, when its rare mainline ferries – one heading towards Rhodes, the other towards Crete – call in. Otherwise, the daily excursion boats from Pigádhia (see p.291) keep a low-key tourist industry, including several tavernas and lodging options, ticking along.

All the **beaches** in northern Kárpathos are made of pebbles. Dhiafáni itself has a reasonable fringe of shingle, or there's a quieter alternative at **Vanánda** cove; follow the pleasant signposted path north through the pines for thirty minutes, short-cutting the road. Naturist **Papá Miná**, with a few trees and cliff-shade, lies an hour's walk distant via the cairned trail taking off from the road to the ferry dock.

Ólymbos

Founded in Byzantine times as a refuge from pirates, the windswept village of **ÓLYMBOS** straddles a long ridge below slopes studded with ruined windmills. Isolated for centuries, the villagers speak a unique dialect, with traces of its Doric and Phrygian origins. Their home has long attracted foreign and Greek ethnologists for **traditional dress**, **crafts**, **dialect and music** that have vanished elsewhere in Greece. Here too the traditions are dwindling by the year; only older women, or those who work in the tourist shops, now wear striking, colourful clothing – while flogging trinkets imported from much further afield.

Women still play a prominent role in daily life, however: tending gardens, carrying goods on their shoulders or herding goats. Nearly all Ólymbos men historically emigrated to Baltimore or work outside the village, sending money home and returning only on holidays.

Live folk music is still played regularly, especially at festival times (Easter and Aug 15), when visitors have little hope of finding a bed.

ACCOMMODATION AND EATING   **THE NORTH**

★ **Gorgona** Dhiafáni ☎ 22450 51509, ⊛ gorgona karpathos.it. Behind the seafront fountain, this Italian-run place is a favourite local rendezvous, featuring light

dishes, wonderful desserts, proper coffees and *limoncello* digestif. Daily 9am–late.

Hotel Aphrodite Ólymbos ☎ 22450 51307. Little hotel,

HIKING IN NORTHERN KÁRPATHOS

Northern Kárpathos is renowned for excellent **hiking**. While the most popular walk of all simply follows the jeep track down from Ólymbos to the superb west-coast beach at **Fýsses**, a sharp drop below the village, most local trails head more gently north or east, on waymarked paths.

Ólymbos to Dhiafáni An easy ninety-minute walk leads back down to Dhiafáni, starting just below the two working windmills. The way is well marked, with water twenty minutes along, and eventually drops to a ravine amid extensive forest. The final half-hour, unfortunately, follows a bulldozed riverbed.

Ólymbos to Vrykoúnda Heading north from Ólymbos, it takes around 1hr 30min to reach sparsely inhabited Avlóna, set on a high upland devoted to grain. From there, less than an hour more of descending first moderately, then steeply, along an ancient walled-in path that takes off from the valley-floor track, will bring you to the ruins and beach at Vrykoúnda. Once you've seen the Hellenistic/Roman masonry courses and rock-cut tombs here, and the remote cave-shrine of John the Baptist on the promontory (focus of a major Aug 28–29 festival), there's good swimming in the pebble coves to one side.

Avlóna to Trístomo Starting just above Avlóna, a magnificent cobbled way leads in 2hr 30min, via the abandoned agricultural hamlets of Ahordhéa and Kílios, to Trístomo, a Byzantine anchorage in the far northeast of Kárpathos. The views en route, and the path itself, are the thing; Trístomo itself is dreary, with not even a beach.

Trístomo to Vanánda If you've already hiked to Trístomo, and would prefer not to retrace your steps to Avlóna, you can hook up, via a shortish link trail east from Trístomo, with a spectacular coastal path back to Vanánda (3hr 30min). Once clear of abandoned agricultural valleys and over a pine-tufted pass, it's often a corniche route through the trees, with distant glimpses of Dhiafáni and no real challenge except at the steep rock-stairs known as Xylóskala.

run by the same management as the nearby Parthenonas restaurant, with just four spacious double rooms, one of which has a kitchen. All have phenomenal views, to the windmills and the sea. **€50**

Hotel Astro Ólymbos ☎ 22450 51421. Smart en-suite rooms, with traditional furnishings, and a warm welcome from its owners, the two sisters who run *Café-Restaurant Zefiros* on the other side of the village, where breakfast is taken. **€55**

Hotel Studios Glaros Dhiafáni ☎ 22450 51501, ⓦ hotel-glaros.gr. Run by the very welcoming George and Anna Niotis, these sixteen huge units, some of which sleep four, are top of the heap in all senses in Dhiafáni, ranged in tiers up the southern slope. Closed Nov–March. **€45**

Pension Olymbos Ólymbos ☎ 22450 51009. This friendly little place, near the village entrance, offers

modern units with baths as well as unplumbed ones with traditional furnishings. It also holds an excellent, inexpensive restaurant, specializing in traditional home cooking, including unusual shellfish. **€30**

Restaurant Avlona Ávlona ☎ 694 60 18 521. On a spur road away from the Dhiafáni–Ólymbos road, this offshoot of the restaurant at *Pension Olymbos* (see above) features artichoke hearts with eggs in spring. The signature dish is *makaroúnes*, home-made pasta with onions and cheese. Four en-suite rooms make it an ideal base for walkers. Daily lunch & dinner.

Studios Delfini Dhiafáni ☎ 22450 51354, ⓦ studiosdelfini.wordpress.com. Very pleasant ground-floor studios, with kitchenettes, bathrooms and air conditioning, just a few metres from the sea. Upstairs, the *Dolphins* restaurant serves vegetables from the garden, and good fish. Closed Nov–March. **€45**

Sými

For sheer breathtaking beauty, the Greek islands can offer nothing to beat arriving at **Sými**. While the island as a whole is largely barren, its one significant population centre, **Sými Town**, is gorgeous, a magnificent steep-walled bay lined with Italian-era mansions.

With its shortage of fresh water and relative lack of sandy beaches, Sými has never developed a major tourist industry. Sými Town however holds a wide range of small hotels, as well as abundant delightful rental properties, while day-trippers from Rhodes – and yachties lured by the wonderful harbour – mean it can support some very good

5

restaurants too. In the height – and searing heat – of summer it can get uncomfortably crowded, with a large influx of Italian visitors as well as mainland Greeks, but in spring and autumn it's wonderful, and even in winter a substantial expat community keeps many businesses open.

Visitors who venture beyond the inhabited areas find an attractive island that has retained some **forest** of junipers, valonea oaks and even a few pines – ideal walking country in the cooler months. Dozens of tiny, privately owned **monasteries** dot the landscape; though generally locked except on their patron saint's day, freshwater cisterns are usually accessible. Near the southern tip of the island, the much larger monastery of **Panormítis** is an important pilgrimage destination.

Little more than a century ago, Sými Town was home to more people than Rhodes Town, thanks to the wealth generated by its twin ancient skills of shipbuilding and sponge-diving. Many of the mansions built during that age of prosperity have long since tumbled into decay – a process hastened in September 1944, when an ammunition blast set off by the retreating Germans levelled hundreds of houses up in Horió. While restoration is gradually bringing them back to life, the scattered ruins lend the island an appealing sense of time-forgotten mystery.

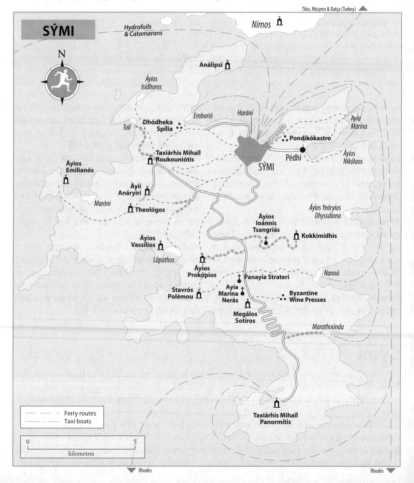

ARRIVAL AND INFORMATION   SÝMI

By ferry Ferries from the following islands use the main harbour in Sými Town: Astypálea (1 weekly; 9hr); Hálki (2 weekly; 2hr 20min); Kálymnos (9 weekly; 2hr 10min–6hr 20min); Kastellórizo (3 weekly; 3hr 20min–6hr); Kos (11 weekly; 1hr 30min–4hr 50min); Léros (6 weekly; 3hr 20min–5hr 50min); Lipsí (6 weekly; 3hr 45min–7hr); Náxos (1 weekly; 14hr); Níssyros (3 weekly; 3–4hr); Páros (1 weekly; 15hr 20min); Pátmos (6 weekly; 5hr 10min–8hr 10min); Pireás (2 weekly; 17–21hr); Rhodes (3–4 daily; 50min–1hr 40min); Tílos (3 weekly; 1hr 30min–3hr 10min). Ferries also call in Panormítis monastery at the island's southern tip, but most stop there en route from Rhodes to Sými Town; only the Proteus sails from Sými Town to Panormítis, three times weekly.

Ticket agents Kalodoukas Holidays at the foot of the Kalí Stráta (☎ 22460 71077, ⓦ kalodoukas.gr), and Sými Tours on the harbourfront (☎ 22460 71307, ⓦ symitours.com).

Tourist office Sými does not have an official tourist office, but Sými Visitor, based above Pahos café by the taxi-boat jetty, sells books and maps of local interest, and runs a very helpful website, ⓦ symivisitor.com.

GETTING AROUND

Boat excursions Between late May and late Sept, taxi-boats from Yialós harbour run south to the beaches detailed on p.300 onwards, and north to Emborió (see p.298). In Aug, several a day make it possible to beach-hop; in lower season, pick a single day-trip destination. Fares range up to €15 for the round-trip to Marathoúnda. Larger boats offer circle-island cruises in summer, with snorkelling and picnic stops, or day-trips to Turkey, for around €40. You can also take a day-trip to Kastellórizo aboard the Dodekanisos Express catamaran (Mon only; €36; ⓦ 12ne.gr). On Saturdays only, the same catamaran makes a day-trip to Datca in Turkey; excursion boats run that route to no fixed schedule in summer.

By bus A year-round bus service operates from a tiny car park on the south side of the harbour. A coach shuttles at regular intervals between Yialós and Pédhi via Horió, while a minibus makes two or three round-trips daily all the way south to Panormítis monastery; both charge €1 flat fare.

By taxi Sými's six taxis, based alongside the bus stop, serve the entire island. Expect to pay €5 to get between Yialós and Horió with baggage.

By car and scooter Scooters and/or cars – not that there's much point renting a car on Sými, with its minimal road network – are available from Glaros (☎ 22460 71926, ⓦ glarosrentacar.gr), Katsaras (☎ 22460 72203) and Sými Tours (ⓦ symitours.com).

Sými Town

SÝMI, the capital and only town, is arrayed around a superb natural harbour in an east-facing inlet on the island's north shore. Inter-island ferries arrive right in the heart of town, while excursion boats jostle for room in summer with mighty Mediterranean cruisers. Immediately behind the straight-line quaysides that enclose the main segment of the port, scattered with sponge stalls and souvenir stores targeted at day-trippers, the lowest row of Italian-era mansions clings to the foot of the hillsides. Each is painted in the officially ordained palette of ochres, terracotta, cream or the occasional pastel blue, and topped by a neat triangular pediment and roof of ochre tiles. The hills are steep enough that the houses seem to stand one above the other, to create a gloriously harmonious ensemble.

The lower level of the town, known as **Yialós**, extends northwards to incorporate the smaller curving **Haráni Bay**. Traditionally this was the island's shipbuilding area, and you'll still see large wooden boats hauled out of the water. Yialós also stretches some way inland from the head of the harbour, beyond the main town square, which is used for classical and popular Greek performances during the summer-long **Sými Festival**.

On top of the high hill on the south side of the port, the old village of **Horió** stands aloof from the tourist bustle below. It's hard to say quite where Yialós ends and Horió begins, however; the massive **Kalí Stráta** stair-path, which climbs up from the harbour, is lined with grand mansions, even if some are no more than owl-haunted shells. Another similar stairway, the **Katarráktes**, climbs the west side of the hill, from further back in Yialós, but it's more exposed, and used largely by locals.

5

Horió

As the 350-plus steps of Kali Stráta deter most day-trippers from attempting to reach **Horió**, the old hilltop village makes a great refuge whenever Yialós is too hot or crowded. It too holds its fair share of Italianate splendours and impressive basilicas. Once you venture away from the main pedestrian lane, it can be quite a tangle to explore – the part you can see from the harbour is just a small portion of the village, which stretches a long way back above Pédhi Bay. At the very pinnacle of things, a **Knights' castle**, largely destroyed by the wartime explosion, occupies the site of Sými's ancient acropolis; you may glimpse a stretch of Classical polygonal wall on one side. The **church of the Assumption**, inside the fortifications, is a modern replacement. One of the bells in the new belfry is the nose-cone of a thousand-pound bomb, hung as a memorial.

A series of arrows leads deep into Horió to the excellent local **museum** (Tues–Sun 8am–2.30pm; €2). Housed in a fine old mansion, its collection highlights Byzantine and medieval Sými, particularly frescoes in isolated, often locked churches. Displays continue in the eighteenth-century **Hatziagapitos mansion** below, with wonderful carved wooden chests and allegorical wall-paintings.

Beaches

There's no beach in Sými Town. Some visitors clamber into the sea from the harbour wall in Haráni Bay, but neither there nor at the tiny, man-made **Sými Paradise** "beach", adjoining a restaurant just around the headland beyond Haráni, is the water clean enough for swimming to be advisable.

Keep walking along the paved coast road from Haráni, however – there's no shade, but the views are nice, and there's seldom any traffic – and in around half an hour you'll come to quiet **Emborió** (Nimborió) Bay. The beach is just a narrow strip of coarse shingle, but it's a great place to while away an afternoon of swimming, snorkelling, and eating at the friendly taverna (see opposite). In summer, the beach is served by regular taxi boats, so you're not obliged to walk both ways.

ACCOMMODATION   SÝMI TOWN

Albatros Marketplace, Yialós ☎22460 71707, ⓦalbatrosymi.gr. This pretty little hotel has five a/c rooms, a pleasant second-floor breakfast salon, and distant sea views. The website is also the booking venue for a number of magnificent Neoclassical villas divided into apartments. **€65**

Aliki Haráni quay, Yialós ☎22460 71665, ⓦhotelaliki .gr. Upscale waterfront hotel, housed in a renovated 1895 mansion, just around the corner from the main harbour. The tasteful rooms have wood floors and some antique furnishings, plus a/c and large bathrooms. All have at least partial sea views, some have balconies, and there's a very nice suite. Closed early Nov to mid-April. **€130**

Fiona Horió ☎22460 72088, ⓦfionahotel.com. Village hotel near the top of the Kalí Stráta; turn left at *George & Maria's*. The large, simply furnished but attractive and airy rooms upstairs enjoy stunning views and have small balconies; breakfast, included in the price, is taken on the bigger shared harbour-view terrace below. Also three studios next door. A three-person room costs €5 extra. **€65**

Iapetos Village Yialós ☎22460 72777, ⓦiapetos -village.gr. Tucked into walled, landscaped grounds just back from the main square at the head of the harbour, this smart complex also includes a roofed-over pool. All its 29

units, variously categorized as rooms, studios and apartments, are exceptionally large, and have kitchens; some sleep up to six. A good buffet breakfast is offered either in cool basement premises or by the pool bar. **€162**

Kalodoukas Holidays ☎22460 71077, ⓦkalodoukas .gr. Rental agents for a wide array of generally irresistible houses and apartments, all with kitchen facilities and many featuring traditional furnishings plus harbour-view balconies and/or courtyard gardens. Some sleep up to six guests. They also offer five beachfront apartments at Marathoúnda Bay; see p.301. Two-person apartments **€100**, four-person houses **€140**

Les Catherinettes north quay, Yialós ☎22460 71671, ⓔmarina-epe@rho.forthnet.r. Spotless en-suite *pension*, above the eponymous restaurant, in a historic harbourfront building. Six simple rooms, with painted ceilings, fridges, fans and sea-view balconies. The same owners also offer three studios in Haráni, plus a family apartment. **€90**

Nireus Hotel Yialós ☎22460 72400, ⓦnireus-hotel .gr. Sými's most conspicuous hotel, in prime position near the clocktower at the harbour entrance, with a lovely waterfront bar and a decent restaurant. The stunning sea views from the adequate but unexceptional

5

seafront rooms just about justify the high prices; don't even consider the cheaper rear-facing ones. Closed mid-Oct to March. **€115**

Niriides Apartments Emborió ☎ 22460 71784, ⓦ niriideshotel.com. Ten simply furnished, spacious and quiet rental units, spread over five hillside buildings on the hillside just above the nice little beach at Emborió, 2km from Yialós in the next bay north. All sleep four, and have a/c; friendly management, on-site "lounge-café", and a good taverna immediately below. **€100**

The Old Markets Kali Stráta, Yialós ☎ 22460 71440, ⓦ theoldmarkets.com. Boutique B&B hotel, housed in an imposing and very elegant converted mansion a short way up the Kali Stráta, with magnificent harbour views. Each of its four en-suite rooms is luxuriously furnished; the Sými Suite, which costs double the rest, is quite superb. **€225**

Opera House Yialós platía ☎ 22460 72034, ⓦ symioperahouse.gr. This unexpectedly large complex, a short walk inland from Yialós' main square, consists of several separate houses, newly built in traditional style, perfunctorily furnished, and owned by a Greek-Australian. They're divided into apartment suites holding from two to six people; few have views to speak of, though they do have balconies, but the rates for the sheer space you get are remarkably low, especially off season. **€70**

★ **Sými Visitor Accommodation** ☎ 22460 71785, ⓦ symivisitor.com. Wendy Wilcox and Adriana Shum offer great-value rental stays in restored houses in Yialós and Horió, with maid service every three days. Ranging from simple studios to family mansions, these are private homes let in their owners' absence, and come with full kitchens, book/DVD collections – and all sorts of idiosyncrasies. Typical four-person house **€115**, two-person **€85**

EATING AND DRINKING

RESTAURANTS

Dhimitris South quay, Yialós ☎ 22460 72207. This family-run ouzerí, with open-air tables near the main island bus stop, offers exotic seafood items like *hokhlióalo* (sea snails), tasty octopus fritters, and the miniature local shrimps, along with grilled local sausages and chops and vegetarian starters. Daily lunch & dinner.

George & Maria's Top of Kalí Stráta, Horió. Jolly, much-loved Sými institution, with summer seating on a pebble-mosaic courtyard. Expect to be invited to inspect the pots in the kitchen before making your choice – perennial dishes, costing around €10, include feta-stuffed peppers, beans with sausage, lemon chicken, and a full range of grills. Dinner daily, plus random lunchtimes in season.

Metapontis Taverna Emborió ☎ 22460 71820. Lovely little taverna, right beside the beach at Emborió, a half-hour walk along the coast from Yialós. Open for all meals daily; some beachgoers hang on to a table all day, with fresh-grilled meat or fish for lunch and then ice creams and snacks later on. Daily 10am–7pm.

★ **Muses** Yialós Platía ☎ 695 87 34 503. The up-and-coming star of the Sými scene, *Muses* offers a distinctive, delicious, very contemporary and rather pricey take on Greek cuisine. The cucumber salad is a deconstructed tsatsiki, while the octopus with ouzo foam and orange is fabulously succulent; like most dishes, it's available as a meze (€10) or a main (€20). They've made the best of their setting on the drab village square, just back from the harbour, with lovely open-air seating beneath trailing vines. Daily 7.30–11.30pm.

★ **Mythos** South quay, Yialós ☎ 22460 71488. This dinner-only, harbour-view roof terrace near the bus stop serves some of the best food on the island. Chef-owner Stavros's specialities include *psaronéfri* with mushrooms

and sweet wine sauce, lamb *stifádho*, feta *saganáki* in fig sauce, and good desserts like lemon pie or panna cotta. Best value of all is the phenomenal meze menu, designed to share and costing around €15 per head; the dishes just keep on coming. Late May to late Sept, daily 7.30–11pm.

Syllogos Platía Syllógou, Horió. Vast but not impersonal place with indoor/outdoor seating, great for taverna standards like *skordhaliá*, *arní lemonáto*, fried fish and aubergine *imám*, with good *hýma* wine on offer – only skimpy portion sizes deprive it of an "author pick" symbol. Daily lunch & dinner.

Tholos Haráni quay ☎ 22460 70203. The last restaurant you come to as you walk around Haráni bay, with waterside tables laid out right on the headland. A fabulously romantic spot for a fine meal of grilled fresh fish; the cheese-topped aubergine is pretty good too. May–Oct, daily lunch & dinner.

Trata Platía Trata, Yialós ☎ 22460 71411. This lively, very informal local hangout fills most of the small square at the foot of the Kalí Stráta. As you might expect from a place called "The Trawler", the fresh seafood is great, but it's also a place to go off piste, and simply see what delights – especially vegetable dishes – may be lurking in the kitchen. Daily 9am–late.

BARS AND CAFÉS

The 2 As Horió. Named for owners Alex and Astrid, but still widely known by its former tag of Jean & Tonic, this convivial place is the heart and soul of the expat bar scene in Horió, and caters to a mixed clientele with 1960s music. Daily 6pm–late.

Bar Tsati Harani quay ☎ 22460 72498. You can't get any closer to the water than this friendly, Italian-run little café-bar, a short walk from the clocktower around Haráni bay. A

5

cluster of pastel-coloured tables and chairs in a harbourfront nook, plus cushions on the seawall itself – people go swimming right here. The wi-fi access reaches to the quayside, while there's a computer inside. Proper Italian espresso and tasty tidbits, and a lively late-night scene. Daily 11am–1am or later.

Evoi Evan Yialós platía. With a large terrace sprawling beneath the spreading ficus trees, and a cavernous interior that includes a pool table upstairs, *Evoi Evan* is open from breakfast onwards, serving coffee, smoothies and juices first thing, and a full drinks menu later on. Daily 8am–late.

Kalí Stráta Horió. The perfect place for a (pricey) sunset cocktail, with its canvas chairs and comfy cushions arrayed where the Kalí Stráta makes its final right-angle bend before reaching Horió. The best views on the island, with a jazz/world soundtrack. Daily noon until late.

Lefteris Top of the Kalí Stráta, Horió. The local characters' *kafenío*, in the second shopfront on Platía Syllógou, and attended by all. Coffee or ice cream at any hour; also simple mezédhes.

Nikolas Yialós. The first-ever *zaharoplastío* on the island, tiucked into a back alley just south of Yialós bridge, and still

the only one making its sweeties on site rather than importing from Rhodes. They also have a freezer-full of the best ice cream on the island.

The Olive Tree Horió ☎ 22460 72683, ⊛ olivetreesymi .eu. Friendly English-run café, across from the *Fiona* hotel (see p.298), that's a meeting place for energetic local expats. Top-quality coffee, really well-priced juices and smoothies using island fruits and Greek yoghurt, sandwiches (including to go), big healthy breakfasts. Also open for dinner on Saturdays in spring and autumn. Daily 8am–3pm.

★ **Pahos** Yialós. Classic *kafenío*, in operation since World War II. Facing the west quay south of Yialós bridge, it's still the spot for an evening ouzo or coffee and people-watching. Pahos himself has retired and can often be found sitting out front as a customer; otherwise it's hardly changed – including the prices, significantly lower than elsewhere. Daily 8am–late.

Sunrise Café/Anatoli Iliou Horió. Cosy English/German-run café, near the windmill on the eastern edge of Horió. Well-priced drinks, breakfasts, good salads and light snacks. Open all day until the small hours.

The rest of the island

Away from Sými Town, the only other settlements on the island are little **Pédhi**, on the shoreline below Horió, and **Panormítis** down at the southern tip. The main attractions for visitors are isolated pebbly **beaches** that stand at the heads of the deeply indented bays along the eastern coast – accessible by taxi-boat in summer – and the tiny scattered **monasteries** that make great targets for hikers.

Pédhi

The hugely indented bay lying south of Sými Town, on the far side of the ridge that stretches away from Horió, is home to the separate little community of **PÉDHI**. Somewhat further than it may look from Horió – it takes about half an hour to walk down the hillside – it's served by regular buses.

Originally a fishing hamlet with a sideline in boatbuilding, Pédhi has slowly expanded over the past twenty years. Much of the waterfront is now lined with new houses built in the standard Italian-influenced Sými style. Even if there's nothing authentic about it, it's reasonably pretty; locals fear the construction of an ugly new marina may spoil things, but there's been little progress so far. While the waterfront holds a hotel and a couple of tavernas, Pédhi doesn't have a beach.

Ayía Marína

A small indentation in the headland that separates Sými Town from Pédhi Bay, known as **Ayía Marína**, has been developed as a miniature beach. With wonderful turquoise water, and a monastery-capped islet within easy swimming distance just offshore, it's an attractive spot, but in summer it tends to fill up (largely with Italians) the moment the day's first taxi boat arrives. The waterfront is an unbroken row of sunbeds, and the one taverna does a brisk trade.

It's possible to beat the crowds by walking here, either along a paint-splodge-marked path from Pédhi or over the top of the ridge from the east end of Horió, but the best time to hike is in low season, when the taxi boats aren't running and you may have the place to yourself.

Áyios Nikólaos

An exposed fifteen-minute footpath along the south side of Pédhi Bay – simply push your way through the gate at the end of the quayside, then follow the cairns along the slope – leads to **Áyios Nikólaos**, the only all-sand cove on Sými. Also served by regular taxi-boats in season, this offers sheltered swimming, shady tamarisks, a bar, beach volleyball and a relaxing taverna.

Áyios Yeóryios Dhyssálona

The first significant bay to interrupt Sými's eastern coastline south of Pédhi is **Áyios Yeóryios Dhyssálona**. This spectacular fjord can only be accessed by boat. No path could find a foothold in the smooth limestone that soars at its inland end. There's no taverna, and the whole place falls into shade in the early afternoon.

Nanoú

The largest east-coast bay, **Nanoú**, holds the most popular beach for boat-trippers. A 200m stretch of gravel, sand and small pebbles, with a scenic backdrop of pines, it offers good snorkelling, and has a decent, seafood-strong **taverna**. Nanoú isn't on a paved road, but it is possible to hike down here, from the main trans-island road; see box below.

Marathoúnda

The southernmost taxi-boat stop, **Marathoúnda**, is a magnificent bay, fringed by a long beach of coarse pebbles and ideal for tranquil swimming. It's also accessible via a paved road, which branches off the main road just after it switchbacks down from the island's central spine towards the monastery at Panormítis. Just back from the beach, the valley floor is flat enough to support a few fields, as well as goats who regularly stroll along the waterfront in search of tidbits.

HIKING ON SÝMI

Sými has become an extremely popular **hiking** destination. With midsummer temperatures high even by Greek-island standards, spring and autumn are much the best seasons to come. Most trails lead through depopulated and waterless areas, so you need to have good equipment and provisions, and ideally relevant experience. Lance Chilton's *Walks in Sými*, sold locally packaged with his "Walker's Map of Sými", is a very good investment for all hikers. Guiding **walking tours**, from €10 per person, can be arranged through ⓦsymidream.com (Neil Gosling, ☎693 64 21 715), ⓦsymivisitor.com, or ⓦkalodoukas.gr.

One excellent trail takes three hours (one-way) to cross the island from Yialós to its westernmost tip, where the tiny monastery of **Áyios Emilianós** is tethered to the mainland by a slender causeway. Some of the route lies through forest. Along the way there, you'll pass Sými's oldest monastery, **Taxiárhis Mihaïl Roukouniótis** (daily 9–11am & 5–6pm), which holds naïve eighteenth-century frescoes. For a shorter walk, you can drop down a dirt track from the monastery to reach small, pebbly **Tolí Bay**, which holds a summer-only taverna. An eastward trail over the hilltop from there drops down to **Emborió**, to complete a potential loop back to Yialós.

Another meaty hike crosses the island from Horió in ninety minutes to scenic **Áyios Vassílios** gulf; for the final forty minutes follow a paint-splodge-marked path from the road's end. Immediately above **Lápathos beach** here, the little monastery (which has accessible water) has some interesting frescoes.

The finest frescoes on the island are at hilltop, 1697-vintage **Kokkimídhis monastery** (usually open), reached by a steep track off the Panormítis road, where a complete cycle shows the acts of the Archangel and the risen Christ.

It's also possible to hike all the way from Horió to **Nanoú beach** (see above) in around three hours. That leaves you with time for a meal and swim before catching the boat back to Yialós. Alternatively, as the route leads first, mostly along an ancient footpath, to the chapel at **Panayía Stateri** on the main road, you could take a scooter that far and only walk the final 45 minutes from there, through a scenic forested gorge, down to the beach.

5

Panormítis monastery

Museums daily 8.30am–2pm & 3–4pm • €1.50 combined admission

In summer, at least one daily inter-island ferry, as well as countless excursion boats from Rhodes, calls in at the large **Taxiárhis Miha
ïl Panormítis** monastery, located in a gorgeous (albeit beachless), almost entirely closed little bay in the far south of Sými. You can also get here by road, with daily buses heading down from Yialós. A shop, bakery and simple taverna cater to the needs of day-trippers.

Built in honour of the Archangel Michael (*Taxiárhis* in Greek), patron saint of the island, the monastery was thoroughly pillaged during World War II, so – except for its lofty belfry – don't expect much of the building or its contents. Away from its spruce main courtyard, which has an attractive pebble-mosaic floor, most of the complex is gently fading. Lit by an improbable number of oil lamps, the central *katholikón* is also graced by a fine *témblon* and of course the cult icon, though frescoes are unremarkable.

The monastery courtyard holds two small **museums**. One, devoted entirely to artefacts related to the monastery's religious significance, contains a strange mix of precious antiques, exotic junk, and votive offerings including bodybuilding and motocross trophies. A small boat is piled with messages-in-bottles carried here by the Aegean currents – the idea is that if the bottle or toy boat arrives, the sender's prayer is answered. In the opposite corner, a folklore museum holds displays on costumes, weaving, and domestic activities.

ACCOMMODATION AND EATING   THE REST OF THE ISLAND

Katsaras Pédhi ☎ 22460 71417. With a shaded terrace right at water's edge, this large taverna, in the middle of Pédhi Bay, makes a great place for a full meal or a sunset drink. Vegetable and seafood mezes cost around €8, grilled meat more like €12. Daily noon–9pm.

Pédhi Beach Hotel Pédhi ☎ 22460 71981, ⓦ pedibeachhotel.gr. Large, simply furnished a/c rooms in the middle of the bay, with a patio laid out with sunbeds. Around ten of the 56 rooms have sea-view balconies; rates include dinner at the on-site restaurant,

and drop significantly outside August. There's no beach here, but for lovers of the quiet life it's not a bad alternative. **€120**

★ **Taverna** Marathoúnda Run by the Kalodoukas family, who also offer rental studios here, and supplied with fresh organic produce from their adjoining fields, this excellent waterfront taverna makes a wonderful lunch spot. Top-quality mezes for around €8, or beautifully prepared fish from around €12.50. Daily lunch & dinner, mid-May to mid-Sept only.

Tílos

Stranded midway between Kos and Rhodes, the small, usually quiet island of **TÍLOS** is among the least frequented and most unpredictably connected of the Dodecanese. For visitors, however, it's a great place simply to rest on the beach, or hike in the craggy hinterland.

Tílos shares the characteristics of its closest neighbours: limestone **mountains** like those of Hálki, plus volcanic lowlands, pumice beds and red-lava sand as on Níssyros. With ample groundwater and rich volcanic soil, the islanders could afford to turn their backs on the sea, and made Tílos the **breadbasket** of the Dodecanese. Until the 1970s, travellers were greeted by the sight of shimmering fields of grain bowing in the wind. Nowadays the hillside terraces languish abandoned, and the population of five hundred dwindles to barely a hundred in winter.

While recent development has turned the port of **Livádhia** ever more towards tourism, Tílos remains low-key. This is still a place where visitors come to get away from it all, often for extended stays. If you're here to **walk**, little may seem striking at first glance, but after a few days you may have stumbled on several small Knights' **castles** studding the crags, or found some of the inconspicuous, often frescoed, often locked **medieval chapels** that cling to the hillsides.

ARRIVAL AND INFORMATION

TÍLOS

By ferry The port of Livádhia is connected with the following islands: Astypálea (1 weekly; 7hr 15min); Hálki (2 weekly; 45min); Kálymnos (1 weekly; 5hr 30min); Kastellórizo (2 weekly; 6hr 35min–10hr); Kos (2 weekly; 2hr–3hr); Náxos (1 weekly; 12hr); Níssyros (3 weekly; 50min); Páros (1 weekly; 13hr 30min); Pireás (2 weekly; 14–19hr); Rhodes (7 weekly; 1hr 20min–2hr 15min); Sými (3 weekly; 1hr 30min–3hr 10min).

Travel agents Buy ferry tickets from Stefanakis, close to

the jetty (☎ 22460 44310, ⊛ tilos-travel.com). English-run Tilos Travel nearby offers boat excursions, accommodation, used-book swap and vehicle rental (☎ 22460 44294 or 694 65 59 697, ⊛ tilostravel.co.uk).

Maps The best maps on Tílos are published by SKAI, while walking guides Iain and Lyn Fulton (☎ 22460 44128 or 694 60 54 593, ⊛ tilostrails.com) offer itineraries geared towards all levels.

GETTING AROUND

By bus A blue-and-white bus, charging €1.20, links Livádhia and Megálo Horió, to coincide with ferry arrivals. It also makes up to five runs daily between Livádhia and the beaches at Áyios Andónios and Éristos, plus a €4 round trip to Ayíou Pandelímona monastery on

Sunday mornings.

By taxi The island has one taxi (☎ 22460 44059).

By car and scooter Tilos Travel (☎ 22460 44294, ⊛ tilostravel.co.uk) and Drive (☎ 22460 44173) in Livádhia.

Livádhia

At its core, the port-cum-resort of **LIVÁDHIA**, at the head of a splendid bay on the island's north shore, is still recognizable as a traditional harbourfront village. A row of little tavernas, hotels and studios stretches away to the east, however, taking advantage of a narrow strip of beach that offers pleasant family swimming. The entire seafront is now lined by a broad pedestrian promenade, which is great for visitors even if it does diminish the "authentic" feel of the place. The bypass road that was supposed to take all vehicles around the back of the village hasn't quite materialized, however, so even the shortest journey by road can require labyrinthine detours. Once you're settled in you'll almost certainly walk everywhere local anyway.

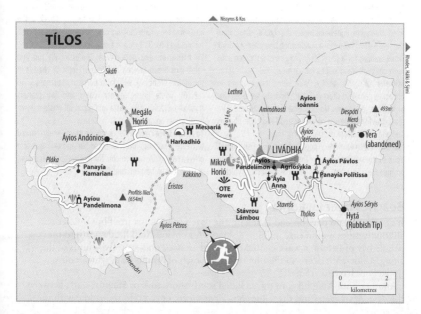

5

Anna's Studios ☎ 22460 44334, ⓦtilosrooms.gr. The immaculate units in this bright whitewashed building, on the west hillside immediately above the jetty, vary in size, but all have pastel-hued furnishings and kitchenettes, and several have enormous sea-view balconies. **€60**

Blue Sky ☎ 22460 44294, ⓦtilostravel.co.uk. Nine well-appointed apartments, right on the harbour just above the ferry jetty, and available year-round through Tilos Travel. Each is designed for three, with a galleried sleeping area, kitchen, and sea-view balcony. **€60**

Dream Island Hotel ☎ 22460 70707, ⓦdreamisland .gr. Assorted very spacious one- and two-bedroom apartments, within a few metres of the water roughly two-thirds of the way around the bay. All have at least partial sea views, and are decorated in cool contemporary colours. Rates include breakfast and sunbeds. **€130**

★ **Eleni Beach Hotel** ☎ 22460 44062, ⓦelenihoteltilos.gr. The best value on the shoreline, about halfway around the bay just as the continuous strip peters out. 36 airy, whitewashed rooms in four separate blocks; 31 have full-on sea views, five partial, and there's wheelchair access. Superbly attentive and sympathetic management. Rates include breakfast and sunbeds. **€60**

Faros Hotel ☎ 22460 44068, ⓔdimkouk@otenet.gr. Friendly hotel-cum-taverna, out on its own at the far east end of the bay. A dozen or so peaceful, well-cared-for three-bedded rooms, plus what's effectively its own beach. It's a ten-minute walk back to the main strip of restaurants, but the food here is perfectly good. **€70**

Ilidi Rock ☎ 22410 44293, ⓦtilosholidays.gr. Tílos' largest and newest hotel, dropping in bright-white tiers to water's edge at the west end of the bay, five minutes' walk from the ferry. State-of-the-art studios and apartments sleeping up to four; one wing has disabled access. Two little private pocket beaches, plus gym facilities. Open all year, breakfast served summer only. A/c available at extra cost. **€100**

Irini Hotel ☎ 22410 44293, ⓦtilosholidays.gr. Lushly landscaped low-rise hotel, 200m inland from the middle of the beach. The large pool, good breakfasts from the onsite café, wi-fi signal and pleasant gardens make up for somewhat small, mock-antique furnished rooms. **€60**

Tilos Fantasy ☎ 22460 44425, ⓦtilosfantasy.gr. Substantial modern complex of studios, in a quiet hillside location 400m back from the sea. They're perfectly presentable, though the furnishings look straight from IKEA and there are two single beds in each room. **€55**

EATING AND DRINKING

CaféBar Georges ☎ 22460 44257. Traditional old bar on the main square, where the outdoor tables are filled nightly with locals watching the world go by. Daily 8am–late.

Iy Omonoia ☎ 22460 44287. Enduringly popular traditional café, also known as *Tou Mihali*, stretching under trees strung with light bulbs beside the square, just up from the sea. A good venue for a sundowner, breakfast or a drink while waiting for a ferry; its inexpensive, tasty, generous mezédhes will stand in for a formal meal. Daily 8am–late.

Mihalis ☎ 22460 44359. Welcoming taverna, set in attractive gardens a short walk back from the sea, 50m east of the central square. No-nonsense fish for around €10, roast goat for a little less, as well as good vegetable platters and non-CAIR bulk wine. Daily 8am–late.

★ **Oneiro/Dream** Very popular "Grill and Fish House", open to the sea breezes near the centre of the beachfront promenade. Excellent grills and spit-roasts, typically costing €8 for meat and €12 for fish. Be prepared to wait for your food in high season. Daily lunch & dinner.

Taverna Trata ☎ 22460 44364. Relaxed taverna, 100m inland from the beach at the first bend in the road, serving good local food on a nice open-air terrace. Check in the kitchen to see what's cooking, or sample grilled meat or fish for around €10. Daily lunch & dinner.

To Armenon ☎ 22460 44134. Professionally run and salubrious beach-taverna-cum-ouzerí, right by the sea in the middle of the bay, with large portions of octopus salad (€8.50), white beans, meaty mains and fish platters (typically €12.50), plus pasta and pizza, all washed down by Alfa beer on tap. Daily 10am–late.

To Mikro Kafé Pretty little shoreline cottage, nicely restored to create a buzzing, music-oriented bar and café that also offers a reasonable snack menu. The rooftop terrace is a great spot for late-night stargazing. Daily 5pm–late.

Beaches near Livádhia

It's easy to spend days on end lazing on the beach at Livádhia itself but quieter alternatives lies within easy walking distance. An obvious trail heads north to the pebble bay of **Lethrá**, a walk that takes around an hour one-way. Two-thirds of the way along, a side-path drops to the tiny red-sand beach of **Ammóhosti**, which you're unlikely to have to yourself.

Another hour-long hike, to the secluded south-shore cove of **Stavrós**, starts between the *Tilos Mare Hotel* and the *Castellania Apartments*; once up to the saddle with its

5

paved road, you've a sharp drop to the beach. Ignore the cairns in the ravine bed; the true path is up on the right bank.

The trail to the similar cove of **Thólos**, also an hour's walk away on the south coast, begins by the cemetery and the chapel of **Áyios Pandelímon**, then curls under the seemingly impregnable castle of **Agriosykiá**. From the saddle on the paved road overlooking the descent to Thólos (25min; also red-marked), a cairned route leads northwest to the citadel in twenty minutes. Head east a couple of curves along that paved road to the trailhead for **Áyios Séryis Bay**, Tílos's most pristine beach but also the hardest to reach (30min from the road).

Mikró Horió

The ghost village of **Mikró Horió**, whose 1200 inhabitants left for Livádhia during the 1950s, is less than an hour's walk west of the port, with some surviving path sections short-cutting the road curves. Its only intact structures are churches (locked to protect their frescoes) and an old house restored as a small-hours **music bar** (July–Aug).

Megálo Horió

Tílos's capital, the village of **MEGÁLO HORIÓ**, lies 7km west of Livádhia along the main road. The only other significant settlement on the island, it enjoys sweeping views over the vast agricultural plain that stretches down to Éristos, and is overlooked in turn by a prominent **Knights' castle**. Reaching the castle requires a stiff thirty-minute climb, which threads its way through a vast jumble of cisterns, house foundations and derelict chapels.

A little **museum** in the town hall (summer only, daily 8.30am–2.30pm; free) displays the bones of midget elephants, found in the **Harkadhió cave** not far east in 1971. Such remains have been found on a number of Mediterranean islands, but Tílos's group may have been the last to survive, until as recently as 4000 BC.

Long, pink-grey-sand **Éristos beach**, 3km south of Megálo Horió, ranks among the island's finest, though swimmers have to cross a reef to reach open sea. The far south end, where the reef recedes, is nudist, as are the two secluded all-naturist coves at **Kókkino** beyond the headland (accessible by path from the obvious military pillbox).

ACCOMMODATION AND EATING — MEGÁLO HORIÓ

Eden Villas Megálo Horió ☏ 22460 44094, ⓦ eden-villas.com. Choice option run by Brits, this comfortable three-bedroom villa, with pool and wi-fi, is nicely located 500m north of Megálo Horió in the valley that leads towards Skáfi beach. Available for extended stays all year round. **€200**

Eristos Beach Hotel Éristos ☏ 22460 44025. Crisp modern complex facing the large, barely developed beach at Éristos on the southwest, with lots of outdoor space, including a pleasant terrace. Hotel rooms with big balconies, and sizeable apartments suitable for four. **€60**

Kastro Megálo Horió ☏ 22460 44232. While the interior of Megálo's only taverna can be a little gloomy, its patio has lovely long-range views, and the food is good, with meat and goat cheese from their own flock, and home-made *dolmádhes*. Daily lunch & dinner.

Milios Apartments Megálo Horió ☏ 22460 44204. Attractive rooms and apartments set in pleasant flowery gardens in the heart of Megálo Horió. All have balconies offering (distant) sea views. **€50**

The far northwest

The main road west of Megálo Horió hits the coast again at somewhat grim **ÁYIOS ANDÓNIOS**, which has an exposed, truncated beach and two tavernas. There's better, warm-water swimming at isolated, sandy **Pláka beach**, another 2km west, where people camp rough despite a total lack of facilities.

5

Ayíou Pandelímona monastery

Daily: May–Sept 10am–7pm, may close briefly at noon; Oct–April 10am–4pm

The paved road ends 8km west of Megálo Horió at fortified **Ayíou Pandelímona monastery**, founded in the fifteenth century for the sake of its miraculous spring, still the best water on the island. A fitfully operating drinks café hosts the island's major **festival** of July 25–27. The monastery's tower-gate and oasis setting, high above the forbidding west coast, are its most memorable features, though a photogenic inner courtyard boasts a *votsalotó* surface, and the church a fine tesselated mosaic floor.

Níssyros

The volcanic island of **Níssyros** is unlike its neighbours in almost every respect. It's much lusher and greener than dry Tílos and Hálki to the south, blessed with rich soil that nurtures a distinctive flora, and it supported a large agricultural population in ancient times. In contrast to long flat Kos to the north, Níssyros is round and tall, with the high walls of its central caldera rising abruptly from the shoreline around its entire perimeter. And Níssyros conceals a startling secret; behind those encircling hills, the interior of the island is **hollow**, centring on a huge crater floor that's dotted with still-steaming vents and cones.

For most visitors, the volcano is Níssyros' main attraction. It's easy enough to see it on a day-trip from Kos, so few bother to spend the night. That's a shame, because it's a genuinely lovely island, very short on beaches but abounding in spectacular scenery. The port and sole large town, **Mandhráki** on the northwest coast, is an appealing tight-knit community with some fine ancient ruins, while two delightful villages, Emboriós and Nikiá, straddle the crater ridge.

These days, much of the island's income is derived from the offshore islet of **Yialí**, a vast lump of pumice, all too clearly visible just north of Mandhráki, that's slowly being quarried away. Substantial concession fees have given the islanders economic security.

Níssyros also offers good **walking**, on trails that lead through a countryside studded with oak and terebinth (pigs gorge themselves on the abundant acorns, and pork figures prominently on menus).

ARRIVAL AND DEPARTURE   NÍSSYROS

By ferry Ferries moor at a concrete jetty a few hundred metres east of Mandhráki, out of sight of town. Níssyros is connected with the following ports: Astypálea (1 weekly; 5hr 30min); Hálki (2 weekly; 1hr 40min); Kálymnos (2 weekly; 2hr 50min); Kastellórizo (2 weekly; 8hr 30min); Kos Kardamena (3 weekly; 40min); Kos Town (8 weekly; 1hr–1hr 40min); Náxos (1 weekly; 10hr); Páros (1 weekly; 12hr); Pireás (1 weekly; 17hr 30min); Rhodes (4 weekly; 3hr 10min–4hr 45min); Sými (3 weekly; 3–4hr); Tílos (3 weekly; 50min).

Travel agencies Dhiakomihalis (☏ 22240 31459) or Kendris (☏ 22420 31227).

GETTING AROUND

By bus Buses from the jetty head up to six times daily to Emboriós and Nikiá, via Páli.

By taxi For fixed-rate taxi service, call ☏ 22420 31460.

By car and scooter Rental outlets include Manos K on Mandhráki harbour (☏ 22420 31029), and Dhiakomihalis in town (☏ 22240 31459).

By coach Several coach trips daily set off from the jetty to visit the volcano. English-run Enetikon Travel, nearby on the road into town (☏ 22420 31180, ✉ agiosnis@otenet .gr), are typical in offering €8 round trips every morning from 10.30am onwards, each of which takes a total of 1hr 45min.

Mandhráki

The ancient harbour of **MANDHRÁKI**, the capital of Níssyros, silted up centuries ago, creating a fertile patch that now serves as the *kámbos* (community orchard), surrounded in turn by the modern town. Nonetheless this remains the island's sole ferry port

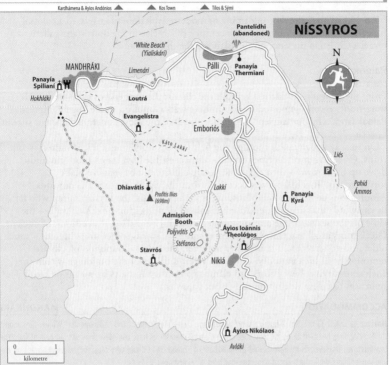

– boats pull in at a concrete jetty to the east, out of sight of the centre. Mandhráki's a nice little place, stretching along the seashore slightly further than appears at first glance. Behind the pedestrianized waterfront promenade, to some extent overwhelmed by poor tavernas and souvenir stores aimed at day-trippers, the tangled narrow lanes are lined with whitewashed houses, whose brightly painted balconies and shutters are mandated by law. The ensemble is punctuated by appealing little squares, and offers repeated glimpses of fruit trees to one side, and blue sea to the other.

At its western end, Mandhráki comes to an abrupt halt at a low bluff that's topped by the stout walls of a **Knights' castle**. Though records have been lost, the Knights Hospitaller occupied Níssyros from 1314 until 1522, and it's thought to have reached its heyday around 1400. You can't access any more of the castle itself than the corner staircase and gateway that leads to the little **Panayía Spilianí monastery**, generally open daylight hours.

Langadháki, the district immediately below the castle, was badly hit by earthquakes in the 1990s, but little damage is now visible. At sea level, an attractive mosaic footpath leads further west around the headland to reach the short, black-rock beach of **Hokhláki**, which is seldom suitable for swimming.

Archeological Museum

Daily 8.30am–3pm • Free

Níssyros's modern **Archeological Museum**, a couple of blocks back from the sea on the main lane, holds assorted treasures from the island's past. The main floor focuses on the pre-Christian era, starting with six-thousand-year-old artefacts created using obsidian from nearby Yialí. Ceramic pieces range from delicate winged figurines of Eros, dating

5

from 350 BC but closely conforming to modern depictions of angels, to a colossal funerary pithos (urn) from the sixth century BC. Stelae in the downstairs galleries reveal a Christian presence on the island in the third century.

Paleókastro

Unrestricted access

From the Langadháki district, beneath the cliffs at the west end of the Mandhráki waterfront, a well-signposted twenty-minute walk climbs up to the hugely impressive **Paleókastro**, a mighty ancient fortress that's one of the most underrated ancient sites in Greece.

On its way up, the path through the fields passes numerous ancient stairways and ruins. Once you meet a cement road – also accessible on a much more circuitous drive up from town – turn right and you're confronted by massive black fortifications. This hilltop was occupied from the eighth century BC onwards. Around four centuries later, Mausolus of Halicarnassus, the Persian satrap who left us the word "mausoleum", enclosed its inland slopes within 3m-thick walls – the cliffs on the seaward side already formed a natural boundary. If you think of ancient Greek ruins as all graceful white marble columns, this is something different – much older and vaster. Slotted chinklessly together, the colossal trapezoid blocks are reminiscent of Inca masonry. Only the barest outlines of the buildings within the enclosure survive, but visitors can clamber onto the ramparts by means of broad staircases to either side of the still-intact gateway.

ACCOMMODATION   MANDHRÁKI

Haritos ☎ 22420 31322. Small hotel, a short walk from the ferry landing; head left along the coast road rather than towards town. Its eleven rooms have marble-trimmed baths and veneer floors, while the seafront across the road holds a terrace restaurant and a hot-spring pool. Open all year. **€60**

Porfyris ☎ 22420 31376, ⊛ porfyris-nisyros.com. Large, somewhat old-fashioned hotel, well back from the sea in the town centre, overlooking the common orchards. Most of the 38 spruce a/c rooms have sea views from private balconies and terraces, and there's also a large swimming pool and breakfast terrace. **€65**

Romantzo ☎ 22420 31340, ⊛ nisyros-romantzo.gr. Good-value family-run hotel, up to the left of the ferry jetty out of sight of the town, with simple but comfortable a/c

en-suite rooms and apartments. While the rooms themselves have rear-view windows, all benefit from the broad, shared and very pleasant sea-view terrace on the first floor. **€35**

★ **Ta Liotridia** ☎ 22420 31580, ⊜ liotridia@nisyrosnet.gr. Two incongruously gorgeous suites, above a rough-and-ready bar just metres from the sea on the oceanfront footpath in the centre of town. Exposed stone walls, incorporating lava boulders; fine wooden furnishings; and head-on sea views. Each sleeps up to four. **€150**

Xenon Polyvotis ☎ 22420 31011. Municipally owned hotel, on the quayside facing the ferry port; its en-suite rooms are large but utterly unremarkable, but there's no faulting the sea views. June–Sept only. **€60**

EATING AND DRINKING

Irini Platía Ilikiomenis ☎ 22420 31365. Lively restaurant, in a busy little tree-shaded square, inland at the west end of town, that's all but entirely filled with bar and taverna tables. Hearty traditional dishes like aubergine and mince, or pepper stuffed with rice for €6–8. In truth the food isn't exceptional, but it's a convivial and involving place to spend an evening. Daily lunch & dinner.

Kali Katsou Cheap and cheerful local specialities poised immediately above the water on the quayside, including seafood such as mussels or squid as well as tasty island sausages for just €6. Daily lunch & dinner.

Kleanthis ☎ 22420 31484. The best seafood restaurant

along the waterfront, with bright blue tables and chairs set out on the quayside, and busy for lunch and dinner. Tasty *pittiá* (chickpea croquettes) and other mezes, followed by fish dishes ranging from fried shrimps for €8 up to stuffed squid with cheese or swordfish for €16. Daily lunch & dinner.

Proveza ☎ 22420 31618, ⊛ proveza.net. Lively café-bar with extensive comfortable seating on the seafront promenade near *Ta Liotridia*. Besides being great for a sunset drink, with an appropriate soundtrack, it also offers free wi-fi and a row of internet-access computers indoors. Daily 11am–late.

5

The coast

Níssyros is almost entirely devoid of **beaches**, and only a small proportion of its coast – along the north and northwest shoreline – is even accessible to visitors. While the coast road east from Mandhráki peters out after barely 10km, it does make a pretty drive – and you'll have to come this way anyway if you're heading for the volcano. The largest structures en route are a couple of huge abandoned spas, dating back to the Italian era.

Four kilometres along, **PÁLLI** is a fishing village turned low-key resort that can be a welcome retreat when Mandhráki fills with trippers. All summer, the little harbour here is busy enough with pleasure boats – which can't moor at Mandhráki – to support several tavernas. Pálli also has an excellent **bakery**, cranking out tasty brown bread and pies. A reasonable tamarisk-shaded **beach** of reddish-grey sand, kept well groomed, extends east to the derelict Pantelídhi spa, behind which the little grotto-chapel of **Panayía Thermianí** is tucked inside the vaulted remains of a Roman baths complex.

Keep going beyond Pálli, along an initially bleak stretch of shore, to the pleasant cove of **Liés**, home to the summer-only Oasis snack-bar. The paved road ends at a car park a little further on, a spot that can also be reached in summer by taxi boats from Mandhráki. There's a grey-sand beach right here, while another fifteen minutes by trail over the headland brings you to the idyllic, 300m expanse of **Pahiá Ámmos**, with grey-pink sand heaped in dunes, limited shade at the far end and a large colony of rough campers and naturists in summer.

ACCOMMODATION AND EATING

THE COAST

Ellinis Pálli ☎ 22420 31397. This long-established taverna is the best in Pálli, serving spit-roasted meat by night and grilled fish in season, all at reasonable prices, and offering a handful of simple rooms upstairs. **€45**

★ **Limenari** Limenari valley ☎ 22420 310233. Excellent traditional cooking, in an attractive location just below the main road 1km west of Pálli, halfway down a terraced valley towards its little namesake bay. Fair prices for big portions of home-style food. Daily lunch & dinner.

Mammis Apartments Pálli ☎ 22420 31453. A dozen tasteful self-contained a/c apartments, capable of sleeping four and equipped with large sea-view balconies and their own separate entrances, perched amid hillside gardens a short walk west of Pálli. **€60**

The interior

If you've come to Níssyros to see the **volcano**, you're already there – the whole island is the volcano. Beyond and behind the steep slopes that climb from the shoreline, the entire centre of the island consists of a vast bowl-shaped depression. The hills end in a slender ridge that's the rim of the caldera, meaning that the two hilltop villages that survive, **Emboriós** and **Nikía**, are long thin strips that enjoy stupendous views both out to sea and down into the maw. The interior is etched almost in its entirety with ancient agricultural terraces, mostly long abandoned but giving a very real sense of the much greater population in antiquity. A side road just beyond Emboriós offers the only road access, and continues south to the craters at the far end.

Emboriós

The road up from Pálli winds first past the all-but-abandoned village of **EMBORIÓS**. As is obvious from the copious ruins that stretch high above the current village centre, the population here once numbered in the thousands; in winter these days it dwindles to just twenty. It's a gorgeous spot though, which not surprisingly is being bought up and restored by Athenians and foreigners. New owners often discover natural volcanic saunas in the basements of the crumbling houses; at the outskirts of the village there's a signposted public **steam bath** in a grotto, its entrance outlined in white paint. It's possible to hike down to the caldera floor from Emboriós; a trail drops from behind the little platía and it's another fifteen-minute walk to the craters.

Some 3km south of Emboriós, a paved drive leads down from the main road to **Panayía Kyrá**, the island's oldest and most venerable monastery, worth a stop for its enchanting, arcaded festival courtyard as much as its church.

5

HIKING ON NÍSSYROS ISLAND

Níssyros is a fabulous destination for hikers, with enticing trails to suit all abilities. The one drawback is that hiking to and from the volcano from Mandhráki is for most walkers too much to attempt in a single day. It's not so much the distance that's the problem as the fact that you have to climb back out of the island interior on your way home. SKAI publish a good topographical **map** (ⓦ shop.skai.gr).

VOLCANO TO MANDHRÁKI

About 1km north of the volcano admission booth, a clear, crudely marked path climbs to a pass, then maintains altitude along the north flank of **Káto Lákki** gulch, emerging after ninety minutes at the important monastery of **Evangelístra** with its giant terebinth tree just outside. Beyond Evangelístra, you have to walk about 1km on the paved access road before the old path kicks in for the final half-hour down to Mandhráki. Look sharp at curves to find the old walled-in path. At first it just short-cuts the road, then for quite a long stretch it loops above the port well away from the road, before finally curling around to emerge above the local school.

NIKIÁ TO EMBORIÓS

Hiking from **Nikiá to Emboriós** takes just under ninety minutes, with a short stretch of road-walking towards the end. Descend from Nikiá towards the volcano and bear right towards Theológos monastery, then take the left fork by the wooden gate before reaching it. The path ambles along through neglected terraces, without much altitude change, occasionally obstructed by debris and vegetation. You eventually emerge after just under an hour by some utility poles on the modern Emboriós–Nikiá road. Follow the road from there for about 1km (15min) to the turn-off for Lakkí, where the onward trail continues conspicuously uphill into Emboriós.

Nikiá

The village of **NIKIÁ**, overlooking the caldera from high on its southeastern rim, is a gorgeous little place that should figure on any island itinerary. Its spectacular location, 14km from Mandhráki, enjoys panoramic views out to Tílos as well as across the volcano. Tiny lanes lead from the bus turnaround at road's end to railed volcano viewpoints as well as to the diminutive, engagingly round central platía called Pórta. Paved in pebble mosaic, ringed by stone seating for folk dances, and facing a pretty little church, it's all so dazzlingly white that it's hard to keep your eyes open.

A 45-minute trail descends from the end of the road to the crater floor. A few minutes downhill, detour briefly to the eyrie-like monastery of **Áyios Ioánnis Theológos**, whose festival grounds come to life at the September 25–26 evening festival.

EATING AND DRINKING   THE INTERIOR

Andriotis Nikiá ☏ 22420 31027. The only taverna in Nikiá, at the village entrance, with huge views out over the sea, serves a good menu of meaty €6 specials, including rabbit or chicken stews, and succulent chocolatey desserts. Summer only, daily lunch & dinner.

★ **Apyria** Emboriós ☏ 22420 31377. Excellent little taverna, which spreads out into the platía by the church in peak season, and otherwise has a couple of tables crammed into a tiny alleyway, and a breezy indoor dining

room. Delicious local food at great prices, including spit-roasted suckling pig in summer as well as grills and mezédhes. The friendly owner is also a beekeeper; be sure to sample fresh honey if you're here in July. Dinner daily all year, lunch daily in summer, Sunday only in winter.

Porta Pangiotis Nikiá ☏ 22420 31285. This welcoming village café, one of a matching pair on Nikiá's tiny, delightful circular platía, is an irresistible spot to pause for a snack, juice or coffee. Daily 10am–8pm.

Visiting the volcano

What's loosely referred to as being the "volcano" is the eerie conglomeration of cinder cones and deep craters at the far southern end of the summit caldera, reached by a single road that drops down beyond Emboriós. Although the volcano is dormant, and you won't therefore see fiery eruptions or flowing lava, it's disconcertingly alive, with sulphurous steam sprouting from holes and fissures on all sides. Access is unrestricted, though occasionally a ticket booth charges €2.50 admission. A snack bar opens at peak times only.

A steady procession of coach trips from Mandhráki (see p.306) usually keeps the area busy between 11am and 3pm; to enjoy it in solitude, make your own way up early or late in the day. Either rent a vehicle, or choose from the hiking possibilities on p.311.

As soon as you follow the short trail from the road's-end car park to the fenced overlook, you realize that while the main crater – officially named **Stéfanos** – may look small from a distance, close-up it's a massive, hissing, stinking pit. Its striated walls, yellow with sulphur, drop straight down 40m to a flat stained floor that's pockmarked with bubbling fumaroles. You can venture down there via an easy trail that winds along a timeworn groove in the crater wall. Don't get too close to the boiling mud-pots, which sound as though there's a huge cauldron bubbling away beneath you. In legend this is the groaning of the titan Polyvotis, crushed by Poseidon under a huge rock torn from Kos.

The hillside immediately west holds several steep-sided cones, accessible via an obvious and undemanding trail. Climbing up lets you escape the crowds, and also offers a greater thrill of discovery. It seems a shame to reveal what awaits you at the top, but rest assured it's worth it.

Kos

After Rhodes, **KOS** ranks second among the Dodecanese islands for both size and visitor numbers. Here too the harbour in **Kos Town** is guarded by an imposing castle of the Knights of St John, the streets are lined with Italian-built public buildings, and minarets and palm trees punctuate extensive Hellenistic and Roman remains. And while its hinterland mostly lacks the wild beauty of Rhodes' interior, Kos is the most fertile island in the archipelago, blessed with rich soil and abundant ground water.

Mass **tourism**, however, has largely displaced the old agrarian way of life; all-inclusive complexes comprising tens of thousands of beds are a blight that contribute little to the local economy, and have forced many restaurants and more modest hotels out of business. Except in Kos Town and Mastihári, there are few independent travellers, and from mid-July to mid-September you'll be lucky to find a room without reserving far in advance, while the tourist industry itself is juxtaposed rather bizarrely with cows munching amid baled hay near olive groves, and Greek Army tanks exercising in the volcanic badlands around the airport. Like Tílos further south, Kos never had to earn its living from the sea and consequently has little in the way of a maritime tradition or a contemporary fishing fleet. All these peculiarities acknowledged, Kos is still worth a few days' time while island-hopping: its few **mountain villages** are appealing, the tourist infrastructure excellent and **swimming** opportunities limitless – about half the island's perimeter is fringed by beaches of various sizes, colours and consistencies.

ARRIVAL AND INFORMATION — KOS

By plane The local airport is just outside Andimahía in the very centre of the island, 24km southwest of Kos Town. Destinations served include Astypálea (2–3 weekly); Athens (5–7 daily); Iráklio, Crete (3 weekly); Léros (2–3 weekly); Rhodes (2–3 weekly); and Thessaloníki (2 weekly). Taxis (☎ 22420 23333, Ⓦ kostaxi.eu) charge around €35 to Kos Town, and more like €20 to Mastihári or Kardhámena. Bus services are detailed below.

By ferry Kos Town is connected by ferry to Agathoníssi (1 weekly; 2hr 40min); Astypálea (1 weekly; 4hr 30min); Hálki (2 weekly; 2hr 45min); Kálymnos (2–5 daily; 30min–1hr); Kastellórizo (1 weekly; 9hr 45min); Léros (1–3 daily; 1hr 25min–3hr); Lipsí (2–3 daily; 2hr 10min–4hr 10min); Níssyros (8 weekly; 1hr–1hr 40min); Pátmos (2–4 daily; 1hr 35min–5hr); Pireás (12 weekly; 10–14hr); Rhodes (1–5 daily; 2hr 10min–6hr 15min); Samos (1 daily; 3hr 30min); Sými (11 weekly; 1hr 30min–4hr 50min); Syros (1 weekly; 5hr 30min); Thíra (2 weekly; 5hr); and Tílos (2 weekly; 1hr 50min–2hr 50min). In addition, Mastihári on the north coast has frequent connections with Kálymnos (6 daily; 20min–1hr), and Kardhámena is connected with Níssyros (2 weekly; 40min).

International ferries Kos Town also has frequent ferry and excursion-boat connections to Bodrum in Turkey (30–45min).

Tourist office Akti Koundouriotou 7 in Kos Town (Mon–Fri 7.30am–2.45pm; ☎ 22420 24460, Ⓦ kosinfo.gr).

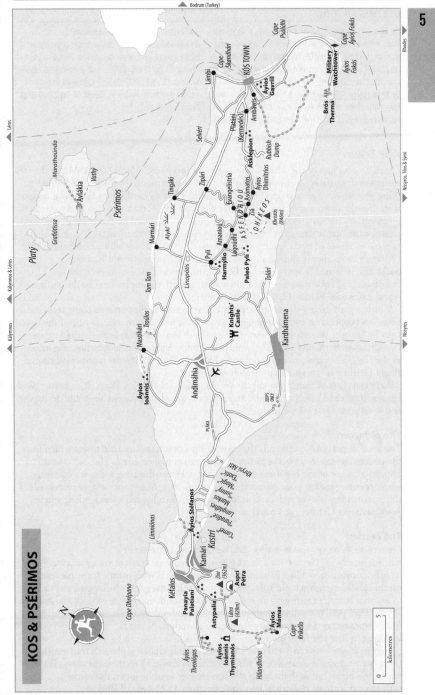

KOS & PSÉRIMOS

Bodrum (Turkey)

Rhodes

Léros

Kálymnos & Léros

Kálymnos

Nissyros

Nissyros, Tílos & Sými

Rhodes

Marathoúnda

Avláki

Vathý

Grafiótissa

PSÉRIMOS

Platý

KÓS TOWN

Cape Skandhári

Cape Psálidhi

Cape Ayíos Fokás

Ayíos Fokás

Military Watchtower

Lámbi

AYÍOS
GAVRIÍL

Brós
Thermá

Platáni
(Kermedé)

Amanioú

Asklepíon

Rubbish
Dump

Selvéri

Tingáki

Zipári

Evangelístria

Ayíos
Dhimítrios

Ayios Asómatos

Zía

Khóstos
(846m)

Marmári

Alykí

A S F E N D H I O U

D H I K E O S

Amanioú

Lagoúdhi

Harmýlio

Paleó Pylí

Pylí

Tóldri

Linopótis

Tam Tam

Troúlos

Mastihári

Knights'
Castle

Kardhámena

Andimáhia

JEEPS
ONLY

PLAKA

Limniónas

Ayíos Stéfanos

Kamári

Kéfalos

Kastrí

"Camel"

"Paradise"

Langádhes

Markos

Magic"

"Sunny"

"Exotic"

Khrysí Aktí

Cape Dhrépano

Panayía
Palatiáni

Astypália

Zíni
(362m)

Aspri
Petra

Ayíos
Theológos

Ayíos Ioánnis
Thymianós

Látra
(428m)

Ayíos
Mámas

Cape
Kríkello

Hiliandhríou

N

0   5
kilometres

5

GETTING AROUND

By bus KTEL buses are based in Kos Town, with several stops around a triangular park 400m back from the water, and an information booth adjacent at Kleopátras 7 (☎ 22420 22292). Buses between Kos Town and the airport also call at Mastihári (3–6 daily; €3.20).

Cycle rental Bicycles make an excellent way to get around Kos; much of the island is very flat, and Kos Town has an extensive system of cycle lanes. George's Bikes, Spetson 48

(☎ 22420 24157), has a good selection.

By car and scooter Cars can be rented at the airport and all the resorts. Kos Town outlets include Budget at Vassiléos Pávlou 31 (☎ 22420 28882) and AutoWay at Vassiléos Yeoryíou 22 (☎ 22420 25326, ⓦ autowaykos.gr). For a scooter, try Moto Harley at Kanári 42 (☎ 22420 27693, ⓦ moto-harley.nl).

Kos Town

Home to over half of the island's population of just over 28,000, **KOS TOWN**, at the far eastern end, radiates out from the harbour and feels remarkably uncluttered. The first thing you see from an arriving ferry is a majestic **Knights' castle**, for once down at sea level, but the town also holds extensive **Hellenistic** and **Roman** remains. Only revealed by an earthquake in 1933, these were subsequently excavated by the Italians, who also planned the "garden suburbs" that extend to either side of the central grid. Elsewhere, sizeable expanses of open space or archeological zone alternate with a hotchpotch of Ottoman monuments and later mock-medieval, Art Deco-ish and Rationalist buildings, designed in two phases either side of the earthquake. As ever, they incorporate a "Foro Italico" – the Italian administrative complex next to the castle – and a Casa del Fascio (Fascist Headquarters).

A little square facing the castle holds the riven trunk of **Hippocrates' plane tree**, its branches propped up by scaffolding; at seven hundred years of age, it's one of the oldest trees in Europe, though it's far too young to have seen the great healer. Adjacent are two **Ottoman fountains** and the eighteenth-century **Hassan Pasha mosque**, also known as the Loggia Mosque; its ground floor – like that of the **Defterdar mosque** on central Platía Eleftherías – is taken up by rows of shops.

Ferry travellers in transit are effectively obliged to stay in Kos Town. It's a pretty good base, with decent hotels, the best restaurants on the island, reasonable public transport, and several car- and bike-rental agencies.

The old town

The liveliest part of Kos Town is the thoroughly commercialized **old town**, which lines the pedestrianized street between the Italian market hall on Platía Eleftherías and Platía Dhiagóras. One of the few areas to survive the 1933 earthquake, today it's crammed with expensive tourist boutiques, cafés and snack-bars. About the only genuinely old thing remaining is a capped Turkish fountain with a calligraphic inscription, where Apéllou meets Eleftheríou Venizélou.

The castle

April–Oct Mon 3.30–8pm, Tues–Sun 8am–7pm; Nov–March Tues–Sun 8.30am–2.30pm • €3

Known locally as "Nerantziás", the **castle** in Kos Town is reached via a causeway over its former moat, now filled in as an avenue and planted with palms. It's a splendid, tumbledown, overgrown old ruin, where once inside the gate, which turns out to lead to another broader moat with an inner fortress beyond, you're free to walk and stumble at your own peril over all sorts of walls, battlements and stairways, as well as the odd much more recent and unattractive concrete accretion. At the far end, you find yourself looking out over the ferry quays.

Built in stages between 1450 and 1514, the double citadel replaced a fourteenth-century fort deemed incapable of withstanding advances in medieval artillery. Few if any of the many cannonballs lying about were ever fired in anger; the castle surrendered without resistance after the marathon 1522 siege of Rhodes.

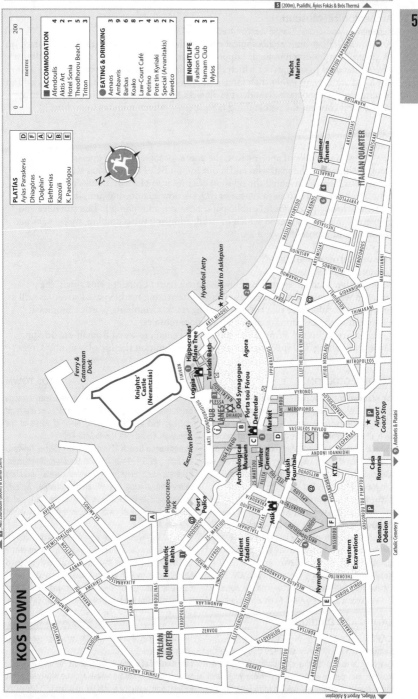

KOS TOWN

PLATÍAS
Ayías Paraskevís	D
Dhiagóras	F
"Dolphin"	A
Eleftherías	C
Kazoúli	B
K. Paeológou	E

■ ACCOMMODATION
Afendoúlis	4
Aktis Art	2
Hotel Sonia	1
Theodhorou Beach	5
Triton	3

● EATING & DRINKING
Aenaos	3
Ambavris	9
Barbas	6
Koako	8
Law-Court Café	1
Petrino	4
Pote tin Kyriaki	5
Special (Arvanitakis)	2
Swedco	7

■ NIGHTLIFE
Fashion Club	2
Hamam Club	3
Mylos	1

0   metres   200

5 (200m), Psalídhi, Áyios Fokás & Brós Thermá

Yacht Marina

ITALIAN QUARTER

Summer Cinema

Hydrofoil Jetty

★ Trenáki to Asklepíon

Ferry & Catamaran Dock

Knights' Castle (Neratziás)

Excursion Boats

Hippocrates' Plane Tree

Turkish Bath

Agora

Old Synagogue

Loggia

Pórta toú Fórou

LANES

Defterdar

Market

PLESSA

DHIAKOU

Archeological Museum

Winter Cinema

Turkish Fountain

KTEL

Casa Romana

Hippocrates Park

Port Police

Asik

Ancient Stadium

Hellenistic Baths

Western Excavations

Nymphaion

Roman Odeion

Catholic Cemetery

★ P Airport Coach Stop

Ambávris & Plátani

Villages, Airport & Asklepíon

Aktí Zouroúdhi (800m) & Lámbi (2km)

ITALIAN QUARTER

ITALIAN QUARTER

5

Archeological Museum

Platía Eleftherías • April–Oct Tues–Sun 8am–8pm; Nov–March Tues–Sun 8.30am–2.30pm • €3

Kos Town's Italian-built **archeological museum** has a predictable Latin bias. Centred on an atrium that holds a mosaic of Hippocrates welcoming Asklepios to Kos, it's almost entirely devoted to statuary, of which the best preserved and most prominently displayed are Roman rather than Greek. That said, the single most famous item, said to be a statue of Hippocrates, is indeed Hellenistic. With no captions to put the displays in historical context, the whole thing takes around fifteen minutes to explore.

The agora

Unrestricted access in daylight hours

The largest single relic of ancient Kos, the **agora**, occupies a huge open site just back from the harbour. The man who laid it out in 366 BC, Hippodamus, was credited by Aristotle as having "invented the division of cities into blocks". Thanks to earthquakes between the second and sixth centuries AD, it's now a confusing jumble of ruins. Scattered through a delightful public park, however, abounding in bougainvillea and palmettos, it's a lovely area in which to stroll, admiring the crumbling walls, standing columns, and exposed mosaics.

The western excavations

Unrestricted access in daylight hours

Set in pit-like gardens up to 4m below the street level of modern Kos Town, the so-called **western excavations** consist of two intersecting marble-paved streets as well as the Xystos or colonnade of a covered running track. Crumbling plastic canopies at either end of the L-shaped complex shelter **floor mosaics**.

Across Grigoríou toú Pémptou to the south, a small, restored Roman-era **odeion**, capable of seating 750 spectators in 14 rows, was built on the site of a similar Greek theatre.

ACCOMMODATION   KOS TOWN

★ **Afendoulis** Evrypýlou 1 ☎22420 25321, ⓦafendoulishotel.com. Large, balconied en-suite rooms – including a few family quads – with fridges, a/c and wi-fi, all at excellent prices. Alexis Zikas, brother Ippokrates and wife Dionysia really look after their guests, winning a loyal repeat clientele; top-quality breakfast at any reasonable hour. Credit cards accepted. Closed mid-Nov to mid-March. **€50**

Aktis Art Vassiléos Yeoryíou 7 ☎22420 47200, ⓦkosaktis.gr. Designer hotel whose futuristic standard doubles or suites, in brown, grey and beige, all face the water. Bathrooms are naturally lit and have butler sinks. There's wi-fi, gym, conference area, seaside bar and affiliated restaurant. All year. **€200**

Hotel Sonia Irodhótou 9, cnr Omírou ☎22420 25594. Popular, friendly little hotel, across from the agora and formerly known as *Pension Alexis*. Its eleven wood-floored

rooms have been thoroughly renovated with en-suite bathrooms, a/c and wi-fi; there's also a pleasant courtyard and bar. Run by the sister and niece of Alexis of the *Afendoulis*. Closed early Nov to April. **€60**

Theodhorou Beach 1200m from the centre, towards Psalídhi ☎22420 22280, ⓦtheodorouhotel.com. Generous-sized units with disabled access, including suites and a wing of self-catering studios. A leafy environment includes a lawn-pool at the back and a small "private" beach with the *Nostos* day-and-night café-bar. **€80**

Triton Vassiléos Yeoryíou 4 ☎22420 20040, ⓦmaritina.gr. Moderately upmarket, town-centre seafront hotel, part of a small local chain, with veneered floored rooms (not all with sea view) in a neutral decor. Bathrooms somewhat small; the ground-floor *Avanti* Italian restaurant and breakfast café is popular. **€80**

EATING AND DRINKING

CAFÉS

Aenaos Platía Eleftherías ☎22420 26044. Join the largely local crowd at this café under the Defterdar mosque, and people-watch while refilling your Greek coffee from the traditional *bríki* used to brew it. They

also serve a range of teas and flavoured hot chocolates. Daily 9am–late.

Law-Court Café Finikon. Some of the cheapest and best-brewed coffees in Kos are available (along with cold drinks) under the arches at the rear of the courthouse, a few paces from Hippocrates' plane tree; no sign outside, mostly civil-servant clientele. Daily 8am–8pm.

Special (Arvanitakis) Vassiléos Yeoryíou ☎ 22420 22087. This tiny hole-in-the-wall pastry and cake shop, right by the sea, also serves dynamite gelato. Daily 10am–7pm.

Swedco Vassiléos Pávlou 20 ☎ 22420 24154. Ultra-sleek outlet of the Rhodes café chain, with (pricey) sandwiches, hot drinks and decadent desserts, as well as internet access. Daily 10am–11pm.

RESTAURANTS

★ **Ambavris** Vourina ☎ 22420 25696, ⓦ ampavris.gr. Top-notch restaurant, 500m south of the edge of town, in the eponymous suburb village. Skip the English-only à la carte menu, take the hint about mezédhes and let the house bring on their best. This changes seasonally but won't much exceed €25 (drink extra) for six plates – typically pinigoúri (bulgur pilaf), pikhtí (brawn), little fish, spicy loukánika, stuffed squash flowers and fáva. May–Oct, dinner only.

Barbas Evrypýlou 6 ☎ 693 71 42 802. Friendly restaurant, opposite Hotel Afendoulis (see opposite). Excellent grills, with giros at €6–7.50 and lamb for €9, as well as the odd seafood choice like octopus salad for €6, all served at cosy outdoor tables. Closed Nov–March. Daily

10am–12.30pm & 5pm–12.30am.

Koako Vassilios Yeoryíou 56 ☎ 22420 25645. This spartan-looking place, with a crisp minimalist terrace just steps from the sea at the south end of Kos Town, is a versatile all-rounder, handling grilled meat and fish, mezédhes and a few daily mayireftá with equal aplomb – all priced below €10 – without the usual multinational flags and photo-menus. Daily lunch & dinner, all year.

Petrino Platía Theológou 1 ☎ 22420 27251, ⓦ petrino .kosweb.com. Elegant garden-set place, which has recently re-invented itself as a "meze restaurant", with a menu that ranges through fish, shellfish, meat and the local hard cheese. Almost nothing costs over €10, though share a few plates and the bill mounts up. As well as the extensive outdoor seating, two cosy indoor salons allow year-round operation (dinner only); large groups should reserve. Dinner only, 6–11pm.

★ **Pote tin Kyriaki** Pissándhrou 9 ☎ 22420 27872. Kos's sole genuine ouzerí, whose creatively assembled menu (painstakingly written out in school exercise books) has delights such as shrimps, fried mussels or gávros, monastiriakí (Cretan "monk's" salad), as well as grilled chops and loukánika. Look out for the couscous-like pinigoúri, served with pork for €4. Summer Mon–Sat evenings only, winter Thurs–Sat evenings plus lunch.

NIGHTLIFE AND ENTERTAINMENT

Kos Town has a hyperactive nightlife. Visitors from all over the island congregate each night in the so-called "Pub Lanes", Nafklírou and Dhiákou, filled with an ever-changing array of generally mediocre bars and clubs. There are newer, better nightlife areas around Platía Dhiagóra (mostly Greeks) and out at Aktí Zouroúdhi towards Lambi.

Fashion Club Kanari 2 ☎ 22420 22592. Beyond its large and very shiny front terrace on the west side of the inner port, this cavernous club is still among the very hottest on the island, noted for its light shows. Daily 8pm–late.

Hamam Club Platía Dhiagóra ☎ 22420 21444. The most stable and classy music bar in town, installed in a former Turkish bath that still holds its original oriental

decor. Chill-out sofas and outdoor seating, until a midnight noise curfew moves everyone indoors. Daily 6pm–late.

Mylos Aktí Zouroúdhi ☎ 22420 23235. Sprawling around an old seafront windmill, with some tables out on Lambi beach, Mylos is Kos Town's top day-and-night-bar, with both live music and DJs. Daily noon–late.

The Asklepion

Tues–Sun: May–Oct 8am–6pm; Nov–April 8.30am–2.30pm • €3

Native son **Hippocrates** is justly celebrated on Kos; not only does he have a tree, a street, a park, a statue and an international medical institute named after him, but his purported **Asklepion**, 4km south of town and one of three in Greece, is a major attraction.

Although the Asklepion was in fact founded just after Hippocrates' death, the methods used and taught here were probably his. Both a sanctuary of Asklepios (god of healing, son of Apollo) and a renowned curative centre, its magnificent setting on three artificial terraces overlooking Anatolia reflects early concern with the therapeutic environment. Little now remains standing, owing to periodic earthquakes and the Knights filching masonry to build their castle. The lower terrace never held many buildings, being instead the venue for the observance of the Asklepieia – quadrennial athletic/musical competitions in honour of the god. Sacrifices to Asklepios were conducted at an **altar**, the oldest structure here, whose foundations are found near the

5

> ## HIPPOCRATES
>
> **Hippocrates** (c.460–370 BC) is generally regarded as the father of scientific medicine, even if the Hippocratic oath, much altered from its original form, may well have nothing to do with him. Hippocrates was certainly born on Kos, probably at Astypalia near present-day Kéfalos, but otherwise confirmed details of his life are few. A great physician who travelled throughout the Classical Greek world, he spent at least part of his career teaching and practising on his native island. Numerous medical writings have been attributed to Hippocrates; *Airs, Waters and Places*, a treatise on the importance of environment on health, is generally thought to be his, but others are reckoned to be a compilation found in a medical library in Alexandria during the second century BC. His emphasis on good air and water, and the holistic approach of ancient Greek medicine, now seem positively contemporary.

middle of the second terrace. Just east, the Corinthian columns of a second-century-AD **Roman temple** were partially re-erected by nationalistic Italians. A monumental **staircase** leads from the altar to a second-century-BC **Doric temple** of Asklepios on the highest terrace, the last and grandest of the deity's local shrines.

The east

The shoreline of the **eastern** half of Kos, in both directions from Kos Town, is fringed with good **beaches**, albeit interspersed with marshlands. The best, around Cape Psalídhi to the east and Lámbi, Tingáki and Marmári to the southwest, have attracted resort development, but with a bike especially (thanks to the coastal bike paths) it's usually possible to find a stretch of sand to yourself. Inland, the rugged **hills** cradle some delightful villages, though many are now sadly empty.

Brós Thermá

East of Kos Town, beyond the huge hotels of Cape Psalídhi, the paved coast road ends after 12km. A dirt track continues for the final kilometre to the massively popular **hot springs** known as **Brós Thermá**. Best experienced at sunset or on moonlit nights, they issue from a grotto and flow through a trench into a shoreline pool formed by boulders, heating the seawater to an enjoyable temperature.

Tingáki and Marmári

The coast southwest of Kos Town is home to the twin beach resorts of Tingáki and Marmári. There's almost always a breeze along this stretch, which makes it popular with windsurfers, while the profiles of Kálymnos, Psérimos and Turkey's Bodrum peninsula all make for spectacular offshore scenery. Heading for either resort from town, especially on a bike, the nicest and safest route is the minor road from the southwest corner of town.

A favourite with British travellers, **TINGÁKI** is 12km west of the harbour. Its long narrow beach of white sand improves, and becomes more separated from the frontage road, the further southwest you go. Thanks to the island of Psérimos just offshore, waves tend to stay small, and the warm shallow waters are ideal for children. There's little accommodation near the beach itself, though medium-sized hotels and studios are scattered amid the fields and cow pastures inland.

MARMÁRI lies another 3km along, beyond the **Alykí** salt marsh, which retains water – and throngs of migratory birds, including flamingos – until June after a wet winter. Marmári has a smaller built-up area than Tingáki, and the beach is broader, especially to the west where it forms little dunes.

The Asfendhioú villages

The inland villages of **Mount Dhíkeos**, a handful of settlements collectively referred to as **Asfendhioú**, nestle amid the island's only natural forest. Together these communities

5

give a good idea of what Kos looked like before tourism arrived, and all have been severely depopulated by the mad rush to the coast. They are accessible via the curvy side road from Zipári, 8km from Kos Town; an inconspicuous minor road to Lagoúdhi; or by the shorter access road for Pylí.

Ziá

There's precious little left of the original village of **ZIÁ**, 7km inland from Tingáki, which now holds barely a dozen resident families. Instead, its heavily commercialized main street and spectacular sunsets make it the target of dozens of tour buses daily, and the general tattiness seems to increase year on year.

Pylí

Both the contemporary village of **Pylí** and the separate ruins of the medieval town can be reached via the road through Lagoúdhi and Amanioú, or from beside the duck-patrolled Linopótis pond on the main island trunk road. Apart from its giant, lion-spouted cistern-fountain (the *piyí*), Pylí's other attraction is the **Harmýlio** ("Tomb of Harmylos"), a fenced-off, subterranean, niched vault that was probably a Hellenistic family tomb. **Paleó** (medieval) **Pylí**, 3km southeast of its modern descendant, was the Byzantine capital of Kos. It's an absolutely wonderful spot, perched on what's now a very isolated peak but still well below the crest of the island's central ridge. Opposite the end of the paved road up, a stair-path leads within fifteen minutes to the roof of the fort. En route you pass the remains of the abandoned town tumbling southwards down the slope.

ACCOMMODATION   THE EAST

Grecotel Kos Imperial Psalídhi ☎ 22420 58000, 🌐 grecotel.com. A superbly designed garden complex with tropical-river novelty pool and spa, where standard doubles and bungalows share decor (including music systems) and size (large). **€160**

Oceanis Beach & Spa Resort Psalídhi ☎ 22420 24641, 🌐 oceanis-hotel.gr. Enormous beachfront hotel, very much geared towards families, with almost four hundred rooms, three pools (two saltwater), kids' club, on-site windsurf school, and an opulent garden environment. **€160**

EATING AND DRINKING

★ **Ambeli** Tingáki ☎ 22420 69682. The "Vineyard" is a great local taverna, in a rural setting 2.5km east of the main beachfront crossroads. Pleasant seating indoors and out, and dishes including *pinigoúri*, *bekrí mezé*, *pikhtí*, *yaprákia* (the local *dolmádhes*) and *arnáki ambelourgoú*, washed down with wine from their own vineyard. Book ahead in peak season. Nov–April Fri & Sat dinner, Sun lunch; May–Oct lunch & dinner daily.

Iy Palia Piyi Pylí ☎ 22420 41510. Excellent taverna, in a superb setting beside a fountain fed by a natural year-round spring in the upper part of Pylí, 100m west of the partly pedestrianized square and church. Inexpensive *soutzoukákia* grilled with onions, home-made *tzatzíki*, fried-vegetable *mezédhes* and local sweet red wine. Daily lunch & dinner.

★ **Oromedon** Ziá ☎ 22420 69983, 🌐 pragmata.info /Oromedon_gb.htm. The best of Ziá's dozen tavernas, this Greek-patronized place serves good *pinigoúri*, mushrooms and local sausage on a roof terrace. Bill Clinton and the Greek and Turkish presidents have all eaten here. May–Oct daily lunch & dinner.

The west

Near the desolate centre of the island, well sown with military installations, a pair of giant, adjacent roundabouts by the airport funnels traffic northwest towards **Mastihári**, northeast back towards town, southwest towards **Kéfalos** and southeast to **Kardhámena**. Most visitors are bound for the south-coast **beaches**, reached from the Kéfalos-bound turning.

Mastihári

The least "packaged" and least expensive of the north-shore resorts, **MASTIHÁRI**, 8km north of the airport, has a shortish, broad beach extending west, with less frequented dunes (and no sunbeds) towards the far end. Ferries and excursion boats from Kálymnos (see p.326) moor close to the centre, which has the feel of a genuine town.

Kardhámena

KARDHÁMENA, 31km from Kos Town and 8km southeast of the airport, is the island's largest package resort after the capital itself. In summer, locals are vastly outnumbered by boozing-and-bonking visitors, predominantly young Brits. A beach stretches to either side – sandier to the southwest, intermittently reefy and hemmed in by a road towards the northeast – but runaway development has banished any redeeming qualities the place might have had. The main reason anyone not staying here would bother to visit is to catch a boat to Níssyros (see p.306).

South-coast beaches

The coastline west of Kardhámena boasts a series of scenic and secluded **south-facing beaches**. Though each has a fanciful English name, they form essentially one long stretch at the base of a cliff, accessed by successive footpaths down from the main road. As the prevailing wind on the island is usually from the north, the water as a rule is gloriously calm.

The longest, broadest and wildest of the beaches, "**Magic**", officially Polémi, has a proper taverna above the car park, no jet-skis and a nudist zone ("**Exotic**") at its eastern end. "**Sunny**", signposted as Psilós Gremmós and easily walkable from "Magic", has another taverna and jet-skis; **Langádhes** is the cleanest and most picturesque, with junipers tumbling off its dunes and more jet-skis. "**Paradise**", alias "**Bubble Beach**" because of volcanic gas-vents in the tidal zone, is small and oversubscribed, with wall-to-wall sunbeds and a large restaurant just above. Jet-ski-free "**Camel**" (Kamíla) is the shortest and loneliest, protected by the steep, unpaved drive in past its hillside taverna; the shore here is pure, fine sand, with good snorkelling to either side.

Kamári

The westernmost resort on Kos, **KAMÁRI**, comes just before the high headland at the island's western tip, and is essentially the shoreline annexe of the old town of Kéfalos. More popular with families and older visitors than Kardhámena, Kamári may look from the main road like a long and rather dispiriting strip, but the beach itself is good.

There's also a very lovely spot at its western end, 3km from the centre, where the tiny **Kastrí** islet, topped by a little chapel, stands just off the **Áyios Stéfanos** headland. A public access road, close to an abandoned Club Med, leads down to beaches either side of a small peninsula, crowned with the remains of two triple-aisled, sixth-century **basilicas**.

The far west

The village of **KÉFALOS**, 43km from Kos Town, covers a bluff looking down the length of the island. Aside from some lively **cafés** at the south end, it's a dull little place mainly of note as a staging point for expeditions into the rugged **peninsula** that terminates at **Cape Kríkello**.

The main highlights of a visit there, along the ridge road south, include **Panayía Palatianí** Byzantine church amid the ruins of a larger ancient temple, 1km beyond the village, and the Classical theatre (unrestricted access) and Hellenistic temple of **ancient Astypalia**, 500m further via the side-path starting from an unlocked gate. A paved road west just beyond Astypalia leads to windy **Áyios Theológos beach**, 7km from Kéfalos.

ACCOMMODATION AND EATING   THE WEST

Ayios Theologos Taverna Ayios Theologos ☏ 697 45 03 556. High-quality taverna at the far western tip of the island, enjoying incredible sunsets. A vast selection of fresh home-grown produce brings in the crowds at weekends. Lunch & dinner daily in summer, weekends only in winter.

Grand Café Kamári ☎ 22420 71290. Large and very comfortable café, at the point where Kamári beach briefly disappears and the sea laps directly against the road, which as well as drinks serves top-quality pastries and sweets from the adjoining bakery. Winter weekends only, summer all day every day.

Kali Kardia Mastihári ☎ 22420 59289. Reliable taverna, facing the ferry jetty, that's good for fresh fish and mezédhes as well as standards like stifádho, and great desserts. Almost all mains cost €8–10. All meals daily.

Panorama Studios Mastihári ☎ 22420 59019, ⓦ kospanorama.eu. Simple studio apartments with a/c, kitchenettes and sea-view balconies, above a nice little restaurant just steps from the beach. **€60**

Psérimos

Were it not so close to Kos and Kálymnos, the little island of **PSÉRIMOS**, filled with remote beaches, might be idyllic. Throughout the season, so many excursion boats arrive that they've had to build a second jetty at little **AVLÁKIA** port. In midsummer, day-trippers blanket the main sandy beach that curves in front of Avlákia's thirty-odd houses and huge communal olive grove; even during May or late September you're guaranteed at least eighty outsiders daily (versus a permanent population of 25). Three other **beaches** are within easy reach: the clean sand-and-gravel strand at **Vathý** is a well-marked, thirty-minute walk east, starting from behind the *Taverna Iy Psérimos*. It takes 45 minutes of walking north along the main trans-island track to get to grubbier **Marathoúnda**, composed of pebbles. Best of all is **Grafiótissa**, a 300m-long beach of near-Caribbean quality half an hour's walk west of town.

ARRIVAL AND DEPARTURE   PSÉRIMOS

By ferry from Kálymnos To spend the entire day on Psérimos, you'll have to take a day-trip from Póthia (Kálymnos); boats usually leave at 9.30am daily, and return at 5–6pm.

By ferry from Kos Boats from Kos Town operate triangle tours to Platý islet and somewhere on Kálymnos with only a brief stop on Psérimos.

ACCOMMODATION AND EATING

Studios Kalliston Avlákia ☎ 22430 51540. Ten reasonable studios, most with sea views and some with a/c, facing a very broad segment of the beach from its eastern end. **€60**

Taverna Manola Avlákia ☎ 22430 51540. Although it looks more like a bar, and stays open late as the island's main social hub, this beachfront taverna, run by the same management as *Studios Kalliston* (see above), serves good Greek standards and fresh seafood. Daily 9am–late.

Tripolitis Avlákia ☎ 22430 23196. Six simple en-suite studio apartments, three of which have sea views, upstairs from English-speaking *Anna's* café/snack-bar and directly across from the beach. Closed Nov–April. **€40**

Astypálea

Geographically, historically and architecturally, **Astypálea** really belongs to the Cyclades – on a clear day you can see Anáfi or Amorgós far more easily than any of the other Dodecanese. Its inhabitants are descended from colonists brought from the Cyclades during the fifteenth century, after pirate raids had left the island depopulated, and supposedly Astypálea was only reassigned to the Ottomans after the Greek Revolution because the Great Powers had such a poor map at the 1830 and 1832 peace conferences.

Astypálea's main visitor attractions include a beautiful old **citadel** – not just the castle itself, but also the whitewashed village of **Hóra** beneath it – as well as several good, easily accessible **beaches**. The island may not immediately strike you as especially beautiful: many beaches along its heavily indented coastline have reef underfoot and periodic seaweed, while the windswept heights are covered in thornbush or dwarf juniper. Hundreds of sheep and goats manage to survive, while citrus groves and vegetable patches in the valleys signal a relative abundance of

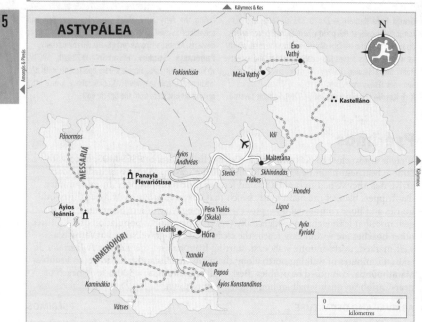

water. Besides the excellent local **cheese**, Astypálea is renowned for its **honey**, **fish** and **lobster**.

There is no **package tourism** on Astypálea, and its remoteness discourages casual trade. During the short, intense **midsummer season** (mid-July to early Sept), however, visitors vastly outnumber the 1500 permanent inhabitants. The one real drawback is that **transport** connections are so poor.

ARRIVAL AND INFORMATION   ASTYPÁLEA

By air Astypálea's tiny airport, 8km east of Hóra and Péra Yialós, has infrequent connections to Athens (1 weekly) and to Léros, Kos and Rhodes, all on the same plane (2–3 weekly). Many hotels will pick up and drop off guests, and buses and taxis are available (see below).

By ferry Astypálea's main ferry port, at Áyios Andhréas, 7km north of Péra Yialós, is extremely inconvenient. There are no facilities whatsoever, and almost all boats arrive and depart in the dead of night. It's connected to Amorgós (2 weekly; 1hr 25min); Dhonoússa (3 weekly; 2hr 20min); Kálymnos (1 weekly; 2hr 15min; Kastellórizo (1 weekly; 15hr 10min); Kos (1 weekly; 3hr 35min); Náxos (3 weekly;

3hr 45min); Páros (3 weekly; 5hr); Pireás (4 weekly; 9hr 45min–11hr 35min); Rhodes (1 weekly; 9hr 10min); Sými (1 weekly; 8hr 25min); Tílos (1 weekly; 6hr 35min). In addition, just one boat, the *Nissos Kalymnos,* calls in at Péra Yialós, with connections to Kálymnos only (3 weekly; 2hr 45min).

Travel agencies Ferry tickets can be bought in Péra Yialós from Astypalea Tours (☏ 22430 61571) and Paradise (☏ 22430 61224).

Tourist office There's an information office in one of the windmills at the approach to Hóra (June–Sept daily 6–9pm; ☏ 22430 61412, ⓦ astypalia.gr).

GETTING AROUND

By bus Ten buses daily connect Péra Yialós with Hóra, Livádhia and Maltezána, and drop passengers at beaches along the way. A connecting bus takes passengers from the airport to Péra Yialós or Maltezána.

By taxi The island's only taxi (☏ 22430 61087) can't cope with passenger numbers in season. Fares are reasonable, at

around €10 from the airport to Péra Yialós.

By car and scooter In Péra Yialós from Lakis and Manolis (☏ 22430 61263), Tomaso (☏ 22430 61000, ⓦ tomaso.gr) and Vergoulis (☏ 22430 61351), or through several island hotels.

The west

The shape of Astypálea is often compared to a butterfly, in that it consists of two separate "wings" joined by a low narrow isthmus. The only major population centre, made up of the built-up strip that joins the waterfront villages of **Péra Yialós** and **Livádhia** by way of hilltop **Hóra**, is on the southeast coast of its **western** half, well away from both the ferry port and the airport.

Péra Yialós

Astypálea was the first Dodecanese island occupied by the Italians, and the little harbour town of **PÉRA YIALÓS**, also known as **SKÁLA**, dates from the Italian era. Set in a deeply indented, steep-sided little bay, it's not where most inter-island ferries arrive (see opposite). Only at the head of the harbour, where a broadish gravel beach – fine for families with young children – fronts a row of seafront cafés and restaurants, is there much life or activity. A broad and uninteresting concrete quayside stretches along its southern shore, below Hóra, while the hillsides are dotted with houses and the odd small hotel.

Archeological museum

June–Sept Tues–Sun 9am–1pm & 6–8.30pm; Oct–May Tues–Sun 8.30am–2.30pm • Free

Just back from the waterfront in the centre of Péra Yialós, the local **archeological museum** consists of a single room. Many of its local finds, spanning the Bronze Age to medieval times, are little more than fragments, but it does hold impressive goblets and vases unearthed from two Mycenaean tombs.

Hóra

The delightful, very photogenic ensemble of **HÓRA**, accessible by road as well as steep stair-paths from Péra Yialós, neatly caps a high headland. Beneath the grey walls of the hilltop castle, the village itself is comprised of dazzling bright houses – many restored as holiday homes – threaded along intriguing narrow alleyways. The main approach road is lined with eight picturesque orange-roofed **windmills**.

Kástro

Unrestricted access • Free

Astypálea's thirteenth-century **kástro**, among the finest in the Aegean, was erected not by the Knights of St John, but by the Venetian Quirini clan, and modified by the Ottomans after 1537. Rather than purpose-built battlements, its unique "walls" consisted instead of the stacked-up frontages of private houses. Until well into the twentieth century more than three hundred people lived inside, but depopulation and a severe 1956 earthquake combined to leave only a shell. Reached via a brightly whitewashed passageway beneath its main church of **Evangelístria Kastrianí**, the interior has been laid out with new pathways.

Livádhia

The little resort village of **LIVÁDHIA** occupies the next bay along from Hóra. A long, straight and pleasant **beach**, albeit scruffy with dried vegetation, lines the waterfront, fringed by cafés, restaurants and low-key hotels. You can walk there from Hóra in fifteen minutes; be sure to take the road that drops down to the sea just beyond the Pylaia Boutique Hotel (see p.324). If you simply go down to the beach you won't realize quite how far this fertile valley stretches inland.

Beyond Livádhia

When the beach at Livádhia is too busy, press on southwest for fifteen minutes on foot to reach the three small fine-pebble coves at **Tzanáki**. Beyond these, **Papoú** is an 80m fine-gravel strand accessible overland by a horrifically steep side track, and then a final path approach around a fenced-off farm.

5

The third large bay beyond Livádhia, **Áyios Konstandínos**, is a partly shaded, sand-and-gravel cove with a good seasonal taverna. Further afield, lonely **Vátses** and **Kaminákia** beaches are visited by a seasonal excursion boat from Péra Yialós. By land, **Vátses** has the easier dirt road and is 25 minutes by scooter from Livádhia; sandy, with a basic *kantína*, it's often windy. The track to **Kaminákia**, 8.5km from Livádhia, is rough and steep for the final 2km – best to go in a jeep – but the sheltered, clean and scenic cove, Astypálea's best, repays the effort.

ACCOMMODATION   WESTERN ASTYPÁLEA

PÉRA YIALÓS

Akti Rooms ☎ 22430 61114, **ⓦ** aktirooms.gr. Rather faded hotel in a beautiful hillside location near the Thalassa, offering cheap but minimally equipped rooms, not all with sea views, above a gorgeous terrace restaurant. **€55**

Hotel Australia ☎ 22430 61275 or 22430 61855, **ⓔ** pmariaki@hotmail.com. Plain but perfectly adequate en-suite rooms, with fans or a/c and balconies, just back from the harbourfront above a friendly little restaurant. **€60**

Hotel Thalassa ☎ 22430 59840, **ⓦ** stampalia.gr. The best accommodation in Péra Yialós, spilling down the hillside across from the castle, where the first access road down to the harbour drops from the coastal road. Open all year, it consists entirely of very comfortable suites and studios, with fabulous views but no direct access to the sea. **€125**

HÓRA

Kalderimi ☎ 22430 59843, **ⓦ** kalderimi.gr. Smart modern complex, just beyond the *Pylaia Boutique Hotel* (see below) on the road out of Hóra, where the eleven impeccably appointed mock-trad a/c cottages (some large enough for families) hold all the lastest electronic gadgets. **€140**

Kallichoron Studios ☎ 22430 61934, **ⓦ** astypalea .com. Tasteful, upscale studios and one-bed apartments, close to the windmills at the edge of Hóra at the start of the road to Livádhia, all with flagstoned terrace and magnificent views of the citadel. Open all year, rates include breakfast. **€120**

Pylaia Boutique Hotel ☎ 22430 61070, **ⓦ** pylaiahotel .gr. Rather sumptuous new hotel, spilling down the hillside

200m out of Hóra towards Livádhia, with friendly young management. Slightly too large to be really "boutique", it holds 25 spacious, stylish rooms and suites, most with outdoor space and great views, plus a pool and summer-only rooftop restaurant. Open all year, rates include breakfast. **€170**

★ **Studios Kilindra ☎** 22430 61131, **ⓦ** astipalea .com.gr. Plush studios and galleried maisonettes, on the quiet west slope of Hóra, with a swimming pool and good breakfasts – units accommodate two to three people. Closed Jan–March. **€150**

LIVÁDHIA

Maganas ☎ 22430 61468, **ⓦ** maganas.gr. Small, neat hotel, directly across from the beach on the frontage road, where the eight stiudios have a/c, kitchenettes and even tiny washing machines. **€60**

Mouras Studios ☎ 697 24 53 571, **ⓔ** mourass @otenet.gr. Very nice little set of individual rental units, right by the beach, each with its own kitchen and balcony, and arranged around a courtyard. Reserve ahead for best rates. **€50**

To Yerani Studios ☎ 22430 61484, **ⓔ** gerani72 @hotmail.com. Ten nicely maintained and very comfortable marble-floored studios, with kitchens and little terraces facing flower-filled gardens, a short walk from the sea behind the village's best taverna. Closed Nov–April. **€60**

Venetos Studios ☎ 22430 61490, **ⓦ** venetosstudios .gr. Several buildings scattered inland from the beach in a pleasant orchard at the base of the westerly hillside, and holding well-furnished studios and apartments of varying sizes. Closed Oct–April. **€60**

EATING AND DRINKING

PÉRA YIALÓS

Akroyiali ☎ 22430 61863. While the food here is pretty good, with a wide range of mezhédes and tasty cheese dishes, the prime reason this beachfront taverna is so full every night is its unbeatable setting, with tables spreading out onto the sand. Daily lunch & dinner.

Australia ☎ 22430 61275. Dependable, long-established favourite, beneath the eponymous hotel (see above) just back from the waterfront, with delicious seafood, and superbly prepared home-grown vegetable dishes. April–Nov daily lunch & dinner.

Dapia Café ☎ 22430 61590. The pick of the waterfront cafés, with a large well-shaded terrace overlooking the harbour and free wi-fi. Good for full breakfasts, crêpes, juices and infusions, as well as sunset drinks. Daily 10am–late.

★ **Maïstrali ☎** 22430 61691. Welcoming, high-quality restaurant, with oblique sea views from the corner of the harbour. As well as rich stews like rabbit with tomato or chicken with yoghurt and mustard, for under €10, they also serve seafood dishes like lobster, scaly fish or shrimp saganaki. Daily lunch & dinner.

HÓRA

Barbarossa ☎ 22430 61577. The only serious taverna in Hóra, just as the main street starts to climb towards the kástro. Popular for its warm, pleasant interior, and nice terrace, it serves hearty but generally unexceptional food, with rich meaty dishes like chicken with okra for €7.50 as well as more substantial seafood; the salads are disappointing. Daily noon–midnight.

LIVÁDHIA

Astropelos ☎ 22430 61473. With its large shaded patio, this beachside taverna is a great place to linger over vegetable dishes like stuffed tomatoes, but the seafood can be expensive. June–Sept daily 11am–late.

★ **To Yerani** ☎ 22430 61484. Livádhia's best food, set inland from the little bridge in the middle of the beach, but still enjoying sea views from its large tiled terrace. Home-cooked specialities range from delicious courgette flowers with cheese for €4 or moussaka for €6 up to large meat grills. May–Oct daily 11am–late.

KAMINÁKIA

Linda ☎ 697 21 29 088. Well-run beach taverna, which as well as offering honest, rustic fare (salads, fresh fish and a dish of the day) oversees a handful of sunbeds. Late June to early Sept, daily noon–6pm.

The east

Astypálea's wilder and less populated **eastern** half is home to the island's airport and a small resort, **Maltezána**. Apart from a couple of south-coast beaches, the only day-trip worth making over here is the bumpy but spectacular drive out to the huge bay at **Mésa Vathý**.

Stenó and Plákes

Two good but isolated beaches stand on the southern shore of Astypálea's slender central isthmus. At **Stenó** (meaning "narrow", in reference to the isthmus), inviting turquoise shallows stretch away from a sandy shore. There's only limited shade, courtesy of a few tamarisks, but a *kantína* opens up in high summer.

Another kilometre east, the much quieter beach at **Plákes** has no facilities and can only be accessed by walking a few hundred metres down from the main road. It's at the end of the airport runways, but with barely a plane a day that's no problem.

Maltezána

The little resort of **MALTEZÁNA**, Astypálea's second-largest settlement, is 9km east of Péra Yialós, under 1km from the airport. Its official name is **ANÁLIPSI**, but it's universally known by the nickname it acquired thanks to medieval Maltese pirates. It's a nice enough spot, with a narrow, exposed, packed-sand beach, a small fishing port at its eastern end, and a good view south to islets.

ACCOMMODATION AND EATING	MALTEZÁNA

Analipsi ☎ 22430 61446. Maltezána's best taverna, also known as *Ilias-Irini's*, is a tranquil little space facing the jetty that doubles as the fishermen's *kafenío*. The food – fried squid, bean soup – is simple but wholesome; confirm prices and portion size of the often frozen seafood. Feb–Dec daily 11am–9pm.

Maltezana Beach ☎ 22430 61558, ⓦ maltezanabeach. gr. Astypálea's largest hotel, with 48 large, well-appointed

bungalow-rooms – five of which are family-sized apartments – plus a pool and on-site restaurant. Closed mid-Sept to Easter. **€100**

Villa Barbara ☎ 22430 61448. A dozen very spruce blue-and-white studios, all with kitchen and balcony and sleeping 2–3, set a short way back from the beach. Closed Oct to mid-May. **€50**

Mésa Vathý

Although the main road turns to dirt east of Maltezána, it remains just about passable in an ordinary car, and snakes its way onwards across the exposed hillsides all the way to **MÉSA VATHÝ**, at the head of an utterly magnificent west-facing bay 23km out from Hóra. Much the best way to arrive at this sleepy fishing hamlet would be by boat; it's a popular anchorage for pleasure yachts in summer. There's no town, just one little taverna; walk onwards from the end of the road to reach a small beach.

5

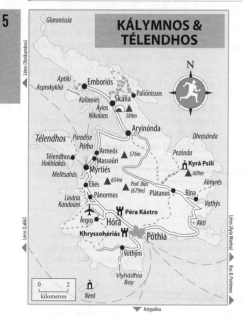

Kálymnos

Despite its size and beauty, the island of **KÁLYMNOS** has long been overshadowed by Kos. Kálymnos fought in the Trojan War as a vassal of its southern neighbour, and to this day its tourist industry remains largely dependent on the overspill – and the airport – of Kos.

In most respects, however, Kálymnos is very unlike Kos. It's much more mountainous, consisting of three high limestone ridges that fan away from the continuous rugged cliffs of its west coast, to create two long sloping valleys that hold most of its settlements and agricultural land.

The island's capital and largest town, the port of **Póthia**, faces Kos from the midpoint of its southern shoreline. Most visitors head instead for the west coast, where a handful of small resorts have struggled to survive the collapse of a short-lived experiment in mass tourism. **Myrtiés**, stands close to some attractive little beaches. This craggy shoreline has found deserved fame among **climbers** and **hikers**, who keep businesses ticking along in the cooler spring and autumn months.

For a beach holiday, you'd do better to head for the separate islet of **Télendhos**, immediately west across a small strait (and a spectacular sight at sunset), or further north up the coast to **Emboriós**.

The prosperity of Kálymnos traditionally rested on its **sponge industry** (see box, p.328), but blights have now wiped out almost all of the eastern Mediterranean's sponges. Only a few boats of the island's thirty-strong fleet remain in use, and most of the sponges sold behind the harbour are imported from Asia and the Caribbean.

ARRIVAL AND INFORMATION   KÁLYMNOS

By air Kálymnos's small airport, 6km northwest of Póthia, is served only by Olympic Air flights to and from Athens (1–2 daily).

By ferry Ferries from Póthia serve the following islands: Agathoníssi (5 weekly; 2hr 15min–5hr 30min); Arkioi (4 weekly; 4hr 20min); Astypálea (3 weekly; 2hr 15min–2hr 45min); Kastellórizo (2 weekly; 10hr 15min–13hr); Kos (Kos Town) (2–5 daily; 30min–1hr); Kos (Mastihari) (6 daily; 20min–1hr); Léros (1–2 daily; 50min–1hr 20min); Lipsi (2–3 daily; 1hr 20min); Náxos (1 weekly; 6hr 55min); Níssyros (2 weekly; 2hr 50min); Páros (1 weekly; 8hr 30min);

Pátmos (2–4 daily; 1hr 40min–3hr 25min); Pireás (5 weekly; 9hr 40min–14hr 10min); Pserimos (3 weekly; 20min); Rhodes (2–4 daily; 2hr 40min–8hr 15min); Sámos (1–2 daily; 2hr 50min–6hr 50min); Sými (11 weekly; 2hr 10min–6hr 20min); Tílos (2 weekly; 4hr 20min). There are frequent ferries to Télendhos from Myrtiés (see p.329).

Travel agents Sofia Kouremeti (☎22430 23700) and Mahias Travel (☎22430 22909).

Tourist office The municipal tourist office faces the ferry jetty in Póthia (Mon–Fri 8am–3pm; ☎22430 50956, ⓦkalymnos-isl.gr).

GETTING AROUND

By bus Buses to the west-coast resorts (6 daily in season; 30min), and also northwest to Emboriós (2 daily; 50min) and east to Vathýs (4 daily; 30min), run from two terminals beside the municipal "palace".

Taxis Shared taxis, available at Platía Kyprou, cost less

than normal taxis.

By car and scooter Car rental outlets along Póthia quay include the recommended Auto Market (☎22430 51780, ⓦkalymnoscars.gr), while for scooters check out Kostas (☎22430 50110), very close to the tourist office.

Póthia

5

The long curving waterfront of **PÓTHIA**, Kálymnos's main town and port, may not be architecturally distinguished, but arrayed around a huge curving bay it looks fabulous at sunset. The town itself remains vibrant year-round, even if it's not really a tourist destination in its own right. With its houses marching up the valley inland or arrayed in tiers along the surrounding hillsides, it forms a natural amphitheatre that readily fills with noise, whether from souped-up motorbikes or summer sound-systems. As well as the usual Italian-era "palace", at the centre of the bay, Póthia also boasts backstreets lined with elegant **Neoclassical houses**, painted the traditional pink or ochre.

Sprawled to either side of the road to the west coast, the built-up area of Póthia stretches northwest up the valley to the suburb of **Mýli**. The whitewashed battlements of the Knights' **Kástro Khryssoheriás** (unrestricted access), 1.2km along, offer wonderful views over town towards Kos. Another 1.5km up, the former island capital, **Hóra**, is still a large, busy village.

Archeological Museum of Kálymnos

Evangelístria • Daily except Mon: May to mid-Sept 8.30am–3pm; mid-Sept to May 9.30am–12.30pm • €3

Tucked away in an unremarkable and hard-to-find new building on Póthia's western hillside, Kálymnos's **Archeological Museum** provides an excellent overview of local history. Everything is beautifully displayed, with very helpful captions in both Greek and English, and many of its artefacts are quite stunning. Its greatest treasures, discovered underwater during the 1990s, are a larger-than-life cast bronze figure of a woman draped in a chiton, thought to date from the second century BC, and the well-preserved bronze head of a ruler, which may have formed part of a colossal equestrian statue.

Municipal Nautical and Folklore Museum

Daily 10am–1pm • €2

Kálymnos's **Municipal Nautical and Folklore Museum**, very near the ferry port on the seaward side of Khristós cathedral, focuses on the sponge-fishing past. A large photo shows Póthia in the 1880s, with no quay, jetty, roads or sumptuous mansions, and with most of the population still up in Hóra. You can also see horribly primitive divers' breathing apparatuses, and "cages" designed to keep propellers from cutting air lines.

Péra Kástro

Hóra • Unrestricted daylight access • Free

The thirteenth-century Byzantine citadel-town of **Péra Kástro**, a magnificent fortified enclave atop the impressive crag that towers over Hóra, originally served as a refuge from seaborne raiders. Appropriated by the Knights of St John, it remained inhabited until the late 1700s. It's now reached by a steep stair-path that climbs from the eastern edge of the village.

Once you've passed through the massive gate and perimeter walls, you're faced with yet more stiff climbing, now through a jumble of overgrown ruins, tumbled stonework, and wildflowers, interspersed with the odd paved walkway. The views are tremendous, but the true highlights are the nine scattered **medieval chapels**, the only complete buildings to survive. Re-roofed and freshly whitewashed, several still hold faded frescoes.

ACCOMMODATION

POTHIA

Arhondiko Áyios Nikólaos ☎22430 24051. Much the most basic option near the port, this refurbished mansion on the southwest quay is the family home of an elderly couple who speak little English, and remains open year-round. Plain rooms with pleasant views. **€45**

Hotel Panorama Amoudhára ☎22430 23138, ⓦpanorama-kalymnos.gr. Simple, well-kept hotel, high on the hillside west of the harbour, where all thirteen en-suite rooms have air conditioning and balconies overlooking the port. There's also a pleasant breakfast salon. Closed Nov–March. **€50**

★ **Villa Melina** Enoria Evangelístria ☎22430 22682, ⓦvilla-melina.com. Póthia's quietest and most elegant hotel, set in attractive gardens near the archeological

5

SPONGES AND SPONGE-DIVING

Sponges are colonies of microscopic marine organisms that excrete a fibrous skeleton. The living sponges that can be seen throughout the Aegean as black, melon-sized blobs, anchored to rocks in three to ten metres of water, are mostly "wild" sponges, impossible to clean or shape with shears. Kalymnian divers seek out "tame" sponges, which are much softer, more pliable, and dwell thirty to forty metres deep.

Sponge-fishers were originally **free divers**; weighted with a rock, they'd collect sponges from the seabed on a single breath before being hauled back up to the surface. Starting in the late nineteenth century, however, divers were fitted with heavy, insulated suits (*skáfandhro*). Breathing through an air-feed line connected to compressors aboard the factory boats, they could now attain depths of up to 70m. However, this resulted in the first cases of the "bends". When divers came up too quickly, the dissolved air in their bloodstream bubbled out of solution – with catastrophic results. Roughly half of those early pioneers would leave with the fleets in spring but fail to return in autumn. Some were buried at sea, others, it's said, buried alive, up to their necks in hot sand, to provide slight relief from the excruciating pain of nitrogen bubbles in the joints.

By the time the malady became understood, during World War I, thousands of Kalymnians had died, with many survivors paralyzed, deaf or blind. Even though the *skáfandhro* was banned elsewhere as the obvious culprit, it remained in use here until after World War II. After the first **decompression chambers** and diving schools reached Greece, in the 1950s, the seabed was stripped with ruthless efficiency, and the sponge fleets forced to hunt further from home.

Even the "tame" sponge is unusable until **processed**. The smelly organic matter and external membrane is thrashed out of them, traditionally by being trodden on the boat deck, and then they're tossed for a day or so in a vat of hot sea-water. Visitors to Póthia's remaining handful of workshops can still watch the sponge-vats spin; in the old days, the divers simply made a "necklace" of their catch and trailed it in the sea behind the boat.

To suit modern tastes, some sponges are bleached to a pale yellow colour with nitric acid. That weakens the fibres, however, so it's best to buy the more durable, natural-brown ones.

museum, just inland from the eastern side of the port. The pink, century-old Italianate villa holds seven high-ceilinged, bug-screened, wood-floored rooms, while a further thirteen studios and apartments, sleeping up to six, are laid out around the large swimming pool behind. There's a friendly and very helpful family atmosphere, especially around the communal, outdoor breakfast table. Open all year. **€60**

EATING AND DRINKING

Kafenes Khristós ☎ 22430 28727. This pavement café, close to the county "palace" in the centre of the harbour, is always full thanks to its generous, tasty salads, seafood, local goat cheese and bulk wine. Be sure to try the €6 "crab balls". Daily 8am–late.

Taverna Pandelis Áyios Nikólaos ☎ 22430 51508. Large but inconspicuous restaurant, tucked into a cul-de-sac behind the waterfront *Olympic Hotel*. Dependably good meat and fish grills – ask for the daily catch – as well as mezédhes. Daily lunch & dinner.

★ **Xefteris Khristós** ☎ 22430 28642. Century-old, family-run restaurant, a block inland from the waterfront east of the Italian "palace". The dining room is utterly plain, more like a large garage, and it's next to the same owners' loud garden-set music bar, but the traditional local food is superb, with dishes including stewed chickpeas, and *mououri*, shredded lamb with rice. Daily lunch & dinner.

Zaharoplastio O Mihalaras Áyios Nikólaos. This wonderful local cake shop, a must for any fan of Greek sweetmeats, has two premises in Póthia. The traditional original is on the harbourfront close to the "palace", while there's *a* modern annexe near the ferry jetty. Daily 8am–6pm.

Vathýs and Rína

Ten kilometres northeast of Póthia, and accessed via an initially dispiriting coastal road, the long, fertile valley known as **VATHÝS** is Kálymnos' agricultural heartland. Its orange and tangerine groves make a startling contrast to the mineral greys and ochres of the surrounding hills, but visitors only pass this way to visit the fjord port of **RÍNA** at its southeastern end. Set at the end of a long slender inlet, Rína remains a popular stopover with yachties, and can also be reached by taxi-boats from Póthia. It's a very scenic spot, with tiny little Christian basilicas perched on the cliffs to either side, while the total lack of a beach keeps the crowds down. This safe anchorage has been in use since Neolithic times; several caves show signs of ancient occupation.

ACCOMMODATION AND EATING   **VATHÝS AND RÍNA**

Galini Hotel Restaurant Rína ☎ 22430 31241, ⓦ galinihotelvathikalymnou.com. Of the three similar, largely open-air seafood restaurants clustered around the harbour at Rína, only the friendly *Galina* also doubles as a hotel, charging bargain B&B rates for its clean, simple sea-view rooms. **€30**

Northern Kálymnos

Northern Kalymnos is fringed with wildflowers, and backed by mighty cliffs, it's great **hiking** and **climbing** territory. **Emboriós** at road's end makes a great overnight stop, or you can simply complete a round-island car or scooter tour by heading inland from **Aryinónda**, further south, and making your way back to Póthia via Vathýs (see opposite).

Aryinónda to Emboriós

ARYINÓNDA itself, 5km beyond Massoúri at the head of its own deeply indented bay, has a clean pebble beach, plus a couple of small tavernas. Keep heading north along the west coast from here to find several more splendid, isolated beaches, including **Áyios Nikólaos** and **Kalamiés**. The village of **EMBORIÓS**, at the end of the bus line 20km out from Póthia, is a pretty little spot that offers a reasonable gravel-and-sand beach, and a scattering of apartments and tavernas. The little jetty in the middle is served by excursion boats from Myrtiés, which only run when demand is high enough.

A hundred metres beyond Emboriós, reached by a detour inland of the church, the next cove along holds the similar, goat-patrolled **Asprokykliá beach**. Follow the rough dirt track above Asprokykliá to the isthmus by the fish farm, then walk fifteen minutes north on path and track to reach **Aptíki**, a smallish but perfectly formed pea-gravel cove.

Paliónissos and around

From Skália, 1km or so short of Emboriós, a newly paved road – signposted only in Greek – switchbacks up the west flank of the island and back down the other side. A steep but safe 5km drive, it stops short of the eastern shoreline, leaving visitors to walk the final couple of hundred metres along a rough track.

Set at the head of another extravagantly indented fjord-like bay, the yacht anchorage of **Paliónissos** is more usually reached by excursion boats from Rína (see opposite). It boasts an ample crescent of shingle beach, with a taverna to either side.

ACCOMMODATION AND EATING   **NORTHERN KÁLYMNOS**

★ **Harry's Paradise** Emboriós ☎ 22430 40062, ⓦ harrys-paradise.gr. This lovely taverna, set behind gorgeous flower-filled gardens a short walk from the beach, serves delicious home-cooked traditional food for all meals, using produce from their own fields. Their small hotel annex alongside offers simple but great-value air conditioned en-suite studios, each individually themed and equipped with a kitchenette and balcony, and they rent out a slightly more expensive renovated cottage. Closed Dec–March. Daily 9am–9pm. **€45**

The west coast

The mountainous headland that fills Kálymnos's southwest corner is largely inaccessible to visitors. From the moment the island's **west coast** can be reached by road, however, the shoreline is lined by a succession of small beach communities. Although several set out to turn themselves into beach resorts around the turn of the millennium, only **Myrtiés** and **Massoúri** have thrived enough to make worthwhile bases.

5

Myrtiés to Armeós

Beach tourism on Kálymnos is most heavily concentrated in the twin resorts of **MYRTIÉS** and **MASSOÚRI**. Occupying neighbouring coves that start 8km northwest of Póthia, they face across to towering Télendhos islet (see below), and enjoy dramatic **sunsets**.

They're easy enough to reach on the island's main road, though once it's crossed the island to Pánormos the road has to climb the Kamári pass before it can zigzag back down to the sea. A lengthy one-way loop then leads drivers through the two resorts. There's no significant gap in the commercial strip of restaurants and hotels that runs through them both, 50m up from the beach, and neither has a historic core or town centre.

The narrow, pebbly **beach** at Myrtiés has a marina at its southern end and the small concrete jetty used by the Télendhos ferries in the middle. The beach at Massoúri, ten minutes' walk north, is broader and sandier; the largest and liveliest on the island, it has a noisy beach-bar vibe in summer. There's also an all-sand beach at **Melitsáhas** cove, 500m south of Myrtiés, but its surroundings have become very run-down; don't reckon on staying there.

Another kilometre north of Massoúri, the coastal village of **Armeós** is the terminus for most local buses. In low season especially, it tends to be dominated by European **rock-climbers**. Several popular cliffs soar overhead – look for the route-inscribed columns at their base – and various businesses cater to climbers' needs.

ACCOMMODATION
THE WEST COAST

★ **Acroyali** Myrtiés ☎ 22430 47521 or 21036 22688, ⓦ acroyali.gr. Six clean, well-designed apartments, right on the beach, with unfussy furnishings and spacious sea-view balconies. Each sleeps two adults and two kids; book well in advance. There's also an on-site restaurant. Closed Dec–March. **€60**

Apollonia Hotel Apartments Massoúri ☎ 22430 48094, ⓦ apollonia-kalymnos.gr. Large, very spruce studio-format hotel, close to the beach at Massoúri. The units are slightly bland, but they're air conditioned, and have nice big balconies with great views. Closed Dec–Feb. **€50**

Hotel Atlantis Myrtiés ☎ 22430 47497, ⓦ atlantis -kalymnos.gr. Eighteen pleasant and well-located studios and apartments, with living room, kitchen and balconies looking across to Télendhos. Closed Nov–March. **€50**

Hotel Philoxenia Armeós ☎ 22430 59310, ⓦ philoxenia-kalymnos.com. Simple but good-value hotel, in prime climbing territory at the foot of the roadside hills ten minutes' walk north of Massoúri. Plain clean rooms with large balconies, plus a nice pool with snack bar; ask in advance if you want dinner. Closed Nov–April. **€50**

EATING AND DRINKING

Kokkinidis Massoúri. Terrace restaurant, perched just above the main road in the centre of Massoúri, with nice views and a good menu of Greek and Mediterranean dishes, including a whole roast chicken for two at €15. Daily lunch & dinner.

To Steki tis Fanis Linária ☎ 22430 47317. Friendly family restaurant, in an old mansion on the hillside overlooking Linária beach. Local specialities such as *mermizéli* (salad of greens, *kopanistí* and barley rusks) and ample vegetarian starters, but mains quality varies. May–Oct, dinner only.

Tsopanakos Armeós ☎ 22430 47929. This friendly meat specialist is the best old-school taverna to survive on the west coast. Whether on the lovely terrace in summer, or in the cosy indoor dining room in winter, feast on fresh meat and cheese dishes from island-grazed goats. Daily noon–9pm.

Télendhos

The towering pyramid-shaped islet of **TÉLENDHOS**, silhouetted at sunset a few hundred metres west of Myrtiés, was severed from Kálymnos by a cataclysmic earthquake in 554 AD. Car-free, home to a mere handful of year-round inhabitants, and blissfully tranquil, it's the single most compelling destination for Kálymnos visitors, and the short row of hotels and restaurants on its east-facing shore makes it a great place to spend a few nights. Regular little boat-buses shuttle across the narrow straits between Myrtiés and Télendhos (every 30min 8am–midnight; €2); it's said that somewhere far below, an ancient town lies submerged.

5

It only takes a few minutes to explore the little built-up strip that stretches in both directions from the boat landing. A narrow beach of reasonable sand runs along the straight seafront, and the calm shallow water is ideal for kids. Kayaks and beach toys are available for rent, while tousled tamarisks provide shade.

To find a more secluded beach, simply keep walking. A few hundred metres north – head right from the boat landing, and keep going after the paved coastal roadway peters out to become a dirt path – nudist **Paradise** beach is peaceful and sheltered, but at its best in the morning, before the sun disappears for good behind the mountain. A ten-minute walk southwest of the village, following a footpath over the ridge, will bring you to the pebble beach at **Hokhlakás**, a scenic but more exposed spot where the sea tends to be much rougher.

While all the shoreline buildings are of modern construction, abundant ruins are scattered slightly further afield. Closest to the village, north of the boat landing, a seafront field holds the ruined outline of the thirteenth-century monastery of **Áyios Vassílios**. On the hillside immediately above Hokhlakás, **Ayía Triádha** was originally an enormous basilica, though now just a few stones survive. Further up the slopes, wherever you look, giant Cyclopean caves burrow deep into the foot of the central massif.

Setting out to hike right round Télendhos would be a mistake; it's a long and exposed walk with little reward. Devote an hour or two, however, to investigating the islet's southwest corner, a little low-lying afterthought. Follow the footpaths through the woods, signed to "Early Christian Necropolis", and in addition to some intact arched sixth-century tombs you'll come to a perfectly sheltered sandy cove that's ideal for swimming and snorkelling.

ACCOMMODATION   TÉLENDHOS

Hotel Porto Potha ☎ 22430 47321, ⓦ telendoshotel.gr. Friendly hotel on the hillside just north of *On The Rocks* (see below), with twelve comfortable and spacious guest rooms, eight self-catering studios alongside, and a large pool, plus what amounts to a private beach. Special offers for hikers and climbers in low season. Closed late Oct to March. **€50**

On the Rocks ☎ 22430 48260, ⓦ otr.telendos.com. Three superbly appointed en-suite rooms, with balconies and sea views, above the beachfront restaurant 200m

north of the ferry jetty. One can hold a family of four. Breakfast – and kayaks – available. The same friendly owners also rent a studio near Hokhlakás beach, with double-glazing, kitchen, bug screens and internet. Free boat connection from Mastihári on Kos. Closed Dec–March. **€50**

Zorba's ☎ 22430 48660. Very simple en-suite rooms at bargain prices, above a reasonable taverna a short walk south from the ferry jetty. **€30**

EATING AND DRINKING

Barba Stathis ☎ 22430 47953. Also known as *Tassia's*, this welcoming place is just behind *Zorba's* (see above) en route to Hokhlakás. Barbecue every night, and daily specials like flounder fillet or fresh-made dolmades. Daily 11am–late.

On the Rocks ☎ 22430 48260, ⓦ otr.telendos.com. Very pleasant restaurant, with a shaded patio overlooking the beach not far north of the ferry jetty, and run by a very friendly Greek-Australian family. A full menu of fresh fish

and meat dishes, typically costing around €10, plus pizzas and burgers, Greek specialities, and lovely home-made desserts. Wednesday night is Greek barbecue, with music and dancing. It also holds a lively bar. Daily 9am–late.

Plaka Next door to, and slightly cheaper than, *On the Rocks* (see above), this large vine-covered terrace, poised just above the beach, is a great place to enjoy inexpensive local dishes such as goat with tomato sauce, or fresh octopus, for under €10. Daily lunch & dinner.

Léros

As the island of **LÉROS** is indented with deep, sheltered bays, lined with little settlements, it doesn't have an obvious "capital". Ferries arrive at both **Lakkí** on the west coast and **Ayía Marína** on the east, but neither is recommended as a place to stay. Instead visitors congregate in the resorts of **Pandélli** and **Álinda**, and in more refined

5

Plátanos up on the hillside. While Léros can be very attractive, however, it doesn't hold spectacular **beaches**, so tourism remains relatively low-key.

The island still bears traces of the **Battle of Léros** of November 1943, when German paratroops displaced a Commonwealth division that had occupied Léros following the Italian capitulation. Bomb nose-cones and shell casings turn up as gaily painted garden ornaments, or do duty as gateposts. After the war, the local economy relied on prisons and sanatoria in former Italian military buildings. During the civil war and the later junta, leftists were confined to a notorious **detention centre** at Parthéni, while **hospitals** warehoused intractable psychiatric cases and mentally handicapped children. In 1989, a major scandal exposed conditions in the asylums; most wards were eventually closed.

ARRIVAL AND DEPARTURE   LÉROS

By air A tiny airport near the island's northern tip is served by twice-weekly flights to Astypálea, Kos and Rhodes.

By ferry Large ferries and the *Dodekanisos Pride* catamaran arrive at Lakkí; smaller ferries and the *Dodekanisos Express* arrive at Ayía Marína. Destinations served: Agathoníssi (5 weekly; 1hr 10min–4hr); Arkí (5 weekly; 2hr 50min); Kálymnos (1–2 daily; 45min–1hr 15min); Kos (1–3 daily; 1hr 25min–3hr); Lipsí (2–3 daily;

20min–1hr); Pátmos (2–4 daily; 40min–1hr 55min); Pireás (3 weekly; 9–11hr); Rhodes (1–2 daily; 4hr–5hr 15min); Samos (1–2 daily; 1hr 55min–5hr 20min); Sými (6 weekly; 3hr 10min–5hr 50min); Syros (2 weekly; 5hr 30min).

Travel agencies Aegean Travel, 9 King George Ave, Lakkí (☎22470 26000, ⓦaegeantravel.gr); Kastis Travel, Ayía Marína (☎22470 22140).

GETTING AROUND

By bus Regular buses from the main taxi rank in Platanós run north via Ayía Marína, Álinda and the airport to Parthéni, and south to Lakkí and Xirókambos.

Car and scooter rental Motoland (Pandélli, ☎22470

24103; Álinda, ☎22470 24584) and Rent A Car Léros (Lakkí, ☎22470 22330). Take care if you rent a scooter – Lerian roads are particularly narrow, potholed and gravel-strewn, and the low-slung, fat-tyred bikes on offer don't cope well.

Lakkí

Set in a hugely indented bay on Léros's southwest coast, the unusual town of **LAKKÍ** is the arrival port for all the island's large **ferries**. Built in the 1930s as a model town to house 7500 civilian dependants of an adjacent Italian naval base, it's now an incongruous under-populated relic. Sweeping boulevards, out of all proportion to the traffic they ever saw, are lined with Stream Line Modern edifices (see box, p.334) including a round-fronted cinema, but the entire seafront tends to be devoid of life even in high season. It does have a handful of hotels and restaurants, but none is worth recommending.

Lakkí's nearest approximation to a beach, sand-and-gravel **Koulóuki** 500m west, holds ample trees for shade and supports a seasonal taverna. A kilometre or so beyond, **Merikiá** is a little nicer, and has two tavernas.

War Museum

Merikiá • Daily 10am–1pm • €3

An interesting little **War Museum**, set in two long arched tunnels that burrow deep into the hillside close to Merikiá beach, 2km west of Lakkí, commemorates the 1943 Battle of Léros. Part of an enormous Italian-built subterranean complex, the tunnels are crammed with barely

5

ITALIAN ARCHITECTURE IN THE DODECANESE

The architectural heritage left by the Italian domination in the Dodecanese has only recently begun to be appreciated. Many structures had been allowed to deteriorate, if not abandoned, by Greeks who would rather forget the entire Italian legacy.

Although the buildings are often dubbed "Art Deco", and some contain elements of that style, most are properly classed as **Rationalist** (or in the case of Léros, **Stream Line Modern**). They drew on various post-World War I architectural, artistic and political trends across Europe, particularly Novecento (a sort of Neoclassicism), the collectivist ideologies of the time, and the paintings of Giorgio di Chirico. The school's purest expressions tended to have grid-arrays of windows (or walls entirely of glass); tall, narrow ground-level arcades; rounded-off bulwarks; and either a uniform brick surface or grooved/patterned concrete. As well as in Italy and Greece, examples can still be found as far afield as Moscow or London (underground stations and blocks of flats), Los Angeles (apartment buildings) and Ethiopia (cinemas).

Italy initially attempted to create a hybrid of Rationalist style and local vernacular elements in the Dodecanese, both real and semi-mythical, to evoke a supposed generic "Mediterranean-ness". Every Italian-claimed island had at least one specimen in this "**protectorate**" style, usually the gendarme station, post office, covered market or governor's mansion, but only on the most populous or strategic islands were plans drawn up for sweeping urban re-ordering.

The years from 1936 to 1941 saw an intensified Fascist imperial ideology, an increased reference to the heritage of the Romans and their purported successors the Knights, and the replacement of the "protectorate" style with that of the "**conqueror**". This involved "**purification**", the stripping of many public buildings in Rhodes (though not, curiously, in Kos) of their orientalist ornamentation, its replacement with a cladding of porous stone to match medieval buildings in the old town, plus a monumental severity – blending Neoclassicism and modernism – and rigid symmetry to match institutional buildings (especially Fascist Party headquarters) and public squares across Italy.

labelled World War II documents, models, machine guns and assorted military hardware. To make sense of it all, head first to the far end and watch the archival footage.

Xirókambos

The fishing port of **XIRÓKAMBOS**, 5km south of Lakkí, is served by regular *kaïki* from Myrtiés on Kálymnos. It's a pretty spot, and many visitors swim, but the beach itself is unremarkable, improving as you head west.

In the hillside village of **LEPÍDHA**, 1km short of Xirókambos, a side turning north of the island's campsite leads up to a tiny **acropolis**. Behind the modern summit chapel, you can admire stretches of restored ancient masonry, while the views across to Kálymnos are superb.

ACCOMMODATION AND EATING   XIRÓKAMBOS

Hotel Efstathia Xirókambos ☏ 22470 24099, ⓦ hotel -efstathia.gr. Studio apartments set 50m back from the beach. Huge, well-furnished doubles (with rather basic bathrooms) as well as family four-plexes facing a large pool. **€60**

To Aloni Xirókambos ☏ 22470 26048. Xirókambos's best waterfront taverna, right of where the road meets the sea. Enjoy *mayireftá*, souvlakí and barbecued meats as well as fish, at beachside tables shaded by jacarandas. Daily 11am–9pm.

Plátanos, Pandélli and around

Five kilometres north of Lakkí, across the island, a continuous built-up strip climbing across a low ridge to connect two east-coast bays nominally consists of three distinct villages. On the shore of the northern bay, **Ayía Marína** stretches along a quayside used

5

by smaller inter-island ferries (see p.333). Immediately above it, older **Plátanos** stands beneath a Knight's castle, while on the bay to the south **Pandélli** is a busy but attractive little resort.

Plátanos

Draped over the saddle between Ayía Marína and Pandélli, a one-minute taxi ride or five-minute walk up from the ferry dock, **PLÁTANOS** is a residential community full of fine Neoclassical and vernacular houses. A good central base for exploring the island, it's short on restaurants or nightlife.

Kástro

May–Oct Mon, Tues, Thurs & Fri 8.30am–12.30pm; Wed, Sat & Sun 8.30am–12.30pm & 2.30–6.30pm; Nov–April daily 8.30am–12.30pm • €1

Atop the mighty headland northeast of Plátanos, Léros's **kástro** overlooks virtually the entire island – which was of course why the Knights sited a castle up here. Reach it either via a steep stair-path from the central square, or along a zigzagging road that starts its climb 100m back from the beach in Pandélli.

Although the castle's walls and staircases have been stabilized and/or restored, there's little to see; the reason to come is to enjoy the stupendous views from the battlements, especially dramatic at sunset.

Archeological Museum

Tues–Sun 8am–2.30pm • Free

Léros's **archeological museum**, a short way down towards Ayía Marína, is little more than a single room. Its few artefacts are however well laid out, with good explanation of where each was found, and a clear account of Lerian history.

Pandélli

Ten minutes' walk down from Plátanos, the former fishing village of **PANDÉLLI** has been transformed into a smart, rather upscale but still very pleasant little resort. In summer, there's little room on its small but reef-free, pea-gravel **beach** for anyone other than guests at its beachfront hotels, but it holds a good crop of cafés and tavernas. A short way east around the bay, a long cement jetty still serves local fishermen rather than yachts, which in high season must anchor offshore.

Southern beaches

Sadly, the prominent coastal footpath that heads south from Pandélli peters out as soon as it curves out of sight. To reach **VROMÓLITHOS**, 1km south, pedestrians and drivers alike have to follow a higher road, through the village of Spília.

Although the **beach** at Vromólithos is usually less crowded than Pandélli, it's no place to linger, consisting of a long narrow strip of exposed gravel squashed up against the high walls of beachfront properties. The sea is clean, but you have to cross rock seabed at most points to reach deeper water. There's a more secluded, sandier cove southeast towards **Tourkopígadho**, and an even better duo at the end of the side-road to **Aï Yiórgi**.

ACCOMMODATION **PLÁTANOS, PANDÉLLI AND AROUND**

Castelo Beach Pandélli beach ☎22470 23030, ⓦcastelo.gr. With its castellated tiers dominating the west end of Pandélli beach, this hotel is an eyesore, but once you're inside – whether in the spacious en-suite rooms, many of which have four-poster beds, or in the terrace café, perched just above water – it's a great place to take it easy. **€120**

★ **Hotel des Couleurs** Plátanos ☎22470 23341, ⓦhotel-des-couleurs.com. This gorgeous Italianate mansion, tucked up on the hillside just a few steps from the centre of Plátanos, holds six irresistibly stylish suites, each decorated in a different colour and featuring antique furnishings such as four-poster beds or clawfoot tubs. Charming and very helpful hosts, and superb breakfasts out on the terrace. **€90**

Panteli Beach Studios Pandélli beach ☎22470 26450, ⓦpanteli-beach.gr. Dutch-owned complex of

5

very tasteful and comfortable studios and apartments, all with balcony or terrace. There's no pool, but it opens directly onto the beach. **€90**

Studios Happiness Pandélli beach ☎ 22470 23498, ⓦ studios-happiness-leros.gr. Attractive blue-trimmed house, just short of the sea, that's been divided into a mixture of good-value rooms, studios and apartments,

with plentiful outdoor space. **€45**

⭐ **Windmills/Anemomyli** Pandélli ☎ 22470 25549, ⓦ leros-windmills.com. Lovely little B&B complex, poised above Pandélli on the road up to the castle, and consisting of two galleried windmill apartments and a long cottage, all with stone floors and great views from rear terraces. Closed Nov–April. **€100**

EATING AND DRINKING

⭐ **Mezedhopolio O Dimitris O Karaflas** Spília ☎ 22470 25626. One of the best-sited ouzerís on the island, adjoining the *Hotel Rodon* up in Spília, between Pandélli and Vromólithos. Ample portions of delicacies such as chunky local sausages, onion rings and *floyéres*, or dairy-based dips like *galotýri* and *batíris*. Daily lunch & dinner, all year.

⭐ **Mylos** Ayía Marína ☎ 22470 24894. Excellent restaurant, with a romantic setting by the wave-lapped windmill at the western edge of Ayía Marína. The menu has a strong Italian leaning, featuring risotto and panacotta as

well as specialities like expertly home-made *garidhopílafo* (shrimp-rice, for €12), grilled *mastéllo* cheese, seasonal fresh fish, and *kolokythokeftédhes* (courgette patties). Reserve in summer. March–Sept only, daily lunch & dinner.

Zorba's Pandélli beach ☎ 22470 22027. Pandélli's best seafront restaurant, with tables on the beach itself, as well as on a long terrace. The food is consistently good, with grills for €8 and steak or fish for €12–15 – choose your own fish in the kitchen – but service can be slow at peak times. Reserve ahead in summer. Daily lunch & dinner.

NIGHTLIFE

Café del Mar Vromólithos ☎ 22470 24766. Stylish, laidback bar, nestling along a shelf in the hillside just above the north end of Vromólithos beach. Very relaxing in the daytime, it hots up at night. Daily noon–late.

Enallaktiko Ayía Marína ☎ 22470 25746. As well as offering a handful of tables right on the quayside, this friendly local café also offers internet access. Daily

10am–midnight.

Savana Pandélli beach ⓦ savanabar-leros.com. Long-standing and very civilized English-Danish bar at the far end of the port, which despite its shaded seafront terrace retains a laidback rural feel. The perfect spot for a late-night musical nightcap (request your favourites); things get going from 10pm nightly. Daily noon–late.

Álinda and around

ÁLINDA, 3km northwest around the bay from Ayía Marína, is the longest-established resort on Léros, with development fringing a long, narrow strip of pea-gravel beach. It's also the first area to open in spring, and the last to shut in autumn.

Historical and Ethnographic Museum

Álinda • May–Sept Tues–Sun 9am–1pm & 6–8pm • €3

Housed in a castle-like seafront mansion, the island's **Historical and Ethnographic Museum** concentrates on the Battle of Léros. Displays include relics from the sunken *Queen Olga*, a wheel from a Junkers bomber, and a stove made from a bomb casing. There's also a grisly mocked-up clinic (mostly gynaecological tools), assorted rural implements, costumes and antiques.

Beaches near Álinda

Beaches near Álinda include **Krithóni**, 1.5km south, where the pretty cove gets very crowded in summer. Several more gravelly inlets lie alongside the road that curves around the bay further north, collectively known as **Dhýo Liskária**. From the dead end of the road, a 25-minute scramble north on a faint path brings you to pebbly **Kryfós** cove.

ACCOMMODATION AND EATING

ÁLINDA AND AROUND

⭐ **Archontiko Angelou** Álinda ☎ 22470 22749, ⓦ hotel-angelou-leros.com. Grand, marvellously atmospheric if slightly faded Italianate villa, a few hundred

metres inland from the beach. Eight pretty and very different rooms, with Victorian bath fittings, beamed ceilings and antique furnishings; some have balconies, but the views are of

the lovely gardens, not the sea. Closed mid-Oct to April. **€100**
Crithoni's Paradise Krithóni ☎ 22470 25120, ⓦ crithonisparadisehotel.gr. Luxurious hotel, halfway between Ayía Marína and Álinda. The low-rise complex holds well over a hundred fair-sized a/c rooms; all have outdoor space, those on the top floor enjoy bay views. The vast common areas include a large pool, gym, sauna and wi-fi zone. **€140**

Hotel Alinda Álinda ☎ 22470 23266. Very friendly family-run hotel, also known as *Xenonas Mavrakis*, set just

back from the middle of Álinda beach behind the good eponymous taverna, and offering good-value well-kept a/c rooms with fridges. **€60**

Vareladiko Dhýo Liskária ☎ 22470 23726. The last beachfront taverna you come to, at road's end east of Álinda. The owners have playfully painted walls and the hillside itself to make it look like it's a hotel, but all the "rooms" are just facades. As a restaurant, with seaside seating, it's fine, with inexpensive options like meatballs or mussels for just €6–7. Daily lunch & dinner.

Goúrna and Dhrymónas

The best beach on Léros's west coast is **Goúrna**, at the head of a large bay 2km southwest of Álinda or 3km north of Lakkí. It's the longest sandy beach on the island, hard-packed and gently shelving, if wind-buffeted and somewhat scruffy. A road along the southern shore of the bay ends beside a jetty at little **Dhrymónas**.

ACCOMMODATION AND EATING   **GOÚRNA AND DHRYMÓNAS**

Gourna Taverna Goúrna ☎ 22470 25120. Friendly taverna, with sunbed rental, slap in the middle of Goúrna beach. Grills include chicken on a spit, wild fish and tasty mezédhes. Summer only, daily noon–7pm.

Ouzerí Sotos Dhrymónas ☎ 22470 24546. This quayside restaurant is so close to the sea that they plant some tables right in the water. Very good food at good prices, with mezédhes at €2–4, unusual shellfish for €8–10, and fresh

fish daily courtesy of owner Sotos himself. May–Oct daily lunch & dinner.

Psilalonia Dhrymónas ☎ 22470 25283, ⓦ psilalonia .com. Lovely French-owned little B&B, up on the hillside above the far end of the bay at Dhrymónas (turn left at the little chapel where the coast road stops). Three nice en-suite rooms, set in a row with fabulous views. **€70**

Pátmos

Arguably the most beautiful, certainly the best known of the smaller Dodecanese, **Pátmos** has a distinctive, immediately palpable atmosphere. In a cave here, St John the Divine (known in Greek as *O Theológos*, "The Theologian", and author of one of the four Gospels) set down the **Book of Revelation**, the final book of the New Testament. The huge fortified **monastery** that honours him remains the island's dominant feature; its monks owned all of Pátmos until the eighteenth century, and their influence remains strong.

For those visitors not motivated by religion, Pátmos's greatest strength is its **beaches**. With so many attractive strands, you can usually escape the crowds even in high season, though you may need a vehicle to do so. **Day-trippers** exceed overnighters, thanks in part to the island's lack of an airport, and Pátmos feels a different place once the last excursion boat has left after sunset. Among those staying, no single nationality predominates, lending Pátmos a **cosmopolitan** feel almost unique in the Dodecanese. The steady clientele can be very **posh** indeed, with assorted royal and ex-royal families among repeat visitors.

ARRIVAL AND INFORMATION   **PÁTMOS**

By ferry All ferries arrive in the heart of Skála. Agathonisi (4 weekly; 1hr 50min–2hr 50min); Arkí (4 weekly; 40min); Kálymnos (2–4 daily; 1hr 35min–4hr); Kos (2–4 daily; 1hr 35min–5hr); Léros (2–4 daily; 40min–1hr 55min); Lipsi (1–3 daily; 25–50min); Pireás (4 weekly; 8hr 10min); Rhodes (1–3 daily; 4hr 45min–9hr 45min); Samos (1–2 daily; 1hr–3hr 10min); Sými (6 weekly; 4hr–8hr); Syros (2 weekly; 4hr).

Travel agencies Astoria Travel (☎ 22470 31324,

ⓦ astoriatravel.com) and Apollon Travel (☎ 22470 31324), both on Skála's main waterfront street.

Tourist office Pátmos has no tourist office, though ⓦ patmos-island.com and ⓦ patmosweb.gr are useful. However, the Orthodox Culture and Information Center facing the ferry landing (Mon, Tues, Thurs & Fri 9am–1pm & 6–9pm, Sat & Sun 6–9pm) aims to make visitors aware of the island's religious sites, and posts current opening hours.

5

GETTING AROUND

By bus Island buses leave from the quayside to Hóra (7 daily), Gríkou (3 daily) and Kámbos (3 daily).

Car and scooter rental Outfits include Tom & Gerry (☎ 22470 31357) and Astoria Travel (☎ 22470 31324,

ⓦ astoriatravel.com).

Excursion boats Boats to Psilí Ámmos and Arkí/Maráthi leave the quayside at 9.30–10am (7.30–10am to Léros and Lipsí depending on day/season).

Skála

Home to most of Pátmos's 3200 official residents, **SKÁLA** seems initially to contradict any solemn image of the island; the commercial district with its gift boutiques is incongruously sophisticated for such a small town. During peak season, the quay and inland lanes throng with trippers, and visitors still tend to be arriving after dark, including from the huge, humming cruisers that weigh anchor around midnight. Skála becomes a ghost town in winter (which here means by early October), when most shops and restaurants close.

Given time, Skála reveals more enticing corners in the residential fringes to its east and west, where vernacular mansions hem in pedestrian lanes creeping up the hillsides. At the summit of the westerly rise, **Kastélli**, masonry courses from an ancient acropolis enclose a more recent chapel. An easy ten-minute walk southwest across the flat isthmus, starting from the central market street, brings you to pebbly **Hokhlakás Bay** on the island's west coast. More of a quiet seafront suburb than a beach, it enjoys wonderful sunset views.

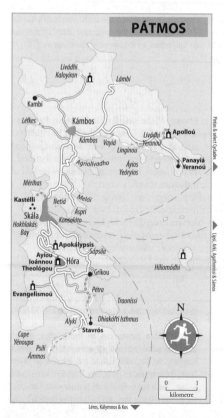

PÁTMOS

ACCOMMODATION   SKÁLA

Asteri near Mérihas cove, Nétia ☎ 22470 32465, ⓦ asteripatmos.gr. The best option in Nétia, set in spacious grounds on a knoll overlooking the bay, just under ten minutes' walk from the ferry. 37 simply furnished en-suite rooms of varying sizes, with sea-view balconies; many have a/c, two have wheelchair access. Breakfasts, available outdoors, feature own-grown produce. Breakfast included. **€80**

Australis Nétia ☎ 22470 31576, ⓦ patmos australis.gr. Very friendly, somewhat spartan en-suite hotel, owned by a helpful Greek-Australian family; an affiliated scooter-rental business saves you traipses into town. Units in the better-standard apartment annexe accommodate up to six. Breakfast included. **€70**

Blue Bay ☎ 22470 31165, ⓦ bluebay.50g.com. Multi-tiered Australian-Greek-run hotel on the hillside just above the sea, a short walk south from the jetty just out of sight of Skála. There's no beach, but all the a/c en-suite rooms have substantial sea-view balconies, and there's a small internet café. Credit cards accepted for stays of over two days. Breakfast included. **€116**

Captain's House Konsoláto ☎ 22470 31793, ⓦ captains-house.gr. A hotel not a house, with 17 a/c rooms, moments from the jetty and facing a tiny beach dotted with café tables. The quiet rooms in the rear wing overlook a fair-sized pool and shady terrace. Friendly management, nice furnishings and on-site car rental. B&B **€85**

5

Galini Skála ☎ 22470 31240, ⓦ galinipatmos.gr. Good-value hotel, at the end of a cul-de-sac just a few metres inland from the jetty, with pleasant furnishings in its eleven large rooms, most of which have balconies. **€75**

Hellenis Netiá ☎ 22470 31275, ⓦ hotelhellinispatmos.gr. This whitewashed 40-room hotel is very close to the sea path (paved at this point) and just north of a new yacht marina, and has bright, airy common areas, a lift (rather superfluous for just two storeys) and rooms offering fridges, balconies and baths. The same management has six superior apartments in contemporary style out back. **€90**

Maria Hokhlakás flatlands ☎ 22470 31201, ⓦ hotelmariapatmos.com. Quietly set small hotel, 150m from the sea, where the pleasant front garden, a/c, lobby internet facility and big sea-view balconies offset tiny bathrooms. Breakfast included. **€80**

★ **Porto Scoutari** Melóï hillside ☎ 22470 33124, ⓦ portoscoutari.com. Pátmos's premier hotel, this bungalow complex overlooks the beach and islets. The common areas and spacious a/c units, with TV and phone, are arrayed around a large pool and small spa. Unparalleled personal service from owner Elina Scoutari and her staff. Rates shown apply for stays of two or more nights. Breakfast included. **€126**

Skala Hotel Skála ☎ 22470 31343, ⓦ skalahotel.gr. Smart, large, bougainvillea-drenched hotel, set a short way back from the quayside and accessed via a flowery gateway-gazebo. 78 comfortable renovated rooms, with sea-view balconies and a large pool. **€130**

Studios Mathios Sápsila beach ☎ 22470 32583, ⓦ mathiosapartments.gr. Superior rural accommodation, ranging from small studios to an entire house, beside an unremarkable beach 2km southeast of Skála, with creative decor and extensive gardens. Owners Iakoumina and Theologos are exceptionally welcoming. **€60**

EATING AND DRINKING

Benetos Sápsila beach ☎ 22470 33089, ⓦ benetosrestaurant.com. High-class Mediterranean fusion, 2km southeast of Skála, with idyllic conservatory seating and a menu encompassing the likes of smoked sardine, bean and salmon croustade, *astakomakaronádha* and decadent desserts; budget €35–40 for three courses plus drink. Reservations recommended. Dinner only, June to early Oct, Tues–Sun from 7.30pm.

Ostria Skála ☎ 22470 33254. The food tends to be run-of-the-mill at this central, mid-priced, year-round ouzerí, facing the excursion-boat quay, but – late ferry arrivals take note – it's the only place serving after 11pm. Daily 10am–late.

To Hiliomodhi Skála ☎ 22470 34080. Cheap and crowded ouzerí, a few metres from the waterfront at the start of the road to Hóra, which offers vegetarian mezédhes (typically €3) and seafood delicacies such as limpets (served live) or grilled octopus (€7.50), plus decent *hýma* wine from Mégara.

There's outdoor seating at the back, in an unremarkable pedestrian lane. Open all year. Daily noon–late.

Tzivaeri Skála ☎ 22470 31170. Quality outfit, facing Theológos town beach a short walk along the quayside from the excursion boats, featuring delicate Cretan-style mezédhes and seafood such as boiled or grilled octopus (€8.50). As well as the enticing tables on the beach itself, seating is on the upstairs sea-view veranda, and there's live music courtesy of the owner in the large room inside. Dinner only, from 6pm nightly all year.

★ **Vegghera** Skála ☎ 22470 32988, ⓦ patmosweb.gr/vegghera.htm. The best all-rounder, opposite the yacht marina, with flawlessly presented stuffed scorpion fish, vegetarian or seafood salads, superb desserts, and per-head bills of €40–45 plus drink. It's the last place you come to as you walk north from the port. Reservations recommended. Easter to early Sept, daily 7.30pm–late.

NIGHTLIFE

Café Arion ☎ 22470 31595. This appealing wood-panelled, barn-like place, in the centre of the quayside, is Pátmos's most durable café-bar; all sorts sit outside, dance inside or prop up the long bar. Daily 9am–late.

Koukoumavla Konsoláta ☎ 22470 32325. The "Owl" is a perennially popular, hippy-ish bar near the foot of the main road up to Hóra. Run by a friendly Italian-Greek couple, it has garden seating, wacky decor and live music, and sells crafts as well as snacks and drinks. Daily noon–late.

Apokálypsis monastery

Daily 8am–1.30pm, also Tues, Thurs & Sun 4–6pm • Free

A ten-minute walk up the hill from Skála, halfway to Hóra, the **Apokálypsis monastery** is built around the cave where St John heard the voice of God issuing from a cleft in the rock, and where he sat dictating to his disciple Prohoros. The cave itself, of course, was once open to the elements, but it's now enclosed within an eleventh-century chapel. In a recess in the rock, the place where the saint is said to have rested his head at night is fenced off and outlined in beaten silver. Only if you come first thing in the morning, before the cacophonous tour groups arrive, can you hope to get a sense of the contemplative peace that inspired St John.

5

Ayíou Ioánnou Theológou monastery

Daily 8am–1.30pm, also Tues, Thurs & Sun 4–6pm • Free, museum €6

In 1088, the soldier-cleric **Ioannis "The Blessed" Khristodhoulos** (1021–93) was granted title to Pátmos by Byzantine emperor Alexios Komnenos. Within three years, he and his followers had completed most of what's now **Ayíou Ioánnou Theológou monastery**. Enclosed within its stout hilltop walls, a warren of courtyards, chapels, stairways, arcades, and roof terraces offers a rare glimpse of a Patmian interior. In antiquity, this site held a temple of Artemis, marble columns from which were incorporated here and there in the monastery.

As most of the complex is closed to outsiders – it remains home to a community of around a dozen monks – few visitors spend more than half an hour up here. The diminutive flower-bedecked courtyard just inside the gate opens onto the church itself, where frescoes depict the Apocalypse. Off to one side, the **museum** has a magnificent array of religious treasures, including medieval icons of the Cretan school, and several later donations from Russia. Manuscripts date as far back as a shrivelled parchment copy of the Gospel of St Mark, from the fifth or sixth century, though pride of place goes to the original chrysobull (edict) signed by Emperor Alexios Komnenos in the eleventh century, granting the island to Khristodhoulos. The upper floor also holds some archeological relics, including a statue of Dionysos from Paros.

Hóra

St John's promise of shelter from pirates spurred the growth of **HÓRA** outside the stout fortifications of the monastery. A magnificent ensemble, it remains architecturally homogeneous, its cobbled lanes sheltering shipowners' mansions from the island's seventeenth to eighteenth-century heyday. High, windowless walls and imposing wooden doors betray nothing of the painted ceilings, *votsalotó* terraces, flagstone kitchens and carved furniture inside. Inevitably, touristic tattiness disfigures the main approaches to the monastery, but by night, when the ramparts are startlingly floodlit, it's hard to think of a more beautiful Dodecanesian village. Neither should you miss the view from **Platía Lótza**, particularly at dawn or dusk.

SAINT JOHN ON PÁTMOS

Pátmos has been intimately associated with Christianity since **John the Evangelist** – later John the Divine – was exiled here from Ephesus by emperor Domitian in about 95 AD. John is said to have written his **Gospel** on Pátmos, but his sojourn is better remembered for the otherworldly voice that he heard coming from a cleft in the ceiling of his hillside grotto, which bid him to set down its words in writing. By the time John was allowed to return home, that disturbing finale to the New Testament, the **Book of Revelation** (aka the Apocalypse), had been disseminated as a pastoral letter to the Seven Churches of Asia Minor.

Revelation followed the standard Judeo-Christian tradition of apocalyptic books, with titanic battles in heaven and on earth, supernatural visions, plus lurid descriptions of the fates awaiting the saved and the damned following the **Last Judgement**. Hugely open to subjective interpretation, Revelation was being wielded as a rhetorical and theological weapon within a century of appearing. Its vivid imagery lent itself to depiction in frescoes adorning the refectories of Byzantine monasteries and the narthexes of Orthodox churches, conveying a salutary message to illiterate medieval parishioners.

John also combated paganism on Pátmos, in the person of an evil wizard, **Kynops**, who challenged him to a duel of miracles. As the magician's stock trick involved retrieving effigies of the deceased from the seabed, John responded by petrifying Kynops while he was under water. A buoy just off Theológos beach in Skála today marks the relevant submerged rock.

Forever after in the Orthodox world, heights amid desolate and especially **volcanic topography** have become associated with John. Pátmos, with its eerie landscape of igneous outcrops, is an excellent example, as is Níssyros, where one of the saint's monasteries overlooks the volcano's caldera.

Numerous "minor" churches and monasteries around Hóra contain beautiful icons and examples of local woodcarving; almost all are locked to prevent thefts, but key-keepers generally live nearby. Among the best are the church of **Dhiasózousa**; the convent of **Zoödhóhou Piyís** (daily except Sat 9am–noon), and the convent of **Evangelismoú**, at the edge of Hóra (daily 9–11am).

ARRIVAL AND INFORMATION   HÓRA

By bus Seven buses from Skála serve Hóra daily, from 7.30am until 7pm.

On foot The 40min walk from Skála to Hóra follows a beautiful old cobbled path. Don't try it in the full heat of the day, and whatever you do, don't walk up the much longer, switchbacking main road. To find the path, head through Skála towards Hokhlakás, then turn left onto a lane that leads

uphill to the main road – you'll see the cobbles ahead of you.

Festivals The best dates to visit, besides the Easter observances, are September 25–26 (Feast of John the Theologian) and October 20–21 (Feast of Khristodhoulos), both featuring solemn liturgies and processions. The annual Festival of Religious Music (late Aug/early Sept) is held in the grounds of the Apokálypsis monastery (see p.339).

ACCOMMODATION AND EATING

★ **Archontariki** Hóra ☎ 22470 29368, ⊛ archontariki -patmos.gr. Very gorgeous B&B, concealed behind high walls in a traditional village house that's been beautifully converted to hold five exquisitely furnished, exceptionally comfortable suites. As well as the lovely central courtyard, there's a garden and roof terrace; rates include a superb breakfast. Closed Oct–Easter. **€200**

Loza Platía Loza, Hóra ☎ 22470 32405. Nicely positioned café/restaurant just below the eponymous platía, close to the main road, where the broad terrace offers sweeping

views, and as well as hot and alcoholic drinks you can get mezédhes for €7–8, salads and pasta dishes for under €10, and pricier steaks. Open for all meals daily.

Pantheon Hóra ☎ 22470 31226. The village's most authentic restaurant, at the start of the monastery approach. Good atmosphere and music, a lovely old interior or terrace views over the village and friendly management offset somewhat run-of-the-mill, pricey mezédhes. Easter–Dec all meals daily, until late.

The rest of the island

Pátmos's **best beaches** are concentrated north of Skála, tucked into the startling eastern shoreline, and accessible from side roads off the main road. Most of the island's west-facing bays are unusable, owing to the prevailing wind and washed-up debris.

Gríkou and Pétra

Not far south of uninspiring Sapsila beach, roads converge at the sandiest part of **Gríkou**. The beach itself, far from the island's best, forms a narrow strip of hard-packed sand, yielding to sand and gravel, then large pebbles at **Pétra** immediately south. It's not possible to drive any further south along the coast.

Melóï and Agriolívadho

A couple of kilometres northeast of Skála, the large crescent beach at **Melóï** is handy and quite appealing, with tamarisks behind the slender belt of sand, and good snorkelling offshore. It's accessible by road at its southern end, which is home to a taverna. North of Melóï, **Agriolívadho** (Agriolivádhi) is another attractive sheltered bay. Most of the beach is pebbly gravel, but there's a reasonable amount of sand at its broad centre.

Kámbos

Hilltop **KÁMBOS**, 4km north of Skála, is the island's only other real village. Originally built to house the wives and children of lay workers at the monastery, it's surrounded by scattered farms.

Kámbos **beach**, 600m downhill to the east, is a strong contender for the best beach on the island, although it fills with local kids in summer. Too deeply indented to be seen from the rest of Pátmos, it offers peaceful sheltered swimming, along with plentiful sunbeds, two tavernas, and beach toys to rent.

5

Beyond Kámbos

A succession of less busy coves lies **east** of Kámbos. **Vayiá** is a little bay where a few trees overhang a beach of pebbles and coarse sand, there's a snack bar, and the sea is a particularly enticing shade of turquoise. The double bay at **Lingínou** can only be reached on foot, but has a *kantína*. **Livádhi Yeranoú** is a long stretch of mingled sand and gravel, shaded by tamarisks, and with a delightful islet offshore as a target for swimmers.

ACCOMMODATION   THE REST OF PÁTMOS

Patmos Aktis Gríkou Beach ☎ 22470 32800, ⓔ patmosasktis.gr. This very upscale, dazzling white 56-room luxury hotel opened in 2011; as a style statement it's incongruous for Pátmos, but there's no disputing the

opulence of its rooms, spa and restaurant. The same management has also taken over and renovated the cheaper *Silver Beach* hotel nearby, bookable via the same website. Closed Oct–Easter. **€200**

EATING AND DRINKING

George's Place Kámbos Beach ☎ 22470 31881. Friendly snack and café bar, spreading out onto the sand at the broader eastern end of Kámbos Beach. Pies and salads €5–7, plus juices, milkshakes and a full bar, and free wi-fi access. Mid-May to Sept, daily 10am–10pm.

★ **Ktima Petra** Petra Beach ☎ 22470 33207. The best rural taverna on Pátmos, set back slightly behind the trees at the north end of Petra beach, with its own large greenhouse. Lush salads, home-made *dolmádhes*, carefully cooked *mayireftá*, plus grills after dark; little on the menu costs over €10. Reservations advised in summer. Easter–Oct daily 1–10pm.

Lambi Lámbi Bay ☎ 22470 31490. Lovely little seafront taverna, founded in 1958, where the roof is held up by

elderly tamarisk trees, and some tables are on the beach itself. The fish is recommended; the menu is very brief off-season. Easter to mid-Oct, daily noon–8pm.

Livádhi Yeranoú Taverna Livádhi Yeranoú Beach ☎ 22470 32046. Good-value taverna, just short of the beach, with a nice terrace and a reasonable menu of seafood, chops, *tzatzíki*, *hórta* and salads. May–Nov daily noon–late.

Tarsanas Patmos Marine boatyard, Dhiakoftí isthmus. The boatyard near the southern tip of the island might not seem the obvious place to find a smart, good-value taverna, but *Tarsanas* is a favourite (all-year) "power lunch" spot for locals. Mountainous salads, quiche-like *píttes* and Greek standards; the nicest tables are in a permanently grounded boat. Daily lunch & dinner.

Lipsí

The largest, most interesting and most populated of the islets north and east of Pátmos, **LIPSÍ** also has the most significant tourist trade. Returning regulars make showing up in peak season without reservations unwise. During quieter months, however, Lipsí still provides an idyllic halt, its sleepy pace almost making plausible a dubious link with **Calypso**, the nymph who held Odysseus in thrall. Once a dependency of the monastery on Pátmos, Lipsí is still conspicuously sown with blue-domed churches. Deep wells water small farms and vineyards, but there's only one flowing spring, and although plenty of livestock can be seen, the non-tourist economy is far from thriving.

ARRIVAL AND DEPARTURE   LIPSÍ

By ferry Agathoníssi (4 weekly; 2hr 45min); Arkí (4 weekly; 1hr 35min); Kálymnos (2–3 daily; 1hr 20min–2hr 50min); Kos (2–3 daily; 1hr 40min–4hr 10min); Léros (2–3 daily; 25min–1hr 5min); Pátmos (2–3 daily; 20min);

Pireás (1 weekly; 9hr 45min); Rhodes (6 weekly; 5hr 10min–8hr 20min); Samos (1 daily; 1hr 30min–4hr 5min); Sými (6 weekly; 4hr 20min–7hr).

Lipsí Village and around

Lipsí's only significant population centre, known as **LIPSÍ VILLAGE**, stretches around its large south-facing harbour. From the ferry jetty at its northwestern extremity, the hilltop centre of town is a 600m walk.

None of the **beaches** is more than an hour's walk from the port. The closest, and sandiest, are crowded **Liendoú** and **Kámbos**, but many prefer attractive **Katsadhiá**

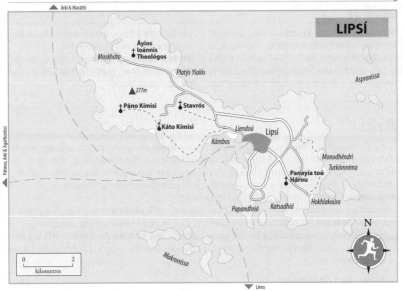

(sand) and **Papandhriá** (coarse sand-and-gravel), adjacent coves 2km south of the port. Another paved road leads 4km west from town to protected **Platýs Yialós**, a shallow, sandy bay, continuing to sumpy Moskháto fjord (no beach).

To reach the isolated east-coast beaches, which lack facilities, rent a **scooter** at the port. **Hokhlakoúra** consists of coarse shingle (finer pebbles at mid-strand); nearby **Turkómnima** is sandy and much shadier, if mercilessly exposed to the *meltémi*.

ACCOMMODATION
LIPSÍ VILLAGE AND AROUND

Aphroditi Lipsí Village ☎ 22470 41000, �🌐 hotel -aphroditi.com. Complex of large, tiled-floor studios and apartments, some with kitchens and two double bedrooms, set slightly back across the road from Liendoú beach. Closed Dec–April. **€75**

Galini Apartments Lipsí Village ☎ 22470 41212. The first building you see on disembarking, right above the ferry jetty, is a prime budget choice in all respects, run by the hospitable Matsouris family. Units have kitchens and balconies. Nikos may take guests fishing on request. Closed Nov–Easter. **€60**

Helios Apartments Lipsí Village ☎ 694 54 60 534, �🌐 helioslipsi.gr. Five variably sized units, just off the road to Hokhlakoúra and Katsadhiá. All have two bedrooms and two bathrooms, and are tastefully decorated with terracotta tiles, rounded corners and quality furnishings like wrought-iron beds and even washing machines. Some have galleries, but there are no sea views. Closed Nov–Easter. **€80**

★ **Nefeli Hotel** Kámbos beach ☎ 22470 41120, ⍵ nefelihotels.com. This modern bungalow-hotel complex, overlooking the beach, offers a range of huge studios plus one- and two-bedroom apartments in the same pastel colours. Ground-floor studios are cave-like, breezier upstairs units are preferable. Open all year. **€100**

★ **Poseidon Apartments** Lipsí Village ☎ 22470 41130, ⍵ lipsi-poseidon.gr. Impeccable, roomy, modern studios with large balconies, 150m from the jetty, as well as a one-bedroom apartment; the decor may be IKEA-on-steroids but everything has been thought of. On the ground floor, handy scooter rental and a convenient *psistariá* with roast chicken. Closed Nov–Easter. **€65**

EATING AND DRINKING

Café du Moulin ☎ 22470 41316. The main daytime hub for travellers, in the central square. Hearty lashings of *mayireftá* at shaded tables, as well as inexpensive breakfasts. Daily 8am–late.

★ **Karnayio** ☎ 22470 41422. This good-value restaurant, adjoining a blue-domed church on the far side of the bay, serves hefty salads and ample helpings of *mayireftá* such as pork with celery and carrots. Daily lunch and dinner, all year.

★ **To Pefko** ☎ 22470 41404. Classic Greek cuisine overlooking the main jetty, strong on baked aubergine recipes and lamb-based hotpots like *ambelourgoú*, and with efficient service. May to late Sept, daily lunch and dinner.

5

NIGHTLIFE

★ **Dilaila** Katsadhiá ☎ 22470 41041. Garden-set beachfront taverna-café, overlooking the strand at Katsadhiá. While pricier than the island norm, it's worth it for such delights as salad with bits of local cheese, chunky aubergine dip or *fáva* and marinated fish dishes; from 11pm until 4am it hots up as a late-night music bar. June to mid-Sept, noon until very late indeed.

The Rock Lipsí's longest-lasting bar, right by the port, with a congenial crowd, boulder-like host Babis and good tunes. Daily 6pm–late.

Arkí

Roughly two-thirds the size of Lipsí, **ARKÍ** is a far more primitive island, lacking proper shops or a coherent village. A mere fifty or so inhabitants eke out a living, mostly fishing or goat/sheep-herding, though servicing yachts attracted by the superb anchorage at Avgoústa Bay – named for the half-ruined Hellenistic/Byzantine **Avgoustínis fortress** overhead – is also important.

Excursion-boat clients swim at the "Blue Lagoon" of **Tiganákia** at the southeast tip, but other **beaches** on Arkí take some finding. The more obvious are the carefully nurtured sandy cove at **Pateliá** by the outer jetty, or tiny **Limnári** pebble-bay (fitting five bathers at a pinch) on the northeast coast, a 25-minute walk away via the highest house in the settlement.

ARRIVAL AND DEPARTURE | | ARKÍ

By ferry Agathoníssi (4 weekly; 1hr); Kálymnos (4 weekly; 4hr 20min); Lipsí (4 weekly; 1hr 35min); Léros (4 weekly; 2hr 50min); Pátmos (4 weekly; 40min); Samos (4 weekly; 2hr 20min).

ACCOMMODATION AND EATING

Nikolas ☎ 22470 32477. Friendly taverna on the flagstoned harbourside platía, where a mother/son team serve home-made puddings and *mayireftá* such as peppers with goat's cheese, and offer pleasant west-facing rooms. **€40**

O Trypas ☎ 22470 32230. Also known as *Tou Manoli*, this waterfront taverna is renowned for its very decent fish meals and *mezédhes*; has mock-trad, stone-floored rental units just up the hillside; and doubles as the island's most happening music bar. Daily 1pm–late.

Maráthi

The nearest large, sandy, tamarisk-shaded beach is a ten-minute boat trip away on **Maráthi**, the only inhabited islet (permanent population 3) of the mini-archipelago around Arkí.

ACCOMMODATION AND EATING | | MARÁTHI

Pantelis ☎ 22470 32609, ⓦ marathi-island.gr. The most elaborate and "resort"-like establishment on Maráthi. The beachfront tables outside make a perfect venue to enjoy local free-range goat, fresh-caught fish, or vegetables from the adjacent garden, while the rooms are spacious, airy and tastefully furnished. Closed Nov–April. **€45**

Piratis ☎ 22470 31580 or 69739 62462, ⓦ marathi-island.com. Full-service taverna with waterside seating and a menu of home-baked classic as well as fresh fish, plus ten simple, adequate a/c en-suite rooms. Barefoot proprietor Mihalis emphasizes his comic-book-pirate persona with a Jolly Roger flag and speedboat named *Piratis*. **€35**

Agathoníssi

The small, steep-sided, waterless islet of **AGATHONÍSSI** is too remote – closer to Turkey than Pátmos, in fact – to be a popular day-trip target. Intrepid Greeks and Italians form its main tourist clientele, along with yachts attracted by excellent anchorage. Even though the *Nissos Kalymnos* (and a summer catamaran) appear regularly, schedules mean you should count on staying at least two days.

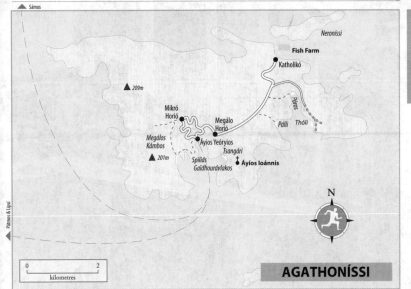

Despite the lack of springs, the island is greener and more fertile than apparent from the sea; lentisc, carob and scrub oak on the heights overlook two arable plains in the west. Fewer than a hundred people live here full time, but they make a go of stock-raising or fishing (or rather, fish-farming), and few dwellings are abandoned or neglected.

Most of the population lives in **Megálo Horió** hamlet, just visible on the ridge above the harbour hamlet of **ÁYIOS YEÓRYIOS** and at eye level with tiny **Mikró Horió** opposite. Except for a small shop and two café-restaurants working peak-season nights only in Megálo Horió, all amenities are in the port.

With no rental scooters, exploring involves **walking** along the cement-road network, or following a very few tracks and paths – bring plenty of water. If you won't swim at the port, home to the largest sandy **beach**, hike ten minutes southwest to shingle-gravel **Spiliás**, or continue another quarter-hour by path over the ridge to **Gaïdhourávlakos**, another gravel cove.

Bays in the east, all reached by paved roads, include tiny **Póros** (45min distant), fine sand with lentisc-tree shade at the back; **Thóli** (25min further) in the far southeast, with good snorkelling and some morning shade; and **Páli** across the same bay, a small but pristine fine-pebble cove reached by a fifteen-minute walk down from the trans-island road.

ARRIVAL AND DEPARTURE   AGATHONÍSSI

By ferry Arkí (4 weekly; 1hr); Kálymnos (4 weekly; 5hr 30min); Lipsí (4 weekly; 2hr 45min); Léros (4 weekly; 4hr); Pátmos (4 weekly; 1hr 50min); Samos (4 weekly; 1hr 5min).

ACCOMMODATION AND EATING

Rooms Maria Kamitsi ☎ 22470 29065, or 693 25 75 121. Thirteen pleasant a/c rooms at the centre of the beach, sharing use of a kitchen and fridges, with a vine-covered patio outside. **€40**

Seagull ☎ 22470 29062. Central taverna, close to the yacht moorings, where the romantic waterside tables are filled every night for a full menu of baked and grilled dishes. Daily lunch & dinner.

To Agnanti ☎ 22470 29019 or 697 48 14 013. Good-value rooms, the newest on the island, above the popular *Memento Bar*, which has a wooden deck reaching out over the water. **€50**

The East and North Aegean

351 Sámos

364 Foúrni

366 Ikaría

372 Híos

382 Inoússes

383 Psará

384 Lésvos

401 Áyios Efstrátios

402 Límnos

408 Samothráki

412 Thássos

PYRGÍ, HÍOS

The East and North Aegean

The seven substantial islands and four minor islets scattered off the Aegean coast of Asia Minor form a rather arbitrary archipelago. While there are similarities in architecture and landscape, the strong individual character of each island is far more striking and thus they do not form an immediately recognizable group, and neither are they all with each other by ferries. What they do have in common, with the possible exception of Sámos and Thássos, is that they receive fewer visitors than other island groups and so generally provide a more authentic Greek atmosphere. Yet the existence of magnificent beaches, dramatic mountain scenery, interesting sights and ample facilities makes them a highly attractive region of Greece to explore.

Verdant **Sámos** ranks as the most visited island of the group but, once you leave its crowded resorts behind, is still arguably the most beautiful, even after a devastating fire in 2000. **Ikaría** to the west remains relatively unspoilt, if a minority choice, and nearby **Foúrni** is (except in summer) a haven for determined solitaries, as are the Híos satellites **Psará** and **Inoússes**. **Híos** proper offers far more cultural interest than its neighbours to the south, but far fewer tourist facilities. **Lésvos** may not impress initially, though once you get a feel for its old-fashioned Anatolian ambience you may find it hard to leave. By contrast, few foreigners visit **Áyios Efstrátios**, and for good reason, though **Límnos** to the north is much busier, particularly in its western half. In the far north Aegean, Samothráki and Thássos are relatively isolated and easier to visit from northern Greece, which administers them. **Samothráki** has one of the most dramatic seaward approaches of any Greek island, and one of the more important ancient sites. **Thássos** is more varied, with sandy beaches, mountain villages and minor archeological sites.

Brief history

Despite their proximity to modern Turkey, only Lésvos, Límnos and Híos bear significant signs of an **Ottoman** heritage, in the form of old mosques, hammams and fountains, plus some domestic architecture betraying obvious influences from Constantinople, Macedonia and further north in the Balkans. The limited degree of this heritage has in the past been duly referred to by Greece in an intermittent **propaganda war** with Turkey over the sovereignty of these far-flung outposts – as well as the disputed boundary between them and the Turkish mainland. Ironically, this friction gave these long-neglected islands a new lease of life from the 1960s onward, insomuch as their sudden **strategic importance** prompted infrastructure improvements to support garrisoning, and gave a mild spur to local economies, engaged in providing goods and services to soldiers, something predating the advent of tourism. Yet the region has remained one of the **poorest regions** in western Europe. Tensions with Turkey have occasionally been aggravated by disagreements over suspected undersea oil

Climbing Mount Kérkis p.363
Walking in western Ikaría p.370
Day-trips from Híos p.374
Mastic mastication p.378
Theophilos Hadzimihaïl: the Rousseau of Greece? p.390
Polikhnítos Spa p.392
The olives of Lésvos p.394
The war cemeteries p.407
The Samothracian mysteries p.410
Climbing the moon p.411

MÓLYVOS, LÉSVOS

Highlights

❶ Vathý, Sámos The two-wing archeological museum is among the best in the islands, while there are atmospheric tavernas in the upper town of Áno Póli. **See p.353**

❷ Foúrni This small fishing island offers numerous deserted coves, a surprisingly lively port and a lovely main street lined with mulberry trees. **See p.364**

❸ Ikaría Western Ikaría has superb beaches and you can participate in the idiosyncratic nocturnal lifestyle of the Ráhes villages. **See p.366**

❹ Southern Híos The architecturally unique *mastihohoriá* (mastic villages) have a distinct Middle Eastern feel. **See p.377**

❺ Mólyvos, northern Lésvos This castle-crowned resort village is undoubtedly the most beautiful on the island, perhaps in the whole island group. **See p.398**

❻ Límnos villages Atmospheric basalt-built villages with lively central tavernas and great local wines to sample. **See p.402**

❼ Sanctuary of the Great Gods, Samothráki With Mount Fengári as a backdrop, the remote Sanctuary of the Great Gods is blessed with a natural grandeur. **See p.409**

❽ Alykí, Thássos A beautifully situated resort, with fine beaches flanked by ancient and Byzantine archeological sites. **See p.417**

HIGHLIGHTS ARE MARKED ON THE MAP ON P.350

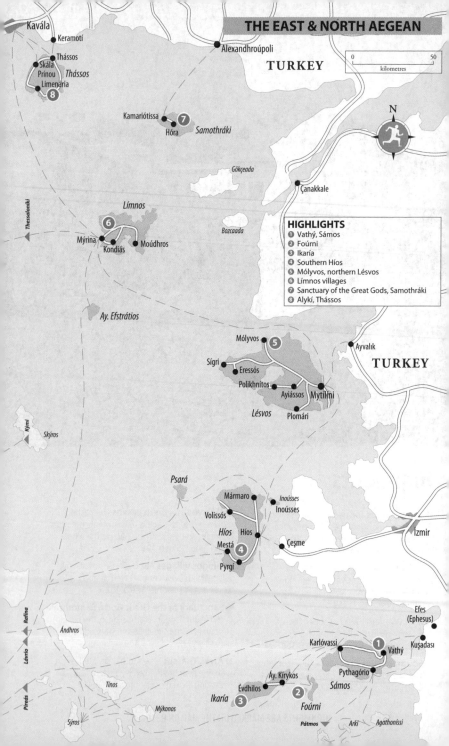

THE EAST & NORTH AEGEAN

TURKEY

HIGHLIGHTS
1. Vathý, Sámos
2. Foúrni
3. Ikaría
4. Southern Híos
5. Mólyvos, northern Lésvos
6. Límnos villages
7. Sanctuary of the Great Gods, Samothráki
8. Alykí, Thássos

Kavála
Keramotí
Thássos
Skála
Prínou
Limenária
Thássos
8

Kamariótissa
Hóra
Samothráki
7

Alexandhroúpoli

Gökçeada

Çanakkale

Thessaloníki

Bozcaada

Límnos
Mýrina
Kondiás
Moúdhros
6

Ay. Efstrátios

Mólyvos
5
Ayvalík
TURKEY
Sígri
Eressós
Polikhnítos
Ayiássos
Mytilíni
Lésvos
Plomári

Kými
Skýros

Psará
Mármaro
Inoússes
Volissós
Inoússes
Híos   Híos
Mestá
4
Çeşme
Pyrgí

İzmir

Ráfina

Ándhros

Lávrio

Piréas

Tínos

Efes
(Ephesus)
Karlóvassi
1
Vathý
Kuşadası
Pythagório
Sámos
Évdhilos
Áy. Kírykos
2
Ikaría
3
Foúrni
Pátmos   Arkí   Agathoníssi
Mýkonos
Sýros

0   50
kilometres

N

deposits in the straits between the islands and Anatolia. The Turks have also persistently demanded that Límnos, astride the sea lanes to the Dardanelles, be demilitarized, and in the last decade Greece has finally complied, with garrisons also much reduced on Sámos and Lésvos, as part of the increasing **détente** between the traditional enemies.

Sámos

Lush, seductive and shaped like a pregnant guppy, **SÁMOS** seems to swim away from Asia Minor, to which the island was joined until Ice Age cataclysms sundered it from Mount Mykáli (Mycale) on the Turkish mainland. The resulting 2.5km strait provides the narrowest maritime distance between Greece and Turkey, except at Kastellórizo. In its variety of mountainous terrain, beaches and vegetation, Sámos has the feel of a much larger island, and despite recent development and wildfires taking their toll, it remains indisputably among the most beautiful in the Aegean.

Brief history

Sámos was during the Archaic era among the **wealthiest** islands in the Aegean and, under the patronage of tyrant Polykrates, home to a thriving intellectual community that included Epicurus, Pythagoras, Aristarcus and Aesop. Decline set in when Classical Athens rose, though Sámos's status improved in Byzantine times when it formed its own imperial administrative district. Late in the fifteenth century, the ruling Genoese **abandoned** the island to the mercies of pirates and Sámos remained almost uninhabited until 1562, when it was repopulated with Greek Orthodox settlers from various corners of the empire.

The new Samians **fought** fiercely for independence during the **1820s**, but despite notable land and sea victories against the Turks, the Great Powers handed the island back to the Ottomans in 1830, with the consoling proviso that it be semi-autonomous, ruled by an appointed Christian prince. This period, known as the **Iyimonía** (Hegemony), was marked by a renaissance in fortunes, courtesy of the hemp, leather-tanning and (especially) tobacco trades. However, union with Greece in 1912, an influx of refugees from Asia Minor in 1923 and the ravages of a bitter World War II occupation followed by mass emigration effectively reversed this recovery until tourism took over during the 1980s.

ARRIVAL AND DEPARTURE   **SÁMOS**

By plane Sámos's airport lies 14km southwest of Vathý and 3km west of Pythagório. There is no airport bus; taxi fares to all points are posted on placards, and in summer taxis to the airport or ferry docks must be booked in advance. There are flights on Olympic Airlines, Aegean or Sky Express to the following destinations (frequencies are for June–Oct):

Destinations Athens (3–4 daily; 50min–1hr 20min); Iráklio, Crete (2 weekly; 1hr); Lésvos (2 weekly; 40min–1hr 20min); Límnos (2 weekly; 1hr 40min–2hr 20min); Rhodes (2 weekly; 45min); Thessaloníki (4 weekly; 1hr 10min).

By ferry/hydrofoil There are three ferry ports: Karlóvassi in the west, plus Vathý and Pythagório in the east, making the island a major travel hub. All ferries between Pireás and Sámos call at both Karlóvassi and Vathý, while those from the northeast Aegean call at one or both. Small boats to Kuşadası in Turkey depart mostly from Vathý, while Karlóvassi has a small ferry to Foúrni and Ikaría. Pythagório offers ferry and hydrofoil connections to the Dodecanese islands. Here is a summary of destinations and summer frequencies:

Karlóvassi to: Áyios Kírykos, Ikaría (8 weekly; 2hr); Évdhilos, Ikaría (3 weekly; 2hr 30min); Foúrni (8 weekly; 1hr 30min–2hr 30min); Híos (1 weekly; 4hr); Kavála (1 weekly; 18hr 30min–19hr 30min); Lésvos (1 weekly; 6hr 30min); Límnos (1 weekly; 12–13hr); Mýkonos (6 weekly; 5hr–5hr 30min); Pireás (6 weekly; 11–12hr); Sýros (6 weekly; 6hr–6hr 30min).

Pythagório to: Agathónissi (4 weekly; 4hr); Lipsí (1–2 daily; 1hr 40min–4hr 30min); Pátmos (1–2 daily; 1hr–3hr 30min); Léros (1–2 daily; 2hr 15min–5hr 30min); Kálymnos (1–2 daily; 3hr 10min–6hr 45min); Kos (1 daily; 3hr 45min); Kuşadası, Turkey (2 weekly; 2hr).

Vathý to: Áyios Kírykos, Ikaría (8 weekly; 3hr); Évdhilos, Ikaría (3 weekly; 2hr 30min); Foúrni (3 weekly; 1hr 30min); Híos (2 weekly; 3hr 30min); Kavála (1 weekly; 18–19hr); Kuşadası, Turkey (1–2 daily; 1hr 30min); Lésvos (2 weekly; 6hr); Límnos (1 weekly; 11hr 30min–12hr 30min); Mýkonos (6 weekly; 5hr–5hr 30min); Pireás (6 weekly; 11–12hr); Sýros (6 weekly; 6hr–6hr 30min); Thessaloníki (1 weekly; 24hr).

6

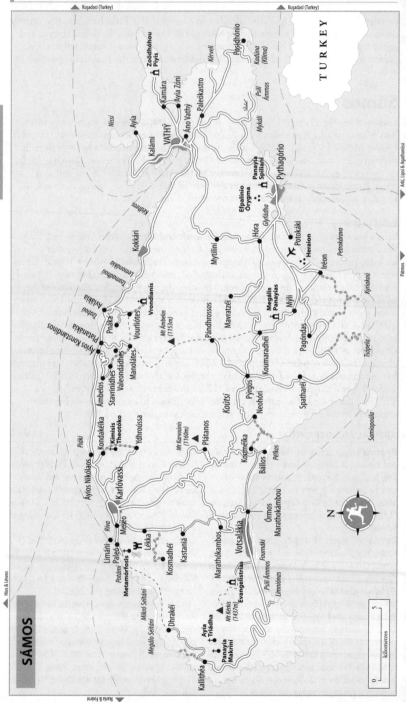

SÁMOS

Travel agents The most comprehensive island-wide travel agents, represented in all three ports and some resorts, are By Ship (☎22730 22116, ✆byshiptravel.gr) and ITSA (☎22730 23605, ✆itsatravelsamos.gr).

GETTING AROUND

By bus The KTEL service is good between Pythagório and Vathý, with 11 services on weekdays, 9 on Saturday and 4 on Sunday, and fair on the Vathý–Kokkári–Karlóvassi route, with 8 weekday services, 5 on Sat and 3 on Sun, but poor for other destinations.

By car or motorbike Of the myriad scooter- and car-rental agencies dotted around the island, three to try are Aramis/Sixt (☎22730 23253), Avis/Reliable (☎22730

80445), both with branches island-wide, and Auto Union (☎22730 27444) at Themistoklí Sofoúli 79 in Vathý, which negotiates good long-term rates and will deliver cars to the airport.

By kaïki There are several weekly *kaïki* day-trips (10am–4pm; from €26) from Órmos Marathokámbou to the nearby islet of Samiopoúla and inaccessible parts of the south coast.

Vathý

Lining the steep northeastern shore of a deep bay, beachless **VATHÝ** (often confusingly referred to as "Sámos") is a busy provincial town which grew from a minor anchorage after 1830, when it replaced Hóra as the island's capital. It's an unlikely, rather ungraceful resort and holds little of interest aside from an excellent museum, some Neoclassical mansions and the hillside suburb of **Áno Vathý**.

Áno Vathý

The best inland target on foot, a twenty-minute walk south from town and 150m above sea level, is the atmospheric hill village of **ÁNO VATHÝ**, a nominally protected but increasingly threatened community of tottering, canal-tile-roofed houses: some buildings are being replaced by bad-taste blocks of flats, others are being defaced with aluminium windows and modern tiles. Best of several venerable **churches** is quadruple-domed **Aï Yannáki**, in the vale separating the village's two hillside neighbourhoods.

Archeological museum

Tues–Sun 8.30am–3pm • €3 • ☎22730 27469

The only real must is the excellent **archeological museum**, set behind the small central park beside the nineteenth-century town hall. The collections are housed in both the old Paschalion building and a modern wing just opposite, constructed for the star exhibit: a majestic, 5m-tall *kouros* discovered out at the Heraion sanctuary. The largest freestanding effigy surviving from ancient Greece, this *kouros* was dedicated to Apollo, but found next to a devotional mirror to Mut (the Egyptian equivalent of Hera) from a Nile workshop.

In the Paschalion, more votive offerings of **Egyptian** design – a hippo, a dancer in Nilotic dress, Horus-as-Falcon, an Osiris figurine – provide evidence of trade and pilgrimage links between Sámos and the Nile valley going back to the eighth century BC. The **Mesopotamian** and **Anatolian** origins of other artwork confirm an exotic trend, most tellingly in a case full of ivory miniatures: Perseus and Medusa in relief; a kneeling, perfectly formed mini-*kouros*; a pouncing lion; and a bull's-head drinking horn. The most famous local artefacts are numerous bronze **griffin-heads**, for which Sámos was the major centre of production in the seventh century BC; they were mounted on the edge of cauldrons to ward off evil spirits. There's also an unlabelled **hoard of gold byzants**, some of more than three hundred imperial coins from the fifth to seventh centuries AD – one of the largest such troves ever discovered.

ARRIVAL AND INFORMATION   VATHÝ

By ferry Ferries dock at the north end of the seafront.
By bus Buses stop on the front, just south of the centre.
By taxi The taxi rank is opposite the fishing harbour.

By car See above for details of car rental around the island. The southern seafront is the best area for free parking.
Tourist office Themistoklí Sofoúli 107 (May–Oct Mon–Fri

6

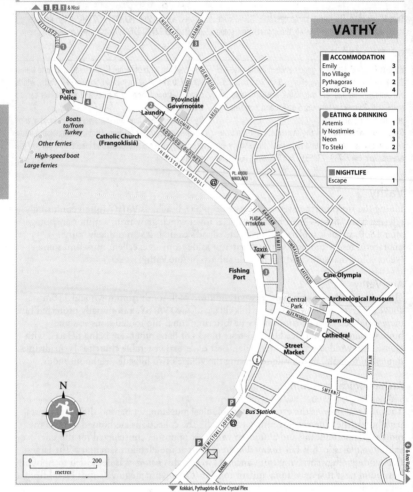

VATHÝ

■ **ACCOMMODATION**
Emily 3
Ino Village 1
Pythagoras 2
Samos City Hotel 4

● **EATING & DRINKING**
Artemis 1
Iy Nostimies 4
Neon 3
To Steki 2

■ **NIGHTLIFE**
Escape 1

Kokkári, Pythagório & Cine Crystal Plex

9am–2pm). The tourist office is minimally helpful.
Services Amenities include the post office, inconveniently remote on Themistoklí Sofoúli. Internet cafés include Net House, on the front near the KTEL.

ACCOMMODATION

Emily Cnr of Grámmou and 11 Noemvríou, Katsoúni ☎ 22730 24691, ✉ emilyhotel@hotmail.com. Small, well-run two-star hotel with cheerful and comfortable rooms – there's even wall art – and a roof garden. Breakfast included. March–Nov. **€60**

Ino Village Kalámi ☎ 22730 23241, ⓦ inovillagehotel.com. Surprisingly affordable three-star hotel about 1.5km north of the ferry dock, with views from most of its large, well-appointed rooms, a big pool and a decent on-site restaurant. Breakfast included. **€65**

Pythagoras Kalistrátou 12 ☎ 22730 28601, ⓦ pythagorashotel.com. This medium-sized hotel, around 600m north of the ferry dock, provides the best value in town with its simple but spotless rooms. There are computers in the friendly bar/restaurant area. **€30**

Samos City Hotel Themistokli Soufóuli 11 ☎ 22730 28377, ⓦ samoshotel.gr. Refurbished behemoth by the ferry dock that's a firm favourite despite the rooms being rather small. Double-glazing against traffic noise, rooftop pool-terrace and popular café out front. Rudimentary breakfast included. **€65**

EATING, DRINKING AND NIGHTLIFE

Vathý's perennial nightlife venue is a "strip" at the start of Kefalopoúlou north of the jetty, with annually changing bars that boast seaside (or sea-view) terraces. Plushly fitted **Cine Olympia**, inland on Yimnasiárhou Katevéni, offers a variable programme of films (subject to unpredictable closure months), in competition with newer **Crystal Plex** at the head of the bay (mostly action films).

★ **Artemis** Kefalopoúlou 4 ☎ 22730 23639. Excellent, affordable seafood and starters like *fáva*, *hórta*, *seláhi* (ray) and *foúskes* as well as the usual mains. Good bulk *robóla* wine from the hill villages. Pleasant indoor/outdoor seating according to season. Mon–Sat 11am–1am.

Escape Kefalopoúlou 9. The most durable of the many clubs in the area that plays a fairly standard mixture of foreign and Greek disco favourites. Pleasant outdoor terrace and a/c dancefloor within. Daily 9pm–late.

Iy Nostimies Áno Vathý; no phone. Popular ouzerí next to the school which features grilled chops and mackerel in summer and more imaginative items at other times. Try

their *bouyiourdí* or pepper-and-cheese hotpot year-round. Mon–Sat 8pm–late; some lunches Oct–May.

Neon Themistoklí Sofoúli, beside Eurobank ☎ 22730 27516. A traditional *kafenío* that's good for an early-evening tipple-with-seafood-mezédhes; the waiter brings a big platter of whatever's cooking for a set price, around €6–8 per head with drink. Daily 10am–midnight.

To Steki ☎ 22730 23580. Family-run *inomayirío* in the shopping centre behind the seafront Catholic church that's tops for dishes like bean soup at lunch; also good fish like *gávros* and decent bulk wine. Daily 11am–1am.

Around Vathý

Around 5km east of Vathý, the ridge-top **Zoödhóhou Piyís convent** (8am–2pm & 5–8pm) is accessible on a climbing zigzag road from Kamára, 3km east of Vathý, and gives superb views across the end of the island to Turkey. The dome of its *katholikón*, where the nuns' chanting is excellent, is upheld by four ancient columns from Miletus in Asia Minor.

Some modest **beaches** around Vathý compensate for lack of same in the capital. Striking **Kérveli Bay**, 8km southeast of Vathý, has a small but popular pebble beach and a fine taverna just inland. On the far southeast coast of the island, almost within spitting distance of Turkey and accessed from a turning 1km west of Paleókastro lie the reasonable beaches of **Mykáli** and **Psilí Ámmos**, both with a mostly mediocre range of facilities. You'll need your own transport to reach both convent and beaches.

ACCOMMODATION AND EATING   AROUND VATHÝ

★ **Iy Kryfi Folia** Kérveli Bay ☎ 22730 25194. This secluded oasis, 300m uphill from the beach, offers simple but inexpensive and sustaining fare such as *kalamári* rings, the best lamb chops on Sámos and roast goat, which you can call to preorder. May to early Oct daily 11am–1am.

Kerveli Village Kérveli Bay ☎ 22730 23006, ⓦ kerveli .gr. One of the best hotels in eastern Sámos, located above the approach road to the beach, with sympathetic architecture, on-site car rental, pool, tennis court and

private lido. April–Oct. €80

Psili Ammos Psilí Ámmos ☎ 693 60 69 325. You can expect excellent service, as well as good seafood, salads and meat grills at this taverna on the far right as you face the sea. May–Oct daily 9am–midnight.

Zefiros Beach Mykáli ☎ 22730 28532, ⓦ zefirosbeach .gr. Decent resort hotel with pleasant rooms, right behind the beach. Good for families, as it has ample watersports facilities off its patch of beach. May–Oct. €60

Pythagório

Originally called Tigani ("frying pan"), a reference to its reputation as a heat trap, the island's premier resort, **PYTHAGÓRIO**, was renamed in 1955 to honour Pythagoras, ancient mathematician, philosopher and initiator of a rather subversive cult. Sixth-century BC tyrant Polykrates had his capital here, whose sporadic excavation has made modern Pythagório expand northeast and uphill. The village core of cobbled lanes and stone-walled mansions abuts a cosy **harbour**, fitting almost perfectly into the confines of Polykrates' ancient jetty, traces of which are still visible, but today devoted almost entirely to pleasure craft and overpriced café-bars. There are, however, several worthwhile sights in the vicinity.

6

Archeological museum

Tues–Sun: June–Sept 8am–8pm; Oct–May 8.30am–3pm • €4 • ☎ 22730 62811

Finally opened to the public in 2010, the splendid new **archeological museum** has a number of fascinating and well-labelled exhibits laid out over two floors. Star billing on the ground floor goes to the stunning collection of **gold coins** from a jar found by a Dutch archeologist at the west end of the island, plus there is a substantial number of votary objects and some Greek, Hellenistic and Roman statuary. Upstairs is the home for larger statues, such as the Roman Emperor Trajan and a fine *kouros* from 540–530 BC, but the most interesting display is on the subject of **ancient Greek dwellings**. The large outdoor site behind the building contains some splendid mosaics but it is not set to open until 2013.

The castle and around

Sámos's most complete **castle**, the nineteenth-century *pýrgos* of local chieftain Lykourgos Logothetis, overlooks both town and the shoreline where he, together with a certain "Kapetan Stamatis" and Admiral Kanaris, oversaw decisive naval and land victories against the Turks in the summer of 1824. The final battle was won on Transfiguration Day (Aug 6) – thus the dedication of the **church** by the castle – with an annual fireworks show commemorating the triumph. Also next to the castle are the remains of an early **Christian basilica**, occupying the grounds of a slightly larger Roman villa.

Efpalínio Órygma

Tues–Sun: June–Sept 8am–8pm; Oct–May 8.30am–3pm • €4 • ☎ 22730 62813

The well-signposted **Efpalínio Órygma** is a 1036m aqueduct bored through the mountain just north of Pythagório. Designed by one Eupalinos of Mégara, and built by slave labour at the behest of Polykrates, it guaranteed the ancient town a siege-proof water supply, and remained in use until late Byzantine times. Even though the work crews started digging from opposite sides of the mountain, the horizontal deviation from true about halfway along – 8m – is remarkably slight, and the vertical error nil: a tribute to the competence of ancient surveyors. Unfortunately, only about the first 120m section of the tunnel is well lit and currently accessible to visitors.

Panayía Spilianí

Cave open daylight hours • Free

On the way up to the Efpalínio Órygma is the well-marked turning for the monastery of **Panayía Spilianí**. The monastery itself, now bereft of nuns or monks, has been insensitively restored and the grounds are crammed with souvenir kiosks, but behind the courtyard the *raison d'être* of the place is still magnificent: a cool, illuminated, hundred-metre **cave**, at the drippy end of which is a subterranean shrine to the Virgin. This was supposedly the residence of the ancient oracular priestess Phyto, and a hiding place from medieval pirates.

Potokáki

The local, variable **beach** stretches several kilometres west of the Logothetis castle, punctuated part-way along by the end of the airport runway and the cluster of nondescript hotels known as **POTOKÁKI**. Although you'll have to contend with the hotel crowds and low-flying jets, the western end of the sand-and-pebble beach is well groomed, the water clean and sports available.

ARRIVAL AND INFORMATION   **PYTHAGÓRIO**

By ferry Ferries and hydrofoils dock at the jetty in the middle of the seafront.

By bus The main bus stop is on the seafront, near the jetty.

By car Street parking is impossible – use the pricey car park near the main T-junction or the free one just west behind the town beach.

Tourist office The information booth is a few paces along from the taxi rank on Lykourgoú Logothéti (June–Sept Mon–Fri 9am–1pm & 5–9pm; ☎ 22730 62274).

Services Several ATMs line Lykourgoú Logothéti; the post office is near the bus stop.

ACCOMMODATION

Doryssa Seaside Resort Potokáki beach ☎22730 61360, ⓦdoryssa-bay.gr. Huge complex including a hotel wing with Philippe Starck-ish rooms and a meticulously concocted fake village; each cosy bungalow is unique and there's even a platía with a pricey café. April to mid-Oct. **€130**

Pension Dryoussa ☎22730 61826, ⓔdryoussa @hotmail.com. Friendly and picturesque guesthouse, two

blocks inland from the town beach, with eight cosy, traditionally decorated rooms, most with small balconies. March–Nov. **€40**

Studios Galini ☎22730 61167. Brightly painted building, four blocks uphill from Lykoúrgou Logothéti, containing high-quality self-catering units, all with balconies and ceiling fans, most with a/c. Kindly English-speaking management. April–Oct. **€35**

6

EATING, DRINKING AND ENTERTAINMENT

Amadeus Popular and enduring club, just in from the jetty, that showcases quality live Greek acts followed by recorded hits. Tues–Sun 9pm–late.

Faros ☎22730 62464. The best of the bunch stretching along from the harbour, where you can get basic seafood and small fish for well under €10. May–Oct daily 10am–1am.

Rex ☎22730 51236. On the outskirts of Mytilini village, 7km northwest, the Rex is one of the best-maintained

outdoor cinemas on the islands, screening quality first-run films, with free *loukoumádhes* (sweet fritters) and cheap pizza at intermission. Late May to mid-Sept.

Souda ☎698 22 79 746. Tucked down an alley off the harbour, this excellent year-round restaurant specializes in oven-baked home cooking such as moussaka and *yiouvétsi* for around €7–8. Check out the dish of the day. Daily 11am–midnight.

Heraion

Tues–Sun: June–Sept 8am–8pm; Oct–May 8.30am–3pm • €3 • ☎22730 95277

Under layers of alluvial mud, plus today's runway, lies the processional Sacred Way joining ancient Sámos with the **Heraion**, a massive shrine of the **Mother Goddess**, 5km west of Pythagório. Much touted in tourist literature, this assumes humbler dimensions – one surviving column and low foundations – upon approach. Yet once inside the precinct you sense the former grandeur of the temple, never completed owing to Polykrates' untimely death at the hands of the Persians. The site chosen, near the mouth of the still-active Imvrassós stream, was Hera's legendary birthplace and site of her trysts with Zeus; in the far corner of the fenced-in zone you can tread a large, exposed patch of the Sacred Way.

Iréon

Modern **IRÉON**, barely a kilometre west of the ancient site, has a coarse-shingle beach and is at first glance a nondescript, grid-plan resort. Nonetheless its characterful pedestrianized waterfront remains popular: there are much better **tavernas** than at Pythagório, and after dark it has a more relaxed feel. The restaurants along the shore are especially busy on summer nights around the **full moon**, when Iréon is the best spot on the island to watch it rise out of the sea.

ACCOMMODATION AND EATING   IRÉON

Aegeon (Markos) ☎22730 95271. Probably the most accomplished and Greek-patronized taverna, halfway along the seafront, with fresh wild fish at normal prices and good starters like potato salad and mushroom soufflé. Book ahead on moonlit nights. April–Oct daily 11am–2am.

Glaros ☎22730 95457. Cult place two-thirds of the way west along the seafront, where the atmosphere and prices

are excellent. Home-cooked delights include fish soup and okra, alongside standard grills, salads, fried vegetables and barrelled wine. May–Oct daily noon–1am.

★ **Kohili** ☎22730 95282. The hotel rooms at *Kohili*, just behind the western seafront, are simple but great value, especially during high season, while the taverna below is a star, offering delights such as urchins, cockles and octopus salad in the shady courtyard (daily 10am–late). **€40**

Southern Sámos

Since island bus routes rarely pass through or near the following places, you really need your own vehicle to explore them. Three Samian "**pottery villages**" specialize, in addition to the usual wares, in the *Koúpa toú Pythagóra* or "Pythagorean cup", supposedly designed by the sage to leak over the user's lap if they were overfilled. Many of the **beaches** in this area are among the most deserted on the island, although it's not worth the effort and time involved in getting to the most remote.

Pottery villages

The biggest concentration of retail outlets is at **KOUMARADHÉÏ**, about 7km west of Hóra, along a route dotted with the odd spot to stop for refreshment and sweeping views. From the village you can descend to the sixteenth-century monastery of **Megális Panayías** (Mon–Sat 10am–1pm & 5.30–8pm; free), containing some recently cleaned frescoes, then carry on to **PAGÓNDAS**, a large hillside community with an unusual communal fountain house on the southerly hillside. From there, a scenic road curls 15km around deforested hillside to **PÝRGOS**, at the head of a ravine draining southwest and the centre of Samian honey production.

Kouméïka and Bállos

The western reaches of the southern Samian shoreline are approached via handsome **KOUMÉÏKA**, which has a massive inscribed marble fountain and a pair of *kafenía*-snack bars on its photogenic square. Below extends the long pebbly bay at **Bállos**, with sand and rock overhangs at the far east end. Bállos itself offers several places to stay and a few tavernas, all on the shore road.

From Kouméïka, the paved side road going west just before the village is a very useful short cut for travelling towards Órmos Marathokámbou (see p.362) and beyond.

Plátanos

From the main road between the south coast and Karlóvassi, it's worth detouring up to **PLÁTANOS**, on the flanks of Mount Karvoúnis; at 520m this is one of Sámos's highest villages, with sweeping views west and south. The name comes from the three stout plane trees (*plátanos* in Greek) on its platía, whose spring-water in the arcaded fountain-house is immortalized in one of the most popular Samian folk songs. The only special sight is the double-naved thirteenth-century **church of Kímisis Theotókou** (key at house opposite west entrance) in the village centre.

ACCOMMODATION, EATING AND DRINKING — SOUTHERN SÁMOS

Amfílissos Bállos ☎22730 31669, 🌐 amfilissos.gr. Friendly medium-sized hotel, a block behind the seafront, with functional, adequately furnished rooms, some with seaview balconies, set behind a nicely landscaped courtyard. Late May to Sept. **€36**

Enalion Bállos ☎22730 36444, 🌐 enalionsamos.gr. The name means "on the sea", and this small white block of fully equipped studios overlooks the beach. Its taverna, *Akrogiali*, does good fish and other fare. April–Oct. **€45**

Koutouki tou Barba Dhimitri Central square, Pýrgos ☎22730 41060. A good range of vegetarian mezédhes, as well as the usual meaty grills, in a surprisingly chic environment for such a remote village. Daily 11am–1am.

Leon Central square, Plátanos ☎22730 39215. Great taverna, popular with the locals, where you can feast on goat in red sauce, *kondosoúvli* or *kokorétsi* for well under €10. Live folk music some nights. Daily noon–late.

O Balos Bállos ☎22730 36339. You can get grills and seafood at this seafront taverna but it's best to stick with the fine traditional baked items, such as *papoutsáki*. Pizza is also available. May to early Oct 10am–1am.

Kokkári

KOKKÁRI, on Sámos's north coast, is the island's second major tourist centre. The town's coastal profile, covering two knolls behind mirror-image headlands called Dhídhymi (Twins), remains unchanged but its identity has been altered by inland expansion across old vineyards and along the west beach. The quaint harbour area is a lively place to hang out, but since the coarse-pebble **beaches** here are buffeted by near-constant winds, locals have made a virtue of necessity by developing the place as a successful **windsurfing** resort.

Tourist office (May–Sept Mon–Sat 8.30am–1.30pm, Mon, Wed & Sat 7–9pm; ☎ 22730 92333). The helpful tourist office is on the main street heading inland.

Activities A windsurfing school thrives just west of town (☎ 22730 92102, ⊛ samoswindsurfing.gr).

ACCOMMODATION, EATING AND DRINKING

Athena Hotel ☎ 22730 92030, ✉ h-athena@otenet .gr. The modern, comfortable rooms are spread over three buildings, set in beautifully landscaped grounds with a large pool, across the road from the south beach. Very helpful Greek-Canadian owner. April–Oct. €45

Cavos ☎ 22730 92436. This perennially popular place on the fishing harbour, run by a Greek/German couple, cranks out breakfast, snacks, coffees and cocktails according to the time of day, though the music can be rather middle-of-the-road. April–Oct daily 8am–late.

Girasole ☎ 22730 92037. Genuine Italian restaurant on the fishing harbour, serving quality pizza, pasta and other classic dishes in the €10–15 range. Chic decor and comfy seating too. May–Oct daily noon–1am.

★ **ly Byra** ☎ 22730 92350. Though the range is limited, the light mezédhes on offer, like *domatokeftédhes* and *keftedhákia* plus maybe seafood titbits, are superbly executed at this old favourite opposite the main church. April–Oct daily 11am–late.

★ **Tarsanas** ☎ 22730 92337. Wonderful terrazzo-floored 1980s throwback, 100m down the lane from the west beach. doing pizzas, a couple of dishes of the day, like *briám* or *dolmádhes*, and their own dynamite red wine. Daily June–Sept 11am–late, Oct–May 8pm–2am.

Tsamadou Hotel ☎ 22730 92314, ⊛ tsamadou.com. Friendly English-run place, towards the south end of the north beach, whose simple a/c rooms have fridges. Asian snacks are available in the garden conservatory. April–Oct. €40

The north coast

The closest sheltered **beaches** to Kokkári are about thirty minutes' walk west, fully carpeted with sunbeds and permanently anchored umbrellas. The further you move away from the resort, however, the wilder and quieter the strands become and the less-touristed the settlements.

Lemonákia and Tzamadhoú

The first beach west of Kokkári, **Lemonákia**, is a bit close to the road, so it is better to carry on 1km to the graceful crescent of **Tzamadhoú**. It can only be accessed by a path, and the eastern third of the beach, made up of saucer-shaped pebbles, is a well-established nudist zone.

Avlákia and Tzaboú

AVLÁKIA, 3km west of Tzamadhoú, is a quiet shoreline hamlet with an excellent taverna and some of the best views on the island. The nearest beach, 2km further west with a steep lane down, is **Tzaboú**, probably the most scenic north-coast beach with its rock formations but mercilessly buffeted by the prevailing wind most days – and the snack-bar tries to charge €6 for parking. There's a nudist annexe, with separate path access from Avlákia, off to the right.

Áyios Konstandínos

Platanákia, the next settlement west of Tzaboú and essentially a handful of buildings at a bridge by the turning for Manolátes, is actually the eastern quarter of **ÁYIOS KONSTANDÍNOS**, whose surf-pounded esplanade has been prettified. However, there are no significant beaches within walking distance, so the collection of mostly warm-toned stone buildings constitutes a peaceful alternative to Kokkári.

Áyios Nikólaos

West of Áyios Konstandínos the mountains hem the road in against the sea, and the terrain doesn't relent until **Áyios Nikólaos**, which is the tiny seaside annexe of more traditional Kondakéïka. A passable pebble beach, **Piáki**, lies ten minutes' walk east past the last studio units.

Kímisis Theotókou

The Byzantine church of **Kímisis Theotókou** (left unlocked) is signposted 2.5km inland along a partly paved road from Kondakéïka. The second oldest and most artistically noteworthy on Sámos, dating from the late twelfth/early thirteenth century, it has extensive frescoes contemporaneous with the building. The deceptively simple exterior gives little hint of the glorious barrel-vaulted interior, its decoration still vivid except where damp has blurred the images.

6

| ACCOMMODATION, EATING AND DRINKING | THE NORTH COAST |

LEMONÁKIA AND TZAMADHOÚ

Arion Lemonákia ☎ 22370 92020, ⊛ arion-hotel.gr. This well-designed bungalow/hotel complex on a flattish patch of hillside 600m inland from the coastal road has dazzlingly white, minimalist rooms and a large pool. Breakfast included. May–Oct. **€100**

★ **Armonia Bay** Tzamadhoú ☎ 22730 92279, ⊛ armoniabay.gr. This hotel directly above the beach has tastefully decorated and sizeable rooms with marble-clad baths, as well as a fine pool and pleasant common areas. Good value. April–Oct. **€75**

AVLÁKIA AND TZABOÚ

To Delfini Avlákia ☎ 22730 94279. Kyra Alexandra is the heart and soul of this welcoming traditional taverna, in the middle of the village, which is strong on fresh little fish, *hórta* and chips. May–Oct daily 10am–1am.

ÁYIOS KONSTANDÍNOS

Aeolos ☎ 22730 94021. Terrific fish or grilled meat for €7–9 and a few daily oven dishes, served at tables adjoining a tiny pebble cove at the far west end of the esplanade. May–Sept daily noon–midnight.

Akroyiali ☎ 22730 94655. Quite pricey all-round mid-quay taverna, with some dishes such as steaks and most fish exceeding €10. Still, a reasonable atmosphere and lovely setting. April to early Oct daily 10am–midnight.

Daphne ☎ 22730 94003, ⊛ daphne-hotel.gr. Set against a leafy backdrop on a hill 500m back from the village, this good-value hotel has smart but compact rooms with baths and great views. Breakfast included. May–Oct. **€50**

Hotel Apartments Agios Konstantinos ☎ 22730 94000, ⊛ hotelagios.gr. Attractive two-storey building on the street linking Platanákia to the sea, with a red tile roof. Its sea-facing rooms are all well equipped and have small balconies. April–Oct. **€40**

ÁYIOS NIKÓLAOS

Iy Psaradhes ☎ 22730 32489. With a terrace lapped by the waves, you'll need to book in season to guarantee a fine meal of fresh fish, salads and good barrelled wine. Easter–Oct daily 11am–1am.

Villa Eva ☎ 22730 30020, ⊛ villaeva-samos.gr. This hotel set in lush grounds, signposted downhill from the main coastal road, is also a thriving New Age retreat centre, with reiki, yoga and Sufi seminars. Breakfast, jacuzzi and exercise session included. May–Oct. **€85**

Northern hill villages

Inland between Kokkári and Kondakéïka, an idyllic landscape of pine, cypress and orchards is overawed by dramatic mountains. Despite bulldozer vandalism, some of the trail system linking the various **hill villages** is still intact, and walkers can return to the main highway to catch a bus back to base. Those with transport should leave it at Vourliótes and execute a **three-hour loop** via Manolátes, north and down to Aïdhónia, then back up east to your starting point. There is some waymarking, and the final stretch of trail has been rehabilitated.

Vourliótes

VOURLIÓTES, closest village to Kokkári, has beaked chimneys and brightly painted shutters sprouting from its typical tile-roofed houses. But restaurateur greed has ruined the formerly photogenic central square by chopping down old mulberries and cramming in more tables.

Manolátes

MANOLÁTES, an hour-plus walk uphill from Vourliótes via a deep river canyon, has several tavernas, as ever with inland locales better value than those at coastal resorts. The two high-quality *raku* ceramic workshops are anything but cheap though.

AAA Manolátes ☎22730 94472. Central taverna that makes a good fist of such dishes as *yiouvarlákia*, grilled *mastéllo*, an idiosyncratic version of aubergine *imám* and dry red wine from Stavrinídhes. March–Nov daily 11am–2am, some winter weekends from 8pm.

Despina Manolátes ☎22730 94043. Warm-hearted Despina whips up dishes of the day, *revythokeftédhes* and good *tzatziki*, which you can enjoy in a gazebo by the central fountain. Daily 10am–10pm.

Galazio Pigadhi Vourliótes ☎22730 93480. Serving up rabbit stew, *soutzoukákia* and aubergine dishes at limited pavement seating under a kangaroo vine up beyond the platía, this is a real locals' favourite. Daily 7pm–late.

★ **ly Pera Vrysi** Vourliótes ☎22730 93277. This taverna at the village entrance offers a huge range of well-priced, imaginative *mezédhes* like spinach croquettes or chicken livers, as well as local *robóla* wine. March–Nov daily noon–1am.

★ **Kallisti** Manolátes ☎22730 94661. Excellent roast goat, courgette pie, grills and some small fish are all available for maximum €7 at this great taverna next to *AAA*, as is fine barrelled wine. Warm welcome assured too. March–Nov daily 11am–1am, some winter weekends from 8pm.

Karlóvassi and the northwest coast

KARLÓVASSI, 31km west of Vathý and Sámos's second town, is sleepier and more old-fashioned than the capital, despite having roughly the same population. It's a useful base for enjoying northwestern Sámos's excellent **beaches** or taking a number of rewarding **walks**. The town divides into five straggly neighbourhoods: **Néo**, well inland, whose growth was spurred by the influx of post-1923 refugees; **Meséo**, across the usually dry riverbed, tilting appealingly off a knoll and then blending to the west with the shoreline district of **Ríva**; picturesque **Paleó** (or **Áno**) lies further west, its hundred or so houses draped either side of a leafy ravine; while below it is **Limáni**, the small harbour district. Most tourists stay at or near Limáni, which has most tourist facilities. The **port** itself is an appealing place with a working boatyard at the west end.

Ríva

On the 1km-long street linking Meséo's Platía 8-Maïoú to **Ríva**, stands a huge, early twentieth-century **church**, topped with twin belfries and a blue-and-white dome, typical of those that dot the coastal plain here. Ríva itself is something of a ghost town, with derelict stone-built warehouses, tanneries and mansions, reminders of the defunct leather industry that flourished here until the 1960s. The epoch is immortalized in the brand-new **Tannery Museum** (Tues–Sat 9am–1pm; free), which has informative displays on the industry, as well as tobacco production.

Potámi and around

The closest decent **beach** to Karlóvassi is **Potámi**, forty minutes' walk away via the coast road from Limáni or an hour by a more scenic, high trail from Paleó. This broad arc of sand and pebbles is presided over on the east by the striking modernist clifftop chapel of Áyios Nikólaos from 1971. A streamside path leads twenty minutes inland from Potámi, past the eleventh-century church of **Metamórfosis** – the oldest on Sámos – to a point where the river disappears into a small gorge. Just above the Metamórfosis church, a clear if precipitous path leads up to the remains of a small, contemporaneous **Byzantine fortress**.

Mikró Seïtáni and Megálo Seïtáni

A couple of daily water-taxi services run in peak season from Karlóvassi port to both beaches

The coast west of Potámi ranks among the most beautiful and unspoilt on Sámos; since the early 1980s it has served as a protected refuge for the rare **monk seal**, still glimpsed occasionally by lucky hikers or bathers. Some twenty minutes along the dirt track at the west end of Potámi Bay takes you to the well-cairned side trail running parallel to the water. After twenty minutes more you'll arrive at **Mikró Seïtáni**, a small pebble cove guarded by sculpted rock walls. A full hour's walk from the trailhead, through olive terraces, brings you to **Megálo Seïtáni**, the island's finest sand beach, at the mouth of the intimidating Kakopérato gorge. Bring food, water and something to shade yourself, though a swimsuit is optional.

ARRIVAL AND DEPARTURE

By ferry Karlóvassi's dock is an inconvenient 3km from the centre. Buses to town are infrequent but do often meet boats.

KARLÓVASSI AND THE NORTHWEST COAST

By bus Most buses call at multiple stops along the seafront before terminating near the port.

ACCOMMODATION

Erato Limáni ☎ 22730 35370. Attractive smallish hotel built in Cretan style 150m east of central Limáni, with compact but spotless rooms and a warm welcome. Breakfast included. May–Oct. **€35**

Samaina Port/Samaina Inn Limáni ☎ 22730 30850, ⓦ samainahotels.gr. Excellent-value place on the pedestrianized old harbour, offering rooms with sea-facing balconies. You can book more luxurious rooms at the nearby sister hotel *Samaina Inn*. Breakfast included at both. April–Oct. *Samaina Port* **€40**, *Samaina Inn* **€60**

EATING, DRINKING AND NIGHTLIFE

★ **Hippy's** Potámi beach ☎ 22730 33796. Laid-back beach bar, set behind a sunflower garden, with a distinct Indian vibe. It does a limited breakfast and meals menu, plus ample coffee and cocktails. Regular parties and musical events. June to early Sept 10am–late.

Iy Platia Platía 8-Maïóu, Meséo ☎ 22730 34600. Busy with locals at lunchtime thanks to plentiful traditional *mayireftá* and a few grills, all served up speedily though quality varies. Daily 11am–midnight.

O Dionysos Platía 8-Maïóu, Meséo ☎ 22730 30120. Offers creative dishes such as asparagus in mushroom sauce and richly cooked meat dishes. Pleasant indoor and outdoor seating, plus a wine list aspiring to Athenian sophistication. Mon–Sat 11am–1am.

Popcorn Ríva ⓦ popcornclub.gr. With DJed events at weekends, this enduring student club, located in an old customs warehouse, has a state-of-the-art sound system pumping out international and Greek hits. 10pm–late: June–Sept daily; Oct–May Fri–Sun.

To Kyma Ríva ☎ 22730 34017. Great ouzerí at the main seafront T-junction, popular with students and townies alike, where you can feast on inexpensive and ample seafood and mezédhes. April–Oct daily noon–late.

Southwestern beach resorts

The southwestern coast of Sámos boasts some of the island's best beaches, stretching in an almost unbroken line between Órmos Marathokámbou and Limniónas. These strands also offer a range of amenities.

The port of Marathókambos, **ÓRMOS MARATHOKÁMBOU**, 18km from Karlóvassi, has become something of a resort, though with ample character in its backstreets. Otherwise, the main focus of attention is the pedestrianized quay, home to several **tavernas** and starting point for excursion boats to the island of Samiopoúla and along the coast.

Two kilometres west of Órmos is **VOTSALÁKIA** (signposted as "Kámbos"), Sámos's most family-pitched resort, straggling a further 2km behind the island's longest beach. The presence of Mount Kérkis (see opposite) looming overhead rarely fails to impress too. Just to the west, **Fournáki**, the collective name for a series of sand-and-pebble **coves** backed by low cliffs, is usually less crowded.

Three kilometres west of Votsalákia, you reach 600m-long **Psilí Ámmos**, not to be confused with its namesake beach in southeastern Sámos. The sea shelves ridiculously gently here – 100m out you're still just knee-deep – but that makes it ideal for families with young children. Access to **Limniónas**, a smaller but superior cove 2km west from Psilí Ámmos, passes the *Limnionas Bay Village Hotel*. Yachts and *kaikia* occasionally call at the protected bay, which offers decent swimming at the east end, away from a rock shelf in the middle.

ACCOMMODATION, EATING AND DRINKING

Evinos Votsalákia ☎ 698 55 68 147, ⓔ elsahiou@gmail .com. Standard clean but smallish rooms above a nice

SOUTHWESTERN BEACH RESORTS

authentic taverna behind the middle of the beach, among the cheapest at this end of the island. May–Sept. **€25**

Hotel Kerkis Bay Órmos Marathokámbou ☎ 22730 37202, ⓦ kerkis-bay.com. Fairly spacious rooms are available at this pleasant spot, one block inland from mid-quay. There are various sports facilities (though no pool) and a decent restaurant. Breakfast included. Mid-April to late Oct. €35

Iy Trata Órmos Marathokámbou ☎ 22730 31859. The most authentic taverna in the resort, at its eastern end just off the pedestrian zone, specializes in fresh local fish, often at under €10 per portion. April–Oct daily 10am–1am.

Limnionas Bay Village Limniónas ☎ 22730 37057, ⓦ hotel-limnionas-bay-village.co.uk. Large rather characterless resort right behind the bay with tiered units arrayed around a garden full of olive trees and a decent pool. Breakfast included. May–Oct. €60

★ **Loukoullos** Fournáki ☎ 22730 37147. This welcoming restaurant with a lovely courtyard overlooking the first cove is better in the evening, when the full range of tasty and inexpensive *mayireftá* and home-grown veg dishes is available. May–Sept daily noon–midnight.

Mount Kérkis and around

A limestone/volcanic oddity in a predominantly schist landscape, **Mount Kérkis** (Kerketévs) – the Aegean's second-highest summit after Mount Sáos on Samothráki – attracts legends and speculation as easily as the cloud pennants that usually wreath it. Hermits colonized and sanctified the mountain's many caves in Byzantine times; resistance guerrillas controlled it during World War II; and mariners still regard it with superstitious awe, especially when mysterious lights – presumed to be the spirits of the departed hermits, or the aura of some forgotten holy icon – are glimpsed at night near the cave-mouths. Gazing up from a supine seaside position, you may be inspired to **climb the peak** (see box below), though less ambitious walkers might want to **circle the mountain's flank**, first by vehicle and then by foot. The road beyond Limniónas through **Kallithéa** is paved all the way to **Dhrakéï**.

Dhrakéï and Megálo Seïtáni

DHRAKÉÏ is a minuscule, back-of-beyond village with views across to Ikaría. A lovely trail – minimally disrupted by a track – descends ninety minutes through forest to **Megálo Seïtáni**, from where it's easy to continue on to Karlóvassi within another two-and-a-half hours. People climbing up from Seïtáni must either retrace their steps, summon a taxi or stay at a few unofficial **rooms** establishments in Dhrakéï.

Kallithéa, Panayía Makriní, Ayía Triádha and around

During term time a vehicle leaves Karlóvassi (Mon–Fri 1.20pm) bound for Kallithéa; during summer it only operates twice a week (Mon to Dhrakéï, Fri to Kallithéa)

From **Kallithéa**, a small village 7km southwest of Dhrakéï with just a simple grill on its tiny square, a newer track (from beside the cemetery) and an older trail both lead up within 45 minutes to a spring, rural chapel and plane tree on the west flank of Kérkis, with path-only continuation for another thirty minutes to a pair of faintly frescoed cave-churches. **Panayía Makriní** stands at the mouth of a high, wide but shallow grotto, whose balcony affords terrific views. By contrast, **Ayía Triádha**, a ten-minute scramble overhead, has most of its structure made up of cave wall; just adjacent, another long, narrow, volcanic cavern can be explored with a torch some hundred metres into the mountain.

CLIMBING MOUNT KÉRKIS

The classic route up Mount Kérkis begins from Votsalákia, along the paved but narrow lane leading inland towards Evangelistrías convent. After a 45-minute walk through olive groves, the path begins, more or less following power lines up to the convent. A friendly nun may proffer an ouzo and point you up the paint-marked trail, continuing even more steeply up to the peak. The views are tremendous, though the climb itself is humdrum once you're out of the trees. About an hour before the top there's a chapel with an attached cottage for sheltering in emergencies, and just beyond, a welcome spring. All told, it's a seven-hour return outing from Votsalákia, not counting rest stops.

Foúrni

The straits between Sámos and Ikaría are speckled with a mini-archipelago – once haunted by pirates from various corners of the Mediterranean – of which only two are inhabited. Of these, the more westerly Thýmena has no tourist facilities but the largest of the group, **FOÚRNI**, has a growing reputation as a great hideaway. Unlike so many small Greek islands, it has a stable population, around 1600, as it is home to a huge fishing fleet and one of the more thriving boatyards in the Aegean.

Apart from remote **Khryssomiliá** hamlet in the north, reached by the island's longest (18km) road, Foúrni's inhabitants are concentrated in the **port** and **Kambí** hamlet just south.

The port

The harbour community is larger than it seems from the sea, with a friendly ambience reminiscent of 1970s Greece; the historical pirate connection is reflected in the municipality's official name, Foúrni Korseón (Fourni of the Corsairs). The central main market street, field-stoned and mulberry-shaded, ends well inland at a little **platía** with two giant plane trees and a Hellenistic sarcophagus found in a nearby field.

Southern Foúrni

From the primary school near the port, it's a fifteen-minute walk south on a flagstone lane, then over the restored windmill ridge, to **KAMBÍ**, a scattered community overlooking a pair of sandy, tamarisk-shaded coves.

A path system starting at Kambí's last house continues south around the headland to other, more secluded **bays** of varying sizes and beach consistencies. These are also favourite anchorages for passing yachts, but unlike Kambí they have substantial summer communities of rough campers and naturists. In order of appearance they are sand-and-pebble **Áspa**, fifteen minutes along, with a tiny spring seeping from the rocks just before, **Pelekanía**, five minutes further, and equidistant **Elidháki** – both of these coarse pebble, the latter also with paved road access. The trail is slippery and steep just before Áspa so some may prefer to employ a taxi-boat service.

The side-road serving Elidháki from the main island ridge-road also has an option for **Petrokopió** (Marmári) cove, named after its role as a quarry for ancient Ephesus in Asia Minor. The quarry itself, with obvious chisel-marks and abandoned half-worked stones down by the shore, proves impressive; the beach is made of the same stone.

Northern Foúrni

North from Foúrni harbour via steps, then path, are a pair of slightly sullied beaches. **Psilí Ámmos**, in front of a derelict fish-processing plant and equally defunct café at the end with tamarisks, is superior to **Kálamos** further along, dominated by a military watchpoint; both now have track access, while the former has a fishermen's jetty and beach bar. In the northeast of the island, **KAMÁRI** too has a beach. Without transport, it's possible to **walk** between town and Kamári on the old *kalderími*, which goes via the ridge-top monastery of Panayía.

ARRIVAL AND GETTING AROUND   FOÚRNI

By ferry Foúrni is surprisingly well connected, with services to: Áyios Kírykos, Ikaría (8 weekly; 1hr 15min); Karlóvassi, Sámos (8 weekly; 1–3hr); Mýkonos (3 weekly; 4hr–4hr 30min); Pireás (3 weekly; 10–11hr); Sýros (3 weekly; 5hr–5hr 30min); Vathý, Sámos (3 weekly; 2hr).

By scooter Although much of the island is walkable, you can rent a scooter from seafront Escape at the port (☎ 22750 51514).

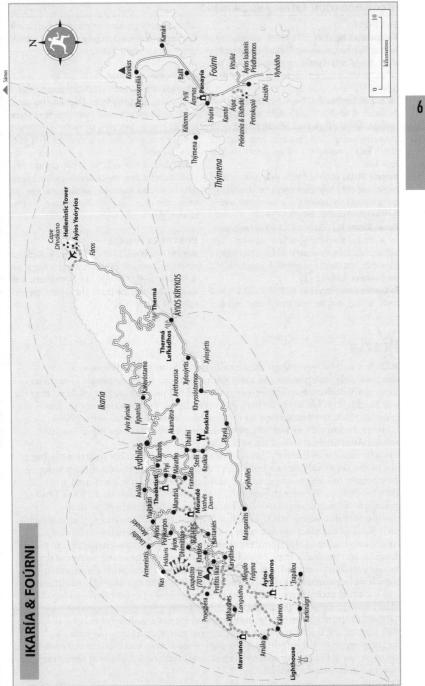

IKARÍA & FOÚRNI

ACCOMMODATION, EATING AND DRINKING

THE PORT

Archipelagos Hotel ☎ 22750 51250, ⊕ archipelagos hotel.gr. This smart modern hotel by the fishing port offers quality fittings in its eighteen doubles and suites, as well as an on-site restaurant during summer. Breakfast included. €45

★ **ly Kali Kardhia** ☎ 22750 51217. The aroma from the superb €8 *kondosoúvli* and *kokorétsi* rotating on the huge spits outside this place just behind the inland square is tempting enough. Some *mayireftá*, fresh salads and decent wine complete the picture. April–Oct daily 7pm–late.

Kafenio Platia ☎ 22750 51678. With tables crowded beneath one of the huge plane tree on the inland square, this traditional *kafenío* doubles up as a restaurant, serving the island's best *souvláki*. Daily 8am–late.

Patras Rooms ☎ 22750 51268, ⊕ fourni-patrasrooms .gr. A choice of wood-floored, antique-bed rooms, some with balconies above the owner's café-bar in the middle of the seafront, and fourteen superb hillside apartments, in a tiered complex. April–Oct. €30

To Koutouki tou Psarrakou ☎ 22750 51670. This local staple, halfway along the main market street, still does

decent *mayireftá* and roasts accompanied by Cretan bulk wine and a Peloponnesian liqueur, despite an enforced change of management. Daily noon–1am.

SOUTHERN FOÚRNI

O Yiorgos Kambí ☎ 22750 51025. With tamarisk-shaded beach seating, the family ferries inexpensive fish plates, Ikarian *soúfiko* and other oven dishes 100m to your table from the premises back along the southern access road. There are a couple of ultra-cheap rooms too (€15). Daily noon–midnight.

Studio Rena Kambí ☎ 22750 51364, ⊕ studio-rena .com. Stacked in three tiers on Kambí's northern hillside, these comfortable apartments, painted island blue and white, offer fully equipped kitchens and sea-view balconies. €40

NORTHERN FOÚRNI

Almyra Kamári ☎ 697 91 41 653. The most accomplished out-of-town taverna on the island rustles up a range of fish at standard prices, goat and various *mezédhes*, with seating right behind the beach. 11am–1am: June–Oct daily; Nov–May Fri–Sun.

Ikaría

IKARÍA, a narrow, windswept landmass between Sámos and Mýkonos, is comparatively little visited and sadly underestimated by many people. The name supposedly derives from Icarus, who in legend fell into the sea just offshore after the wax bindings on his wings melted. For years the only substantial tourism was generated by a few **hot springs** on the southeast coast; since the early 1990s, however, tourist facilities of some quantity and quality have sprung up in and around **Armenistís**, the only resort of note.

Ikaría, along with Thessaly, Lésvos and the Ionian islands, has traditionally been one of the **Greek Left**'s strongholds. This dates from long periods of right-wing domination in Greece, when, as in Byzantine times, the island was used as a place of **exile** for political dissidents, particularly Communists, who from 1946 to 1949 outnumbered native islanders. This house-arrest policy backfired, with the transportees (including Mikis Theodhorakis in 1946–47) favourably impressing their hosts as the most noble figures they had ever encountered, worthy of emulation. Earlier in the twentieth century, many Ikarians had emigrated to North America and ironically their capitalist remittances kept the island going for decades. Yet anti-establishment attitudes still predominate and local pride dictates that outside opinion matters little. Thus many Ikarians exhibit a lack of obsequiousness and a studied **eccentricity**, which some visitors mistake for hostility, making the island something of an acquired taste.

Except for forested portions in the northwest, it's not a strikingly beautiful island, with most of the landscape being scrub-covered granite and schist put to use as building material. The mostly desolate south coast is overawed by steep cliffs, while the less sheer north face is furrowed by deep canyons creating hairpin road-bends extreme even by Greek-island standards.

ARRIVAL AND DEPARTURE

By plane Ikaría airport, which can only handle small domestic planes, is around 12km northeast of Áyios Kírykos. There is just one daily flight to Athens (50min) year-round and 1–5 weekly to Iráklio (Crete; 40min), Límnos (35min) and Thessaloníki (1hr 45min).

By ferry Ikaría lies on the main Pireás–Sámos route and ferries alternate between calling at Áyios Kírykos and Évdhilos. Áyios Kírykos also has a weekly service on the northeast Aegean route to Kavála, as well as a small seasonal boat to Foúrni and Karlóvassi on Sámos.

IKARÍA

Áyios Kírykos to: Foúrni (9 weekly; 1hr); Híos (1 weekly; 5hr); Karlóvassi, Sámos (9 weekly; 2hr–2hr 30min); Kavála (1 weekly; 21hr); Lésvos (1 weekly; 7hr 30min); Límnos (1 weekly; 13hr 30min); Mýkonos (3 weekly; 3hr); Pireás (3 weekly; 9hr–9hr 30min); Sýros (3 weekly; 4hr 30min); Vathý, Sámos (4 weekly; 2hr 30min–3hr).

Évdhilos to: Karlóvassi, Sámos (3 weekly; 2hr); Mýkonos (3 weekly; 2hr 30min); Pireás (3 weekly; 8hr 30min–9hr); Sýros (3 weekly; 4hr); Vathý, Sámos (3 weekly; 2hr 30min).

GETTING AROUND

By bus There are 1–2 cross-island bus services between Áyios Kírykos, Évdhilos and Armenistís, with occasional erratic onward services to Khrístos. Unfortunately, the most reliable year-round service usually leaves Áyios Kírykos early morning and does not link with ferry arrivals.

By car or motorbike Aventura (☎ 22750 71117) and Dolihi Tours/Lemy (☎ 22750 71122) are the most prominent rental agencies, with branches in Armenistís,

Évdhilos and Áyios Kírykos.

Taxi Taxis can be elusive, as well as expensive, and are best booked through one of the agencies above, especially if you have a ferry or flight from the other side of the island – budget on at least €50.

Hitching For more leisurely travel, note that hitching is a common practice on this unconventional island.

Áyios Kírykos and around

The south-coast port and capital of **ÁYIOS KÍRYKOS** has little to detain foreign tourists, at least until the modest archeological museum reopens in 2014. The spa of **Thérma**, just over 1km northeast of the port, saw its heyday in the 1960s, and now relies on a mostly elderly, health-service-subsidized clientele from July to early October. Of more general interest is the *spílio* or **natural sauna** on the shore (8am–8pm; €4.50), co-housed with plunge pools under the cave roof. Other good bets for informal soaks are the seaside, open-air pool (35–40°C) of the **Asklipioú hot springs**, reached by steps down from the Áyios Kírykos courthouse, or better still the natural, shoreline hot springs at **Thérma Lefkádhos**, 2km southwest of Áyios Kírykos, where 50–58°C water mixes with the sea to a pleasant temperature inside a ring of giant volcanic boulders. A further 3km brings you to another pleasant cove, below the small hamlet of **Xylosýrti**.

Fáros and around

The longest **beach** on the south coast is at **Fáros**, 12km northeast of Áyios Kírykos along a good road which also serves the airport. A colony of summer cottages shelters under tamarisks along the sand-and-gravel strand, with a reefy zone to cross before deep water. From a signposted point just inland from Fáros beach, a dirt track leads 2km to the trailhead for the round **Hellenistic watchtower** at **Cape Dhrákano**, much the oldest and most impressive ancient ruin on the island (closed for restoration). It's part of a much larger, now mostly crumbled fort extending halfway to the cape and its pretty rustic chapel of **Áyios Yeóryios**. Right below this to the north, perfectly sheltered in most weathers, is a fantasy-image sand **beach**, with assorted rocks and islets off the cape-tip for contrast.

ACCOMMODATION

ÁYIOS KÍRYKOS AND AROUND

★ **Agriolykos Pension** Thérma ☎ 22750 22433, ⓦ agriolykos.gr. Wonderful and welcoming place on the eastern bluff with original artwork, delightfully decorated rooms, use of kitchen, extensive shady grounds and direct access to a hidden cove. Breakfast included. April–Oct. **€45**

Akti Áyios Kírykos ☎ 22750 22694, ⓦ pensionakti.gr. Pleasant spot on a knoll above the east quay, with comfy a/c rooms, wi-fi, fluent English-speaking management and views of Foúrni from the café-garden. Breakfast included. **€40**

Evon's Rooms Fáros ☎ 22750 32580, ⓦ evonsrooms
.com. Attractively appointed and well-equipped a/c
rooms, especially the pricier galleried top-floor units. Right
on the beach, with a pleasantly landscaped garden and
private parking. **€40**

Marina Hotel Thérma ☎ 22750 22188, ⓦ marina
-hotel.gr. All the rooms at this friendly little hotel, just

above the western end of the bay, have fridges, a/c and
either balconies or verandas. March–Oct. **€40**

Pension Ikaria Áyios Kírykos ☎ 22750 22108,
ⓔ gmoulas@chi.forthnet.gr. Compact but cosy a/c rooms
with small balconies, some above the seafront café. The
entrance is on the first parallel street behind the front. **€25**

EATING AND DRINKING

Arodhou Xylosýrti ☎ 22750 22700. This taverna on the
shore, next to Ayía Paraskeví church, does excellent
mezédhes and a full selection of meat and fish grills. Daily
2.30pm–midnight, closed Mon Oct–May.

Avra Thérma ☎ 22750 23805. The best of the handful of
mostly fish tavernas set back from the beach, offering a
number of seafood items for under €10, as well as fine
wine. April–Oct daily 10am–midnight.

Iy Klimataria Áyios Kírykos ☎ 22750 23686. With

tables tucked on a pedestrianized alley beneath climbing
vines, two blocks back from the seafront, this old favourite
does various grills, salads, dips and the odd oven dish.
April–Oct daily 11am–midnight.

To Synapandi Áyios Kírykos ☎ 22750 22287. A new
ouzerí at the start of the Évdhilos road, which serves a wide
range of seafood, meat and vegetable mezédhes in a
pleasant courtyard. May–Oct daily 1–11pm.

SHOPPING

Studio Pelagos Áyios Kírykos ☎ 697 28 45 546,
ⓦ studio-pelagos.com. You might want to take a peek or
purchase one of the unique hand-painted marbles at this

gallery, a block back from the seafront square. July–Sept
daily 11am–2pm & 6–10pm.

Évdhilos and around

The north-coast port of **ÉVDHILOS** is the island's second town, with most of its
facilities packed around the picturesque fishing harbour, separated by a headland
from the busy port. Barely 1km west, the tiny hamlet of **Fýtema** offers better dining
options. There are some decent beaches and places of interest in the villages around
Évdhilos.

The twisting, 37km road from Áyios Kírykos, on the south coast, to Évdhilos is one
of the most hair-raising in the islands, especially as a passenger, and Ikaría's longitudinal
ridge often wears a streamer of cloud, even when the rest of the Aegean is clear. So it
comes as quite a relief when you reach the north coast at the pleasant fishing village of
Karavóstamo, 8km short of Évdhilos.

Kámbos

KÁMBOS, 1.5km west of Fýtema, offers a small hilltop **museum** (Tues–Sun 8.30am–
3pm; €2; ☎ 22750 31300) with finds from nearby ancient Oinoe; the twelfth-century
church of **Ayía Iríni** stands adjacent, with column stumps and mosaic patches of a
fourth-century basilica defining the entry courtyard. Lower down still are the sparse
ruins of a **Byzantine palace** used to house exiled nobles, signposted as "odeion", which
earlier structure it encloses. An unmarked track below the palace leads to a 250m-long
sandy **beach** with sunbeds and refreshments available.

Monastery of Theóktisti

Ikaría's outstanding medieval monument is the **monastery of Theóktisti**, 4km up
from Kámbos along a twisty road (and an easier 3km road from the cute coastal
village of Avláki). The monastery looks over pines to the coast from its perch under
a chaos of slanted granite slabs, under one of which is tucked the much-
photographed chapel of Theoskepastí. The *katholikón* features damaged but
worthwhile frescoes dated to 1688.

ACCOMMODATION AND EATING

Coralli Évdhilos ☎ 22750 31924. On the west quay, this is a good place to feast on large portions of inexpensive oven-cooked meat, such as goat done as *yiouvétsi* or *kokkinistó*, plus ample salads, dips and so on. April–Oct daily 1pm–midnight.

★ **Karimalis Winery** Piyí, 5km southwest of Évdhilos ☎ 22750 31151, ⓦ ikarianwine.gr. Several luxuriously restored ancient, family-sized cottages make for perhaps the classiest accommodation on the island. Half-board, bottle of wine and port/airport transfer included. Cooking courses and seminars also offered. The winery is near the junction of the two access roads to the monastery of Theóktisti. May–Sept. **€100**

Kerame Évdhilos ☎ 22750 31426, ⓦ atheras-kerame.gr. On the hill behind the harbour, this is the best of Évdhilos's three hotels. There are more spacious studio units 1km east

ÉVDHILOS AND AROUND

overlooking the eponymous beach. April–Oct. **€45**

★ **Mandouvala** Karavóstamo ☎ 22750 61204. With a delightful patio set above wave-lapped schist rock, this popular taverna at the far right of the seafront provides a range of average-priced fish, *mezédhes* and veg delights such as *soúfiko* (Ikarian ratatouille). May–Oct daily noon–midnight.

★ **Mezedopolio tou Ilia** Avláki ☎ 22750 71009. Some 300m up the road towards Theóktisti, this is the only real ouzeri on the north coast, and very proud of its own produce and self-caught fish. Has a lovely sea-view courtyard. Noon–1am: June–Sept daily, Oct–May Fri–Sun.

Sto Fytema Fýtema ☎ 22750 31387. Across the coastal road from the beach, *Sto Fytema* draws crowds to its shady courtyard from all over the island for its excellent vegetable dishes and fish, most under €10. May–Oct daily 11am–1am.

Armenistís and around

Most visitors congregate at **ARMENISTÍS**, 51km from Áyios Kírykos via Évdhilos, and for good reason: this little resort lies below Ikaría's greatest, if slightly fire-diminished, forest, with two enormous sandy **beaches** battered by seasonal surf – **Livádhi** and **Messaktí** – five and fifteen minutes' walk east respectively, the latter with several reed-roofed *kantínas*. The sea between here and Mýkonos is the windiest patch in the Aegean, generating a fairly consistent summer surf. The waves, which attract Athenian boogie-boarders, are complicated by strong lateral currents, and regular summer drownings have (at Livádhi) prompted a lifeguard service and a string of safety buoys.

Armenistís itself is spectacularly set, facing northeast along the length of Ikaría towards sun- and moonrise, with Mount Kérkis on Sámos visible on a clear day. A dwindling proportion of older, schist-roofed houses and ex-warehouses, plus boats hauled up in a central sandy cove, lend the place the air of a Cornish fishing village, though in fact it started out as a smuggler's depot, with warehouses but no dwellings. Just east of Messaktí, the fishing settlement of **Yialiskári** offers alternative facilities and looks out past pines to a picturesque jetty church.

Nas

Three kilometres west of Armenistís, **NAS**, a river canyon ending at a deceptively sheltered sand-and-pebble beach, remains a rather hippyish hangout, though it is no longer a naturist's paradise. This little bay is almost completely enclosed by weirdly sculpted rock formations, but again it's unwise to swim outside the cove's natural limits – marked here with a line of buoys. The crumbling foundations of the fifth-century BC temple of **Artemis Tavropoleio** (Artemis in Bull-Headdress) overlook the permanent deep pool at the mouth of the river. Sadly the delightful former riverside forestation further inland was swept away by heavy flooding in 2011.

ACCOMMODATION

ARMENISTÍS

★ **Daidalos** ☎ 22750 71390, ⓦ daidaloshotel.gr. This smart place on the western edge of town has a distinct artistic flavour, with a blob-shaped pool, unusually appointed rooms and a shady breakfast terrace. Breakfast included. May–Oct. **€60**

Erofili Beach ☎ 22750 71058, ⓦ erofili.gr. Considered

ARMENISTÍS AND AROUND

the island's best hotel, though the common area and pool, perched dramatically over Livádhi beach, impress more than the rooms. Breakfast included. April–Oct. **€90**

Valeta Apartments ☎ 22750 71252, ⓦ valeta.gr. The attractive and comfortable studios and quads here above the harbour offer a comparable standard and setting to the hotels, at better rates. May–Oct. **€40**

6

NAS

Artemis ☎ 22750 71485, ✉ artemis-studio@ikaria.gr. With rooms overlooking the river canyon from the cliff above, this rambling place provides great-value, comfortable and well-appointed accommodation. May–Sept. **€30**

EATING, DRINKING AND NIGHTLIFE

ARMENISTÍS

Casmir Livádhi beach. One of the island's most enduring clubs acts as a beach bar during the day and pumps out foreign and Greek hits by night. June–Sept daily 11am–late.

★ **Kiallaris (aka tis Eleftherias)** Yialiskári ☎ 22750 71227. Mid-seafront taverna that's tops for well-executed *mayireftá* and the freshest fish, all caught locally. Especially good for fish soup and *melitzanosaláta*. May to early Oct daily 11am–2am.

Paradhosiaka Glyka (Kioulanis) ☎ 22750 71150. On the road down to the harbour, this is one of the Aegean's star *zaharoplastía*, featuring addictive *karydhópita* (walnut cake) with goat's-milk, mastic-flavoured ice cream and other sweet delights. May–Oct daily 8am–1am; reduced winter hours.

★ **Paskhalia** ☎ 22750 71302. With a few inexpensive rooms above (€30), this friendly taverna on the harbour approach road has a sea-view terrace, open for breakfast, where you can enjoy tasty home-cooking such as rabbit *stifádho* and roast lamb. Great barrelled wine too. April–Oct daily 8am–1am.

NAS

O Nas ☎ 22750 71486. With a huge terrace on the cliff that has the best bay views, this place offers pasta, grills and oven-baked dishes, plus there's a good bakery. May–Sept daily noon–midnight.

Thea ☎ 22750 71491, ⊛ theasinn.com. On the east cliff, this long-standing favourite has lots of vegetarian options like *soufikó* and pumpkin-filled *pítta*. Also has a few rooms. 6pm–1pm: May–Oct daily, Nov–April weekends; from noon in late July & Aug.

The Ráhes villages

Armenistís was originally the port of four inland hamlets – Áyios Dhimítrios, Áyios Polýkarpos, Kastaniés and Khristós – collectively known as **Ráhes**. Curiously, these already served as "hill station" resorts during the 1920s and 1930s, with three hotels, since long-gone, and the only tourism on the island. Despite the modern, paved access roads through the pines, the settlements retain a certain Shangri-La quality, with older residents speaking a positively Homeric dialect.

On an island not short of foibles, these villages are particularly strange in that most locals sleep until 11am or so, move around until about 4pm, then have another nap until 8pm, whereupon they rise and spend most of the night shopping, eating and drinking, in particular excellent home-brewed **wine** traditionally kept in goatskins.

EATING AND DRINKING
THE RÁHES VILLAGES

Kapilio Khristós ☎ 22750 41517. Right in the main pedestrian zone, this good, inexpensive carnivorous supper option serves mainly grills, with the odd dish from the oven and some simple salads. Daily 6pm–4am.

WALKING IN WESTERN IKARÍA

Although bulldozers and forest fires have reduced the number of attractive possibilities, **walking** between Ráhes and both coasts on old paths is a favourite visitor activity. A locally produced, accurate map-guide, *The Round of Ráhes on Foot*, shows most asphalt roads, tracks and trails in the west of the island, as well as a **loop-hike** taking in the best of the Ráhes villages. The well-marked route sticks partly to surviving paths; the authors suggest a full day for the circuit, with ample rests, though total walking time won't exceed six hours. The highlight is the section from Khristós to Kastaniés, which takes in the Hárakos ravine with its Spanédhon watermill.

Those wishing to traverse across Ikaría are best advised to keep on a "Round of Ráhes" sub-route from Khristós to Karydhiés, from where a historic path crosses the lunar Ammoudhiá uplands before dropping spectacularly southeast to Managanítis on the south coast, a generous half-day's outing from Armenistís.

Platanos Áyios Dhimítrios ☎ 22750 41472. Underneath the deep shade of the eponymous plane tree on the square, this local favourite is renowned for its *mayireftá*, like beef in wine sauce and moussaka. Daily 5pm–4am.

Ydrohöos Áyios Dhimítrios ☎ 22750 41526. Typically off-beat art café on the square, which has a relaxed atmosphere and showcases frequent live rock, jazz, techno or Latin bands. Wed–Sun 5pm–4am.

The south coast

The well-paved route south from Évdhilos via Akamátra crosses the island watershed before dropping steadily towards the **south coast**; with your own vehicle this is a quicker and much less curvy way back to Áyios Kírykos compared to going via Karavóstomo. It's an eminently scenic route worth taking for its own sake, the narrow road threading corniche-like through oaks at the pass, and then olives at **Playiá** village on the steep southern slope of the island. Out to sea the islands of Pátmos and Dhonoússa are generally visible, and on really clear days Náxos and Amorgós as well. The principal potential detour, 2km past the castle turning, is the road right (west) to the secluded pebble beach of **Seÿhélles** ("Seychelles"), the best on this generally inhospitable coast, with the final approach by ten-minute hike.

With your own transport, you can visit several villages at the southwest tip of the island. **Vrahádhes** enjoys a natural-balcony setting, while a sharp drop below it, the impact of the empty convent of **Mavrianoú** lies mostly in its setting amid gardens overlooking the sea. Nearby **Langádha** is not actually a village but a lush hidden valley. Note that facilities are scarce over the whole south-coast area, with just the odd erratically opening *kafenío* or seasonal taverna providing refreshment.

Híos

"Craggy Híos", as **Homer** aptly described his putative birthplace, has a turbulent history and a strong identity. This large island has always been prosperous: in medieval times through the export of **mastic resin** – a trade controlled by Genoese overlords between 1346 and 1566 – and later by the Ottomans, who dubbed the place Sakız Adası ("Resin Island"). Since union with Greece in 1912, several shipping dynasties have emerged here, continuing to generate wealth, and someone in almost every family still spends time in the merchant navy.

Unfortunately, the island has suffered more than its share of **catastrophes** since the 1800s. The Ottomans perpetrated their most infamous, if not their worst, anti-revolutionary atrocity here in March 1822, massacring 30,000 Hiots and enslaving or exiling even more. In 1881, much of Híos was destroyed by a violent earthquake, and throughout the 1980s the island's natural beauty was compromised by devastating forest fires, compounding the effect of generations of tree-felling by boat-builders.

Until the late 1980s, the more powerful ship-owning dynasts, local government and the military authorities discouraged **tourism** and even now it is concentrated mostly in the capital or the nearby beach resorts of Karfás and Ayía Ermióni. Despite this, various foreigners have discovered a Híos beyond its rather daunting port capital: fascinating **villages**, important **Byzantine monuments** and a respectable, if remote, complement of **beaches**. English is widely spoken courtesy of numerous returned Greek-Americans and Greek-Canadians.

ARRIVAL AND DEPARTURE   HÍOS

By plane There are flights to the following destinations (frequencies given for June–Oct): Athens (4–5 daily; 45–50min); Lésvos (2 weekly; 30min); Límnos (2 weekly; 1hr 30min); Rhodes (2 weekly; 1hr–1hr 45min); Thessaloníki (4 weekly; 1hr 10min–2hr 45min).

By ferry Híos is the only stop on the daily superfast service between Pireás and Lésvos and is also on the much slower northern mainland to Sámos/Ikaría route, while smaller boats connect it with the satellite islands of Psará and Inoússes, as well as Çeşme in Turkey. Nearly all boats leave from Híos Town but some Psará and all Lávrio sailings go from the port of Mestá.

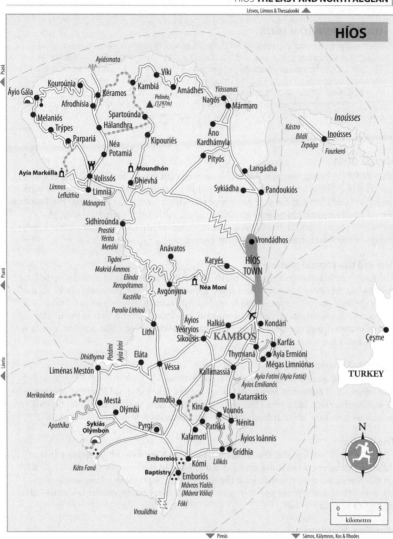

Híos Town to: Áyios Kírykos, Ikaría (1 weekly; 5hr); Çeşme (1–2 daily; 30–45min); Inoússes (1–2 daily; 30min); Karlóvassi, Sámos (1 weekly; 4hr); Kavála (2 weekly; 16hr); Lésvos (2 weekly; 3hr); Límnos (2 weekly; 9hr); Pireás (1 daily; 6hr 30min); Psará (6 weekly; 3hr); Thessaloníki (1 weekly; 19hr 45min); Vathý, Sámos (1 weekly; 4hr). Mestá to: Lávrio (3 weekly; 6hr 30min); Psará (3–4 weekly; 1hr 15min).

GETTING AROUND

By bus While services to the major destinations in the south run quite frequently (Mon–Sat 3–5, Sun 1–2), those bound for the north are much less frequent (1–4 daily) and the northwest is especially poorly served, with no schedules on Sun.

By car or motorbike To explore properly you'll need to rent a powerful motorbike or a car. Of the many rental agencies around the island, the best is Vassilakis/Reliable Rent a Car (☎ 22710 29300, ⊛ rentacar-chios.com), with branches at Evyenías Handhrí 3 in Híos Town (behind the eyesore *Chandris Hotel*), Karfás and Mégas Limniónas.

> ### DAY-TRIPS FROM HÍOS
> The most popular boat excursions from the main port of Híos Town are to the nearby satellite island of Inoússes (see p.382) and to the Turkish coast, as Psará is too far for a comfortable day-trip. Trips to **Inoússes** usually depart twice a week, on Thursday and Sunday, at 8.30am, returning by 6pm at a cost of €20. The longer excursions to Turkey leave daily at 8am for the port of **Çeşme**, where an optional bus transfer takes you to the city of Izmir, returning by 7.15pm. Prices vary according to demand but are often as low as €35; Kanaris Tours at Leofóros Egéou 12 (☎ 22710 42490, ⓦ kanaristours.gr) sell tickets for both.

Híos Town

HÍOS TOWN, a brash, concrete-laced commercial centre with little predating the 1881 quake, will come as a shock after modest island capitals elsewhere. Yet in many ways it's the most satisfactory of the east Aegean ports, with a large and fascinating **marketplace**, several **museums**, an **old quarter** and some good, authentic **tavernas**. Although a sprawling place of about 30,000 souls, most things of interest lie within a few hundred metres of the water, fringed by Leofóros Egéou.

Around the central platía

The town's small triangular central **platía**, officially Plastíra but known universally as **Vounakíou**, lies only a block inland from the seafront, up by the main dock. To the south extends the marvellously lively tradesmen's **bazaar**, where you can find everything from parrots to cast-iron woodstoves. Inland to the west is the urban sprawl's single lung, the attractively lush central **park**, whose most notable feature is an Ottoman fountain.

Byzantine Museum

Opposite the Vounakíou taxi rank • Tues–Sun 8.30am–3pm • €3 • ☎ 22710 26866

The refurbished **Byzantine Museum**, occupying the renovated old **Mecidiye Mosque** with its leaning minaret, has a small but interesting collection, with sections on religious and secular architecture, some splendid murals and icons, as well as various ceramics.

The Kástro

Until the 1881 earthquake, the Byzantine-Genoese **Kástro** stood completely intact; thereafter developers razed the seaward walls, filled in the moat to the south and sold off the real estate thus created along the waterfront. Nevertheless, large sections of imposing ramparts remain and the most dramatic entry to the citadel is via the **Porta Maggiora** behind the town hall.

Maritime Museum

Stefánou Tsoúri 20 • Mon–Sat: May–Oct 9am–2pm; Nov–April 9am–1pm • Donation • ☎ 22710 44139, ⓦ chiosnauticalmuseum.gr

The **Maritime Museum** consists principally of model ships and nautical oil paintings, all rather overshadowed by the mansion containing them. In the foyer are enshrined the knife and glass-globe grenade of Admiral Kanaris, who partly avenged the 1822 massacre by ramming and sinking the Ottoman fleet's flagship, thus dispatching Admiral Kara Ali, architect of the atrocities.

Argenti Folklore Museum

Koraï 2 • Mon–Thurs 8am–2pm, Fri 8am–2pm & 5–7pm, Sat 8am–12.30pm • €2 • ☎ 22710 28256

The central **Argenti Folklore Museum**, on the top floor of the Koraïs Library, features ponderous genealogical portraits of the endowing family, an adjoining wing of costumes and rural impedimenta, plus multiple replicas of Delacroix's *Massacre at Hios*, a painting which did much to arouse sympathy for the cause of Greek independence.

Archeological museum

Mihálon • June–Aug daily 8am–7pm; Sept–May Tues–Sun 8.30am–3pm • €3 • ☎ 22710 44239

The **archeological museum** has a wide-ranging, well-lit collection from Neolithic to Roman times. Highlights include limestone column bases from the Apollo temple at Faná in the shape of lions' claws; numerous statuettes and reliefs of Cybele (an Asiatic goddess especially honoured here); Archaic faience miniatures from Emborió in the shape of a cat, a hawk and a flautist; a terracotta dwarf riding a boar; and figurines (some with articulated limbs) of *hierodouloi* or sacred prostitutes, presumably from an Aphrodite shrine. Most famous is an inscribed edict of Alexander the Great from 322 BC, setting out relations between himself and the Hiots.

6

ARRIVAL AND GETTING AROUND

HÍOS TOWN

By air The poky airport lies 3km south of the capital at Kondári, a €4 taxi-ride away; otherwise any blue urban bus on the Híos Town–Karfás route should pass the stop opposite the airport.

By ferry Ferry agents cluster along the north end of waterfront Egéou and its continuation Neoríon.

By bus Blue city buses radiate out from the terminal on the north side of Híos Town's central park and serve some nearby beaches, principally Vrondhádhos and Karfás, but also as far as Ayía Ermióni. For anywhere further afield, long-distance KTEL buses leave from just behind the passenger waiting-room on seafront Egéou.

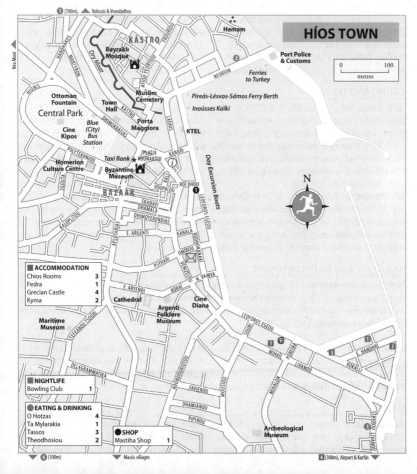

HÍOS TOWN

ACCOMMODATION
Chios Rooms	3
Fedra	1
Grecian Castle	4
Kyma	2

NIGHTLIFE
Bowling Club	1

EATING & DRINKING
O Hotzas	4
Ta Mylarakia	1
Tassos	3
Theodhosiou	2

SHOP
Mastiha Shop	1

By car or motorbike Parking in town is possible only on the southern fringes and in the moat west of the kástro.

By taxi For shorter distances around the capital, the main taxi rank is on the central platía.

INFORMATION

Tourist office Kanári 18 (Mon–Fri 7.30am–3pm; ☎ 22710 44389, ⓦ chioscity.gr).

Online A good general online resource for the whole island is ⓦ chiosonline.gr.

Services Commercial maps and a few English-language books are found at Newsstand, at the first "kink" in Egéou. The most reliable internet café is Enter, just seaward of the *Fedra Hotel*. The post office is on Omírou.

ACCOMMODATION

Híos Town has a fair quantity of affordable accommodation, rarely full. Most places line the front or the perpendicular alleys and parallel streets behind, and almost all are plagued by traffic noise – we've listed the more peaceful establishments.

★ **Chios Rooms** Egéou 110 ☎ 22710 20198, ⓦ chiosrooms.gr. Don and Dina's lovingly restored tile- or wood-floored, high-ceilinged rooms are relatively quiet for a seafront location. Some en suite; best is the penthouse "suite" with private terrace. **€25**

Fedra Mihaïl Livanoú 13 ☎ 22710 41129. Well-appointed pension in a nineteenth-century mansion, with stone arches in the downstairs winter bar; in summer the bar operates outside, so get a rear room to avoid nocturnal noise. **€35**

Grecian Castle Bélla Vísta shore avenue ☎ 22710 44740, ⓦ greciancastle.gr. Converted factory towards the airport with lovely grounds and a sea-view pool, but the smallish main-wing rooms, despite their marble floors, wood ceilings and bug screens, are inferior to the rear "villa" suites. Breakfast included. **€100**

★ **Kyma** Evyenías Handhrí ☎ 22710 44500, ✉ kyma @chi.forthnet.gr. Variable rooms in a Neoclassical mansion or modern extension, with huge terraces on the sea-facing side; most units have new handmade wood-and-leather furniture. Owner Theo's knowledgeable service really makes the place. Breakfast included. **€65**

EATING AND DRINKING

★ **O Hotzas** Yeoryíou Kondhýli 3 ☎ 22710 42787. Oldest and most popular taverna in town, with an old-style interior and delightful summer garden. Menu varies seasonally, but expect a mix of vegetarian dishes and *lahanodolmádhes*, sausages, baby fish and *mydhopílafo* (rice and mussels) accompanied by own-brand ouzo or retsina. Mon–Sat 7pm–late.

Ta Mylarakia Tambákika district ☎ 22710 40412. A large seafood selection, every kind of Hiot ouzo (Tetteri Penindari is the best) and limited seating at the island's most romantic waterside setting at the four restored windmills. Reservations advisable in summer. Daily: April–Oct 11am–2am; Nov–May 8pm–1am.

Tassos Stávrou Livanoú 8, Bélla Vísta district. Good all-rounder with creative salads, better-than-average bean dishes, *dolmádhes*, snails, good chips, a strong line in seafood and decent barrelled wine. There's sea-view summer garden seating and a heated gazebo for winter. Daily noon–1am.

Theodhosiou Neoríon 33. The oldest of three ouzerís on this quay, occupying a domed, arcaded building. There's a fair range of meat grills for this type of place, plus various seafood standards. Generally, avoid the fried platters in favour of grilled or boiled ones. Dinner only; closed Sun.

NIGHTLIFE AND ENTERTAINMENT

Some 1400 local university students help keep things lively, especially along the waterfront between the two "kinks" in Egéou. Shooting **pool** is big here; many bars have several tables. **Film** fans are well served by Cine Kipos (late June to early Sept), in one corner of the central park, with quality/art-house first-run screenings; from October the action shifts to Cine Diana, under the eponymous hotel.

Bowling Club Leofóros Egéou 120 ☎ 22710 28517. This popular bar has a multitude of pool tables and seven bowling alleys as well. Daily 10am–late.

Homerion Cultural Centre Iroón Polytekhníou 5 ☎ 22710 44391, ⓦ homerion.gr. This large events hall on the south side of the park hosts changing exhibitions, and big-name acts, including some foreign ones, often come here after Athens concerts. Hours vary.

SHOP

Mastiha Shop Egéou 36 ☎ 22710 81600, ⓦ mastihashop.com. Home base of a chain with nine branches in Greece plus others in New York, Paris and even Jeddah. Sells all things mastic from chewing gum to shower gel. Daily: July–Sept 8.30am–midnight; Oct–June 8.30am–10pm.

Around Híos Town

Vrondádhos is served by Blue urban buses from Híos Town; most buses heading here are labelled "the Teacher's Rock"

North of Híos Town, **VRONDÁDHOS** is an elongated coastal suburb that's a favourite residence of the many local seafarers. Homer is alleged to have lived and taught here, and in terraced parkland just above the little fishing port and pebble beach you can visit his purported lectern, more likely an ancient altar of Cybele.

The locals swim at the tiny pebble coves near here or from the grubby town beach in Bélla Vísta, but really the closest decent option is at **Karfás**, 7km south beyond the airport. However, as most large Hiot resort hotels are planted here, the 500m-long beach itself, sandy only at the south end, has limited appeal. The nearby inland village of **Thymianá** offers a more authentic atmosphere and better dining options.

Some 2km further along the coast from Karfás, **Ayía Ermióni** is a fishing anchorage, adjoining the next proper beach at **Mégas Limniónas**, a few hundred metres further on, smaller than Karfás but more scenic, with low cliffs as a backdrop. Some 4km further south is the turning for **Ayía Fotiní**, also known as Ayía Fotiá, a 600m pebble **beach** with exceptionally clean water. Cars are excluded from the shore area and the pedestrian esplanade is lined with various rooms and tavernas. Five kilometres further south, back via the main road, the small fishing village of **Katarráktis** is a pleasant spot where locals in the know go to eat.

ACCOMMODATION   AROUND HÍOS TOWN

Apartments Iro Ayía Ermióni ☎ 22710 51166. Large self-catering studios on the seafront beside the access road, with sea views from the balconies. Nicely furnished, with a/c and dedicated parking. April–Oct. **€40**

Karatzas Karfás ☎ 22710 31221. Typically compact but decent-value rooms above a taverna at the northern end of the seafront, which offers pricey fish but much more reasonable meat dishes. April–Oct. **€35**

★ **Markos' Place** Karfás ☎ 22710 31990, ⊛ marcos -place.gr. Markos Kostalas has lovingly created a peaceful,

leafy environment on the hillside behind the bay out of a beautiful deconsecrated monastery. Guests stay in the former pilgrims' cells, with a kitchen available or superior breakfasts provided by arrangement. April–Nov. **€35**

Mavrokordatiko 1.5km south of the airport ☎ 22710 32900, ⊛ mavrokordatiko.com. With enormous wood-panelled rooms and spacious communal areas, including a fine café/restaurant, this renovated mansion, 1.5km south of the airport, oozes atmosphere. Breakfast included. **€70**

EATING AND DRINKING

Ankyra Mégas Limniónas ☎ 22710 32178. All-round reliable *psarotaverna* behind the middle of the beach, serving fish of all categories and an accompanying range of meat, veg and salads, as well as a fine ouzo selection. May–Oct daily 11am–midnight.

O Tsambos Katarráktis ☎ 22710 61601. Long-established favourite taverna on the centre of the seafront, with friendly management and a wide menu, including the cheapest pork chops on Híos at only €5. April–Oct daily 11am–1am.

★ **To Talimi** Thymianá ☎ 22710 32940. Serves excellent home-style *mayireftá* like *yiouvarlákia*, *kókoras krasáto* or bean-and-artichoke salad at friendly prices in a lovely shady courtyard in the centre of the village. Daily noon–midnight.

The Twins Ayía Fotiní ☎ 22710 51630. At the seaward end of the access road, this is easily the best taverna in the resort, excelling in shrimp fritters and other seafood delights, mostly for under €10. May–Oct daily 10am–2am.

The mastihohoriá

Besides olive groves, southern Híos's gently rolling countryside is home to the **mastic bush**, and the twenty or so *mastihohoriá*, or mastic villages (see box, p.378). Since the decline of the mastic trade, the *mastihohoriá* live mainly off their tangerines, apricots and olives, though the villages, the only settlements on Híos spared by the Ottomans in 1822, retain their architectural uniqueness, designed by the Genoese but with a distinctly Middle Eastern feel. The basic plan involves a rectangular warren of tall houses, with the outer row doubling as perimeter fortification, and breached by a limited number of gateways. More recent additions, whether in traditional architectural style or not, straggle outside the original defences. Of the surviving villages, three stand out: **Pyrgí**, **Olýmbi** and **Mestá**.

6

MASTIC MASTICATION

The **mastic bush** (*Pistacia lentisca*) is found across much of Aegean Greece but only in southern Híos – pruned to an umbrella shape to facilitate harvesting – does it produce aromatic resin of any quality or quantity, scraped from incisions made on the trunk during summer. For centuries it was used as a base for paints, cosmetics and the chewable jelly beans that became an addictive staple in Ottoman harems. Indeed, the interruption of the flow of mastic from Híos to Istanbul by the revolt of spring 1822 was a main cause of the brutal Ottoman reaction. The wealth engendered by the mastic trade supported twenty *mastihohoriá* (mastic villages) from the time the Genoese set up a monopoly in the substance during the fourteenth century, but the demise of imperial Turkey and the development of petroleum-based products knocked the bottom out of the mastic market.

Now it's just a curiosity, to be chewed – try the sweetened Elma-brand gum – or drunk as *mastíha* liqueur. It has had medicinal applications since ancient times; contemporary advocates claim that mastic boosts the immune system and thins the blood. High-end cosmetics, toothpaste and mouthwash are now sold at the Mastiha Shop in Híos Town (see p.376).

Pyrgí

PYRGÍ, 25km south of Híos Town, is the most colourful of the *mastihohoriá*, its houses elaborately embossed with *xystá*, patterns cut into whitewash to reveal a layer of black volcanic sand underneath; in autumn, strings of sun-drying tomatoes add a further splash of colour. On the northeast corner of the central square the twelfth-century Byzantine church of **Áyii Apóstoli** (erratic hours), embellished with much later frescoes, is tucked under an arcade.

Olýmbi and around

OLÝMBI, 7km west of Pyrgí along the same bus route, is one of the less visited mastic villages but not devoid of interest. The characteristic **tower-keep**, which at Pyrgí stands half-inhabited away from the modernized main square, here looms bang in the middle of the platía.

The Sykiás Olýmbon cave

Tues–Sun: June–Aug 10am–8pm; Sept 11am–6pm • Admission every 30min • €5

From Olýmbi, a paved road leads 6km to the well-signed cave of **Sykiás Olýmbon**. For years it was just a hole in the ground where villagers disposed of dead animals, but from 1985 on speleologists explored it properly. The cavern, with a constant temperature of 18°C, evolved in two phases between 150 million and 50 million years ago, and has a maximum depth of 57m (though tours only visit the top 30m). Its formations, with fanciful names like Chinese Forest, Medusa and Organ Pipes, are among the most beautiful in the Mediterranean.

Mestá

Sombre, monochrome **MESTÁ**, 4km west of Olýmbi, is considered the finest of the villages; despite more snack-bars and trinket shops than strictly necessary, it remains just the right side of twee. From its main square, dominated by the **church of the Taxiárhis** with its two icons of the Archangel – one dressed in Byzantine robes, the other in Genoese armour – a maze of dim lanes with anti-seismic tunnels leads off in all directions. Most streets end in blind alleys, except those leading to the six portals; the northeast one still has its original iron gate.

ACCOMMODATION AND EATING   **THE MASTIHOHORIÁ**

Tourist facilities are relatively sparse in the mastic villages. Apart from the establishments listed below, you will find a smattering of cafés, the odd tiny taverna and some signs for private rooms, usually available on spec.

Chrysanthi Apartments Olýmbi ☏ 22710 76196, ⓦ chrysanthi.gr. Three units suitable for two to five persons near the central platía – nicely furnished with smart kitchens – retaining many original features such as stone alcoves. **€55**

★ **Medieval Castle Suites** Mestá ☏ 22710 76345, ⓦ mcsuites.gr. Superbly refurbished medieval mansion on a lane just off the main square, with much of the original stone exterior, yet lavishly furnished and equipped with all modern facilities inside. Easter–Oct. **€80**

★ **Mesaionas (Kyra Dhespina)** Mestá ☏ 22710 76050. Excellent home-cooked dishes, such as stewed octopus, moussaka and various veg in sauces for well under €10 each, served on the square. The welcoming owner can put you in touch with places offering rooms. Daily 11am–midnight.

6

The mastic coast

The most popular **beaches** at the southern end of Híos are in the vicinity of **Emboriós**, tucked in the southeast corner. Over on the southwest coast, the closest good, protected beach to Mestá lies 4.7km southwest at **Apothíka**. Others, east of ugly but functional **Liménas Mestón** port, include **Dhídhyma**, 4km away, a double cove guarded by an islet; **Potámi**, with a namesake stream feeding it; and less scenic **Ayía Iríni**, 8km distant, with a reliably open taverna.

Emboriós

EMBORIÓS, an almost landlocked harbour, is 6km southeast of Pyrgí. Ancient **Emboreios**, on the hill to the northeast, has been rehabilitated as an "archeological park" (summer daily 8.30am–3pm, winter closed Mon; €2). Down in modern Emboriós a cruciform early Christian **baptistry** is signposted in a field just inland; it's protected by a later, round structure, which remains locked but everything's visible through the grating.

Beaches around Emboriós

For **swimming**, follow the road a short way south from Emboriós to an oversubscribed car park and the beach of **Mávros Yialós**, better known as Mávra Vólia, then continue by flagstoned walkway over the headland to more dramatic **Fóki**. Twice as long and backed by impressive cliffs, this pebble strip of purple-grey volcanic stones is part nudist. If you want sand (and amenities) go to **Kómi**, 3km northeast of Emboriós, which is the main (albeit low-key) resort for the area.

ACCOMMODATION AND EATING	THE MASTIC COAST

Bella Mare Kómi ☏ 22710 71228. Classic beach taverna-cum-rooms-combo towards the southern end of the beach, which offers a fair selection of seafood and meat as mezédhes or main dishes, as well as simple sea-view accommodation. Restaurant May–Oct 9am–2am. **€30**

Nostalgia Kómi ☏ 22710 70070. Good all-round taverna behind the northern end of the beach, specializing in grilled fish and meat but also offering a line in veg dishes and some decent barrelled wine. April to mid-Oct daily noon–2am.

Porto Emborios Emboriós ☏ 22710 71306. The best of the four tavernas clustered around the harbour offers good seafood at fair prices, a range of salads and dips, plus home-made desserts. March–Oct daily 10am–1am.

Central Híos

The inland portion of Híos extending west and southwest from Híos Town matches the south in terms of interesting **monuments**, and good roads make touring under your own steam an easy matter. The flat **Kámbos** leads to more mountainous terrain to the west and north.

The Kámbos

The **Kámbos**, a vast fertile plain carpeted with citrus groves, extends southwest from Híos Town almost as far as the village of Halkió. The district was originally settled by the Genoese during the fourteenth century, and remained a preserve of the local aristocracy until 1822. Exploring by two-wheeler may be less frustrating than going by car, since the web of narrow, poorly marked lanes sandwiched between high walls guarantees disorientation and frequent backtracking. Behind the walls you catch fleeting glimpses of ornate old mansions built from locally quarried sandstone, whose courtyards are paved in pebbles or alternating light and dark tiles.

Néa Moní

Daily 8am–1pm & 4–8pm, 5–8pm in summer • ☎ 22710 79370

Almost exactly in the middle of the island, the monastery of **Néa Moní** was founded by the Byzantine Emperor Constantine Monomahos ("The Dueller") IX in 1042 on the spot where a wonder-working icon had been discovered. It ranks among the most important monuments on any of the Greek islands; the mosaics, together with those of Dháfni and Ósios Loukás on the mainland, are the finest surviving art of their era in Greece, and the setting – high in partly forested mountains 15km west of the port – is equally memorable. Once a powerful community of six hundred monks, Néa Moní was pillaged in 1822 and most of its residents, including 3500 civilians sheltering here, were put to the sword. The 1881 tremor caused comprehensive damage, wrecking many of its outbuildings, while exactly a century later a forest fire threatened to engulf the place until the resident icon was paraded along the perimeter wall, miraculously repelling the flames.

The site

Just inside the **main gate** stands a **chapel/ossuary** containing some of the bones of the 1822 victims; axe-clefts in children's skulls attest to the savagery of the attackers. The restored *katholikón* has a cupola resting on an octagonal drum, a design seen elsewhere only in Cyprus; the famous **mosaics** within have now been returned to their former glory. The narthex contains portrayals of various local saints sandwiched between *Christ Washing the Disciples' Feet* and the *Betrayal*, in which Judas's kiss has unfortunately been obliterated, but Peter is clearly visible lopping off the ear of the high priest's servant.

Avgónyma

Some 5km west of Néa Moní sits **AVGÓNYMA**, a cluster of dwellings on a knoll overlooking the coast; the name means "Clutch of Eggs", an apt description when viewed from the ridge above. Since the 1980s, the place has been restored as a summer haven by descendants of the original villagers, though the permanent population is fewer than ten.

ACCOMMODATION AND EATING   CENTRAL HÍOS

★ **Arhondiko Perleas** 3km south of the airport, Kámbos ☎ 22710 32217, ⓦ perleas.gr. Set in a huge organic citrus ranch, with a well-regarded in-house restaurant, this extremely classy converted mansion boasts dark wood interiors and original artwork, as well as lavish furnishings. Gourmet breakfast included. **€90**

0 Pyrgos Avgónyma ☎ 22710 42175, ⓔ pyrgosrooms @chiosnet.gr. In an attractive arcaded mansion on the main square, with ample courtyard seating, this taverna run by Greek-Americans offers both oven-cooked dishes and grills. There are some simple but adequate rooms too. **€40**

Spitakia Avgónyma ☎ 22710 20513, ⓦ spitakia.gr. A cluster of small stone cottages sleeping up to five people, plus some rooms, all lovingly restored and tastefully decorated, with good heating for the winter months. **€50**

The west coast

The central section of the island's **west coast** offers a couple of picturesque villages and some not-too-crowded beaches, given that they are so easily accessible from Híos Town by way of Avgónyma, from where the main road descends 6km to the sea in well-graded loops.

Tigáni and Makriá Ámmos

On the northern stretch of the central west coast, bypass Elínda, alluring from afar but rocky and often murky up close, in favour of the more secluded coves to either side of Metóhi – best of these are **Tigáni** and **Makriá Ámmos**, the latter nudist.

Lithí and Paralía Lithioú

Friendly **LITHÍ** village perches on a forested ledge overlooking the sea towards the southern end of the central west coast. You can eat here but most visitors head 2km downhill to **Paralía Lithioú**, a popular weekend target of Hiot townies thanks to its large but hard-packed, windswept beach.

Véssa

Some 5km south of Lithí, valley-bottom **VÉSSA** is an unsung gem: more open and less casbah-like than Mestá or Pyrgí, but still homogeneous, its tawny buildings are arrayed in a vast grid punctuated by numerous belfries and arcaded passages.

ACCOMMODATION AND EATING	THE WEST COAST
Almyriki Apartments Paralía Lithioú ☏ 22710 73124, ⓦ almiriki.gr. Smart new complex behind the middle of the beach, with modern well-appointed rooms sporting modern furniture, LCD TVs and fridges. Chic café-bar on site too. April–Oct. €65	**To Akroyiali** Paralía Lithioú ☏ 22710 73286. The best of the handful of tavernas here, behind the beach's north end, providing fresh fish, a variety of seafood, simple grilled meat and some tasty mezédhes. May–Sept daily 11am–1am.

Northern Híos

Northern Híos never really recovered from the 1822 massacre, and between Pityós and Volissós the forest's recovery from 1980s **fires** has been partly reversed by a bad 2007 blaze. Most villages usually lie deserted, with about a third of the former population living in Híos Town, returning occasionally for major festivals or to tend smallholdings; others, based in Athens or North America, visit their ancestral homes for just a few midsummer weeks.

Langádha and around

Some 16km north of Híos Town, **LANGÁDHA** is probably the first point on the eastern coast road you'd be tempted to stop, though there is no proper beach nearby. Set at the mouth of a deep valley, this attractive little harbour settlement looks across its bay to a pine grove, and beyond to Turkey.

Just beyond Langádha a side road leads 5km up and inland to **Pityós**, an oasis in a mountain pass presided over by a small, round castle; continuing 4km further brings you to a junction that allows quick access to the west of the island.

Mármaro and around

Káto Kardhámyla, 37km out of Híos Town, is the island's second town. Better known as **MÁRMARO**, it's positioned at the edge of a fertile plain rimmed by mountains, which comes as welcome relief from the craggy coastline. However, there is little to attract casual visitors other than some Neoclassical architecture; the mercilessly exposed port is strictly businesslike and offers only a limited range of tourist facilities and mediocre beach. Swimming is much more enjoyable at the pebble bay of **Nagós**, 5km west, or at **Yióssonas**, a much longer and rockier beach, 1km further on.

Volissós and around

VOLISSÓS, 42km from Híos Town, was once the market town for a dozen remote hill villages beyond. The buildings around the main square are mostly modern but a host of old stone houses still curl appealingly beneath a crumbling hilltop Byzantine-Genoese **fort**. These upper quarters, known as **Pýrgos**, are in the grip of a restoration mania, most in good taste, with ruins changing hands for stratospheric prices and usually being turned into quality accommodation.

Beaches around Volissós

LIMNIÁ (or Limiá), the port of Volissós, lies 2km south of town, bracketed by the local beaches. A 1.5km drive or walk southeast over the headland brings you to **Mánagros**, a seemingly endless sand-and-pebble beach. More intimate, sandy **Lefkáthia** lies just a ten-minute stroll along the cement drive over the headland north of the harbour.

Límnos, the next protected cove 400m east of Lefkáthia, can also be accessed by a direct road from Volissós. **Ayía Markélla**, 5km further northwest of Límnos, has another long beach, fronting the eponymous, barracks-like pilgrimage **monastery** of Híos's patron saint (festival on July 22).

6

Monastery of Moundhón

For access, seek out the warden, Yiorgos Fokas, in nearby Dhievhá village (☎ 22740 22011)

The engagingly set sixteenth-century **monastery of Moundhón** was second in rank to Néa Moní before its partial destruction in 1822. Best of the naïve interior frescoes of the (locked) church is one depicting the *Ouranódhromos Klímax* (Stairway to Heaven, not to be confused with Led Zeppelin's): a trial-by-ascent, in which ungodly priests are beset by demons hurling them into the mouth of a great serpent symbolizing the Devil, while the righteous clergy are assisted upwards by angels. The monastery is reached on a 2km detour north of the main Hios Town–Volissós road.

ACCOMMODATION, EATING AND DRINKING · NORTHERN HÍOS

LANGÁDHA AND AROUND

★ Makellos Pityós ☎ 22720 23364. Renowned all over the island for its splendid home-style lamb and beef dishes, as well as the likes of rabbit and free-range rooster. Great barrelled wine too. Noon–1am: May–Sept daily, Oct–April most weekends.

Pandoukios (Kourtesis) Pandoukiós ☎ 22710 74262. Excellent if rather pricey waterside taverna towards the south end of the beach, where lobster can often be had, as well as less expensive seafood, some meat dishes and plenty of salads and dips. May–Oct daily 10am–2am.

T'Ayeri Langádha ☎ 22710 74813. The cheapest and most traditional taverna here, serving a combination of small fish and excellent *mayireftá* for €7–8, as well as very palatable barrelled wine. Noon–2am: April–Oct daily, Nov–March Fri–Sun.

MÁRMARO AND AROUND

Hotel Kardamyla Mármaro ☎ 22720 23353. Co-managed with Híos Town's *Hotel Kyma*, this friendly central hotel offers spacious, fan-equipped rooms and a few suites, all pleasantly furnished and some with sea views. The restaurant is good too. Breakfast included. April–Oct. **€50**

Thalasses Mármaro ☎ 22720 23888. Slightly upmarket but still good value, this *psarotavérna* on the northern seafront specializes in fresh fish and seafood, with delights such as crab and octopus salads. Daily noon–2am.

VOLISSÓS AND AROUND

Aigiali Límnos ☎ 22740 21856, ⓦ aigiali.gr. Attractive, comfortably furnished apartments at the beach end of the access road, with well-equipped kitchens and sea-view balconies in a sturdy modern stone building. The café does great sweets too. May–Sept. **€35**

★ Fabrika Volissós ☎ 22740 22045. Just behind the square, this converted factory, hence the name, does superb *kondosoúvli* and *kokorétsi*, as well as a range of daily-changing oven-baked dishes. Seating in the attractive interior or leafy courtyard. Daily noon–2am.

Limnos Límnos ☎ 22740 22122. Good all-round taverna in the corner of the beach (near the access road) that dishes up fish grills and specials like *kókoras krasáto*, as well as delicious mezédhes and highly drinkable wine. May to mid-Oct daily 10am–midnight.

★ Moneos A & B/Theias Pýrgos district, Volissós ☎ 22740 21413, ⓦ volissostravel.gr. Three skilfully converted stone houses accommodating two people each – all have terraces, fully equipped kitchens, a/c and features such as tree trunks upholding sleeping lofts, reflecting proprietress Stella's background as a sculptor. May–Oct. **€45**

★ O Zikos Limniá ☎ 22740 22040. Popular local spot on the quay with good grills and a fine house salad featuring sun-dried tomatoes, plus occasional seafood, all at prices under €10, except for top-quality fish. Daily 11am–1am.

Ta Petrina Pýrgos district, Volissós ☎ 22740 21228, ⓦ tapetrina.gr. Half a dozen unique properties, expertly renovated by the British co-owners. They vary in size and character from a tiny stone house to a converted church. **€80**

Inoússes

Inoússes, the closer and more easily accessible of Hios' two satellite islands, has a permanent population of about three hundred, less than half its 1930s figure. For generations this islet, first settled around 1750 by Hiot shepherds, provided Greece with many of her wealthiest shipping families: various members of the Livanos, Lemos and Pateras clans were born here.

Inoússes town

Two church-tipped, privately owned islets guard the unusually well-protected harbour of **Inoússes town**, which is surprisingly large, draped over hillsides enclosing a ravine. Its illustrious maritime connections help explain the presence of large villas and visiting summer gin-palaces in an otherwise sleepy Greek backwater. Near the quay, the island's only specific sight, the impressive **Marine Museum** (daily 10am–1pm; €2), also has a nautical theme and was endowed by various shipping magnates. At the west end of the quay, the bigwigs have also funded a nautical academy, which trains future members of the merchant navy.

Around the island

The southern slope of this tranquil island is surprisingly green and well tended; there are no springs, so water comes from a mix of fresh and brackish wells, as well as a reservoir. The sea is extremely clean and calm on the sheltered southerly shore; among its beaches, choose from **Zepága**, **Biláli** or **Kástro**, respectively five, twenty and thirty minutes' walk west of the port. More secluded **Fourkeró** (or Farkeró) lies 25 minutes east.

ARRIVAL AND DEPARTURE   INOÚSSES

By ferry Inoússes can be reached from Híos Town either on a day-trip (see box, p.374) or on the daily ferry (30min), which usually departs from Híos in the afternoon and returns in the morning.

ACCOMMODATION, EATING AND DRINKING

Naftikos Omilos ☎ 22710 55596. This yachtie near the jetty hangout provides a steady stream of coffee and snacks during the day before morphing into a fairly lively bar by night, as the music volume ramps up. May–Sept daily 9am–2am.

Oinousses Studios ☎ 22710 55255, ✉ oinousses studios@gmail.com. Smart modern apartments overlooking the harbour with fully equipped kitchens and large balconies facing the sea. May–Sept. **€35**

Pateronisso ☎ 22710 55311. At the base of the disembarkation jetty, this is the best of the small bunch of tavernas dotted on or around the seafront. All the usual fish, meat and salad staples are available at average prices. June–Sept daily 8am–midnight.

Thalassoporos ☎ 22710 55475. This modest establishment, on the main easterly hillside lane in town, is the island's only bona fide hotel, with basic clean rooms, mostly affording sea views. May–Sept. **€45**

Psará

Remote **Psará** lies a good 20km west of the northwest tip of Híos and is too far from it to be visited on a day-trip. The birthplace of revolutionary war hero Admiral Konstandinos Kanaris, the island devoted its merchant fleets – the third largest in 1820s Greece – to the cause of independence, and paid dearly for it. Vexed beyond endurance, the Turks landed overwhelming forces in 1824 to stamp out this nest of resistance. Perhaps 3000 of the 30,000 inhabitants escaped in small boats to be rescued by a French fleet, but the majority retreated to a hilltop powder magazine, blowing it and themselves up rather than surrender. Today, it's a sad, bleak place fully living up to its name ("the mottled things" in ancient Greek), never really having recovered from the holocaust. The official population now barely exceeds four hundred, and, despite some revitalization since the 1980s, it has never seen a tourist boom.

The harbour

Since few buildings in the east-facing harbour community predate the twentieth century, a strange hotchpotch of ecclesiastical and secular architecture greets you on disembarking. There's a distinctly southern feel, more like the Dodecanese or the Cyclades, and some peculiar churches, no two alike in style.

Around the island

Psará's **beaches** are decent, improving the further northeast you walk from the port. You quickly pass **Káto Yialós**, **Katsoúni** and **Lazarétto** with its off-putting power station, before reaching **Lákka** ("narrow ravine"), fifteen minutes along, apparently named after its grooved rock formations. **Límnos**, 25 minutes from the port along the coastal path, is big and attractive, but there's no reliable taverna here, or indeed at any of the beaches.

The only other thing to do on Psará is to follow the paved road north across the island to **Kímisis (Assumption) monastery**. Uninhabited since the 1970s, it comes to life only in early August, when its revered icon is carried in ceremonial procession to town and back on the eve of August 5.

ARRIVAL AND DEPARTURE   PSARÁ

By ferry Psará has decent ferry links with Híos Town (6 weekly; 3hr), Mestá in southwest Híos (3–4 weekly; 1hr 15min) and Lávrio (1–2 weekly; 6hr) during the summer months; frequencies drop drastically off season.

ACCOMMODATION

Kato Gialos Apartments Behind Káto Yialós beach ☎ 22740 61201. A mixture of spotless rooms and larger apartments with kitchen facilities, all with sea views and only a minute from the water. June–Sept. **€50**

Psara Studios At the back of the harbour village ☎ 22740 61233. The rooms here are large and furnished well enough, and have functional kitchenettes, plus there's a pleasant garden fringed with palms. May–Sept. **€50**

EATING AND DRINKING

Iliovasilema Behind Káto Yialós beach ☎ 22470 61121. As the name suggests, sunset is the best time to dine here on seafood delights such as fried kalamári or octopus with aubergines. A friendly welcome is guranteed. June–Sept daily 11am–midnight.

★ **Spitalia** Behind Katsoúnis beach ☎ 22740 61376. Located in a restored medieval hospital, this great taverna

comes up with specialities such as stuffed goat and other home-style dishes, plus grills, salads and good wine. May–Sept daily 11am–1am.

Ta Delfinia In the middle of the harbour ☎ 22740 61352. Probably the top place for simply but expertly grilled fish and seafood, such as lobster, *tsipoúra* and *barboúni*. Also does various *pikilíes*. May–Oct daily 7am–1am.

Lésvos

LÉSVOS (Mytilíni), the third-largest Greek island after Crete and Évvia, is the birthplace of the ancient bards Sappho, Aesop, Arion and – more recently – primitive artist Theophilos and Nobel Laureate poet Odysseus Elytis. Despite these **artistic associations**, the island may not initially strike one as particularly beautiful or interesting: much of the landscape is rocky, volcanic terrain, encompassing vast grain fields, saltpans or even near-desert. But there are also oak and pine forests as well as endless olive groves, some more than five centuries old. With its balmy climate and suggestive contours, Lésvos tends to grow on you with prolonged exposure. Lovers of medieval and Ottoman **architecture** certainly won't be disappointed, and castles survive at Mytilíni Town, Mólyvos, Eressós, Sígri and near Ándissa.

Social and political **idiosyncrasies** add to the island's appeal: anyone who has attended one of the village *paniyíria*, with hours of music and tables groaning with food and drink, will not be surprised to learn that Lésvos has the highest alcoholism rate (and some of the worst driving habits) in Greece. There is a tendency to **vote Communist**

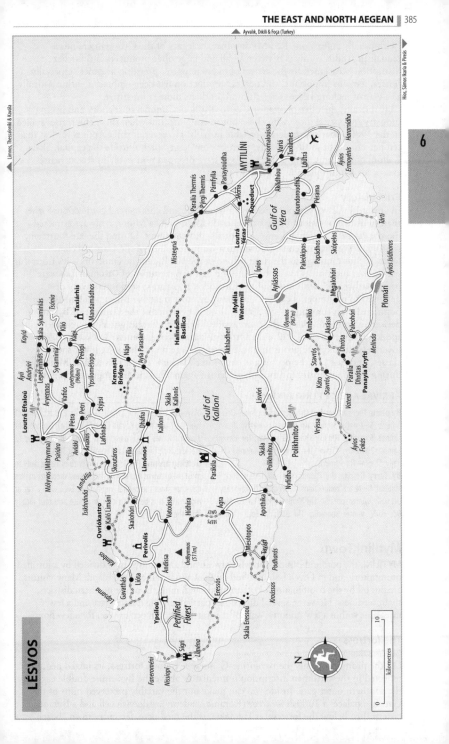

LÉSVOS

(with usually at least one Red MP in office), a legacy of the Ottoman-era quasi-feudalism, 1880s conflicts between small and large olive producers and further disruption occasioned by the arrival of many refugees. Breeding livestock, especially horses, remains important, and organic production has been embraced enthusiastically as a way of making Lésvos's agricultural products more competitive.

Historically, the olive plantations, ouzo distilleries, animal husbandry and fishing industry supported those who chose not to emigrate, but when these enterprises stalled in the 1980s, **tourism** made appreciable inroads. However, it still accounts for less than ten percent of the local economy: there are few large hotels outside the capital, Skála Kallóni or Mólyvos, and visitor numbers have dropped noticeably in recent years, except for a mini-boom in Turkish weekenders.

Brief history

In antiquity, Lésvos's importance lay in its artistic and commercial connections rather than in historical events: being on the trade route to Asia Minor, it always attracted merchants and became quite wealthy during **Roman times**. During the late fourteenth century, Lésvos was given as a dowry to a Genoese prince of the Gattilusi clan following his marriage to the sister of one of the last Byzantine emperors – it's from this period that most of its castles remain. The first two centuries of **Ottoman rule** were particularly harsh, with much of the Orthodox population sold into slavery or deported to the imperial capital – replaced by more tractable Muslim colonists, who populated even rural areas – and most physical evidence of the Genoese or Byzantine period demolished. Out in the countryside, Turks and Greeks got along, relatively speaking, right up until 1923; the Ottoman authorities favoured Greek *kahayiádhes* (overseers) to keep the peons in line. However, large numbers of the lower social classes, oppressed by the pashas and their Greek lackeys, fled across to Asia Minor during the nineteenth century, only to return again after the exchange of populations.

ARRIVAL AND GETTING AROUND

LÉSVOS

By plane There are services (frequencies for June–Oct) to Athens (5–7 daily; 50min–1hr); Híos (2 weekly, 30min); Límnos (5 weekly; 30min); Rhodes (2 weekly; 1hr 40min); Sámos (2 weekly; 45min–1hr 30min); Thessaloníki (1–2 daily; 55min–1hr 50min).

By ferry Despite the island's size, all ferries dock in Mytilíni; there are connections to: Ayvalık (Turkey; May–Oct daily, winter sporadic; 1hr 20min); Dikili (Turkey; May–Oct daily, winter sporadic; 1hr 30min); Foça (Turkey;

May–Oct 4 weekly; 1hr); Híos (1–2 daily; 2–3hr); Ikaría (1 weekly; 7hr 30min); Kavála (2 weekly; 12hr); Límnos (6hr 30min); Pireás (1–2 daily; 8hr 30min–9hr); Sámos (2 weekly; 7hr); Thessaloníki (1 weekly; 14hr 30min).

Getting around Public buses run once or twice daily to most major towns and resorts, but Lesvos' sheer size makes day-trips from the capital impractical. Even with a car or motorbike, it is better to choose a base and tour locally from there.

Mytilíni Town

MYTILÍNI, the port and capital, sprawls between and around two bays divided by a fortified promontory, and in Greek fashion often doubles as the name of the island. Many visitors are put off by the combination of urban bustle and, in the humbler northern districts, slight seediness. However, several diversions, particularly the marketplace and a few museums within a few minutes' walk of the waterfront, can occupy you for a few hours.

The fortress

Tues–Sun 8.30am–3pm • €2

On the promontory sits the Byzantine-Genoese-Ottoman **fortress**, its mixed pedigree reflected in the Ottoman inscription immediately above the Byzantine double eagle at the southern outer gate. Inside you can make out the variably preserved ruins of the Gattilusi palace, a Turkish *medresse* (Koranic academy), a dervish cell and a Byzantine cistern. Just below the fortress, at **Tsamákia**, is the mediocre, fee-entry town "beach".

The bazaar area

Inland, the town skyline is dominated in turn by the Germanic-Gothic belfry spire of **Áyios Athanásios cathedral** and the mammary dome of **Áyios Therápon**, both expressions of the (post)-Baroque taste of the nineteenth-century Ottoman Greek bourgeoisie. The interior decor of Áyios Therápon in particular seems more appropriate to an opera house than a church, with gilt aplenty in the vaulting and ornate column capitals. They stand more or less at opposite ends of the **bazaar**, whose main street, Ermoú, links the town centre with the little-used north harbour of **Epáno Skála**.

The old town

Between the bazaar and Epáno Skála, Ermoú passes various expensive antique shops near the roofless, derelict **Yéni Tzamí** at the heart of the old Muslim quarter, just a few steps east of a superb Turkish **hammam**, restored to its former glory but – like the mosque – closed

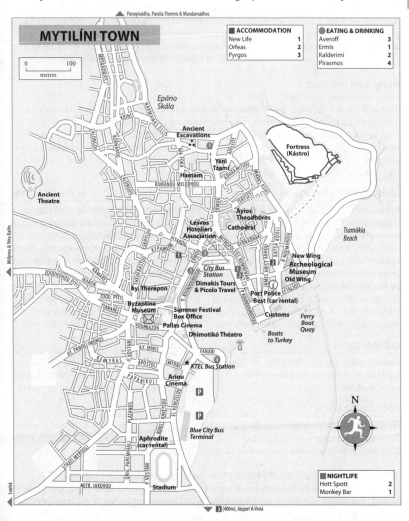

unless a special exhibition is being held. Between Ermoú and the castle lies a maze of atmospheric lanes lined with *belle époque* mansions and humbler vernacular dwellings.

Archeological museum

New wing 8-Noemvríou • ☎ 22510 40223 • Old wing Eftalióti 7 • ☎ 22510 28032 • Tues–Sun 8.30am–3pm • €3

Mytilíni's excellent **archeological museum**, the only real must-see, is housed in two separate galleries, a few hundred metres apart. The **newer wing** is devoted to finds from wealthy Roman Mytilene, in particular three rooms of well-displayed mosaics from second/third-century AD villas. Highlights include a crude but engaging scene of Orpheus charming all manner of beasts and birds, two fishermen surrounded by clearly recognizable (and edible) sea creatures, and the arrival of baby Telephos, son of Auge and Hercules, in a seaborne box, again with amazed fishermen presiding.

Earlier eras are represented in the **older wing**, located in a former mansion just behind the ferry dock. The ground floor has Neolithic finds from Áyios Vartholoméos cave and Bronze Age Thermí, but the star exhibits are the minutely detailed late Classical terracotta figurines upstairs: a pair of acrobats, two *kourotrophoi* figures (goddesses suckling infants, predecessors of all Byzantine *Galaktotrofoússa* icons), children playing with a ball or dogs, and Aphrodite riding a dolphin. A rear annexe contains stone-cut inscriptions of various edicts and treaties, plus a Roman sculpture of a drunken satyr asleep on a wineskin.

Byzantine Museum

Aríonos • Mon–Sat 9am–1pm • €2 • ☎ 22510 28916

The well-lit and well-laid-out **Byzantine Museum**, just opposite the entrance to Áyios Therápon, contains various icons rescued from rural island churches. The most noteworthy exhibit, and the oldest, is a fourteenth-century icon of Christ *Pandokrátor*; other highlights include a sultanic *firmáni* or grant of privileges to a local bishop, a rare sixteenth-century three-dimensional icon of *The Crucifixion* and a canvas of the *Kímisis* (*Assumption*) by Theophilos (see box, p.390).

ARRIVAL AND DEPARTURE   MYTILÍNI TOWN

By air There's no bus link with the airport, so you may need to take a taxi the 7km into Mytilíni Town.

By ferry Nearly all agencies can make bookings for ferries within Greece, while Dimakis Tours at Koundouriótou 73 (☎ 22510 27865) or Picolo Travel at no. 73a (☎ 22510 27000) are best for tickets to Turkey.

By bus There are two bus terminals: the long-distance KTEL buses leave from a small station near Platía Konstandinopóleos at the southern end of the harbour, while the blue town buses depart from a stand at the top of the harbour, or the dedicated terminal near the stadium.

By car Car rental is arrangeable through reputable franchises like Best at Koundouriótou 87–89 (☎ 22510 37337, ⓦ best-rentacar.com) or excellent local agency Aphrodite at the corner of Elýti & Karapanayióti (☎ 22510 48100, ⓦ aphroditehotel.gr). Drivers should use the enormous free public car park a few blocks south of the KTEL or the oval plaza near the new wing of the archeological museum. If you're driving out, 8-Noemvríou, starting just behind the ferry quay, is the quickest way.

INFORMATION

Tourist office James Aristárhou 6 (Mon–Fri 8am–2.30pm). Provides excellent town and island maps, plus other brochures.

Online The website ⓦ lesvos.com is highly useful.
Services Amenities include the post office behind the central park, and numerous ATMs starting just outside the port gate.

ACCOMMODATION

Finding accommodation can be frustrating: waterfront hotels are noisy and overpriced, but supply usually exceeds demand for the better-value rooms in the backstreets. The Lesvos Hoteliers Association at Koundouriótou 47A (☎ 22510 41787, ⓦ filoxenia.net) can book rooms in town and around the island.

★ **New Life** Olýmbou, cul-de-sac off Ermoú ☎ 22510 23400, ⓦ new-life.gr. Moderate-sized, comfy en-suite rooms (some a/c) with polished wood floors, in an old eccentrically

decorated mansion with a garden. Great value. €30
Orfeas Katsakoúli 3 ☎ 22510 28523, ⓦ orfeas-hotel .com. Probably the quietest of the town hotels, this

well-restored nineteenth-century building has somewhat small a/c doubles with cheerfully hued modern furnishings. Some balconies; lift; breakfast included. **€50**
Pyrgos Eleftheríou Venizélou 49 ☎ 22510 25069, ⓦ pyrgoshotel.gr. Premier in-town restoration, with utterly over-the-top kitsch decor in the common areas. Most rooms have a balcony, some have bath tubs and there are three round units in the tower. **€100**

EATING, DRINKING AND NIGHTLIFE

The trendy northeast quay is the main venue for buzzing café-bars. The summer **cinema**, Pallas, is on Vournázon near the park; the winter cinema, Arion, is near the KTEL.

Averoff Koundouriótou 33 ☎ 22510 22180. Its handy location on the west quay makes this old-fashioned *estiatório* a popular venue for *mayireftá* (including early-morning *patsás*). Most dishes €5–8. Daily 6am–11pm.

★ **Ermis** Ermoú, Epáno Skála ☎ 22510 26232. Best-value, and friendliest, of the ouzerís in this district. *Belle époque* decor (panelled ceiling, giant mirrors, faded oil paintings) inside and a pleasant courtyard. Best check what the "crap salad" involves though. Daily noon–2am.

Hott Spott Koundouriótou 63 ☎ 22510 22200. Named after its wi-fi connection, this perennially popular hangout also offers flashing pop videos and increasing volume as the night wears on. Daily 10am–2am.

Kalderimi Thássou 2 ☎ 22510 46577. One of the few surviving bazaar ouzerís, occupying three picturesque buildings with seating under the shade of vines; the food is abundant if a bit plainly presented. Mon–Sat 11am–2am, Sun 11am–4pm.

Monkey Bar Koundouriótou 57 ☎ 22510 37717. A favourite meeting place for students and townies alike, where fashionably dressed waitresses ferry high-quality coffees and elaborate cocktails to their equally trendy customers. Daily 10am–3am.

Pirasmos Fanári quay ☎ 22510 54970. Better value than the fish tavernas surrounding it, this unpretentious grill house specializes in delicious meat such as *kondosoúvli* and *kokorétsi*, as well as simple salads and starters. Daily 1pm–1am.

Around Mytilíni

The road heading **north** from Mytilíni towards Mandamádhos follows a rather nondescript coastline, but offers startling views across the straits to Turkey. South of the capital, there are two fine museums at **Variá** and a couple of decent beaches further down the peninsula.

Paralía Thermís

Just 500m beyond Pýrgi Thermís, at **PARALÍA THERMÍS**, the Roman/Byzantine **hammam** has been allowed to decay in favour of an ugly, sterile modern facility adjacent, though it still supplies the hot water, and you can stick your head in to admire the vaulted brickwork. At 12km, you're a bit far from town, but there is a decent accommodation option here.

Loutrá Yéras

Baths daily: April–May & Oct 8am–6pm; June–Sept 8am–7pm; Nov–March 9am–5pm • €3

For a lovely warm bath near Mytilíni, make for **Loutrá Yéras**, 8km along the main road to Kalloní. These **public baths** are just the thing if you've spent a sleepless night on a ferry, with two ornate spouts that feed 38°C water to marble-lined pools in vaulted chambers; there are separate facilities for men and women (the ladies' pool is a tad smaller but has lovely masonry), and skinny-dipping is, unexpectedly in prudish Greece, obligatory.

If you take the more northerly route via Mória to Loutrá Yéras, you will pass close by the impressive remains of a second-century **Roman aqueduct**, signposted down a fertile valley.

Variá

Accessible by hourly buses

The most rewarding sights to be visited near Mytilíni are a pair of museums at **VARIÁ**, 5km south of town, which between them hold much of the island's artistic legacy.

6

THEOPHILOS HADZIMIHAÏL: THE ROUSSEAU OF GREECE?

The "naïve" painter **Theophilos Hadzimihaïl** (1873–1934) was born and died in Mytilíni Town, and both his eccentricities and talents were remarkable from an early age. After wandering across the country from Pílio to Athens and the Peloponnese, Theophilos became one of *belle époque* Greece's prize eccentrics, dressing up as Alexander the Great or various revolutionary war heroes, complete with pom-pommed shoes and pleated skirt. Theophilos was ill and living as a recluse in severely reduced circumstances back on Lésvos when he was introduced to Thériade in 1919; the latter, virtually alone among critics of the time, recognized his peculiar genius and ensured that Theophilos was supported both morally and materially for the rest of his life.

With their childlike perspective, vivid colour scheme and idealized mythical and rural subjects, Theophilos's works are unmistakeable. Relatively few of his works survive today, because he executed commissions for a pittance on ephemeral surfaces such as *kafenío* counters, horsecarts, or the walls of long-vanished houses. Facile comparisons are often made between Theophilos and Henri Rousseau, the roughly contemporaneous French "primitive" painter. Unlike "Le Douanier", however, Theophilos followed no other profession, eking out a precarious living from his art alone. And while Rousseau revelled in exoticism, Theophilos's work was principally and profoundly rooted in Greek mythology, history and daily life.

Theophilos Museum

Tues–Sun 10am–4pm • €2 • ☎ 22510 41644

The **Theophilos Museum** honours the painter (see box above), born here in 1873, with four rooms of wonderful, little-known compositions commissioned by his patron Thériade (see below) during the years immediately preceding Theophilos's death. A wealth of detail is evident in elegiac scenes of fishing, reaping, olive-picking and baking from the pastoral Lésvos which Theophilos obviously knew best. The *Sheikh-ul-Islam* with his hubble-bubble (Room 2) seems drawn from life, as does a highly secular Madonna merely titled *Mother with Child* (also Room 2). But in the museum's scenes of classical landscapes and episodes from wars historical and contemporary Theophilos seems on shakier ground.

Thériade Museum

Tues–Sun: April–Sept 9am–2pm & 5–8pm; Oct–March 9am–5pm • €2 • ☎ 22510 23372

Next to the Theophilos Museum, the imposing **Thériade Museum** is the legacy of another native son, Stratis Eleftheriades (1897–1983). Leaving the island aged 18 for Paris, he Gallicized his name to Thériade and eventually became a renowned avant-garde art publisher, enlisting some of the leading artists of the twentieth century in his ventures. The displays comprise two floors of lithographs, engravings, ink drawings, wood-block prints and watercolours by the likes of Miró, Chagall, Picasso, Giacometti, Matisse, Le Corbusier, Léger, Rouault and Villon, either annotated by the painters themselves or commissioned as illustrations for the works of prominent poets and authors: an astonishing collection for a relatively remote Aegean island, deserving leisurely perusal.

South of Variá

Heading **south** beyond the airport and Krátigos village, the paved road loops around the peninsula to **Haramídha**, 14km from town and the closest decent (pebble) **beach**; the eastern bay has a few **tavernas**. **Áyios Ermoyénis**, 3km west and directly accessible from Mytilíni via Loutrá village, is more scenic and sandy. The patron saint's chapel perches on the cliff separating two small, sandy coves from a larger, less usable easterly bay accessed by a separate track.

ACCOMMODATION AND EATING   AROUND MYTILÍNI

Loriet/Laureate Variá, 4km south of Mytilíni ☎ 22510 43111, ⊛ loriet-hotel.com. A nineteenth-century mansion with modern wings, gardens, fine restaurant and 25m saltwater pool. Rooms vary from blandly modern, marble-trimmed studios to massive suites with retro decor and big bathrooms. April–Oct. **€80**

Theodora Glava (Grioules) Haramídha ☎ 22510 46417. Right on the beach, legendary Theodora dishes up a great range of lovingly prepared vegetarian and seafood *mezédhes*, as well as more substantial meat and fish items. April–Oct daily 11am–1am.

★ **Votsala** Paralía Thermís ☎ 22510 71231, ⓦ votsalahotel.com. This comfortable and relaxing place offers watersports off the (somewhat scrappy) beach and well-tended gardens. It prides itself on having no TV in the rooms and no "Greek nights". May–Oct. **€45**

6

Southern Lésvos

Southern Lésvos is indented by two great inlets, the gulfs of **Kalloní** and **Yéra**, the first curving in a northeasterly direction, the latter northwesterly, creating a fan-shaped peninsula at the heart of which looms 967m **Mount Ólymbos**. Both shallow gulfs are landlocked by very narrow outlets to the open sea, which don't – and probably never will – have bridges spanning them. This is the most verdant and productive olive-oil territory on Lésvos, and stacks of pressing-mills stab the skyline.

Pérama

A regular kaïki service (no cars carried) links Pérama with Koundoroudhiá, which has a blue city bus service to/from Mytilíni on the far side

PÉRAMA, disused olive-oil warehouses dotting its oddly attractive townscape, is one of the larger places on the Gulf of Yéra. Although it feels rather forlorn and end-of-the-road, it is easily accessible by public transport from Mytilíni and offers great eating.

Plomári and around

Due south of Mount Ólymbos, at the edge of the "fan", **PLOMÁRI** is the only sizeable coastal settlement hereabouts, and indeed the second-largest municipality on Lésvos. It presents an unlikely juxtaposition of scenic appeal and its famous ouzo industry, courtesy of several local **distilleries**. Despite a resounding lack of good **beaches** within walking distance, Plomári is popular with Scandinavian tourists; most actually stay at **Áyios Isídhoros**, 3km east.

Varvayianni Distillery

May–Oct Mon–Fri 9am–7pm, Sat 9am–1pm; Nov–April Mon–Fri 8am–4pm • Free • ☎ 22520 32741, ⓦ barbayanni-ouzo.com

The largest and oldest of Plomári distilleries, **Varvayianni**, offers free tours and tasting, plus a fascinating display of old alembics, presses, storage jars and archival material. Best venues for a tipple afterwards are the old *kafenía* on central Platía Beniamín.

Melínda

Melínda, a 700m sand-and-shingle beach at the mouth of a canyon lush with olive trees, lies 6km west of Plomári by paved road. It's an alluring place, with sweeping views west towards the Vaterá coast and the cape of Áyios Fokás, and south (in clear conditions) to northern Híos, Psará and the Turkish Karaburun peninsula.

Panayía Kryftí hot springs

One of the best excursions beyond Melínda is to the **Panayía Kryftí hot springs**. From the first curve of the paved road up to Paleohóri, a dirt track goes 2.8km to a dead-end with parking space, with the final 400m on a downhill path to the little chapel just above a protected inlet. On the far side of this you'll see a rectangular cement tank, just big enough for two people, containing water at a pleasant 37–38°C.

Ayiássos and around

AYIÁSSOS, 26km from Mytilíni, nestled in a remote, wooded valley under the crest of Mount Ólymbos, is the most beautiful hill town on Lésvos, its narrow cobbled streets lined by ranks of tiled-roof houses, built in part from proceeds of the trade in *tsoupiá*

6

(olive sacks). On the usual, northerly approach, there's no hint of the enormous village until you see huge knots of parked cars at the southern edge of town. Most visitors proceed past endless ranks of kitsch wooden and ceramic souvenirs or carved "Byzantine" furniture, aimed mostly at Greeks, and the central church of the **Panayía Vrefokratoússa** – built in the twelfth century to house an icon supposedly painted by the Evangelist Luke – to the old bazaar, with its *kafenía*, yoghurt/cheese shops and butchers' stalls. With such a venerable icon as a focus, the local August 15 *paniyíri* is one of the liveliest on Lésvos.

Mount Ólymbos

From the southern side of Ayiássos, keen walkers can follow a network of marked paths and tracks for three hours to the **Ólymbos summit**. Approaching from Plomári, there's asphalt road and public transport only up to Megalohóri, with a good dirt surface thereafter up to some air-force radar balls, where paving resumes. The area between Megalohóri and the summit ridge was damaged by a 1994 forest fire, though once over the other side dense woods of unscathed oak and chestnut take over from the recovering pine growth.

Mylélia water mill

Daily 9am–6pm • Ⓦ mylelia.gr

Six kilometres northeast of Ayiássos, signposted along a track near the turning for Ípio, you can visit the **Mylélia water mill**. The name means "place of the mills", and there were once several hereabouts – this is the last survivor, restored to working order in the 1990s. The keeper will show you the millrace and paddle-wheel, as well as the flour making its spasmodic exit, after which you can browse the gourmet pastas and other products at the shop, including cheeses, jams, vinegar and salted fish. They also do cooking courses.

Polikhnítos and around

The largest settlement in the southwestern part of southern Lésvos is **POLIKHNÍTOS**, a rather dull, workaday rural centre. It is, however, the point of access to magnificent **Vaterá** beach, the seaside villages of **Skála Polikhnítou** and and **Nifídha**, each with its own smaller beach, and the Natural History Museum of **Vrýssa**.

Vrýssa: Natural History Museum

May & June daily 9.30am–3.30pm; July–Sept daily 9.30am–3pm & 4–8pm; Oct–April Wed–Sun 9.30am–3.30pm • €2 • ☎ 22520 61890

VRÝSSA, 4km south of Polikhnítos, has a mildly diverting **Natural History Museum** documenting local paleontological finds. In 1997 Athenian paleontologist Michael Dermitzakis confirmed what farmers unearthing bones had long suspected when he pronounced the area a treasure-trove of **fossils**, including those of two-million-year-old gigantic horses, mastodons, monkeys and tortoises the size of a Volkswagen Beetle. Until 20,000 years ago, Lésvos (like all other east Aegean islands) was joined to the Asian mainland, and the gulf of Vaterá was a subtropical freshwater lake; the animals in question came to drink, died nearby and were trapped and preserved by successive volcanic flows.

Vaterá and around

VATERÁ, 9km south of Polikhnítos, is a 7km-long sand beach, backed by vegetated hills; the sea here is delightfully calm and clean, the strand itself among the best on

---

POLIKHNÍTOS SPA

If you're after a hot bath, head for the vaulted, well-restored **Polikhnítos Spa** complex (daily: April–Oct 9am–8pm; Nov–March 2–7pm; €4; ☎ 22520 41229, Ⓦ hotsprings.gr) 1.5km east of the town of **Polikhnítos**; there are separate, warm-hued chambers for each sex. The water actually gushes out at temperatures up to 87°C, so needs to be tempered with cold.

Lésvos. Development, mostly seasonal villas and apartments for locals, straggles for several kilometres to either side of the central T-junction but is nicely spread out, so the strip does not feel overtly commercialized.

Some 3km west at the cape of **Áyios Fokás** only the foundations remain of a temple of Dionysos and a superimposed early Christian basilica. The little tamarisk-shaded anchorage here has a superb taverna.

ACCOMMODATION AND EATING   SOUTHERN LÉSVOS

PÉRAMA

★ **Balouhanas** Pérama ☎ 22510 51948. The northernmost establishment on the front, with a wooden, cane-roofed deck jutting out over the water. Seafood is a strong point, whether grilled or as croquettes, as are regional mezédhes and home-made desserts. Daily 11am–2am.

PLOMÁRI AND AROUND

Maria's Melínda ☎ 22520 93239. Right where the access road reaches the sea; the restaurant is excellent, serving a range of fish, meat and mezédhes, while the rooms are simple but extremely cheap. May–Oct. **€25**

Melinda Studios Melínda ☎ 22520 93282, ✉ melindastudios@gmail.com. Two doors along from *Maria's*, this small pension has clean, bright studios with small kitchenettes and sea-facing balconies. May–Sept. **€30**

Pebble Beach Áyios Isídhoros ☎ 22520 31651. Many of the rooms here, which are adequate in size and comfort, overlook a slightly reefy section of beach – though avoid those near the bar if you value sleep. Breakfast included. May–Oct. **€60**

Pension Lida Near Platía Beniamín, Plomári ☎ 22520 32507. An attractive restoration inn occupying two old mansions, with sea-view balconies for most units. Some of the high-ceilinged rooms share bathrooms. **€30**

★ **Taverna tou Panaï** Áyios Isídhoros ☎ 22520 31920. Set in an olive grove just beyond the northerly town limits sign; here you'll find salubrious meat, seafood and *mayireftá* dishes, and mostly Greeks in attendance. Most produce is home-grown and organic. Daily 10am–late.

AYIÁSSOS AND AROUND

Dhouladhellis Ayiássos ☎ 22520 22236. Near the fork at the village's southern end, this family taverna with a huge courtyard serves various soups, meat dishes for €6–7 and plenty of *glyká koutalioú*. March–Nov daily 9am–midnight.

Ouzerí To Stavri Ayiássos ☎ 22520 22936. At the extreme north end of the village in Stavrí district, this quirky little place offers a warm welcome and great home-style mezédhes such as cheese croquettes and octopus in vinegar. Daily 11am–late.

POLIKHNÍTOS AND AROUND

★ **Akrotiri/Angelerou** Áyios Fokás ☎ 22520 61465. Top-notch little taverna, specializing in seafood delights such as shrimp salad or *sardhélles Kallonís*, plus starters like cheese croquettes. All cost well under €10 and can be washed down with aromatic wine. April–Oct daily noon–1am.

★ **Aphrodite Beach** Vaterá ☎ 22520 61288, ⓦ aphroditehotel.gr. Sparkling blue-and-white complex of comfortable units with a/c, fridges and small balconies. The extremely welcoming family restaurant features tasty dishes like lamb, *briám*, very palatable wine and occasional live music sessions. Breakfast included. May to early Oct. **€30**

O Grigoris Nifídha ☎ 22520 41838. Good seafront *psarotavérna* with the usual range of fish and seafood, backed up by some salads and veg dishes. Noon–1am: March–June & mid-Sept to Nov Fri–Sun; July to mid-Sept daily.

Western Lésvos

The area from the Gulf of Kalloní to the island's west coast is a mostly treeless, craggy region whose fertile valleys offer a sharp contrast to the bare ridges. River mouths form little oases behind a handful of **beach resorts** like Skála Kallonís, Sígri and Skála Eressoú. A few **monasteries** along the road west of Kalloní, plus the occasional striking **inland village**, provide monumental interest.

Ayía Paraskeví and around

A rewarding detour en route to Kalloní is to **AYÍA PARASKEVÍ** village, midway between two important and photogenic monuments from diverse eras: the Paleo-Christian, three-aisled basilica of **Halinádhou**, its dozen basalt columns amid pine-and-olive scenery, and the large medieval bridge of **Kremastí**, the largest and best preserved such in the east Aegean, 3km west of Ayía Paraskeví.

THE OLIVES OF LÉSVOS

No other Greek island is as dominated by **olive production** as Lésvos, which is blanketed by approximately 11 million olive trees. Most of these vast groves date from after a lethal frost in 1851, though a few hardy survivors are thought to be over five hundred years old. During the first three centuries after the Ottoman conquest, production of olive oil was a monopoly of the ruling pasha, but following eighteenth-century reforms in the Ottoman Empire, extensive tracts of Lésvos (and thus the lucrative oil trade) passed into the hands of the new Greek bourgeoisie, who greatly expanded the industry.

Museum of Industrial Olive Oil Production in Lésvos

Daily except Tues 10am–6pm, closes 5pm mid-Oct to Feb • €3 • ☎ 22530 32300, ⓦ piop.gr

On the southern outskirts of Ayía Paraskeví stands the eminently worthwhile **Museum of Industrial Olive Oil Production in Lésvos** (Mousío Viomihanikís Elaeouryías Lésvou), housed in a restored communal olive mill. The mill, built by public subscription in the 1920s, only ceased working under the junta; the industrial machinery has been lovingly refurbished and its function explained, while former outbuildings and warehouses are used as venues for secondary exhibits and short explanatory films.

Kallorí and around

KALLONÍ is a lively agricultural and market town in the middle of the island. Some 3km south lies the town's seaside package resort, **Skála Kallonís**, backing a long, sandy but absurdly shallow beach on the lake-like gulf whose water can be turbid. It's mainly distinguished as a **birdwatching** centre during the nesting season (March–May) in the adjacent salt marshes. The local speciality is the gulf's celebrated, plankton-nurtured **sardines**, best eaten fresh-grilled from August to October, although they're available salt-cured all year round.

ACCOMMODATION AND EATING

KALLONÍ AND AROUND

Aegeon Kallorí ☎ 22530 22398, ⓦ aegeon-lesvos.gr. Set in a leafy garden, with above-average furnishings for its class, a large pool and friendly owners, this is the best option among the hotels grouped on the west side of town. **€45**

Medusa Skála Kallonís ☎ 697 22 01 813. Top restaurant for sardines done Kallorí style; and other super-fresh fish and seafood, much of it under €10. Pleasant location in a renovated stone house on the seafront. April–Oct daily 10am–1am.

Limónos monastery

Museum daily 9.30am–6.30pm, may close 3pm off-season • €2

West of Kallorí, the road winds 4km uphill to **Limónos monastery**, founded in 1527 by the monk Ignatios, whose cell is maintained in the surviving medieval north wing. It's a rambling, three-storey complex around a vast, plant-filled courtyard, home to just a handful of monks and lay workers. The *katholikón*, with its ornate carved-wood ceiling and archways, is traditionally off-limits to women; a sacred spring flows from below the south foundation wall. Only the ground-floor **ecclesiastical museum** is currently functioning, with the more interesting ethnographic gallery upstairs still closed.

Hídhira

Seven kilometres south of the beautiful settlement of **Vatoússa**, which boasts a classic plane-shaded square and some fine architecture, stands the hilltop village of **HÍDHIRA**, with a fine winery and interesting museum. The village is a dead end unless you have a jeep capable of continuing across the rough track to Eressós by way of Ágra.

Methymneos Winery

Daily July–Sept 9am–6pm, otherwise by appointment • ☎ 22530 51518, ⓦ methymneos.gr

Just below the entrance to Hídhira, the **Methymneos Winery** has successfully revived the local ancient grape variety, decimated by phylloxera some decades ago. Because of the altitude (300m) and sulphur-rich soil (you're in a volcanic caldera), their velvety, high-alcohol, oak-aged red can be produced organically; 2007 saw the introduction of bottled white wines. Proprietor Ioannis Lambrou gives a highly worthwhile twenty-minute tour of the state-of-the-art premises in English.

Digital Art Museum of George Jakobides

Tues–Sun: July & Aug 11am–7pm; Sept–June 9am–5pm • €2 • ☎ 22530 51128, ⓦ jakobides-digital-museum.gr

The fancy name of the **Digital Art Museum of George Jakobides** is a slight misnomer in that it is not about anything hi-tech and the artist to whom it is dedicated, a native of Hídhira who lived from 1853 to 1932, predated the computer age. Yet the short digital film and copies of seven of his most famous works, such as *Children's Concert* and *Naughty Grandson*, are worth a peep.

Monastery of Perivolís

Daily 10am–1pm & 5–6pm • Donation • No photos

Some 8km beyond Vatoússa, a short track leads down to the thirteenth-century monastery of **Perivolís**, built amid a riverside orchard (*perivóli*), with fine if damp-damaged sixteenth-century frescoes in the narthex. An apocalyptic panel worthy of Bosch (*The Earth and Sea Yield up their Dead*) shows the Whore of Babylon riding her chimera and assorted sea monsters disgorging their victims; just to the right, towards the main door, the Three Magi are depicted approaching the Virgin enthroned with the Christ Child. On the north side there's a highly unusual iconography of Abraham, the Virgin, and the penitent thief of Calvary in paradise, with the four heavenly rivers gushing forth under their feet; just right are assembled the Hebrew kings of the Old Testament.

Ándissa and around

ÁNDISSA, 11km west of Vatoússa, nestles under this parched region's only substantial pine grove; at the edge of the village a sign implores you to "Come Visit Our Square", not a bad idea for the sake of a handful of refreshment options sheltering under three sizeable plane trees.

Gavathás and around

Directly below Ándissa a paved road leads 6km north to **GAVATHÁS**, a village with a shortish, partly protected **beach** and a few places to eat and stay. A side road leads one headland east to huge, dune-dominated, surf-battered **Kámbos** beach, which you may well have to yourself, even in August.

ACCOMMODATION AND EATING	**ÁNDISSA AND AROUND**
Paradise Gavathás ☎ 22530 56376. This pension-cum-restaurant, 300m back from the seafront, has simple but adequate rooms and serves good fish and locally grown vegetables. May–Sept. **€30**	oldest and best taverna, shaded by the largest plane tree, is very friendly and rustles up excellent *mayireftá*, such as lamb fricassee and okra. You may even run into local octogenarian poet Panayiótis Petréllis. Daily 10am–midnight.
★ **Pedhinon** Ándissa ☎ 22530 56106. The village's	

Monastery of Ypsiloú

Museum daily 8.30am–3pm • Donation

Two kilometres west of Ándissa there's an important junction. Keeping straight leads you past the still-functioning, double-gated monastery of **Ypsiloú**, founded in 1101 atop an outrider of extinct Órdhymnos volcano. The *katholikón*, tucked in one corner of a large, irregular courtyard, has a fine wood-lattice ceiling but has had its frescoes repainted to detrimental effect. Exhibits in the upstairs **museum** encompass a fine collection of *epitáfios* (Good Friday) shrouds, ancient manuscripts, portable icons and – oddest of all – a *Deposition* painted in Renaissance style by a sixteenth-century Turk.

6

The petrified forest

Daily: June–Sept 8am–sunset; Oct–May 8am–4pm · €2

To the west of Ypsilóu begins the 5km side road to the main concentration of Lésvos's overrated **petrified forest**, a fenced-in "reserve" toured along 3km of walkways. For once, contemporary Greek arsonists cannot be blamed for the state of the trees, created by the combined action of volcanic ash from Órdhymnos and hot springs some fifteen to twenty million years ago. The mostly horizontal sequoia trunks average 1m or less in length, save for a few poster-worthy exceptions; there's another more accessible (and free) cluster south of Sígri.

Sígri

SÍGRI, near the western tip of Lésvos, has an appropriately end-of-the-line feel; its bay is guarded both by an Ottoman castle and the long island of **Nissiopí**, which protects the place somewhat from prevailing winds. The eighteenth-century **castle**, built atop an earlier one, sports the reigning sultan's monogram over the entrance, something rarely seen outside Istanbul, evidence of the high regard in which this strategic port with a good water supply was held. The odd-looking church of **Ayía Triádha** is in fact a converted **mosque**, with a huge water cistern taking up the ground floor; this supplied, among other things, the half-ruined **hammam** just south.

Natural History Museum of the Lésvos Petrified Forest

Daily: July–Sept 8am–8pm; Oct–May 8am–5pm · €5 · ☎ 22530 54434, ⓦ lesvosmuseum.gr

At the top of town stands the well-executed but overpriced **Natural History Museum of the Lésvos Petrified Forest**, which covers pan-Aegean geology with samples and maps (including, ominously, seismic patterns), as well as the expected quota of petrified logs and plant fossils from when the surrounding hills were far more vegetated.

The beaches

The nearest of several **beaches**, south of the castle headland, is somewhat narrow but is the only one with amenities. The far superior strand of **Faneroméni** lies 3.5km north by a coastal dirt track from the northern outskirts of town. A shorter but equally good beach, **Liména**, can be found 2km south of Sígri at another creek mouth, just off the rough, one-lane, 15km track to Eressós, passable with care in an ordinary car, in 35 minutes.

ACCOMMODATION, EATING AND DRINKING | SÍGRI

Cavo d'Oro/Blue Wave (no sign) ☎ 22530 54221. The only taverna on the harbour itself is a classic for lobster and scaly fish; most of the restaurants around the nearby platía are run-of-the-mill in comparison. Daily 11am–2am.

Notia The hippest place in town, with frequent live jazz sessions and offering the usual range of refreshments. Daily 8pm–late.

Pyrgospito/Towerhouse ☎ 22530 22909, ⓦ lesvos-towerhouse.gr. Four spacious antique-furnished apartments in a *belle époque* folly, 500m outside of the village, in a landscaped hillside setting with pool. May–Oct. **€70**

Skála Eressoú

Most visitors to western Lésvos park themselves at **SKÁLA ERESSOÚ**, reached via a southerly turning between Ándissa and Ypsilóu. Its 3km **beach** almost rivals Vaterá's as the best on the island. Behind stretches the largest and most attractive agricultural plain on Lésvos, a welcome green contrast to the volcanic ridges above.

There's not much to central Skála – just a roughly rectangular grid of perhaps five streets by twelve, angling up to the oldest cottages on the slope of Vígla hill above the east end of the beach. The waterfront pedestrian lane is divided midway by a café-lined, circular platía with a bust of **Theophrastos**. This renowned botanist hailed from **ancient Eressós** atop Vígla hill – the remaining citadel wall is still visible from a distance, and though the ruins themselves prove scanty, the views reward a scramble up.

CLOCKWISE FROM TOP THÁSSOS (P.412); SEAFOOD, MÓLYVOS, LÉSVOS (P.398); ARCHEOLOGICAL MUSEUM, VATHÝ, SÁMOS (P.353) >

Another famous native of ancient Eressós, honoured by a stylized statue on the platía, was **Sappho** (c.615–562 BC), poetess and reputed lesbian. There are thus always conspicuous numbers of gay women about (especially during the annual September festival), particularly in the clothing-optional zone of the **beach** west of the river mouth, also home to a small community of terrapins.

ACCOMMODATION   SKÁLA ERESSOÚ

For accommodation, it's wise to entrust the search to Sappho Travel (☎ 22530 52202, ⓦ sapphotravel.com) who can arrange something to suit your needs; they also rent out cars.

ly Galini ☎ 22530 53138, ⓦ hotel-galinos.gr. Three blocks inland, this welcoming, slightly old-fashioned hotel with a colourful yard outside has cosy, spotlessly clean rooms with little balconies. Wi-fi in lobby. Breakfast included. **€40**

Sappho the Eressia ☎ 22530 53233, ⓦ sappho-hotel .com. With wi-fi and a pleasant ground-floor snack bar, this central seafront hotel has been spruced up to attract all comers, having dropped its previous women-only policy. **€40**

EATING, DRINKING AND NIGHTLIFE

With about seven clubs/bars to choose from in peak season, local **nightlife** is the best on the island and all are gay-friendly. There's also a central, open-air **cinema** (July to early Sept), predictably called Sappho.

Ioannis & Gabi ☎ 22530 53272. Run by a Greek-Austrian couple, this garden taverna is a delightful spot to sample simple home-style cooking with a range of meat, fish and vegetarian dishes, washed down by fine barrelled wine. May–Oct daily noon–midnight.

Kyani Sardhini/Blue Sardine ☎ 22530 53503. A creditable seafood ouzeri at the far west end of the front, where the engaging manager will provide anything from lobster and crab at market rates to more modest small fish. April–Oct daily 11am–1am.

Parasol Ethnic sounds abound and exotic cocktails flow at one of the resort's most enduring café-cum-bars,

with an attractive central seafront location under a thatched bamboo roof. May to early Oct daily 10am–late.

Samadhi ☎ 697 62 00 799. On the east quay, this trendy and upmarket newcomer does steaks for €17, plus pitsa, curries, unusual salads such as niçoise and some innovative desserts. May–Sept daily 10am–2am.

Sappho Garden ☎ 22530 53682. Relaxed garden bar a couple of blocks inland, largely frequented by lesbians, often with live performances from poetry to music, and events like yoga sessions. April–Oct daily 11am–2am.

Northern Lésvos

The northern part of Lésvos is largely fertile and green countryside stippled with poplars and blanketed by olive groves. Occupying the prime position on a promontory in the middle of the coast is one of the northeast Aegean's most attractive resorts, **Mólyvos**, whose castle's cockscomb silhouette is visible for many kilometres around. On either side of it, a number of **coastal resorts** offer superior bathing.

Mólyvos (Míthymna)

MÓLYVOS (officially Míthymna after its ancient predecessor), 61km from Mytilíni, is the island's most beautiful village, with tiers of sturdy, red-tiled houses, some standing with their rear walls defensively towards the sea, mounting the slopes between the picturesque harbour and the Byzantine-Genoese **castle**. A score of weathered Turkish fountains, a mosque and hammam grace flower-fragrant, cobbled alleyways, reflecting the fact that before 1923 Muslims constituted more than a third of the local population and owned many of the finest dwellings.

Modern dwellings and hotels have been banned from the old core, but this hasn't prevented a steady drain of all authentic life from the upper **bazaar**; perhaps four or five "ordinary" shops ply their trade among souvenir shops vastly surplus to requirements. The shingly **town beach** is mediocre, improving considerably as you head towards the sandy southern end of the bay, called **Psiriára**.

The castle

Daily 8.30am–3pm • €2

The imposing ramparts of the **Byzantine castle** of Mólyvos, later repaired by Genoan Francesco Gattelusi, are visible from many kilometres around. Sections can now be accessed from the inside, affording splendid views of the harbour and beyond. Entrance is via the impressive main gate, through which a set of steps leads up to the largely open interior, where a wooden **amphitheatre** is used for occasional summer performances.

The Komninaki Kralli mansion

Daily 9am–3pm • Free

The **Komninaki Kralli mansion**, high up in the town, is worth the climb; the lower floor houses a well-signposted "School of Fine Arts", and the wall- and ceiling-murals on the upper storey (dated 1833) compare with those of the Vareltzídena mansion in Pétra (see p.400). Panels in the smallest room portray dervish musicians and women dancing to shawm and drum, while other murals depict stylized versions of Constantinople and Mytilíni Town.

6

ARRIVAL AND INFORMATION

MÓLYVOS (MÍTHYMNA)

By bus and taxi The bus stop and taxi rank are at the southeast edge of town.

By car and motorbike There are numerous motorbike and car rental places near the tourist office, including Kosmos (☎ 22530 71710) and Best (☎ 22530 72145), both offering the option of pick-up here and drop-off in Mytilíni or the airport. The main car park is at the southeast edge of town;

there are further car parks above the port and up by the castle.

Tourist office (May–Oct Mon–Sat 10am–5pm; ☎ 22530 71347, ⓦ mithymna.gr). The municipal tourist office, near the main junction on the south side of town, keeps lists of rented rooms.

Services The main post office is near the top of the upper commercial street; ATMs and wi-fi spots abound.

ACCOMMODATION

Delfinia ☎ 22530 71315, ⓦ hoteldelfinia.com. Luxury resort hotel, 1km south of town, set in 87 acres of greenery, with rooms and bungalows, a castle-view pool, tennis courts and direct access to Psiriára beach. Breakfast included. €70

Hermes ☎ 22530 71250, ⓦ hermeshotel-molivos.com. Modern beachside single-storey hotel with variable, marble-floored rooms, all fitted with bright contemporary furnishings and set in quite lush grounds. May–Oct. €50

Molyvos I ☎ 22530 71496, ⓦ molyvos-hotels.com.

On the main town beach, with large balconied and comfortably furnished rooms. Complimentary breakfast served on the flagstoned terrace under the palms. Sister *Molyvos II* on nearby Eftaloú beach. April–Oct. €60

★ **Sun Rise Hotel** ☎ 22530 71713, ⓦ sunrisehotel -lesvos.com. High-class hotel that sprawls in startling white tiers over a hillside 2km east of town. The rooms come in varying sizes but all are well appointed. Two pools, tennis courts, gym, sauna and classy restaurant. Breakfast included. April–Oct. €75

EATING, DRINKING AND NIGHTLIFE

Apart from a selection of lively bars, there's also an outdoor **cinema** (June–Sept) next to the taxi rank.

Bazaar The main indoor dance hall, hidden behind an inconspicuous door on the road down to the quay, pumps out a mixture of foreign and Greek disco hits. Daily midnight–late.

★ **The Captain's Table** ☎ 22530 71241. Splendid quayside taverna offering squirmingly fresh seafood, including great octopus and *gávros pastós*, meat grills, plus vegetarian moussaka and mezédhes, washed down with their very palatable, own-label wine. May–Oct daily noon–2am.

Molly's Bar ☎ 22530 71772. Popular hangout, with taped music at a conversational level during the day and louder music videos by night. The cosy balcony has atmospheric harbour views. May–Oct daily 10am–late.

To Ouzadhiko tou Baboukou ☎ 22530 71776. On the south quay, this joint has an impressive array of ouzos, a bohemian atmosphere and competent, well-priced renditions of the usual mezédhes. Daily 11am–1am.

Around Mólyvos

West of Mólyvos there is a string of decent beaches with varying degrees of commercialization, most rampant at **Pétra**. To the east, coastal development is more measured, with some appealing beaches and yet another spa. Inland and southeast, the main paved road via Vafiós curves around 968m, poplar-tufted **Mount Lepétymnos**. You can complete a scenic loop of the mountain via Kápi and Ypsilométopo on its southern flank.

Pétra

Given political and practical limits to expansion in Mólyvos, many package companies have shifted emphasis to **PÉTRA**, 5km due south. The modern outskirts sprawl untidily behind its broad, sandy beach, but two attractive nuclei of old stone houses, some with Levantine-style balconies overhanging the street, extend back from the part-pedestrianized seafront square. Pétra takes its name from the giant, unmissable rock monolith inland, enhanced by the eighteenth-century church of the **Panayía Glykofiloússa**, reached via 114 rock-hewn steps. Other local attractions include the sixteenth-century church of **Áyios Nikólaos**, with three phases of well-preserved frescoes up to 1721, and the intricately decorated **Vareltzídhena mansion** (Tues–Sun 8am–3pm; free), with late eighteenth-century naïve wall paintings of courting couples, a bear being trained, sailing ships and a stylized view of a naval engagement at Constantinople.

Ánaxos

ÁNAXOS, 3km south of Pétra, is a higgledy-piggledy package resort fringing by far the cleanest **beach** and seawater in the area: 1km of sand well sown with sunbeds and a handful of tavernas. From anywhere along here you enjoy beautiful sunsets between and beyond three offshore islets.

Loutrá Eftaloú

Daily: May & Oct 9am–1pm & 3–7pm; June–Sept 10am–2pm & 4–8pm; Nov–April variable access • €3.50 for group pool • Occasional summer shuttle-bus service from Mólyvos

The **Loutrá Eftaloú** thermal baths lie 5km east of Mólyvos, at the end of the paved road. Patronize the hot pool under the Ottoman-era domed structure, rather than the sterile modern tub-rooms. The spa is well looked after, with the water mixed up to a toasty 43°C, so you'll need to cool down regularly; outside stretches the long, good pebble beach of **Áyii Anáryiri**, broken up by little headlands, with the two remotest coves nudist.

Sykaminiá

The exquisite hill village of **SYKAMINIÁ** (Sykamiá, Skamniá), just under 10km from Mólyvos, is the birthplace in 1892 of novelist Stratis Myrivilis. One of the imposing basalt-built houses below the platía, from which there are views north to Turkey, is marked as his childhood home.

Skála Sykaminiás

A marked trail short-cuts the twisting road from just east of Sykaminiá down to **SKÁLA SYKAMINIÁS**, easily the most picturesque fishing port on Lésvos. Myrivilis used it as the setting for his best-known work, *The Mermaid Madonna*, and the tiny rock-top **chapel** at the end of the jetty will be instantly recognizable to anyone who has read the book. The only local **beach** is the one of Kayiá 1.5km east, which has a pebble-on-sand base.

Klió and Tsónia

Some 5km east from upper Sykaminiá is **KLIÓ**, whose single main street leads down to a platía with a plane tree, fountain and more views across to Turkey. The village is set attractively on a slope, down which a wide, paved road descends 6km to **Tsónia** beach, 600m of beautiful pink volcanic sand.

ACCOMMODATION AND EATING

PÉTRA

Hotel Michaelia ☎ 22530 41730. Good-value hotel behind the south waterfront, with smart if slightly cramped rooms, most with balconies facing the sunset. Decent buffet breakfast included. May–Sept. **€35**

Mermaid ☎ 22530 41275. At the far north end of the seafront, this all-round taverna provides heaps of inexpensive small and more upscale fish, as well as some meat dishes and a variety of starters. April to mid-Oct daily 9am–1am.

Women's Agricultural Tourism Cooperative ☎ 22530 41238, ⓦ lesvos-travel.com/womens -cooperative. The downstairs office arranges rooms or studios (from €30) in scattered premises, while the rooftop restaurant serves up tasty grills and *mayireftá*. Proceeds go to the organization's efforts. Daily 10am–midnight.

ÁNAXOS

Klimataria ☎ 22530 41864. Tucked under the cliff at the beach's northern end, the best local restaurant has a large shady courtyard, where you can enjoy healthy portions of fresh fish, meat and salads. Mid-May to Sept daily 11am–midnight.

LOUTRÁ EFTALOÚ

Iy Eftalou ☎ 22530 71649. With a shady courtyard, large meat grills, fish and *mayireftá*, if sometimes glum service, this is the nearest location to the spa to grab a snack or fuller meal. April–Oct daily 9am–midnight.

AROUND MÓLYVOS

Khrysi Akti ☎ 22530 71879. Typical taverna plus rooms combo in the converted old spa-patrons' inn, built around a church. The en-suite rooms are quite small, while the menu offers a mixture of grills and the odd oven-baked dish. May–Sept. **€30**

SKÁLA SYKAMINIÁS

Anemoessa ☎ 22530 55360. By the chapel, this taverna has the local edge quality-wise, with imaginative starters like stuffed squash blossoms complementing fresh seafood, much of which costs under €10. April–Oct daily, some winter weekends (Fri–Sun) noon–1am.

★ **Gorgona** ☎ 22530 55301, ⓦ gorgonahotel.gr. Small, centrally located hotel run by a friendly old couple, whose simple but clean rooms have wrap-around balconies. There's a shaded terrace for the complimentary breakfast and meals are available too. May–Sept. **€35**

Iy Mouria tou Myrivili ☎ 22530 55319. Picturesque taverna named after the mulberry tree in which Myrivilis used to sleep on hot summer nights. You can sit under said tree and tuck into a standard range of *mezédhes*, salads, meat and fish dishes. May–Oct daily 11am–1am.

KLIÓ AND TSÓNIA

Maria Tsónia ☎ 22530 93662. No sign, oddly enough, but the first restaurant as you reach the southern end of the beach from the access road cannot be accused of serving anonymous food, as the home-style *mayireftá* are quite delicious. May–Sept daily 10am–midnight.

Áyios Efstrátios

ÁYIOS EFSTRÁTIOS (Aï Strátis) is one of the quietest and loneliest islands in the Aegean, with a registered population of under 400, only half of whom live here all year round. It was only permanently settled during the sixteenth century, and land is still largely owned by three monasteries on Mount Áthos. Historically, the only outsiders to visit were those compelled to do so – political prisoners were exiled here both during the 1930s and the civil war years.

Áyios Efstrátios village

ÁYIOS EFSTRÁTIOS village – the island's only habitation – is among the ugliest in Greece. Devastation caused by an earthquake on February 20, 1968, which killed 22 and injured hundreds, was compounded by the reconstruction plan: the contract went to a junta-linked company, who prevented survivors from returning to their old homes and used army bulldozers to raze even those structures – comprising one of the more beautiful ports in these islands – that could have been repaired. From the hillside, some two dozen surviving houses of the old village overlook grim rows of prefabs, a sad monument to the corruption of the junta years.

Architecture apart, Áyios Efstrátios still functions as a traditional fishing and farming community, with the prefabs set at the mouth of a wooded stream valley draining to the sandy harbour beach. There are scant tourist amenities.

Around the island

Beyond the village – there are few vehicles and no paved roads – the hilly **landscape**, dotted with a surprising number of oak trees, is deserted apart from rabbits, sheep and the occasional shepherd. **Alonítsi**, on the north coast – ninety minutes' walk from the port following a track due east and over a low ridge – is the island's best **beach**, a 1.5km stretch of sand with rolling breakers and views across to Límnos. South of the harbour lies a series of grey-sand beaches, most with wells and drinkable water, accessible by roundabout tracks. **Áyios Dhimítrios**, an hour-plus distant, and **Lidharió**, ninety minutes away at the end of a wooded valley, are the most popular.

ARRIVAL AND DEPARTURE   ÁYIOS EFSTRÁTIOS

By ferry There are ferry connections with Lávrio (4 weekly; 8hr 30min), Límnos (4 weekly; 1hr 30min) and Kavála (4

weekly; 5hr). You can also visit from Límnos on one of the overpriced day-trips (2–3 weekly; €35 return).

ACCOMMODATION AND EATING

Veranda ☎ 69470 50153. The best of the island's handful of tavernas, near the port, has super-fresh though rather pricey fish and seafood, plus a limited range of salads and starters. June–Sept daily noon–midnight.

Xenonas Aï-Stratis ☎ 22540 93329. The only bona fide pension on the island (otherwise just look for rooms signs) offers cosy and comfortable lodgings on the north side of the village. May–Sept. €45

Límnos

Bucolic **Límnos** is a sizeable agricultural and military island that has become positively trendy of late: there are upscale souvenir shops, old village houses restored by mainlanders as seasonal retreats and music bars during summer at nearly every beach. For all that, the island's remoteness and peculiar ferry schedules protected it until the mid-1990s from most aspects of the holiday trade, and conventional tourism was late in coming because hoteliers lived primarily off the visiting relatives of the numerous soldiers stationed here. Most summer visitors are still Greek, particularly from Thessaloníki, though some Brits and other Europeans now arrive by charter flights.

The island has often been the focus of **disputes** between the Greek and Turkish governments, with frequent posturing over invaded airspace, although the détente of recent years has seen such incidences cease. As a result, Límnos's **garrison** of 25,000 soldiers – at the nadir of Greco-Turkish relations during the 1970s and 1980s – is now down to about 6000, and set to fall further if, as expected, the remaining bases close.

The **bays** of **Bourniá** and **Moúdhros**, the latter one of the largest natural harbours in the Aegean, divide Límnos almost in two. The west of the island is dramatically hilly, with abundant basalt put to good use as street cobbles and house masonry. The east is low-lying and speckled with seasonal salt marshes where it's not occupied by cattle, combine harvesters and vast corn fields. There are numerous sandy **beaches** around the coast – mostly gently shelving – and it's easy to find a stretch to yourself.

Like most volcanic islands, Límnos produces excellent **wine** – good dry white, rosé and retsina – plus ouzo. The Limnians proudly tout an abundance of **natural food products**, including thyme honey and sheep's cheese, and indeed the population is almost self-sufficient in foodstuffs.

ARRIVAL AND DEPARTURE   LÍMNOS

By plane The airport lies 18km east of Mýrina, almost at the geographic centre of the island; a few taxis always linger outside, there being no shuttle bus into town. Frequencies below are for June–Oct.
Destinations Athens (1–3 daily; 50min); Híos (2 weekly; 1hr 30min); Ikaría (6 weekly; 1hr 40min); Lésvos (5 weekly;

30min); Rhodes (5 weekly; 2hr–3hr 30min); Sámos (2 weekly; 1hr 45min–2hr 30min); Thessaloníki (6 weekly; 40min).
By ferry Límnos lies on two ferry routes, the one from Lávrio to Kavála and from the northern mainland ports down through the eastern Aegean.
Destinations Áyios Efstrátios (4 weekly; 1hr 30min); Híos

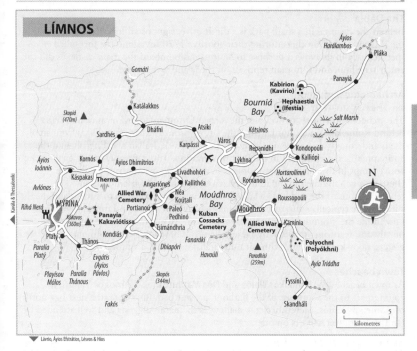

LÍMNOS

 Áyios
Harálambos
Pláka
Gomáti
Panayiá
Kabírion
(Kavírio)
Bourniá   Hephaestia
Bay   (Ifestía)
Katálakkos
Skopíd
(470m)
Sardhés   Dháfni   Atsikí   Kótsinas   Salt Marsh
Város
Karpássi   Repanídhi   Kondopoúli
Kornós   Lýkhna   Kallíópi
Áyios
Ioánnis   Áyios Dhimítrios   Livadhohóri   Romanoú   Hortarolímni
Káspakas   Thermá   Kallithéa   Kéros
Avlónas   Angariónes   Néa   Moúdhros
Allied War   Koútali   Bay
Rihá Nerá   Cemetery   Paleó
MÝRINA   Portianoú   Pedhinó   Moúdhros
Panayía   Kuban   Allied War
Kókavos   Kakaviótissa   Cossacks   Kamínia
(360m)   Tsimándhria   Cemetery
Platý   Kondiás   Roussopoúli
Paralía   Thános   Fanaráki
Platý   Dhiapóri   Havoúli   Polyochni
Evgátis   (Polyókhni)
Playísou   (Áyios   Paradhísi   Ayía Triádha
Mólos   Paralía   Pávlos)   (259m)
Thánous   Skopós
(344m)   Fyssíni
Fakós   Skandháli

N

0 ___ 5
kilometres

6

(3 weekly; 10hr); Ikaría (1 weekly; 16hr 30min); Kavála (6 weekly; 4hr–4hr 30min); Lávrio (4 weekly; 9hr 30min); Lésvos (3 weekly; 6hr 30min); Sámos (3 weekly; 14–15hr); Thessaloníki (1 weekly; 8hr 30min).

GETTING AROUND

By bus Buses are fairly infrequent on Límnos, with only afternoon departures from Mýrina to many of the more distant villages and only 1–2 daily to those nearer the capital.

By motorbike A vehicle is required for touring; a motorbike is quite sufficient for the more touristed western third of the island, which is a blessing as cars are expensive.

Mýrina

MÝRINA (aka Kástro), the port-capital on the west coast, has the ethos of a provincial market town rather than of a resort. With about five thousand inhabitants, it's pleasantly low-key, if not especially picturesque, apart from a core neighbourhood of old stone houses dating from the Ottoman era, and the ornate Neoclassical mansions backing **Romeïkós Yialós**, the town's beach-lined esplanade. Shops and amenities are mostly found along Kydhá and its continuation Karatzá – which meanders north from the harbour to Romeïkós Yialós – or Garoufalídhi, its perpendicular offshoot, roughly halfway along.

Mýrina castle

Unrestricted access

Mýrina's main attraction is its Byzantine **castle**, perched on a craggy headland between the ferry dock and Romeïkós Yialós. Ruinous despite later Genoese and Ottoman additions, the fortress is flatteringly lit at night and warrants a climb towards sunset for views over the town, the entire west coast and – in clear conditions – Mount Áthos, 35 nautical miles west. Skittish miniature deer, imported from Rhodes and fed by the municipality, patrol the castle grounds to the amusement of visitors.

The Dápia

Behind the hospital in a small park is a diminutive, signposted fort, the **Dápia**, built by the Russian Orloff brothers during their abortive 1770 invasion. The fort failed spectacularly in its avowed purpose to besiege and bombard the main castle, as did the entire rebellion, and Ottoman reprisals on the island were severe.

Archeological museum

Tues–Sun 8.30am–3pm • €2 • ☎ 22540 22900

6

The **archeological museum** occupies the former Ottoman governor's mansion right behind Romeïkós Yialós, not far from the site of Bronze Age **Mýrina**. Finds from all of the island's major sites are assiduously labelled in Greek, Italian and English, and the entire premises is exemplary in terms of presentation. The star upper-storey exhibits are votive lamps in the shape of sirens, found in an Archaic sanctuary at Hephaestia (Ifestía), much imitated in modern local jewellery. There are also numerous representations of the goddess Cybele/Artemis, who was revered across the island; her shrines were typically situated near a fauna-rich river mouth – on Límnos at Avlónas, now inside the grounds of the *Porto Myrina* resort. An entire room is devoted to metalwork, featuring impressive gold jewellery and bronze objects, both practical (cheese graters, door-knockers) and whimsical-naturalistic (a snail, a vulture).

Town beaches

As town beaches go, **Romeïkós Yialós** and **Néa Mádhitos** (ex-Toúrkikos Yialós), its counterpart to the southeast of the harbour, are not bad. **Rihá Nerá**, the next bay north of Romeïkós Yialós, is even better – shallow as the name suggests and well attended by families, with watersports on offer.

ARRIVAL AND INFORMATION　　　　　　　　　　　　　　　　　　　　　　MÝRINA

By bus The bus station is on Platía Eleftheríou Venizélou, at the north end of Kydhá.

By ferry The new jetty is on the far side of the bay. The most efficient agency for tickets is Maria Kantara Travel on Platía Eleftheríou Venizélou (☎ 22540 29570).

By car and motorbike Cars and motorbikes can be rented from central Limnos Car Rental (☎ 22540 23777) or Myrina Rent a Car (☎ 22540 24476), while Rent a Moto

(☎ 22540 25419), on the north side of town at Leofóros Dhimokratías 89, has good rates on two-wheelers.

Online information There is no tourist office but a useful site is ⊕ limnosisland.gr.

Services Most banks with ATMs cluster around a platía about halfway along Kydhá; the post office is around the corner on Garoufalídhi. Several cafés on the old harbour and Kydhá have wi-fi.

ACCOMMODATION

Despite Límnos's steady gentrification, some room owners still meet arriving ferries. Otherwise the most fruitful area to search is in the northern beach suburb of Rihá Nerá.

Apollo Pavilion Frýnis ☎ 22540 23712, ⊕ apollopavilion.gr. In a peaceful cul-de-sac about halfway along Garoufalídhou, this mock classical hotel offers three-bed a/c studios with TV and mini-kitchen. Most have balconies, with castle or mountain views. **€60**

Arhondiko Cnr of Sakhtoúri and Filellínon, Romeïkós Yialós ☎ 22540 29800, ⊕ arxontikohotel.gr. Límnos's first hotel, this 1851-built mansion has three floors of small-to-medium-sized wood-trimmed rooms with all mod cons but no balconies. There's a pleasant ground-floor

bar/breakfast lounge. **€50**

Hotel Lemnos Limáni Mýrinas ☎ 22540 22153, ⊜ lemnos-hotel@yahoo.gr. Standard 1960s-style hotel with average-sized, simply decorated rooms, but the balconies overlooking the fishing harbour and price make it good value. **€35**

Ifestos Ethnikís Andístasis 17, Andhróni ☎ 22540 24960. Quiet, professionally run two-star hotel with pleasant common areas. Slightly small rooms have a/c, fridges, balconies and a mix of sea or hill views. Breakfast included. **€65**

EATING, DRINKING AND NIGHTLIFE

Karagiozis Romeïkós Yialós 32. The most established watering hole on the island transforms from laidback café

by day to buzzing bar by night, which sometimes holds theme parties or hosts live bands. Daily 11am–late.

Kosmos Romeïkós Yialós ☎ 22540 22050. The most reasonable of the establishments on this popular but mostly overpriced strip of seafront offers fresh fish, a range of mezédhes and glorious sunsets across Mt Áthos. April–Oct daily noon–1am.

★ **0 Platanos** Kydhá ☎ 22540 22070. Excellent traditional *mayireftá* such as *papoutsáki* and highly quaffable aromatic Limniot wine draw big crowds to the atmospheric little square beneath two plane trees. Daily 11am–6pm, until midnight June–Sept.

Western Límnos

Nearly all the tourist amenities are concentrated in the western third of the island, mostly in and around the coastal stretch between Mýrina and the vast Moúdhros Bay. This area includes many of the best **beaches** and most picturesque inland **villages**.

Coast north of Mýrina

Beyond Mýrina's respectable town beaches, the closest good sand lies 3km north at **Avlónas**, unspoilt except for the local power plant a short way inland. Just beyond, the road splits: the right-hand turning wends its way through **Káspakas**, its north-facing houses in neat tiers and a potable spring on its platía, before plunging down to **Áyios Ioánnis**, also reached directly by the left-hand bypass from the capital. The furthest of its three **beaches** is the most pleasant, a curved cove punctuated by a tiny fishing harbour and offshore islet named Vampire Island.

Thérma and around

Daily 10am–2pm & 5–9pm • ⓦ thermaspa.gr

Six kilometres northeast of Mýrina, the old Ottoman baths at **Thérma**, complete with calligraphic plaques, have been restored as an eye-wateringly expensive contemporary health spa, with all conceivable treatments available – or you can just have a hydromassage soak (€12). Unusually for a hot spring, the water is non-sulphurous and is the tastiest on the island, so there is always a knot of cars parked nearby under the trees while their owners fill jerry cans with warm water from a **public fountain**, which has a bilingual Greek/Ottoman Turkish inscription.

Just south of Thérma is the iconic poster image of Límnos: the **chapel of Panayía Kakaviótissa**, tucked into a volcanic cave on the flank of Mt Kákavos (360m).

Sardhés

Some 7km north of Thérma, **SARDHÉS** is the highest village on the island, with wonderfully broody sunsets and a celebrated central taverna. The handsome local houses are typical of mountain villages on Límnos in having an external staircase up to the first floor, as the ground floor was used for animals.

Gomáti

Beyond Sardhés and 5km below Katálakkos lies the spectacular, well-signposted **dune** environment at **Gomáti**, one of the largest such in Greece. There are two zones, reached by separate dirt tracks: one at a river mouth, with a bird-rich marsh, and the other to the northwest, with a beach bar and sunbeds. Despite wind exposure, the latter portion especially is a popular outing.

Platý

PLATÝ, 2km southeast of Mýrina, has had its traditional profile somewhat compromised by modern villa construction, but it does have two nocturnal tavernas. The long sandy **beach**, 700m below, is popular, with non-motorized **watersports** available at the south end through Babis, below the *Lemnos Village* complex.

Thános and its beaches

THÁNOS has more architectural character than smaller Platý, 2km southeast. **Paralía Thánous**, 1.5km below, is among the most scenic of southwestern beaches, flanked by volcanic crags and looking out to Áyios Efstrátios island. Beyond Thános, the road curls over to the enormous beach at **Evgátis** (**Áyios Pávlos**), reckoned the island's best, with more igneous pinnacles for definition and Áyios Efstrátios on the horizon.

Kondiás and around

Eleven kilometres east of Mýrina, **KONDIÁS** is the island's third-largest settlement, cradled between hills tufted with Límnos's biggest pine forest. Stone-built, often elaborate houses combine with the setting to make Kondiás an attractive inland village, a fact not lost on the Greeks and foreigners restoring those houses with varying degrees of taste. Cultural interest is lent by the central **Balkan Art Gallery** (daily except Fri 10am–2pm & 7.30–9.30pm; €2), featuring works by prominent painters from across the Balkans – especially Bulgarian Svetlin Russev. **Tsimándhria**, 2.5km further east, has better dining options.

ACCOMMODATION, EATING AND DRINKING   WESTERN LÍMNOS

COAST NORTH OF MÝRINA

Aï Yiannis Áyios Ioánnis ☎22540 61669. Featuring seating in the shade of piled-up volcanic boulders at the end of the first beach, this modest *psarotavérna* has fresh fish at very reasonable prices. June–Aug daily 11am–midnight.

Aliotida Apartments Áyios Ioánnis ☎22540 24406, ⓦ aliotida-apartments.gr. Bright, well-furnished studios with kitchenettes on nicely landscaped grounds up behind the third beach. May–Sept. €40

SARDHÉS

★ **Man-Tella** ☎22540 61349. Portions of rural delights such as rabbit *stifádho* and village rooster are huge, the local barrelled wine is superb and the location in the vine-trellised courtyard is atmospheric. Daily noon–1am.

PLATÝ

★ **O Sozos** ☎22540 25085. Just off the main platía, this local favourite serves up huge portions of succulent *kondosoúvli* and *kokorétsi*, salads and a few *mayireftá* like *dolmádhes*, washed down by *tsípouro* and local barrelled wine. Daily noon–late.

Studios Magda ☎22540 25370. Set about 100m back from the sea, this block of modern studios is well designed, with moderate-sized, comfortable rooms and friendly management. May–Sept. €40

★ **Villa Afroditi** ☎22540 23141, ⓦ afroditi-villa.gr.

With its spectacular topiary, welcoming owners, pleasant pool bar and mixture of spotless doubles and studios spread over two wings, this is one of the best resorts on Límnos. Free port pick-up and buffet breakfast included. Mid-May to early Oct. €65

THÁNOS AND ITS BEACHES

Evgatis Hotel Evgátis ☎22540 51700. Behind the main road some way back from the beach, this functional hotel has decent rooms, a pool and a full-service taverna serving home-cooked food. May–Oct. €40

Petradi Studios Paralía Thános ☎22540 29905, ⓦ petradistudios.gr. Modern but tastefully designed two-storey building, warm ochre in colour, with spacious and comfortable rooms. There's a pleasant, relaxed beach bar on the premises. May–Sept. €30

Yiannakaros Paralía Thános ☎22540 22787. Reliable taverna that covers all the bases, with simple fish and some meat dishes and a fair range of starters and salads. May to late Sept daily noon–midnight.

KONDIÁS AND AROUND

O Hristos Tsimándhria ☎22540 51278. Old-favourite taverna with a new name on the central square that dishes up cheap, salubrious grills and a few seafood dishes, plus great dips, salads and wine. Daily 10am–midnight.

Eastern Límnos

The shores of **Moúdhros Bay**, glimpsed south of the trans-island road, are muddy and best avoided by serious bathers. The bay itself enjoyed strategic importance during World War I, culminating in Allied acceptance of the Ottoman surrender aboard the anchored British warship HMS *Agamemnon* on October 30, 1918. The huge chunk of Límnos east of the bay is little visited but offers some deserted **beaches** and interesting reminders of the island's recent and more distant past.

Moúdhros

MOÚDHROS, the second-largest town on Límnos, is rather a dreary place, with only the wonderfully kitsch, two-belfried **Evangelismós church** to recommend it. The closest

THE WAR CEMETERIES

About 800m along the Roussopoúli road from Moúdhros is an unlocked **Allied military cemetery** maintained by the Commonwealth War Graves Commission, its neat lawns and rows of white headstones incongruous in such parched surroundings. During 1915, Moúdhros Bay was the principal staging area for the disastrous Gallipoli campaign. Of approximately 36,000 Allied dead, 887 are buried here – mainly battle casualties, who died after having been evacuated to the base hospital at Moúdhros. Though the deceased are mostly British, there is also a French cenotaph, and – speaking volumes about imperial sociology – a mass "Musalman" grave for Egyptian and Indian troops in one corner, with a Koranic inscription.

There are more graves at another immaculately maintained cemetery behind the hilltop church in **Portianoú**, a little over 1km from the west side of Moúdhros Bay. Among the 348 buried here are two Canadian nurses, three Egyptian labourers and three Maori soldiers. East of Portianoú and Paleó Pedhinó, signposted on a headland, lies the last and strangest of Límnos's military cemeteries: about forty 1920–21 graves of **Kuban Cossacks**, White Army refugees from the Russian civil war.

6

decent beaches are at **Havoúli**, 4km south by dirt track, and **Fanaráki**, 4km west, but both have muddy sand and don't really face the open sea. Until recently Moúdhros was quite literally a God-forsaken place, owing to an incident late in Ottoman rule. Certain locals killed some Muslims and threw them down a well on property belonging to the Athonite monastery of Koutloumousioú; the Ottoman authorities, holding the monks responsible, slaughtered any Koutloumousiot brethren they found on the island and set the local monastery alight. Two monks managed to escape to Áthos, where every August 23 a curse was chanted, condemning Moúdhros's inhabitants to "never sleep again"; the Athonite brothers finally relented in July 2001.

Polyochni (Polyókhni) and around
Tues–Sun 8.30am–3pm • Free

Traces of the most advanced Neolithic Aegean civilization have been unearthed at **Polyochni (Polyókhni)**, 10km east of Moúdhros, on a bluff overlooking a long, narrow beach. Since 1930, Italian excavations have uncovered five layers of settlement, the oldest from late in the fourth millennium BC, predating Troy on the Turkish coast opposite. The town met a sudden, violent end from war or earthquake in about 2100 BC. The **ruins** are mostly well labelled but mostly of specialist interest, though a small, well-presented **museum** behind the entrance helps bring the place to life.

The only really decent beach in the area is **Ayía Triádha**, accessed off the Polyókhni road, with blonde sand heaped in dunes.

Kótsinas
Some 10km north of Moúdhros, reached via Repanídhi, the hard-packed beach at **KÓTSINAS** is set in the proteted western limb of Bourniá Bay. The nearby anchorage offers two busy, seafood-strong tavernas. On a knoll overlooking the jetty stands a corroded, sword-brandishing statue of **Maroula**, a Genoese-era heroine who briefly delayed the Ottoman conquest, and a large church of **Zoödhóhou Piyís** (the Life-Giving Spring), with intriguing kitsch icons, a vaulted wooden ceiling and antique floor tiles. Out front, 63 steps lead down through an illuminated tunnel in the rock to the potable (if slightly mineral) spring in question, oozing into a cool, vaulted chamber.

Kerós beach
Kalliópi, 8km northeast of Moúdhros via attractive Kondopoúli, is a pleasant little village, giving direct access to **Kéros beach**, a 1.5km stretch of sand with dunes and a small pine grove, plus shallow water. It remains popular despite being exposed and often dirty, and attracts plenty of windsurfers and foreigners with camper vans.

Hephaesia and Kabirion

Both sites Tues–Sun 8.30am–3pm • Free

Aside from Polyochni (Polyókhni), Hephaestia and Kabirion are Límnos's other significant **ancient sites**, only reachable with your own transport. **Hephaestia** (present-day Ifestía), 4.5km from Kondopoúli by rough, signposted track, offers an admirably reconstructed theatre overlooking its former harbour. The name comes from the god Hephaestos, rescued and revered by the ancient Limnians after he crash-landed on the island, hurled from Mt Olympos by Hera.

Kabirion, also signposted as "Kabeiroi" (modern Kavírion), on the opposite shore of Tigáni Bay and accessed by a paved road, is more evocative. The **ruins** are of a sanctuary connected with the cult of the Samothracian Kabiroi (see box, p.410), though the site here is probably older. Little survives other than eleven column stumps staking out a *stoa*, behind the *telestirio* or shrine where the cult mysteries took place. A nearby **sea grotto** has been identified as the Homeric Spiliá toú Filoktíti, where Trojan war hero Philoktetes was abandoned by his comrades-in-arms until his stinking, gangrenous leg had healed by application of *límnia yí*, a poultice of volcanic mud still prized on the island. Landward access to the cave is via steps leading down from the caretaker's shelter, though final access (from a little passage on the right as you face the sea) involves some wading.

ACCOMMODATION AND EATING　　　　　　　　　　　**EASTERN LÍMNOS**

Keros Kalliópi ☎ 22540 41059. At the start of the road down to Kéros beach, this is one of the few accommodation options in the far east of Límnos. Pleasant rooms with balconies but very remote. June to mid-Sept. **€30**

To Mourayio Kótsinas ☎ 22540 41065. Easily the better, if slightly pricier, of the two tavernas here, worth the extra for the higher quality of both food and service. Good for fish, meat and veg dishes. May–Sept daily noon–midnight.

Samothráki

SAMOTHRÁKI (Samothrace) has one of the most dramatic profiles of all the Greek islands, second only to Thíra (Santorini): its dark mass of granite rises abruptly from the sea, culminating in the 1611m **Mount Fengári**. Seafarers have always been guided by its imposing outline, clearly visible from the mainland, and its summit provided a vantage point for Poseidon to watch over the siege of Troy. Landing is subject to the notoriously unpredictable weather, but that did not deter pilgrims who, for hundreds of years in antiquity, journeyed to the island to visit the **Sanctuary of the Great Gods** and were initiated into its mysteries. The sanctuary remains the main archeological attraction of the island, which, too remote for most tourists, combines earthy simplicity with natural grandeur. The tourist season is relatively short – essentially (late) July and August – but you will find some facilities open as early as Easter and one or two all year round.

Kamariótissa

Ferries dock at the dull village of **KAMARIÓTISSA**. While you're unlikely to want to spend much time here, it does make a convenient base, as some of Samothráki's best hotels lie along or just behind the tree-lined seafront and various rooms for rent can be found in the maze of streets behind; owners often meet incoming vessels.

Hóra

HÓRA, also known as **Samothráki**, is the island's capital. Far larger than the portion visible from out at sea would suggest, it's an attractive town of Thracian-style stone houses, some whitewashed, clustered around a hollow in the western flanks of Mount Fengári. It is dominated by the Genoese **Gateluzzi fort**, of which little survives other than the gateway. Half an hour or so can be whiled away at the charming **folklore museum** (late May to late Sept daily 9am–2pm & 6–10pm; €1), which contains a motley collection of clothing, domestic items and miscellany.

The Sanctuary of the Great Gods

Daily 8.30am–3pm; museum Tues–Sun only • €3 combined ticket • ☎ 22510 41474

Hidden in a stony but thickly wooded ravine between the tiny hamlet of **PALEÓPOLI** – 6km northeast from Kamariótissa, and 3km directly north from Hóra – and the plunging northwestern ridge of Mount Fengári, lie the remains of the **Sanctuary of the Great Gods**. From the late Bronze Age (around the eighth century BC) until the early Byzantine era (fifth century AD), the mysteries and sacrifices of the cult of the Great Gods (see box, p.410) were performed on Samothráki, in ancient Thracian, until the second century BC. Little is known of this dialect except that it was a very old Indo-European tongue, related to and eventually replaced by ancient Greek. The spiritual focus of the northern Aegean, the importance of the island's rituals was second only to the Mysteries of Eleusis in all the ancient world. The well-labelled site strongly evokes its proud past while commanding views of the mountains and the sea.

Archeological museum

Closed Mon

For an explanatory introduction, it is best first to visit the **archeological museum**, whose exhibits span all eras of habitation, from the Archaic to the Byzantine. Highlights include a frieze of dancing girls from the propylaion of the Temenos, entablatures from different buildings, and Roman votive offerings such as coloured glass vials from the necropolis of the ancient town east of the sanctuary. You can also see a reproduction of the exquisitely sculpted marble statue, the *Winged Victory of Samothrace*, which once stood breasting the wind at the prow of a marble ship in the Nymphaeum. Discovered in 1863 by a French diplomat to the Sublime Porte, it was carried off to the Louvre, where it remains a major draw.

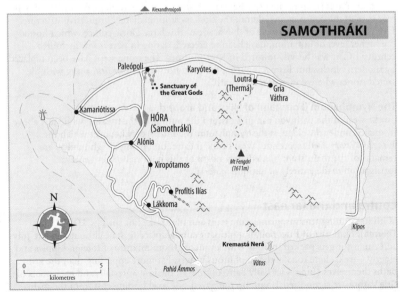

6

THE SAMOTHRACIAN MYSTERIES

The **religion of the Great Gods** revolved around a hierarchy of ancient Thracian fertility figures: the Great Mother Axieros; a subordinate male deity known as Kadmilos; and the potent and ominous twin demons the Kabiroi, originally the local heroes Dardanos and Aeton. When the Aeolian colonists arrived (traditionally c.700 BC) they simply merged the resident deities with their own – the Great Mother became Cybele, while her consort Hermes and the Kabiroi were fused interchangeably with the *Dioskouroi* Castor and Pollux, patrons of seafarers. Around the nucleus of a sacred precinct the newcomers made the beginnings of what is now the sanctuary.

Despite their long observance, the mysteries of the cult were never explicitly recorded, since ancient writers feared incurring the wrath of the Kabiroi (who could reputedly brew up sudden, deadly storms), but it has been established that two levels of initiation were involved. Both ceremonies, in direct opposition to the elitism of Eleusis, were open to all, including women and slaves. The lower level of initiation, or *myesis*, may, as is speculated at Eleusis, have involved a ritual simulation of the life, death and rebirth cycle; in any case, it's known that it ended with joyous feasting, and it can be conjectured, since so many clay torches have been found, that it took place at night. The higher level of initiation, or *epopteia*, carried the unusual requirement of a moral standard – the connection of theology with morality, so strong in the later Judeo-Christian tradition, was rarely made by the early Greeks. This second level involved a full confession followed by absolution and baptism in bull's blood.

The Anaktoron and Arsinoeion

The **Anaktoron**, or hall of initiation for the first level of the mysteries, dates in its present form from Roman times. Its inner sanctum was marked by a warning stele, now in the museum, and at the southeast corner you can make out the **Priestly Quarters**, an antechamber where candidates for initiation donned white gowns. Next to it is the **Arsinoeion**, the largest circular ancient building known in Greece, used for libations and sacrifices. Within its rotunda are the fourth-century BC walls of a double precinct where a rock altar, the earliest preserved ruin on the site, has been uncovered.

The Temenos and Hieron

A little further south, on the same side of the path, you come to the **Temenos**, a rectangular area open to the sky where the feasting probably took place, and, edging its rear corner, the conspicuous **Hieron**, the site's most immediately impressive structure. Five columns and an architrave of the facade of this large Doric edifice, which hosted the higher level of initiation, have been re-erected; dating in part from the fourth century BC, it was heavily restored in Roman times. The stone steps have been replaced by modern blocks, but Roman benches for spectators remain *in situ*, along with the sacred stones where confession was heard.

The Nymphaeum (Fountain) of Nike and around

To the west of the path you can just discern the outline of the **theatre**, while just above it, tucked under the ridge, is the **Nymphaeum (Fountain) of Nike**, over which the *Winged Victory* used to preside. West of the theatre, occupying a high terrace, are remains of the main **stoa**; immediately north of this is an elaborate medieval fortification made entirely of antique material.

Loutrá and the far east

With its running streams, giant plane trees and namesake hot springs, **LOUTRÁ** (aka **Thermá**), 6km east of Paleópoli, is a pleasant enough place to stay, although in late July and August it gets packed, mainly with an incongruous mixture of foreign hippies and elderly Greeks, here to take the sulphurous waters. Far more appealing than the grim **baths** themselves (June–Oct daily 8am–6pm; €5), the low waterfalls and rock pools of **Gría Váthra** are signposted 1.5km up the paved side road leading east from the main

---

CLIMBING THE MOON

Loutrá is the prime base for the tough six-hour climb up the 1611m **Mount Fengári** (known to the ancients as **Sáos**, a name found on some maps to this day), the highest peak in the Aegean islands; the path starts at the top of the village, beside a concrete water tank and a huge plane tree. Tell your accommodation proprietors that you're going. Fengári is Greek for "moon" and, according to legend, if you reach the top on the night of a full moon your wish will come true – most of those foolhardy enough to attempt this will just hope to get back down safely.

6

Thermá access drive. Loutrá is ghostly quiet for most of the year and its miniature harbour, built as an alternative to Kamariótissa, is never used at all.

Beaches on Samothráki's north shore are mostly clean but uniformly pebbly and exposed. Some 15km from Loutrá along a fine corniche road is **Kípos beach**, a long strand facing the Turkish island of Gökçeada (Ímvros to the Greeks) and backed by open pasture and picturesque crags. The water is clean and there's a rock overhang for shelter at one end, a spring, shower and seasonal *kantína* for refreshments.

The south coast

The warmer south flank of the island, its fertile farmland dotted with olive groves, boasts fine views out to sea – as far as Gökçeada on a clear day. On the way south, beyond sleepy **Lákkoma**, the attractive hill village of **Profítis Ilías** is worth the brief detour.

From Lákkoma itself, it's less than 2km down to the eponymous **beach**. A further 6km east lies **Pahiá Ámmos**, a long, clean beach. The nearest (meagre) supplies are in Lákkoma but this doesn't deter big summer crowds who also arrive by excursion *kaïkia*. These continue east to **Vátos**, a secluded nudist beach, the **Kremastá Nerá** coastal waterfalls and finally round to Kípos beach (see above).

ARRIVAL AND INFORMATION

SAMOTHRÁKI

By ferry The only current connection with Samothráki is the ferry from Alexandhroúpoli (2hr 30min); frequency varies from 2–3 daily in July & Aug to 4–5 weekly in winter.

By kaïki In peak season 1–2 daily excursions run from Kamariótissa to the south-coast beaches.

By bus There are plenty of buses from Kamariótissa along the north coast to Loutrá (6–7 daily; 20min) and inland to Hóra in season (5–6 daily; 10min), though far fewer in winter.

By motorbike or car You can only get to the south and

far east of the island with your own transport. The best places to rent wheels are Niki Tours (☎25510 41465, ✉niki_tours@hotmail.com) and Kyrkos car rental (☎25510 69728, ✉akis1kirkos@gmail.com), both on the seafront at Kamariótissa; best book in advance in high season, as supply is short. The only fuelling station on the entire island is 1km above the port, en route to Hóra.

Services There is no official tourist office on Samothráki. Kamariótissa has two banks with ATMs and the island's only post office.

ACCOMMODATION, EATING AND DRINKING

KAMARIÓTISSA

Aeolos ☎25510 41595, ⊛hotelaiolos.gr. Samothráki's most comfortable accommodation has a large pool and quiet, spacious rooms. There are good half-board deals in the low season. June–Sept. **€50**

ly Klimataria ☎25510 41535. Towards the northeast end of the seafront, with a huge summer terrace, this enduring taverna serves dishes like fried aubergines, oven-baked goat and *soutsoukákia*, plus palatable barrelled wine. June–Sept daily noon–2am.

Kyrkos Apartments ☎25510 41620, ✉akis1kirkos @gmail.com. Spacious modern studios with well-equipped kitchens, in a rural setting 500m from the port,

just off the road to Hóra. April–Oct. **€30**

To Mouragio ☎694 58 94 107. New restaurant at the southwestern end of the seafront, where you can get pizza, sandwiches and *souvláki*, as well as a range of typical taverna items. Daily 11am–1am.

HÓRA

★ **1900** ☎25510 41222. Boasting a lovely vine-shaded terrace with stunning views of the Kástro and the valley below, this friendly taverna serves stuffed goat (€8) and spicy aubergines. Mid-May to mid-Sept daily noon–1am.

THE SANCTUARY OF THE GREAT GODS

Samothraki Village Paleópoli ☎25510 42300, ⓦsamothrakivillage.gr. Smart new resort, handily placed for the Sanctuary of the Great Gods, with manicured grounds, neatly furnished rooms, two pools and a bar-restaurant. **€60**

LOUTRÁ AND THE FAR EAST

Camping Platia ☎25510 98244. Around1.5km east of the village, this beachside municipal campsite is very basic, with toilets only. May–Sept. Adult plus tent **€5.50**

Camping Voradhes ☎25510 98258. Some 3km east of the village, the island's prime municipal campsite has hot-water showers, electricity, a minimarket, restaurant and bar. July & Aug. Adult plus tent **€8**

O Paradhisos ☎697 57 75 997. This place has the advantage of the village's best location, up under the plane trees. The traditional cuisine and barrelled wine also hit the spot. Mid-May to mid-Sept daily noon–1am.

To Fengari ☎25510 98321. Small set of adequately furnished studios, tucked in a lane east of the centre, which maintains at least a low level of operation all year, including a home-style taverna on site. **€25**

★ **To Perivoli T'Ouranou** ☎25510 98313. "Heaven's Orchard" aptly describes this leafy taverna on the lane to Gría Váthra. Various dips, types of *saganáki* and spaghetti dishes supplement the usual grills and salads. Regular live traditional music. June to mid-Oct daily 11am–2am.

THE SOUTH COAST

Delfini Pahiá Ámmos ☎25510 94235. Classic taverna-cum-rooms enterprise at the west end of the beach. The rooms are fairly basic but habitable enough and the taverna is a friendly hangout with a decent range of staples. May–Sept. **€30**

Paradisos Profítis Ilías ☎25510 95267. Atmospheric rustic taverna, with a lovely terrace facing sunsets over Thássos. The house speciality is a selection of meats such as lamb, goat and *kondosoúvli* roast on the spit, accompanied by fiery *tsípouro* or soothing wine. June to mid-Sept daily 10am–2am.

To Akroyiali Lákkoma beach ☎25510 95123. Simple but clean rooms with seaview balconies are available above a friendly taverna, which serves fresh fish, some meat and a standard menu of *mezédhes* and salads. June–Sept. **€35**

Thássos

Just 12km from the mainland, **Thássos** has long been a popular resort island for northern Greeks, and since the early 1990s has also attracted a cosmopolitan mix of tourists, particularly Germans and Scandinavians on packages, as well as an increasing number of people from eastern Europe. They are all entertained by vast numbers of *bouzoúkia* (music halls) and music tavernas, while nature-lovers can find some areas of outstanding beauty, especially inland. Moreover, the island's traditional industries have managed to survive the onslaught of modernity. The elite of Thássos still make a substantial living from the pure-white **marble** that constitutes two-thirds of the landmass, found only here and quarried at dozens of sites in the hills between Liménas and Panayía. Olives, especially the oil, honey, nuts and fruit (often sold candied) are also important products. The spirit *tsípouro*, rather than wine, is the main local tipple; pear extract, onions or spices like cinnamon and anise are added to home-made batches.

Brief history

Inhabited since the Stone Age, Thássos was settled by Parians in the seventh century BC, attracted by **gold** deposits between modern Liménas and Kínyra. Buoyed by revenues from these, and from **silver** mines under Thassian control on the mainland opposite, the ancient city-state here became the seat of a medium-sized seafaring empire. Commercial acumen did not spell military invincibility, however; the Persians under Darius swept the Thassian fleets from the seas in 492 BC, and in 462 BC Athens permanently deprived Thássos of its autonomy after a three-year siege. The main port continued to thrive into Roman times, but lapsed into Byzantine and medieval obscurity.

Sadly, the salient fact of more recent history has been a series of devastating, deliberately set **fires** in the 1980s and 1990s. Only the northeastern quadrant of the island, plus the area around Astrís and Alykí, escaped, though the surviving forest is still home to numerous pine martens.

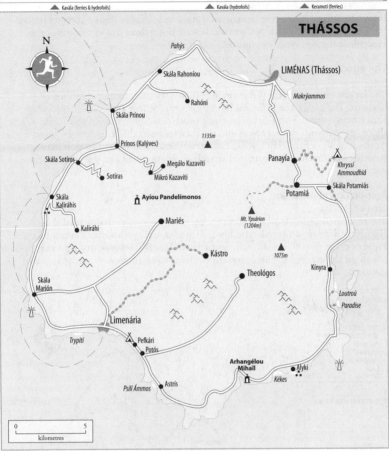

△ Kavála (ferries & hydrofoils)   △ Kavála (hydrofoils)   △ Keramotí (ferries)

THÁSSOS

N

Pahýs

Skála Rahoníou

LIMÉNAS (Thássos)

Rahóni

Makrýammos

Skála Prínou

Prínos (Kalýves)

1135m

Panayía

Skála Sotíros

Megálo Kazavíti

Khryssí
Ammoudhiá

Sotíras

Mikró Kazavíti

Skála Potamiás

Skála
Kaliráhis

Ayíou Pandelímonos

Potamiá

Kaliráhi

Mariés

Mt. Ypsárion
(1204m)

Kástro

1075m

Kínyra

Theológos

Skála
Marión

Loutroú
Paradise

Limenária

Trypití

Pefkári
Potós

Psilí Ámmos

Astrís

Arhangélou
Mihaïl

Kékes

Ályki

0   5
kilometres

ARRIVAL AND GETTING AROUND   THÁSSOS

By ferry/hydrofoil Kavála-based ferries (2–6 daily; 1hr 15min) arrive at Skála Prínou, in the northwest of the island. Ferries to Liménas (8–12 daily; 40min) leave from Keramotí on the mainland opposite. Depending on the economic situation, there may be high-season hydrofoils from Kavála to Liménas.

By bus The service is fairly good, with frequent buses to Panayía and Skála Potamiás (7–8 daily; 15–20min), Limenária (7 daily; 45min) via Skála Prínou and Potós,

Theológos (5 daily; 1hr) and Alykí (3 daily; 30min) via Kínyra.

By car or motorbike Thássos is small enough to circumnavigate in one full day by rented motorbike or car. Car rental is offered by the major international chains and local Potos Car Rentals (☎25930 23969, ⓦ www .rentacarpotos.gr), with seven branches around the island; try bargaining in the shoulder seasons.

Water taxi In peak season there are 2 daily services from Liménas to Khryssí Ammoudhía.

Liménas

Largely modern **LIMÉNAS** (also signposted as Limín or Thássos) is the island's capital, though not the only port. Although it's plagued with surprisingly clogged traffic, it is partly redeemed by its picturesque fishing harbour and the impressive remains of the **ancient city**. Thanks to its mineral wealth and safe harbour, ancient Thássos prospered from Classical to Roman times. There are substantial remains which appear above and below the streets, plus a fine archeological museum. Thássos hosts a **summer festival** (ⓦthassos-festival.gr), with performances of anything from jazz to comedy at the Hellenistic theatre, funds permitting.

The agora

Free

The largest excavated area is the **agora**, a little way back from the fishing harbour. The grassy site is fenced but not always locked, and is most enjoyably seen towards dusk. Two Roman *stoas* are prominent, but you can also make out shops, monuments, passageways and sanctuaries from the remodelled Classical city. At the far end, a fifth-century BC passageway leads through to an elaborate sanctuary of Artemis, a substantial stretch of Roman road and a few seats of the *odeion*.

Archeological museum

Tues–Sun 8.30am–3pm • €2

The renovated **archeological museum**, close to the agora, contains small but absorbing displays on prehistoric finds, archeological methods and ancient games. Pride of place goes to the 4m-tall, seventh-century BC *kouros* carrying a ram, found on the acropolis. The courtyard contains some impressive sarcophagi and statuary.

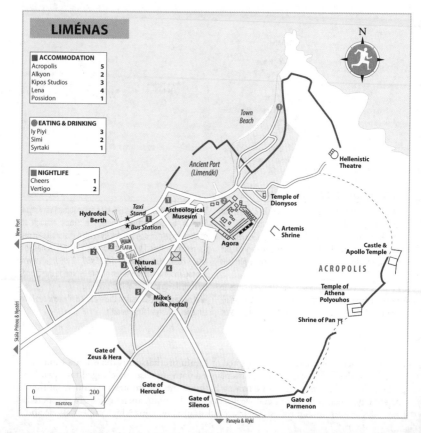

Other ancient remains

Free

From a **temple of Dionysos** behind the fishing port, a path curls up to a **Hellenistic theatre**, fabulously positioned above a broad sweep of sea. Sadly, it's only open for performances of the summer festival (see opposite). From just before the theatre, the trail winds on the right up to the **acropolis**, where a Venetian-Byzantine-Genoese fort arose between the thirteenth and fifteenth centuries, constructed from recycled masonry of an Apollo temple. You can continue, following the remains of a massive circuit of fifth-century walls, to a high terrace supporting the foundations of the **Athena Polyouhos** (Athena Patroness of the City) temple, with Cyclopean walls.

From the temple's southern end, a short path leads to a cavity in the rock outcrop that was a **shrine of Pan**, shown in faint relief playing his pipes. Following the path to the left around the summit brings you to a precipitous rock-hewn stairway with a metal handrail, which provided a discreet escape route to the **Gate of Parmenon**, the only gate in the fortifications to have retained its lintel. From here a track, then a paved lane, descend through the southerly neighbourhoods of the modern town, completing a satisfying one-hour circuit.

6

ARRIVAL AND INFORMATION

LIMÉNAS

By bus Buses arrive and leave from the KTEL office on the front, opposite the hydrofoil berth.

By ferry Ferries from Keramotí dock towards the west end of the seafront at the New Port. Hydrofoils dock much more centrally.

By taxi The taxi rank is just in front of the bus stop.

By bike Bikes can be rented from Mike's (☎ 25930 71820), opposite the *Acropolis* hotel. Car rental is also available (see p.413).

Services There is no official tourist office. Thassos Tours (☎ 25930 22546, ⊛ thassostours.gr) provide various services. Several banks have ATMs.

ACCOMMODATION

Acropolis ☎ 25930 22488, ⊛ acropolis-hotel.com. Occupying a fine traditional house with flagstone floors, comfortable rooms decorated in traditional style and a rear garden-bar but subject to traffic noise. **€40**

Alkyon ☎ 25930 22148. Certainly the most pleasant harbour hotel with cosy rooms; voluble management make it a home away from home for independent British travellers. Breakfast, with English tea, included. **€40**

Kipos Studios ☎ 25930 22469, ⊛ kipos.gr. In a quiet cul-de-sac next to *Iy Piyi* taverna, this has cool lower-ground-floor doubles and four-person galleried

apartments, plus a small pool in the garden. Late May–Sept. **€30**

★ **Lena** ☎ 25930 22933, ✉ hotel_lena@hotmail .com. The best-value budget hotel in town, with compact but clean and comfy rooms; run by a welcoming Greek-American family and young British in-law. May–Oct. **€30**

Possidon ☎ 25930 22690, ⊛ thassos-possidon .com. Unattractive concrete block on the seafront with a spacious lobby café and nicely refurbished rooms. The only place absolutely guaranteed to be open all year. **€50**

EATING AND DRINKING

Iy Piyi ☎ 25930 22941. At the south corner of the main square, this classic *estiatório* has a small terrace and is a dependable favourite for meaty *mayireftá* at only €6–7. April–Oct daily 6.30pm–midnight.

Simi ☎ 25930 22517. Reliable taverna behind the ancient port, offering a full menu of fish, meat and mezédhes, along with memorably good wine. Daily

11am–2am.

★ **Syrtaki** ☎ 695 53 04 897. At the far eastern end of the town beach, this just edges *Simi* as the town's most accomplished taverna, dishing up some fine seafood, an imaginative selection of dips and salads, plus the usual grills and fine barrelled wine. Daily 10am–1am.

NIGHTLIFE

★ **Cheers** ☎ 25930 22689. Behind the ancient port, this friendly Brit-run café-bar is open for cooked breakfasts and all the way through to late-night beers or cocktails. Decent music and football on TV too. Daily 8.30am–late.

Vertigo Popular with trendy young Greeks and assorted tourists alike for its rocking ambience, with touches of techno and more dancy vibes as the evening draws on. Plenty of shots downed every night. Daily 10am–4am.

The east coast

The busy **east coast** between Liménas and Alykí, occupying roughly a third of the clockwise circuit of the island – the logical way to conduct an island tour if you want to maximize the sun's presence on the beaches – contains many of the more attractive coves and best alternative bases to the capital.

Panayía

6

The first place worthy of a halt southeast from Liménas is **PANAYÍA**, the attractive hillside village overlooking Potamiá Bay. It's a large, thriving place where life revolves around the central square with its huge plane trees, fountain and slate-roofed houses. Up above the village towers the island's highest peak, **Mount Ypsárion**.

Potamiá

POTAMIÁ, much lower than Panayía in the river valley, is far less prepossessing – with modern red tiles instead of slates on the roofs – though it has a lively winter carnival. It also offers the modest **Polygnotos Vayis Museum** (May–Oct daily 10am–1pm & 6–8pm; €2), devoted to the locally born sculptor; though Vayis emigrated to America when young, he bequeathed most of his works to the Greek state.

Skála Potamiás

The road from Potamiá towards the coast is lined with rooms for rent and apartment-type accommodation. A side road some 12km from Liménas takes you down to **SKÁLA POTAMIÁS**, at the southern end of the bay. From the harbourfront a road off to the left brings you to sand dunes extending all the way to the far northern end of the bay.

Khryssí Ammoudhiá

Water taxis ply between Liménas and Khryssí Ammoudhiá twice daily in summer (10am & 4.30pm; €8)

The north end of Skála Potamiás beach, **Khryssí Ammoudhiá** – often anglicized to "**Golden Beach**" for the benefit of tourists – is quite built-up but edges the southern end in the quality of both sand and sea; it can also be approached by a direct road that spirals for 5km down from Panayía.

Kínyra and its beaches

The dispersed hamlet of **KÍNYRA**, some 24km south of Liménas, marks the start of the burnt zone which overlooks it, though recovery is under way. Although not having much to recommend it per se, Kínyra is convenient for the superior **beaches** of Loutroú (1km south) and partly nudist Paradise (3km along) – officially called Makrýammos Kinýron – both of which can be reached down poorly signposted dirt tracks. The latter ranks as the most scenic of all Thassian beaches.

ACCOMMODATION, EATING AND DRINKING — THE EAST COAST

PANAYÍA

★ **Hotel Thassos Inn** ☎ 25930 61612, ⓦ thassosinn.gr. Up in the Tris Piyés district near the Kímisis church, with fine views over the rooftops, this hotel's bright yellow walls mirror the colour of the mature carp in its fishpond. The rooms are fine and the terrace cafeteria very relaxing. April–Oct. €35

Iy Thea ☎ 25930 61265. Excellent *psistariá* at the southeast edge of town en route to Potamiá, with fine views from the terrace, where you can enjoy simple but succulent grills and aromatic local wine. Daily noon–midnight.

SKÁLA POTAMIÁS

Eric's ☎ 25930 61554, ⓦ erics.gr. On the main road 400m inland and so called after the owner who advertises his resemblance to footballer Eric Cantona widely. The rooms and studios are spotless, and there are Premiership matches on satellite TV and a swimming pool with bar. €45

Hera ☎ 25930 61467. Just inland from the far south end of the beach, this four-storey cream-coloured building contains neat rooms and larger studios, set behind a small, well-tended garden. June–Sept. €50

Theagenis ☎ 25930 61481. Popular local taverna by the fishing harbour, which serves some oven-baked meat and veg dishes, grilled meat and fish, plus decent wine. May–Oct daily 10am–midnight.

KHRYSSÍ AMMOUDHIÁ
Camping Golden Beach ☎ 25930 61472, ⓦ camping
-goldenbeach.gr. The only official campsite on this side of
the island has plenty of shaded pitches, clean baths and
laundry facilities and a minimarket. May to mid-Oct. Adult
plus tent **€8.40**
Enavlion ☎ 25930 58222, ⓦ enavlionhotel.com.
Cream-and-pastel-blue mock-Classical hotel on the
main road, somewhat resembling a wedding cake. Still,
the rooms are luxurious, with all mod cons. Breakfast
included. Late April–Sept. **€75**
Golden Sand ☎ 25930 61771, ⓦ hotel-goldensand.gr.
Backing onto the sand after which it is named, this mid-
sized resort hotel has smart rooms, most with sea-facing
balconies, and a café-bar. April–Oct. **€60**
Sotiris ☎ 25930 61478. Best of the tavernas dotted along
the beachfront, serving a large selection of mezédhes such as

crab salad and small cheese pies, plus more substantial
grilled fish and meat courses. May–Sept daily noon–1am.

KÍNYRA AND ITS BEACHES
Agorastos ☎ 25930 41225, ⓔ agorastoskinira
@yahoo.de. On the main road behind the village, this
colourful pension with a leafy terraced garden has cosy,
well-furnished rooms at very reasonable prices. April–
Oct. **€30**
Paradise Beach ☎ 25930 41248. Pleasant daytime
restaurant on the eponymous beach south of Kínyra,
serving filling breakfasts, good coffee and a full menu with
meat dishes (€8–12). May–Oct daily 8am–8pm.
Studios Niki ☎ 25930 25930, ⓦ studios-niki.gr.
Sparking white building just below the main road 3km
south of Kínyra, whose smart rooms have balconies
overlooking Paradise beach. May–Oct. **€35**

Southern Thássos

The south-facing coast of Thássos has the balance of the island's best beaches, starting
with the prettiest resort, in the shape of **Alykí**. In the southwest corner, by way of
contrast, **Limenária** is rather dull and functional, although its greater local population
means it has more authentic dining choices.

Alykí and around
ALYKÍ hamlet, 35km from Liménas and just below the main road, faces a perfect double
bay which almost pinches off a headland. Uniquely, it retains its original whitewashed,
slate-roofed architecture, since the presence of extensive antiquities here has led to a
ban on any modern construction. Those **ruins** include an ancient temple to an
unknown deity, and two exquisite early Christian basilicas out on the headland, with a
few columns re-erected.

Of the **beaches**, the sand-and-pebble west bay gets oversubscribed in peak
season, though you can always head off to the less crowded, rocky east cove, or
snorkel in the crystal-clear waters off the marble formations on the headland's far
side. Alternatively, head for secluded **Kékes** beach, in a pine grove 1km further
southwest.

Convent of Arhangélou Mihaïl
Open during daylight hours
Some 5km southwest of Alykí, the **convent of Arhangélou Mihaïl** clings spectacularly to
a cliff on the seaward side of the road. Though founded in the twelfth century above
the spot where a spring had gushed forth, the convent has been hideously renovated by
the nuns, resident here since 1974. A dependency of Filothéou on Mount Áthos, its
prize relic is a purported nail from the Crucifixion.

Potós and around
Just 1km west of the island's southern tip is a good but crowded beach, **Psilí Ámmos**,
with watersports on offer. A few kilometres further, **POTÓS** is the island's prime
German-speaking package venue, its centre claustrophobically dense, with the few
non-block-booked rooms overlooking cramped alleys. Although the kilometre-long
beach is decent enough, there is little to warrant lingering here. **Pefkári**, with its
manicured beach and namesake pine grove, 1km west, is essentially an annexe of Potós,
with a few mid-range places to stay and better eating options.

Limenária and around

LIMENÁRIA, the island's second town, was built to house German mining executives brought in by the Ottomans between 1890 and 1905. Their remaining mansions, scattered on the slopes above the harbour, lend some character, but despite attempts at embellishing the waterfront, it's not the most attractive place on Thássos.

The nearest good beach is **Trypití**, a couple of kilometres west – turn left into the pines at the start of a curve right. The broad, 800m-long strand is rather marred by the massed ranks of umbrellas and sun loungers for rent. The cleft to which the name refers (literally "pierced" in Greek) is a slender tunnel through the headland at the west end of the beach, leading to a tiny three-boat anchorage.

6

ACCOMMODATION, EATING AND DRINKING   SOUTHERN THÁSSOS

ALYKÍ AND AROUND

Beautiful Alice ☎ 25930 31574. The oldest taverna in the village, with a lovely terrace, where you can choose from a bewildering array of reasonably priced seafood and fish, including sardines cooked in four different ways. May–Oct daily 11am–1am.

Skidhia ☎ 25930 31528, ⓦ kekesbeach.gr. On Kékes beach, 3km south, this traditional seaside taverna, which serves good seafood and grills, has a set of simple but adequate bungalow-style rooms. May–Sept. **€35**

POTÓS AND AROUND

Camping Pefkari Beach Pefkári ☎ 25930 51190, ⓦ camping-pefkari.gr. With its attractive wooded location and clean facilities, this is undoubtedly the best campsite on Thássos. June–Sept. Adult plus tent **€8.80**

Thassos Pefkári ☎ 25930 51596, ⓦ hotel-thassos.gr. Accomplished resort hotel just behind the beach with refreshingly colourful and contemporary decor, from its spacious lobby to the well-appointed rooms. Pool, tennis and watersports available too. Breakfast included. **€65**

LIMENÁRIA AND AROUND

Mouragio ☎ 25930 51178. The most authentic of the main seafront tavernas, serving a mixture of tasty oven-baked items and grilled meat or fish, while its Street Café behind is a colourful hangout. Mid-April to mid-Oct daily noon–1am.

Must ☎ 25930 34795. Hip new bar with imaginative decorations and a surprisingly cutting-edge line in both rock and dance sounds, plus the usual battery of beers and spirits. May–Sept daily noon–late.

Sgouridis ☎ 25930 51241, ⓦ hotelsgouridis.gr. Set one block back from the seafront, this refurbished hotel, with vines creeping up the exterior, has nicely furnished if rather cramped rooms. April to mid-Oct. **€40**

★ **To Limani ☎** 25930 52790. This old-style *tsipourádhiko* is the preferred gathering place for the savvy locals, who accompany the fiery spirit from the mainland with freshly caught fish from the adjacent sea. Daily 11am–midnight.

The west coast

The western coast, between Limenária and Liménas, is Thrassós's most exposed and scenically least impressive, and the various *skáles* (harbours) such as Skála Kaliráhis and Skála Sotíros – originally the ports for namesake inland villages – are bleak, straggly and windy. **SKÁLA MARIÓN**, 13km from Limenária, is the exception: an attractive little bay, with fishing boats hauled up on the sandy foreshore, and the admittedly modern low-rise village arrayed in a U-shape all around. There are, most importantly, two fine beaches on either side.

SKÁLA PRÍNOU has little to recommend it, other than ferry connections to Kavála. **SKÁLA RAHONÍOU**, between here and Liménas, has a smattering of facilities, as well as proximity to **Pahýs beach**, 9km short of Liménas, by far the best strand on the northwest coast. Narrow dirt tracks lead past various tavernas through surviving pines to the sand, partly shaded in the morning.

ACCOMMODATION AND EATING   THE WEST COAST

Brian's Restaurant Skála Prínou ☎ 25930 71445. In a huge new building 500m east of the port, this all-round taverna does daily specials and a wide standard menu. It also hosts live music every Saturday night in season. May–

Sept daily 10am–1am.
Pefkospilia Pahýs beach, Skála Rahoníou ☎ 25930 81051. One of the oldest and most picturesque tavernas on the island, located on Pahýs beach. Great traditional cuisine

is served outside the tiny whitewashed building, almost hidden by firs, as the name ("Fir cave") suggests. May–Sept daily noon–1am.

Pension Dimitris Skála Maríon ☎ 694 45 05 064, ⓦ pension-dimitris.gr. Perched on a hilltop behind the port, this attractively designed modern building offers smart rooms, a communal kitchen and optional breakfast for a small extra charge. May to mid-Oct. €40

Ploumis Skála Rahoníou ☎ 25930 81442. Right on the main beach, this café-taverna provides everything from breakfast through light snacks to full-blown meals of freshly grilled fish, seafood and meat. Good for sunsets especially. May to mid-Oct daily 9am–midnight.

The interior

Few people get around to exploring inland Thássos – with the post-fire scrub still struggling to revive, it's not always rewarding – but there are several worthwhile excursions to or around the **hill villages**, which, as usual, portray a very different lifestyle to the coastal resorts.

Theológos

THEOLÓGOS, 10km along a well-surfaced but poorly signposted road from Potós, was founded in the sixteenth century by refugees from Constantinople and became the island's capital under the Ottomans. Its houses, most with oversized chimneys and slate roofs, straggle in long tiers to either side of the main street, surrounded by generous kitchen gardens or walled courtyards. A stroll along the single high street, with its couple of *kafenía*, a soldiers' bar, a sandalmaker and traditional bakery, is rewarding.

Kástro

KÁSTRO is the most naturally protected of the island's anti-pirate redoubts: thirty ancient houses and a church surround a rocky pinnacle, fortified by the Byzantines and the Genoese, which has a sheer drop on three sides. Summer occupation by shepherds is becoming the norm after total abandonment in the nineteenth century, when mining jobs at Limenária proved irresistible. Despite its proximity to Theológos as the crow flies, there's no straightforward route to it; especially with a car, it's best to descend to Potós before heading up a rough, 17km dirt track from Limenária.

Sotíras

SOTÍRAS, a steep 3.5km up from Skála Sotíros, is the only interior village with an unobstructed view of sunset over the Aegean, and is thus popular with foreigners, who've bought up about half of the houses for restoration. On the ridge opposite are exploratory shafts left by the miners, whose ruined lodge looms above the church.

The Kazavíti villages

From Prínos (Kalýves) on the coast road, it's a 6km journey inland to the **Kazavíti villages**, which are shrouded in greenery that escaped the fires; they're (poorly) signposted and mapped officially as Megálo and Mikró Prínos but still universally known by their Ottoman name. **MIKRÓ KAZAVÍTI** marks the start of the track for **MEGÁLO KAZAVÍTI**, where the magnificent platía is one of the prettiest spots on the whole island.

EATING AND DRINKING	THE INTERIOR
★ **Kleoniki/Tou Iatrou** Theológos ☎ 25930 31000. In the village centre, this excellent traditional taverna is at its best in the evening when the roasting spits, loaded with goat and suckling pig, start turning. Great barrelled wine too. Daily noon–1am.	★ **Opos Palia** Sotíras ☎ 697 96 35 703. Wonderfully re-created old-style village *mezedhopolío* on the plane-shaded square below the old fountain, serving original recipes for dishes such as octopus in tomato sauce, *strapatsádha* and *bekri mezé*. Daily noon–midnight, except occasional winter closing.

The Sporades and Évvia

422 Skiáthos
429 Skópelos
434 Alónissos
439 Skýros
445 Évvia

VIEW FROM ALÓNISSOS

The Sporades and Évvia

The Sporades lie close off Greece's eastern coast, their hilly terrain betraying their status as extensions of Mount Pílio, right opposite on the mainland. The three northern islands, Skiáthos, Skópelos and Alónissos, are archetypal Aegean holiday venues, with wonderful beaches, lush vegetation and transparent sea; they're all packed out in midsummer and close down almost entirely from October to April. Skýros, the fourth inhabited member of the group, lies well southeast, and is much more closely connected – both physically and historically – to Évvia than to its fellow Sporades. These two have less obvious attractions, and far fewer visitors.

Skiáthos, thanks to its international airport and extraordinary number of sandy beaches, is the busiest of the islands, though **Skópelos**, with its *Mamma Mia!* connections, extensive pine forests and idyllic pebble bays, is catching up fast. **Alónissos**, much quieter, more remote and less developed, lies at the heart of a National Marine Park, attracting more nature-lovers than night owls. Traditional **Skýros** sees fewer foreign visitors, partly because it's much harder to reach, though plenty of domestic tourism means no shortage of facilities. Between Skýros and the mainland, **Évvia** (classical Euboea) extends for nearly 200km alongside central Greece. Although in spots one of the most dramatic of Greek islands, with forested mountains and rugged stretches of little-developed coast, its sheer size and proximity to the mainland means that it rarely has much of an island feel; mainlanders have holiday homes around numerous seaside resorts, but foreigners are very thin on the ground.

An indented coastline full of bays and coves to moor in, relatively steady winds and the clear waters of the National Marine Park, also make the northern Sporades, rightly, a magnet for **yacht flotillas** and charters. Many companies have bases in Skiáthos, in particular.

GETTING THERE

By plane The airports on Skiáthos and at Vólos on the nearby mainland (see p.74) receive regular international charters as well as scheduled domestic flights. Skýros has a domestic airport, but only about three flights a week from Athens and Thessaloníki.

By ferry Frequent ferries and hydrofoils run from Vólos (p.74) and Áyios Konstandínos (p.69) to Skiáthos, Skópelos and Alónissos. Skýros is accessed from the port of Kými on

THE SPORADES AND ÉVVIA

Évvia (p.448), where ferries connect with buses from Athens. Two or three times a week in midsummer, this same ferry runs between Kými and Alónissos and Skópelos. For Évvia, local ferries shuttle from various strategic points on the mainland.

By bus and train Évvia is joined to central Greece by two bridges. Buses from Athens run to various points on the island, and there are trains to the island capital, Halkídha.

Skiáthos

Undulating green countryside, some fine rural monasteries and a labyrinthine old town notwithstanding, the real business of **Skiáthos** is **beaches**: by far the best, if also the most oversubscribed, in the Sporades. There are over fifty strands (plus a few more on

Skiáthos's top ten beaches p.427
Walking on Skópelos p.433
Hiking on Alónissos p.436

The Mediterranean Monk seal p.439
Carnival on Skýros p.440
Skyrian horses p.444

SKÓPELOS TOWN

Highlights

❶ Lalá28ria beach, Skiáthos Glistening white pebbles and turquoise waters, backed by steep cliffs and a natural rock arch, form a photogenic contrast to the island's other, mostly sandy, bays. **See p.427**

❷ Skópelos Town Wooden shutters, ornate balconies, domed churches and atmospheric passageways make this one of the most alluring island towns in Greece. **See p.430**

❸ National Marine Park of Alónissos-Northern Sporades Spend a day – or longer – on a boat exploring the islets of this pristine reserve, with their wildlife, monasteries and secluded bays. **See p.439**

❹ Skýros An outrageously pagan carnival, a striking hillside Hóra and traditional interiors are all found on one of the least spoiled islands in the Aegean. **See p.439**

❺ Dhimosári Gorge, southern Évvia Traverse the wildest corner of the island on a mostly cobbled path descending from Mount Óhi. **See p.451**

❻ Límni, northern Évvia A proud port with beautiful horizons to the west and clean pebble beaches either side. **See p.451**

HIGHLIGHTS ARE MARKED ON THE MAP ON P.424

satellite islets), most with fine, pale sand, though still barely enough room for the legions of visitors; Italians and Greeks in summer, Brits and Scandinavians in spring and autumn. The main road along the south and southeast coasts serves an almost unbroken line of villas, hotels, minimarkets and restaurants; although they've not impinged much on Skiáthos's natural beauty, they make it difficult to find anything particularly Greek here. But by **hiking** or using a **4WD vehicle**, you can find relative solitude, refreshing vistas and charming medieval monuments in the island's north.

ARRIVAL AND DEPARTURE SKIÁTHOS

By plane As well as international charters, there are regular Olympic flights to Athens (April–Oct 1 daily, otherwise 2 weekly; 45min; ⓦ olympicair.com). Skiáthos airport is a tourist attraction in itself; built on reclaimed

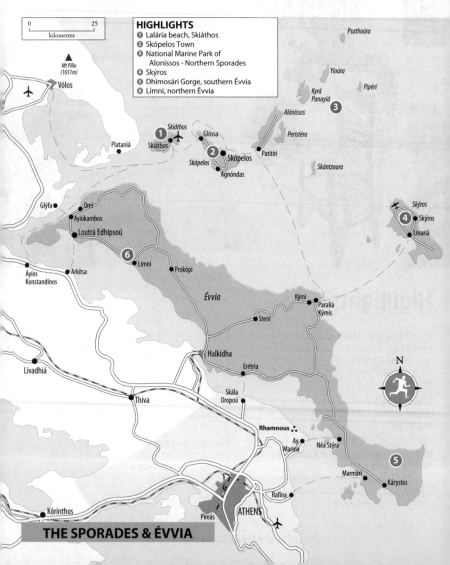

HIGHLIGHTS
1. Lalária beach, Skiáthos
2. Skópelos Town
3. National Marine Park of Alonissos - Northern Sporades
4. Skýros
5. Dhimosári Gorge, southern Évvia
6. Límni, northern Évvia

THE SPORADES & ÉVVIA

land immediately outside Skiáthos Town, it has an extremely short runway, and planes come in incredibly low over the harbour. On Friday, the busiest day for charters, hundreds of people gather by the road at the end of the runway where landing planes pass just a few metres overhead, and the jet blast from those taking off can knock you over; check it out on YouTube.

By ferry Hellenic Seaways (Ⓦhsw.gr) flying dolphins and ferries run twice daily for most of the year – more in mid-summer – to and from Vólos (1hr 30min–2hr 30min), Skópelos (50min–1hr) and Alónissos (1hr 25min–1hr 45min). Flying dolphins and, in summer, a ferry (NEL Lines; Ⓦnel.gr) also connect Skiáthos daily with Áyios Konstandínos (1hr 35min–2hr 45min), and with Skópelos and Alónissos. On Fridays especially it is worth booking in advance; Friday mornings into Skiáthos and evening departures to the islands are frequently full.

Tickets and agencies There are ticket booths on the dock at busy times; otherwise the Hellenic Seaways agent (Ⓣ24270 22209) is directly opposite the jetty at the base of Papadhiamándi; NEL is handled by Panos Andritsopoulos (Ⓣ24270 22018), 100m round the new harbour to the right.

INFORMATION

Services In Skiáthos Town, the National Bank is on Papadhiamándi, and there are numerous others nearby and around the harbour, many with ATMs. The post office is also on Papadhiamándi. Many cafés and bars have wi-fi; i-Net internet café, on the first floor overlooking the new harbour opposite the taxi stand, has plenty of terminals and fast connections.

Useful website Ⓦskiathos.gr has extensive accommodation listings.

GETTING AROUND

By bus A superb bus service runs along Skiáthos's coast road, from town to Koukounariés at the western end of the island, daily from 7am to midnight, with departures every fifteen minutes for most of the day (€2); the entire run takes about thirty minutes most of the time, much longer in August when traffic is chaotic. In town the terminus is at the eastern (airport) end of the new port, with further stops on the ring road. There are 26 numbered stops in all, and these numbers are often used when giving directions to a beach or restaurant. In summer a small bus also runs up to Evangelistrías monastery (8 times daily in Aug, otherwise 4 daily; 15min), departing from the car park near the Health Centre at the top of the old town.

By taxi The main taxi rank (Ⓣ24270 24461) is at the new port just east of the ferry jetties.

By car or scooter Numerous rental outlets offering bicycles, motorbikes, cars and motorboats are based around the new port; Aegean Car Rental (Ⓣ24270 22430, Ⓦaegeancars.gr), virtually opposite the ferries, is recommended. Parking in town is impossible, except out past the yacht anchorage and at the southwest edge near the health centre.

By boat Dozens of boat trips are on offer, ranging from shuttles to various beaches (for example Kanapítsa roughly hourly all day; 15min; €2.50) to day-trips round the island (around €15 a head) or round Skópelos (€20). Most of these depart from the old port, but there are various interesting alternatives, on small sailing yachts for example, around the new harbour. The island tour is well worth doing – an excellent way to get your bearings and check out the beaches, including a few that can only be reached by boat.

Skiáthos Town

SKIÁTHOS TOWN, the only real population centre on the island, is set on a couple of low hills around a point, with the ferry harbour and new town to the east, the picturesque old port, with the old town rising above it, in the west. You can easily get lost among the maze-like backstreets and shady platíes of the old town, but heading downhill will swiftly bring you back, either to the water or the flatter new town, where the main drag, Alexándhrou Papadhiamándi, runs directly inland from the ferry jetties.

Alexándros Papadiamántis Museum

Just off Alexándhrou Papadhiamándi • Daily 9.30am–1.30pm & 5–7.30pm • €1.50

There are few specific sights in Skiáthos, though the **Alexándros Papadiamántis Museum**, housed in the nineteenth-century home of one of Greece's best-known writers, is worth a look. The upper storey – basically two tiny rooms – has been maintained as it was when the writer lived (and died) here, plainly enjoying a remarkably ascetic lifestyle. The ground floor operates as a bookshop-cum-exhibition area.

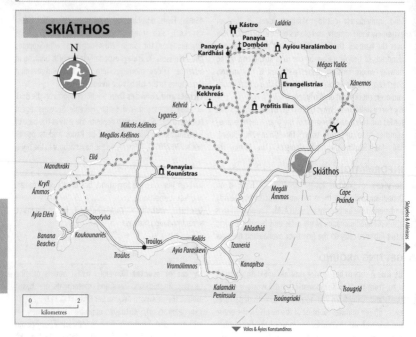

The Boúrtzi

The peninsula that separates the two harbours, the **Boúrtzi**, makes for an enjoyable stroll. Surrounded by crumbling defences and a few rusty cannon – there was a castle in this obvious defensive position from at least the thirteenth century – it is today a peaceful setting for occasional exhibitions, a café with great views, and an open-air municipal theatre, with regular summertime music and drama performances.

The rest of the island

Skiáthos's south coast is lined with beach after beach after beach, almost all of them easily accessible on the bus. If you want to explore the mountainous area north of town, though, or get to the north-coast beaches, you'll need to have your own transport or be prepared for some very hot hiking. Be warned that a moped simply won't make it up some of the exceptionally steep tracks, especially around Kástro. Thanks to the humid climate and springs fed from the mainland, the interior is exceptionally green, thick with pine, lentisc, holm oak, heather and arbutus even where (as is all too common) it has been ravaged by forest fires over the years. There are plenty of villas and tourist facilities on the coast and chapels and farms in the interior, but only **Troúlos** (with another excellent beach) really counts as a village, and even that a tiny one.

Evangelistrías monastery

Monastery Daily 10am–sunset · Free **Museum** 10am–2pm · €2

From town, you can drive up to eighteenth-century **Evangelistrías monastery** in ten minutes, or walk it in just over an hour; the path takes various short-cuts from the road, mostly well signed, starting out from the ring road close to bus stop 2. A beautiful and much revered spot and the scene of major pilgrimages at Easter and on August 15, it was here that the modern Greek flag was first unfurled in 1807. Inside it's alive with the

OPPOSITE KOUKOUNARIÉS BEACH (SEE OPPOSITE) >

SKIÁTHOS'S TOP TEN BEACHES

Although almost all the island's beaches are sandy, some of them are very narrow. On the south coast every one will have loungers and at least one bar or taverna, often pumping out loud music; most have watersports too. If you want to get away from it all, the harder to reach sands on the north coast offer more chance of escape. These (listed clockwise from town) are our favourites:

Tsougriá An islet in the bay opposite Skiáthos Town, with excursion boats shuttling back and forth from the old port three or four times daily. A favourite of locals, it has two spectacular sand beaches, each with a taverna.

Vromólimnos The prettiest of the beaches on the Kalamáki peninsula, fine-sand Vromólimnos is a bit of a walk from bus stop 13, and hence a little quieter than many south-coast sands – it still has several cafés from which to enjoy the sunset views, though, and a busy water-ski operation.

Koukounariés Huge stretch of sand – at the end of the bus route – which is arguably the island's finest beach, and certainly one of its busiest. Wooden walkways traverse the sand to a series of *kantínas*, there's a harbour for excursion boats and every imaginable form of watersport including snorkelling and diving with Skiathos Diving, one of the island's best outfits (☎697 70 81 444, ⓦskiathosdiving.gr). Behind the beach a small salt lake, Strofyliá, sits in the midst of a grove of pine trees – all of it a protected reserve. There's horseriding, too, in the forested dunes to the north, with Skiathos Riding Centre (☎24270 49548, ⓦskiathos-horse-riding.gr).

Big Banana Reached by a short track over the headland from bus stop 26 at Koukounariés, Big Banana is announced before you arrive by the thumping bass tracks from three competing beach bars. It's beautifully sandy but absolutely packed, with a young crowd and a clubbing atmosphere, plus ski boats, kayaks, pedaloes and more.

Small Banana In the next cove beyond Big Banana, this beach is almost entirely nudist yet still thoroughly commercialized, with a café and loungers occupying almost every centimetre. Like its neighbour, it is named not for the appendages on display but for its perfect yellow crescent of sand.

Ayía Eléni About 600m from bus stop 25 in Koukounariés, Ayía Eléni is a stunning, broad, sandy beach looking west towards the mountainous mainland. It is bigger and more family-oriented than the neighbouring Banana beaches, with a couple of beach bars and pedaloes and kayaks to rent.

Mandhráki Dunes and a protected pine forest back Mandhráki, a sandy beach with views of Mount Pílio and an exceptionally friendly snack bar serving *souvláki*, salads and omelettes. One of the island's least developed, it is accessed either by a walking path from bus stop 23 in Koukounariés, or a driveable track that follows the coast round past Ayía Eléni beach.

Megálos Asélinos From Troúlos village, a side-road leads 3.5km north through a lush valley to Megálos Asélinos, a large and exposed beach of gritty sand. There's a big taverna where many excursion boats stop for lunch, but it's a lovely, unspoilt spot at the end of the day when they've all headed home.

Kástro A small cove set steeply below Kástro (see p.428), Kástro can be very crowded in the middle of the day when the tour boats arrive, but is delightful early or late – though it loses the sun early. There's a wonderfully ramshackle snack bar with a shower of cold river water.

Lalária Famous beach nestling near the northernmost point of Skiáthos, and only accessible by taxi- or excursion-boat from town. With steep cliffs rising behind a white-pebble shore and an artistic natural arch, it's undeniably beautiful; three sea-grottoes just east rate a stop on most round-the-island trips.

7

sound of caged songbirds, there's a shop selling local wine and preserves, and an eclectic **museum** comprising ecclesiastical and rural-folklore galleries plus a vast collection of documents, posters and photos from the independence struggle and Balkan wars.

Below the monastery, another signed **path** leads north, past restored **Ayíou Haralámbou** monastery, full of cats and chickens kept by the caretaker, and on past **Panayía Dombón** chapel and then to **Panayía Kardhási** on the way to Kástro (see below).

Kástro

Daily sunrise–sunset • Free

Kástro, occupying a windswept headland at the northernmost tip of Skiáthos, was the island's main population centre throughout the Middle Ages. The fortified settlement, established for security from pirate raids, thrived under Byzantine, Venetian and Turkish control until its abandonment around 1830, when the new Greek state stamped hard on piracy and the population left to build the modern capital. Most of the buildings were dismantled and the materials reused elsewhere, so all that's left now are the remains of the defences, half a dozen churches (there were once 20) and a mosque. You enter the rocky outcrop across a narrow, stone ridge – a superb natural defence once enhanced by walls and a drawbridge; inside, the remains are beautifully maintained and well signed, with tables where you can picnic and fresh spring water.

If you come by boat you're unlikely to escape the crowds; driving or walking involves an exceptionally steep, narrow cobbled track, but does give the chance to arrive early or late, and perhaps get the place to yourself.

ACCOMMODATION   SKIÁTHOS

Much of the accommodation on Skiáthos, especially villas and places out of town with pools, is block-booked by package companies. You may find it easier to check the island's website (see p.425) or go through a local agent such as Dolphin of Skiathos (☎ 24270 29910, ⓦ dolphin-skiathos.gr). There are also two local room-owners' association kiosks on the quayside (☎ 24270 22990 or 21488), operating long hours in high season. Everywhere is heavily booked in August; at other times, rates dip by as much as half.

SKIÁTHOS TOWN

Bourtzi Moraḯtou 8 ☎ 24270 21304, ⓦ hotelbourtzi.gr. Boutique hotel just off Papadhiamándi with designer decor and a courtyard pool; rooms boast marble floors, flat-screen TVs and all mod-cons. Impressive, though the atmosphere is more business than island. **€170**

Meltemi New harbour ☎ 24270 22493, ⓦ meltemi skiathos.com. The waterfront position is unbeatable, and rooms at the front have great sea views. Simple, island-style rooms are a bit dated, but scrupulously clean and with an exceptionally friendly welcome. Wi-fi and a/c included, and breakfast is available in the snack-bar out front. **€90**

Pension Nikolas Evangelistrías ☎ 24270 23062, ⓦ nikolaspension.gr. Very central place, off Papadhiamándi close to the port, in two buildings facing each other across an internal courtyard, tucked away from the street so reasonably quiet. The simple rooms all have a/c, fridge and TV, with balconies overlooking the courtyard. **€70**

Thymi's Home ☎ 24270 22817, ⓦ thymishome.gr. Modern studio complex in the heart of town (signed off Papadhiamándi) with classy modern decor and every facility including wi-fi, flat-screen TVs, quiet a/c, internal balcony and tiny kitchenette. Some rooms are pretty small, and the pool is tiny. **€80**

KOUKOUNARIÉS

Mandraki Village ☎ 24270 49301, ⓦ mandraki -skiathos.gr. Delightful garden complex near the lake, at bus stop 23, with tasteful, modern pastel-coloured rooms, family quads and junior suites (worth the small price difference), all very well equipped, spacious grounds and pool. **€140**

EATING AND DRINKING

By Greek standards – just about any standards in fact – eating in Skiáthos is expensive. The best places also get very busy so, unusually, booking is often advisable.

SKIÁTHOS TOWN

★ **Alexandhros** ☎ 24270 22431. Traditional Greek restaurant in the old-town backstreets; signposted from Platía Trión Ierarhón but still hard to find, in an alley behind restaurant *1901*. Packed every night thanks to some of the lowest prices in town, with live Greek music most nights; service can suffer from the crowds, and book or be prepared to wait. Daily, evenings only.

★ **Amfiliki** ☎ 24270 22839. This restaurant sits opposite the health centre, high on the west side of the old town. Walk through the house and past the kitchen to find a gorgeous terrace, high above the sea. All the standard taverna recipes, skilfully prepared – and excellent seafood dishes like *seláhi* (skate), parsley and onion salad, or *bráska kípo*, monkfish covered in spicy tomato sauce. Just forty seats overlooking the sea, so book to be sure of the view (or come for breakfast). They also have some very simple rooms to rent. Daily all day. Rooms **€80**

Bakaliko ☎ 24270 24024. Probably the best of the restaurants here in a strip (the coast road beyond the new harbour) more known for nightlife, with mock decor of a traditional Greek grocer's, unimprovable seating on a deck cantilevered over the water and decently priced, Turkish-influenced food (*yogurtlu* kebab at €9.50, for example); live acoustic Greek music some nights. Daily, evenings only.

Maria's ☎ 24270 22292. Enjoy excellent pizza, pasta and creative salads at this restaurant behind Trís lereárhes church, up the steps from the old port. Check out the riotously eclectic decor inside, though in summer you'll prefer to sit out on the balcony, or down in the courtyard, and menus handwritten in old accounting books. The downside is price; simple pasta and pizza

dishes start from around €12, though portions are large. Daily, dinner only.

Mesoyia ☎ 24270 21440. Cheap-and-cheerful outfit (though still around €40 for two, with house wine) in the old-town backstreets featuring the usual grilled and *mayireftá* suspects, plus daily changing seafood, such as prawn *yiouvétsi*. Tables in the lane in summer (they can usually squeeze in one more when busy); indoors during the cooler months. Daily, evenings only.

PROFÍTIS ILÍAS

Platanos ☎ 693 24 13 539. Close to the island's highest point, about 4km from town, *Platanos* has fabulous views over town and towards Skópelos and Évvia. The food is almost beside the point, but there's a decent taverna menu, plus breakfast, omelettes, sandwiches or simply coffee and baklává; it's wise to book if you want a decent view in the evening. Daily 10.30am–11pm.

KOLIÓS

Infinity Blue Koliós Bay ☎ 24270 49750. Hop off at bus stop 15 to get to *Infinity Blue*, with its lovely vistas from a romantic, hillside setting. The restaurant has a Greek/Mediterranean menu and a more refined ambience than most, with proper linen and wine glasses. Fine steaks (as they should be for around €23), pasta and risotto, plus Greek dishes standard and exotic (rabbit with plums) for €9 –14. Daily, evenings only.

NIGHTLIFE

There are plenty of bars and pubs on Papadhiamándi and the nearby old-town backstreets, but the coolest places are overlooking the old port or out on the "club strip" at the start of the coast road beyond the yacht marina. The summer open-air cinema, Attikon, is at the bottom of Papadhiamándi by the museum; it has been showing *Mamma Mia!* three or four times a week since the film's release.

BBC ☎ 695 72 62 167. Club strip venues seem to be annually changeable, and operate only in July and August, but *BBC* – on the coast road – is bigger and longer-lived than most: riotous crowd inside and a deck jutting out over the shallows to chill out. Seasonal; from 11pm.

Kentavros Mitropolítou Ananíou ☎ 24270 22980. An evergreen, much-loved rock, jazz and blues bar right in the

centre of town, just a few paces from the new harbour near the Papadiamántis Museum. Nightly 9.30pm–4am.

Rock'n'Roll Old Port ☎ 24270 22944. The busiest of four neighbouring, essentially identical bars on the steps leading up to Platía Trión Ierarhón, *Rock'n'Roll* has outdoor seating with sofas and scatter cushions; inside a DJ serves up mainstream rock, Latin and dance music. Nightly 7pm–4am.

Skópelos

SKÓPELOS is bigger and more rugged than Skiáthos and its concessions to tourism are lower-key and in better taste, despite a boom in recent years fuelled by the filming here of the *Mamma Mia!* film. Much of the countryside, especially the southwest coast, really is as spectacular as it appears in the film, with a series of pretty cove beaches backed by extensive pine forests as well as olive groves and orchards of plums (**prunes** are a local speciality), apricots, pears and almonds. **Skópelos Town (Hóra)** and **Glóssa**, the two main towns, are among the prettiest in the Sporades, their hillside houses distinguished by painted wooden trim and grey slate roofs.

ARRIVAL AND DEPARTURE

SKÓPELOS

By ferry Hellenic Seaways (w hsw.gr) flying dolphins and ferries run three times daily for most of the year – more in midsummer – to and from Alónissos (20–35min), and to Skiáthos (50min–1hr) and either Vólos (2hr 45min–3hr 45min) or Áyios Konstandínos (2hr 15min–4hr); some of these call at Loutráki, the port for Glóssa (and known as Glóssa on ferry and hydrofoil schedules), as well as Skópelos Town. In summer NEL Lines (w nel.gr) also have a ferry with daily connection to Alónissos, Skiáthos and Áyios Konstandínos, and Skyros Shipping (w sne.gr) go twice a

week to Alónissos and Kými on Évvia (3hr 20min). Connections to flights in Skiáthos can be very busy: try to book in advance.

Tickets and agencies There are ticket booths on the dock in Skópelos Town at busy times; otherwise the Hellenic Seaways agent (☎ 24270 22767) is directly opposite the harbour gate, and NEL and Skyros Shipping are handled by Lemonis Travel (☎ 24270 22363), by the National Bank, on the far side of the harbour close to the old port. The harbour agent in Loutráki is Triandafyllou (☎ 24240 33435).

INFORMATION

Services Several banks with ATMs are on the quayside in Skópelos Town; the post office is on Dhoulídhi, just off Platía Plátanos ("Souvláki Square"), which lies directly up from the ferry harbour. Cafés all along the front have wi-fi; Blue Sea, the very last place at the northern (old port) end of the harbour, is a large internet café.

Useful websites w skopelos.net, w skopelosweb.gr and w skopelos.com. There's no tourist office on the island.

Newspapers English-language newspapers are sold at a shop just off Souvláki Square.

GETTING AROUND

By bus Services run from Skópelos Town, across to the island's south coast, and then along the south and west coast past all the major beaches; in summer at least a dozen buses a day ply to Miliá – just over half of them continue as far as Glóssa. The bus stop is immediately to the left as you leave the ferry dock in Hóra.

By car and scooter There are numerous car and scooter rental outlets near the ferry dock in Hóra, around the corner of the coast road and the main road heading inland, and along this inland road; they include Magic (☎ 22420 23250, w skopeloscars.com) and Discovery (☎ 24240

23033, w skopelosweb.gr/discovery).

By taxi The central taxi stand is to the left as you leave the ferry dock in Hóra.

By bicycle Skópelos Cycling (☎ 22420 22398), based at Stáfylos beach, rents out mountain bikes.

Boat trips A huge variety of boat trips is on offer around the harbour, at prices ranging from around €10, for a return shuttle to Glystéri beach, to €30 for a trip to Alónissos; island circuits, many of them *Mamma Mia!* themed, go for around €20.

Skópelos Town

SKÓPELOS TOWN (Hóra) pours off a hill on the west flank of a wide, oval bay: a cascade of handsome mansions and slate-domed churches below the ruined Venetian **kástro**. Away

from the waterside commercial strip, the hóra is endearingly time-warped – indeed among the most unspoilt in the islands – with wonderfully idiosyncratic shops of a sort long vanished elsewhere, and vernacular domestic architecture unadulterated with tasteless monstrosities.

The folklore museum

June–Sept Mon–Sat 10am–2pm & 7–10pm • €3

The disorganized **folklore museum** musters a motley collection of weaving, embroidery and costumes; detailed panels explaining local customs and the religious calendar redeem it.

Old Skopelitian Mansion Museum

Tues–Sun 10am–2pm & 6–9pm • €3

The **Old Skopelitian Mansion Museum**, former home of the island's doctor – subsequently occupied by his three daughters, all spinsters and all doctors – was left to the town by the last surviving daughter and is displayed much as it was when they lived here. It's a comfortable, bourgeois home full of everyday items: furniture, clothing, books and ephemera.

ACCOMMODATION   SKÓPELOS TOWN

There are numerous rooms for rent in the backstreets, as well as entire houses, but in high season everything is very booked up. In mid-summer a Rooms Association office (☎ 24240 24567) opens in the lane leading up to Souvláki Square; a wider choice, including apartments and hotels across the island, can be arranged through helpful Madro Travel, by the old port (☎ 24240 22145, ⓦ madrotravel.com). August prices are roughly halved the rest of the year.

Adonis ☎ 24240 22231. Old-fashioned establishment above a taverna, whose central waterfront position (above the the the ferry quay, reached via Souvláki Square) means noise can be a problem. A couple of the simple wooden-floored, a/c rooms at the front have huge terraces. **€80**

Georgios L ☎ 24240 24625, ⓦ www.skopelos-hotels .gr. The last building at the northern end of the harbour, above the *Blue Sea* café, houses this small hotel with basic, old-fashioned, stone-floored rooms with a/c and TV; those at the front have great views. **€80**

Kir Sotos ☎ 24240 22549, ⓦ skopelos.net/sotos. Rambling old-house *pension*, set back from the middle of the harbour, behind the giant plane trees, whose wood-floored, a/c, en-suite rooms are justifiably a favourite budget option, though perhaps due for a revamp. Go for the quieter rear units, especially no. 4, with its fireplace; there's a communal kitchen and sunny courtyards. **€45**

Mylos ☎ 24240 24034, ⓦ skopelosweb.gr/milos. White-painted studios and apartments behind the kástro (all the way round the ring road, or a steep climb up from the harbour) with flagstone floors and mini kitchens. They enjoy great views towards Alónissos. **€45**

Skopelos Village ☎ 24240 22517, ⓦ skopelosvillage .gr. Pricey, self-catering complex, 600m east around the bay, with luxurious studios and suites set among landscaped grounds with two pools and a restaurant. The Seabreeze studios are worth the extra for their modern design and sleek bathrooms, though it's only good value if you get a good off-season deal. **€125**

★ **Thea Home** Ring road ☎ 24240 22859, ⓦ skopelosweb.gr/theahome. Lovely rooms and a family apartment with sweeping views from the top of the town; accommodation is cosy but very comfortable, with fridge and a/c. Bikes are available (free) and there's an excellent home-made breakfast (extra); new studios and a pool are being added. **€55**

EATING AND DRINKING

The seafront is lined with cafés and tavernas, the best of which are up at the old port end; for something rather more modest, aptly nick-named Souvláki Square is packed with decent fast-food outfits.

Englezos Harbour ☎ 24240 22230. Greek food with a slight edge, served with a view towards the old port end of the harbour. There are plenty of straightforward dishes and great, spit-roasted lamb, pork and chicken (around €10 a portion), but also some more inventive recipes such as aubergine (eggplant) millefeuille, feta with chili and tomato, or beetroot salad. Daily lunch & dinner.

Gorgones ☎ 24240 24709. Popular ouzerí in town (beside the well-signed *Oionos Blue Bar*), with tables in a stepped alley, garden courtyard and indoors. The usual meat and seafood at fair prices (prawn pasta €15, *soutsoukákia* €7), though occasionally erratic service. Daily lunch & dinner.

Klimataria Harbour ☎ 24240 22273. Good standard taverna, just a couple of doors from *Englezos*, with plenty of

local customers. Menu includes a good selection of fish by the kilo and local specialities like pork with plums; best to stick to the simpler dishes. Daily lunch & dinner.

Perivoli ☎ 24240 23758. A beautiful spot in the garden courtyard of an old house, up an alley just above Souvláki Square. The upmarket Greek/Mediterranean menu includes pasta and risotto as well as inventive Greek dishes like rolled pork with apple and plum in wine sauce (€11) or stuffed zucchini (€7.50) – plus a selection of wines by the glass. Evenings only, from 7.30pm.

★ **Ta Kymata (Angelos)** Old port ☎ 24240 22381. About the oldest taverna on Skópelos, a shrine of quality *mayireftá* such as *exohikó* (a local speciality of lamb and vegetables in a filo triangle) and *mezédhes* like fresh beets with their own greens. Daily lunch & dinner.

7

NIGHTLIFE

Anatoli Kástro ☎24240 22851. Veteran rembétika musician Yiorgos Xintaris performs at this tumbledown place on top of the kástro; music from late June to early Sept, when his sons (who accompany him) return from university in Athens. By day there's a café with incomparable views. Daily 10am–late.

Bardon Old Olive Factory ☎24240 24494. Vast lounge bar in this food-and-nightlife complex, occupying a restored industrial area directly opposite the harbour car park. Cocktails, dance music and occasional live bands. Daily 6pm–3am.

Merkourio (Mercurius) ☎24240 24593. Cool bar, just up from the ferry jetty between Souvláki Square and the Folklore Museum, with views over the harbour action. Cocktails are served on candle-lit terraces, to a soft-rock and Latin soundtrack; also open during the day for breakfast and coffee. Daily 10am–2am.

Oionos Blue Bar ☎694 24 06 136. Old-house bar, well signed inland from the centre of the harbour, with a jazz, blues and world-music playlist, plus a staggering variety of imported beers and whiskies. Daily 10am–2am.

Platanos Harbour ☎24240 23661. Evergreen bar on the northwest quay, just past *Englezos* restaurant, with jazz and world-music soundtrack. Great too for a morning coffee or breakfast and people-watching under the namesake plane tree outside. Daily 9am–3am.

South and west coast

Many of the island's best, and certainly the most accessible, **beaches** lie just off the main road and bus route, which heads south across the island from Hóra and then up the west coast.

Stáfylos

Barely 4km from Hóra, **Stáfylos** is the closest decent beach, though it gets very crowded in season. There's a noisy beach bar, so if it's peace you're after walk to the end of the beach and climb over the headland to larger, more scenic, sand-and-fine-gravel **Velanió**, with a summer-only *kantína* and a bit of a nudist scene.

Agnóndas and Limnonári

The beautiful bay of **AGNÓNDAS** has very much the feel of traditional old Greece, with yachts moored and a pretty fishing harbour where the water laps right up to the tables of several tavernas. There's not much of a beach, though, so for that follow the side road to **LIMNONÁRI**, about 1km west, 300m of white sand in a steep-sided bay.

Pánormos and around

PÁNORMOS is the biggest resort outside Skópelos Town, though still very understated and low-key. An extensive pebble beach lines the expansive bay, with plenty of tavernas (most offering free loungers for customers), shops and rooms. Adjoining **Blo** inlet is a beautiful, quiet anchorage, though there's no beach here.

The wide-open spaces of **Miliá**, immediately beyond Pánormos, comprise two 400m sweeps of grey sand and pebbles opposite Dhassía islet, divided by a headland with a sometimes obtrusively noisy beach bar at the south cove. Having found fame as the *Mamma Mia!* beach, **Kastáni**, almost adjacent to Miliá, has become very crowded, with a big beach bar pumping out dance music. Nonetheless it's a beautiful place, with fine sand and crystal-clear water. Beyond unattractive **Élios (Néo Klíma)**, isolated **Armenópetra** boasts two spectacular beaches either side of a point. There's no shade and no facilities, but great views of Glossá on the hillside above.

ACTIVITIES
SOUTH AND WEST COAST

Watersports In Pánormos you can rent motorboats (☎24240 24788, ⊚holidayislands.com/boathire) or kayaks (☎694 70 44 870) to explore the surrounding bays.

ACCOMMODATION AND EATING

Adrina Beach 1km north of Pánormos ☎24240 23371, ⊚adrina.gr. Beautiful, ivy-clad, four-star bungalow complex tumbling down a hillside to its own private beach. Wonderful sea views from the rooms and duplex

---

WALKING ON SKÓPELOS

Away from the main roads there's plenty of **walking** on Skópelos. Long-time resident Heather Parsons battles to maintain paths and leads spring/autumn walks along what remains (❶694 52 49 328, ⓦskopelos-walks.com), as well as publishing a hiking guide, *Skopelos Trails*. Among the better walks are those east of Skópelos Town, where three historic **monasteries**, Metamórfosis, Evangelistrías and Prodhrómou (all open approx 8am–1pm & 5–8pm daily), stand on the slopes of Mount Paloúki. Near Glóssa there's a beautiful 45-minute trail to the renovated village of **Palió Klíma**, via the island's oldest settlement, **Athéato** (Mahalás), slowly being restored by outsiders, and the foreign-owned hamlet of **Áyii Anáryiri**.

---

maisonettes, plus seawater pool and taverna. **€175**

Limnonari Beach Restaurant Limnonári ❶24240 23046, ⓦskopelos.net/limnonarirooms. An excellent taverna serving simple but delicious food, such as a rich goat *kokkinísto* and delicious local spiral *tyrópittes*. Above there are pleasant rooms, also simple and mostly with inland views. Open all day, breakfast to dinner. Rooms **€55**

★ **Mando** Stáfylos ❶24240 23917, ⓦwww.mando-skopelos.gr. Some of the best accommodation on the island, very friendly and quiet with stone-floored, a/c rooms (and a family suite) set among manicured lawns, with steps leading down to a private swimming platform. There are fridges and tea- and coffee-making equipment in the rooms, plus an outdoor communal kitchen area. **€80**

Milia Studios Miliá ❶24242 23998, ⓦskopelosweb .gr/milia. Studio complex with doubles and galleried quads; breakfast can be supplied to the rooms and there's a decent taverna nearby. Before the crowds arrive, you have your own private beach. **€70**

Panormos Beach Hotel Pánormos ❶24240 22711, ⓦpanormos-beach.com. Looking down over Pánormos from its hillside setting, *Panormos Beach Hotel* offers comfortable stone-floored, a/c rooms with fine views set amid a huge lawn studded with fruit trees. Breakfast included. **€80**

★ **Pavlos** Agnóndas ❶24240 22409. The most popular of the simple harbourside tavernas here, *Pavlos* is an unpretentious place with fair prices for fish and plenty of well-prepared Greek dishes (mains €7.50–9), plus decent house wine. They also have simple rooms (**€60**). Daily lunch & dinner.

Glóssa and around

Skópelos's second town, **GLÓSSA**, 26km from Hóra near the northwest tip of the island, is spectacularly arrayed in stepped, hillside tiers, high above the coast. A traditional, rural place where many of the vernacular houses have overhanging balconies and lush gardens, it is explored along narrow, steep, mostly car-free lanes (there's an unsigned car park behind the church on the main road), with breathtaking views around almost every corner. Apart from wandering the photogenic alleys and visiting the excellent tavernas, there's not a great deal to do here, and the only official accommodation in town is in rented houses (rarely available locally); there is a small **Folklore Museum** just above the main square, though (Tues, Wed & Fri–Sun 10am–2.30pm & 5.30–9pm, Thurs 10am–2.30pm; free).

LOUTRÁKI, some 3km steeply down a serpentine road from Glóssa (or on foot by a shorter, well-signed *kalderími*), is a pretty little place with views of Skiáthos. The port of the larger town, it has a line of cafés and tavernas around the dock, an archeological kiosk with information on local sites and island history, lots of **yachts** at anchor and a narrow pebble beach.

ACCOMMODATION AND EATING

★ **Agnanti** ❶24240 33606. Traditional taverna, well signposted in the centre of Glóssa, with upmarket takes on traditional recipes – pork with prunes or *hortokeftédhes* (vegetable croquettes) – served indoors and on a terrace with spectacular views. Only marginally pricier than average, and well worth it. Daily lunch & dinner.

Selenunda Hotel ❶24240 34073, ⓦhotelselenunda .com. High above the harbour at Loutráki, the peaceful

Selenunda has stunning views from every room. All the tile-floor rooms come with a/c, TV and kitchenette; also bigger family apartments. Steps lead down to the waterfront, but with luggage you may want to call to be picked up. **€80**

To Steki tou Mastora ❶24240 33563. Café-restaurant by the church on the main road in Glóssa, with wonderful views of Loutráki, Skiáthos and the mainland. It does a brisk trade in coffee and sandwiches as well as fabulous charcoal-grilled meats, including whole roast lamb or goat on the spit (daily in midsummer, weekends only off-season). Daily all day.

Northeast coast

The island's northeast coast is tricky to reach; just a few paved roads go there, from Skópelos to Glystéri, and from Glóssa to Perivolioú or Áyios Ioánnis Kastrí.

Perivolioú

A narrow, winding road through mature pine forest leads to beautiful little **Perivolioú** beach, some 7km from Glóssa close to the island's northern tip. There's ice-clear water and no development at all at this sandy cove, nor at nearby **Hondroyiórgis** beach, reached along a driveable track. Continue on this track, and you'll join the road down to Áyios Ioánnis Kastrí.

Áyios Ioánnis Kastrí

The tiny sand cove at **Áyios Ioánnis Kastrí** is one of the busiest on the island, thanks to its position at the base of the *Mamma Mia!* wedding chapel. Perched on a rock monolith (steps lead up), the chapel is almost ridiculously photogenic, and attracts tour boats from Skiáthos as well as an essential halt on the round-island trip. Late afternoon, when they've all left, is generally the quietest time; there's an excellent snack bar here, serving a mean Greek salad.

Glystéri

Less than 4km northwest of Skópelos Town, **Glystéri** is a small sand-and-pebble beach at the base of an almost completely enclosed bay. Plenty of people brave the narrow, steep road and many more arrive by boat – there's a regular shuttle from town – so it can get busy, especially at weekends when locals pack out the taverna here.

EATING AND DRINKING NORTHEAST COAST

Palio Karnayio Glystéri ☎ 694 43 54 705. Locals rate the taverna at Glystéri beach one of the island's best, while *Mamma Mia!* fans are drawn by the reconstructed arch from the film's *Villa Donna*, so on summer weekends it's extremely busy. Their speciality is blackfish or Alónissos tuna stifádo. Daily lunch & dinner.

Alónissos

ALÓNISSOS is the largest and only permanently inhabited member of a mini-archipelago at the east end of the Sporades. It's more rugged and wild than its neighbours, but no less green; pine forest, olive groves and fruit orchards cover the southern half, while a dense maquis of arbutus, heather, kermes oak and lentisc cloaks the north. In part thanks to its marine park status (see p.439), some of Greece's cleanest sea surrounds Alónissos – the **beaches** rarely match those of Skópelos or Skiáthos for sand or scenery, but the white pebbles on most of them further enhance the impression of gin-clear water. Remoteness and limited ferry connections mean that **Alónissos** attracts fewer visitors than its neighbours. There is, however, a significant British and Italian presence (the latter mostly in all-inclusive hotels), while Greeks descend in force all summer.

ARRIVAL AND DEPARTURE ALÓNISSOS

By ferry Hellenic Seaways (ⓦ hsw.gr) flying dolphins and ferries run three times daily for most of the year – more in midsummer – to and from Skópelos (20–30min), Skiáthos (1hr 25min–1hr 45min) and either Vólos (3hr 15min–4hr 30min) or Áyios Konstandínos (3hr–5hr). In summer NEL Lines (ⓦ nel.gr) also have a ferry with daily connection to Skópelos, Skiáthos and Áyios Konstandínos, and Skyros Shipping (ⓦ sne.gr) go twice a week to Skópelos and to Kými on Évvia (2hr 30min). Connections to flights in Skiáthos can be very busy: try to book in advance.

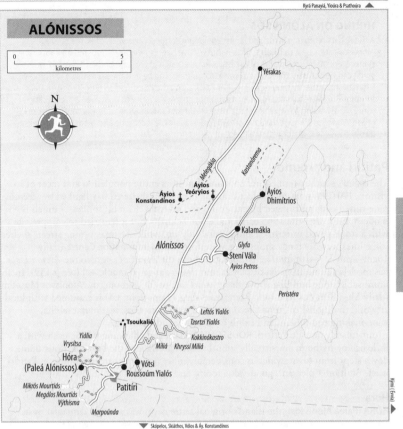

Kyrá Panayiá, Yioúra & Psathoúra

ALÓNISSOS

0 — 5
kilometres

N

Yérakas

Melegákia

Kastanórema

Áyios
Konstandínos

Áyios
Yeóryios

Áyios
Dhimítrios

Kalamákia

Alónissos

Glyfa
Steni Vála

Ayios Petros

Peristéra

Leftós Yialós
Tzortzí Yialós

Tsoukaliá

Kokkinókastro

Yiália
Vrysítsa

Miliá Khryssí Miliá

Hóra
(Paleá Alónissos)

Vótsi
Roussoúm Yialós

Mikrós Mourtiás
Megálos Mourtiás
Výthisma

Patitíri

Marpoúnda

Skópelos, Skiáthos, Vólos & Áy. Konstandínos

Kými (Évvia)

7

Operators and tickets The Hellenic Seaways agent is Alkyon Travel (☎ 24240 65220, ⓦ alkyon-travel.gr), under the *Alkyon Hotel* on the harbourfront at the bottom of the first (eastern) inland street; NEL is handled by Albedo Travel (☎ 24240 65804, ⓦ albedotravel.com), at the bottom of the second (western) inland street, and Skyros Shipping by Alonnisos Travel (☎ 24240 66000, ⓦ alonnisostravel.gr), between the two.

INFORMATION

Services There's a bank with an ATM on the eastern shopping street leading up from the harbour in Patitíri. The post office is also up here, while Play internet café is close to the post office.

Newspapers English-language newspapers are sold near the bottom of the western shopping street in Patitíri.

GETTING AROUND

By bus There are just two bus routes on Alónissos: from Patitíri up to Hóra (11 daily, including hourly from 7pm–midnight; €1.60) and to Steni Vála (3 daily; €1.70). In Patitíri the bus stop is on the harbour at the bottom of the eastern inland street.

By taxi The taxi stand in Patitíri is on the harbour opposite the bus stand.

By car and scooter There are numerous car and scooter rental outlets near the harbour, including Albedo Travel (see above) and others in the inland street immediately beyond it.

Boat trips and excursions Various boat trips are on offer around the harbour; the best marine park tours cost around €30 a head (including lunch and drinks), but check their itineraries as some don't go far in; walking (see p.436) and sea kayak excursions can be arranged through Albedo Travel.

> ## HIKING ON ALÓNISSOS
>
> Although its often harsh, rugged landscape might suggest otherwise, of all the Sporades Alónissos caters best to **hikers**. Fifteen routes have been surveyed, numbered and admirably signposted: many provide just short walks from a beach to a village or the main road, but some can be combined to make meaty circular treks. The best of these are trail #11 from Áyios Dhimítrios, up the Kastanórema and then back along the coast on #15 (2hr 30min), or trails #13 plus #12, Melegákia to Áyios Konstandínos and Áyios Yeóryios (just over 2hr, including some road-walking to return to start). Island resident Chris Browne's comprehensive walking guide, *Alonnisos Through the Souls of Your Feet*, is available locally; he also leads guided treks (☎ 697 91 62 443, ⊛ alonnisoswalks.co.uk).

Patitíri and around

The island's southeastern corner contains almost its entire population and most of its visitors. **PATITÍRI**, port and de facto capital, occupies a sheltered bay flanked by steep, pine-tufted cliffs and ringed by bars, cafés and tavernas. It's a bit soulless – much is modern, built after the 1965 earthquake (see below) – but it has tried to compensate with a stone-paved waterfront and general tidy-up, while the unassuming streets shelter some unexpectedly fancy shops. The waterfront **MOM Information Centre** (daily 10am–4pm & 6–10pm; free; ⊛ mom.gr), above the *Avra* café, next to the *Alkyon Hotel*, has models and multimedia displays about the endangered **monk seal** (see p.439). In an unmissable stone building above the western side of the harbour, the **Alonissos Museum** (daily May, Sept & Oct 11am–7pm, June–Aug 11am–9pm; €4) is crammed with local artwork, traditional costumes, reconstructed island interiors, war memorabilia, wine-making equipment, and exhibits on piracy and seafaring.

Immediately outside Patitíri, **ROUSSOÚM YIALÓS** and adjoining **VÓTSI**, each with a little fishing harbour, are virtually suburbs. You can walk to the beach at Roussoúm, down steps from town, which is considerably more pleasant than swimming in Patitíri itself. Both offer pleasant, good-value rooms and tavernas.

Hóra

HÓRA (Paleá Alónissos), the island's original settlement, was severely damaged by a Sporades-wide earthquake in March 1965, after which most of the reluctant population was compulsorily moved to Patitíri (see above); the issue was essentially forced in 1977 by the school's closure and cutting off of electricity. Outsiders later acquired the abandoned houses for a song and restored them in variable taste; only a few locals still live here, which gives the village a very twee, un-Greek atmosphere, abetted by multiple knick-knack and crafts shops. But it's stunningly picturesque, with great views as far as Mount Áthos in clear conditions. For much of the year, and indeed for much of most days, there are more hedgehogs than people about; the place only really comes to life – noisily so – on midsummer evenings. As an alternative to the bus ride, you can walk up on a well-preserved *kalderími* (45min uphill, 30min down), signposted off Patitíri's western inland street, almost at the edge of town.

Southern beaches

Numerous small cove beaches surround Alónissos's southern tip. Closest to Patitíri is **Výthisma** – less than 1km down a track off the road to **Marpoúnda** beach (monopolized by an all-inclusive Italian complex) and then a scramble down into the cove. Look out for the latest signs, as the paths down are regularly washed out. The grey sand-and-pebble beach is pretty, and part nudist, but without facilities or shade. **Megálos Mourtiás** is just a short swim further round, and there is a path which continues that way, but most people get here on the steep paved road from Hóra. With bright white pebbles and two tavernas, it's a complete contrast; crowded and noisy. **Mikrós Mourtiás**, just west, is served by a well-maintained footpath from Hóra (#1), or you can get most of the way down on a driveable dirt track. Another enclosed cove, it has graffiti proclaiming it a nudist beach – though in practice it doesn't seem to be. Immediately north of Hóra, visible tucked into their respective finger-like inlets, compact **Vrysítsa** and **Yiália** (with a picturesque windmill) both have more sand than pebbles, but no facilities.

ACCOMMODATION   PATITÍRI AND AROUND

Most Alónissos accommodation is in Patitíri or immediately around; you may be approached with offers as you disembark at the port. Albedo Travel (☎ 24240 65804, ⓦ albedotravel.com) handles hotels, studios and villas across the island, while the local room-owners' association booth (☎ 24240 66188, ⓦ alonissos-rooms.gr), on the waterfront, can also find you a room.

PATITÍRI

Nereides Hotel Paliohoráfina ☎ 24240 65643, ⓦ nereides.gr. Classy place high above the western edge of town, with stunning views, small pool and recently refurbished rooms, studios and family apartments, all with free wi-fi, flat-screen TVs, modern wooden furniture, and quality bathrooms. Very good deals out of season. Breakfast included. **€100**

Paradise Hotel ☎ 24240 65213, ⓦ paradise-hotel .gr. Two-star hotel above the eastern side of the harbour, overlooking Roussoúm, with pool, bar, and an exceptionally friendly welcome. Plain rooms have a/c and balcony but no TV; many have views over the bay. Breakfast included. **€70**

Pension Pleiades ☎ 24240 65235, ⓦ pleiadeshotel .gr. Fairly simple studio rooms, plus a couple of apartments available year-round (with a/c and heating), above the harbour in a backstreet behind Albedo Travel. Few have unobstructed views from their balconies, but you can enjoy those from the restaurant downstairs – there's also a washing machine and free wi-fi for guest use. **€50**

HÓRA

Elma's Houses ☎ 24240 66108, ⓦ elmashouses.com. Two exquisitely restored studios (a one-bed and a two-bed) and two houses in the upper part of the village. They accommodate up to four people, and are beautifully furnished from the owner's Gorgona antique shop; upmarket, but worth it. **€75**

Fantasia House ☎ 24240 65186. Beamed ceilings and a terrace with amazing views to the south and east are the big attractions of these simple, a/c rooms, off the main square at the bottom of the village. **€60**

Konstantina's Studios ☎ 24240 66165, ⓦ konstantina studios.gr. A renovated building in the lower part of the village, past *Fantasia*, with eight fully equipped studios and one apartment, all enjoying exceptional views. There's a lovely garden, and Konstantina will collect you from the port on request. **€80**

VÓTSI

Hippocampus ☎ 24240 65886, ⓦ hippocampus.com .gr. Modern block of studios and apartments on the road down to the bay whose balconies have fine views down over Vótsi and out to sea. Comfortable tiled-floor rooms have a/c, TV and functional kitchenettes. **€70**

EATING AND DRINKING

Though there's no shortage of places to eat in Patitíri, only a couple stand out from the crowd; nightlife here consists of a few music bars over on the western side of the harbour, below the museum. There's generally better, if pricier, food, and more night-time activity, up in Hóra. Hóra's main street is lined with restaurants, mostly with wonderful views, but few that are good value or particularly high quality. Locals and those in the know tend to eat further down, or in the backstreets.

PATITÍRI

Archipelagos Harbour ☎ 24240 65031. The waterfront restaurants are generally nothing special; an exception, popular with locals, is *Archipelagos*, at the bottom of the western street, with good mezédhes, fish and traditional Greek cooking – plus excellent home-made chips. Daily lunch & dinner.

Pleiades ☎ 24240 65235. On a terrace overlooking the harbour (signed uphill behind Albedo Travel), *Pleiades* makes a conscious attempt to offer something different, with more elegant than usual tableware and dishes such as seafood chowder, chicken in lemon and ginger, and a choice of puddings; there's a daily special for €10. Regular events including live music, barbecues and quizzes make it

popular with expats. Daily from 7.30pm.

To Kamaki ☎ 24240 65245. Authentic, welcoming ouzerí on the eastern street, 150m from the waterfront. Portions are not huge but the seafood-heavy menu encompasses unusual dishes like crab croquettes, skate and *tsitsírava* shoots. Meze €4–5, mains €7.50–9. Dinner daily, plus lunch at weekends.

HÓRA

Acquasanta ☎ 693 28 32 748. An elegant hideaway (signed off the main street, just above the square) with a predominantly Italian menu, not badly priced considering the sophisticated food, swish surroundings and sparkling vistas from the terrace; pasta and fish are the specialities but not all they serve, and there's also a children's menu. Daily, evenings only.

Astrofeyia ☎ 24240 65182. Unusual (for Greece) dishes like chicken curry or chile con carne (each €10) as well as vegetarian options and more ambitious offerings such as calamari with a cream, garlic and saffron wine sauce, all served on a terrace with a friendly welcome and great view, not far from the lower square. Daily, evenings only.

★ **Hayiati** Right at the end of the main street, *Hayiati* has probably the best view in Hóra (which is saying something); an unbeatable setting for coffees and traditional sweets like *kazandibí*. In the evening it's a piano bar with occasional live music. Cocktail prices are steep, but otherwise not too bad considering the location, though it

can be very busy. Daily all day.

Peri Orexeos ☎ 24240 65186. Not a very glamorous setting, on the lower square, by the bus stop, but the food is a great deal better than you might guess from the fast-food style menu. Snacks, sandwiches and burgers as well as Greek standards, but also delicious, innovative salads and dishes like honey-and-lemon pork belly, or paella-like fried rice with tuna. Daily lunch & dinner.

ROUSSOÚM

Remezzo ☎ 24240 65123. Tranquil spot by the little fishing harbour and beach serving coffee and breakfast early, taverna standards and spit-roast meat at lunch and dinner. Good value, and frequent live music in the evenings. Daily all day.

Northern Alónissos

A single road runs northeast from Patitíri up the spine of the island, giving access to beaches, almost exclusively on the east coast. The first turning, though, heads westwards to **Tsoukaliá**, a scruffy cove signed as an archeological site; there was an ancient kiln here, and pottery continued to be made until recently, so thousands upon thousands of potsherds strew the closed, fenced site and beach.

First of the east-coast beaches are **Miliá** and **Khryssí Miliá**: the former is busy, with white pebbles, piney cliffs, a *kantína* and watersports in summer; the latter sandy and beautiful, and hence very busy, with loungers and beach bars. Next up is scenic **Kokkinókastro**, named for the red-rock cliffs which overlook it. Pebbles on a red-sand base extend both sides of a promontory, and there's a seasonal bar,. Another road leads to **Leftós Yialós** and **Tzórtzi Yialós**: the pretty white-pebble beach at Leftós, with its tavernas and loud beach bars, attracts plenty of day-trip boats; Tzórtzi is smaller and less attractive, but much quieter.

STENÍ VÁLA, about halfway up the east coast, is the biggest settlement away from the island's southern corner, though still barely a village. There are plenty of rooms, while the harbourfront shops and tavernas attract yachts and day-trip boats. A long pebble beach – **Glýfa** – lies immediately north, and a better, partly sandy one, **Áyios Pétros**, is a ten-minute walk south. **KALAMÁKIA**, the next hamlet north, has no beach but does have a timeless fishing-port feel and some great waterfront **tavernas**. At **Áyios Dhimítrios**, the final beach easily accessible by road, brilliantly white pebbles stretch around both sides of a narrow point; the south-facing side has loungers and a couple of café/bars, the other is quite undeveloped. **Yérakas**, almost at the island's northern tip, is the end of the road and feels like it; there's a tiny fishing harbour in the deep bay and a dirty-white pebble beach where a snack truck parks in summer – the water, however, is spectacularly clean and clear.

ACTIVITIES   NORTHERN ALÓNISSOS

Scuba diving There's a good diving outfit, Ikion Diving (☎ 24240 65158, 🌐 ikiondiving.gr), at Stení Vála.

ACCOMMODATION AND EATING

Eleonas Leftós Yialós ☎ 24240 66066. Set in an olive grove immediately behind the beach, this is the better of the popular tavernas at Leftós Yialós. Alónissos pies (from €8) are their speciality, from excellent plain cheese to more exotic octopus and goat varieties. Prices are relatively high but portions big – a single pie and a salad makes a substantial lunch for two. Daily lunch & dinner.

Margarita Kalamákia ☎ 24240 65738. The best of four

tavernas lined up along the quayside, each with its own fishing boat, *Margarita* serves excellent fish and mezédhes. They also have simple a/c rooms out back. Daily lunch & dinner. Rooms **€50**

Milia Bay Hotel Apartments Miliá ☎ 24240 66032, 🌐 milia-bay.gr. Great position above Miliá beach, where the modern studios and apartments have views out to sea over the landscaped grounds as well as being handy for

THE MEDITERRANEAN MONK SEAL

The **Mediterranean monk seal** (*Monachus monachus*) has the dubious distinction of being the most endangered European mammal – fewer than 600 survive, almost half or them here, the rest elsewhere in the Aegean or around islands off the coast of West Africa.

Females have one **pup** about every two years, which can live for 45 years, attaining 2m in length and over 200kg as **adults**. Formerly pups were reared in the open, but disturbance by man led to whelping seals retreating to isolated sea caves with partly submerged entrances. Without spending weeks on a local boat, your chances of seeing a seal are slim (marine-park cruises are far more likely to spot dolphins); if seals are spotted (usually dozing on the shore or swimming in the open sea), keep a deferential distance.

Monk seals can swim 200km a day in search of food – and compete with fishermen in the overfished Aegean, often destroying nets. Until recently fishermen routinely killed seals; this occasionally still happens, but the establishment of the **National Marine Park of Alónissos-Northern Sporades** has helped by banning September–November fishing northeast of Alónissos and prohibiting it altogether within 1.5 nautical miles of Pipéri. These measures have won local support through the efforts of the **Hellenic Society for the Protection of the Monk Seal** (Ⓦmom.gr; see p.436), even among Sporadean fishermen, who realize that the restrictions should help restore local fish stocks. The society has reared several abandoned seal pups (bad weather often separates them from their mothers), subsequently released in the sea around Alónissos.

town. There's a pool and pool-bar. **€110**
Sossinola Sténi Vála ☎24240 65776, Ⓦsossinola.gr. Harbourfront taverna that also has modern, a/c studios and two-room apartments, with balconies looking out over the harbour or out to sea. Plenty of fish on the menu, plus Alónissos pies and a meaty goat in tomato sauce. Daily lunch & dinner. Studios & apartments **€80**

The National Marine Park of Alónissos-Northern Sporades

Ⓦalonissos-park.gr

Founded in 1992, the **National Marine Park** protects monk seals, dolphins, wild goats and rare seabirds in an area encompassing Alónissos plus a dozen **islets** speckling the Aegean to the east. None of these (save one) has any permanent population, but a few can be visited by excursion boats, weather permitting. **Pipéri** islet forms the core zone of the park – an off-limits seabird and monk-seal refuge, approachable only by government-authorized scientists. **Peristéra**, opposite Alónissos, is uninhabited, though some Alonissans cross to tend olive groves in the south; it's little visited by excursion craft except for a brief swim-stop at the end of a cruise. Well-watered **Kyrá Panayiá**, the next islet out, has a tenth-century monastery whose old bakery and wine/olive presses, restored in the 1990s, are maintained by one farmer-monk. Nearby **Yioúra** has a stalactite cave which mythically sheltered Homer's Cyclops, plus the main wild-goat population, but you won't see either as *kaïkia* must keep 400m clear of the shore. Tiny, northernmost **Psathoúra** is dominated by its powerful lighthouse, the tallest in the Aegean; some excursions stop for a swim at a pristine, white-sand beach.

Skýros

Despite its natural beauty, **SKÝROS** has a relatively low profile. There are few major sites or resorts, and access, wherever you're coming from, is awkward. Those in the know, however, realise it's worth the effort, and there are increasing numbers of trendy Athenians and Thessalonians taking advantage of domestic flights – and making Skýros Town a much more cosmopolitan place than you might expect – plus steadily growing international tourism. The New Age Skyros Centre, pitched mostly at Brits, has also effectively publicized the place. There are plenty of **beaches**, but few that can rival the sand of

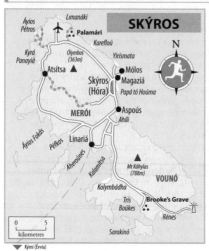

Skiáthos or film-set scenery of Skópelos. There's also a substantial air-force presence around the airport in the north, and a big naval base in the south; almost all the accommodation and tourist facilities cluster around Skýros Town in the centre of the island.

A position bang in the centre of the Aegean has guaranteed the island a busy **history**: it was occupied from prehistory, with a truly impressive Bronze Age settlement currently being excavated, was a vital Athenian outpost in the Classical era, and an equally important naval base for the Byzantines and under Venetian and Turkish rule, when it was an important staging post on the sea-lanes to Constantinople.

ARRIVAL AND DEPARTURE
SKÝROS

By plane Sky Express (ⓦ skyexpress.gr) operate three flights a week (2 only Oct–April) from Athens (40min) to Skýros to Thessaloníki (40min) and back. The airport is about 10km from town; there's no public transport, so you'll have to take a taxi or rent a car – a Pegasus car rental booth opens at flight times (see p.442).

By ferry Skyros Shipping (ⓦ sne.gr) sail daily from Kými, on Évvia (see p.448), to Linariá, Skýros's port. The crossing takes around 1hr 45min and leaves Kými every evening, returning from Skýros early in the morning. In July and August there are additional daytime crossings several times a week (especially at weekends), and a twice-weekly connection via Kými to

Alónissos and Skópelos. To get to Kými there are direct KTEL buses from Athens' Liossion bus station, with early afternoon departures connecting with the ferry, or Skyros Travel (ⓣ 22220 91600, ⓦ skyrostravel.com) organizes two transfers a week direct from Athens airport (Mon & Fri early afternoon, €58 per person including ferry ticket).

Agents and tickets Skyros Travel, about 100m above the platía on the main street in Skýros Town, is the local agent for both plane and ferry tickets (Mon–Sat 9.15am–1.30pm & 6.45–10pm, Sun 9.45am–1.45pm & 7–10pm; timetables and other useful info displayed outside); they also have a ticket office in Linariá that opens an hour before departures.

INFORMATION

Services The post office and National Bank (with ATM) are on the platía in Skýros Town, and there's a further ATM higher up the main street; the most reliable internet café is Xanthoulis (ⓦ Mano.com), also on the main street.

Useful website ⓦ skyros.gr.

Newspapers English-language newspapers are sold from a hut opposite the platía in Skýros Town.

CARNIVAL ON SKÝROS

Skýros has a particularly outrageous *apokriátika* (pre-Lenten) **carnival**, featuring its famous **goat dance**, performed by groups of masked revellers in the streets of Hóra. The leaders of each troupe are the **yéri**, menacing figures (usually men but sometimes sturdy women) dressed in goat-pelt capes, weighed down by huge garlands of sheep bells, their faces concealed by kid-skin masks, and brandishing shepherds' crooks. Accompanying them are their "brides", men in drag known as **korélles** (maidens), and **frángi** (maskers in assorted "Western" garb). When two such groups meet, the *yéri* compete to see who can ring their bells longest and loudest with arduous body movements, or even get into brawls using their crooks as cudgels.

These rites take place on each of the four weekends before Clean Monday (see p.43), but the final one is more for the benefit of tourists, both Greek and foreign. The Skyrians are less exhausted and really let their (goat) hair down for each other during the preceding three weeks. Most local hotels open for the duration, and you have to book rooms well in advance.

SNORKELLING NEAR LALÁRIA BEACH, SKIÁTHOS (P.427) >

GETTING AROUND

By bus Buses run five times daily between Skýros Town and Liniariá (€1.60), connecting with the ferries; in town the bus stop is near the bottom of the main street, by the school. In summer there are also four buses daily from Liniariá to Magaziá and Mólos via town, and two daily from Skýros Town to Kalamítsa.

By taxi There are plenty of taxis (☎ 22220 91666) to meet the ferries, with taxi stands by the main square in town, and close to the bus stop.

By car and scooter Skyros Travel (see p.440) rent cars (trading as Pegasus; ☎ 22220 91600, ⓦ skyrosrentacar .com), or you can get scooters from several places including Vagios (☎ 22220 92957), in a side street just below the main square in town.

Skýros Town and around

Once through the rather scruffy outskirts, **SKÝROS TOWN (Hóra)** is a beautiful place, its Cycladic-style white, flat-roofed, red-tiled houses clinging to the inland slope of a pinnacle rising precipitously from the coast. In legend, King Lykomedes raised the young Achilles in his palace here, and also pushed Theseus to his death from the summit. A single main street leads up to a central platía; beyond that, cobbled and increasingly narrow and traffic-free, lies a 150m stretch lined with almost everything you'll need – shops, many of them selling classy jewellery, crafts and antiques, restaurants, banks and sophisticated bars. Wander off the main street and the place is suddenly bigger than it first seemed. It's easy to become momentarily lost, but there are always fascinating glimpses – covered passageways, churches and front doors open to reveal traditional house interiors with gleaming copperware, antique embroideries and the proud local crafts of painted ceramics and elaborately carved wooden furniture.

Kástro

The Byzantine-Venetian **kástro** atop the ancient **acropolis** above town is a very steep climb, so unless you're interested in seeing the picturesque old quarter along the way, you may want to check that it is open following reconstruction – it was badly damaged by an earthquake in 2001. Even from outside there are great views; inside is the Byzantine **monastery of Áyios Yeóryios**.

Rupert Brooke memorial

The British poet Rupert Brooke is always associated with Skýros, though in fact he spent only a few days here, arriving as a naval officer off the south of the island on April 17, 1915, and dying six days later of blood poisoning on a French hospital ship. He lies buried in an olive grove above the bay of Trís Boúkes (see p.445). The **Rupert Brooke memorial** comprises a nude bronze statue of "Immortal Poetry", in a quiet square overlooking the coast; it's right on the edge of town, reached by following the main street uphill and taking the signed left fork, or by steps up from Magaziá.

The archeological museum

Below the Rupert Brooke memorial • Tues–Sun 8.30am–3pm • €2

Skýros's two-room **archeological museum** is far better than you might expect, with the added bonus of a lovely setting above the sea. The highlights are Early Bronze Age pottery, obsidian axe-heads and stone blades and tools from Palamári (see p.444); later artefacts include a Geometric-era ceramic rhyton in the form of a Skyrian pony and a vase with eight ducks being beset by snakes. There's also a side room in the form of a traditional Skyrian house, with carved wooden screen and furniture.

Manos Faltaïts Museum

Below the Rupert Brooke memorial • Daily 10am–2pm & 6–9pm • €2 • ⓦ faltaits.gr

An early nineteenth-century mansion built over a bastion in the ancient walls houses the eccentric **Manos Faltaïts Museum**, in the family home of a prolific local painter. Along with his own works it's an Aladdin's cave of local history and folklore, with traditional furnishings and costumes, curios and books.

Magaziá and Mólos

Immediately below Skýros Town, reached by a direct stairway or more roundabout roads, is the beach hamlet of **MAGAZIÁ**. From here a long sandy beach extends to **MÓLOS**; these days the two are pretty much joined by low-key, low-rise development – much of the island's accommodation is down here, along with plenty of restaurants and a couple of lively beach bars. Around the point beyond Mólos, a much more exposed beach is punctuated by rock outcrops, whose weird, squared-off shapes are the result of Roman (and later) quarrying rather than natural erosion; one monolith, by the cape with its snack-bar/windmill, has a rock-hewn chapel inside.

Linariá

LINARIÁ, where the ferries dock, is a pleasant enough place, with plenty of options for eating and drinking if you're waiting for a boat, but little reason to stay. In high season, **excursion boats** (€30 including lunch) offer trips to the islet of **Sarakinó**, with its white-sand beach, stopping at various sea-caves en route. Should you want to stay around here, the next little bay, **Aheroúnes**, is a peaceful spot with a much better beach, only about fifteen minutes' walk away.

ACCOMMODATION	SKÝROS TOWN AND AROUND

SKÝROS TOWN

★ **Nefeli** ☎ 22220 91964, ⊛ skyros-nefeli.gr. The island's plushest hotel, on the main road as you enter town, has a range of lovely designer rooms, studios and apartments, arrayed around a large salt-water pool. Breakfast (included) on an outdoor terrace and free wi-fi in the lobby. **€120**

Pension Nikolas ☎ 22220 91778, ✉ pension_nicholas @hotmail.com. Located on the edge of town, this friendly rooms establishment offers doubles and quads; many have traditional wooden sleeping platforms, and all have a/c and TVs. **€60**

MAGAZIÁ/MÓLOS

Angela Mólos ☎ 22220 91764, ⊛ angelahotelskyros .com. Large complex of two-storey rooms and studios, close to the beach at the northern end of Mólos, beyond the harbour, in extensive gardens around a pool. All with a/c, TV and fridge, some with kitchenette. **€90**

★ **Perigiali** Magaziá ☎ 22220 92075, ⊛ perigiali .com. Sparkling new rooms, studios and family apartments

around a good-sized pool, in a narrow lane behind the beach at the southern end of Magaziá. A few have sea views, though most look over the gardens, and there are a few simpler, cheaper rooms in the original wing; all have a/c, wi-fi and cooking facilities. **€100**

Yeoryia Tsakami Magaziá ☎ 22220 91357, ✉ gtsakamis@yahoo.gr. Simple, old-fashioned rooms with fridge and electric ring, in a great position directly behind the beach. Most have private balcony at the back, with communal terrace at the front. **€50**

LINARIÁ/AHEROÚNES

King Lykomides Linariá ☎ 22220 93249, ✉ soula @skyrosnet.gr. Spotless *dhomátia* with wooden-shuttered balconies overlooking the harbour; all have a/c and tv, some with cooking facilities. **€60**

Pegasus Aheroúnes ☎ 22220 93442, ⊛ skyrosvillas .com. A variety of studios and apartments, most with good views, in a tranquil spot behind the beach. All come with a/c, TV and a friendly welcome. **€70**

EATING, DRINKING AND NIGHTLIFE

SKÝROS TOWN

Akamatra Main square ☎ 22220 29029. Large, fancy bar on two floors, with leather seating and terraces overlooking both platía and street. Open during the day for coffee, and regular DJ events till the early hours. Daily 10am–2am.

Kalypso Main street ☎ 22220 92696. The last of the places as you climb the street, *Kalypso* is a long-established café-bar with a jazz and blues soundtrack, attracting a slightly older, more touristy crowd than the places around the platía, though it can get lively later on. Daily from around 7pm.

Maryetis Main street ☎ 22220 91311. Much the most

popular place in town, with only a few tables on the street-side terrace, opposite Skyros Travel, so you may well have to wait. Simple Greek oven dishes and grilled meat or fish at reasonable prices are the attraction, washed down with decent house wine. Daily lunch & dinner.

MAGAZIÁ/MÓLOS

Asterias Mólos ☎ 22220 93008. Excellent restaurant on the waterfront platía with a pretty beachfront terrace and sunbeds below for customer use. There's no printed menu – usually a good sign – just half a dozen daily specials reeled off by the waiter, plus the usual salads and sides. Daily lunch & dinner.

7

7

SKYRIAN HORSES

Skýros has a race of **native pony**, related to the breeds found on Exmoor and Dartmoor. They are thought to be the diminutive steeds depicted in the Parthenon frieze; according to legend, Achilles went off to fight at Troy mounted on a chestnut specimen. In more recent times they were used for summer threshing; communally owned, they were left to graze wild ten months of the year on Vounó, from where each family rounded up the ponies they needed. Currently only about 150 individuals survive, and the breed is **threatened** by the decline of local agriculture, indifference and cross-breeding. To be classed as a true Skyrian pony, the animal must be 98–115cm in height, and 130cm maximum from shoulder to tail. They're elusive in the wild, but you can see (and ride) them at the centre opposite *Mouries* restaurant opposite.

★ **ly Istories tou Barba** Mólos ☎22220 91453. Lovely setting with blue chairs on a blue terrace above the Magaziá end of Mólos beach. The food is traditional and interesting – crab salad, or cuttlefish with fennel sauce and leeks – the atmosphere also, with black-and-white photos of old island life in the menu. Daily lunch & dinner.

Juicy Beach Bar Magaziá ☎22220 93337. Beach bar with loungers and umbrellas, plus a terrace with food (sandwiches, crêpes, pasta), free wi-fi and a bar. Quiet music by day, cranked up at night with summer events such as a full moon party. Daily all day, breakfast till the early hours.

Stefanos Magaziá ☎22220 91272. Attractive, traditional taverna with wooden tables on a terrace hanging out over the sand at the southern end of Magaziá beach. Standard dishes like stifádo (€9) or lamb with potatoes (€7.50) are deliciously prepared. Daily all day.

Thalassa Mólos beach ☎22220 92044. Beach bar by day, with wi-fi, sunbeds, bar and snacks, cocktail bar and club at night, when there's a huge dance space, though that is only really busy in August. Daily 9am–3am.

LINARIÁ

Kavos All-day bar tumbling down a rocky cliff on a series of terraces, with steps down to a private swimming area below. Quiet daytime sounds which are often turned up loud to greet the evening ferry; wi-fi, drinks and light meals, plus late-night revelry in mid-season. Daily 10am–late.

Psariotis ☎22220 93250. Probably the best of the tavernas around Linariá's harbour, Psariotis has its own boat to catch fish, which is marginally less expensive than elsewhere. Also a good fish soup (€10) or lobster spaghetti (€20), plus plenty of standard Greek dishes at regular prices. Daily lunch & dinner.

Merói

A single paved road loops around Skyros's northern half, **Merói**. Heading anticlockwise from Hóra the first possible stop is at secluded **Kareflóu** beach, 1.5km down a poorly signed rough track. Sandy and extensive, it's also exposed with no facilities at all.

Palamári

Mon–Fri 7.30am–2.30pm • Free

The early Bronze Age settlement of **Palamári**, inhabited from around 2800 to 1600 BC, and then lost for 3500 years, is set on the ridge of a low cape at the northeastern edge of the island, above a beach and a river which once formed a lagoon and natural harbour. The site, still being excavated, is extraordinary: you can make out the houses, streets, drainage and walls of a well-organized city, which must have been at the heart of Aegean trading in the Minoan era. Informative signage and a small exhibition fill in the background.

Atsítsa and around

Past the airport at the island's northern tip, the west coast is infinitely greener, heavily forested in pine. Around 2.5km of rough track leads to a couple of the island's most scenic and remote beaches: nudist **Áyios Pétros**, more respectable **Limanáki**, right by the airport almost at the end of the runway, and still more isolated **Agalípa**. **Atsítsa** itself is well-known as the home of the Skyros Centre; its attractive, pine-fringed bay is sheltered by an islet and has lovely clear water for swimming, but not much of a beach.

Beyond Atsítsa, you can head back across the centre of the island on a good dirt road through the woods, or carry on around the coast, through an area devastated by forest fire in 2007 and still characterized by charred stumps. **Áyios Fokás**, in the heart of this area, is a quiet, sandy beach that makes a great lunch spot; the descent through woods to deeply indented **Péfkos**, the best of the southwest-coast bays with a fine, long, sandy beach, offers spectacular views.

EATING AND DRINKING   MERÓI

Perasma ☎ 22220 92911. Excellent, reasonably priced taverna at the junction of the airport road not far from Palamári; apparently in the middle of nowhere, but with plenty of custom from local air-force families. Family-style cooking based on local produce, much of it organic and produced in the taverna's own fields, served beneath a shady awning. Daily lunch & dinner.

Taverna tis Kira Kalis Áyios Fokás. A wonderfully out-of-the-way lunch spot, with octopus and sardines thrown on a charcoal grill on the beach and simple Greek home-style cooking. Lush vines and pot plants compensate for the burnt slopes roundabout. Daily lunch & dinner.

Vounó

South of Skýros Town you turn off at **Aspoús**, where there's a decent, grey-sand beach, to reach **Vounó**. Much of this southern half of the island, especially as you ascend **Mount Kóhylas**, is almost eerily barren, home only to goats and a few stunted trees, but it's here also – high on the mountain – that you're most likely to see wild Skyrian horses and other wildlife, including abundant Eleonora's falcon. En route there's a narrow pebble strand at **Kalamítsa**, and a slightly better beach at **Kolymbádha**. The one sight down here is Rupert Brooke's grave at **Trís Boúkes**, a simple marble tomb inscribed with his most famous poem, *The Soldier* ("If I should die, think only this of me/That there's some corner of a foreign field/That is for ever England…"). The grave is very hard to spot: follow the turning to the naval base for just over 1km and it lies in an olive grove off to the left of the road.

EATING AND DRINKING   VOUNÓ

Mouries Fléa ☎ 22220 93555. Big, traditional taverna in this tiny hamlet on the road between Aspoús and Kalamítsa, serving local lamb and wine under the namesake mulberries. It's very popular at weekends when they often have live Greek music, and over the road they run a Skyrian Horse Centre, with riding and pony-and-trap rides. Daily lunch & dinner.

★ **O Pappous ki Ego** ☎ 22220 93200. "My Grandfather and I", on the road approaching Kalamítsa, serves traditional Skyrian dishes such as fried bread with Skyrian cheese, and at weekends spit-roasted lamb and *kokorétsi*, plus fish, grills, pastas and risotto. Classier than your average Greek taverna, with mains around €10. Daily lunch & dinner.

Évvia

The second largest of the Greek islands after Crete, **ÉVVIA (Euboea)** – separated only by a narrow gulf from central Greece – often feels more like an extension of the mainland than an entity in its own right. At **Halkídha**, the old drawbridge spans a mere 40m channel where Évvia was mythically split from Attica and Thessaly by a blow from Poseidon's trident. Easy access from Athens means that in summer Évvia can seem merely a beach annexe for Athens and the mainland towns across the Gulf.

Nevertheless, Évvia *is* an island, often a very beautiful one, and in many ways its problems – long distances to cover, poor communications, few concessions to tourism – are also its greatest attractions, ensuring that it has remained out of the mainstream of tourism. Exceptionally fertile, Évvia has always been a quietly prosperous place that would manage pretty well even without visitors. The classical name, Euboea, means "rich in cattle", and throughout history it has been much coveted. Today agriculture still thrives, with plenty of local goat and lamb on the menu, along with highly rated local retsina.

Évvia divides naturally into three sections, with just a single road connecting the northern and southern parts to the centre. The **south** is mountainous, barren and rocky; highlights are low-key Kárystos and hiking the nearby mountains and gorges. The **centre**, with the sprawling island capital at Halkídha, is green, wealthy and busy with both industry and agriculture, but for visitors mainly a gateway, with the bridges at Halkídha and onward transport to Skýros from the easterly port of Kými. In the **north**, grain fields, olive groves and pine forest are surrounded by the bulk of the island's resorts, most dominated by Greek holiday homes.

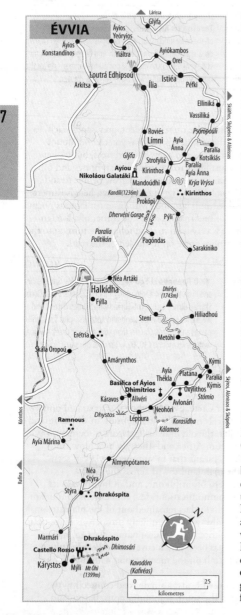

ARRIVAL AND DEPARTURE   ÉVVIA

By ferry Ferries make the short crossing from the mainland to Évvia at various points all the way up the coast: from Ráfina to Marmári, Ayía Marína to Néa Stýra, Skála Oropoú to Erétria, Arkítsa to Loutrá Edhipsoú and Glýfa to Ayiókambos. Which you choose depends on where you are heading on Évvia; most run very frequently – details are given under the individual ports.

By car Two bridges link Évvia to the mainland, the old drawbridge right in the heart of Halkídha and a suspension bridge on the outskirts. If you are driving you can use these or any of the ferries (more expensive, but the mainland motorway is far faster than roads on the island if you're heading to the north or south).

By bus KTEL buses run direct from Athens' Liossion bus station to many destinations on Évvia including Halkídha, Kárystos, Kými, Límni and Loutrá Edhipsoú. There are also buses from Athens to all of the mainland ports above.

By train Frequent trains connect Athens with Halkídha.

GETTING AROUND

By bus Most places in Évvia can be reached by bus, but services tend to run just a couple of times a day, so if you hope to explore you'll really need a car. All the major rental companies have offices in Halkídha, and there are local operations in the resorts.

Halkídha

Évvia's capital, **HALKÍDHA** (ancient Chalkis), has a population of around 100,000, making it one of the ten biggest cities in Greece. So it's not entirely surprising if it often has an urban feel, rather than an island one. Nonetheless the centre is compact and easy to explore, and the busy waterfront thoroughly attractive. Right at the centre, beneath the drawbridge across the narrow **Évripos channel** to the mainland, the gulf-water swirls by like a river; every few hours the current reverses.

Aristotle is said to have thrown himself into the waters in despair at his inability to understand what was happening; there is still no entirely satisfactory explanation for the capricious currents.

An impressive **fortress**, floodlit at night, protects Halkídha from the mainland side. Across the bridge, Odhós Kótsou heads directly uphill towards the centre through the old **Kástro** district, where a few relics of an older city survive. Chief of these is a handsome fifteenth-century **mosque** (locked), now a warehouse of Byzantine artefacts, with an exceptionally ornate carved **Ottoman fountain** out front. Off to the right further up Kótsou you'll find the **Folklore Museum** (Wed 10am–1pm & 6–8pm, Thurs–Sun 10am–1pm; €3). Housed in the old jail, it has a jumbled collection of costumes, furniture and local traditions in a series of reconstructed rooms. Higher up still, then left on the main street, the **archeological museum** at Venizélou 13 (Tues–Sun 8.30am–3pm; €2) offers a pleasant escape from the raucous surrounds; a tortoise roams the statuary in the shady garden, while inside there's a good display of finds from across the island.

ARRIVAL AND DEPARTURE HALKÍDHA

7

By train The train station is very close to the bridge on the mainland side, with at least sixteen services to and from Athens daily (6am–11pm; 1hr 25min).

By bus The KTEL bus station is almost 2km from the centre at Stíron 1, on the ring road at the east edge of town; local buses will take you in to the market area, but it's much easier to use a taxi (about €5). Very frequent departures to Athens (every 30min 5am–10pm; 1hr 15min), less often along all the island's main routes including to Erétria (18 daily; 30min); Kárystos (2 daily; 3hr); Kými (8 daily; 2hr); Límni (3–4 daily; 2hr); Loutrá Edhipsoú (3–4 daily; 2hr 30min).

ACCOMMODATION

Kentrikon Angéli Govíou 5 ☎22210 22375, ⊛hotel -kentrikon.com. Rather forbidding nineteenth-century mansion, just up from the bridge, which conceals unexpectedly modern a/c rooms, with wi-fi and satellite TV. No real views, though. **€55**

Kymata Liáska 1 ☎22210 74724, ⊛kimata.com.gr. Simple, minimally furnished rooms above a busy main road overlooking the port; modern double glazing and a/c keep out most of the noise, and it's very good value. **€45**

Lucy Voudoúri 10 ☎22210 23831, ⊛lucy-hotel.gr. Big, high-rise Best Western hotel with luxurious rooms, many with great views across the water; all with wi-fi and cable TV. **€75**

EATING AND DRINKING

A long line of cafés and restaurants extends along the waterfront to the north of the bridge; there are plenty of fancy seafood restaurants and elegant café-bars (most with wi-fi) but also a number of simpler places. Prices are lower inland towards the centre, though.

Apanemo Ethníkis Symfíliosis 78, Fanári ☎22210 22614. Very popular, decent-value seafood restaurant with tables on the sand; it's a good half-hour walk from the centre, just before the lighthouse at the far north end of the shoreline, so you may want to book, and/or take a taxi. Daily lunch & dinner.

Paralia Voudoúri 10 ☎22210 87932. Long-established, old-fashioned, waterfront *psistariá*, serving up large portions of grilled meat at very reasonable prices; salads and oven-baked dishes too. Daily lunch & dinner.

Tsaf Papanastasíou 3 ☎694 81 80 857. An imposing stone building, off Platía Agorás near the top of Kótsou, houses this bustling ouzerí, with good fish and mezédhes. It's busiest late in the evening. Daily, evenings only.

Central Évvia

The **coast road** southeast of Halkídha heads through industrial suburbs to a coastline of second homes, small hotels and beaches which make popular escapes from the city. At **Lépoura** it forks, to the right for the south of the island, left to curl around towards the east coast and **Kými**. Beyond Kými you can cut back across the mountainous heart of the island via **Metóhi** and **Stení**, a spectacular road with a short unpaved section.

Erétria

Modern **ERÉTRIA** is a dull-looking resort on a grid plan; for most travellers its main asset is a ferry service across to Skála Oropoú. The place deserves a closer look, though. For a start it boasts some of the best **beaches** on this stretch of coast, to the east of the harbour, and more importantly it preserves the remains of **Ancient Eretria**, the most impressive on the island. Eretria was an important city from the eighth century BC to the sixth century AD, flourishing above all around 400 BC following the decline of Athens. First stop on your exploration should be the **museum** (Tues–Sun 8.30am–3pm; €2), on the edge of town by the main road, where you can pick up a leaflet with a map showing all the main sites around town. Among the museum's displays of ceramics, statues and jewellery, labelled mainly in Greek and French, the tenth-century BC Lefkandi Centaur stands out – a lovely piece and one of the earliest known examples of figurative pottery. There are also fascinating models of the ancient city.

It's worth crossing the road from the museum to see the overgrown West Gate and **theatre**, but of the other sites, many of them locked, the unarguable highlight is the **House of Mosaics**. Here, under a modern cover, four magnificent mosaic floors dating from around 370 BC have been preserved, vividly depicting animals and mythical scenes.

ARRIVAL AND DEPARTURE ERÉTRIA

By ferry Ferries shuttle the short crossing to Skála Oropoú roughly every 20min (6.30am–9.30pm; 25min; ☎ 22290 62201 or 64990).

By bus Erétria is linked to Halkída (18 daily; 30min).

ACCOMMODATION

Eviana Beach Oníron ☎ 22290 62113, ⓦ evianabeach .gr. Smart hotel at the start of the beach road, right behind the beach, handy for town and with great sea views; all the rooms have balcony, wi-fi and attractive modern decor. €60

Kálamos

The most accessible of a number of beautiful coves on the west coast is **Kálamos**, about 7km down narrow lanes from Neohóri on the main road. This stretch of the main road is dotted with medieval remains – Byzantine chapels and watchtowers which gave warning of approaching pirates. Kálamos itself is a tiny but stunning cove enclosing a sandy beach, surrounded by half a dozen tavernas and rooms establishments. In August it's packed; the rest of the year often deserted.

ACCOMMODATION AND EATING KÁLAMOS

Tota Marinou ☎ 22230 41881. One of many simple rooms places right behind the beach, with a welcoming waterfront taverna too. Restaurant open lunch & dinner. €50

Kými

KÝMI consists of two parts: the ferry port, properly known as Paralía Kýmis, and the upper town, 4km up a spectacularly winding road. The port offers plenty of accommodation and a long row of harbourfront restaurants and cafés should you be waiting for a ferry, but the upper town is far more attractive, with great views towards Skýros from its lush, green hillside location. There's a small **folklore museum** (daily 10am–1pm & 6–8.30pm; €2) with costumes, rural implements and old photos recording the doings of Kymians both locally and in the US, home to a huge emigrant community. Among them was Dr George Papanikolaou, deviser of the "Pap" cervical smear test, who is honoured with a statue up on the platía.

ARRIVAL AND DEPARTURE

KÝMI

By bus Buses generally drop off in the upper town, except for those connecting with Skýros ferries; there are 8 daily to Halkídha (2hr) and 5 to Athens (4hr).

By ferry Skyros Shipping (☎ 22220 22020, ⓦ sne.gr) sail every evening to Linariá on Skýros (1hr 45min), returning

from Skýros early in the morning. In July and August there are additional daytime crossings several times a week (especially at weekends), and a twice-weekly connection to Alónissos (2hr 30min) and Skópelos (3hr 20min). The ticket office is on the quayside; Athens buses connect with all the ferries.

ACCOMMODATION AND EATING

Hotel Beis Waterfront ☎ 22220 22604, ⓦ hotel-beis .gr. A straightforward, good-value four-storey hotel, very handy for the ferries, whose a/c rooms have balconies overlooking the harbour. **€60**

Ouzeri Skyros Waterfront ☎ 22220 22641. 150m north

of the jetty, past the *Hotel Beis*, so quieter than the places right by the harbour. A terrace over the water and blue-and-white decor lend a classic island look. Good mezédhes. Daily lunch & dinner.

Stení

7

At bustling Néa Artáki, 5km north of Halkídha, a side road leads east to **STENÍ**, a village-cum-hill-station at the foot of Mount Dhírfys. There are marked hiking trails up the mountain, Évvia's highest summit where traces of snow survive till early summer, and it's a beautiful place, cool in summer and full of rushing streams. It's also pretty much the halfway point of a wonderfully scenic **road link to Kými**, all paved except for 8km just before Metóhi; it's 51km or 95 minutes' drive (follow signposting for Metóhi if starting from Kými).

ACCOMMODATION AND EATING

STENÍ

Steni ☎ 22280 51221. Cosy, welcoming hotel towards the top of the village with spectacular views from its sumptuous common areas and simple, comfortable if rather small rooms with modern bathrooms. **€60**

Vrahos ☎ 22280 51546. Numerous tavernas specializing

in meaty fare line the road as it passes through Steni, all popular for weekend outings. *O Vrahos*, on the village-centre platía, is the most atmospheric, with seating under a mulberry tree and views of the village goings-on. Daily lunch & dinner.

Southern Évvia

So narrow that you sometimes spot the sea on both sides, mountainous **southern Évvia** is often barren, bleak and windswept. The single road from the north is winding and tortuous – most people who come here arrive by ferry, and though Greeks have holiday homes in numerous coastal spots there's really just one attractive resort, at **Kárystos**.

Heading south by road you'll pass what maps mark as **Lake Dhýstos**; these days it has been largely reclaimed as farmland, and there's barely any water. Atop conical Kastrí hill on the east shore are sparse fifth-century BC ruins of **ancient Dystos** and a medieval citadel. At **STÝRA**, 35km from Lépoura, three **dhrakóspita** ("dragon houses") are signposted and reachable by track. So named because only dragons were thought capable of installing the enormous masonry blocks, their origins and purpose remain obscure. The shore annexe of **NÉA STÝRA**, 3.5km downhill, is a dull, Greek-frequented resort, worth knowing about only for its handy ferry connection to Ayía Marína. Much the same is true of **MARMÁRI**, 20km south, except here the link is with Rafína. Both have plenty of food and accommodation should you be stuck waiting for a bus or ferry.

ARRIVAL AND DEPARTURE

SOUTHERN ÉVVIA

By ferry There are at least a dozen ferries daily shuttling between Néa Stýra and Ayía Marína (45min; information ☎ 22240 41533), and five to eight a day linking Marmári and Rafína (4–6 Oct–April; 1hr; information ☎ 22240 32340). Tickets are sold on the quayside.

By bus Most ferries in Marmári are met by a bus to Kárystos (4 daily). In Néa Stýra buses (3 daily) stop on the main street, inland from the front. Connecting buses link Athens Mavrommatéon terminal with both Rafína (see p.73) and Ayía Marína.

Kárystos

KÁRYSTOS is a delightfully old-fashioned, thoroughly Greek resort, strung out along a broad bay flanked by good (if often windy) beaches. It's a quiet place – even in August, when thousands of Greeks descend, they're a fairly staid crowd – but its attractions grow on you; graceful Neoclassical buildings in the centre, endearingly old-fashioned shops and tavernas, and a magnificent setting. On the main town **beach**, west of the centre, there are beach bars, sunbeds and kayak rental; further out this way, and around the bay to the east, there are plenty of empty patches of sand.

Though a place of some importance in antiquity, mentioned by Homer and a rival of Athens, there's very little trace now of this history: only a fenced-in **Roman heroön** or mausoleum, a block from the water at the corner of Kotsíka and Sakhtoúri, and the thirteenth-century, waterfront **Boúrtzi** (locked except for special events), all that's left of once-extensive fortifications. Just uphill from this small Venetian tower, a small but well-explained **archeological museum** (Tues–Sun 8.30am–3pm; €2) displays statues, temple carvings and votive objects from the region.

ARRIVAL AND INFORMATION KÁRYSTOS

By bus The bus station is on Amerikís to the east of the Town Hall, about three blocks in and one east from central, waterfront Platía Amalías. Departures to Halkídha (2 daily, 3hr), Marmári (4 daily, 30min) and Néa Stýra (3 daily, 1hr).
Taxis There's a taxi office (☎ 22240 26500) on Platía Amalías.
Services The post office and ATMs lie within sight of Platía Amalías.

Travel agency There's no tourist office, but helpful South Evia Tours at Platía Amalías 7 (☎ 22240 26200, ⓦ eviatravel.gr) sells ferry tickets, rents cars and bikes, finds lodging, arranges excursions and also has a shop selling souvenirs, maps and foreign newspapers.
Useful websites ⓦ southevia.gr and ⓦ in-karystos.gr.

ACCOMMODATION

★ **Galaxy** Odysséos 1 ☎ 22240 22600, ⓦ galaxy hotelkaristos.com. Big old hotel at the western end of the waterfront with a friendly, family atmosphere. The rooms are gradually being upgraded with stylish furnishings and new bathrooms; get one of the new ones with a view and it's excellent value. **€50**

Karystion Kriezótou 3 ☎ 22240 22391, ⓦ karystion .gr. A lovely spot on a quiet, pine-covered promontory with direct access to the adjacent beach. The rather old-fashioned rooms are not quite what the modern exterior and public areas would lead you to expect, though. **€70**

EATING, DRINKING AND NIGHTLIFE

Seafront Kriezótou is lined with cafés and touristy tavernas, though you'll generally find better value away from the front. Theohári Kótsíka, one of the lanes leading inland from here to parallel Sakhtoúri, just to the west of the platía, has several *psistariés* and takeaway kebab places, as does I. Kótsika, between Platía Amalías and the Town Hall.

Aeriko West beach ☎ 22240 22365. Lounge bar behind the beach and a beach bar area on it; probably the best of a selection of bar/clubs behind the beach here. Live music and club nights in summer. Daily all day till late.

★ **Cavo D'oro** Paródos Sakhtoúri ☎ 22240 22326. Despite the name, this is an absolutely traditional Greek taverna, always busy, serving the likes of cheese-stuffed peppers, home-made tzatziki and goat in tomoto sauce. There's no menu, so choose from the bubbling pots or raw ingredients in the kitchen. You'll find it in the first alley off the waterfront west of the square. Lunch & dinner; closed Tues & 4.30–7pm.

Hovolo Kriezótou 118. Elegant café on the waterfront

serving coffee and sweets by day, wine by the glass and beer at night; somewhat pricey, but offset by the delicious traditional snacks that come with each drink. Daily all day till late.

Marinos Kriezótou 106 ☎ 22240 24126. Waterfront taverna with an enticing display of fish out front, sold by the kilo at reasonable prices. Also all the usual meat and traditional dishes, including good stuffed vegetables. Daily lunch & dinner.

To Kyma Káto Aetós ☎ 22240 23365. Big seaside restaurant 2km east of town, with a terrace above the water and another further up; popular weekend excursion for big parties so it's safest to book. Fri–Sun lunch & dinner.

Mount Óhi

Mount Óhi (1399m), inland from Kárystos, is Évvia's third-highest peak and the focus of trails of sufficient quality to attract overseas trekkers. **MÝLI**, a fair-sized village around a spring-fed oasis with a few tavernas, is a natural first stop. Medieval **Castello Rosso (Kokkinókastro)** lies a twenty-minute climb above the village; inside, the castle is ruinous, except for an Orthodox **chapel** built over the water cistern, but sweeping views make the trip worthwhile.

From Mýli, it's a three-hour-plus **hike** up the bare slopes of Óhi, mostly by a good path short-cutting the road; about forty minutes along are various finished and half-finished cipollino marble **columns**, abandoned almost two thousand years ago. The Romans loved the stuff and extensively quarried southern Évvia, shipping the marble back to Italy. The path reaches an alpine club shelter just below the summit (springwater outside; ☎22240 24414 to get the keys), and a **dhrakóspito**, more impressive than the Stýra trio (see p.449), seemingly sprouting from the mountainside.

The Dhimosári Gorge

The one unmissable excursion in southern Évvia is the three-hour hike down the **Dhimosári Gorge**. The descent northeast, mostly in deep shade past various springs and watermills, follows a path (often *kalderími*) as far as the farming hamlet of Lenoséi, then a track to **Kallianós** village, with another path just before the latter down to a beach. South Evia Tours (see opposite) organize a weekly guided trek here in summer as well as other walking trips; otherwise you'll have to arrange a taxi transfer back, or hitch.

Northern Évvia

Leaving Halkídha to the north, the main road snakes steeply over a forested ridge, with spectacular views back over the city and the narrow strait, and then down through the Dhervéni Gorge, gateway to Évvia's northwest.

ARRIVAL AND DEPARTURE	NORTHERN ÉVVIA
By ferry Ten or more ferries a day shuttle between Loutrá Edhipsoú and Arkítsa (45min; ☎22260 23330 or 22395, ⓦferriesedipsos.gr), and between Ayiókambos and Glýfa (25min; ☎22260 31680, ⓦferriesglyfa.gr). Tickets are sold on the quayside, and buses from Athens' Liossíon 260	terminal serve both mainland ports. **By bus** Buses run from Halkídha to most points; there are three or four daily to Límni and Roviés, to Loutrá Edhipsoú and to Istiéa, the hub for north- and west-coast beaches.

Prokópi

PROKÓPI, in a broad wooded upland where the road emerges from the gorge, is famous for its hideous 1960s pilgrimage **church of St John the Russian**, actually a Ukrainian soldier captured by the Ottomans early in the eighteenth century and taken to central Anatolia, where he died. His mummified body began to work miracles, leading to canonization; the saint's relics were brought here in the 1923 population exchange. A vast pilgrimage in late May sees people walking from Halkídha (and beyond) and camping all around the church.

The large manor house overlooking the village is home to Philip Noel-Baker, a descendant of English Philhellene nobleman Edward Noel, a relative of Lady Byron, who bought the estate from the Turks in 1832 in order to support the new Greek state. The house (ⓦcandili.gr) now operates as a tranquil centre for conferences and courses (yoga, art, etc).

Límni and around

LÍMNI, a well-preserved Neoclassical town and sheltered port, with magnificent views west to the mainland, rivals Kárystos as the most characterful resort on Évvia. The main drawback is a lack of decent beaches, though there are plenty of pebble strands all around. Behind the waterfront is a maze of unnamed alleys; on one such is the little **museum** (Mon–Fri 9am–1pm, Sat 10am–1pm, Sun 10.30am–1pm; €2). This traces the history of the place from Mycenaean times – ancient Elymnia was an important city in Euboea – to the twentieth century, with some wonderful old photos, and it's a fun visit, where you're likely to get a personal tour from the curator, who speaks little English.

Immediately west of Límni, the hamlets of **Sipiádha** and **Khrónia** are virtually suburbs, each with good pebbly beaches and a choice of accommodation. **ROVIÉS**, 7km from Límni, is a bigger place, famous for its olives and with a picturesque, ruined medieval tower at its heart.

Ayíou Nikoláou Galatáki

Daily: winter 9am–noon & 2–5pm; summer 9am–noon & 5–8pm; knock and wait for entry • Free • Strict clothing rules apply

Around 7km southeast of Límni, the beautiful monastery of **Ayíou Nikoláou Galatáki** perches on the wooded slopes of Mount Kandíli, overlooking the Evvian Gulf. Though much rebuilt since its original Byzantine foundation atop a temple of Poseidon, the convent retains a thirteenth-century anti-pirate tower and a crypt. One of the six nuns will show you **frescoes** dating from a sixteenth-century renovation. Especially vivid, on the right, is the *Entry of the Righteous into Paradise*: the virtuous ascend a perilous ladder to be crowned by angels and received by Christ, while the wicked miss the rungs and fall into the maw of Leviathan.

There are pebble-and-sand **beaches** scattered along the road to the monastery, and more that can only be reached on foot immediately below it.

ARRIVAL AND DEPARTURE   LÍMNI AND AROUND

By bus Buses stop on Límni's central waterfront near the bottom of the main street, Angéli Govioú. Tickets are sold at the nearby Kafenío Neon.

ACCOMMODATION

Dennis House Khrónia ☎ 22270 31787, ⓦ dennishotel .gr. Apartment block in lush gardens, 500m out of the village towards Límni, with its own bar and restaurant; studios and two-room apartments with a/c, tv and great sea views. **€55**

★ **Eleonas** Roviés ☎ 22270 71619, ⓦ eleonashotel .com. Classy, peaceful place in a secluded olive grove outside town, with ground-floor a/c garden rooms or first-floor ones with balconies. Set back some way from the sea, but still with fine views. Breakfast included. **€80**

Graegos Studios Límni ☎ 22270 31117, ⓦ graegos .com. Just four comfortable a/c studios, with well-equipped kitchens, right at the eastern end of the waterfront. The two at the front have fabulous big balconies with views of the fishing port. **€70**

Livaditis Beach Sipiádha ☎ 22270 31640, ⓦ livaditis beach.com. Modern-looking beachfront apartment complex; the units are not as new as you might think, but spotless and in a great location, with a playground, taverna, kayaks and pedaloes on the beach, and a van for transfers to town. **€60**

EATING AND DRINKING

7 Anemous Límni ☎ 22270 32121. Unexpectedly fancy, though not overly expensive restaurant in a restored stone building in a backstreet behind the eastern seafront. Mediterranean menu includes pizza, pasta with salmon, salads and a few grills served in a garden or (in winter) inside by a roaring fire. Dinner only; closed Tues Oct–May.

Kalderimi Límni. Café ouzerí in an alley above the plaza, behind the *Plaza Hotel*, serving everything from omelettes for breakfast to octopus and fish in the evenings. Great for a morning coffee, but better in the evening when there's ouzo and excellent mezédhes. Daily all day, till late.

Lamaros Límni ☎ 22270 31351. Immaculate setting with a waterfront terrace and steps down to the water in an absolutely tranquil spot, 500m out of town, on the road to the monastery. Food is the regular Greek taverna array, with plenty of fish, cooked with care. Daily, evenings only.

To Pikandiko Límni ☎ 22270 31300. Simple, inexpensive grill-and-*souvláki* place with a great seafront position. *Yíros* pita and kebabs as well as more substantial meat dishes, with seating indoors and out. Daily lunch & dinner.

Loutrá Edhipsoú

LOUTRÁ EDHIPSOÚ is one of Greece's most popular **spa** towns, with a line of grand hotels gracing the front. If your wallet doesn't stretch to services at the *Thermae Sylla Spa* (see opposite), you can bathe for free at the adjacent public **beach**, where geothermal water pours into an artificial set of cascades. There are more free, open-air **hot springs** at **Ília**, 8km east, where sulphurous water boils up at 65°C on the pebble beach, then is channelled at more bearable temperatures into ad hoc pits dug by shovel-wielding locals.

ARRIVAL AND DEPARTURE   LOUTRÁ EDHIPSOÚ

By ferry Ferries arrive on the central seafront.
By bus The bus station is a couple of blocks south on Thermopotámou, which runs inland by the *Aegli* hotel.

Taxis The taxi stand (☎ 22260 23280) is directly opposite where the ferry docks.

ACCOMMODATION

Aegli Waterfront ☎ 22260 22215. A rather magnificent 1930s hotel that has clearly seen better days – they claim that Greta Garbo and Winston Churchill were among former guests. If faded grandeur is your thing, look no further. It's just north of the ferry dock, and also has a good waterfront terrace restaurant. **€50**
Avra Waterfront ☎ 22260 22226, ⓦ avraspahotel.gr. Grand old hotel, similar in style to the next-door *Aegli* (see above) if rather less interesting. Here the rooms have been

recently refurbished, however, and there's a variety of treatments on offer. **€70**
Thermae Sylla Waterfront ☎ 22260 60100, ⓦ thermaesylla.gr. Five-star pentagonal complex at the northern end of the seafront promenade that's by far the grandest of the surviving hotels, with indoor and outdoor pools. Pricey treatments, available to non-guests too, include a 45min "oriental bath" for €131 or 90min mud therapy for €95. **€250**

The north and west coasts

Northern Évvia's north and west coasts are home to most of the island's resorts – none, however, that is particularly attractive or sees many foreign visitors. On the whole they consist of long, exposed pebble beaches, backed by scrappy hamlets of second homes and small hotels. Heading clockwise from Loutrá Edhipsoú, you come first to **AYIÓKAMBOS**, with regular **ferry** connections to Glýfa on the mainland. **OREÍ** and **NÉOS PÝRGOS**, next up, pretty much merge together into a single resort; the former with good restaurants around its harbour, the latter quieter, but with only a tiny beach. **PÉFKI** is another small, pleasant resort with extensive beaches either side. At **Psaropoúli**, steeply below the town of **VASILIKÁ**, there's a vast, barely developed bay of grey sand and pebbles. **PARALÍA AYÍA ÁNNA**, by contrast, is a substantial resort on a couple of kilometres of brownish sand, with showers and loungers at the resort end, and plenty of empty space beyond. Finally, at the tiny hamlet of **KRÝA VRÝSSI**, there's a lovely brown-sand beach with the ruins of ancient Kirinthos at its southern end.

ACCOMMODATION AND EATING   NORTH AND WEST COASTS

Agali Hotel Paralía Ayía Ánna ☎ 22260 41208, ⓦ hotelagali.gr. Modern hotel at the northern end of the beach with an attractive, designer look. Rooms are less fancy than the exterior might lead you to expect, but comfortable and well equipped. Buffet breakfast included. **€70**
Galini Hotel Péfki ☎ 22260 41208, ⓦ pefkigalinihotel .gr. Right in the centre of the beach area, this is the largest and, in yellow and dark red, most brightly coloured of the beachfront hotels here, with a café-bar and restaurant out

front. Standard, modern a/c rooms. **€60**
To Pirofani Néos Pýrgos ☎ 22260 71448. A good *psarotavérna* overlooking the fishing harbour, serving all the usuals at waterfront tables and on a substantial roof terrace across the road. Daily lunch & dinner.
To Steki tis Yiannas Oreí ☎ 22260 71540. Excellent taverna with a lovely seaside setting by the harbour, serving fresh fish, octopus and calamari, plus daily oven-baked specials. Daily lunch & dinner.

7

The Ionian islands

459 Corfu

476 Paxí and Andípaxi

479 Lefkádha

488 Kefaloniá

498 Itháki

502 Zákynthos

510 Kýthira

MYRTOS BEACH, KEFALONIÁ

The Ionian islands

The six core Ionian islands, shepherding their satellites down the west coast of the mainland, float on the haze of the Ionian Sea, their lush green contours, a result of heavy winter rains, coming as a shock to those more used to the stark outlines of the Aegean. The west coasts of the larger islands also boast some of Greece's most picturesque cliff-backed beaches, whose sands are caressed by a band of milky turquoise water leading to the deeper azure sea.

Tourism is the dominant influence these days, as it has been for decades on **Corfu** (Kérkyra), which was one of the first Greek islands established on the package-holiday circuit, though the continuing downturn means it does not feel as swamped as in the past. And while parts of its coastline are among the few stretches in Greece with development to match the Spanish *costas*, the island is large enough to contain parts as beautiful as anywhere in the group. The southern half of **Zákynthos** (Zante) has also gone down the same tourist path, but elsewhere the island's pace is a lot less intense. Little **Paxí** lacks the water to support large-scale hotels and has limited facilities tucked into just three villages, meaning it gets totally packed in season. Perhaps the most rewarding trio for island-hopping are Kefaloniá, Itháki and **Lefkádha**. The latter is connected to the mainland by a causeway and iron bridge but still has quite a low-key straggle of tourist centres and only two major resorts, despite boasting some excellent beaches, strung along its stunning west coast. **Kefaloniá** offers a series of "real towns" and more stunning beaches, as well as a selection of worthwhile attractions, while **Itháki**, Odysseus's rugged capital, is protected from a tourist influx by an absence of sand. Finally, although officially counted among the Ionians and constituting the seventh of the traditional *eptánisos* (heptanese or "seven islands"), rugged **Kýthira** is quite separate from the six main islands on several counts. It is geographically 200km removed and only accessible from the southern Peloponnese, it shares the drier and warmer climate of southern Greece, and it remains quite a touristic backwater.

Brief history

The Ionian islands were the Homeric realm of Odysseus, centred on Ithaca (modern Itháki), and here alone of all modern Greek territory the Ottomans never held sway – except on Lefkádha. After the fall of Byzantium, possession passed to the **Venetians**, and the islands became a keystone in Venice's maritime empire from 1386 until its collapse in 1797. Most of the population remained immune to the establishment of Italian as the official language and the arrival of Roman Catholicism, but Venetian influence remains evident in the architecture of the island capitals, despite damage from a series of earthquakes.

The Ionian School of painting p.463
Mount Pandokrátor p.466
Boat trips from Paleokastrítsa p.471
Walking the Corfu Trail p.475
Walks around Lákka p.478
Lefkádha's summer festivals p.482

Boat trips from Nydhrí p.484
Lover's leap p.487
Odysseus sights around Vathý p.499
Boat trips from Zákynthos Town p.502
Loggerhead turtles p.506

THE LISTÓN, CORFU TOWN

Highlights

❶ Corfu Town Venetian fortresses, beautiful churches, fine museums and appealing Venetian architecture. **See p.459**

❷ Longás beach, Corfu Shaded till early afternoon and backed by sheer vertical red cliffs, this beach is an excellent hangout. **See p.472**

❸ Andípaxi Some of the Ionians' best swimming and snorkelling is on offer at the exquisite beaches of Paxí's little sister. **See p.478**

❹ Lefkádha's west coast Between Áï Nikítas and Pórto Katsíki lie some of the archipelago's finest and least crowded beaches. **See p.487**

❺ Melissáni Cave, Kefaloniá See dappled sunlight on the water amid rock formations on a boat trip inside this once-enclosed underwater cave. **See p.495**

❻ Mount Énos, Kefaloniá The highest point in the Ionians has stunning vistas of sea and distant land, plus a unique species of pine. **See p.492**

❼ Itháki's Homeric sites Relive the myths on Odysseus's island by visiting locations described by Homer. **See p.499**

❽ Boat tour around Zákynthos The best way to see the impressive coastline, including the Blue Caves and Shipwreck Bay, is to cruise from Zákynthos Town. **See p.502**

HIGHLIGHTS ARE MARKED ON THE MAP ON P.458

On Corfu, the Venetian legacy is mixed with that of the **British**, who imposed a military "protectorate" over the Ionian islands at the close of the Napoleonic Wars, before ceding the archipelago to Greece in 1864. There is, however, no question of the islanders' essential Greekness: the poet Dhionyssios Solomos, author of the national anthem, hailed from the Ionians, as did Nikos Mantzelos, who provided the music, and the first Greek president, Ioannis Kapodhistrias.

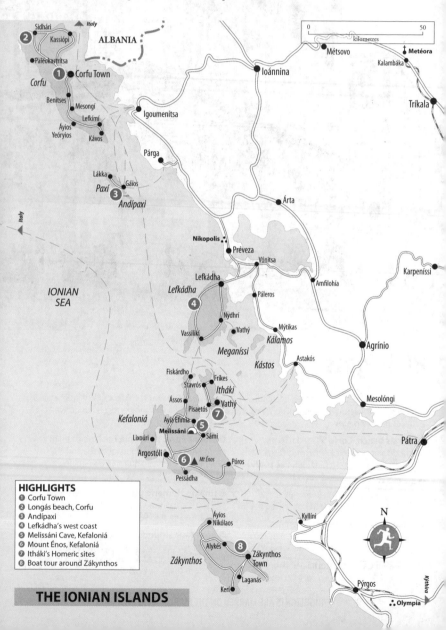

HIGHLIGHTS
1. Corfu Town
2. Longás beach, Corfu
3. Andípaxi
4. Lefkádha's west coast
5. Melissáni Cave, Kefaloniá
6. Mount Énos, Kefaloniá
7. Itháki's Homeric sites
8. Boat tour around Zákynthos

THE IONIAN ISLANDS

Corfu

Dangling between the heel of Italy and the west coast of mainland Greece, green, mountainous **CORFU (Kérkyra)** was one of the first Greek islands to attract mass tourism in the 1960s. Indiscriminate exploitation turned parts into eyesores but a surprising amount of the island still consists of olive groves, mountains or woodland. The majority of package holidays are based in the most developed resorts and unspoilt terrain is often only a few minutes' walk away.

Corfu is thought to have been the model for Prospero and Miranda's place of exile in Shakespeare's *The Tempest*, and was certainly known to writers such as Spenser, Milton and – more recently – Edward Lear and Henry Miller, as well as Gerald and Lawrence Durrell. Lawrence Durrell's *Prospero's Cell* evokes the island's "delectable landscape" still evident in some of its beaches, the best of the whole archipelago.

The staggering amount of accommodation on the island means that competition keeps prices down even in high season, at least in many resorts outside of Corfu Town. Prices at restaurants and in shops also tend to be a little lower than average for the Ionians.

ARRIVAL AND DEPARTURE — CORFU

By plane Corfu receives seasonal charter flights from all over northern Europe but only has year-round scheduled services to Athens (4–6 daily; 1hr).

By ferry The vast majority of domestic services and all those to Italy run from Corfu Town, although there are a few boats to the mainland from Lefkímmi. Most of the ferry offices are on the main road opposite the New Port; ferries to Italy or south towards Pátra become very busy in summer and booking is advisable. The port authority (domestic ☎ 26610 32655, international ☎ 26610 30481) can advise on services. There are buses that board the ferry

from the island capital to Greece's two largest cities, Athens (3 daily; 9–10hr) and Thessaloníki (2 daily; 8–9hr); schedules are year-round. For the additional destinations below, frequencies given are for the summer season and are greatly reduced in winter.

Corfu Town to: Ancona (1–2 daily; 14hr); Bari (2–3 daily; 11hr); Brindisi (3–5 daily; 4–9hr); Eríkoussa/Mathráki/Othoní (3 weekly; 2–4hr); Igoumenítsa (every 10–45min; 1hr 15min); Pátra (6–10 daily; 6–9hr); Venice (3–4 weekly; 25hr).

By hydrofoil Services run from Corfu Town to Gáïos (Paxí; May–Oct 1–3 daily; 50min).

GETTING AROUND

By bus Corfu's bus service radiates from the capital. Islandwide services stop operating between 6 and 9pm, suburban ones at between 9 and 10.30pm. Printed English timetables are available for both and can be picked up at the respective terminals.

By car or motorbike Many people rent vehicles to get around the island and there are numerous international and local companies in the capital (see p.464) and around the resorts.

Corfu Town

The capital, **CORFU TOWN**, has been one of the most elegant island capitals in the whole of Greece since it was spruced up for the EU summit in 1994. Although many of its finest buildings were destroyed by Nazi bombers in World War II, two massive forts, the sixteenth-century church of Áyios Spyrídhon and some buildings dating from French and British administrations remain intact. As the island's major port of entry by ferry or plane, Corfu Town can get packed in summer.

Corfu Town comprises a number of distinct areas. The **Historic Centre**, the area enclosed by the Old Port and the two forts, consists of several smaller districts: **Campiello**, the oldest, sits on the hill above the harbour; **Kofinéta** stretches towards the Spianádha (Esplanade); **Áyii Apóstoli** runs west of the Mitrópolis (Orthodox cathedral); while tucked in beside the Néo Froúrio is what remains of the old **Jewish quarter**. These districts and their tall, narrow alleys conceal some of Corfu's most beautiful architecture. The **New Town** comprises all the areas that surround the Historic Centre.

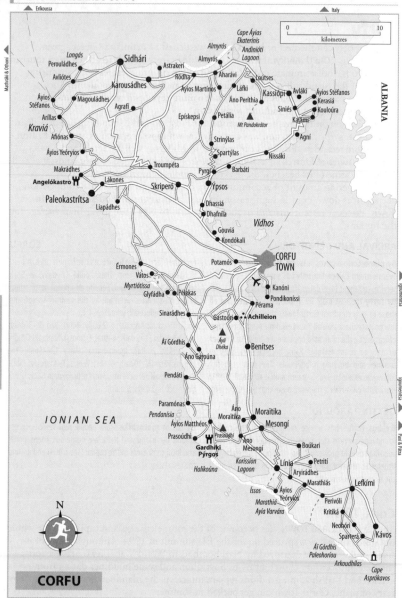

The Historic Centre

The most obvious sights are the forts, the **Paleó Froúrio** and **Néo Froúrio**, whose designations (*paleó* – "old", *néo* – "new") are a little misleading, since what you see of the older structure was begun by the Byzantines in the mid-twelfth century, just a hundred years before the Venetians began work on the newer citadel. They have both been damaged and modified by various occupiers and besiegers, the last contribution being the Neoclassical shrine of St George, built by the British in the middle of Paleó Froúrio during the 1840s.

Néo Froúrio

Daily: April–Oct 9am–9pm (or sunset if earlier); Nov–March 8am–3pm • €3

Looming above the Old Port, the **Néo Froúrio** is the more architecturally interesting of the two forts. The entrance, at the back of the fort, gives onto cellars, dungeons and battlements, with excellent views over the town and bay; there's a small gallery and seasonal café at the summit.

Paleó Froúrio

April–Oct Mon–Sat 8am–8pm, Sun 8.30am–3pm; Nov–March daily 8.30am–2.30pm • €4 • ☎ 26610 48310

The **Paleó Froúrio** is not as well preserved as the Néo Froúrio and contains some incongruous modern structures, but has an interesting **Byzantine Museum** just inside the gate, and even more stunning views from the central Land Tower. It also hosts daily son et lumière shows.

The Listón and Spianádha

Just west of the Paleó Froúrio, the focus of town life is the **Listón**, an arcaded café-lined street built during the French occupation by the architect of the Rue de Rivoli in Paris, and the green **Spianádha** (Esplanade) it overlooks. The cricket pitch, still in use at the northern end of the Spianádha, is another British legacy, while at the southern end the **Maitland Rotunda** was built to honour the first British High Commissioner of Corfu and the Ionian islands. The neighbouring statue of Ioannis Kapodhistrias celebrates the local hero and statesman (1776–1831) who led the diplomatic efforts for independence and was made Greece's first president in 1827.

Palace of SS Michael and George

Listón • **Asiatic Museum** Tues–Sun: May–Oct 8.30am–8pm; Nov–April 8.30am–3pm • €3 **Modern Art Gallery** Wed–Sun 9am–3pm • €4

At the far northern end of the Listón is the nineteenth-century **Palace of SS Michael and George**, a solidly British edifice built as the residence of their High Commissioner (one of whom was the future British prime minister William Gladstone) and later used as a palace by the Greek monarchy. The former state rooms house the **Asiatic Museum**, a must for aficionados of Oriental culture. Amassed by Corfiot diplomat Gregorios Manos (1850–1929) and others, it includes Noh theatre masks, woodcuts, wood and brass statuettes, samurai weapons and artworks from Thailand, Korea and Tibet. The adjoining **Modern Art Gallery** holds a small collection of contemporary Greek art.

Solomos Museum

3rd Párodhos Arseníou • Mon–Fri 9.30am–2pm • €1 • ☎ 26610 30674

This hidden museum is dedicated to modern Greece's most famous nineteenth-century poet, **Dhionysios Solomos**. Born on Zákynthos, Solomos was author of the poem *Amnos stín Eleftheria* ("*Hymn to Liberty*"), which was to become the Greek national anthem. He studied at Corfu's Ionian Academy, and lived in a house on this site for much of his life. On display are a number of his personal effects and manuscripts of some works.

CORFU TOWN COMBINATION TICKET

There is a handy **combination ticket** that covers four of Corfu Town's main attractions: the Paleó Froúrio, Byzantine Museum, Archeological Museum and Asiatic Museum. The ticket costs €8 and is available at any of the four sights.

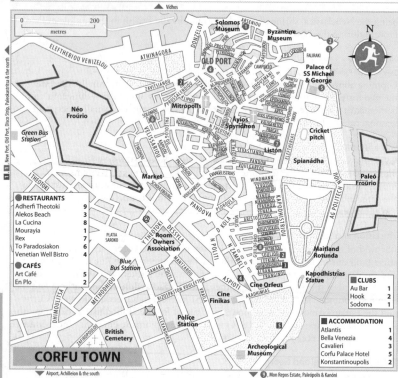

CORFU TOWN

Byzantine Museum

Arseníou • Tues–Sun 9am–3pm • €2 • ☎ 26610 38313

Up a short flight of steps on Arseníou, the **Byzantine Museum** is housed in the restored church of the Panayía Andivouniótissa. It houses church frescoes and sculptures and sections of mosaic floors from the ancient site of Paleópolis, just south of Corfu Town. There are also some pre-Christian artefacts, and a collection of icons dating from between the fifteenth and nineteenth centuries.

Church of Áyios Spyrídhon

Spyrídhonos • Daily 8am–9pm

A block behind the Listón is the sixteenth-century **church of Áyios Spyrídhon**, whose maroon-domed campanile dominates the town. Here you will find the silver-encrusted coffin of the island's patron saint, **Spyrídhon** – Spyros in the diminutive – after whom seemingly half the male population is named. Four times a year (Palm Sunday and the following Sat, Aug 11 and the first Sun in Nov), to the accompaniment of much celebration and feasting, the relics are paraded through the town streets. Each of the days commemorates a miraculous deliverance of the island credited to the saint – twice from plague, once from a famine and, in the eighteenth century, from the Turks.

The Mitrópolis

Platía Mitropóleos • Daily 8am–7pm

After Áyios Spyrídhon the next most important of the town's many churches, the **Mitrópolis** (Orthodox cathedral), is perched at the top of its own square opposite the Old Port. It also houses the remains of a saint, in this case St Theodora, the ninth-century wife of Emperor Theophilos. The building dates from 1577, and the plain exterior conceals a splendid iconostasis, as well as some fine icons, including a sixteenth-century image of *Saint George Slaying the Dragon*.

The New Town

There are a couple of noteworthy sights in the New Town that surrounds the Historic Centre. This area also encompasses much of Corfu Town's commercial heart, centred around busy **Platía Saróko**.

Archeological Museum

Bráïla 1 • Tues–Sun 8.30am–3pm • €3 • ☎ 26610 30680

Corfu Town's **Archeological Museum**, just round the coast from the southern end of the Spianádha, is the best in the archipelago. The most impressive exhibit is a massive (17m) Gorgon pediment excavated from the Doric temple of Artemis at Paleópolis, just south of Corfu Town; this dominates an entire room, the Gorgon flanked by panthers and mythical battle scenes. The museum also has fragments of Neolithic weapons and cookware, and coins and pots from the period when the island was a colony of ancient Corinth.

The British cemetery

Cnr of Zafiropoúlou and Kolokotróni • Open access

Just south of Platía Saróko, the well-maintained **British cemetery** features some elaborate civic and military memorials. It's a quiet green space away from the madness of Saróko and, in spring and early summer, comes alive with dozens of species of orchids and other exotic blooms.

8

The outskirts

Each of the sights on the sprawling outskirts of the city can easily be seen in a morning or afternoon, and you could conceivably cover several in one day.

Mon Repos and around

Estate daily 8am–7.30pm • Free • ☎ 26610 41369

About1.5km around the bay from the Rotunda and Archeological Museum, tucked behind Mon Repos beach, the area centred on the **Mon Repos** estate contains the most accessible archeological remains on the island, collectively known as **Paleópolis**. Within the estate, thick woodland conceals two **Doric temples**, dedicated to Hera and Poseidon. The Neoclassical **Mon Repos villa**, built by British High Commissioner Frederic Adam

---

THE IONIAN SCHOOL OF PAINTING

The Ionian islands have a strong tradition of excellence in the fine arts, particularly iconography. Having been occupied by the Venetians and later the British, the islands spent centuries more in touch with developments in western Europe than in the Ottoman empire.

Until the late seventeenth century, religious art in the Ionians, as elsewhere, was dominated by the stylistic purity and dignified austerity of the Cretan School. The founder of the **Ionian School of painting** is considered to be **Panayiotis Dhoxaras**, who was born in the Peloponnese in 1662 but, after studying in Venice and Rome, moved to Zákynthos and later lived and worked in Lefkádha and Corfu until his death in 1729. From his travels Dhoxaras absorbed the spirit of Italian Renaissance art, and brought a greater degree of naturalism into iconography by showing his subjects, usually saints, in more human poses amid everyday surroundings. He is also credited with introducing the technique of **oil painting** into Greece in place of the older method of mixing pigments with egg yolk.

Dhoxaras's work was carried on by his son, **Nikolaos** (1710–1775), and over the next two centuries the tradition flourished through the skilled brushwork of a host of talented artists, such as Corfiot **Yioryios Khrysoloras** (1680–1762), Zakynthian **Nikolaos Kandounis** (1768–1834) and three generations of the Proselandis family, starting with **Pavlos Proselandis** (1784–1837).

in 1824 and handed over to Greece in 1864, is the birthplace of Britain's Prince Philip and has been converted into the **Paleópolis Museum** (daily 8.30am–7.30pm; €3). As well as various archeological finds from the vicinity, including some fine sculpture, it contains period furniture *in situ*, and temporary modern art exhibitions.

Other remains worth a peek outside the confines of the estate include the **Early Christian Basilica** (Tues–Sun 8.30am–3pm; free) opposite the entrance, the **Temple of Artemis**, a few hundred metres west, and the eleventh-century church of **Áyii Iáson and Sosípater**, back towards the seafront on Náfsikas.

Vlahérna and Pondikoníssi

Bus #2 leaves Platía Saróko every 30min for Vlahérna convent • Boats leave the dock at Vlahérna for Pondikoníssi (€3 return)

The most famous excursion from Corfu Town is to the islets of Vlahérna and Pondikoníssi, 2km south of town below the hill of Kanóni, named after the single cannon trained out to sea atop it. Reached by a short causeway, the tiny, white convent of **Vlahérna** is one of the most photographed images on Corfu. **Pondikoníssi**, tufted by greenery from which peeks the small chapel of Panayía Vlahernón, is identified in legend with a ship from Odysseus's fleet, petrified by Poseidon in revenge for the blinding of his son Polyphemus.

Vídhos

Hourly shuttle *kaïkia* run from the Old Port (€1.50 return, last boat back 1.30am)

Vídhos, the wooded island visible from the Old Port, is a quieter destination then Vlahérna or Pondikoníssi. It makes a particularly pleasant summer evening excursion, when there is live music at the municipal restaurant near the jetty.

The Achilleion

Daily: May–Oct 8am–7pm; Nov–April 8am–4pm • €7 • ☏ 26610 56245

Some 6km south of Corfu Town, past the resort sprawl of Pérama, is the bizarre **Achilleion**, a palace built in a mercifully unique blend of Teutonic and Neoclassical styles in 1890 by Elizabeth, Empress of Austria. Henry Miller considered it "the worst piece of gimcrackery" that he'd ever laid eyes on and thought it "would make an excellent museum for surrealistic art". The house is predictably grandiose but the gardens are pleasant to walk around and afford splendid views in all directions.

ARRIVAL AND INFORMATION   CORFU TOWN

By plane The airport is 2km south of the town centre. A dedicated bus connects with central Corfu Town 8 times daily or blue city buses #5 and #6 can be flagged at the junction 500m north of the terminal. Taxis charge a rather steep €10 into town.

By bus There are two terminals: the islandwide green bus service is based on Avramíou (also for Athens and Thessaloníki), and the suburban blue bus system, which also serves nearby resorts such as Benítses and Dhassiá, is based in Platía Saróko.

By ferry or hydrofoil All vessels dock at the New Port (Néo Limáni), just west of the Néo Froúrio. The Old Port (Paleó Limáni), east of the New Port, is used only for day excursions.

By car For car rental, try Avis, Ethnikís Andístasis 42 (☏ 26610 24404, airport ☏ 26610 42007), behind the New Port; Budget, Venizélou 22 (☏ 26610 28590; airport ☏ 26610 44017); or Hertz, Ethnikí Lefkímis (☏ 26610 38388, airport ☏ 26610 35547). Among local companies, Sunrise, Ethnikís Andístasis 14 (☏ 26610 44325), is reliable.

By motorbike or scooter Motorbikes and scooters can be rented from Easy Rider, Venizélou 4 (☏ 26610 43026), or Atlantis, Xenofóndos Stratigoú 48 (☏ 26610 40580), both in the New Port.

Services There is no official tourist office, amazing for such a touristic island. The post office (Mon–Fri 7.30am–8pm) is on the corner of Alexándhras and Zafirópoulou. Many regular cafés have wi-fi and there are some internet cafés dotted around, such as X-plore, N. Lefteríti 4, two blocks north of Platía Saróko.

ACCOMMODATION

Accommodation in Corfu Town is busy all year round and expensive in comparison to the rest of the island. For rooms you can try the Room Owners' Association at D. Theotóki 2A (Mon–Fri 9am–1.30pm, plus summer Tues, Thurs & Fri 6–8pm; ☏ 26610 26133, ✉ oitkcrf@otenet.gr).

Atlantis Xenofóndos Stratigoú 48 ☎ 26610 35560, ⓦ atlantis-hotel-corfu.com. Large and spacious a/c hotel in the New Port; with its functional 1960s ambience it rather lacks character but the rooms are perfectly adequate. **€68**

★ **Bella Venezia** Zambéli 4 ☎ 26610 46500, ⓦ bellaveneziahotel.com. Smart, yellow Neoclassical building, blending elegance with a cosy atmosphere. The elegant rooms are furnished and decorated in warm hues. Breakfast in the airy conservatory included. **€107**

Cavalieri Kapodhstríou 4 ☎ 26610 39041, ⓦ cavalieri -hotel.com. Classy and large yet still welcoming, with all mod cons in the lavishly decorated rooms, great views and a roof bar open to non-residents. Breakfast included. **€90**

Corfu Palace Hotel Leofóros Dhimokratías 2 ☎ 26610 39485, ⓦ corfupalace.com. The most luxurious hotel on the island, with sweeping staircases up from the lobby, indoor and outdoor pools, landscaped gardens and well-appointed rooms, each with a marble bath. Breakfast included. **€220**

Konstantinoupolis Zavitsiánou 1 ☎ 26610 48716, ⓦ konstantinoupolis.com.gr. Classy hotel in the Old Port with tasteful decoration and comfortable rooms, most with fine harbour views. Good discounts out of high season. **€75**

EATING AND DRINKING

RESTAURANTS

Adherfi Theotoki M. Athanassíou, Garítsa ☎ 26610 45910. By far the best of the several establishments tucked behind the seafront park, this popular family taverna serves excellent mezédhes, meat and good-value fish dishes. March–Oct daily noon–2am.

Alekos Beach Faliráki jetty ☎ 26610 31030. Set in the tiny harbour below the palace, with great views, this place offers simple, mostly grilled meat and fish dishes at good prices. May–Sept daily 11am–midnight.

La Cucina Guildford 15 ☎ 26610 80011. The town's most authentic Italian food, including fine antipasti and meat or seafood spaghetti dishes at around €10–15. Two separate locations on the same block. Daily noon–1am.

Mourayia Arseníou 15–17 ☎ 26610 33815. This unassuming, good-value ouzerí near the Byzantine Museum does a range of tasty mezédhes, including sausage or seafood such as mussels and shrimp in exquisite sauces. Also boasts views of passing ferries and Vídhos island. March–Nov daily noon–midnight.

Rex Kapodhstríou 66 ☎ 26610 39649. Slightly pricey, owing to its location just behind the Listón, but this place has some of the best food in town, especially the delicious oven dishes, such as pork stuffed with plum and fig (€12). Daily 11am–1am.

To Paradosiakon Solomoú 20 ☎ 26610 37578. Behind the Old Port, this friendly place serves good inexpensive fresh food, especially home-style oven dishes such as *stifádho* and *kokkinistó*. April–Oct daily 10.30am–midnight.

★ **Venetian Well Bistro** Platía Kremastí ☎ 26610 44761. Tucked in a tiny square a few alleys north of the cathedral, this is the place for Greek nouvelle cuisine, with exotic main courses such as Iraqi lamb and Albanian calves' livers in ouzo for around €16–22. Easter–Oct daily 7pm–midnight.

CAFÉS

Art Café In a delightful garden behind the art gallery of the Palace of SS Michael and George, this is a great relaxed spot to take in some refreshment in between sightseeing. Daily 9am–midnight.

En Plo Faliráki jetty ☎ 26610 27000. This popular café boasts an unbeatably brilliant, breezy setting, with views of the Paleó Forúrio. Fine spot for a pre-prandial ouzo or late night brandy. Daily 10am–late.

NIGHTLIFE AND ENTERTAINMENT

There are some hip youth bars in town and a few remaining clubs on the "disco strip" of Ethnikís Andistáseos, a couple of kilometres north of town, past the New Port, though much of the action has shifted to the resorts. There are two cinemas, both showing mostly English-language films.

CLUBS

Au Bar Emborikó Kéndro, Ethnikís Andistáseos ☎ 26610 80909, ⓦ aubarcorfu.com. Happening club in a shopping centre that has regular theme nights, mixing mainstream international dance and Greek hits, plus occasional live shows. Daily 9pm–late.

Hook Kapodhstríou 14. Along with *Base* next door but one, this bar features cutting-edge sounds, ranging from indie to house and techno. Popular with students in term and locals plus a few tourists in summer. Daily 10pm–late.

Sodoma Ethnikís Andistáseos ☎ 26610 37227. Club with a large dancefloor, where an impressive light show accompanies techno, trance, some rock and Greek sounds. Daily 10pm–late.

CINEMAS

Cine Finikas Akadhimías ☎ 26610 39768. Down the cul-de-sac extension of Akadhimías, the town's open-air summer cinema is a lovely place to take in a film. June–Sept, showings usually 9pm & 11pm.

Cine Orfeus Cnr of Akadhimías and Aspióti ☎ 26610 39768. Corfu's winter cinema has comfy seats and a big screen. Oct–May, times vary.

8

The northeast

The **northeast**, at least beyond the suburban resorts near Corfu Town, is the most typically Greek part of Corfu – it's mountainous, with a rocky coastline chopped into pebbly bays and coves, above wonderfully clear seas.

Dhassiá and Ýpsos

Six kilometres from Corfu Town the coastline begins to improve at **Dhafníla** and **DHASSIÁ**, set in adjacent wooded bays with pebbly beaches. The latter, the first worthwhile place to stop in this direction, is much larger and contains nearly all the area's facilities, including a trio of **watersports** enterprises.

ÝPSOS, 2km north of Dhassiá, can't really be recommended to anyone but hardened bar-hoppers, though it is home to a diving centre (see opposite). The thin pebble beach lies right beside the busy coast road, and the resort is generally pretty tacky.

Barbáti

At **BARBÁTI**, 4km north of Ýpsos, you'll find the sandiest beach on this coast, though its charm has been somewhat diminished recently by the construction of the gargantuan *Riviera Barbati* apartment complex. The beach is a favourite with families and much accommodation is prebooked in advance.

Agní, Kalámi and Kouloúra

The first of three unmissable pebbly coves you encounter when travelling north from largely missable Nissáki is **AGNÍ**, a favourite mooring spot for yachties, largely because of its well-established reputation as something of a gourmet's paradise.

KALÁMI, around 3km north of Agní, is somewhat commercialized, but the village is still small and you can imagine how it would have looked in the year Lawrence Durrell spent here on the eve of World War II. The **White House**, where Durrell wrote *Prospero's Cell*, is now split in two: the ground floor is an excellent taverna, while the upper floor houses exclusive accommodation.

The tiny harbour of **KOULOÚRA**, barely a kilometre north of Kalámi, has managed to keep its charm intact, set at the edge of an unspoilt bay with nothing to distract from the pine trees and *kaïkia* apart from its idyllically located taverna.

MOUNT PANDOKRÁTOR

Mount Pandokrátor, Corfu's highest mountain, is crowned by the moderately interesting **Pandokrátoras monastery**, whose main sanctuary, built in the seventeenth century, is open to visitors; nothing remains of the original buildings from three centuries earlier.

The most direct route from the south is signposted via Spartýlas and then the village of **Strinýlas**, a popular base for walkers served by buses from Corfu Town. An alternative approach from the north coast goes via Loútses to the charming ghost village of **Áno Períthia**, from where you are a steep 5km from the summit and can only climb any higher on foot or in a four-wheel drive. Apart from taking a quick peek at the crumbling remains of half a dozen churches, there is good eating in the village. The main westerly route ascends via **Láfki** to **Petália**, just south of which a paved road leads the final 5km east to the summit.

Anyone interested in walking the Pandokrátor paths is advised to get the **map** of the mountain by island-based cartographer Stephan Jaskulowski or one of Hilary Whitton-Paipeti's walking books, available from the better English-language bookshops in Corfu Town.

RESTAURANT

★ **Old Perithia** Áno Perithia ☎ 26630 98055. Worth climbing any mountain for, this traditional taverna is renowned for succulent goat and home-produced feta cheese. The views are splendid too, of course. Noon–midnight: May–Sept daily; Oct–April Sat & Sun.

Áyios Stéfanos

The most attractive resort on this stretch of coast, 3km down a lane from Siniés on the main road, is **ÁYIOS STÉFANOS** (officially Áyios Stéfanos Sinión to distinguish it from its namesake in northwestern Corfu). The delightful bay bends almost at a right angle, the northern section of which contains the beach, beyond the string of restaurants.

ARRIVAL AND GETTING AROUND
THE NORTHEAST

By bus Green buses between Corfu Town and Kassiópi serve all resorts, along with some blue suburban buses as far as Dhassiá.

By boat In Áyios Stéfanos, Giannis Boats (☎ 26630 81322, ⓦ giannisboats.gr) rents out vessels of varying sizes from €50 per day.

ACTIVITIES

Diving Ýpsos is home to one of the island's major diving centres, Waterhoppers (☎ 26610 93867, ⓔ diverclub @hotmail.com).

Watersports Corfu Ski Club, the most established watersports outfit in Dhassiá (☎ 694 28 52 188, ⓦ corfuskiclub.com), claims to be the world's first paragliding operator.

ACCOMMODATION

In **Agní**, various high-quality studios and villas can be booked through Kalami Tourist Services, based in the eponymous village. Kalami Tourist Services (☎ 26630 91062, ⓦ kalamibay.com) in **Kalámi** has a range of rooms in the area on their books.

DHASSIÁ AND ÝPSOS

Corfu Camping Ipsos Ýpsos ☎ 26610 93579, ⓦ corfucampingipsos.com. The only campsite on this coast apart from the superior *Dionysus* at Dhafníla has a bar and restaurant, and offers standing tents. May–Oct. Adult plus tent **€9**

Dassia Beach/Dassia Margarita Dhassiá ☎ 26610 93224, ⓦ dassiahotels.gr. Two almost adjacent sister hotels, the best options on the beach itself, with large dining rooms and adequate balconied guest rooms. Breakfast included. April–Oct. **€50**

Dassia Chandris/Corfu Chandris Dhassiá ☎ 26610 97100, ⓦ chandris.gr. These twin luxury hotels dominate the resort imperiously from the main road, and have extensive grounds, pools and beach facilities, as well as huge stylish rooms and suites. Breakfast included. **€120**

★ **Dionysus Camping Village** Dhassiá ☎ 26610 91417, ⓦ dionysuscamping.gr. The best campsite on Corfu, where tents are pitched under terraced olive trees. There are also bungalow huts, a pool, shop, bar and a restaurant. Adult plus tent **€9.70**

BARBÁTI

Paradise ☎ 26630 91320. Up above the main road set amid a colourful tiered garden, this place offers decent-sized rooms with balconies, offering bird's-eye sea views. April–Oct. **€35**

ÁYIOS STÉFANOS

Kochili ☎ 26630 81522. This fine family taverna, which serves good home-style oven food and grills, also has the only independently bookable rooms in the village, simply furnished but with lovely bay views. May–Oct. **€40**

EATING, DRINKING AND NIGHTLIFE

DHASSIÁ AND ÝPSOS

B52 Ýpsos. One of the most enduring clubs that line the northern end of the seafront, popular for its large outdoor dancefloor, where you can shake it to pop, soul, funk and reggae. May to mid-Oct 8pm–late.

EDEM Dhassiá ☎ 26630 93013, ⓦ edemclub.com. Corfu's prime beach nightclub draws revellers from far and wide. International DJs play cutting-edge techno, trance and other latest genres to a lively crowd. Occasional rock and other theme nights. May–Sept daily 9pm–late.

Karydia Dhassiá ☎ 26630 93562. A good restaurant on the main road, with a pleasant garden, serving well-prepared versions of Corfiot specialities such as *sofrito* and *pastitsadha*, accompanied by decent barrelled wine. April–Oct 2pm–midnight.

AGNÍ, KALÁMI AND KOULOÚRA

★ **Nikolas** Agní ☎ 26630 91243. The oldest taverna of the excellent trio here. Superb home-style dishes such as lamb *kléftiko* are served with a smile and there are plenty of tasty mezédhes to choose from. April–Oct daily 9am–1am; Nov–March Fri–Sun noon–1am.

Toula's Agní ☎ 26630 91350. Rather upmarket restaurant with a grand terrace, where the huge menu includes a range of home-made pies and even Black Angus Argentinian steaks (upwards of €20). May–Sept 12.30–11pm.

White House Kalámi ☎ 26630 91040. Located in the old Durrell house and recommended for its specials – mussels and swordfish with garlic – but also good for simple grills, salads and a variety of mezédhes. April–Oct daily, Nov–March Fri–Sun, noon–1am.

8

ÁYIOS STÉFANOS
★ **Fagopotion** ☎ 26630 82020. With a deck right on the quay, this place offers finely prepared seafood, dishes such as rabbit *stifádho* and unusual items such as a *zogorítiki* soufflé with four cheeses. Most main dishes €10–13. Noon–1am: April–Oct daily; Nov–May Fri–Sun.

The north coast

The north coast between **Kassiópi** and **Sidhári** is blessed with some of the island's best stretches of sand and, as a direct result, is also home to a few of Corfu's most crowded package tourism resorts, varying in degrees of development but still with plenty to offer the independent traveller.

Kassiópi

At the far east end of the north coast is **KASSIÓPI**, a fishing village that's been transformed into a major party resort. The Roman emperor Tiberius had a villa here, and the village's sixteenth-century Panayía Kassópitra church is said to stand on the site of a temple of Zeus once visited by Nero. Little of Kassiópi's past survives, apart from an abandoned Angevin *kástro* on the headland – most visitors come for the nightlife and the five **pebbly beaches**, the largest of which is Kalamiónas, close to the coast road.

Almyrós beach and around

Little-developed **Almyrós beach**, around 10km west along the marshy, overgrown coastline from Kassiópi, is one of the longest on the island, with only a few apartment buildings and one huge new resort dotted sporadically behind it. The **Andinióti lagoon**, a haven for birds and twitchers, backs Cape Ayías Ekaterínis to the east, which marks the northern end of the Corfu Trail (see box, p.475).

Aharávi

At the western end of Almyrós beach, **AHARÁVI**'s old village is tucked on the inland side of the busy main road in a quiet crescent. The village serves as a base for those seeking alternative routes up onto **Mount Pandokrátor** (see p.466). Roads to small hamlets such as Áyios Martínos and Láfki continue onto the mountain, and even a stroll up from the back of Aharávi will find you on the upper slopes in under an hour.

Ródha

RÓDHA, barely 3km west of Aharávi, has tipped over into overdevelopment, and is certainly not the place to come for a quiet time. The resort does, however, offer some handy facilities. "Old Ródha" is a small warren of alleys between the main road and the seafront, where you'll find the best restaurants and bars.

Sidhári

At the west end of the north coast, **SIDHÁRI** is totally dominated by British package tourists; its small but pretty town square, with a bandstand set in a small garden, is lost in a welter of restaurants, bars and shops. The beach is sandy but not terribly clean, and many people tend to head just west to the curious coves, walled by wind-carved sandstone cliffs, around the vaunted Canal d'Amour. Sidhári also has its own modest water park (free entry), a good place to keep the kids happy.

GETTING AROUND   **THE NORTH COAST**

By car or motorbike Vlasseros Travel (☎ 26630 95695) is Sidhári's biggest general tourist agency and handles car rental. In Ródha, Myron offers good rates for motorbike rental (☎ 26630 63477).
By boat Voyager in Ródha (☎ 693 29 08 173) has boat rental from €15/hr.

ACTIVITIES

Diving Kassiópi is home to one of the island's most reliable diving operations, Corfu Divers (☎ 26630 81218, ⓦ corfu-divers.com), which is partly British-run.

Horseriding Costas in Ródha offers horseriding (☎ 694 41 60 011; €20/2hr), as does Vlasseros Travel in Sidhári (see opposite).

ACCOMMODATION

KASSIÓPI

★ **Kastro** ☎ 26630 81045, ⓦ kastrokassiopi.com. Overlooking the beach behind the castle, these smart a/c apartments have balconies with sweeping views, as does the attached restaurant, which does excellent fresh food. May to mid-Oct. **€50**

Panayiota Apartments ☎ 26630 81063, ⓦ panayotakassiopi.com. Bargain studios, quite small and simply furnished, one block behind Kalamíones beach on the west side of the castle's peninsula. April–Oct. **€35**

ALMYRÓS BEACH AND AROUND

Villa Maria ☎ 26630 64284. The ideal place for a peaceful escape, this attractively designed two-storey block sits on a grassy plot close to the quiet beach and has sea-facing balconies. May–Oct. **€40**

AHARÁVI

Dandolo ☎ 26630 63557, ⓦ dandolo.gr. Set in lush grounds on the edge of the old village, the refurbished complex contains fair-sized studios with well-equipped kitchens and verandas. April–Oct. **€45**

RÓDHA

Roda Camping ☎ 26630 93120, ⓦ rodacamping.gr. Around 2km east of the resort, one of the island's best campsites offers a plethora of amenities, including a pool, restaurant and minimarket. May–Sept.

Roda Inn ☎ 26630 63358, ⓦ rodainn.com. On the seafront at the edge of the old town, the oldest hotel in the resort (dating from 1975) is one of the few places not exclusively rented by package companies. May–Oct. **€40**

EATING, DRINKING AND NIGHTLIFE

8

KASSIÓPI

Eclipse The liveliest and most established of the cluster of bars around the only junction in the resort, which shows DVDs before assuming full-on club mode as the night wears on. April–Oct daily 11am–late.

Janis ☎ 26630 81082. Where Kalamíones beach meets the coast road, this huge taverna has an equally extensive menu, or, for a splurge, you can choose a live lobster from the tank (€70/kg). April–Oct daily 9am–2am.

Porto ☎ 26630 81228. Fish restaurant at the harbour, which has plenty of smaller fry for €7–9 per generous portion, plus meat dishes, salads and all the standard dips. May–Oct daily 11am–1am.

AHARÁVI

★ **Theritas** ☎ 26630 63527. This taverna in the old village is the most authentic in the area, serving good home-cooked dishes such as beef in a rich red sauce or *sofríto*, grills and various starters, as well as very palatable wine. May–Oct daily noon–1am.

Votsalakia ☎ 26630 63346. At the western end of the beach, this is the best seaside restaurant, serving fresh fish and seafood at reasonable prices, as well as the usual array of salads and mezédhes. May–Oct daily 10am–midnight.

RÓDHA

Crusoe's ☎ 693 22 50 487. Cheerful British-run pub which has decent snacks and features pub games, quizzes and Sky Sports on TV, as well as a range of music. May–Oct daily 9am–2am.

Dolphin ☎ 26630 63431. This seafront taverna in Old Ródha is the best place for fish or seafood, which you can enjoy with some good local barrelled wine beside the waves that lap below the patio. May–Oct daily 11am–1am.

SIDHÁRI

Babylon ☎ 26630 95065. Fairly typical of the resort's numerous bars in appearance and ambience but one of the most popular, getting livelier the later it gets, with a mixture of pop and disco hits. May–Oct daily noon–late.

Kavvadias ☎ 26630 99032. Reliable taverna on the eastern stretch of beach, which dishes up all the Greek favourites and has the odd foray into Asian cuisine. Three-course specials for €7.50. April–Oct daily 10am–midnight.

Kohenoor ☎ 26630 95111. One of Corfu's best curry houses, serving a wide range of subcontinental favourites from tandoori to vindaloo for as little as €7–8. May–Sept daily 6pm–midnight.

Corfu's satellite islands

Only three of Corfu's quintet of **Dhiapóndia islands**, scattered up to 20km off the northwest coast, are inhabited: Eríkoussa, Othoní and Mathráki. Each of them supports a tiny year-round community but they only really come alive in summer and even then the islands remain a relaxed backwater.

Flattish **Eríkoussa** is the sandiest and most visited of the three. There is an excellent golden sandy beach right by the harbour and quieter **Bragíni beach**, reached by a path across the wooded island interior. **OTHONÍ** is the largest island and has a handful of places to stay and eat in its port, **Ámmos**, which has two pebbly beaches. The village of **Horió** in the island's centre and sandy but deserted **Fýki Bay** are worth visiting if you stay. Hilly, densely forested and with long, almost invariably deserted **Portéllo beach**, beautiful **MATHRÁKI** has the fewest inhabitants, though it is gradually gearing up towards visitors.

ARRIVAL AND DEPARTURE — CORFU'S SATELLITE ISLANDS

Day-trips Some travel agencies in the northern resorts offer day-trips just to Eríkoussa, while a trip taking in all three islands from Sidhári or Áyios Stéfanos is excellent value. Vlasseros Travel in Sidhári (T 26630 95695) offer trips, while on the west coast, day-trips run several times a week in season (€20 per person) from Áyios Stéfanos to all three islands.

By kaïkia and ferry You can travel independently between the islands on regular *kaïkia* from Sidhári; there are also passenger services on the Aspiotis lines *kaïki* (3–5 weekly; €10–12 return; T 26630 41297, W aspiotislines.gr) from Áyios Stéfanos. The thrice-weekly ferry from Corfu Town (2–4hr) is the least efficient way to get there.

ACCOMMODATION, EATING AND DRINKING

The only rooms are those rented by locals such as Tassos Kassimis (T 26630 71700; €30) and Khristos Aryiros (T 26630 71652; €40), both on Portéllo beach.

8

Erikousa Eríkoussa T 26630 71110, W hotelerikousa.gr. Busy throughout the season by virtue of being the island's sole hotel, with simple but adequate rooms, it also boasts the only bona fide taverna. Breakfast included. May–Sept. €60

Hotel Calypso Othoní T 26630 72162. Some 200m east of the jetty, Othoní's only hotel has pleasant, comfortably furnished rooms with balconies plus a small bar. May–Sept. €40

La Locanda dei Sogni Othoní T 26630 71640. Quality but not unreasonably priced Italian restaurant, which does a line in authentic antipasti, pasta and pizza dishes, plus plenty of Greek items. Also has some rooms. Restaurant May–Sept daily noon–1am. €35

Port Centre Mathráki. Good restaurant on the harbour that specializes in freshly caught fish at very decent prices, plus a few simple salads and mezédhes. Late May to Sept daily noon–midnight.

Paleokastrítsa

PALEOKASTRÍTSA, a sprawling village 23km west of Corfu Town, surrounded by dramatic hills and cliffs, has been identified as the Homeric city of Scheria, where Odysseus was washed ashore and escorted by Nausicaa to the palace of her father Alkinous, king of the Phaeacians. It's a stunning site, as you would expect, with a delightful centre, though it's one that's long been engulfed by tourism.

Beaches

The focal point of the village is the largest and least attractive of three **beaches**, home to sea taxis and *kaïkia* (see box opposite). The second beach, to the right, is stony with clear water, but the best of the three is a small, unspoilt strand reached along the path by the *Astakos Taverna*. Protected by cliffs, it's almost entirely undeveloped.

Theotókou monastery

7am–1pm & 3–8pm • Free, donations welcome

On the rocky bluff above the village, the **Theotókou monastery** is believed to have been established in the thirteenth century. There's also a museum, resplendent with icons, jewelled Bibles and other impedimenta of Greek Orthodox ritual, though the highlight is the gardens, from which there are spectacular coastal views.

BOAT TRIPS FROM PALEOKASTRÍTSA

From Paleokastrítsa's first beach you can get a boat trip to some nearby seawater caves, known as the **'blue grottoes'** (€10 for a 30min trip), which is worth taking for the spectacular coastal views. Boats also serve as a taxi service to three neighbouring **beaches**, Áyia Triánda, Palatákia and Alípa, which all have snack bars.

Angelókastro
June–Oct daily 8.30am–2pm • €2

Paleokastrítsa's ruined Byzantine castle, the **Angelókastro**, is around 6km up the coast; only approachable by a path from the hamlet of **Kríni**, en route to which there are a couple of outstanding spots around the village of **Makrádhes** for a snack or drink while taking in the whole vista of Paleokastrítsa's promontory. The fortress itself has been partially restored for visitor safety and is worth the steep climb for the stunning, almost circular views of the surrounding sea and land from the battlements.

ACCOMMODATION AND EATING	PALEOKASTRÍTSA

Accommodation isn't hard to find but sprawls a long way back from central Paleokastrítsa, often leaving quite a walk to the beach. Nightlife is pretty low-key, mostly comprising similar garden bars dotted along the main road.

Astacos Taverna ☎ 26630 41068, ⓦ astacos.biz. Just behind the second beach, highlights at this friendly taverna include the lobster after which it's named or more pocket-friendly moussaka. There are also some well-appointed studios just behind. May–Sept. **€40**

Dolphin Snackbar ☎ 26630 41035. Just down some steps from the main road and above Alípa beach, the simple rooms here are adequate, with easy beach access, and the food on offer (April–Oct 8.30am–midnight) is more substantial than the name suggests. **€35**

Odysseus ☎ 26630 41209, ⓦ odysseushotel.gr. On the road into town, this 65-room hotel has a pool, snack bar, a/c restaurant and balconies facing either the garden or the sea. Breakfast included. April–Oct. **€50**

Paleo Camping ☎ 26630 41204, ⓦ camping paleokastritsa.com. Just off the main road, almost a 30min walk from the centre, this campsite has good facilities, shady if slightly cramped tent pitches and a mini-market. May–Sept. Adult plus tent **€7.50**

Vrahos ☎ 26630 41128. Upmarket taverna with starched tablecloths and rather stiff service but offering pricey top-of-the-range fish and some unusual dishes like artichokes. Reckon on at least €25–30 per head. April to mid-Oct noon–1am.

The northwest coast

The northwest conceals some of the island's most dramatic coastal scenery, the violent interior mountainscapes jutting out of the verdant countryside. North of Paleokastrítsa, the densely olive-clad hills conceal good sandy beaches, such as **Áyios Yeóryios** and **Áyios Stéfanos**. Public **transport** between west coast resorts is difficult: virtually all buses ply routes from Corfu Town to single destinations and rarely link resorts.

Áyios Yeóryios

Like many of the west-coast resorts, **ÁYIOS YEÓRYIOS**, around 9km north of Paleokastrítsa, isn't actually based around a village, though it is sometimes referred to as Áyios Yeóryios Pagón after the inland village of Payí to avoid confusion with its southern namesake. The resort has developed in response to the popularity of the large sandy bay, and it's a major **windsurfing** centre, especially towards the northern end, where boats can also be rented.

Afiónas

The village of **AFIÓNAS**, perched high above the north end of Áyios Yeóryios bay, has been suggested as the likely site of **King Alkínous's castle** – there are vestigial Neolithic remains outside the village – and the walk up to the lighthouse on Cape Aríllas affords excellent views over Áyios Yeóryios and Aríllas Bay to the north.

Áyios Stéfanos

The northernmost of the west coast's resorts, **ÁYIOS STÉFANOS** is low-key, popular with families and a quiet base from which to explore the northwest and the Dhiapóndia islands (see p.469), visible on the horizon. The small harbour lies a good kilometre south of the long sandy beach.

Avliótes and around

In the northwest corner of Corfu stands **AVLIÓTES**, a handsome hill town with the odd *kafenío* and tavernas but few concessions to tourism. The town is useful for its accessibility to the small, quiet village of **Perouládhes** in the very northwest and stunning **Longás beach** below, bordered by vertical reddish layer-cake cliffs that make for shady mornings.

ACCOMMODATION, EATING AND DRINKING   **THE NORTHWEST COAST**

ÁYIOS YEÓRYIOS

★ **Ostrako** ☎ 26630 96028. Gaily painted taverna with a terrace overlooking the southern end of the beach, unbeatable for seafood such as squid and octopus. The eclectic recorded folk music helps create a pleasant atmosphere. May–Oct 11am–1am.

Pension Vrahos ☎ 26630 96366, ⓦ pension-vrachos .com. At the far northern end of the beach, under the eponymous cliff, this pension offers bright, good-value rooms in the building behind its taverna, which serves Greek and international cuisine. May–Oct. **€40**

Studio Eleana ☎ 26630 96366. Smart modern studios with crisp white linen, nice kitchenettes and some sea-view balconies, 50m behind the central section of beach. Late May–Sept. **€35**

AFIÓNAS

To Panorama ☎ 26630 51846, ⓔ panorama_afionas @hotmail.com. Friendly family restaurant which serves tasty meals made from organic produce and has great views from its terrace; it has also some good-value rooms. May–Sept. **€30**

ÁYIOS STÉFANOS

Nafsika ☎ 26630 51051, ⓦ nafsikahotel.com. Behind the southern strip of beach, the resort's oldest hotel has comfy rooms, a popular restaurant and gardens with a pool and bar. April–Oct. **€40**

★ **O Manthos** ☎ 26630 52197. The oldest taverna, behind the southern beach, is still the best, and serves Corfiot specialities such as *sofríto* and *pastitsádha*. Ask the venerable owner to show you his memorabilia. Music and dance every Sat. May–Oct noon–1am.

Restaurant Evinos ☎ 26630 51766. Has small apartments above the northern end of the village and serves up wholesome food, a mixture of *mayireftá* and grilled meat or fish. May to mid-Oct. **€35**

AVLIÓTES AND AROUND

Panorama Longás beach ☎ 26630 51846. The taverna's name gives the game away – perched on the cliff above the beach, its garden terrace is a great spot for a sunset dinner or cocktail at the attached *7th Heaven Café*. May–Sept daily 11am–midnight.

Central Corfu

Much of central Corfu is occupied by the **plain of Rópa**, whose fertile landscape backs onto some of the best beaches on the west coast, such as delightful **Myrtiótissa**, as well as the island's only mountain resort, **Pélekas** – all a quick bus ride across the island from Corfu Town. The only place of note on the central east coast is **Benítses**.

Érmones and around

ÉRMONES, around 15km south of Paleokastrítsa by road, is one of the busiest resorts on the island, its lush green bay backed by the mountains above the Rópa River but rather marred by the ugly tiered *Ermones Beach Hotel* and its private funicular. Just inland is the **Corfu Golf and Country Club** (☎ 26610 94220, ⓦ corfugolfclub.com), the only golf club in the archipelago, and reputed to be one of the finest in the Mediterranean.

Myrtiótissa

Far preferable to the gravelly sand of Érmones is the idyllic strand of **MYRTIÓTISSA**, about 3km south. In *Prospero's Cell*, Lawrence Durrell described Myrtiótissa as "perhaps the loveliest beach in the world"; it was for years a well-guarded secret but is now a firm favourite, especially with nudists, and gets so busy in summer that it supports three *kantínas*, meaning it's at its best well out of high season. Above the north end of the beach is the tiny, whitewashed **Myrtiótissa monastery**, dedicated to Our Lady of the Myrtles.

Pélekas and around

PÉLEKAS, inland and 5km southeast of Érmones, has long been popular for its views – the **Kaiser's Throne** viewing tower, just above the town, was Wilhelm II's favourite spot on the island. On the small square the **Odhiyítria church**, renovated in 1884, is worth a peek. Pélekas's sandy **beach** is reached down a short path, though sadly it's been rather spoilt by the monstrous *Pelekas Beach* hotel that now looms over it.

The inland area around Pélekas holds some of Corfu's most traditional villages. This atmosphere of days gone by is best reflected in **SINARÁDHES**, around 4km away, which has the **Folk Museum of Central Corfu** (Tues–Sun 9.30am–2.30pm; €2). The museum comprises an authentic village house, complete with original furniture, fittings and decoration and full of articles and utensils that formed an intrinsic part of daily rural life.

Áï Górdhis and around

Around 7km south of Pélekas, **Áï GÓRDHIS** is one of the major party beaches on the island, largely because of the activities organized by the startling *Pink Palace* complex (see p.474), which dominates the resort.

Inland from the resort is the south's largest prominence, the humpback of **Áyii Dhéka** (576m), reached by path from the hamlet of Áno Garoúna; it is the island's second-largest mountain after Pandokrátor. The lower slopes are wooded, and it's possible to glimpse buzzards wheeling on thermals over the higher slopes. The monks at the tiny monastery just below the summit lovingly tend a bountiful orchard.

Áyios Matthéos

The town of **ÁYIOS MATTHÉOS**, 3km inland, is still chiefly an agricultural centre, although a number of *kafenía* and tavernas offer a warm welcome to passers-by. On the other side of Mount Prasoúdhi, 2km by road, is the **Gardhíki Pýrgos**, the ruins of a thirteenth-century castle built in this unlikely lowland setting by the despots of Epirus.

Benítses

South of Corfu Town on the east coast, there's nothing to recommend before **BENÍTSES**, a once-notorious bonking-and-boozing resort, whose old centre at the north end has long since reverted to a quiet bougainvillea-splashed Greek village. There are a couple of minor attractions, namely the modest ruins of a **Roman bathhouse** at the back of the village and the small but impressive **shell museum** (March–May & Oct daily 10am–6pm; June–Sept 9am–8pm; €4; ☏ 26610 72227, ⍉ corfushellmuseum.com).

ACCOMMODATION, EATING AND DRINKING	CENTRAL CORFU

ÉRMONES

Nafsica ☏ 26610 94911. Perched just above the southern end of the beach, with a huge terrace, *Nafsica* provides good, filling mezédhes and main courses of both meat and fish. April–Oct 11am–1am.

Philoxenia ☏ 26610 94091, ⍉ hotelphiloxenia.gr. Far better value than the *Ermones Beach*, this spacious modern hotel on the south side of the creek has two pools, a bar and all the rooms face the sea. May to mid-Oct. **€60**

MYRTIÓTISSA

★ **Myrtia** ☏ 26610 94113, ✉ sks_mirtia@hotmail

.com. Delightful taverna with an olive-shaded garden, which serves tasty home-style cooking and offers a few simple but clean and cosy rooms. May–Oct. **€40**

PÉLEKAS AND AROUND

Alexandros Pélekas ☏ 26610 94215, ⍉ alexandros pelekas.com. Lots of the usual Greek favourites, plus pizza and pasta dishes, can be sampled here and the studios above are reasonably sized and comfortably furnished. April–Oct. **€50**

Pension Paradise Pélekas ☏ 26610 94530, ⍉ paradisepelekas.com. On the road in from Vátos, this ochre-tinted year-round *pension* run by a friendly old couple has simple homely rooms at bargain rates. €30

★ **Pink Panther** Pélekas ☎ 26610 94360. Serves quite a few imaginative dishes, with a refreshing array of peppery sauces, all at under €10, which can be enjoyed along with a glass or two of aromatic local wine while gazing at the splendid view from the lofty terrace. Easter–Oct.

AÏ GÓRDHIS AND AROUND

★ **Elena's** ☎ 26610 53210, ⓦ elenasapartments.com. A variety of rooms and apartments in the village is available through the seafront taverna, which is painted marine blue and white and serves excellent home-style cuisine at low prices, like beef in mustard sauce. April–Oct. €30

Pink Palace ☎ 26610 53103, ⓦ thepinkpalace.com. Legendary year-round backpackers' haunt, with pools, games courts, internet access, restaurants, a shop and a disco. Apart from the dorms for up to ten a night, which include breakfast and an evening buffet, there are compact singles and doubles. Dorms from €18; doubles €50

BENÍTSES

Benitses Arches ☎ 26610 72113, ⓦ hotelbenitsesarches .com. Pleasant bougainvillea-adorned hotel, just south of the centre of the resort, with quiet rooms set a couple of blocks back from the main road. April–Oct. €45

O Paxinos ☎ 26610 72339. Intimate taverna in the old village, specializing in Corfiot dishes such as *sofríto* and *pastitsádha*, not cheap at €12 a pop but expertly prepared and washed down with fine barrelled wine. Daily noon–1am.

Stadium Huge club at the southern end of the main strip. The interior opens only occasionally, hosting concerts or big dance nights, but the lively outdoor pool bar is open throughout the season. May–Sept daily noon–late.

Southern Corfu

Corfu's southwest coast offers perhaps the island's finest stretches of sand, from the peaceful **Korissíon lagoon** on down, almost unbroken to the island's tip. On the east side, there is a mixture of resorts, ranging from peaceful enclaves like **Boúkari** to the full-on party antics of **Kávos**, by way of Corfu's second-largest settlement, traditional **Lefkími**.

Moraïtika and Mesongí

On the east coast roughly 20km south of the capital, the first real development after Benítses is **MORAÏTIKA**, whose main street is an ugly strip of bars, restaurants and shops, but its beach is the best between Corfu Town and Kávos. The original village, **ÁNO MORAÏTIKA**, is signposted a few minutes' hike up the steep lanes inland and is virtually unspoilt, its tiny houses and alleys practically drowning in dazzling bougainvillea. The resort has become very popular with eastern Europeans.

Commencing barely a hundred metres on from the Moraïtika seafront and separated only by the Mesongí River, **MESONGÍ** continues this stretch of package-tour-oriented coast but is noticeably quieter and has a range of accommodation deals.

Boúkari and around

BOÚKARI, linked to Mesongí by a quiet road that follows the seashore for about 3km, often only a few feet above it, comprises little more than a handful of tavernas, a shop and a few small, family-run hotels. Out of the way, it's an idyllic little strip of unspoilt coast for anyone looking to relax. It is also handily placed for the unspoilt wooded region inland around **Aryirádhes**, rarely visited by tourists and perfect for quiet walks.

Petrití and around

Four kilometres south of Boúkari, the village of **PETRITÍ**, only created in the 1970s when geologists discovered the hill village of Korakádhes was sliding downhill, fronts onto a small but busy harbour. It is mercifully free of noise and commerce, with a beach of rock, mud and sand set among low olive-covered hills. Barely 2km south of Petrití, the picturesque rocky coves of **Nótos beach** are little visited.

Korissíon lagoon and around

Over on the southwest coast, one of the island's most distinctive geographical features is the **Korissíon lagoon**, home to turtles, tortoises, lizards and numerous indigenous and

WALKING THE CORFU TRAIL

The **Corfu Trail**, 200km in length and open since 2001, covers the whole island from **Cape Asprókavos** in the south to Áyios Spyrídhon beach, next to **Cape Ayías Ekaterínis** in the far north. The route avoids roads as much as possible and takes walkers across a variety of terrain – from beaches to the highest peaks – passing by Lefkími, Korissíon lagoon, Áyii Dhéka, Pélekas, Myrtiótissa, Paleokastrítsa, Áyios Yeóryios Pagón, Spartýlas and Mount Pandokrátor.

Paths along the entire route are **waymarked** with yellow aluminium signs. As usual, ramblers are advised to wear headgear and stout footwear and carry ample water and provisions, as well as all-weather kit in all but the high summer months. It is reckoned that strong walkers can cover the route in ten days.

Those interested in attempting all or part of the trail should pick up Hilary Whitton Paipeti's excellent *Companion Guide to the Corfu Trail* (ⓦ corfutrailguide.com; €10), which contains detailed **maps** and descriptions of the route, divided into ten daily sections. A proportion of the profits goes towards maintenance of the trail, and anyone using the trail is asked to contribute €3 for the same reason. You can also log on to ⓦ travelling.gr/corfutrail for information on organized walking packages, including accommodation.

migratory birds. Its northern section, which is over 5km long and 1km wide at its centre, is separated from the sea by the dunes of **Halikoúna beach**, an idyllic spot for swimming and rough camping, while more touristic **Íssos beach** borders the southern end.

Áyios Yeóryios, Marathiá and Ayía Varvára

Far pleasanter than **Áyios Yeóryios**, the main Brit-dominated but rather brash resort on the coast south of the Korissíon lagoon, are **MARATHIÁ** and **AYÍA VARVÁRA**, both essentially forming a single resort further southeast along the same continuous strand. They are separated only by a stream that you can easily cross on the beach but each settlement must be approached by different roads. The most direct route to Marathiá beach is signposted from the tiny village of **Marathiás**, a couple of kilometres southeast of Aryirádhes on the main road, while **AYÍA VARVÁRA** is signposted from the village of Perivóli further south.

Lefkími

Anyone interested in how a Greek town works away from the bustle of tourism shouldn't miss **LEFKÍMI**, towards the island's southern tip. The second-largest settlement after Corfu Town, it's the administrative centre for the south of the island as well as the alternative ferry port for Igoumenítsa. The town has some fine architecture, including several striking churches: **Áyii Anáryiri** with a huge double belfry, **Áyios Theódhoros**, on a mound above a small square, and **Áyios Arsénios**, with a vast orange dome that can be seen for miles.

Kávos

There are no ambiguities in **KÁVOS**, 6km south of Lefkími: either you like 24-hour drinking, clubbing, bungee-jumping, go-karts and chips with almost everything, or you should avoid the resort altogether. Kávos stretches over 2km of decent sandy beach, with watersports galore. As numbers have dropped in recent years, unbelievable accommodation bargains can be had, should you choose to stay.

South of Kávos

Beyond the limits of Kávos, where few visitors stray, a path leaving the road south to the hamlet of Sparterá heads through unspoilt countryside; after around thirty minutes of walking it reaches the cliffs of **Cape Asprókavos** and the crumbling **monastery of Arkoudhílas**. The cape looks out over the straits to Paxí, and down over deserted **Arkoudhílas beach**, which can be reached from Sparterá, a pleasant village 5km by road but only 3km by the signed path from Kávos. Even wilder is **Aï Górdhis Paleohoríou beach**, 3km further on from Sparterá, one of the least visited on the island and not to be confused

8

with the eponymous beach further north; a municipal café provides the only refreshment. The Cape is also the southern starting point for the **Corfu Trail** (see box, p.475).

ARRIVAL AND DEPARTURE — SOUTHERN CORFU

By ferry Lefkími has a year-round ferry connection to Igoumenítsa (6 daily; 40min).

By bus Lefkími is on the frequent bus route from Corfu Town to Kávos (11 Mon–Fri, 8 Sat, 4 Sun; 1hr 20min).

ACCOMMODATION, EATING AND DRINKING

MORAÏTIKA AND MESONGÍ

Bella Vista Áno Moraïtika ☎ 26610 75460. The menu is fairly basic but wholesome, with grills and fresh salads, but the place justifies its name with a lovely garden, sea views and breezes. March–Nov daily noon–midnight.

Charlie's Moraïtika. The village's oldest bar, which opened in 1939, is a meeting place for locals and tourists alike, with a central location on the main road. Light snacks are available and the music consists of old pop favourites. Daily noon–late.

Firefly Moraïtika ☎ 26610 75850. On one of the northernmost lanes down to the beach, this taverna has a good range of meat, fish, salads and dips, plus it rents those rooms not booked by Romanian tour operators. May–Sept. €30

Hotel Gemini Mesongí ☎ 26610 75221, ⓦ geminihotel.gr. This rather elegant hotel boasts a large pool and manicured gardens, plus sizeable en-suite rooms with balconies. Breakfast included. May–Sept. €65

Spiros on the Beach Mesongí ☎ 26610 75285. Beachfront restaurant with two premises 20m apart, good for tasty €8 fish soup plus other offerings from the deep, plus various carnivorous or vegetarian options. May to mid-Oct daily 11am–2am.

BOÚKARI AND AROUND

★ **Boukari Beach** Boúkari ☎ 26620 51791, ⓦ boukaribeach.gr. Right on the sea 1km north of Boúkari's harbour, one of Corfu's best tavernas offers delicious home cooking, and fresh fish and live lobster. The friendly family also run the smart and comfortable *Penelopi* and *Villa Alexandra*, with huge self-catering suites. Breakfast included. April–Nov. €40

PETRITÍ AND AROUND

★ **Panorama Villas** Nótos beach ☎ 26620 51707, ⓦ panoramacorfu.gr. A wonderfully friendly haven worth making the detour to, whether to stay or for its fine shady restaurant, renowned for its excellent home cooking. Breakfast included. April–Oct. €40

Pension Egrypos Petrití ☎ 26620 51949, ⓦ egrypos .gr. Pleasantly landscaped complex with a pool, bar and a restaurant. The rooms are smart, modern and fully equipped. Breakfast included. May to mid-Oct. €50

Stamatis Petrití ☎ 26620 51920. The best of the bunch clustered around the harbour, this year-round local taverna rustles up goodies like mussels and small fish for around €7–8. Daily noon–1am.

ÁYIOS YEÓRYIOS, MARATHIÁ AND AYÍA VARVÁRA

Akroama Marathiá ☎ 26620 52736. Good family-run taverna with treats like swordfish and local sausage, which can be enjoyed from the low-lying cliff terrace. They also rent some comfortable rooms. May–Sept. €30

LEFKÍMI

Cheeky Face ☎ 26620 22627. The old couple who run this simple year-round *estiatório*, by the bridge over the canal in the lower part of town, provide inexpensive staples and a few equally basic rooms upstairs. €40

KÁVOS

Future The most lively club of the dozens that line the main drag, with imported north European DJs, state-of-the-art sound-and-light systems, shots galore and a constant parade of the scantily clad. May–Oct daily 10pm–late.

Paxí and Andípaxi

Unusually verdant and still largely unspoilt, **PAXÍ (Paxos)** has established a firm niche in Greece's tourist hierarchy, despite being the smallest of the main Ionian islands at barely 12km by 4km, with only mediocre beaches and no historical sites. Yet it has become so popular it is best avoided in high season. It's a particular favourite of yachting flotillas, whose spending habits have brought the island an upmarket reputation, making it just about the most expensive place to visit in the Ionian islands. The capital, **Gáios**, is quite cosmopolitan, with delis and boutiques, but northerly **Lákka** and tiny **Longós** are where hardcore Paxophiles head, while by far the best swimming is at Paxí's little sister island, **Andípaxi**.

Gáïos

The island's capital, **GÁÏOS**, is a pleasant town built around a small square in the middle of an elongated seafront overlooking two islands, Áyios Nikólaos and Panayía. Nearly all the town's facilities are to be found on the seafront or within little over 100m of it.

Folk Museum

June to mid-Sept daily 10am–2pm & 7–11pm • €2

The island's only museum, the **Folk Museum**, is housed in an old school building on the seafront about 200m south of the main square. One room is set up as an eighteenth-century bedroom with some period furniture and costumes. Other items on display from different epochs include kitchen implements, musical instruments, china, stationery and guns.

Around Gáïos

Inland are some of the island's oldest settlements, such as Oziás and Vellianitátika, in prime walking country but with scarcely any facilities. The **coast south** of Gáïos is punctuated by the odd shingly cove, none ideal for swimming, until matters improve towards the tip at **Mogoníssi beach**, which shares some of Andípaxi's sandier geology.

Longós and around

LONGÓS is the prettiest village on the island, though it's dominated by the upmarket villa crowd. Its scruffy beach is favoured by local grannies for the sulphur springs, so most people swim off **Levrehió beach** in the next bay south. Longós is at the bottom of a steep winding hill, making **walking** a bit of a chore, but the short circuit around neighbouring **Dhendhriátika** provides spectacular views and allows access to the small

8

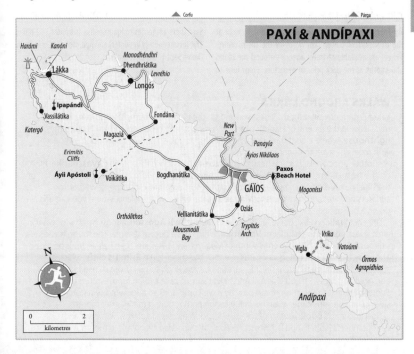

but excellent **Monodhéndhri beach**. You can also walk to **Fondána** and the former capital of **Magaziá**, back on the main road.

Lákka and around

Buses run 3–4 times Mon–Sat between Gáïos and Lákka, most diverting through Longós; taxis between Gáïos and Lákka cost around €10

Approached from the south, **LÁKKA** is an unprepossessing jumble of buildings, but once in its maze of alleys and neo-Venetian buildings or on the quay with views of distant Corfu, you do get a sense of its charm. Lákka's two **beaches**, Harámi and Kanóni, are none too brilliant for swimming or sunbathing, but there's a sense of community about the place and overall it's the best place to hang out on the island, with plenty of great dining and local walking.

Andípaxi

Frequent seasonal *kaïkia* shuttle between Gáïos and Andípaxi (€10 return); the glass-bottomed boat from Gáïos to Andípaxi (€15 return) also takes you to its sea stacks and caves

Less than 2km south, Paxí's tiny sibling **ANDÍPAXI** has scarcely any accommodation and no facilities beyond several beach tavernas open during the daytime in season. Andípaxi's sandy, blue-water coves have been compared with the Caribbean, but you'll have to share them with *kaïkia* and sea taxis from all three villages on Paxí, plus larger craft from Corfu and the mainland resorts.

Boats basically deposit you either at the sandy **Vríka beach** or the longer pebble beach of **Vatoúmi**, although quieter bays are accessible to the south. Paths also lead inland to connect the handful of homes and the southerly lighthouse, but there are no beaches of any size on Andípaxi's western coastline and thick thorny scrub makes access difficult.

ARRIVAL AND DEPARTURE   PAXÍ AND ANDÍPAXI

By ferry/hydrofoil Both ferries and hydrofoils dock at the new port of Gáïos, 1km north of the town centre. Tickets are available at travel agencies around the island and booths at the dock prior to departure. From June to Sept there are ferries to Igoumenítsa (summer 1–2 daily; 1hr; less frequently in winter) and hydrofoils to Corfu Town (May–Sept 1–3 daily; 50min).

WALKS AROUND LÁKKA

Lákka is perfectly sited for the finest walking on the island. For a simple, short hike, take the track leaving the far end of Harámi beach. This mounts the headland and leads on to the **lighthouse**, where a goat track descends through tough scrub to a sandy open-sea beach with rollers best left to confident swimmers.

Another good walking route heads west into the hills above the village to **Vassilátika**, high on the west-coast cliffs, which has stunning views out to sea. From here, the path to the left of the blue-painted stone archway leads on to the most dramatic cliff-edge views (vertigo sufferers beware) and continues to **Magaziá** in the centre of the island, where you can flag down a bus or taxi.

The best **walk** on Paxí, however, is to the church at **Áyii Apóstoli**, almost halfway down the west coast, next to the hamlet of **Voïkátika**, which has a decent taverna. The rough track is signposted a few hundred metres south of Magaziá, and takes less than half an hour on foot. The church and surrounding vineyards overlook the sheer 150m **Erimítis cliffs**, which at sunset are transformed into a seaside version of Ayers Rock, turning from dirty white to pink and gold and brown. If you visit Áyii Apóstoli at sunset, take a torch for the return trip. The *Sunset* **bar**, next to the church, can provide a welcome drink to augment the natural splendour and sometimes even hosts full-moon parties during the warmer months.

Noel Rochford's **book**, *Landscapes of Paxos*, lists dozens of walks on the island; this and cartographers Elizabeth and Ian Bleasdale's *Paxos Walking Map* are on sale in most travel agencies.

ACCOMMODATION, EATING, DRINKING AND NIGHTLIFE

As there are only three hotels and most accommodation on Paxí is booked by foreign tour companies, rooms and villas are best arranged in advance through one of the island's travel agencies: Gaïos Travel (☎ 26620 32033, ⊛ gaiostravel.co.uk) and Bouas Tours (☎ 26620 32401, ⊛ bouastours.gr), both on the capital's seafront; or Routsis (☎ 26620 31807, ⊛ routsis -holidays.com) and British-owned Planos Holidays (☎ 26620 31744 or UK +44 1373 814200, ⊛ planos.co.uk), both based in Lákka, for northern Paxí.

GAÏOS

Dodos ☎ 26620 32265. Set in a garden inland from the Anemoyiannis statue towards the southern end of the seafront, this old favourite has a full range of mezédhes and main courses, mostly under €10. May to early Oct daily noon–midnight.

★ **Genesis** ☎ 26620 32495. Convivial, brightly decorated taverna-cum-café, by far the best of the seafront establishments, right opposite the Anemoyiannis statue, serving great wine and home-cooked dishes such as several types of *stifádho*, including octopus. May–Oct daily 10am–1am.

★ **Paxos Beach Hotel** ☎ 26620 32211, ⊛ paxosbeachhotel.gr. Attractive en-suite bungalows with balconies on a hillside above a pebbly beach 2km south of town; amenities include a saltwater pool, yoga sessions, tennis court and mini-golf. Free shuttle bus. Breakfast included. May–Oct. **€120**

Paxos Club ☎ 26620 32450, ⊛ paxosclub.gr. Nearly 2km inland from Gáïos, this luxury resort set in lavish gardens offers large, well-furnished rooms and suites with kitchens, as well as a classy restaurant, pool and bar. Breakfast included. May–Sept. **€110**

PhoenixDisco ☎ 26620 32210. On a hill overlooking the bay, with a large outdoor dancefloor and the usual mix of foreign and Greek disco hits, this is the island's premier nightclub. June–Sept daily 10pm–late.

LONGÓS AND AROUND

O Gios ☎ 26620 31735. A simple and cheap taverna in the middle of the harbour, where you can get great grills, the odd oven dish and some basic salads and dips. June–Sept daily noon–midnight.

★ **Vassilis** ☎ 26620 30062. Friendly portside restaurant, where the bus has to squeeze past the pavement tables. Terrific fish dishes and tasty starters, outlined on a memorable newspaper-style menu. May–Oct daily 11am–1am.

LÁKKA AND AROUND

★ **Alexandros** Platía Edward Kennedy ☎ 26620 30045. Very friendly taverna tucked in the southwest corner of the village, great for fresh fish, *gourounópoulo* (roast suckling pig), creamed mushrooms and pork roll for €10. May–Oct daily 1pm–1am.

Amfitriti Hotel ☎ 26620 30011, ⊛ amfitritihotel.gr. Hidden among olive groves behind Harámi beach, the least expensive of Paxí's three hotels offers comfortable rooms with private balconies and kitchenettes. May–Oct. **€65**

Harbour Lights ☎ 26620 31412. Perennial favourite bar in the middle of the harbour, most likely to stay open the longest hours. Good range of drinks and mostly well-known pop and rock sounds. May–Oct daily noon–late.

La Rosa di Paxos ☎ 26620 31471. Slightly upmarket seafront restaurant, which does good risottos and ravioli, a variety of salads and some more standard Greek favourites. Mid-May to mid-Oct daily noon–1am.

Nionios ☎ 26620 31315. Serving a fine range of Hellenic favourites on the main square, from fish and meat grills to some tasty oven-baked veggie options, as well as fine barrelled wine. May–Oct daily noon–midnight.

ANDÍPAXI

Bella Vista Vatoúmi beach ☎ 26620 31766. Perched on a cliff overlooking the cove, this taverna justifies its name and also dishes up fresh fish and meat grills, plus a suitable range of salads and mezédhes. June–Sept noon–6pm.

Spiros Vríka beach ☎ 26620 31172. The oldest taverna on the island has great grilled and oven food. They can also arrange self-catering accommodation up in Vígla, the island's hilltop settlement, on a weekly basis. Late May to mid-Sept 11am–7pm.

Lefkádha

LEFKÁDHA (Lefkás) is an oddity, which is exactly why it is some people's favourite Ionian island. Connected to the mainland by a long causeway through lagoons and a 30m pontoon swivel bridge, it barely feels like an island, at least on the busier eastern side. Lefkádha was long an important strategic base and approaching the causeway you pass a series of fortresses, climaxing in the fourteenth-century castle of **Santa Maura** – the Venetian name for the island. These defences were too close to the mainland to avoid an Ottoman tenure, which began in 1479, but the Venetians wrested back control a couple of centuries later. They were in turn overthrown by Napoleon in 1797 and then the British took over as Ionian protectors in 1810 until reunification with Greece in 1864.

The whiteness of its rock strata – *lefkás* has the same root as *lefkós*, "white" – is apparent on its partly bare ridges. While the marshes and boggy inlets on the east coast can lead to a mosquito problem, the island is a fertile place, supporting cypresses, olive groves and vineyards, particularly on the western slopes. The rugged west coast, however, is the star attraction, boasting some of the finest beaches in the archipelago.

Lefkádha remains relatively undeveloped, with just two major resorts: **Vassilikí**, in its vast bay in the south, claims to be Europe's biggest windsurfing centre; **Nydhrí**, on the east coast, overlooks the island's picturesque set of satellite islets, including laidback **Meganíssi**. The capital's superb **marina** also appeals to yachties in large numbers.

ARRIVAL AND INFORMATION LEFKÁDHA

By plane Lefkádha itself does not have an airport but is less than 20km from the one at Préveza, served by charter flights from northern and eastern Europe, as well as domestic connections to Athens (1–2 daily; 50min). There is no airport bus but KTEL services from Préveza stop at the terminal entrance and taxis are readily available.

By bus The new bus station is out past the marina, around 1km from the centre of Lefkádha Town.

Destinations Athens (4 daily; 5hr 30min); Igoumenítsa (5 weekly; 3hr); Pátra (2 weekly; 3hr); Préveza (4 Mon–Sat, 3 Sun; 30min); Thessaloníki (2 weekly; 8–9hr).

By ferry Apart from the shuttle ferry from Nydhrí to Meganíssi (see p.486), the only ferries departing from Lefkádha now leave from Vassilikí; the summer schedules below are reduced drastically in the low season.

Destinations Fiskárdho (Kefaloniá; 1–2 daily; 1hr); Fríkes (Itháki; 1 daily; 1hr 30min).

Information There is no tourist office on Lefkádha but for further information you can check out ⓦ lefkasgreece.com, the most comprehensive site on the island.

GETTING AROUND

By bus There are services from Lefkádha Town to almost every village on the island, with frequent daily schedules to Nydhrí, Vassilikí and Áyios Nikítas/Káthisma, especially in summer.

By car or motorbike Two outlets for car and motorbike rental in the capital are EuroHire, Golémi 5 (ⓣ 26450

26776, ⓦ eurohire.gr), near the bus station, and Santas (ⓣ 26450 25250, ⓦ ilovesantas.gr), next to the *Ionian Star* hotel. There are numerous other rental agencies throughout the island, especially Nydhrí, Vassilikí and Áyios Nikítas.

Lefkádha Town

LEFKÁDHA TOWN sits at the island's northernmost tip, right where the causeway joins it to the mainland. Like other capitals in the southern Ionian, it was hit by the earthquakes of 1948 and 1953 and the town was devastated, with the exception of a few Italianate churches. It's a small town – you can cross it on foot in little over ten minutes – and still very attractive, especially around the main square, **Platía Ayíou Spyridhónos**, and the arcaded high street of Ioánnou Méla. The largely pedestrian-only centre boasts over half a dozen richly decorated private family **churches**, best visited around services as they are usually locked at other times. Many contain rare works from the Ionian School of painting, including work by its founder, Zakynthian Panayiotis Doxaras.

Phonograph, Radio and Tradition Museum

Panayióti Políti 1–3 • May–Oct daily 10am–2pm & 7pm–midnight • Free • ⓣ 26450 21088

You can catch a glimpse of the old way of life at the quaint little **Phonograph, Radio and Tradition Museum**, which is dedicated to antique phonographs, radios and an astounding array of bric-a-brac. It also sells recordings of rare traditional music and a few assorted souvenirs.

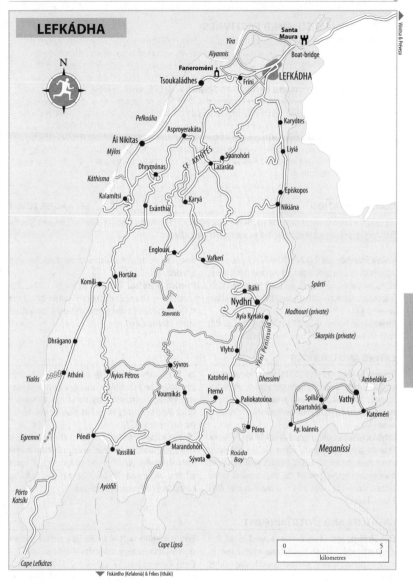

Fiskárdho (Kefaloniá) & Fríkes (Itháki)

Archeological museum

Cnr of Sikelianoú & Svorónou • Tues–Sun 8.30am–3pm • €2 • ☏ 26450 21635

On the northwestern seafront the modern cultural centre houses the newly expanded **archeological museum**, which contains interesting, well-labelled displays on aspects of daily life, religious worship and funerary customs in ancient times, as well as a room on prehistory dedicated to the work of eminent German archeologist Wilhelm Dörpfeld.

LEFKÁDHA'S SUMMER FESTIVALS

Lefkádha has been home to various literati, including two prominent Greek poets, Angelos Sikelianos and Aristotelis Valaoritis, and the American writer Lafcadio Hearn. Fittingly then, each summer for over fifty years, Lefkádha has hosted two parallel and wide-ranging cultural festivals, which these days attract performers and visitors from around the world. These are the **International Folklore Festival** and **Speech & Arts Events**. Originally only lasting for two to three weeks in August, they now extend from June to September, and troupes come from eastern and western Europe, South America and elsewhere, performing mainly at Santa Maura castle near Lefkádha Town, but also in villages around the island. The island and mainland Greece respond with troupes of their own musicians, dancers and theatrical companies. You can usually enjoy occasional performances of world music and jazz too, as well as art exhibitions and special cinema showings. For details, contact ☎ 26450 26711 or see ⓦ lefkasculturalcenter.gr.

ACCOMMODATION   LEFKÁDHA TOWN

The Lefkádha Room Owners Association (☎ 26450 21266; from €30) can help find rooms in Lefkádha Town, mostly in the dormitory area northwest of Dörpfeld, and around the rest of the island.

Ionian Star Panágou 2 ☎ 26450 24672, ⓦ ionian-star.com. With its own pool, a games room and free internet access for guests, the island's top hotel has comfortable spacious rooms, many with sea-view balconies. Breakfast included. €85

Nirikos Ayías Mávras ☎ 26450 24132, ⓦ nirikos.gr. This fairly standard four-storey block contains fairly spacious rooms that are stylish in a minimalist sort of way. Breakfast included. April–Oct. €65

Pension Pyrofani Dörpfeld ☎ 26450 25844. This smallish deep ochre-coloured *pension*, just on the sea side of the main square, offers warmly decorated, comfortable rooms. May–Oct. €60

EATING AND DRINKING

Burano Golémi ☎ 26450 26025. Smart *mezedhopolío* on the seafront almost opposite the marina, which has candlelit tables within, as well as pavement seating to enjoy the wide range of items available. May–Oct daily noon–1am.

Eftyhia Alley just off Dörpfeld ☎ 26450 24811. A fine little old-fashioned *estiatório* where you can make your choice from the mostly baked delights such as stuffed marrow once you've perused the glass window in the kitchen. April–Oct daily, plus occasional winter days 11am–11pm.

Ev Zin Filarmonikís 8 ☎ 697 46 41 160. Self-proclaimed "soul food place" with a slightly bohemian atmosphere, imaginative decor and unusual dishes such as Tex-Mex, risotto and Roquefort steak for €14. April–Oct daily noon–1am.

★ **Regantos** Dhimárhou Venióti ☎ 26450 22855. Well-established local favourite, serving a delicious array of meat like stuffed pork, fish and starters such as baked octopus, all around €6–8. Often has live Lefkadan *kantádhes*. Feb–Nov daily 7pm–2am.

NIGHTLIFE AND ENTERTAINMENT

Cäsbäh Platía Ayíou Spyridhónos ☎ 26450 25486. One of the most enduring café-bars in town, which echoes its name by playing some ethnic sounds and having touches of eastern decor. Daily 11am–late.

Coconut Sikelianoú ☎ 26450 23341. Airy and relaxed café on the seafront west of the bridge, which turns into a lively club as the night wears on. Sip a cocktail or down shots to the latest dance tunes. May–Oct noon–late.

Eleni Faneroménis 51 ☎ 26450 24550. The town's outdoor cinema has two showings of mostly English films, with programmes changing daily. May to mid-Oct daily from 9pm.

Around Lefkádha Town

Lefkádha has the best swimming close to town of any Ionian capital, thanks to the sandy borders to the lagoon at **Yíra** and **Aïyánnis**. Inland, there is also the attractive **Faneroméni monastery** and some traditional mountain villages centred around **Karyá**.

Yíra and Aïyánnis

There is a decent and lengthy shingle-and-sand beach west of the lagoon at **YÍRA**, a thirty-minute walk from the centre of Lefkádha Town. Roughly 4km long, the beach is often virtually deserted even in high season. Its western extension, **AÏYÁNNIS**, is a popular yet relaxed spot with several restaurants.

Faneroméni monastery

Daily 8am–2pm & 4–8pm • Free

The uninhabited **Faneroméni monastery** is reached by any of the west-coast buses or by a steep 45-minute hike on foot from town through the hamlet of Fríni. There's a small museum and chapel, and an ox's yoke and hammer, used when Nazi occupiers forbade the use of bells.

Karyá and the interior

The island's **interior** offers imposing mountainscapes and excellent walking between villages only a few kilometres apart. **KARYÁ** is at the centre of the interior, and offers some rooms. This is the centre of the island's lace and weaving industry, with a small but fascinating **folklore museum** set in a lacemaker's home (April–Oct daily 9am–9pm; €2.50). The historic and scenic villages of **Vafkerí** and **Englouví** are within striking distance, with the west-coast hamlets of **Dhrymónas** and **Exánthia** a hike over the hills.

ACCOMMODATION, EATING AND NIGHTLIFE   AROUND LEFKÁDHA TOWN

For rooms in Karyá, contact the Kakiousis family (📞 26450 61136; €30) or Haritini Vlahou (📞 26450 41634; €25).

Club Milos Yíra 📞 26450 21332. This lively club in a disused windmill is so far from any other buildings that it can pump out the hottest disco sounds at full volume far into the night. May–Sept daily 10pm–late.

Ta Platania Karyá 📞 26450 41247. The best of the trio of tavernas that fringe the beautiful plane-shaded square

dishes up ample portions of mostly meat dishes such as *frigadhéli*, for around €5–7. Daily 11am–1am.

Tilegraphos Aïyánnis 📞 26450 24881. Good restaurant with a shady elongated garden, serving a decent range of mezédhes and seafood, and also has some simple rooms. May–Oct. **€40**

The east coast

Anchored by the island's busiest resort of **Nydhrí**, Lefkádha's east coast is the most accessible and the most developed part of the island, much more so, in fact, than the nearby mainland coast. The beaches are mostly shingly and unspectacular, with the exception of **Dhessími** and **Rouda** bays, until you reach the long strand on the bay of **Vassilikí**.

Northeast coast

The stretch of the **northeast coast** between the capital and Nydhrí is a rather unprepossessing sprawl of seaside villages linked by almost unbroken development. Unless you choose to camp at **Karyótes**, there's little point stopping before the small fishing port of **Liyiá**. Further on lies **Nikiána**, another reasonably picturesque fishing village. Beaches all along this part of the coast tend to be pebbly and small.

Nydhrí

Most package travellers will find themselves in **NYDHRÍ**, the island's biggest resort by far and also the jumping-off point for Meganíssi (see p.486). It's an average resort but has a lovely setting and a reasonable pebble beach offering watersports. The town's focus is the Aktí Aristotéli Onássi **quay**, where most of the restaurants and bars are found. The German archeologist **Wilhelm Dörpfeld** is honoured with a statue here for promoting the theory that Nydhrí, rather than Itháki, was the site of Odysseus's capital, while his tomb is tucked away at Ayía Kyriakí on the opposite side of the bay. The turning signposted Ráhi leads to Nydhrí's modest **waterfall**, a 45-minute walk inland.

BOAT TRIPS FROM NYDHRÍ

Nydhrí is the base for myriad **boat trips** around the nearby satellite islands and further afield to Itháki and Kefalloniá. The boats line up along the quay each morning, ready for departure between 9 and 10am, returning late afternoon. Tickets are around €12 per person for the local trips, €20–25 for the longer distances. Most craft to the nearby islets are interchangeable: small fibreglass *kaïkia*, with bars and toilets, and open seating areas on the top deck or aft. Where they do differ, however, is in their itinerary – some will take in the sea caves of Meganíssi, others not, so it's advisable to check.

Dhessími Bay, Roúda Bay and around

Just south of Nydhrí, beyond somnolent **Vlyhó**, the neck of the Yéni peninsula to the east joins the main body of the island. Across this thin but steep strip of land, sizeable **Dhessími Bay** is perhaps the prettiest spot on the whole east coast, carved out by deep pine-ridged promontories.

South of Vlyhó, the coast road turns inland and climbs the foothills of Mount Stavrotás, through the hamlets of Katohóri and Paliokatoúna to the quiet village of **Póros**. Just south of here is the increasingly busy beach resort of **Roúda Bay**, officially Mikrós Yialós, some 10km from Nydhrí.

Sývota

Around 14km south of Nydhrí, the fjord-like inlet of **SÝVOTA**, 2km down a steep hill from the main road, cuts a deep gash into the coastline. This is one of the most popular stops for yachting flotillas. There's no beach except for a remote cove, but some fine tavernas, mostly specializing in fish.

Vassilikí, Póndi and around

Around 5km due west of Sývota but longer by the winding road, **VASSILIKÍ**, the island's premier watersports resort, lies at the east end of a huge bay, cut off from the rest of the east coast by the barren peninsula of Cape Lipsó. Winds in the huge bay draw vast numbers of windsurfers, with light morning breezes for learners and tough afternoon blasts for advanced surfers.

The beach at Vassilikí is stony and poor but improves 1km west at tiny **Póndi**. Most non-windsurfers, however, use the daily *kaïki* trips to superior beaches on the sandy west coast (see p.487).

ACTIVITIES   THE EAST COAST

Windsurfing In Vassilikí, the largest of the three beach windsurf centres, British-run Club Vassiliki (☎ 26450 31588, ⓦ clubvass.com) offers all-in windsurfing tuition and accommodation deals; Wildwind is another UK-based operation (☎ 697 91 10 665, ⓦ wildwind.co.uk).

ACCOMMODATION, EATING AND DRINKING

NORTHEAST COAST

Camping Kariotes Beach Karyótes ☎ 26450 71103, ⓦ campingkariotes.com. The nearest campsite to Lefkádha Town has shady pitches, a small shop and a nice pool, handy as the local beach is poor. May–Oct.

★ **Limni** Liyiá ☎ 26450 72013. Excellent and friendly taverna with a newly landscaped terrace garden and a range of tasty dishes such as *spartiátiko* (pork, peppers, mushroom and cheese in a wine and cognac sauce) and lamb *ladhókolla*. May–Sept daily noon–midnight.

Pantazis Nikiána ☎ 26450 71211. A good fish restaurant at the south end of the small curved beach, which also has simple rooms to let in a row of adjoining bungalows at the back. May–Sept. **€35**

NYDHRÍ

★ **Ionian Paradise** ☎ 26450 92268, ⓦ ionianparadise .gr. Set in a lush garden only a minute along the Ráhi turning from the main road. The rooms have been recently refurbished with smart furniture and kitchenettes. May–Oct. **€50**

Mamma Mia ☎ 26450 93102. Towards the south end of the resort, this restaurant has a huge patio, where you can

8

enjoy a wide range of mezédhes and some unusual main courses such as swordfish in sweet lemon sauce. Noon–1am: Easter–Nov daily, Dec–Easter Fri–Sun.

DHESSÍMI BAY, ROÚDA BAY AND AROUND

Camping Santa Maura Dhessími Bay ☎ 26450 95007, Ⓦ campingsantamaura.nl. This is marginally the better of the two huge campsites that dominate the olive groves behind Dhessími Bay. May–Oct.

Pirofani Dhessími Bay. This beach taverna in between the two Dhessími Bay campsites is very good, dishing up exquisite mezédhes such as octopus in wine sauce and *koloukythopittákia* (little courgette pies). May to mid-Oct daily 11am–midnight.

Poros Beach Camping Roúda Bay ☎ 26450 95452, Ⓦ porosbeach.com.gr. One of the smartest campsites in the archipelago, with a bar, post office, shop, pool, vehicle rental and forty spanking new studios. May–Oct. Studios **€40**

★ **Rouda Bay** Roúda Bay ☎ 26450 95634, Ⓦ roudabay.gr. Taverna-cum-studios venture right opposite the beach. The food includes excellent home-cooked dishes and the accommodation is in luxurious and spacious suites. Breakfast included. May–Oct. **€80**

SÝVOTA

★ **Palia Apothiki** ☎ 26450 31895. By far the most attractive of Sývota's tavernas, located in an old storehouse as the name indicates, and serving unique dishes such as giant shrimps wrapped in bacon. May–Oct 11am–midnight.

Sivota Apartments ☎ 26450 31347. Just above the middle of the harbour, these pleasant rooms are of varying sizes and most have balconies overlooking the bay. May–Sept. **€40**

VASSILIKÍ, PÓNDI AND AROUND

Akroyiali Póndi ☎ 26450 31569. A welcoming old couple run this taverna, which has a beachside seating and offers delights such as garlic prawns and steak Diane, as well as fine barrelled wine. May–Oct daily 11am–1am.

Alexander Vassilikí ☎ 26450 31355. Well-established taverna on the western quay, which dishes up pizza and pasta and has a massive menu of Greek cuisine and a variety of wines. April–Oct daily 10am–1am.

Grand Nefeli Póndi ☎ 26450 31378, Ⓦ grandnefeli .com. Right on the beach, this smart block has comfortably furnished rooms, many with sea-view balconies, and some luxury suites. Arranges windsurfing lessons. Breakfast included. May to mid-Oct. **€60**

Pension Holiday Vassilikí ☎ 26450 31011, Ⓔ pensionholidays@hotmail.com. Round the corner from the ferry dock, this remains the best value option, with a/c and TV in all the cosy rooms. May–Oct. **€35**

Volero Club Vassilikí ☎ 26450 31859. The resort's liveliest club, a short way back from the seafront, provides post-windsurfing dancefloor frolics to the predominantly young crowd that spend the summer here. May–Sept daily 7pm–late.

Lefkádha's satellites

Lefkádha has four satellite islands clustered off its east coast, although only one, **Meganíssi**, the largest and most interesting, is accessible. **Skorpiós**, owned by the Onassis family, fields armed guards to deter visitors. **Madhourí**, owned by the family of poet Nanos Valaoritis, is private and similarly off-limits, while tiny **Spárti** is a large scrub-covered rock. Day-trips from Nydhrí skirt all three islands (see box, p.484), and some stop to allow swimming in coves. Though officially a dependency of Lefkádha, the more remote island of **Kálamos** is only accessible from the mainland.

Meganíssi

Ferries run from Nydhrí (7 daily; 20min)

Meganíssi is a sizeable island with a growing number of facilities and a magical, if somewhat bleak and scrubby, landscape. The locals – many returned émigrés from Australia – live from farming and fishing and are genuinely welcoming. There are actually two ports, the main one of **Vathý** in the north, and **Spiliá** on the west coast, ten minutes' steep walk below **Spartohóri**, an immaculate village with whitewashed buildings and an abundance of bougainvillea. The walk between the two docks takes little over an hour, by way of the attractive inland village of **Katoméri**. From here, paths lead from Katoméri to remote beaches, including popular **Ambelákia**.

ACCOMMODATION, EATING AND DRINKING   MEGANÍSSI

Different Studios Vathý ☎ 26450 22170, Ⓦ different-studios.com. This small complex of six studios and two 2-bedroom apartments stands right on the harbour. All units are nicely furnished and well

---

LOVER'S LEAP

Fourteen kilometres south along the main road from Atháni, barren **Cape Lefkátas** drops abruptly 75m into the sea. Byron's Childe Harold sailed past this point, and "saw the evening star above, Leucadia's far projecting rock of woe: And hail'd the last resort of fruitless love". The fruitless love is a reference to Sappho, who in accordance with the ancient legend that you could cure yourself of unrequited love by leaping into these waters, leapt – and died. In her honour the locals termed the place Kávos tis Kyrás ("lady's cape"), and her act was imitated by the lovelorn youths of Lefkádha for centuries afterwards. And not just by the lovelorn, for the act (known as *katapondismós*) was performed annually by scapegoats – always a criminal or a lunatic – selected by priests from the Apollo temple whose sparse ruins lie close by. This purification rite continued into the Roman era, when it degenerated into little more than a fashionable stunt by decadent youth. These days, in a more controlled modern re-enactment, Greek hang-gliders hold a tournament from the cliffs every July.

---

equipped. May–Sept. €40

Meganissi Katoméri ☏ 26450 51240. The island's longest-established hotel is a comfortable place with decent-sized, comfortable rooms, a restaurant and pool, and is handily located for exploring. May–Sept. €45

Rose Garden Vathý ☏ 26450 51216. Popular place tucked into the corner of the square and seafront, where

you can get good fresh fish or a few meat or veg options from the oven. May–Sept daily noon–midnight.

Tropicana Spartohóri ☏ 26450 51486. This simple summertime restaurant (daily noon–11pm) offers a variety of pizzas and some other basic snacks and meals, plus they are the point of contact for good-value rooms in the village. May–Sept. €30

The west coast

Lefkádha's **west coast** vies with anywhere in Greece in displaying coastal scenery at its most dramatic. On both sides of **Áï Nikítas**, the only real resort, mountainous roads rise and descend from the sea, offering tantalizing glimpses of the stunning sandy beaches that are sandwiched between imposing cliffs and lapping waves of turquoise.

Áï Nikítas and around

Jammed into a picturesque gorge 12km southwest of Lefkádha Town is **ÁÏ NIKÍTAS**, the prettiest resort on Lefkádha, a jumble of lanes and small wooden buildings. To add to its appeal, the village itself is now a pedestrian zone, at least in theory. Sea taxis (€3 one-way) ply between Áï Nikítas and **Mýlos beach**, the delightful cove just round the southern promontory. A couple of kilometres back north, sand-and-pebble **Pefkoúlia beach** is one of the longest on the island.

Káthisma beach

It's a 45-minute walk (or a short bus ride) from Áï Nikítas to the most popular beach on the coast, **Káthisma**, a shadeless kilometre of fine sand, which becomes nudist and a lot less crowded beyond the large jutting rocks halfway along – freelance camping still goes on at this end too.

Atháni and around

South of Kalamítsi, past the hamlets of Hortáta and Komíli, the landscape becomes almost primeval. At 38km from Lefkádha Town, **ATHÁNI** is the island's most remote spot to stay. Three of the Ionian's choicest **beaches**, where azure and milky turquoise waves buffet strands enclosed by dramatic cliffs, are accessible from Atháni: the nearest, reached by a 4km paved road, is **Yialós**, followed by **Egremní**, down a steep incline unpaved for the last 2km. Further south, an asphalted road leads to the dramatic and popular twin beach of **Pórto Katsíki**.

8

ACCOMMODATION, EATING AND DRINKING
THE WEST COAST

AΪ NIKÍTAS AND AROUND

Captain's Corner ☎ 26450 97493. Near the beach, this is the liveliest drinking venue in the village, with a pub-style atmosphere, a decent selection of drinks, snacks and mostly rock tunes. May to mid-Oct daily 10am–late.

Deck Pefkoúlia beach ☎ 26450 97070, ⊚ mydeck.gr. Buzzing café-restaurant halfway along the huge beach, with a selection of coffees, cocktails and full meals to choose from, plus some well-equipped studios. May–Sept. **€50**

O Lefteris ☎ 26450 97495. Simple grilled fish and meat dishes for €7–8, accompanied by the expected choice of salads, dips and starters, and washed down with quaffable local wine. May to mid-Oct daily 11am–midnight.

★ **Pension Ostria** ☎ 26450 97483. A beautiful blue-and-white building above the village, decorated in a mix of beachcomber and ecclesiastical styles, with compact but comfortable rooms and a snack bar with terrace. Breakfast included. May–Oct. **€85**

T'Agnantio ☎ 26450 97383. Just above and south of the main street, this place serves excellent traditional cuisine, much of it oven baked such as *pastítsio* or *hirinó krasáto* (pork in wine sauce) and nearly all under €10. May–Sept daily noon–1am.

KÁTHISMA BEACH

Club Copla ☎ 26450 29411. This beach bar-cum-club has long established itself as a favourite with the night-time crowd, holding regular parties and raves to a techno soundtrack. May–Sept daily 11am–late.

Kathisma ☎ 26450 97050, ⊚ kathisma.com. Vast taverna at the north end of the beach, with an equally extensive menu of Greek staples and some smart apartments. May–Oct. **€50**

ATHÁNI AND AROUND

★ **Lygos** Hortáta ☎ 694 85 91 543, ⊚ amadryades -villas.gr. Good local taverna, serving up simple home recipes such as moussaka or *briám*, expertly cooked and accompanied by inexpensive barrelled wine. Nicely designed stone villas available too. May–Sept. **€70**

★ **Panorama** Atháni ☎ 26450 33291. One of the most welcoming tavernas on the island (daily 10am–midnight), where you can enjoy excellent fresh local dishes while gazing towards the distant sea from the terrace. Great-value rooms also available. May–Oct. **€30**

★ **Serenity** Atháni ☎ 698 18 53 064, ⊚ serenity-th .com. Wonderful new retreat and health spa run by two Israeli women, beautifully constructed in stone on the hillside 500m south of the village. The five rooms are decorated in ethnic style, and there are chill-out tents and an infinity pool. May–Oct. **€100**

Kefaloniá

KEFALONIÁ (also known in English as Cephalonia) is the largest of the Ionian islands, a place that has real towns as well as resorts. Kefaloniá was overrun by Italians and Germans in World War II; the "handover" after Italy's capitulation in 1943 led to the massacre of over five thousand Italian troops on the island by invading German forces, as chronicled by Louis de Bernières in his novel, *Captain Corelli's Mandolin*. Virtually all of its towns and villages were levelled in the 1953 earthquake and these masterpieces of Venetian architecture had been the one touch of elegance in a severe, mountainous landscape.

Until the late 1980s, the island paid scant regard to tourism; perhaps this was partly due to a feeling that Kefaloniá could not be easily marketed. A more likely explanation, however, for the island's late emergence on the Greek tourist scene is the Kefalonians' legendary reputation for insular pride and stubbornness, plus a good measure of eccentricity. There are, however, definite attractions here, with some **beaches** as good as any in Greece and the fine local wines of Robola. Moreover, the island seems able to soak up a lot of people without feeling at all crowded and the magnificent scenery speaks for itself.

ARRIVAL AND DEPARTURE
KEFALONIÁ

By plane Kefaloniá airport lies 7km south of Argostóli. Apart from international charters, the only domestic scheduled flights are to Athens (2 daily; 1hr).

By ferry Kefaloniá has no fewer than four ports that provide ferry connections with neighbouring islands and the mainland. The following are summer schedules, which are reduced drastically in winter; any services that stop altogether are indicated by months of operation.
Argostóli to: Kyllíni (1 daily; 2hr 15min).
Pessádha to: Áyios Nikólaos (Zákynthos; 2 daily May–Sept; 1hr 30min). Be warned that the pathetic bus service from Argostóli to Pessádha is no good for connecting with the boats. You'll have to hitch or take an expensive taxi in most cases.

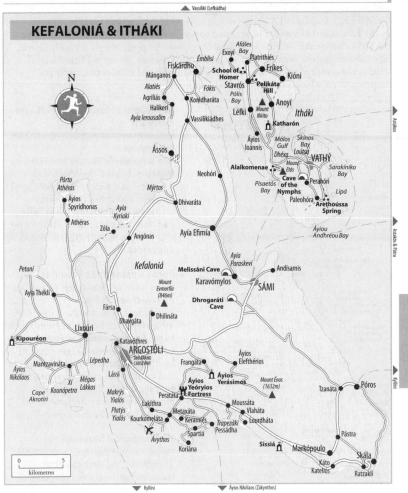

KEFALONIÁ & ITHÁKI

8

Póros to: Kyllíni (3–5 daily; 1hr 15min).
Sámi to: Astakós (1 daily; 2hr 30min); Pátra (1–2 daily; 3hr 30min); Pisaetós (Ithakí; 2–3 daily; 40min); Vathý (Ithakí; 1–2 daily; 1hr).

By bus There are buses from Argostóli via Sámi to Athens (2–3 daily; 7hr); and from Póros to Athens (1 daily; 6hr 30min) and to Pátra (1 daily; 4hr).

GETTING AROUND

By bus Kefaloniá's basic KTEL bus network radiates out from Argostóli (see above). There are 2–3 services to all the main island destinations on Mon–Fri, 1–2 on Sat but no buses on Sun. KTEL also runs a seasonal tour of the island from Argostóli every Thurs and Sat (9am–6pm; €18).
By car or motorbike The island-wide Sunbird agency (☎ 26710 23723, ⊛ sunbird.gr) is a reliable rental agency.

Argostóli

ARGOSTÓLI, Kefaloniá's capital, is a large and thriving town – virtually a city – with a marvellous position on a bay within a bay. The causeway connecting the two sides of the inner bay, known as Dhrápano owing to its sickle shape, was initially constructed by the British in 1813 and is now closed to traffic. The town was totally rebuilt after the 1953 earthquake, but has an enjoyable atmosphere that remains defiantly Greek, especially during the evening *vólta* around **Platía Valianou** (formerly Platía Metaxá) – the nerve centre of town – and along the pedestrianized **Lithóstroto**, the main shopping street which runs parallel to the seafront.

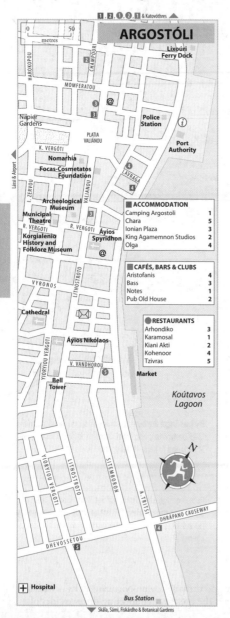

Korgialenio History and Folklore Museum

Ilía Zervoú 12 • Mon–Sat 9am–2pm • €3 • ☎ 26710 28835, ⓦ corgialenios.gr

The **Korgialenio History and Folklore Museum**, behind the Municipal Theatre, has a rich collection of local religious and cultural artefacts, including photographs taken before and after the earthquake. At the time of writing it was closed due to staffing difficulties.

Focas-Cosmetatos Foundation

Valiánou 1 • Mon–Sat 9.30am–12.30pm, plus June–Sept 7–9.30pm • €3 • ☎ 26710 26595

Insight into how the island's nobility used to live can be gained from a visit to the **Focas-Cosmetatos Foundation**, opposite the provincial government building. It contains elegant furniture and a collection of lithographs and paintings, including works by nineteenth-century British artists Joseph Cartwright and Edward Lear.

Archeological Museum

Y. Vergóti • Tues–Sun 8.30am–3pm • €3 • ☎ 26710 28300

The refurbished **Archeological Museum** has a sizeable collection of pottery, jewellery, funerary relics and statuary from prehistoric, through Mycenaean to late Classical times. It is well laid out and labelled, rivalling Corfu Town's (see p.463) as the best such museum in the Ionians.

Botanical Gardens

Tues–Sat 9am–2.30pm • Free • ☎ 26710 26595

Around 2km south of the town centre, the pleasantly relaxing **Botanical Gardens** have been transformed under the stewardship of the Focas-Cosmetatos Foundation into a diverse collection of the island's flora, arranged in a natural fashion with a stream running through the middle.

ARRIVAL AND INFORMATION

By plane There are no airport buses, so taxis (at least €10) are the only way into town.

By bus The KTEL bus station is 100m south of the Dhrápano causeway in the south of town. A city bus links the centre of town with Lássi at least hourly in season (30min).

ARGOSTÓLI

By ferry There are frequent flat-bottomed boats to Lixoúri (Mon–Sat every 30min, Sun hourly; 20min).

Tourist office Andoníou Trítsi, at the north end of the seafront next to the port authority (Mon–Fri 7.30am–2.30pm; ☎ 26710 22248).

ACCOMMODATION

The Kefalonia & Ithaca Federation of Lodgings (☎ 26710 29109, ⓦ kefalonia-ithaca.gr) can arrange rooms in Argostóli and around the island, as can travel agencies such as Ainos Travel (☎ 26710 22333, ⓦ ainostravel.gr).

Camping Argostoli ☎ 26710 23487, ⓦ camping argostoli.gr. Although it's an inconvenient 2km north of the centre, just beyond the Katavóthres sea mills, this campsite has decent facilities, including a minimarket. May–Sept. One person plus tent . **€11.50**

Chara Cnr Dhevossétou/Y. Vergóti ☎ 26710 22427. Small house very close to the bus station with extremely simple rooms with shared bathrooms, whose friendly owner offers coffee in the leafy courtyard. The only budget hotel left in town. **€23**

★ **Ionian Plaza** Platía Valiánou ☎ 26710 25581, ⓦ ionianplaza.com. One of the ritziest hotels on the island and surprisingly reasonable for what it is – designer decor from the lobby up to the chic bathroom fixtures. Breakfast included. **€85**

King Agamemnon Studios A. Trítsi ☎ 26710 24260, ⓔ kathya@europe.com. Good-value modern studios with kitchenettes in a brightly painted block north of the Lixoúri ferry dock, all with a/c and TV, some with sea-facing balconies. **€35**

Olga A. Trítsi 82 ☎ 026710 24981, ⓦ olgahotel.gr. Imposing seafront hotel with a/c and TV in all rooms, which are fairly compact and do not match the grandeur of the lobby. Sizeable off-season discounts. **€45**

EATING, DRINKING AND NIGHTLIFE

RESTAURANTS

★ **Arhondiko** Rizospastón 5 ☎ 26710 27213. Classy stone building with a small patio out front, where the *kandádhes* from pricey *The Captain's Table* next door can often be heard. The friendly proprietress serves tasty dishes such as *exohikó*, *strapsádha* and *biftéki* in Roquefort sauce. Daily noon–1am.

Karamosal A. Trítsi ☎ 26710 28590. Good ouzerí, with an artistic touch in the bright decor and a fair bit of imagination in the preperation of the *mezédhes*, which include cheese croquettes, pickled anchovies, meatballs and various veg options. Daily noon–1am.

★ **Kiani Akti** A. Trítsi ☎ 26710 26680. Unmissable dining experience on a large wooden deck jutting out over the water by the new cruise-ship dock, about 400m north of Platía Valianou. Specializes in seafood such as razor clams in mustard sauce and shrimps in ouzo. Friendly service and reasonable prices. Daily 1pm–2am.

Kohenoor Lavrága ☎ 26710 26789. Just southeast of Platía Valiánou, this British-run curry house has an Indian chef and is one of the most authentic in the Ionians. Daily 6pm–midnight; closed Mon Nov–April.

Tzivras V. Vandhórou 1. A classic daytime-only *estiatório* with an impressive range of staples from the oven, including a lot of vegetarian options such as *briám*, helpings of which tend to be large. Daily 10am–5pm.

CAFÉS, BARS AND CLUBS

Aristofanis A. Trítsi ☎ 26710 28012. Right by the Dhrápano bridge, this simple old-style *kafenío* might have a limited repertoire of coffee and basic booze but it enjoys one of the best locations in town, ideal for some gentle people-watching. Daily 8am–midnight.

Bass P. Valiánou ☎ 26710 25020, ⓦ bassclub.gr. Opposite the archeological museum, this is the town's main late-night indoor club, whose hi-tech interior shakes to the latest vibes of various dance genres and hosts occasional live acts. Daily 10pm–late.

Notes ☎ 26710 23597. Argostóli's big summer *bouzoúki* club, nearly 2km north of town before the Katavóthres sea mills, is the place to head if you want to join the Greeks in rose-throwing and whiskey-drinking escapades. June–Sept daily 10pm–late.

★ **Pub Old House** Harboúri 13–15 ☎ 26710 23532. Tucked behind the kids' playground, the most relaxed and welcoming hangout on the island is a great place to have a drink in the magical garden and unwind to an eclectic range of mostly rock sounds. Daily 7pm–late.

8

The Livathó peninsula

The bulge of land southeast of Argostóli known as the **Livathó peninsula** is a patchwork of small villages and agricultural land bordered by some attractive coastline. Many package travellers will find themselves staying in **Lássi**, a short bus ride or half-hour walk from town. The only other reason you might come to this corner of the island is for the summer ferry link with Zákynthos from **Pessádha** (see.p.488).

Áyios Yeóryios

The best inland excursion from Argostóli is to **ÁYIOS YEÓRYIOS**, the medieval Venetian capital of the island, 7km southeast of Argostóli but not connected by public transport. The old town here supported a population of fifteen thousand until its destruction by an earthquake in the seventeenth century: substantial ruins of its **castle** (Tues–Sun 8.30am–3pm; free) can be visited on the hill above the modern village of Peratáta, a steep 1km walk below on the main southeast bus routes.

Mount Énos and around

At 15km from a point halfway along the Argostóli–Sámi road, **Mount Énos** isn't really a walking option but roads nearly reach the official 1632m summit. The mountain has been declared a national park, to protect the *Abies cephalonica* firs named after the island, which clothe the slopes. There are absolutely no facilities on or up to the mountain but the views from the highest point in the Ionian islands out over Kefaloniá's neighbours and the mainland are wonderful. Out of summer, watch the weather, which can deteriorate with terrifying speed.

Áyios Yerásimos monastery and around

Áyios Yerásimos monastery Daily 9am–1pm & 4–8pm **Robola winery** April–Oct daily 7am–8.30pm, Nov–March Mon–Fri 7am–3pm • ⓦ robola.gr

Not far west of the mountain turning, taking a detour towards Frangáta is doubly rewarded, firstly by the huge and lively **Áyios Yerásimos monastery**, which hosts two of the island's most important festivals (Aug 15 and Oct 20); the most interesting feature is the double cave beneath the back of the sanctuary, where the eponymous saint meditated for lengthy periods. Right behind the monastery, the **Robola winery** offers a free self-guided tour and generous wine tasting.

Lixoúri and its peninsula

Ferries run to Lixoúri from Argostóli till well after midnight (summer Mon–Sat every 30min, Sun hourly; winter hourly; 20min)

Across the water from Argostóli, the town of **LIXOÚRI** was flattened by successive earthquakes and hasn't risen much above two storeys since. It's a little drab but has good restaurants, quiet hotels and is favoured by those who want to explore the eerie quake-scapes left in the south and the barren north of the peninsula.

Beaches around Lixoúri

Xi and Mégas Lákkos are served by bus from Lixoúri

Lixoúri's nearest beach, a 2km walk south, is **Lépedha**, composed of rich-red sand and backed by low cliffs, as are **Xi** and **Mégas Lákkos** (the name means "big hole") beaches, both of which have good facilities. Around 4km southwest lies the quieter beach at **Kounópetra**, site of a curious rock formation. Until the 1953 earthquake, this "rocking stone" (as the name signifies in Greek) had a strange rhythmic movement that could be measured by placing a knife into a gap between the rock and its base. However, after the quake the rock became motionless. Some 2km further west, in an area known as Vátsa, the last beach of any size on the southern tip of the peninsula is sandy **Áyios Nikólaos**, a very quiet and scenic strand.

The western coast

Those with transport can also strike out for the rugged western coast of the peninsula, first visiting the monastery at **Kipouréon** (daily 8am–6pm; free), now home to just a single monk, then heading north to the spectacular beach at **Petaní**, one of the best in the Ionians. Tucked in the fold of the **Áyios Spyrídhonas** inlet further north, the beach of **Pórto Athéras**, which serves the traditional village of Athéras, a short way inland, is another fine strip of sand with shallow water.

ACCOMMODATION AND EATING	LIXOÚRI AND ITS PENINSULA

★**Akrogiali** Lixoúri ☎26710 92613. Wonderful unpretentious taverna on the seafront, which draws admirers from all over the island for its excellent and inexpensive grilled and baked meat, fish and seafood. Daily noon–1am.

★**La Cité** Lixoúri ☎26710 92701, ⓦlacitehotellixouri .gr. Four blocks back from the front, this great-value hotel has a uniquely shaped pool in its exotic garden, while the rooms are spacious and colourfully furnished. April–Oct. **€45**

★**Spiaggia** Áyios Nikólaos ☎697 76 31 053, ⓦvatsa .gr. Atmospheric restaurant with an attractive wood and bamboo deck, where you can tuck into excellent pasta, seaweed salad and seafood. There are four well-equipped

luxury chalets behind. May–Oct; restaurant daily 11am– late. **€80**

Xouras Petaní ☎26710 97128, ⓔpetanoi@gmail.com. By far the better of the two tavernas here, whose friendly Greek-American owner Dina serves a fine selection of grills, salads and some oven-cooked dishes. There are comfortable studios attached too. May–Oct; restaurant daily 11am–midnight. **€50**

Yialós Pórto Athéras. Good all-round taverna at the back of the beach, which serves mostly grills and whose garden acts as home for families with camper vans and could be used for camping. May–Sept daily noon–1am.

Southeast Kefaloniá

8

Southeast Kefaloniá contains some fine beaches and much of the island's package tourism, from smaller resorts such as **Lourdháta** and **Káto Kateliós** east via the busiest foreign enclave of **Skála** to the port resort of **Póros**. One or two of the villages strung along the main Argostóli–Póros road, which follows the southern contours of Mt Énos, are also worth a brief halt, especially **Markópoulo**.

Lourdháta and around

From the pleasant village of Vlaháta, around 15km east of Argostóli, a couple of turnings bear 2km down the mountainside to **LOURDHÁTA**, which has a kilometre-long shingle beach, mixed with imported sand. Another fine beach, reached by a turning from Moussáta, 2km west of Vlaháta, is **Trapezáki**, a relatively slim but appealing strand with just one restaurant by the small jetty.

Markópoulo

The inland village of **MARKÓPOULO** witnesses a bizarre snake-handling ritual every year on August 15, on the occasion of the **Assumption of the Virgin festival**, when a swarm of harmless snakes "appears" in commemoration of a legend that the nuns of the former convent here prayed to be turned into snakes to avoid an attack by pirates. The church at which the ritual is enacted is well worth visiting at any time of year.

Káto Kateliós and around

Some of the finest sandy beaches on the island are to be found around the growing micro-resort of **KÁTO KATELIÓS**, which already has a couple of hotels, and below the village of **Ratzaklí** just before the resort of Skála. The coast around Káto Kateliós is also Kefalonia's key breeding ground for the loggerhead **turtle** (see p.506); camping on the nearby beaches is therefore prohibited.

Skála

SKÁLA is a low-rise resort set among handsome pines above a few kilometres of good sandy beach. A **Roman villa** (daily 10am–2pm & 5–8pm, longer hours in summer;

free) and some mosaics were excavated here in the 1950s, near the site of the *Golden Beach Palace* rooms, and are open to the public.

Póros

Connected to Skála by a lovely 12km coastal route that at times seems to skim across the shallow sea, **PÓROS** was one of the island's earliest developed resorts, though it definitely gives the impression of having seen better days. The town's small huddle of hotels and apartment blocks is almost unique on Kefaloniá, and not enhanced by a scruffy seafront and thin pebbly beach. Póros is actually made up of two bays: the northern one, where most tourists are based, and the harbour bay, a few minutes over the headland, with connections to Kyllíni on the Peloponnesian coast.

ACCOMMODATION, EATING AND DRINKING

SOUTHEAST KEFALONIÁ

LOURDHÁTA AND AROUND

Christina Studios Lourdháta ☎ 26710 31130, ⓦ christinastudio.gr. Fully equipped kitchen-studios with side views to the sea are available at this lovely building set into the lush vegetation behind the beach. May–Oct. **€40**

★ **Denis** Trapezáki ☎ 26710 31454. This friendly taverna does not abuse its monopoly, instead maintaining a fine level of quality in the typical Greek menu of grills with salads and dips, plus good service when especially busy around lunchtime. May–Oct daily 11am–11pm.

★ **Lorraine's Magic Hill** Lourdháta ☎ 26710 31605. With a lovely airy terrace on the hill just behind the beach, this relaxed joint serves a wide range of home produce, including tender calves' liver. Also does cocktails in its alter ego as a bar. May–Oct daily noon–late.

Trapezaki Bay Hotel Trapezáki ☎ 26710 31503, ⓦ trapezakibayhotel.com. Luxury hotel 500m uphill from the beach, offering all mod cons, including spa and beauty treatments. The fixed price all summer means good value in peak season and the rate includes airport transfer and breakfast. May–Oct. **€115**

KÁTO KATELIÓS

Blue Sea ☎ 26710 81122. Seafront taverna renowned for the freshness and quality of its fish, though much of it is pricey. Also does the usual accompanying dishes, plus pizza and pasta. April–Oct daily 11am–1am.

Cozy ☎ 26710 81031. This little bar with a fitting name is the prime drinking location, where you can enjoy a beer or cocktail to the accompaniment of some laidback summer sounds. May–Oct daily 10am–late.

Galini Resort ☎ 26710 81582, ⓦ galini.de. This spacious complex with a pool and manicured grounds, around 500m back from the beach, has good deals on fully

equipped rooms and larger apartments. May–Sept. **€50**

Ostria ☎ 26710 81765. At the western end of the front, this ouzerí-cum-taverna offers a wide selection of dishes such as stuffed pork or baked swordfish for around €8. May–Oct daily noon–1am.

SKÁLA

Captain's House ☎ 26710 83389, ⓦ captainshouse .net. On the road parallel to the main street to the east, the good Captain can steer you towards a warmly decorated room or studio. April–Oct. **€40**

The Old Village ☎ 26710 83513. A standard range of Greek and continental cuisine, including large steaks for around €10–12, and very palatable local wine from the barrel. May–Oct daily 10am–1am.

Paspalis ☎ 26710 83140. The well-established beachside frontrunner serves fish and home-cooked meat and vegetable dishes. Especially popular during the day, as it has a pool for patrons. May–Oct daily 11am–midnight.

Tara Beach Hotel ☎ 26710 83250, ⓦ tarabeach.gr. The best of the large seafront hotels has smart rooms and individual bungalows in lush gardens on the edge of the beach. Breakfast included. April–Oct. **€60**

PÓROS

Fotis Family ☎ 26710 72972. Tucked into the rocky corner of the northern bay, this taverna serves an array of grilled meat and fish, plus plenty of salads and mezédhes. April–Oct daily 11am–midnight.

Santa Irina ☎ 26740 72017, ⓔ maki@otenet.gr. By the crossroads inland, this medium-sized *pension* has basic but clean rooms that offer superb value. Breakfast included. Mid-May to Sept. **€40**

Sámi and around

Most boats to the island dock at the large and functional port town of **SÁMI**, near the south end of the Itháki straits, more or less on the site of ancient Sami. This was the capital of the island in Homeric times, when Kefaloniá was part of Ithaca's maritime kingdom. Ironically, today the administrative hierarchy is reversed, with Itháki being considered the backwater. In more recent times, Sámi was used as the set for much of the filming of *Captain Corelli's Mandolin*. The long sandy beach that stretches round the bay to the village of **Karavómylos** is perfectly adequate, but 2km further east, beyond ancient Sami, lies a more dramatic pebble beach, **Andísamis**, set in a stunning curved bay.

Dhrogaráti cave
April–Oct daily 9am–8pm • €4

Five kilometres from Sámi, signposted just off the Argostóli road, lies a very impressive stalagmite-bedecked chamber, known as **Dhrogaráti**. The cave, which reaches a depth of 60m and was discovered over 300 years ago, is occasionally used for concerts thanks to its marvellous acoustics.

Melissáni cave
Daily 8am–7pm • €7

Three kilometres north of Sámi towards Ayía Efimía, **Melissáni** is partly submerged in brackish water, which, amazingly, emerges from an underground fault extending the whole way underneath the island to a point near Argostóli. At that point, known as Katavóthres, the sea gushes endlessly into a subterranean channel – the fact that the water ends up in the cave has been shown with fluorescent tracer dye. The beautiful textures and shades created by the light pouring through the collapsed roof of the cave make the short boat excursion into it a must.

Ayía Efimía
AYÍA EFIMÍA, 9km north of Sámi along a scenic coastal drive that includes coves such as **Ayía Paraskeví**, is a small fishing harbour popular with package operators, yet with no major developments. Its main drawback is its beaches, or lack thereof – the largest, risibly named Paradise beach, is a pathetic 20m of shingle. It is, however, home to one of the island's few **scuba diving** enterprises.

ARRIVAL AND GETTING AROUND
SÁMI AND AROUND

By ferry The dock is towards the southern end of the long seafront.

By bus Island buses congregate outside the KTEL office about 100m from the dock.

By car and motorbike The seafront Sami Center (☎26740 22254) rents out motorbikes at fair rates, and Island (☎26740 23084, ✉islecars@otenet.gr) is a reliable local car rental company.

ACTIVITIES

Diving The Aquatic Scuba Diving Club in Ayía Efimía (☎26740 62006, ⊛aquatic.gr) is the island's premier scuba diving outfit. It runs courses, does wreck diving and offers introductory dives.

ACCOMMODATION, EATING AND DRINKING

SÁMI AND AROUND
Akrogiali Sámi ☎26740 22494. At the far northern end of the seafront, this family taverna with seating right above the beach offers a range of fish and meat dishes for around €7. May–Sept daily noon–midnight.

Camping Karavomilos Beach Karavómylos ☎26740 22480, ⊛camping-karavomilos.gr. Just 1km along the beach from Sámi, the better of the island's two campsites has over three hundred well-shaded spaces, a taverna, shop and bar. May–Oct. One person plus tent **€12.50**

Kastro Sámi ☎26740 22282. Smart two-storey hotel in the middle of the seafront, with compact but comfy rooms and a small café on the ground floor. June–Sept. **€50**

Melissani Sámi ☎26740 22464. Up a couple of blocks behind the main dock, this slightly old-fashioned but welcoming hotel has cosy, good-value rooms, many with good views from their balconies. May–Sept. **€35**

Mermaid Sámi ☎26740 22202. With a decent selection of vegetable and meat dishes, including the famous local meat pie, this is the best of the central bunch of portside tavernas. April–Oct daily 11am–2am.

AYÍA EFIMÍA
Amalia Ayía Efimía ☎26740 61088. Round the headland past the harbour, this is the place for moderately priced island cuisine such as small fried fish and local sausage. May–Sept daily noon–1am.

★ **Ayía Paraskeví** Ayía Paraskeví ☎26740 23061.

Named after the tiny cove it sits above, this taverna with a huge sunken terrace is famous for its delicious spaghetti with mussels. There is a separate chill-out beach bar on the premises too. May–Sept daily 10am–midnight.

Captain Corelli's Ayía Efimía ✆ 26740 61955. Predictably renamed after the film crew and cast who spent hours unwinding here, this café-restaurant is nonetheless a good spot right on the harbour for a refreshing drink or light snack. April–Oct daily 8am–2am.

Moustakis Ayía Efimía ✆ 26740 61030, 🌐 moustakishotel.com. Around 100m along the main road inland, the resort's only bona fide hotel has old-fashioned yet comfortable rooms, all with small balconies. April–Oct. **€50**

To Steki Ayía Efimía ✆ 26740 61025. A wide range of island specialities such as meat pie and standard Greek dishes from pork chops to beef in red sauce, all under €10 at this mid-harbour taverna. May–Sept daily noon–1am.

Northern Kefaloniá

Northern Kefaloniá offers some splendid beaches, an architecturally attractive village in **Fiskárdho**, and some amazing coastal scenery. Indeed, the northern half of the road between Argostóli and Fiskárdho, starting at the point where a side road peels off to the long sandy beach of **Ayía Kyriakí**, is the most spectacular ride in the Ionian archipelago.

Mýrtos beach and around

Four kilometres by paved road below the main north–south artery, stunningly photogenic **Mýrtos** is regarded by many as the most dramatic beach in the Ionian islands – a splendid strip of pure-white sand and pebbles. Sadly, it has no natural shade for most of the day and gets mighty crowded in high season, with just a couple of seasonal snack-shacks for refreshment.

Back at the crossroads, the small settlement of **Dhivaráta** has the nearest amenities to Mýrtos.

Ássos

Six kilometres beyond Dhivaráta is the turning for the atmospheric village of **ÁSSOS**, clinging to a small isthmus between the island and a huge hill crowned by a ruined fort. It can get a little claustrophobic, but there's nowhere else quite like it in the Ionians. Ássos has a small pebble beach, and three tavernas on a plane-shaded village square backed by mansions, mostly now restored after being ruined in the 1953 quake.

Fiskárdho

Boats from Ith-ki and Lefkádha dock on the far side of the small bay; island buses terminate in the car park up at the back of the village

FISKÁRDHO, on the northernmost tip of the island, sits on a bed of limestone that buffered it against the worst of the quakes. Two **lighthouses**, Venetian and Victorian, guard the bay, and the ruins on the headland are believed to be from a twelfth-century chapel begun by Norman invader Robert Guiscard, who gave the place its name. The nineteenth-century harbour frontage is intact, and is nowadays occupied by smart restaurants and chic boutiques. There is an **Environmental and Nautical Museum** (summer Mon–Fri 10am–6pm, Sun 10am–2pm; donation; ✆ 26740 41182), housed in a renovated Neoclassical mansion on the hill behind the village. The volunteers who curate it conduct valuable ecological research and can also arrange **scuba diving**.

Around Fiskárdho

There are two good pebble beaches close to Fiskárdho – **Émblisi** 1km back out of town and **Fókis** just to the south – and a nature trail on the northern headland. It is worth making the effort to explore the coastal region west of **Mánganos: Alatiés** has a tiny beach tucked in between folds of impressive white volcanic rock, but the real gem is the small bay of **Ayía Ierousalím**, whose gravel-and-sand beach remains quiet even in August.

CLOCKWISE FROM TOP LEFT ARGOSTÓLI, KEFALONIÁ (P.489); SHIPWRECK BAY, ZÁKYNTHOS (P.510); MELISSÁNI CAVE, KEFALONIÁ (P.495) >

8

ACCOMMODATION, EATING AND DRINKING

MÝRTOS BEACH AND AROUND

Mina Studios Dhivaráta ☎ 26740 61716, ✉ markela1@hol.gr. Just above the main junction, these large and well-appointed studios with kitchenettes are the best accommodation close to Mýrtos beach. April–Oct. **€50**

ÁSSOS

Cosi's Inn ☎ 26740 51420, ⊛ cosisinn.gr. Brightly decorated and well-furnished, good-value rooms are the attraction at this pleasant hill on the approach road to the centre. Breakfast included. April–Oct. **€50**

Kanakis Apartments ☎ 26740 51631, ⊛ kanakis apartments.gr. Very smart studios and spacious maisonettes, all equipped with all mod cons and sharing a pool. Only 100m from the heart of the village. April–Oct. **€65**

Nefeli ☎ 26740 51251. With its prime location on the quay beside the beach, this taverna does a nice line in seafood, mezédhes and salads. Most main courses around €9–10. April–Oct daily 10am–1am.

Platanos Grill Set just back from the seafront, as the name suggests, this place is good for grilled meat and fish. There's also a wide selection of salads and starters, plus aromatic local wine. April–Oct daily 11am– midnight.

FISKÁRDHO

Archontiko ☎ 26740 41342. Beautiful traditional stone mansion that has been converted to luxurious rooms above and behind a harbourfront minimarket. The furniture is period style but all the equipment, such as TVs, is cutting edge. April–Oct. **€100**

Kastro Club ☎ 26740 41010. Up behind the main bypass road, the oldest club in northern Kefaloniá has tiered

NORTHERN KEFALONIÁ

terraces and a big outdoor dancefloor. The isolated location allows the volume to be jacked up on the usual mix of international and Greek hits. July–Sept daily 10pm–late.

Lagoudera ☎ 26740 41275. With two premises, one on the harbour, the other just off the small square, *Lagoudera* specializes in tasty oven food for €7–9 but also does grills and all the usual side dishes. April–Oct daily noon–2am.

Lord Falcon ☎ 26740 41072. One block back from the harbour, the Ionians' first Thai restaurant does a fine array of soups, stir-fries and red, green and Penang curries for around €10–12. May–Oct Mon–Sat 6.30pm–midnight, Sun 1–4.30pm.

Panormos ☎ 26740 41203. Just round the headland with a great location, offering sweeping bay views from its outdoor terrace, this taverna does simple grills, salads and starters at very reasonable prices. April–Oct daily noon–1am.

★ **Regina's** ☎ 26740 41125. Up by the car park, these friendly family-run studios are compact but great value. Some have balconies looking over the village to the bay and there's a lovely courtyard. Can arrange motorboat rental too. April–Oct. **€30**

AROUND FISKÁRDHO

★ **Odisseas** Ayía Ierousalím ☎ 26740 41133. Extremely friendly brother-sister-mum trio serve up exquisite traditional dishes from free-range meat and do a line in olive bread and other baked goodies, plus jams and preserves. They also allow camping on their grounds. April–Oct daily noon–midnight.

Ith–áki

Rugged **ITHÁKI**, Odysseus's legendary homeland, has yielded no substantial archeological discoveries but it fits Homer's description to perfection: "There are no tracks, nor grasslands … it is a rocky severe island, unsuited for horses, but not so wretched, despite its small size. It is good for goats." Despite its proximity to Kefaloniá, relatively little tourist development has arrived to spoil the place. This is doubtless accounted for in part by a dearth of beaches beyond a few pebbly coves, though the island is good walking country, and indeed the interior with its sites from **The Odyssey** is the real attraction. In the scheme of modern Greek affairs, the island is a real backwater and its inhabitants rather resentful that it is officially a subsection of Kefaloniá prefecture.

ARRIVAL AND DEPARTURE
ITHÁKI

By ferry For such a small island, Itháki perhaps surprisingly has three active ports. The following are summer schedules, which are often reduced drastically in winter; any services that stop altogether are denoted by months of operation.
Fríkes to: Fiskárdho (Kefaloniá; May–Oct 4 weekly; 1hr).
Vassilikí (Lefkádha; May–Oct 1 daily; 1hr 30min).

Pisaetós to: Astakós (1–2 daily; 2hr 30min); Pátra (1–3 daily; 3hr 45min); Sámi (Kefaloniá; 4 daily; 45min); Vathý (1–2 daily; 1hr).
Vathý to: Astakós (1–2 daily; 1hr 30min); Pátra (1–3 daily; 2hr); Pisaetós (1–2 daily; 1hr); Sámi (Kefaloniá; 1–3 daily; 1hr 45min).

GETTING AROUND

By bus There is effectively no public transport on the island, though you might be able to flag down the school bus during term.

By taxi Taxis are available, especially at Vathý's square.

By car and motorbike Cars and motorbikes can be rented through the two main travel agencies, based in Vathý, Polyctor Tours (☎26740 33120, ⌨ithakiholidays .com) and Delas Tours (☎26740 32104, ⌨ithaca.com.gr).

Vathý and around

Itháki's main port and capital is **VATHÝ**, enclosed by a bay within a bay so deep that few realize the mountains out "at sea" are actually the north of the island. This snug town is compact, relatively traffic-free and boasts the most idyllic seafront setting of all the Ionian capitals. Like its southerly neighbours, it was heavily damaged by the 1953 earthquake but some fine examples of pre-quake architecture remain. Vathý has a small **archeological museum** on Kalliníkou (Tues–Sun 8.30am–3pm; free), a short block back from the quay. Near the corner of the quay behind the Agricultural Bank, there is also the moderately interesting **Folklore & Cultural Museum** (April–Oct Mon–Fri 10am–2pm & 7.30–9.30pm; €1).

Beaches around Vathý

There are two reasonable pebble **beaches** within fifteen minutes' walk of Vathý: **Dhéxa**, over the hill above the ferry quay, and tiny **Loútsa**, opposite it around the bay. The better beaches at **Sarakíniko** and **Skínos** are an hour's trek along paved roads leaving the opposite side of the bay. In season, daily *kaïkia* ply between the quay and remote coves.

8

ODYSSEUS SIGHTS AROUND VATHÝ

Three of the main **Odysseus** sights are just within walking distance of Vathý: the Arethoússa Spring, the Cave of the Nymphs and ancient Alalkomenae, although the last is best approached by **moped** or **taxi**.

THE ARETHOÚSSA SPRING

The walk to the **Arethoússa Spring** – allegedly the place where Eumaeus, Odysseus's faithful swineherd, brought his pigs to drink – is a three-hour round trip along a track signposted next to the seafront telecoms office. The unspoilt but shadeless landscape and sea views are magnificent but some of the inclines can be slippery.

Near the top of the lane leading to the spring path, a signpost points up to what is said to have been the **Cave of Eumaeus**. The route to the spring continues for a few hundred metres, and then branches off onto a narrow footpath through steep gorse-covered cliffs. Parts of the final downhill track involve scrambling across rock fields (follow the splashes of green paint), and care should be taken around the small but vertiginous ravine that houses the **spring**. The ravine sits below a crag known as **Kórax** (the raven), which matches Homer's description of the meeting between Odysseus and Eumaeus. In summer it's just a dribble of water.

THE CAVE OF THE NYMPHS

The **Cave of the Nymphs** (Marmarospíli) is about 2.5km up a rough but navigable road signposted on the brow of the hill above Dhéxa beach. The cave is atmospheric, but it's underwhelming compared to the caverns of neighbouring Kefaloniá and, these days, is illuminated by coloured lights. The claim that this is *The Odyssey*'s Cave of the Nymphs, where the returning Odysseus concealed the gifts given to him by King Alkinous, is enhanced by the proximity of Dhéxa beach.

ALALKOMENAE

Alalkomenae, Heinrich Schliemann's much-vaunted "Castle of Odysseus", is signposted on the Vathý–Pisaetós road, on the saddle between Dhéxa and Pisaetós, with views over both sides of the island. The actual site, however, some 300m uphill, is little more than foundations spread about in the gorse, and in fact the most likely contender for the site of Odysseus's castle is above the village of Stavrós (see p.500).

Pisaetós

The harbour of **PISAETÓS**, around 5km west of Vathý via a steep route across the island's neck, has a fair-sized rocky beach that's all right for a pre-ferry swim and popular with local rod-and-line fishermen. Little goes on here except during the busy period around ferry arrivals, when a small canteen on the quay is the focus of activity.

INFORMATION   **VATHÝ AND AROUND**

Services There is no tourist office but a smattering of banks, a post office, police and a medical centre. An excellent website on the island is ⓦithacagreece.com.

ACCOMMODATION

The best source of rooms, studios or villas around the capital or all over the island are the two main quayside travel agencies (see p.499).

★ **Captain Yiannis** ☎ 26740 33311, ⓦcaptain yiannis.com. Complete with tennis court and pool with bar, this great-value resort round the east side of the bay is spread over several blocks of modern rooms and apartments. Breakfast included. Mid-May to Sept. **€55**

Mentor ☎ 26740 32433, ⓦhotelmentor.gr. In the southeast corner of the harbour, the town's oldest hotel was refurbished a few years ago and its comfortable rooms have balconies either with direct or side views of the water. **€45**

Omirikon ☎ 26740 33596, ⓦomirikonhotel.com. Stylish boutique hotel, yet with a personal, family-run touch. All its rooms are classed as suites, and are spacious and well furnished with sea-view balconies. Breakfast included. May–Oct. **€70**

EATING AND DRINKING

O Nikos ☎ 26740 33039. Just off the square, this is a good old-fashioned *estiatório*, where you can feast on heaps of oven-baked goodies, on show behind the glass panel within. Pavement seating in summer. Daily 11am–midnight.

Paliocaravo (aka Gregory's) ☎ 26740 32573. Popular for its lamb and fish, with a good range of accompanying dishes and beverages, plus the occasional impromptu music session. April–Oct daily noon–1am.

★ **To Kohili** ☎ 26740 33565. By far the best of the half-dozen harbourside tavernas, serving a good range of *mezédhes* as well as tasty meat dishes such as lamb *kléftiko*, *yiouvétsi* and *soutsoukákia*, plus grills and pasta. Daily 11am–1am.

Northern Itháki

The main road out of Vathý continues across the isthmus and takes a spectacular route to the northern half of Itháki, based around **Stavrós**. This is excellent scooter country, and the close proximity of the settlements, small coves and Homeric interest also make it good rambling terrain. As with the rest of Itháki there are only limited tourist facilities, concentrated mostly in **Fríkes** and **Kióni**.

Stavrós

STAVRÓS, the second-largest town on the island, is a steep 2km above the nearest beach at Pólis Bay. It's a pleasant enough town, with *kafenía* edging a small square dominated by a rather fierce statue of Odysseus. There is even a tiny **museum** (Tues–Sun 8.30am–3pm; free) off the road to Platrithriés, displaying local archeological finds. Most of these come from the early Helladic site on the side of **Pelikáta Hill**, where remains of roads, walls and other structures have been suggested as the possible site of Odysseus's palace.

Anoyí

Some 5km southeast of Stavrós along a scenic mountain road is **ANOYÍ**, which translates roughly as "upper ground". Once the second-most important settlement on the island, it is almost deserted today. The centre of the village is dominated by a freestanding Venetian campanile, built to serve the church of the **Panayía**, which features heavily restored Byzantine frescoes. The church comes alive for the annual *paniyíri* on August 14, the eve of the Virgin's Assumption; at other times enquire at the *kafenío* about access. In the surrounding countryside are some extremely strange rock formations, the biggest being the 8m-high Iraklis (Hercules) rock, just east of the village.

Monastery of Katharón

The **monastery of Katharón**, 3km south of Anoyí, boasts stunning views down over Vathý and the south of the island. It houses an icon of the *Panayía* discovered by peasants clearing scrubland in the area. The monastery celebrates its festival on September 8 with services, processions and music.

Afáles Bay area

Local British expat Katrina (☎ 697 59 28 240) offers expert guided rambles in the area

Afáles, the largest bay on the entire island, with an unspoilt and little-visited pebble-and-sand beach, can be accessed by a track down from the outskirts of **Platrithriés**. This quiet yet rather spread-out village lies on the less direct westerly route from Stavrós to Fríkes, which first loops below the hill village of Exoyí. Just off the start of the road up to Exoyí a signpost points about 1km along a rough track to the supposed **School of Homer**, where excavations still in progress have revealed extensive foundations, a well and ancient steps. The site is unfenced and well worth a detour for its views of Afáles Bay as much as the remains.

Fríkes

Wedged in a valley between two steep hills, **FRÍKES** was only settled in the sixteenth century and emigration in the nineteenth century almost emptied the place – as few as two hundred people live here today – but the protected harbour is a natural port. There are no beaches in the village, but plenty of good, if small, pebble coves a short walk away towards Kióni; it also offers superior dining options to its neighbour. When the ferries and their cargoes have departed, Fríkes falls quiet and this is its real charm.

Kióni

KIÓNI sits at a dead end 5km southeast of Fríkes. On the same geological base as the northern tip of Kefaloniá, it avoided the very worst of the 1953 earthquake and so retains some fine examples of pre-twentieth-century architecture. It's an extremely pretty village, wrapped around a tiny harbour, and tourism here is dominated by British blue-chip travel companies and visiting yachts. The bay has a small **beach**, 1km along its south side, a sand-and-pebble strand below a summer-only snack-bar.

ACCOMMODATION AND EATING   NORTHERN ITHÁKI

STAVRÓS

Margarita ☎ 26740 31229. This large, friendly *zaharoplastío* is a good place for a coffee, a refreshing drink or to sample the local sweet *rovaní* (syrupy rice cakes). Daily 8am–11pm.

Petra ☎ 26740 31596. Popular village taverna that serves grilled and oven dishes, plus some pizza and pasta. It also offers basic but clean and good-value rooms above the restaurant. March–Nov noon–midnight. **€35**

FRÍKES

Aristotelis Apartments ☎ 26740 31079, ⓦ aristotelis-ithaca.gr. Smart apartments only 100m or so back from the harbour, with attractive wooden eaves in the upper rooms and colourful rustic decoration throughout. May–Oct. **€50**

Nostos ☎ 26740 31644, ⓦ hotelnostos-ithaki.gr. Around 100m from the seafront, the only conventional

hotel in northern Itháki has a pool in its relaxing grounds and smart, spacious rooms. Buffet breakfast included. May to mid-Oct. **€80**

★ **Rementzo** ☎ 26740 31719. Friendly taverna in the corner of the quay, offering a selection of fresh fish, baked meat and vegetable dishes, salads and pizza, plus good wine and ouzo. April–Oct daily 10am–1am.

Ulysses ☎ 26740 31733. Specializing in succulent home-style cuisine, this popular restaurant in the middle of the seafront also provides plenty of snacks, sweets and beverages. May–Oct daily 11am–midnight.

KIÓNI

Calypso ☎ 26740 31066. Pleasant taverna in the middle of the tiny bay, which has imaginative dishes like pork with artichokes and some very drinkable aromatic wine. May–Oct daily noon–midnight.

8

Captain's Apartments ☎ 26740 31481, ⓦ captains -apartments.gr. Set up above the village with sweeping views of the village, these roomy apartments are decorated in warm rustic colours. May–Sept. **€50**

Maroudas Apartments ☎ 26740 31691, ⊕ maroudas @greek-tourism.gr. Just a couple of blocks from the harbour, these compact, convenient and comfortable apartments offer modern amenities and a warm welcome. May–Sept. **€40**

Oasis ☎ 26740 31317. Harbourside taverna that offers the usual selection of fresh salads, some dips and a good choice of mainly grilled meat and fish courses. May–Sept daily noon–1am.

Zákynthos

ZÁKYNTHOS (Zante), southernmost of the six core Ionian islands, is somewhat schizophrenically divided between relative wilderness and indiscriminate commercialization. Much of the island is still green and unspoilt, with only token pockets of tourism, however, and the main resorts seem to be reaching maximum growth without encroaching too much on the quieter parts. The island has three distinct zones: the barren, mountainous northwest; the fertile central plain; and the eastern and southern resort-filled coasts. The biggest resort is **Laganás**, on Laganás Bay in the south, a 24-hour party venue that doesn't give up from Easter until the last flight home in October. There are smaller, quieter resorts north and south of the capital, and the southerly Vassilikós peninsula has some of the best countryside and beaches, including exquisite **Yérakas**.

The island still produces fine wines, such as the white Popolaro, as well as sugar-shock-inducing *mandoláto* nougat, whose honey-sweetened form is best. Zákynthos is also the birthplace of *kantádhes*, the Italianate folk ballads which can be heard in tavernas in Zákynthos Town and elsewhere. In addition, the island harbours one of the key breeding sites of the endangered **loggerhead sea turtle** at Laganás Bay (see box, p.506).

ARRIVAL AND DEPARTURE ZÁKYNTHOS

By plane Zákynthos' airport is 4km southwest of the capital. It receives mostly European charters, plus a seasonal daily easyJet flight from London and year-round domestic flights from Athens (1–2 daily; 55min).

By bus Buses from Zákynthos Town to the following mainland destinations are timed to connect with ferry sailings:

Destinations Athens (4–6 daily; 5hr 30min); Pátra (3–4 daily; 3hr); Thessaloníki (2 weekly; 11–12hr).

By ferry The island is well connected year-round with Kyllíni on the Peloponnesian coast and has a seasonal ferry link with Kefaloniá from the northern Áyios Nikólaos (aka Skinári).

Áyios Nikólaos to: Pessádha (Kefaloniá; 2 daily May–Sept; 1hr 30min).

Zákynthos Town to: Kyllíni (5–7 daily; 1hr 30min).

GETTING AROUND

By bus The local KTEL network radiates out from Zákynthos Town with frequent summer services to the busiest tourist resorts, especially Argási, Kalamáki and Laganás, but few or no buses to the far north or the west coast.

By cars and motorbike There are many rental outlets around the island, such as Eurosky (☎ 26950 26278, ⓦ eurosky.gr), whose head Zákynthos Town office is at Makrí 6, two blocks south of the main square.

By taxi Taxis are widely available and can be called on ☎ 26950 48400.

BOAT TRIPS FROM ZÁKYNTHOS TOWN

At least ten pleasure craft offer **day-trips** around the island from the quay in Zákynthos Town (around €20). All take in sights such as the **Blue Caves** at Cape Skinári, and moor in **Tó Naváyio (Shipwreck Bay)** and at the Marathiá caves at **Cape Kerí** in the southwest. You might want to shop around for the trip with the most stops, as eight hours bobbing round the coast can become a bore. Check also that the operators actually take you into the caves. There are also shorter trips to Kerí and turtle-spotting in Laganás Bay for €15, including on one vessel with underwater seating. **Cavo Grosso** at Lombárdhou 22 (☎ 26950 48308, ⓦ cavogrosso.gr) offers a range of excursions.

Zákynthos Town

The town, like the island, is known as both **ZÁKYNTHOS** and Zante. This former "Venice of the East" (*Zante, Fior di Levante*, "Flower of the Levant", in an Italian jingle), rebuilt on the old plan after the 1953 earthquake, has bravely tried to re-create some of its style, though reinforced concrete can only do so much.

The town stretches beyond the length of the wide and busy harbour, its main section bookended by the grand **Platía Solomoú** at the north, and the church of **Áyios Dhionýsios**, patron saint of the island, at the south. Zákynthos is a working town with limited concessions to tourism, although there are sufficient facilities and it's the only place to stay if you want to see the island by public transport.

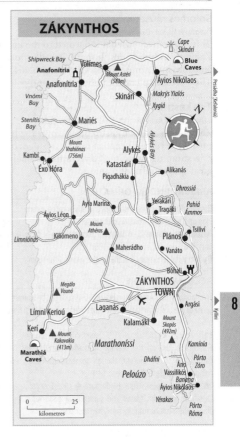

Áyios Dhionýsios

Church Daily 8am–1pm & 5–10pm **Museum** Daily May–Sept 8am–11pm, Oct–April 9am–noon & 5–8pm • €2

The church of **Áyios Dhionýsios** is well worth a visit for the dazzling giltwork and fine modern murals inside, which were completely repainted at the turn of the millennium. Behind the church there is also a **museum**, which has some fine paintings and icons.

Platía Solomoú

Platía Solomoú is named after the island's most famous son, the poet Dhionysios Solomos, the father of modernism in Greek literature, who was responsible for establishing demotic Greek (as opposed to the elitist *katharévousa* form) as a literary idiom. He is also the author of the lyrics to the national anthem, an excerpt from which adorns the statue of Liberty in the square.

Platía Solomoú is home to the town's **library**, which has a small collection of pre- and post-quake photography, and the massive **Byzantine Museum**, sometimes referred to as the Zákynthos Museum. On the seaward corner of the square stands the squat restored church of **Áyios Nikólaos tou Mólou**, where the vestments of St Dhionysios are kept.

Byzantine Museum

Platía Solomoú • Tues–Sun 8.30am–3pm • €3 • ☎ 26950 42714

The **Byzantine Museum** is most notable for its collection of artworks from the Ionian School (see box, p.463), the region's post-Renaissance art movement, spearheaded by Zakynthian painter Panayiotis Doxaras. The movement was given impetus by Cretan refugees, unable to practise their art under Turkish rule. It also houses some secular painting and a fine model of the town before the earthquake.

Solomos museum

Platía Ayíou Márkou • Daily 9am–2pm • €3

This impressive **museum** is devoted to the life and work of **Solomos** and other Zakynthian luminaries. It shares its collection of manuscripts and personal effects with an eponymous museum on Corfu (see p.461), where Solomos spent most of his life. There are also plenty of photographs and paintings of notable islanders.

The kástro

Daily: June–Sept 8am–8pm; Oct–May 8.30am–3pm • €1.50

Zákynthos's massive **kástro** broods over the hamlet of Bóhali on its bluff above the town. The ruined Venetian fort has vestiges of dungeons, armouries and fortifications, plus stunning views in all directions. Its shady carpet of fallen pine needles makes it a great spot to relax or picnic.

ARRIVAL AND INFORMATION   ZÁKYNTHOS TOWN

By bus The bus station is inconveniently located nearly 2km up from the seafront, near the hospital.
Destinations Athens (5–6 daily; 5hr 30min); Pátra (4 daily; 3hr); Thessaloníki (3 weekly; 12–13hr).
By ferry The ferry quay is at the southern end of the town's

seafront.
Services The tourist police is in the main police station, halfway along the seafront. They can supply basic information and keep a list of accommodation (May–Oct daily 8am–10pm; ☎ 26950 24482).

ACCOMMODATION

The Room Owners Association (☎ 26950 49498) can be contacted for accommodation around town and all over the island. Some of the best hotels are in the quiet Repára district, just north of the centre.

Egli Loútzi ☎ 26950 28317. Smallish hotel whose entrance is just off the seafront, tucked in beside the gargantuan *Strada Marina*, though some of its clean, compact rooms face the harbour. **€40**
★ **Palatino** Kolokotróni 10, Repára ☎ 26950 27780, ⓦ palatinohotel.gr. Classy and surprisingly good-value place, which has beautifully furnished rooms with all mod

cons and ritzy common areas. Ample buffet breakfast included. **€70**
Plaza Kolokotróni 2, Repára ☎ 26950 45733, ⓦ plazazante.gr. Barely 50m from the town beach, this pleasant four-storey hotel has comfortable, modern rooms, some with sea-facing balconies, and a relaxing lobby café. Breakfast included. **€60**

EATING AND DRINKING

★ **Arekia** Dhionyssíou Romá ☎ 26950 26346. Beyond the town beach, this cosy, welcoming taverna offers a succulent range of fresh grilled meat and fish, but the real reason to come is for the best nightly *kantádhes* to be heard anywhere. Daily 8pm–2am.
Iy Padella Dhessylá 15 ☎ 26950 23356. Just a couple of blocks inland south of the main square, this simple *estiatório* offers wholesome home cooking at the best prices in town. Daily 11am–midnight.

Iy Thymalos Lombárdhou 78 ☎ 26950 26732. Huge seafront taverna with a nautical theme and pavement seating, where you can feast on imaginative prawn and crab salad, plenty of quality fish and some Cypriot dishes such as *seftaliá*. March–Nov daily noon–2am.
Komis Bastoúni tou Ayíou ☎ 26950 26915. Across the quay from Áyios Dhionýsios, this upmarket favourite serves unusual seafood dishes like clams and urchins, along with multiple *mezédhes* and good barrelled wine. Daily noon–2am.

NIGHTLIFE

Base Platía Ayíou Márkou ☎ 26950 42409. Perennially busy favourite, in a prime location, which plays an eclectic dance mix at night, while its daytime café mode is more prone to rock and ethnic sounds. Daily 11am–late.

Iy Proza 21 Maïou 23. Lively upstairs rock bar where black is the colour apart from the startling metallic pipework, the drinks are fairly cheap and the soundtrack is mostly punkish and indie. Daily 10pm–late.

The Vassilikós peninsula

The busy southern end of the island's most noticeable feature is the **Vassilikós peninsula**, which points in somewhat phallic mimicry of Florida towards the

Peloponnese. It is headed by the package resort of **Argási** but its treasures really lie in the succession of sandy beaches, mostly on the eastern side, which culminate in the stunning strand of **Yérakas**.

Argási

Barely 4km south of Zákynthos Town, **ARGÁSI** is the busiest resort on this coast, sprawling for over a kilometre behind a beach that is scarcely a few feet wide in parts. Although the rest of the peninsula is far more appealing, it does offer a wide choice of facilities, including a popular concentration of clubs, and is a closer base for exploring the rest of the island.

The east coast

The first two coves south of Argási are **Kamínia** and the more scenic **Pórto Zóro**. The main road dips and dives along the east coast of the peninsula, with short access roads descending to these and other longer beaches further south, such as **Iónio** and **Banana**. Above these contiguous strands, the only real facilities away from the coast are to be found at the rather formless village of **Áno Vassilkós**.

The coast ends up at **ÁYIOS NIKÓLAOS**, which has a good beach and lures day-trippers from Argási, Kalamáki and Laganás with a free bus service in season. It's a fast-emerging hamlet with a fair range of amenities.

The west coast

At the very southwestern tip of the peninsula, **Yérakas** is the star attraction: a sublime crescent of golden sand. It's also a key loggerhead turtle breeding ground, and is therefore off-limits between dusk and dawn, as well as being subject to strict rules on the number and placement of umbrellas. The excellent open-air **Turtle Information Centre** (ⓦearthseasky.org) provides interesting background on these and other sea creatures, some of which are on display in its recently acquired aquarium.

Further north along the rugged west coast of the peninsula, accessed by the only (partly unpaved) road which crosses it, is **Dháfni**, home to a couple of tavernas.

8

ACTIVITIES

THE VASSILIKÓS PENINSULA

Watersports St Nicholas Beach Watersports in Áyios Nikólaos (☎ 693 71 07 652) rents equipment for a range of activities, including windsurfing, parasailing and scuba diving.

ACCOMMODATION, EATING AND NIGHTLIFE

ARGÁSI

Barrage ☎ 693 24 52 020. One of the big outdoor clubs that line the road from Zákynthos Town into Argási, where well-known DJs play house, techno and other dance vibes to a crowd of gyrating bodies. May to mid-Oct daily 10pm–late.

Locanda ☎ 26950 45386, ⓦlocanda.gr. Smart seafront hotel with a choice of standard doubles or larger studios, all with kitchenettes and balconies facing the sea or mountain. Also pool and bar. Breakfast included. April–Oct. **€60**

Pension Vaso ☎ 26950 44599. Just off the main road entering the village from Zákynthos Town, this simple guesthouse has basic but clean rooms and you can be sure of a warm welcome from the owner whose name it bears. May–Oct. **€30**

Three Brothers ☎ 26950 44479. One of the oldest tavernas in the resort, with a wide but familiar menu and the cute claim that the fish is "caught by two brothers and cooked by the third". May–Oct daily 10am–1am.

THE EAST COAST

Christina's Áyios Nikólaos ☎ 26950 39474, ☻ christina _law8@hotmail.com. One of the best deals on the island: The neat, brilliant-white studios with cooking facilities are comfortably furnished and the welcome adds to an all-round cosy atmosphere. May–Oct. **€30**

★ **Levantino Studios & Apartments** Kamínia ☎ 26950 35366, ⓦlevantino.gr. Well-equipped units of varying size, set in carefully manicured grounds at the back of the beach. Also a snack bar and free sunbeds with umbrellas. May–Oct. **€30**

Logos Áno Vassilkós ⓦlogosbar.com. Legendary rustic club which occupies a large space in the pine woods, where night owls dance to a mixture of rock and disco sounds and sip exotic cocktails. June–Sept Mon, Wed, Fri & Sat 9pm–late.

Porto Zorro Pórto Zóro ☎ 26950 35304, ⓦportozorro .gr. This good-value hotel, right on the eponymous beach, has decent-sized rooms whose stark white linen is tempered by the brown wood-panelling. The attached taverna offers a full menu. **€40**

Vasilikos Beach Áyios Nikólaos ☎ 26950 35325, ⓦ hotelvasilikosbeach.gr. Huge beach-resort complex that has a variety of rooms but also offers a pool, jacuzzi and watersports among its many amenities. Buffet breakfast included. May–Oct. **€65**

THE WEST COAST

Antonis Dháfni ☎ 26950 26989. Fine taverna-cum-bar, where you can have a full meal of fresh fish or home-cooked meat, a lighter snack or just sip a sunset cocktail. June–Sept daily 10am–10pm.

★ **To Triodi** Yérakas ☎ 26950 35215. Excellent taverna with a leafy garden, where you can sample fresh fish or well-prepared meat dishes, plus all the usual salads, dips and good local wine. May–Oct daily 11am–1am.

Laganás Bay

The large sweep of **Laganás Bay**, anchored on the major party resort of **Laganás** itself, dominates southern Zákynthos. **Kalamáki** is another busy resort at the eastern end, while delightful **Límni Kerioú** in the southwest completes the picture. As the bay is also a prime home to the loggerhead turtle, there has long been an uneasy coexistence between mass tourism and conservation (see box below).

Laganás

The majority of the hundreds of thousands of people who visit Zákynthos each year find themselves in **LAGANÁS**. Set amid the fine 9km beach that runs almost the entire length of the bay, it offers entertainments from watersports to ballooning, and even an occasional funfair. Beachfront bars and restaurants stretch for well over 1km, the bars and restaurants on the main drag another kilometre inland. Some stay open around the clock; others just play music at deafening volume until dawn. The competing video and music bars can make Laganás at night resemble the set of *Blade Runner* but that's how its predominantly English visitors like it.

8

LOGGERHEAD TURTLES

The Ionian islands harbour the Mediterranean's main concentration of **loggerhead sea turtles**, a sensitive species which is, unfortunately, under direct threat from the tourist industry. These creatures lay their eggs at night on sandy coves and, easily frightened by noise and lights, are therefore uneasy cohabitants with rough campers and late-night discos. Each year, many turtles fall prey to motorboat injuries, nests are destroyed by bikes and the newly hatched young die entangled in deckchairs and umbrellas left out at night.

The Greek government has passed laws designed to protect the loggerheads, including restrictions on camping at some beaches, but local economic interests tend to prefer a beach full of bodies to a sea full of turtles. On **Laganás**, nesting grounds are concentrated around the 14km bay, and Greek marine zoologists are in angry dispute with those involved in the tourist industry. The turtles' nesting ground just west of **Skála** on Kefaloniá is another important location, although numbers have dwindled to half their former strength and now only about eight hundred remain. Ultimately, the turtles' best hope for survival may rest in their potential draw as a unique tourist attraction in their own right.

While capitalists and environmentalists are still at, well, loggerheads, the **World Wildlife Fund** has issued guidelines for visitors:

- Don't use the beaches of Laganás and Yérakas between sunset and sunrise.
- Don't stick umbrellas in the sand in the marked nesting zones.
- Take your rubbish away with you – it can obstruct the turtles.
- Don't use lights near the beach at night – they can disturb the turtles, sometimes with fatal consequences.
- Don't take any vehicle onto the protected beaches.
- Don't dig up turtle nests – it's illegal.
- Don't pick up the hatchlings or carry them to the water.
- Don't use speedboats in Laganás Bay – a 9kph speed limit is in force.

Kalamáki

Neighbouring Laganás to the east, **Kalamáki** has a better, much wider beach than its westerly neighbour and is altogether quieter, with a slightly more family-oriented feel. Even the bars are more laidback, although it does suffer from some airport noise.

Límni Kerioú

Límni Kerioú, at the southwestern end of Laganás Bay, has gradually evolved into a relaxing and picturesque resort, and has a couple of diving operations. It's reached by a turning that branches off the main road before it climbs up towards the west coast, after the hill village of **Lithákia**.

ACTIVITIES

LAGANÁS BAY

Diving Límni Kerioú is home to the Turtle Beach Diving Centre (☎ 26950 49424, ⓦ diving-center-turtle-beach .com).

Horseriding Nana's Horses (☎ 26950 23195), just outside Kalamáki, can arrange riding trips.

ACCOMMODATION, EATING, DRINKING AND NIGHTLIFE

LAGANÁS

Ionis ☎ 26950 51141, ⓦ zante-ionis-hotel.com. On the main drag towards the beach, one of the few places not block-booked is this surprisingly classy boutique hotel with tastefully designed rooms and a huge pool. Breakfast included; open May–Oct. If they're full try the local Union of Room Owners (daily 8.30am–2pm & 5–8pm; ☎ 26950 51590), which has a range of accommodation. €80

Rescue Club ☎ 26950 51612. Proclaiming itself to be the biggest club on the island, this place has an outdoor bar area and huge indoor dancefloor with top sound and lighting equipment to enhance the nonstop dance favourites. May–Oct daily 10pm–late.

★ **Sarakina** ☎ 26950 51606. Best taverna in the area, serving tasty dishes such as pork in wine sauce and featuring nightly *kantádhes*. There's a free minibus to convey diners to its leafy location nearly 2km inland. May–Oct 6pm–2am.

Zeros ⓦ zerosclubzante.com. Massive club with state-of-the-art sound systems and top DJs, which hosts various big events through the summer and regular foam parties and other themes. May–Oct daily 9pm–late.

KALAMÁKI

Cave Club ☎ 26950 48278. Set into a real cave on the hillside above the village, with a pleasantly leafy patio garden where you can enjoy a cocktail to the mostly laid-back rock sounds. May–Oct daily 9pm–3am.

Crystal Beach ☎ 26950 42788, ⓦ crystalbeach.gr. Large resort hotel, which has smart rooms for independent

as well as package holiday-makers, plus restaurant, bar, pool and watersports on the beach. Breakfast included. May–Oct. €70

Stanis ☎ 26950 26374. Both branches of this well-established taverna have extensive menus of Greek and international dishes, although the one by the beach is predictably busier during the day. May–Oct daily 11am–1am.

LÍMNI KERIOÚ

Camping Tartaruga ☎ 26950 51967, ⓦ tartaruga -camping.com. Easily the best campsite on the island, though reaching it requires a vehicle as it's on a remote stretch of Laganás Bay below Lithákia. Shady pitches, a pebble beach and minimarket all to hand. May–Oct. Adult plus tent €7.40

★ **Pansion Limni** ☎ 26950 48716, ⓦ pansionlimni .com. Disarmingly friendly family guesthouse, with comfortable self-catering rooms and a shared wraparound balcony with sea views. Their wonderful stone *Porto Tsi Ostrias* pension nearby has huge, beautifully designed apartments. May–Oct. €40

Poseidon ☎ 26950 48708. Overlooking the bay from the hill at the east end, and serving a variety of grilled meat and fish, plus good daily specials. May–Oct daily noon–1am.

Rock Café ☎ 26950 23401. Chilled-out joint with an airy wooden balcony overlooking the beach, a well-stocked bar and, as the name suggests, a decent line in rock sounds. May–Oct daily noon–2am.

Western Zákynthos

At the far southwest end of Laganás Bay, the landscape ascends into the mountains around **Kerí**, the first of a series of pretty villages along the sparsely inhabited **west coast**. The bus system does not reach the wild western side of the island, so a rental car or sturdy motorbike is required to get there.

Kerí

Hidden in a fold above the cliffs at the island's southernmost tip, the village of **KERÍ** retains several pre-quake Venetian buildings, including the **Panayía Kerioú** church; the Virgin is said to have saved the island from marauding pirates by hiding it in a sea mist. A road leads 1km on to the lighthouse, with spectacular views of the sea, rock arches and stacks.

Maherádho

MAHERÁDHO boasts impressive pre-earthquake architecture set in beautiful arable uplands, surrounded by olive and fruit groves. The church of **Ayía Mávra** has an impressive freestanding campanile and, inside, a splendid carved iconostasis and icons. The town's major **festival** – one of the biggest on the island – is the saint's day, which falls on the first Sunday in June. The other notable church in town, that of the **Panayía**, commands breathtaking views over the central plain.

Kilíómeno and around

KILÍÓMENO is the best place to see surviving pre-earthquake domestic architecture, in the form of the island's traditional two-storey houses. The town was originally named after its church, **Áyios Nikólaos**, whose impressive campanile, begun over a hundred years ago, still lacks a capped roof. The road from Kilíómeno passes through the nondescript village of Áyios Léon, from where two turnings lead through fertile land and down a paved loop road to the impressive rocky coast at **Limniónas**, where there is a tiny bay.

Kambí

The tiny clifftop hamlet of **KAMBÍ** is popular with day-trippers, who come to catch the sunset over the sea; there are extraordinary views to be had of the 300m-high cliffs and western horizon from Kambí's three clifftop tavernas.

Mariés and around

Set in a wooded green valley 5km north of Kambí, the tiny village of **MARIÉS** is the only other place with coastal access on this side of Zákynthos: a 7km track leading down to the rocky inlet of **Stenítis Bay**, where there's a taverna and yacht dock. Another steep road leads to the uninspiring **Vrómi Bay**, from where speedboats run trips to Shipwreck Bay (see p.510), while the main road continues north towards Volímes (see p.510).

ACCOMMODATION AND EATING   **THE WEST COAST**

KERÍ

Apelati ☎ 26950 43324. Just off the main road before the incline east of the village, this farm-like taverna serves home-style dishes from fresh ingredients and has a few simple rustic rooms. May–Oct 11am–midnight. **€30**

Keri Lighthouse ☎ 26950 43384. Scenically situated taverna, 1km west of the village, where people flock for sunset dinners in the large and lush patio garden. The food is standard fare but the view unsurpassed. May–Sept daily noon–midnight.

KILÍÓMENO AND AROUND

★**Alitzerini** Kilíómeno ☎ 26950 48552. At this beautifully restored eighteenth-century stone house with a terrace the friendly owner serves up traditional cuisine with a twist, such as *sfigadoúra* – beef in tomato sauce with cheese and red pepper. 7pm–1am: May–Sept daily, Oct–April Sat & Sun; also some Sun lunches.

Porto Limnionas Limniónas. Perched on a rocky outcrop just above the tiny harbour, this *psarotavérna* is known for its high-quality if rather pricey fish and also has a huge selection of tasty mezédhes. May–Oct daily noon–11pm.

The northeast

A few kilometres north of the capital the amalgamated resorts of **Tsiliví** and **Plános** are the touristic epicentre of this part of the island. Further north they give way to a series of tiny beaches, while picturesque villages punctuate the lush landscape inland. Beyond **Alykés**, as you approach the island's tip at **Cape Skinári**, the coast becomes more rugged, while the mountains inland hide the weaving centre of **Volímes**.

Tsiliví, Plános and around

North and inland from Zákynthos Town, the roads thread their way through luxuriantly fertile farmland, punctuated with tumulus-like hills. **TSILIVÍ**, 5km north of the capital, is the first beach resort here and is in effect one with the hamlet of **PLÁNOS**, the resultant conglomeration rivalling Argási for development.

The beaches further along this stretch of coast become progressively quieter and more pleasant, and all have at least some accommodation and restaurants to choose from. Good choices include **Pahiá Ámmos** and **Dhrossiá**.

Alykés Bay

Alykés Bay, 12km north of Tsiliví, is a large sandy bay with lively surf and the northeast's two largest resorts. The first, **ALIKANÁS**, is a small but expanding village, much of its accommodation being foreign-owned villa rentals. The second, **ALYKÉS**, named after the spooky saltpans behind the village, has the best beach north of the capital.

Makrýs Yialós and around

Tiny **Xygiá beach**, cut into a deep cove 4km north of Alykés, has sulphur springs flowing into the sea – follow the smell – which provide the odd sensation of swimming in a mix of cool and warm water. The next, somewhat longer, beach of **Makrýs Yialós** also makes for an extremely pleasant break on a tour of the north. Just to the north of Makrýs Yialós you come to a pretty promontory with a small harbour, called **Mikró Nissáki**.

Áyios Nikólaos and around

Just over 20km from Zákynthos Town, **ÁYIOS NIKÓLAOS**, known to locals as **Skinári** (after the nearby inland village) to avoid confusion with its namesake on the Vassilikós peninsula, is a small working port with a daily summer ferry connection to Pessádha on Kefaloniá but unfortunately there is no bus service, so travellers using the crossing without their own transport are forced to fork out for a taxi or hitch a ride south.

The Blue Caves

Boat trips €7.50; €15 combined with Shipwreck Bay

The **Blue Caves** are some of the more realistically named of the many contenders in Greece; ignore scams claiming that Áyios Nikólaos is the last place from which you can catch a boat. They're terrific for snorkelling and when you go for a dip here your skin will appear bright blue. To reach them, follow the road as it snakes onwards from Áyios Nikólaos through a landscape of gorse bushes and dry-stone walls until it ends at the lighthouse of **Cape Skinári**, from below which the cheapest **boat trips** operate.

Katastári

Two kilometres inland from Alykés, **KATASTÁRI** is the largest settlement after the capital. Precisely because it's not geared towards tourism, it's the best place to see Zakynthian life as it's lived away from the usual racket. Its most impressive edifice is the huge rectangular church of Iperáyia Theotókos, with a twin belfry and small new amphitheatre for festival performances.

Pighadhákia

A couple of kilometres south of Katastári, the tiny hamlet of **PIGHADHÁKIA** is the unlikely setting for the **Vertzagio Cultural Museum** (March to early Nov Mon–Fri & Sun 9am–2pm & 6–8pm, Sat 9am–2pm; €3), which houses an interesting array of agricultural and folk artefacts. There is also the diminutive **Áyios Pandeléïmon** chapel, which has the unusual feature of a well, hidden beneath the altar.

8

Ayía Marína

AYÍA MARÍNA, a few kilometres southwest of Katastári, has a church with an impressive Baroque altar screen, and a belfry that's being rebuilt from the remnants left after the 1953 earthquake. As in most Zákynthos churches, the bell tower stands detached, in Venetian fashion. In the upper part of the village is the new **Helmi's Natural History Museum** (May–Oct 9am–6pm, Nov–April 9am–2pm; €2; ⊚museumhelmis.gr), which displays plenty of stuffed birds and mammals, seashells and the largest ammonite found in Greece, as well as showing an informative film about turtles.

Volímes and around

Divided into three contiguous parts, **VOLÍMES** is the centre of the island's embroidery industry and numerous shops sell artefacts produced here. With your own transport, you could make it to the **Anafonítria monastery**, 3km south, thought to have been the cell of the island's patron saint, Dhionysios, whose festivals are celebrated on August 24 and December 17.

Shipwreck Bay

A paved road leads on from Volímes to the cliffs overlooking **Shipwreck Bay** (Tó Naváyio), with hair-raising views down to the shipwreck, a cargo ship which was mistaken for a drug-running vessel and run aground by the coastguard in the 1960s.

ACCOMMODATION AND EATING

THE NORTHEAST

TSILIVÍ, PLÁNOS AND AROUND

Anetis Hotel ☎26950 44590, ⊚anetishotel.gr. Comfortable, good-value hotel with sizeable a/c rooms, many with sea-facing balconies overlooking the lively beach bar. April–Oct. **€35**

The Olive Tree ☎26950 62834. The best of the predictably touristy bunch, with a huge menu, including grilled meat and fish, a host of starters and perfectly acceptable wine by the kilo. May–Oct daily noon–1am.

Passage to Asia ☎26950 43788. One of the best oriental restaurants on the island, serving authentic enough versions of both Indian and Chinese cuisine. Has meal deals for two people at around €20. May–Oct daily noon–midnight.

ALYKÉS BAY

Eros Piccadilly ☎26950 83606, ⊚piccadilly.com.gr. Near the beginning of the road to Katastári, this hotel often has super deals going on its studios and compact but comfortable rooms. April–Oct. **€25**

Fantasia ☎26950 83249. Fairly standard tourist fare with a dash of flair makes this one of the better options in the resort. Also does full English breakfasts for €3.50. May–Oct daily 9am–1am.

MAKRÝS YIALÓS AND AROUND

Pilarinos ☎26950 31396. This good taverna on the flattish hillock behind the beach does a decent line in grills, fish and the usual accoutrements, plus there's a makeshift campsite on the grounds. May–Oct daily 11am–midnight.

ÁYIOS NIKÓLAOS AND AROUND

★ **Anemomilos** Cape Skinári ☎26950 31241, ⊚potamitisbros.gr. Two expertly converted windmills make for a unique place to stay. There are also some more conventional rooms, a snack bar, and the same family run the excellent *To Faros* taverna nearby. May–Oct. **€50**

Panorama Áyios Nikólaos ☎26950 31013, ✉panorama -apts@ath.forthnet.gr. Great if you are leaving on the morning ferry to Kefaloniá or want a northern base, these friendly studios are a good-value option. Breakfast included. April–Oct. **€35**

PIGHADHÁKIA

★ **Kaki Rahi** ☎26950 83670. Traditional family-run taverna, which serves tasty local cuisine from home-grown ingredients, its own barrelled wine and provides transportation on its little train twice daily from Alykés. €12.50 including set mixed plate. Live music Sat evenings. May–Oct daily 11am–midnight.

Kýthira

Isolated at the foot of the Peloponnese, the island of **KÝTHIRA** traditionally belongs to the Ionian islands, and shares their history of **Venetian** and, later, British rule; under the former it was known as Cerigo. For the most part, the similarities end there: the island architecture of whitewashed houses and flat roofs looks more like that of the Cyclades; the landscape is different, too, with wild scrub- and gorse-covered hills, or moorland sliced by deep valleys and ravines; and most summer visitors are Greeks. For the few foreigners who reach Kýthira, it remains something of a refuge, with its undeveloped **beaches** a principal attraction. Note that some accommodation does not open until June and closes early in September.

Kýthira was never a rich island, but, along with Monemvasiá, it did once have a military and economic significance – which it likewise lost with Greek independence and the opening of the Corinth Canal. Since then, emigration (almost entirely to **Australia**, which islanders refer to as "Big Kýthira") has reduced the permanent population significantly. In summer many Greek Australians return to here to visit family (Greeks call it "**Kangaroo Island**"), which is why the English spoken on the island usually has a distinct Down Under lilt.

ARRIVAL AND DEPARTURE KÝTHIRA

By air The airport is deep in the interior, 8km southeast of Potamós; the few Olympic Airways flights, from Athens only, are met by taxis, as are most high-season boats.

By ferry The huge all-weather harbour at Dhiakófti is the arrival point for the daily Neápoli ferries (cars €50 one-way, foot passenger €12; ⓦkythira-kithira-kythera.com).

Dhiakófti has a sandy beach and a few places to stay but most people move on quickly.

Destinations Andikýthira (2 weekly in season, 2hr); Kalamáta (1 daily; 4hr 30min); Kissamos (Crete; 1 daily; 3hr 40min); Neápoli (up to 4 daily, 1hr); Pireás (2 weekly in season; 6hr); Yíthio (1–5 weekly in season; 2hr 30min).

INFORMATION AND ACTIVITIES

Travel agents For booking and buying both ferry and air tickets, Kithira Travel has two locations on the island, one on the main street of Hóra and the other in Potamós (ⓣ27360 31390 or 27360 31848).

Services Potamós town has tavernas, a bank ATM, a post office and petrol stations, as well as an Olympic Airways office (ⓣ27360 33362). Hóra has a couple of banks with

ATMs and a post office on the main square.

Guided walks The Mare Nostrum camping and outdoor shop in Potamós (ⓣ27360 33573, ⓔchronisdiver@ hotmail.com) can organize guided walks from Paleohóra down through the Káki Langádha Gorge to the coast 2km south of Ayía Pelayía.

GETTING AROUND

By bus A single daily service runs between Ayía Pelayía– Kapsáli–Dhiakófti, starting at 9am Mon–Sat, returning Dhiakófti–Kapsáli–Ayía Pelayía late mornings or mid-afternoon, depending on the ferry times.

By taxi Taxis from the port charge around €25 to Kapsáli and €17 to Potamós, but establish a price beforehand.

Car and motorbike rental Panayotis, based in Hóra

(ⓣ27360 31004, ⓦpanayotis-rent-a-car.gr) but with offices in Kapsáli, Ayía Pelayía, Dhiakófti and at the airport, rents cars, motorbikes, mountain bikes and scooters. The roads are generally well surfaced and there are petrol stations on the central road at Potamós, Kondoliánika and Livádhi.

Potamós and the north

Inland, northwest of the ferry port, is **POTAMÓS**, Kýthira's largest town. It's a pleasant, unspoilt place, which makes a perfect lunch stop when you're exploring the island, though you should choose to stay at one of the towns on or near a beach. The **Sunday market** here is the island's biggest event – local cafés provide live music to coincide.

Paleohóra

Open access • Free

About 3km east of Potamós lies **Paleohóra**, the ruined **medieval capital** of Kýthira (then called Áyios Dhimítrios). Few people seem to know about or visit these remains, though they constitute one of the best Byzantine sites around and boast a spectacular setting, surrounded by a sheer 100m drop on three sides. The 4.5km mostly rough dirt road to Paleohóra is signposted off the main road south from Potamós just north of Aroniádhika.

8

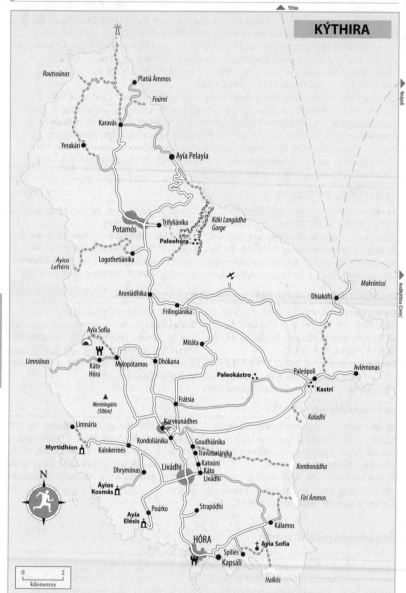

KÝTHIRA

The town was built in the thirteenth century, and when Mystra fell to the Turks, many of its noble families sought refuge here. Despite its seemingly concealed and impregnable position, the site was discovered and sacked in 1537 by Barbarossa, commander of the Turkish fleet, and the island's seven thousand inhabitants were killed or sold into slavery. The principal remains are of the surviving **churches**, some still with traces of **frescoes** (but kept firmly locked, so peer in through the windows), and the **castle**.

Ayía Pelayía

About 4km northeast of Potamós is the resort of **AYÍA PELAYÍA**, with a good choice of **rooms** and **tavernas**; the main beaches are cleaner since the ferries stopped coming here, but the beach at **Kalamítsa**, a 2km dirt track away to the south, is better – the track continues on to the mouth of the Káki Langádha gorge which offers excellent hiking (see p.511).

ACCOMMODATION AND EATING	**POTAMÓS AND THE NORTH**

POTAMÓS

Panaretos ☎ 27360 34290. Traditional taverna, dominating the central platía, with indoor seating in the main restaurant down below. Excellent home-made bread and juicy olives. Daily breakfast, lunch & dinner.

AYÍA PELAYÍA

★ **Kaleris** ☎ 27360 33461. The chef here specializes in inventive, original takes on a whole range of traditional dishes, such as "feta french fries". Expect about €20/person. Daily lunch and dinner.

Moustakias ☎ 27360 33519. A classic seafood taverna, with portside seating and very friendly service. Catch-of-the-day is always a good choice, along with whatever is in season – green beans, artichokes or courgettes. Live music Sat eve. Daily lunch and dinner.

★ **Venardos** ☎ 27360 34100, ⓦ venardos-hotels.gr. Extensive hotel complex boasting hilltop views and located just a short walk from the beach. Facilities include a large pool, gym, sauna and spa. Rooms range from standard doubles to suites and studios. Discounts for Rough Guide readers. Breakfast included. **€80**

Mylopótamos and around

Some 6km south of Potamós it is worth making a detour 4km west off the main road for **MYLOPÓTAMOS**, a lovely traditional village and a shady oasis in summer, set in a wooded valley with a small stream. Follow the signs for "Katarráktis Neraïdha" to find a **waterfall**, hidden from view by lush vegetation, next to a long-closed café.

The Ayía Sofía cave

Mid-June to mid-Sept Mon–Fri 3–8pm, Sat & Sun 11am–5pm • €3 • Guided tour (30min) in Greek and English

Most visitors come to Mylopótamos to see the **cave of Ayía Sofía**, the largest and most impressive of a number of caverns on the island, a half-hour signposted walk from the village, or a short drive along a paved road off the Limniónas road. When the cave is closed, you can probably find a guide in Mylopótamos. The cave's entrance has been used as a church and has an iconostasis carved from the rock, with important Byzantine frescoes on it. Beyond, the cave system comprises a series of chambers, which reach 250m into the mountain, although the tour only takes in the more interesting outer chambers.

EATING	**MYLOPÓTAMOS**

Platanos ☎ 27360 33397. This shady café-taverna makes a pleasant stop for a freshly squeezed orange juice or a full meal, above the village's springs. About €12/ person. Inside, there's an appealing music bar. May–Oct daily noon–midnight and beyond.

Kapsáli and the south

KAPSÁLI on the south coast is largely devoted to summer tourism, and is where most savvy foreign visitors to Kýthira stay – particularly yachties, as it's sheltered from the strong north winds. Set behind double coved beaches, overlooked by Hóra castle, and backed by high grey cliffs on which the tiny white monastery of Áyios Ioánnis Éngremmos perches, it is certainly memorable.

Hóra

HÓRA (or Kýthira Town), the island's picturesque capital, is a steep 2km haul above Kapsáli, and is quite somnolent in comparison. It does enjoy an equally dramatic position, however, its Cycladic-style houses tiered on the ridge leading to its very own

Venetian **castle**. Below the castle are both the remains of older Byzantine walls and, in Mésa Vouryó, numerous well-signed but securely locked Byzantine churches. The Stavros **bookshop**, on the town's main street, sells a book of **walks** (mainly around the southern half of the island).

Hóra castle

Daily 8am–7pm • Free

Hóra's **castle** is a must mostly for the breathtaking 360-degree **panorama** it affords over the entire area – on a clear enough day you can even see Crete. Access to the fortress is up a modern pathway, but, to the right of this, the original narrow tunnel entrance is still usable. Within the castle walls, most of the buildings are in ruins, except for the paired churches of Panayía Myrtidhiótissa and the smaller Panayía Orfáni (Catholic and Orthodox respectively, under the Venetian occupation). There are spectacular **views** down to Kapsáli and out to sea to the chunk of inaccessible islet known as **Avgó** (Egg), legendary **birthplace of Aphrodite**. On its cliffs grow the yellow-flowered everlasting (*sempreviva*), used locally for making small dried flower arrangements, which you see for sale in every shop, symbol of the goddess's eternal beauty.

ACCOMMODATION AND EATING   **KAPSÁLI AND THE SOUTH**

In high season, it goes without saying that you must book ahead if you want accommodation in Kapsáli. Finding a hotel in Hóra is easier, since it's well away from the beach. Both towns have plenty of good places to eat.

KAPSÁLI

★ **Afrodite Apartments** ☎ 27360 31328, ⓦ hotel -afrodite.gr. This white complex stands above the town, with good views, a pleasant rear garden, and (slow) internet facilities for guests. A few really choice apartments are on the seaward side of the road, just above the beach. **€70**

Chýtra Named after the island offshore, the Kettle (aka the Egg), where Aphrodite is said to have been born, this appealing harbourside taverna offers all the best of Greek traditional cookery – extraordinary stewed broad green beans in season – with beachfront seating. May–Sept daily lunch and dinner.

Hydragogio ☎ 27360 31065. Located at the Hóra end of the beach, facing the water, this choice serves up good veggie options, such as *briam*, as well as fish (€20–70/kg). Main dishes average about €8. May–Sept daily lunch and dinner.

Vasili Spitia ☎ 27360 31125, ⓦ kythirabungalows vasili.gr. Located a short way up the hill amid an old olive grove, this place offers comfortable rooms and studios, all with a/c, balconies and sea views. Breakfast included. April–Oct. **€80**

HÓRA

Belvedere Overlooking both the castle and the twin bays of Kapsáli, the main draw here is the impressive terrace seating. Traditional Greek dishes plus pizzas. Daily lunch and dinner.

Castello Apartments ☎ 27360 31869, ⓦ castello apts-kythera.gr. On the Kapsáli side of town, with great views all around, this cheerful structure is off the street, in a garden setting. The nine self-catering rooms, studios and apartment are simple, and some have balconies and views. **€45**

★ **Margarita** ☎ 27360 31711, ⓦ hotel-margarita .com. This beautiful, immaculately maintained 1840s house is down just below the main street. There are wonderful views of the coast and the castle, and very friendly and helpful staff. Buffet breakfast €10/person. **€80**

Zorba's 34 on the lane that leads down from the platía ☎ 27360 31655. By far the best taverna in town, as both locals and travellers concur. Only €10–15 for a full meal, with grilled meats a speciality, served on a beautiful terrace. Tues–Sun lunch and dinner; Mon dinner only.

Avlémonas

The prettiest destination on the east coast is **Avlémonas**, on a rocky bay at the top of this coast. It's a small fishing port with an end-of-the-world feel as you approach from a distance. It becomes much more attractive once reached, and has a remarkable coordination of colour schemes throughout the village. There is a small Venetian fortress and little coves with some of the clearest water around, fine for swimming.

ACCOMMODATION AND EATING — AVLÉMONAS

Maryianni ☎ 27360 33316, ⓦ maryianni.kythera.gr. This bright, pleasantly landscaped complex is the closest one to the sea. Most rooms are fully self-catering and offer great views from private terraces. **€70**

Sotiris This taverna, with seating overlooking the sparkling little cove, offers a wide selection of fresh, well-prepared and reasonably priced fish dishes (around €10). Daily lunch and dinner.

Andikýthira

Thirteen kilometres to the south of Kýthira, the tiny, wind-blown 22-square-kilometre island of **ANDIKÝTHIRA** (ⓦ antikythira.gr) is linked to its bigger sister by a sporadic ferry service. Rocky and poor, and a site of political exile until 1964, the island only received electricity in 1984, but it has one remarkable claim to fame: the **Andikythera Mechanism** now in the National Archeological Museum in Athens (p.61). Local attractions include good birdlife (a bird observatory has been built in the old school at Lazianá) and flora, but it's not the place if you want company: with only 45 residents divided among a scattering of settlements – mainly in **Potamós**, the harbour, and **Sohória**, the village. Ferries-permitting, the **festival of Áyios Mýron** is held here on August 17– an annual reunion jamboree for the Andikytheran diaspora.

Recent excavation work above Xeropótamos has revealed the site of ancient **Aigila**, a 75-acre fortress city of the Hellenistic period. At the harbour below are the remains of one of ancient Greece's best-preserved warship slipways, a *neosoikos*, carved out of the rock. Archeologist Aris Tsaravopoulos (☎ 697 30 50 204) can sometimes arrange volunteer excavation work at the sites.

ARRIVAL AND DEPARTURE — ANDIKÝTHIRA

By ferry Andikýthira has, theoretically, a twice-weekly summer connection with Kýthira (2hr) on the Pireás–Kýthira–Kastélli (Crete) run, but landings are often impossible due to adverse weather.

ACCOMMODATION AND EATING

Antikythera Rooms Potamós ☎ 27360 33004, ⓦ antikythera.gr. The only official accommodation on the island, this set of rooms is run by the local community. There are a couple of tavernas and a village shop at Sohória but you'd be wise to bring plenty of supplies with you. **€40**

8

MINOAN VASES, IRÁKLION MUSEUM

Contexts

517 History

542 Archeology

546 Wildlife

550 Music

555 Books

561 Greek

History

The history of the Greek Islands is, broadly, the history of Greece, and it is that which follows. However, in the context of well over five thousand years of civilization on the islands, and of constant trade between them and the wider world, it is not surprising that individual islands have their own unique histories. What is consistent is that their position at the crossroads of Europe, Asia and Africa has made them a prize much fought over. The islanders have also played a full part in Greece's unparalleled impact on Western society in the fields of politics, philosophy, literature, science and art.

Prehistoric Greece: to 2100 BC

Evidence of human habitation in Greece goes back half a million years, as demonstrated by the skeleton of a **Neanderthal** youth in the **Petralóna Cave**, 50km east of the northern city of Thessaloníki, along with the earliest known site of a man-made fire in Europe.

Only very much later, about 40,000 years ago, did **Homo sapiens** make his first appearance in Greece after migrating out of Africa. At several sites in **Epirus** in northwest Greece (including some on what are now the Ionian islands, then attached to the mainland), *Homo sapiens* used tools and weapons of bone, wood and stone to gather wild plants and hunt. Even between 20,000 and 16,000 years ago, when the Ice Age was at its peak, **Stone Age man** continued to make a home in Greece, though only in around 10,000 BC did a considerably warmer climate set in and the glaciers retreat, raising sea levels and finally separating many of the islands from the mainland.

The Neolithic period

Agricultural communities first appeared in northern Greece around **6500 BC**. Whether agriculture developed indigenously or was introduced by migrants from Asia Minor is much debated: what is certain, however, is its revolutionary effect.

An assured supply of food enabled the Stone Age inhabitants of Greece to settle in fixed spots, building mud-brick houses on stone foundations. Though still reliant on stone implements, this new farming culture marked a significant break with the past, so a "new stone age" or **Neolithic period** is said to have begun. As the flint needed for weapons and tools was rare in Greece, mainlanders imported obsidian from the island of **Melos** (Mílos) in the southern Cyclades. The earliest **seaborne trade** known anywhere in the world, this clearly involved a mastery of building and handling boats, skills that were to define the Greek islanders throughout their history.

Cycladic culture and the beginnings of the Greek Bronze Age

Around **3000 BC** a new people settled in the **Cyclades**, probably from Asia Minor,

c.40,000 BC	c.6500 BC	c.3000 BC	c.2100 BC
Stone Age Homo sapiens arrives in Greece.	Permanent communities and the world's earliest sea-borne trade herald the Neolithic era.	In the Cycladic islands, a new people introduce striking new art forms. The dawn of the Bronze Age.	The Greek language is heard in Greece for the first time.

bringing with them the latest metallurgical techniques. While continuing the old trade in obsidian, they also developed a **trade in tin** and were making prodigious voyages westwards as far as Spain by 2500 BC. The mining of **gold and silver** in the Cyclades may have dated from this period, too. Long before Crete or the Greek mainland, these new islanders became specialists in **jewellery-making**, **metalwork** and **stone-cutting**. From the abundant marble of the Cyclades, they sculpted statuettes, mostly of female figures. Slender, spare and geometric, these **Cycladic sculptures** are startlingly modern in appearance, and were exported widely, to Crete and mainland Greece.

In about 3000 BC, the introduction of bronze technology to the mainland, also from the Cyclades, marked the start of the **Bronze Age** in Greece. By **2500 BC** the widespread use of bronze had transformed farming and fighting throughout the Eastern Mediterranean and the Middle East. Because **tin** (which when alloyed with copper creates bronze) came from so far afield – in the east from the Caucasus, Persia and Afghanistan, in the west from Cornwall, Brittany, northwest Spain and northern Italy – the Aegean became an important trade route. Hence the burst of development that now took place along the eastern coast of **central Greece** and the **Peloponnese**, and on the **Aegean islands** which linked the Greek mainland to Asia Minor and the Middle East.

It is uncertain what **language** was spoken at this time, but one thing is clear: it was not yet Greek. Indeed, when **Greek-speaking people** did arrive on the mainland in about 2100 BC, their destructive impact paralyzed its development for five hundred years, while the large and secure island of **Crete** – which they did not invade or settle – flourished and dominated the Aegean.

The coming of the Greeks

The destruction of numerous mainland sites in about **2100 BC**, followed by the appearance of a new style of pottery, has suggested to archeologists the violent arrival of a **new people**. They domesticated the horse, introduced the potter's wheel and possessed considerable metallurgical skills. These newcomers replaced the old religion centred on female fertility figures with **hilltop shrines**, thought to have been dedicated to the worship of male sky gods like Zeus. And with them came a new language, an early form of **Greek**, though they were obliged to adopt existing native words for such things as olives, figs, vines, wheat and the sea, suggesting that these new migrants or invaders may have come from distant inland steppes where they had been pastoral highlanders, not farmers, fishermen or sailors.

Minoan and Mycenaean civilizations: 2100–1100 BC

The history of the Aegean during the second millennium BC can be seen as a struggle between the **Mycenaean culture** of the Greek mainland and the **Minoan culture** of Crete. Situated halfway between mainland Greece and Egypt, Crete exploited the Bronze Age boom in trade, to become the dominant power in the Aegean by the start of the second millennium BC. Its influence was felt throughout the islands and also on the mainland, where the Greek-speaking invaders were "Minoanized", gradually developing a culture known as Mycenaean (after Mycenae, a principal mainland Bronze Age site) that owed a lot to Crete.

c.2000 BC	c.1700 BC	c.1650 BC	c.1500 BC
On Crete, the great Minoan palaces are built.	Knossos and the other palaces are destroyed by earthquake, but rebuilt even more grandly.	Thíra (Santorini) devastated by a massive volcanic explosion, whose effects spread across the region.	Mainland Mycenaeans gain control of Crete.

THE TROJAN WAR

For the Greeks, the story of the **Trojan War** was the central event in their early history, and in their minds Homer's **Iliad** was not just a poem of heroic deeds sung at noble courts, but the epic of their first great national adventure.

Excavations in the late nineteenth century by Heinrich Schliemann (see p.543) uncovered many Troys of several periods, but the layer known as **Troy VIIa** clearly suffered violent destruction in about 1220 BC. The Mycenaeans are the likeliest perpetrators, though the abduction of a Greek beauty called **Helen** would not have been the only reason they launched a thousand ships against the Trojans. Mycenaean prosperity greatly depended on trade with the Eastern Mediterranean, where increasingly unsettled conditions made it imperative that the Mycenaeans secure their lines of **trade and supply**. Troy commanded a strategic position overlooking the Hellespont, the narrow waterway (today called the Dardanelles) dividing Europe and Asia and linking the Aegean to the Black Sea, where it controlled important trade routes. Trade was especially important to island peoples, which is why so many were involved in the expedition: Ithaca, Rhodes, Kos, Symí, Évvia, Kálymnos and Crete all sent ships to Troy.

The capture of Troy was the last great success of the Mycenaeans, and perhaps for that reason it was long remembered in poetry and song. It inspired later generations of Greeks to dream of overseas expansion, culminating in the fourth century BC when Alexander the Great carried a copy of the Iliad as he marched across Asia.

Minoan Crete

Living on a large and fertile island with good natural harbours, the people of **Crete** raised sufficient crops and livestock to export surplus quantities of oil and wool. Among their most impressive tools, literally at the cutting edge of new technology, was a metre-long bronze saw that readily converted the forest-clad mountains into an ample source of **timber for ships**. Some timber was probably also exported, most likely to treeless Egypt, while metalwork, jewellery and pottery of superb Cretan craftsmanship were shipped to the mainland and beyond. **Kamares ware**, as Cretan pottery of this period is known, was especially valued; it has been found all along the Cretans' 875km-long maritime trade route to the East – on the Aegean islands of Rhodes and Sámos, on the coast of Asia Minor at Miletus, and in Syria and Egypt.

On Crete itself, Minoan power was concentrated on three vast **palace complexes** – at **Knossos**, **Phaestos** and **Malia**, all in the centre of the island. First built around 2000 BC, their similarity of plan and lack of defences suggest that some form of confederacy had replaced any regional rivalries on the island, while Minoan sea power induced a sense of security against foreign invasion. Crete's maritime supremacy was consolidated by a network of **colonies**, or close allies throughout the islands – most famously **Thíra** (Santoríni), but also Kýthira, Mílos, Náxos, Páros, Mikonós, Delos, Rhodes and others. On Crete, prosperity was not confined to the palace centres; the numerous remains of villas of the Minoan gentry, and of well-constructed villages, show that the wealth generated by the palaces was redistributed among the island's population. Following an **earthquake** around 1700 BC, the palaces at Knossos and Phaestos were rebuilt, and a more modest palace constructed at **Zakros** on the east coast. This activity coincided with an apparent centralization of power at Knossos, giving rise to a **Minoan golden age**.

c.1220 BC	c.1150 BC	c.1100 BC	900–700 BC
Trojan War, whose events are immortalized by Homer and enter the realm of myth.	The so-called Sea Peoples sweep across Greece, ushering in a new Dark Age.	The first iron tools and weapons begin to transform agriculture and warfare.	Geometric Period.

Mycenaean dominance

Suddenly, however, around **1500 BC**, the Mycenaeans gained control of the palace of Knossos and were soon in full possession of Crete. How this happened is unknown, but it probably marked the culmination of a growing rivalry between the Mycenaeans and the Minoans for control of the Aegean trade, which perhaps coincided with a **volcanic explosion** on the island of Thíra (Santoríni) and its consequent **tsunami**.

Greek now became the language of administration at Knossos and the other former Minoan palaces, as well as on the mainland – indeed this is the earliest moment that Greek language can definitely be identified, as the palace records on Crete are from now on written in a script known as **Linear B**, which when deciphered in 1953 was shown to be a form of Greek. Having wrested control of the Aegean trade from the Minoans, the **Mycenaeans** were dominant for another three hundred years. At the end of that period in about 1220 BC, they famously laid siege to, and destroyed, yet another rival, the city of **Troy**.

Yet within a generation the Mycenaean world was overwhelmed by a vast **migration** of northerners from somewhere beyond the Black Sea. Probably victims of a catastrophic change in climate that brought drought and famine to their homelands, these **Sea Peoples**, as the ancients called them, swept down through Asia Minor and the Middle East and also crossed the Mediterranean to Libya and Egypt, disrupting trade routes and destroying empires as they went. With the palace-based Bronze Age economies destroyed, the humbler **village-based economies** that replaced them lacked the wealth and the technological means to make a mark in the world. Greece was plunged into a Dark Age, and knowledge of the Minoan and Mycenaean civilizations slipped into dim memory.

The Dark Age and the rise of the city-state: 1150–491 BC

The poverty and isolation that characterized Greece for the next five hundred years did have one lasting effect, **emigration**. Greeks spread to the Dodecanese islands, to Cilicia along the south coast of **Asia Minor**, and to **Cyprus**, which became Greek-speaking. Later, around 1000 BC, they also settled in large numbers along the western coast of Asia Minor. Even in the Dark Age there were a few glimmers of light: **Athens**, for example, escaped the destruction that accompanied the fall of Mycenaean civilization and maintained trading links abroad. It became the route through which the **Iron Age** was introduced to mainland Greece with the importation of iron weapons, implements and technological know-how around 1100 BC.

A new cultural beginning was also made in the form of pottery painted in the **Geometric style**, a highly intricate and controlled design that would lie at the heart of later Greek architecture, sculpture and painting. But it was the **Phoenicians**, sailing from Sidon and Tyre in present-day Lebanon, who really re-established trading links between the Middle East and the Aegean world in the eighth century BC, and Greeks followed swiftly in their wake.

With wealth flowing in again, Greek civilization developed with remarkable rapidity; no other people achieved so much over the next few centuries. The institution most responsible for this extraordinary achievement, the **city-state** or **polis**, came into being at a time of rapidly growing populations, greater competition for land and resources, increasing productivity and wealth, expanding trade and more complex relationships

800–700 BC	776 BC	750–650 BC	c.725 BC
Revival of trade between Greece and the Middle East kick-starts an economic revival.	The first Olympic Games staged at Olympia.	Greeks colonize the Eastern Mediterranean, from Italy to Asia Minor.	The Iliad and Odyssey, hitherto retold as oral sagas, are set down in writing.

THE ILIAD AND THE ODYSSEY

The **Iliad** and the **Odyssey**, the oldest and greatest works in Greek literature, were the brilliant summation of five centuries of poetic tradition, first developed by nameless bards whose recitations were accompanied by music. Completed by 725 BC, they are far older than the *Pentateuch*, the first five books of the Old Testament, which achieved their finished form only around 400 BC. The whole Greek world knew the Homeric epics, and their influence upon the subsequent development of Greek literature, art and culture in general cannot be overstated. Few works, and probably none not used in worship, have had such a hold on a nation for so long.

The Iliad is the story of a few days' action in the tenth and final year of the Trojan War, which in its tales of heroic exploits recalls the golden age of the Mycenaeans. The Odyssey begins after the war and follows the adventures of Odysseus, who takes ten years to return to his island home of Ithaca (usually taken to be Itháki, in the Ionian islands) on the western side of Greece. The story of his voyages demonstrates the new Greek interest in the area around the Black Sea and in Italy and Sicily to the west. They are also a celebration of an emerging hellenic identity, of a national adventure encompassing both shores of the Aegean and beyond.

with neighbouring states. The birthplace of **democracy** and of equality before the law, the city-state became the Greek ideal, and by the early seventh century BC it had spread throughout Greece and wherever Greeks established colonies overseas, with important centres growing up throughout the islands.

Trade also acted as a cultural stimulus; contact with other peoples made the Greeks aware of what they shared among themselves, and led to the development of a **national sentiment**, notably expressed and fostered by the **panhellenic sanctuaries** that arose during the eighth century BC, of **Hera** and **Zeus** at **Olympia**, and of **Apollo** and **Artemis** on **Delos**, as well as the **oracles** of **Zeus** at **Dodona** and of **Apollo** at **Delphi**.

Expansion and colonization

Around 750 BC, Greeks began to found **colonies** in the Western Mediterranean – in **Sicily** and **southern Italy** especially – while a century later, around 650 BC, further colonies were established round the shores of the **Black Sea**. By the fifth century BC Greeks seemed to sit upon the shores of the entire world, in Plato's words like "frogs around a pond". The islands were vital staging points en route to the new colonies, and thrived on the trade they brought.

One impetus for expansion was competition between the Greeks and the Phoenicians over trade routes; but there was also rivalry between the Greek city-states themselves. **Chalkis**, **Eretria** and **Corinth** were the major colonizers in the West, while the **Ionian Greeks** were the chief colonizers around the Black Sea. When the Spartans needed more land, they conquered neighbouring Messenia in 710 BC, but generally land shortage drove Greeks overseas. Thus colonists were sent from Thera (Thíra) to found Cyrene in North Africa, and were forbidden to return on pain of death. Whatever the reason for their foundation, however, most colonies kept up close relations with their mother cities.

Democracy, tyranny and slavery

Meanwhile, at home in the city-states, political tensions were building between the

700–480 BC	621 BC	c.620–570 BC	498 BC
Archaic period.	Draco's reforming "draconian" law code is published in Athens.	The literary zenith of Lésvos, where Sappho, one of the greatest poets of the ancient world, and Aesop both live.	Rebellious Ionian Greeks burn the city of Sardis, provoking a Persian invasion of Greece.

aristocratic rulers and the **people**. A large class of farmers, merchants and the like was excluded from political life but forced to pay heavy taxes. The pressure led to numerous reforms and a gradual move towards **democracy**. Ironically, the transition was often hastened by **tyrants**. Despite the name – which simply means they seized power by force – many tyrants were in fact champions of the people, creating work, redistributing wealth and patronizing the arts. **Peisistratos**, tyrant of Athens during the sixth century BC, is perhaps the archetype. Successful and well-liked by his people, his populist rule ensured Athenian prosperity by gaining control of the route into the Black Sea. He also ordered that Homer's works be set down in their definitive form and performed regularly, and encouraged the theatrical festivals where Greek drama would be born.

City-states also flourished on islands throughout the Aegean, and they too had their tyrants and their artists. On **Lésvos**, for example, the poet **Sappho**, part of a long tradition of poetry on the island, was writing around the turn of the sixth century BC; some claim that her contemporary Aesop (of Fables fame) was also from Lésvos. Not long after their time, the island, along with other nearby territories, was captured by **Polycrates**, tyrant of **Sámos**, who built up his island's navy to establish himself as a regional power, at various times in alliance with the Egyptian pharaoh, the king of Persia and with Lygdamis, tyrant of **Náxos**. **Lygdamis**, in turn, was a close ally of Peisistratos.

Athens and the Golden Age: 490–431 BC

Democracy was a very long way from universal. The population of **Athens** and surrounding Attica amounted to some 400,000 people, of whom about 80,000 were slaves, 160,000 foreigners, and another 160,000 free-born Athenians. Out of this last category came the **citizens**, those who could vote and be elected to office, and their number amounted to no more than 45,000 adult men.

Yet if the powers of democracy were in the hands of the few, the energy, boldness and creative spirit that it released raised Athens to greatness. Throughout the **fifth century BC** the political, intellectual and artistic activity of the Greek world was centred on the city. In particular Athens was the patron of **drama**, both tragedy and comedy. Athenian tragedy always addressed the great issues of life and death and the relationship of man to the gods. And the Athenians themselves seemed to be conscious of living out a high drama as they fought battles, argued policy, raised temples and wrote plays that have decided the course and sensibility of Western civilization.

The Persian Wars

The wars between Greece and Persia began with a revolt against Persian rule by Ionian Greeks in Asia Minor. Athens and Eretria (on Évvia) gave them support, burning the city of Sardis in 498 BC. Provoked by their insolence, **Darius**, the Persian king, launched a punitive expedition. The **Persians'** unexpected repulse at **Marathon** in 490 BC persuaded Darius to hurl his full military might against Greece, to ensure its subjection once and for all to the Persian Empire.

After Darius died in 486 BC, his son **Xerxes** took over. In 483 BC, he began preparations that lasted two years and were on a fabulous scale. Bridges of boats were built across the Hellespont for Persia's vast imperial army to parade into Europe, and a canal was cut through the peninsular finger now occupied by the Mount Áthos monasteries, so that

490 BC	480 BC	480 BC
After the Battle of Marathon, a runner is despatched to Athens to relay the good news; having run the first marathon, Pheidippides drops dead.	Greek defeat at the Battle of Thermopylae, scene of heroic Spartan defiance.	Persians sack and burn Athens.

the Persian fleet could avoid storms while rounding the headlands of the Halkidhikí. Though the Greek historian **Herodotus** claimed that Xerxes' army held one million eight hundred thousand soldiers, his figure is probably a tenfold exaggeration. Even so, it was a massive force, an army of 46 nations, combined with a fleet of eight hundred triremes carrying almost as many sailors as there were soldiers in the army.

Despite their numerical superiority, the might of Asia was routed at sea off **Salamis** in 480 BC (see p.81). A significant part of the Greek fleet came from the islands: above all from Égina, then a major rival of Athens, but with ships from Náxos, Lefkádha, Styra on Évvia, Kýthnos, Kéa, Mílos, Sífnos and Sérifos (there were also ships from Rhodes and others in the Persian fleet). The following year the Persians were also defeated on land, at **Plataea**. Within a few days of that second battle came another naval victory at **Mycale**, off Sámos, where the battle was won when Xerxes' subject Ionians went over to their fellow Hellenes. Xerxes could do no more than return to Susa, his capital deep in Persia, leaving the entire Aegean free.

Despite occasional reversals, this sudden shift in the balance of power between East and West endured for the next 1500 years. Within 150 years, Alexander the Great achieved in Asia what Xerxes had failed to achieve in Europe, and the Persian Empire succumbed to a Greek conqueror.

The rise of the Athenian Empire: 478–431 BC

The first consequence of the Greek victory against the Persians was not, as might have been expected, the rise of **Sparta**, the pre-eminent Greek military power, whose soldiers had obediently sacrificed themselves at Thermopylae and won the final mainland battle at Plataea. Instead, many Greek city-states voluntarily placed themselves under the leadership of Athens.

This Aegean confederation was named the **Delian League**, after the island of **Delos** where the allies kept their treasury; it included cities on virtually every island in the Aegean, plus many on the eastern coast Greece and western coast of Asia Minor. Its first task was to protect the Greeks of Asia Minor against a vengeful Xerxes. This was the opposite of the policy proposed by Sparta and its Peloponnesian allies, which called for the abandonment of Greek homes across the Aegean and the resettlement of Asian Greeks in northern Greece.

That typified the Spartan attitude throughout the Persian crisis, in which Sparta had shown no initiative and acted only at the last minute. Its policy was provincial, protecting its position in the Peloponnese rather than pursuing the wider interests of Greece. Thus over the coming decades Sparta lost prestige to Athens, which Themistocles had established as a maritime power and whose imperial potential was realized under Pericles.

This was the **Athenian golden age**, and indeed a golden age for all Greece. The fifty years following Salamis and Plataea witnessed an extraordinary flowering in architecture, sculpture, literature and philosophy whose influence is felt to this day. Greeks of the time recognized the historical importance of their experience and gave it realization through the creative impulse. Just as **Herodotus**, the "father of history", made the contest between Europe and Asia the theme of his great work, so **Aeschylus**, who fought at Marathon, made Xerxes the tragic subject of *The Persians* and thereby brought the art of drama to life. Indeed in the intoxicating Athenian atmosphere the warriors who

480 BC	480–323 BC	479 BC	447–438 BC
Naval victory at Salamis, involving fleets from many islands, marks the beginning of the end of the invasion.	Classical Period.	Persians defeated at the Battle of Plataea and are forced out of Greece.	Parthenon constructed, the symbol of Athens' Golden Age.

turned back the Persian tide seemed to have fought in the same cause as Homer's heroes at Troy. In thanksgiving and celebration the temples upon the Acropolis that the Persians had destroyed were rebuilt – most notably with the building of the **Parthenon**.

Yet Athens was still just one among numerous city-states, each ready to come together during a common danger but reasserting its sovereignty as the foreign threat receded. This was illustrated by the ten-year struggle from 461 BC onwards between Athens (and her island allies in the Delian League) and various **Peloponnesian states**, itself a warning of a yet greater war to come between Athens and Sparta. Perhaps 451 BC marks the fatal moment when Athens passed up the opportunity to create an institution more generous, and more inclusive, than the city-state. Instead Pericles (c.495–429 BC), Athens' greatest leader, supported the parochial and populist demand that **Athenian citizenship** should not be extended to its allies, thereby stoking up the flames of envy and foregoing the chance of creating a genuine and enduring Greek confederacy.

The decline of the city-state: 431–338 BC

The **Peloponnesian War** that began in **431 BC** was really a continuation of earlier conflicts between Athens and its principal commercial rivals, Corinth and Aegina (though technically a member of the Delian League, ancient Aegina – Égina – was also a jealous rival of Athens) and their various allies in the Peloponnese. Sparta had earlier stood aside, but by 432 BC when Corinth again agitated for war, the **Spartans** had become fearful of growing Athenian power.

The Athenian empire was built on trade, and the city was a great sea power, with 300 triremes. The members of Sparta's **Peloponnesian League**, meanwhile, had powerful armies but no significant navy (though from time to time various islands, particularly in the Dodecanese, would ally themselves with Sparta). Just as Themistocles had sought to fight the Persians by sea, so Pericles followed the same strategy against Sparta and its allies, avoiding major battles against superior land forces. Athens and Piraeus were protected by their walls, but the Peloponnesians and their allies were allowed to invade Attica with impunity nearly every year, and Thrace saw constant warfare. On the other hand the Peloponnesians lacked the sea power to carry the fighting into Asia Minor and the Aegean islands or to interfere with Athens' trade, while the Athenians used their maritime superiority to launch attacks against the coasts of the Peloponnese, the Ionian islands and the mouth of the Gulf of Corinth, hoping to detach members from the Peloponnesian League. So long as Athens remained in command of the sea, it had every reason to expect that it could wear down its enemies' resolve.

Pericles' death in 429 BC was an early blow to the Athenian cause. Although **Kleon**, his successor, is widely blamed for Athens' eventual defeat, after Pericles the city was in fact always divided into a peace party and a military one, unable to pursue a consistent policy. The final straw came in 415 BC, when a bold operation designed to win Sicily to the Athenian cause turned into a catastrophic debacle. Though not entirely defeated, Athens was never to be a major power again.

City-state rivalries

The Peloponnesian War left **Sparta** the supreme power in Greece, but those whom the Spartans had "liberated" swiftly realized that they had simply acquired a new and

431–415 BC	408 BC	399 BC	380 BC
Peloponnesian War marks the end of Athens' ascendancy.	Rhodes town founded.	Socrates tried and condemned to death for corrupting the minds of the youth of Athens.	Plato establishes his Academy in Athens.

THUCYDIDES: THE FIRST MODERN HISTORIAN

The writing of history began among the Greeks, first with **Herodotus**, then with Thucydides. Whereas Herodotus gives the feeling that he prefers telling a good story, that he still inhabits Homer's world of epic poetry, with **Thucydides** the paramount concern is to analyze events. In that sense Thucydides is the first modern historian; wherever possible he seeks out primary sources, and his concern is always with objectivity, detail and chronology. Not that there is anything dry about his writing; its vividness and insight make reading him as powerful an experience as watching a Greek drama.

Thucydides began writing his history at the outset of the **Peloponnesian War**, intending to give an account of its whole duration. For reasons unknown, however, he abruptly stopped writing in the twentieth year, though he is thought to have survived the war by a few years, living until about 400 BC. Born into a wealthy, conservative Athenian family around 455 BC, he was a democrat and an admirer of Pericles; his reconstruction of Pericles' speeches presents the most eloquent expression of the Athenian cause. But when Thucydides was exiled from his city seven years into the war, this was the making of him as a historian. As he put it, "Associating with both sides, with the Peloponnesians quite as much as with the Athenians, because of my exile, I was thus enabled to watch quietly the course of events".

Thucydides was himself a military man, who understood war at first hand. Hence his concern for method in his research and analysis in his writing, for he intended his book to be useful to future generals and statesmen. For these reasons we have a better understanding of the Peloponnesian War than of any ancient conflict until Julius Caesar wrote his own first-hand accounts of his campaigns. And for these reasons too, Thucydides' history stands on a par with the greatest literature of ancient Greece.

inferior master, one that entirely lacked the style, the ability and the intelligence of Athens. Meanwhile Athens had lost its empire but not its trade, so its mercantile rivals faced no less competition than before. During the first decade of the fourth century, Athens managed to restore much of its naval power in the Aegean.

Adding to the intrigues between Persia, Athens and Sparta was a bewildering and unstable variety of alliances involving other Greek states. The most important of these was **Thebes**, which had been an ally of Sparta during the Peloponnesian War but came round to the Athenian side, and then for a spectacular moment under its brilliant general **Epaminondas** became the greatest power in Greece, in the process dealing Sparta a blow from which it never recovered. Theban supremacy did not survive the death of Epaminondas, however, and Greece subsequently found itself free for the first time in centuries from the dictates of Persia or any over-powerful Greek city-state. Exhausted and impoverished by almost continuous war, it was an opportunity for Greece to peacefully unite. But the political and moral significance of the city-state had by now eroded, and with the **rise of Macedonia** came the concept of an all-embracing kingship.

The Macedonian Empire

Despite its large size and population, **Macedonia** played little role in early Greek affairs. Many in Greece did not consider the Macedonians to be properly Greek; not in speech, culture or political system. They did not live in city-states, which Aristotle said was the mark of a civilized human being, but as a tribal people, led by a king, and were closer to

371 BC	359 BC	338 BC	336 BC
Sparta defeated by Thebes at the Battle of Leuctra.	Philip II becomes king of Macedonia.	Philip II's victory at Chaeronia unites Greece under Macedonian rule.	Alexander the Great succeeds his father, and within six years has conquered all of Persia.

BIG IDEAS: SOCRATES, PLATO AND ARISTOTLE

The Golden Age of Athens under Pericles, and the city-state rivalry after the Peloponnesian War, saw the **birth of Western philosophy** under the towering figures of Socrates, Plato and Aristotle.

SOCRATES (c.470–399 BC)

The son of an Athenian sculptor, Socrates was for a time a sculptor himself. Though he fought bravely for Athens as a hoplite in the Peloponnesian War, much earlier, in his twenties, he had turned to philosophy, which he practised in his own peculiar style. Promoting no philosophical position of his own, he asserted, ceaselessly, the supremacy of reason. Often this was done in the streets of Athens, buttonholing some self-regarding Athenian of the older generation, asking him questions, picking his answers to pieces, until he came up with a definition that held water or, more likely, the spluttering victim was reduced to confess his own ignorance before crowds of Socrates' mirthful young supporters.

By this "Socratic method" he asked for definitions of familiar concepts such as piety and justice; his technique was to expose the ignorance that hid behind people's use of such terms, while acknowledging his own similar ignorance. Indeed when the Delphic oracle proclaimed that no man was wiser than Socrates, he explained this by saying wisdom lies in knowing how little one really knows. Because he valued this question-and-answer process over settling on fixed conclusions, Socrates never wrote anything down. Yet his influence was pivotal; before his time philosophical inquiry concerned itself with speculations on how the natural world was formed and how it operates; afterwards it looked to the analysis of concepts and to ethics.

Socrates' method could be irritating, especially when he questioned conventional morality, and this, coupled with powerful friendships with unpopular oligarchs, led to a backlash. Having tried him for impiety and corrupting the young, and sentenced him to death, the city gave him the option of naming another penalty, probably expecting him to choose exile. Instead Socrates answered that if he was to get what he deserved, he should be maintained for life at public expense. At this the death penalty was confirmed, but even then it was not to be imposed for two months, with the tacit understanding that Socrates would escape. Instead Socrates argued that it was wrong for a citizen to disobey even an unjust law, and in the company of his friends he drank the cup of hemlock. "Such was the end," wrote Plato, "of our friend; of all the men of his time whom I have known, he was the wisest and justest and best."

PLATO (c.427–347 BC)

As a young man, Plato painted, composed music and wrote a tragedy, as well as being a student of Socrates. He intended a career in politics, where his connections would have ensured success, but Socrates' death made Plato decide that he could not serve a government that had committed such a crime, and instead his mission became to exalt the memory of his teacher. In Plato's writings, many of them dialogues, Socrates is frequently the leading participant, while at the Academy in Athens, which Plato founded, the Socratic question-and-answer method was the means of instruction.

the barbarians (such attitudes still rankle today, and inform some of the bitter debate over the name and status of FYROM, the Former Yugoslav Republic of Macedonia).

Towards the middle of the fourth century, however, the power of Macedonia grew under the leadership of **Philip II**. Philip was determined to Hellenize his country; borrowing from Greek ways and institutions, he founded the city of **Pella** as his capital and lured teachers, artists and intellectuals to his court, among them **Aristotle** and **Euripides** (the latter originally from the island of Salamis). An admirer of Athens, Philip

335 BC	323 BC	c.300 BC	226 BC
Aristotle founds the Lyceum in Athens.	Death of Alexander.	Euclid's Elements published, its 13 volumes creating the basis or much of modern maths and science.	The vast statue known as the Colossus of Rhodes, one of the wonders of the Ancient World, collapses in an earthquake.

Plato's philosophy is elusive; he never sets out a system of doctrines, nor does he tell us which of his ideas are most basic, nor rank them in hierarchical order, nor show how they interrelate. Nevertheless, certain themes recur. He believed that men possess immortal souls separate from their mortal bodies. Knowledge, he believed, was the recollection of what our souls already know; we do not gain knowledge from experience, rather by using our reasoning capacity to draw more closely to the realm of our souls. The true objects of knowledge are not the transient, material things of this world, which are only reflections of a higher essence that Plato called Forms or Ideas. Forms are objects of pure thinking, cut off from our experience; but also Forms motivate us to grasp them, so that the reasoning part of us is drawn to Forms as a kind of mystic communion.

Plato's notion of a mystic union with a higher essence would play an important role in later religious thought. But more immediately his teachings at the Academy concerned themselves with logic, mathematics, astronomy and above all political science, for its purpose was to train a new ruling class. Prominent families sent him their sons to learn the arts of government. Plato taught that the best form of government was a constitutional monarchy, at its head a wise and just philosopher-king. Though it was a utopian vision, Plato's political philosophy helped prepare the intellectual ground for the acceptance of an absolutist solution to the increasing uncertainties of fourth-century BC Greece.

ARISTOTLE (384–322 BC)

Aristotle grew up in Pella, the capital of an increasingly powerful Macedonia, where his father had been appointed doctor to King Amyntas II; it is therefore not unlikely that Amyntas' son, the future Philip II, and Aristotle were boyhood friends. Aged seventeen, Aristotle was sent to Plato's Academy at Athens to continue his education, and he remained there, first as a student, then as a teacher, a faithful follower of Plato's ideas. His independent philosophy matured later, during the years he spent, again at Pella, as tutor to Alexander the Great, and later still, after 335 BC, when he founded his own school, the Lyceum, in Athens.

Aristotle came to reject Plato's dualism. He did not believe that the soul was of a substance separate from the body, rather that it was an aspect of the body. Instead of Plato's inward-looking view, Aristotle sought to explain the physical world and human society from the viewpoint of an outside observer. Essentially a scientist and a realist, he was bent on discovering the true rather than establishing the good, and he believed sense perception was the only means of human knowledge. His vast output covered many fields of knowledge – logic, metaphysics, ethics, politics, rhetoric, art, poetry, physiology, anatomy, biology, zoology, physics, astronomy and psychology. Everything could be measured, analyzed and described, and he was the first to classify organisms into genera and species.

The exactitude of Aristotle's writings does not make them easy reading, and Plato has always enjoyed a wider appeal owing to his literary skill. All the same, Aristotle's influence on Western intellectual and scientific tradition has been enormous.

sought an alliance that would make them joint-masters of the Greek world. But the Athenians opposed him, and he took matters into his own hands.

In **338 BC** Philip defeated the Theban and Athenian forces at **Chaeronia**, and effectively brought the whole of Greece including virtually all the islands (though not Crete) under one rule for the first time. His success was built on one of the most formidable fighting units the world has ever seen, the **Macedonian phalanx**. Armed with the *sarissa*, an eighteen-foot pike tapering from butt to tip, its infantrymen were

c.287	215–213 BC	200–197 BC	146 BC
Mathematician, inventor and scientist Archimedes is born on the Greek colony of Sicily.	First Macedonian War extends Roman influence in Greece.	Second Macedonian War, culminating in the Roman victory at Cynoscephalae.	Greece divided into Roman provinces.

trained to move across a battlefield with all the discipline of a parade ground drill. Instead of relying on a headlong charge, its effectiveness lay in manipulating the enemy line – seeking to open a gap through which the cavalry could make its decisive strike.

Alexander's conquests

After Chaeronia, Philip summoned the Greek states to Corinth, and announced his plans for a panhellenic conquest of the Persian Empire. But Philip was murdered two years later and to his son **Alexander** fell his father's plans for an **Asian campaign**.

In the East too there was an assassination, and in 335 BC the Persian throne passed to **Darius III**, namesake of the first and doomed to be the last king of his line. Using essentially his father's tactics, Alexander led his army through a series of astonishing victories, usually against greater numbers, until he reached the heart of the Persian Empire. Alexander crossed the Hellespont in May of **334 BC**, with thirty thousand foot soldiers and five thousand horses. By autumn all the Aegean coast of **Asia Minor** was his; twelve months later he stood on the banks of the Orontes River in **Syria**; in the winter of 332 BC **Egypt** hailed him as pharaoh; and by the spring of 330 BC the great Persian cities of **Babylon**, **Susa**, **Persepolis** and **Pasargadae** had fallen to him in rapid succession until, at **Ecbatana**, he found Darius in the dust, murdered by his own supporters. Alexander wrapped the corpse in his Macedonian cloak, and assumed the lordship of Asia.

Hellenistic Greece

No sooner had **Alexander** died at Babylon in 323 BC, aged 33, than Athens led an alliance of Greeks in a **war of liberation** against Macedonian rule. But the Macedonians had built up a formidable navy which inflicted heavy losses on the Athenian fleet. Unable to lift the Macedonian blockade of Piraeus, Athens surrendered and a pro-Macedonian government was installed. The episode marked the end of the city as a sea power and left it permanently weakened.

Greece was now irrevocably part of a new dominion, one that entirely altered the scale and orientation of the Greek world. Alexander's strategic vision had been to see the Mediterranean and the East as two halves of a greater whole. Opened to Greek settlement and enterprise, and united by Greek learning, language and culture, if not always by a single power, this **Hellenistic Empire** enormously increased international trade and created unprecedented prosperity.

Asked on his deathbed to whom he bequeathed his empire, Alexander replied "To the strongest". Forty years of warfare between his leading generals gave rise to three dynasties: the **Antigonid** in Macedonia, which ruled over mainland Greece, the Ionian islands and most of those in the western Aegean; the **Seleucid** which ultimately centred on Syria and Asia Minor, including most of the Dodecanese and eastern Aegean islands; and the **Ptolemaic** in Egypt, ruled from Alexandria, founded by Alexander himself, which in wealth and population, not to mention literature and science, soon outshone anything in Greece. **Rhodes** in particular was caught up in the battles between the dynasties, enduring a long and ultimately unsuccessful siege in 305 BC – the Colossus of Rhodes was constructed to commemorate the event and the island became one of the leading powers of the succeeding age.

Meanwhile, in the Western Mediterranean, **Rome** was a rising power. **Philip V** of

86 BC	31 BC	49–52 AD	95 AD
Romans, led by Sulla, sack Athens.	Defeat of Antony and Cleopatra at the Battle of Actium brings all of Greece and the Middle East under Roman sway.	St Paul lives and preaches in Corinth and Athens, first introducing Christianity to Greece.	St John the Divine is exiled to Pátmos, where he compiles the Bible's Book of Revelation.

Macedonia had agreed a treaty of mutual assistance against Rome with Hannibal. After Hannibal's defeat, Rome's legions marched eastwards, and routed Philip's army at **Cynoscephalae** in Thessaly in 197 BC.

Roman Greece: 146 BC–330 AD

Rome was initially well disposed towards Greece, which they regarded as the originator of much of their culture, and granted autonomy to the existing city-states. However, after a number of uprisings, the country was divided into **Roman provinces** from 146 BC.

During the first century BC Rome was riven by civil wars, many of whose climactic battlefields were in Greece: in 49 BC **Julius Caesar** defeated his rival Pompey at **Pharsalus** in Thessaly; in 42 BC Caesar's assassins were beaten by **Mark Antony** and **Octavian** at **Philippi** in Macedonia; and in 31 BC **Antony** and his Ptolemaic ally **Cleopatra** were routed by **Octavian** in a sea battle off **Actium**, just north of Lefkádha in western Greece. The latter effectively marked the birth of the **Roman Empire** – an empire that in its eastern half continued to speak Greek.

By the first century AD Greece had become a **tourist destination** for well-to-do Romans; they went to Athens and Rhodes to study literature and philosophy, and toured the country to see the temples with their paintings and sculpture. They also visited the by now thoroughly professional **Olympic Games**. When the emperor **Nero** came to Greece in AD 67, he entered the Games as a contestant; the judges prudently declared him the victor in every competition, even the chariot race, in which he was thrown and failed to finish.

Greece had an early taste of **Christian teaching** when **Saint Paul** came to preach in 49–52 AD. Brought before the Court of the Areopagus in Athens, he was asked to defend his talk of the death and resurrection of his foreign god, and dismissed as a crank. Paul then spent eighteen months in **Corinth**; he made some converts, but as his subsequent Epistles to the Corinthians show, their idea of Christianity often amounted to celebrating their salvation with carousing and fornication. His journeys also took him to Crete, and to other islands. In the last decades of the century, **Saint John the Divine**, who was proselytizing at Ephesus, was exiled by the Romans to Pátmos, where in a cave still shown to visitors today he is said to have written Revelation, the apocalyptic last book of the Bible.

Byzantine and medieval Greece: 330–1460 AD

The **Byzantine Empire** was founded in May 330 when the **emperor Constantine** declared Nova Roma (as he called the city of Byzantium – known today as Istanbul) the new capital of the Roman Empire. Founded on the banks of the Bosphorus by Greek colonists in the seventh century BC, Byzantium occupied a commanding point from where the entire trade between the Black Sea and the Mediterranean could be controlled. **Constantinople**, the city of Constantine, as it became popularly known, was perfectly positioned for the supreme strategic task confronting the empire: the defence of the Danube and the Euphrates frontiers. Moreover, the new capital stood astride the flow of goods and culture from the East, that part of the empire richest in economic resources, most densely populated and rife with intellectual and religious activity.

117–138	267	395
The reign of Emperor Hadrian, a hellenophile who left many monuments, above all his great library and triumphal arch in Athens.	Barbarians pillage Athens.	Roman empire splits; Greece becomes part of the eastern, or Byzantine, empire; Olympic Games suppressed.

THE ORIGINS OF THE ORTHODOX CHURCH

The split between the Orthodox and Catholic churches is traditionally dated to the "Great Schism" of 1054, but in practice the Churches had been diverging for centuries, and arguably the final break came much later. The causes of the split were as much linguistic – following the division of the Roman Empire, the language of the Church in Rome was Latin, while in the East it was Greek – and political as they were doctrinal, though there were certainly significant theological differences. Chief among these were the iconoclastic controversy – over the use of images in worship – the use of leavened (in the East) or unleavened bread (in the West) in the liturgy, and the Roman adjustment of the Creed, in 1014, to include the word "filioque" (and the Son).

The final schism was precipitated by the pope's claim to supremacy over the Church. While the patriarch in Constantinople and other Orthodox leaders accepted the bishop of Rome as "first among equals", they were not prepared to accept his ultimate authority over all the Church – or his subsequent claims to infallibility. In 1054, papal legates went to Constantinople to press the patriarch, Michael Celaurius, to accept Rome's claims. When he refused, Cardinal Humbert, leader of the Latin contingent, excommunicated Celaurius, who responded by in turn excommunicating Humbert and his colleagues.

Any hope of reconciliation disappeared with the sacking of Constantinople during the Fourth Crusade, when Orthodox churches were looted by Catholic crusaders, and forcibly converted to Catholic worship, and by the centuries of separation which followed the fall of Constantinople, when much of the Orthodox East came under Ottoman rule.

The Christian empire

Constantine's other act with decisive consequences was to **legalize** and patronize the **Christian Church**. Here again Constantinople was important, for while Rome's pagan traditions could not yet be disturbed, the new capital was conceived as a Christian city. Within the century Christianity was established as the religion of state, with its liturgies (still in use in the Greek Orthodox Church), the Creed and the New Testament all in Greek.

In 391 emperor **Theodosius I** issued an edict banning all expressions of **paganism** throughout the empire. In Greece the mysteries at Eleusis ceased to be celebrated the following year, and in 395 the Olympic Games were suppressed, their athletic nudity an offence to Christianity. Around this time too the Delphic oracle fell silent. The conversion of pagan buildings to Christian use began in the fifth century. Under an imperial law of 435 the Parthenon and the Erechtheion on the Acropolis, the mausoleum of Galerius (the Rotunda) in Thessaloníki and other temples elsewhere became churches. Even this did not eradicate pagan teaching: philosophy and law continued to be taught at the Academy in Athens, founded by Plato in 385 BC, until prohibited by the emperor Justinian in 529.

In 395 the Roman Empire split into **Western and Eastern empires**, and in 476 **Rome fell** to the barbarians. As the Dark Ages settled on Western Europe, Byzantium inherited the sole mantle of the empire. Latin remained its official language, though after the reign of Justinian (527–565) the emperors joined the people in speaking and writing Greek.

Thessaloníki, the second city of the Byzantine Empire, was relatively close to Constantinople, yet even so the journey by land or sea took five or six days. The rest of Greece grew decidedly provincial, and conditions worsened sharply in the late sixth century when the country was devastated by **plague**. In Athens after 580 life almost came

435	730	824 –961	1071
The Parthenon and other Greek temples converted to churches.	Icons and other images banned in the Orthodox Church for being idolatrous; the height of the iconoclastic controversy.	Arab occupation of Crete; a warning of things to come.	Byzantine army defeated by the Turks.

to an end, as the remaining inhabitants withdrew to the Acropolis, while at Corinth the population removed itself entirely to the island of Égina. The islands, especially those of the eastern Aegean closer to Byzantium, perhaps suffered less, though as central authority broke down so the threat of **piracy** grew. Remnants of very **early Christian churches**, from the sixth and seventh centuries onward, are scattered widely across the islands.

The Crusades

In 1071 the **Byzantine army** was destroyed at **Manzikert**, a fortress town on the eastern frontier, by the **Seljuk Turks** who went on to occupy almost all Asia Minor. After the Byzantine emperor turned to the West for help, the Roman Catholic pope replied by launching the **First Crusade** in 1095. Together, the Crusaders and the Byzantines won a series of victories over the Seljuks in Asia Minor, but the Byzantines, wary of possible Crusader designs on the empire itself, were content to see their Latin allies from the West advance alone on Jerusalem, which they captured in 1099.

The worst fears of the Byzantines were borne out in 1204 when the **Fourth Crusade** attacked and sacked **Constantinople** itself. Greece and its islands were shared out and endlessly changed hands between Franks, Venetians and many others in a bewildering patchwork of feudal holdings; for the maritime empires of Venice and Genoa, the islands held special appeal. Amid this endless infighting in the West, a new Turkish dynasty, the **Ottomans**, emerged in the late thirteenth century. By 1400 they had conquered all of mainland Byzantine Greece except Thessaloníki and the Peloponnese. In 1452 they invaded the Peloponnese as a diversion to the main attack on **Constantinople**, which fell on May 23, 1453. In 1456 the Ottomans captured **Athens** from the Venetians and turned the Parthenon church into a mosque, and in 1460 they conquered the **Peloponnese**. **Trebizond** fell the following year, and the Byzantine empire was no more.

The fates of the islands were more varied. **Crete** enjoyed a spectacular cultural renaissance after the fall of Constantinople as a stream of refugees arrived from the east. Though increasingly embattled, it held out as a Venetian-ruled outpost for over two hundred years, before Iráklion was finally surrendered in 1669. In the **Dodecanese**, meanwhile, Rhodes and Kos had been built up as formidable fortresses during the Crusades, home to the **Knights Hospitallers of St John**. The Knights held out until 1522 before Süleyman the Magnificent finally drove them out; the trigger for the last Venetian islands in the Aegean, **Évvia** and **Égina**, to succumb not much later. In the west, closer to Venice, **Corfu** and the other Ionian islands were occasionally fought over, but never submitted for long – they remained in Venetian hands through most of the Turkish occupation, passing to France in the eighteenth century when Napoleon conquered Venice.

Greece under Turkish occupation: 1460–1821

Although the Greeks refer to the Turkish occupation as *sklavía* – "slavery" – in practice, in exchange for submitting to Muslim rule and paying tribute, the Greeks were free to pursue their religion and were left very much in charge of their own religious and civil affairs. The essence of the Turkish administration was **taxation**; collection was often farmed out to the leaders of the Greek communities, and some local magistrates profited sufficiently to exercise a dominant role not only within their own region but

1095	1204	1453	1522
First Crusade drives back the Turks.	Fourth Crusade sacks Constantinople; many of the islands taken over by western European powers.	Constantinople falls to the Ottoman Turks, followed by much of Greece.	Knights of St John driven from Rhodes.

also in the Ottoman Empire at large. On the mainland and larger islands, the Ottomans controlled the towns and the plains but left the mountains almost entirely to the Greeks. The fate of smaller islands depended largely on their resources; where there were none, they saw little interference.

The other important institution within Greece was the **Orthodox Church**. The Church was wealthy and powerful; Greeks preferred to give their lands to the monasteries than have them occupied by the Turks, while the Muslims found it easier to work with the Church than to invent a new administration. Though often corrupt and venal, the Church did at least preserve the traditional faith and keep alive the written form of the Greek language, and it became the focus of Greek nationalism.

Western resistance

In 1570 Ottoman troops landed on **Cyprus**. Nicosia was swiftly captured, and 30,000 of its inhabitants slaughtered. Turkish brutality in Cyprus horrified Europe, and the **Holy League** was formed under the aegis of the pope. Spain and Genoa joined Venice in assembling a fleet led by Don John of Austria, the bastard son of the Spanish king, its lofty aim not only to retake the island but to recapture all Christian lands taken by the Ottomans. In the event, it was utterly ineffectual; no serious attempt was made even to launch an expedition to relieve Cyprus. Yet out of it something new arose – the first stirrings of **Philhellenism**, a desire to liberate the Greeks, whose ancient culture stood at the heart of Renaissance thought.

There was, too, the encouragement of a naval victory, when in 1571 Don John's fleet surprised and overwhelmingly defeated the much larger Ottoman fleet, at its winter quarters at **Lepanto** on the Gulf of Corinth in western Greece. Two hundred and sixty-six Ottoman vessels were sunk or captured, fifty thousand sailors died, and fifteen thousand Christian galley slaves were freed. Throughout Europe the news of Lepanto was received with extraordinary rejoicing; this was the first battle in which Europe had triumphed against the Ottomans, and its symbolic importance was profound. Militarily and politically, however, the Ottomans remained dominant. The fall of **Crete**, in 1669, marked the end of the last bastion of Byzantine culture.

Greek nationalist stirrings

During the eighteenth century the islanders of **Ýdhra** (Hydra), **Spétses** and **Psará** built up a Greek merchant fleet that traded throughout the Mediterranean, where thriving colonies of Greeks were established in many ports. The fleets were to form the basis of the Greek naval forces in the struggle for independence, and these islands produced many of the movement's early leaders. Greek merchant families were also well established, often in important administrative positions, throughout the Ottoman Empire.

These wealthier and more educated Greeks enjoyed greater than ever opportunities for advancement within the Ottoman system, while the Greek peasantry, unlike the empire's Muslim inhabitants, did not have to bear the burden of military service. Nevertheless the Greeks had their grievances against the Ottoman government, mostly concerning the arbitrary, unjust and oppressive system of taxation. Among the Greek peasantry it was primarily religion that set them against their Muslim neighbours – as much as one-fifth of the population – and their Ottoman overlords. Muslim leaders had long preached hatred of the infidel, a view reciprocated by the priests and bishops of the Orthodox Church.

1571	1669	1715	1821
Battle of Lepanto – the first significant military defeat for the Ottoman Empire.	Iráklion falls to the Ottomans – the end of a brutal 25-year conquest of Crete.	Tínos is finally taken by the Ottomans, the last of the Cyclades to succumb.	Rebellion breaks out in various parts of the Empire; much of Greece liberated.

The War of Independence: 1821–32

The **ideology** behind the **War of Independence** came from the Greeks of the diaspora, particularly those merchant colonies in France, Italy, Austria and Russia who had absorbed new European ideas of nationalism and revolution. Around 1814, assorted such Greeks formed a secret society, the **Filikí Etería** (Friendly Society). Their sophisticated political concepts went uncomprehended by the peasantry, who assumed the point of an uprising was to exterminate their religious adversaries. And so when war finally broke out in **spring 1821**, almost the entire settled **Muslim population of Greece** – farmers, merchants and officials – was **slaughtered** within weeks by roaming bands of Greek peasants armed with swords, guns, scythes and clubs. They were often led by Orthodox priests, and some of the earliest Greek revolutionary flags portrayed a cross over a severed Turkish head.

The war

While the Greeks fought to rid themselves of the Ottomans, their further aims differed widely. Landowners sought to reinforce their traditional privileges; the peasantry saw the struggle as a means towards land redistribution; and westernized Greeks were fighting for a modern nation-state. Remarkably, by the end of **1823** the Greeks appeared to have won their independence. Twice the sultan had sent armies into Greece; twice they had met with defeat. Greek guerrilla leaders, above all **Theodoros Kolokotronis** from the Peloponnese, had gained significant military victories early in the rebellion, which was joined by a thousand or so **European Philhellenes**, almost half of them German, though the most important was the English poet, **Lord Byron**.

But the situation was reversed in 1825, when the Peloponnese was invaded by formidable Egyptian forces loyal to the sultan. Thus far, aid for the Greek struggle had come neither from Orthodox Russia, nor from the Western powers of France and Britain, both wearied by the Napoleonic Wars and suspicious of a potentially anarchic new state. But the death of Lord Byron from a fever while training Greek forces at **Mesolóngi** in 1824 galvanized European public opinion. When Mesolóngi fell to the Ottomans in 1826, Britain, France and Russia finally agreed to seek autonomy for certain parts of Greece, and sent a combined fleet to put pressure on the sultan's army in the Peloponnese and the Turkish-Egyptian fleet harboured in Navaríno Bay. Events took over, and an "accidental" naval battle at **Navaríno** in October 1827 resulted in the destruction of almost the entire Ottoman fleet. The following spring, Russia itself declared war on the Ottomans, and Sultan Mahmud II was forced to accept the existence of an autonomous Greece.

At a series of conferences from 1830 to 1832, **Greek independence** was confirmed by the Western powers, and borders were drawn in 1832. These included just 800,000 of the six million Greeks living within the Ottoman Empire, and territories that were largely the poorest of the classical and Byzantine lands: **Attica**, the **Peloponnese** and the islands of the **Argo-Saronic**, the **Sporades** and the **Cyclades**. The rich agricultural belt of **Thessaly**, **Epirus** in the west and **Macedonia** in the north remained in Ottoman hands, as did the Dodecanese and Crete. Meanwhile after the Napoleonic Wars the **Ionian islands** had passed to British control.

1824	1825	1827	1826–28
Lord Byron dies, becoming a Greek national hero in the process.	Egyptian armies reconquer most of Greece.	Ottoman fleet destroyed at the Battle of Navaríno, encouraging Great Power intervention.	The first capital of independent Greece is on the island of Égina.

The emerging state: 1832–1939

Modern Greece began as a **republic**, with its first capital on the island of Égina. **Ioannis Kapodistrias**, the first president, a native of Corfu, concentrated his efforts on building a viable central authority. Almost inevitably he was assassinated, and perhaps equally inevitably the "Great Powers" – Britain, France and Germany – stepped in. They created a **monarchy**, setting a Bavarian prince, Otto (Otho), on the throne with a new capital at Athens. By 1834, Greece also had its own national, state-controlled **Orthodox Church**, independent from the Patriarchate in Constantinople; at the same time, two-thirds of the monasteries and convents were closed down.

Despite the granting of a constitution in 1844, **King Otto** proved autocratic and insensitive, filling official posts with fellow Germans and ignoring all claims by the landless peasantry for redistribution of the old estates. When he was forced from the country by a popular revolt in 1862, the Europeans produced a new prince, this time from Denmark. The accession of **George I** (1863–1913) was marked by Britain's decision to hand over the **Ionian islands** to Greece. During his reign, Greece's first roads and railways were built, its borders were extended, and land reform began in the Peloponnese.

The Great Idea and expansionist wars

From the start, Greek foreign policy was motivated by the **Megáli Idhéa** (Great Idea) of redeeming ethnically Greek populations outside the country and incorporating the old territories of Byzantium into the new kingdom. There was encouragement all around, as Ottoman control was under pressure across the Balkans.

In 1881, revolts broke out among the Greeks of **Crete**, **Thessaly** and **Epirus**, aided by guerrillas from Greece. Britain forced the Ottoman Empire to cede Thessaly and Arta to Greece, but Crete remained Ottoman. When Cretan Greeks set up an independent government in 1897, declaring *énosis* (union) with Greece, the Ottomans responded by invading the mainland and came within days of reaching Athens. The Great Powers came to the rescue by warning off the Turks and placing Crete under an international protectorate. Only in 1913 did **Crete** unite with Greece.

It was from Crete, nonetheless, that the most distinguished modern Greek statesman emerged: **Eleftheríos Venizélos**, having led a civilian campaign for his island's liberation, was elected as Greek prime minister in 1910. Two years later he organized an alliance of Balkan powers to fight the **Balkan Wars** (1912–13), campaigns that saw the Ottomans virtually driven from Europe, and the Bulgarian competition bested in the culmination of a bitter, four-decade campaign for the hearts and minds of the **Macedonian** population. With Greek borders extended to include the **northeast Aegean islands**, **northern Thessaly**, **central Epirus** and parts of **Macedonia** (though not the Dodecanese, which had been seized by Italy in 1912), the Megáli Idhéa was approaching reality.

World War I

Division, however, appeared with the outbreak of **World War I**. Although Venizélos urged Greek entry on the Allied side, hoping to liberate Greeks in Thrace and Asia Minor, the new king, **Constantine I**, who was married to the German Kaiser's sister, imposed neutrality. Eventually Venizélos set up a revolutionary government in Thessaloníki, polarizing the country into a state of **civil war**. In 1917 Greek troops entered the war to join the French, British and Serbians in the Macedonian campaign against Bulgaria and

1829	1832	1834	1864
Náfplio, on the mainland, becomes the official capital.	Cyclades become part of the new Greek state.	Capital transferred to Athens.	Control of the Ionian islands is granted to the Greek state.

Germany. Upon the capitulation of Bulgaria and the Ottoman Empire, the Greeks occupied **Thrace**, and Venizélos presented demands at Versailles for predominantly Greek **Smyrna** (modern Izmir), on the Asia Minor coast, to become part of the Greek state.

The Catastrophe and its aftermath

The demand for Smyrna triggered one of the most disastrous episodes in modern Greek history, the so-called **Katastrofí** (Catastrophe). Venizélos was authorized to move forces into Smyrna in 1919, but a new Turkish nationalist movement was taking power under Mustafa Kemal, or **Atatürk**. After monarchist factions took over when Venizélos lost elections in 1920, the Allies withdrew support for the venture. Nevertheless the monarchists ordered Greek forces to advance upon Ankara, seeking to bring Atatürk to terms. The Greeks' **Anatolian campaign** ignominiously collapsed in summer 1922 when Turkish troops forced the Greeks back to the coast. As the Greek army hurriedly evacuated from **Smyrna**, the Turks moved in and **massacred** much of the **Armenian and Greek** population before burning most of the city to the ground.

For the Turks, this was the successful conclusion of what they call their War of Independence. The borders of modern Turkey, as they remain today, were established by the **1923 Treaty of Lausanne**, which also provided for the **exchange of religious minorities** in each country – in effect, the first large-scale regulated ethnic cleansing. Turkey was to accept 390,000 Muslims resident on Greek soil. Greece, with a population of under five million, was faced with the resettlement of over **1.3 million Christian refugees** from Asia Minor; significant numbers were settled across Macedonia, western Thrace, Epirus and in Athens, as well as on Límnos, Lésvos, Híos, Sámos, Évvia and Crete.

The Katastrofí had intense and far-reaching consequences. The bulk of the agricultural estates of **Thessaly** were finally redistributed, to Greek tenants and refugee farmers, and huge shanty towns grew into new quarters around **Athens, Pireás** and **Thessaloníki**, spurring the country's then almost non-existent industry. Politically, reaction was even swifter. By September 1922, a group of Venizelist army officers "invited" King Constantine to abdicate and executed six of his ministers held most responsible for the debacle. Democracy was nominally restored with the proclamation of a **republic**, but for much of the next decade changes in government were brought about by factions within the armed forces. Meanwhile, among the urban refugee population, unions were being formed and the **Greek Communist Party (KKE)** was established.

The rise of Metaxás

In 1935 a plebiscite restored the king, **George II**, to the throne, and the next year he appointed **General Ioánnis Metaxás** as prime minister. Metaxás had opposed the Anatolian campaign, but had little support in parliament, and when KKE-organized strikes broke out, the king dissolved parliament without setting a date for new elections. This blatantly unconstitutional move opened the way for five years of ruthless and at times absurd **dictatorship**. Metaxás proceeded to set up a state based on the fascist models of the era. Left-wing and trade-union opponents were imprisoned or forced into exile, a state youth movement and secret police were set up, and rigid censorship, extending even to passages of Thucydides, was imposed. But it was at least a Greek dictatorship, and while Metaxás was sympathetic to fascist organizational methods and economics, he utterly opposed German or Italian domination.

1896	1912–13	1923	1924
First modern Olympics are held in Athens.	Balkan Wars extend Greece's borders close to its modern extent; Crete also becomes part of the new nation.	Following a disastrous campaign against Turkey, over one million Christian refugees are resettled in Greece.	Plebiscite abolishes the monarchy and establishes a republic.

GREEK JEWS AND WORLD WAR II

Following the German invasion of Greece, Jews who lived in the Italian zone of occupation were initially no worse off than their fellow Greeks. But after Italy capitulated to the Allies in September 1943 and German troops took over from the Italians, the Jewish communities in Rhodes and Kos in the Dodecanese, as well as in Crete, Corfu, Vólos, Évvia and Zákynthos, were exposed to the full force of Nazi **racial doctrine**. The Germans applied their "final solution" in Greece during the spring and summer of 1944 with the deportation of virtually the entire Jewish population, about 80,000 in all, to extermination camps in Poland.

Greek Christians often went to extraordinary lengths to protect their persecuted countrymen. Thus when the Germans demanded the names of the Jews of Zákynthos prior to a roundup, Archbishop Khrysostomos and Mayor Loukas Karrer presented them with a roster of just two names – their own – and secretly oversaw the smuggling of all the island's 275 Jews to remote farms. Their audacious behaviour paid off, as every Zakynthian Jew survived the war. In Athens, the police chief and the archbishop arranged for false identity cards and baptismal certificates to be issued. Elsewhere, others were warned in good time of what fate the Germans had in store for them, and often took to the hills to join the partisans.

World War II and civil war: 1939–1950

When World War II broke out, the most immediate threat to Greece was **Italy**, which had invaded Albania in April. Even so, Metaxás hoped Greece could remain neutral, and when the Italians torpedoed the Greek cruiser *Elli* in Tínos harbour on August 15, 1940, they failed to provoke a response. **Mussolini**, however, was determined to have a war with Greece, and after accusing the Greeks of violating the Albanian frontier, he delivered an ultimatum on October 28, 1940, to which Metaxás famously if apocryphally answered "**ohi**" (no). Galvanized by the crisis, the Greeks not only drove the invading Italians out of Greece but managed to gain control over the long-coveted and predominantly Greek-populated area of northern Epirus in southern Albania. ("Ohi Day" is still celebrated as a national holiday.)

Mussolini's failure, however, only provoked Hitler into sending his own troops into Greece, while the British rushed an expeditionary force across the Mediterranean from Egypt. Within days of the **German invasion**, on April 6, 1941, the German army was pouring into central Greece. Outmanoeuvred by the enemy's highly mechanized forces and at the mercy of the Luftwaffe, resistance was soon broken. When the Germans occupied Crete in May, King George and his ministers fled to Egypt and set up a government-in-exile. Metaxás himself had died before the German invasion.

Occupation and resistance

The joint Italian-German-Bulgarian **occupation of Greece** was among the most bitter experiences of the European war. Nearly half a million Greek civilians starved to death over the winter of 1941–42, as all food was requisitioned to feed the occupying armies. In addition, entire villages throughout the mainland, but especially on Crete, were burned at the least hint of resistance and nearly 130,000 civilians were slaughtered up to autumn 1944. In their northern sector, which included Thássos and Samothráki, the Bulgarians demolished ancient sites and churches to support any future bid to annex "Slavic" Macedonia.

1935	1936–41	1940	1941
Monarchy restored.	Fascist-style dictatorship of Ioánnis Metaxás.	Italian invasion of Greece is successfully repelled.	German invasion rapidly overruns the country; mass starvation in the Greek cities in the winter.

No sooner had the Axis powers occupied Greece than a spontaneous resistance movement sprang up in the mountains. The National Popular Liberation Army, known by its initials **ELAS**, founded in September 1941, quickly grew to become the most effective resistance organization, working in tandem with **EAM**, the National Liberation Front. Communists formed the leadership of both organizations, but opposition to the occupation and disenchantment with the prewar political order ensured they won the support of many non-communists. By 1943 ELAS/EAM controlled most areas of the country, working with the British Special Operations Executive (SOE), against the occupiers.

But the Allies were already eyeing the shape of postwar Europe, and British prime minister **Winston Churchill** was determined that Greece should not fall into the communist sphere. Ignoring advice from British agents in Greece that ELAS/EAM were the only effective resistance group, and that the king and his government-in-exile had little support within the country, Churchill ordered that only right-wing groups like **EDES**, the National Republican Greek Army, should receive British money, intelligence and arms. In August 1943 a resistance delegation asked the Greek king, George, in Cairo, for a postwar coalition government in which EAM would hold the ministries of the interior, justice and war, and requested that the king himself not return to Greece without popular consent expressed through a plebiscite. Backed by Churchill, King George flatly rejected their demands.

Liberation and civil war

As the Germans began to withdraw from Greece in September 1944, most of the ELAS/EAM leadership agreed to join an interim government headed by the liberal anti-communist politician **George Papandréou**, and to place its forces under that government's control, which effectively meant under command of the British troops who landed in Greece that October. But many partisans felt they were losing their chance to impose a communist government and refused to lay down their arms. On December 3, 1944 the police fired on an EAM demonstration in Athens, killing at least sixteen. The following day, vicious **street fighting** broke out between members of the Greek Communist Party (KKE) and British troops which lasted throughout the month, until eleven thousand people were killed and large parts of Athens destroyed. In other large towns, ELAS rounded up its most influential and wealthy opponents and marched them out to rural areas in conditions that guaranteed their deaths.

After Papandréou resigned and the king agreed not to return without a plebiscite, a **ceasefire** was signed on February 12, 1945, and a new British-backed government agreed to institute democratic reforms. Many of these were not implemented, however. The army, police and civil service remained in right-wing hands, and while collaborators were often allowed to retain their positions, left-wing sympathizers were excluded. A KKE boycott of elections in March 1946 handed victory to the parties of the right, and a **rigged plebiscite** followed that brought the king back to Greece. Right-wing gangs now roamed the towns and countryside with impunity, and by the summer of 1946 eighty thousand leftists who had been associated with ELAS had taken to the mountains.

By 1947 guerrilla activity had again reached the scale of a **full civil war**, with ELAS reorganized into the Democratic Army of Greece (DSE). In the interim, King George had died and been succeeded by his brother Paul, while the Americans had taken over

1943	1944–49	1948	1952
Massacre of Italian troops on Kefalloniá by the Germans, following the island's "handover".	German withdrawal is promptly followed by the outbreak of bitter civil war.	Dodecanese islands finally become part of the Greek state.	Greece, now firmly part of the Western bloc, joins NATO.

the British role and began implementing the Cold War **Truman Doctrine**, in which massive economic and military aid was given to an amenable Greek government. In the mountains American military advisors trained the initially woeful Greek army for campaigns against the DSE, while the cities saw mass arrests, courts martial and imprisonments. From their stronghold on the slopes of Mount Grámmos on the border of Greece and Albania, the partisans waged a losing guerrilla struggle. At the start of 1948 Stalin withdrew Soviet support, and in the autumn of 1949, after Tito closed the Yugoslav border, denying the partisans the last means of outside supplies, the remnants of the DSE retreated into Albania and the KKE admitted defeat by proclaiming a supposedly temporary suspension of the civil war. Also in 1948, the **Dodecanese** islands finally became an official part of the Greek state.

Reconstruction and dictatorship: 1950–74

After a decade of war that had shattered much of Greece's infrastructure (it is said that not one bridge was left standing by 1948), and had killed twelve percent of the 1940 population, it was a demoralized, shattered country that emerged into the Western political orbit of the 1950s. Greece was **American-dominated**, enlisted into the **Korean War** in 1950 and **NATO** not long after. The US embassy – still giving the orders – foisted an electoral system on the Greeks that ensured victory for the Right for the next twelve years. Overt leftist activity was banned (though a "cover" party for communists was soon founded), and many of those who were not herded into political "re-education" camps or dispatched by firing squads, legal or vigilante, went into exile throughout Eastern Europe, to return only after 1974. The 1950s also saw the wholesale **depopulation of remote villages** and the virtual emptying of many of the smaller islands as migrants sought work in Australia, America and Western Europe, or the larger Greek cities.

Constantine Karamanlís and Cyprus

The American-backed right-wing **Greek Rally** party, led by **General Papágos**, won the first decisive post-civil-war elections in 1952. After the general's death, the party's leadership was taken over – and to an extent liberalized – by **Constantine Karamanlís**. Under his rule, stability of a kind was established and some economic advances registered, particularly after the revival of Greece's traditional German markets.

The main ongoing crisis in foreign policy was **Cyprus**, where Greek Cypriots demanding *énosis* (union) with Greece waged a long terrorist campaign against the British. Turkey adamantly opposed *énosis* and said that if Britain left Cyprus it should revert to Turkish rule. A 1959 compromise granted independence to the island and protection for its Turkish Cypriot minority but ruled out any union with Greece.

By 1961, unemployment, the Cyprus issue and the presence of US nuclear bases on Greek soil were changing the political climate, and when Karamanlís was again elected there was strong suspicion of intimidation and fraud carried out by right-wing elements and the army. After eighteen months of strikes and protest demonstrations, Karamanlís resigned and went into voluntary exile in Paris.

George Papandréou and the colonels

New elections in 1964 gave the **Centre Union Party**, headed by **George Papandréou**, an

1952	1959	1964	1964
New constitution establishes a parliamentary democracy, with king as Head of State.	Cyprus gains independence.	The film of *Zorba the Greek*, shot on Crete, released, its soundtrack going on to grace (or blight) every Greek restaurant ever since.	King Constantine II succeeds his father, Paul.

outright majority and a mandate for social and economic reform. The new government was the first to be controlled from outside the right since 1935 and, in his first act as prime minister, Papandréou sought to heal the wounds of the civil war by **releasing political prisoners** and allowing exiles to return. When King Paul died in March and his son came to the throne as **Constantine II**, it seemed a new era had begun.

But soon **Cyprus** again took centre stage. Fighting between Turkish and Greek Cypriots broke out in 1963, and only the intervention of the United States in 1964 dissuaded Turkey from invading the island. In the mood of military confrontation between Greece and Turkey – both NATO members – Papandréou questioned Greece's role in the Western alliance, to the alarm of the Americans and the Greek right. When he moved to purge the army of disloyal officers, the army, with the support of the king, resisted.

Amid growing tension, elections were set for May 1967. It was a foregone conclusion that Papandréou's Centre Union Party would win, but **King Constantine**, disturbed by the party's leftward shift, was said to have briefed senior generals for a coup. True or not, the king, like almost everyone else in Greece, was caught by surprise when a group of unknown **colonels** staged their own **coup** on April 21, 1967. In December the king staged a counter-coup against the colonels, and when it failed he went into exile.

The junta announced itself as the **Revival of Greek Orthodoxy** against corrupting Western influences, not least long hair and miniskirts. Political activity was banned, independent trade unions were forbidden to recruit or meet, the press was so heavily censored that many papers stopped printing, and thousands of communists and others on the left were arrested, imprisoned and often tortured. Culturally, the colonels put an end to popular music and inflicted ludicrous censorship on literature and the theatre, including a ban on the production of classical tragedies. In 1973, chief colonel **Papadópoulos** abolished the monarchy and declared Greece a republic with himself as president.

Restoration of democracy

The colonels lasted for seven years. Opposition was voiced from the start by exiled Greeks in London, the US and Western Europe, but only in 1973 did demonstrations break out openly in Greece – the colonels' secret police had done too thorough a job of infiltrating domestic resistance groups and terrifying everyone else into docility. After students occupied the **Athens Polytechnic** on **November 17**, the ruling clique sent armoured vehicles to storm the gates. A still-undetermined number of students (estimates range from 24 to 300) were killed. Martial law was tightened and Colonel Papadópoulos was replaced by the even more noxious and reactionary **General Ioannídes**, head of the secret police.

The end came within a year when the dictatorship embarked on a disastrous adventure in **Cyprus**. By attempting to topple the Makários government, the junta provoked a **Turkish invasion** and occupation of forty percent of Cypriot territory. The army finally mutinied and **Constantine Karamanlís** was invited to return from Paris to resume office.

Karamanlís swiftly negotiated a ceasefire in Cyprus, and in November 1974 he and his **Néa Dhimokratía** (New Democracy) party were rewarded by a sizeable majority in elections. The chief opposition was the new Panhellenic Socialist Movement (**PASOK**), led by **Andréas Papandréou**, son of George.

1967	1973	1974	1975
Colonels' coup marks the start of seven years of repressive military rule.	Monarchy abolished and a republic declared.	Greek-backed attempted coup in Cyprus leads to Turkish invasion and the division of the island; and to the end of the colonels' regime.	New constitution provides for parliamentary government with president as Head of State.

Europe and a new Greece: 1974–2000

To Karamanlís's enduring credit, his New Democracy party oversaw an effective return to **democratic stability**, even legalizing the KKE (the Greek Communist Party) for the first time. Karamanlís also held a **referendum on the monarchy**, in which seventy percent of Greeks rejected the return of Constantine II. So a largely symbolic presidency was instituted instead, occupied by Karamanlís from 1980 to 1985, and again from 1990 to 1995. In 1981, Greece joined the **European Community**.

In the same year the socialist party, **PASOK**, and its leader, Andréas Papandréou, swept to power. The new era started with a bang as long-overdue **social reforms** were enacted: peasant women were granted pensions; wages were indexed to the cost of living; civil marriage was introduced; family and property law was reformed in favour of wives and mothers; and equal rights legislation was passed. By the time PASOK was returned to power in 1985, it was apparent the promised economic bonanza was not happening: hit by low productivity, lack of investment (not helped by anti-capitalist rhetoric from the government) and world recession, unemployment rose, inflation hit 25 percent and the national debt soared.

In the event it was the European Community, once Papandréou's *bête noire*, which rescued him, with a huge loan on condition that an austerity programme was maintained. Forced to drop many of his populist policies, the increasingly autocratic Papandréou turned on his former left-wing allies. Combined with the collapse of Soviet rule in Eastern Europe, his own very public affair with an Olympic Airways hostess half his age and a raft of economic scandals, PASOK's hold on power was not surprisingly weakened. Since 1989, when New Democracy was elected once more, the two parties have exchanged power on a regular basis.

The 1990s were not easy, with an economy riven by unrest and division, and huge foreign policy headaches caused by the break-up of the former Yugoslavia and the ensuing wars on Greece's borders. Meanwhile, alone among NATO members, Greece was conspicuous for its open support of **Serbia**, ostentatiously supplying trucks to Belgrade via Bulgaria.

By the end of the 1990s, the economy was apparently stabilizing, with inflation consistently in single figures, and in 1997 national morale was further boosted with the award of the 2004 Olympic Games to Athens. Abroad, a dramatic and unexpected change in Greece's always distrustful **relations with Turkey** came when a severe **earthquake** struck northern Athens on September 7, 1999, killing scores and rendering almost 100,000 homeless. Coming less than a month after a devastating earthquake in northwest Turkey, it spurred a thaw between the two historical rivals. Greeks donated massive amounts of blood and foodstuffs to the Turkish victims, and were the earliest foreign rescue teams to reach Turkey; in turn they saw Turkish disaster-relief squads among the first on the scene in Athens. Soon afterwards, foreign minister George Papandréou (son of Andréas, later prime minister) announced that Greece had dropped its opposition to EU financial aid to Turkey and would no longer oppose Turkish candidacy for the EU.

The twenty-first century: boom … and bust?

Greece entered the twenty-first century on a high; entry to the **eurozone** in 2001 was seen as hugely prestigious, while the **2004 Olympic Games** were considered a

1981	1982	1991	1999
Greece joins the EU.	*Rough Guide to Greece*, the first ever Rough Guide, published; first *Greek Islands* book follows in 1995.	Yugoslav Republic of Macedonia declares independence; Greece objects to use of the name Macedonia.	Athens earthquake; rapprochement between Greece and Turkey.

IMMIGRATION – AND THE ALBANIAN INFLUX

Greece may continue to occupy the EU's economic cellar, but it's still far wealthier than many of its neighbours. This has acted as a magnet for a permanent underclass of **immigrants**. Since 1990 they have arrived in numbers estimated at over a million, a huge burden for a country of just over ten million citizens. These days your waiter, hotel desk clerk or cleaning lady is most likely to be Albanian, Bulgarian or Romanian, to cite the three largest groups. There are also significant communities of Pakistanis, Egyptians, Poles, Bangladeshis, Syrians, Filipinos, Ukrainians, Russians, Equatorial Africans, Kurds and Georgians, not to mention ethnic Greeks from the Caucasus – a striking change in what had hitherto been a homogeneous and parochial culture.

The Greek response has been decidedly mixed. **Albanians**, who make up roughly half the influx, are almost universally detested, and blamed for all manner of social ills. For the first time, crime – especially burglaries – is a significant issue. The newcomers have also prompted the first significant anti-immigration measures in a country whose population is more used to being on the other side of such laws. A member of the Schengen visa scheme, Greece sees itself, as in past ages, as the first line of defence against the barbarian hordes from the East. The Aegean islands regularly receive boatloads of people from every country in Asia.

triumph – which, in sporting and public relations terms, they probably were. EU funds and Olympic investment kick-started widespread infrastructure improvements, and the future seemed rosy. Both these events, however, turned out to be symptomatic of Greece's **problems**. Even at the time of adoption of the euro, it was an open secret that the figures had been massaged to ensure Greece met the strict criteria – the extent of that fix only became apparent later. And behind the successful facade of the Olympics were vast cost overruns in the desperate rush to complete the facilities, and a complete lack of legacy planning that has left many venues to rot.

In December 2008, **rioting** broke out in Athens, provoked by the police shooting of a 15-year-old student. The weeks of unrest that followed – as young people, in particular, protested their lack of opportunities – were the first sign that the wider world had of Greece's deep-rooted troubles and impending **crisis**. When PASOK was returned to power in 2009, now led by George Panpandreou, the extent of the economic problems began to be fully revealed, with a **national debt** of €262 billion and a deficit running at 12.7 percent of GDP (against a euro limit of 3 percent). As Greece's huge public sector, lax tax collection and allegedly widespread corruption came increasingly into the spotlight, government attempts to cut spending and increase revenue ran into the double whammy of popular opposition and economic downturn. As we went to press at the end of 2011, Papandréou had stood down in favour of a government of "national unity", while the latest of a series of **EU bailouts** again failed to make much impact on the financial markets, or on Greece's ever-growing debt. Default or a humiliating departure from the eurozone seemed inevitable. Whatever the outcome, Greece's short-term economic future looks bleak.

2001	2004	2008	2011
Greece adopts the euro, consigning the drachma, to history.	Athens Olympics pass off triumphantly, though their legacy is less happy.	Rioting breaks out in Athens, bringing the country's economic crisis to world attention.	Debt crisis threatens to engulf the whole of Europe.

Archeology

Until the second half of the nineteenth century, archeology was a very hit-and-miss, treasure-hunting affair. The early students of antiquity went to Greece to draw and make plaster casts of the great masterpieces of Classical sculpture. A number soon found it more convenient or more profitable to remove objects wholesale, and might be better described as looters than scholars or archeologists.

Early excavations – and pillaging

The **British Society of Dilettanti** was one of the earliest promoters of Greek culture, financing expeditions to draw and publish antiquities. Founded in the 1730s as a reputedly drunken club for young aristocrats who had completed the Grand Tour and fancied themselves arbiters of taste, its leading spirit was **Sir Francis Dashwood**, a notorious rake who also founded the infamous Hellfire Club. Nevertheless, the society was the first body organized to sponsor systematic research into Greek antiquities, though it was initially most interested in Italy, as Greece was then still a backwater of the Ottoman Empire.

In the 1740s, two young artists, **James Stuart** and **Nicholas Revett**, formed a plan to produce a scholarly record of ancient Greek buildings. With the support of the society they spent three years in Greece, principally in and around Athens, drawing and measuring the antiquities. The publication of their exquisite illustrations and the 1764 publication of **Johann Winckelmann**'s *History of Art*, in which the **Parthenon** and its sculptures were exalted as the eternal standard by which beauty should be measured, gave an enormous boost to the study (and popularity) of Greek sculpture and architecture; many European Neoclassical town and country houses date from this period.

While most of the early excavations were carried out on the mainland, in 1811, a party of English and German travellers, including the architect **C.R. Cockerell**, uncovered the **Temple of Aphaea** on **Égina** and shipped away the pediments. They auctioned off the marbles for £6000 to Prince Ludwig of Bavaria, and, inspired by this success, returned to Greece for further finds. This was a huge sum for the time but they were also pioneering archeology for the period. Besides, removing the finds was hardly surprising: Greece, after all, was not yet a state and had no public museum; antiquities discovered were sold by their finders – if they recognized their value.

The new nation

The Greek War of Independence (1821–28) and the establishment of a modern Greek nation changed all this. As a result of the selection of Prince Otto of Bavaria as the first king of modern Greece in 1832, the **Germans**, whose education system stressed Classical learning, were in the forefront of archeological activity. One dominant Teutonic figure during the early years of the new state was **Ludwig Ross**, who in 1834 began supervising the excavation and restoration of the **Acropolis**. Dismantling the accretion of Byzantine, Frankish and Turkish fortifications, and reconstructing Classical originals, began the following year.

The Greeks themselves had begun to focus on their ancient past when the first stirrings of the independence movement were felt. In 1813 the **Philomuse Society** was formed, aiming to uncover and collect antiquities, publish books and assist students and foreign philhellenes. In 1829 an orphanage on the island of Égina became the first **Greek archeological museum.**

In 1837 the **Greek Archeological Society** was founded "for the discovery, recovery and restoration of antiquities in Greece" under the auspices of **Kyriakos Pittakis**, who played a major role in the attempt to convince Greeks of the importance of their heritage; antiquities were still being looted or burned for lime.

The great Germans: Curtius and Schliemann

Although King Otto was deposed in 1862 in favour of a Danish prince, Germans remained in the forefront of Greek archeology in the 1870s. Two men dominated the scene: Heinrich Schliemann and Ernst Curtius.

Curtius was a traditional Classical scholar. He had come to Athens originally as tutor to King Otto's family and in 1874 returned to Greece to secure permission to excavate at **Olympia**. He set up a **German Archeological Institute** in Athens and negotiated the **Olympia Convention**, under the terms of which the Germans were to pay for and have total control of the dig; all finds were to remain in Greece, though the excavators could make copies and casts; and all finds were to be published simultaneously in Greek and German.

This was an enormously important agreement, which almost certainly prevented the treasures of Olympia and Mycenae following that of Troy to a German museum. But other Europeans were still in acquisitive mode: **French consuls**, for example, had been instructed to buy any "available" local antiquities in Greece and Asia Minor, and had picked up the Louvre's great treasures from separate islands, the **Venus de Milo** and **Winged Victory of Samothrace**, in 1820 and 1863 respectively.

While Curtius was digging at Olympia, a man who represented everything that was anathema to orthodox Classical scholarship was standing archeology on its head. **Heinrich Schliemann**, who had amassed a private fortune through various Midas-like enterprises, had embarked on the **search for Troy** and the vindication of his lifelong belief in the truth of Homer's tales of prehistoric cities and heroes. Although all his work was on the Greek and Turkish mainlands, almost single-handedly, and in the face of continuing academic obstruction, Schliemann had revolutionized archeology and pushed back the knowledge of Greek history and civilization a thousand years. Although some of his results have been shown to have been deliberately falsified in the sacrifice of truth to beauty, his achievement remains enormous.

Evans and Knossos

The early twentieth century saw the domination of Greek archeology by an Englishman, **Sir Arthur Evans**. An egotistical maverick like Schliemann, he too was independently wealthy, with a brilliantly successful career behind him when he started his great work and recovered another millennium for Greek history. Evans excavated what he called the "Palace of Minos" at **Knossos** on **Crete**, discovering one of the oldest and most sophisticated Mediterranean societies, which he christened Minoan.

The son of a distinguished antiquarian and collector, Evans read history at Oxford and travelled whenever he could. It was in 1893, while in Athens, that his attention was drawn to Crete. In a vendor's stall he came upon some small drilled stones with tiny engravings in a hitherto unknown script; he was told they came from Crete. He had seen Schliemann's finds from Mycenae and had been fascinated by this prehistoric culture. Crete, the crossroads of the Mediterranean, seemed a good place to look for more.

Evans visited Crete in 1894 and headed for the legendary site of Knossos, which had earlier attracted the attention of Schliemann (who had been unable to agree a price with the Turkish owners of the land) and where a Cretan, appropriately called Minos, had already done some impromptu digging, revealing massive walls and a storeroom

TOP TEN ARCHEOLOGICAL SITES

In a country with such a wealth of ancient remains as Greece, it's hard to pick out a definitive list of highlights but here are some of the most famous and unmissable sites on the islands, along with a few of the more obscure but equally worthy ones.

Temple of Aphaea, Égina One of the most complete Classical temples in Greece stands on a pine-covered ridge. See p.85

Knossos, Crete The lava-preserved Minoan palace contains some beautiful ancient frescoes. See p.209

Eretria, Évvia Extensive remains such as an agora, Apollo temple and ancient theatre are spread around town. See p.448

Delos Guarded by majestic stone lions, the treasury of the Athenian Empire occupied the entire island. See p.146

Sanctuary of the Great Gods, Samothráki Idyllically located site that was a major centre of an ancient mystery cult. See p.409

Akrotíri, Santoríni Structures as high as two and three storeys, plus frescoes on display in Athens were unearthed here. See p.193

Paleopolis, Corfu Relatively few people visit the scattering of temples and basilicas in the suburbs of Corfu Town. See p.463

Palace of Phaestos, Crete A complex network of foundations sits amid some splendid mountain scenery. See p.213

Ancient Thassos, Thássos The lush agora in the modern town centre is overlooked by various temples on the hill behind. See p.413

Líndhos, Rhodes The splendid ancient acropolis contains remains from prehistoric to medieval times. See p.278

filled with jars. Evans succeeded in buying the site and in March 1900 began excavations. Within a few days, evidence of a great complex building was revealed, along with artefacts that indicated an astonishing cultural sophistication. The huge team of diggers unearthed elegant courtyards and verandas, colourful wall-paintings, pottery, jewellery and sealstones – the wealth of a civilization which dominated the eastern Mediterranean 3500 years ago.

Evans continued to excavate at Knossos for the next thirty years, during which time he established, on the basis of changes in the pottery styles, the **system of dating** that remains in use today for classifying **Greek prehistory**: Early, Middle and Late Minoan (Mycenaean on the mainland). Like Schliemann, Evans attracted criticism and controversy for his methods – most notably his decision speculatively to reconstruct parts of the palace in reinforced concrete – and for many of his interpretations. Nevertheless, his discoveries and his dedication put him near the pinnacle of Greek archeology.

Into the twentieth century: the foreign institutes

In 1924 Evans gave the **British School at Athens** the site of **Knossos** along with his on-site residence, the Villa Ariadne, and all other lands within his possession on Crete (it was only in 1952 that Knossos became the property of the Greek State). At the time the British School was one of several foreign archeological institutes in Greece; founded in 1886, it had been preceded by the **French School**, the **German Institute** and the **American School**.

Greek archeology owes much to the work and relative wealth of these foreign schools and others that would follow. They have been responsible for the excavation of many of the most famous sites in Greece: the **Heraion** on **Sámos** (German); the sacred island of **Delos** (French); sites on **Kos** (Italian) and in central **Crete** (Italian, American, British); and **Samothráki** (American), to name but a few.

The years between the two World Wars saw an expansion of excavation and scholarship, most markedly concerning the prehistoric civilizations. Having been shown by Schliemann and Evans what to look for, a new generation of archeologists was uncovering numerous **prehistoric sites** on the mainland and Crete, and its members were spending proportionately more time studying and interpreting their finds.

One of the giants of this era was **Alan Wace** who, while director of the British School at Athens from 1913 to 1923, conducted excavations at **Mycenae** and proposed a new chronology for prehistoric Greece, which put him in direct conflict with Arthur Evans. Evans believed that the mainland citadels had been ruled by Cretan overlords, whereas Wace was convinced of an independent Mycenaean cultural and political development. Wace was finally vindicated after Evans's death, when in the 1950s it emerged that Mycenaean Greeks had conquered the Minoans in approximately 1450 BC.

Classical archeology was not forgotten in the flush of excitement over the Mycenaeans and Minoans. The period between the wars saw the continuation of excavation at most established sites, and many new discoveries, among them the sanctuary of **Asklepios** and its elegant Roman buildings on **Kos**, excavated by the Italians from 1935 to 1943.

More recent excavations

A number of postwar excavations were as exciting as any in the past. In 1961 the fourth great **Minoan palace** (following the unearthing of Knossos, Phaestos and Malia) was uncovered by torrential rains at the extreme eastern tip of the island of Crete at **Káto Zákros** and cleared by Cretan archeologist **Nikolaos Platon**. Its harbour is now thought to have been the Minoans' main gateway port to and from southwest Asia and Africa, and many of the artefacts discovered in the palace storerooms – bronze ingots from Cyprus, elephants' tusks from Syria, stone vases from Egypt – seem to confirm this. Greek teams have found more Minoan palaces at **Arhánes** and **Galatás**, and possibly at **Haniá** in the west and **Petrás** and **Palékastro** in the east of the island. Challenging previous orthodoxy, many of the new generation of scholars believed that these were ceremonial buildings and not the seats of dynastic authority, as Evans proposed. American excavations at **Kommós**, in central Crete, have uncovered another gateway site with an important harbour, like Káto Zákros, of the Minoan and Mycenaean periods.

At **Akrotíri** on the island of **Thíra** (Santoríni), **Spyros Marinatos** revealed, in 1967, a Minoan-era site that had been buried by volcanic explosion sometime between 1650 and 1550 BC – scientists (using carbon dating evidence) and archeologists (relying on dating of discovered artefacts) are still deliberating its exact date. Its buildings were two or three storeys high, and superbly frescoed. Marinatos was later tragically killed while at work on the site when he fell off a wall, and is now buried there.

At the beginning of this century the various foreign schools, recently joined by the Australian, Austrian, Belgian, Canadian, Danish, Dutch, Finnish, Georgian, Irish, Norwegian, Spanish, Swedish and Swiss, along with Greek universities and the 25 *ephorates*, or inspectorates, of Prehistoric and Classical Antiquities, are still at work in the field, although the emphasis today is as concerned with **conserving and protecting** what has been revealed as unearthing new finds. All too often newly discovered sites have been inadequately fenced off or protected, and a combination of the elements, greedy developers and malicious trespassers – sometimes all three – has caused much damage and deterioration.

Wildlife

For anyone who has first seen Greece at the height of summer with its brown parched hillsides and desert-like ambience, the richness of the wildlife – in particular the flora – may come as a surprise. As winter warms into spring, the countryside (and urban waste ground) transforms itself from green to a mosaic of coloured flowers, which attract a plethora of insect life, followed by birds.

Plants

Whereas in temperate northern Europe plants flower from spring until autumn, the arid summers of Greece confine the main **flowering period** to the spring, a narrow climatic window when the days are bright, the temperatures not too high and the groundwater supply still adequate. **Spring** starts in the southeast, in Rhodes, in early March, and then travels progressively westwards and northwards. Rhodes, Kárpathos and eastern Crete are at their best in March, western Crete in early April, the eastern Aegean mid- to late April, and the Ionian islands in early May, though a cold dry winter can cause several weeks' delay. In the high mountains the floral spring arrives in the chronological summer, with the alpine zones of central and western Crete in full flower in June and July.

The delicate flowers of early spring – orchids, fritillaries, anemones, cyclamen, tulips and small bulbs – are replaced as the season progresses by more robust shrubs, tall perennials and abundant annuals, but many of these close down completely for the fierce **summer**. A few tough plants, like shrubby thyme and savory, continue to flower through the heat and act as magnets for butterflies.

Once the worst heat is over, and the first showers of **autumn** arrive, so does a second "spring", on a much smaller scale but no less welcome after the brown drabness of summer. Squills, autumn cyclamen, crocus and other small bulbs all come into bloom, while the seeds start to germinate for the following year's crop of annuals. By the new year, early spring bulbs and orchids are flowering in the south.

Coastal species

Plants on the **beach** grow in a difficult environment: fresh water is scarce, salt is in excess, and dehydrating winds are often very strong. Feathery **tamarisk** trees are adept at surviving this habitat, and consequently are often planted to provide shade. On hot days or nights you may see or feel them sweating away surplus saltwater from their foliage.

Meadow and hill plants

Arable fields can be rich with colourful weeds, and small, unploughed **meadows** may be equally colourful, with slower-growing plants such as orchids in extraordinary quantities. The rocky earth makes cultivation on some hillsides difficult and impractical, so agriculture is often abandoned and areas regenerate to a rich mixture of

---

THE FIRST NATURALISTS

Despite an often negative attitude to wildlife, Greece was probably the first place in the world where it was an object of study. **Theophrastos** (372–287 BC) from Lésvos was the first recorded botanist and a systematic collector of general information on plants, while his contemporary, **Aristotle**, studied the animal world. During the first century AD the distinguished physician **Dioscorides** compiled a herbal study that remained a standard work for over a thousand years.

TOURISM AND THREATS TO WILDLIFE

Since the 1970s, tourist developments have ribboned along island **coastlines**, sweeping away both agricultural plots and wildlife havens as they do so. These expanding resorts increase local employment, often attracting inland workers to the coast; the generation that would once have herded sheep on remote hillsides now works in tourist bars and tavernas. Consequently, the pressure of domestic animal grazing, particularly in the larger islands, has been significantly reduced, allowing the regeneration of tree seedlings; Crete, for example, has more woodland now than at any time in the last five centuries. However, **forest fires** remain a threat everywhere. Since 1980 blazes have destroyed much of the tree cover in Thássos, southern Rhodes, Kárpathos, Híos, Sámos and parts of the Peloponnese; the trees may well regenerate eventually, but by then the complex shade-dependent ecology is irrecoverably lost.

shrubs and perennials – known as **garigue**. With time, a few good wet winters and in the absence of grazing, some shrubs will develop into small trees, intermixed with tough climbers – the much denser **maquis** vegetation. The colour yellow often predominates in early spring, followed by the blues, pinks and purples of bee-pollinated plants. An abundance of the pink and white of *Cistus* rockroses is usually indicative of an earlier fire, since they are primary recolonizers. A third vegetation type is **phrygana** – smaller, frequently aromatic or spiny shrubs, often with a narrow strip of bare ground between each hedgehog-like bush. Many aromatic herbs such as lavender, rosemary, savory, sage and thyme are native to these areas.

Orchids

Nearly 140 species of **orchid** are believed to occur in the Greek islands; their complexity blurs species' boundaries and keeps botanists in a state of taxonomic flux. In particular, the *Ophrys* bee and spider orchids have adapted themselves, through subtleties of lip colour and false scents, to seduce small male wasps. These insects mistake the flowers for a potential mate, and unintentionally assist the plant's pollination. Though all species are officially protected, many are still picked.

Mountains and gorges

The **limestone peaks** of islands such as Corfu, Kefaloniá, Crete, Rhodes, Sámos and Thássos hold rich collections of attractive **rock plants**, flowers whose nearest relatives may be from the Balkan Alps or the Turkish mountains. **Gorges** are another spectacular habitat, particularly rich in Crete. Their inaccessible cliffs act as refuges for plants that cannot survive the grazing, competition or more extreme climates of open areas. Many of Greece's endemic plants are confined to cliffs, gorges or mountains.

Birds

Migratory species which have wintered in East Africa move north, through the eastern Mediterranean, from around **mid-March to mid-May**. Some stop in Greece to breed; others move on into the rest of Europe. The southern islands are the first landfall after a long sea crossing, and smaller birds recuperate for a few days before moving on. Larger birds such as storks and ibis often fly very high, and binoculars are needed to spot them as they pass over. In autumn birds return, but usually in more scattered numbers.

Larger raptors occur in remoter areas, preferring mountain gorges and cliffs. Buzzards are the most abundant, and often mistaken by optimistic birdwatchers for the rarer, shyer eagles. Griffon vultures, however, are quite unmistakable, soaring on broad, straight-edged wings, whereas the lammergeier is a state-of-the-art flying machine with narrower, swept wings, seen over mountaintops by the lucky few; the remaining nine or ten pairs in Crete are now the Balkan's largest breeding population.

TOP FIVE WILDLIFE SPOTS

Samariá Gorge, Crete Crete's most famous ravine is not only one of Europe's longest but hides some of Greece's rarest plants. See p.251

Korissíon Lagoon, Corfu This serene patch of water bordered by sand dunes hosts various waterfowl. See p.474

Laganás Bay, Zákynthos Though much of it is touristic, the bay is still a prime breeding ground for the loggerhead turtle. See p.506

Petaloúdhes, Rhodes A delightful canyon is home to thousands of tiger moths during summer. See p.281

Mount Énos, Kefaloniá The highest point in the Ionians is home to much flora, including its own species of fir. See p.492

In areas of **wetland** that remain undrained and undisturbed, such as saltmarshes, coastal lagoons, estuaries and freshwater ponds, ospreys, egrets, ibis, spoonbills, storks, pelicans and many waders can be seen feeding. Flamingos sometimes occur, as lone individuals or small flocks, particularly in the eastern Aegean saltpans between December and May.

Mammals

The islands' small **mammal** population ranges from rodents and shrews to hedgehogs and hares, and the dark-red Persian squirrel on Lésvos. Medium-sized mammals include badgers, foxes and the persecuted golden jackal, but the commonest is the ferret-like stone (or beech) marten, named for its habit of decorating stones with its droppings to mark territory.

Occasionally seen running wild in Crete's White Mountains, but more often as a zoo attraction, is an endemic ibex, known to hunters as the *agrími* or *krí-krí*. Formerly in danger of extinction, a colony of them was established on the offshore islet of Dhía, where they thrived, exterminating the rare local flora.

Reptiles and amphibians

Reptiles flourish in the hot dry summers of Greece, the commonest being **lizards**. Most of these are small, agile and wary, rarely staying around for closer inspection. Nocturnal **geckos** are large-eyed, short-tailed lizards. Their spreading toes have claws and ingenious adhesive pads, allowing them to cross house walls and ceilings in their search for insects, including mosquitoes. The rare **chameleon** is a swivel-eyed inhabitant of eastern Crete and some eastern Aegean islands such as Sámos, but hard to spot as its coloration and slow movement enable it to blend into the surroundings.

Once collected for the pet trade, **tortoises** can be found on some islands, though not Crete. Usually their noisy progress through hillside scrub vegetation is the first signal of their presence, as they spend their often long lives grazing the vegetation. Closely related **terrapins** are more streamlined, freshwater tortoises which love to bask on waterside mud by streams or ponds. Shy and nervous, omnivorous scavengers, usually only seen as they disappear under water, their numbers have recently declined steeply on many islands.

Sea turtles occur mostly in the Ionian Sea, but can be seen in the Aegean too. The least rare are the loggerhead turtles (*Caretta caretta*), which nest on Zákynthos and Kefaloniá, and occasionally in Crete. Their nesting grounds are disappearing under tourist resorts, although they are a protected endangered species (see box, p.506).

By contrast, **snakes** are abundant in Greece and many islands; most are shy and non-venomous. Several species, including the Ottoman viper, the nose-horned viper and the localized Cycladic lebetina viper, do have a venomous bite, though they are not usually aggressive; they are adder-like and often have a very distinct, dark zigzag stripe down the back. Snakes are only likely to bite if a hand is put in the crevice of a wall or

FLORA AND FAUNA FIELD GUIDES

FLOWERS

Marjorie Blamey and Christopher Grey-Wilson *Mediterranean Wild Flowers*. Comprehensive field guide, with coloured drawings; recent and taxonomically reasonably up to date.

Lance Chilton *Plant Check-Lists*. Small booklets that also include birds, reptiles and butterflies, for a number of Greek islands and resorts. Available direct at ⓦ marengowalks.com).

Pierre Delforge *Orchids of Britain and Europe*. A comprehensive guide, with recent taxonomy.

John Fielding & Nicholas Turland *Flowers of Crete*. Large volume with 1900 coloured photos of the Cretan flora, much of which is also widespread in Greece.

BIRDS

George Handrinos and T. Akriotis *Birds of Greece*. A comprehensive guide that includes island birdlife.

Lars Jonsson *Birds of Europe with North Africa and the Middle East*. The ornithologist's choice for the best coverage of Greek birds, with excellent descriptions and illustrations.

MAMMALS

Corbet and Ovenden *Collins Guide to the Mammals of Europe*. The best field guide on its subject.

REPTILES

Arnold, Burton and Ovenden *Collins Guide to the Reptiles and Amphibians of Britain and Europe*. A useful guide, though it excludes the Dodecanese and east Aegean islands.

INSECTS

Michael Chinery *Collins Guide to the Insects of Britain and Western Europe*. Although Greece is outside the geographical scope of the guide, it will provide generic identifications for many insects seen.

Lionel Higgins and Norman Riley *A Field Guide to the Butterflies of Britain and Europe*. A thorough and detailed field guide that illustrates nearly all species seen in Greece.

MARINE LIFE

B. Luther and K. Fiedler *A Field Guide to the Mediterranean* (o/p). Very thorough; includes most Greek shallow-water species.

a rock-face where one of them is resting. Leave them alone, and they will do the same for you, but if bitten, seek immediate treatment. Most snakes are not only completely harmless to humans, but beneficial since they keep down populations of pests such as rats and mice.

Frogs and toads are the commonest and most obvious amphibians throughout much of Greece, particularly during the spring breeding season. Frogs prefer the wettest places, and the robust marsh frog revels in artificial water-storage ponds, whose concrete sides magnify their croaking impressively. Tree frogs are tiny emerald green jewels, with huge and strident voices at night, and can sometimes be found in quantity on the leaves of waterside oleanders.

Insects

Greece teems with insects: some pester, like flies and mosquitoes, but most are harmless to humans. From spring through to autumn, the islands are full of **butterflies**. Swallowtail species are named for the drawn-out corners of the hindwings, in shades of cream and yellow, with black and blue markings. The unrelated, robust brown-and-orange pasha is Europe's largest butterfly. Tiger moths, with their black-and-white forewings and startling bright orange hindwings, are the "butterflies" occurring in huge quantity in sheltered sites of islands such as Rhodes, Níssyros and Páros.

Other insects include the camouflaged **praying mantis**, holding their powerful forelegs in a position of supplication until another insect comes within reach. The females are notorious for eating the males during mating. Corfu is famous for its extraordinary **fireflies**, which flutter in quantities across meadows and marshes on May nights, speckling the darkness with bursts of cold light to attract partners; look carefully in nearby hedges, and you may spot the less flashy, more sedentary and more widespread glow-worm.

Music

Music is ubiquitous in modern Greek culture; even the most indifferent visitor will notice it in tavernas and other public spaces. Like so many aspects of the country, it amalgamates "native" and Eastern styles, with occasional contributions from points West, and flourishes alongside and often in preference to Western pop. Music and dance form an integral part of weddings, betrothals, baptisms, elections, saints' days and name-days.

Don't be shy about asking people where you can hear *ta paradhosiaká* (traditional music); a few words of Greek go a long way towards inclining locals to help foreign travellers. Learn the Greek names of the instruments you would like to hear, or find someone to translate for you. Once it's clear that you're a budding *meraklís* (untranslatable, but roughly, aficionado), people will be flattered by the respect paid to "real" music, and doors will open for you.

Island styles

Island musical **traditions** are wonderfully **diverse**, so only a general overview will be attempted here. Each archipelago has its dances, songs and customs which vary between islands and even between towns on the same island. Different dances go by the same name (eg *syrtós*) from place to place, while different lyrics are set to many of the same melodies and vice versa. The same tune can be played so idiosyncratically between neighbouring island groups as to be barely recognizable to an outsider. Compared to Western styles, Aegean music is more circuitous than linear, as would be expected from its Byzantine origins and later Ottoman influences. Although transcriptions exist, and there are some who teach with written notes, most folk pieces are learned by ear.

Traditional island folk songs – *nisiótika* – feature melodies which, like much folk music the world over, rely heavily on the pentatonic scale. Lyrics, especially on smaller islands, touch on the perils of the sea, exile and (in a society where long separations and arranged marriages were the norm) thwarted love. In Crete, **rhyming couplets** called *mantinádhes* are sung in alternation with instrumental interludes; similar satirical couplets are found in the Dodecanese (such as *pismatiká* on Kálymnos), while on Náxos such couplets are called *kotsákia*, and the short repeating melody to which they are set is called a *kotsátos*. Singers improvise such rhymed couplets on the spot, thinking of new lines during the short instrumental breaks and coming in again when ready with new lines. These often tease the wedding couple, praise the in-laws, lament the

---

WEDDINGS AND RELIGIOUS MUSIC

Many pieces, which vary from island to island, are specifically associated with **weddings**. Some are processional songs/tunes (*patinádhes*), sung/played while going to fetch the bride from her home, or as the wedding couple leave the church, plus there are specific dances associated with different stages of the wedding ritual. It was common in the past for the music and dancing that followed a wedding to last for up to three days – nowadays overnight into the next day is more common. Some songs are heard only at **pre-Lenten Carnival** (*Apókries* in Greek), accompanied by the wearing of animal skins or costumes and, in some places such as Skýros, by the shaking of large goat-bells roped together. Such rituals, widespread across Europe, date back to pre-Christian times. Music also accompanies informal, unpublicized **private gatherings** in homes, *kafenía* and tavernas with facilities for musicians and patrons.

loss of a community member or chide a politician. There are also "set" couplets, sometimes mixed in with newly improvised material.

The **Sporades** – linked in many cultural ways to the Magnesian peninsula opposite – never had a *nisiótika* tradition, according to Yiorgos Xintaris, owner/main soloist of a successful rembétika (urban underground music) ouzerí on Skópelos. The soundtrack of his mid-twenieth-century youth was not only rembétika but *laïká* (popular songs), operatic arias and tangos.

Alone of all modern Greek territory, the **Ionian Islands** (except Lefkádha) were never occupied by the Ottomans, but instead by the Venetians, and thus have a predominantly Western musical tradition. The indigenous song-form is both Italianate in names (*kantádhes, ariétes, arékia*), instrumentation (guitar and mandolin – as in Captain Corelli's) and vocals (harmonized choir). Style and nomenclature differ subtly between the various islands: the equivalent of *ariétes* on Kefaloniá is known as *arékia* on Zákynthos. All of the Ionians, especially Corfu, have a tradition of formal musical instruction and excellence.

The **rizítika** of Crete, slow elegies for historic events and personages with a bare minimum of instrumentation, are confined to the foothill villages of the Lefká Óri (White Mountains); over six hundred bodies of lyrics have been collected, but it's claimed that there are only 34 distinct melodies. Also Cretan are *tragoúdhia tís strátas* or travelling songs, sung a capella in pre-motor-car days to ease the boredom of long journeys between villages.

Many songs (except for the slow table songs, or *epitrapézia*, of which Cretan *rizítika* are a type) are in **dance rhythm**, with a vital interaction between dancers and musicians/ singers. Dancers and listeners may also join in the song (solo or as a chorus), or even initiate verses. It is customary for the lead dancer to tip the musicians, often requesting a particular tune and/or dance rhythm for his party to dance to. Fairly similar dances for couples are called *soústa* in Crete but *bállos* across the rest of the Aegean. The *pendozális* of Crete ("five-step", *zála* being Cretan dialect for step) is an easy, slow-starting dance for all abilities, though the *pidhiktós* "jumping" dance requires more acrobatic ability.

The instruments

The violin (**violí** in Greek) supposedly appeared in Greece during the seventeenth century, migrating from Western Europe (followed some decades later by the clarinet, featuring mainly in mainland Greek music). Although the violin is also played on the Greek mainland, it is the principal melody instrument of the Aegean islands, with the striking exceptions of Crete, Kárpathos, Kássos and Hálki in the southern Aegean, where two kinds of *lýra* prevail (see p.552). The violin bridge may be sanded in Greece to a less highly arched form than that used for Western classical music (this is also done in Western folk traditions). An alternative **tuning** known as "*álla Toúrka*", more widespread in the past, is still used by some musicians on certain islands (eg Sífnos, Kýthnos and Kos). From high to low, its string values are D, A, D and G, with a fourth between the two higher-pitched strings instead of the typical all-fifths arrangement. The lowered high string is slacker and "sweeter", and the violin's tonality altered by the modified tuning.

Playing **styles** vary widely within island groups (or even between villages) but Greek violin technique differs radically from both classical and Western folk styles. Modes (related to both the Byzantine and Ottoman musical systems) are used rather than Western scales, there's a range of ornamentation techniques, and, in some places, unmetered solos (called *taxímia*) based upon the mode of the melody and subject to modulation into other modes. Idiosyncratic violin styles are still found on Sífnos or Kýthnos in the Cyclades, and on Kálymnos or Kos in the Dodecanese, with a few of the finest old-style performers only fairly recently deceased (eg Andonis Xanthakis and Andonis Mougadhis Komis in Sífnos). Bowing patterns in these places can be swift and angular, resulting in a more "fiddle"-like sound than styles that rely on smoother, longer bow-strokes.

The **laoúto** is a member of a family of instruments generally referred to as long-necked lutes. It has a fat, gourd-like back like the oud (*oúti* in Greek, *al-ud* in Arabic) from which the *laoúto* (and lute) derives its name and basic form, but a long fretted neck (the oud has a short, unfretted one) and four sets of double metal strings (the oud has gut ones). The Greek *laoúto* is tuned in fifths (C, G, D, A from lowest to highest), but the G actually has the lowest pitch, since the C is anomalously tuned a fourth higher than the G. On Sífnos and Kýthnos the heavier of the lowest-pitched doublet is removed to accentuate the treble, and make the *laoúto*'s sound less "thunderous".

In most of the Aegean, the *laoúto* is played with the *violí* or *lýra* and sometimes also with the island bagpipe, the *tsamboúna* (see below). Typical duos are *violí/laoúto* in the Cyclades or *lýra/laoúto* in Crete and the Dodecanese. In north Aegean islands (such as Lésvos and Samothráki) the *laoúto* may be played with violin and *sandoúri* or even in large ensembles which include brass instruments and accordion. In the hands of a competent player, the *laoúto* doesn't merely "accompany" a *violí* or *lýra*, but forms part of a true duo by virtue of well-chosen rhythmic patterns and melodic phrases in chime-like tones.

The **sandoúri** is a member of the zither family, resembling the hammered dulcimer and played with the *violí* (or *violí* plus *laoúto*) in many of the Dodecanese and also the northeast Aegean islands, where it may also appear in much larger ensembles. It entered these island groups from nearby Asia Minor, especially after 1923 when it was (re)introduced by refugees, especially on Lésvos. The *sandoúri* plays both chords and melody, as well as introductory *taxímia*. While at times only basic chords are played to complement the violin, it can fill in with arpeggios, scale runs or melodic tags, and occasionally serves as a solo instrument, especially on Lésvos.

The term **lýra** refers to a family of small, pear- or bottle-shaped instruments which are held upright on the player's thigh with strings facing forward and bowed with the palm facing away from the body. Greek-island types are pear-shaped and have three metal strings, with notes played by pressing the fingernails laterally against the strings. The **Dodecanesian lýra** has a loose bow which can touch all three gut strings (the middle one a drone) simultaneously, making double chords possible; the bow in some cases has little bells on it which provide rhythmic accompaniment. Its tonal range matches that of the *tsamboúna* played in the Dodecanese and can be played alone, with *laoúto*, with *tsamboúna*, or both of these together, often accompanying vocalists. The **Cretan lýra** is a relatively modern instrument, having supplanted the Dodecanesian type which was used on Crete before the 1930s. The contemporary *lýra* is larger and fatter, lacks a drone string and is tuned lower and in successive fifths, thus extending the melodic range by a fifth beyond that of the older instrument. A fingerboard was added to make fingering easier, as well as a longer, narrow neck, and a modern violin bow replaced the older, more convex bow. Yet despite all these violin-like innovations, the *lýra* retains a very different tonal quality; even a skilled violinist can never entirely imitate its sound.

The **tsamboúna** (in Crete, *askomandoúra*) is a Greek-island bagpipe made of goatskin, with no drone and two chanters made of calamus reed. The left chanter never varies, having five holes which allow an incomplete diatonic scale from "do" to "fa". The right chanter is of three types, with anywhere from two to five holes depending on the locale. In the Dodecanese this bagpipe may be played alone, with another *tsamboúna*, or with a *laoúto* and *lýra*; many songs are accompanied by these various combinations. In the Cyclades (and formerly Híos) the *tsamboúna* is (or was) played with a **toumbáki** or two-headed drum, only one side of which is struck with two wooden (or bone) drumsticks. It is suspended to one side of the player's torso by a strap. The *tsamboúna* and *toumbáki* are quintessential shepherds' instruments, their skins taken from their flocks. Along with the *lýra*, they are the oldest of the instruments played on the islands, though rare now except in some of the places mentioned above. On Náxos the *tsamboúna-toumbáki* duo is still heard during the pre-Lenten Carnival.

Accordion, clarinet, guitar and *bouzoúki*, all **imported** from the Greek mainland or urban traditions, are sometimes played along with the more traditional instruments on the islands.

Discography

The following CDs are among the best available for the island genres detailed above: ★ denotes a particularly strong recommendation. Unless otherwise specified, all are Greek pressings. Athens has numerous good Greek CD stores. Online, you'll find some of our choices at Amazon, but rather more at Thessaloníki-based Studio 52 (⊕www.studio52.gr), which operates a worldwide online order service.

COLLECTIONS

★**Avthentika Nisiotika tou Peninda** (Lyra CD 0168). Good Cretan and Dodecanesian material recorded during the 1950s, from the collection of the late Ted Petrides, musician and dance master.

Ellines Akrites (FM Records). FM's folk pressings are generally to be approached with caution, but Vol. 1 of this 12-CD series (FM 801, "Híos, Mytilíni, Sámos, Ikaría"), Vol. 2 (FM 802, "Límnos, Samothráki, Ímvros, Ténedhos") and Vol. 9 ("Pátmos, Kálymnos, Léros, Kos, Astypálea") feature excellent local musicians (violí/lýra) and singers such as Stratis Rallis of Lésvos, as well as violinist Kyriakos Gouvendas of Thessaloníki and the late Gavriel Yiallizis of Kos.

Kalimera Theia – Samothrakiki Skopi ke Tragoudia/Good Morning Auntie – Tunes and Songs of Samothraki (Arheio Ellinikis Musikis-AEM 014). The local repertoire from this north Aegean island, as well as pieces from neighbouring islands and Asia Minor.

Kasos: Skopi tis Lyras/Lyra Tunes (Lyra 0113; may be deleted). A 1990s collection from the bleakest, but one of the more musical, of the Dodecanese.

★**Tis Kritis ta Polytima** (MBI 7056). Double box-set showcasing the best Cretan talent since the 1980s by Lyra/MBI artists, all the more valuable given that many of the source discs are now out of circulation. Mostly big names whom you're likely to see in concert: Vasilis Skhoulas, Yiorgo Xylouris, Lizeta Kalimeri, Psarantonis. Avoid the inferior single-disc offering.

Tis Lerou ta Tragoudhia/Songs of Leros (Politistikós ké Morfotikós Sýllogos Néon Lérou/Instructive & Cultural Lerian Youth Society), double CD produced by Music Folklore Archive. Live field recordings from 1996–98 of Lerian musicians and singers; violí, sandoúri, laoúto and bagpipes in various combinations, plus unaccompanied singing.

★**Lesvos Aiolis: Tragoudhia ke Hori tis Lesvou/ Songs & Dances of Lesvos** (Panepistimiakés Ekdhóseis Krítis/University Press of Crete, double CD 9/10). Two decades (1974–96) of field recordings of this island's last traditional music, a labour of love supervised by musicologist Nikos Dhionysopoulos. Expensive, but the quality and uniqueness of the instrumental festival tunes and dances especially, and the illustrated booklet, merit the expense (typically around €30).

Lesvos: Mousika Stavrodhromia sto Egeo/Musical Crossroads of the Aegean (University of the Aegean).

Pricey five-CD set with an accompanying fat, illustrated booklet. Everything from originally Asia Minor music to carols and wedding songs.

★**ly Protomastores, 1920–1955** (⊕www.aerakis .net; 10-CD set). Some of the artists on this massive retrospective of early Cretan recordings are a bit arcane, but the following four standout discs justify the price tag: Disc 1, Baxevanis, on lýra with small orchestra; Disc 4, Stelios Fousaleris, last master of the voúlgari, knowledge of which died with him; Disc 5, Yiannis Demirtzoyiannis, guitarist and epic singer; and Disc 6, Yiorgis Kousourelis, melodic laoúto.

Seryiani sta Nisia Mas, Vol. 1 (MBI 10371). An excellent retrospective of various nisiótika hits and artists, mostly from the 1950s. The highlight of Vol. 1 (2 doesn't exist) is Emilia Hatzidhaki's rendering of "Bratséra".

Skopi tis Kalymnou/Kalymnian Folk Music (Lýkio tón Ellinídhon E2-276-97). Double CD with excellent notes and song translations. Traditional Kalymnian repertoire and native musicians featuring Mikes Tsounias on violin, his grandson playing unison violin on some pieces, plus tsamboúna accompaniment.

Skopi kai Tragoudhia apo tin Apirantho tis Naxou (Aperathítikos Sýllogos TC-CP957). 1983 recording from the famous Náxos mountain village of Apíranthos, featuring Yiannis Zevgolis (violin) with singer Koula Klironomou-Sidheri, Yiorgos Karapatis on laoúto, plus others on guitar and tsamboúna. Beautiful renditions of traditional Naxian music, with many wistful and nostalgic songs from a past era.

Songs of ...(Society for the Dissemination of National Music, Greece). A thirty-disc-plus series of field recordings from the 1950s–70s, each covering traditional music of one region or type. Lyrics in English, all available in CD form, especially at the Museum of Greek Popular Instruments in Athens. The best island discs, besides Amorgos, Kythnos and Sifnos (SDNM105), are:

Songs of Kassos and Karpathos (SDNM 103). The Kárpathos side is unremittingly poignant (or monotonous, depending on your tastes), enlivened by passages on the tsamboúna. You'll still hear material like this at Ólymbos festivals. The Kássos side is more sweetly melodic, closer to Crete musically and geographically.

Songs of Rhodes, Chalki and Symi (SDNM 104). The pieces from Sými are the most accessible, while those from Rhodes and Hálki show Cretan influence. All material was recorded in the early 1970s; you're unlikely to hear similar pieces today, though Sými retains the instrumentation (*violí, sandoúri*) heard here.

★ **Songs of Mytilene and Chios** (SDNM 110), **Songs of Mytilene and Asia Minor** (SDNM 125). The Mytilene (Lésvos) sides are the highlight of each of these discs. Sublime instrumental and vocal pieces, again from the mid-1970s. Most selections are from the south of the island, particularly Ayiássos, where a tradition of live festival music was – and still is – strong.

Songs of Ikaria & Samos (SDNM 128). Much older material, from the 1950s; even then it was obvious that indigenous styles were dying out, as there is extensive reliance on cover versions of songs common to all the east Aegean and Anatolian refugee communities, and the music – mostly choral with string accompaniment – is executed by the SDNM house band of the time, directed by Simon Karas. The Ikarian side is more distinctive, though marred by an irritating voice-over.

Songs of the North and East Aegean (SDNM CD7). Features music of Límnos, Thássos, Samothráki, Lésvos and Híos including local dances (*pyrgoúsikos, kehayiádhikos*) using local musicians recorded during the early 1970s.

★ **Thalassa Thymisou/Sea of Memories: Tragoudhia ke Skopi apo tis Inousses** (Navtikó Mousío Inoussón-En Khordais CD 1801/1802). The result of a "field trip" by the En Khordais traditional music school of Thessaloníki to Inoússes, a small islet northeast of Híos, to rescue vanishing material with the help of the islanders' long memories; the result's superb, a mix of live sessions in Inoussan tavernas and some studio recordings. Thorough, intelligent notes, but no lyrics translations.

Tragoudhia ke Skopi tis Patmou/Songs and Melodies of Patmos (Politistikón Ídhryma Dhodhekanísou 201). Live 1995 field recordings of well-edited pieces, as raw but compelling as you'd hear them at an old-time festival. Local singers and instrumentalists on *violí, tsamboúna* and *sandoúri*.

INDIVIDUAL ARTISTS/GROUPS

Anna Karabesini & Efi Sarri CD reissues from old LPs: *Yialo Yialo Piyeno* (Lyra 0102067), *Tis Thalassas* (Lyra 10777) and *Ena Glenti* (Lyra 10717). Two singing sisters from the island of Kos, who were for the Dodecanese what the **Konitopoulos family** (see next entry) was for the Cyclades; that they performed only for private gatherings added to their cachet.

Irini Konitopoulou-Legaki *Athanata Nisiotika 1* (Tzina-Astir 1020). A 1978 warhorse, beloved of bus drivers across the islands. *Anefala Thalassina* (Lyra 4693) from 1993 is far less commercial than the usual Konitopoulous-clan offerings and one of the finest recordings from Náxos, featuring Naxian *lautiéris* Dhimitris Fyroyenis and Yiannis Zevgolis, one of the last old-style violinists. Then aged 61, Irini sung her heart out in a richer, deeper voice than she was known for on club stages.

★ **Argyris Kounadis** *Kefalonitikes Arietes* (Philips 526 492-2). Sweet without being syrupy, this is one of the very few still in-print collections of traditional vocal music from Kefaloniá (indeed from any of the Ionians); largely songs composed by Kounadis.

★ **Nikos Oikonomidis** *Perasma stin Amorgo/Passage to Amorgos* (Keros Music CD 101). A native of Skhinoússa islet, violinist and *lautiéris* Oikonomidis plays and sings traditional pieces from nearby Amorgós on this 2001 recording, with guest appearances by Yiasemi Saragoudha, wife of the great oudist, and folklorist Domna Samiou. His latest (2006) outing, *Antikeri*, is all-acoustic, with Oikonomidis's own compositions and lyrics.

★ **Andonis Xylouris (Psarantonis)** *Palio Krasi In'ïy Skepsi Mou* and *Idheon Antron* (both Lyra MBI). Psarantonis – shunned by other Cretan musicians as too "out there" – has an idiosyncratically spare and percussive *lýra* style, but here unusual instruments are well integrated into a densely textured whole. Daughter Niki, now a star in her own right, executes a gorgeous rendition of "Meraklídhiko Poulí" on *Idheon Antron*, and also proves a highlight of Psarantonis's 2008 latest, *Mountain Rebels* (Network/Raki 495123), especially on "Kimáte o Ílios sta Vouná" and "Neraïdhas Yié", with brothers Yiorgos and Lambis on *laoúto* and oud respectively.

Nikos Xylouris *O Arkhangelos tis Kritis, 1958–1968* (MBI 10376); *Ta Khronia stin Kriti* (2CD, MBI 10677/78). The best two retrospectives of the sweet-voiced Cretan singer (Andonis's brother), in traditional mode, with copious notes; the first covers his initial decade of recordings before he became a noted *éntekhno* (art music) star, with self-accompaniment on the *lýra*.

★ **Ziyia** (now reformed as **Edessa**) Fine arrangements and singing, by a five-member American group who simply run rings around most native-Greek session musicians. Their first outing, *From the Mountains to the Islands* (AgaRhythm, 1992), has more island music than *Travels with Karaghiozis* (AgaRhythm, 1995), which does, however, include a lovely song from Kálymnos. Available through ⓦ www.edessamusic.com or ⓦ www.ziyia.com.

Books

The best books in this selection are marked by a ★ symbol; titles currently out of print are indicated as "o/p". Recommended specialist Greek booksellers include, in the UK, the Hellenic Bookservice (ⓦhellenicbookservice.com) and, in Canada, Kalamos Books (ⓦkalamosbooks.com).

TRAVEL/IMPRESSIONS

James Theodore Bent *Aegean Islands: The Cyclades, or Life Among the Insular Greeks*. Originally published in 1881, this remains an authoritative account of Greek island customs and folklore, gleaned from a long winter's travel in the archipelago.

Charmian Clift *Mermaid Singing* (o/p). Clift and family's experiences living on 1950s Kálymnos – among the first postwar expats to do so. Last reissued around the millennium, it's easily found; her *Peel Me a Lotus*, about a subsequent sojourn on Ýdhra, may also appeal, and is often co-bound with *Mermaid Singing*.

Charles Cockerell *Travels in Greece*. Cockerell arrived in Greece in 1810, stayed four years, engaged in archeological pillaging typical of the era – which he recounts with extraordinary insouciance – and had more adventures on islands and mainland than he bargained for.

★ **Gerald Durrell** *My Family and Other Animals*. Delightful evocation of Durrell's 1930s childhood on Corfu, where his family settled, and where he developed a passion for the island's fauna while elder brother Lawrence entertained Henry Miller and others.

Lawrence Durrell *Prospero's Cell* and *Reflections on a Marine Venus*. The former constitutes Durrell's Corfu memoirs, from his time there as World War II loomed. *Marine Venus* recounts his 1945–47 colonial-administrator experiences of Rhodes and other Dodecanese islands.

Peter France *A Place of Healing for the Soul: Patmos*. A former BBC film-maker, France settled on Pátmos with his Greek Orthodox wife, and slowly adopted her faith. More spiritual than travel journey – albeit marred by unsound theology – but island life is nicely observed, too.

★ **Roger Jinkinson** *Tales from a Greek Island*. Twenty-eight related tales, long and short, set in and around Dhiafáni, Kárpathos (identified cryptically as "The Village"), by turns poignant, revisionist about World War II heroics or blackly funny. The We (The Villagers, among whom part-time resident Jinkinson counts himself) vs. Them (tourists) tone can grate, but he's been there and done it, with special insight into the mysterious craft of Aegean fishing.

★ **Elias Kulukundis** *The Feasts of Memory: Stories of a Greek Family*. A journey back through time and genealogy by a diaspora Greek two generations removed from Kássos, poorest of the Dodecanese. A 2003 re-release, with an extra chapter, of his 1967 classic *Journey to a Greek Island*.

Edward Lear *The Corfu Years and The Cretan Journal*. Highly entertaining journals from the 1840s and 1850s, beautifully illustrated with watercolours and sketches.

John Lucas *92 Acharnon Street*. Beautifully told tale of a British poet who moves to Athens in the mid-Eighties to teach literature, and gets hooked – not on the glories of the ancients, but on modern Greece, specifically its poets, tavernas, politics and foibles; plenty on Égina, his preferred island retreat, as well.

★ **Willard Manus** *This Way to Paradise: Dancing on the Tables*. American expat's memoir of nearly four decades in Líndhos, Rhodes, beginning long before its submersion in tourism. Wonderful period detail, including bohemian excesses and cameos from such as S.J. Perelman, Germaine Greer and Martha Gellhorn.

Christopher Merrill *Things of the Hidden God: Journey to the Holy Mountain*. Merrill, an accomplished poet and journalist, first came to Áthos in the wake of a traumatic time reporting on the breakup of Yugoslavia. With fine black-and-white photographs, this is probably the best contemporary take on Áthos, and Orthodoxy.

Henry Miller *The Colossus of Maroussi*. Corfu, Crete, Athens and the soul of Greece in 1939, with Miller completely in his element; funny, sensual and transporting.

Dilys Powell *The Villa Ariadne*. 1950s account of the British in Crete, from Arthur Evans to Patrick Leigh Fermor, viewed through the prism of the villa at Knossos which hosted all of them. Brings early archeological work to life, but rather syrupy style.

Tom Stone *The Summer of My Greek Taverna*. Enjoyable cautionary tale for those fantasizing about a new life in the Aegean sun. Moving to Pátmos in the early 1980s, Stone tries to mix friendship and business at a beach taverna, with predictable (for onlookers anyway) results.

Richard Stoneman, ed *A Literary Companion to Travel in Greece*. Ancient and medieval authors, plus Grand Tourists – an excellent selection.

★ **Patricia Storace** *Dinner with Persephone*. A New York poet, resident for a year in Athens (with forays to the provinces, including Corfu) puts the country's 1990s psyche on the couch. Storace has a sly humour and an interesting take on Greece's "imprisonment" in its imagined past.

John L. Tomkinson, ed *Travellers' Greece: Memories of an Enchanted Land*. Seventeenth- to nineteenth-century (mostly English) travellers' impressions of islands and mainland, ranging from the enraptured to the appalled; ideal for dipping into.

William Travis *Bus Stop Symi* (o/p). Chronicles three years' residence there in the mid-Sixties; fairly insightful (if rather resented on the island itself for its inaccuracies), though Travis erroneously prophesied that Sými would never see tourism.

Sarah Wheeler *Evia: Travels on an Undiscovered Island*. Entertaining, re-issued chronicle of a five-month ramble through Évvia, juxtaposing meditations on culture and history with an open approach to nuns, goatherds or academics. The main quibble is her success in making the island seem more exotic than it really is.

FICTION

FOREIGN FICTION

★ **Louis de Bernières** *Captain Corelli's Mandolin*. Set on Kefaloniá during the World War II occupation and aftermath, this accomplished 1994 tragi-comedy acquired cult, then bestseller, status in the UK and US. But in Greece it provoked a scandal, once islanders, Greek Left intellectuals and surviving Italian partisans woke up to its virulent disparaging of ELAS. It seems the novel was based on the experiences of Amos Pampaloni, an artillery captain on Kefalonià in 1942–44 who later joined ELAS, and who accused De Bernières of distorting the roles of both Italians and ELAS on the island. The Greek translation was abridged to avoid causing offence.

Meaghan Delahunt *To The Island* Novel of an Australian woman travelling with her young son to Náxos, to meet the father she has never met, and encountering also his past, as a political activist tortured by the junta. Not your usual travelogue.

Oriana Fallaci *A Man* (o/p). Gripping tale of the junta years, based on the author's involvement with Alekos Panagoulis, the army officer who attempted to assassinate Colonel Papadopoulos in 1968 – and who himself died in mysterious circumstances in 1975.

★ **John Fowles** *The Magus*. Fowles' biggest and best tale of mystery and manipulation – plus Greek island life – based on his stay on Spétses as a teacher during the 1950s. A period piece that repays revisiting.

Peter Green *The Laughter of Aphrodite*. Historical novel, originally published in 1965, by a distinguished classicist, which re-creates the life and times of Sappho on ancient Lesbos.

Victoria Hislop *The Island; The Thread*. The former leper colony of Spinalonga forms the backdrop to *The Island*, a huge-selling novel about a young woman discovering her Cretan roots. A potentially good story is marred by the cloying, derivative nature of its telling. *The Thread* attempts a similar uncovering of little-known history interwoven with family secrets, set in Thessaloníki.

Olivia Manning *The Balkan Trilogy, Volume 3: Friends and Heroes*. Wonderfully observed tale, in which Guy and Harriet Pringle escape from Bucharest to Athens, in the last months before the 1941 invasion.

Steven Pressfield *Gates of Fire; Alexander: The Virtues of War*. Two of several Greek-set historical novels by Pressfield. *Gates of Fire*, his bestselling first, is a stirring tale of the Spartans at Thermopylae; later books, including *The Virtues of War* – in which Alexander the Great recounts his warrior's life to brother-in-law Itanes in a first-person narrative – are rather more measured.

Evelyn Waugh *Officers and Gentlemen*. This second volume of Waugh's brilliant, acerbic wartime trilogy includes an account of the Battle of Crete and subsequent evacuation.

GREEK FICTION

★ **Apostolos Doxiadis** *Uncle Petros and Goldbach's Conjecture*. Uncle Petros is the disgraced family black sheep, living reclusively in outer Athens; his nephew discovers that Petros had staked everything to solve a theorem unsolved for centuries. Math-phobes take heart; it's more a

GREEK POETRY

Modern Greece has an intense and dynamic poetic tradition. Two Greek poets – George Seféris and Odysseus Elýtis – have won the Nobel prize for literature; along with C.P. Caváfy, from an earlier generation, and Yiánnis Rítsos they are the great names of modern Greek poetry. Good English translations of pretty much all of their work are widely available, or try these anthologies:

Peter Bien, Peter Constantine, Edmund Keeley, Karen Van Dyck, eds *A Century of Greek Poetry, 1900–2000* (o/p). Superb bilingual anthology, with some lesser-known surprises alongside the big names.

Nanos Valaoritis and Thanasis Maskaleris, eds *An Anthology of Modern Greek Poetry*. English-only text, but excellent biographical info on the poets and good translations by two native Greek-speakers.

THE CLASSICS

Many of the classics make excellent companions for a trip around Greece; reading Homer's Odyssey when battling the vagaries of island ferries puts your own plight into perspective. Most of these good beginners' choices are published in a range of paperback editions. Particularly outstanding translations are noted.

★ **Mary Beard and John Henderson** *The Classics: A Very Short Introduction.* Exactly as it promises: an excellent overview.

Herodotus *The Histories.* Revered as the father of narrative history – and anthropology – this fifth-century BC Anatolian writer chronicled both the causes and campaigns of the Persian Wars, as well as the assorted tribes and nations inhabiting Asia Minor.

★ **Homer** *The Iliad* and *The Odyssey.* The first concerns itself, semi-factually, with the late Bronze Age war of the Achaeans against Troy in Asia Minor; the second recounts the hero Odysseus's long journey home, via seemingly every corner of the Mediterranean. The best prose translations are by Martin Hammond, and in verse Richmond Lattimore. For a stirring, if very loose, verse *Iliad*, try also Christopher Logue's recent version, *War Music.*

Ovid *The Metamorphoses.* Ovid was a first-century AD Roman poet, but his masterpiece includes accessible renditions of the more piquant Greek myths, involving transformations as divine blessing or curse. Excellent verse translation by David Raeburn; prose version A.D. Melville.

Pausanias *The Guide to Greece.* Effectively the first-ever guidebook, intended for Roman pilgrims to central mainland and Peloponnesian sanctuaries. Invaluable for later archeologists in assessing damage or change to temples over time, or (in some cases) locating them at all. The two-volume Penguin edition is usefully annotated with the later history and nomenclature of the sites.

★ **Thucydides** *History of the Peloponnesian War.* Bleak month-by-month account of the conflict, by a cashiered Athenian officer whose affiliation and dim view of human nature didn't usually obscure his objectivity.

Xenophon *The History of My Times.* Thucydides' account of the Peloponnesian War stops in 411 BC; this eyewitness account continues events until 362 BC.

meditation on how best to spend life, and what really constitutes success.

Vangelis Hatziyannidis Hatziyannidis' abiding obsessions – confinement, blackmail, abrupt disappearances – get a workout in his creepy debut novel *Four Walls*, set on an unspecified east Aegean isle, where a reclusive landowner takes in a fugitive woman and convinces him to revive his father's honey trade – with unexpected consequences. His next novel, *Stolen Time*, revisits the same themes as an impoverished student gets a tidy fee from a mysterious tribunal for agreeing to spend two weeks in the Hotel from Hell.

★ **Panos Karnezis** Karnezis has become the most accessible, and feted, Greek writer since the millennium. He grew up in Greece but now lives in London, writing in English; however, his concerns remain utterly Greek. *Little Infamies* is a collection of short stories set in his native Peloponnese during the late 1950s and early 1960s; *The Maze* is a darker-shaded, more successful novel concerning the Asia Minor Catastrophe. More recent works include *The Birthday Party*, based on events in the life of Aristotle Onassis and daughter Christina, and *The Convent*, a gentle whodunnit with nuns.

Nikos Kazantzakis *Zorba the Greek; The Last Temptation of Christ; Christ Recrucified/The Greek Passion; Freedom and Death; The Fratricides; Report to Greco.* Kazantzakis can be hard going, yet the power of his writing shines through.

Zorba the Greek is a dark, nihilistic work, worlds away from the two-dimensional film. By contrast, the movie version of *The Last Temptation of Christ* – specifically Jesus's vision, once crucified, of a normal life with Mary Magdalene – provoked riots among Orthodox fanatics in Athens in 1989. *Christ Recrucified* (*The Greek Passion*) resets the Easter drama against the backdrop of Christian/Muslim relations, while *Freedom and Death*, perhaps his most approachable, chronicles the rebellions of nineteenth-century Crete. *The Fratricides* portrays a family riven by the civil war. *Report to Greco* is an autobiographical exploration of his Cretan-ness.

Artemis Leontis (ed) *Greece: A Traveler's Literary Companion.* A nice idea, brilliantly executed: various regions of the country as portrayed in (very) short fiction or essays by modern Greek writers.

Alexandros Papadiamantis *Tales from a Greek Island; The Murderess.* The island is Skiáthos, Papadiamantis' birthplace. These quasi-mythic tales of grim fate come from a nineteenth-century writer ("the inventor of modern Greek fiction") comparable to Hardy and Maupassant.

★ **Dido Sotiriou** *Farewell Anatolia.* A perennial favourite since publication in 1962, this chronicles the traumatic end of Greek life in Asia Minor, from World War I to the 1922 catastrophe, as narrated by a fictionalized version of Sotiriou's father.

ANCIENT GREECE

A.R. Burn *Penguin History of Greece*. A classic account; packed and informative on everything from philosophy to military history.

Paul Cartledge *Cambridge Illustrated History of Ancient Greece* or *Ancient Greece: A Very Short Introduction*. Two excellent general introductions to ancient Greece; choose between brief paperback or large illustrated tome.

★ **Paul Cartledge** *The Spartans: The World of the Warrior-Heroes of Ancient Greece*. Reassessment of this much-maligned city-state, secretive and a source of outsider speculation even in its own time.

Paul Cartledge *Alexander the Great: The Hunt for a New Past*. An evocative, meticulous and accessible biography, stinting neither on the man's brutality nor his achievements.

Simon Hornblower *The Greek World 479–323 BC*. An erudite, up-to-date survey of ancient Greece at its zenith, from the end of the Persian Wars to the death of Alexander.

★ **M.I. Finley** *The World of Odysseus*. Reprint of a 1954 warhorse, pioneering in its investigation of the historicity (or not) of the events and society related by Homer. Breezily readable and stimulating.

Oswyn Murray *Early Greece*. The story of Greece from the Minoans and Mycenaeans through to the beginning of the Classical period.

Robin Osborne *Greece in the Making 1200–479 BC*. Well-illustrated paperback on the rise of the city-state.

F.W. Walbank *The Hellenistic World*. Greece under the sway of the Macedonian and Roman empires.

MEDIEVAL AND MODERN GREECE

Timothy Boatswain and Colin Nicolson *A Traveller's History of Greece*. Well-written overview of crucial Greek periods and personalities, from earliest times to the end of the twentieth century.

★ **Richard Clogg** *A Concise History of Greece*. If you read only one title on "modern" Greek history, this should be it: a remarkably clear account, from the decline of Byzantium to 2000, with numerous maps and feature captions to the well-chosen artwork.

C.M. Woodhouse *Modern Greece: A Short History*. Woodhouse was a key liaison officer with the Greek Resistance during World War II, and later a Conservative MP. Writing from a more right-wing perspective than Clogg, his account – from the foundation of Constantinople to 1990 – is briefer and drier, but scrupulous with facts.

BYZANTINE, MEDIEVAL AND OTTOMAN GREECE

David Brewer *Greece, the Hidden Centuries: Turkish Rule from the Fall of Constantinople to Greek Independence*. Readable yet authoritative history of this little-explored era of Greek history.

Nicholas Cheetham *Medieval Greece* (o/p). A general survey of the period's infinite convolutions in Greece, with Frankish, Catalan, Venetian, Byzantine and Ottoman struggles for power.

★ **Roger Crowley** *Constantinople: The Last Great Siege, 1453*. Thrillingly readable narrative of perhaps the key event of the Middle Ages, and its repercussions throughout Europe and the Islamic world.

Paul Hetherington *The Greek Islands: Guide to Byzantine and Medieval Buildings and Their Art*. A readable, well-illustrated and authoritative gazetteer to most island monuments of the period, though there are some peculiar omissions.

★ **John Julius Norwich** *Byzantium: The Early Centuries; Byzantium: the Apogee* and *Byzantium: The Decline*. Perhaps the main surprise for first-time travellers to Greece is the fascination of its Byzantine monuments. This is an astonishingly detailed yet readable – often witty – trilogy of the empire that produced them. There's also an excellent, one-volume abridged version, *A Short History of Byzantium*.

INDEPENDENT GREECE

★ **John S. Koliopoulos and Thanos M. Veremis** *Greece: The Modern Sequel, from 1831 to the Present*. Thematic rather than chronological study that pokes into corners rarely illuminated by conventional histories; especially good on Macedonian issues, brigandage and the Communists.

David Brewer *The Flame of Freedom: The Greek War of Independence 1821–1833* (o/p). The finest narrative of revolutionary events (with some black-and-white illustrations), strong on the background of Ottoman Greece as well as the progress of the war.

★ **Michael Llewellyn Smith** *Ionian Vision: Greece in Asia Minor, 1919–22*. Still the best work on the disastrous Anatolian campaign, which led to the population exchanges between Greece and Turkey.

WORLD WAR II AND THE CIVIL WAR

★ **Antony Beevor** *Crete: The Battle and the Resistance*. The historian best known for his Stalingrad and Berlin epics actually made his debut with this short 1992 study, which first aired the theory that Crete was allowed to fall by the British to conceal the fact that they'd cracked the Germans' Enigma code, in order to win the more strategic campaign in North Africa.

Winston Churchill *The Second World War, Vol. 5: Closing the Ring*. Includes the Allied Aegean campaigns, with detailed coverage of battles on and around Rhodes, Léros, Sámos and Kos.

Alan Clark *The Fall of Crete*. Racy and sensational military history by the late maverick English politician, if less

BOOKS FOR KIDS

The Greek myths and legends are perfect holiday reading for kids; they're available in a huge number of versions aimed at all ages, often lavishly illustrated.

Terry Deary *Groovy Greeks; Greek Tales* and the *Fire Thief* trilogy. The first of these is from Deary's familiar Horrible Histories series; the three books of *Greek Tales* take a sideways look at famous myths; the *Fire Thief* is a comedy-fantasy series based on Prometheus, who stole fire from the gods.

Caroline Lawrence *The Roman Mysteries*. The final two volumes of this authentically detailed series of Roman-era mystery books for 8- to 11-year-olds, *The Colossus of Rhodes* and *Fugitive from Corinth*, are set in Greece.

Mary Renault *The King Must Die; The Last of the Wine; The Masks of Apollo; The Praise Singer; The Alexander*

Trilogy. The style may be a tad dense and dated, but these retellings of great Greek stories remain classics of historical fiction.

Rick Riordan *Percy Jackson* series. A modern setting infused with Greek mythology as Percy Jackson, twelve years old and dyslexic, discovers he is the modern-day son of a Greek god. Gripping, best-selling tales.

Franzcesca Simon *Helping Hercules*. Fans of *Horrid Henry* will enjoy this clever retelling of Greek myths by the same author, where young heroine Susan sorts out the not-so-heroic heroes.

---

thorough than Beevor's tome (and lacking maps). Detailed on the battles, and more critical of the command than you might expect from a former cabinet minister.

★ **David H. Close** *The Origins of the Greek Civil War*. Excellent, even-handed study that focuses on the social conditions in 1920s and 1930s Greece that made the country so ripe for conflict; draws on primary sources to overturn various received wisdoms.

★ **Mark Mazower** *Inside Hitler's Greece: The Experience of Occupation 1941–44*. Eccentrically organized, but the scholarship is top-drawer and the photos magnificent. Demonstrates how the utter demoralization of the country

and incompetence of conventional politicians led to the rise of ELAS and the onset of civil war.

Adrian Seligman *War in the Islands* (o/p). Collected oral histories of a little-known Allied unit: a flotilla of kaïkia organized to raid the Axis-held Aegean islands. Boy's Own stuff, with service-jargon-laced prose, but lots of fine period photos and detail.

★ **C.M. Woodhouse** *The Struggle for Greece, 1941–49*. Masterly, well-illustrated account of the so-called "three rounds" of resistance and rebellion, and how Greece emerged without a communist government.

RELIGION, ART AND ARCHEOLOGY

John Boardman *Greek Art*. An evergreen study in the *World of Art* series, first published in 1964. For more detailed treatment, there are three period volumes entitled *Greek Sculpture: Archaic Period, Classical Period* and *The Late Classical Period*.

★ **Walter Burkert** *Greek Religion: Archaic and Classical*. Superb overview of deities and their attributes and antecedents, the protocol of sacrifice and the symbolism of festivals. Especially good on relating Greek worship to its predecessors in the Middle East.

A.R. and Mary Burn *The Living Past of Greece: A Time Traveller's Tour of Historic and Prehistoric Places* (o/p). This wide-ranging guide covers sites from Minoan through to Byzantine and Frankish, with clear plans and lively text.

Costis Davaras *Guide to Cretan Antiquities* (Eptalofolos, Athens). A fascinating guide to the antiquities of Crete, by a distinguished archeologist. Cross-referenced in gazetteer form, it has authoritative articles on all major sites up to the Ottoman era, as well as topics as diverse as Minoan toilet articles and the disappearance of Cretan forests. Widely available at Cretan museums.

Reynold Higgins *Minoan and Mycenaean Art*. Concise, well-illustrated round-up of the culture of Mycenae, Crete and the Cyclades, again part of the *World of Art* series.

Mary Lefkowitz *Greek Gods, Human Lives: What We Can Learn from Myths*. Rather than being frivolous, immoral or irrelevant, ancient religion and its myths, in their bleak indifference of the gods to human suffering, are shown as being more "grown up" than the later creeds of salvation and comfort.

J. Alexander Macgillivray *Minotaur: Sir Arthur Evans and the Archaeology of the Minoan Myth*. Excellent monograph by a Crete-based archeologist showing how Evans fitted the evidence at Knossos to his own preconception of the Minoans as peaceful, literate and aesthetic second-millennium BC Victorians.

★ **Constantine E. Michaelides** *The Aegean Crucible: Tracing Vernacular Architecture in Post-Byzantine Centuries*. It's difficult to pigeonhole this sprawling, interdisciplinary study by a Greek-American architecture professor on how island settlements – especially the Cycladic *kástra*, Ýdhra, Santoríni, fortified monasteries – came to be as they are, drawing on history, geology, climatic influences, agriculture and popular religion. The text, erudite without being technical, is directly keyed to copious illustrations and maps.

★ **Oliver Rackham and Jennifer Moody** *The Making of the Cretan Landscape*. An impressive academic-press tome written for the casual visitor. It takes in geology, natural history, agricultural practices, place names, architecture and demography, all arranged by topic.

R.R.R. Smith *Hellenistic Sculpture*. Appraisal of the art of Greece under Alexander and his successors; yet another *World of Art* title.

James Witley *The Archaeology of Ancient Greece*. An excellent overview of current scholarship, not overly academic.

PEOPLE AND CULTURE

Juliet du Boulay *Portrait of a Greek Mountain Village*. Ambéli village on Évvia, during the 1960s: habits and customs of a bygone way of life in an absorbing narrative.

★ **Bruce Clark** *Twice a Stranger: How Mass Expulsion Forged Modern Greece and Turkey*. The build-up to and execution of the 1923 population exchanges, and how both countries are still digesting the experience eight-plus decades on. Compassionate and readable, especially the encounters with elderly refugees and oral histories.

Adam Hopkins *Crete: Its Past, Present and People* (o/p). Excellent general introduction to Cretan history and society with interesting detail on diverse topics like the Battle of Crete, daily life, mass tourism and herbology, though beginning to show its age (1977).

John Cuthbert Lawson *Modern Greek Folklore and Ancient Greek Religion: A Study in Survivals*. Exactly as it says: a fascinating, thorough study still applicable a century after first publication.

Michael Llewellyn Smith *The Great Island: A Study of Crete* (o/p). Long before he became a known scholar (and twice ambassador to Greece), Llewellyn Smith debuted with this fine volume emphasizing folk traditions, including a lengthy analysis of Cretan song.

Anthony J. Papalas *Rebels and Radicals: Icaria 1600–2000*. The lowdown on that most peculiar of mid-Aegean islands, delving into its Ottoman past, American diaspora links, unexpected Communist affiliations and recent touristic development.

David Sutton *Memories Cast in Stone: The Relevance of the Past in Everyday Life*. A 1990s ethnology of Kálymnos, where tenacious "traditional" practices such as dynamite-throwing *paniyíria* and dowry-collecting confront the new, pan-EU realities.

★ **John L. Tomkinson** *Festive Greece: A Calendar of Tradition*. Copiously photographed gazetteer by date of festivals and events; Christian, pagan, political or plain bizarre.

FOOD AND WINE

★ **Rosemary Barron** *Flavours of Greece*. The leading Greek cookbook – among many contenders – by an internationally recognized authority. Constantly reprinted, with over 250 recipes and background info.

Andrew Dalby *Siren Feasts: A History of Food and Gastronomy in Greece; Tastes of Byzantium: The Cuisine of a Legendary Empire*. *Siren Feasts* demonstrates just how little

Greek cuisine has changed in three millennia; also excellent on the introduction and etymology of common vegetables and herbs. *Tastes of Byzantium* adds the influences of Rome, Turkey and the Middle East.

Konstantinos Lazarakis *The Wines of Greece*. An excellent, up-to-2005 overview of what's happening in Greece's eleven recognized wine-producing regions.

ACTIVITIES

See also the Wildlife guides (p.549).

Lance Chilton Various walking pamphlets (ⓦ marengowalks.com). Small but thorough guides to the best walks on several islands, accompanied by three-colour maps.

★ **Loraine Wilson** *The High Mountains of Crete*. Nearly a hundred walks and treks, from easy to gruelling, by the doyenne of foreign trekking guides in Crete. Mostly in the White Mountains, but also Psilorítis and the Lasíthi range. Reliable directions, clear maps, enticing photos – but no index.

Rod Heikell *Greek Waters Pilot*. An indispensable reference for yachting in the Aegean or Ionian seas, updated in 2011; various regional sub-guides are available.

Greek

So many Greeks have lived or worked abroad that you will find English-speakers in the tiniest island village. Add the thousands attending language schools or working in the tourist industry – English is the lingua franca of most resorts – and it's easy to see how so many visitors return home having learned only minimal restaurant vocabulary. You can certainly get by this way but it isn't very satisfying, and the willingness and ability to say even a few words will transform your status from that of dumb "tourístas" to the more honourable one of "xénos/xéni", which can mean foreigner, traveller and guest all combined.

Learning basic Greek

Greek is not an easy language for English-speakers but it is a very beautiful one, and even a brief acquaintance will give you an idea of the debt owed to it by Western European languages. Greek **grammar** is predictably complicated; **nouns** are divided into three genders, all with different case endings in the singular and in the plural, and all adjectives and articles have to agree with these in gender, number and case. To simplify things, all adjectives are cited in the neuter form in the lists on the following pages. **Verbs** are even more complex; they're in two conjugations, in both active and passive voices, with passively constructed verbs often having transitive sense. As a novice, it's best to simply say what you want the way you know it, and dispense with the niceties.

TEACH-YOURSELF GREEK COURSES

Alison Kakoura and Karen Rich *Talk Greek* (book and 2 CDs). Probably the best in-print product for beginners' essentials, and for developing the confidence to try them.

Anne Farmakides *A Manual of Modern Greek, 1, for University Students*. If you have the discipline and motivation, this is among the best for learning proper, grammatical Greek.

Hara Garoufalia et al *Read & Speak Greek for Beginners* (book & CD). Unlike many quickie courses, this provides a good grammatical foundation.

David Holton et al *Greek: A Comprehensive Grammar of the Modern Language*. A bit technical, so not for rank beginners, but it covers almost every conceivable construction.

Aristarhos Matsukas *Teach Yourself Greek* (book and optional cassettes or CDs). Another complete course, touching on idiomatic expressions too.

PHRASEBOOKS AND DICTIONARIES

Rough Guide Greek Phrasebook Current, accurate and pocket-sized, with phrases that you'll actually need. The English–Greek section is transliterated, though the Greek–English part requires mastery of the Greek alphabet.

The Pocket Oxford Greek Dictionary J. T. Pring. A bit bulky for travel, but generally considered the best Greek–English, English–Greek paperback dictionary.

Collins Pocket Greek Dictionary Harry T. Hionides. Very nearly as complete as the *Pocket Oxford* and probably better value for money. The inexpensive *Collins Gem Greek Dictionary* (UK only) is palm-sized but identical in contents – the best day-pack choice.

The Greek alphabet: transliteration and accents

Besides the usual difficulties of learning a new language, Greek has an entirely separate **alphabet**. Despite initial appearances, this is in practice fairly easily mastered – a skill that will help enormously in getting around independently. In addition, certain combinations of letters have unexpected results. This book's **transliteration system** (see below) should help you make intelligible noises, but remember that the correct **stress** (marked throughout the book with an acute accent or sometimes dieresis) is crucial. With the right sounds but the wrong stress people will either fail to understand you, or else understand something quite different.

The **dieresis** (¨) is used in Greek over the second of two adjacent vowels to change the pronunciation; often in this book it can function as the primary stress. In the word *kaïki* (caique), the use of a dieresis changes the pronunciation from "keh-key" to "ka-ee-key". In the word *païdhákia* (lamb chops), the dieresis changes the sound of the first syllable from "peh" to "pah-ee", but in this case the primary stress is on the third syllable. It is also, uniquely among Greek accents, used on capital letters in signs and personal-name spellings in Greece, and we have followed this practice on our maps.

GREEK	TRANSLITERATION	PRONOUNCED
A, α	a	a as in father
B, β	v	v as in vet
Γ, γ	y/g	y as in yes except before consonants or a, o or ou when it's a breathy g, approximately as in gap
Δ, δ	dh	th as in then
E, ε	e	e as in get
Z, ζ	z	z sound
H, η	i	i as in ski
Θ, θ	th	th as in theme
I, ι	i	i as in ski
K, κ	k	k sound
Λ, λ	l	l sound
M, μ	m	m sound
N, ν	n	n sound
Ξ, ξ	x	ks sound, never z
O, o	o	o as in box
Π, π	p	p sound
P, ρ	r	r sound, lightly rolled as in Scottish
Σ, σ, ς	s	ss sound, except z before m or g
T, τ	t	t sound
Y, υ	y	i as in ski
Φ, φ	f	f sound
X, χ	h before vowels, denoted kh before consonants but pronounced the same	harsh h sound, like ch in loch
Ψ, ψ	ps	ps as in lips
Ω, ω	o	o as in box, indistinguishable from o

COMBINATIONS AND DIPHTHONGS

ΑΙ, αι	e	e as in get
ΑΥ, αυ	av/af	av before voiced consonants and vowels af before voiceless consonents
ΕΙ, ει	i	i as in ski
ΕΥ, ευ	ev/ef	ev before voiced consonants and vowels ef before voiceless consonents
ΟΙ, οι	i	i as in ski
ΟΥ, ου	ou	ou as in tourist
ΓΓ, γγ	ng	ng as in angle; always medial
ΜΠ, μπ	b/mb	b at start of a word, mb if medial
ΝΤ, ντ	d/nd	d at start of a word, nd if medial

THE QUEST FOR "PURE" GREEK

When Greece achieved independence in 1832, its people were mostly illiterate, and the spoken language – **dhimotikí**, "demotic" or "popular" Greek – had undergone enormous change since the Byzantine and Classical eras. The vocabulary had numerous loan-words from the languages of the various invaders and conquerors – especially Turks, Venetians and Slavs – and the grammar had been considerably streamlined since ancient times.

The leaders of the new Greek state, filled with romantic notions of Greece's past glories, set about purging the language of foreign words and reviving its Classical purity. They accordingly created what was in effect an artificial language, **katharévoussa** (literally "cleansed" Greek). Long-forgotten words and phrases were reintroduced and complex Classical grammar reinstated. *Katharévoussa* became the language of the schools, government, business, the law, newspapers and academia. Everyone aspiring to membership in the elite strove to master it.

The split between *katharévoussa* and *dhimotikí* quickly took on a **political** dimension with intellectuals and left-wing politicians championing the demotic form, while the right, notably the colonel's junta of 1967–74, insisted on the "purer" *katharévoussa*. *Dhimotikí* returned permanently after the fall of the colonels, though the Church and the legal profession still persist with *katharévoussa*.

All this has reduced, but not eliminated, confusion. The Metaxás dictatorship of the 1930s changed scores of village names from Slavic, Turkish or Albanian words to Greek ones – often reviving the name of the nearest ancient site. These official **place names** still hold sway on most road signs and maps – even though the local people may use the *dhimotikí* or non-Greek form. Thus for example you will see "Plomárion" or "Spétsai" written, while everyone actually says "Plomári" or "Spétses".

Polite forms and questions

Greek makes the distinction between the **informal** (*essý*) and **formal** (*essís*) second person, like the French "tu" and "vous". Young people and country people often use *essý* even with total strangers, though it's best to address everyone formally until/unless they start using the familiar with you, to avoid offence. By far the most common greeting, on meeting and parting, is *yiásou/yiásas* (literally "health to you").

To ask a **question**, it's simplest, though hardly elegant, to start with *parakaló* (please), then name the thing you want in an interrogative tone.

GREEK WORDS AND PHRASES

ESSENTIALS

Hérete/Yiássas	Hello
Kaliméra	Good morning
Kalíspéra	Good evening
Kaliníkhta	Goodnight
Adío	Goodbye
Tí kánis/Tí kánete?	How are you?
Kalá íme	I'm fine
Ké essís?	And you?
Né	Yes
Óhi	No
Parakaló	Please
Efharistó (polý)	Thank you (very much)
Sygnómi	Sorry/excuse me
Miláte angliká?	Do you speak English?
(Dhén) Katalavéno	I (don't) understand
Parakaló, na milísate pió sigá	Speak slower, please
Pós léyete avtó stá Elliniká?	How do you say it in Greek?
Pós se léne?	What's your name?
Mé léne ...	My name is ...
Kýrios/Kyría	Mr/Mrs
Dhespinís	Miss
Parakaló, o ...?	Where is the ...?
Dhén xéro	I don't know
Thá sé dhó ávrio	See you tomorrow
Kalí andhámosi	See you soon
Páme	Let's go
Parakaló, ná mé voithíste	Please help me
(Dhen) Trógo/píno	I (don't) eat/drink
(Dhen) Mou aréssi	I (don't) like
Málista	Certainly
Endáxi	OK, agreed
Anikhtó	Open
Klistó	Closed
Méra	Day
Nýkhta	Night
Edhó	Here

Ekí	There
Grígora	Quickly
Sigá	Slowly
Poú?	Where?
Pós?	How?
Póte?	When?
Yiatí?	Why?
Tí óra … ?	At what time … ?
Tí íne/Pió íne … ?	What is/Which is … ?

ACCOMMODATION

Parakaló, éna dhomátio	We'd like a room
yiá éna/dhýo/tría	for one/two/three
átoma	people
yiá mía/dhýo/trís	for one/two/three
vradhiés	nights
mé dhipló kreváti	with a double bed
mé doús	with a shower
Xenodhohío	Hotel
Xenón(as)	Inn
Xenónas neótitas	Youth hostel
Zestó neró	Hot water
Krýo neró	Cold water
Klimatismós	Air conditioning
Anamistíra	Fan
Boró ná tó dhó?	Can I see it?
Boroúme na váloume	Can we camp here?
ti skiní edhó?	
Kámping/Kataskínosi	Campsite

SHOPPING AND SERVICES

Póso (káni)?	How much (does it cost)?
Tí óra aníyi/ klíni?	What time does it open/ close?
Parakaló, éna kiló portokália?	May I have a kilo of oranges?
Póssi, pósses or póssa?	How many?
Aftó	This one
Ekíno	That one
Kaló	Good
Kakó	Bad
Megálo	Big
Mikró	Small
Perisótero	More
Ligótero	Less
Lígo	A little
Polý	A lot
Ftinó	Cheap
Akrivó	Expensive
Mazí (mé)	With (together)
Horís	Without
Foúrnos	Bakery
Farmakío	Pharmacy
Tahydhromío	Post office

Gramatósima	Stamps
Venzinádhiko	Petrol station
Trápeza	Bank
Leftá/Khrímata	Money
Toualéta	Toilet
Astynomía	Police
Yiatrós	Doctor
Nosokomío	Hospital

ON THE MOVE

Parakaló, ó dhrómos yiá … ?	Can you show me the road to … ?
Aeropláno	Aeroplane
Leoforío, púlman	Bus, coach
Aftokínito, amáxi	Car
Mihanáki, papáki	Motorbike, scooter
Taxí	Taxi
Plío/vapóri/karávi	Ship
Tahyplöö, katamarán	High-speed boat, catamaran
Dhelfíni	Hydrofoil
Tréno	Train
Sidhirodhromikós stathmós	Train station
Podhílato	Bicycle
Otostóp	Hitching
Mé tá pódhia	On foot
Monopáti	Trail
Praktorío leoforíon KTEL	Bus station
Stási	Bus stop
Limáni	Harbour
Ti óra févyi?	What time does it leave?
Ti óra ftháni?	What time does it arrive?
Póssa hiliómetra?	How many kilometres?
Pósses óres?	How many hours?
Poú páte/pás?	Where are you going?
Páo stó …	I'm going to …
Thélo ná katévo stó …	I want to get off at …
O dhrómos yiá …	The road to …
Kondá	Near
Makriá	Far
Aristerá	Left
Dhexiá	Right
Katefthía/ísia	Straight ahead
Éna isitírio yiá …	A ticket to …
Éna isitírio aplí/mé epistrofí	A ticket one-way/ return
Paralía	Beach
Spiliá	Cave
Kéndro	Centre (of town)
Eklissía	Church
Thálassa	Sea
Horió	Village

NUMBERS

énas/éna/mía	1
dhýo	2
trís/tría	3
tésseris/tésseres/téssera	4
pénde	5
éxi	6
eftá	7
okhtó	8
ennéa (or, in slang, enyá)	9
dhéka	10
éndheka	11
dhódheka	12
dhekatrís	13
dhekatésseres	14
íkossi	20
íkossi éna	21
triánda	30
saránda	40
penínda	50
exínda	60
evdhomínda	70
ogdhónda	80
enenínda	90
ekató	100
ekatón penínda	150
dhiakóssies/ dhiakóssia	200
pendakóssies/ pendakóssia	500
hílies/hília	1000
dhlo hiliádhes	2000
próto	first
dhéftero	second
tríto	third

TIME AND DAYS OF THE WEEK

Tóra	Now
Argótera	Later
Símera	Today
Ávrio	Tomorrow
Khthés	Yesterday
Tó proï	In the morning
Tó apóyevma	In the afternoon
Tó vrádhi	In the evening
Kyriakí	Sunday
Dheftéra	Monday
Tríti	Tuesday
Tetárti	Wednesday
Pémpti	Thursday
Paraskeví	Friday
Sávato	Saturday
Tí óra íne?	What time is it?
Mía íy óra/dhýo iy óra/trís íy óra	One/two/three o'clock
Tésseres pará íkossi	Twenty minutes to four
Eftá ké pénde	Five minutes past seven
Éndheka ké misí	Half past eleven
Sé misí óra	In half an hour
S'éna tétarto	In a quarter-hour
Sé dhýo óres	In two hours

MONTHS AND SEASONS

Yennáris	January
Fleváris	February
Mártis	March
Aprílis	April
Maïos	May
Ioúnios	June
Ioúlios	July
Ávgoustos	August
Septémvris	September
Októvris	October
Noémvris	November
Dhekémvris	December
Therinó dhromolóyio	Summer schedule
Himerinó dhromolóyio	Winter schedule

A food and drink glossary

BASICS

Katálogos, menoú	Menu
O logariasmós	The bill
Zestó	Hot
Krýo	Cold
(Horís) ládhi	(Without) oil
Hortofágos	Vegetarian
Kréas	Meat
Lahaniká	Vegetables
Neró	Water
Psári(a)	Fish
Thalassiná	Seafood
Aláti	Salt
Avgá	Eggs
Méli	Honey
Psomí....	Bread...
Olikís	Wholemeal
Sikalísio	Rye
Kalambokísio	Corn
Tyrí	Cheese
Yiaoúrti	Yoghurt
Záhari	Sugar

GREEK'S GREEK

There are numerous words and phrases which you will hear constantly, even if you don't have the chance to use them. These are a few of the most common.

Éla!	Come (literally) but also Speak to me! You don't say! etc.	**Po-po-po!**	Expression of dismay or concern, like French "O là là!"
Oríste!	Literally, Define!; in effect, What can I do for you?	**Pedhí moú**	My boy/girl, sonny, friend, etc.
Embrós!/Léyete!	Standard phone responses	**Maláka(s)**	Literally "wanker", but often used (don't try it!) as an informal term of address
Tí néa?	What's new?		
Tí yínete?	What's going on ?		
Étsi k'étsi	So-so	**Sigá sigá**	Take your time, slow down
Ópa!	Whoops! Watch it!	**Kaló taxídhi**	Bon voyage

COOKING TERMS

Akhnistó	Steamed
Frikasé	Stew, either lamb, goat or pork, with celery
Iliókafto	Sun-dried
Kokkinistó	Cooked in tomato sauce
Kourkoúti	Egg-and-flour batter
Krasáto	Cooked in wine sauce
Makaronádha	Any spaghetti/ pasta-based dish
Pastó	Fish marinated in salt
Petáli	Butterflied fish, eel, shrimp
Psitó	Roasted
Saganáki	Cheese-based red sauce; also fried cheese
Skáras	Grilled
Sti soúvla	Spit-roasted
Stó foúrno	Baked
Tiganitó	Pan-fried
Tís óras	Grilled/fried to order
Yakhní	Stewed in oil and tomato sauce
Yemistá	Stuffed (squid, vegetables, etc)

SOUPS AND STARTERS

Avgolémono	Egg and lemon soup
Bouréki, bourekákia	Courgette/zucchini, potato and cheese pie
Dolmádhes, yaprákia yalantzí	Vine leaves stuffed with rice and mince; with vegetables
Fasoládha	Bean soup
Fáva	Purée of yellow peas
Féta psití	Baked feta cheese slabs with chilli
Galotýri	Curdled creamy dip
Hortópitta	Pastry stuffed with greens

Kápari	Pickled caper leaves
Kopanistí, khtypití	Pungent, fermented cheese purée
Lahanodolmádhes	Stuffed cabbage leaves
Mavromátika	Black-eyed peas
Melitzanosaláta	Aubergine/eggplant dip
Piperiés florínes	Marinated sweet peppers
Rengosaláta	Herring salad
Revythokeftédhes	Chickpea/garbanzo patties
Skordhaliá	Garlic dip
Soúpa	Soup
Strapatsádha	Eggs scrambled with tomato and onions
Taramosaláta	Cod roe pâté
Tiganópsomo	Toasted oiled bread
Trahanádhes	Crushed wheat and milk soup, sweet or savoury
Tyrokafterí	Cheese dip with chilli
Tzatzíki	Yoghurt and cucumber dip
Tzirosaláta	Cured mackerel dip

VEGETABLES

Ambelofásola	Runner beans
Angináres	Artichokes
Angoúri	Cucumber
Ánitho	Dill
Bámies	Okra/ladies' fingers
Briám, tourloú	Ratatouille
Domátes	Tomatoes
Fakés	Lentils
Fasolákia	French (green) beans
Fasóles	Small white beans
Horiátiki (saláta)	Greek salad (with olives, feta, etc)
Hórta	Steamed greens
Kolokythákia	Courgette/zucchini
Koukiá	Broad fava beans

Maroúli	Lettuce
Melitzánes imám/ Imám baïldí	Aubergine/eggplant slices baked with onion, garlic and copious olive oil
Patátes	Potatoes
Piperiés	Peppers
Pligoúri, pinigoúri	Bulgur wheat
Radhíkia	Wild chicory
Rókka	Rocket, arugula
Rýzi/Piláfi sáltsa	Rice (usually with sauce)
Saláta	Salad
Spanáki	Spinach
Yígandes	White haricot beans

FISH AND SEAFOOD

Ahini, foúskes	Sea urchins
Astakós	Lobster
Bakaliáros	Cod or hake, usually latter
Barbóuni	Red mullet
Fangrí	Common bream
Galéos	Dogfish
Garídhes	Shrimp, prawns
Gávros	Mild anchovy
Glóssa	Sole
Gónos, gonákia	Any hatchling fish
Gópa	Bogue
Hokhlí	Sea snails
Kalamarákia	Baby squid
Kalamária	Squid
Karavídhes	Crayfish
Koliós	Chub mackerel
Koutsomoúra	Goatfish (small red mullet)
Lakérdha	Light-fleshed bonito, marinated
Lithríni	Red bream, pandora
Melanoúri	Saddled bream
Ménoula	Sprat
Mýdhia	Mussels
Okhtapódhi	Octopus
Petalídhes	Limpets
Platý	Skate, ray
Sardhélles	Sardines
Sargós	White bream
Seláhi	Skate, ray
Sfyrídha	White grouper
Skáros	Parrotfish
Skathári	Black bream
Skoumbrí	Atlantic mackerel
Soupiá	Cuttlefish
Strídhia	Oysters
Thrápsalo	Large, deep-water squid
Tónos	Tuna
Tsipoúra	Gilt-head bream
Xifías	Swordfish

Yermanós	Leatherback
Yialisterés	Smooth Venus; common ouzerí shellfish

MEAT AND POULTRY

Arní	Lamb
Bekrí mezé	Pork chunks in spicy pepper sauce
Biftéki	Hamburger
Brizóla hiriní	Pork chop
Brizóla moskharísia	Beef chop
Exohikó	Lamb baked in tin foil or in pastry
Hirinó	Pork
Keftédhes	Meatballs
Kókoras krasáto	Coq au vin
Kokorétsi	Liver/offal roulade, spit-roasted
Kondosoúvli	Spit-roasted pork
Kopsídha	(Lamb) shoulder chops
Kotópoulo	Chicken
Kounéli	Rabbit
Loukánika	Spicy course-ground sausages
Manári	Spring lamb
Moskhári	Veal
Moussakás	Aubergine/eggplant, potato and lamb-mince casserole with béchamel topping
Païdhákia	Rib chops, lamb or goat
Papoutsákia	Stuffed aubergine/eggplant "shoes"
Pastítsio	Macaroni "pie" baked with minced meat
Pastourmás	Cured, highly spiced meat; traditionally camel, nowadays beef
Patsás	Tripe soup
Patsitsádha	beef with pasta in wine sauce
Provatína	Female mutton
Psaronéfri	Pork tenderloin medallions
Salingária	Garden snails
Sofríto	beef fried in garlic sauce
Soutzoukákia	Minced meat rissoles/ beef patties
Spetzofáï	Sausage and pepper stew
Stifádho	Meat stew with tomato and boiling onions
Sykóti	Liver
Tiganiá	Pork chunks fried with onions
Tziyéro sarmás	Lamb's liver in cabbage leaves

| Yiouvétsi | Baked clay casserole of meat and pasta |
| Zygoúri | 1- to-2-year-old lamb |

SWEETS AND DESSERT
Baklavás	Honey and nut pastry
Bergamóndo	Bergamot
Bougátsa	Salt or sweet cream pie served warm with sugar and cinnamon
Galaktoboúriko	Custard pie
Glykó koutalioú	Spoon sweet (syrupy fruit preserve)
Halvás	Semolina- or sesame-based sweet meat
Karydhópita	Walnut cake
Kréma	Custard
Loukoumádhes	Dough fritters in honey syrup and sesame seeds
Pagotó	Ice cream
Pastélli	Sesame and honey bar
Ravaní	Sponge cake, lightly syruped
Ryzógalo	Rice pudding

FRUITS
Akhládhia	Big pears
Aktinídha	Kiwis
Fistíkia	Pistachio nuts
Fráoules	Strawberries
Himoniátiko	Autumn (cassava) melon
Karpoúzi	Watermelon
Kerásia	Cherries
Krystália	Miniature pears
Kydhóni	Quince
Lemóni	Lemon
Míla	Apples

Pepóni	Melon
Portokáli	Orange
Rodhákino	Peach
Sýka	Figs
Stafýlia	Grapes
Yiarmádhes	Autumn peaches

CHEESE
Ayeladhinó	Cow's-milk cheese
Féta	Salty, creamy white cheese
(Kefalo)graviéra	(Extra-hard) Gruyère-type cheese
Katsikísio	Goat cheese
Kasséri	Medium-sharp cheese
Myzíthra	Sweet cream cheese
Próvio	Sheep cheese

DRINKS
Alisfakiá	Island sage tea
Boukáli	Bottle
Býra	Beer
Gála	Milk
Galakakáo	Chocolate milk
Kafés	Coffee
Krasí	Wine
áspro/lefkó	white
kokkinélli/rozé	rosé
kókkino	red
Limonádha	Lemonade
Metalikó neró	Mineral water
Portokaládha	Orangeade
Potíri	Glass
Stinyásas!	Cheers!
Tsáï	Tea
Tsáï vounoú	"Mountain" (mainland sage) tea

Glossary

Acropolis Ancient, fortified hilltop.
Agora Market and meeting place of an ancient Greek city; also the "high street" of a modern village (**agorá** in modern Greek).
Amphora Tall, narrow-necked jar for oil or wine.
Áno Upper; common prefix of village names.
Apse Curved recess at the east end of a church nave.
Archaic period Late Iron Age period, from around 750 BC to the start of the Classical period in the fifth century BC.
Arhondikó A lordly stone mansion, often restored as boutique accommodation.
Astikó (Intra) city, municipal, local; adjective applied to phone calls and bus services.

Ayíasma A sacred spring, usually flowing out of church foundations.
Áyios/Ayía/Áyii (m/f/plural). Saint or holy. Common place-name prefix (abbreviated Ag or Ay), often spelled **Agios** or **Aghios**.
Basilica Colonnaded, "hall-" or "barn-" type church adapted from Roman models, most common in northern Greece.
Bema Rostrum for a church oratory.
Bouleuterion Auditorium for meetings of an ancient town's deliberative council.
Capital The flared top, often ornamented, of a column.
Cavea Seating curve of an ancient theatre.
Cella Sacred room of a temple, housing the cult image.
Classical period From the end of the Persian Wars in

DIALECTS AND MINORITY LANGUAGES

Greece exhibits considerable linguistic diversity, both in its **regional dialects** and minority languages. Ancient dialects survive in many remote areas, some quite incomprehensible to outsiders. Examples include the dialect of Sfákia in Crete, and those of Náxos and Lésvos, which are influenced by immigration from Crete and Asia Minor respectively. The dialects of Sámos and adjacent Híos are completely different from one another, Híos being considered a more pure "Ionian" (and this thousands of years after the Ionians arrived from the mainland), while the rough "Samian" variant owes much to the diverse origins of its settlers. Arvanítika – a form of medieval Albanian – was until well into the twentieth century the first language of many villages of southern Évvia, northern Ándhros, and much of the Argo-Saronic area; it is still (just barely) spoken or at least understood among the oldest generation. Lately the clock has been turned back, so to speak, as Albanian immigrant communities have been established on almost every island of the Aegean. On Rhodes and Kos there is a dwindling Turkish-speaking population, probably less than six thousand.

480 BC until the unification of Greece under Philip II of Macedon (338 BC).

Conch Concave semi-dome surmounting a church apse, often frescoed.

Corinthian Decorative columns, festooned with acanthus florettes; any temple built in this order.

Dhimarhío Town hall.

Dhomátia Rooms for rent in purpose-built block, without staffed reception.

Dorian Northern civilization that displaced and succeeded the Mycenaeans and Minoans through most of Greece around 1100 BC.

Doric Minimalist, unadorned columns, dating from the Dorian period; any temple built in this order.

Drum Cylindrical or faceted vertical section, usually pierced by an even number of narrow windows, upholding a church cupola.

Entablature The horizontal linking structure atop the columns of an ancient temple; same as **architrave**.

Eparhía Subdivision of a modern province, analogous to a county.

Exedra Display niche for statuary.

Exonarthex The outer vestibule or entrance hall of a church, when a true **narthex** is present.

Forum Market and meeting place of a Roman-era city.

Frieze Band of sculptures around a temple. Doric friezes consist of various tableaux of figures (**metopes**) interspersed with grooved panels (**triglyphs**); Ionic ones have continuous bands of figures.

Froúrio Medieval citadel; nowadays, can mean a modern military headquarters.

Garsoniéra/es Studio villa/s, self-catering apartment/s.

Geometric period Post-Mycenaean Iron Age era named for its pottery style; starts in the early eleventh century BC with the arrival of Dorian peoples. By the eighth century BC, with development of representational styles, the **Archaic period** begins.

Hammam Domed "Turkish" bath, found on Rhodes and

certain northeast Aegean islands.

Hellenistic period The last and most unified "Greek empire", created in the wake of Alexander the Great's Macedonian empire and finally collapsing with the fall of Corinth to the Romans in 146 BC.

Heroön Shrine or sanctuary-tomb, usually of a demigod or mortal; war memorials in modern Greece.

Hóra Main town of an island or region; literally it means "the place". A hóra is often known by the same name as the island.

Ierón The sanctuary between the altar screen and the apse of a church, reserved for priestly activities.

Ikonostási Wood or masonry screen between the nave of a church and the altar, supporting at least three icons.

Ionic Elaborate, decorative development of the older **Doric** order; Ionic temple columns are slimmer, with deeper "fluted" edges, spiral-shaped capitals and ornamental bases.

Kafenío Coffee house or café.

Kaïki (plural **kaïkia**) Caique, or medium-sized boat, traditionally wooden and used for transporting cargo and passengers; now refers mainly to island excursion boats.

Kalderími A cobbled mule-track or footpath.

Kámbos Fertile agricultural plain, usually near a river mouth.

Kantína Shack, caravan or even a disused bus on the beach, serving drinks and perhaps sandwiches or quick snacks.

Kástro Any fortified hill, but most often the oldest, highest, walled-in part of an island hóra, intended to protect civilians.

Katholikón Central church of a monastery.

Káto Lower; common prefix of village names.

Kendrikí platía Central square.

Kouros Nude Archaic statue of an idealized young man, usually portrayed with one foot slightly in front of the other.

Megaron Principal hall or throne room of a Mycenaean palace.

Meltémi North wind that blows across the Aegean in summer, starting softly from near the mainland and hitting the Cyclades, the Dodecanese and Crete full on.

Metope see **Frieze**.

Minoan Crete's great Bronze Age civilization, which dominated the Aegean from about 2500 to 1400 BC.

Moní Formal term for a monastery or convent.

Moreas Medieval term for the Peloponnese; the peninsula's outline was likened to the leaf of a mulberry tree, *mouriá* in Greek.

Mycenaean Mainland civilization centred on Mycenae and the Argolid from 1700 to 1100 BC.

Naos The inner sanctum of an ancient temple; also, the central area of an Orthodox Christian church.

Narthex Western vestibule of a church, reserved for catechumens and the unbaptized; typically frescoed with scenes of the Last Judgement.

Neolithic Earliest era of settlement in Greece; characterized by use of stone tools and weapons together with basic agriculture. Divided arbitrarily into Early (c.6000 BC), Middle (c.5000 BC) and Late (c.3000 BC).

Néos, Néa, Néo "New" – a common prefix to a town or village name.

Nomós Modern Greek province – there are more than fifty of them. Village bus services are organized according to their borders.

Odeion Small theatre, used for musical performances, minor dramatic productions or councils.

Orchestra Circular area in a theatre where the chorus would sing and dance.

Palaestra Gymnasium for athletics and wrestling practice.

Paleós, Paleá, Paleó "Old" – again a common prefix in town and village names.

Panayía Virgin Mary.

Pandokrátor Literally "The Almighty"; generally refers to the stern portrayal of Christ in Majesty frescoed or in mosaic in the dome of many Byzantine churches.

Paniyíri Festival or feast – the local celebration of a holy day..

Paralía Beach, or seafront promenade.

Pediment Triangular, sculpted gable below the roof of a temple.

Pendentive Triangular sections of vaulting with concave sides, positioned at a corner of a rectangular space to support a circular or polygonal dome; in churches, often adorned with frescoes of the four Evangelists.

Períptero Street kiosk.

Peristereónes Pigeon towers, in the Cyclades.

Peristyle Gallery of columns around a temple or other building.

Pinakothíki Picture gallery, ancient or modern.

Pithos (plural **pithoi**) Large ceramic jar for storing oil, grain, etc. Very common in Minoan palaces and used in almost identical form in modern Greek homes.

Platía Square, plaza.

Polygonal masonry Wall-building technique of Classical and Hellenistic periods, using unmortared, closely joined stones; often called "Lesvian polygonal" after the island where the method supposedly originated. The much-(ab)used term **Cyclopean** refers only to Bronze Age mainland sites such as Tiryns and Mycenae.

Propylaion Monumental columned gateway of an ancient building; often used in the plural, **propylaia**.

Pýrgos Tower or bastion; also tower-mansions found in the Máni or on Lésvos.

Skála The port of an inland island settlement, nowadays often larger and more important than its namesake, but always younger since built after the disappearance of piracy.

Squinch Small concavity across a corner of a column-less interior space, which supports a superstructure such as a dome.

Stele Upright stone slab or column, usually inscribed with an edict; also an ancient tombstone, with a relief scene.

Stoa Colonnaded walkway in Classical-to-Roman-era marketplaces.

Távli Backgammon; a favourite café pastime, especially among the young. There are two more difficult local variations (*févga* and *plakotó*) in addition to the standard international game (*pórtes*).

Témblon Wooden altar screen of an Orthodox church, usually ornately carved and painted and studded with icons; more or less interchangeable with **ikonostási**.

Temenos Sacred precinct of ancient temple, often used to refer to the sanctuary itself.

Theatral area Open area found in most of the Minoan palaces with seat-like steps around. Probably a type of theatre or ritual area.

Tholos Conical or beehive-shaped building, eg a Mycenaean tomb.

Triglyph see **Frieze**.

Tympanum The recessed space, flat or carved in relief, inside a pediment.

Votsalotó Mosaic of coloured pebbles, found in church or house courtyards of the Dodecanese and Spétses.

Yperastikó Long-distance – as in bus services.

ACRONYMS

ANEK Anónymi Navtiliakí Etería Krítis (Shipping Co of Crete, Ltd), which runs most ferries between Pireás and Crete, plus many to Italy.

EAM National Liberation Front, the political force behind ELAS.

ELAS Popular Liberation Army, the main Resistance group during World War II and predecessor of the Communist army during the civil war.

ELTA Postal service.

EOT Ellinikós Organismós Tourismoú, National Tourist Organization.

KKE Communist Party, unreconstructed.

KTEL National syndicate of bus companies; also refers to individual bus stations.

LANE Lasithiakí Anónymi Navtiliakí Etería (Lasithian Shipping Company Ltd), based in eastern Crete.

ND Conservative (Néa Dhimokratía) party.

NEL Navtiliakí Etería Lésvou (Lesvian Shipping Co).

OTE Telecommunications company.

PASOK Socialist party (Pan-Hellenic Socialist Movement).

SYRIZA Synaspismós tis Rizospastikís Aristerás (Coalition of the Radical Left) – alternative, "Euro"-Socialist party.

Small print and index

573 Small print
576 Index
586 Map symbols

A ROUGH GUIDE TO ROUGH GUIDES

Published in 1982, the first Rough Guide – to Greece – was a student scheme that became a publishing phenomenon. Mark Ellingham, a recent graduate in English from Bristol University, had been travelling in Greece the previous summer and couldn't find the right guidebook. With a small group of friends he wrote his own guide, combining a highly contemporary, journalistic style with a thoroughly practical approach to travellers' needs.

The immediate success of the book spawned a series that rapidly covered dozens of destinations. And, in addition to impecunious backpackers, Rough Guides soon acquired a much broader readership that relished the guides' wit and inquisitiveness as much as their enthusiastic, critical approach and value-for-money ethos.

These days, Rough Guides include recommendations from budget to luxury and cover more than 200 destinations around the globe, as well as producing an ever-growing range of eBooks and apps.

Visit **roughguides.com** to see our latest publications.

Rough Guide credits

Editors: Lucy White, Andy Turner and Edward Aves
Layout: Pradeep Thapliyal
Cartography: Deshpal Dabas and Lokamata Sahu
Picture editor: Nicole Newman
Proofreader: Jan McCann
Managing editor: Monica Woods
Assistant editor: Dipika Dasgupta
Production: Rebecca Short
Cover design: Nicole Newman, Michelle Bhatia and Pradeep Thapliyal
Photographers: Chris Christoforou and Michelle Grant
Editorial assistant: Eleanor Aldridge

Senior pre-press designer: Dan May
Marketing, Publicity & roughguides.com: Liz Statham
Design director: Scott Stickland
Travel publisher: Joanna Kirby
Digital travel publisher: Peter Buckley
Reference director: Andrew Lockett
Operations coordinator: Becky Doyle
Operations assistant: Johanna Wurm
Publishing director (Travel): Clare Currie
Commercial manager: Gino Magnotta
Managing director: John Duhigg

Publishing information

This eighth edition published May 2012 by
Rough Guides Ltd,
80 Strand, London WC2R 0RL
11, Community Centre, Panchsheel Park,
New Delhi 110017, India
Distributed by the Penguin Group
Penguin Books Ltd,
80 Strand, London WC2R 0RL
Penguin Group (USA)
375 Hudson Street, NY 10014, USA
Penguin Group (Australia)
250 Camberwell Road, Camberwell,
Victoria 3124, Australia
Penguin Group (NZ)
67 Apollo Drive, Mairangi Bay, Auckland 1310,
New Zealand
Rough Guides is represented in Canada by Tourmaline
Editions Inc. 662 King Street West, Suite 304, Toronto,
Ontario M5V 1M7
Printed in Singapore by Toppan Security Printing Pte. Ltd.
© Rough Guides 2012

Maps © Rough Guides
No part of this book may be reproduced in any form
without permission from the publisher except for the
quotation of brief passages in reviews.
592pp includes index
A catalogue record for this book is available from the
British Library
ISBN: 978-1-40538-599-2
The publishers and authors have done their best to
ensure the accuracy and currency of all the information
in **The Rough Guide to The Greek Islands**, however,
they can accept no responsibility for any loss, injury, or
inconvenience sustained by any traveller as a result of
information or advice contained in the guide.
1 3 5 7 9 8 6 4 2

Help us update

We've gone to a lot of effort to ensure that the eighth
edition of **The Rough Guide to The Greek Islands** is
accurate and up-to-date. However, things change – places
get "discovered", opening hours are notoriously fickle,
restaurants and rooms raise prices or lower standards. If
you feel we've got it wrong or left something out, we'd like
to know, and if you can remember the address, the price,
the hours, the phone number, so much the better.

Please send your comments with the subject line
"**Rough Guide Greek Islands Update**" to ✉ mail
@uk.roughguides.com. We'll credit all contributions and
send a copy of the next edition (or any other Rough Guide
if you prefer) for the very best emails.
Find more travel information, connect with fellow
travellers and book your trip on ⓦ roughguides.com

ABOUT THE AUTHORS

Nick Edwards Since graduating in Classics & Modern Greek from Oxford, Nick spent many years living in Athens and travelling widely, especially in India. He later settled in Pittsburgh with spouse Maria, until they returned to his native south London in 2008. He's a lifelong Spurs fan, psych music aficionado and believer in universal Oneness.

John Fisher co-wrote the first edition of this book – the first ever Rough Guide – and has been inextricably linked with Rough Guides ever since, much of the time stuck in the office. Now living in London with his wife, Adrienne, and two boys, he is a freelance writer and editor.

John Malathronas was born in Athens but has spent most of his life in London where he has written three travelogues and contributed to nine guidebooks. He is a member of the Guild of Travel Writers and the Society of Authors, as well as a social media addict and a compulsive blogger.

Carol Palioudakis has lived in Greece since 1986; she runs a tourism agency in western Crete, publishes a website about living in Crete and is a freelance writer and author. She lives near Haniá with her Greek husband and two children.

Greg Ward, who covered the Dodecanese islands for this book – and chose Sými for his honeymoon – is a London-based author and photographer specializing in history, music and travel. He has written more than a dozen travel guides to different parts of Europe and the US, including France, Spain, Italy and Greece. His latest book is the Rough Guide to the Titanic; for more details, visit ⓦgregward.info

Readers' letters

Thanks to all the readers who have taken the time to write in with comments and suggestions (and apologies if we've inadvertently omitted or misspelt anyone's name):

Douglas Adler; Gabriela Barbosa de Oliveira; Dinah Bear; Gillian Billington; John Bishop; David Black; Kathy Blandin; Pete Chambers; Ian Chandler; Gerald Chapman; Adrian Clement; Alison Culshaw; Laura Czebotar; Bob Dent; Chris Deviaene; Katerina Dikaiou; Igor Fabjan; Annabell Go; Pauline and Gordon Hinson; Xenia Kataki; Kirsty Mackenzie; Ann, Ian and James Mason; Wendy and Diran Meghreblian; Rhiannon Monks; John Newstead; M. Ostler; Marianna Patané; Linda J. Reynolds; M. Rosenthal; Carola Schupham; Brian Shepherd; Neville Spencer-Lewis; James A. Stefan; Danielle Stewart; Will Straw; Rachel Taylor; Donna Thornton; Michaela Urben; Alexander Zawadzki.

Acknowledgements

Nick Edwards would like to thank all the people who offered help, hospitality and harmony along the way, including too many to mention in Macedonia and Thrace. On the islands, thanks especially to Kostas Vlachopulos at Boúkari Beach; Mariana in Horepiskopi/Gosport; Vasso and Yiorgos in Agrinio; Maria at Ionian Paradise in Nydhrí; Odisseas, Memi, Panayiotis, Andronikos and Lefteris on Kefaloniá; the *Villa Afrodite/Aphrodite Beach* hotel families of Límnos and Lésvos; Theo of To Kyma in Híos Town; Stella in Volissós and the Archipelagos Hotel on Foúrni. Many thanks for useful tips to Matt Barrett, but the greatest bundle of thanks for eastern Aegean help, advice, contacts, company, chauffeuring and accommodation on Samos goes to Marc Dubin. Finally cheers to old friends Kate for the overnight in Athens, Yiannis and Eleftheria, Makarios and Robert and Roudi for *parea* on Híos and Ikaría, plus bravo to Robert for steering the rent-a-wreck across the mountain. As ever, thanks to Maria for love and support from afar and bearing long absences in difficult circumstances.

John Fisher would like to thank all those who helped in Athens, the Argo-Saronics Islands and Sporades, especially Eleni Vardaki; Makis Bitzios; Kostas and Bessie Efstathiou on Alónissos; Rosy Agianozoglou and Kostas Antoniou on Angistri; Iannis Goumas, Bruce and Vassos on Égina; Kostas, Andrew and Marion on Skiáthos; Mathi and Vangelis on Skópelos; Lefteris Trakos and Maria Hadjipaniyiri on Skýros; Anastasios Naoum on Spetses; Irini Tavladoraki on Ýdhra; and Vangelis Lagoutaris, Dorina Stathopoulou James Monteith and Kate Donnelly in Athens; not forgetting the team at Rough Guides and, as ever, A & the two Js for love, support and disrupting the research.

John Malathronas would like to thank NEL Lines, Kyklades Fast Ferries, Efthimios Athanasias and Makis Bitzios from MTC Group Greece, Kostas Skayas on Mýkonos, Alexandros Konstantinou and the staff of GNTO London, as well as what seems in retrospect the whole population of the Cyclades for their help.

Carol Palioudakis Thanks to Kostas, Lia, Tolis and my friends and colleagues for their help and support, especially Lyn Protopsaltis and Lynn Malleli, and to all who offered their time and hospitality during my travels around Crete.

Greg Ward Thanks to Sam for all her love and support, in the hope we'll be back on Sými soon; aloha to Donna Young and Chef Mavro, for a serendipitous meeting; and thanks to everyone who helped to make my Dodecanese trip so memorable, including Antonios Antonoglu; Yiorgos Berdos and Maria Martzoukou; Maria Christofi; Ian Hoop on Tilos; Annie Kalogianni and Christine at *Archontoriki*; George Koulouris; Alex Marshall and all the family at the *Spirit of the Knights*; Tom Panagos and Chloe Buchanan; Stella Sandaltzopoulou, Liz, and everyone at the *Hotel des Couleurs*; Dimitris Vlachos; Kayleen Vourtsis; Wendy Wilcox and Adriana Shum on Sými; Marina F. Zawaher; and Alexis Zikas. At Rough Guides, thanks to Andy Turner for setting it all up, and to Lucy White for another enjoyable collaboration.

Photo credits

Index

Maps are marked in grey

A

accommodation...............33–36
Achilleion.............................464
Adhámas.............................125
Aegina.....................see Égina
Afáles Bay...........................501
Afándou..............................275
Agathoníssi.........................344
Agathoníssi........................ 345
Agathopés...........................152
Agístri......................see Angístri
Agní....................................466
Agnóndas............................432
Agriolívadho........................341
Agriosykiá............................305
Aharávi...............................468
Áï Górdhis (Corfu)...............473
Áï Górdhis Paleohoríou (S Corfu)
....475
Aï Nikítas............................487
Aï Strátis........see Áyios Efstrátios
air conditioning................... 34
airlines, international.............. 25
Aïyannis (Lefkádha)..............483
Akrotíri (Santoríni)...............193
Akrotíri peninsula (Crete)......250
Alalkomenae.......................499
alcohol................................ 39
Alexander the Great..............528
Alexandhroúpoli.................. 68
Alikanás.............................509
Álinda.................................336
Almyrós (Corfu)...................468
Alónissos.................... 435–439
Alónissos........................ 435
Alonítsi...............................402
Aloprónia............................181
alphabet, Greek...................562
Alykés (Zákynthos)...............509
Alykí (Kímolos).....................130
Alykí (Kos)...........................318
Alykí (Thássos)....................417
Amári valley........................242
Ambelás (Páros)...................159
Ambéli (Folégandhros)..........184
Ammopí...............................292
Ammouá.............................288
Ammoúdhi (Santoríni)...........191
Amorgós.................. 173–177
Amorgós........................ 174
Anáfi...................................194
Anáfi............................. 194
Anafonítria monastery..........510

Análipsi..............................325
Anáryiros, Sotírios...............100
Ánaxos...............................400
Ándhros.................... 132–136
Ándhros......................... 133
Andikýthira.........................515
Andinióti lagoon...................468
Andíparos............................161
Andíparos....................... 155
Andípaxi.................. 476–479
Andípaxi......................... 477
Andísamis............................495
Ándissa...............................395
Angáli (Folégandhros)...........184
Angelókastro........................471
Angístri............................87–89
Angístri........................... 88
Áno Méra (Mýkonos)............146
Áno Meriá (Folégandhros).....184
Áno Moraïtika......................474
Áno Sýros............................150
Áno Vathý (Sámos)...............353
Anoyí.................................500
Anóyia................................218
Antipaxos ....see Andípaxi
Apalírou.............................168
Ápella.................................294
Aperáthou...........................169
Aphaea, Temple of (Égina)..... 85
Apokálypsis monastery (Pátmos)
....339
Apóllonas (Náxos)................170
Apollonía (Sífnos)................120
Apónissos........................... 89
archeology.................. 542–545
architecture, Italian..............334
Aréta..................................287
Arethoússa spring................499
Argási.................................505
ARGO-SARONIC ISLANDS, THE
.................................**78–103**
Argo-Saronic Islands, the... 80
Argostóli.................... 489–491
Argostóli......................... 490
Arhangélou Mihaïl convent
(Thássos).........................417
Aristotle.............................527
Arkádhi, Monastery of (Crete)
....238
Arkássa...............................292
Arkhoudhílas.......................475
Arkí....................................344
Armathiá............................288
Arméni................................191
Armenistís...........................369

Armeós (Kálymnos) 330
Armeós (Sýros) 152
Artemis Tavropoleio temple
(Ikaría)..............................369
Artemónas...........................120
Aryinónda...........................329
Asfendhioú villages...............318
Askéli.................................. 92
Asklepion (Kos)....................317
Asklipió (Rhodes)..................279
Aspoús...............................445
Ássos.................................496
Assumption of the Virgin
.............................17, 51, 136
Astakós............................... 69
Astypálea.................... 321–325
Astypálea........................ 322
Astypalia, ancient (Kos).........320
Atávyros, Mount 282
Atháni................................487
Athéato..............................433
Athens...........................56–68
Athens 62–63
Athens and the ports 58–59
ATMs.................................. 50
Atsítsa................................444
Avgónyma...........................380
Avlákia (Psérimos)................321
Avlémonas...........................514
Avliótes..............................472
Avlóna................................295
Axis occupation 536
Ayía Anastasía Romeá...........279
Ayía Ánna (Amorgós)............175
Ayía Ánna (Évvia).................453
Ayía Ánna (Náxos)................167
Ayía Efimía..........................495
Ayía Eléni (Skiáthos)............427
Ayía Ermióni.......................377
Ayía Fotiní..........................377
Ayía Galíni..........................242
Ayía Iríni (Híos)...................379
Ayía Iríni gorge....................255
Ayía Marína (Crete)..............251
Ayía Marína (Égina)...............86
Ayía Marína (Kássos).............289
Ayía Marína (Léros)..............334
Ayía Marína (Spétses)...........103
Ayía Marína (Sými)...............300
Ayía Markélla......................382
Ayía Paraskeví (Lésvos)........393
Ayía Paraskeví (Spétses)........102
Ayía Pelayía........................217
Ayía Pelayía (Kýthira)...........513
Ayía Rouméli.......................254

Ayía Sofía (Kárpathos)............292
Ayía Triáda (Crete).................214
Ayía Triáda (Límnos)..............407
Ayía Triáda (Sámos)................363
Ayía Triáda (Télendhos)........330
Ayía Triáda monastery..........250
Ayiássos (Lésvos)...................391
Áyii Anáryiri (Lésvos)..............400
Áyii Anáryiri (Páros)...............156
Áyii Anáryiri (Skópelos)..........433
Áyii Anáryiri (Spétses)............102
Áyii Dhéka (Corfu).................473
Áyii Dhéka (Crete)..................212
Ayiókambos.............................453
Áyios Andónios (Tílos)............305
Áyios Dhimítrios (Aï Strátis)
....402
Áyios Dhimítrios (Alónissos)...438
Áyios Efstrátios (Aï Strátis)......401
Áyios Emilianós (Sými)............301
Áyios Fokás (Lésvos)...............393
Áyios Fokás (Skýros)................445
Áyios Fokás (Tínos)..................138
Áyios Ioánnis (Límnos)............405
Áyios Ioánnis (Mýkonos)........145
Áyios Ioánnis (Sérifos).............117
Áyios Ioánnis Kastrí.................434
Áyios Ioánnis Theológos
(Níssyros)...............................311
Áyios Kírykos...........................367
Áyios Konstandínos (Astypálea)
....324
Áyios Konstandínos (Sámos)
....359
Áyios Konstandínos.................69
Áyios Matthéos (Corfu)...........473
Áyios Nektários (Égina)...........85
Áyios Nikólaos 220
Áyios Nikólaos (Anáfi)............194
Áyios Nikólaos (Crete)
.... 220–222
Áyios Nikólaos (Kálymnos).....330
Áyios Nikólaos (Kárpathos)
....292
Áyios Nikólaos (N Zákynthos)
....509
Áyios Nikólaos (S Zákynthos)
....505
Áyios Nikólaos (Sámos)..........359
Áyios Nikólaos (Sými)............301
Áyios Nikólaos (Ýdhra)............98
Áyios Nikólaos Foundouklí 282
Áyios Pétros (Ándhros)...........132
Áyios Pétros (Alónissos).........438
Áyios Pétros (Skýros)..............444
Áyios Prokópios......................167
Áyios Sóstis (Mýkonos)..........146
Áyios Stéfanos (Mýkonos).....144
Áyios Stéfanos (NE Corfu)......467
Áyios Stéfanos (NW Corfu).....472

Áyios Theológos (Kos)............320
Áyios Vassílios (Sými) 301
Áyios Vassílios (Télendhos)
....330
Áyios Yeóryios (Agathoníssi)
....345
Áyios Yeóryios (Andíparos)
....162
Áyios Yeóryios (Crete)............225
Áyios Yeóryios (Folégandhros)
....184
Áyios Yeóryios (Irakliá)...........171
Áyios Yeóryios (Kefaloniá) 492
Áyios Yeóryios (Náxos)...........166
Áyios Yeóryios (NW Corfu) 471
Áyios Yeóryios (S Corfu).........475
Áyios Yeóryios Dhyssálona....301
Áyios Yerásimos.......................492
Ayíou Haralámbou (Skiáthos)
....428
Ayíou Ioánnou Prodhrómou
(Hálki)...................................287
Ayíou Ioánnou Theológou
(Pátmos)....................20, 340
Ayíou Nikoláou Galatáki 452
Ayíou Pandelímona (Tílos)
....306
Ayíou Yeoryíou Hadhión........289

B

backpackers............................35
Balí..218
Bállos.......................................358
Banana Beach (Skiáthos) 427
Banana Beach (Zákynthos) 505
banks..50
Barbáti.....................................466
bars...39
Batsí...132
beer...39
Benítses...................................473
Big Blue, The...........................173
Biláli..383
birds...547
Bísti...98
Blue Caves...............................509
Bonátsa....................................130
books 555–560
Boúka.......................................288
Boúkari....................................474
bouzoúki music......see rembétika
breakfast...................................36
Brooke, Rupert........................442
Brós Thermá 318
buses...31
Byron..533
Byzantine Greece....................529

C

cafés 38
camping....................................35
Captain Corelli's Mandolin......488,
495, 556
car rental..................................32
Castello Rosso.........................451
catamarans 30
Cave of the Nymphs (Itháki) ...499
cellphones................................52
cemeteries, war.......................407
Cephallonia............see Kefaloniá
Chania....................see Haniá
chemists...............see pharmacies
children, travelling with........53
Chios .... see Híos
civil war...................................537
climate.............................11, 48
climbing.........................16, 239
coffee 38
colonels' junta........................539
Constantine I, King.................534
Constantine II, King.................539
contraception 40
Corfu (Kérkyra) 459–476
Corfu 460
Corfu Town..............20, 459–465
Corfu Town 462
Corfu Trail...............................475
costs..46
credit cards..............................50
CRETE (Kríti) 10, 198–259
Crete 200–201
crime...47
Crusades..................................531
Curtius, Ernst...........................543
CYCLADES, THE 104–195
Cyclades, The...................... 108
Cyclades, Lesser 170–173
Cyclades, Lesser 171
cycling.............................33, 45
Cyprus crises...........................538

D

Delos...............................16, 146
Delos 147
democracy, ancient................521
Dháfni......................................505
Dhafníla...................................466
Dhassiá....................................466
Dhervéni gorge.......................451
Dhessími Bay...........................484
Dhéxa.......................................499
Dhiafáni...................................294
Dhiapóndia islands.................469

Dhídhyma..............379
Dhíkeos, Mount..............318
Dhiktean Cave..............225
Dhílos..............see Delos
Dhimosári Gorge..............451
dhimotikí..............563
Dhodhekánisos
..............see Dodecanese
debt crisis..............541
dhomátia..............34
Dhonoússa..............173
Dhragonéra..............89
Dhrákano, Cape..............367
Dhrakéï..............363
dhrakóspita..............449, 451
Dhrogaráti cave..............495
Dhrossiá..............509
Dhrymónas..............337, 483
Dhryopídha..............115
Dhýo Liskária..............336
Dhýstos, Lake..............449
dialects..............569
disabilities, travellers with
..............52
discography..............553
discounts..............47
diving..............45, 328
doctors..............40
DODECANESE, THE......260–345
Dodecanese, the..............264
dovecotes..............139
Dovecote Trail (Tínos).......13, 139
dress codes..............45
driving in Greece..............31
driving to Greece..............28
drugs..............47
Dystos, ancient..............449

Émblisi..............496
Émbona..............282
Emborió (Hálki)..............286
Emborió (Sými)..............301
Emboriós (Híos)..............379
Emboriós (Kálymnos)..............329
Emboriós (Kássos)..............288
Emboriós (Níssyros)..............310
emergencies..............52
Englouví..............483
Énos, Mount..............492
entrance fees..............47
entry requirements..............47
Eptá Piyés..............282
Eressos, ancient..............396
Erétria..............448
Eríkoussa..............470
Erimítis cliffs..............478
Éristos..............305
Érmones..............472
Ermoúpolis..............150
Ermoúpolis..............151
estiatória..............37
etiquette..............45
Euboea..............see Évvia
Eumaeus, Cave of..............499
Evangelistrías monastery
(Skiáthos)..............426
Evans, Sir Arthur..............543
Évdhilos..............368
ÉVVIA..............445–453
Évvia..............446
Exánthia..............483
Exóbourgo..............140
Eyiáli..............176

Falásarna..............257
Faliráki..............275
Fanaráki..............407
Faneroméni monastery
(Lefkádha)..............483
Fáros (Ikaría)..............367
Fáros (Sífnos)..............122
fast food..............36
Fengári, Mount..............411
ferries..............27, 29
festivals..............42–44
Filérimos..............281
Fínikas (Koufoníssi)..............172
Fínikas (Sýros)..............152
Finíki (Kárpathos)..............292
Firá (Thíra)..............188–190
Firá..............189
Firipláka..............128
Firostefáni..............188
fish..............37
Fiskárdho..............496

Fléa..............445
Flério..............169
flights, domestic..............30
flights, international..............25
flying dolphins..............see hydrofoils
Fódheli..............217
Fóki..............379
Fókis..............496
Folégandhros..............182–186
Folégandhros..............181
food and drink..............36–40
Fourkeró..............383
Fournáki (Sámos)..............362
Foúrni..............364–366
Foúrni..............365
Foúrni (Rhodes)..............281
Frangokástello (Crete)..............253
Fríkes..............501
Frý..............288
Fylakopí..............128
Fýsses..............295
Fýtema..............368

G

Gaïdhourávlakos..............345
Gaidhouronísi..............233
Gáïos..............477
galaktopolía..............39
Galissás..............152
Gardhíki Pýrgos..............473
Gavathás..............395
Gávdhos..............259
Gávrio..............132
gay travellers..............48
George I, King..............534
George II, King..............535
Glóssa..............433
glossary..............568
Glýfa (Alónissos)..............438
Glýfa (Andíparos)..............162
Glystéri..............434
goat dance, Skyrian..............440
gods, Greek..............12
Golden Age of Athens..............522
Gomáti..............405
Górtys..............212
Goúrna (Léros)..............337
Goúrnes..............216
Gourniá, ancient..............227
Gouvernétou monastery..............251
Grafiótissa..............321
Gramvoússa (Amorgós)..............176
Grazia-Barozzi Tower..............169
Greek Islands..............6–7
Greek language..............561–568
Gría Váthra..............410
Gríkou..............341
Grótta..............166

E

East and north Aegean
..............348–419
East and north Aegean......350
Easter..............42
ecotourism (Crete)..............256
Efpalínio Órygma..............355
Égina (Aegina)..............81–87
Égina..............82
Égina Town..............83
Egremní..............487
Ekatondapylianí, Church of
(Páros)..............17, 156
Elafonísi..............258
electricity..............47
Eleoússa (Rhodes)..............282
Eliá (Mýkonos)..............145
Élios..............432
Eloúnda (Crete)..............222–225
embassies, Greek..............48

F

H

Hadzimihaïl, Theophilos 390
Halikoúna beach......................475
Hálki 285–287
Hálki.................................... 286
Halkí (Náxos) 169
Halkídha..................................446
Haniá 18, 244–250
Haniá..................................... 245
Haráki......................................276
Harkadhió cave 305
Harmýlio 319
health...40
Hellenistic Greece....................528
Hephaestia, ancient................408
Heraion, ancient......................357
Hersónissos..............................216
Hídhira....................................394
hiking..................... see walking
Híos 372–382
Híos 373
Híos Town 374–376
Híos Town 375
Hippocrates.............................318
history........................ 517–541
Hivadholímni 128
Hokhlakás (Télendhos)...........330
Hokhlakás Bay (Pátmos)
....338
Hokhláki (Níssyros) 307
Hokhlakoúra (Lipsí)................343
holidays, public 51
Homer...................180, 521, 557
Hondroyiórgis.........................434
Hóra (Alónissos)......................436
Hóra (Amorgós).......................175
Hóra (Anáfi).............................194
Hóra (Ándhros).......................134
Hóra (Astypálea) 323
Hóra (Folégandhros)
....183
Hóra (Íos) 178
Hóra (Kálymnos) 327
Hóra (Kímolos)........................129
Hóra (Koufoníssi) 172
Hóra (Kýthira)..........................513
Hóra (Kýthnos)........................114
Hóra (Pátmos).........................340
Hóra (Samothráki)...................408
Hóra (Sérifos)..........................118
Hóra (Síkinos)..........................181
Hóra (Skhinoússa) 172
Hóra (Skýros)..........................442
Hóra Sfakíon (Crete) 253
Horió (Hálki).............................287
Horió (Sými)............................298
horses, Skyrian........................444
hospitals...................................40
hostels 35
hotels 33
Hotzoviótissas monastery
....176
Hydra....................... see Ýdhra
hydrofoils...................................30

I

Ía..190
Ialyssos, ancient 281
ice cream 39
Idean cave (Crete) 219
Ierápetra..................................232
Igoumenítsa 69
Ikaría 366–372
Ikaría 365
Ília...453
Iliad, The 521, 557
Imerovígli 188
immigration.............................541
Independence, War of 533
Inoússes...................................382
insects.....................................549
insurance...................................48
internet cafés 49
IONIAN ISLANDS,THE... 454–515
Ionian Islands, The............. 458
Iónio 505
Íos 177–180
Íos 178
Ioulídha...................................111
Irakliá......................................171
Iráklion........................ 201–208
Iráklion 203
Iréon 357
Íssos 475
Ítanos 230
Itháki (Ithaca) 498–502
Itháki.................................... 489
itineraries.................................. 22

J

jellyfish 41
junta, colonels'.......................539

K

Kabirion, ancient 408
kafenía 38
Kaïki beach 102
kaïkia 30
Kalafáti....................................146
Kalamáki (Zákynthos).............507
Kalamákia (Alónissos).............438
Kalamáta....................................70
Kalámi (Corfu).........................466
Kalamiés (Kálymnos)...............330
Kalamiótissa 195
Kalamítsi (Kímolos) 130
Kálamos (Évvia) 448
Kalandó....................................169
Kaláva 70
Kalávria.....................................92
Kallérgi hut 253
Kallianós..................................451
Kallithéa (Sámos) 363
Kalloní......................................394
Kalotarítissas 175
Kálymnos................16, 326–332
Kálymnos 326
Kamáres (Sífnos) 120
Kamári (Kos) 320
Kamári (Santoríni) 191
Kamariótissa 408
Kambí (Foúrni).........................364
Kambí (Zákynthos)...................508
Kámbos (Crete)........................257
Kámbos (Híos)..........................379
Kámbos (Ikaría)........................368
Kámbos (Lipsí).........................342
Kámbos (Pátmos).....................341
Kameiros, ancient....................280
Kaméni islets (Santoríni).........193
Kaminákia................................324
Kamíni (Ýdhra) 97
Kamínia (Zákynthos)...............505
Kanála......................................115
Kanáli..92
Kapodistrias, Ioannis 534
Kapsáli.....................................513
Karamanlís, Constantine
....538, 539
Karamanlís, Kostas (younger)
....630
Karávi (Sérifos)........................117
Karavóstamo...........................368
Karavostási (Folégandhros) ...183
Kardhámena.............................320
Karfás......................................377
Karlóvassi.................................361
Kárpathos........ 10, 19, 289–295
Kárpathos 290
Kárpathos Town 291
Karterádhos 188
Karthaia, ancient.....................111
Karyá (Lefkádha)......................483
Kárystos...................................450
Káspakas..................................405
Kassiópi...................................468
Kássos 287–289
Kássos 288
Kastáni (Skópelos).............13, 432
Kastélli (Kíssamos)............... 257

Kastélli (Pátmos) 338
Kastéllo (Ýdhra) 97
Kastellórizo **282–285**
Kastellórizo **283**
Kastellórizo Town 283
Kastrí (Kos) 320
Kástro (Inoússes) 383
Kástro (Léros) 335
Kástro (Sífnos) 121
Kástro (Skíathos) 428
Kástro (Thássos) 419
Kástro Kritinías 281
Kástro tís Oriás (Kýthnos) 115
Katápola 175
Katarráktis 377
Katastári 509
katastrofí 535
Kateloumátsa 194
Katergó (Folégandhros) 183
katharévoussa 668
Káthisma beach 487
Katholikó monastery 251
Káto Kateliós 493
Káto Lákki 311
Katoméri 486
Katsadhiá 342
Kavála 70
Kávos 475
Kazavíti, Mikró/Megálo 419
Kéa (Tzía) **109–112**
Kéa **110**
Kéa, lion of 112
Kefaloniá **488–498**
Kefaloniá **489**
Kéfalos (Kos) 320
Kekés 417
Kéndros (Dhonoússa) 173
Kerí 508
Kérkis, Mount 363
Kérkyra ....see Corfu
Kéros beach (Límnos) 407
Kérveli Bay 355
Khíos .... see Híos
Khrónia 452
Khryssí Aktí (Páros) 161
Khryssí Ammoudhiá 416
Khryssí Miliá (Alónissos) 438
Khryssomiliá (Foúrni) 364
Khryssopiyí monastery 122
Khryssoskalítissa 258
Kiliómeno 508
Kímisis monastery (Psará) 384
Kímisis Theotókou (Rhodes) ...279
Kímisis Theotókou (Sámos) 360
Kímolos **129–132**
Kímolos **124**
Kínyra 416
Kióni (Itháki) 501
Kiónia (Tínos) 138
Kípos (Samothráki) 411

Kipouréon monastery 493
Kíssamos ....see Kastélli
Kíthnos ....see Kýthnos
Kléftiko (Mílos) 16, 128
Klió 400
Klisídhi 194
Knossós **15, 209–211**
Knossós **210**
Kokkári 358
Kokkimídhis 301
Kókkini Ámmos 194
Kókkino 305
Kokkinókastro 438
Kolofána 175
Kolymbíthra (Tínos) 140
Kómi 379
Kondiás 406
Kórfos (Thirassía) 193
Korissía (Kéa) 111
Korissíon lagoon 474
Koronídha 170
Kos **312–321**
Kos **313**
Kos Town 314
Kos Town **315**
Kótsinas 407
Koufoníssi 172
Koukounariés 427
Kouloúra 466
Koumaradhéï 358
Kouméïka 358
Kournás lake 239
Kremastá Nerá 411
Kremastí (Lésvos) 393
Kríkello, Cape 320
Krithóni 336
Kríti ....see Crete
Kritsá 226
Krýa Vrýssi 453
Kykládhes ....see Cyclades
Kyllíni 71
Kými 448
Kyrá Panayiá (Sporades) 439
Kýthira **19, 510–515**
Kýthira **512**
Kýthnos **112–115**
Kýthnos **113**

L

Ladhikó 275
Laganás 506
Lahaniá 279
Lákka (Paxí) 478
Lákka (Psará) 384
Lakkí (Léros) 333
Lalária 427
Langádha (Híos) 381

Langádhes (Kos) 320
Langéri 159
Lápathos 301
Lárdhos 279
Lasíthi plateau 225
Lássi 492
Lato, ancient 226
laundries 49
Lávrio 71
Lefkádha **479–488**
Lefkádha **481**
Lefkádha Town **480–482**
Lefkátas, Cape 487
Lefkáthia 382
Lefkími 475
Lefkós 293
Leftós Yialós 438
Lemonákia 359
Léndas 215
Lépedha 492
Lepídha 334
Léros **332–337**
Léros **333**
Lesser Cyclades **170–173**
Lesser Cyclades **171**
Lésvos **10, 384–401**
Lésvos **385**
Lethrá 304
Levrehió 477
Lidharío 402
Liendoú 342
Liés (Níssyros) 310
Limenária (Angístri) 89
Limenária (Thássos) 418
Liménas (Thássos) **413–415**
Liménas (Thássos) **413**
Limnári (Arkí) 344
Límni (Évvia) 451
Límni Kerioú 507
Limniá (Híos) 381
Limniónas (Sámos) 362
Limniónas (Zákynthos) 508
Limnonári 432
Límnos **402–408**
Límnos **403**
Límnos (Híos) 382
Límnos (Psará) 384
Limónos monastery 394
Linariá (Skýros) 443
Líndhos **20, 276–278**
Lindos, ancient 278
Lingínou 342
lion of Kéa 112
Lipsí **342–344**
Lipsí **343**
Lissos, ancient 255
Lithí 381
Livadhákia (Sérifos) 117
Livádhi (Folégandhros) 183
Livádhi (Ikaría) 369

Livádhi (Irakliá)................................171
Livádhi (Sérifos)............................116
Livádhi Yeranoú...........................342
Livádhia (Astypálea)..................323
Livádhia (Tílos).............................303
living in Greece.............................49
Lixoúri...492
Liyiá..483
Longás beach (Corfu)................472
Longós (Paxí)..................................477
Lourdháta.......................................493
Loutrá (Kýthnos)..........................114
Loutrá (Samothráki)..................410
Loutrá (Tínos)...............................140
Loutrá Eftaloú..............................400
Loutrá Ehipsoú............................452
Loutrá Yéras..................................389
Loutráki (Skópelos).....................433
Loutró..254
Loútsa (Itháki)..............................499
Love Bay (Póros).............................92

M

Magaziá...443
magazines...41
Maherádho.....................................508
mail..49
Makrá...288
Makrá Ámmos (Híos)..................380
Makryialós (Crete)......................233
Makrýs Yialós (Zákynthos)......509
Mália, modern..............................216
Mália, Palace of............................217
Maltezána.......................................325
Mamma Mia!.............13, 429, 430,
    432, 434
Managrós...381
Mandhráki (Níssyros)...............306
Mandhráki (Skiáthos)...............427
Mandhráki (Ýdhra)........................97
Manganári......................................180
Manolás (Thirassía).....................193
Manolátes.......................................360
maps...50
Maráthi..344
Marathónas (Égina)........................86
Marathoúnda (Psérimos)..........321
Marathoúnda (Sými)...................301
Mariés (Zákynthos).....................508
Marinatos, Spyros.......................545
Markópoulo....................................493
Marmári (Évvia)............................449
Marmári (Kos)................................318
Mármaro (Híos).............................381
Massoúri...330
mastic bush....................................378
Mastihári..319

Mastihohoriá (mastic villages)
   377
Mátala...214
Mathráki..470
Mávros Yialós................................379
mayireftá...37
meats..37
media..41
Megáli Ámmos (Mýkonos).....145
Megális Panayías.........................358
Megálo Horió (Agathoníssi)...345
Megálo Horió (Tílos)...................305
Megálo Neório..................................92
Megálos Asélinos.........................427
Meganíssi..486
Mégas Lákkos................................492
Mégas Limniónas........................377
Melínda..391
Melissáni cave (Kefaloniá)
    ....21, 495
Melitsahás.......................................329
Melöï..341
Melos, ancient.............................127
meltémi.......................11, 106, 570
Mérihas..114
Merikiá..333
Merói..444
Mersíni (Dhonoússa)..................173
Mésa Vathý....................................325
Mesaktí..369
Mesohóri...293
Mesongí...474
Mestá..378
Metamórfosis church (Sámos)
   361
Metaxás dictatorship.................535
Metóhi (Angístri)............................88
Meyísti..................see Kastellórizo
mezédhes...37
mezedhopolía....................................39
Míkonos....................see Mýkonos
Mikró Horió (Tílos)......................305
Miliá (Alónissos)..........................438
Miliá (Skópelos)...........................432
Mílos........................... 124–129
Mílos.. 124
Mílos, ancient (Amorgós).......127
Minoan era.....................................518
Minotaur, the...................12, 209
Míres..214
mobile phones.................................52
Mogoníssi..477
Mókhlos...227
Mólos (Skýros)..............................443
Mólyvos..398
Mon Repos.....................................463
Monastíri (Anáfi)..........................195
Monastiríou (Póros)........................93
money..50
Moní (Égina).....................................87

Monólithos (Rhodes)................281
monsters, Greek..............................12
Moraïtika...474
mosquitoes.......................................41
motorbike rental.............................32
Moúdhros..406
Moundhón monastery..............382
Mount Zas......................................169
Mourtiás, Megálos/Mikrós
   436
music............................... 550–554
Mýrthios...240
Mýrtos..233
Mycenaean era.............................520
Mykáli..355
Mýkonos.......... 10, 15, 140–146
Mýkonos............................... 141
Mýkonos Town............. 142–144
Mýkonos Town.................... 143
Mylélia...392
Mýli (Évvia)....................................451
Mylopótamos (Kýthira)...........513
Mylopótas (Íos)............................178
Mýlos (Angístri).............................89
Mýlos beach (Lefkádha).........487
Mýrina..403
Myrtiés..330
Mýrthios (Crete)..........................240
Myrtiótissa.....................................472
Mýrtos beach (Kefaloniá).......496
mysteries of Samothráki........410
mythology, Greek....12, 148, 209,
    499, 521, 557
Mytilíni Town.............. 386–389
Mytilíni Town..................... 387

N

Nagós...381
name days...42
Nanoú...301
Náoussa (Páros)...........................159
Nás..369
National Marine Park of
    Alónissos-Sporades........21, 439
Návlakas...285
Náxos..................... 15, 162–170
Náxos...................................... 163
Náxos Town....................................164
Náxos Town........................ 165
Néa Dhimokratía (New
    Democracy)...............................539
Néa Moní...380
Neápoli...72
Néa Stýra...449
Néo Klíma.......................................432
Neolithic Greece..........................517
Néos Pýrgos...................................453

newspapers 41
Nídha plateau 219
Nikiá 311
Nikiána 483
Níssyros **13, 306–312**
Níssyros **307**
Nótos beach 474
Nydhrí 483

O

Odyssey, The 499, 521, 557
Óhi, Mount 451
olives, Lésvos 394
Olýmbi 378
Ólymbos (Kárpathos) 19, 294
Olympia, wreck of 176
Olympic Games (2004) 630
Omalós 253
opening hours 51
Oreí 453
orektiká 37
Órmos Marathokámbou 362
Órmos Ysterníon 139
Ornós 145
Orthodox church 531
Othoní 470
Óthos 294
Otto, King 534
Ottoman Greece 531
Otziás 112
outdoor pursuits 44
ouzerís 39
oúzo 39

P

Pagóndas 358
Pahiá Ámmos (Níssyros) 310
Pahiá Ámmos (Samothráki) ... 411
Pahiá Ámmos (Zákynthos) 509
Palamári 444
Paleá Alónissos 436
Palékastro 230
Paleó Klíma 433
Paleó Pylí (Kos) 319
Paleohóra (Crete) 254
Paleohóra (Égina) 85
Paleohóra (Kýthira) 511
Paleohóri (Mílos) 127
Paleokastrítsa (Corfu) 470
Paleókastro (Ándhros) 136
Paleókastro (Kímolos) 130
Paleókastro (Níssyros) 308
Paleópolis (Ándhros) 134
Paliónissos 329

Pálli (Agathoníssi) 345
Pálli (Níssyros) 310
"Palm Beach" (Crete) 240
Panayía (Irakliá) 171
Panayía (Thássos) 416
Panayía Dombón 428
Panayía Episkopí (Santoríni) 193
Panayía Kardhási 428
Panayía Katholikí 275
Panayía Kyrá (Crete) 226
Panayía Kyrá (Níssyros) 310
Panayía Makriní 363
Panayía Palatianí 320
Panayía Panakhrándou 135
Panayía Protóthronis 169
Panayía Spilianí (Níssyros) ... 307
Panayía Spilianí (Sámos) 356
Panayía Thermianí 310
Pandélli 335
Pandokrátor, Mount 466
Panormítis 302
Pánormos (Mýkonos) 146
Pánormos (Skópelos) 432
Papá Miná 294
Papafránga 128
Papandhriá 343
Papandréou, Andreas 539
Papandréou, George (younger)
.... 630
Papandréou, George senior ... 537
Paradise beach (Mýkonos) 145
Paralía Kaláthou 276
Paralía Kopriá 281
Paralía Kýmis 448
Paralía Lefkoú 293
Paralía Lithíou 381
Paralía Thánous 405
Paralía Thermís 389
Paránga 145
Parikía **155–158**
Parikía **157**
Páros **154–161**
Páros **155**
PASOK 539
Pateliá 344
Patitíri 436
Pátmos **337–342**
Pátmos **338**
Pátra 72
Paxí (Paxos) **476–479**
Paxí **477**
Paxos .... see Paxí
Pédhi 300
Péfki (Évvia) 453
Péfki (Rhodes) 279
Péfkos (Skýos) 445
Pefkoúlia 487
Pélekas 473
Pelikáta hill 500
Peloponnesian wars 524

Péra Kástro (Kálymnos) 327
Péra Yialós 323
Pérama (Lésvos) 391
Perastá 285
Pérdhika (Égina) 86
Veríssa 191
Peristéra (Sporades) 439
Perivolioú (Skópelos) 434
Perivolís monastery 395
Perouládhes 472
Persian wars 522
Pessádha 492
Petaloúdhes (Páros) 156
Petaloúdhes (Rhodes) 281
Petaní beach 493
Pétra (Lésvos) 400
Pétra (Pátmos) 341
petrified forest, Lésvos 96
Petrití 474
Petrokopió 364
Phaestos 213
Phaestos **213**
pharmacies 40
philosophy 526
phones 51
photography 51
Pigadhákia 509
Pigádhia (Kárpathos) 291
Pipéri (Páros) 159
Pipéri (Sporades) 439
Piraeus .... see Pireás
Pireás **64–68**
Pireás **65**
Pisaetós 500
Píso Livádhi 160
Pisses 112
Pityós 381
Piyés Kallithéas 275
Pláka (Crete) 224
Pláka (Mílos) 126
Pláka (Náxos) 167
Pláka (Tílos) 305
Plákes (Astypálea) 325
Plákes (Ýdhra) 97
Plakiás (Crete) 240
Plános 509
plants 41, 546
Plátanos (Léros) 335
Platiá Poúnda 172
Plato 526
Platon, Nikolaos 545
Platrithiés 501
Platý (Límnos) 405
Platýs Yialós (Lipsí) 343
Platýs Yialós (Sífnos) 123
Plomári 391
poetry 556
police 47
Polikhnítos spa 392
Pollónia (Mílos) 128

Polyochni.............................407
Póndamos.......................286
Póndi.................................484
Pondikoníssi....................464
population exchange.............535
Porí...................................172
Póros 90–93
Póros 90
Póros (Kefaloniá)...................494
Póros Town............................91
Pórtes (Égina)......................86
Pórto Katsíki.....................487
Pórto Zóro.........................505
Poseidon, temple of (Póros)....93
Posidhonía (Sýros)................152
postal services.....................49
Potámi (Híos).....................379
Potámi (Sámos)..................361
Potamiá (Thássos).................416
Potamós (Kýthira)................511
Póthia...............................327
Potokáki...........................356
Potós...............................417
Poúnda..............................161
Pouthená............................288
Prassoníssi........................279
Préveli monastery (Crete).......240
Profítis Ilías (Rhodes).........282
Profítis Ilías (Samothráki)....411
Profítis Ilías (Ýdhra)...........98
Prokópi.............................451
Provatás...........................128
Psará...............................383
Psaralíki..........................162
Psaroú..............................145
Psathoúra...........................439
Psérimos...........................321
Psérimos 313
Psilí Ámmos (E Sámos)..........355
Psilí Ámmos (Sérifos)...........117
Psilí Ámmos (W Sámos).........362
Psilorítis, Mount.................219
psistariés..........................37
Psykhró.............................225
Pylés (Kárpathos)..................294
Pylí (Kos).........................319
Pyrgí (Híos).......................378
Pýrgos (Sámos).....................358
Pýrgos (Tínos).....................139
Pýrgos Himárrou...................169
Pythagório.........................355

R

radio.................................41
Rafína................................73
Ráhes...............................370
rembétika...................149, 551

reptiles.............................548
restaurants..........................36
Réthymnon 234–238
Réthymnon.......................235
Rhodes..........................264–282
Rhodes...............................267
Rhodes Town 266–274
Rhodes Town 268
Rhodes Old Town 270
Rína.................................328
Ríva.................................361
rock climbing..................16, 329
Ródha...............................468
Roman Greece.......................529
rooms, private......................34
Ross, Ludwig.......................542
Rossikós Nafstathmós..............92
Roúda Bay..........................484
Roúkounas..........................194
Roussoúm Yialós...................436
Roviés..............................452

S

sailing..............................45
St John monastery, Pátmos..........
    see Ayíou Ioánnou Theológou
    (Pátmos)
St John the Evangelist............340
St Paul's harbour..................278
Salamína..............................80
Salamis ....see Salamína
Salamis, battle of..................81
Samariá Gorge 251–253
Samariá Gorge 252
Sámi................................494
Sámos 351–363
Sámos 352
Samothrace .... see Samothráki
Samothráki 408–412
Samothráki.......................409
Sanctuary of the Great Gods
   409
Sánta María (Páros)...............159
Santoríni..............13, 186–194
Santoríni.........................187
Sarakíniko (Itháki)................499
Sarakíniko (Mílos).................128
Sarakinó (Skýros).................443
Sardhés.............................405
Schliemann, Heinrich..............543
School of Painting, Ionian......463
scooter rental.......................32
scuba diving.........................45
sea urchins...........................41
seafood...............................37
seals, Mediterranean monk....439
Seïtáni, Mikró/Megálo 361

Sérifos 115–118
Sérifos...............................116
Seyhélles...........................372
Sfinári..............................257
Shipwreck Bay (Zákynthos)
    ....18, 510
Sidhári.............................468
siesta...............................46
Sifnos 118–124
Sifnos 119
Sígri...............................396
Síkinos 180–182
Síkinos 181
Síros ....see Sýros
Sitía 227–229
Sitía 228
Skála (Angístri)...................88
Skála (Astypálea)
    ....see Péra Yialós
Skála (Kefaloniá).................493
Skála (Pátmos)....................338
Skála Eressoú.....................396
Skála Kallonís....................394
Skála Kamírou.....................281
Skála Marión......................418
Skála Potamiás....................416
Skála Prínou......................418
Skála Sykaminiás..................400
Skhinoússa.........................172
Skiáthos 422–429
Skiáthos 426
Skiáthos Town......................425
Skinári, Cape......................509
Skinós..............................499
Skíros ....see Skýros
Skópelos 10, 429–434
Skópelos 430
Skópelos Town 430–432
Skýros 439–445
Skýros 440
Skýros Town 442–444
smoking..............................46
snacks...............................36
Socrates............................526
Sorós...............................162
Sotíras (Thássos)..................419
Soúyia..............................254
Spartohóri.........................486
Spétses 99–103
Spétses 99
Spétses Town.......................100
Spiádha.............................452
Spíli...............................242
Spiliás.............................345
Spinalónga.........................224
Spóa................................294
sponges.............................328
SPORADES, THE.............422–445
Sporades, the 424
sports...............................44

Stáfylos....................................432
stamps.......................................49
Stavrós (Crete)......................251
Stavrós (Dhonoússa)...........173
Stavrós (Hálki)......................287
Stavrós (Itháki).....................500
Stavrós (Tílos).......................304
Stefanos crater (Níssyros)
....13, 312
Stegná......................................276
Stení (Évvia)..........................449
Stení Vála................................438
Stenó...325
Strinýlas...................................466
Stýra..449
Super Paradise beach (Mýkonos)
....145
Sykamiá
.... see Sykaminiá (Lésvos)
Sykaminiá (Lésvos)................400
Sykiás Olýmbon cave.............378
Sými....................17, 295–302
Sými.. 296
Sými Town................................297
Sýros........................... 149–154
Sýros 149
Sývota (Lefkádha)..................484

T

tavernas.......................................37
taxi boats...................................30
Taxiárhis Mihaïl Panormítis....302
taxis..32
Télendhos...............................330
Télendhos........................... 326
telephones...............................51
television...................................42
Thános (Koufoníssi)...............172
Thános (Límnos).....................405
Thárri monastery...................282
Thássos...................... 412–419
Thássos 413
Thássos Town........... see Liménas
theft...47
Theóktisti monastery..............368
Theológos................................419
Theophilos Museum (Lésvos)
....390
Theotókou monastery (Corfu)
....470
Thériade Museum (Lésvos)....390
Thérma (Ikaría)........................367
Thérma (Límnos).....................405
Thermá (Samothráki)..............410
Thérma Lefkádhos..................367
Thermiá.....................see Kýthnos

Thessaloníki..............................73
Thira, ancient...........................191
Thirassía islet..........................193
Thóli (Agathoníssi)...............345
Thólos (Tílos)...........................305
Thucydides................................525
Thymianá...................................377
Tiganákia (Arkí).......................344
Tigáni (Híos)...........................380
Tílos............................. 302–306
Tílos... 303
time..51
Tingáki.......................................318
Tínos............................. 136–140
Tínos 137
Tínos Town.................................137
tipping..46
toilets, public.............................52
tomb, Homer............................180
Toploú monastery....................229
tour operators...........................28
tourist information...................52
tourist police............................47
Tourkopígadho.........................335
Tragéa, the.................................168
Trahiá...287
trains..27
transliteration..........................562
Trapezáki..................................493
travel agencies..........................28
travellers' cheques...................50
Trís Boúkes...............................445
Trojan war..................................519
Truman Doctrine......................538
Trypití (Mílos).........................126
Tsambíka....................................275
Tsigoúri.....................................172
Tsigrádho.................................128
Tsiliví...509
tsípouro.....................................39
Tsónia...400
Tsougriá....................................427
Turkómnima.............................343
turtles, loggerhead..................506
Týlissos.....................................218
Tzaboú.......................................359
Tzamadhoú...............................359
Tzanáki......................................323
Tzermiádho..............................225
Tziá...............................see Kéa
Tzórtzi Yialós..........................438

V

Vafkerí......................................483
Váï beach (Crete)..............14, 230
Vanánda....................................295

Vardhiá......................................183
Vári...152
Variá...389
Vassilikí (Lefkádha)................484
Vassilikós peninsula (Zákynthos)
....504
Vaterá...392
Vathý....................................... 354
Vathý (Itháki)...........................499
Vathý (Meganíssi)...................486
Vathý (Psérimos)......................321
Vathý (Sámos).........................353
Vathý (Sífnos)...........................123
Vathýs (Kálymnos)..................328
Vátos (Samothráki)..................411
Vatoúmi.....................................478
Vátses...324
Vayiá..342
Vayioniá......................................93
vegetarians.................................38
Velanió......................................432
Venizelos, Eleftherios.............534
Véssa..381
Vídhos.......................................464
villa rental...................................34
visas..47
Vlahérna....................................464
Vlyhó (Lefkádha)......................484
Vlyhós (Ýdhra)...........................97
Voládha......................................294
Vólax..140
Volímes.......................................510
Volissós.....................................381
Vólos..74
Votsalákia..................................362
Vótsi...436
Vouņó (Skýros)........................445
Vourkári....................................112
Vourliótes.................................360
Vréllos.......................................102
Vríka...478
Vromólimnos (Skiáthos)
....427
Vromólithos (Léros)................335
Vrondádhos...............................377
Vróndi Bay................................291
Vrykoúnda.................................295
Vrysítsa.....................................437
Vrýssa..392
Výthisma...................................436

W

Wace, Alan................................545
walking.....................45, 103, 295,
   301, 311, 370, 433, 436, 466,
   475, 478, 560

War of Independence.............533
water.................................... 40
watersports............................... 44
weather............................ 11, 48
wildlife........................ **546–549**
windsurfing..................13, 44, 280
wine...................19, 38, 192, 214
women travellers.......................46
working in Greece.....................49
World War I...............................534
World War II..............................536

X

Xi...492
Xinára......................................140
Xirókambos 334
Xygiá beach (Zákynthos)........509
Xylokériza.................................103

Y

Ýdhra (Hydra) **13, 93–99**
Ýdhra...................................... **94**
Ýdhra Town..............................95
Ýdhra Town.......................... **95**
Yennádhi...................................279
Yeoryoúpoli 239
Yérakas (Zákynthos) 505
Yialí (Hálki)..............................439
Yiália (Alónissos) 437
Yialiskári (Ikaría)....................369
Yialiskári (Kéa)..........................111
Yialós (Íos)...............................178
Yialós (Lefkádha)....................487
Yialós (Sými) 297
Yióssonas.................................381
Yioúra......................................439
Yíra...483
Yíthio...................................... 75
youth hostels 35

Ypsárion, Mount 416
Ypsiloú monastery..................395

Z

zaharoplastía.............................. 39
Zákros, Palace of......................231
Zákros, Áno...............................230
Zákros, Káto...............................230
Zákynthos **502–510**
Zákynthos **503**
Zákynthos Town.......................503
Zante......................see Zákynthos
Zas, Mount...............................169
Zepága 383
Ziá 319
Zoödhóhou Piyís (Anáfi) 195
Zoödhóhou Piyís (Límnos).....407
Zoödhóhou Piyís (Síkinos) 182
Zoyeriá......................................102

Map symbols

The symbols below are used on maps throughout the book

Post office	Mosque	Viewpoint	Boat
Information office	Monastery/convent	Spring/spa	Metro/subway
Hospital	Campsite	Waterfall	Tram stop
Parking	Cave	Winery	Helipad
Point of interest	Synagogue	Archeological site	Church
Internet café	Gorge	Mountain range	Building
Gardens/fountain	Steep slope	Peak	Stadium
Bridge	Marshland	Shipwreck	Park
Gate	Windmill	Airport	Beach
Castle	Lighthouse	Bus/taxi stop	Cemetery

Listings key

- Accommodation
- Eating & Drinking
- Nightlife
- Shop